A Companion to Stuart Britain

A COMPANION TO STUART BRITAIN

Edited by

Barry Coward

THE
HISTORICAL
ASSOCIATION
THE VOICE FOR HISTORY

Blackwell
Publishing

350 Main Street, Malden, MA 02148–5018, USA
108 Cowley Road, Oxford OX4 1JF, UK
550 Swanston Street, Carlton South, Melbourne, Victoria 3053, Australia
Kurfürstendamm 57, 10707 Berlin, Germany

First published 2003 by Blackwell Publishers Ltd

Library of Congress Cataloging-in-Publication Data

A companion to Stuart Britain / edited by Barry Coward.
    p. cm. – (Blackwell companions to British history)
Includes bibliographical references and index.
    ISBN 0-631-21874-2 (alk. paper)
    1. Great Britain–History–Stuarts, 1603-1714–Handbooks, manuals, etc. 2. Great Britain–Civilization–17th century–Handbooks, manuals, etc. I. Coward, Barry. II. Series.
    DA375. C684 2003
    941.06–dc21

                                                                                    2002005622

A catalogue record for this title is available from the British Library.

Set in 10/12pt Galliard by Kolam Information Services Pvt. Ltd, Pondicherry, India
Printed and bound in the United Kingdom
by TJ International, Padstow, Cornwall

For further information on
Blackwell Publishing, visit our website:
http://www.blackwellpublishing.com

BLACKWELL COMPANIONS TO BRITISH HISTORY
Published in association with The Historical Association

This series provides sophisticated and authoritative overviews of the scholarship that has shaped our current understanding of British History. Each volume comprises up to forty concise essays written by individual scholars within their area of specialization. The aim of each contribution is to synthesize the current state of scholarship from a variety of historical perspectives and to provide a statement on where the field is heading. The essays are written in a clear, provocative and lively manner, designed for an international audience of scholars, students and general readers.

The *Blackwell Companions to British History* is a cornerstone of Blackwell's overarching Companions to History series, covering European, American and World History.

Published

A Companion to Britain in the Later Middle Ages
Edited by S. H. Rigby

A Companion to Stuart Britain
Edited by Barry Coward

A Companion to Eighteenth-Century Britain
Edited by H. T. Dickinson

A Companion to Early Twentieth-Century Britain
Edited by Chris Wrigley

In preparation

A Companion to Roman Britain
Edited by Malcolm Todd

A Companion to Britain in the Early Middle Ages
Edited by Pauline Stafford

A Companion to Tudor Britain
Edited by Robert Tittler and Norman Jones

A Companion to Nineteenth-Century Britain
Edited by Chris Williams

A Companion to Contemporary Britain
Edited by Paul Addison and Harriet Jones

The Historical Association is the voice for history. Since 1906 it has been bringing together people who share an interest in, and love, for the past. It aims to further the study and teaching of history at all levels. Membership is open to everyone: teacher and student, amateur and professional. Membership offers a range of journals, activities and other benefits. Full details are available from: The Historical Association, 59a Kennington Park Road, London SE11 4JH, enquiry@history.org.uk, www.history.org.uk.

Other Blackwell History Companions include:

BLACKWELL COMPANIONS TO HISTORY

Published
A Companion to Western Historical Thought
Edited by Lloyd Kramer and Sarah Maza

In preparation
A Companion to Gender History
Edited by Teresa Meade and Merry E. Weisner-Hanks

BLACKWELL COMPANIONS TO EUROPEAN HISTORY

Published
A Companion to the Worlds of the Renaissance
Edited by Guido Ruggiero

In preparation
A Companion to the Reformation World
Edited by R. Po-chia Hsia

A Companion to Europe Since 1945
Edited by Klaus Larres

A Companion to Europe 1900–1945
Edited by Gordon Martel

BLACKWELL COMPANIONS TO AMERICAN HISTORY

Published
A Companion to the American Revolution
Edited by Jack P. Greene and J. R. Pole

A Companion to 19th-Century America
Edited by William L. Barney

A Companion to the American South
Edited by John B. Boles

A Companion to American Indian History
Edited by Philip J. Deloria and Neal Salisbury

A Companion to American Women's History
Edited by Nancy A. Hewitt

A Companion to Post-1945 America
Edited by Jean-Christophe Agnew and Roy Rosenzweig

A Companion to the Vietnam War
Edited by Marilyn B. Young and Robert Buzzanco

In preparation
A Companion to Colonial America
Edited by Daniel Vickers

A Companion to 20th-Century America
Edited by Stephen J. Whitfield

A Companion to the American West
Edited by William Deverell

A Companion to American Foreign Relations
Edited by Robert Schulzinger

BLACKWELL COMPANIONS TO WORLD HISTORY

In preparation
A Companion to the History of Africa
Edited by Joseph Miller

A Companion to the History of the Middle East
Edited by Youssef M. Choueiri

Contents

List of Plates   ix

Notes on Contributors   x

Introduction   xiii
Barry Coward

PART I   Stuart Britain and the Wider World   1

1   The Multiple Kingdoms of Britain and Ireland: The
     'British Problem'   3
     Allan I. Macinnes

2   The Making of Great Britain and Ireland   26
     Toby Barnard

3   Asia, the Atlantic and the Subjects of the British Monarchy   45
     Nicholas Canny

PART II   The Changing Face of Stuart Britain   67

4   The Rise of the Fiscal State   69
     Michael J. Braddick

5   The Press and Popular Political Opinion   88
     Ian Atherton

6   Gender Relations   111
     Elizabeth Foyster

7   Crime and Popular Protest   130
     Steve Hindle

8   Economic and Urban Development   148
     Craig Muldrew

9   Literature and History   166
     Thomas N. Corns

10   Art, Architecture and Politics   187
     Tim Wilks

11   Scientific Change: Its Setting and Stimuli   214
     Michael Hunter

PART III   Stuart Britain, 1603–1642   231

12   Politics in Early Stuart Britain, 1603–1640   233
     David L. Smith

13   Religion in Early Stuart Britain, 1603–1642   253
     Tom Webster

14   Political Thought in Early Stuart Britain   271
     Malcolm Smuts

15   The Outbreak of the Civil Wars in the Three Kingdoms   290
     Jason Peacey

PART IV   Stuart Britain, 1642–1660   309

16   The Wars of the Three Kingdoms, 1642–1649   311
     David Scott

17   Unkingship, 1649–1660   331
     Sean Kelsey

18   Religion, 1640–1660   350
     Ann Hughes

19   Political Thought During the English Revolution   374
     J. C. Davis

PART V   Stuart Britain, 1660–1714   397

20   Politics in Restoration Britain   399
     John Miller

21   Religion in Restoration England   416
     John Spurr

22   The Revolution of 1688–1689   436
     Colin Brooks

23   Politics after the Glorious Revolution   455
     Mark Knights

24   Political Thinking between Restoration and Hanoverian Succession   474
     Justin Champion

Bibliography   492

Index   530

Plates

1 Samuel Cooper (attributed), *Oliver Cromwell*,
   watercolour on vellum, *c.*1655.   189

2 François Dieussart, Thomas Howard,
   earl of Arundel.   192

3 Robert van Voerst, *Charles I*, 1636, engraving
   after François Dieussart.   195

4 Inigo Jones, Queen's Chapel, St James's Palace (west front),
   London, 1623–5.   197

5 William Dobson, *Portrait of the artist with Nicholas Lanier
   and Sir Charles Cotterell*, oil, *c.*1645–6.   200

6 Sir Peter Lely, *Princess Mary* (later Mary II),
   oil on canvas, 1677.   203

7 Romeyn de Hooghe, *Sir Itur ad Astra Scilicet*
   ('This is the way to the stars, of course'), etching, 1688.   206

8 Inigo Jones, Banqueting House, Whitehall, 1619–22.   208

9 Sir Christopher Wren, St Paul's Cathedral (west, upper),
   London, 1675–1710.   210

Contributors

Ian Atherton is Lecturer in History at Keele University. He has co-edited *Norwich Cathedral: Church, City and Diocese 1096–1996* (1996) and written *Ambition and Failure in Stuart England: The Career of John, First Viscount Scudamore* (1999). He has also published work on the manuscript circulation of news in seventeenth-century England.

Toby Barnard is Fellow and Tutor in Modern History at Hertford College, University of Oxford. He has written widely on early modern Irish history. His *Cromwellian Ireland: English Government and Reform in Ireland 1649–1660* was reissued in paperback in 2000.

Michael J. Braddick is Professor of History at the University of Sheffield. His previous publications include *Parliamentary Taxation in Seventeenth Century England: Local Administration and Response* (1994), *The Nerves of State: Taxation and the Financing of the English State, 1558–1714* (1996) and *State Formation in Early Modern England* (2000). He is also co-editor (with John Walter) of *Negotiating Power in Early Modern Society: Order, Hierarchy and Subordination in England and Ireland* (2001) and (with David Armitage) of *The British Atlantic World, 1500–1800* (2002).

Colin Brooks is Senior Lecturer in History at the University of Sussex. He has taught there since 1970 and has been Dean of the School of English and American Studies and Pro-Vice-Chancellor. His research interests are in British politics in the late seventeenth and early eighteenth centuries. He is completing a book on the government of Britain from the sixteenth to the nineteenth centuries.

Nicholas Canny is Professor of History and Academic Director of the Centre for the Study of Human Settlement and Historical Change at National University of Ireland, Galway. He has edited *The Origins of Empire* which is volume 1 of the Oxford History of the British Empire (paperback edition, 2001) and his most recent book is *Making Ireland British, 1580–1650* (2001). He is a Member of the Royal Irish Academy and of Academia Europaeia.

Justin Champion is Reader in the History of Early Modern History of Ideas at Royal Holloway, University of London. His previous publications include *The Pillars of Priestcraft Shaken* (1992) and *John Toland's Nazarenus* (1999). His book on the *Great Plague of London 1665: London's Dreaded Visitation* (1995) was turned into an award-winning television programme for Channel 4 in 2001. His study of the life and thought of John Toland, *Republican Learning: John Toland and the Crisis of Christian Culture 1696–1722*, is forthcoming.

Thomas N. Corns is Professor of English and Head of the School of Arts and Humanities at the University of Wales, Bangor. His principal publications include *The Development of Milton's Prose Style* (1982), *Milton's Language* (1990), *Uncloistered Virtue: English Political Literature 1640–1660* (1992), *Regaining 'Paradise Lost'* (1994) and the

Twayne Guide to Milton's Prose (1998). He edited *The Cambridge Companion to English Poetry: Donne to Marvell* (1993), *The Royal Image: Representations of Charles I* (1999) and the *Blackwell Companion to Milton* (2001).

Barry Coward is Reader in History at Birkbeck College, London. His previous publications include *The Stanleys, Lords Stanley and Earls of Derby: The Origins, Wealth and Power of a Landowning Family, 1385–1672* (1983), *Oliver Cromwell* (1991), *The Stuart Age: England 1603–1714* (second edition, 1994) and, with Christopher Durston, *The English Revolution: A Sourcebook* (1997). He is the President of the Cromwell Association.

J. C. Davis is Professor of English History at the University of East Anglia. His previous publications include *Utopia and the Ideal Society* (1981), *Fear, Myth and History: The Ranters and the Historians* (1986), *Oliver Cromwell* (2001) and numerous articles and essays on political, religious and utopian thought in the early modern period.

Elizabeth Foyster is Lecturer in History in the Department of History, University of Dundee. She has published *Manhood in Early Modern England: Honour, Sex and Marriage* (1999), and a number of articles and chapters on the themes of marriage, childhood and gender relations in seventeenth- and eighteenth-century England. She is currently writing a book about marital violence in England between the Restoration and the mid-nineteenth century.

Steve Hindle is Senior Lecturer in History at the University of Warwick. He is the author of *The State and Social Change in Early Modern England, c.1550–1640* (2000) and co-editor (with Adam Fox and Paul Griffiths) of *The Experience of Authority in Early Modern England* (1996). He has also published several articles on social relations in English rural communities and is currently writing a book on the local politics of poor relief in seventeenth-century England.

Ann Hughes is Professor of Early Modern History at the University of Keele and worked previously at Manchester University and the Open University. She is the author of *Politics, Society and Civil War in Warwickshire 1620–1660* (1987) and *The Causes of the English Civil War* (2nd edition, 1998), and co-editor (with Richard Cust) of *Conflict in Early Stuart England* (1989) and *The English Civil War* (1997). She won the Alexander Prize of the Royal Historical Society in 1980.

Michael Hunter is Professor of History at Birkbeck College, University of London. He has written or edited many books on science and its milieu in late seventeenth-century England, and is the principal editor of the definitive edition of *The Works of Robert Boyle* (14 vols, 1999–2000) and *The Correspondence of Robert Boyle* (6 vols, 2001).

Sean Kelsey is the author of *Inventing a Republic: The Political Culture of the English Commonwealth, 1649–1653* (1997). He has written several essays and articles on the revolution of 1649, and is currently preparing a book on the death of Charles I.

Mark Knights is a Senior Lecturer in British History at the University of East Anglia, Norwich. His previous publications include *Politics and Opinion in Crisis, 1678–1681* (1994) and a number of articles about the political culture and thought of the Restoration period. He has contributed to the History of Parliament volumes for 1690–1714 and is currently writing a book about *Representation and Misrepresentation: Politics and Language in Later Stuart Britain, c.1660–1720* (forthcoming), which develops a number of the themes outlined in his chapter. He is General Editor of the Parliament History Record Series.

Allan I. Macinnes holds the Burnett-Fletcher Chair of History at the University of Aberdeen. He has written extensively on clanship, covenants and confederal union in the seventeenth century. His monographs include *Charles I and the Making of the Covenanting Movement, 1625–1641* (1991) and *Clanship, Commerce and the House of Stuart, 1603–1788* (1996, reprinted 2000). His (jointly) edited works include *Ships, Guns and Bibles in North Sea and the Baltic States, c.1350–c.1700* (2000) and *The Stuart*

Kingdoms in the Seventeenth Century: Awkward Neighbours (2002). He is a founder and initial convenor of the Northern European Historical Research Network, which now contains 25 affiliated institutions in 18 states.

John Miller is Professor of History at Queen Mary, University of London. His most recent book is *After the Civil Wars: English Politics and Government in the Reign of Charles II* (2000). Earlier works include *James II* (first published 1978, republished 2000), *Popery and Politics in England, 1660–88* (1973) and *Charles II* (1991). He has also edited collections of essays on European Protestantism and absolutism in seventeenth-century Europe. He is currently working on a study of politics and religion in English provincial towns, 1660–1722. He is chairman of the Editorial Board of the History of Parliament.

Craig Muldrew is a University Lecturer in the Faculty of History, Cambridge University and a fellow of Queens' College, Cambridge. His research has focused primarily on investigating the economic and social role of trust in the development of the market economy in England between 1500 and 1700. He has published a monograph on the subject entitled *The Economy of Obligation: The Culture of Credit and Social Relations in Early Modern England* (1998).

Jason Peacey is a Senior Research Fellow at the History of Parliament Trust, London. He is the editor of *The Regicides and the Execution of Charles I* (2001), and co-editor (with Chris R. Kyle) of *Parliament at Work: Parliamentary Committees, Political Power and Public Access in Early Modern England* (2002). His main area of interest is the political culture and polemical literature of the seventeenth century, and he is currently completing a book on *Politicians and Pamphleteers in the British Civil Wars* (forthcoming).

David Scott is a Research Fellow at the History of Parliament Trust, London. He has

written several articles and essays on Quakerism and on British politics in the 1640s. He was also joint editor of the *Juxon Journal* (Camden Society, 1999). Among his forthcoming publications is a study of politics, power and government in mid-seventeenth century Britain and Ireland.

David L. Smith is Fellow and Director of Studies in History at Selwyn College, Cambridge. His previous publications include *Oliver Cromwell: Politics and Religion in the English Revolution, 1640–1658* (1991), *Louis XIV* (1992), *Constitutional Royalism and the Search for Settlement, c.1640–1649* (1994), *A History of the Modern British Isles, 1603–1707: The Double Crown* (1998) and *The Stuart Parliaments, 1603–1689* (1999).

Malcolm Smuts is Professor of History at the University of Massachusetts, Boston. His previous publications include *Court Culture and the Origins of a Royalist Tradition in Early Stuart England* (1987; paperback 1999) and *Culture and Power in England* (1999). He also edited *The Stuart Court and Europe* (1996).

John Spurr is Reader in History at the University of Wales, Swansea. He is the author of *The Restoration Church of England, 1646–1689* (1991), *English Puritanism, 1603–89* (1998) and *England in the 1670s* (2000). He is writing a history of oaths and swearing and a survey of seventeenth-century English religion.

Tom Webster is Lecturer in British History at the University of Edinburgh. His works include *Godly Clergy in Early Stuart England* and he is editor of the *Diary of Samuel Rogers 1634–38*. He specializes in English spirituality and the philosophy of history.

Tim Wilks is a Senior Lecturer at Southampton Institute where he teaches fine arts valuation and the history of collecting. His current research is focused on patronage and collecting at the early Stuart court. He has published on leading patrons including Henry, Prince of Wales, Anne of Denmark, the earl of Somerset and the earl of Clanricard.

Introduction

BARRY COWARD

When I was asked to edit this book, I was very happy to accept because it seemed to me that the time was ripe for a group of experts in various fields of seventeenth- and early eighteenth-century British history to stand back and synthesize the current state of scholarship in their areas of expertise. During the last thirty years of the twentieth century the flow of new and conflicting interpretations of many aspects of British history during the Stuart age has been rapid. As new books and articles have appeared in bookshops, libraries and historical journals, for those deeply involved in the study of this period the high level of excitement and interest that has always surrounded it has been sustained and perhaps even increased. But for scholars, students and general readers who have not had the time to keep abreast of this new work, the result has been to make the period difficult to get to grips with. Indeed some hard-pressed schoolteachers have told me that they are thinking of abandoning teaching courses on this period in favour of 'easier' periods about which historical interpretations have been less frequently and bitterly contested. This is primarily why I accepted the invitation to edit a book that would both reflect the intrinsic excitement and importance of the Stuart age and help to dispel the confusion caused by the kaleidoscopic and changing nature of historical interpretations about it.

The excitement and importance of the period are not in doubt. Just a brief list of a few historical questions and themes connected with its political–religious core demonstrates that they demand attention by anyone interested in the historical development of England, Wales, Scotland and Ireland. Why were all four countries embroiled in civil wars by the early 1640s? What impact did the War of Three Kingdoms[1] have throughout the British Isles? Why were the principal outcomes of the war the execution of the king of Britain and Ireland and the establishment of republican regimes (the Commonwealth, 1649–53, and the Cromwellian Protectorate, 1653–9) that were the first to be in effective control of all the British Isles? What impact did these regimes have on the British Isles in the 1650s? Why was republican rule short-lived and monarchy restored? Did the revolutionary events of the mid-century change fundamentally the structure of government and society in the British Isles? How strong was the restored monarchy of Charles II in Britain? Why did major political and religious tensions continue under the later Stuarts, Charles II and James II? Why did a second Stuart monarch lose his throne (if not his life) in 1688–9? Were the events of 1688–9 a 'Glorious Revolution' and what impact did they have on England and Wales, Scotland and Ireland? What were the origins of the bitter party rivalries between Whigs and Tories that raged in the last decades of Stuart rule under William III, Mary II and Queen Anne? To what extent and why did Britain and Ireland change during 'the long seventeenth century' of the Stuart age? A similar list of questions could easily be compiled about the social, economic, cultural and intellectual history of the period. Indeed many such questions will be raised and addressed in this book. So, too, will the exacting challenge of reflecting the importance of some of the individuals who were actors in the fascinating events of the period.

In order to bring out as many as possible of these important themes and questions, this book is divided into five parts. Parts I and II have chapters on themes that are important throughout the whole of the Stuart age. Parts III, IV and V divide the long seventeenth century into three chronological periods: 1603–42, 1642–60 and 1660–1714.

Revisionism: Its Value and Limitations

If the Stuart age is so exciting and important, why has it become confusing? A major part of the explanation is the impact of 'revisionism', the name given to much historical writing on this period in the 1970s and 1980s that cast serious doubts on many assumptions that had long been held by historians of seventeenth-century England. Revisionism is discussed in later chapters by David Smith, Jason Peacey, David Scott and others, and so there is no need to deal with it in detail here. But since I am going to argue that it has been a source of confusion about the period for some people, I ought to make clear that its impact has not been totally negative. When revisionist writings by G. R. Elton, Conrad Russell and others on England before 1640 first appeared in the 1970s, their impact was refreshing and stimulating (e.g. Elton 1979; Russell 1976). Their methodological emphasis that historians should avoid the danger of hindsight when looking at historical periods and should differentiate between 'necessary' and 'sufficient' causes was timely. Too often in the past historians had allowed their interpretations of periods before episodes like the English Civil War or the Glorious Revolution to be shaped by assumptions that they were the inevitable outcomes of deep-seated, long-term causes. Revisionists persuasively questioned assumptions often made by Marxist historians that political changes were directly related to social and economic developments like 'the rise of the gentry'. They also made a persuasive case for abandoning a Whig interpretation of history that portrayed the long seventeenth century as a lineal and inevitable progress towards 'modernity'. Revisionists effectively demolished Whig assumptions that the seventeenth 'century of revolution' was caused by a long-term rise of a constitutionally aggressive parliament harnessed to a subversive revolutionary creed, Puritanism. Historical writings that sought to play down the extent and seriousness of religious and constitutional ideological differences among the English in the early seventeenth century were stimulating (e.g. Tyacke 1973; Collinson 1983; Burgess 1992, 1996; Sharpe 1983, 1991). So, too, were attempts to rehabilitate the historical reputation of the first Stuart monarch of Britain, James VI and I, and rescue him from 'the wisest fool in Christendom' image with which he had long been associated (Wormald 1983).

The revisionist onslaught on the period after 1640 was equally successful in breathing fresh life into the historical study of the mid-seventeenth century and beyond. In a major work that is still of great value, Anthony Fletcher (1981) stressed the accidental nature of the outbreak of the English Civil War, a war that no one wanted. The fact that in the subtitles of their books on the Civil War Robert Ashton and John Morrill put 'conservatism' before 'revolution' was significant. Instead of emphasizing the 'revolutionary' aspects of the period, as had Christopher Hill and others, Ashton and Morrill brought out the importance of non-commitment and neutralism as reactions to the war (Ashton 1976; Morrill 1976). In an important book published in 1975 Mark Kishlansky couched his explanation for the explosion of the parliamentary New Model Army onto the political stage in 1647 in functional terms that had little to do with religious or political ideologies. Moreover, Colin Davis argued that the Ranters, far from being exponents of one of Hill's 'radical beliefs in the English Revolution', had never existed (Davis 1986; Hill 1972). Revisionism on the period after 1660 also took an interesting anti-Whig line that departed from a common belief that after 1660 England was on a 'high road' that led inevitably to constitutional monarchy, and stressed the growing authoritarianism of the monarchy of Charles II and James II (Western 1972). This was a line that was taken furthest by J. C. D Clark in two ultra-revisionist books that depicted England by the eighteenth century as an *ancien régime* state 'dominated politically, culturally and ideologically by the three pillars of early-modern social order, monarchy, aristocracy and church, which were the landmarks of eighteenth-century England, not the end of divine right monarchy, Lockeian contractualism and constitutional monarchy [and] economic and social changes of a nation about to be transformed into the First Industrial Nation' (Clark 1985, 1986).

These revisionist writings that shifted the focus of historians away from political, religious, economic, social and intellectual change were provocative, stimulating and exciting. But by the late 1980s and early 1990s they had also begun to bring some confusion in their wake. The main reason for this is that the explanations that were put forward, to replace those they had demolished, did not seem powerful enough to bring about great events like the Civil War and regicide. Revisionist arguments that the mid-century crisis was brought about by factors like the impact of war in the late 1620s and late 1630s on an unreformed state structure (Russell 1979; Sharpe 1983, 1991), the ineptness of Charles I (Russell 1990), the rise of a novel theology, Arminianism, imposed on the English church (Tyacke 1973) and the active political role of the nobility (Adamson 1990) are not unimportant. But they were far less persuasive than the arguments used by revisionists to demolish Whig and Marxist explanations. The revisionist tendency to squeeze 'revolution' out of the English Revolution and the role of ideology and beliefs out of political activism also made the major changes that occurred in the British Isles in the long seventeenth century very difficult to understand. The revisionist emphasis on continuity, too, was difficult to fit into a pattern of fundamental changes that undoubtedly did occur between 1603 and 1714 in many aspects of life in the three kingdoms of the British Isles. By the late 1980s these and other limitations of revisionism had become apparent (Cust and Hughes (1989) is the best analysis of these limitations that led to not a little dissatisfaction and much confusion).

The result was that a sustained 'post-revisionist' search was begun for alternative approaches to the history of this period that avoid discredited Whig and Marxist assumptions and yet provide more satisfying and persuasive interpretations of it than the rather narrow 'functional' explanations offered by revisionism of the 1970s and 1980s. In reality, in the writings of many historians, as in the chapters of this book, these new approaches intermingle and overlap. But in what follows four principal approaches are discussed separately – the 'British' context, the 'cultural' context, the social and economic context, and the ideological context – before this introduction ends with the case for putting the main historical emphasis back on the important changes that came about in Stuart Britain.

Reactions to Revisionism (1): The 'British' Context

Building on pioneering work by J. G. A. Pocock and Conrad Russell, some historians during the last few years have advocated this approach with an evangelical fervour (Pocock 1975; Russell 1987; Morrill in Bradshaw and Morrill 1996; Asch 1993; Grant and Stringer 1995; Ellis and Barber 1995). Such has been the vigour with which the virtues of 'new British history' have been championed that it has become almost *de rigueur* to avoid writing English history that is not set in a British and Irish context. Those who write merely the history of England stand in danger of being castigated as 'anglocentric' and, by definition, hopelessly outdated and old-fashioned.

There is much force in these criticisms. Consequently, great care has been taken in structuring this book to ensure that it has a 'British' dimension. The most obvious examples are the first two chapters by Allan Macinnes and Toby Barnard, which survey the interaction between England (and Wales) and Scotland and Ireland, and also deal with the complexities of writing history from a 'British' dimension. Further-more, many other contributors to this book, even when the main focus of their topics is England, take account of developments in the British Isles when the nature of the subject demands it. For example, Michael Hunter in his chapter on scientific thought makes the important point that 'the institution which formed the focus of scientific activity for the last fifty years of the Stuart period, the Royal Society, was always a British rather than an essentially English one'. David Smith, in giving his chapter on early seventeenth-century politics a British context, points out that it is crucial to a full understanding of the early Stuart court that it was 'a British one'. As befits an historian from the University of Edinburgh, Tom Webster emphasizes the import-ance of taking a Scottish, as well as Irish and English, perspective on religion in the early part of the century. He shows that one useful by-product is to qualify the generally complimentary assessment of James VI and I's ecclesiastical policies by some recent revisionist and anglocentric historians. The 'British' context, too, is given a great deal of attention in the three chapters by Jason Peacey, David Scott and Sean Kelsey on the outbreak of the War of Three Kingdoms and its aftermath in the 1640s and 1650s, by John Miller in his contribution on politics after the Restoration, by Colin Brooks in his chapter on the Glorious Revolution, and by other contributors to the book.

All that is as it should be. Most of the following chapters demonstrate the value of taking account of 'the British context'. A key question, though, is whether historians should endeavour to do more than take account, whenever possible, of the intercon-nections between England, Scotland and Ireland. For some of the more vociferous proponents of the 'new British history', like John Morrill, the answer is 'yes' and that those who do not attempt to do so are guilty of writing merely 'enhanced English history'. Others, however, are doubtful whether the kind of holistic British history advocated by Morrill can ever be written. In addition to the chapters by Allan Macinnes and Toby Barnard, those by Tom Webster and David Scott are especially interesting in the different attitudes they take on this issue. Webster forthrightly comments that 'an immediately holistic analysis of the three kingdoms [is] to be performed at the expense of comprehension: cohesion would join with incoherency, as it were'; while Scott is much more positive about the value of the attempt to take more than merely 'an enhanced English history' approach to his topic. Even Scott, though, does not go as far as Morrill appears to advocate, and many historians believe that the value of 'the new British history' suffers from various limitations (Gaunt 1997, 2000).

The first such limitation is that (before 1707) 'Britain' did not exist, making a history of Britain difficult to write. As Tony Claydon (1997) points out in a powerful critique of the 'new British history', the fact that England and Wales, Scotland and Ireland did not have common political institutions, cultures and ideologies, let alone economic and social structures, makes such a venture a near impossibility. The chapters by Macinnes and Barnard, too, show that very few people at the time had a vision of creating 'Britain' or thought of themselves as being 'British'. Certainly most English people did not often put Scotland or Ireland at the centre of their thoughts and, when they did, their main aim seems to have been to make these countries as much like England as they could (Canny 2001). 'Most [English] pamphleteers', in Barnard's striking words, 'aspired to make Ireland "West England", though not "West Britain"'. The anglicization policies of the Cromwellian Protectorate in Scotland and Ireland were but an extreme example of that phenomenon (Coward 2002, ch. 7). Furthermore, it is highly likely that undue stress on the British context can lead to an exaggeration of the impact of the Scottish and Irish context on England. Conrad Russell is probably guilty of this in his account of the period immediately before the outbreak of civil war in England in 1642. By the late 1630s and early 1640s there were enough purely English issues to divide English people and bring about the serious polarization that took place before the outbreak of war in 1642 (Russell 1991; Fletcher 1993). Moreover, as John Adamson has argued, to give equal weight to all three kingdoms may be 'politically correct, but it is far from clear that it is also correct historically'. His point is that England was by far and away the most powerful and wealthy of the three kingdoms and that what happened there was therefore more important than events in Scotland and Ireland. 'If reaching that conclusion [that the outcome of civil war in England had more important consequences than the outcome of conflicts elsewhere in the British Isles] seems culpably anglocentric, then so perhaps were the seventeenth-century British Isles' (Adamson 1998: 25, 19).

Contributors to this book were asked to bear in mind where their fields of history were heading. My editorial contribution to the debate on the 'new British history' is to make the point that during the last ten years its influence has been very beneficial in forcing historians of England to take full account of the British context, as contributors to this book have done. Perhaps, though, that is the limit of its usefulness, and historians, instead of pursuing the Holy Grail of a holistic British history, ought now to be widening their horizons even further by putting English history in a European context, as has been done by some historians (see, for example, Murdoch 2001;

Smuts 1996). This is a point made by some contributors to this book, including Michael Braddick, Sean Kelsey and Colin Brooks, as well as by Allan Macinnes and Toby Barnard. Equally important is the need for British historians to cast their gazes even further than that, by taking account of the 'Atlantic and Asian context', which is just one of the many lessons to be drawn from Nicholas Canny's chapter.

Reactions to Revisionism (2): The 'Cultural' Context

A second prominent trend in recent writings on this period has been an attempt to integrate the history of the Stuart age with intellectual, literary and cultural developments. If anything, the benefits of taking this so-called 'cultural (or linguistic) turn' have been trumpeted with even more evangelical fervour than has been shown by those proclaiming the virtues of the 'new British history'. One of its most ardent proponents has urged historians 'to pay attention to the representations that contemporaries presented of (and to) themselves: to urge a move from politics concerned (anachronistically) as the business of institutions, bureaucracies and officers to the broader politics of discourse and symbols, anxieties and aspirations, myths and memories' (Sharpe 2000: 3). Clearly there is a danger that historians might get too carried away by the potential value of this approach. It is far from certain that, when it has been fully followed, the history of the early modern period will be totally 're-mapped' or (in the words of Ronald Hutton) that 'soon the traditional preoccupation [of seventeenth-century historians] with Civil War soldiers and statesmen will seem . . . part of a lost world' (Hutton 1999: 57, in a review of Sharpe and Zwicker 1998).

But there is no doubt that the history of the Stuart age has already benefited (and that it will continue to do so in the future) from the work of those who bridge the gap between history and other disciplines, principally the history of art and of literature. (For an excellent illustration of what has already been achieved, see the essays in Sharpe and Lake 1994). That is why this book includes two contributions from specialists in those two disciplines, Thomas Corns and Tim Wilks, whose chapters on 'literature and history' and 'art, architecture and politics' explain the ways in which the cultural context can open up new and exciting aspects of the history of Stuart Britain. Corns makes the point that not all historians have neglected to use literary sources in the past. 'There is nothing new in a hermeneutic that reads seventeenth-century literature in terms of its relationship to seventeenth-century political history', he writes, at the same time paying a well-deserved compliment to the pioneering work of historians like Christopher Hill. Corns quite rightly reminds historians that 'in the ascendancy of revisionist historiography the contribution of the Marxist tradition in this field is too lightly set aside'. Yet his chapter shows that in recent years the main drive to treat seventeenth-century literature in its historical context and vice versa has come from literary scholars in a process known as 'the new historicism'. Corns points to the limitations as well as the value of this approach, an analysis from which historians have much to learn. The lists of references at the end of the chapters by Corns and Wilks are excellent illustrations of the valuable influence on the study of the history of Stuart Britain of the 'cultural turn'.

One major effect of this approach has been to encourage historians to follow art historians and literary scholars in using, not only the work of artists and writers long considered to be part of the 'great' canons of artistic and literary tradition, but also a much wider range of contemporary texts and images than ever before. Many of the chapters in this book reflect the valuable influence of this approach. This is especially true of the three chapters on political thought by Malcolm Smuts on the early seventeenth century, Colin Davis on the mid-seventeenth century and Justin Champion on the period between 1660 and 1714 . None of them, of course, ignores the importance of the 'great' political thinkers of the seventeenth century, like Thomas Hobbes and John Locke. Indeed Davis writes of Hobbes that 'however much we integrate him with the debates of the 1640s and 1650s, there are still a number of respects in which he remains a novel thinker'. Yet the importance of the 'cultural turn' is explicitly apparent in his chapter, as it is in those by Smuts and Champion. Smuts's chapter begins with an excellent paragraph that illustrates the way that work by literary and cultural historians has brought about a reconceptualization of 'the history of political thought' 'We need', he writes,

> to reconstruct the vocabularies and linguistic rules through which political discourse was conducted in the past, rather than concentrating only on a few canonical thinkers . . . [Historians of political thought] have paid too little attention to the vocabularies and assumptions revealed by sources like diplomatic correspondence, policy memoranda and newsletters. Nor have they made extensive use of imaginative literature, representational culture and political ritual, although literary scholars and cultural historians have examined ideas expressed through these genres.

Champion, too, echoes this theme in his chapter: 'To understand the nature of political thought between 1660 and 1714 is not ultimately to engage with the great canonical figures . . . It can best be reconstructed by charting the cut and thrust of political and religious exchanges amongst the minor figures, the priests, the pamphleteers, the editors and re-publishers of the canons of earlier texts.'

Another striking example of the influence of the 'cultural turn' on the history of Stuart Britain seen in this book is its impact on the history of the practice of politics, as well as on the history of political thought. Ian Atherton's keynote essay on 'the press and popular political opinion' is a wide-ranging survey of work that has been done recently on manuscript and printed sources that were once considered to be ephemeral and unimportant by historians, but which have now been exploited by historians to splendid effect. Atherton's chapter leaves no room for doubt that the political process in Stuart Britain spread widely outside the court to include many more people in the country than was once imagined. As Atherton's chapter shows, much about popular involvement in politics and the influence of 'public opinion' remains uncertain: for example, how relevant to what happened is the concept of 'the public sphere' developed by the German sociologist Jürgen Habermas? Did popular political awareness grow in a linear way in seventeenth-century Britain? But what is certain is that definitions of 'politics' and 'political culture' have been widened by political historians in order to take account of 'public opinion' and 'popular' involvement in politics. 'The existence in early Stuart England of a politically well-informed and engaged public' and 'the growth of political awareness and assertiveness of the people' (in the words of David Scott in his chapter) are now well-established features of the history of early Stuart Britain. Moreover, later chapters on political and religious debates in the mid-seventeenth century (for example, the chapter by Ann Hughes) and in the later Stuart period (for example, the chapters by John Miller, Colin Brooks and Mark Knights) all bring out the same theme.

Reactions to Revisionism (3): The Social and Economic Context

A third post-revisionist historiographical trend has been the revitalization of social and economic approaches to the history of Stuart Britain. One of the most welcome aspects of this trend is the way in which the gap between religious–political history and economic–social history has begun to be bridged. One unfortunate side-effect of the revisionist onslaught on teleological history noted above was that political historians neglected the social and economic context. Significantly, although his influence remained strong with the wider reading public, the reputation in the academic world of Christopher Hill, the man who had done more than anyone else to develop a Marxist, socio-economic interpretation of the history of Stuart Britain, declined rapidly. Indeed, as Michael Hunter's criticism of Hill's work on the history of scientific thought shows (chapter 11, this volume), the backlash against Hill is still strong. (See also a critique of Hill in Morrill 1993.) Keith Wrightson (1993), in an influential essay, identified other reasons than the reaction against Marxist economic and social determinism that accounted for the way in which economic and social history lost its place at the centre of interest of many historians of the Stuart age.

There is still a long way to go, but there are encouraging signs that this situation is now being remedied. Works on the social and economic causes of the English Revolution and on the social and economic impact of the War of Three Kingdoms that have been published recently have gone some way towards reintegrating social and economic history into the mainstream history of Stuart Britain (e.g. Brenner 1993; Carlton 1992; Bennett 2000). As yet the impact of this is not as noticeable as the influence of 'the new British history' and 'the cultural turn'. Yet it is having an effect. Craig Muldrew's keynote chapter on 'economic and urban development' surveys recent themes on this topic; while Michael Braddick's and Steve Hindle's chapters, just like their recent books on the formation of the English state, are impossible to categorize as either 'social' or 'political' history (Braddick 2000; Hindle 2000).

Elizabeth Foyster's essay on 'gender relations' also demonstrates that social historians are beginning to force historians of Stuart Britain to revise their conception of 'politics' in even more fundamental ways than are historians who advocate 'the cultural turn'. Her chapter puts a powerful case for the 'need to adjust our notion of what is "political" history, and to examine the exercise of power and authority beyond the central institutions of church and state . . . [and to] include the family, household and neighbourhood into our definition of political arenas'. Foyster also claims that 'gender history lets us look at aspects of the past in new ways, and suggests a very different narrative to Stuart history from that which has been traditionally taught'. Whether future research will bear out that claim remains to be seen, but there is no doubt that there is much scope for reinterpreting and revising the history of this period in light of the social and economic context.

Reactions to Revisionism (4): The Ideological Context

Perhaps the most important post-revisionist historiographical trend is the renewed emphasis on the importance of beliefs and ideas in the historical process. There is fairly general agreement that a principal weakness of revisionism was to play 'far too little attention to ideas and ideology in an era when men spoke passionately about values and beliefs' (Sharpe 2000: 10). This is why this book includes chapters on political thought and religion in all three of its chronological parts. Taken together with the chapters on the political history of the period, they explain why and how historians have successfully reinstated ideology at the centre of the politics and society of Stuart Britain. So strong is this theme in most of the chapters in this book, that it needs little editorial emphasis.

One aspect of it, though, is worthy of comment here. This is the continuity in the nature of ideological debates and discussions throughout the whole of the Stuart period. The chapters on religion by Tom Webster on the early seventeenth century, by Ann Hughes on the mid-century and John Spurr on the period after 1660 demonstrate how religion retained its central position in the lives of most people in Stuart Britain. Unsurprisingly, therefore, religion was always at the heart of political debates in this period. This point is made forcefully in the chapters on the history of political thought by Malcolm Smuts, Colin Davis and Justin Champion. As Colin Davis writes, 'consolidating the Reformation remained a central theme of political discourse throughout the period'. Moreover, as is apparent from those chapters and the chapters on political practice, there was also a great deal of continuity in the ideas and issues that formed the staple of political debates throughout the whole of the Stuart age.

Reactions to Revisionism (5): Change

These elements of continuity are extremely important aspects of the history of this period. Yet it is important to stress, as do many of the chapters in this book, that the Stuart age witnessed seismic change in most areas of life. One of the important conclusions of Ann Hughes's chapter on religion in the mid-century is that the period marked a major change towards religious plurality and diversity. 'It transpired', writes Hughes, 'that the revolutionary decades had fractured Protestant unity once and for all. In the place of the godly church most parliamentarians had expected in the early 1640s, a religious market-place had emerged.' Michael Braddick's chapter shows clearly the decisive changes that affected the nature of the government of Britain in the long seventeenth century. During the Stuart age Britain was transformed from a personal monarchy into an impersonal state in which the role of parliament was now immeasurably strengthened in comparison with the start of the century. 'Before the Civil War', according to Braddick, 'perhaps three quarters of [government] revenues were not under the control of parliament, and the proportion was declining. After the Civil War non-parliamentary revenues provided only about 10 per cent of total income and by the 1690s that figure had dwindled to around 3 per cent.'

As Braddick's chapter shows, this was paralleled by the changed position by the end of the period of Britain in world affairs. The emergence of Great Britain in 1707 after the reluctant union of England and Scotland in 1707 denoted much more than a change in name. By this stage, in comparison with its weak position in European affairs for much of the seventeenth century (apart from the period of the Common-wealth and Cromwellian Protectorate in the 1650s), Britain was a Great Power in the world. Nicholas Canny's and Craig Muldrew's chapters also point to important changes that affected the economy and society of the British Isles between 1603 and 1714. Canny stresses that what happened after 1660 'can be attributed to experience gained and strategy decisions taken in preceding decades'. But both he and Muldrew bring out the more prosperous state of all the major sections of the economy (agriculture, manufacturing and, above all, trade) by the end of this period, as well as the improvements that had taken place in the standards of living enjoyed by many (though obviously not all) inhabitants of Britain and Ireland. Another major change is emphasized in Michael Hunter's important chapter on scientific thought. 'Late seventeenth-century Britain' he concludes, 'played a key role in the emergence of a recognizably modern experimental method.'

As was pointed out earlier in this introduction, revisionist historians quite rightly reacted against those who interpreted historical development as a series of changes towards 'modernity'. One of the fascinating challenges faced nowadays by students of seventeenth-century Britain is how to analyse changes like those touched on in the last paragraph without falling into that particular Whig trap. One way of doing this is to acknowledge that 'recognizably modern' aspects of government, beliefs, and so on, coexisted (quite often comfortably) with those that are alien to 'modern' life and ideas. Michael Hunter succeeds in showing how the 'recognizably modern experi-mental method' that emerged in the seventeenth century was quite consistent with a traditional religious-based world view. Ian Atherton in his chapter wrestles with a related problem of how to interpret the changes in popular awareness of political issues without seeing them simply as part of 'the Whig trajectory from manuscript to print'. Indeed one of Atherton's most striking conclusions is that in Stuart Britain 'manuscript news was more highly prized and held to be more reliable than its printed cousin'.

In other areas of life in Stuart Britain that saw major changes, too, one can see the persistence of many traditional features: for example, the continued importance of patrimonialism, patronage and the personality of the monarch in government, along-side the growing power of parliaments and impersonal bureaucracy; illiteracy and ignorance of and indifference to politics alongside the appearance of an informed 'public opinion'; poverty and economic instability alongside 'the commercial revolu-tion'; and evidence of religious intolerance alongside the emergence of religious diversity and plurality. Clearly, as the chapters in this book demonstrate, Stuart Britain was undergoing a profound period of change. But perhaps a better map to use to chart what was happening is not one that traces a 'high road' to 'modernity', but one that reflects the country as it was: a country that was neither 'medieval' nor 'modern'. Stuart Britain developed a distinctive polity, distinctive political and religious mental-ities, and a distinctive economic and social order that, when taken together, are best described as 'early modern'.

NOTE

1 'Three Kingdoms', not 'Four Kingdoms', is preferred here because by the seventeenth century the integration of England and Wales into one kingdom was all but total.

REFERENCES

Adamson, J. 1990: 'The baronial context of the English Civil War', *Transactions of the Royal Historical Society*, 5th series, vol. 40 (reprinted in R. Cust and A. Hughes, eds, *The English Civil War*, London, 1997).

Adamson, J. 1998: 'The English context of the British Civil Wars', *History Today*, vol. 48.

Asch, R. (ed.) 1993: *The Three Nations – a Common History?* Bochum.

Ashton, R. 1976: *The English Civil War: Conservatives and Revolution, 1603–41*: London.

Bennett, M. 2000: *The Civil Wars Experienced: Britain and Ireland, 1638–51*: London.

Braddick, M. 2000: *State Formation in Early Modern England*: London.

Bradshaw B. and Morrill, J. (eds) 1996: *The British Problem c.1534–1707: State Formation in the Atlantic Archipelago*: Basingstoke.

Brenner, R. 1993: *Merchants and Revolution: Commercial Change, Political Conflict and London's Overseas Traders, 1550–1653*: Cambridge.

Burgess, G. 1992: *The Politics of the Ancient Constitution: An Introduction to English Political Thought*: London.

Burgess, G. 1996: *Absolute Monarchy and the Stuart Constitution*: New Haven, CT.

Canny, N. 2001: *Making Ireland British, 1580–1650*: Oxford.

Carlton, C. 1992: *Going to the Wars: The Experience of the British Civil Wars, 1638–51*: London.

Clark, J. C. D. 1985: *English Society: Social Structure and Political Practice during the Eighteenth Century*: Cambridge.

Clark, J. C. D. 1986: *Revolution and Rebellion: State and Society in England in the Seventeenth and Eighteenth Centuries*: Cambridge.

Claydon, T. 1997: 'Problems with the British Problem', *Parliamentary History*, vol. 16.

Collinson, P. 1983: *The Religion of Protestants*: Oxford.

Coward, B. 2002: *The Cromwellian Protectorate 1653–59*: Manchester.

Cust, R. and Hughes, A. (eds) 1989: *Conflict in Early Stuart England: Studies in Reform and Politics 1603–42*: Harlow.

Davis, J. C. 1986: *Fear, Myth and History: The Ranters and Historians*: Cambridge.

Ellis S. and Barber, S. (eds) 1995: *Conquest and Union: Forming a British State, 1485–1725*: Harlow.

Elton, G. R. 1979: 'Parliament and the Tudors: its functions and fortunes', *Historical Journal*, vol. 22.

Fletcher, A. 1981: *The Outbreak of the English Civil War*: London.

Fletcher, A. 1993: 'Power, myth and realities', *Historical Journal*, vol. 36.

Gaunt, P. 1997: *The British Civil Wars, 1637–51*: London.

Gaunt, P. (ed.) 2000: *The English Civil War*: Oxford.

Grant, A. and Stringer, K. (eds) 1995: *Uniting the Kingdom*: London.

Hill, C. 1972: *The World Turned Upside Down: Radical Beliefs during the English Revolution*: London.

Hindle, S. 2000: *The State and Social Change in England, 1558–1640*: London.

Hutton, R. 1999: *History Today*, vol. 49 (5).

Kishlansky, K. 1975: *The Rise of the New Model Army*. Cambridge.

Morrill, J. 1976: *The Revolt of the Provinces: Conservatives and Revolutionaries in the English Civil War 1603–42*: Harlow.

Morrill, J. 1993: *The Nature of the English Revolution*: Harlow.

Morrill, J. 1999: 'The war(s) of the three kingdoms.' In G. Burgess, ed., *The New British History: Founding a Modern State 1603–1715*: London.

Murdoch, S. 2001: *Scotland and the Thirty Years' War*. Leiden.

Pocock, J. G. A. 1975: 'British history: a plea for a new subject', *Journal of Modern History*, vol. 4.

Russell, C. (ed.) 1973: *The Origins of the English Civil War*. Basingstoke.

Russell, C. 1976: 'Parliamentary history in perspective, 1604–29', *History*, vol. 61.

Russell, C. 1979: *Parliaments and English Politics, 1621–29*: Oxford.

Russell, C. 1987: 'The British Problem and the English Civil War', *History*, vol. 72.

Russell, C. 1990: *The Causes of the English Civil War*. Oxford.

Russell, C. 1991: *The Fall of the British Monarchies*. Oxford.

Sharpe, K. 1983: 'The personal rule of Charles I.' In H. Tomlinson, ed., *Before the English Civil War*. London.

Sharpe, K. 1991: *The Personal Rule of Charles I*: New Haven, CT.

Sharpe, K. 2000: *Remapping Early Modern England: The Culture of Seventeenth-Century Politics*. Cambridge.

Sharpe, K. and Lake, P. (eds) 1994: *Culture and Politics in Early Modern England*: Basingstoke.

Sharpe, K. and Zwicker, S. (eds) 1998: *Refiguring Revolutions: Aesthetics and Politics from the English Revolution to the Romantic Revolution*: Berkeley, CA.

Smuts, R. M. (ed.) 1996: *The Stuart Court and Europe: Essays in Politics and Political Culture*: Cambridge.

Tyacke, N. R. N. 1973: 'Puritans, Arminians and counter-revolution.' In C. Russell, ed., *The Origins of the English Civil War*. Basingstoke.

Western, J. R. 1972: *Monarchy and Revolution: The English State in the 1680s*. London.

Wormald, J. 1983: 'James VI and I: two kings or one?', *History*, vol. 68.

Wrightson, K. 1993: 'The enclosure of English social history.' In A. Wilson, ed., *Rethinking Social History: English Society and its Interpretations*. Manchester.

PART I

Stuart Britain and the Wider World

The Multiple Kingdoms of Britain and Ireland: The 'British Problem'

ALLAN I. MACINNES

The 'British Problem' in the seventeenth century is as much historiographic as historic. The Whig tradition of progressive empiricism, grounded on the 'Glorious Revolution' (1688–91), dominated the historiography of Britain and Ireland as multiple kingdoms well into the twentieth century. The recent concerns of the 'new British histories' with the Stuart court and baronialism, with religious establishments and with the resolution of divergence through institutional union, have verged not so much on revisionism as neo-Whiggery. Indeed, the primacy accorded to national identities, civil wars and, above all, state formation seriously questions whether the 'new British histories' have marked a distinctive shift in focus away from Whiggish concerns with nation building. For the problematic nature of 'New British Histories' is rooted in an overwhelmingly insular and introspective historiography.

I

Within the closed ambit of England, Scotland and Ireland as multiple kingdoms, comparative history has tended towards multifarious discussions on identity. Seemingly divergent identities within the multiple kingdoms have been resolved constructively by multi-polar or multi-layered approaches (Kidd 1998: 321–42), which carry added resonance when applied to the wider Stuart world of the seventeenth century. But such wider contextualizing must take account of apocalyptic visions as well as baronial politics, commercial networks as well as confessional allegiances, representative images as well as written texts. The 'new British histories' have given particular focus to the civil wars 'in' and 'of' the three kingdoms during the mid-seventeenth century (Pocock 1996: 172–91), albeit Irish links to Spain and France have questioned the validity of this insular construct (cf. Ohlmeyer 1993). However, the Scottish Covenanters, as later the Commonwealth, viewed the civil wars as a fight 'for' the three kingdoms. From this perspective, civil wars within the British Isles were part of the wider European theatre of the Thirty Years' War (cf. Murdoch 2001). Through the Covenanting Movement, which emerged in opposition to the prerogative rule of Charles I throughout the British Isles, the Scots adopted a proactive role in promoting federative alliances with the United Provinces and Sweden as well as England between 1640 and 1645. Covenanting Scotland, as the new Israel, was preparing the ground for not just European but global reordering once the forces of godliness had vanquished those of the Antichrist (Williamson 1989: 7–30).

The 'new British histories', no less than their Whig predecessors, have tended to view political unification as part of a grand narrative, if not a manifest British destiny. State formation in early modern Europe, driven by sustained geopolitical competition, was characterized by the emergence of regimes which were absolutist or constitutional and supported by infrastructures that were bureaucratic or patrimonial (Ertman 1997: 6–34). While the composition of early modern states can be explained in terms of these four variables, the actual process of state formation was achieved usually by one of two methods described either as acquisition and association (Elliot 1992: 48–71) or conquest and coalescence (Greengrass 1991: 1–24). Thus, England had effectively absorbed Cornwall and Wales by 1543 through parliamentary incorporation, administrative cohesion in church and state, and the political if not the cultural integration of the ruling elites. However, Ireland, despite being declared a subordinate kingdom in 1541, was not incorporated into a composite English kingdom. Successive Tudor monarchs failed to effect conquest and achieved little integration outwith the Pale. The limited advent of the Protestant Reformation in Ireland further compounded this failure (Ellis 1995: 40–63). The alternative 'new British' narrative of state formation has cast the multiple kingdoms on a transitional stage from a composite England to a unified kingdom of Britain and Ireland marked by parliamentary incorporation, administrative and religious uniformity, and elite integration. The accession of James VI of Scotland to the English throne in 1603 paved the way for the United Kingdom of Great Britain in 1707, to which Ireland was added in 1801 (cf. Murdoch 1998).

Yet the move from regal union to parliamentary union in the seventeenth century was neither inevitable nor seamless. The English parliament rejected full union with Scotland in 1607 and 1670, and overtures for Irish political incorporation in 1703 (cf. Smyth 2001). For their part, the Scottish Estates resisted incorporating overtures in 1689 and 1702, albeit, like the Irish parliament, they were forced into an unwanted union at the behest of the English Commonwealth in 1651, repackaged as the Protectorate from 1654. During the Restoration era, Scottish moves towards commercial union initiated in 1664 were rebuffed in 1668. A similar English initiative never got off the drawing board in 1674.

II

The determination of James VI of Scotland to project himself as James I of Great Britain and Ireland laid the foundations for the Stuarts viewing themselves as an imperial British dynasty, not just as rulers of multiple kingdoms. This dynastic resolve had firm intellectual roots in his ancient and native kingdom, not least because tangible British harmony enabled the Scots to counter traditional English claims to suzerainty. Indeed, aspirations for union, which were given a particular fillip by the Protestant Reformation in both Scotland and England, had a long pedigree founded on the concept of empire that had exclusive sovereignty within the British Isles (Mason 1998: 242–69). At the same time, traditional English dominance of the three kingdoms, characterized by the interchangeability of Britain for England, was a contemporaneous historiographic problem rooted in medieval myth refocused by Renaissance scholarship.

The anglocentric dominance of British history rested on Norman–Welsh myth-making of the twelfth century. The construct of Britain was derived from Brut, the epic Trojan hero who moved to Rome before progressing through Gaul from where he and his followers settled the whole of the British Isles. Although Britain was divided up among the successors of Brut during the first millennium BC, anglocentric dominance was reasserted under Roman occupation. Constantine the Great, who spread Christianity throughout the Roman Empire and transferred the capital from Rome to Byzantium at the outset of the fourth century AD, was both born and acclaimed emperor in Britain. Following the fall of Rome, the Britons were subject to invasions from Picts, Scots and Saxons that forced them to the margins in Wales and Cornwall. However, King Arthur had led a British revival in the early sixth century, which expanded his dominion throughout the British Isles and into France. Successive conquests by the Saxons, Danes and Norsemen tied epic British heroism to the march of civility as institutionalized through kingship, the common law and post-Reformation Protestantism. This mythical perception of Britain was reinforced by Welsh antiquarians, keen to identify Wales as the enduring heartland of the original Britons, as well as by English chroniclers like Raphael Holinshed during the sixteenth century. The construct of a territorially expansive Britain was rationalized by the antiquarian William Camden, in his final version of *Britannia* prepared in 1607 (Woolf 1990: 55–64, 115–25).

Camden's concept of Britain underwrote English claims to be an exclusive empire, that the English were an elect Protestant nation with a Christian tradition under an Erastian episcopacy unbeholden to Rome, and that its civilizing mission had been refined by conquest and invasion. Thus, London, the old Roman foundation, was now the metropolitan capital of a composite British Empire whose territories encompassed the Anglo-Saxon heptarchy as well as Wales and Cornwall. This composite empire could not only lay claim to Ireland but also to that part of Scotland formerly held by the Picts. Though barbarians, they were not of Gothic strain, as alleged for the Irish and the Scots, but actually Britons who had lived outwith the boundaries of Roman civilization; the classical demarcation which ensured that such Gothic influences as the Saxons, Danes and Norsemen enriched rather than destroyed Britain. These northern boundaries, which were settled at the Forth–Clyde division of Scotland, conformed to the division between the ancient Scottish kingdom of Alba and the Saxon kingdom of Northumbria. Following his accession to the English throne, the founder of the Stuart dynasty's imperial vanity was certainly enhanced by the notion that he was the fabled heir to both Constantine the Great and King Arthur, as well as the more prosaic Tudors. At the same time, the repeated print runs of Camden's *Britannia* throughout the seventeenth century fuelled rather than dispelled English claims to superiority over Scotland and Ireland as well as Wales.

That the multiple kingdoms were actually an imperial composite was illustrated graphically by the cartographer John Speed, whose *Theatre of the British Empire*, first published in 1611, remained the template for the subsequent mapping of Britain and Ireland for much of the seventeenth century. Following Camden, England was depicted as a composite kingdom based on the Anglo-Saxon heptarchy. Scotland was also a composite of the Scots, the Picts and the Isles; Ireland of its four provinces of Munster, Leinster, Connacht and Ulster together with Meth; even Wales had a tripartite division of North, South and Powys. Subsequent abridged versions of his maps, though purportedly depicting Britain and Ireland as multiple kingdoms, still adhered to the basic structure of a composite empire. The barbarous, if noble, representation of a male Britannia was refined by Romans, Saxons, Danes and Normans in the guise of classical heroes (Moreland and Bannister 2000: 213–16). The composite representation of Camden and Speed, which effectively appended Scotland, Ireland and the rest of the British Isles onto detailed topographical descriptions of the English and Welsh shires, was accorded international recognition by the leading Dutch cartographer, Wilhelm Blaeu. His map of *Britannia* was published posthumously in 1645 (Goss 1990: 72–3).

While James I glorified in portraying himself as Constantine *redivivus*, he also brought into play Scottish origin myths to consolidate his shaping of a composite British Empire (Mason 1987: 60–84). Largely the product of the Wars of Independence in the late thirteenth and fourteenth centuries, these Scottish myths borrowed heavily from the Irish origin mythology, the first to be articulated within the multiple kingdoms from the eleventh century. In contrast to the Roman imperial element, which the English shared with other aggressive northern powers in early modern Europe, such as the Swedes and the Lithuanians (Rowell 2000: 65–92), the Scottish myths stressed civic origins. Gathelus of Athens, having sojourned to Egypt, married Scota, daughter of the Pharaoh, shortly before Moses led the Israeli exodus. In the wake of the Pharaoh's destruction in the Red Sea, Gathelus and Scota wandered to Iberia, from whence their heirs moved to Ireland and then to Scotland, where an autonomous kingdom was established in 330 BC under Fergus son of Ferchar, a contemporary of Alexander the Great. Around AD 403, having overcome an alliance of the Romans and the Picts which temporarily forced their return to Ireland, Fergus son of Earc re-established the kingdom of the Scots which was expanded under Kenneth MacAlpine in 843 to include that of the Picts. Despite continuing English hostility, their descendants went on to consolidate the borders of Scotland from the Solway to the Tweed in the eleventh century. This legend not only underwrote Scottish pretensions to the longest unbroken line of kings in Europe, but also the imperial aspirations of their Stewart monarchy. For Achaius, the sixty-fifth king of Scots, was leagued in friendship, not clientage, with Charlemagne, the Holy Roman Emperor, around 790; a league which had laid the foundation of the 'auld alliance' between Scotland and France that was consolidated by the Wars of Independence. The advent of the Reformation gave added significance to the legend, for the spread of Christianity from the Scots to the Picts by Columba and his followers during the sixth century was viewed as proto-Presbyterianism untrammelled by an Erastian episcopate or by Rome.

Fergus MacEarc, who actually ruled around AD 500, was the first authentic king of Scots. His designation as fortieth in line from Fergus MacFerchar was a fabrication notably embellished by Hector Boece in his *Scotorum Historiae* of 1527, when Anglo-Scottish relations had degenerated towards the real prospect of English conquest of Scotland. Six years earlier, Boece's fellow countryman and Sorbonne scholar John Mair had proposed an alternative strategy offering permanent resolution for Anglo-Scottish conflict. His *Historia Maioris Britannia* discounted the mythical origins of both countries, rejected English claims to superiority and distanced him from his country's xenophobia towards England. Mair was an eloquent advocate of British union through dynastic alliance, as that between James IV of Scotland and Margaret

Tudor of England in 1503, an alliance that eventually brought their great-grandchild James VI to the English throne. James VI was notably indebted to Mair's imperial vision of a composite British Empire. However, this vision requires wider international contextualizing, not least for Spanish copyright on the sole status of superpower having established an Iberian world empire when the Stuarts commenced their British dynasty (McGinnis and Williamson 2002: 70–93).

Mair was the principal Iberian apologist within the three kingdoms. However, the main opponents of world empire within the three kingdoms were also Scots, especially John Knox from a biblical and apocalyptic British perspective and George Buchanan as an exponent of aristocratic republicanism. Both viewed post-Reformation Scotland as a virtuous commonwealth that should be open to wider federative arrangements to counter universal monarchy. Buchanan had firmed up Boece's fabricated line of kings in order to demonstrate the capacity of the Scottish Commonwealth to remove tyrannical monarchs. This right of resistance to monarchy, which upheld trusteeship over sovereignty in *De Iure Regni* (1579), made the book a ready target for proscription by successive Stuarts. The foremost classical humanist within the three kingdoms in the sixteenth century had afforded an incisive critique of hierarchic kingship that was to prove receptive to Scottish Covenanters and British Whigs as the seventeenth century unfolded (Mason 1994: 3–16)

When seeking a distinctive counterpoint to the composite delineation of Great Britain by Camden and Speed, Dutch typographers and cartographers turned to Buchanan, supplemented by Boece. In 1627 Bonaventure and Abraham Elzevirus published at Leiden a topographical compilation, *Respublica, sive Status Regni Scotiae et Hiberniae*. Their selective representation, together with a summative history of the 'auld alliance' with France, underlined Scotland's status as a commonwealth independent of England. For Ireland, however, the evidence drawn predominantly from Camden and Speed was loaded in favour of its status as an English dependency. This differentiation was sustained by the publication of Joan Blaeu's *Grand Atlas* in which Scotland was covered in book 12 of the edition first published in Amsterdam in 1654. (Ireland, though recognized as a distinct European entity in book 13, was published as a supplement.) The accompanying topographical sections were prepared primarily by Sir Robert Gordon of Stralloch, an Aberdeenshire laird firmly wedded to the Graeco-Egyptian origins of the Scots, to the antiquity of the Scottish kingdom and to the emphatic rebuttal of Camden (Goss 1990: 84–5). Neither Blaeu nor his contributors to the volumes for all three kingdoms had ready access to the one work of Renaissance scholarship that served as a corrective to both the antiquarian pretensions of the Scots and the hegemonic claims of the anglocentric Britons. *Foras Feasa ar Éirinn* by Séathrún Céitinn (Geoffrey Keating) was a history purged of fable but written in Irish around 1634 and subsequently circulated in manuscript only.

Keating's refutation of the kingship line fabricated by Boece and Buchanan was part of his wider rejection that Irish kings were ever dependent on Arthur or any other king of the Britons. Ireland was never part of any foreign dominion prior to the incursion of the Normans from England at the behest of the papacy in the twelfth century. At the same time, his underlying historical purpose was to demonstrate that Ireland was not a barbaric backwater requiring civilization through conquest. In the common classical Gaelic tradition both the native Irish and the Scots who migrated from Ireland were designated the *Gael* and all other inhabitants and invaders within

Britain and Ireland were deemed the *Gall*. The Gael was associated with epic heroism, scholarship and fidelity and the Gall with the foreign and alien cultures that had come initially through the Gallic sojourns of Brutus and were perpetuated in Britain by the invasions of the Romans, Saxons, Danes and Normans. Thus, Camden's civilizing mission of the Britons against the Irish and Scottish Goths was turned on its head. The Irish were comparable to any nation in Europe in relation to valour, learning and steadfastness in the Catholic faith. But Keating, as befitting a descendant of an Old English family, was also concerned to ensure that due place was given to the contribution of the *Sean-Gallaibh* ('old-foreigners': the Old English who came in from the time of Henry II) as well as the Gaelic Irish in sustaining Catholicism. Both groups should be designated *Eireannaigh*, that is, the Catholic Irish in contrast to the *Nua-Gallaibh*, effectively the Protestant settlers who arrived as New English under the Tudors and as New British under the Stuarts. Nonetheless, this Catholic nation building remained located within the contexts of Britain and Ireland as multiple kingdoms. Although validating the national dynamic that gave rise to the Irish Confederation of Catholics during the 1640s, Keating was primarily concerned to legitimize the Irish acceptability of the Stuart dynasty through such traditional mechanisms as providence, prophecy and legitimacy (Ó Buachalla 1987: 1–8). Indeed, these same mechanisms ensured that the Catholic Confederation sought *rapprochement* with Charles I as the legitimate king of Ireland throughout the 1640s (Clarke 2000: 35–55).

The shift from a Tudor to a Stuart dynasty in 1603 had been particularly welcomed in Ireland. Unlike the Tudors whose rights to Ireland were due to conquest, James could claim direct descent not only from Fergus MacEarc who had arrived from Ulster as first king of the Scottish Gaels, but also from the kings of the other provinces of Muster, Leinster and Connacht. His right to the high kingship of Ireland was endorsed theologically. Under the leadership of Peter Lombard, Archbishop of Armagh, the Roman Catholic Church in Ireland taught that James, despite his Protestantism, was *de iure* king of Ireland and entitled to temporal allegiance (Ó Buachalla 1996: 148–94). This allegiance was eagerly affirmed by the Irish parliament in 1613, notwithstanding the writings of continental Jesuits that a heretical monarch could be deposed at papal instigation; writings which moved James to a vigorous defence of his independent empire to which unequivocal allegiance was owed by all subjects, whether Catholic or Protestant. Plantations in Ulster and Connacht dashed the hopes of Irish Catholics that allegiance to the Stuart dynasty would be reciprocated by liberty of conscience. Nonetheless, Keating and other clerical agents of the Counter-Reformation endorsed the aims of the Catholic political elite for an accommodation with the crown to ensure that Ireland would be treated as an equal partner – not as a confessionally disadvantaged, satellite kingdom – within a composite British Empire (Clarke 1978: 57–72).

III

Non-anglocentric sensibilities were partially accommodated on the flags, seals and emblems projecting the Stuarts as an imperial British dynasty. Thus, the maps drawn by Speed and reproduced subsequently for the Blaeu family were embossed with a composite imperial emblem representing the multiple kingdoms of Britain and

Ireland as well as the Stuarts' inherited English claim on France: the royal standard featured three English lions set against three French lilies on both the top left and bottom right quarterings; the lion rampant of Scotland was placed on the top right and the Irish harp on the bottom left (Goss 1990: 90–1). Conversely, rather than retain the Scottish Stewart as the founding surname of the first encompassing British dynasty, James I took over the Francophile adaptation of Stuart first patented by his mother, Mary Queen of Scots. His first issue of coinage proclaimed him as Emperor of Great Britain.

As a firm advocate that monarchy was divinely interposed between God and civil society, James I of Great Britain viewed dynastic consolidation as the first step towards perfect union under an imperial monarchy. Such a union opened up the prospect of British leadership in a Protestant Europe battling to resist Antichrist in the form of the papacy and the whole panoply of the Counter-Reformation. This imperial vision of godly monarchy could draw on traditional English claims to be an empire free from papal control and, simultaneously, counter Presbyterian claims to the autonomy of the Scottish Kirk (Wormald 1991: 36–54). Albeit warranted discretely in his capacity as monarch of multiple kingdoms rather than a composite British empire, the Authorised Version of the Bible produced under the imprimatur of King James in 1611 endorsed his imperial vision of godly monarchy and his resolve that English should be the prescribed language of Reformed civility throughout his dominions.

British union was endorsed with varying degrees of enthusiasm by the Protestant episcopate in the multiple kingdoms (Jenkins 1995: 115–38). James Thornborough, bishop of Bristol, viewed the providential reunification of the British Empire under a godly monarch as an occasion of great happiness that would be perfected by the eventual merging of the constituent identities of England and Scotland into a composite British nation. Confidence in the ultimate victory of the godly over Antichrist, which inspired Calvinists throughout Britain, stood in marked contrast to Protestant perceptions in Ireland, that in the last few days Antichrist was at its strongest and the godly were threatened with their greatest sufferings and persecution (Ford 1987: 194–242). Accordingly, the imperial vision of a godly monarchy was endorsed as a matter of urgency by James Ussher, who became the Anglican primate in Ireland as archbishop of Armagh. His work on biblical chronology reputedly undermined the mythic line of Scottish kings and in the process Buchanan's staunch advocacy of a contractual rather than an organic bond between monarchy and civil society (Ferguson 1998: 138–9). But Buchanan's vibrant intellectual legacy, manifest in the contractual interpretation of fundamental law favoured by the Scottish Estates in 1604, resurfaced in the National Covenant of 1638.

Having ridiculed any supposition in the English parliament that Scotland should be garrisoned like a Spanish province, James I rather tactlessly made comparisons with Sicily and Naples, which provoked the Scottish Estates to temper their support for a British empire if it resulted in their governance by a Viceroy or Deputy. The more obvious, albeit implicit, exemplar was not Spain's Italian provinces but the English dependency of Ireland. On the same occasion James had interpreted the fundamentals of *jus regis* to apply only to laws governing his succession, but the Scottish Estates insisted *jus* fundamentally related to the whole framework of government for the kingdom. Without *jus*, the key to civility as the natural bond of human society, Scotland could not be an independent kingdom. Such fundamental law, issued usually with the consent of the political nation or sustained by immemorial custom, was differentiated from specific acts, statutes or customs made in different societies by the magistrates or ruler that, as *lex regis*, were alterable when required for the common welfare. The integral distinction between *jus* as a universal and *lex* as a relative concept was grounded in civil (or Roman) law. Its principal propagator was Sir Thomas Craig of Riccarton, the leading Scottish jurist and one of the joint parliamentary commissioners charged to negotiate the actual terms for union from 1604. As close agreement was apparent on the fundamentals of *jus* in both Scotland and England, Riccarton contended that there need be no insurmountable obstacle to the harmonizing of civil and common laws. James had admonished the English parliament in 1607 that the civil framework of government in Scotland should not be sacrificed by an imperial construct in which English common law would invariably predominate (Levack 1994: 213–40).

Despite Riccarton's promptings on the joint commission, perfect union tended to be interpreted on the English side as the full integration of both government and laws. The more gradualist position in favour of political and commercial integration also came under sustained attack from vested legal and mercantile interests in the English parliament of 1606–7. The English had been required, when extending their authority in Ireland as later when arguing for closed seas around the king's British dominions, to temper common law with civil law. Nonetheless, there was a marked aversion to accepting any innovative arrangement for union that neither accorded supremacy nor deferred ultimately to common law, the basis of their parliamentary privileges, religious liberties and rights of property (Peck 1996: 80–115). Four years of fitful negotiations by the joint commissioners foundered on the back of English concepts of political hegemony and parliamentary supremacy.

The strained resolution of Calvin's Case under English law in 1608 accorded common nationality to all born within Britain since the regal union. In promoting this objective as attorney general for England, Sir Francis Bacon argued before the House of Commons that the benefit of conceding naturalization to the Scots was the undoubted association of the multiple kingdoms on English terms: that is, by assimilation through the spread of the common law rather than an accommodation with the civil law of Scotland (Wormald 1993: 154–8). In establishing the *jus imperium* of the Stuarts, James had propounded such an accommodation, which leavened the relativism of common law with Scottish legal fundamentalism. Bacon was arguing for an expansion of the composite English kingdom, not the creation of a composite British empire. The spread of the common law to Scotland would enhance the security of England by making permanent the sundering of the 'auld alliance' with France. In arguing that British civility was tied strategically to English security, he was underscoring the case made by Camden's antiquarian associate Sir John Davies, as Attorney General for Ireland, that the imposition of the common law would reduce that kingdom to obedience and cut off the threat of invasion from Spain (Pawlish 1985: 55–64, 84–100). Indeed, for Bacon, having Scotland united and Ireland reduced through the common law was the constitutional bedrock of English greatness as an elect kingdom capable of global expansion.

The extent to which non-anglocentric interests could be accommodated within the English body politic was the historic nub of the British problem (Macinnes 1999b: 33–64). The Stuart *jus imperium* was exclusive in asserting sovereignty free from the interference of the papacy or other foreign power, but inclusive in the organic sense of involving not just England, but also Scotland and Ireland. The proponents of English greatness through the supremacy of the common law placed contractual emphasis on rights, liberties and privileges which were applicable to all freeborn Englishmen, but which were exclusively English at the expense of differing Scottish legal traditions or Irish customs. Both these perspectives were underwritten by antiquarianism that derived from Britannic legend. However, the formative role of the Anglo-Saxons in the constitutional history of England led Camden's associate, Sir Henry Spelman, to play down British continuity from the Romans to the Normans. The rehabilitation of the Anglo-Saxon contribution, which could be represented chronologically rather than mythologically, led Richard Verstegan (alias Rowlands) to stress the positive civilizing influence of the post-Roman Goths in shaping the nebulous but ancient constitution of England (Kidd 1999: 77–87). Both the Britannic perspective favoured by the Stuarts and the Gothic perspective favoured by common lawyers and parliamentarians were undoubtedly anglocentric. But only the Stuarts, whose imperial vision ensured that Britain was always something more than England, sought a meaningful accommodation with the other constituent multiple kingdoms. For the English common lawyers who regulated government and parliamentarians who voted supply, Britain was England. The British problem, thus identified as rival Britannic and Gothic perspectives, remained a recurrent feature linking political thought to the political process throughout the seventeenth century.

IV

The Britannic perspective favoured by James I and continued by his son Charles I faced several obstacles. The rejection of full union in 1607 meant that there was no formal British executive or legislative to effect public policy for all three kingdoms; albeit the bedchambers of the early Stuarts afforded a measure of informal policy coordination which ensured that neither James nor Charles was uncounselled in British affairs (Russell 1994: 238–56). At the same time, the lack of a unified legal system required patents for honours to be issued separately for England, Ireland and Scotland which, in turn, inhibited the creation of a British aristocracy, notwithstanding the growing tendency of courtiers to hold titles in more than one kingdom. Despite the continuing hostility of the English parliament to the designation 'Great Britain' in its dealings with the crown, James I was notably intent on demonstrating his *jus imperium* by land and sea through foreign, frontier and colonial policies.

Treaties and marriage alliances were contracted on behalf of the crown of Great Britain and Ireland, not England; a pattern maintained by Charles after 1625 and only broken by the emergence of the Covenanting Movement in Scotland. With respect to the conduct of diplomatic affairs, James rationalized his ambassadorial service. Scots were accorded primacy in the crown's dealings with Scandinavia and Northern Europe, while Russia and the rest of Europe remained the leading preserve of English diplomats; a division of labour also sustained until the emergence of the Covenanting Movement (Murdoch 2000: 44–89). Simultaneously, the espionage service became British. Sir James Hay, the Scot who headed the espionage service under James I, was ennobled in England as earl of Carlisle. Likewise, Charles I furthered the Britannic perspective of the Stuarts – not the process of anglicization

(Brown 1999: 238–65) – by awarding Scottish titles to English career diplomats such as Walter Aston, created Lord Forfar. Military contingents, licensed initially for Bohemia in 1620 and Germany in 1625 and then recruited formally for Danish and Swedish service in 1627 and 1631, intervened in the Thirty Years' War as British expeditionary forces. Although the forces raised were predominantly Scottish and were led respectively by two Scottish courtiers, Robert Maxwell, 1st earl of Nithsdale and James Hamilton, 3rd marquis of Hamilton, they served willingly under British command.

Concerted executive action in London, Dublin and Edinburgh led to the implementation of four projects to civilize frontier areas: on the Anglo-Scottish Borders, Ulster, the adjacent western seaboard in the Highlands and Western Isles and in the Northern Isles of Orkney and Shetland. The cross-border policing of the Middle Shires which commenced in 1605 was reputed a pronounced success within four years; yet border disturbances were a continuous, if localized, feature over the next three decades. The plantation of Ulster, though not formally launched as a British endeavour on the forfeited estates of exiled Gaelic lords until 1610, had actually commenced on escheated lands in the east of the province at the behest of Scottish adventurers in 1606. The paramount need to promote economic recovery after decades of continuous warfare ensured that there was limited displacement of the native Irish outwith the ranks of the landed classes. The Gaelic lord, Randal Mac-Donnell of the Glens, ennobled as viscount Dunluce in 1618 (later as earl of Antrim), became a planter in East Ulster. The Scottish Catholic recusant James Hamilton, 1st earl of Abercorn, took his Irish title as viscount Strabane from his plantation in West Ulster. Their participation in the showpiece endeavour of frontier policy suggests the inclusion as much as the marginalization of Ireland in the Stuart empire (Canny 1991: 35–66).

The essence of frontier policy within Scottish, as Irish, Gaeldom was not to promote expropriation but primarily to expedite the pace at which the clan elite on the western seaboard would become assimilated into Scottish landed society. At the same time, James had clearly pointed the way for political advancement in Scotland and Ireland through acceptance of his British vocabulary. The principal beneficiary of the crown's offensive on the western seaboard was the house of Argyll which was to the fore from 1607 in using the term 'North British' for Scotland and 'British' for colonists settling in Ulster. The British influence at court of Archibald Campbell, 7th earl, had been cultivated from 1604 by Richard Burke, 4th earl of Clanricarde, the head of the prominent Old English family, later an acclaimed if absentee governor of Galway opposed to the plantation of Connacht (Macinnes 1996: 56–87).

The annexation of Orkney and Shetland in 1612 was partly an extension of frontier policy, in that culturally distinctive Norse customs were eradicated in favour of the standardized administration of common laws throughout Scotland. There was un-doubted imperial symmetry in the imposition of Scots law over the Northern Isles to complement the imposition of the common law throughout Ulster. However, there was a wider imperial concern in annexing islands mortgaged to Scotland by the Danish–Norwegian crown in the mid-fifteenth century. Residual territorial claims on the Northern Isles gave Christian IV, the brother-in-law of James, the opportunity to claim exclusive jurisdiction over fishing in the northeastern Atlantic and to license access of English and Scottish whaling ventures to Greenland and Arctic waters.

Above all, the consolidation of the territorial waters around the British Isles into the Stuarts' imperial dominions served as a practical rebuttal to the claims from *mare liberum* articulated by the Dutch jurist Grotius (alias Hugo de Groot) in 1609. It is also noteworthy that James preferred to rely on two Scottish jurists, William Wellwood and Craig of Riccarton, to sustain his intellectual case for *mare clausum* around his British empire (Fulton 1911: 338–75).

As the Americas were 'beyond the line' of international regulation in the first half of the seventeenth century, colonial policy was especially amenable to a British projection (Armitage 1997: 34–63). During the initial phase of American colonization there was a declared preference both within governmental and entrepreneurial circles for an identifiable Scottish venture to expand the colonial dominions of the Stuart monarchy. Thus, New England was to be complemented by a New Scotland to bolster the British cause against the French in North America. At the same time, Nova Scotia offered a distinct British alternative to Ulster, in which Scots law was utilized to implement and direct plantations at the former French base of Port Royal and in Cape Breton from 1627. Albeit the latter plantation produced the first pamphlet published in America extolling the virtues of British colonialism, Scottish entrepreneurs had one manifest disadvantage. Their interests were deemed expendable when their commercial aspirations conflicted with international diplomacy. Five years after the initial settlements, Charles I withdrew his support as the price of peace exacted by Louis XIII of France for abortive British efforts to relieve the Huguenots in La Rochelle (Reid 1981: 20–51).

Despite its abandonment as a plantation by 1634, the proprietorial model under which Sir William Alexander of Menstrie (later earl of Stirling) was authorized to colonize Nova Scotia became the favoured means for promoting colonies outwith Virginia and Massachusetts. Thus, Barbados and the Leeward Islands were assigned under the proprietary control of the 1st earl of Carlisle from 1629. Although these Caribbean colonies were certainly English in terms of government, the character of their settlement can be viewed as British. Carlisle's principal factor was his Scottish kinsman, Peter Hay of Hayston. Scots also featured in the London merchant syndicate favoured with leases of the best land in Barbados. The designation of a Scotland district on that island would suggest that place names related as much to settlers' backgrounds as to geographic features; likewise more than English settlement is indicated by the subsequent naming of parishes in the Caribbean after the constituent saints of the British Isles (Dunn 1972: 49–53).

Notwithstanding his continuance of his father's foreign, frontier and colonial policies, the Britannic perspective of the Stuarts tilted in a distinctive anglocentric direction under Charles I, a direction first signalled in Scotland by his promotion of social and administrative uniformity through his proved ill-conceived, technically complex and financially unproductive Revocation Scheme. His supplementary pursuit of economic uniformity through tariff reform induced recession in Scotland by 1635. At the same time, his common fishing policy provoked an outcry against Charles's use of his British imprimatur, which the privy council in Edinburgh deemed particularly prejudicial since no union had as yet been negotiated with England (Macinnes 1991: 49–76, 108–13). As a further point of departure from his father, Charles preferred to rely on English lawyers, most notably Sir John Borough and John Selden, to uphold his *jus imperium* over the seas surrounding the British Isles. There were, however, two representational difficulties. All maps accompanying the texts of Camden and Speed, as those by Blaeu and other Dutch cartographers, only recognized the waters of the Channel as 'the British Seas'. Moreover, contemporaneous English maps were Dutch engraved, with the result that Dutch ships were depicted as sailing freely around the British Isles on open rather than closed seas! (Moreland and Bannister 2000: 217–23.)

The common fishing was an integral aspect of British uniformity associated with William Laud's promotion of 'thorough' in church and state. Above all, the authorization of religious uniformity by Charles under the direction of his archbishop of Canterbury unleashed pent-up dissatisfaction in Scotland that culminated in the termination of his prerogative rule in all three kingdoms. Religious and constitutional protest was not so much a reaction against misunderstood congruity (Morrill 1994: 209–37) as a concerted rejection of the perceived imposition of anglicization, Counter-Reformation and authoritarianism. Scotland, like Ireland, was being used as a political laboratory for the perfection of 'thorough' prior to its more rigorous enforcement in England. While Laud made no formal claims to ecclesiastical or political superiority, the court's endorsement of British uniformity provoked the National Covenant of 1638. The willingness of the emergent Covenanting Movement to effect revolution through warfare, not only offered a radical corrective to imperial monarchy, but also initiated the one momentous Scottish check to the prevailing Britannic and Gothic perspectives in the seventeenth century.

V

The National Covenant established a written constitution that prioritized parliamentary supremacy within a religious and constitutional compact between God, king and people. It made a fundamental distinction between the office of the monarch and the person of the king which sustained loyalty to the house of Stuart, but not necessarily to Charles I. Buchanan's anti-imperial notions of an aristocratic republic were also given force by the most radical aspect of the National Covenant: the oath of allegiance and mutual association. This oath, which was a positive act of defiance in reserving loyalty to a covenanted king, upheld the corporate right of the people to resist a lawful king who threatened to become tyrannical. Such resistance was to be exercised by the natural leaders of society through a centralized governmental structure that was dominated by the nobility but included representatives from the gentry, burgesses and clergy. As the corporate embodiment of the national interest, the Covenanting Movement, which was as much oligarchic as aristocratic or even baronial, reduced the power of the Stuart monarchy in Scotland to that of a cipher by 1641 (Macinnes 2000: 191–220).

Reinforced ideologically by French and Dutch advocates of the right to resist from the later sixteenth century, the Covenanting Movement was supported militarily and materially by Sweden from whose service Scottish forces were released to form Europe's second national army (Grosjean 2000: 115–38). Adapting the Swedish model, the Covenanters created an army serviced by a centralized state structured to enforce ideological commitment, military recruitment and financial supply within Scotland and to seize the political initiative throughout the multiple kingdoms by direct intervention in England and Ireland. Implemented during the Bishops Wars of

1639–40, this structure provided a model for revolution in the other two kingdoms and remained in operation until 1651, when overtaken by the no less organized, if somewhat derivative, New Model Army effected in 1645, which later brought Oliver Cromwell to power in England. The Covenanting determination to effect the reconfiguration of the multiple kingdoms by replacing regal with confederal union was notably supported by John Pym, the parliamentary leader in the House of Commons, and formalized by the Solemn League and Covenant of 1643, which exported Scottish constitutional fundamentalism to England and Ireland. In effect, the Solemn League represented an extension of confessional confederation to achieve common spiritual and material aims while maintaining distinctive national structures in church and state.

At the same time, the Solemn League and Covenant signposted a British confederal commitment by Scottish Covenanters and English parliamentarians to win the War for the Three Kingdoms, a commitment initially welcomed by Marchamont Nedham in his first edition of *Mercurius Britanicus* that August. In strategic terms, British unity entailed convergence of public policy rather than institutional incorporation; albeit one British institution did arise out of the Solemn League and Covenant. The short-lived Committee of Both Kingdoms, which projected itself internationally from 1644–6 as *Concilium Amborum Magnae Britanniae*, served as the co-ordinating confederal agency for British union charged to channel diplomatic dealings between the Covenanters and the parliamentarians (Macinnes and Ohlmeyer 2002: 15–35). To effect this diplomatic remit, redefined in November 1645 to include oversight of the war in Ireland as well as military collaboration in England, the committee would have required to operate as a federal executive – a role the increasingly Gothic English parliament was palpably not prepared to concede, as evident from the distinction it drew between supplies for the British and the Scottish forces fighting against the Catholic Confederates (Adamson 1995: 128–59).

The making of peace within the multiple kingdoms marked a further step away from confessional confederation. English intransigence, and internal divisions between the New Model Army and parliament, compounded tensions between the parliamentarians and Covenanters that were aggravated by the endemic hostility generated in the north of England by Scottish occupations during the 1640s (Scott 1999: 347–75). However, the Covenanting Movement was itself divided over continued intervention in England prior to the complication of Charles I handing himself over to its army in 1646. A radical element advocated withdrawal from England and alignment with Sweden against Christian IV of Denmark to open up trade through the Baltic Sound. The driving force behind British confederation, Archibald Campbell, marquis of Argyll, attempted to transcend such divisions in a celebrated speech to the Grand Committee of Both Houses in June 1646. The imperative of confederal action was maintained steadfastly. The English parliament should not negotiate unilaterally with Charles I, and the Scottish armies in England and Ireland should be supplied promptly.

Escalating public indebtedness, as well as the patent mistrust engendered by Charles I, were primary considerations moving Argyll and his associates to transfer the king from the custody of the Covenanting army to the English parliament for £400,000 sterling in January 1647. This transfer revived the Movement's conservative element that covertly concluded the Engagement with Charles I to defend and restore monarchical authority. The Engagement, which was the first Scottish-instigated effort to promote incorporating union, was terminated at Preston after a disastrous invasion of England in September 1648 (Macinnes 1999a: 43–55). The Covenanting Movement having effectively conceded the political initiative within the British Isles, Marchamont Nedham reported the resultant period of political transition through the pages of *Mercurius Pragmaticus*. With support from Oliver Cromwell, the radical Covenanters staged a successful revolt that culminated in the exclusion of the Engagers from public office.

News of the execution of Charles I, on 30 January 1649, sundered this collabor-ation. The immediate proclamation of Charles II not just as King of Scots but as King of Great Britain and Ireland, reasserted the international identity of the house of Stuart within the context of confederal union. Charles II was duly obliged to subscribe both the National Covenant and the Solemn League and Covenant prior to his coronation on 1 January 1651. However, his proclamation provoked the Cromwellian occupation of Scotland after the parliamentary forces had taken full advantage of the factional disarray among royalists and Catholic Confederates to conquer Ireland. With the Cromwellian forces triumphant in all three kingdoms by the autumn of 1651, enforced union all round was marked first by the Common-wealth, then the Protectorate of England, Scotland and Ireland. The deliberate avoidance of Great Britain for this incorporation denoted an emphatic rejection of both the Stuart vision of empire and the confederal conception of multiple kingdoms united by covenanting (Hirst 1996: 192–219).

The emergence of the New Model Army in England had not only marked a shift away from reliance on provincial forces, but also constituted a key moment in the establishment of an assertive English national consciousness (Wheeler 1999: 191–7). This sense of identity was enhanced through the conquest of Ireland and Scotland, conquests necessitated by the refusal of both kingdoms to accept the accomplishment of an English republic through regicide. Whereas the Irish were viewed as uncivilized and deluded, the Scots were chided as misled, even false, brethren who had strayed from the path of godliness. A sense of English superiority seems to have resonated throughout the New Model Army, particularly as the mutinous soldiers in 1647 viewed themselves as freeborn Englishmen placed between the people and parliament to mediate for justice and righteousness. While most of the English forces had accepted the invasion of Ireland in 1649, the Levellers had contended that this was a tyrannical measure of the type they had fought against in the civil wars. Others in the Army considered that England was not fully settled as a republic. With the quashing of Leveller mutinies and a formidable force of Covenanters and royalists uniting in a patriotic accommodation to support Charles II, there were few dissenting English voices to the invasion of Scotland in 1650 (Barber 1995: 195–221).

In projecting an exclusive Englishness, Cromwell went further than Elizabeth Tudor in pushing the frontiers of English hegemony to include all three kingdoms. Indeed, his regime's recourse to Borough and Selden to assert dominion over the British seas surrounding the multiple kingdoms, his imposition of Navigation Laws in 1651, his treaties of commercial confederation with Northern European powers, his waging of the First Dutch War in 1652–4 and his seizure of Jamaica in 1655, denote Cromwell as England's Gothic emperor (Woolrych 1986: 274–311). Propagandists with integrity such as John Milton and those without such as George Waller, claimed that the Commonwealth, as later the Protectorate, was the true heir to British loyalty originally vested in the Stuarts and then in the Solemn League and Covenant of 1643. The refusal of the Irish and the Scots to accept the regicide were manifestations of their selfish sectional interests that ran against the commonweal to which England alone remained providentially committed. No matter their aggressive behaviour as conquerors, which Marchamont Nedham glossed over in *Mercurius Politicus*, republican commentators were shielded from self-criticism by the godly reason with which the English under Cromwell had reconstructed themselves not just as a superior but as a chosen people (Barber 1998: 174–201).

VI

The restoration of Charles II produced a constitutional settlement in all three kingdoms, which revived the Stuarts' *jus imperium*, but ruled out the confederal conception of Britain and Ireland united by covenanting. The supplanting of confessional by commercial politics was signposted by the imposition of the English Navigation Laws (1660, 1671, 1681) and the resurgence of European mercantilism. Although its political independence had been regained formally, Scotland, like Ireland, operated effectively as a satellite state over the next three decades. The Scottish and Irish parliaments, like the Caribbean colonies, awarded a substantive annuity from their excise to Charles II for life, an award that obviated the need for regular parliaments to vote supply. While the continuity of military governors-general and colonial administration has been well attested with respect to Ireland (Webb 1979: 329–466), Scotland became a training ground for the oppressive use of the militia as well as regular forces. The ruling regime, most notably under James Maitland, duke of Lauderdale, manufactured and exploited a climate of disorder over religious dissent in the Lowlands and purported banditry among the clans, to promote the beginnings of a military–fiscal state that served as a model for absolutism on the cheap throughout the Stuart dominions (Macinnes 1996: 122–58). The revival of the Stuart concept of British imperialism was more proclaimed than implemented, however. Proposals for an incorporating union instigated by Charles II in October 1669 were but one in a series of political diversions to facilitate secret dealings for an alliance with Louis XIV of France.

In reality, restored Stuart rule over the multiple kingdoms represented a compromise between Britannic and Gothic perspectives. The former was highlighted by the Dutch academic Rutgerius Hermannides in his *Britannia Magna* of 1661, which chronicled English hegemony over Scotland and Ireland. The latter was articulated forcibly by the Swedish jurist Samuel von Pufendorf who, in his *Introduction to the History of the Principal Kingdoms and States of Europe*, came to view England as a composite monarchy with Scottish and Irish dependencies. Charles II was carrying on the mantle of Cromwell in maintaining English greatness through dominion over the seas and the promotion of commerce. John Ogilby, a Scot who made his reputation as a theatrical impresario in Ireland, stage-managed the coronation of Charles II as King of England in 1661. Triumphal arches built by the city of London celebrated Britain's monarchy by buttressing loyalty to the Stuarts with the commercial clout of the metropolis flanked by Edinburgh to the right and Dublin to the left. During the actual ceremonial, the interests of Scotland and Ireland were discreetly represented by the respective presence of Lauderdale and James Butler, 1st duke of Ormonde (Montaño 1995: 31–51). Subsequently moving on to cartography, Ogilby financed through public subscriptions a detailed survey of the main roads of England and Wales, which was published under the rubric of *Britannia* in 1675 (Moreland and Bannister 2000: 157–8). The anglocentric appropriation of Britain was further evident in the defence of the restored Erastian episcopacy bolstered by the purity of Anglican tradition and untainted by popery. The instigator of renewed claims for the spiritual and temporal supremacy of the English monarchy throughout the British Isles was William Prynne who, after a career as a religious and political agitator, was reconciled to Anglicanism at the Restoration (Lamont 1996: 119–45).

The prospect of Charles II being succeeded by his brother James, duke of York – an avowed Catholic intent on using his prerogative powers to remove penal restrictions on his co-religionists throughout the multiple kingdoms – instigated a further round of hegemonic Anglicanism. In vindicating Erastian episcopacy and the royal supremacy, William Lloyd, bishop of St Asaphs and William Stillingfleet (the future bishop of Worcester) were essentially attempting to reconcile Anglican advocates of nonresistance, who had become identified with the Tories in the course of the Exclusion Crisis of 1679–81. At the same time, they were serving notice to the future James II, under sustained attack from Whig proponents of a contractually limited monarchy, that passive obedience should not be taken as political endorsement (Harris 1993: 9–27). However, their associated dismissal of the mythical progenitors of Fergus MacEarc provoked outrage in Scotland led by the Lord Advocate, Sir George Mackenzie of Rosehaugh, and the polymath Sir Robert Sibbald, for whom the unrivalled antiquity of the Scottish kings was the bedrock of Scottish independence. The Irish joined in this controversy. Roderic O'Flaherty, a dispossessed landowner, rebutted the Scottish interpretation of classical Irish sources and argued that Ireland, no less than Scotland, should be an independent kingdom in the Stuarts' empire of the British Isles (Ferguson 1998: 144–72). Unfortunately, James continued to view Ireland as a political dependency despite his wholesale reliance on Catholic Ireland's support in his struggle against William of Orange from 1688 to 1691.

As duke of York, James had played a key public role in upholding a Britannic perspective. The association of the Levellers with the 'Norman yoke theory' of arrested English constitutionalism had served to associate the Gothic with popular insurrections and civil wars at the Restoration. Nonetheless, the imposition of the Navigation Laws and the rise of London to global significance had facilitated a Gothic mercantilism as well as the English appropriation of the British Empire by cartographers like Richard Bloome (alias Nathaniel Crouch). Giving added force to the debate over the Stuarts' *jus imperium* was the changing intellectual context. In contrast to the situation that prevailed in the aftermath of the union of the crowns in 1603, this debate was conducted primarily within the context of political economy rather than jurisprudence (Pincus 1998: 705–36). James was instrumental in using the prerogative powers his dynasty claimed by divine right to suspend or dispense with laws restricting Scottish and Irish participation in English ventures, whether in the Americas or the East Indies. The pressing of Scots into service in the Royal Navy and the conscription of Scots seamen to serve in the Second (1666–7) and Third (1672–4) Dutch Wars against their main commercial partner further encouraged a laxity in applying trading prohibitions. Having been awarded New York as a proprietary colony on its wresting from the Dutch in 1664, James had been an assiduous and tolerant promoter of a durable Scottish and Dutch commercial network from 1673 that was based in Albany, named after his Scottish ducal title (Landsman 1998: 351–74). His opening up of participation from the multiple kingdoms in the Hudson's Bay Company was reflected in the naming of the Bay's eastern shore as North and South Wales and its western shore as New Britain (Moreland and Bannister 2000: 158–60).

The duke of York also attempted to moderate the Gothic mercantilism that sought to secure the fishing resources around the British Isles for English benefit. The Company of the Royal Fishery of Great Britain and Ireland established in 1661, which drew upon the expertise of agents involved in the common fishing of Charles I, was a Thames-led initiative regulated by the English common law. Having attracted criticism from the diarist Samuel Pepys that the money realized by lottery as well as public subscription proved more corrupting than remunerative, the company was remodelled in 1664. Its continuing operation was compromised by the existence of a separate Scottish initiative operating through provincial associations from 1661 that were recast in 1670 as the Royal Company for Fishery in Scotland. This venture, which stuttered on until 1690, remained distinct from and detrimental to the viability of the complementary Company of the Royal Fishery of England established under the duke's leadership in 1677. Regardless of any resolution on respective territorial waters claimed for Scotland and England, neither company could operate independently of Dutch fishing expertise (Scott 1912 II: 361–82).

Whereas fishing was part of the debate on national improvement through commerce in England, it was integral to the debate on national survival in Scotland. As in Ireland, overtures for union with England also featured as issues of political economy. Scotland, however, had no equivalent to Sir William Petty who promoted union with England in order to facilitate social engineering, if not ethnic and cultural assimilation, through the transplantation of peoples (Kelly 1987: 236–63). When James established his court in Edinburgh during his retreat from the Exclusion Crisis in England, he reinvigorated Scottish endeavours for the targeted pursuit of colonies as the commercial alternative to union (Brown 1994: 58–87). In 1681 the Scottish Council of Trade reported that the only effective way for the country to cope with mercantilism and growing dependence on English markets was either to seek closer union or develop overseas colonies. James duly authorized Scottish ventures to South Carolina in 1682 and East New Jersey from 1685. The future James II (like his grandfather, he viewed his nomenclature as King of Great Britain) was the only Stuart monarch not to sponsor political incorporation – an understated issue in assessing subsequent Scottish support for Jacobitism after 1688–91.

VII

The 'Glorious Revolution' in England can be viewed as a triumph of Gothic constitutionalism and mercantilism: the Anglican ascendancy was confirmed, limited monarchy was consolidated and the Navigation Laws were reasserted comprehensively and exclusively. In Ireland, the replacement of James II by William and Mary established an Anglican ascendancy for the English interest which rigorously excluded Irish Catholics and Ulster-Scottish Presbyterians from public life. In Scotland, the parliamentary deposition of James was unequivocably Whiggish. Notwithstanding the re-establishment of Presbyterianism, the Revolution was marked especially by the resurgence of radical constitutional activity as the unicameral Scottish Estates attempted to secure permanent checks on the executive power wielded on behalf of the British court. In turn, politicians favourable to the court used the prospect of union as a diversionary ploy to root and branch constitutional reform (Riley 1979: 27–33, 48–54). Albeit distinctive in each of the multiple kingdoms (Harris 1997: 97–117), the Revolution settlements effectively empowered baronial sectarianism in alliance with military engagements that were predominantly Francophone and with commercial opportunism on a global scale. The proclaimed Gothic achievement of constitutional monarchy in place of Stuart autocracy glossed over the continuation of the fiscal–military state instigated in the Stuarts' dominions outwith England in the Restoration era. Ostensibly under parliamentary control from the Revolution, imperialism was moderated rather than contained by votes of supply and fructified by the creation of the National Debt in 1693 that was financed through the Bank of England from 1694 (Braddick 1996: 27–45).

The Revolution transformed a British empire based on the Stuarts' royal prerogative into an English empire subject to constitutional oversight by the English parliament. Notwithstanding their establishment of the Bank of Scotland and their warranting of the Company of Scotland trading to Africa and the Indies in 1695, William and Mary could not endorse the Darien colonial venture as a rival to the English East India Company. William's need for parliamentary supply, his desire to appease Spain and the expendable nature of Scottish interests as he sought to broker a military alliance against Louis XIV, conspired to reduce Darien from a confederation of Scottish, English, Dutch and Hanseatic commercial interests to a separatist endeavour. Though funded as a national enterprise, as a commercial compact between God and the Scottish people, surveying and provisioning were deficient. While English polemicists declared open season in ridiculing the audacity of Scottish enterprise, Spanish tenacity on the Panama Isthmus was wholly underestimated. Indeed, the Darien fiasco, which came to grief in 1700, was in no small measure due to misplaced British – not just Scottish – disrespect for Spain as 'the sick man of Europe' (Storrs 1999: 5–38).

The political fall-out from Darien was the mobilization of Scottish public opinion against the court, which imperilled the continuation of regal union following the accession of Anne in 1702. Anglo-Scottish antipathy was compounded by a legislative war instigated by the Act of Settlement, which the English parliament had imposed unilaterally in favour of the house of Hanover in 1701. Scottish retaliation was two-pronged. The Act Anent Peace and War provided for an independent Scottish foreign policy on Anne's death. The Act of Security threatened to dissolve the regal union unless the sovereignty of Scotland, the power of its parliament and the freedom of its religion and commerce were secured from English interference by Anne's successor. Scottish retaliation was trumped by the Alien Act of 1705 and by the mobilizing of troops on the Borders and across the North Channel in Ireland. Along with the threat of subjecting the Scots to the same punitive tariffs as foreigners was an invitation to treat for incorporating union (Young 1999 24–53).

The understated issue during the legislative war was the relative standing of the Irish parliament, which had accepted the Act of Settlement only to have its overture for parliamentary union rejected by the English in 1703 (Smyth 1993: 785–96). Overt English interference post-Revolution that had damaged the wool trade, asserted the jurisdictional superiority of the Lords at Westminster and threatened the redistribution of forfeited Jacobite estates, had provoked William Molyneux's *The Case of Ireland* in 1698. His assertion that Ireland was as separate and distinct a kingdom as Scotland from England, instigated a polemical debate which initially differentiated the independence of Scotland from that of Ireland, but then challenged the sovereignty of Scotland in relation to England as an imperial monarchy. Such were Scottish antipathies that the hangman in Edinburgh publicly burned pamphlets advocating English claims of suzerainty. The Scottish Estates remunerated published rebuttals. Alexander Fletcher of Saltoun, as a committed opponent of English influence on Scottish affairs, made much of the constitutional and economic slavery of Ireland (Robertson 1995: 198–227). Notwithstanding such polemical rhetoric, Scottish politicians generally preferred confederation or a federal arrangement. But the English were intent on parliamentary incorporation, which was facilitated by the Scottish sense of defeatism occasioned by the Darien fiasco. The failure of the Scots to break out of the mercantilist prism made them more reliant on access to English domestic and colonial markets.

The accomplishment of parliamentary union signposted a collective crisis of political will among Scots to pursue a separate commercial agenda, not an entrepreneurial lack of ambition. The British nature of the empire was reasserted through Scottish networks within an English governmental framework. While the coalescence of political elites lay in the future, and full integration was never achieved with respect to the church, the law and local government (Brown 2001: 363–84), the Gothic realities of British state formation were expressed appositely eight days after the Treaty of 1707 became operative. On 9 May, Governor Thomas Handasyd of Jamaica was notified by the Council of Trade and Plantations 'that Scotchmen are thereby to be looked upon for the future as Englishmen to all intents and purposes whatsoever' (Macinnes 2001: 67–94).

REFERENCES

Adamson, J. 1995: 'Stafford's ghost: the British context of Viscount Lisle's lieutenancy of Ireland.' In J. Ohlmeyer, ed., *Ireland from Independence to Occupation, 1641–1660*: Cambridge.

Armitage, D. 1997: 'Making the empire British; Scotland in the Atlantic world 1542–1717', *Past and Present*, 155.

Barber, S. 1995: 'Scotland and Ireland under the Commonwealth: a question of loyalty.' In S. G. Ellis and S. Barber, eds, *Conquest and Union: Fashioning a British State, 1485–1725*: London.

Barber, S. 1998: *Regicide and Republicanism: Politics and Ethics in the English Revolution, 1646–1659*: Edinburgh.

Braddick, M. J. 1996: *The Nerves of State: Taxation and the Financing of the English State, 1558–1714*: Manchester.

Brown, K. M. 1994: 'The vanishing emperor; British kingship in decline.' In R. A. Mason, ed., *Scots and Britons: Scottish Political Thought and the Union of 1603*: Cambridge.

Brown, K. M. 1999: 'Seducing the Scottish Clio: has Scottish history anything to fear from the New British History?' In G. Burgess, ed., *The New British History: Founding a Modern State, 1603–1715*: London.

Brown, K. M. 2001: 'The Scottish nobility and the British multiple monarchy (1603–1714).' In R. G. Asch, ed., *Der Europäishe Adel im Ancien Régime: Von der Krise der Ständischen Monarchien bis zur Revolution (ca.1600–1789)*: Böhlau.

Canny, N. 1991: 'The marginal kingdom: Ireland as a problem in the first British empire.' In B. Bailyn and P. D. Morgan, eds, *Strangers within the Realm: Cultural Margins of the First British Empire*: Chapel Hill, NC.

Clarke, A. 1978: 'Colonial identity in early seventeenth-century Ireland.' In T. W. Moody, ed., *Nationality and the Pursuit of National Independence*: Belfast.

Clarke, A. 2000: 'Patrick Darcy and the constitutional relationship between Ireland and Britain.' In J. H. Ohlmeyer, ed., *Irish Political Thought in the Seventeenth Century*: Cambridge.

Dunn, R. S. 1972: *Sugar and Slaves: The Rise of the Planter Class in the English West Indies, 1624–1713*: Chapel Hill, NC.

Elliot, J. H. 1992: 'A Europe of composite monarchies', *Past and Present*, 137.

Ellis, S. G. 1995: 'Tudor state formation and the shaping of the British Isles.' In S. G. Ellis and S. Barber, eds, *Conquest and Union: Fashioning a British State, 1485–1725*: London.

Ertman, T. 1997: *Birth of the Leviathan: Building States and Regimes in Medieval and Early Modern Europe*: Cambridge.

Ferguson, W. 1998: *The Identity of the Scottish Nation: An Historic Quest*: Edinburgh.

Ford, A. 1987: *The Protestant Reformation in Ireland, 1590–1641*: Frankfurt am Main.

Fulton, T. W. 1911: *The Sovereignty of the Sea: An Historical Account of the Claims for Dominion of the British Seas*: Edinburgh.

Goss, J. 1990: *World Historical Atlas, 1662*: London.

Greengrass, M. 1991: 'Introduction: conquest and coalescence.' In M. Greengrass, ed., *Conquest and Coalescence: The Shaping of the State in Early Modern Europe*: London.

Grosjean, A. 2000: 'General Alexander Leslie, the Scottish Covenanters and the Riksråd debates, 1638–1640.' In A. I. Macinnes, T. Riis and F. G. Pedersen, eds, *Ships, Guns and Bibles in the North Sea and Baltic States, c.1350–c.1700*: East Linton.

Harris, T. 1993: 'Tories and the rule of law in the reign of Charles II', *The Seventeenth Century*, 8.

Harris, T. 1997: 'Reluctant revolutionaries? The Scots and the revolution of 1688–89.' In H. Nenner, ed., *Politics and the Political Imagination in Later Stuart Britain: Essays Presented to Lois Green Schwoerer*: Rochester.

Hirst, D. 1996: 'The English republic and the meaning of Britain.' In B. Bradshaw and J. Morrill, eds, *The British Problem, c.1534–1707*: Basingstoke.

Jenkins, P. 1995: 'The Anglican church and the unity of Britain: the Welsh experience, 1560–1714.' In S. G. Ellis and S. Barber, eds, *Conquest and Union: Fashioning a British State, 1485–1725*: London.

Kelly, J. 1987: 'The origins of the act of union: an examination of unionist opinion in Britain and Ireland, 1650–1800', *Irish Historical Studies*, 25.

Kidd, C. 1998: 'Protestantism, constitutionalism and British identity under the later Stuarts.' In B. Bradshaw and P. Roberts, eds, *British Consciousness and Identity: The Making of Britain, 1533–1707*: Cambridge.

Kidd, C. 1999: *British Identities before Nationalism: Ethnicity and Nationhood in the Atlantic World, 1600–1800*: Cambridge.

Lamont, W. M. 1996: 'The Puritan revolution: a historiographical essay.' In J. G. A. Pocock, ed., *The Varieties of British Political Thought, 1500–1800*: Cambridge.

Landsman, N. C. 1998: 'The middle colonies: new opportunities for settlement, 1660–1700.' In N. Canny, ed., *The Oxford History of the British Empire, vol. 1: The Origins of Empire: British Overseas Empire to the Close of the Seventeenth Century*: Oxford.

Levack, B. 1994: 'Law, sovereignty and the union.' In R. A. Mason, ed., *Scots and Britons: Scottish Political Thought and the Union of 1603*: Cambridge.

McGinnis, P. and Williamson, A. 2002: 'Britain, race, and the Iberian world empire.' In A. I. Macinnes and J. Ohlmeyer, eds, *The Stuart Kingdoms in the Seventeenth Century: Awkward Neighbours*: Dublin.

Macinnes, A. I. 1991: *Charles I and the Making of the Covenanting Movement, 1625–1641*: Edinburgh.

Macinnes, A. I. 1996: *Clanship, Commerce and the House of Stuart, 1603–1788*: East Linton.

Macinnes, A. I. 1999a: 'Politically reactionary Brits?: The promotion of Anglo-Scottish union, 1603–1707.' In S. J. Connolly, ed., *Kingdoms United? Great Britain and Ireland since 1500*: Dublin.

Macinnes, A. I. 1999b: 'Regal union for Britain, 1603–38.' In G. Burgess, ed., *The New British History: Founding a Modern State, 1603–1715*: London.

Macinnes, A. I. 2000: 'Covenanting ideology in seventeenth-century Scotland.' In J. H. Ohlmeyer, ed., *Political Thought in Seventeenth-Century Ireland: Kingdom or Colony*: Cambridge.

Macinnes, A. I. 2001: 'Union for Ireland failed (1703), Union for Scotland accomplished (1706–7).' In D. Keogh and K. Whelan, eds, *Acts of Union: The Causes, Contexts, and Consequences of the Act of Union of 1801*: Dublin.

Macinnes, A. I. and Ohlmeyer, J. 2002: 'International setting: awkward perspectives.' In A. I. Macinnes and J. Ohlmeyer, eds, *The Stuart Kingdoms in the Seventeenth Century: Awkward Neighbours*: Dublin.

Mason, R. A. 1987: 'Scotching the Brut: politics, history and national myth in sixteenth-century Britain.' In R. A. Mason, ed., *Scotland and England, 1286–1815*: Edinburgh.

Mason, R. A. 1994: 'Imagining Scotland: Scottish political thought and the "problem" of Britain, 1560–1650.' In R. A. Mason, ed., *Scots and Britons: Scottish Political Thought and the Union of 1603*: Cambridge.

Mason, R. A. 1998: *Kingship and the Commonweal: Political Thought in Renaissance and Reformation Scotland*: East Linton.

Montaño, J. P. 1995: 'The quest for consensus: the Lord Mayor's Day Show in the 1670s.' In G. Maclean, ed., *Culture and Society in the Stuart Restoration: Literature, Drama and History*: Cambridge.

Moreland, C. and Bannister, D. 2000: *Antique Maps*: London.

Morrill, J. 1994: 'A British patriarchy: ecclesiastical imperialism under the early Stuarts.' In A. Fletcher and P. Roberts, eds, *Religion, Culture and Society in Early Modern Britain: Essays in Honour of Patrick Collinson*: Cambridge.

Murdoch, A. 1998: *British History, 1660–1832: National Identity and Local Culture*: Basingstoke.

Murdoch, S. 2000: *Britain, Denmark–Norway and the House of Stuart, 1603–1660*: East Linton.

Murdoch, S. (ed.) 2001: *Scotland and the Thirty Years' War, 1618–1648*: Leiden.

Ó Buachalla, B. 1987: *Foras Feasa ar Éirinn, History of Ireland: Foreword*: Dublin.

Ó Buachalla, B. 1996: *Aisling Ghearr: Na Stiobhartaigh Agus an tAos Leinn 1603–1788*: Dublin.

Ohlmeyer, J. 1993: *Civil War and Restoration in the Three Stuart Kingdoms: The Political Career of Randal MacDonnell First Marquis of Antrim, 1609–83*: Cambridge.

Pawlish, H. S. 1985: *Sir John Davies and the Conquest of Ireland: A Study in Legal Imperialism*: Cambridge.

Peck, L. L. 1996: 'Kingship, counsel and law in early Stuart Britain.' In J. G. A. Pocock, ed., *The Varieties of British Political Thought, 1500–1800*: Cambridge.

Pincus, S. 1998: 'Neither Machiavellian moment nor possessive individualism: commercial society and the defenders of the English Commonwealth, *American Historical Review*, 103.

Pocock, J. G. A. 1996: 'The Atlantic archipelago and the war of the three kingdoms.' In B. Bradshaw and J. Morrill, eds, *The British Problem, c.1534–1707*: Basingstoke.

Reid, J. G. 1981: *Acadia, Maine and New England: Marginal Colonies in the Seventeenth Century*: Toronto.

Riley, P. W. J. 1979: *King William and the Scottish Politicians*: Edinburgh.

Robertson, J. 1995: 'An elusive sovereignty: the course of the Union debate in Scotland 1698–1707.' In J. Robertson, ed., *A Union for Empire: Political Thought and the Union of 1707*: Cambridge.

Rowell, S. C. 2000: 'The Grand Duchy of Lithuania and Baltic identity, c.1500–1600.' In A. I. Macinnes, T. Riis and F. G. Pedersen, eds, *Ships, Guns and Bibles in the North Sea and Baltic States, c.1350–c.1700*: East Linton.

Russell, C. 1994: 'The Anglo-Scottish Union of 1603–43: a success?' In A. Fletcher and P. Roberts, eds, *Religion, Culture and Society in Early Modern Britain: Essays in Honour of Patrick Collinson*: Cambridge.

Scott, D. 1999: 'The "Northern Gentlemen", the parliamentary Independents and Anglo-Saxon relations in the Long Parliament', *Historical Journal*, 42

Scott, W. R. 1912: *The Constitutions and Finance of English, Scottish and Irish Joint-Stock Companies to 1720*, 3 vols: Cambridge.

Smyth, J. 1993: ' "Like amphibious animals": Irish Protestants, Ancient Britons, 1691–1707', *Historical Journal*, 36.

Smyth, J. 2001: *The Making of the United Kingdom, 1660–1800*: Harlow.

Storrs, C. 1999: 'Disaster at Darien: 1698–1700? The persistence of Spanish imperial power on the eve of the demise of the Spanish Habsburgs', *European History Quarterly*, 29.

Webb, S. S. 1979: *The Governors-General: The English Army and the Definition of Empire, 1569–1681*: Chapel Hill, NC.

Wheeler, J. S. 1999: *Cromwell in Ireland*: Dublin.

Williamson, A. 1989: 'The Jewish dimension of the Scottish apocalypse: climate, covenant and world renewal.' In Y. Kaplan, H. Mechoulan and R. H. Popkins, eds, *Menasseh Ben Israel and His World*: New York.

Woolf, D. R. 1990: *The Idea of History in Early Stuart England: Erudition, Ideology, and 'The Light of Truth' from the Accession of James I to the Civil War*: Toronto.

Woolrych, A. 1986: *Commonwealth to Protectorate*: Oxford.

Wormald, B. H. G. 1993: *Francis Bacon: History, Politics and Science, 1561–1626*: Cambridge.

Wormald, J. 1991: 'James VI and I, *Basilikon Doron* and *The Trew Law of Free Monarchies*: the Scottish context and the English translation.' In L. L. Peck, ed., *The Mental World of the Jacobean Court*: Cambridge.

Young, J. R. 1999: 'The Parliamentary Incorporating Union of 1707: political management, anti-Unionism and foreign policy.' In T. M. Devine and J. R. Young, eds, *Eighteenth Century Scotland: New Perspectives*: East Linton.

FURTHER READING

Barnard, T. and Fenlon, J. (eds) 2000: *The Dukes of Ormonde, 1610–1745*: Woodbridge.

Bennett, M. 1997: *The Civil Wars in Britain and Ireland, 1638–1651*: Oxford.

Brewer, J. 1989: *The Sinews of Power: War, Money and the English State, 1688–1783*: London.

Brown, K. M. 2000: *Noble Society in Scotland: Wealth, Family and Culture from Reformation to Revolution*: Edinburgh.

Burgess, G. 1992: *The Politics of the Ancient Constitution: An Introduction to English Political Thought, 1603–1641*: University Park, PA.

Burns, J. H. 1996: *The True Law of Kingship: Concepts of Monarchy in Early Modern Scotland*: Oxford.

Calder, A. 1998: *Revolutionary Empire: The Rise of the English-Speaking Empires from the Fifteenth Century to the 1780s*: London.

Carlton, C. 1994: *Going to the Wars: The Experience of the British Civil Wars, 1638–51*: London.

Downing, B. M. 1992: *The Military Revolution and Political Change: Origins of Democracy and Autocracy in Early Modern Europe*: Princeton, NJ.

Evans, R. J. W. and Thomas, T. V. (eds) 1991: *Crown, Church and Estates: Central European Politics in the Sixteenth and Seventeenth Centuries*: London.

Kupperman, K. O. (ed.) 1995: *America in European Consciousness, 1493–1750*: Chapel Hill, NC.

Lee, M., Jr, 1990: *Great Britain's Solomon: King James VI and I in his Three Kingdoms*: Urbana, IL.

Levack, B. P. 1987: *The Formation of the British State: England, Scotland and the Union, 1603–1707*: Oxford.

McEachern, C. 1996: *The Poetics of English Nationhood, 1590–1612:* Cambridge.

Pagden, A. 1995: *Lords of all the World: Ideologies of Empire in Spain, Britain and France c.1500–c.1800*: New Haven, CT.

Pincus, S. A. 2001: *Restoration*: Cambridge.

Raymond, J. (ed.) 1993: *Making the News: An Anthology of the Newsbooks of Revolutionary England, 1641–1660*: Moreton-in-Marsh.

Sharpe, K. and Zwicker, S. N. (eds) 1987: *Politics of Discourse: The Literature and History of Seventeenth-Century England:* Berkeley, CA.

Spruyt, H. 1996: *The Sovereign State and Its Competitors*: Princeton, NJ.

Whatley, C. A. 2001: *Bought and Sold for English Gold? Explaining the Union of 1707*: East Linton.

CHAPTER TWO

The Making of Great Britain and Ireland

TOBY BARNARD

I

On 24 March 1603, James VI of Scotland succeeded not just to the English throne but to that of Ireland as well. The inhabitants of Ireland exercised no choice in this matter. Since 1541, the king of England had also been designated as king of Ireland. The powerlessness of those in Ireland to choose their ruler again showed in 1689. When William III and Mary II took James II's crown, they too became rulers of Ireland, as well as of England and Wales. Ireland's political and constitutional subjection had begun long before 1689, or even 1541. In 1169, Henry II invaded and conquered part of the island. Thereafter he and his successors ruled as lords of Ireland. Their authority fluctuated. The lordship of Ireland embraced Dublin, the adjacent countryside, and a few ports. Henry VIII's assumption of the kingly title announced an ambition to rule all Ireland. It arose from the same urge which had recently incorporated Wales into the English monarchy. In Ireland it proved a frustrating ambition. In pursuing it successive monarchs deployed large armies, spent much and were rebuffed humiliatingly.

Much that happened in seventeenth-century Ireland could be regarded as a simple continuation of Tudor policies. This has become clearer as the assumptions behind and the details of governing sixteenth-century Ireland have been uncovered (Ellis 1998). Prestige, security and money all meant that no English government could allow Ireland to slip into practical let alone legal independence. Yet twice – after 1641 and again between 1689 and 1691 – it threatened to do so. In consequence, much English and Scottish activity was directed to reconquest. Earlier patterns recurred. Troops were shipped into Ireland. In the aftermath of defeat, the properties of the vanquished Irish were confiscated and bestowed on others (Bottigheimer 1971; Simms 1956). A second great gain from the writings of the last twenty-five years has been to clarify each uprising, both its causes and course (MacCuarta 1993; Perceval-Maxwell 1994; Simms 1969). Each varied in its geographical location and in its precise occasions; all provoked broadly similar responses from the English (and Scots) conquerors. Recent work has also explained the theory and practice of subsequent responses. The standard reaction was to forfeit the insurgents' property and substitute new proprietors for the old (Bottigheimer 1971; Canny 2001; MacCarthy-Morrogh 1986).

Underlying continuities linked Stuart with Tudor (and earlier) engagement with Ireland. Yet, in 1603, the monarchy itself changed with the regal union of England and Scotland under James VI and I. In the past, Scotland no less than England, as a near neighbour, had concerned itself with Ireland. The question naturally arises as to what difference the regal union made to the treatment of Ireland. A second question is suggested by the frequency and ferocity with which Ireland resisted English (and Scottish) rule. Despite the costs and trouble of consolidating, extending and re-establishing English power, England apparently never contemplated relinquishing the island. Security, reputation and possible profit combined to persuade England that it must uphold its jurisdiction over Ireland. In addition, successive sovereigns and their advisers were assured that public benefits would soon flow from the westerly possession. Meanwhile, private profits could be amassed quickly.

Simple proximity meant that Ireland had been settled by migratory English, Welsh and Scots, long before official schemes were invented. Northeastern Ireland was clearly visible from the southwestern extremities of Scotland and its islands. On a calm day, the sea voyage took only hours. Shared culture and language also united Gaelic peoples on either shore of the Northern Sea. What changed under James VI and I was the decision of the governments in London and Dublin to sponsor settlement in Ulster. The king, baulked of his hopes to achieve a legislative union of England and Scotland, turned instead to less formal devices. One was a joint enterprise in which English and Scots would work together to bring civility, prosperity and peace to his third kingdom. The main method was to import into Ireland Protestant peoples from outside (Gillespie 1985; McCavitt 1998; Perceval-Maxwell 1973).

Such projects of plantation were not new. They had been tried since the mid-sixteenth century, most ambitiously in the southern province of Munster in the 1580s and 1590s. But the promising beginnings were destroyed by fresh rebellion. The insurgents were decisively defeated at Kinsale in 1601, shortly before James succeeded Elizabeth. In Ireland, the agents of the new king had to reconstruct what had been shattered. Debates developed about the best courses. There was a tradition of disputing whether severity or generosity was to be preferred. But these were matters of emphasis and timing rather than fundamental disagreements about the desirability of replacing the disloyal and supposedly idle and barbarous locals with more biddable strangers. Concerning Munster, no one in government, whether in London or Dublin, dissented from the proposition that the plantation should be resumed as quickly as possible. Munster, because of its geography, had long been the destination, temporary or permanent, of immigrants from further east. It was not conveniently situated to act as a magnet for itinerant Scots. Consequently, the Munster plantation remained resolutely an English and Welsh, not a British, enterprise (MacCarthy-Morrogh 1986).

Meanwhile Ulster, pacified after the Nine Years' War (1594–1603), was unsettled in 1607, when its two leading peers, Tyrconnell and Tyrone, suddenly sailed away to Catholic Europe. Next, the O'Dohertys rebelled. These disturbances provided the pretext for extending into Ulster a similar programme to that in Munster of engineered resettlement. Yet in one essential the Ulster project differed. Scots and English were involved as equal partners (McCavitt 1998). Peers and lairds from the northern kingdom like the Hamiltons, McClellands and Murrays of Broughton, undertook to establish colonies of the industrious on their freshly granted estates. Where they did so, they implanted habits carried over from Scotland. In time the distinctiveness of these communities was smudged as they took on colouration from Irish and English neighbours. However, differences – in diet, dress, housing, dialect, techniques and tools – persisted. Religious beliefs ensured that these variations not only survived but deepened. In Scotland itself, James VI was trying to add an episcopalian element to the established Presbyterian system. Under his son, Charles I, efforts to tilt the Kirk further towards the doctrine and rituals of the episcopal Church of England were angrily resisted. Many of the Scots who emigrated to the north of Ireland brought Presbyterianism with them. Subjected late in the 1630s to the same pressures towards conformity felt in Scotland, the Ulster Scots resisted (Canny 2001: 205–42, 347–61, 469–91; Gillespie in MacCuarta 1993; Kearney 1959). From the 1640s onwards, Covenanting generals and soldiers protected and advanced Presbyterianism in Ulster. So far from being eradicated, it was entrenched. A tacit toleration during the Cromwellian Interregnum allowed a formal Presbyterian organization to be created. A further influx of Scottish settlers, notably in the 1690s, strengthened this Presbyterian presence and ensured that the Scots of Ulster diverged in their worship from Protestants elsewhere in Ireland.

The manners in which Scots and English mainly in the north of Ireland worshipped accentuated other differences. On their estates, the separate communities had adopted practices which told of origins either in southwestern Scotland or northern England. The upheavals of the late 1630s and 1640s, which drove some settlers back to their places of origin and brought armies into the province, tightened ancestral bonds and widened cultural rifts. Inevitably, on the ground in the north of Ireland some fusion of Scots and English occurred. Also, when, in 1641, the settlers were attacked by the aggrieved indigenes, the distinction between English and Scottish ceased to mean much. All faced the same threat; all must co-operate against a danger which clearly came from the Irish and Catholics. It was at this moment of crisis that it looked as if James VI and I's dream of creating a British people had been achieved in the north of Ireland. Yet it remained largely a fiction that 'British Protestants' now peopled the region (Canny 2001: 301–401)

Conceived as a British venture, the Ulster plantation in the 1640s looked to a British alliance for salvation. During the civil wars the Scottish Covenanters united with the English and Welsh parliament through the Solemn League and Covenant. These allies co-operated uneasily; nowhere more so than in Ireland. The military co-operation resembled the uneasy alliances into which the distinct Scottish and English communities of Ulster had been driven owing to the emergency of 1641. Scottish soldiers were despatched to Ireland. Defending their compatriots and co-religionists, they seldom ventured outside the areas of earlier Scottish settlement. In this way, the tendency of Ireland to be divided into distinct English and Scottish spheres of interest was confirmed. As Scottish influence within the northeast increased, the contrast with other regions of Ireland was deepened and problems stored up for the future.

II

Early Stuart designs to import large contingents of English, Welsh and Scots into Ireland remind us of the official insistence that Ireland be retained – and if possible improved – as a possession of the English monarch. Reputation mattered greatly to sixteenth- and seventeenth-century rulers. Just as with lesser lords on their holdings, so sovereigns knew that it was incumbent on them to pass to heirs a patrimony intact or enlarged, but certainly not diminished. It was damaging to allow a rebellious territory to secede, since it lessened standing in the monarchical club, strengthened adversaries and might embolden other subjects to rise. The rulers of England, far from extricating themselves from the costly and awkward entanglement with Ireland, proclaimed through the Act for the kingly title of 1541 an intention to prove their claims to control the entire island. As well as the prestige of the Tudor monarchy, its security and prosperity were at stake. Ireland had a long history of hosting bids by pretenders and foreign adversaries to unseat the king from England. In the sixteenth century, as dynastic rivalries were backed by confessional differences, the potential of Ireland as a beach-head from which challengers might attack England and Wales increased. Ireland worried military and political strategists. As an island, it lacked the common frontier which England enjoyed with Wales and Scotland. Its long and often inaccessible coasts were well-nigh impossible to guard. Apparently open to foreign invaders, it was also inhabited with many thought at best tenuously linked with Christianity and civility and hostile to rule by England. The fundamental for both Tudors and Stuarts was to minimize the threat from the island. More ambitious advisers went beyond this minimalism. In an age of aggressive dynasticism, grandiloquent designs and spiralling costs, it was not enough simply to keep a territory inert. Ireland, so often a liability and a danger, could be transformed into an asset. These schemes varied from the utopian to the ruthlessly mercenary.

By 1603 the costs of English intervention were clearer than the profits. The numbers of soldiers in Ireland had regularly to be increased. A force of about 2,000 in the late 1550s grew to 8,000 during the 1580s. Most recently, the uprising of Tyrone, which had engulfed much of Ulster and spread into Munster, was reckoned to have cost England £1,845,696. Coinciding and indeed connected with the war against Spain, it was an unwelcome complication which aggravated the financial, social and political problems during the last decade of Elizabeth I's reign. Once England had ended these heavy commitments, its rulers hoped to avoid any more. Accordingly, at the start of James I's reign, government in Ireland reverted to its more modest form. The army was scaled down. By 1606 it was planned that no more than 880 soldiers should serve there (McCavitt 1998: 23–4, 36–9, 48). At the same time, if open threats receded, more subtle but equally dangerous ones persisted. In particular, the unwillingness of most in Ireland to embrace the state religion of England, Wales and Scotland perplexed the government. It was a universally accepted axiom that non-conformity in religion all too easily shaded into and sustained political dissidence. Catholics in Ireland, unwilling to abandon their confession, expected sympathy from the new monarch. This hope turned out to be mistaken. Instead, highly placed recusants, especially in Dublin, were harassed. So far from pressures for conformity being moderated, they intensified. Within the administration, both in London and Dublin, councillors argued about the wisdom of penalizing stubborn Catholics. These arguments resurrected disagreements which had bedevilled policy towards Ireland since Henry VIII had broken with Rome and since his successors had adopted Protestantism. Some contended that Ireland would not be brought to Protestantism until the writ of the English government was obeyed throughout Ireland. Accordingly, any push to convert the bulk of the Irish should be delayed. Others were not prepared to wait so long. Rather, they cast Protestant evangelists as the agents who would spread English ways among the local elites and into the Irish hinterlands. Any such dynamic approach was hindered by the scarcity of ministers, especially those able to preach and instruct in the Irish language, still spoken by the bulk of the population (Barnard 1975: 90–82; Ford 1997).

Councillors in London and Dublin routinely argued. These wrangles in high places were reminders that Irish policy was largely decided outside Ireland. Needs other than those of Ireland often determined what was done there. The council boards in both Dublin and London were attended by veterans deferred to as old Ireland hands. Throughout the seventeenth century, former Irish viceroys and commanders, such as Mountjoy (earl of Devonshire), Carew (earl of Totness), Chichester, Charles Fleetwood, Ormond and Essex, advised on Irish policy after they had relinquished their Irish stations. Astute Irish Catholics and later the Irish Protestants sought to play on these divergences. The recognition that most important questions were decided not in Dublin but in London shaped the way in which Irish politics developed. Unpalatable policies might be reversed or unpopular officials still in Dublin could be recalled if their Irish opponents could undermine them at the English court. The sophisticated Catholic politicians, increasingly excluded from the counsels of the viceroy and from parliament in Dublin, worked on the king, sometimes directly but more often through his favourites. Brokers at court offered to smooth the path. Especially when Charles I and his eldest son married Catholics, the entourage of the queen consort gave considerable leverage. In the 1670s both Sir Richard Bellings, a Catholic loyalist, and Lord Ossory, a Protestant grandee and heir to the lord lieutenant, Ormond, used their places within the household of Queen Catherine to promote the interests of kinsfolk and clients in Ireland. Then, too, during the 1650s, Catholics from Ireland shared exile with the future Charles II and James II. These privations created an intimacy which would be exploited after 1660 by the ambitious or disgruntled, such as Richard Talbot, future earl of Tyrconnell (Barnard in Ohlmeyer 1995: 265–91; Clarke in Moody, Martin and Byrne 1976: 187–242).

The interdependence of Irish and English politics had been evident almost from the moment when England first intervened in Ireland. However, the instability of the groupings around the monarch bemused outsiders anxious to discover the surest routes to royal favour. Immediately after James was installed as king in London, Catholics from Ireland were at a loss how to bring their case before the king. Subsequently, when some were summoned into his presence following opposition in the Dublin parliament, they were roughly handled. This lack of sympathy and limited access contrasted with the apparent ease with which Scots and even Irish Protestants moved through the passages of Whitehall and Theobalds. Neither James I nor Charles I was much interested in Ireland. Projectors depicted it – at least in prospect – as El Dorado. Seventeenth-century historians showed it to be a crowded Golgotha. Yet voracious courtiers discerned how Ireland might be turned to advantage. As the civil and military establishments of the kingdom grew, so too did the opportunities to gratify followers. Monarchs stuffed suppliants into Irish jobs and gave titles and lands there to absentees. Soon councillors, courtesans and courtiers strove to add Ireland to their spheres of patronage. These predators encouraged a tendency, already in train, to turn office and property in Ireland into the exclusive preserves of Protestants from England and Scotland. Protests that this venality was inimical to good government and ultimately to the king's revenues and power in Ireland were brushed aside. So, too, were the complaints of those in Ireland cheated of the preferments which they believed were rightly theirs (Treadwell 1998).

English rulers attended to Ireland, and to what its inhabitants desired, only when factors external to Ireland demanded it. Foreign warfare usually explained the attentiveness. Charles I, inheriting and expanding wars from his father in 1625, urgently needed troops and cash. His adversaries, France and Spain, might invade Ireland. Charles, therefore, explored how Ireland could help. His Catholic subjects, so much more numerous, offered the better prospect. But before they would agree to assist, they named their price. In 'the Graces', leading Catholics set out a programme to check and reverse their recent losses. The military crisis passed before they could extort their price. Nevertheless, 'the Graces' remained the clearest statement of Irish Catholic grievances and what they would require in return for any future help (Clarke 1965). In the 1640s civil war once more turned Charles into a supplicant. In Ireland he now faced a Catholic force, based in the inland town of Kilkenny, which governed much of the kingdom. The king, desperate for reinforcements in his struggle with the Westminster parliament and the Scottish Covenanters, was prepared to barter away Protestant privileges accumulated over recent years. Twice he sanctioned truces with the Confederate Catholics at Kilkenny, seeing these cessations as the prelude to solid treaties. However, Charles's advisers, mainly English and Protestant, knew the virulence of anti-Catholic and anti-Irish feelings throughout England, Wales and Scotland. They warned that any gain from the Irish troops despatched to his side would be offset by the alienation of Protestants in all three of his kingdoms (Ó Siochrú 1999; Little in Ó Siochrú 2001). This same need to conciliate Protestants throughout Britain and Ireland inhibited Charles II when tempted to treat the Irish Catholics better. Even his brother James, although an avowed Catholic, retained some of the conventional English prejudices against Ireland. As king after 1685, James proceeded more slowly towards righting old wrongs (Barnard in Ohlmeyer 1995: 277–81; Simms 1969).

These disappointments emphasized how the Stuarts had to balance concern for their subjects in Ireland with humouring those in their other kingdoms. These were the predictable problems of composite monarchies, but aggravated in the case of the Stuarts by confessional diversity. The Protestants of England, Scotland and Wales were at once more numerous than the Catholics of Ireland and better placed to make trouble when affronted. Irish interests were usually subordinated to those of the other kingdoms. Ironically, this did not always work to the detriment of Ireland. So long as Ireland did not obtrude itself onto the attention of the monarch and his (or her) ministers, much control was delegated to those on the spot. Increasingly, this habit favoured cliques of Irish Protestants, and so angered the Catholics who felt pushed aside. These realities rendered supererogatory much of the learned discussion – at the time and since – about how Ireland was most appropriately treated. Yet discussions of Irish policy ranged over the justifications for English sovereignty in Ireland, where precisely it resided (in the king alone or the king in parliament) and what rights the inhabitants of Ireland possessed. Occasionally, impatient with the insensitivity of England's handling, the irritated advocated complete constitutional union. More rarely still, the angry wanted completely to sunder the ties with England

(Ó hAnnracháin in Ó Siochrú 2001: 176–91). Most pamphleteers aspired to make Ireland 'West England', though not 'West Britain'. Features seemingly unique to Ireland, or at least different from lowland England and Scotland, were universally decried. The terminology of barbarism, incivility and primitivism was easily applied to an island which in so many aspects deviated from Britain. The scholarly investigated the history and antiquities of Ireland. Others reported on terrain and indigenous Gaelic societies. The gloomy and cheerful alike lamented the frequent failures to tap the human and inanimate resources. Where they differed was on how to correct these failures: whether by cajolery or coercion. Optimists contended that once the right structures and institutions – modelled on English originals – were in place across Ireland, then it would take on a decidedly more amiable aspect. Pessimists could reasonably remind that many of these desiderata had been introduced long before. English law, manors, walled and chartered towns, English systems of tenure, inheritance and trading guilds had featured in Angevin and Plantagenet Ireland. Under the early Stuarts, it was nevertheless true that only recently and even then incompletely had the whole of Ireland bowed to a nominal English authority. Much consequently remained to be done before the norms of English administration prevailed throughout the entire country.

Economy and policy alike recommended a shift from the heavily militarized regime maintained throughout much of the sixteenth century to one in which the army and martial law figured less conspicuously. Faith was placed in the uniform and supposedly impartial operations of the law. Under James VI and I, the whole island was divided into counties. Already, chartered boroughs had been created, and these were increased. There magistrates would dispense English law. Their endeavours were seconded at a more local level by courts leet and baron held by lords of manors, and at a higher level by the judges sent twice yearly from Dublin to preside over the county assizes. This deeper penetration of legal process into the Irish provinces was intended to lessen the allegedly arbitrary powers hitherto wielded by the chiefs of the Gaelic septs (or clans). Soon enough, it was alleged that the ancient tyranny had simply been replaced by a modern one, exercised by a different group of mainly Protestant officials and property-owners (Gillespie 1985; MacCarthy-Morrogh 1986; McCavitt 1998).

Linked with this wish to conform Ireland more closely to English legal procedures was the drive to ensure that the western kingdom also forsook Catholicism. These secular and religious aims were thought most likely to be advanced by reinvigorating the earlier plantations. In planning how to plant Munster and Ulster with the skilled and active from Britain, few dissented from the wisdom of the age: that settlements of chosen immigrants would enrich and anglicize Ireland. Inducements were offered to those who would undertake new settlements and who could entice tenants, artificers and craftsmen to Ireland. The results, disappointing to many, were not derisory. By the 1630s Ulster had a population of Protestant newcomers, some Scots, some English, totalling perhaps 15,000, which may have doubled by 1660. In Munster there were approximately 22,000 settlers by 1641. This total may have recovered and modestly increased to about 30,000 in 1660 (Barnard in Canny 1998: 309–27). Elsewhere, smaller colonies of Protestants were established. Often these communities focused on a town, such as Parsonstown (later Birr) or Mountrath. More immigrants were attracted through less formal methods. Counties Antrim and Down, for example, drew over Scots seeking a better life. Canny proprietors, like Sir John

Clotworthy in the environs of Antrim town, encouraged these settlers. The Welsh, particularly from the maritime counties, readily moved to the neighbouring island. Grandees from inland counties, notably the Herberts of Cherbury, granted lands in the remote county of Kerry, established Welsh tenants around Castleisland (Canny 2001: 233–9, 254–5, 371–5; MacCarthy-Morrogh 1986; Perceval-Maxwell 1973).

Everywhere, towns were viewed as vital to this industrious and godly society. Centres and seminaries, they set out to lure those with rare and specialized skills. They also had political functions. Most blatantly, they ensured that, between 1613 and 1634, Protestants became the majority in the lower house of the Irish parliament. Some boroughs did function as more than devices to deposit two members in the Dublin legislature. They offered lessons in and outlets for fraternity and public spirit. Protestants were deliberately concentrated in urban strongholds. Before 1641 this programme brought conflict with the established Catholic townspeople who resisted – often successfully – any Protestant takeover. Defeat of the Catholics between 1649 and 1653 allowed a much more comprehensive advance of the Protestants into the government and trade of the towns. By then, confessional tests excluded Catholics from national and local government (Barnard 1975: 50–89). These exclusions emphasized the centrality of the towns to the English and Protestant mission in Ireland. At the same time, by debarring Catholics from urban life, the authorities contradicted their professed aim of tutoring Catholics in civility (as conceived by the English). This contradiction ran through much of English action in Ireland; for example, debarring Catholics from the lettered professions (other than medicine), from county office as magistrates and sheriffs, from national positions as judges and councillors and (after 1661) from membership of the lower house of parliament.

The opening years of James VI and I's reign, far from heralding a recovery by Catholics of much that they had recently forfeited, inaugurated the tougher measures which would soon squeeze Catholics from the little that they still enjoyed. Leading Dubliners who failed to attend worship according to the rites of the Protestant Church of Ireland, as enjoined by a law of 1560, were fined, imprisoned and humiliated. The ancient port of Waterford, intended as an Irish equivalent of Bristol with which it kept strong trading links, was stripped of its charter in 1618, and temporarily ruled by a governor (Clarke in Moody, Martin and Byrne 1976: 189, 224). Bit by bit, Protestant newcomers infiltrated the large towns, but the incumbent Catholics, although intimidated by the government, were courageous and ingenious in their resistance. Only the Catholics' comprehensive defeat after 1649 allowed the English authorities to expel the surviving Catholic townspeople and transfer civic government, the bulk of property and monopolies over intramural trade to Protestants. The latter were not always substantial enough in means and international contacts to sustain the commercial dynamism of ports like Limerick, Galway, Waterford and Wexford. As a result, Charles II, convinced by economic reasoning as well as by sentiment, relaxed the prohibitions (Barnard in Ohlmeyer 1995: 272–7). James VII and II restored Catholics to their former urban dominance. The principal motive was political. Corporations were the key to an amenable parliament. With James and his Catholic ministers planning to summon a new assembly, its tractability depended on restoring the Catholic majority. In the event, the parliament was elected only in 1689 – after James had abandoned England and Scotland, and arrived, as a welcome refugee, in Ireland. Although furnished with an overwhelmingly Catholic body, he – like his predecessors – hesitated to grant all that the Catholics desired. Too great concessions to the Irish Catholics, above all by returning the lands that they had lost over the past century, would alarm and estrange potential supporters in his other kingdoms (Simms 1969).

III

The main effect of English actions towards Ireland was to transfer property and power from the incumbent majority to a small minority. Over the seventeenth century the achievement was most clearly visible in the stark statistics of landownership. In 1641, on the eve of the Confederate War, Catholics owned 59 per cent of the profitable acreage of the kingdom; by 1703 this percentage had dropped to 14 (Simms 1956: 195–6). During the same period Catholics had been edged from high office, the judicial bench, the lower house of parliament and from most local positions of profit and authority. The trend had in some measure been disguised by the reverses of the 1640s and 1680s. James II's defeat ruined his Irish Catholic supporters. After 1690 they were excluded from full citizenship, office and (often) property. In 1704 a Test Act, copied from an earlier English measure, confined most prestigious places in government to members of the established Church of Ireland (Connolly 1992: 263–313; Dickson 1987: 29–61).

This reservation of office and political rights to the adherents of the state confession was the norm across much of seventeenth- and eighteenth-century Europe. Recent writing reminds us that Ireland was not unique in being a confessional state (Connolly 1992: 103–43). At the same time, detailed studies have softened the impression of universal and total ruin. The amounts of land which Catholics succeeded in keeping varied from region to region. West of the Shannon, in counties such as Galway and Clare, it proved easier for some Catholic proprietors to survive. Even nearer the heart of English government in Ireland, wily Catholics in Louth, Meath and County Dublin evaded the bans. Important as these successes were, they hardly altered a situation in which land, the conventional determinant of status and key to entry into public affairs, had become largely a Protestant possession. Catholics showed flexibility in adjusting to these conditions. Some, especially in the upper reaches of society, converted to Protestantism and by doing so preserved their inheritances and the traditional power of their dynasties. Since the sixteenth century, through a mixture of blandishments and threats, the English authorities had worked for these conversions. Especially among the peerage, the policy claimed remarkable triumphs. In turn, the Butlers, earls, marquesses and dukes of Ormonde, the Burkes (marquesses of Clanricarde), the Barrys (earls of Barrymore), the O'Briens (earls of Thomond and of Inchiquin) and the Macdonnells (marquesses of Antrim) abandoned their ancestral Catholicism. By the 1720s so numerous were the defections that of a lay peerage of approximately 130 in Ireland fewer than 10 remained Catholic (Barnard and Fenlon 2000: 1–54).

Financial and social pressures also worked to persuade lawyers to defect to Protestantism. Practice at the bar, a calling in Ireland which Catholics had dominated before 1641, was legally closed to them by the 1690s. However, it was suspected that Catholics were circumventing the ban. Because of these suspicions, delight at the Catholics who deserted their church was tempered by fear that this was a cunning ploy through which a fifth column might enter and in time undermine the Protestant interest in Ireland. So what had once been a favourite objective of English policy – to bring over to Protestantism as many Irish Catholics as possible – by the early eighteenth century was regarded ambivalently. Anxiety about the sincerity of conversions told of continuing worries among the Protestants of Ireland. Their recent history alternated between tribulations and triumphs. Unnerved by the speed and completeness of the Catholic *revanche* under James II, Irish Protestants remained sceptical well into the eighteenth century that the pattern of the previous 150 years, in which rebellions recurred regularly after forty years, had indeed been broken. The winners watched the vanquished warily. As in the aftermath of previous defeats, the victors had quarrelled over whether it was best to show magnanimity or severity. From the 1690s into the 1730s the harsher attitude prevailed. The past taught that Protestant clemency had been repaid by the Catholics with fresh insurrections. In the 1650s moves were made to disable the losers. The leaders of Confederate Ireland – the landowners, the military commanders, the lawyers and the priests – were singled out as the villains. When not killed, they were banished and expropriated. However, the punitive measures had been relaxed soon after Charles II's restoration and were reversed in 1685. After 1691 the triumphant Protestants vowed not to repeat these mistakes. A series of statutes elevated the proclamations of the 1650s into a discriminatory system, which created in all but name a Protestant (and after 1704, Church of Ireland) ascendancy (Barnard 1975; Barnard in Ohlmeyer 1995: 218–40; Dickson 1987: 62–95; Connolly 1992: 307–17).

The novelty of this exclusive confessional state, it has been suggested, vanishes when it is compared with the similar regimes in Britain and continental Europe. Yet in one vital particular it differed: power inevitably flowed towards the propertied and privileged. Everywhere the lucky were few. But at least notionally, any who subscribed to the state cult had a chance to prosper within these confessional regimes. In Scotland, Wales and England, as in Western Europe, the state cult comprehended the bulk of the population. This was not the case in Ireland. During the seventeenth century the number of Protestants grew, both absolutely and proportionately. Planned settlements, colonial spread and unplanned movement strengthened the Protestant interest – and with it the English and Scottish presence – in Ireland. Even so, early in the eighteenth century, by most reckonings no more than 25 per cent – perhaps 300,000 to 400,000 – of Ireland's inhabitants were Protestants. Furthermore, they were divided between conformist members of the Church of Ireland and dissenters, mainly the Scottish Presbyterians of Ulster. The latter, under the terms of the Test Act of 1704, were denied many rights; indeed, they were relegated to the same depressed legal status as the Catholic majority. These proscriptions meant that the English – or (after 1707) British – state in Ireland rested on a dangerously narrow base.

Other than in its meagre size, the Protestant community of Ireland was not unusual in the ways in which it was favoured. Contemporary statecraft taught that a people which diverged from its rulers in religion might readily engage in other sorts of defiance. The uprising of 1641 and the war of 1689–91 were most easily explained as religious in origin. This line of reasoning then justified the use of confession as the surest guide to political reliability (Barnard in Ó Siochrú 2001: 20–43). Charles II and – even more – the Catholic James II were reluctant to accept a doctrine expounded by their fervently Protestant advisers. Instead they approved a fealty offered to them personally, and in which questions of confessional affiliation looked irrelevant. However, once unequivocally Protestant monarchs were enthroned, first with William and Mary in place of the departed James and then with George I in preference to a Catholic Stuart, it seemed wise – especially in Ireland – to confine civil rights to those who publicly affirmed their Protestantism. Many Catholics protested. Had they not bravely demonstrated their loyalty? Unavailingly, they insisted that they could and would obey a Protestant. Their rivals, particularly the Protestants settled in Ireland, pointed to what they believed to be contrary evidence: the wars of the 1640s and 1689–91.

No more than the Protestant community were the Catholics ever homogeneous. However, it suited their adversaries to demonize them as such. Among the Catholics some groups were readier to fight than to negotiate in order to reclaim what they thought their own. Few, other than those who spent many years as exiles on the Continent, wanted to exchange their English overlord for another. Most, still looking for help from Charles I and James II, helped them (Clarke 1965; Simms in Moody, Martin and Byrne 1976: 478–508). The Irish Catholics were unlucky twice to choose a loser. Implicated in the Stuarts' defeats, Irish Catholics were easily cast as enemies by the victorious Cromwellians and the Williamites. James VII and II's arrival in Ireland in 1689 – the first of an English ruler since Richard II – delighted Irish Catholics, but it all too soon disclosed the disparity between the king's concern to regain his other two kingdoms, and those of his Irish subjects. Tensions beset the Jacobite camp and contributed to the defeats on the battlefields of the Boyne and Aughrim (Simms 1969). Yet the Irish, sharing defeat and foreign exile, could hardly repudiate their Stuart monarch. Just as James himself had been obliged to seek the backing of his more powerful cousin Louis XIV, becoming his pensionary, so after 1691 pragmatic Irish entered the service of continental rulers, including both Louis and his enemies in Spain and the Empire. These refugees had certainly not abandoned hope that both they and the Catholic Stuarts would be restored to their hereditary possessions within Ireland. Until that bright day dawned, they had livings to earn.

Events in Ireland belonged to the complex interactions within and between the Stuarts' several territories. They were also part of European and North Atlantic developments. Of late, historians have stressed that Ireland was not sealed hermetically against outside influences. Nor did the Irish operate only in the Stuarts' dominions. Even before the defeated were dispossessed and forced into exile in the seventeenth century, Catholics from Ireland had traded with and campaigned on the Continent. As the authorities put greater obstacles in the way of Catholic worship and teaching, so more resorted to convents and seminaries overseas (O'Connor 2001). Propitious circumstances in Ireland after 1641 and 1660 tempted some refugees to return. Often they came back with attitudes at variance with those who had collaborated and colluded with the Dublin government. Schooled to uphold absolutism, those Catholics who would allow the Stuarts virtually unlimited power and who had no patience with representative institutions confirmed Protestant fears about the danger of this alliance between the Stuarts and the Irish Catholics. Despite what the Protestant alarmists sometimes alleged, not all Catholics thought in these terms. Those who had remained in Ireland, battling to contain or repel Protestant encroachments, shared many tactics and ideals with Scottish and

English critics of James I and Charles I. This was hardly surprising, since the Irish had been trained in the same London Inns of Court, in parliamentary procedures borrowed from England, and sometimes even in the English universities. They had also read the same humanist manuals and legal texts. This common culture could have created an elite at ease – as the Old and New English of Ireland – with the values of Stuart England and Wales. Wilfully, it seemed, the English government turned the adder's ear to the protestations of loyalty from the Catholic Old English, so straining and eventually breaking their patient loyalty (Clarke 1965; Cunningham 2000).

The English government acted provocatively because it could not ignore the awkwardness that the traditional elite in Ireland, a hybrid of the native Irish and the descendants of earlier settlers from England and Wales, seemingly amenable to so much that England intended for Ireland, gagged on one detail. It uncompromisingly rejected Protestantism. There was no inherent reason why Ireland – or at least the bulk of its property-owners – should not embrace Protestantism. Already by 1603 the likelihood of their doing so had receded, and by 1660 had wholly disappeared (Barnard 1975: 298–9; Ford 1997). A lack of money and clergy weakened an evangelical campaign at the time – early in Elizabeth's reign – when it might have succeeded. In addition, uncertainties over and the discontinuities in ecclesiastical policy in England itself affected what could be attempted in Ireland. Even after English policy had been clarified and become unequivocally Protestant, the authorities in Ireland disagreed as to how best to act. By the time disagreements were resolved, the field was crowded with Catholic competitors. Catholic priests and monks easily outnumbered their Protestant rivals, by two or three to one. They enjoyed more than a simple numerical advantage. Members of Irish families, conversant with the terrain and the vernacular, they fitted more easily into the society from which – in most instances – they had been recruited. In time, Protestant clergy would be supplied from families born in Ireland. However, it was not until the end of the seventeenth century that many had those local roots, and by then the Catholics had dug in more deeply (Connolly 1992: 144–97).

The government of Stuart Ireland, by treating Catholicism as tantamount to treason, may have created the problem it affected to control. It is a vexed issue as to why and when an Irish Catholic nationalism developed, and whether in its seventeenth-century manifestations it resembled – let alone connected with – its nineteenth-century equivalent. As the difficulty of and penalties for worshipping as a Catholic were increased under the early Stuarts, so a grievance was aggravated. Its redress became an ambition of Catholic activists. In the uprising of 1641 Protestant clergy, Bibles and churches were singled out for attack. Protestant propagandists may have exaggerated the sufferings, but enough occurred to lend veracity to their claims. At the same time the Confederation of Kilkenny brought the Catholic bishops into its deliberations, took back church buildings, patronized Catholic rituals and demanded an end to discriminations based on confession. In so far as any single force united the fissiparous Confederation it was Catholicism. Ranged against it – in Ireland, but also in England and Scotland – were forces which were almost exclusively and assertively Protestant. Belatedly, some would say that the wars of religion which had engulfed sixteenth- and early seventeenth-century Europe had reached Ireland (MacCuarta 1993: 93–158; Ó Siochrú 1999).

Catholics protested in vain against the way in which the Protestants of Ireland portrayed them. It suited Protestants, scheming to grab the remainder of Catholic property and power, to promote themselves as the only firm supports of the English interest in Ireland. Henceforward all Catholics were labelled and treated as subversives, even when unswervingly loyal to their Stuart kings. In large measure excluded from the state which 150 years earlier they had controlled, the Catholic majority was reluctant to shed its ingrained habits of loyalty. However, it was increasingly difficult to identify with an order from which Catholics were excluded and which denied them many of the most lucrative and prestigious employments. Again, what recent accounts have tended to stress is the resilience of these despised and rejected Catholics. Tactics included the outward conformity mentioned already or the retention of old livelihoods by surreptitious means. The title to lands might have passed to others, but sometimes the supplanted stayed on as tenants and occupiers. Protestants were soon disconcerted by the Catholics' capacity for survival. They were also worried by the frequency with which Catholics acted as agents for Protestant landowners either absent from or uninterested in their Irish holdings. Further fears were excited by the success as merchants of Catholics, forbidden to invest in freehold property. This activity built on the remnants of the Catholics' former dominance over urban and overseas trade and their excellent links with the ports around the littoral of the north Atlantic. Catholic survivals were remarkable; but, as so often, the fortunate leave clearer traces than the failures.

In Ireland, as in Scotland, a pastoral economy afforded scant opportunities for exciting and remunerative careers (Dickson 1987: 96–127). As a result, the Irish had long followed the trade of arms. European rulers welcomed soldiers of fortune. A few from Ireland flourished. More typical were the exhausted and destitute who sought charity from foreign monarchs and churches or ended in the Hôtel des Invalides. Even these veterans constituted a lucky minority. For those still in Ireland, life was usually short and grim. The savagery of warfare there shocked those accustomed to the gentler conduct in England and Scotland. Vengeance added to the fatalities through the fighting itself. Divine retribution, it was widely believed, then unleashed pestilence and famine on already weakened populations, especially after 1649. Some estimate that as many as a third of Ireland's inhabitants died. After the shorter Jacobite War no pandemics scythed through the surviving population. Even without these shocks Ireland remained alarmingly vulnerable to dearth, disease and massive mortality (Connolly 1992: 41–59; Dickson 1987: 96–127). Contemporaries who sought explanations other than divine disfavour returned to the theme of underdevelopment and the evident gap between potential and achievement. In order to address these problems many of the preferred methods of the English in Ireland were sanctioned. The transfer of property, the planting of newcomers with specialist skills, the outlawing of Gaelic practices and techniques, even the promotion of Protestantism and the proscription of Catholicism would speed the spread of industry and prosperity. Hopes as to what could be accomplished by these means rose and fell. At the very least it was expected that a quickening economy would ensure that the locals might be gainfully employed as hewers of wood and drawers of water.

IV

It is in the nature of defeat that the experience of individuals on the losing side can seldom be retrieved. Only the few grandees, the nimble who escaped to Europe and reconstructed some sort of career, or the recipients of institutional philanthropy, survive as something other than a statistic of the dead or as a name on a list of the taxed or enlisted. Poetry, prose and propaganda have been ingeniously analysed to recover something of Irish Catholic attitudes, but at best they hint at the daily round of the humble (Cunningham 2000; O'Riordan in Ohlmeyer 1995: 112–27; Ó Ciardha in Barnard and Fenlon 2000: 177–93). The Protestants, in contrast, dominated the record. They were keen to descant on what they and their forebears suffered in establishing themselves in Ireland. They stressed how hard they had struggled to bring the recalcitrant mass into conformity with English, Scottish and Protestant norms. The sufferings, most meticulously itemized and preserved for 1641, give incidental insights into the affairs of the modestly circumstanced, although not of the propertyless labourer who even then existed in Protestant Ireland (Barnard in Ó Siochrú 2001: 20–43).

A Protestant society, recognizably modelled after English, Welsh and Scottish prototypes, had come into being in Ireland. Fashioned in part from elements to hand, as some within the indigenous Catholic communities switched confession, it relied heavily on replenishment from Britain. It also welcomed refugees from Protestant Europe. In 1641 it was distributed unevenly across the island and between different social and occupational groups. It was strongest in the areas of planned settlement, notably Munster and Ulster, and in those eastern maritime counties most accessible from Britain. It was densest in the larger towns, of which Dublin was the chief. One seventeenth-century observer supposed that half the Protestants in Ireland were town dwellers. Furthermore, it was top-heavy. Those with pretensions to be gentlemen and merchants were disproportionately well represented. These imbalances may not have been corrected as the century passed. Nevertheless, the number of Protestants increased and with it the availability of the craftsmen and specialists needed if Ireland was to thrive. The authorities were disconcerted that larger numbers brought a problem of the Protestant poor. As in England, Wales and Scotland, this was tackled at the parochial level and through private benefactions and initiatives. In communities polarized around the different confessions, the Church of Ireland parishes tended to look after their own. Others were left either without any obvious aid or with what their kindred, neighbours and the Catholic church could offer (Barnard in Canny 1998: 309–27; Dickson 1987: 169).

The Catholic majority in Ireland might reasonably feel estranged from the English Protestant state. However, estrangement was less obvious than indifference to or evasion of its authority. The insurgents of the 1640s and 1680s declared their adherence to their English monarch. In 1689, with James II briefly in Ireland, this was not empty rhetoric. In these wars opportunities were taken to avenge themselves on the local representatives and beneficiaries of Stuart rule. Relative newcomers to Ireland were, on occasion, savagely assaulted (Simms in MacCuarta 1993: 107–38).

During times of peace, agrarian disorders and even atrocities happened. On their side, Protestant notables in the provinces hunted trouble-makers – tories, rapparees and brigands – with the same zeal as they pursued wolves and game. Rulers in Dublin acknowledged that Ireland was too unsettled for it to be possible to stand down the army or rely altogether on civil processes. Yet there was reluctance to use soldiers for routine policing and law enforcement. Nor was it felt – except in rare emergencies – that the incidence or seriousness of violence demanded army intervention. Whatever the Protestants of Ireland might allege in efforts to discredit their Catholic neighbours, the island did not teeter constantly on the brink of chaos.

Two periods of warfare, one protracted, the other briefer, have to be balanced against the longer periods of relative quiet. The passivity did not mean that Ireland had supinely accepted English authority and been assimilated to English ways. Nor did the wars involve a total rejection of English rule; indeed, rather the reverse: the insurgents proclaimed their allegiance to and affection for their Stuart king. Undoubtedly many Catholics formerly important in Ireland were dismayed by and wished to reverse recent policies. So far from being reversed, the discriminatory measures were intensified. The profiteers were the English, Scots and Welsh substituted for the Catholic Irish. Favoured because they seemed the best hope of pacifying and enriching Ireland, they imprinted the kingdom with a stamp rather different from what had been intended. Furthermore, they continued, even after settling in Ireland, to think of themselves still as English, Welsh or Scots, seldom as British and only slowly – in the mid-eighteenth century – as Irish. Throughout the seventeenth century these planters were mortified that they had not grown as rich as had been predicted and that the government had not assisted them as much as they had expected. Such disappointments embittered relations between the Protestants in Ireland and the government in London. Sometimes the agents of English rule in Ireland sounded more critical of the Stuarts than did the Catholics. In particular, they were annoyed that England, whether in the shape of king or parliament, did less than they wanted to disable and – in the 1640s and 1689–90 – to defeat their Catholic adversaries. Yet, as these Protestants discovered to their embarrassment, alone they could not stave off a Catholic assault. Ultimately, their only saviours were England and Scotland. That truth accepted, many Protestants in Ireland were brutally pragmatic when deciding whom to support. During the 1640s the increasing unlikelihood of Charles I being able to help his beleaguered subjects in Ireland and his willingness to entertain kindly thoughts towards the Confederates inclined more Protestants towards the Westminster parliament or the Scottish Covenanters. Similarly, James II's eagerness to liberate his co-religionists in Ireland from the worst of their disabilities made Protestants, especially when pushed from their army commands and patentee offices, reconsider their allegiance. They differed in the alacrity with which they rallied to the side of William of Orange, but few in Protestant Ireland after 1691 dissented from the credo that he was indeed their deliverer to whom they owed liberty and property.

V

Analysts have disagreed as how best to characterize the society which emerged in seventeenth-century Ireland. Some liken the large and sudden exodus from England,

Wales and Scotland to Ireland to that which took Spaniards and Portuguese to America and the subjects of the Tudors and Stuarts in the same direction. The motives for so many so suddenly uprooting themselves in order to settle in Ireland are also disputed: whether for betterment or simple subsistence. What then resulted has sometimes been seen as a colony (or group of colonies) comparable to those in New England. Others regard the Protestant settlements in Ireland as variants of the provincial societies which abounded in the peripheries and uplands of Scotland, Wales and western England (Canny 2001; Connolly 1992; Gillespie 1985; MacCarthy-Morrogh 1986). What is clearer is that, while Protestant Ireland gained its unique privileges between 1603 and 1731, its formation was a considerably slower process. It was made up of earlier vintages of settlers, chiefly from Wales and England, who switched to Protestantism after 1560. Between the 1530s and 1650s they were overlaid by the numerous soldiers and officials whose service in Ireland was rewarded with lands. In turn, these servitors and servants of the Tudors were in danger of being swamped by those attracted to Ireland by the expanding army, bureaucracy and Protestant church and by the schemes of assisted settlement under the Stuarts. These elements did not always knit together. Moreover, many retained traces of the regions from which they had originated and with which they often stayed in contact. This helped to explain the distinctive characters of the Ulster and Munster plantations (Gillespie 1985; Perceval-Maxwell 1973; MacCarthy-Morrogh 1986).

Hybrids sprang up in Protestant Ireland, neither truly English, Welsh or Scots, nor indisputably Irish. Identities constantly mutated, as loyalty focused on kindred, neighbourhood, confession, craft, county and country. Most Protestants, inserted in place of Catholics, inevitably defined themselves in opposition to the latter. However, the feelings of difference and antagonism varied. There was a loyalty towards England or Scotland, and towards those deputed to rule on their behalf in Ireland, but this obedience was far from unconditional, and might – as in the 1640s – move from the English monarch to the English parliament. At other times, famously in 1689–91, William and Mary were regarded as a better embodiment of Irish Protestant values than James II. This selective approach to what constituted their Englishness and Protestantism strained the relations of the Protestants in Ireland with England. As the Irish Protestants increased in numbers, so they gained in confidence and became more disputatious.

By 1714, although still a minority, the Protestants had benefited from continuing immigration and natural increase. By then the stock of land which might still be transferred from Catholics to Protestants was virtually exhausted. The ending of enforced redistributions posed problems for landowners: how to supplement the usually disappointing yield of their estates or, for the cadets, how to buy into the landed orders. These difficulties made more galling the policy of England towards Ireland. The best jobs, from the lord lieutenancy itself through judgeships, bishoprics, army commissions and patentee offices, were reserved for strangers from Britain. The policy spoke of contempt for the natives of Ireland, including now not just Catholics but Protestants, regarded as inferior in culture and doubtful in loyalty. It told also of the continuing use of Irish lands and patronage to gratify the important in England and Wales. In addition, it was part of an approach which subordinated a still potentially wayward kingdom more ruthlessly to English control. Although government in Ireland had been turned into a Protestant monopoly, the latitude allowed to that government in deciding fiscal, military and religious policy had been progressively curtailed. So, too, had its freedom to legislate for itself and even to trade. Briefly, during the Cromwellian interlude, Ireland had been united with England and Scotland. The experiment left few, either in England or Ireland, with much enthusiasm for repeating it. In an imperial diet, Irish voices were scarcely heard and seldom heeded. Benefits, such as admission to the trade of an expanding empire, were strictly rationed.

The trend, particularly from the 1630s, was to subject Ireland demeaningly to England. Simultaneously, Protestant communities were built up. By the later seventeenth century Irish Protestants had become as vehement as once the Catholics had been when the Westminster parliament or English privy council arrogated to itself the right to decide matters of consequence for Ireland. In 1642 the English parliament had legislated for the future settlement once the current rising was suppressed. In 1690, without reference to Ireland, it decided who should rule there as well as in England and Wales – William and Mary. During the 1660s and 1690s it stopped two of Ireland's most valuable exports. Irish complaints simply provoked more far-reaching English assertions of legislative sovereignty. Indicative too of the disregard of Irish Protestant sensitivities was the ruse by which, from 1698, 12,000 of the troops needed for William III's European enterprises in future would be stationed in and paid by Ireland (Dickson 1987: 29–61).

Coupled with other examples of English control over important Irish matters, these developments might suggest that Ireland was being drawn into a more uniform system of administering the Stuarts' multiple kingdoms. In practice, what Ireland felt bore little resemblance to the measures adopted for Scotland, or indeed for the United Provinces and (after 1714) Hanover. Furthermore, the resulting friction between the Irish Protestants and their English rulers fostered an incipient Irish Protestant particularism which resisted assimilation to unitary British policies. Many of the arrangements which irritated the important in Ireland resulted from the fiscal and military needs of a state drawn deeper into European and global affairs. William III's international ambitions and commitments had first brought him to England, and made Ireland a part of his grand strategy. Protestants might subsequently lament that their sacrifices on William's behalf had been meagrely rewarded. Indeed, with the quartering of the large force there, Ireland seemed little better than an offshore garrison: the more so as its own denizens were debarred from serving in the army on the island. In other respects, however, the growing dominion of the English king bestowed benefits. These in the end reconciled the testy Irish Protestants to their lot as subjects of England.

The most attractive posts in Ireland often went to interlopers. However, as government expanded, so did the number of jobs with adequate salaries and standing. These generally went to locals. Moreover, Protestants from Ireland found work in the Stuarts' and Hanoverians' other possessions. In particular, the War of Spanish Succession during Queen Anne's reign, notable for the employment it offered often indigent Scots, performed the same function for Irish Protestants. Thus, although Protestants from Ireland complained that their kingdom was being run primarily for the benefit of England, they overlooked their own gains. If access to the British army and navy was one, a second was the acquisition of a regular parliament. Between 1603 and 1688 the Dublin parliament had been summoned four times. An occasional event, it had little chance to develop cohesiveness. Paradoxically, this situation altered at the very time when England was curtailing Irish independence. From 1692, under the same financial pressures which had turned the English parliament into a fixture, the Irish assembly was convened regularly. Its members, subject to numerous irksome and some substantial constraints, skilfully used it to create a tax regime highly favourable to themselves as landowners and to direct those taxes into ventures from which they and – arguably – all Ireland profited (McGrath 2000). By doing so the Protestant interest in Ireland confirmed its reputation – among contemporaries and later commentators – for self-interest. A minority of Protestants, with influence, authority and salaries, were reconciled to English rule; others, the majority in Ireland, submitted more grudgingly.

REFERENCES

Barnard, T. C. 1975: *Cromwellian Ireland: English Government and Reform in Ireland, 1649–1660*: Oxford. Reprinted with new introduction, 2000.
Barnard, T. C. and Fenlon, J. (eds) 2000: *The Dukes of Ormonde, 1610–1745*: Woodbridge.
Bottigheimer, K. S. 1971: *English Money and Irish Land*: Oxford.
Canny, N. P. (ed.) 1998: *The Oxford History of the British Empire*, vol. 1: Oxford.
Canny, N. P. 2001: *Making Ireland British, 1580–1650*: Oxford.
Clarke, A. 1965: *The Old English in Ireland, 1625–1642*: London. Reprinted Dublin, 2000.
Connolly, S. J. 1992: *Religion, Law and Power: The Making of Protestant Ireland, 1659–1760*: Oxford.
Cunningham, B. 2000: *The World of Geoffrey Keating*: Dublin.
Dickson, D. 1987: *New Foundations: Ireland, 1600–1800*: Dublin. 2nd edn 2000.
Ellis, S. G. 1998: *Ireland in the Age of the Tudors, 1447–1603*: Harlow.
Ford, A. 1997: *The Protestant Reformation in Ireland, 1590–1641*, 2nd edn: Dublin.
Gillespie, R. 1985: *Colonial Ulster: The Settlement of East Ulster, 1600–1641*: Cork.
Kearney, H. F. 1959: *Strafford in Ireland, 1633–1641*: Manchester. Reprinted Cambridge, 1989.
MacCarthy-Morrogh, M. 1986: *The Munster Plantation: English Migration to Southern Ireland, 1583–1641*: Oxford.
McCavitt, J. 1998: *Sir Arthur Chichester: Lord Deputy of Ireland, 1605–16*: Belfast.
MacCuarta, B. (ed.) 1993: *Ulster 1641: Aspects of the Rising*: Belfast.
McGrath, C. I. 2000: *The Making of the Eighteenth-Century Irish Constitution: Government, Parliament and the Revenue, 1692–1714*: Dublin.
Moody, T. W., Martin, F. X. and Byrne, F. J. (eds) 1976: *A New History of Ireland, vol. 3: Early Modern Ireland, 1534–1691*: Oxford.
O'Connor, T. (ed.) 2001: *The Irish in Europe, 1580–1815*: Dublin.
Ohlmeyer, J. H. (ed.) 1995: *Ireland from Independence to Occupation, 1641–1660*: Cambridge.
Ó Siochrú, M. 1999: *Confederate Ireland, 1642–1649: A Constitutional and Political Analysis*: Dublin.
Ó Siochrú, M. (ed.) 2001: *Kingdoms in Crisis: Ireland in the 1640s*: Dublin.
Perceval-Maxwell, M. 1973: *The Scottish Migration to Ulster in the Reign of James I*: London.
Perceval-Maxwell, M. 1994: *The Outbreak of the Irish Rebellion of 1641*: Dublin.
Simms, J. G. 1956: *The Williamite Confiscation in Ireland, 1690–1703*: London.
Simms, J. G. 1969: *Jacobite Ireland, 1685–1691*: London. Reprinted Dublin, 2000.
Treadwell, V. 1998: *Buckingham and Ireland, 1616–1628: A Study in Anglo-Irish Politics*: Dublin.

FURTHER READING

There is no recent and reliable single-volume history of Ireland throughout the seventeenth century. The chapters by A. Clarke, P. J. Corish and J. G. Simms in T. W. Moody, F. X. Martin and F. J. Byrne, eds, 1976: *A New History of Ireland Vol. 3: Early Modern Ireland, 1534–1691*: Oxford, provide authoritative introductions. Newer work (not all focused on the seventeenth century) can be sampled in C. Brady and R. Gillespie, eds, 1986: *Natives and Newcomers: The Making of Irish Colonial Society 1534–1641*: Dublin; B. MacCuarta ed., 1993: *Ulster 1641: Aspects of the Rising*: Belfast; S. G. Ellis and S. Barber, eds, 1995: *Conquest and Union: Fashioning a British State, 1485–1725*: Harlow; and J. H. Ohlmeyer, ed., 1995: *Ireland from Independence to Occupation, 1641–1660*: Cambridge. Irish Catholic outlooks are illuminated by B. Cunningham 2000: *The World of Geoffrey Keating*: Dublin. The organizations and habits of the natives are treated in K. Nicholls 1972: *Gaelic and Gaelicized Ireland in the Later Middle Ages*: Dublin (new edition promised in 2002). For the years after 1660 there are excellent guides in D. Dickson 1987: *New Foundations: Ireland, 1600–1800*: Dublin (2nd edn 2000) and J. G. Simms 1969: *Jacobite Ireland, 1685–1691*: London (reprinted Dublin, 2000). Recent writing is considered in T. Barnard, 'British History and Irish History' in G. Burgess, ed., 1999: *The New British History: Founding a Modern State, 1603–1715*: London; and in the introduction to T. C. Barnard 1975: *Cromwellian Ireland: English Government and Reform in Ireland, 1649–1660*: Oxford (reprinted 2000). Of efforts to integrate as well as to compare Irish experience with that of the British state, the most ambitious and successful is M. J. Braddick 2000: *State Formation in Early Modern England, c. 1550–1700*: Cambridge. Several essays in B. Bradshaw and J. Morrill, eds, 1996: *The British Problem, c. 1534–1707: State Formation in the Atlantic Archipelago*: Basingstoke, attempt the same feat with uneven success.

CHAPTER THREE

Asia, the Atlantic and the Subjects of the British Monarchy

NICHOLAS CANNY

Introduction

It is widely appreciated that the relationship of England, and to a lesser degree that of Scotland and Ireland, with the world beyond Europe was altered fundamentally during the course of the seventeenth century. This essay will explain how this transformation was the outcome of several incremental changes rather than the result of any master plan, and that the outcome remained in doubt until the close of the century.

The title suggests that there were two distinct aspects to Britain's trans-oceanic involvement, and while enterprises in the Atlantic and in Asia were indeed discrete in management and purpose, they were also interconnected. For example, trading and exploratory activities in both areas were primarily sponsored from London, and larger-scale operations were launched by companies even if private individuals sometimes proved more resilient. Companies were generally favoured for trans-oceanic business because they provided the best possibility both to aggregate scarce capital, and to spread risks in speculative ventures.

Cautious London merchants engaged in uncertain operations principally because they were losing their traditional European market for manufactured woollen goods, at the same time as they were being excluded from access to exotic commodities for which there was a demand in England. In that sense the cluster of English ventures in the Atlantic and Asia which emerged at the outset of the seventeenth century comprised several responses to a crisis which beset English trade. On the positive side, fresh ventures to remote places were possible because merchants were well informed of market opportunities throughout the world and could draw upon the extensive pool of maritime and geographic knowledge which existed in all English ports. The most important information was that concerning the wind systems and currents of the Atlantic ocean. This knowledge was as vital to trade with Asia as to voyages to Africa and the Americas, because ships bound for Asia had to skirt the coast of South America to take advantage of the trade winds which would then carry them back across the Atlantic and south of the Cape of Good Hope.

Enterprise in all three continents was to some degree inspired by a missionary imperative, and all overseas activity also relied upon the same material and human resources that went into making, repairing, navigating and manning British ships which, at different stages in their working lives, were employed to traverse several seas and oceans and to engage in a variety of trades. However, for the first half of the century, profits open to English merchants in Asia, Africa and across the Atlantic remained modest, and involvement in distant trade was always qualified by doubt and uncertainty. Therefore it was not until the later decades of the seventeenth century, when overseas engagements were producing serious financial returns, that colonial and imperial endeavours came to be considered vital to British interests.

More important than the common characteristics of ventures to different continents, is the fact that contemporaries considered them to be interlinked. Thus, in April 1602, when it was proving difficult for the East India Company to raise capital for its first voyage, the directors assigned £100 to George Weymouth, a well-known Atlantic explorer, to facilitate the 'discovery of a nearer passage into the . . . East Indies . . . by way of the Northwest' because the known route by the Cape of Good Hope was 'long and tedious' (Birdwood and Foster 1893: 21–5).

While members of the board of the East India Company considered their undertaking to be exploratory they also showed that they, like Columbus, believed the prime extra-European contact to be that with the fabulous continent of Asia. They proved themselves more determined than Columbus's reluctant sponsors because their normal access to Asian goods had been disrupted. The prime disruption stemmed from the 1498 achievement of Vasco da Gama in steering 'an all water route' to Asia (Prakash 1998). Following on that, the Portuguese crown (which in 1580 had become an integral part of an Iberian composite monarchy) had striven, through an agency known as Estado da India, to impose a trading levy upon indigenous merchants in the Indian Ocean, while they themselves carried some Asian goods, especially pepper, directly to the European market. Consequently, the cost of Asian products, most of which were still conveyed to Europe by the centuries-old land-cum-sea route, rose sharply.

This increase in the price of Asian commodities was partially redressed in Western Europe once Dutch, and then English, traders began to sail to the eastern Mediterranean to purchase goods directly from Asian merchants rather than wait for them to be brought overland to trans-Alpine markets by Venetian middlemen. However, in England, the benefit of this trade, enjoyed principally by the Levant Company, was threatened during the 1590s, when Dutch merchants began to sail directly to Asia around the Cape of Good Hope in well-armed ships. By doing so, they were defying the Portuguese dominance over the indigenous Asian trade, and were bringing Asian commodities to European markets at a significantly lower price. These developments which, in 1602, were to culminate in merchants from several cities of the United Provinces constituting themselves into a single united trading company with Asia, the Verenigdne Oost-Indische Compagnie (VOC), left London merchants with the choice between becoming reliant on Dutch traders for the commodities of the East or competing with them for access to markets in Asia.

Asia, pre-1640

This background to the formation of the English East India Company (EIC) on 31 December 1600 shows that London merchants who then commenced direct trade with Asia proceeded from a double disadvantage. First, they, like the Dutch, had to defy the Portuguese stranglehold on trade in the Indian Ocean, but they now also

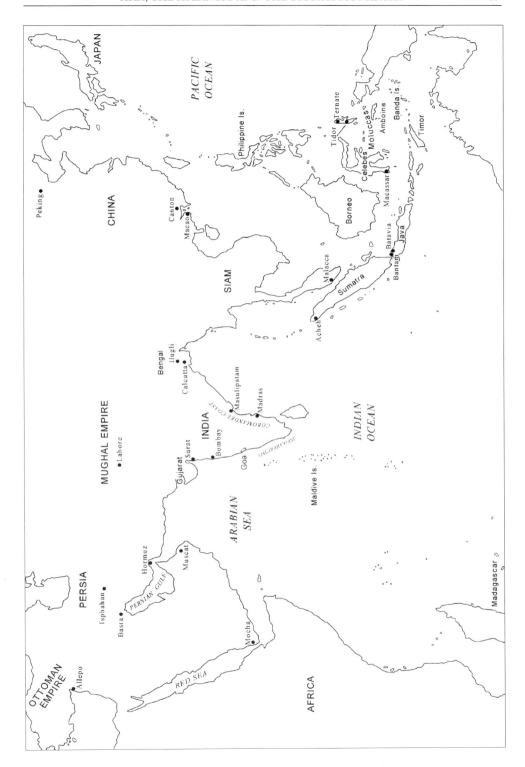

had to contend with the forceful efforts of Dutch merchants to monopolize trade with the Moluccan islands of the East Indian archipelago, from which came the spices most coveted by Europeans: cloves, nutmeg, mace and cinnamon.

As well as seeking access to Asian spices which they might market in Europe, London merchants hoped to sell English woollen textiles in Asia. This latter was critical because English merchants had been losing their market for woollen goods, which constituted the basis of English manufacturing. Their immediate problem was that their customary outlet in Antwerp had been closed both by Spanish blockade and by a natural silting of the Schelde. Independently of this, the heavy fabrics which England had customarily produced had been losing sales to lighter cloths, known as the New Draperies, which were being fashioned primarily on Flemish and Dutch looms.

Their concern to counteract such shrinking of opportunity explains why it was London's established merchants in chartered companies who were most prominent in the quest for fresh opportunities in Asia. Because they were experienced traders, they were aware of the uncertainty and the costs that would necessarily be associated with new ventures. The principal initial outlays concerned the purchase, manning, provisioning and the fitting out of ships which, in effect, had to be floating fortresses capable of combating possible challenges from European rivals or pirates in the Atlantic or Indian oceans. Then, if they were to match the Portuguese and the Dutch they would have to construct and staff 'factories'; that is, fortified trading posts located in strategic coastal locations throughout Asia. And before they could engage in any trade they had to procure an outward cargo to exchange for the desired Asian products.

These various challenges and uncertainties explain why the EIC had difficulty in persuading the initial shareholders to come forward with their promised investment in the first voyage and why, in the early years, capital as well as dividends were distributed at the end of each successful expedition. This necessitated attracting fresh capital investment for each early voyage. On the other hand, merchants were confident they could do as well in Asia as their Dutch competitors. Moreover, as is clear from the directions given to the commanders of the early voyages, most directors, including those who had never been outside Europe, had a relatively accurate mental map of Asia and its trading possibilities, and had a ready-made response to all contingencies that might arise except for shipwreck (Birdwood and Foster 1893: 114–36). Some of this knowledge was probably current in all European trading communities, but more precise details of opportunities in different locations frequently came from Dutch people who had been to Asia, including Jan Huygen van Linschoten, part of whose *Itinerario*, as a servant to the Portuguese archbishop of Goa, had become available in English translation in 1598 (Linschoten 1955–7, 1884).

At the outset, company officials admired the achievements of the Dutch and they expected that fellow Protestants who had been supported by the English in their struggle against Spain would now become their trading partners. In this they were quickly disillusioned because by 1618–19, after a brief experiment at sharing factories, Dutch and English traders in Asia were in open conflict. Ultimately, the EIC was forced to concede control of the spice islands to the Dutch after the 'Amboina massacre' of 1623, when ten English merchants were summarily put to death by their supposed Dutch partners. Another occasion for disenchantment was that clients from whom the EIC had purchased Asian goods were unwilling to become their customers, both because European woollen cloth was inappropriate as human attire in the warm climates of Southeast Asia, and because European textiles could not compete in price and quality with more technologically advanced Asian production. Therefore the Company had to pay for Asian commodities principally in silver which, as a commodity, was more prized in Asia than in Europe. Their Dutch competitors had encountered this same difficulty but it proved more acute for the EIC because the language of political economy in Britain was hostile to the export of bullion. Therefore, the EIC launched a printed propaganda campaign, associated initially with Thomas Munn but continued by other authors to the end of the century, which argued that the export of bullion should be regarded positively whenever it contributed to an increase in foreign trade through the promotion of re-exports (McCulloch 1954).

Despite these various difficulties the EIC persisted because, despite initial uncertainty, the early voyages reaped handsome dividends, and because the Company's agents discovered fresh opportunities for business in Asia even as the Dutch were attempting to exclude them from the spice islands. Thus the third voyage of 1607 sailed for the Red Sea with a view to gaining access to Persian silk together with the range of gums, drugs and precious stones customarily associated with the caravan trade. At the same time, English traders learnt that fine calicoes and other textiles available in Surat, the principal port of Gujarat, could be sold profitably in Europe. Then, in 1610, the EIC was advised by two Dutchmen on how to engage in the 'country trade' of exchanging textile goods from Gujarat or from the Coromandel coast of India for pepper which was available on the islands of Java and Sumatra. The EIC also used its bases at Bantam in Java and at Macassar in Celebes to exchange Indian goods for spices, especially cloves, which Indonesian traders were able to smuggle to them in defiance of the wishes of the VOC. The willingness of Asians to circumvent Dutch restrictions shows that they and their political rulers welcomed the English, while European rivals attempted to hinder the EIC in its effort both to acquire goods in Asia and to dispose of them in Europe. Essentially, all Europeans – regardless of their arguments for free trade – were monopolists at heart, while Asians found the EIC less exacting than the Estado da India, and recognized that each new Western trader would expand and diversify their markets.

These initial gains of the EIC were contested by the Portuguese who, from their bases at Goa, on the Malabar coast of India, and at Hormuz, at the mouth of the Persian Gulf, still dominated the western sector of the Indian Ocean. Therefore, while they struggled with the VOC for trading advantage in Indonesia, the EIC also, and without any sanction from the English crown, joined forces with the ruler of Persia in 1622, to expel the Portuguese from Hormuz. At this point, the ambition of the EIC was to become carriers of the commodities which, customarily, had been conveyed by caravan to Aleppo and thence to Europe. While the English failed in this, their destruction of Hormuz ended Portuguese dominance over trade in Asia, while they did gain a share of the trade which had previously gone through Aleppo. Thus, as Niels Steensgaard has phrased it, where the King of Portugal had been the 'world's biggest tax gatherer' the traders associated with both the EIC and the VOC became 'the world's biggest smugglers' (Steensgaard 1973: 151).

The proven ability of the EIC to establish and retain a profitable niche in Asian trade through the use of what K. N. Chaudhuri has called 'Mediterranean-style warfare' meant that, in England, capital for continuing ventures became more readily available (Chaudhuri 1985: 14). Thus the Company moved from treating individual expeditions in isolation, and between 1613 and 1620 the Company attracted subscriptions to the first and second joint stocks drawing investment from courtiers and landed gentry and even Dutch speculators, as well as from the still dominant London merchant community. The joint stock facility gave the Company money in hand both to develop an Asian infrastructure, and to commission ships which would remain in Asia where they would both defend the Company's interests and, through involvement in the 'country trade', have cargoes of varied Asian commodities awaiting outgoing trading vessels for their return journey.

The appointment of factors and presidents in its various Asian factories lent an appearance of permanency to the EIC. Then, in Europe, the Company also regularized its business affairs. Instead of issuing dividends in kind, which individual investors might dispose of as they saw fit, all imports were now retained by the company and were studiously released to prevent glutting on the domestic and export markets. Masters of vessels were also urged to reach port in London ahead of the VOC vessels returning to Amsterdam, both to forestall the Dutch on the English and continental markets. This produced England's first experiment with a re-export trade, as merchants from several different companies who had invested in the EIC used their contacts, reaching from the Baltic to the Levant, to exchange the Asian imports of the EIC for Spanish rials which would meet their debts in Asia.

In pointing to these very real achievements it is easy both to exaggerate the success of the EIC and to overlook the difficulties it still experienced. The Company certainly did make spices, pepper, textiles, dyestuffs and many other luxury products of the East more plentifully available throughout Europe at more affordable prices. This, however, was but import substitution and the Company could never conceive of a mass market for luxury products. On the other hand, cheap calicoes did capture the popular imagination, as can be seen from the fact that the 100,000 pieces imported to England in 1620 had risen to 221,500 pieces by 1625. However, the hope that they had gained access to a limitless supply of saleable goods was shattered in 1631 through the dismemberment by famine of the artisan community of Gujarat.

The activity of the EIC certainly generated employment in England's shipbuilding and armaments sectors, and new employment was also created in London and its vicinity in providing salted and barrelled provisions which would remain edible during a return voyage lasting up to thirty-two months through a variety of climates. However, whatever job increases were thus achieved were offset in the textile sector where linen goods and linen/wool fabrics lost ground to imported calicoes. The real economic benefits went, therefore, to a narrow segment of established merchants who profited principally from the re-export trade which was the Company's crowning achievement during its early phase. Even this was threatened by a European-wide economic crisis which persisted beyond the duration of the Thirty Years' War (1618–48). At this point, the governors of the EIC sought to reduce both their fixed costs and the supply of Asian exports, first by cutting back on the number of its factories and then by sponsoring fewer outward sailings. Even then they confronted fresh difficulties when, in 1637, rival merchants and courtiers persuaded King Charles I to license the competing Courteen Company to trade in Asia. At this point the governors of the EIC gave serious thought to terminating its operations, and this remained an option while Britain and Ireland were beset by war and political instability in 1639–60.

This brief summary of England's early involvement with direct trading in the East will have shown that its role in Asia was principally a parasitic one, driven mainly by the concern of London merchants not to be deprived of their livelihood by their European competitors. Once they reached Asia, they had to establish niches within indigenous trading networks which already stretched from the Persian Gulf to the coast of Japan and which employed such sophisticated devices as contracts, credit, coinage, tables of currency exchange, and weights and measures (Prakash 1998: 2–4). The military endeavours of the EIC were, of necessity, directed against other Europeans and pirates, and their agents succeeded in establishing coastal trading rights usually only with the consent of political rulers who always remained more powerful than they on land. These rulers, and indigenous merchants, welcomed these new traders into what were already multi-ethnic trading communities both because they extended their trading possibilities and supplied them with silver. Therefore, in retrospect, it seems that the positive contribution of the EIC up to mid-century was, with its European competitors, to link the existing trading world of the East into 'a global network of exchange' which brought Asian commodities to European markets, principally in return for coins minted from the silver which had been extracted by an American labour force in the mines of Potosi (Prakash 1998: 337).

The Atlantic, pre-1640

Atlantic achievements contrast with those in Asia because they were the product of English effort. Until the mid-seventeenth century, English mariners and adventurers forged new trading connections or expanded upon those already developed in previous generations. The part of the Atlantic best known to English sailors was that linking England with the Continent. These were rapidly extended, as English merchants, threatened by the loss of their wool trade, scoured for opportunity in the North Sea and the Baltic, even as far as Russia, and southwards along the coasts of France, and Iberia and even to the eastern shore of the Mediterranean. London merchants, like their Dutch counterparts, sponsored explorers to track a northeast passage to Asia, while some venturesome sailors and traders proceeded southwards in the wake of the Portuguese, and identified trading potential in dye woods, hides, wax, gold and even in slaves (the four ventures of John Hawkins, 1562–8) that existed along the African coast, especially in the vicinity of Senagambia and Sierra Leone. After 1618 some traders to Africa constituted themselves into companies, although their desire for a monopoly was regularly challenged by rivals and interlopers. Nonetheless, from the 1630s ventures for red wood and gold proved highly profitable (Nicholas Crispe claimed to have imported gold to the value of £500,000 during the years 1633–44) and as many as five English 'factories' had been established at various points along the Gold Coast by 1644 (Hair and Law in Canny 1998: 251–3).

Mariners from the west of England, but also some from England's northeast ports, were also intrepid seekers after fishing grounds in the north Atlantic. Their ancestors with their small but sturdy craft had long maintained trading and fishing contacts with Iceland, and Bristol fishermen, seeking for fresh stocks, had possibly discovered the Newfoundland banks before Columbus's first Atlantic crossing of 1492 (Quinn 1974). Certainly, thereafter, they (as well as Basque, Breton, Norman and Dutch fishermen) exploited the Newfoundland banks systematically, and new English trading connections with Mediterranean ports, especially Leghorn, opened markets for dried and salted Atlantic fish. Thus the 40 English ships which fished off Newfoundland in 1578 had risen to 150 by 1604, and possibly to 300 by the 1620s (Wrightson 2000). Many of these ships sailed with full holds from the fishing grounds directly to Mediterranean destinations, and returned to their home ports in England with cargoes of Mediterranean products or with salt or wine from Southern Europe or the wine islands of the Atlantic.

Success in Newfoundland and contact with the native populations of North America produced a continuing quest for new resources – furs as well as fish – while a growing familiarity with the coast of North America encouraged some English sponsors to continue the quest for a northwest passage to Asia. To some degree the English Puritan settlements of the 1620s and 1630s, in New England, were an outgrowth of these previous exploits in northern waters. Merchants who partly funded the Puritan initiatives had previous experience with these ventures, and were confident that godly communities, which aimed at agricultural self-sufficiency, would be able to exchange fish and furs for English manufactured goods. A continuing quest for fishing grounds by European fishermen of many nations improved general understanding of the North American coastline, and as mariners traversed waterways, such as the Gulf of the St Lawrence and Hudson Bay, which seemed to extend endlessly westwards, they considered themselves to be on the way to Asia.

Parallel with this activity was the intrusion of another group of English mariners into the south Atlantic which, until the middle of the sixteenth century, had been accepted as the preserve of the Iberian monarchies. Those leading the way, in the 1560s, were militant Protestants allied with co-religionists from France and the Low Countries who sought to attack both the Spanish silver fleet and Spanish settlements in the Caribbean and Central America. These marauders justified their actions on the premise that New World silver was making it possible for King Philip II of Spain to tyrannize over Protestantism in Europe. What was an extreme attitude became commonplace in England from 1585 to 1604, when formal hostilities with Spain raged on land and sea. Then Queen Elizabeth granted formal licences to scores of English privateers to raid Iberian shipping and settlements and to sell their prizes and cargoes (whether from America or Asia) on English markets. This enhanced a taste in England for exotic goods, while it enriched both many English merchants whose business was being ruined by Spanish blockades, and adventurers, principally from the English west country, who had never been involved with legitimate trade. Bolder privateers got to know the coast of Iberian America, and they became even more familiar with North American inlets and fringe islands of the Caribbean from which to attack the silver fleet.

Far-sighted adventurers, such as Walter Ralegh, his half-brother Humphrey Gilbert, and their associates, concluded that privateering would persist only as long as the war and they sought to move beyond plundering to establish English settlements in America. One purpose behind such settlement was to demonstrate that English Protestants were more sincere than Spanish Catholics in bringing Christianity to

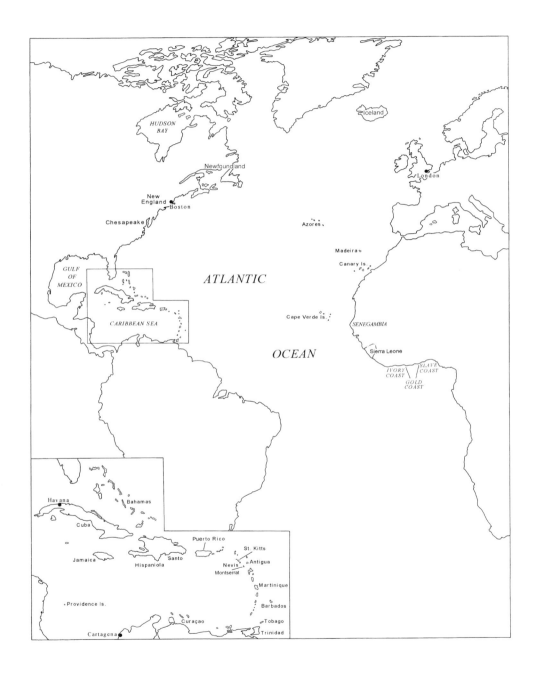

HUDSON
BAY

Iceland

Newfoundland

London

New
England
Boston

Chesapeake

Azores

Madeira

Canary Is.

GULF
OF
MEXICO

ATLANTIC

Cape Verde Is.

SENEGAMBIA

CARIBBEAN SEA

Sierra Leone

OCEAN

IVORY
COAST

SLAVE
COAST

GOLD
COAST

Havana

Bahamas

Cuba

Puerto Rico

St. Kitts

Jamaica

Santo

Antigua

Nevis

Hispaniola

Montserrat

Providence Is.

Martinique

Curaçao

Barbados

Tobago

Cartagena

Trinidad

native Americans, and much publicity was given in England, and elsewhere in Protestant Europe, to the destruction by the conquistadores of the native population of Hispanola. This had been complained of in Spain by Fra Bartoloemé de Las Casas, whose reports were eagerly translated and broadcast. The desire to evangelize natives while making England richer explains the enthnographic study of the population of Roanake island conducted in the 1580s by Thomas Hariot, at the direction of Ralegh. Enrichment was to be achieved principally through import substitution, which was the prime concern of Richard Hakluyt's *Discourse of Western Planting* (1584).

Ralegh, and most English promoters of colonization until the eighteenth century, appreciated that the principal benefit which Spain had derived from the New World derived from its discovery of precious metal. Therefore, while on the one hand propagandists envisioned those who would settle in England's colonies joining with Christianized natives to produce commodities such as wine or silk which were not available in England, on the other hand they also imagined themselves in the role of Cortéz or Pizarro overcoming insuperable odds and placing untold wealth at the disposal of the English crown. Propagandists made much of the moral zeal of their countrymen, and stories of daring achievements and glorious failures were quickly absorbed into English historical memory. However, during his years in prison, when Ralegh reflected upon these actions, he concluded that 'discourse of magnanimity, of National Virtue, of Religion, of Liberty, and whatsoever' had counted for little with England's 'common soldiers' when fighting the Spaniards in the Indies. Rather, they fought 'in hope of their reyals of plate and pistolets' and they would, if they had 'been put to it upon the like disadvantages in Ireland, or in any poor country... have turned their pieces and pikes against their commanders' (Ralegh 1971: 260). Base motives were not confined to soldiers, and even promoters and leaders of expeditions, and even clergy who had justified colonization on moral grounds, shifted to recommending draconian treatment of natives whenever they threatened the security or profitability of the various ventures which were got underway after 1604, when peace was restored between England and Spain.

Some of those who had been privateers now turned to piracy, but other adventurers, and the merchants who had sponsored them, enlisted in the many syndicates being established to promote settlement in, and the exploitation of the resources of, several of the lesser islands of the Caribbean and on several points along the American coastline ranging from the extreme north to the Amazon basin. Most such ventures came to nothing and it was only the more promising, such as the Virginia Company of London, which attracted investment from wealthier London merchants. This and other companies also attracted gentry or even noble involvement, but the driving force behind transatlantic investment was lesser merchants, many of whom had previously been involved with privateering.

The sluggish performance of these companies is explained by the fact that most hoped that precious metals would be discovered, or that exotic crops (sometimes of Mediterranean or Asian origin) could be grown successfully in a new location. Another reason is that organizers were torn between recruiting a native labour force, which usually proved futile, and importing labourers from England. This, wherever it was attempted, proved uncertain and costly, and in some cases (notably the Chesapeake and the Caribbean) mortality rates among recently arrived labourers proved extraordinarily high. These two problems exacerbated the third more fundamental problem of attracting investment capital which, as with the EIC, remained scarce during the seventeenth century.

The fact that most Atlantic projects were primarily reliant upon the support of lesser merchants, and that the few prominent merchants who supported the Virginia Company had become discouraged long before it was dissolved in 1624, meant that sponsors had to resort to extraordinary measures to advertise for support. In the case of the Virginia Company, when initial capital was exhausted, pleas for financial support, as well as for emigrants, were made through pamphlets, through popular ballads, and resort was had even to a lottery. Thus, in 1620, one London correspondent explained the especially severe shortage of capital as caused by the outbreak of war in Bohemia, the export of bullion by the EIC, and 'the bewitching lotteries for Virginia the last two years in all the good cities of England, and this year... in all great market towns that they will pick from such a town as Chester, Eversham, or Bath, a match of three thousand pounds before they move' (Chatsworth, Lismore, XI, 45).

This particular correspondent was writing to a client in Ireland, which reminds us that the efforts of trans-oceanic projectors to raise funds coincided with a state-sponsored effort to establish major plantations in Ireland. London merchant companies were then required by King James I, against their own better judgement, to 'undertake' the settlement of County Londonderry within the early seventeenth-century plantation of Ulster. British migration to Ulster (within and without the plantation effort) reached about 30,000 people by 1622, and perhaps as many more again by the late 1630s, but the element of the scheme in which the merchant companies were involved required them to construct walled towns in Derry and Coleraine, and to develop a sequence of plantation estates. Mayor Sebright, who had been persuaded by King James to lend support, justified merchant participation principally on the grounds that Ulster was ideally situated for exploiting the resources of the Atlantic. While hypothetically true, their involvement with Ulster seems to have dissuaded the London companies from further dealings in the Atlantic because collectively they invested about £100,000 in their Ulster acquisition only to find, in 1635, that their estates had been recalled to the crown and they themselves fined £70,000 because they had not complied with plantation conditions (Canny 2001: 214–15, 297).

If London's leading merchants were thus disenchanted, lesser merchants from London, Bristol and smaller western ports were prominent in the commercial exploitation of the natural resources of Munster, the most southerly Irish province, during the first half of the seventeenth century. They and the landowners with whom they associated established a highly skilled artisan and farming population (principally from England and Wales and reaching a figure of 25,000 before 1640) in, or close to, the urban settlements which they dominated. Then, while enjoying rents from the tenants who occupied their urban and rural properties, proprietors and merchants exported the fruits of their dependants' labour, especially timber and smelted iron ore, to meet orders in England or the Netherlands, and they also sent barrel staves to the wine-producing areas of Southern Europe, Madeira and the Canaries. Some far-sighted planters in Munster visualized it becoming a resource base, from which they might transport English settlers, as well as cattle and provisions, to nascent transatlantic colonies. Their aspirations worked out in practice and men of modest means who succeeded as planters, merchants, fishing entrepreneurs, timber processors and manufacturers in Munster established new trading paths in the Atlantic which linked ports on the southern coast of Ireland both with those in the south of England and Western Europe, and with the Wine Islands, Newfoundland, New England, Virginia and the British West Indies (Canny 2001: 312).

This appraisal suggests that English merchants did succeed in establishing various nodes of settlement on all coasts of the Atlantic during the first half of the seventeenth century. However, none of these, other than the fishing stations on the coast of Newfoundland, and state-sponsored Irish plantations, seemed permanent. Aspirations to discover precious metals and to produce exotic crops in the settlements sponsored by the Virginia Company and its successors in Chesapeake Bay proved illusory, and the colony would have been abandoned in the 1620s were it not that people recognized the possibility of growing and harvesting tobacco to satisfy a cultivated European taste for pipe smoking, after the fashion of native Americans. Also, in 1622, after English settlers in the Chesapeake had endured an onslaught from the native population, the promoters believed themselves justified in seeking the expulsion of Amerindians from their midst and seizing land suited to tobacco cultivation.

These efforts of mostly marginal traders and planters resulted by 1640 in a straggling settlement along the waterways of the Chesapeake. The residences of the settlers were crude; their society was predominantly male; the product which sustained them was subject to fluctuating prices in London; and the vast majority of the English residents were indentured servants who lived and worked as tobacco cultivators in the hope that, on the expiry of their indentures, they would become tobacco planters in their own right. This expectation was in sharp contrast with the demographic reality where heavy mortality rates, principally from malaria, made it necessary for planters to import between 8,000 and 9,000 indentured servants throughout each of the 1630s and 1640s to sustain a population of 8,000 English inhabitants (Horn in Canny 1998: 177).

By comparison, settlers in New England seemed at mid-century more successful. There were then approximately 23,000 people of English birth settled about Massachusetts Bay. Their sex ratio was fairly evenly balanced, which enabled most people to reside in a family household dedicated to agriculture or agriculture-related manufacturing, and their demographic experience was remarkably favourable. Their leaders also organized them into town-based godly communities, thus fulfilling the stated ambition behind the migration. The fact that Amerindians of the area in which they chose to settle succumbed to European-borne diseases was taken as evidence of God's favour, but the future of the colony nonetheless remained uncertain. One problem was that those natives who survived were generally unwilling to be absorbed into an English and Protestant community, and the expansion of Puritan settlement brought them into bloody conflict with some tribes, especially the Pequots. Economically, the Puritans achieved near self-sufficiency in food, but it quickly became apparent that fishing and fur trapping, which would help meet the costs of imports from England, seemed incompatible with communal living of the type which Puritans believed had been decreed by God. And, most frightening of all, discord over the interpretation of the godly life both provoked schisms and discouraged a continuing out-migration from the British monarchies which New England Puritans considered necessary to their survival (DeJohn Anderson in Canny 1998).

The settler population on those islands of the West Indies which were settled by Englishmen from 1624 forward – St Christopher (St Kitts), Barbados, Nevis, Montserrat and Antigua – was by 1640 as large as that of New England. However, the background of the promoters of these various island settlements was more akin to that of those who succeeded as tobacco planters in the Chesapeake, and like the Chesapeake settlers they too looked to tobacco production to sustain them. However, they were able to supplement this through the production of cotton and indigo; the latter considered of better quality for dyeing than what could be procured in Gujarat by the EIC. To meet labour requirements the planters, like their counterparts in the Chesapeake, imported indentured servants, principally from England, and these faced the same dangers to life and health as did white settlers there. Those who went to the lesser islands had also to confront strident opposition from the indigenous population, and settlers in the West Indies, many of whom were former pirates or privateers, realized that, in the event of renewed war with Spain, they would be especially vulnerable (Beckles in Canny 1998).

When we aggregate factories on the African Gold Coast, plantations in Ireland, fisheries in Newfoundland and New England, Puritan settlements in New England, and tobacco plantations in the West Indies and the Chesapeake, it becomes apparent that Atlantic endeavours must have added considerably to England's wealth and brought some individuals from modest circumstances to considerable wealth. Collectively these ventures resulted in a dramatic increase in the hundreds of small English ships that regularly traversed the Atlantic, most still travelling between London and a particular overseas destination. Some individuals invested in many companies but most operations were independent, and it is only the appearance of Winthrops and Downings in Ireland, New England and the West Indies, or the transfer by Daniel Gookin of his interests from Munster to Virginia and then to New England, or the involvement of Maurice Thompson, minor London merchant, Virginia planter, and investor in the EIC, with almost every Atlantic venture, which suggests that England's interest in the Atlantic was integrated. It was not so, and the survival of most ventures remained uncertain during the Wars of Three Kingdoms.

Scottish and Irish Involvement

The low population level of the kingdoms of Scotland and Ireland (both about 1 million people as opposed to 4.25 millions in England and Wales at the outset of the seventeenth century), their rigid social divisions and their limited urban development explain why Irish and Scots were more poorly placed to engage in overseas adventures of the seventeenth century than in subsequent centuries. The fact that their seventeenth-century role was but minor does not mean that some Scots and Irish people could not visualize themselves as analogues to the Portuguese. Scots had, for centuries, been active fishers of the North Sea, they had maintained continuous trading contacts with Scandinavian countries, and perhaps as many as 75,000 Scots were to become pedlars in Poland and fighting men in the Protestant armies of Northern Europe in 1600–50 (Smout, Landsman, and Devine in Canny 1996: 85). It is therefore not at all surprising that a Scottish author was the first to challenge Dutch pretensions, articulated by Hugo Grotius in 1609, to enjoy free access to all seas (Armitage 2000: 208–13).

Such discourse would not have seemed relevant to Irish authors because coastal and freshwater fish were so plentifully available in Ireland that fishermen there developed no significant fleets. Instead, lords with estates abutting the southern and western coasts had customarily licensed foreign – usually Spanish – fishermen to use their shores for fishing and curing. Then, at the outset of the seventeenth century, both coastal stations and inland fisheries were eagerly sought out by English and Scots adventurers, usually through the process of plantation.

While indigenous Irish merchants might have fallen short in taking commercial advantage of fishing, they were neither inept nor unadventurous. Those on the south and east coasts had maintained regular trading contacts with ports on the west coasts of England and Wales, while merchants from western ports, notably Galway, ventured to southwest Europe in search of wine and salt. Some must have been bolder, as is suggested by the gift of a lion made by Prince Henry the Navigator to the town of Galway in recognition of the service to Portuguese geographic exploration made by a son of the town. Some of Galway's dynamism survived into the seventeenth century, since some merchants from there featured as planters in the West Indies during the 1630s, while an Irish conglomerate, which included men with Old English Catholic names and an O'Brien from neighbouring County Clare, were active in colonization ventures in both St Christopher and the Amazon basin down to the mid-1640s (Cullen in Canny 1996). However, the enduring Irish experience of the seventeenth century was that of being colonized, and those with Irish associations who were most dynamic in long-distance ventures were those English, or even Dutch, settlers with Munster interests who we noted venturing deep into Atlantic waters.

Account has also been taken of the Scottish energies expended in planting Ulster, which attracted nobles, lairds, artisans and tenants, while Scottish merchants extended loans to several grantees who required capital to become successful planters. In return, Ulster provided a home for up to 30,000 Scots in the years before 1640. Estate ownership there proved beneficial for landowners who could manage their acquisitions as an extension of their property in Scotland, and the province provided Calvinist clergy with an opportunity to extend their spiritual empire. On the negative side this was a costly undertaking for a poor community, and investment in Ulster obviously reduced the possibility of Scots playing any major role in the exploitation of new opportunities in Asia and the Atlantic.

However, while collectively Scots were not seriously committed to any major overseas ventures, individuals in Scotland were clearly conscious of their entitlements and how these might be turned to profit. They could petition for royal trading charters from the Scottish crown to parallel the monopolies granted by a common monarch to his English subjects but which, in practice, forced the English grantees to come to terms with the Scots. Thus, in 1617, King James granted Sir James Cunningham the right to establish a Scottish East India Company with a charter identical to that of the EIC, and, in 1634, a Scottish Guinea Company was similarly chartered and actually sponsored two voyages to Africa (Birdwood and Foster 1893: 490–1; Hair and Law in Canny 1998: 253). Sir William Alexander in the 1620s seems to have been more committed to establishing Nova Scotia as a Scottish equivalent to New England, not least because he sought assurance that any children within his colony would have British nationality with a right to reside in any of the three kingdoms of the British monarchy. While, with this one exception, Scottish entrepreneurs displayed scant interest in distant trade and plantation, it is clear from the petition of the Committee of Estates of Scotland in 1641 that they saw the potential in such traffic and demanded equal rights with English and Irish merchants in 'any outtrade and dealing in any foreign places' (Armitage 1997: 51; Canny 1998: 17).

Conflict and Crisis, 1639–1660

The difficulties which British trans-oceanic ventures had been facing prior to 1640 were exacerbated by the conflict which beset all three jurisdictions of King Charles I in 1639–60. These domestic wars coincided with continental conflict which persisted until 1655, and with naval warfare between the government of Oliver Cromwell and that of the United Provinces in 1652–4. Trade was but a minor issue in these wars, except that with the Dutch, but political uncertainty, military disturbance and destruction of property took its inevitable toll on business, while the government of Oliver Cromwell was interventionist in overseas affairs to an extent that was previously inconceivable.

It was fortunate for the EIC that it had undertaken a retrenchment of its activities just as these disturbances broke out, and unpromising trading conditions persuaded the rival Courteen Company to desist from trading in Asia. Reduced dividends from the EIC also resulted in the withdrawal of many investors, leaving the Company to the elite London merchants who had always been its driving force. This, however, left the EIC exposed to the charge that it was royalist in sympathy, and the English parliament, which was opposed to monopolies in principle, did nothing to hinder English interlopers from trading in Asia. Thus, the ubiquitous Maurice Thomson, having made money in the Atlantic, sought to trade also in Asia, and in 1650 he was authorized by the Rump Parliament to establish an entirely new Asian trading monopoly based on the island of Assada, close to Madagascar. When Thomson failed in this venture, Cromwell considered abandoning all English claims to trade in Asia to the VOC if the Dutch would leave Atlantic trading to the British. Then, in the absence of Dutch agreement, Cromwell decided in 1657 to reconstitute the EIC as a joint stock company similar to that chartered by Queen Elizabeth. Thus reconstituted, the company concentrated on trade with India, now acquiring calicoes on the Coromandel coast as well as in Gujurat, and purchasing raw silk, silk fabrics and saltpetre in Bengal.

Civil war and Cromwellian rule also proved destabilizing for English settlement throughout the Atlantic basin, not least because revolution at home allowed discontented elements overseas to challenge political elites appointed by King Charles I. The Guinea Company, which had always had difficulty in preserving its trading monopoly on the African coast, suffered the indignity of having its management passed by the English parliament to previous interlopers, including Maurice Thomson. Then it had its activities harassed successively by the Dutch and the Royal fleets, and finally, in 1657, when it was heavily in debt, the Company and its remaining factories were passed to the reconstituted EIC, which had an interest in marketing African gold, ivory and cloth in Asia (Hair and Law in Canny 1998).

The collapse of political authority in Britain also provided an opportunity to extreme Puritans to revive an anti-Spanish policy in Atlantic waters. One group headed by such notables as Lord Saye and Sele and the earl of Warwick, and again including Maurice Thomson, established a colony on Providence island, off the coast of Nicaragua, with the intention of its becoming both an exemplary community which would inspire the native population on the mainland to desert their Spanish oppressors, and a base from which English attacks upon Spanish interests might be renewed. When the Spaniards destroyed the settlement the survivors immediately transferred their anti-papal zeal to Ireland, where they hoped to participate in the transfer of land and trade from Catholic to Protestant hands in revenge for the attack upon the Protestant interest in the Irish insurrection of 1641. The grand ambition to pursue war specifically against Spain was revived in Cromwell's Western Design of 1655–6, when he employed the state's navy to advance colonial interests and the Protestant faith. The only gain to Britain from this campaign was the island of Jamaica, which did not then seem an important acquisition.

The Civil War and Interregnum also proved testing for the Puritan settlers in New England because would-be emigrants from England, and also from Scotland and Ireland, now anticipated achieving a godly Commonwealth at home rather than across the Atlantic. Worse still for Massachusetts Bay, some settlers returned to participate in the conflict in Britain, or transferred their allegiances to the new Puritan settlements being promoted on Providence island and in Connecticut.

On the positive side, social dislocations in Europe meant that fish became an even more consequential source of cheap protein, with a consequent boost for fishing both off Newfoundland and on the coast of New England. Also, perhaps due to the influence of armies, tobacco became widely consumed at all social levels throughout Western Europe. The ensuing demand meant that Chesapeake tobacco cultivation became more profitable and more extensive, and during the single decade of the 1650s, planters imported 16,000 indentured servants. Even more dramatic was the sudden switch during the 1640s from tobacco to sugar production in Barbados. Planters there were persuaded by experienced Dutchmen with capital to invest that they had an opportunity to become sugar producers because Portuguese Brazil, previously the principal source of Atlantic sugar, was beset by conflict. The apparently inexhaustible European demand for sugar brought immediate prosperity to Barbados planters, but also a commensurate demand for workers. Labour requirements were but partly met by an increased importation of indentured servants from England and by the employment of significant numbers of Scottish and Irish soldiers who were forced to the West Indies in the aftermath of Cromwellian military victory in both countries. The continuing shortfall was made good when English planters, following the practice of the Dutch and the Portuguese, began to employ West African slaves to cultivate and process sugar. The parlous position of the Guinea Company meant that it could not immediately respond to this demand for labour. However, the tentative resort to slavery pointed to an opportunity which could become profitable in more settled times. These came with the Restoration of 1660, but it was again apparent that it would be English, rather than Scots or Irish, merchants who would benefit from trading in slaves because both Scotland and Ireland had been chastened by Cromwellian conquest, and because Irish Catholic merchants had been forced to give way to English supporters of the Lord Protector.

Transformation

Readers will be aware that the benefit which England, and indeed Britain, derived from its trans-oceanic interests increased out of all proportion in the years following the Restoration of 1660. What is not so well understood is the extent to which this can be attributed to experience gained and strategic decisions taken in the preceding decades.

In Asia the EIC was alert for new trading opportunities and sought to eliminate unprofitable activities. In making decisions the Company relied increasingly on advice from its agents, who directed it towards maintaining but a few bases each of which would be supplied by satellite factories. The outcome of this rationalization was the continued existence of Surat (until it was superseded by Bombay) controlling trade both on the west coast of India (which included both Gujarat and the Malabar coast) and oceanic trade between India and the Persian Gulf; the establishment of Madras as a depot which would foster trade on the Coromandel coast and reach out to Bantam on the island of Java; and the maintenance of a trading position, initially at Hugli and later at Calcutta, to draw upon the resources of Bengal and to reach across the Bay of Bengal to Malaysia. These quickly became 'English' towns with Asian or Eurasian populations resident on their fringes, and the Company fortified them whenever this was permitted by the neighbouring potentate. Linked with this rationalization was the decision to withdraw from the 'country trade' (although Company agents still made handsome profits from local trading), and instead to have ships from England sail directly to designated towns in Asia from where they would quickly return with full holds. This practice made it possible for the Company to lease rather than to own the vessels it used, and it now also strove to equalize the number of outgoing and returning voyages, and to effect a quick turn-about to avoid expensive demurrage charges.

The outgoing cargo was still predominantly bullion with some copper and African ivory, while return cargoes were comprised of hundreds of commodities from the several regions of Asia, with the principal value attaching to textiles: calicoes from Coromandel and Gujurat, and raw silk or silk fabrics from Bengal. Spices were still cherished, but the pepper which the Company imported came increasingly from the Malabar coast, as did coarse cinnamon and cardamom. Saltpetre from Bengal frequently served as ballast with a commercial value. This inventory points to a declining interest in Indonesia, and while the Company maintained a post at Bantam until they were expelled by the Dutch in 1682, they appreciated the archipelago increasingly for the staging posts it offered on their route to Japan and China. Such exploratory voyages provided more information than profit, and the EIC again experienced difficulty because it had so little to sell which interested the Chinese. Nonetheless, by the end of the seventeenth century, some people in England had acquired a taste for Chinese tea although, as yet, there was nothing to point to tea importation becoming a commercial success story during the next century.

English experience with Asian trade during the late seventeenth century was not an unqualified success; trouble with the Dutch persisted; European wars from 1689 to 1713 threatened orderly trade and brought the French to prominence as a major presence in Asia; and from the 1680s to 1709 (when a new United East India

Company was formed) the EIC had to contend with rivals and interlopers. However, its successes were remarkable, and these were the consequence of a focus on India rather than Indonesia; of a shift from spices to textiles; and, within India, of a willingness to draw successively upon the resources of Gujurat, Madras and Bengal. Success was above all explained by the ability of the Company's agents in Europe to cultivate a taste for an amazing range of Asian commodities so that, by the end of the seventeenth century, London matched, or even surpassed, Amsterdam as a European entrepôt for Asian commodities.

The benefit that England derived from its contacts in the Atlantic was also related to the extent to which more valued imports could be sold on the Continent; first fish, then also tobacco, to which was added sugar and sugar derivatives. This enumeration reveals that it was the achievements of those associated with Newfoundland fishing, Chesapeake tobacco and West Indian sugar that contributed most to Britain's economic success in the Atlantic. However, as well as generating considerable profits these three products, and the entrepreneurs associated with them, contributed to the integration of Britain's various interests to the point where, towards the end of the seventeenth century, people could conceive of an English empire in the Atlantic.

The first evidence of integration was the development of innumerable triangular and cross-hatched trading contacts. These, as was mentioned, existed in the fishing business from an early stage, and similar multiple points of contact emerged as a consequence of the commercial success of sugar production, initially on Barbados and later on Jamaica. Sugar planters continued to rely on England (and increasingly also on Scotland and Ireland) for indentured servants and manufactured goods, but white servants had to be augmented by African slaves who, after 1660, were usually supplied by one of a succession of companies (the most enduring being the Royal African Company) which were granted monopoly trading rights with West Africa by the British authorities. The need of sugar planters for slaves thus gave rise to trading connections between London, slave ports on the coast of West Africa, and the West Indies. Just as the demand for slaves in the West Indies provided a life-line for faltering English interests on the coast of West Africa, so also did population increase on the islands create a market for the food surpluses of New England farmers. Ports on the south coast of Ireland, now securely in Protestant hands, also emerged as centres for the provision of barrelled meat and butter, not only for West Indian plantations, and the British navy, but also for slave ports in West Africa. The Chesapeake, despite an increase of the white population to about 85,000 by 1700, was by comparison more self-sufficient. However, many English vessels bound there had first stopped off in the West Indies and conveyed sugar, rum and slaves in exchange for the tobacco being exported to London.

Another striking feature of the Atlantic trading world was that success bred success. Thus the proven ability of New England to survive as a food-producing economy, and that of the Chesapeake to achieve near self-sufficiency in food while cultivating a commercial crop, encouraged government officials and private speculators to promote plantation of the entire eastern coastline of North America. This objective had been largely attained by the end of the seventeenth century. The vast tracts of land which thus came into crown possession were eagerly sought after by the adventurous, who aspired variously, as had projectors of previous generations, to discover mineral wealth, or to cultivate crops that would facilitate import substitution. Now people could proceed more confidently because it had become clear that labour deficiencies could be satisfied through slavery, and that profits could be made even from the promotion of a European-style agronomy aimed at supplying the needs of other colonies in the Atlantic or even European markets.

Such considerations explain the dedication of the promoters of settlement to the felling of tall trees in northern New England for ship masts, the tapping of the pine forests of the Carolinas for pitch and tar, the establishment in 1670 of the Hudson's Bay Company to promote fur trading in the frozen Arctic, but also the creation of colonies of primarily white settlement along the Hudson and Delaware river valleys dedicated to European-style agriculture in a transatlantic setting. Some, such as Quakers in Pennsylvania and New Jersey and Huguenots in Carolina, sought a place of religious refuge as had Puritans of the early seventeenth century. Most voluntary settlers seem, however, to have perceived America as a place where farmers and artisans might better their condition, and this explains the growing numbers of English and Scots, as well as German speakers, who crossed the Atlantic in the late seventeenth century.

The integration of the emerging English interests in the Atlantic, which was resulting from the actions of merchants and adventurers, was consolidated by government intervention. Much of the new territory that became available for development had been prised from European competitors through war or diplomacy, and a sequence of English parliamentary enactments of 1651, 1660, 1663, 1673 and 1696 (known as the Navigation Acts) lent a sense of unity to heterogeneous colonies. These Acts aimed to have trade between England and its Atlantic colonies conducted in English ships which would be manned by English seamen; to have colonial commodities (not including fish) brought directly to England rather than to markets in continental Europe; and also to have imports to England from the European continent carried either in English ships or those of the country of origin. The legislation intended to exclude the Dutch (against whom the British government went to war in 1652–4, 1665–7 and 1672–4) from the English carrying trade, but governments also valued it as an instrument to assist in the collection of customs and excise duties which became an increasingly important element of government revenue after 1660. Another consequence of the importance which Atlantic colonies assumed in the official mind was the establishment of commissions (notably the Council for Trade and Plantations of 1660) to oversee Atlantic affairs, and more controversially to devise common forms of governance for very different colonial societies.

The fact that Atlantic interests were given more attention than Asian ones by government officials reflects the fact that trade on the Atlantic was the single most dynamic sector of the English economy during the second half of the seventeenth century. Like the Asian trade, that on the Atlantic supplied commodities which satisfied domestic requirements and left a considerable surplus for re-export. However, where Asian goods had still to be paid for principally in bullion, Atlantic settlements created a demand for English manufactured goods, for commodities imported from Asia, and for provisions produced in Ireland. In statistical terms, imports from the American colonies constituted 18.5 per cent of London's total imports in 1700, where imports from Asia amounted to 16.2 per cent; in each case these figures represented an increase over time, with goods from the Atlantic colonies rising in value from £334,915 in 1663 to £863,000 by 1699. Many of these imports stimulated employment in processing, refining and packaging them for the re-export trade which, by 1700, accounted for something between 34 per cent and 45 per cent of the total exports passing through the port of London. How American re-exports balanced with those of Asia is uncertain, but trade on the Atlantic came to be perceived as contributing more positively to the domestic economy than the Asian trade. Essentially, Atlantic trading boosted exports while trade with Asia was still lubricated by bullion exports. Exports to Atlantic destinations from London had increased four-fold, from £105,910 to £410,000 in 1663–1700, and some impression of the boost which this provided to domestic employment can be gleaned from the fact that, in 1686, London exported 598 different commodities in 329 different ships to various American colonies (Zahedieh 1998: 54; Wrightson 2000: 238–9). It is also evident from contemporary diaries that English people began to adopt a possessive attitude towards their settlements on the Atlantic. This is not at all surprising given that an outward journey took but six to seven weeks and many English people corresponded with relatives among the tens of thousands of English people who had made their homes in American settlements.

The new term being employed to describe the new socio-economic unit that was emerging in the Atlantic basin was the English Empire in America (Canny 1998: 22). This reflects the fact that Scots and Irish people had played little part in its development, other than as subordinates to English planters in the West Indies. Scots did contribute significantly to the shaping of the settler society in the valleys of the Delaware and Hudson rivers, but the principal outlet for Scots people still remained the province of Ulster, where a further 50,000 people found refuge after the Scottish harvest failures of the 1690s (Smout, Landsman, and Devine in Canny 1996: 88). This shows that Ireland continued to be colonized, by Scots as well as English, to the close of the seventeenth century, and the only significant benefit it derived from developments on the Atlantic was through the involvement of Protestant merchants in Munster ports with the provisioning trade. Authors from the now dominant Protestant community did articulate grievances over the inferior position that was forced upon them by English parliamentary Acts, but their principal concern was over the exclusion of some Irish-produced commodities from the English market. Scots who addressed the same subject wanted the recognition of Scots as equals with English in colonial trade, whether in the Atlantic or to Asia.

This, as it transpired, was to be one of the principal lures to bring Scotland into union with England in 1707. Before then, and in response to the Scottish economic calamity of the 1690s, William Paterson, in his proposal for the establishment of a Scottish business free-trading port at Darien on the isthmus of Panama, demonstrated that a Scotsman could think more globally than any Englishman. He chose Darien as the location for his dream settlement because it would dominate trade on the Pacific as well as the Atlantic, thus drawing the wealth of the entire world towards Scotland (Armitage 2000: 159–61). The failure of the scheme left those Scots who wanted access as equals to colonial trade to seek it in partnership with the English in a trading world that had been shaped by English adventurers. However, once Scots became involved as equals with the English after 1707 they would make a major contribution to the future evolution of that world, especially in its Atlantic context. In doing so they would also draw upon the human resources of the province of Ulster, where so many of their kin and co-religionists had made their home during the course of the seventeenth century, thus ultimately providing all subjects of the British monarchy with access to what, after 1707, became a British colonial empire.

REFERENCES

Andrews, K. N. 1984: *Trade, Plunder and Settlement: Maritime Enterprise and the Genesis of the British Empire, 1480–1630*: Cambridge.

Armitage, D. 1997: 'Making the British Empire: Scotland in the Atlantic world, 1542–1717', *Past and Present*, no. 155, May, 99, 34–63.

Armitage, D. 2000: *The Ideological Origins of the British Empire*: Cambridge.

Birdwood, G. and Foster, W. (eds) 1893: *The First Letterbook of the East India Company*: London.

Canny, N. 1996: *Europeans on the Move: Studies on European Migration, 1500–1800*: Oxford.

Canny, N. (ed.) 1998: *The Origins of Empire: British Overseas Enterprise to the Close of the Seventeenth Century*, vol. 1 of *The Oxford History of the British Empire*: Oxford.

Canny, N. 2001: *Making Ireland British, 1580–1650*: Oxford.

Chatsworth House, Lismore Papers, vol. XI, no. 45.

Chaudhuri, K. N. 1985: *Trade and Civilisation in the Indian Ocean: An Economic History from the Rise of Islam to 1750*: Cambridge.

Linschoten, J. H. van 1884: *The Voyage of John Huygen van Linschoten to the East Indies from the Old English Translation of 1598*, ed. A. C. Burnell and P. A. Tiele: London.

Linschoten, J. H. van 1955–7: *Itinerario: voyage ofte schipvaert von Jan Huygen van Linschoten naer oost ofte Portugaeles Indien, 1579–92*, 3 vols, ed. H. Kern and H. Terprstra: the Hague.

McCulloch, J. R. 1954: *Early English Tracts on Commerce*: Cambridge.

Prakash, O. 1998: *The New Cambridge History of India: European Commercial Life in Pre-Colonial India*: Cambridge.

Quinn, D. B. 1974: *England and the Discovery of America, 1481–1620*: New York.

Quinn, D. B. 1977: *North America from Earliest Discovery to First Settlement*: New York.

Ralegh, Sir Walter 1971: *The History of the World*, ed. C. A. Partrides: London.

Steensgaard, N. 1973: *Carracks, Caravans and Companies: The Structural Crisis in the European Asian Trade in the Early Seventeenth Century*: Copenhagen.

Wrightson, K. 2000: *Earthly Necessities: Economic Lives in Early Modern Britain*: New Haven, CT.

Zahedieh, N. 1998: 'Credit, risk and reputation in late seventeenth-century colonial trade', *Research in Maritime History*, no. 15.

FURTHER READING

Andrews, K. N. 1984: *Trade, Plunder and Settlement: Maritime Enterprise and the Genesis of the British Empire, 1480–1630*: Cambridge.

Armitage, D. 1997: 'Making the British Empire: Scotland in the Atlantic world, 1542–1717', *Past and Present*, no. 155, May, 99, 34–63.

Armitage, D. 2000: *The Ideological Origins of the British Empire*: Cambridge.

Birdwood, G. and Foster, W. (eds) 1893: *The First Letterbook of the East India Company*: London.

Bittereli, U. 1986: *Cultures in Conflict: Encounters between European and Non-European Cultures, 1492–1800*: Stanford, CA.

Bruijn, J. and Gaastra, F. 1993: *Ships, Sailors and Spices: East India Companies and their Shipping in the 16th and 18th Centuries*. Amsterdam.

Canny, N. 1996: *Europeans on the Move: Studies on European Migration, 1500–1800*. Oxford.

Canny, N. (ed.) 1998: *The Origins of Empire: British Overseas Enterprise to the Close of the Seventeenth Century*, vol. 1 of *The Oxford History of the British Empire*. Oxford.

Canny, N. 2001: *Making Ireland British, 1580–1650*. Oxford.

Chaudhuri, K. N. 1965: *The English East India Company: The Study of an Early Joint Stock Company*. London.

Chaudhuri, K. N. 1978: *The Trading World of Asia and the English East India Company, 1660–1760*. Cambridge.

Chaudhuri, K. N. 1985: *Trade and Civilisation in the Indian Ocean: An Economic History from the Rise of Islam to 1750*. Cambridge.

Davis, R. 1972: *The Rise of the English Shipping Industry in the Seventeenth and the Eighteenth Centuries*. Newton Abbot.

Hancock, D. 1995: *Citizens of the World: London Merchants and the Integration of the British Atlantic Community, 1735–85*. Cambridge.

Linschoten, J. H. van 1884: *The Voyage of John Huygen van Linschoten to the East Indies from the Old English Translation of 1598*, ed. A. C. Burnell and P. A. Tiele. London.

Linschoten, J. H. van 1955–7: *Itinerario: voyage ofte schipvaert von Jan Huygen van Linschoten naer oost ofte Portugaeles Indien, 1579–92*, 3 vols, ed. H. Kern and H. Terprstra. the Hague.

McCulloch, J. R. 1954: *Early English Tracts on Commerce*. Cambridge.

Prakash, O. (ed.) 1997: *European Commercial Expansion in Early Modern Asia*. London.

Prakash, O. 1998: *The New Cambridge History of India: European Commercial Life in Pre-Colonial India*. Cambridge.

Quinn, D. B. 1974: *England and the Discovery of America, 1481–1620*. New York.

Ralegh, Sir Walter 1971: *The History of the World*, ed. C. A. Partrides. London.

Scammell, G. V. 1981: *The World Encompassed: The First European Maritime Empires c.800–1650*. London.

Steensgaard, N. 1973: *Carracks, Caravans and Companies: The Structural Crisis in the European Asian Trade in the Early Seventeenth Century*. Copenhagen.

Wrightson, K. 2000: *Earthly Necessities: Economic Lives in Early Modern Britain*. New Haven, CT.

Zahedieh, N. 1998: 'Credit, risk and reputation in late seventeenth-century colonial trade', *Research in Maritime History*, no. 15.

PART II

The Changing Face of Stuart Britain

CHAPTER FOUR

The Rise of the Fiscal State

MICHAEL J. BRADDICK

The structure of English national finances underwent a profound transformation during the seventeenth century, and the new structure was markedly more productive than the old. Before 1640 the crown struggled to meet the increasing demands for expenditure, particularly military expenditure, using an increasingly complex set of financial arrangements. This elaborate structure collapsed in the political crisis of the 1640s, but the demands of mobilization for the subsequent wars led to the creation of new forms of revenue which were of lasting significance. Before the Civil War perhaps three-quarters of revenues were not under the control of parliament, and the proportion was declining. After the Civil War non-parliamentary revenues provided only about 10 per cent of total income and by the 1690s that figure had dwindled to around 3 per cent (Braddick 1996: 13). This transformation was associated also with a great increase in the scale of public revenues which, according to the best current estimate, doubled as a proportion of national wealth during the 1640s (O'Brien and Hunt 1993: chart 1). This double transformation of the revenues in the 1640s was of lasting significance for the development of the English (and subsequently British) state. It also provided the basis for a further increase of the revenues during the wars of the 1690s. For the second time in fifty years the proportion of national wealth being taxed appears to have doubled (ibid.). In that decade, too, the final stage in the transformation of royal debt into a national debt was reached, symbolized in the foundation of the Bank of England. The result was a vastly increased capacity for fiscal–military mobilization. By the 1690s England was a significant European power and the eighteenth-century British state continued to expand across the globe, consolidating the empire of trade and settlement in the Atlantic and expanding into the Indian Ocean. This military and imperial power was founded on a transformation of finances which clearly had deeper roots than an exclusive concentration on measures taken during the 1690s would suggest.

The Pressure to Increase Revenues

The long-term pressures behind the transformation of the finances is clear: the escalating cost of war led to a fairly continuous pressure to raise money and secure credit in order to procure the necessary materials. The adoption of hand-held gunpowder weapons transformed the role of infantry in battle, shifting the balance between cavalry and infantry. The result was a pressure to increase the numbers of infantrymen and to improve their training and equipment. This was increasingly expensive because weaponry and tactics continually evolved. At sea the (admittedly hesitant) adoption of broadside fire led to the construction of specialized warships, with many internal decks and much-reduced cargo space. Under Elizabeth it had been fairly easy to convert an ordinary merchant ship for warfare, but by the early seventeenth century there was pressure to establish a specialized royal navy comprised of fighting ships (Braddick 2000: 202–13). Although there were increasing pressures for impressive court establishments, the really innovative pressure was for new, expensive and specialized military resources. Down to 1640 the crown sought ways of achieving this improvement of military resources by pushing the costs onto the localities in the form of demands for military service in various forms. Over the century as a whole, however, it is possible to discern a consistent pressure to create specialized military forces, and that created a consistent need to raise cash.

The costs of the court, by contrast, did not necessarily have to be paid in cash. The crown had legal powers that could be made to yield a monetary return, either to the crown or to someone licensed by the crown to exercise those powers. Courtiers then, did not need to be paid – they could be put into a position to make money at no cost to the crown but to their own considerable benefit. Similarly, court consumption was met partly by demanding the supply of goods to the crown at the 'king's price' rather than the market price. This right to demand 'purveyance' therefore also provided a means by which to meet the demands of the royal household without raising cash. Early modern governments were, on the whole, cash-poor but they were in this sense asset-rich: they could not easily lay their hands on large sums of money, but they were in a position either to bully or to offer inducements to people to offer services to government. Among the principal creditors of the early Stuarts, for example, were city merchants who paid a rent in return for the right to collect the customs duties. They paid large cash advances to the crown and an annual rent in return for this right. The crown received immediate lump sums and an annual income, but the cost of this was hidden, literally, in the profits of the farmers – whatever profit they made was money that the crown might have had if the money had been collected directly. Although, at the end of each lease, the size of the advance and the level of rent could be negotiated upwards, the crown was, in effect, alienating a principal asset. Merchants only entered these agreements because they could get more from collecting the customs than they were paying the crown. In other words, the crown was losing out in the long term in order to secure short-term gain, and this arose from the overall weakness of the crown's financial position.

There was, then, an institutional logic behind the process by which crown assets were alienated or mortgaged in return for service or for cash in the short term. It resulted in the creation of a twilight world of concessions and leases in which particular individuals were able to make a considerable profit. A prime example of this was the system of monopolies and patents which allowed the recipient to collect fines or payments from those who breached their legal privileges. The logic of the system was to reward innovation or to encourage production of some particular item. Of course, the crown also made money by charging the monopolist or receiving services from them, but there was a persistent suspicion that these people were taking the government for a ride. There was an elaborate political rhetoric of patronage and benefit with which contemporaries could justify such exchanges, but there was also a counter-rhetoric of corruption. A number of Jacobean financiers fell foul of the opposition of those excluded from these and other benefits and, paradoxically, the hostility aroused hampered financial reform which might have made these measures unnecessary.

As a result of this policy it is difficult to say where the boundaries of public revenue lay, since measures of regulation or licensing might actually have been designed to generate cash, or to reward service. However, if we are interested in the reasons for the great increase in the amount of cash paid to the government in taxation over the long term, the explanation lies in the increased pressure for military spending. War was increasingly complex and large-scale, and it had to be paid for in cash. The Stuart state performed other functions, and paid for some of them in cash, but the principal pressure on the development of public revenues over the century as a whole was clearly military. Once state finances were unambiguously based on cash payment, of course, the temptation to resort to these various concessions and licences was much reduced.

The Financial System of the Early Stuarts

Historians categorize the sources of revenue available to the early Stuarts in a number of ways. Following contemporary practice, it is common to distinguish between ordinary revenues which supported the crown's normal business, and extraordinary revenues, which were designed for exceptional purposes, especially war. Ideally, the ordinary account should be run with an accumulating surplus so that there was something in the war chest should extraordinary expenses arise. These ordinary revenues were not, on the whole, granted by parliament and those that parliament did grant were given for the lifetime of the monarch. As a result the grants of taxation made by parliaments during the reign of a monarch represented marginal additions (albeit crucial ones) to the royal finances as a whole.

The bureaucratic resources available to locate wealth were limited, and these constraints were the same for all revenues – ordinary and extraordinary, parliamentary and non-parliamentary. As a result, the costs of government fell on the same range of commodities. The most obvious and easily measured form of wealth was land, of course, and landholders bore the burden of many revenues of the period. Income was (and is) extremely difficult to measure, but those with high incomes and little land might bear the burden of exactions falling on moveable wealth. Over time the range of forms of moveable wealth successfully taxed was quite wide and included, for example, windows and chimneys. Internal trade was very difficult to tax, but overseas trade was successfully monitored since the bulk of it flowed through a relatively small number of ports. Under the early Stuarts the trade revenues were the most dynamic element of the finances, and customs revenues of various kinds seem to have made up 30–40 per cent of total revenues throughout the century – they expanded at least as quickly as the revenues as a whole, therefore (Schnabel forthcoming; Braddick 1994: 49).

The crown's ordinary revenue was made up from a variety of sources. Its own landholdings were very substantial and with careful management might be made to yield a considerable annual income. There were a number of reasons why this did not happen, however. Paternal obligations inhibited the crown from maximizing the revenues from its land, for example, and the need for cash at short notice led to sales which reduced the long-term revenues from land (Hoyle 1992). In addition to these landholdings the crown could raise money as a result of its tenurial relationship with leading landholders – a number of revenues usually referred to as the feudal dues. For example, people who held land from the crown under particular terms might be liable to wardship – if they inherited while under age the lands might revert to the crown and they might have to pay sums of money to receive their lands on achieving adulthood. In the meantime the crown could milk the lands for profit, or grant them to an individual who would do that. Wardship, therefore, was another resource which might be used to meet the costs of government without the need for the crown to raise cash. Of crucial importance to overall finances were the various duties imposed on overseas trade known collectively as the customs. Some of them were granted by parliament to the king for life (tonnage and poundage), others belonged to the crown by ancient right and still others were raised as a result of prerogative power (the impositions). These latter arose from the right of the crown to regulate trade and so they were not, in the technical legal sense, taxes.

As we have seen, it was not always necessary to raise cash in order to meet the costs of government and in a number of cases the crown was able to commute forms of service into cash payments. We have already mentioned the provision of goods to the royal household in the form of purveyance, for example. This was an unpopular duty and the people who went into the country to take up the goods were widely resented. As a result the officials of the household were able to offer a deal to the counties whereby they would accept a sum of money in place of goods, the money being sufficient to cover the difference between the king's price and the market price for the goods that were said to be due from the county. As a result, the duty to provide purveyance was transformed into a cash payment – effectively a service had been commuted into a form of taxation. The most notorious of these commutations was the demand for ship money, associated particularly with the 1630s but with precedents from the earlier period. Port towns had an ancient obligation to provide ships in time of war, but this duty of service was commuted into a payment with which the crown could secure ships of its own, and this payment was extended to inland ports. Again, a duty of service was thereby commuted into a cash payment.

The principal parliamentary revenues were the subsidy and the fifteenth and tenth. Subsidies required local officers to assess the wealth of eligible taxpayers, returning their valuation to the exchequer. Another set of officials were then charged with the collection of a tax at a fixed rate of that valuation. Subsidies were the only form of taxation in the sixteenth and early seventeenth centuries which required this valuation of personal wealth (although the later seventeenth-century hearth taxes attempted something similar, as we will see) and their voluminous records provide an invaluable source for social and economic historians. However, as a result of local evasion, the valuations on which the tax was raised became increasingly inaccurate with the result that their value to the crown was falling. James inherited the subsidy just after a period in which the effects of multiple grants had been offset by extensive under-reporting of wealth in the localities and the crown never managed to make up this shortfall. The fifteenth and tenth was more characteristic of early modern taxation, in England and abroad, in that it imposed a fixed sum on each local jurisdiction. This kind of quota (or partition) tax was extremely attractive to early modern governments because the overall yield was predictable and the administration imposed fewer demands on the central government. The fifteenth and tenth, however, was of limited value because the overall burden was fixed by custom. The division of the burden within the localities was also customary and, often, very unequal. As a result local disputes were fairly common and each time the tax was granted particularly harshly treated localities or groups secured exemption. The result was a steadily declining yield, with increasing exemptions, and a local distribution of the burden which bore little relation to the actual distribution of wealth.

To make up for gaps between income and expenditure, governments borrow. Early Stuart borrowing was rudimentary. Kings could call on favours, of course, and intimidate people into lending, but royal credit was generally poor. To get debts repaid was a tricky political business and monarchs seem to have felt no particular need to conform to the notions of fair dealing held by their subjects. As a result of this, and the constant shortage of funds available to make repayments, the crown found it increasingly difficult to borrow directly. A second difficulty was the absence of a well-established money market. Most credit was designed to facilitate trade – extending relatively small amounts of credit for relatively short periods of time in order to allow for the completion of transactions. This credit was advanced in the form of written obligations – bonds and bills of exchange in particular – which promised payment of a particular sum at a particular date. These pieces of paper did have an intrinsic value, of course, since the bearer could collect some money at some date in the future, and they circulated as a form of money as well as simply facilitating trade. Some individuals in the City of London with good credit might be able to raise substantial sums on behalf of the crown using these instruments, but it was a complex business and not an attractive commercial proposition. The City of London itself might be induced to raise money on behalf of the crown, however, and particular merchants might raise large cash advances in return for the right to collect the customs revenues, as we have seen. One of the most striking developments of seventeenth-century finances was the emergence of a money market in which the government could raise money directly, rather than through these intermediaries, but under the early Stuarts this was a distant prospect indeed. The nearest they came, in fact, was to raise benevolences or privy seal loans – essentially forcing individuals into lending to the crown with uncertain prospects of repayment and poor rates of return. This was not, therefore, a strategy that met with universal approval. Credit took the form mainly of the anticipation of revenue – running an overdraft – or of leasing or mortgaging assets in return for cash payments.

Revenue raising produced political frictions of course. As we have seen, a consequence of military change was to monetize more functions of government. This was something with more than simply financial implications, of course, since it affected the way in which the relationship between crown and subject operated. Private property was taken by the government for some public service – a quite different transaction from a duty of service of some kind on demand. Governments needed to enter into a process of negotiation in order to secure the necessary participation. Commuting services into cash payments frequently produced legal disputes and the crown was taken to court on a number of occasions in order to test the legality of these commutations or applications of the prerogative. The famous cases brought by John Bate and John Hampden, for example, tested these powers.

A crucial element in the latter case was the legal question of whether Hampden was being asked for money or a service (Russell 1990). These disputes were expressed in formal legal terms, of course, and so their political importance is difficult to discern. The political motives of the litigants (if there were any) are even more obscure for the same reason.

Resort to parliament required the crown to persuade parliament of the necessity for the grant of taxation. Parliament was frequently reluctant to grant money and never gave as much as the crown claimed was necessary. On this debate most modern historians have thought that the crown had the better case, but parliament was influenced in part by a belief that the crown was extravagant. An early attempt to break this circle was the Great Contract in 1610, which sought, effectively, to augment the ordinary revenue through permanent parliamentary grants. In return some of the more imaginative uses of crown authority to make up for a lack of cash would be abandoned. The failure of the Great Contract condemned parliament and the crown to further wrangling over these issues, wrangles that were made more difficult by the suspicion generated by the policy of mortgaging and alienation of crown resources. Granting more money to the crown was, it was feared, simply another way of feeding the apparently insatiable appetite of shady City figures and corrupt courtiers for royal largesse. It was understood too that parliaments were not simply supposed to provide money but also a forum for the resolution of problems in the commonwealth. Whether there was a contract implied (that supply depended on redress), or an agreed sequential relationship (that supply followed redress), was unclear. It is possible that for some members of parliament this was a fairly conscious contest for political power, although that is a controversial issue (Smith 1999: 51–3).

The Elizabethan and early Stuart financial 'system' was actually a complicated web of rights and resources which offered the possibility of *ad hoc* solutions to particular problems. In this web the role of parliament was relatively limited (although still crucial) and the finances are best described as being royal, rather than national.

The Financial History of the Early Stuart Period

Although sources are available with which to establish a clear picture of royal finances they have, until now, been rather under-utilized. We have good administrative accounts of the financial system for the whole period and a thorough knowledge of revenue and expenditure after 1660 (Dietz 1964; Chandaman 1975). The confused picture of the 1640s and 1650s has recently been very helpfully elucidated (Wheeler 1999), but our knowledge of the financial position of the early Stuarts remains surprisingly sketchy. Happily this lack is soon to be remedied (Schnabel forthcoming). What follows is based on the current state of our knowledge, therefore, and may eventually be overtaken by further research. What seems clear is that by the later 1630s this financial system had reached a degree of elaboration and productiveness that should command respect.

Under the early Stuarts a series of *ad hoc* solutions were sought to the revenue problem which built on the policies pursued under Elizabeth. Elizabeth had been prudent, or perhaps parsimonious, aiming to trim expenditure and to reward court-iers in ways that did not impose a cash cost on the crown – they were rewarded with licences, patents or wardships, or were fobbed off with the promise of these things.

The later sixteenth century was a period of rapid inflation, but the royal household was protected from its effects by the imposition of purveyance – the king's price, naturally, did not rise nearly as quickly as the market price. Even in the case of military reform measures were taken which preserved the crown from the dire necessity of having to raise cash directly.

The principal military resource on land was the militia – the citizens armed in response to call for service from the monarch. All adult males were liable for service and could be required to attend a general muster in their county each year. Although this might produce large numbers of men, however, it was difficult, in fact unrealistic, to expect private individuals to keep up with the rapidly changing weaponry of the period. Under Elizabeth a core of specialized troops had been developed from within the general muster – the trained bands – made up of men particularly apt for military service. They were armed and trained at the expense of the county, the charges being passed on in the form of local rates raised by the lieutenancy. For many people the effect of this was to transform the duty of service into a duty to pay a rate to support the activities of the trained bands. The crown was able to achieve a degree of military reform, therefore, without bearing a direct cash cost, but the price was a dependence on local co-operation in the raising and equipping of the trained bands. Troops for service abroad were also raised from among the general muster – again the crown did not bear a cash cost but depended instead on the right to demand service. It seems, however, that local officeholders generally thought the trained bands too valuable a resource on which to draw for this purpose. The standard of recruits and equipment for foreign expeditions was notoriously bad and this contributed to the fairly dismal record of English military expeditions prior to 1640. The expeditions to Ireland during the 1590s, however, did re-establish English authority and the feared Spanish invasion never arrived.

At sea the problem was, at least under Elizabeth, less acute. Merchants trading in overseas markets generally had to protect their boats and so many of them were relatively well-suited to use in wartime. The standard naval tactic was to bear down on the enemy and fire shots which cleared the decks. The attacker could then come alongside and board. This required only that a gun could be mounted in the bow and had few implications for the internal architecture of the ships – there was as yet no very clear distinction between the design of merchant ships and warships. This harmony of design was matched during the 1590s by a coincidence of interest which allowed the crown to persuade large numbers of merchants to pursue their fortunes by attacking Spanish shipping. A major part of the war effort was privateering: merchants' ships were issued with letters of marque which allowed them to attack enemy ships in reprisal for attacks on English shipping. The fiction was stretched to an impressive degree, with the result that during the 1590s about a hundred privateers set out each year to attack Spanish ships with the blessing of the English crown (Andrews 1964: 32–4).

The costs of the expensive wars of the last fifteen years of Elizabeth's reign were also, largely, covered. The military record of these forces was far from shameful, and the financial position that James I inherited was not desperate, in part because the war had not consumed cash. But although Elizabeth had left him relatively healthy finances, he also inherited pent-up demand for spending. Court expenditure had a direct political value, in creating friends for the crown, but it was also an important component of the representation of political authority, and some rise in court expenditures was probably inevitable for the new king. He also had a family to support and he brought with him a Scottish entourage which was widely suspected of devouring English resources. Increased spending was clearly not the result of war, since James pursued a peace policy until the last years of his reign, and so he has been accused of extravagance by modern historians, who can find plenty of contemporary comment to support that view. The increased spending pushed Jacobean finances into deficit – rather than accumulating a surplus on the ordinary account the king faced deficits which were met by anticipating future revenue. As future revenue was mortgaged the problem was, potentially at least, an escalating one, and the crown had no protection from short-term shocks, such as warfare.

The Great Contract failed as a result of mutual mistrust and from then on financial policies revolved around attempts to restrict expenditure. The principal success here was to avoid war, at least until the 1620s, but there were also periods of retrenchment in royal expenditure which promised to reduce the deficit. There were political problems associated with this attack on inefficiencies and extravagances, as Lionel Cranfield was to discover to his cost. On the revenue side, new duties on imports and exports were introduced (impositions) and monopolies and other concessions were granted in order to secure service at no immediate cash cost, or to secure cash payments. The value of the leases of the customs farms were consistently increased and pressure was applied to the management of wardship in order to realize a greater annual income. Crown lands were sold in order to raise immediate cash, but the effect of this on annual revenue was offset to some extent by improved management of the lands that remained. Parliamentary taxation was by no means the most important element of crown finances for much of this period.

The outbreak of European war in 1618 made these policies appear increasingly fragile. The future of Protestantism was at stake; so too the dynastic interests of James's son-in-law, and to remain on the sidelines was politically unacceptable. But the costs of participation were horrendous and there had been no accumulating ordinary surplus on which to draw in this time of need. Expeditions required cash for wages, transport and equipment. At sea the willingness of merchants to put their ships to service was reduced, and in any case ship design had begun to become more specialized with the result that fewer merchant ships were likely to be useful in war. Parliaments were unrealistic about the financial implications of active warfare, perhaps misled by the memory of the success of the Elizabethan effort. Frictions between crown and parliament over other issues added to the reluctance of parliament to grant subsidies and fifteenths and tenths. The value of the subsidies that were granted was eroded by evasion in the localities. As a result the crown was caught in a bind: it could not really afford to fight, financially, but could not afford not to, politically. The forced loan of 1626 was one solution – to raise money using the subsidy as a guide but without parliamentary consent, but this was a very controversial measure (Cust 1987).

The return of peace during the 1630s allowed for some recovery of the financial position. Militia reform was urged with renewed vigour and ship money was used as a means to begin to establish a specialized royal navy, suitable to meet the demands of modern warfare. The effects of these reforms are unclear, however, and the material measures necessary to support them provoked legal challenge once again. The ordinary costs of government were addressed by more thorough exploitation of feudal and other legal rights and the import duties were of crucial importance – impositions had continued to expand during the 1620s and Charles raised tonnage and poundage without parliamentary sanction. As a result of these measures, and the coming of peace, the crown was by the late 1630s approaching solvency (Schnabel forthcoming), although it had paid a political price for the success with which this complex of rights and revenues had been manipulated.

Under James I and Charles I (and under Elizabeth) this pattern of revenue raising had proved adequate to meeting the needs of peace-time expenditure. During the 1620s war caused acute financial and political difficulties and it was war that brought the Caroline financial system crashing down in the late 1630s. The financial record of the early Stuarts was not great, but they had managed to keep the show on the road. The price of their relative failure had been that they had fallen off the pace of European military reform. And even though they had not kept up with the military reforms of their most powerful neighbours, they had taken measures in that direction that were unpopular. The result was a regime that was weakened in two ways: it was both militarily enfeebled and unpopular at the same time.

Public Finances in the Civil Wars and After

The collapse of the Caroline regime was part cause and part consequence of financial problems, therefore. During the civil wars that followed both sides faced acute financial and military demands and measures of lasting significance were taken – in the extreme conditions of civil war many earlier constraints were broken, with permanent effect. Both sides paid for most of their military resources in cash, and developed new instruments of taxation in order to do that. Parliament developed the more durable system of money raising, which rested on three principal pillars. Land was taxed by means of a quota tax, the assessment, which was highly productive and long-lasting: with the exception of a brief interlude in the early 1690s, quota taxation was to be the principal means of taxing landed wealth until the late eighteenth century. The collection of customs duties continued and their yield continued to expand as quickly as that of the revenues as a whole. The most striking innovation of the period was the excise, a tax on domestic consumption which provided a means to reach taxpayers with disposable income but not much land. As a result, over the coming century and a half the excise was to prove very popular with the landed interest. These sources of revenue provided the financial basis of the state until the late eighteenth century, and two of them date from the early years of the Civil War. In 1640 control of the customs had passed to parliament, which now determined the rates and set about increasing them. All these revenues remained under parliamentary control after the return of the monarchy in 1660. Other kinds of crown revenue, outlawed in the early years of the Long Parliament, were never restored. As a result, overall, there was a profound shift in the nature of royal finances – parliamentary sources of income now dominated.

Despite this very productive tax regime the governments of the 1640s and 1650s still accumulated debts, but they were able to raise credit in new ways. By offering to repay debts in strict order, and as a result of the existence of very productive taxes, credit was raised quite readily from suppliers and other intermediaries were willing to operate on behalf of the government because of the potential profits to be had (Wheeler 1999: ch. 3; Braddick 1996: 37–40). Men like Martin Noell took up farms of the excise or customs and advanced other sums secure in the knowledge that they would get their money back. This had, potentially, important political implications: the security for this credit was the regime, not the word of the king, and we might discern here an important further step in the long-term depersonalization of political power. But this borrowing remained largely short-term and was undertaken for particular reasons – there was as yet no long-term funded national debt. It was not until the 1690s that the royal debt was decisively transformed into a national one.

Much of the financial system established during the wars was retained at the Restoration and there were further developments in public borrowing. Even the excise, the collection of which had sometimes caused riot and whose officers were pilloried in pamphlets of the period, was retained. Indeed the excise and the customs were the basis of Charles II's ordinary revenue. Added to this was the hearth tax, another attempt to tax non-landed wealth by fixing upon an easily measured form of disposable income. Chimneys were a luxury and there was a broad correlation between their numbers and the wealth of the inhabitants of a house. Here was a dramatic shift, then: the ordinary revenue of the king was derived not from inherited property or legal rights but from parliamentary grants.

When describing the Restoration financial settlement historians usually concentrate on its financial inadequacy: the ordinary revenue was funded at too low a level, and the productiveness of its component parts was overestimated. That the king did not have enough money is clear enough, but the capacity to raise money was much improved, and the military capacity of the state likewise. The ordinary revenue exceeded the hard-won achievements of Charles I in the 1630s and huge additional amounts of money were raised to fight the Dutch wars of the 1660s and 1670s. It did not deliver military dominance, but it was a great improvement on the military record of the period prior to the civil wars. Most importantly, however, there had been a long-term, never-to-be-reversed shift in the basis of government finance. This was to some extent reflected in the security for borrowing. Parliament achieved control over the disposal of moneys raised, appropriating them to particular purposes and auditing them in order to ensure that they had in fact been used for those purposes. A system for the repayment of debts in strict order was introduced, reducing the power of the king to exercise political preference and, in response to a short-term disaster, long-term forms of borrowing were introduced. In 1672 government credit became over-extended, with the result that payments on some forms of borrowing were suspended in the notorious Stop of the Exchequer. This was not a bankruptcy, since many forms of credit were honoured, but it was the ruin of some influential bankers. Their compensation came in the issue of annuities: the debt was deemed to be a long-term investment in the government on which there was an annual return. It was a small but successful measure, which effectively transformed small-scale short-term credit into long-term funded debt. Once again, the security was the health of the state, not the word of the king (Roseveare 1991: ch. 2).

These financial innovations paid for a standing army and specialized navy. Up to one in eight adult males bore arms during the Civil War and a significant number of men were in arms throughout the 1650s. Rather than an intermittent expense the army was now a permanent military presence. And it was a professional, specialized body dependent on wages too – the militia was no longer the basis of the army but a kind of local defence and police force. At the same time there was a dramatic transformation of the navy. From the 1650s onwards, in particular, the role of private ships in wartime was dramatically reduced and action at sea increasingly depended on the effectiveness of the specialized state navy. The navy and the customs administration became tools of national policy – binding trade in the burgeoning empire into the protective shell of the navigation system, which had its origins in the measures of the early 1650s. After 1660 the army was the object of much suspicion, of course, but a small permanent force was maintained nonetheless. More than that, the capacity to mobilize substantial numbers of men remained. The navy was not prey to quite the same kind of suspicion and its retention at the Restoration was less problematic. In effect, the state was now a major employer and by 1688 Gregory King was able to recognize soldiers and sailors as distinct social groups.

Although England was not the principal military power in Europe after the Restoration it was a much more significant military power than it had been before the civil wars. The small standing army and the increasingly impressive, professional and effective state navy represented a significant change in the nature of the military resources of the state. It would be quite wrong, therefore, to suggest that the civil wars had only a short-term effect on the development of the military resources of the state. These new military and fiscal resources were, self-evidently, the consequences of civil war. They supported a level of military mobilization hitherto unimagined and were to support English military dominance of Britain and Ireland.

New taxes and a new financial system created new political issues, of course. During the 1640s and 1650s the legitimacy of the regimes was questionable, for obvious reasons, and there were constitutional challenges to the power of the Cromwellian regimes to collect the assessment and the customs. But these were the last legal challenges to their revenue rights that governments faced in the seventeenth century; after the Restoration, parliamentary grants with the royal assent were of unimpeachable legality. Constitutional fears now centred on the possibility that parliament might grant away its independence by over-funding the crown – a too-generous grant of customs and excise duties might free the crown from the need to resort to parliament again. Another new issue arose as a result of the nature of the administration of some of these taxes, particularly the excise. The taxes of the Tudor and early Stuart period had been collected by local officeholders – magistrates and constables – acting in response to particular commissions. The tax administration drew upon, but did not create, their political role in the locality. This continued to be true of land taxes: the assessment and the land tax were in the hands of gentry commissioners and local officeholders. The excise, by contrast, was in the hands of a separate, specially constituted administration – excisemen made a career from taxing the localities. This personal interest made them the objects of acute suspicion, and they were often described in terms of a biblical plague – arriving from outside and devouring local crops to their own benefit. At some points in its history the hearth tax too was in the hands of a specialized administration and similar concerns were expressed. In response to these pressures a new emphasis was placed on precision; whereas the power of a magistrate was justified with reference to his discretion, the power of an exciseman was acceptable only because he had no discretion. A kind of bureaucratic legitimacy was asserted by these people, more recognizable to modern eyes than the paternal or patriarchal model of political authority drawn upon by local officeholders (Braddick 2000: 260–3).

Alongside this concern about the constitution, and the powers of the state, a more coherent debate was emerging about the economic effects of taxation – there was a much more self-conscious discussion of the political economy of taxation and the national debt. In part this probably reflected the increasing impact of government on the economy. We are used to modern governments being the largest spenders and consumers in national economies – the income of the British state in 2001 represents just under 40 per cent of GNP. How governments choose to raise and spend money has implications for demand and supply throughout the economy and can have a profound impact on overall patterns of production and economic growth. The tax regime can be deliberately manipulated in order to discourage smoking or to encourage saving, for example. The seventeenth-century English state was not in this position – its income by the 1690s probably represented only 10 per cent of national wealth – but contemporaries had nonetheless begun to recognize the possibility that the fiscal system could be used to encourage or discourage particular kinds of production or consumption. The overall pattern of import duties was manipulated to encourage domestic manufacture and discourage imports of finished goods, and a system of tariffs was used to tie the trade of the colonies to the metropolitan economy. Debate about how to tax domestic wealth took account of the effects of taxes on the distribution of wealth between social groups and on patterns of consumption. By modern standards these debates were crude, but in the thinking of William Petty and others we can see the origins of the ambition to manage the economy by fiscal means, although that was clearly something much beyond the technical and financial capacity of the state in 1700 (Braddick 1996: chs 6–7). It seems, too, that in building up the necessary coalitions of support for warfare a new language of national interest came to prominence alongside more established dynastic or religious arguments – the national interest might, according to these arguments, lie in the preservation of trade in order to secure the necessary financial resources to maintain independence. In the wars against the Dutch in the later seventeenth century, arguments about national trading interests were certainly more prominent than in earlier periods of warfare (Pincus 1996).

The Glorious Revolution led to diplomatic and military entanglement on the Continent. This called forth a massive military mobilization and necessitated the raising of huge sums of money. The money was spent abroad, since troops on the Continent secured supplies locally, and this massive export of demand had serious economic effects, especially in the acute shortage of coin at home. It was not least for this reason that the 1690s were a golden age for coining: good coin had been taken abroad and there was little domestic alternative other than to undertake clipping and coining (Jones 1988). Although the scale of taxation had again increased, however, this mobilization was achieved by familiar means: the customs, the excise and the land tax (which quickly became much like the assessment in its organization). This took the financial system established during the civil wars to a new level of effectiveness – it was mobilization much like that of the 1640s and 1650s, but completely unlike that of the 1590s – but it did not establish a new one. By contrast, neither the

Cromwellian nor Williamite mobilization bears much relationship to the financial and military system presided over by Elizabeth and the early Stuarts.

Despite the massive sums of money raised, however, the government rapidly accumulated debt and this is where the real novelty of the 1690s lies. Much borrowing was short-term in nature but during that decade a permanent national debt was established: individuals bought instruments of credit that were not redeemable but offered either an annual return or the possibility of sale for a profit at a future date. This is quite different from short-term credit designed to cover a gap between spending and the arrival of the sum which will cover that expenditure. The security for these sums was not the word of the king, but the financial health of the state, and the credit was extended for an open-ended period of time. In 1694 the Bank of England was founded, initially as a money-raising operation, but in time it was the Bank that undertook to make these credit arrangements. In the future government credit would be raised directly on the London money market by a specialized institution (Dickson 1967). This change rested on the security offered by dependable tax revenues under parliamentary control, and on the increasing sophistication of the London money market. Clearly, both had roots in the period before the Glorious Revolution.

The Reaction of Taxpayers

Looking at the century as a whole it is possible to see a dramatic transformation of the scale and nature of the finances. In histories of particular periods there is an inevitable concentration on the political difficulties that attended these developments, but that should not obscure the successes. Over the long term it is the compliance of taxpayers that commands attention and it is something that eludes simple explanation. However, the long-term success of the state in these matters should caution us against using stark dichotomies to discuss the politics of taxation. In particular, it is clear that taxpayers rarely felt that they were making a choice about whether or not to pay, but did frequently address more specific questions about the administration and impact of the tax. Secondly, the apparently commonsense distinction between centre and locality does not appear to capture the reality of the politics of taxation. The centre was a resource for the resolution of local disputes of the first kind, and there were local benefits as well as costs arising from the imposition of taxation. Imposing taxes did not represent a simple exercise of power by the centre, over and at the expense of, the localities.

When confronted by someone carrying a tax demand the willingness of an individual actually to pay was undoubtedly affected by debates about constitutional powers and abstract issues relating to property rights. But the effect of these things is difficult to chart because opposition was expressed through formal channels. Refusal to pay might be justified with reference to particularities – local liberties, or the precise powers of collectors or assessors, for example – but whether that was the 'real' reason for the refusal must remain an open question. The effect on local compliance of these issues of grand political principle is impossible to gauge because we can talk only about behaviour, not motivation. It is clear, however, that there were more specific local concerns raised by taxation. If governments could answer or remove these objections they would remove one set of plausible objections to payment, whatever the reasons that actually motivated people to make these complaints. That, in itself, would therefore help to increase revenue yields.

Prominent among these kinds of objection was the issue of the fairness of the local distribution of the burden. This was raised in response to almost all the revenues discussed here. Quota taxes were inevitably challenged on the grounds that the quotas were unfairly apportioned. Boroughs complained about the ease of the burden on the surrounding county, and counties habitually complained that they were under-taxed. The subsidy was criticized because it was unfairly assessed, falling particularly heavily on specific social groups or allowing assessors to favour their friends. Various levies were said to burden the poor unfairly, but the richer sort habitually claimed that they underwent all sorts of unpaid service on behalf of the crown which should allow them some relief from supplying cash. A refusal to allow accurate assessment (some-thing thought to be incompatible with liberty) meant that there was no effective means to set authoritative quotas either. Related to these issues of distributive fairness was the concern to preserve local liberties. The English financial regime was much more uniform than, for example, that of *ancien régime* France, but there were a number of privileges and rights which were jealously preserved. Exemptions were sought for property in cathedral chapters or the lands of dissolved monasteries, and corporate bodies like the universities were keen to preserve their liberties. Someone arguing on these grounds might have been motivated by quite different concerns, of course.

We cannot easily say, then, what actually motivated tax refusal. It is possible, though, to be clear about the strategies available to those who might want to limit or remove a tax liability. There was a range of responses from taxpayers to the raising of taxation, from evasion to riot. For example, all forms of financial obligation might be avoided. Since the powers of revenue agents and the forms of liable wealth were all legally defined, it was always possible to avoid obligation by claiming either that the agents were exceeding their powers or that the particular item being rated was not legally liable. Similarly the excise and the hearth taxes included various categories of exemption that might be exploited by reluctant taxpayers. This kind of avoidance shades into evasion when the spirit or letter of the law is exceeded. Chimneys were bricked up while the hearth tax was being assessed, levels of beer production were concealed from excise collectors and goods were smuggled into or out of the country. A notable success of government in response to this was to impose compositions – rather than actually to measure wealth a deal was struck with which both sides could be happy. Thus, brewers agreed to pay a certain amount to the excise collectors which was below their full liability but which was sufficient to satisfy the bureaucracy. The adoption of quotas for land taxes represents a kind of compos-ition on a grand scale – rather than actually rate the wealth of the country a deal was struck, effectively, between the exchequer and each particular locality (Braddick 1996: ch. 8).

Those unable to avoid or evade their liabilities might simply refuse to pay. In that case they were likely to be liable to distraint and that distraint might then become the subject of a legal dispute. Physical or verbal resistance might attend the attempt to assess forms of wealth or to take distraint, but it was not the only or natural resort of the reluctant taxpayer. Riot was very unusual and largely confined to resistance to the excises on meat and salt in the 1640s and 1650s, and the hearth tax in the mid-1660s. In general, the possibility of paying less, or differently, allowed for a degree of local negotiation which largely eliminated any conflict between centre and locality. Indeed, as noted above, people seeking to shift the burden of taxation onto another local group resorted to the institutions of central government as allies, rather than enemies, in that attempt. Increasing levels of taxation did not, therefore, automatically increase levels of violence or prompt provincial revolt (Braddick 1996: ch. 8).

Even the payment of taxation seems to have served to integrate centre and locality, since the transmission of funds was related to the credit networks of the private economy. Collectors of direct taxes entered personal bonds to the exchequer for the sum of money due from the areas under their jurisdiction. If they defaulted they were able to name their own creditors as reasons for that default, and these processes sometimes reveal the connection between tax collection and private credit networks (Braddick 1994: 33–4). To enter a personal bond for such large sums was an intimidating prospect of course. Humphrey Chetham, an important local provincial cloth merchant with bases in London and Manchester, seems to have been an attractive man to run parliamentary finances in the 1640s because of his credit connections: he could return money to London by paper transaction rather than carting large sums of money around the country, and his financial expertise was obviously attractive in such a position (Guscott 2000: 216–17). In the 1660s money was returned by bill of exchange rather than in cash, reducing the risks and delays of moving coin. It also reduced the possibility that tax would create shortages of coin locally (Braddick 1994: 162–3).

The fiscal–military state was not just a tax collector, of course, but also a customer. At the national level, at each stage of the transformation outlined above, opportunities arose from which individuals might make considerable fortunes. Under the early Stuarts successful merchants such as Lionel Cranfield might spread their risks by taking up licences and concessions under the crown (Prestwich 1966). In the mid-century, London financiers like Martin Noell, Robert Vyner or Edmund Backwell could advance cash to the government and take up tax farms or offices as a means of diversifying their investments (Braddick 1994: 37–8; Roseveare 1991: 11–12). Perhaps the most successful such figure was Sir Stephen Fox, who rose from being a virtually penniless servant of Charles II in exile in the 1650s to become one of the richest commoners in England and the longest-serving lord treasurer of his day. During the 1660s he undertook to supply wages to the army at a discount, relieving the army of the frustrating and disappointing business of trying to get the money from the exchequer. His profits rapidly escalated and at one point he was able to take control of the excise too, bidding for the farm in 1674 (Clay 1978). Lesser offices also provided opportunities, of course. The excise was by the late seventeenth century a reliable employer, offering regular pay, a career structure and pension rights. Customs collection, too, offered a safe employment, as did the increasingly complex bureaucracy associated with the management of the financial and military resources of the state. The army and navy themselves, of course, were sufficiently attractive employers to attract volunteers. The imperial administration represented an opportunity state for military men and colonial governments around the Atlantic world offered positions for soldiers (Armitage 1999: 442). From the 1690s onwards large numbers of people were investing in the national debt: 10,000 by 1709, 30,000 by 1719, 60,000 by 1756 (quoted from Brewer 1989: 126). This, clearly, created a vested interest in the perpetuation of these financial arrangements.

Behind all this lay an increased willingness to pay taxation – this was the fundamental fact of English political life allowing the creation of this fiscal–military structure. It is easy to demonstrate that tax burdens increased and that tax resistance did not, but it is very difficult to explain why. In the 1640s, but not at other times, it might have been the result of the presence of soldiers. Even then, the presence of soldiers seems sometimes to have caused rather than prevented violence (Braddick 1994: 180–1, 278). In part, fiscal success resulted from the reduction of possibilities of avoidance and evasion, or the limitation of their effects. The transformation of the constitutional basis of finances also foreclosed particular kinds of legal resistance. But these changes might simply have displaced resistance, leading to an even greater parliamentary reluctance to grant taxation or to a greater incidence of riot, for example. In fact, the greater weight of financial demands does not seem to have met with an equal and opposite reaction. Parliament granted ever larger sums of taxation, raised by means which were difficult to evade and avoid, and which could not be resisted through the courts. There was no provincial rebellion, however. In part this was because, as we have seen, all this was not simply a cost to the country but might also offer opportunities. It was also, no doubt, enabled by the increasingly persuasive case that these military and fiscal instruments could be deployed in the national interest in commercial war and imperial expansion. But it was also, surely, due to the memory of the experience of the 1640s – a greater awareness of the financial needs of the state and the consequences of failing to meet them. The regimes of the 1630s and 1640s laid increasing stress on arguments of necessity and reasons of state in seeking consent to taxation and the persuasiveness of these arguments was greatly increased as a result of the Civil War and revolution (Tuck 1993: ch. 6). Both sorts of argument were widely accepted as a useful currency of politics thereafter. These arguments, and those relating to the national interest, are striking features of eighteenth-century political life, but their origins clearly lie in the mid-seventeenth century political crisis.

Conclusion: The Rise of the Fiscal State

In 1588 England possessed no distinct military profession and hardly any specialized revenue officers. The basis of the land forces was the muster of able-bodied men rather than full-time soldiers and action at sea was undertaken by privateers and merchant ships as much as by the ships of a specialized royal navy. Tax revenues were small and parliamentary revenue only a minor part of the overall financial system. Taxes were largely administered by local officeholders rather than a special-ized bureaucracy and payment was likely to be justified with reference to a personal obligation to the monarch. Many government services were paid for in kind, rather than with cash. Borrowing was avoided as far as possible and, when it was undertaken, depended on the co-operation of intermediaries since royal credit was so poor.

According to Gregory King's social accounts 44,000 families were headed by military officers in 1688, and their dependants numbered around 106,000 if his estimates of household size were accurate. In 1690 there were 1,311 customs officers and 1,211 excise officers. Applying King's multiplier of 6 heads per household for lesser officers, there were another 15,000 people dependent for their livelihood on the fiscal–military state. A crude guess, then, is that at that date 120,000 people, 2.4 per cent of the population, were directly dependent on the financial and military activities of the state for their livelihood. A substantial proportion of the 150,000 people in the families of common seamen could be added to that figure (Laslett 1983: 32–3; Brewer 1989: 66). The use of these instruments to foster and protect overseas trade secured the material well-being of many others. During the Nine Years' War (1688–97) there were, on average, 119,000 men in arms each year. Tax revenues, which ultimately supported all this, may have represented about 10 per cent of national wealth during the 1690s (Brewer 1989: 30; O'Brien and Hunt 1993: 159). The tax burden was absolutely higher than any other European country other than France and the only country which paid more per head was the United Provinces (Jones 1988: 29). Tens of thousands of people were persuaded to invest in the national debt, giving them a direct material interest in the financial health of the regime.

In many areas of national life, over the century between the Armada and the Glorious Revolution, service had been commuted into cash payments and this had important consequences for the way in which political authority was perceived and justified. There was a marked depersonalization of political authority as royal finances and obligations were transformed into public finances. In the management of the debt, in particular, the significance of royal will declined markedly as political preference was removed from the repayment of debts. By the 1690s practices and specialized institutions with which we are familiar – parliamentary taxation, the Bank of England, the Treasury, the national debt – were the financial pillars of the state. The role of the monarch had been, accordingly, reduced. This was, of course, a difference in degree rather than kind, but this is clearly a very significant stage in that longer-term process.

The contrast is not complete, of course. Some areas of government were still conducted as a matter of service, in particular the social and economic regulation of local life undertaken by the unpaid officeholders of county and borough administration. The business of the fiscal–military state did not by any means represent the totality of government activities. Indeed some important aspects of the fiscal and military activity remained in the hands of local gentlemen. The land tax, in particular, was not entrusted to professional agents and local defence and policing remained in the hands of the militia which, in turn, remained in the hands of local gentlemen acting voluntarily. In these wider aspects of government, dynastic or religious arguments remained extremely important to the legitimation of political power. Nonetheless, the emergence of a powerful English fiscal–military state in the seventeenth century was of long-term significance for the economic, imperial and political development of the British state thereafter. The importance of the 1690s to that development is now well known, but clearly there were very significant developments prior to that date. In fact the real breach with the past seems to have come in the 1640s, in the crisis of civil war and revolution. The changes introduced in those years were not reversed and as a result they represent the closure of one chapter in English fiscal and military history and the opening of another.

REFERENCES

Andrews, K. R. 1964: *Elizabethan Privateering: English Privateering during the Spanish War, 1585–1603*: Cambridge.

Armitage, D. 1999: 'Greater Britain: a useful category of historical analysis?' *American Historical Review*, 104, 427–45.

Braddick, M. J. 1994: *Parliamentary Taxation in Seventeenth-Century England: Local Administration and Response*, Royal Historical Society, Studies in History, 70: Woodbridge.

Braddick, M. J. 1996: *The Nerves of State: Taxation and the Financing of the English State, 1558–1714*: Manchester.

Braddick, M. J. 2000: *State Formation and Social Change in Early Modern England c.1550–1700*: Cambridge.

Brewer, J. 1989: *The Sinews of Power: War, Money and the English State, 1688–1783*: London.

Chandaman, C. D. 1975: *The English Public Revenue, 1660–1688*: Oxford.

Clay, C. 1978: *Public Finance and Private Wealth: The Career of Sir Stephen Fox, 1627–1716*: Oxford.

Cust, R. 1987: *The Forced Loan and English Politics 1626–1628*: Oxford.

Dickson, P. G. M. 1967: *The Financial Revolution in England: A Study in the Development of Public Credit 1688–1756*: London.

Dietz, F. C. 1964: *English Public Finance 1485–1641, vol. 2: 1558–1641*: London.

Guscott, S. J. 2000: 'Humphrey Chetham (1580–1653): fortune, politics and mercantile culture in seventeenth-century England.' Unpublished Ph.D. thesis: Sheffield University.

Hoyle, R. W. (ed.) 1992: *The Estates of the English crown, 1558–1640*: Cambridge.

Jones, D. W. 1988: *War and Economy in the Age of William III and Marlborough*: Oxford.

Laslett, P. 1983: *The World We Have Lost – Further Explored*, 3rd edn: London.

O'Brien, P. K. and Hunt, P. A. 1993: 'The rise of a fiscal state in England, 1485–1815', *Historical Research*, 66: 129–76.

Pincus, S. C. A. 1996: *Protestantism and Patriotism: Ideologies and the Making of English Foreign Policy, 1650–1668*: Cambridge.

Prestwich, M. 1966: *Cranfield: Politics and Profits under the Early Stuarts*: Oxford.

Roseveare, H. 1991: *The Financial Revolution 1660–1760*: London.

Russell, C. 1990: 'The ship money judgements of Bramston and Davenport', reprinted in C. Russell, *Unrevolutionary England, 1603–1642*: London.

Schnabel, F. forthcoming: 'English crown finance, 1603–42.' Unpublished Ph.D. thesis, Harvard University.

Smith, D. L. 1999: *The Stuart Parliaments 1603–1689*: London.

Tuck, R. 1993: *Philosophy and Government 1572–1651*: Cambridge.

Wheeler, J. S. 1999: *The Making of World Power: War and the Military Revolution in Seventeenth-Century England*: Stroud.

FURTHER READING

Andrews, K. R. 1991: *Ships, Money and Politics: Seafaring and Naval Enterprise in the Reign of Charles I*: Cambridge.

Boynton, L. O. 1967: *The Elizabethan Militia 1558–1638*: London.

Braddick, M. J. 1996: *The Nerves of State: Taxation and the Financing of the English State, 1558–1714*: Manchester.

Braddick, M. J. 2000: *State Formation and Social Change in Early Modern England c.1550–1700*: Cambridge.

Brewer, J. 1989: *The Sinews of Power: War, Money and the English State, 1688–1783*: London.

Capp, B. 1989: *Cromwell's Navy: The Fleet and the English Revolution 1648–1660*: Oxford.

Chandaman, C. D. 1975: *The English Public Revenue, 1660–1688*: Oxford.

Childs, J. 1976: *The Army of Charles II*: London.

Childs, J. 1980: *The Army, James II and the Glorious Revolution*: Manchester.

Childs, J. 1987: *The British Army of William III, 1689–1702*: Manchester.

Childs, J. 1991: *The Nine Years' War and the British Army 1688–1697: The Operations in the Low Countries*: Manchester.

Cruickshank, C. G. 1966: *Elizabeth's Army*, 2nd edn: Oxford.

Davies, J. D. 1991: *Gentlemen and Tarpaulins: The Officers and Men of the Restoration Navy*: Oxford.

Dickson, P. G. M. 1967: *The Financial Revolution in England: A Study in the Development of Public Credit 1688–1756*: London.

Dietz, F. C. 1964: *English Public Finance 1485–1641, vol. 2: 1558–1641*: London.

Harding, R. 1995: *The Evolution of the Sailing Navy, 1509–1815*: London.

Jones, D. W. 1988: *War and Economy in the Age of William III and Marlborough*: Oxford.

O'Brien, P. K. and Hunt, P. A. 1993: 'The rise of a fiscal state in England, 1485–1815', *Historical Research*, 66: 129–76.

Western, J. R. 1965: *The English Militia in the Eighteenth Century: The Story of a Political Issue 1660–1802*: London.

Wheeler, J. S. 1999: *The Making of World Power: War and the Military Revolution in Seventeenth-Century England*: Stroud.

CHAPTER FIVE

The Press and Popular Political Opinion

IAN ATHERTON

Stuart Britain witnessed an information revolution with profound consequences for the political, religious, social, cultural and intellectual life of its citizens. That revolution affected England first, from the early seventeenth century; its effects were slower in coming in Scotland and Ireland, but nowhere escaped its impact. The volume and circulation of printed material increased considerably. Furthermore, the seventeenth century saw the invention of a new technology of information dissemination (the newspaper), the creation of new sites for reading, hearing and *discussing* the news (the coffee house) and the development of a new occupation for circulating the news (the news-monger, news-writer or journalist). The effect of this revolution was far-reaching – on the organization of the print trade, on habits of reading, on social life and pre-eminently (according to most historians) on the politics of Stuart Britain.

Some scholars have made explicit comparison between the information revolution of Stuart Britain and the internet revolution of the 1990s (Sommerville 1996a, 1996b; Halasz 1997: 205–6). As such comparisons suggest, much of the work on the Stuart press has been present-centred and written under the modernization motif. Not only the search for the first newspapers, but also what scholars saw when they found them, were conducted in the shadow of the authors' attitude towards the press of their own day. Nineteenth- and early twentieth-century studies tended to see the Stuart press as the press of liberal democracies in embryonic form, defending freedoms and pushing back the dark frontier against ignorance and tyranny. As attitudes to the twentieth-century press changed, as the modern media industry began to be viewed as manipulative and serving commercial interests, so attitudes to seventeenth-century news media have altered. The change is clearest in Sommerville's account of the 'news revolution' which traces many of the 'dysfunctional characteristics of modern societies' back to the invention of a periodical press in seventeenth-century England (Sommerville 1996a, esp. pp. vii–viii).

Academic study of this revolution began in the 1790s with the work of George Chalmers and a consensus quickly emerged of the broad outlines of early modern press history, an approach that held sway until its transformation in the last decade (Raymond 1999a: 1–5). A standard trajectory for the development of news and the press was described: from manuscript to print; from the reporting of foreign news to a preoccupation with the domestic; of increasing sophistication and growing regularity and frequency; and of battles with, and eventual triumph over, the evils of censorship and the securing of 'that great principle, "The freedom of the Press"' (Cranfield 1978: 226). It was a great and often exciting story of the 'progress' of the press and of how newspapers 'improved' (Bourne 1887 I: 15, 26, 54). It was also an *English* story: Scotland and Ireland were both late comers and bit players.

The story unfolded in such accounts was Whiggish. It searched for the origins of the 'free press' of the nineteenth and early twentieth centuries, and it saw newspapers pitted in a great constitutional clash with absolute monarchy in the fight for democracy. A similar story has been told and retold, often by nineteenth- and twentieth-century journalists and newspapermen (Hunt 1850; Grant 1871; Bourne 1887; von Stutterheim 1934; Herd 1952; Williams 1977).

That traditional story opens with the single news pamphlets of the late sixteenth century, typically reporting foreign battles or domestic signs, wonders and prodigies. It moves quickly to 1620 and the first English-language news serials, published in Amsterdam (then the centre of European journalism) and imported into England, and to 1621 and the first news serials published in England, known as corantos. These were first intensively studied and catalogued by Dahl (1950, 1952). For all that the traditional Whig view trumpets these corantos as the first English newspapers, they have been severely censured for immaturity. Bourne called them 'Faulty and slight' and condemned them for dealing with 'foreign events of importance . . . very superficially' while 'trivial concerns often received inordinate notice'; Frank criticized their 'haphazard' arrangement and lack of editorial organization and reckoned them 'plodding and impersonal' (Bourne 1887 I: 6; Frank 1961: 4). Such comments betray both the Whig understanding of the steady 'maturation' of the Stuart press and the judging of seventeenth-century news by the concerns and standards of the nineteenth and twentieth centuries.

The next stage of the Whig view comes with the civil wars and the supplanting of corantos and their diet of foreign news with the domestic news that filled the pages of the newsbooks of the 1640s. The first English weekly of home news, *The Heads of Severall Proceedings in this Present Parliament*, began at the end of November 1641. Within weeks it had up to seven rivals. In all accounts the collapse of effective censorship in the early 1640s and the abolition of the prerogative courts of Star Chamber and High Commission in July 1641 (the main bodies which had been used to control the press) are seen as crucial to what is usually regarded as the natural progression from foreign to domestic news, from coranto to English newsbook (Birley 1964: 7–8; Cranfield 1978: 10). Most works tell essentially the same story of evolution and development of the newsbook in the 1640s. Bourne (1887 I: 10) wrote that though the newsbooks of 1641–2 were 'bald and often clumsily written chronicles' they were 'far in advance of the earlier newspapers, and they in their turn were soon improved upon'. Frank used the metaphor of the ages of man to chart their progress, from 'childhood' and 'early adolescence' through 'growing pains' and 'late adolescence' to 'coming of age' and 'maturity', before the tightening of press controls in 1649 led to 'decline and fall' (Frank 1961: ix).

The press of the 1650s received little attention in the standard Whig accounts (e.g. Williams 1908: 157). Partly, no doubt, that is because the stricter censorship of the Cromwellian regimes sat uncomfortably alongside Whiggish championing of Oliver as the victor against Stuart tyranny. Partly it is that the resulting contraction in the numbers of newsbooks published, from the myriads of the 1640s to just two authorized newsbooks between 1655 and 1659, *Mercurius Politicus* on a Thursday and *The Publick Intelligencer* on a Monday, both produced by Marchamont Nedham, did not fit the lineal story of growth and development that historians wanted to tell. And partly it was that, in Frank's revealing phrase, the later 1650s 'have a certain inevitable quality' and so can be considered 'newsless' (Frank 1961: 253).

A new chapter is usually considered to have opened either at the Restoration or in 1665 with the foundation of the *Oxford Gazette* (retitled the *London Gazette* the following year). Frank (1961) finished in 1660 where Sutherland (1986) later began, and Williams (1908) closed his account with the beginning of the *Gazette*. The *Gazette* adopted a new format – a half sheet in folio creating a two-page newspaper set in double columns – which later became the standard for Stuart newspapers. The *Gazette* was an official twice-weekly publication managed by the principal secretaries of state (Fraser 1956: 48–56) which was, between 1666 and 1679, the only licensed newspaper in England. It published mainly foreign news and has received comparatively little scholarly attention. Even Sutherland's account of the Restoration newspaper devotes almost as much space to the *Impartial Protestant Mercury*, which lasted for thirteen months in 1681–2, as it does to the *Gazette*, which hardly missed an edition from 1665 (Sutherland 1986). Scholars have generally been content to dismiss the *Gazette* as a thin and vapid government organ. Macaulay (1913–14 I: 380–1) parodied its contents and Bourne (1887 I: 41) considered that there was 'nothing notable' in it except 'its emptiness and worthlessness'; all echo contemporary criticisms such as that of Richard Steele, its editor from 1707 to 1710, that it was both 'very innocent and very insipid' (quoted in Sutherland 1986: 125; see also Cranfield 1978: 20).

Suppression of any rivals to the *Gazette* was achieved under the 1662 Licensing Act (initially passed for only two years, but regularly renewed), which lapsed in 1679 when the political impasse caused in parliament by the Exclusion Crisis meant that neither could it be renewed nor could any new legislation be passed. Censorship was reimposed by royal prerogative in 1682 (backed up by a revived Licensing Act in 1685), but the years of the Exclusion Crisis saw a 'remarkable outburst of newspapers' (Sutherland 1986: 20). That short-lived freedom is typically seen as prefiguring what was to come two decades later, after the 'dismal period' of James II's reign when 'Newspaper history...is almost a blank' (Bourne 1887 I: 50), and the brief publishing surge during the Glorious Revolution, with four new (but short-lived) titles starting up in December 1688. In 1695 the 1685 Licensing Act was once again due for renewal, but parliament declined and the Act lapsed, not with resounding claims about liberty and freedom, but with muted agreement about the practical defects of the Act (Astbury 1978).

The lapsing of the Licensing Act is often seen as one of the signal moments in press – indeed English – history: a 'great event', the emancipation of English literature (Macaulay 1913–14 V: 2483); the opening of the way for 'far more progress of newspaper enterprise' than hitherto (Bourne 1887 I: 53); an advance for 'the pursuit of the common welfare' (De Beer 1968: 129); 'the first major step towards the freedom of the Press' (Cranfield 1978: 30); or the assurance, 'at last', of 'the liberty of the Press' (Muddiman 1920: 13) – although that accolade is occasionally accorded to 1641 (Birley 1964: 7). The constraints on what could be printed after 1695 have, however, been restated (Gibbs 1992).

The twenty years following 1695 are seen in most histories as a period of rapid innovation in the form of the press (e.g. Sutherland 1986: 29–32). New newspapers 'sprang up almost overnight' (Cranfield 1978: 31). Several, notably those Walker (1974: 698–9) has christened the 'Big Three' (the *Post Boy*, the *Flying Post* and the *Post Man*) moved to thrice-weekly publication in what Sutherland (1986: 27) calls 'a genuine advance'. The first evening paper appeared in 1696, *Dawks's News-Letter*. The first provincial newspaper, the *Norwich Post*, began in 1701, followed by twelve others in nine towns by 1710 (Cranfield 1962: 13–17). The first daily newspaper came out in 1702, the *Daily Courant*. The periodicals of the early eighteenth century have attracted considerable attention, not least because the glittering names of Defoe, Addison and Steele are attached to them. Journalism and literature, it is sometimes claimed, merged (e.g. von Stutterheim 1934: 30). It is the case, indeed, that scholars based in departments of English literature have undertaken at least as much research into the Stuart press as their colleagues in departments of history.

The early eighteenth century is also seen as witnessing the birth of party-political journalism and the government manipulation of the press. Despite the Stamp Act of 1712, a form of regulation which taxed newspapers (imposing a duty on each one) rather than reimposing pre-publication censorship, at the end of Queen Anne's reign it was through the press, and especially the newspaper press, that readers were politically educated and ideologically polarized between Whigs and Tories (de Krey 1985; Downie 1979; Ellis 1985). Harley's management of the press is thus seen as prefiguring the more intense news management in the 1720s and 1730s of the ministry of Walpole, which has attracted greater attention from historians (Harris 1987; Targett 1994a, 1994b). Accounts of the early eighteenth-century press, especially Whig ones, contain a number of unresolved (and sometimes un-acknowledged) tensions. On the one hand the press is the glorious victor of the battle against tyranny, the creator of a public sphere and civil society, and the precursor of the modern age. On the other hand it is corrupt, venal, in the pocket of the government and therefore impotent and unable to influence public opinion. More-over, public opinion and the newspapers, the former seen as growing but inchoate, and led by the latter which are seen as wretchedly produced, plodding and vapid, are able to bring down the whole edifice of Stuart censorship and absolutism and bear the fruit of modernity.

The maturation of the Stuart press which unfolds in the Whig account is heavily dependent on evidence and assumptions about increasing frequency of publication, growing numbers of titles, and rising circulation. Until the monumental biblio-graphic efforts of Dahl (1952) and of Nelson and Seccombe (1987), however, any figures for numbers of titles were provisional estimates. Their recent work has established that over 700 newspapers and serials were issued between 1641 and 1700, with over 31,000 separate issues, compared with 90–100,000 books, tracts and broadsides published in the same period (Nelson and Seccombe 1987: vii). A chronological analysis shows a growing press, but a fluctuating output. In 1642 64 periodical titles were published, the highest number for any year in the seven-teenth century, but producing only 367 issues. Of these titles 30 appeared in only one issue, and only 6 managed more than 20 issues; periodical publishing was a very volatile trade. By 1700 the trade was more secure: there were fewer titles (just over 30) but many more issues (nearly 1,400).

Figures for newspaper circulation have generally been seen as providing a similar picture. Various estimates and claims were made by publishers and their critics for circulation, but more secure evidence is available for the very end of the period from two sources. There are a few surviving accounts for stamp duty imposed on each newspaper under the Act of 1712. These show that about 70,000 newspapers were sold each week in the autumn of 1712, immediately after the Stamp Act came into force, falling to around 46,000 a week in the summer of 1713. The accounts also show the circulation of individual titles: in 1712 the *Daily Courant* sold 900–1,000 copies per issue, the *Flying Post* sold 1,400–1,650 copies, and the *Post Man* 3,800–4,450. Figures for the *London Gazette* have also survived for some years, showing that in 1705–6 its circulation was between 7,000 and 9,000, falling to around 2,400 by 1714 (Sutherland 1934; Price 1958; Snyder 1968, 1976).

From these relatively firm footings historians are on increasingly shaky ground the further back they go. There is agreement that although the fortunes of individual titles fluctuated, the general trend was upwards. An estimate of current circulation made in 1704 is generally accepted as reliable. In that year it was said that 43,800 newspapers were sold every week (Price 1958). Earlier estimates of circulation are more or less intelligent guesswork, for there are no reliable statistics. The most sophisticated are those of Frank and Cotton for the newsbooks of the 1640s, based on what the former calls 'semicircumstantial evidence': estimates about typesetting speed, profit and average print-runs for books. Based on such calculations, both conclude that the average print-run for a 1640s newsbook was 500, with 200 or 250 as the minimum and 1,000 as the maximum for the most popular newsbooks (Frank 1961: 57, 314 n. 54; Cotton 1971: 8–13). The most recent study (Raymond 1996: 233–8) broadly accepts these minima but suggests a maximum of 3,000 copies an issue, based on a fresh calculation of typesetting speed. Calculations of print-runs for corantos are similarly fraught with difficulties. Dahl suggested 400 copies an issue, others 250–850 copies or even more (Dahl 1952: 22; Frearson 1993a, 1993b; Raymond 1996: 237). If the lower figures are taken, then there was a dramatic increase in the volume and circulation of printed news from the mid-seventeenth to the early eighteenth century. If the higher figures are accepted, then 1640s news-books compare favourably with early eighteenth-century newspapers and, as will be seen, theories of an expanding public sphere are harder to maintain.

Two further points about circulation are often made. First, practices of reading meant that each issue had several readers. The provision of newspapers was a feature of coffee houses and one of the principal reasons for their popularity, and each copy could expect to be read and discussed many times. Addison estimated that there were twenty readers of the *Spectator* for each copy sold. It was also a common practice to read the news aloud, so that for every reader there might be several hearers (Sutherland 1934: 116; Pincus 1995; Raymond 1996: 242–5). Second, it is also said that the influence of a newspaper was not necessarily proportionate to its circulation (e.g. Snyder 1968: 209), although such historians also claim increasing circulation over the Stuart period and want to see that as proof of an expanding public opinion.

Three further aspects of the standard view should be noted: Anglo-centricity, censorship and public opinion. First, the story that is told is an English one. Scotland and Ireland are left out of the narrative, and little work has been done on the early newspaper press of either country. In part these lacunae are because of the slow development of a native press in either country.

Although there were two short-lived Irish newspapers at the Restoration, and another at the beginning of the reign of James II and VII, the principal study of the Irish newspaper concludes that 'Irish newspaper history dates from the conquest of Ireland by William III'. A small number of newspapers were published in Dublin from 1690 (including reprints of London papers), but until the 1720s their purpose was to furnish their readers with news of England and continental Europe, just as London manuscript newsletters had circulated in Ireland previously (Fraser 1956: 141–3; Munter 1967: 6–17, 116; Nelson and Seccombe 1987: 695). The situation regarding the history of the Scottish newspaper is similar, although the story begins earlier. London newsbooks and newspapers were occasionally reprinted in Edinburgh from 1641, with the first native newsbooks published at Leith in 1651–2. The centre of the news trade soon moved to Edinburgh (although one newspaper was published in Glasgow in the 1690s) where a number of newspapers were published during the Exclusion Crisis and again from 1689. In addition, London newsletters and London printed news circulated in the major Scottish burghs from the 1640s; a number of Scottish towns also secured the services of newsletter writers in Edinburgh. Although pre-publication censorship remained on the Scottish statute book, it was increasingly ignored from 1710. Like the Irish press, early eighteenth-century Scottish news-papers have been regarded as a branch of the English provincial press which began at about the same time, for they performed similar functions, relating news culled from London papers for an apparently limited readership. In the case of Scotland the slow development of a newspaper press compared with England has been blamed on the restricted nature of Scottish urban development; a similar argument could be made for Ireland (Couper 1908; Kelsall and Kelsall 1986; Nelson and Seccombe 1987: 695; Harris 1996). As Raymond has suggested, 'an "archipelagic" history of the newsbook . . . would actually be a study of the impact of the English newsbook on those places' (Raymond 1996: 80). Studies of news in Stuart America and the West Indies are conceived in just these terms (Steele 1985; Nelson 1993).

Second, the development of the press is written in terms of censorship. It is the freedom of the press which is the goal and that freedom gradually unfolds, despite reverses, from 1620 as demands for an end to censorship build up (Muddiman 1920: 3–15; Siebert 1952; Linton and Boston 1987: 321–34). The Whig story of the seventeenth-century press is a reflection of the Whig struggle between king and parliament for English liberties, the newspaper a key player in the defeat of Stuart tyranny. A cast of familiar characters and martyrs is deployed in the battle – and a long line of authors and publishers tread what one writer has called the '*via dolorosa* which only too often led to the pillory or into prison' (von Stutterheim 1934: 25), and are canonized for their sufferings.

The censorship on which the standard accounts are predicated was wide-ranging, harsh and thoroughly effective at controlling print for much of the seventeenth century; Hill has even compared the Stuart regime with those of late twentieth-century Eastern Europe (Siebert 1952; Hill 1985). It is not, however, an uncontested view. A number of studies, influenced by early Stuart revisionism, stress instead that censor-ship was muddled, less clear cut, in many cases possible to evade, and generally not very effective in controlling what was published (Lambert 1992; Worden 1987). The field remains divided, with the most recent contributions continuing to contest the effect-iveness and degree of repression in Stuart press controls. Cogswell (1989) sees the Jacobean regime as tightly controlling what could be published during the Bohemia crisis at the end of the king's reign, while Thompson (1998) argues that Charles increasingly sought to curtail the power of the press in the 1630s. Two recent studies have rejected simplistic notions of a monolithic censorship and instead have argued for the importance of paying attention both to detailed chronologies in the rigour of controls and to competing interests within the regime in the operations of censorship. They still come to different conclusions, Milton (1998) stressing the possibility of tight control of what was printed and Clegg (2001) positing a permissive government line. As will be seen, however, while issues of censorship are central to the Whig case, other work suggests that press controls do not hold the key to opening the press and political opinion.

The final salient point of the standard account, and the other motor of the development of the press, is the growth of public opinion. The coincidence between the first corantos and the beginning of the Thirty Years' War, or between the first English newsbooks and the English civil wars – indeed between wars and increased public news hunger – has often been noted (Williams 1908: 30; Dahl 1950: 178; Cust 1986: 69; Black 1992). Each new conflict is seen as cranking up the appetite for news and building up the pressure against censorship until in 1695 either the dam bursts or the English government realizes the inevitable and opens the floodgates (Schwoerer 1992). Historians' use of the term 'public opinion' has tended to be very unsystematic and impressionistic, it meaning whatever each individual historian chooses. Bourne saw public opinion growing in the 1670s and 1680s, while in Cranfield's account public opinion exists in the early sixteenth century and the government uses the printing press to 'inform' it, but its growth in the seventeenth century lies behind most of the signal moments of press history until the demand for news made the existing press laws 'increasingly futile' (Bourne 1887 I: 42; Cranfield 1978: 2, 10, 21, 25–6, 29). By contrast a recent account of the circulation of news has public opinion as the effect not the cause. The 'ever increasing' appetite for news was stimulated by developments in professional journalism, the emergence of a postal service, the increasing commercialization of printing, and gradually loosening censorship; together they created by 1700, in England at least, 'public opinion' (Fox 2000: 336, 405).

The most significant attempt to formulate and theorize the usually amorphous concept of public opinion, done with specific reference to the development of English newspapers in the 1690s, is the concept of the 'bourgeois public sphere' of the German philosopher and sociologist Jürgen Habermas, originally published in 1962 but not translated into English until 1989, although a brief version of the idea appeared in English in 1974 (Habermas 1974, 1989, 1992a). In Habermas's account, pre-modern societies had a very limited state-governed public sphere in which the power and authority of the ruler was represented and demonstrated before and in front of the people; this he called 'representative publicness'. In Western Europe, however, as a product of the clash between an emerging bourgeoisie and absolute states, a new bourgeois or political public sphere gradually emerged in which the authority of the state was publicly monitored and checked through critical, informed debate by the bourgeoisie of state policies. The bourgeois public sphere is situated in concrete social spaces, in debate in coffee houses and salons, in newspapers and periodicals, and there 'public opinion' is formed. One account of political opinion calls coffee houses the 'architecture for the emergence of the public sphere' (Pincus 1995: 822). The public sphere had a number of defining characteristics. As its underlying Marxist dialectic suggests, the model is confrontational: the public of the public sphere was the opponent of the public authority and the public sphere was the arena for the criticism of the government's rule. Within the public sphere, however, matters are more harmonious. The public sphere is, in principle, both rational and inclusive. All have a theoretical right of access to the sphere and within it no notice is taken of rank or status.

Habermas's real interest is not so much the beginnings of the bourgeois public sphere in eighteenth-century Western Europe as what he calls its 'structural trans-formation' or 'collapse' in the nineteenth and twentieth centuries, a 'refeudalization of the public sphere' in which liberal, critical debate of the state was replaced with state-sponsored manipulation of the public itself and the promotion of consumer culture. A 'culture-debating public' became a 'culture-consuming public' (Habermas 1989, esp. pp. 4, 159, 195). Nevertheless, he seeks to root his work firmly in a historical epoch. His first and 'model' case is Britain (by which he means England) and he dates its inception precisely to 1694–5, with the elimination of the institution of censorship as a key moment (ibid.: 57–67). His model therefore fits with the predominant (though not uncontested) Whig view of the Glorious Revolution as one of the key turning points of British history. It fits neatly into the standard account of newspaper history. It fits with claims for the revolutionary impact of the printing press on Western society (e.g. Eisenstein 1968, 1979). It also broadly accords with the work of a number of historians who have seen the birth of public opinion as a significant force within politics at some point in the last two decades of the seventeenth century. Goldie's study of the 192 polemical pamphlets published in 1689–94 on the allegiance controversy and the works of Harris and Knights on the Exclusion Crisis all suggest that popular opinion or politics 'out-of-doors' both exerted an influence on, and were influenced by, the politics of government (Goldie 1980; Harris 1997; Knights 1994). Though they give slightly different chronologies and though their work does not explicitly engage with that of Habermas, their ideas resonate with his interpretation of the rise of the public sphere.

Although some scholars have ignored Habermas's work as (presumably) irrelevant, the over-theorizing of a historical-sociologist with little to say to empirical historians (Fox 2000; Mendle 2001a, 2001b), many (particularly scholars of English literature or historians who have taken the literary turn) have taken up the notion of a public sphere enthusiastically, while silently abandoning Habermas's economic determinism. There have been a number of attempts to adapt the idea and push it back further into the seventeenth century, or even earlier. Such work, however, runs up against Haber-mas's own assertion that the development of a bourgeois public sphere is historically situated and cannot be transferred or 'idealtypically generalized, to any number of historical situations that represent formally similar constellations'. Habermas has reiterated the point: 'I have some doubts about how far we can push back the very notion of the public sphere into the sixteenth and seventeenth centuries without somehow changing the very concept of the public sphere to such a degree that it becomes something else' (Habermas 1989: xvii–xviii; 1992b: 465). Despite such caveats, Pincus (1995) has argued that a public sphere existed in the coffee houses of not only Restoration London and provincial English towns, but Scotland and Ireland too – though coffee houses appear to have been few in number in the latter two kingdoms. Achinstein (1994) has suggested that a non-rational public sphere was created in 1640s pamphlet wars. Norbrook (1994) and Raymond (1999b) have proposed that a significant expansion in the political public sphere occurred from the 1620s, culminating in the 1640s, while Clegg thinks that a 'nascent public sphere' emerged in England during the Bohemia crisis of 1619–24 (Clegg 2001: 162, 229).

Halasz (1997) has pushed the birth of the public sphere back further, to the late sixteenth century, called into being by the 'marketplace of print'. In her reworking of the idea, the public sphere emerged in the arena of discourse and was opened up by the capitalistic production of pamphlets. Like Habermas she works within a broadly Marxist tradition, but whereas he thinks that commercial interests precipitated the structural transformation of the public sphere in the nineteenth century, she sees those interests as both creating and constituting the public sphere from the very beginning. Two problems with Halasz's presentation are immediately apparent for historians of Stuart Britain. First, her explicit eschewal of empirical argument, claiming that the evidence does not exist for a consideration of readership or distribution of the pamphlets she discusses (ibid.: 8–13), means that the size and composition of the public sphere does not matter to her. Indeed, her public sphere of discourse probably consisted of only a handful of readers and writers. Second, her public sphere is entirely removed from the realm of politics and lacked impact beyond the world of publishing.

The most detailed claims for a public sphere in mid-seventeenth-century England are contained in the work of Zaret. In his model, popular political participation before the 1640s was limited and restricted by norms of secrecy, deference and privilege in matters of political communication. It was print, and in particular the printing of petitions in the 1640s, that ushered in public opinion as a force in English politics (Zaret 1992, 2000). Reason remains a key feature of the public sphere, and he emphasizes the importance of scientific ideas and natural religion or Latitudinarianism, although these are features more usually associated with the Restoration period than the 1640s. Despite treating Habermas's theory as an ideal type, he significantly modifies the model, particularly by disassociating the public sphere from the Habermasian preoccupation with bourgeois society and economic change: 'the use of printed petitions to constitute and invoke public opinion in politics occurs in the middle of the seventeenth century, when it was neither limited to urban areas, reliant on a state bureaucracy, nor orientated principally to economic debates' (Zaret 2000: 32).

Zaret's focus on the printing of petitions, rather than the emergence of newspapers, is also novel. Most accounts of public opinion in the 1640s have stressed the role of printing and even petitions, but have done so in terms of the facility of print to disseminate ideas faster and more widely. Printed petitions, for example, have been studied as 'public utterances intended for general consumption', designed to appeal to public opinion (e.g. Fletcher 1981: 198; Underdown 1985: 138). What Zaret argues is for the novel use of print, particularly in petitions, to reorientate 'political discourse so that its production increasingly involved simultaneous constitution and invocation of public opinion', what he calls 'printing's imposition of dialogic order on conflict' (Zaret 2000: 177). Printed petition was met by printed counter-petition, which could itself be rebuffed once again in print, often in the space of only a few days, and the whole process could be reported the following week in the newsbooks.

Zaret's work is important in analysing some of the ways in which print changed the political landscape in the 1640s, but his work is open to a number of criticisms. It may underestimate the extent of political communication and discussion before the 1640s. It is based on the traditional model of a move from the closed worlds of manuscript to the open ones of print, a model which has met sustained criticism from students of scribal publication (Love 1993). Moreover, while he notes the existence of religious controversies before the civil wars, he sees these as only a 'prototype' of the political public sphere he describes (Zaret 2000: 165–73). To many historians such a distinction between religion and politics in Stuart Britain is overdrawn. Indeed, Lake and Questier (2000) have analysed aspects of those religious controversies in late sixteenth-century England and have argued that they constituted a fully-fledged public sphere. Nonetheless, their public sphere is explicitly emptied of all 'normative and conceptual Habermasian baggage'. They show clearly that polemicists and politicians were using a very wide range of media – printed tracts, proclamations, circulating manuscripts, and a variety of public performances from sermons to trials, disputations and executions – to appeal to a public audience and shape a public debate about religion and politics in late Elizabethan England. Forms of public opinion clearly existed in the late sixteenth century, but it is not clear whether these differed from those of previous centuries sufficiently to deserve the special appellation of 'public sphere'.

Habermas, Zaret, Halasz and others are all searching for *the* public sphere, a single, unified arena of debate. A further approach to the problem is to posit the existence of several smaller, separate public spheres. Since early modern society was stratified, so, the argument runs, there would be a number of stratified publics, what O'Callaghan calls a 'plurality of publics' (O'Callaghan 2000: 7; see also Fraser 1992). Raymond has raised the issue for the 1640s, for some newsbooks were apparently targeted at specific audiences (Raymond 1999b: 125, 130). Moreover, it was a trope of early seventeenth-century satire of the circulation of news that there was, as Ben Jonson put it, 'Puritan', 'Protestant' and 'Pontifical newes' as well as 'Barbers newes / And Taylors Newes, Porters, and Watermens newes' (quoted in Atherton 1999b: 49, 56).

Scholars are currently left with either a multiplicity of public spheres in the seventeenth century or one overarching public sphere with a multiplicity of dates for its inception. In part, disagreement is a product of the fact that scholars are not studying public opinion itself but a particular event or period in which they see the operation of something they call public opinion. In part, it occurs because of the narrow chronological focus of most scholars, who, less familiar with work on earlier periods, assume that public opinion began in the period under review. In fact, medievalists have employed the concept of 'public opinion' in fourteenth- and fifteenth-century England, although they construe it differently (Maddicott 1978; Ross 1981; Doig 1998). The impression given from all the studies is that public opinion was forever rising. One might sympathize with the subtitle of a study of early modern readers of the news: 'are we having a public sphere yet?' (Dooley 2001).

Most of these studies appear to be playing a modern academic parlour game: 'hunt the public sphere'. They are concerned to uncover its inception and then to delineate certain of its features. Once created and analysed, however, many of these public spheres appear to do little except wait around for their Habermasian structural transformation several centuries later. Authors are often little interested in the subsequent fate of their public sphere. Some of them have bought into the modernization motif of so much writing about the press and are, as Zaret candidly admits, seeking 'the roots of modernity in the soil of seventeenth-century history' (Zaret 2000: 19). Knights (2000) has cautioned against such an approach: 'the public sphere was not an entity, but had to be constantly renewed through the process of public debate; it therefore enlarged but also contracted at certain times. Structural change could not be a one-off process in the 1640s.'

Studies of the public sphere have privileged establishing its existence over the form and content of public opinion. They have little to say about what public opinion was at any given time, the nature of the pressures exerted on and by popular political opinion, what could (and could not) be said within the public sphere. For such matters less theoretical and more empirical studies of public opinion are more revealing.

Some historians are unwilling to countenance the existence of public opinion in Stuart Britain. Hill has written that 'in normal times illiteracy plus the censorship effectively excluded the majority of the population from being able to take part in politics, probably even from contemplating the possibility of participation' (Hill 1985: 32; see also Hill 1998). Hill not only posits a draconian and effective censorship in the seventeenth century; he also reckons literacy to have been much lower than most other historians would accept, many analyses of reading (a much more widespread skill than writing) suggesting that in England half of all men and a sixth of women could read in 1642, rising to two-thirds of men and two-fifths of women in 1714. In London literacy was even higher; in Scotland male literacy was similar to that in England, but female literacy was considerably lower (Schofield 1968: 324; Spufford 1979; Cressy 1980; Houston 1982; Fox 2000: 17–19).

Most historians do accept that public opinion existed in the seventeenth century, if not continuously then at times of crisis such as the 1620s, 1640s, and from the late 1670s, and that it can be subject to historical enquiry. Public opinion found expression in and could be subject to manipulation by (historians are often unable to distinguish one from the other) a wide variety of forms. In addition to newspapers and pamphlets historians have analysed discussion in coffee houses and taverns, personal communication, manuscripts, preaching, playing cards, plays, pope-burning processions, prints and woodcuts, ballads, libels, graffiti, addresses, petitions and elections (see especially T. Harris 1987: 101–7). In his analysis of public opinion in the reign of Charles II, Miller focuses particularly on parliamentary elections and asserts that the House of Commons 'did represent "public opinion"' (Miller 1995: 376). The late seventeenth-century English electorate was particularly large, perhaps 200,000 in the 1690s and 250,000 in 1714, with a greater proportion of adult males possessing the vote in the early eighteenth century than after the great Reform Act of 1832; moreover, it has been suggested that the English electorate under the early Stuarts was even larger (Plumb 1969: 111, 116; Hirst 1975: 104–5).

While most are agreed that the English political nation was large, analysing popular opinion is beset by a number of problems. The ambiguities in the word 'popular', both as meaning pertaining only to common (as opposed to elite) people, the crowd, the vulgar, and as expressing the views of the majority of all sorts of people (including the elite), have muddied waters already murky through the problems of sources. Many polemicists of widely differing views claimed to speak for the people; as Knights has noted, 'the question of determining the true sense and representation of the people was central to the political crisis' between 1679 and 1681. In addition, as contemporaries remarked, opinions expressed in printed and manuscript tracts – key sources for any study – may have been considerably more bitter or extreme than the temper of many of their readers (Knights 1994: 155). Goldie too has warned of the danger of assuming that polemical pamphlets directly and accurately reflect public opinion (Goldie 1980: 474). Against these problems of approach and source, two linked issues in particular about public opinion have divided historians: the extent to which popular opinion was different from elite opinion, and the extent to which public opinion was inherently oppositionist and the circulation of political news therefore politically divisive.

The move from news to action is a key question lying behind much work on the Stuart press, scribal publication and propaganda. Much of the work on manuscript news and libels in England in the first three decades of the seventeenth century is predicated on the idea that it circulated in a 'literary underground', in some accounts divorced from elite opinion, in others a zone of critical discussion in which people from all stations of society participated, but in most accounts one that was oppositional. Cogswell (1995) argues that scandalous songs and ballads in early Stuart England formed an 'underground verse' in which an autonomous popular voice can be heard, which was characterized by political polarization and which 'facilitated the abrupt formation' of opposing sides in the early 1640s. Cust (1986), in a very influential study of news and politics in the period, while arguing that verses and ballads operated on two levels – entertaining the literate and disseminating news and opinion to the illiterate – has claimed that the news, by emphasizing conflict, polarized political debate and, by being slanted against the court, supported an oppositionist line. In a similar vein Bellany has called early Stuart 'news culture' a 'politically dangerous form' (Bellany 2002: 132). Much of this concentration on the conflictual nature of news has undoubtedly arisen because of a concern to overthrow revisionist notions of early Stuart politics as consensual, but it also (although not explicitly) accords with both the Whig notion of the press pitted against the forces of Stuart absolutism, and Habermas's depiction of the public sphere ranged against the government.

Against such work Atherton (1999b) has argued for the capacity of news circulation to heal divisions and ease the political process, while Sharpe has criticized arguments about 'the move from sharp words to sharper swords' as simplistic, ignoring the 'popular' circulation of conformist and loyalist verse (Sharpe 2000: 401–2). Work on the printed propaganda of the 1640s has shown how a very close reading of texts is necessary, for very different viewpoints could be encoded in only subtle differences of language (Shagan 1997). While 1640s newsbooks allowed no rhetorical space for moderation or neutrality between the opposing sides, and so have been held up as examples of the alleged polarizing propensity of the press, a more subtle account of reading practices which does not merely imprint the views on the page to the supposed *tabula rasa* of the reader is needed, one which allows for the interaction of readers with their reading matter. The parliamentary commander Sir Samuel Luke, for example, busily distributed copies of the royalist newsbook *Mercurius Aulicus* to his many correspondents during the first civil war, but neither they nor Luke were likely to have agreed with any of the opinions contained within (Raymond 1996: 243, 247, 253–4).

The work of Lake and Questier has important implications here too. They eschew simplistic notions of government and opposition and show how any study of public opinion has to be set in the context of 'an ideologically, politically, and even institutionally variegated establishment' and the struggles to gain the ideological and political initiative both against and within that regime (Lake and Questier 2000: 591). Public opinion was called into being not only by opponents of the governing regime but also by elements within it, and was as much about elements within that regime exploring ways in which their policies could be developed as it was about elements outside the regime seeking to contain or influence that regime. Meanwhile the most sophisticated analyses of popular political opinion in late Stuart England reject both the manipulation of crowds by the elite and a division between popular and elite politics. In their place they stress a convergence of interests between different levels of society, and see politics 'out-of-doors' as an unofficial and extra-institutional means of carrying on political struggles also conducted in the formal institutions of central government, parliament and the court (e.g. T. Harris 1997).

Avenues for future research to produce a 'more nuanced model of popular political opinion' have recently been sketched by Raymond: plurality of arenas of debate, including public spheres in the three kingdoms rather than Habermas's London-centred view; the heterogeneous material culture of newspapers, noting how the juxtaposition of diverse items in the news, from accounts of battles and parliamentary debates to monstrous births, book adverts and bills of mortality, made the reader instrumental in construing 'a view of the world from the page before them'; and attention to the history of reading (Raymond 1999b: 129–33). Such an approach is promising, for it draws on three developments which have characterized recent scholarship on the news and politics in Stuart Britain: an awareness of the vibrancy of news media other than newspapers; studies of the form and content of the news and public opinion; and a consideration of how the news was read and understood. All have helped not only to transform our understanding of the press and popular political opinion but also to overthrow Whig and indeed all modernizing interpretations of news.

The hallowed place of newspapers as defenders of nineteenth-century liberty has, until recently, obscured the vital and long-lived role of other forms of news media in Stuart Britain, where most news was not spread by newspapers and probably not even by print. Oral, scribal and printed forms of communication were interwoven in Stuart England (Fox 2000), and scholars have begun to study some of the other media which may have constituted a 'public sphere', by which news was circulated and in which it was discussed: rumour and gossip (Fox 1997; 2000: 335–405); ballads, doggerel, libels and songs (Croft 1991, 1995; Bellany 1994, 2002; Fox 1994, 2000: 299–334; Cogswell 1995); manuscript newsletters and 'separates' (Levy 1982; Cust 1986;

Love 1993; Atherton 1999b; Baron 2001); petitions (Maltby 1998; Zaret 2000: 217–65); plays (Wiseman 1999); and sermons (Claydon 2000).

Collectively, such work has five important implications for the study of Stuart news and politics. First, and most obviously, it shows the vibrancy and diversity of media in which the inhabitants of Stuart Britain heard of and reflected on events. The narrowness of older histories that looked only at newspapers is patent. Work on news circulation in the 1620s, for example, shows the volume of news, the variety of news media and the interaction between those media that circulated in the English provinces (Cust 1986; Mousley 1991).

Second, it completely falsifies the Whig trajectory from manuscript to print which underlies the traditional story of the evolution of the newspaper. The minor role played by manuscript there, merely as the precursor to print, is now shown to be a serious devaluation of its role. Manuscript was not the inferior and private forebear of print's superior publicness. A number of studies have analysed the production of manuscript news in newsletters – those written by professional newsletter writers like John Pory and Edmund Rossingham and those written more informally by friends and relatives – and 'separates' – scribally produced copies of political texts such as speeches and treaties. Manuscript news was more highly prized and held to be more reliable than its printed cousin; study of manuscript news also allows analysis of the relationship between writer and reader (Muddiman 1923; Powell 1977; Love 1993; Atherton 1999b; Baron 2001). The sources of information and correspondents of one avid reader of newsletters, viscount Scudamore, have been studied. At least forty-five correspondents who sent Scudamore news can be identified, ranging from friends and relatives who might send a line or two of news buried in their domestic and familiar correspondence, to courtiers and government officials and professional news-writers, all of whom might send long, weekly newsletters. Newsfactors were a vital point of contact for local governors like Scudamore. In addition to newsletters they would send separates, corantos and newsbooks, bills of mortality and other published books, plays and verses. Through the range of contacts they kept they were also useful for networking, keeping open channels of communication between recipient, writer, central government, London society and local elites (Atherton 1999a: 153–7; 1999b). Manuscript newsletters survived the development of newspapers and persisted into the eighteenth century, although they have been little studied (Snyder 1977).

The third implication of recent work on the variety of news media is that the Whiggish concentration on the battle against censorship is wrong. The history of censorship does not hold the key to understanding news, popular political opinion and the public sphere in Stuart Britain. There were, of course, controls and forms of censorship applied to oral and scribal communication as well as to printed, but the chronologies of the battle against censorship in the traditional histories of the winning of the freedom of the press rarely stretch to encompass them. Moreover, they did not prevent the circulation of news, or its eager discussion, in Stuart Britain. The year 1695 no longer seems such a signal moment in British history, although it remains a convenient starting point for histories of the newspaper in the eighteenth century (Barker 1999).

Raymond's account of the outbreak of the English newsbook bears out these points. In place of previous explanations which stressed the collapse of censorship in 1641 and saw the first newsbooks as the children of corantos, he argues that the appearance was not a release of old pressures, but a response to the new situation of 1641, and that its immediate predecessor was a manuscript account of proceedings in parliament (Raymond 1996: 80–108).

Fourth, the audience for all types of news was 'large, geographically broad and socially varied' (Bellany 2002: 132). News and politics were discussed far down the social scale in Stuart Britain, and although there were important gender differences in the way that news was produced and consumed, women and men were involved in all stages of manuscript and print production, circulation and reading (Freist 1997: 278–98; McDowell 1998; Atherton 1999b: 49–50). Freist has shown how in 1640s London and elsewhere 'ordinary people' – blacksmiths, victuallers, maids, tailors, watermen and the like – discussed political and religious issues (Freist 1997: 209–38). Studies of petitioning have shown that both women and the relatively humble could be involved as organizers and signatories. Maltby, for example, has correlated signatories of a pro-episcopacy petition from Cheshire in 1641 with local tax records to show that the petition received significant support from the lower levels of parish society (Higgins 1973; McEntee 1992; Maltby 1998). Her work on mid-century petitions is echoed by Knights's (1993) analysis of London's 'monster' petition to the king of 1680: among the nearly 16,000 signatories he found a wide cross-section of London society. The notion of a *bourgeois* public sphere has been severely dented.

Fifth, recent work has focused attention on the content of the news and the languages in which it was written. This has been a further move from the concentration on the rational and the narrowly political that characterized much earlier study of the news. In particular, recent scholarship has looked at court scandal such as the Overbury affair and the Castlehaven trial (Herrup 1999; Bellany 2002). Where once the details of early Stuart court scandal were dismissed as distractions from the business of real politics (Morrill 1975), they are now seen as the very stuff of that politics. A wider analysis of the full variety of news media has been coupled with a wider definition of the political and an interest in the culture of politics. What constituted news is no longer seen as an ahistorical given – wars, treaties, parliamentary proceedings, court intrigue and the like – but as a culturally determined construct framed, in the seventeenth century, in an often porno-political language (Wiseman 1992). Much interest has been shown in the scatological, pornographic, satirical and ribald discourses of some Stuart news, such as in Underdown's study of John Crouch's royalist newsbook, *The Man in the Moon* (Underdown 1996: 90–111).

This last trend is also a part of the wider recent concern with the material culture of Stuart news. Studies of particular publications or journalists have long been a standard means of analysis but recent work, particularly that by Raymond (1996) on the newsbooks of the 1640s, has played close attention to what was published as news and how those stories and items were written up. Black's recent history of the English press opens not with the standard litany of the freedom of the press, but with vignettes of the diverse heterogeneity of eighteenth-century newspapers, with their stories of crimes, marriages, bankruptcies, quack doctors and popular superstitions, and the 'abrupt transition from one thing to another' (Black 2001: vii, 3). Viewed holistically, Stuart newspapers were 'both informative and polemical, idealistic and instrumental, accessible and discriminating, reasoned and Babelish' (Raymond 1999b: 133).

The third broad trend in modern scholarship has been a consideration of how the news was read and understood. Influenced by work on the history of reading, scholars have begun to consider not just how the news was put together and circulated in Stuart Britain, but how it was digested by its audience. Scholars have long been interested in how the new news media of Stuart England were received by contemporaries, and studies which turn to the many satirical descriptions of news-mongers and corantos and stale Stuart jokes about the untrustworthy and lying news are legion. Many have focused on two of Ben Jonson's dramatic productions, *News from the New World Discovered in the Moon* (1620) and *The Staple of News* (1626), and use them either as a treasure-house of quips about the news (Bourne 1887 I: 2–3; Williams 1908: 18–20; Frank 1961: 12, 275–7), or ponder what they have to say about early Stuart news- and print-culture more seriously (McKenzie 1973; Muggli 1992; Sanders 1998).

More detailed analyses of the readership of Stuart news have recently been attempted, despite the lack of annotations in Stuart newsbooks and newspapers and the reticence of some newsletter-writers to comment upon the news (Raymond 1996: 241–68; Atherton 1999b). Although little is therefore known about how particular newsbooks were read, analogies drawn from early modern reading habits suggest that readers of the news, whether elite or only partially educated, would be active and manipulative, capable of reading against the grain of a text and reworking its meaning. In Sommerville's pessimistic account of the reading of news in Stuart England, periodicity appears as the great evil, encouraging unreflective reading and predisposing readers to take an atomized and disintegrative view of reality (Sommerville 1996a). Other studies have suggested the opposite, that despite the apparently transient nature of news and newsbooks, they were often read in the seventeenth century as part of a vital attempt to discern the hidden hand of God intervening in human affairs. In the ephemeral details of news journals, contemporaries sought eternal truths (Atherton 1999b: 45–7). It has also been suggested that the reading of news altered the conception of the present. The discussion of news prolonged the present moment and altered the relationship between past and present. What constituted both news and history was redefined, as the former shaded into the latter, and histories of the civil wars, for example, were written from the materials of the newsbooks (Raymond 1996: 267, 280–4; Woolf 2001). There is still much work to be done on how the news was read in Stuart Britain. Paradoxically, we know more about how one poor London woodturner and Puritan (Nehemiah Wallington) consumed published news than we do about almost any other individual. He described the piles of newsbooks lying about his house as 'so many thieves that had stolen away my money before I was aware of them', but out of them he transcribed passages that confirmed his apocalyptic world view (Seaver 1985, esp. pp. 156–81).

So much of the history of the Stuart press has been written with an eye to the present. Too often, what is privileged in accounts of the Stuart press are the features that the author sees as most resembling the modern world. Even those who have argued against the modernity of the Stuart press are writing under the influence of the modernization motif. So much has been written about seventeenth-century news as a way of explaining features of the present-day world. Newspapers are seen as ushering in a modern public sphere in the accounts of Habermas and his followers. In the accounts of the Whigs and the work of Zaret, news and the printing press are lauded for defeating Stuart tyranny and bringing in liberty and democracy. News, the newspaper press and the spread of periodicity are seen as responsible in no small way for the birth of the novel (Hunter 1990: 167–94; Sommerville 1996a: 109–18), the diary and modern notions of time (Woolf 2001: 84), the secularization of religion (Mousley 1991: 162) or the decline of religious observance and belief (Sommerville 1996a: 135–45). Moreover, Stuart news culture is also blamed for what the author sees as the failings of the modern world: eroding powers of sustained thinking and replacing it with 'a giddy politics, puerile culture, and irresponsible social relations' (ibid.: 118, 168). Accounts of the Stuart press have thus been conditioned by the authors' views of the newspaper press of their own day, and have been written as reflections of modern understandings of and attitudes to the media industry. The future directions that scholarship takes are, therefore, as likely to be governed by future attitudes to print, radio, television, journalism and the Internet (and any other new media technologies) as by what new discoveries in archives and libraries reveal about the operation of the press and popular political opinion in Stuart Britain.

REFERENCES

Achinstein, S. 1994: *Milton and the Revolutionary Reader*. Princeton, NJ.

Astbury, R. 1978: 'The renewal of the Licensing Act in 1693 and its lapse in 1695', *The Library*, 33, 296–322.

Atherton, I. J. 1999a: *Ambition and Failure in Stuart England: The Career of John, first Viscount Scudamore*: Manchester.

Atherton, I. J. 1999b: 'The itch grown a disease: manuscript transmission of news in the seventeenth century'. In J. Raymond, ed., *News, Newspapers, and Society in Early Modern Britain*: London.

Barker, H. 1999: *Newspapers, Politics and English Society, 1695–1855*: Harlow.

Baron, S. A. 2001: 'The guises of dissemination in early seventeenth-century England: news in manuscript and print.' In B. Dooley and S. Baron, eds, *The Politics of Information in Early Modern Europe*: London.

Bellany, A. 1994: '"Raylinge rymes and vaunting verse": libellous politics in early Stuart England, 1603–1628.' In K. Sharpe and P. Lake, eds, *Culture and Politics in Early Stuart England*: Basingstoke.

Bellany, A. 2002: *The Politics of Court Scandal in Early Modern England: News Culture and the Overbury Affair, 1603–1660*: Cambridge.

Berry, H. 1997: '"Nice and curious questions": coffee houses and the representation of women in John Dunton's *Athenian Mercury*', *The Seventeenth Century*, 12, 257–76.

Birley, R. 1964: *Printing and Democracy*: London.

Black, J. 1992: 'War and the English press during the eighteenth century', *Journal of Newspaper and Periodical History*, 8 (2), 65–70.

Black, J. 2001: *The English Press 1621–1861*: Stroud.

Bourne, H. R. F. 1887: *English Newspapers: Chapters in the History of Journalism*, 2 vols: London.

Claydon, T. 2000: 'The sermon, the "public sphere" and the political culture of late seventeenth-century England'. In L. A. Ferrell and P. McCullough, eds, *The English Sermon Revised: Religion, Literature and History 1600–1750*: Manchester.

Clegg, C. S. 2001: *Press Censorship in Jacobean England*: Cambridge.

Cogswell, T. 1989: *The Blessed Revolution: English Politics and the Coming of War, 1621–1624*: Cambridge.

Cogswell, T. 1995: 'Underground verse and the transformation of early Stuart political culture. In M. Kishlansky and S. Amussen, eds, *Political Culture and Cultural Politics in Early Modern England*: Manchester.

Cotton, A. N. B. 1971: 'London newsbooks in the Civil War: their political attitudes and sources of information.' Unpublished D.Phil. thesis: Oxford University.

Couper, W. J. 1908: *The Edinburgh Periodical Press: Being a Bibliographical Account of the Newspapers, Journals, and Magazines issued in Edinburgh from the Earliest Times to 1800*, 2 vols: Stirling.

Cranfield, G. A. 1962: *The Development of the Provincial Newspaper 1700–1760*: Oxford.

Cranfield, G. A. 1978: *The Press and Society from Caxton to Northcliffe*: London.

Cressy, D. 1980: *Literacy and the Social Order: Reading and Writing in Tudor and Stuart England*: Cambridge.

Croft 1991: 'The reputation of Robert Cecil: libels, political opinion and popular awareness in the early seventeenth century', *Transactions of the Royal Historical Society*, 6th series, 1, 43–69.

Croft 1995: 'Libels, popular literacy and public opinion in early modern England', *Historical Research*, 68, 266–85.

Cust, R. 1986: 'News and politics in early seventeenth-century England', *Past and Present*, 112, 60–90.

Dahl, F. 1950: 'Amsterdam – cradle of English newspapers', *The Library*, 5th series, 4, 166–78.

Dahl, F. 1952: *A Bibliography of English Corantos and Periodical Newsbooks 1620–1642*: London.

De Beer, E. S. 1968: 'The English newspapers from 1695 to 1702.' In R. Hatton and J. S. Bromley, eds, *William III and Louis XIV: Essays 1680–1720 by and for Mark A. Thomson*: Liverpool.

de Krey, G. S. 1985: *A Fractured Society: The Politics of London in the First Age of Party 1688–1715*: Oxford.

Doig, J. A. 1998: 'Political propaganda and royal proclamations in late medieval England', *Historical Research*, 71, 253–80.

Dooley, B. 2001: 'News and doubt in early modern culture: or, are we having a public sphere yet?' In B. Dooley and S. Baron, eds, *The Politics of Information in Early Modern Europe*: London.

Downie, J. A. 1979: *Robert Harley and the Press: Propaganda and Public Opinion in the Age of Swift and Defoe*: Cambridge.

Eisenstein, E. L. 1968: 'Some conjectures about the impact of printing on western society and thought: a preliminary report', *Journal of Modern History*, 40, 7–29.

Eisenstein, E. L. 1979: *The Printing Press as an Agent of Change*: Cambridge.

Ellis, F. H. (ed.) 1985: *Swift vs. Mainwaring: The Examiner and The Medley*: Oxford.

Fletcher, A. 1981: *The Outbreak of the English Civil War*: London.

Fox, A. 1994: 'Ballads, libel, and popular ridicule in Jacobean England', *Past and Present*, 145, 47–83.

Fox, A. 1997: 'Rumour, news, and popular political opinion in Elizabethan and early Stuart England', *Historical Journal*, 40, 597–620.

Fox, A. 2000: *Oral and Literate Culture in England 1500–1700*: Oxford.

Frank, J. 1961: *The Beginnings of the English Newspaper 1620–1660*. Cambridge, MA.

Fraser, N. 1956: *The Intelligence of the Secretaries of State and their Monopoly of Licensed News 1660–1688*: Cambridge.

Fraser, N. 1992: 'Rethinking the public sphere: a contribution to the critique of actually existing democracy.' In C. Calhoun, ed., *Habermas and the Public Sphere*: Cambridge, MA.

Frearson, M. 1993a: 'London corantos in the 1620s', *Studies in Newspaper and Periodical History*, 1, 3–17.

Frearson, M. 1993b: 'The distribution and readership of London corantos in the 1620s.' In R. Myers and M. Harris, eds, *Serials and their Readers 1620–1914*: Winchester.

Freist, D. 1997: *Governed by Opinion: Politics, Religion and the Dynamics of Communication in Stuart London 1637–1645*. London.

Gibbs, G. C. 1992: 'Press and public opinion: prospective.' In J. R. Jones, ed., *Liberty Secured? Britain before and after 1688*: Stanford, CA.

Goldie, M. 1980: 'The revolution of 1689 and the structure of political argument: an essay and an annotated bibliography of the pamphlets on the allegiance controversy', *Bulletin of Research in the Humanities*, 83, 473–564.

Grant, J. 1871: *The Newspaper Press: Its Origin – Progress – and Present Position*, 2 vols: London.

Habermas, J. 1974: 'The public sphere: an encyclopedia article', *New German Critique*, 3, 49–55.

Habermas, J. 1989: *The Structural Transformation of the Public Sphere: An Inquiry into a Category of Bourgeois Society*: Cambridge.

Habermas, J. 1992a: 'Further reflections on the public sphere.' In C. Calhoun, ed., *Habermas and the Public Sphere*: Cambridge, MA.

Habermas, J. 1992b: 'Concluding remarks.' In C. Calhoun, ed., *Habermas and the Public Sphere*: Cambridge, MA.

Halasz, A. 1997: *The Marketplace of Print: Pamphlets and the Public Sphere in Early Modern England*: Cambridge.

Harris, B. 1996: *Politics and the Rise of the Press: Britain and France, 1620–1800*: London.

Harris, M. 1987: *London Newspapers in the Age of Walpole*. Rutherford.

Harris, T. 1987: *London Crowds in the Reign of Charles II: Propaganda and Politics from the Restoration until the Exclusion Crisis*: Cambridge.

Harris, T. 1997: 'The parties and the people: the press, the crowd and politics "out-of-doors" in Restoration England.' In L. K. J. Glassey, ed., *The Reigns of Charles II and James VII and II*: Basingstoke.

Herd, H. 1952: *The March of Journalism: The Story of the British Press from 1622 to the Present Day*: London.

Herrup, C. B. 1999: *A House in Gross Disorder: Sex, Law, and the 2nd Earl of Castlehaven*: Oxford.

Higgins: 1973: 'The reactions of women, with special reference to women petitioners.' In B. Manning, ed., *Politics, Religion, and the English Civil War*: London.

Hill, C. 1985: 'Censorship and English literature.' In C. Hill, ed., *Collected Essays Volume I: Writing and Revolution in Seventeenth-Century England*: Brighton.

Hill, C. 1998: 'Protestantism, pamphleteering, patriotism and public opinion.' In C. Hill, ed., *England's Turning Point: Essays on 17th Century English History*: London.

Hirst, D. 1975: *The Representative of the People? Voters and Voting in England under the Early Stuarts*: Cambridge.

Houston, R. A. 1982: 'The literacy myth? Illiteracy in Scotland 1630–1760', *Past and Present*, 96, 81–102.

Hunt, F. K. 1850: *The Fourth Estate: Contributions towards a History of Newspapers, and of the Liberty of the Press*: London.

Hunter, J. P. 1990: *Before Novels: The Cultural Contexts of Eighteenth-Century English Fiction*: New York.

Kelsall, H. M. and Kelsall, R. K. 1986: 'How people and news got around.' In H. M. Kelsall and R. K. Kelsall, *Scottish Lifestyle 300 Years Ago: New Light on Edinburgh and Border Families*: Edinburgh.

Knights, M. 1993: 'London's "monster" petition of 1680', *Historical Journal*, 36, 39–67.

Knights, M. 1994: *Politics and Opinion in Crisis, 1678–81*: Cambridge.

Knights, M. 2000: Review of D. Zaret, *Origins of Democratic Culture*, H-Albion, H-Net Reviews, September 2000. URL: http://www.h-net.msu.edu/reviews/showrev.cgi?path =23451969480497.

Lake, P. and Questier, M. 2000: 'Puritans, papists, and the "public sphere" in early modern England: the Edmund Campion affair in context', *Journal of Modern History*, 72, 587–627.

Lambert, S. 1992: 'State control of the press in theory and practice: the role of the stationers' company before 1640.' In R. Myers and M. Harris, eds, *Censorship and the Control of Print in England and France 1600–1900*: Winchester.

Levy, F. J. 1982: 'How information spread among the gentry, 1550–1640', *Journal of British Studies*, 21 (2), 11–34.

Linton, D. and Boston, R. 1987: *The Newspaper Press in Britain: An Annotated Bibliography*: London.

Love, H. 1993: *Scribal Publication in Seventeenth-Century England*: Oxford.

Macaulay, T. B. 1913–14: *The History of England from the Accession of James the Second*, 6 vols, ed. C. H. Firth: London.

McDowell, P. 1998: *The Women of Grub Street: Press, Politics, and Gender in the London Literary Marketplace 1678–1730*: Oxford.

McEntee, A. M. 1992: ' "The [un]civill-sisterhood of oranges and lemons": female petitioners and demonstrators, 1642–53.' In J. Holstun, ed., *Pamphlet Wars: Prose in the English Revolution*: London.

McKenzie, D. F. 1973: '*The Staple of News* and the late plays.' In W. Blissett, J. Patrick and R. W. van Fossen, eds, *A Celebration of Ben Jonson*: Toronto.

Maddicott, J. R. 1978: 'The county community and the making of public opinion in four-teenth-century England.' *Transactions of the Royal Historical Society*, 5th series, 28, 27–43.

Maltby, J. 1998: *Prayer Book and People in Elizabethan and Early Stuart England*: Cambridge.

Mendle, M. 2001a: Review of J. Raymond, ed., *News, Newspapers, and Society in Early Modern Britain*, H-Albion, H-Net Reviews, April 2001. URL: http://www.h-net.msu.edu/reviews /showrev.cgi?path=23833987187733.

Mendle, M. 2001b: 'News and the pamphlet culture of mid-seventeenth-century England.' In B. Dooley and S. Baron, eds, *The Politics of Information in Early Modern Europe*: London.

Miller, J. 1995: 'Public opinion in Charles II's England', *History*, 80, 359–81.

Milton, A. 1998: 'Licensing, censorship, and religious orthodoxy in early Stuart England', *Historical Journal*, 41, 625–51.

Morrill, J. S. 1975: 'William Davenport and the "silent majority" of early Stuart England', *Journal of the Chester Archaeological Society*, 58, 115–29.

Mousley, A. 1991: 'Self, state, and seventeenth-century news', *Seventeenth Century*, 6, 149–68.

Muddiman, J. G. 1920: *Tercentenary Handlist of English and Welsh Newspapers, Magazines and Reviews*: London.

Muddiman, J. G. 1923: *The King's Journalist, 1659–1689*: London.

Muggli, M. Z. 1992: 'Ben Jonson and the business of news', *Studies in English Literature*, 32, 323–40.

Munter, R. 1967: *The History of the Irish Newspaper 1685–1760*: Cambridge.

Nelson, C. 1993: 'American readership of early British serials.' In R. Myers and M. Harris, eds, *Serials and their Readers 1620–1914*: Winchester.

Nelson, C. and Seccombe, M. 1986: *Periodical Publications 1641–1700: A Survey with Illustrations*. Bibliographical Society, Occasional Paper, no. 2: London.

Nelson, C. and Seccombe, M. 1987: *British Newspapers and Periodicals 1641–1700. A Short-Title Catalogue of Serials Printed in England, Scotland, Ireland, and British America*: New York.

Norbrook, D. 1994: '*Areopagitica*, censorship, and the early modern public sphere.' In R. Burt, ed., *The Administration of Aesthetics: Censorship, Political Criticism, and the Public Sphere*: Minneapolis.

O'Callaghan, M. 2000: *The 'Shepheards Nation': Jacobean Spenserians and Early Stuart Political Culture, 1612–1625*: Oxford.

Pincus, S. C. A. 1995: ' "Coffee politicians does create": coffeehouses and Restoration political culture', *Journal of Modern History*, 67, 819–20.

Plumb, J. 1969: 'The growth of the electorate in England from 1600 to 1715', *Past and Present*, 45, 90–116.

Powell, W. S. 1977: *John Pory 1572–1636: The Life and Letters of a Man of Many Parts*: Chapel Hill, NC.

Price, J. M. 1958: 'A note on the circulation of the London press, 1704–1714', *Bulletin of the Institute of Historical Research*, 31, 215–24.

Raymond, J. 1996: *The Invention of the Newspaper: English Newsbooks 1641–1649*: Oxford.

Raymond, J. 1999a: 'Introduction: newspapers, forgeries, and histories.' In J. Raymond, ed., *News, Newspapers, and Society in Early Modern Britain*: London.

Raymond, J. 1999b: 'The newspaper, public opinion, and the public sphere in the seventeenth century.' In J. Raymond, ed., *News, Newspapers, and Society in Early Modern Britain*: London.

Ross, C. 1981: 'Rumour, propaganda and popular opinion during the Wars of the Roses.' In R. A. Griffiths, ed., *Patronage, the Crown and the Provinces in Later Medieval England*: Gloucester.

Sanders, J. 1998: 'Print, popular culture, consumption and commodification in *The Staple of News*.' In J. Sanders, K. Chedgzoy and S. Wiseman, eds, *Refashioning Ben Jonson: Gender, Politics and the Jonsonian Canon*: Basingstoke.

Schofield, R. S. 1968: 'The measurement of literacy in pre-industrial England.' In J. Goody, ed., *Literacy in Traditional Societies*: Cambridge.

Schwoerer, L. G. 1992: 'Liberty of the press and public opinion 1660–1695.' In J. R. Jones, ed., *Liberty Secured? Britain before and after 1688*: Stanford, CA.

Seaver, S. 1985: *Wallington's World: A Puritan Artisan in Seventeenth-Century London*: Stanford, CA.

Shagan, E. H. 1997: 'Constructing discord: ideology, propaganda, and English responses to the Irish rebellion of 1641,' *Journal of British Studies*, 36 (1), 4–34.

Sharpe, K. 2000: 'Celebrating a cultural turn: political culture and cultural politics in early modern England.' In K. Sharpe, ed., *Remapping Early Modern England: The Culture of Seventeenth-Century Politics*: Cambridge.

Siebert, F. S. 1952: *Freedom of the Press in England 1476–1776: The Rise and Decline of Government Controls*: Urbana, IL.

Snyder, H. L. 1968: 'The circulation of newspapers in the reign of Queen Anne', *The Library*, 5th series, 23, 206–35.

Snyder, H. L. 1976: 'A further note on the circulation of newspapers in the reign of Queen Anne', *The Library*, 5th series, 31, 387–9.

Snyder, H. L. 1977: 'Newsletters in England, 1689–1715: with special reference to John Dyer – a byway in the history of England.' In D. H. Bond and W. R. McLeod, eds, *Newsletters to Newspapers: Eighteenth-Century Journalism*: Morgantown, WV.

Sommerville, C. J. 1996a: *The News Revolution in England: Cultural Dynamics of Daily Information*: New York.

Sommerville, C. J. 1996b: 'Surfing the coffeehouse', *History Today*, 47 (6), 8–10.

Spufford, M. 1979: 'First steps in literacy: the reading and writing experiences of the humblest seventeenth-century spiritual autobiographers', *Social History*, 4, 407–35.

Steele, I. K. 1985: 'Communicating the English Revolution to the colonies, 1688–1689', *Journal of British Studies*, 24, 333–57.

Sutherland, J. R. 1934: 'The circulation of newspapers and literary periodicals, 1700–30', *The Library*, 4th series, 15, 110–24.

Sutherland, J. R. 1986: *The Restoration Newspaper and its Development*: Cambridge.

Targett, S. 1994a: 'Government and ideology during the age of Whig supremacy: the political arguments of Walpole's newspaper propagandists', *Historical Journal*, 37, 289–317.

Targett, S. 1994b: ' "The premier scribbler himself ": Sir Robert Walpole and the management of public opinion', *Studies in Newspaper and Periodical History*, 2, 19–33.

Thompson, A. B. 1998: 'Licensing the press: the career of G. R. Weckherlin during the personal rule of Charles I', *Historical Journal*, 41, 653–78.

Underdown, D. 1985: *Revel, Riot and Rebellion: Popular Politics and Culture in England 1603–1660*: Oxford.

Underdown, D. 1996: *A Freeborn People: Politics and the Nation in Seventeenth-Century England*: Oxford.

von Stutterheim, K. 1934: *The Press in England*, trans. W. H. Johnson: London.

Walker, R. B. 1974: 'The newspaper press in the reign of William III', *Historical Journal*, 17, 691–709.

Williams, J. B. (pseudonym of Muddiman, J. G.) 1908: *A History of English Journalism to the Foundation of the Gazette*: London.

Williams, K. 1977: *The English Newspaper: An Illustrated History to 1900*: London.

Wiseman, S. 1992: ' "Adam, the father of all flesh": porno-political rhetoric and political theory in and after the English Civil War.' In J. Holstun, ed., *Pamphlet Wars: Prose in the English Revolution*: London.

Wiseman, S. 1999: 'Pamphlet plays in the Civil War news market: genre, politics, and "context".' In J. Raymond, ed., *News, Newspapers, and Society in Early Modern Britain*: London.

Woolf, D. 2001: 'News, history, and the conception of the present in early modern England.' In B. Dooley and S. Baron, eds, *The Politics of Information in Early Modern Europe*: London.

Worden, B. 1987: 'Literature and political censorship in early modern England.' In A. C. Duke and C. Tamse, eds, *Too Mighty to be Free: Censorship and the Press in Britain and the Netherlands*: Zutphen.

Zaret, D. 1992: 'Religion, science, and printing in the public spheres in seventeenth-century England.' In C. Calhoun, ed., *Habermas and the Public Sphere*: Cambridge, MA.

Zaret, D. 2000: *Origins of Democratic Culture: Printing, Petitions, and the Public Sphere in Early-Modern England*: Princeton, NJ.

FURTHER READING

There is no single volume that covers the entire subject in depth. Introductory surveys of newspaper history are Black, J. 2001: *The English Press 1621–1861*: Stroud; and Cranfield, G. A. 1978: *The Press and Society from Caxton to Northcliffe*: London. The latter's Whig approach also characterizes Siebert, F. S. 1952: *Freedom of the Press in England 1476–1776: The Rise and Decline of Government Controls*: Urbana; while Barker, H. 1999: *Newspapers, Politics and English Society, 1695–1855*: Harlow, is a good textbook introduction to the later Stuart period. Good analyses of particular short periods are: Cust, R. 1986: 'News and politics in early seventeenth-century England. *Past and Present*, 112, 60–90, on news in the 1620s; Frank, J.

1961: *The Beginnings of the English Newspaper 1620–1660*: Cambridge, MA, on the 1640s; Sutherland, J. R. 1986: *The Restoration Newspaper and its Development*: Cambridge; and Downie, J. A. 1979: *Robert Harley and the Press: Propaganda and Public Opinion in the Age of Swift and Defoe*: Cambridge. Essential for any understanding of newspapers is the bibliographic listing in Nelson, C. and Seccombe, M. 1987: *British Newspapers and Periodicals 1641–1700. A Short-Title Catalogue of Serials Printed in England, Scotland, Ireland, and British America*: New York. The most sophisticated analysis of news is that of Raymond, J. 1996: *The Invention of the Newspaper: English Newsbooks 1641–1649*: Oxford, which illuminates much more than its title and supersedes most earlier work. See also Raymond, J., ed., 1993: *Making the News: An Anthology of the Newsbooks of Revolutionary England 1641–1660*: Moreton-in-Marsh. Knights, M. 1994: *Politics and Opinion in Crisis, 1678–81*: Cambridge, is a good study of the varieties and force of popular political opinion in one narrow moment of political crisis. For arguments about the existence of a public sphere in Stuart Britain see Habermas, J. 1989: *The Structural Transformation of the Public Sphere: An Inquiry into a Category of Bourgeois Society*: Cambridge; Calhoun, C., ed., 1992: *Habermas and the Public Sphere*: Cambridge, MA; and, for the detailed claim that a public sphere emerged in the 1640s, Zaret, D. 2000: *Origins of Democratic Culture: Printing, Petitions, and the Public Sphere in Early-Modern England*: Princeton, NJ. Many of the essays in Dooley, B. and Baron, S., eds, 2001: *The Politics of Information in Early Modern Europe*: London, and Raymond, J., ed., 1999: *News, Newspapers, and Society in Early Modern Britain*: London, are well worth reading.

CHAPTER SIX

Gender Relations

ELIZABETH FOYSTER

When Margaret Cavendish, duchess of Newcastle, recalled her childhood in Stuart Britain she described how her brothers would 'exercise themselves with fencing, wrestling, shooting, and such like exercises...and very seldom or never dance, or play on music, saying it was too effeminate for masculine spirits'. In marked contrast, she and her sisters would 'read, work, walk, and discourse with each other' (Cavendish 1906: 159). The upbringing which Cavendish experienced was one which was profoundly different from that of her brothers. She may have been born with a body which had been identified as being of the female sex, but she and her sisters had to learn how to be feminine. Her brothers, meanwhile, were occupied with developing their masculine qualities by pursuing manly sporting pursuits which would test their physical strength, agility and courage. As men in the making, her brothers spent much of their childhood apart from their sisters, but as Cavendish astutely observed, the upbringing of her brothers was informed by ideas of what were feminine activities. Dancing and music were unsuitable pastimes for boys who aspired to be manly because of their association with women, and engaging in them ran the danger of leaving a boy 'effeminate'. In this family, and in wider society, masculinity and femininity were relational categories which were defined in opposition to the 'other'. From their birth, the lives of women and men were shaped by their gender in Stuart Britain, and it is only by studying both sexes that we can make sense of gender identity and relations in this period.

As a focus for historical investigation, gender is a relatively new area which developed from women's history in the 1980s. It operates from the premise that men's as well as women's lives were shaped by their gender in the past. Gender historians seek to recover and understand the meanings which were given to femininity and masculinity. They believe that an individual's gender identity is a result of nurture not nature, and is constructed and shaped by the social and cultural context in which they live. Hence ideas about gender may be specific to particular points in time, and are capable of change over time. As this chapter will show, gender history has added much to our understanding of Stuart history by providing new information on the lives of women, who were rarely studied in traditional histories of this period. New histories of men which focus on their personal lives are also beginning to be written. But as well as contributing to our knowledge of the period, gender history is also demonstrating an exciting and radical potential, which is to challenge the very definition of what constitutes Stuart history. The significance of the traditional economic, political and religious turning points in seventeenth-century history have been questioned in the light of the research of gender historians. Gender has also shown to have had meaning in areas of life where women were frequently absent, such as in war and high politics. In fact, gender was everywhere, and has relevance for each of the topics in the chapters of this book. This is because ideas about gender did not just influence the relationships between women and men, but they also shaped the way that people described, ordered and understood their world. The speech, writing and images used by early modern individuals were laden with gendered language and metaphors. Most frequently, the language of gender was used to signify relationships of power, whether in the household, church or state (Scott 1986; Roper and Tosh 1991). As this chapter will demonstrate, gender history lets us look at aspects of the past in new ways, and suggests a very different narrative to Stuart history from that which has been traditionally taught. For a form of history which has been practised only for the past twenty or so years, this is no mean achievement.

Gender Relations by the Book

The sources which are most readily available to the historian of gender relations are the printed advice or conduct books and manuals which were published in large numbers, particularly in the period before the civil wars. These gave instruction on marital, family and household relationships, and prescribed an ideal form of gender relations. Their authors, Puritan clergy such as William Gouge, William Whateley, Henry Smith, John Dod and Robert Cleaver, often based their work on the sermons they had delivered to their congregations. Although much of their advice was the repeated wisdom of Catholic writers, it is thought that their work did contain new emphases, and was more widely distributed and read in the post-Reformation period (Davies 1981; Fletcher 1994). Potted versions of their advice were printed in many other forms, such as popular ballads and chapbooks (the songs and cheap books of the period), and was repeated on the stage in Renaissance and Restoration drama (Spufford 1981: ch. 7; Foyster 1993). Whether learnt in oral or written form, it is difficult to believe that anyone could have remained ignorant of the main tenets of their advice.

According to these male writers, God had created men and women to be different. From the point at which Eve had led to the Fall of mankind, women had become subordinate to men. Biblical passages were employed by these writers to demonstrate that God had intended women to be inferior to men in all areas of life. In marriage, it was argued that wives should be submissive and obedient to their husbands. Wives were advised to guard their tongues, since silence among women was praiseworthy, and to centre their lives in their homes with their families. Sexual chastity and fidelity to their husbands was of crucial importance. Men also had duties in this gender order. Whereas women were expected to remain in the 'private' sphere of the home, men were expected to work in the 'public' sphere outside it, so that they could materially provide for and support their wives and children. As the heads of households, they were told to rule their wives with mildness, respect and justice. Both sexes were enjoined to love each other, and marriage was often described as a yoke which husbands and wives shared and should draw together.

But the importance which was placed on companionship in marriage never amounted to equality. For what these writers were articulating was a 'patriarchal' system of gender relations. Patriarchy is the term that historians have given to the ways in which men, as husbands, brothers, sons, as well as fathers, dominated over and subordinated women, within and beyond the household. Patriarchy assumed a new political importance in the seventeenth century. Political theorists such as Sir Robert Filmer drew analogies between the power of the king in the state and that of the father in the family. This analogy was extended by royalists when they argued that the contract between a king and his subjects was as irrevocable as the marriage contract between husband and wife. Ideas about gender and a gendered language were serving a clear political purpose here. By the end of the seventeenth century the political theory of patriarchy was being challenged by John Locke, but by this time its implications for domestic conduct had become the mainstay of advice books. The comparisons between order in the household and stability in society were commonplace, and in popular thinking gender and social order were inseparable. For Gouge, the family was 'a little Commonwealth . . . a school wherein the first principles and grounds of government and subjection are learned'. Society was conceived as a collection of households, and the godly, orderly household where men had authority over women was upheld as a model for all to follow (Gouge 1634: 17; Amussen 1988: ch. 2).

The ideas of male superiority and female inferiority were supported by contemporary medical thinking about the body. Many people derived their ideas about the body from the writer Galen of Pergamum (c. AD 130–200). He established a humoural model for the body, in which the different combinations and temperature of the four humours – blood, phlegm, yellow bile and black bile – determined male and female characteristics. It was believed that women's humoural balance was colder and moister than men's, and that this made them naturally less rational and strong. Women and men, it was thought, had the same reproductive organs, with the chief difference being that a woman's sexual organs were inverted inside her body. A woman's anatomy was simply an imperfect version of the male. According to this model of the 'one-sex body' both women and men had to produce 'seed' during sexual relations for conception to occur, but it was generally believed that it was the man's semen which contained the vital qualities which would determine the characteristics of the child. Again, these ideas did not remain unchallenged through our period. Nevertheless, the notion that women's bodies rendered them the 'weaker sex', and that the gender order was one which was natural, as well as ordained by God, remained intact (Laqueur 1990; Fletcher 1995: chs 2 and 3).

Since women and men were believed to have bodies with both male and female attributes, childhood and youth were seen as vital periods for gender construction and socialization. Parents could be anxious to instil into their children the conduct and values which they perceived to be appropriate for their gender. We know from their letters and diaries that middling and elite women and men experienced an upbringing and education which were designed to train them for their future gender roles. For girls, this could involve them learning how to be chaste, silent and obedient so that they would make good wives. Hence, in 1704, John Evelyn instructed his grandson to teach any daughters that he might have to be 'humble, modest, moderate', and 'good housewives' (Pollock 1989: 242). For boys, childhood was a training which was more likely to include formal schooling away from the effeminizing influence of mothers. The Stuart grammar school and university imposed a curriculum and regime upon boys which demanded self-control and discipline, and involved a process of physical and emotional hardening. The aim was to produce men with the qualities suited to family and social leadership (Fletcher 1995: chs 15 and 16).

Marriage and the setting up of a household allowed women and men to put what they had learnt to the test. The advice about married life contained in the conduct books was taken very seriously by some. Nehemiah Wallington, a Puritan artisan living in London, was so convinced by what he read in Gouge's conduct book, *Of Domesticall Duties* (first published in 1622), that he drew up rules for his family based on what he had read, and got his wife, servants and apprentice to sign them (Fletcher 1994: 165). It is clear that the prescribed patriarchal model of gender relations set a spotlight upon the marital household. Men could be acutely sensitive to how their abilities as husbands and heads of household could reflect upon their honour, reputation or credit in the wider community. The parallels drawn between gender and the social order meant that the man who could not govern his household was thought incapable of public office. 'My house', declared the earl of Huntingdon in a set of household regulations of the early seventeenth century, 'doth nearest resemble the government in public office which men of my rank are often called unto . . . if I fail in the lesser . . . I shall never be capable of the greater' (Cust 1995: 82).

Those who could not or did not conform to their gender roles could be mocked, humiliated or persecuted. The heterosexual model of gender relations meant that although the idea of homosexuality as an identity had no meaning in this period, sexual relationships between men were abhorred and subject to the death penalty (Bray 1982). Erotic and sexual relationships between women were not criminalized, and a dearth of sources makes it difficult for us to know how these relationships were interpreted, but the notion that women could find sex satisfying without the presence of a man was profoundly threatening to the patriarchal system of gender relations (Mendelson and Crawford 1998: 20–1, 242–51).

Heterosexual marital relationships which did not appear to follow the prescribed pattern could also be subject to censure. For men in married relationships, the insult of 'cuckold' was given to those whose lack of sexual dominance had led their wives to adultery. Animal horns, the symbol of the cuckold, could be attached to the property of men suspected of being cuckolded, and mocking ballads and libellous rhymes were targeted at these men who had failed to fulfil their duties as husbands (Foyster 1999). Wives who did not conform to their prescribed roles of silence and obedience could be subjected to a range of punishments as 'scolds' or 'shrews'. Bridles or branks – iron collars with bits which cut into the tongue to prevent the woman from talking – and the cucking or ducking stool were used in an attempt to enforce gender roles throughout our period (Underdown 1985). According to some feminists, witchcraft accusations reflected the most extreme expression of concerns about rebellious women (Hester 1992). Rituals aimed at publicly shaming married couples who had offended gender norms included 'charivari', which were loud mocking demonstrations (Ingram 1984). Such was the concern for sexual chastity among women that throughout the seventeenth century large numbers of married women went to the church courts to defend their names (and their husband's honour) against sexual defamation or slander. The law courts may have punished both male and female sexual deviance, but they appear to have supported a double sexual standard whereby women were usually subjected to greater penalties (Gowing 1996). Fear of being shamed or punished for not conducting gender relations 'by the book' pressurized many to maintain at least the outward appearance of conformity to the standards which were set.

Historians are agreed that the ideal pattern of gender relations which was pre-scribed by many writers in the seventeenth century had an impact on the ways in which women and men in practice thought about themselves and their relationships with each other. People's expectations of their relationships were affected, and there is little doubt that many aspired to fulfil the ideals which were set for their gender. However, the very existence of records of measures taken against those who did not conform to the ideal model should warn us that this system was one which was not easily achieved, and could be open to challenge. Certainly, early modern people were not in the habit of accepting all that they were told by figures in authority. The parishioners of Blackfriars in London fiercely objected when Gouge preached that wives should have limited control over property within marriage, so that he had to justify his views in the advice book which he subsequently published (Amussen 1988: 44–5). It seems likely that many who listened to the views of Puritan ministers such as Gouge, or read their books, viewed their advice as contributing to the overall debate about gender relations, rather than offering definitive solutions to the prob-lems which the relationships between women and men raised. Perhaps, as Jacqueline Eales (1998) has suggested, the Puritan models for married life were understood to be only fully achievable within the exceptional conditions of clergy marriages. In more ordinary households, relationships may have been 'complementary and com-panionate' in private, while adhering to the behaviour of male dominance and female subordination in public (Wrightson 1982: 92). Certainly, any attempt to apply the advice of ministers to real life must have made individuals aware of the contradictions which were inherent in their writing. How was a man to be both an authoritarian patriarch and a loving companion to his wife? Could women be expected to be silent, submissive and obedient and yet govern their families and households wisely and competently when required (Pollock 1989)? The writers of conduct literature them-selves could not resolve these paradoxes, and instead must have caused further confusion as they struggled to reach some clarity. This was shown by Whateley's changing position over whether men's authority over women within marriage could extend to a right to correct their wives physically. After denying that husbands should beat their wives in the 1617 version of his conduct book, *A Bride Bush*, he had decided by the time the 1619 edition was published that there were some circumstances when physical correction was justified (Eales 1998: 168–9).

The study of prescriptive literature has only been the starting point for historians interested in gender within this period. The analysis of a wide range of other sources from the period, including diaries and personal correspondence, law court and poor relief records, popular literary texts, account books, inventories and wills, has consid-erably increased our knowledge about the lives of women and men in this period. This chapter will now turn to consider three areas of life in which gender relations operated: the economy, politics and religion. This will demonstrate that conduct literature was far from being descriptive of most people's lives in the Stuart period. However, it will also show that women and men were adept at using the ideology and rhetoric of gender difference which was contained in this literature for their own ends. Women and men were aware that they were different, whatever elite medical theorists liked to think. Women's recorded experiences of their own bodies, especially of menstruation, pregnancy, childbirth and the menopause, lends little support to the idea of the one-sex body. But awareness of physical difference did not mean that women and men felt restricted to the female and male roles which society set for them. Gender was not something that just happened to people, or was imposed upon them in the past. Instead, Stuart women and men were active in shaping both their gender identities and their relationships with each other.

Gender Relations and the Economy

One of the pioneers of the history of women, Alice Clark, believed that the seventeenth century marked a crucial turning point in the working lives of women and men. Clark labelled the early Stuart period as a 'golden age' for women in which they worked alongside men in their families to produce the goods that they and their household would consume or sell. Women were able to combine motherhood with an active and valued role in the economy, whatever their social position, and whether they worked in the rural or urban economy. According to Clark, all this changed in the late seventeenth century with the advent of capitalism, mechanization and industrialization. The location of work moved from the home to the workshop and factory, and a 'sexual division of labour' took place, in which women's work was confined to the home, and men worked outside it for wages. Rather than being economically productive, the focus of women's lives became their reproductive capacities, as childbearers and carers. Middling women were increasingly excluded from the skilled trades, and labouring women were no longer equal contributors to the household economy, but intermittently worked for low wages in home-based industries such as spinning. Wealthy women in the middling and upper ranks did not have to work and became primarily consumers in this economy, living idle lives which centred on the pursuit of pleasure (Clark 1992).

Clark's work has provoked much interest and debate from more recent historians. But the Stuart period has continued to be seen as an important transition point between the medieval and modern economies, in which the notion that work should be differentiated according to gender can be detected. Certainly, key features of Clark's chronology of change can be questioned, as mechanization and the movement of work to the factories has been shown to have only begun in the late eighteenth and nineteenth centuries. In the seventeenth century, historians have found only limited evidence of husbands and wives working as partners in family businesses. What was far more common was for women to work in occupations which were separate from their husbands. Hence Peter Earle found that of the 256 wives who stated that they were employed when they appeared as witnesses before the London church courts between 1695 and 1725, only 26 were working with their husbands (Earle 1989: 338). Even when women and men were engaged in the same area of economic activity, there was a hierarchy of tasks which was assigned according to gender. William Waterman's wife may have worked in the same location as her husband when he was made keeper of the Salisbury workhouse in 1623, but she was made a 'laundress and nurse' of the institution, while her husband was employed in the managerial tasks of supervision and control (Wright 1985: 107). In the rural economy the harvest provided an annual occasion when there was a visible demarcation of gender roles in the fields. This was so particularly when farmers began to rely more upon male workers who could use the heavier scythe to collect their harvests, than the use of the sickle, a tool which had traditionally been utilized by female workers (Roberts 1979). So it is clear that the sexual division of labour preceded the changes which Clark labelled as capitalism or industrialization.

Like men, the types of work in which women were employed depended on their social rank, where they lived and the point in time (both within each calendar year, as much work had a seasonal basis, and the date within the Stuart period). However, unlike men, women's work depended on their marital status, could be interrupted by childbearing, and endured some long-term continuities. Theoretically, women's role in the economy changed with their marital status, as the law imposed restrictions on the ability of married women to operate as independent economic agents. Married women could not trade, make contracts, sue and be sued like men, unmarried or widowed women, because their legal identity was subsumed into their husband's. Under this system of 'coverture' a woman lost all her control over her personal and real property upon marriage (Erickson 1993). Whatever economic role women played, childbearing and rearing, and housework were seen as their primary and most 'natural' duties. Over time, women's work continued to be rewarded with less pay than men, and was more likely to be casual and intermittent. Without equal access to training through schooling and apprenticeships, women's work had less tendency to be labelled as 'skilled' work. The majority of working women were occupied in a limited number of occupations such as domestic service, retailing, laundering, nursing, needlework, haymaking, dairy and poultry work (Bennett 1993; Earle 1989).

Clark focused her attention on married women, but we know that a significant proportion of between 10 per cent and 20 per cent of women in Stuart England never married. As the seventeenth century progressed the rate of remarriage declined, with widows less likely to remarry than widowers. How did spinsters and widows survive when wages for women were always lower than for men, and when much of the early modern economy was structured and founded upon the multiple contributions of household members rather than on the labour of lone workers? There is little doubt that those women who were not married could experience impoverishment, and were more likely to become a burden on the poor rates. The Norwich Census of the Poor conducted in 1570 revealed that 15 per cent of those claiming relief were widows (Mendelson and Crawford 1998: 262). However, around one-fifth of households in early modern England were headed by women, either as spinsters or widows, and more recent research has shown that life as a single or widowed woman could be economically rewarding. The wills and inventories of spinsters in early eighteenth-century rural Wales, for example, demonstrate that unmarried women were able to avoid financial dependence upon men, and make decisions about the inheritance of their property which reflected their own interests (Davison 2000). Hester Pinney was born in Dorset in 1658, but moved to London and worked initially supplying lace to a network of wealthy clients. Remaining unmarried, by the time she was in her forties she was a successful money lender and business woman (Sharpe 1999). Like spinsters, widows could also be in an ambiguous position within an economy and society which held expectations of female subordination to men. Few widows in the middling groups inherited their husband's businesses or had the skills to continue to operate them on their own, and some widows were restricted in their economic opportunities by the terms of their husband's wills, or by the existence of children from their former marriages. It was elite women from landed families who could be in the most advantageous position upon widowhood. Elizabeth Talbot, countess of Shrewsbury, popularly known as Bess of Hardwick, made a career out of widowhood and remarriage until her death in 1608.

Recent work by historians of the early modern economy has seen attention turn from macro-economic forces to studies of how individuals functioned and made economic decisions in their daily lives. This shift in focus has been accompanied by a new interest in the purchase or consumption of goods as the end point of the early modern economy. Inventories, the list of moveable goods which was made just after a person's death, are valuable sources which allow us to gain a picture of the material lives of people in the Stuart period. For historians studying gender relations, these approaches and sources have produced two main areas of interest. The first centres upon determining who within a household made the purchasing decisions. It is becoming clear that as household managers, and with limited legal rights to pledge their husband's credit to purchase 'necessary' goods, married women could hold a powerful position. What is more, there was a series of legal expedients which allowed wives to avoid the strictures of coverture and own property which was 'separate' from their husband's control. Historians have shown that ordinary women, quite far down the social scale, had more command over the property which they inherited or acquired through their labour than the theory of the law might seem to indicate (Erickson 1993). The decisions which women made concerning their property could have widespread implications. There is much to support the argument that it was consumer demand led by women that in the long term stimulated change and development in the early modern European economy (De Vries 1993). With rising real incomes and a greater range and better quality of goods to purchase from the Restoration period onwards, gender could be one of a number of factors which had an influence upon the ownership of goods. The meaning which women and men invested in the goods that they possessed is the second main area of the consumer economy which interests gender historians. But in contrast with a growing body of research based on the eighteenth century, for our period, this is a topic that is only just beginning to be explored (Weatherill 1986).

What did work mean for women and men in this period? Work had a qualitative as well as quantifiable or monetary value for people in the past, but it is possible that its value varied according to gender. The evidence outlined above shows that expectations of gender roles meant that work for women and men in the Stuart period was not often a shared experience. At first sight, the ways in which contemporaries described work may appear to indicate that the work which engaged women was less valued than men's work. Male early modern record keepers tended to note the occupation of men against their names, but only the marital status of women. Men's economic contribution was identified as their 'calling' or 'art'; terms which were rarely applied to women's work. Instead, many of the tasks in which women were engaged were labelled as the duties or obligations of the wife, rather than as 'work' or as an 'occupation' (Roberts 1985). Men's work could give them a collective as well as individual identity, and the honour of certain trades and occupations was often proudly asserted. The large numbers of young men who migrated to towns to learn the skills of a trade celebrated their apprenticeship status during festivals such as Shrove Tuesday. Civil pageants and processions gave the male-dominated guilds an opportunity to display their worth and foster ties of loyalty between their members. Records of such occasions demonstrate the importance of work to early modern notions of masculinity.

The organization and structure of women's work gave them less opportunity for such formal displays of occupational and institutional identity. But there is much to suggest that their work gave them both a measure of self-identity and esteem, and was respected by others. A key contribution of gender historians to our understandings of early modern economy has been to recognize the importance of women's unpaid work as mothers and housewives, and hence widen the definition of work used more traditionally by historians. Bearing and raising children, collecting and carrying water, lighting fires, cooking, laundry and cleaning was intensive and physically demanding work, and could provide employment opportunities for other women as midwives, wetnurses, teachers and domestic servants. Although for many women work within and outside the household was a necessity and essential to survival, it could also be a source of pride. The insult of 'idle housewife' was damaging to women because so much of their self-respect and social status rested upon their ability to carry out their work in a competent and efficient manner (Walker 1996). The competition among men for wives who had the reputation for being able and hard workers, or higher up the social scale, for marriages which would bring dowries, and wives who had the business acumen and social contacts to support their husbands, shows that the potential for women to make a significant economic contribution within marriage was more widely recognized and respected. Whatever their marital or social status, through their engagement in the economy as producers and consumers, Stuart women gained variable degrees of autonomy and very occasionally authority over the men with whom they lived and worked.

Gender Relations and Politics

Women's active participation in the early modern economy, working in the fields, travelling to markets, as street sellers and as consumers, clearly shows that few adhered to the advice contained in conduct books that women should concentrate their lives within the 'private' sphere of the home. The boundaries between the household and the neighbourhood were crossed on a daily basis by most women and men. In practice the worlds of the private and public, the personal and the political, overlapped. As this section will demonstrate, relationships between women and men were politicized at every level, and power was employed in everyday interactions and exchanges. As feminists have recognized, the personal was political. To understand fully the operation of politics in this period, we therefore need to adjust our notion of what is 'political' history, and examine the exercise of power and authority beyond the central institutions of the church and state (Wrightson 1996).

Once we include the family, household and neighbourhood into our definition of political arenas, we can see how women were able to exercise power even in a patriarchal society. We have seen how many women had some control over the expenditure of the household budget. The rituals surrounding childbirth, sickness and death tended to be managed by women and gave them occasions of special authority. As mistresses of households women also exercised daily authority over individuals, in particular servants and children. When historians have studied the politics of the parish, local community or neighbourhood, the importance of net-works of female friends to women becomes clear. These networks of friends, or 'gossips' as contemporaries liked to call them, shared information about people in their community, and importantly, passed judgement upon their behaviour. In the close-knit communities of Stuart Britain, where houses were often packed closely together, sharing backyards, alleyways and thin adjoining walls, notions of what was 'private' behaviour must have been very different from today. Talk about other people's behaviour allowed women to be the moral guardians of their communities, and because most people wanted to avoid being the subject of gossip, a considerable source of power (Capp 1996).

As historians we know how women's talk operated because going to the law courts was one way of attempting to stop gossip. Persistent gossips could be labelled as scolds. Scolding was an offence which could be punished in a range of ways, including the use of a ducking or cucking stool. A more common response was to go to the church courts and accuse the gossip of defamation, for which the punishment was penance, in which the offender would have to publicly declare that they had done wrong. The records of hundreds of defamation cases survive, and these give us valuable insights into the everyday workings of Stuart communities. They reveal that fear of gossip and the loss of a 'good name' or reputation served to regulate both female and male behaviour.

Married women were the group who were most likely to bring defamation cases to the church courts. An examination of the insults which were used shows that these women were most frequently slandered using sexual insults which centred on the word 'whore'. In contrast, the few men who brought defamation cases to the church courts, or slander cases to the secular courts, complained mainly of the non-sexual insults which questioned their business honesty, such as 'thief', 'cheat' or 'liar'. This might seem to suggest that notions of morality, of what was acceptable or deviant, differed according to gender (Gowing 1996). What is telling is how often sexual insults were used by women to further or settle disputes which had little to do with sex. In March 1618, for example, during a quarrel with Jane Garnett's husband over the weight of some flax in county Durham, Mary Dobson called Jane a 'quean, drunken bitch, and said that she thought that the devil was in her, she the said Jane being then great with child'. Sexual language was also used in arguments over household noise, leaking drains and broken fences and walls (Foyster 1999: 150). What we are seeing here is evidence of what some historians have called 'women's agency'. Women were deploying sexual insult, and using the system of the church courts, to further their own interests. In a similar way, the study of cases of witchcraft has shown that they often revolved around stories of women's anxieties about food production, childbearing and childcare. Antagonisms between women over these issues could lead to accusations of witchcraft (Purkiss 1995). The labels of 'whore' or 'witch' may have originally been created by men to fit a male political agenda designed to restrict and confine women's behaviour. But women were able to use those terms to their own ends. In so doing they were engaging in a political process of negotiating access to power, and disputing and sometimes resolving the place of individuals on the otherwise invisible hierarchies of power within local communities.

Women generally used gossip, insult and accusations of deviant behaviour to control the conduct of other women, but there were occasions when they questioned male behaviour. Individually, this could be a dangerous course of action, as Margaret Knowsley, a maidservant in Nantwich, found when she spread gossip in the late 1620s that her master, the preacher Stephen Jerome, had harassed her sexually, and had attempted to rape her. On three market days she was whipped through the town, placed in a cage above the market bearing papers with the words, 'for unjustly slandering Mr Jerome a preacher of God's word', and then carted through the town still holding this message (Hindle 1994). But collectively women's disapproval could have more effect. The cruelty of William Bullocke towards his wife so outraged his neighbours in Bristol that he had to employ a constable 'to guard him from the fury of the people and especially the women who knew him to be a base fellow'. Knowledge of his behaviour spread to Bath 'and many miles about', and he was 'much cried shame of'. Finally, in February 1667 as William walked through Bristol, a large crowd gathered around him and pelted him with mud. Women's talk had led William to be socially ostracized from his community, and to become the victim of a loud mocking demonstration characteristic of charivari (Foyster 1996: 222). But it is important to note that these Bristol women were not questioning male authority *per se*. Instead, by their speech and actions, they were shaming a man who had abused his authority, and seeking a restoration of harmonious gender relations in which a husband ruled over his wife, but without the recourse to excessive violence.

Women's collective action did not just focus upon the familial relationships of their neighbours. Instead, contemporary commentators often remarked upon women's participation in riots and other economic, political and religious protests. As workers in the early modern economy, and with responsibility for the purchase and preparation of food, women may have been acutely sensitive to changes in the price or access to food. Hence women were involved in both grain riots and protests over the enclosure of common land. On occasion, women were the leaders and instigators of protest. In 1629 in Maldon, Essex, Ann Carter acted as one of the ringleaders when a crowd of two to three hundred people boarded grain ships to try and prevent the export of grain. In Northamptonshire in October 1693, bad harvests led women to come to the markets with knives 'to force corn at their own rates'. Some believed that by the rules of coverture, married women had an immunity from corporal punishment, since within marriage it was thought a husband became responsible for his wife's actions. The mistaken nature of these popular beliefs was shown by the public hanging of women such as Ann Carter. In the eyes of the authorities women were capable of independent action, and should bear the consequences (Walter 1980; Houlbrooke 1986; Mendelson and Crawford 1998: 427).

There is little doubt that the world of 'high politics' was perceived by contemporaries as primarily a male arena. This was made clear in the highly sexualized language and images of politics and warfare. The royalist standard in the Civil War, for example, portrayed a naked soldier with a sword which was unsheathed, an erect penis, and in Latin, the words 'ready to use both' (Mendelson and Crawford 1998: 394). There was no question that women, like the majority of ordinary men at this time, should play a formal role in politics by standing for parliament or being permitted to vote in elections. But this did not prevent women from having a political voice. Women shared the belief that governors should listen and respond to their concerns. Hence we have surviving examples of petitions, sometimes signed by hundreds of women, and submitted to parliament and those in authority. The numbers of petitions submitted to parliament in the 1640s and 1650s were unprecedented. Some of these petitions were part of campaigns for peace, and it is possible that women were more able to take this pacifist stance, because unlike men, their gender identity did not rest upon physical strength and courage on the battlefield. The way in which female petitions were worded showed a keen awareness of gender ideology. Each began with an acknowledgement of female inferiority and an explanation as to why the women felt compelled to abandon their traditional submissive roles. Women's motivation to act was usually described as a consequence of their position as wives and mothers, and thus was couched as a suitably 'feminine' response to events that might destabilize the familial as well as the social order (Higgins 1973; Mendelson and Crawford 1998: 403).

Elite women had the wealth, time and social contacts throughout the Stuart period to engage in political activities. Some were tireless campaigners in the elections of their kinsmen. Lady Brilliana Harley's letters to her son in the summer of 1642 show her using her family connections to win him support in the Hereford by-election. She later became an exemplar for female courage when she defended the family home at Brampton against the royalists (Eales 1990). Whom wealthy women chose to patronize could be a highly significant political act. Hence Lady Joan Barrington (aunt to Oliver Cromwell) made her sympathies clear when she patronized a number of Puritan divines (Willen 1992: 570–4). But women could also act in more surreptitious ways by acting as the collectors and carriers of political information. At times, the popular belief that women were not political agents could act to their advantage. In 1654 it was reported that a letter of intelligence which had been written in a 'woman's hand' was not intercepted, because it was not expected that it would contain any 'business' (Mendelson and Crawford 1998: 414).

Women may have influenced the shape of political events in the Stuart period, but we must remember that women who did use political power were always liable to hostile criticism and satire for transgressing their 'natural' gender roles. Elite women were not always free to choose their political allegiances. At times, these women were little more than pawns in the political alliances which were cemented in marriages at court. Arguably, the Civil War gave women unique opportunities for political involvement, but with peace women were expected to resume their traditional activities of home and childcare. While Mary II and Queen Anne may have attracted less attention than the Tudor queens because of their sex, their reigns did revive political questions of female authority and rule (Weil 1999).

The sources for the study of popular and elite political culture in this period reveal that women at all levels of Stuart society were not passive recipients of authority, but instead were active participators and commentators of their political worlds, whether that was the neighbourhood or the royal court. Women shared with men a political consciousness and a sense of common rights, but the way they expressed their political beliefs was shaped by their gender. In this period women did not collectively campaign for equality with men, although there were some prominent individuals who can be labelled as 'feminists', such as the writer Mary Astell (1668–1731). An examination of the politics of neighbourhoods instead reveals that women could be deeply divided against each other, and that women were as likely to wield the tools of political power against their own sex, as against men.

Gender and Religion

Religious beliefs were what frequently motivated women to become involved in political protests in the Stuart period. Although considered inferior to men in other aspects of their lives, women were thought spiritual equals before God. Physically, mentally and emotionally women were believed to have a greater propensity than men to religious conviction. As the 'weaker sex', who were inclined to be less rational and more passionate than men, women were constructed as individuals who were more open to the influences of both God and the devil. Piety was seen as a 'feminine' virtue; ''tis not to be denied', wrote Richard Allestree, Professor of Divinity at Oxford, and author of *The Ladies Calling* (1673), 'that the reputation of Religion is more kept up by women than men' (Gregory 1998: 244).

Yet preaching and administering the sacraments were seen as tasks in the established church which only men had the qualities to perform. It is in this context that the appeal to women of the separatist churches and sects, which in the period before and during the Civil War broke away from the church, can begin to be understood. By allowing women to preach, prophesy and act as missionaries, these groups gave women a platform and opportunity publicly to voice their religious beliefs. In the lists which survive of congregations of groups such as the Quakers, Fifth Monarchists, Familists and Ranters, women outnumbered men, and the historian Phyllis Mack has identified nearly 300 women who were preachers, writers or missionaries in the period between 1640 and 1665 (Crawford 1993; Mack 1992). These religious groups attracted women across Britain from a wide range of social backgrounds. What is rewarding for the historian is that the details of these women's spiritual experiences were so often recorded by themselves or by others. Hence we have six publications which are attributed to Anna Trapnel, the Fifth Monarchist, who in a trance prophesied against the Protectorate; records relating to Katherine Chidley whose religious beliefs also led her to involvement with the Levellers during the 1640s and 1650s; and hundreds of tracts and letters between Quaker women, who meticulously recorded their own histories from the early days of the movement (Graham et al. 1989; Crawford 1993; Peters 1998).

However, we must not exaggerate the impact of these religious groups upon women's lives. Only a minority of all women were ever members of the sects, and a close examination of the organization and beliefs of each Nonconformist group reveals that they offered only limited opportunities for women to break free of their conventional roles. Even if missionary work engaged husbands and wives together, studies of the Quaker movement in Wales have shown that wives still faced the additional burden of housework and motherhood on their own. Patently, spiritual equality did not amount to worldly equality with men. Kate Peters has shown that although key leaders of the Quaker movement such as Margaret Fell and George Fox may have been publicly advocating women's spiritual authority and rights to preach, from as early as 1652 strategies were being developed to control and contain women's role within the movement. Increasingly, male religious radicals saw women's presence as a source of weakness and even embarrassment. Divisions within the Quakers about the role of women meant that by the 1650s there were separate meetings for women. Such was the strength of contemporary wisdom about appropriate gender roles for women, that the sight of ecstatic and prophesying women was thought to attract more critics than converts, especially in the years after the 'crisis' period of the Civil War. Many questioned the motivation of women to leave the established church, and unable to conceive that women could be governed by anything other than their sexual desires, believed that they must be yearning for sexual as well as spiritual freedoms. The leaders of the radical sects had to face frequent accusations of sexual impropriety. Ultimately the presence of women prophets and preachers was seen as challenging to manly control over religious affairs both within and outside the established church (Thomas 1958; Allen 2000; Peters 1998; Crawford 1993).

Sexual politics influenced the institutions and practical organization of religious life in our period, but ideas about gender also affected the way in which religious beliefs were expressed. When women prophesied, Mack (1992) has argued, they may have been engaging in an act which was radical for their sex, but the language which they used was rooted in conservative notions of gender difference. They described their spiritual experiences using metaphors of motherhood and daughter-hood, and relied on images of marriage in which the wife was subordinate to her husband. Negative female stereotypes were applied by all religious groups to their enemies. Hence Protestants frequently labelled the Catholic church as the 'whore of Babylon', and in the Restoration period dissenting ministers were scorned for having the feminine characteristics of being 'giddy' and 'volatile' in their beliefs (Crawford 1993: 16; Gregory 1998: 249). At the same time, the Reformation had seen a reconceptualization of the divine so that the masculine qualities of God were emphasized to contrast with the passive and dependent feminine qualities of the church and the believer. The spiritual experience was understood as the marriage between 'Christ the husband' and the 'brides of Christ' who were his believers. The church was 'the mother' who gave sustenance to her followers. The result of this thinking was that gendered and even sexualized language was often used to describe religious beliefs. Stephen Marshall told the House of Commons in 1645 that the church to believers was 'their Mother, in whose womb they have laine, whose breasts they have sucked'. The prophet Anne Bathurst wrote of the fiery kisses she received after her marriage with Christ, and recorded in September 1679, 'O Jesus, I am thine, thou hast ravished me ... O the sweetness and full Satisfaction' (Crawford 1993: 14–15). Men also saw themselves as 'brides of Christ', allowing for a kind of 'spiritual gender-reversal'. As Susan Hardman Moore has argued, it may be that it was only by seeing piety as a feminine practice that men could find a way of expressing emotions which would otherwise be seen as unmanly. But men's use of these feminine metaphors was based on negative interpretations of women's nature and role. They saw themselves as brides in a marriage with Christ only because this was assumed to be analogous to the submission of the weak and inferior bride to the superior strength of her husband. The result was that the gender order was reinforced rather than subverted (Hardman Moore 1998).

The exploration of the relationship between gender and religion has left historians of this period with a number of issues which remain to be explored. First, because of the quantity of primary material which survives, histories of Stuart women and religion have tended to focus on either the godly or the radical female believer. We know far less about the religious beliefs of those who conformed, or about the women and men who, in the minister Ralph Josselin's words, were the 'sleepy hearers' of many congregations. Secondly, the assumption by contemporaries that men were naturally less inclined towards religion than women has rarely been challenged by historians, leaving us with accounts of masculinity which portray men with only secular concerns. In this context, the work of Jeremy Gregory (1998, 1999) has been important in beginning to reclaim the significance of religion in the construction of masculinity for this period.

Conclusions

This chapter has shown that a person's gender played a significant part in determining how they experienced and made sense of their lives in the Stuart period. Of course, there are many other aspects of Stuart history which have been explored from a gendered perspective, which for reasons of space cannot be discussed here. But through an exploration of gender and economy, politics and religion what this chapter has demonstrated is that other components of identity such as social status, marital status, geographical location, religious faith, occupation and age, interacted with gender to constitute experience. As a result, it makes a nonsense of any attempt by historians of women to attempt to make generalizations about whether women's position 'improved' or 'declined' through the Stuart period. It is perhaps telling of the gendered perspective of traditional historians that no such task has ever been mounted to examine men's lives in this period. What the historians of women have revealed is that women's lives were similarly complex, and that they cannot be studied as a homogeneous group.

Gender history has presented a series of challenges to the historian of Stuart Britain. First is the question of sources. The most numerous are the conduct books with which this chapter began. But it has been shown that there was often a significant difference between the theory and the practice of gender relations. Since women were less likely to be able to write than men throughout our period, we have less direct evidence of their views. When historians want to study the lives of ordinary women and men, historians are often reliant upon the incidental references made about them by their social superiors, or upon the archives of the church or secular courts. The problem with court records is that the words of the women and men who testified were mediated and perhaps altered as they were written down, and because courts by their nature dealt with those who had been labelled as 'deviant', they can give us a distorted view of the past. Historians are often left with the difficult task of 'reading against the text' to try and determine what was considered the 'normal' pattern of gender relations. It remains the case that fewer histories of men have been written from a gendered perspective than of women, and that we still know little about the personal, emotional and sexual lives of Stuart men. But in an attempt to reach for the inner lives of men and women, gender historians have often been innovatory in their search for and approach to sources. To take just one example, historians of gender have recently started to analyse records of the dreams of early modern men and women (Bray 1996; Crawford 2000).

Secondly, gender historians have exposed some of the limitations of traditional approaches to Stuart history. They have questioned the definitions which historians have used, such as the meaning of the words 'work' and 'politics', by showing that such terms had a different applicability when they were applied to women's lives. Gender historians have widened the parameters of Stuart history by introducing new topics for historical research such as childhood, parenting, sexual practices and sexual identities. Slowly, but surely, gender history is becoming part of mainstream history. A chapter such as this one would have been unthinkable in an equivalent collection twenty years ago.

Finally, what remains undecided and an area for debate among historians is the relationship between gender history and the chronology of Stuart history. Many historians argue that there is no necessary link between the chronologies of women's and men's lives. The turning points which historians have marked out in the Stuart period such as the revolutionary years which marked the mid-century, or the Restoration which followed, may have only been significant to some men's lives. In this context, Patricia Crawford's question 'did women have a revolution?' is a very valid one (Crawford 1993: 5). For ordinary women and men the chronology or pattern of their individual life-cycles may have had more meaning than the types of national events which historians usually study. There is little doubt that the way gender relations were understood and expressed changed in our period, but how change came about remains unclear. Some have argued that periods of gender crisis, when women threatened to overturn the gender order, were instrumental to change. But the term 'crisis' suggests that sudden and dramatic change disrupted formerly static and stable gender relations. Instead, what this chapter has shown is that underlying an enduring patriarchal ideology, gender relations involved women and men continually negotiating, accommodating and adjusting their access to the dynamics of power which lay between them.

ACKNOWLEDGEMENTS

I would like to thank Helen Berry and Anthony Fletcher for their helpful comments on this chapter.

REFERENCES

Allen, R. 2000: '"Taking up her daily cross": women and the early Quaker movement in Wales, 1653–1689.' In *Women and Gender in Early Modern Wales*: Cardiff.

Amussen, S. D. 1988: *An Ordered Society: Gender and Class in Early Modern England*: New York.

Bennett, J. M. 1993: 'Women's history: a study in continuity and change', *Women's History Review*, 2, 2, 173–84.

Bray, A. 1982: *Homosexuality in Renaissance England*: London.

Bray, A. 1996: 'To be a man in early modern society: the curious case of Michael Wigglesworth', *History Workshop Journal*, 41, 155–65.

Capp, B. 1996: 'Separate domains? Women and authority in early modern England.' In P. Griffiths, A. Fox and S. Hindle, eds, *The Experience of Authority in Early Modern England*: London.

Cavendish, M. 1906: *The Life of William Cavendish, Duke of Newcastle: To which is added The True Relation of my Birth, Breeding and Life; by Margaret, Duchess of Newcastle*, ed. C. Harding Firth: London.

Clark, A. 1992: *Working Life of Women in the Seventeenth Century*, 3rd edn, with an introduction by A. L. Erickson: London.

Crawford, P. 1993: *Women and Religion in England 1500–1720*: London.

Crawford, P. 2000: 'Women's dreams in early modern England', *History Workshop Journal*, 49, 129–41.

Cust, R. 1995: 'Honour and politics in early Stuart England: the case of Beaumont *v.* Hastings', *Past and Present*, 149, 57–94.

Davies, K. M. 1981: 'Continuity and change in literary advice on marriage.' In R. B. Outhwaite, ed., *Marriage and Society: Studies in the Social History of Marriage*: London.

Davison, L. 2000: 'Spinsters were doing it for themselves: independence and the single woman in early eighteenth-century rural Wales.' In M. Roberts and S. Clarke, eds, *Women and Gender in Early Modern Wales*: Cardiff.

De Vries, J. 1993: 'Between purchasing power and the world of goods: understanding the household economy in early modern Europe.' In R. Porter and J. Brewer, eds, *Consumption and the World of Goods*: London.

Eales, J. 1988: 'Gender construction in early modern England and the conduct books of William Whateley (1583–1639).' In R. N. Swanson, ed., *Gender and Christian Religion*, Studies in Church History, vol. 34: Woodbridge.

Eales, J. 1990: *Puritans and Roundheads: The Harleys of Brampton Bryan and the Outbreak of the English Civil War*: Cambridge.

Eales, J. 1998: *Women in Early Modern England, 1500–1700*: London.

Earle, P. 1989: 'The female labour market in London in the late seventeenth and early eighteenth centuries', *Economic History Review*, 42, 328–53.

Erickson, A. L. 1993: *Women and Property in Early Modern England*: London.

Ewan, E. and Meikle, M. M. (eds) 1999: *Women in Scotland c.1100–c.1750*: East Linton.

Fletcher, A. 1994: 'The Protestant idea of marriage in early modern England.' In A. Fletcher and P. Roberts, eds, *Religion, Culture and Society in Early Modern Britain: Essays in Honour of Patrick Collinson*: Cambridge.

Fletcher, A. 1995: *Gender, Sex and Subordination in England 1500–1800*: New Haven, CT.

Foyster, E. 1993: 'A laughing matter? Marital discord and gender control in seventeenth-century England.' *Rural History*, 4, 1, 5–21.

Foyster, E. A. 1996: 'Male honour, social control and wife beating in late Stuart England', *Transactions of the Royal Historical Society*, 6th series, 6, 215–24.

Foyster, E. A. 1999: *Manhood in Early Modern England: Honour, Sex and Marriage*: London.

Gouge, W. 1634: *Of Domesticall Duties: Eight Treatises*, 3rd edn: London.

Gowing, L. 1996: *Domestic Dangers: Women, Words, and Sex in Early Modern London*: Oxford.

Graham, E., Hinds, H., Hobby, E. and Wilcox, H. (eds) 1989: *Her Own Life: Autobiographical Writings by Seventeenth-Century Englishwomen*: London.

Gregory, J. 1998: 'Gender and the clerical profession in England, 1660–1850.' In R. N. Swanson, ed., *Gender and Christian Religion*, Studies in Church History, vol. 34: Woodbridge.

Gregory, J. 1999: '*Homo religiosus*: masculinity and religion in the long eighteenth century.' In T. Hitchcock and M. Cohen, eds, *English Masculinities 1660–1800*: London.

Hardman Moore, S. 1998: 'Sexing the soul: gender and the rhetoric of Puritan piety.' In R. N. Swanson, ed., *Gender and Christian Religion*, Studies in Church History, vol. 34: Woodbridge.

Hester, M. 1992: *Lewd Women and Wicked Witches: A Study of the Dynamics of Male Domination*: London.

Higgins, P. 1973: 'The reactions of women with special reference to women petitioners.' In B. Manning, ed., *Politics, Religion and the English Civil War*: London.

Hindle, S. 1994: 'The shaming of Margaret Knowsley: gossip, gender and the experience of authority in early modern England', *Continuity and Change*, 9, 3, 391–419.

Houlbrooke, R. A. 1986: 'Women's social life and common action in England from the fifteenth century to the eve of the Civil War', *Continuity and Change*, 1, 2, 171–89.

Ingram, M. 1984: 'Ridings, rough music and the "reform of popular culture" in early modern England', *Past and Present*, 105, 79–113.

Laqueur, T. 1990: *Making Sex: Body and Gender from the Greeks to Freud*: Cambridge, MA.

MacCurtain, M. and O'Dowd, M. (eds) 1991: *Women in Early Modern Ireland*: Edinburgh.

Mack, P. 1992: *Visionary Women: Ecstatic Prophecy in Seventeenth-Century England*: Berkeley, CA.

Mendelson, S. and Crawford, P. 1998: *Women in Early Modern England 1550–1720*: Oxford.

Peters, K. 1998: ' "Women's speaking justified": women and discipline in the early Quaker movement, 1652–56.' In R. N. Swanson, ed., *Gender and Christian Religion*, Studies in Church History, vol. 34: Woodbridge.

Pollock, L. 1989: ' "Teach her to live under obedience": the making of women in the upper ranks of early modern England', *Continuity and Change*, 4, 2, 231–58.

Purkiss, D. 1995: 'Women's stories of witchcraft,' *Gender and History*, 7, 3, 408–32.

Roberts, M. 1979: 'Sickles and scythes: women's work and men's work at harvest time', *History Workshop Journal*, 7, 3–28.

Roberts, M. 1985: ' "Words they are women and deeds they are men": images of work and gender in early modern England.' In L. Charles and L. Duffin, eds, *Women and Work in Pre-Industrial England*: London.

Roper, M. and Tosh, J. 1991: 'Introduction: historians and the politics of masculinity.' In M. Roper and J. Tosh, eds, *Manful Assertions: Masculinities in Britain Since 1800*: London.

Scott, J. 1986: 'Gender: a useful category of historical analysis', *American Historical Review*, 91, 5, 1053–75.

Sharpe, P. 1999: 'Dealing with love: the ambiguous independence of the single woman in early modern England', *Gender and History*, 11, 2, 209–32.

Spufford, M. 1981: *Small-Books and Pleasant Histories: Popular Fiction and its Readership in Seventeenth-Century England*: London.

Thomas, K. V. 1958: 'Women and the Civil War sects', *Past and Present*, 13, 42–62.

Underdown, D. 1985: 'The taming of the scold: the enforcement of patriarchal authority in early modern England.' In A. Fletcher and J. Stevenson, eds, *Order and Disorder in Early Modern England*: Cambridge.

Walker, G. 1996: 'Expanding the boundaries of female honour in early modern England', *Transactions of the Royal Historical Society*, 6th series, 6, 235–45.

Walter, J. 1980: 'Grain riots and popular attitudes to the law: Maldon and the crisis of 1629.' In J. Brewer and J. Styles, eds, *An Ungovernable People: The English and their Law in the Seventeenth and Eighteenth Centuries*: London.

Weatherill, L. 1986: 'A possession of one's own: women and consumer behaviour in England, 1660–1740', *Journal of British Studies*, 25, 131–56.

Weil, R. 1999: *Political Passions: Gender, the Family and Political Argument in England*: Manchester.

Willen, D. 1992: 'Godly women in early modern England: Puritanism and gender', *Journal of Ecclesiastical History*, 43, 4, 561–80.

Wright, S. 1985: ' "Churmaids, huswyfes and hucksters": the employment of women in Tudor and Stuart Salisbury.' In L. Charles and L. Duffin, eds, *Women and Work in Pre-Industrial England*: London.

Wrightson, K. 1982: *English Society 1580–1680*: London.

Wrightson, K. 1996: 'The politics of the parish in early modern England.' In P. Griffiths, A. Fox and S. Hindle, eds, *The Experience of Authority in Early Modern England*: London.

FURTHER READING

Bray, A. 1982: *Homosexuality in Renaissance England*: London.

Crawford, P. 1993: *Women and Religion in England 1500–1720*: London.

Eales, J. 1998: *Women in Early Modern England, 1500–1700*: London.

Ewan, E. and Meikle, M. M. (eds) 1999: *Women in Scotland c.1100–c.1750*: East Linton.

Fletcher, A. 1995: *Gender, Sex and Subordination in England 1500–1800*: New Haven, CT.

Foyster, E. A. 1999: *Manhood in Early Modern England: Honour, Sex and Marriage*: London.

Gowing, L. 1996: *Domestic Dangers: Women, Words, and Sex in Early Modern London*: Oxford.

Hitchcock, T. and Cohen, M. (eds) 1999: *English Masculinities 1660–1800*: London.

Houston, R. A. 1989: 'Women in the economy and society of Scotland, 1500–1800.' In R. A. Houston and I. D. Whyte, eds, *Scottish Society 1500–1800*: Cambridge.

MacCurtain, M. and O'Dowd, M. (eds) 1991: *Women in Early Modern Ireland*: Edinburgh.

Mendelson, S. and Crawford, P. 1998: *Women in Early Modern England 1550–1720*: Oxford.

Roberts, M. and Clarke, S. (eds) 2000: *Women and Gender in Early Modern Wales*: Cardiff.

Sharpe, P. (ed.) 1998: *Women's Work: The English Experience 1650–1914*: London.

Shoemaker, R. and Vincent, M. (eds) 1998: *Gender and History in Western Europe*: London.

Sommerville, M. R. 1995: *Sex and Subjection: Attitudes to Women in Early-Modern Society*: London.

CHAPTER SEVEN

Crime and Popular Protest

STEVE HINDLE

On 28 June 1607, King James I issued a royal proclamation 'as well for suppressing of riotous assemblies about inclosures, as for reformation of Depopulations' (Larkin and Hughes 1973: 154–8). The context for this lengthy statement of the regime's attitudes towards civil commotion was the Midland Rising, a series of anti-enclosure protests which had spread throughout the counties of Leicestershire, Northampton-shire and Warwickshire in the late spring and early summer of 1607, and which had culminated in a pitched battle at Newton in Rockingham Forest. On 8 June the deputy-lieutenant of Northamptonshire had confronted over a thousand 'levellers' who had assembled to dig out enclosures, ordered them to disperse in the king's name, and (when they refused) routed them, slaying fifty men in the field, and capturing many others who were later hanged, drawn and quartered in accordance with the terrifying logic of exemplary punishment (Gay 1905; Martin 1983: 159–215; Manning 1988: 229–46).

James's proclamation was entirely characteristic of the ambivalent response of the early Stuart regime to episodes of popular protest. In the first place, he insisted on the paramount need for the execution of severe justice against the rebels:

> We will prefer the safetie, quiet and protection of our subjects in generall, and of the body of our State, before the compassion of any such offenders, bee they more or less, and howsoever misled: and must forget our natural clemency by pursuing them with all severity for their so hainous Treasons, as well by our Armes as Lawes, knowing well, that We are bound (as the head of the politike body of our Realme) to follow the course which the best Phisitians use in dangerous diseases, which is, by a sharpe remedy applyed to a small and infected part, to save the whole from dissolution and destruction. (Larkin and Hughes 1973: 156)

Yet James also determined to redress the grievances – covetousness in the country-side, and the depopulating enclosure which was its most visible symptom – which had initially provoked the levellers' insurrection:

> We doe notifie and declare to all our loving Subjects, That We are resolved, not out of any apprehension or regard of these tumults and disorders . . . nor to satisfie disobedient people, be they rich or poore: But meerely out of love of Justice [and] Christian compassion of other of our Subjects . . . As also out of our Princely care and providence to preserve our people from decay or dimunition, To cause the abuses of Depopulations

and unlawfull Inclosures to be further looked into, and by peaceable and orderly meanes to establish such a reformation thereof, as shall bee needfull for the just reliefe of those that have just cause to complaine, and therin neglect no remedy, which either the lawes of our realme doe prescribe, or our owne Royall Authority, with the advice of our Councell can supply. (Ibid.: 157)

In denouncing to the rioters 'the same severe punishment which belongeth to Rebels in the highest degree' yet simultaneously resolving 'graciously to lend our eares to humble and just complaints and to afford our people Justice and favour', James not only provided posterity with a classic statement of the self-image of Renaissance monarchy, he also articulated the binary oppositions – quiet rather than commotion, safety rather than danger – which together constituted the Stuart ideology of order (ibid.: 158).

In this antithesis of order and disorder lies the key to understanding the pattern of seventeenth-century popular protest. Commonplace statements about the desirability of order belie the confidence of the Stuart regime. England from the 1590s, arguably even from the 1530s, may well have been a police state, but if so it was a police state without police. Popular awareness of a tradition of disorder, a custom of disobedience, enabled the populace if not to dictate, then at least to influence, the terms of their subordination. For if there was one set of dichotomies in James's proclamation, there was also another: while violent protest would inevitably lead to punishment, peaceful complaint might lead to redress. In what follows, the pattern of crime and popular protest in seventeenth-century England will be contextualized within this participatory political culture, in which authority was not only experienced, but actually often exercised by, relatively humble people. Nowhere is this degree of participation more clearly evident than in the prosecution of crime.

Crime and Criminal Justice

In early modern England the successful prosecution of criminal behaviour within a system of common law depended very largely upon the victims of crime: 93 per cent of criminal prosecutions in East Sussex were brought by victims in the period 1592–1640 (Herrup 1987: 93–130). This system of private prosecution by definition renders the measurement of the frequency of disorder extremely difficult. As we shall see, quantitative analyses of indictments are vulnerable to the possibility, arguably even a probability, that crimes prosecuted were only a small proportion of those committed. As an alternative, historians have engaged in qualitative, though not invariably impressionistic, analysis of the behaviour of specific social groups, a tendency which has resulted in interpretative polarization, especially in the historiography of violent crime. Lawrence Stone long ago portrayed the jangling nerves, intemperate language and retributive rage which characterized the conduct of the Elizabethan and early Stuart nobility, a picture which was only slightly modified by the sophisticated reading of the honour complex of Tudor aristocrats provided in a seminal essay by Mervyn James (Stone 1965; James 1986: 308–415). Alan Macfarlane (1980), by contrast, sought to demonstrate that the yeomanry of England were by comparison relatively restrained, generally unmoved by the kind of irrational anger and fury to which their social superiors so often fell prey. Both views are of course partial and blinkered, and extrapolate a picture of social behaviour in general from that of particular social groups. There were admittedly special cases: some areas, especially the Scottish and Welsh borders, and some social groups, were especially disorderly even at the end of the sixteenth century, and the civilizing process of pacification seems to have taken longer in these regions and for these groups than elsewhere (Reinmuth 1970: 231–50). The taming of the nobility was not, however, achieved exclusively by conciliar policing of lawless aristocrats in the court of Star Chamber. The social values of the elite had undoubtedly shifted by the early seventeenth century as the martial and chivalric codes of a warrior caste were transmogrified into the civic and humanist ethos of a service nobility (James 1986: 375–91). The decline of outright lawlessness also probably owed much to the changing technology of brawling, as weapons were carried less frequently. Pacification, however, came at a price: pacific forms of combat found expression in the law courts, which during the late Elizabethan and early Stuart period experienced an astonishing degree of 'hyperlexis', an unprecedented and unsurpassed increase of litigation which was fuelled partly by gentry instincts to retaliation and partly by the desire for distributive justice among the middling sort (Brooks 1986, 1998; Muldrew 1998: 299–371). Characterizing early modern society as 'lawless' is not, therefore, appropriate: 'popular legalism', that general sense of law-mindedness which inevitably came to pervade a society in which so many social and economic relationships were engrossed on parchment and sealed in wax, seems to have been a fact of life for the governors of Stuart England, and the rule of law was part of the political creed of all Englishmen (Sharp 1985). This recognition poses in particularly acute form the problem of how to interpret the simultaneous coexistence of, on the one hand, a sophisticated popular legal culture and, on the other, a behavioural pattern that suggests that criminal and disorderly conduct was, if not more widespread, at least more frequently prosecuted at the turn of the sixteenth century.

Much scholarly controversy over the profile of *violent* crime in early modern England has turned on what has turned out to be a *question mal posée*: 'how violent was a violent society?' Indeed, this issue has itself provoked something of a historiographical brawl (Sharpe 1981; Stone 1983, 1985; Sharp 1985; Cockburn 1991). Although the controversy over the 'violence-we-have-lost' debate seems to have died down since the mid-1980s as more sophisticated readings have been offered of the place of violence within English society, it is important to recognize that homicide may not in fact be the most sensitive or even the most appropriate index of violence. The plenitude of evidence for homicide in judicial records is itself, moreover, a function of the very sophisticated law of homicide, in which murder and manslaughter had long been distinguished and which was effectively policed by coroners and their juries (Gaskill 2000: 206–9). Even so, when the first generation of historians of crime engaged in positivist fashion in the serial analysis of indictments to measure the incidence of crime, it is unsurprising that they turned first to homicide, a crime that was by definition difficult to conceal and therefore likely to be relatively unaffected by the problems of under-recording and of the 'dark figure' of unprosecuted deviance. These investigations 'proved' that the homicide rate was three times higher in the seventeenth century than in the twentieth. In turn, it was argued that the seventeenth century was a decisive turning point in the transition from crimes of violence to crimes against property, a transition which, it is argued, characterized most societies experiencing the growth of capitalism. The fall in the homicide rate between the sixteenth and eighteenth centuries, argued Stone (1983), was entirely consistent with such a transition from *violence* to *vol*. There were also intriguing characteristics of the profile of serious violent crime as it was reconstructed on the basis of these researches: what slaughter there was seems to have been rather more (though by no means exclusively) *casual* than is the case today. While over half the homicides committed so far in twenty-first century England are domestic, only 21 per cent of those committed in early seventeenth-century Essex were committed by a member of the household (Sharpe 1981). This picture of a relatively high degree of spontaneous violence is reinforced to a certain extent by what seems to have been a general absence of psychological trauma that criminologists have taught us to expect in the aftermath of murder. It was, apparently, very uncommon for murderers to commit suicide (MacDonald and Murphy 1990). Part of the reason for this may lie in the most common circumstances that resulted in violent death: most were simply episodes of aggravated assault between quarrelling neighbours in an alehouse (Sharp 1985). Most homicide trials ended, accordingly, in manslaughter verdicts. Women, intriguingly, were very rarely indicted. All these insights are drawn from a body of evidence which is notoriously unsuited to long-term comparison over time, not least because of the changing levels of medical care since the early modern period, which implies that many episodes of aggravated assault resulted in death in the seventeenth century which could be resolved with a speedy (although doubtless time-consuming) visit to an accident and emergency ward in the twenty-first (Cockburn 1991).

It follows that the distinction between serious and less serious violent crime is rather more difficult to draw than might at first be thought. Assault was far less well defined in English law than might be expected: it might be tried in manorial courts, at quarter sessions or in the civil courts (King 1996). Prosecutions were brought privately by the victim, and expense was inevitably a deterrent: hence the 'dark figure' of unprosecuted assault must have been very high indeed. One far less expensive and more flexible alternative was the practice of swearing the peace against an opponent: the antagonist was then bound by recognizance with sureties not to break the peace towards the victim, or indeed to anybody within the community. This system of binding over – a quasi-formal prosecution that might be initiated whether or not an assault had actually taken place – was extremely popular, especially among the 'middling sort' of people (Hindle 1996). Although there were some 652 assault indictments at Essex quarter sessions between 1620 and 1680, there were some 1,688 peace bonds, a ratio of over 3 : 1 (Sharpe 1983: 116–17). Despite magistrates' insistence on an oath that the intended victim was genuinely in fear of his life, swearing the peace in this manner was doubtless open to abuse, and bonds were often insisted upon rather out of 'malice' than of any genuine 'matter'. At least one magistrate, the Cheshire JP Sir Richard Grosvenor, thought it 'tow common a way of revenge upon the least unkindnes' (Cust 1996: 37).

The overall picture of crimes against the person in the seventeenth century, then, appears to be one in which a fair degree of petty violence was tolerated. There was a general familiarity within the populace of the practice of corporal punishment, which found expression not only in the whippings of petty offenders at public courts, but also in the discipline and correction of faults by husbands, fathers and masters within the little commonwealth of the household (Amussen 1995). The key

distinction which might be made is between *violence*, which was in certain circumstances regarded as a desirable means of exercising authority; and *violation*, the
illegitimate or excessive use of force in maintaining social and political relations.
Homicide, by extension, was never condoned and was accordingly treated with
severity.

Serious crimes of violence seem, however, to have been far less common than
serious crimes against property. Indeed the criminal justice system is most plausibly
described as an apparatus for the protection of private property rather than of the
public peace (Hay 1975; Lawson 1988). Theft was very neatly defined in English law,
but two fundamental distinctions affected the sentencing and punishment that might
result from conviction. In the first place, the law distinguished between the 'felony'
(or capital crime) of grand larceny, involving the theft of goods worth more than
1 shilling, on the one hand, and the 'misdemeanour' (for which the death penalty by
definition did not apply) of petty larceny, the theft of any goods worth less than
1 shilling, on the other (Cockburn 1985: 66). It should be noted, however, that
long-run sixteenth-century price inflation had driven the value of many stolen goods
across the 12–pence threshold, with the result that more and more thefts were likely
by definition to have been felonious. In the second place, some serious property
crimes, especially grand larceny, were subject to 'benefit of clergy' – the judicial fiction
whereby the ability to read the so-called 'neck verse' (Psalm 51.1) would preclude
the punishment of a convicted felon by hanging and restrict the judge to issuing the
sentence of a public branding on the thumb – while others, especially burglary
and horse theft, were not (Cockburn 1985: 117–21). Women were also entitled to
'plead the belly', a claim tested by the physical examination of her body for signs of
pregnancy by a jury of matrons, although this too was probably a form of judicial
mitigation which was in practice derived more from readings of female reputation
than of the actual existence of an unborn child (Cockburn 1985: 121–3; Oldham
1985). This suggestion is confirmed in the most surprising judicial fiction of all, that
women were allowed to plead clergy in some cases of larceny from 1623 and universally from 1693 (Cockburn 1985: 118).

As might be expected there has been considerable historiographical controversy
over the incidence of property crime in seventeenth-century England. The classic
contemporary pessimistic statement about the scale of unprosecuted theft was provided in 1596 by the Somerset magistrate and MP Sir Edward Hext, who thought
that one-fifth of the victims of property crime were deterred from prosecution by the
'trouble' of travelling to the assizes and the 'charge' of legal fees (Tawney and Power
1924: II, 340). This assessment has proved to be the foundation of the so-called
'interactionist' position in the historiography of criminal justice, which implies that it
is impossible to allow for the numerous fluctuating variables that might have influenced decision-making by the various protagonists in the criminal justice system –
victims, witnesses, constables, magistrates – to reveal a plausible measure of the scale
of property crime that was actually committed (Lenman and Parker 1980).

On the other hand, the striking rise in the *prosecution* of property crime in the
period 1580–1630, so skilfully documented in Peter Lawson's (1986) painstaking
analysis of the records of the Hertfordshire assizes and quarter sessions, not only
exceeded the rate of population growth but also fluctuated dramatically in the
immediate aftermaths of the harvest failures of 1586–7, 1594–7 and 1622–4. This

trend has plausibly been taken to imply the widespread and increasing indictment both of vagrants and of the respectable poor for petty theft, in turn a function of the prominence of opportunistic pilfering in the makeshift economy of the poor, a survival strategy which might genuinely justify crimes of necessity in years of poor harvest or industrial depression (ibid.). These speculations are lent further credence by Jim Sharpe's detailed analysis of the different profiles of theft prosecutions in two Essex villages in the period 1620–80: while the trend of prosecution for larceny in the context of the stable poverty of agrarian Heydon was low and even, it was high and fluctuating amid the unstable poverty of industrial Coggeshall (Sharpe 1983: 199–201). The attractions of this 'neo-positivist' reading of the archives of criminal justice notwithstanding, it is abundantly clear that prosecutions for property crime were associated with the very significant element of discretion within the system: both the victims of theft, and those law officers – constables and magistrates – responsible for helping to bring these indictments to court generally preferred out-of-court settlement wherever that was possible. From the traditional perspective, which idealized mercy and charity as the twin pillars of the Christian commonwealth, the various informal or quasi-formal steps in the disputing process – forgiveness, composition, mediation and arbitration – were infinitely preferable than the 'pick-purse lawing' associated with formal indictment (Roberts 1983; Hindle 1996; Muldrew 1996). Even magistrates themselves recognized the desirability of acting rather as chancellors, pacifying differences, than as judges, formally adjudicating disputes (Cust 1996: 37).

Discretion was, however, probably most potent in the hands of criminal trial jurors, whose verdicts generally suggest that these conscientious county freeholders often (though by no means invariably) found it possible to be merciful (Herrup 1987: 131–64; Lawson 1988). Indeed, some contemporary comment suggests that both grand and trial jurors were exercising their prerogative of clemency rather too blatantly: 'lawless juries', it was argued, were frequently returning verdicts against the evidence, their 'fond and foolish pity' serving to usurp the powers of judicial mitigation which should arguably reside only with judges and magistrates (Hindle 2000b: 133–4). There is some evidence in the archives of the criminal justice system to bear out this allegation: some 24 per cent of indictments were thrown out by the grand jurors of early seventeenth-century East Sussex; and 'pious perjury' (the artificial devaluing of goods stolen to ensure that the accused would be convicted of misdemeanour rather than of felony) seems to have been not only widespread but actually increasing across the whole home circuit in the early seventeenth century. Perhaps one in five grand larcenists were actually convicted only of petty larceny. (Herrup 1987: 114; Hindle 2000b: 134). A combination of these 'partial verdicts' at the behest of jurors and of benefit of clergy exercised by judges helps explain why as few as 6 per cent of sheep stealers were hanged in Elizabethan Essex (Samaha 1978). 'Clergy' was, moreover, emphatically not the final opportunity for a criminal to benefit from judicial discretion; there was also the possibility of either a judicial reprieve or a royal pardon even after conviction for felony (Beattie 1987). The likelihood that mercy would season justice in this way evidently varied according to the crime committed: while only 15 per cent of those convicted of the theft of foodstuffs hanged in early seventeenth-century East Sussex, the equivalent figure for convicted horse thieves was as high as 94 per cent. Judges as well as juries were apparently perfectly at ease with a distinction between crimes of necessity on the one hand and crimes of profit on the other (Herrup 1987: 169). The letter and spirit of the law were therefore differentiated in seventeenth-century England, but that differentiation was probably not an accidental by-product of the inefficiency of an amateur system of law enforcement.

On the contrary, the flexibility of the criminal law as it was applied was a direct product of the structural characteristics of the system. Historians argued in the 1970s that the eighteenth-century criminal justice system was a vengeful tool of a landed elite that was determined to exercise its discretionary power to enforce a fat and swelling sheaf of felony statutes in the interests of private property (Hay 1975). There has, however, been much more emphasis in the recent literature on the relatively broad social base from which discretion was exercised: by victims, by constables, and by jurors, as well as by judges (Herrup 1987). The seventeenth-century criminal justice system was therefore characterized by a significant degree of participation. Lest this system be thought benevolent and sympathetic to those who were huddled through the dock by the half dozen at assizes, it should be remembered that clemency could never be guaranteed. Exemplary punishment was often necessary, and was applied most commonly to those who were not settled members of the community in either a moral or geographical sense, especially at times of instability (King 1984; Lawson 1988); hence the judicial carnage of the period 1580–1630 which saw a penal death rate of quite shocking proportions (Jenkins 1986). Although the precise mechanics of discretion remain controversial among those historians who have debated the balance of power in the seventeenth-century criminal trial, there seems to be little doubt about the principles upon which such discretion was exercised (Herrup 1987: 131–64; Lawson 1988; Hindle 2000b: 131–4).

The system of criminal justice in seventeenth-century Englishmen was, therefore, harsh if not downright ferocious. Assizes were bloody when they had to be and were undoubtedly ghastly by twenty-first century standards; the accused enjoyed no right to defence counsel; criminal trials lasted only a matter of minutes; jurors delivered their verdicts in batches in an atmosphere which was conducive at the very least to haste if not to partiality (Cockburn 1988). This was not, then, an insensitive, brutal age but one whose range of sympathy could be extremely limited. The popularity of those 'last dying speeches' recited by repentant felons on the scaffold amid the spectacle of ritualized public executions, and subsequently published to serve the wider polemical purposes of moralists on either side of the confessional divide, is a powerful reminder that the bottom line of the English criminal law was the apparatus of social discipline which came to litter the streets and marketplaces of communities across the land: the stocks, pillories, whipping posts and scaffolds which symbolized the monopoly of violence claimed by the Stuart state (Sharpe 1985; Lake and Questier 1996).

Popular Protest

By contrast, it has become clear that seventeenth-century popular culture in general, and popular protest in particular, were characterized by relatively *low* levels of violence. As Edward Thompson famously demonstrated, eighteenth-century food riots were emphatically not violent outrages conducted by wild mobs (Thompson 1991:

185–258). In a manifesto for the study of 'crown actions' which has subsequently been adopted by students of popular protest not only in early modern England but also throughout the historical and contemporary world, Thompson emphasized that interpretations of the behaviour of the rioting crowd have been constrained by two historical influences. In the first place, he insisted, the rhetoric of contemporary elites, who conventionally described the rioting crowd as a 'many-headed monster' animated only by desperation and blind folly, should not necessarily be taken at face value. In the second, the very wide technical definition of riot in England as any unlawful act committed by three or more individuals should sensitize historians to the dangers of an exclusively legalistic reading of crowd behaviour. Once the rhetorical agenda of elite, especially judicial, descriptions of riots had been stripped away, Thompson argued, a more nuanced and realistic image of the riot could be reconstructed. Thus, rather than being mindless 'rebellions of the belly', grain riots were collective crowd actions, which expressed deeply felt and widely shared grievances, saturated with customary expectations of paternalism. These grievances 'operated within a popular consensus as to what were legitimate and what were illegitimate practices in marketing, milling, baking, etc. This in turn was grounded upon a traditional, consistent view of social norms and obligations, of the proper economic functions of several parties within the community, which taken together, can be said to constitute the moral economy of the poor' (ibid.: 188). This enormously influential argument emphasizes that the common people themselves were capable of developing sophisticated economic attitudes, even if they were less formally articulated than those of political economists like Adam Smith.

These twin principles of the right to subsistence and the respect for custom, it has been argued, not only characterized crowd behaviour in the eighteenth century, but played a fundamental role in constructing the popular mentalities of subordination over the preceding centuries (Sharp 1980; Wrightson 1982: 172–80). In large measure, the historiography of early modern popular protest has been dominated by the retrospective application of Thompson's eighteenth-century model to the rather richer depositional evidence generated in the course of prosecuting food rioters in the seventeenth century and earlier (Walter and Wrightson 1976; Walter 1980; Sharp 2000). Indeed, as we shall see, several aspects of the 'moral economy' thesis have been extrapolated not only to protests over subsistence but also to that other great manifestation of popular protest, the enclosure riot.

Seventeenth-century grain riots, it seems, characteristically occurred in years of harvest failure or industrial depression, though they were by no means an automatic response when standards of living fell. The most striking thing about the chronology and distribution of these episodes is not that there were so many outbreaks of food rioting, but so few. Rioting was evidently not an immediate reflex in times of hunger (Walter and Wrightson 1976; Walter 1989). Painstaking work in the judicial and administrative archives of central and local government has revealed that there were 'only' forty-five outbreaks between 1585 and 1660, despite the fact that these decades included several periods of prolonged dearth (Walter and Wrightson 1976: 26). Equally interesting is their geography. The protests appear to have been distributed in the context of a developing pattern of regional trade, and in particular they occurred as a result of local inequalities of supply created by an inadequately developed marketing system. Hence they were generally focused in heavily populated areas, in areas of industrial wage dependence, in ports or other centres from whence food was exported, and in urban markets. Overwhelmingly, it seems, they were characterized by discipline and restraint, and are best described as *demonstrations* rather than as *insurrections*. Crowds engaged in direct action only as the very last resort, as the last step in a ritual dance of complaint in which their grievances had previously been expressed in grumbling, in appealing and in petitioning (Walter 2001). Only very rarely did they involve violence.

Convinced of their own rectitude, rioters saw themselves as enforcing the king's good laws, as mimicking (perhaps even *mocking*) the magistrates' responsibility to regulate the grain market by ensuring that corn was sold from the expected hour, in customary measures, and at fair prices. These, then, were *taxations populaires* in which grain or other foodstuffs were rarely, if ever, stolen, and were frequently sold to the protesters at what was popularly considered to be a 'just' price. Accordingly, the most frequent targets of the rioting crowd were those who abused the grain market in order to profit from high prices: middle-men, millers, corn-factors and badgers, and less commonly the magistrates who failed to fulfil their quasi-legal obligations to punish them. The intention was that magistrates would be induced to enforce the marketing regulation stipulated not only by the mid-sixteenth century statutes on engrossing and forestalling, but also the marketing regulation stipulated under the royal prerogative in the 'books of orders' of the period 1577–1631 (Slack 1980, 1992). Indeed, food riots were generally, if not invariably, successful in this respect. Local magistrates very frequently fined the participants in food riots, but then proceeded to rectify the grievances which had actually provoked their moral outrage. The *locus classicus* are the two grain riots in the Essex port of Maldon in March and May 1629, the second and more violent of which is effectively the exception that proves the rule, in the sense that it took place when the local magistrates proved themselves either unwilling or incapable of remedying the distress which had provoked the first. In turn, the regime showed its ruthlessness, and four of the rioters – including a woman, 'Captain' Ann Carter – were hanged, an extremely unusual fate for those convicted of riot (Walter 1980).

A not dissimilar pattern of restraint and respect for the law has been suggested for enclosure riots. Their chronology is rather more unevenly spread. Anti-enclosure protest does seem to have played a role in the great uprisings of the early and mid-Tudor period, especially in the late 1540s when opposition to fiscal seigneurialism led to hedges being thrown down in commotions which spread outwards from the Hertfordshire villages of Cheshunt and Northaw across the whole of southern, eastern and midland England (Beer 1982: 140–63; Jones 2002). Overall, however, the pattern appears to be that enclosure riots were numerous and sporadic. Analysis of the archives of Star Chamber, admittedly a problematic source in the sense that allegations of riot were often legal fictions designed to bring a dispute within the cognizance of the prerogative courts, suggests a peculiar concentration of enclosure riots in the period 1590–1610 (Manning 1988). There certainly were geographical clusters: as we have seen, a series of anti-enclosure protests across Leicestershire, Northamptonshire and Warwickshire crystallized as the Midland Rising in the spring and summer of 1607 (Gay 1905). The crown's policies of disafforestation provoked protracted enclosure rioting in the wood-pasture zones of Gloucestershire and Worcestershire in the so-called Western Rising of 1628–32 (Sharp 1980). 'Levelling' fenmen organized large-scale opposition to the drainage policies of the crown across south Lincolnshire, Cambridgeshire and the Isle of Ely in the late 1630s and early 1640s (Lindley 1982). Characteristically these riots expressed respect for a normative agrarian order structured by customary rights. Like grain riots, they were frequently a matter of last resort and had often been preceded by the prior appeals and complaint, sometimes involving mediation by clergymen. Although cross-dressing (for reasons of symbolism or disguise) was not unknown in grain riots, enclosure riots seem to have more characteristically employed the informal sanctions of ridicule and reproach, involving anonymous threats, seditious libels and the use of synonyms to lend even greater mystique to charismatic – perhaps even entirely fictional – leaders: Captain Pouch at Newton (Northamptonshire) in 1607, Thomas Unhedgeall at Ladbroke (Warwickshire) in 1604, Lady Skimmington in the western forest in the 1620s (Gay 1905; Walter 2001; Sharp 1980). Anti-enclosure protest was often festive, sometimes arising from the affirmation of communal solidarity in the roga-tiontide perambulation, occasionally employing the rough music that characterized the popular shaming rituals or charivari to which those who had breached community norms were subjected (Underdown 1985: 115–16; Walter 1999: 101–2). Although, as this suggests, there was little attempt at stealth, rioters were often strategic, organizing the levelling of hedges by two persons at a time, or by women, or even by men dressed as women. This element of inversion was further elaborated in the ritualized treatment of the enclosures themselves; enclosed ground might be ritually ploughed up and sown; fences, gates and hedges might be burned, or (in a more poignant expression of agricultural symbolism) buried. Although enclosing landlords might be hanged in effigy, there was generally very little violence against persons (Hoyle 1997: 41). These inversion rituals notwithstanding, enclosure riots often embodied a significant degree of order within disorder: despite the fantasies of the elites that they were risings against the crown which merited full-scale prosecution under the treason statutes, they were not overtly aimed at overthrowing the social order or at rebellion. Indeed, they often took place with the complicity of other gentlemen or clergy, and in some cases were apparently stage-managed in order to provoke a hearing in the royal courts where the paternalistic instincts of the crown might be mobilized against aggressive landlords (Manning 1988).

All the evidence suggests that government response to enclosure protest was in fact rather moderate. In large measure, the early Stuart regime subscribed to the same view of the proper ordering of social and economic relations within the common-wealth as did the rioters (Slack 1999: 53–76). Although the agrarian policies of the Caroline period ultimately became smeared with the trail of finance, the active policing of seigneurial abuses served to restore the credibility, even to vindicate the paternalistic credentials, of the government. Cumulatively, then, riots served to establish the terms on which the poor based their obedience. In the context of the field-of-force of seventeenth-century social relations, relations of paternalism and deference were perforce not only *reciprocal* but *conditional*, and both patricians and plebs were only too aware that the tradition of riot – the widely recognized 'custom of disobedience' – might contain within itself an element of tacit negotiation (Thompson 1991: 73; Hindle 1996: 178). Where the rioting crowd did succeed in provoking sympathetic intervention from the government, however, it is important to recognize the limitations of state action. Government policies never succeeded in reversing economic trends, although they might well moderate their rigour. By the end of the seventeenth century the moral authority of traditional economic values had been eroded by the sheer weight of practice, and economic activity had gradually been separated from social morality (J. Appleby 1978; Clay 1984: II, 236–50; Wrightson 2000: 202–26). Although the government ultimately recognized its duty as the amelioration of distress attendant upon enclosure, its immediate priority was almost invariably the enforcement of the law.

By the mid-1980s, students of popular protest were in broad agreement on this reading of the social and political dynamics of bread and enclosure riots in particular and crowd actions in general (Sharp 1985). Apart from an ongoing debate among historians about the profile of social participation on rural protest (to which we shall return), the historiography of riot had become so dominated by the Thompsonian paradigm that there was effectively no debate to be had. More recently, however, the cultural hegemony of the moral economy paradigm has come under scrutiny from a number of different directions (Stevenson 1985; Wood 2001). In the first place, there is growing disquiet about the plausibility of reconstructing the popular mental-ities of subordination from crowd behaviour rather than from their expressed thoughts. Although, as we have seen, there were several occasions on which crowd action was preceded by the presentation of formal petitions, there are obvious dangers in ascribing a set of attitudes to the rioting crowd in the majority of instances in which explicit evidence is conspicuous by its absence. To this we might add the related question of the extent to which 'the crowd' had a single homogeneous set of attitudes at all. The sense that we should recognize the existence of individual faces within the rioting crowd has also raised anxieties about the ability of the Thompso-nian model to explain why some members of the community rioted and why others did not (Woods 1983). There has also been more general scepticism about the dangers of an *ex post facto* reading of riots, which emphasizes, possibly even exagger-ates, the tradition of 'order within disorder'. After all, it is abundantly clear that elites were very often terrified.

Finally, although Thompson emphasized the public, even the theatrical, nature of postures of paternalism and deference, historians have come to realize the desirability of reconstructing the 'hidden transcript' of popular mentalities of subordination. This last direction has proved to be among the more fruitful lines of historical enquiry into the tradition of riot as students of protest have drawn upon the insights of the rural anthropologist James C. Scott to think more broadly about the weapons that the weak might employ as they confronted the forces of authority (Scott 1985, 1990). Sensitive analysis of the ballads and libels composed and transcribed in alehouses, and of the rumours and rhymes broadcast in churchyards and market-places, has done much to disclose the contours of a semi-concealed dissident subculture, a saturnalia of power, in which the plebeian voice was rather less deferential than ruling elites might have liked to have heard (Fox 1994, 1997, 2000). From this perspective we can see that there was in fact a continuum of popular protest extending from gossip to mockery to full-scale insurrection, a spectrum whose range and depth is only dis-torted by refracting it through the evidential prism of riot (Rollison 1992: 202).

As historians have probed deeper into the customary consciousness that informed crowd actions, the question of local and regional geography and peculiar chronology of rioting has become all the more urgent. In the first place, it is abundantly clear that there is a fundamental lack of symmetry between the chronologies of enclosure rioting on the one hand and of the development of capitalist property rights on the other. J. R. Wordie would have us believe that the enclosure rate peaked in England in the late seventeenth century, a period in which the tradition of rural disorder appears to have been dying (Wordie 1983; Hindle 2000a). The nature and scale of anti-enclosure protest seems to have changed markedly after the Restoration, a particularly significant development in the light of the rapidly expanding acreage of enclosed land. Although the scarcity of enclosure rioting might in part be an optical illusion caused by the disappearance of the archival resources of the court of Star Chamber (abolished in 1641) in which it had once been so visibly represented, 'the scattered evidence that exists suggests that although the English rural population continued to defend their common rights when they were threatened, they did so less often and with less determination' (Underdown 1996: 123). In part, the retreat from open opposition to enclosure reflects the stance of the regime itself. Because riot was often a continuation of litigation by other means, both formal and informal protests were vulnerable to the law of diminishing returns. When the courts were notoriously ambivalent about the injustices of enclosure, there was little point in attempts to mobilize the support of judges and crown lawyers. The relative quiescence of enclosed fields and wastes probably also reflects the 'local re-coalescence of elite power after the Restoration' (Wood 1999: 296). Not only were the yeomen who had once been the natural leaders of communal protests over access to the perquisites of waste now fully persuaded of the benefits of enclosure, but the consolidation of the 'social economy' of dearth in the form of discretionary parish relief and gentry paternalism also perforce inhibited freedom of political action among the poor. The 'social economy' not only offered the poor protection from famine, it endowed the propertied with both 'protection from the fear of disorder and the validation of their authority'. In conferring upon rural elites the right to define eligibility, parish relief in particular ensured that although the poor of Restoration England 'escaped a "crisis of subsistence", many fell victim to a "crisis of dependence"' (Walter 1989: 127–8).

Although the lack of any systematic study of popular protest in the 1660s and 1670s renders dangerous any generalization about the scale, nature and significance of grain riots in the late seventeenth century, it is nonetheless clear that the years of marginal surplus in food production immediately after the Restoration saw fewer food riots than the 1620s and 1630s. When the harvest failed so spectacularly in the 1690s, dearth did not lead to starvation as it had done in the 1590s, but it nonetheless seems there was a rediscovery of the tradition of social turbulence, with perhaps as many as twenty-four separate episodes of riot clustering in the years 1693–5 (Appleby 1979; Underdown 1996: 122–3). These crowd actions exhibited a marked similarity to those *taxations populaires* of 1629–31 that had emulated government policy in preventing exports and selling grain at what was considered to be a just price. In several respects, therefore, the long-term legacy of the 'book of orders' was the popular recognition of the desirability of market regulation.

Although, therefore, broad understandings of the significance of the ideology of custom now inform understandings of riot, it remains the case that the 'moral economy' paradigm cannot in and of itself explain the geography of rioting. As more nuanced understandings of custom have emerged in the literature, recognition of the local particularlism of customary consciousness has come to the fore (Thompson

1991: 97–184; Wrightson 1996: 22–5; Wood 1997, 1999). Custom was by definition *lex loci*, and customary consciousness was above all local. This has led historians
into very precise investigations of the *local* configurations of interest, which in turn
created unusual 'loops of association' in the pattern of rural protest (Hindle 1998;
Wood 1999; Hipkin 2000). This represents a considerable advance on the relatively
unsophisticated class-based readings of the social profile of participation adopted by
the first students of rural protest, who felt able to characterize the riots of the 1620s
and 1630s as artisanal in the west country and gentrified in the east (Sharp 1980;
Lindley 1982).

The proliferation of these local studies of seventeenth-century social protest
is surely to be welcomed. Despite recent scepticism that we cannot hope to generalize
from individual episodes, no matter how well documented they might be, it remains
true that local circumstances were almost certainly decisive in influencing the experience of, and responses to, change. The problem lies, rather, in the nature of the
generalizations about social relations that early modernists have drawn from
these case studies. One promising line of enquiry recognizes that, despite Oliver
Cromwell's idealized vision of a definitive 'good and great interest of the nation'
embodied in the static 'ranks of orders and men whereby England has been known for
hundreds of years', 'interest' was a compound of the fluctuating perceptions and
attitudes not only of those noblemen, gentlemen and yeomen to whom the lord
protector referred, but also of those husbandmen and labouring men who were
no less capable of social and political action. Shifting configurations of *interest*
within the social order of individual communities are therefore crucial, and will
repay further investigation. Although historians have a general sense of the social
order that conditions our understanding of the 'mediate structuration' of class
relationships in early modern England, it is the intimacies of 'proximate structuration'
that really matter on the ground: that is to say that the same social components
might well be reconfigured in different, often highly localized, economic and political
situations. Certain specific issues might therefore cause the crystallization of powerful solidarities within one local hierarchy while simultaneously creating conflict
elsewhere.

Conclusion

The investigation of the particular geographies and sociologies of protest has focused
attention in particular on those communities where a long-standing and highly
localized tradition of protest appears to have developed over time. It is abundantly
clear that the reputation for disorderliness enjoyed by certain areas was not entirely
manufactured by elites distrustful – or blindly uncomprehending – of the economic
sophistication implicit in the exploitation of common rights (Neeson 1993: 32–4;
Wood 1999: 1–8). In the forest parishes of Northamptonshire or the lead-mining
communities of the Peak District, there really was a custom of disobedience,
a tradition of disorder which was an unconscionable time dying long after lowland
arable fielden England had been pacified. In this sense, perhaps, Andrew Appleby's
famous insight captures an essential truth: there really were 'two Englands', characterized not simply as Appleby thought by differing patterns of market integration, but
also by divergent experiences of governance (Appleby 1979).

The governance of rural parishes did not, after all, inhere in one class or another, but developed from the tension between different groups both within and beyond the social field of the local community. It is overwhelmingly clear that pastoral and arable regions were characterized by significantly different degrees of participation in the process of governance. The political geography of pastoral areas was relatively independent of gentry influence, and the associational life of the community was dominated by men of more humble status. In some cases, at least, this might permit the appropriation by the middling sort of the vestry – an arena which, after all, was potentially gentry-controlled – as a body within which a sophisticated political culture of rights might develop. In the arable areas, by contrast, participation was moulded, if not directly controlled, by landholding gentry who asserted their private interests through patronage and through the authority of such public institutions as quarter sessions. This had very substantial significance for the meaning of the rule of law in the two types of community: in the pastoral regions, as at Caddington in the Chiltern hills, vestries might exercise their responsibilities to guarantee the rights not only of their members but also of their subordinates (Hindle 1998). In the arable regions, as at Terling, parish governance was much more likely to be a matter of social control by local elites, acting in the interests of their gentry patrons (Wrightson and Levine 1995). Such an analysis is obviously predicated upon the 'ideal types' of community which have become familiar as conceptual tools in early modern historiography. Although there were obviously more subtle complexities at play in the process by which ten thousand parishes became integrated into a single political society, it is to these micro-sociologies of power that historians must look in seeking to explain the shifting patterns of crime and disorder in seventeenth-century England.

REFERENCES

Amussen, S. 1995: 'Punishment, discipline and power: the social meanings of violence in early modern England', *Journal of British Studies*, 34 (January), 1–34.

Appleby, A. B. 1978: *Famine in Tudor and Stuart England*: Liverpool.

Appleby, A. B. 1979: 'Grain prices and subsistence crises in England and France, 1590–1740', *Journal of Economic History*, 39, 4 (December), 865–87.

Appleby, J. 1978: *Economic Thought and Ideology in Seventeenth Century England*: Princeton, NJ.

Beattie, J. M. 1987: 'The royal pardon and criminal procedure in early modern England', *Historical Papers/Communications Historiques*, 1–14.

Beer, B. L. 1982: *Rebellion and Riot: Popular Disorder During the Reign of Edward VI*: Kent, OH.

Bossy, J. 1983: 'Postscript.' In J. Bossy, ed., *Disputes and Settlements: Law and Human Relations in the West*: Cambridge.

Brooks, C. W. 1986: *Pettyfoggers and Vipers of the Commonwealth: The 'Lower Branch' of the Legal Profession in Early Modern England*: Cambridge.

Brooks, C. W. 1998: *Lawyers, Litigation and English Society Since 1450*: London.

Clay, C. 1984: *Economic Expansion and Social Change: England, 1500–1700*, 2 vols: Cambridge.

Cockburn, J. S. 1985: 'Introduction.' In J. S. Cockburn, ed., *Calendar of Assize Records: Home Circuit Indictments, Elizabeth I and James I, Introduction*: London.

Cockburn, J. S. 1988: 'Twelve silly men? The trial jury at assizes, 1560–1670.' In J. S. Cockburn and T. A. Green, eds, *Twelve Good Men and True: The Criminal Trial Jury in England, 1200–1800*: Princeton, NJ.

Cockburn, J. S. 1991: 'Patterns of violence in English society: homicide in Kent 1560–1985', *Past and Present*, 130 (February), 70–106.

Cust, R. (ed.) 1996: *The Papers of Sir Richard Grosvenor, 1st Bart. (1585–1645)*. Record Society of Lancashire and Cheshire 134.

Dean, D. 1996: *Law-Making and Society in Late Elizabethan England: The Parliament of England, 1584–1601*: Cambridge.

Fox, A. 1994: 'Ballads, libels and popular ridicule in Jacobean England', *Past and Present*, 145 (November), 47–83.

Fox, A. 1997: 'Rumour, news and popular political opinion in Elizabethan and early Stuart England', *Historical Journal*, 40, 3, 597–620.

Fox, A. 2000: *Oral and Literate Culture in England, 1500–1700*: Oxford.

Gaskill, M. 2000: *Crime and Mentalities in Early Modern England*: Cambridge.

Gay, E. F. 1905: 'The Midland revolt and the inquisitions of depopulation of 1607', *Transactions of the Royal Historical Society*, new series, 18, 195–244.

Hay, D. 1975: 'Property, authority and the criminal law.' In D. Hay, P. Linebaugh, J. G. Rule, E. P. Thompson and C. Winslow, eds, *Albion's Fatal Tree: Crime and Society in Eighteenth-Century England*: London.

Herrup, C. B. 1987: *The Common Peace: Participation and the Criminal Law in Seventeenth-Century England*: Cambridge.

Hindle, S. 1996: 'The keeping of the public peace.' In P. Griffiths, A. Fox and S. Hindle, eds, *The Experience of Authority in Early Modern England*: London.

Hindle, S. 1998: 'Persuasion and protest in the Caddington common enclosure dispute, 1635–39', *Past and Present*, 158 (February), 37–78.

Hindle, S. 2000a: 'The growth of social stability in Restoration England', *The European Legacy*, 5, 4 (August), 563–76.

Hindle, S. 2000b: *The State and Social Change in Early Modern England, c.1550–1640*: London.

Hipkin, S. 2000: '"Sitting on his penny rent": conflict and right of common in Faversham Blean, 1595–1610', *Rural History*, 11, 1, 1–35.

Hoyle, R. W. 1997: 'The forest under the Dynhams.' In J. Broad and R. Hoyle, eds, *Bernwood: The Life and Afterlife of a Forest*: Preston.

James, M. 1986: 'English politics and the concept of honour, 1485–1642.' In M. James, *Society, Politics and Culture: Studies in Early Modern England*: Cambridge.

Jenkins, P. 1986: 'From gallows to prison? The execution rate in early modern England', *Criminal Justice History*, 7, 51–71.

Jones, A. C. 2002: 'Commotion time: the English risings of 1549.' Unpublished Ph.D. thesis: University of Warwick.

King, P. 1984: 'Decision-makers and decision-making in the English criminal law, 1750–1800', *Historical Journal*, 27, 1, 25–58.

King, P. 1996: 'Punishing assault: the transformation of attitudes in the English courts', *Journal of Interdisciplinary History*, 27, 1 (summer), 43–74.

Lake, P. and Questier, M. 1996: 'Agency, appropriation and rhetoric under the gallows: Puritans, Romanists and the state in early modern England', *Past and Present*, 153 (November), 64–107.

Larkin, J. F., and Hughes, P. L. (eds) 1973: *Stuart Royal Proclamations, Vol. 1: Royal Proclamations of King James I, 1603–1625*: Oxford.

Lawson, P. G. 1986: 'Property crime and hard times in England, 1559–1624', *Law and History Review*, 4, 95–127.

Lawson, P. G. 1988: 'Lawless juries? The composition and behaviour of Hertfordshire juries, 1573–1624.' In J. S. Cockburn and T. A. Green, eds, *Twelve Good Men and True: The English Criminal Trial Jury, 1200–1800*: Princeton, NJ.

Lenman, B. and Parker, G. 1980: 'The state, the community and the criminal law in early modern Europe.' In V. A. C. Gatrell, B. Lenman and G. Parker, eds, *Crime and the Law: The Social History of Crime in Western Europe Since 1500*: London.

Lindley, K. 1982: *Fenland Riots and the English Revolution*: London.

MacDonald, M. and Murphy, T. R. 1990: *Sleepless Souls: Suicide in Early Modern England*: Oxford.

Macfarlane, A. 1980: *The Justice and the Mare's Ale: Law and Disorder in Seventeenth-Century England*: Cambridge.

Manning, R. B. 1988: *Village Revolts: Social Protest and Popular Disturbances in England 1509–1640*: Oxford.

Martin, J. E. 1983: *Feudalism to Capitalism: Peasant and Landlord in English Agrarian Development*: London.

Muldrew, C. 1996: 'The culture of reconciliation: community and the settlement of economic disputes in early modern England', *Historical Journal*, 39, 4, 915–42.

Muldrew, C. 1998: *The Economy of Obligation: The Culture of Credit and Social Relations in Early Modern England*: London.

Neeson, J. M. 1993: *Commoners: Common Right, Enclosure and Social Change in England, 1700–1820*: Cambridge.

Oldham, J. C. 1985: 'On pleading the belly: a history of the jury of matrons', *Criminal Justice History*, 6, 1–64.

Reinmuth, H. S. 1970: 'Border society in transition.' In H. S. Reinmuth, ed., *Early Stuart Studies: Essays in Honour of David Harris Wilson*: Minneapolis.

Roberts, S. 1983: 'The study of dispute: anthropological perspectives.' In J. Bossy, ed., *Disputes and Settlements: Law and Human Relations in the West*: Cambridge.

Rollison, D. 1992: *The Local Origins of Modern Society: Gloucestershire, 1500–1800*: London.

Samaha, J. 1978: 'Hanging for felony: the rule of law in Elizabethan Colchester', *Historical Journal*, 21, 763–82.

Scott, J. C. 1985: *Weapons of the Weak: Everyday Forms of Peasant Resistance*: New Haven, CT.

Scott, J. C. 1990: *Domination and the Arts of Resistance: Hidden Transcripts*: New Haven, CT.

Sharp, B. 1980: *In Contempt of All Authority: Rural Artisans and Riot in the West of England, 1586–1660*: Los Angeles, CA.

Sharp, B. 1985: 'Popular protest in seventeenth-century England.' In B. Reay, ed., *Popular Culture in Seventeenth-Century England*: London.

Sharp, B. 2000: 'The food riots of 1347 and the medieval moral economy.' In A. Randall and A. Charlesworth, eds, *Moral Economy and Popular Protest: Crowds, Conflict and Authority*: London.

Sharpe, J. A. 1981: 'Domestic homicide in early modern England', *Historical Journal*, 24, 29–48.

Sharpe, J. A. 1983: *Crime in Seventeenth-century England: A County Study*: Cambridge.

Sharpe, J. A. 1985a: 'Debate: the history of violence in England, some observations', *Past and Present*, 108 (August), 206–15.

Sharpe, J. A. 1985b: '"Last dying speeches": religion, ideology and public execution in seventeenth-century England', *Past and Present*, 107 (May), 144–67.

Sharpe, J. A. 1985c: 'The people and the law.' In B. Reay, ed., *Popular Culture in Seventeenth-century England*: London.

Slack, P. 1980: 'Books of orders: the making of English social policy, 1577–1631', *Transactions of the Royal Historical Society*, 5th series, 30, 1–22.

Slack, P. 1992: 'Dearth and social policy in early modern England', *Social History of Medicine*, 5, 1, 1–17.

Slack, P. 1999: *From Reformation to Improvement: Public Welfare in Early Modern England*: Oxford.

Stevenson, J. 1985: 'The moral economy of the English crowd: myth and reality.' In A. Fletcher and J. Stevenson, eds, *Order and Disorder in Early Modern England*: Cambridge.

Stone, L. 1965: *The Crisis of the Aristocracy, 1558–1641*: Oxford.

Stone, L. 1983: 'Interpersonal violence in English society, 1300–1980', *Past and Present*, 101 (February), 22–33.

Stone, L. 1985: 'Debate: the history of violence in England, a rejoinder', *Past and Present*, 108 (August), 216–24.

Tawney, R. H. and Power, E. (eds) 1924: *Tudor Economic Documents*, 3 vols: London.

Thompson, E. P. 1991: *Customs in Common*: London.

Underdown, D. 1985: *Revel, Riot and Rebellion: Popular Politics and Culture in England, 1603–1660*: Oxford.

Underdown, D. 1996: *A Freeborn People: Politics and the Nation in Seventeenth-Century England*: Oxford.

Walter, J. 1980: 'Grain riots and popular attitudes to the law: Maldon and the crisis of 1629.' In J. Brewer and J. Styles, eds, *An Ungovernable People: The English and Their Law in the Seventeenth and Eighteenth Centuries*: London.

Walter, J. 1989: 'The social economy of dearth in early modern England.' In J. Walter and R. Schofield, eds, *Famine, Disease and the Social Order in Early Modern Society*: Cambridge.

Walter, J. 1999: *Understanding Popular Violence in the English Revolution: The Colchester Plunderers*: Cambridge.

Walter, J. 2001: 'Public transcripts, popular agency and the politics of subsistence in early modern England.' In M. Braddick and J. Walter, eds, *Negotiating Power in Early Modern Society: Order, Hierarchy and Subordination in Britain and Ireland*: Cambridge.

Walter, J. and Schofield, R. 1989: 'Famine, disease and crisis mortality in early modern society.' In J. Walter and R. Schofield, eds, *Famine, Disease and the Social Order in Early Modern Society*: Cambridge.

Walter, J. and Wrightson, K. 1976: 'Dearth and the social order in early modern England', *Past and Present*, 71 (May), 22–42.

Wood, A. 1997: 'The place of custom in plebeian political culture: England, 1550–1800', *Social History*, 22, 1 (January), 46–60.

Wood, A. 1999: *The Politics of Social Conflict: The Peak Country, 1520–1770*: Cambridge.

Wood, A. 2001: *Riot, Rebellion and Popular Politics in Early Modern England*: London.

Woods, R. L. 1983: 'Individuals in the rioting crowd: a new approach', *Journal of Interdisciplinary History*, 14, 1, 1–24.

Wordie, J. R. 1983: 'The chronology of English enclosure, 1500–1914', *Economic History Review*, 2nd series, 36, 4, 483–505.

Wrightson, K. 1982: *English Society, 1580–1680*: London.

Wrightson, K. 1996: 'The politics of the parish in early modern England.' In P. Griffiths, A. Fox and S. Hindle, eds, *The Experience of Authority in Early Modern England*: London.

Wrightson, K. 2000: *Earthly Necessities: Economic Lives in Early Modern Britain*: New Haven, CT.

Wrightson, K. and Levine, D. 1995: *Poverty and Piety in an English Village: Terling, 1525–1700*, 2nd edn: Oxford.

Wrigley, E. A. and Schofield, R. S. 1981: *The Population History of England, 1541–1871*: Cambridge.

FURTHER READING

Braddick, M. and Walter, J. (eds) 2001: *Negotiating Power in Early Modern Society: Order, Hierarchy and Subordination in Britain and Ireland*: Cambridge.

Brooks, C. W. 1986: *Pettyfoggers and Vipers of the Commonwealth: The 'Lower Branch' of the Legal Profession in Early Modern England*: Cambridge.

Cockburn, J. S. 1985: 'Introduction.' In J. S. Cockburn, ed., *Calendar of Assize Records: Home Circuit Indictments, Elizabeth I and James I, Introduction*: London.

Cockburn, J. S. and Green, T. A. (eds) 1988: *Twelve Good Men and True: The English Criminal Trial Jury, 1200–1800*: Princeton, NJ.

Fletcher, A. and Stevenson, J. (eds) 1985: *Order and Disorder in Early Modern England*: Cambridge.

Griffiths, P., Fox, A. and Hindle, S. (eds) 1996: *The Experience of Authority in Early Modern England*: London.

Herrup, C. B. 1987: *The Common Peace: Participation and the Criminal Law in Seventeenth-Century England*: Cambridge.

Sharpe, J. A. 1985: 'The people and the law.' In B. Reay, ed., *Popular Culture in Seventeenth-Century England*: London.

Sharpe, J. A. 1999: *Crime in Early Modern England, 1550–1750*, 2nd edn: London.

Thompson, E. P. 1991: *Customs in Common*: London.

Underdown, D. 1985: *Revel, Riot and Rebellion: Popular Politics and Culture in England, 1603–1660*: Oxford.

Wood, A. 2001: *Riot, Rebellion and Popular Politics in Early Modern England*: London.

Wrightson, K. 1996: 'The politics of the parish in early modern England.' In P. Griffiths, A. Fox and S. Hindle, eds, *The Experience of Authority in Early Modern England*: London.

Wrightson, K. 2000: *Earthly Necessities: Economic Lives in Early Modern Britain*: New Haven, CT.

CHAPTER EIGHT

Economic and Urban Development

CRAIG MULDREW

When James I arrived in England from Scotland in the late spring of 1603 it would not yet have been apparent that the following summer would produce the best harvest since 1592, and that the next three years would see the best harvests before 1618. Bread prices in London fell 100 per cent from their great height in 1596, so in terms of cost of living this marked a fortunate beginning to the new reign. Had Elizabeth died a few years earlier, however, the transition might have been more difficult, for the decade of the 1590s was not only one of war and political instability, but also witnessed one of the most severe economic depressions in English history, which cast a shadow over the first three decades of the new century. Understanding the nature and legacy of this crisis is crucial, as it highlights a number of themes central to any attempt to describe the early modern British economy. These are: population, the growth of the market, credit, rising food prices and the problem of growing poverty as a result.

The population of Tudor England had been expanding since the 1520s, which meant that a continually growing number of mouths to feed, and bodies to clothe and house, created more demand for goods than in any period hitherto. As a result, prices rose and created an incentive for farmers and artisans to produce more. Larger farmers and yeomen who had sizeable crops became wealthier by selling on the market to townsmen and to agricultural labourers, and the farmers used their new wealth to increase the size of their holdings by purchasing land from small-holders who were unable to survive as independent producers. Networks of distribution and marketing became more complex as traders took advantage of the profits which could be made by shipping goods to places where prices were high because demand was greatest. At the same time, purchasing power based on credit increased more rapidly than the technology of production and the organization of distribution, and this resulted in more than a century of constant inflation. In southern England, for example, food prices increased at least five-fold between 1530 and 1640, and the prices of industrial goods more than doubled (Clay 1984: I, 29–52). The purchase of land by larger farmers led to a reduction in the size and number of smallholdings, which in turn increased the number of landless agricultural labourers and those who did not have enough land to support themselves as producers, and who had to buy food on the market. This led to a growing cycle of demand as profits made from the increased sales of food as well as basic commodities such as clothing were invested in the purchase of more refined goods by wealthier individuals, in turn opening up more opportunities for employment in local manu-facturing trades.

As a result of this, consumption on the part of the middling sort, generally the wealthiest 20 per cent of society – yeomen, husbandmen, wealthy tradesmen and merchants – increased rapidly until the 1580s. The amount of goods recorded in samples of probate inventories (from Southampton, the parish of Chesterfield, and Lincolnshire) for this segment of the population roughly doubled between 1540 and 1585, while at the same time inflation drove up the prices of what was being bought. Although contemporaries blamed the import of American gold and silver into Europe for the continual inflation of the period, arguing that reduced scarcity led to a lowering of the value of gold and silver, and hence to higher prices for the same quality of goods, it has been argued by J. R. Wordie that little of this new gold and silver found its way into monetary circulation in England for any great length of time, because of bullion outflows (Wordie 1997: 49–61). The value of the circulating medium at the end of the sixteenth century might have been as low as only £1.5 mil-lion, but between 1540 and 1600 food prices also more than trebled, while industrial prices doubled. As a result, by the end of the sixteenth century the demand for money had probably increased by something like 500–600 per cent, while the supply of coins hardly expanded at all. This lack of cash, combined with the absence of sophisticated banking services, meant that the economy expanded on a web of sales credit. Wher-ever possible, reciprocal debts contracted between as many interested parties as possible would be 'reckoned' and cancelled against each other after a certain number of months, and then only the remaining balance would be paid in money.

This vast expansion of credit, however, contributed to the economic crisis of the 1590s, which was brought about by a combination of plague in the early years of the decade followed by a run of bad harvests from 1594–7. As a result, prices and the cost of living jumped more after 1594 than at any time since before 1560. In addition the 1590s saw a great outflow of money from England to pay for war and trade imbalances, which would have compounded debt repayment enormously because the number of times reckonings could be settled in cash would have been limited, and a large number of unpaid debts would have had a domino effect along chains of credit affecting more and more households. It is easy to see how this would have led to a depression, as losses mounted, and shopkeepers, merchants and artisans cut back on the amount of credit they could realistically extend if they were to meet their own debts, while not being paid by others. This would have reduced demand for con-sumer goods, providing less employment, thus causing a downward spiral of rapidly falling demand, continuing loss of purchasing power, and more unemployment. The difference in the rate of inflation between agricultural goods and industrial products bears this out. While prices of foodstuffs rose by 25 per cent over the course of the decade, demand for industrial products was so low that prices only rose by .03 per cent in comparison (Muldrew 1998: chs 1, 4).

During this decade population growth also slowed to almost half of what it had been in the preceding two decades, but recovered quickly in the first decade of the seventeenth century as mortality fell and birth rates rose. At the beginning of the new century the population of England stood at just over 4 million, having grown from 3 million in 1550. The population would reach 5,283,000 in the mid-1650s before beginning to decline for most of the rest of the century, and it would not reach the same level as the 1650s until about 1720. The population of Wales grew by around 60 per cent, from 250,000 in 1550 to 400,000 by 1650, while Scotland's population grew from 700,000 to around 1,000,000 by the mid-seventeenth century. The population of Ireland is more difficult to determine before the late seventeenth century, but by that time there were 800,000 Catholics and 300,000 Protestants. In England inflation between 1600 and 1650 rose at about the same rate as the preceding 50 years, but with the decline in population, the rise in prices ended and average real wages of labourers actually rose somewhat by the beginning of the eighteenth century.

It is difficult to know what happened to living standards in England between the depression of the 1590s and the beginning of the Civil War, but work being done on a sample of 8,000 probate inventories drawn from Kent and Cornwall by Overton and Whittle (forthcoming) shows that in Kent, in terms of household furnishings, while there are indications of rising standards of living before the Civil War, the value of household goods rose more rapidly after 1640. Between 1600 and 1640 the average inventoried value of goods in Kent only rose about 10 per cent above the rate of inflation of industrial goods. But if the value of household goods did not rise very much in the first half of the century, the heating and glazing of houses, as well as the consumption of imported groceries, was expanding. This can be seen from trade statistics which demonstrate a generally buoyant trend of rising overall consumption through the first half of the century (ibid.). Annual production of pig iron rose from 15,000 tons in the 1580s to 24,000 tons in the 1650s, and imports of Swedish iron bars also increased concurrently. Derbyshire's lead mines increased production from 34,000 loads of ore in 1600 to 95,000 in 1636 for use in glazing, roofing and pewter vessels (Clay 1984: II, 55; Wood 1999: 73). But perhaps the most dramatic rise in consumption in terms of scale and economic and social impact was the rise in the use of what contemporaries called 'seacoal', which was coal mined largely along the Tyne and shipped out of Newcastle (some was shipped out of Sunderland and Scotland) south to London and other coastal ports. A proportion of this was consumed in industry, but the vast majority was bought by households to be burnt in hearths for warmth, as wood supplies became more expensive. Coastal exports from Newcastle grew from about 140,000 tons per year in 1590 to around 400,000 tons in the 1630s, and 500,000 tons by the late seventeenth century. From 1566 to 1685 the northeast coasting trade grew at an average compound rate of 2.3 per cent a year, which was comparable to growth during the Industrial Revolution (Hatcher 1992: 487–92).

The tonnage of English shipping also went up from 50,000 tons in 1572 to 115,000 tons in 1629 as consumption of foreign luxuries such as wine, Italian silk, spices, sugar and fruit increased dramatically in the late Elizabethan and early Stuart period. Between 1563 and 1620 the amount of wine, currants, raisins and spices imported into London increased over five-fold, and by the mid-1590s over a million pounds of currants were being imported into London alone from the Levant, which rose again to between 3 and 5 million pounds by 1620, or almost a pound per person in England. This caused the Venetian ambassador to claim, hyperbolically, that poor men would hang themselves if they did not have enough money to buy currants during popular festivals (Brenner 1983: 43). Imports of fresh fruit also rose dramatically. In 1581, 21,000 oranges and lemons reached Norwich in time for Bartholomew Fair, and possibly over 1,000 tons of foreign fruit, spices and groceries were being shipped into East Anglia each year by the 1590s. The popularity of foreign groceries is shown by the fact that this represents possibly between 7–8.5 pounds per person in Lincolnshire, Norfolk, Suffolk and Cambridgeshire. In 1660 there were also 200,000–300,000 pounds of pepper being imported into London per year, or about 6 ounces for every household in England. Even more striking was the growth in tobacco production which, as we shall see, provided the impetus for the development of the North American colonies. The amount of tobacco imported went up 36 times in just 20 years, from 50,000 pounds in 1618 to 1,800,000 pounds in 1638, and then rose to 9,000,000 pounds in 1668 (Davis 1969: 80–3).

The total value of all imports into London rose from about £1,000,000 to possibly as much as £3,000,000 between 1600 and 1640, while the value of England's traditional export, woollen cloth, which had remained buoyant until 1614, declined precipitously thereafter. The decline began in 1614 as a result of what has come to be known as Alderman Cokayne's project, in which he and other projectors convinced the crown that they could create a cloth finishing industry in England. Previously most of England's exports had been of heavy undyed woven short staple wool known as the old draperies, which were finished by dyeing and dressing in the low countries. In order that this could be done, James I ordered an embargo on the Merchant Adventurer's export of unfinished cloth in hopes of gaining increased tax revenue from Cokayne and his partners. Since most of the price of finished cloth came from the dyeing process this was economically attractive, but because skilled workers were not present in large enough numbers to match the quality of cloths finished in the Lowlands, it simply meant that foreign merchants sought new suppliers, and English cloths sat unsold in warehouses and many business contracts were broken. As a result, by 1617 exports had dropped by a third which, combined with changes in market demand towards lighter cloths and a general saturation of the European market, meant that English exports continued to decline. Although increasingly English cloth manufacturers, especially in East Anglia, where skills were learned from Dutch immigrant cloth workers fleeing religious warfare, began making lighter new draperies, it has been estimated that by 1640 English cloth exports totalled just over £1,000,000 in value, much less than that of imports.

This meant that there was a continuing negative balance of payments in foreign trade. Since cloth formed over 90 per cent of exports, as these declined and imports of foreign groceries expanded, currency was increasingly drawn out of the country to pay for this imbalance. It was estimated by Edward Misselden in 1622 that the value of imports was already about £300,000, a figure which was much higher by the 1630s. Although gold was attracted into England as a result of the Mint making it more valuable in relation to silver, much of what was minted was needed to finance the trade deficit. This decision also had the effect of chasing silver out of the country, and by the 1620s there was a great shortage of small coins, resulting in the production of tokens and farthings. Although it is doubtful that the shortage of coin ever reached the severity of the 1590s, it is also unlikely that the amount of circulating currency expanded very much beyond £2–3 million, which made the 1620s a very difficult decade. In the 1630s, however, a deal was made with the Spanish government which eased the problems of the increasing trade imbalance. Under this arrangement Spanish silver was imported into England and minted there to protect it from Dutch warships, and then Spanish armies in the Lowlands would be paid in bills of exchange drawn on London. This increased the value of the circulating coinage in England to about £10 million by 1640, but before this England was chronically short of specie (Wordie 1997: 54–6; Challis 1992: 308–17).

For middling-sort tradesmen this problem was overcome by the extensive use of credit, and in fact the vast majority of buying and selling, whether commercial wholesaling or consumer purchases made in shops or the market-place, was done on credit. Such credit was often remarkably informal, consisting only of memory of oral agreements, but it formed the basis of the country's financial system, making trust and reputation for honesty in paying one's debts a crucial component of social relations. For the increasingly large number of poor wage earners, though, such trust was problematic, as their earnings were variable depending on the availability of work, and had also been eroded by inflation. This was especially true in the cloth industry, which together with agriculture, employed the largest number of wage earners. In many areas, most notably the West Country and East Anglia, cloth making existed in tandem with agricultural work. Carding, spinning and stocking knitting were done by women and children as household by-employment, while weaving was done by labourers who also might spend some of the year working as agricultural labourers or tending to a few of their own animals. In Gloucestershire, for instance, a militia list from 1608 shows that 15 per cent of the men listed were engaged in the production of textiles, of whom the largest number were weavers (Tawney and Tawney 1934–5: 59–63).

The symbiosis of the cloth-making industry and agriculture is an important one because despite the growth of trade and artisanal manufacturing, the majority of England's population was rural. Although the percentage of people living in towns of 2,000 people or more rose from 17 per cent in 1600 to 25 per cent in 1700, much of this growth was accounted for by the tremendous expansion of London. Most people remained engaged in food production, growing wheat, oats and barley for sale on the market and raising sheep and cattle for milk, wool and slaughter. There were improvements in agricultural technology in the seventeenth century, often resulting from enclosure, such as better animal breeding, improved drainage of land and improved fertilization, but crop rotation remained very traditional, and weeds and animal pests placed severe restrictions on the productivity of land. This meant that agriculture could not support many more than 5 million people without grain imports (Overton 1996: chs 2–3). Although the basic staple was wheaten bread, vegetables and salads grown in gardens were eaten, as was a surprisingly large amount of meat, especially by the wealthy who consumed much more per capita than is common today. This meat consumption was linked to the leather industry, as there was a continual demand for shoes, gloves, saddles and jerkins.

Most rural families lived in villages on manors, all of which still had lords who rented out land in various forms of tenure, and while the authority of the national common law administered through the quarter sessions and assizes had become more important than manorial courts by the seventeenth century, the latter dealt with regulatory matters by enforcing communal customs and by-laws affecting such aspects of co-ordination of the common fields as ploughing, sowing, harvesting and drainage, as well as administering fines for behaviour which hurt neighbours, such as letting cattle into a close or garden, or throwing garbage on the street. Manorial custom also dominated the English land law and forms of tenure, and manorial courts baron dealt with land transfers of copyhold land, which became increasingly common as the land market developed in the sixteenth century. The sale of land, enclosure and agricultural improvement were all motivated by the profit which could be made as food prices continued to rise until mid-century, and when prices stabilized and fell after this, improvement was motivated in order to maintain profits through improved efficiency. This meant that agriculture was very commercialized, with grain and meat being sold not only to local towns and labourers, but also to grain merchants in regional market towns who then shipped it by river and coastal shipping to places where demand was high, such as London or the northern counties where sheep grazing was common and the land was too poor to support the population. There were about 760 market towns in England and Wales by the seventeenth century. Most were small regional centres of 500–1,000 people which served an agricultural hinterland, but there were also about 250 chartered boroughs which had been granted rights of self-government by mayors and aldermen outside the jurisdiction of manorial authority, and many of these were regional trading centres.

By 1688 Gregory King estimated that the numbers of households which had to be paid wages or poor relief (labouring people, out-servants, cottagers and paupers) had reached about 50 per cent of the population. These households faced the dual problem of a general shortage of work, and the fact that the lack of cash meant it was difficult actually to pay the wages for what work was done, and many poor families had to survive on credit and charity for long periods of time. Donald Woodward has estimated that by the beginning of the seventeenth century labourers in Lincoln and Hull would have had to work many more days than there were in the year to feed a family of five. Many of these families, though, were those of either agricultural day labourers or what were termed servants in husbandry who bargained for terms of employment of usually a year or half-year for board and wages. Here payment was less of a problem as wages could be cancelled against sales of foodstuffs. For all labourers, though, work by wives and older children together with the keeping of animals was a necessary part of earning a living (Laslett 1983: 32–3; Woodward 1995: ch. 7).

As a result of this lack of employment the proportion of the population estimated to have been poor by tax officials and town governments became increasingly high. In the late sixteenth century various town governments took censuses of the poor living within their jurisdictions. These ranged from 12 per cent to 22 per cent of the population, the latter being the percentage in Norwich, the second largest town in the kingdom at the time and a centre of cloth weaving. These percentages reflect the numbers of people who might at some time in their lives need public assistance. At any one time about 5 per cent of such towns' populations were likely to be receiving relief in the form of cash doles or other forms of assistance from the town authorities. By the time of the Restoration, when the government introduced a tax on the number of hearths in households, commonly 30–40 per cent of those on such tax lists were exempted as being too poor to pay, although exemptions could reach higher levels, such as in the cloth-making parish of Coggeshall in Essex or the pasture and woodland parish of Eccleshall in Staffordshire, where the proportions exempt were 60 per cent and 69 per cent respectively, or in the coal-mining parish of

Wickham in 1666, where a huge 79 per cent were exempt. Although those exempt from the hearth tax are not directly comparable to those counted in urban censuses, as they were not considered to be in direct danger of going on relief, they were still considered unable to afford to pay a tax of 1 shilling for their single hearths (Spufford and Went 1995: 18–19; Slack 1985: 41, 73).

Such figures, however, tend to give an impression of a static society segmented into a pyramid composed of a few very rich households with the next 20–25 per cent of the population composed of middling-sort households and an increasingly broad base of poor families. While this might be true for an historian looking back over a large expanse of time, for those at the time engaged in getting and spending, wealth and financial security could be very volatile, and status was often precarious. This was increasingly an economy based on households competing for work and income on the market, whose wealth consisted not of stored cash or bank accounts, but purchasing power in the form of credit in their community. This meant being owed more than what was owed to others by successfully selling enough goods or labour. But it was also based on moral standing, as the more honest and chaste husbands and wives were considered, the more they were likely to be trusted by their neighbours. Both husbands and wives as well as older children and servants and apprentices were all active members of the household economy and their reputation mattered, even if legally under the laws of coverture, wealth and authority (apart from female inheritance protected by marriage contracts and customary rights) were invested in the husband. In shopkeepers' households wives and servants worked in the shop preparing goods, while farmers' wives tended some animals and looked after the feeding of farm servants, and both wives and servants made bargains and transacted reckonings.

Reputation also involved being hospitable and charitable to one's neighbours, but this had to be balanced against thrift to prevent households spending too much and going into debt further than their potential earning power could support. Thrift became one of the bywords of the age because over-spending became increasingly common as consumption increased. It was advocated as being necessary for the rich as well as the poor, and after the example of Queen Elizabeth's fiscal restraint even the Stuart kings were often chided for being unthrifty. For many small as well as large tradesmen going too far into debt from over-spending or loss of business was all too common. Peter Earle has estimated that in the 1710s and 1720s 10–15 per cent of the very wealthiest tradesman and citizens in London had commissions of bankruptcy sued out against them at some point in their careers. Also, in various samples of probate accounts, which listed all liabilities on an estate after death, between 22–39 per cent of those who died had more liabilities in the form of unpaid debts than the value of their movable assets (Earle 1991: 128–30). The defaults of others could also be damaging, especially for poor tradesmen who might be more in need of the funds because their earning potential limited their ability to raise more credit, which would result in a domino effect of defaults. The wine merchant John Paige described how easy it was for such a situation to come about. In April of 1651 he reported that in two months the price of wine in London had fallen from £25 to £21 a pipe (112–20 gallons) because of 'sad times and little money going' in England, causing men to 'give over' drinking wine. The result of this was that the vintners could only pay their debts to the importers 'very slowly', with precipitous effects:

I never knew men break so fast as now, insomuch that makes all trade at a stand. One man durst not trust another... Mr. Isaac Ellis is broken for near £15,000, they having his person in prison, upon which here broke 2 merchants of this city; men that were engaged for him deeply are now utterly undone.

A month later he was still reporting that 'here is such breaking abroad and at home every week and I protest I am fearful to trust any man... you may see the danger of these uncertain times that where a man thinketh himself most secure commonly is in most danger' (Muldrew 1998: 290–1).

Many poorer households were continually in debt and had to have their debts continually forgiven. In order to try to meet their obligations they existed in what has come to be called 'the economy of makeshifts' with the husband, wife and children all doing as many jobs as possible, such as weaving, cleaning streets, looking after animals, nursing, etc., in addition to perhaps keeping a few cows to sell milk and butter, or running a small alehouse. But bad harvests which caused bread prices to increase, or lack of work, could impoverish such families very rapidly, causing them to default on their debts or to seek assistance. The institutional response to growing structural poverty was the development of a national system of relief. With the loss of monastic charity after the dissolution of religious houses in the 1540s, relief of poverty was a problem tackled initially by private charity and individual responses on the part of town governments. There were also numerous statutory initiatives ordering severe punishment for vagrancy. But it was the crisis years of the 1590s which caused the statute for the relief of the poor to be passed in 1598, which gave churchwardens and the newly created office of overseers of the poor the power to rate wealthier parishioners for a tax to be expended on the relief of those they considered in need. These were the impotent poor – widows with children, the lame and those too old to work. For those who were termed 'lusty' or 'sturdy beggars', or those of sound body who would not work, parish officers were given the power to put them to work weaving or doing other labour for wages. Initially most parishes concentrated on helping those who could not work. Work schemes largely failed because most of the able bodied who were not working were in fact in such a position because of a lack of demand. This meant it was usually more expensive for parishes to provide uneconomical work than to supply a minimum of relief when necessary, and workhouses did not become common until the eighteenth century, when the cost of outdoor relief was much higher. As a result poor law payments came to be integrated into the economy of makeshifts with families applying for relief to augment their income from other sources when work was short, or when sickness or death of a husband caused hardship. The amount collected by poor rates rose from £10,000 in 1610 to £100,000 in 1650, to £400,000 in 1700 and £689,000 in 1750. Private bequests in wills to set up schools, almshouses and to pay for apprenticeships for poor children also increased in this period, but the poor law became a structural component within the economy which helped to maintain a body of people who relied on searching for wages to make their living (Slack 1985).

One notable feature of this situation was that it promoted a high level of geographical mobility in the search for work and better opportunity. Families continued to rely on kin relations for loans or residence to help them if they were in trouble, but searching for work on the market was the main way in which families sought to deal with economic hardship, or to attempt to improve their lot. We know that many people migrated between villages and local market and county towns within roughly a 25-mile radius to get married, or to take positions as servants or to take up apprenticeships in towns. Higher child mortality rates in larger towns of over 5,000 people due to insanitary living conditions and the importation of pathogens because of trade meant that there was always a net inflow of young people moving into towns to begin careers to maintain their population. In 1600 most of England's provincial towns were small, with only Norwich, York, Bristol and Newcastle having over 10,000 inhabitants. Outside of London the urban population of England continued to grow in the seventeenth century, but while such growth was steady, it was hardly spectacular. The population of Norwich went up from about 15,000 to 30,000 and Bristol expanded from 12,000 to 21,000, but the population of York remained steady at about 12,000. Other towns such as Manchester and Birmingham grew from small market towns to medium-sized towns of about 8–9,000 people, but most other county towns only grew from about 4–5,000 people to about 5–7,000. In contrast to this London, which had already grown from about 55,000 people in the mid-sixteenth century to 200,000 in 1600, continued to expand rapidly, reaching 575,000 by 1700, making it the largest city in Europe. This pattern of growth was the result of an integrated marketing system where the county towns served as distribution points for goods shipped to and from London by the coasting trade. As a result of this, most of the infrastructure growth to facilitate such trade took place in the capital rather than the provincial towns because of efficiencies of scale.

Between 1550 and 1650 the population of the capital increased by about 3,300 inhabitants per year, which given that there were 2,500 more deaths than births within London, meant that a net annual average immigration of around 6,000 people was required. Since it has been estimated that about 25 per cent of children born in country parishes died before reaching their tenth birthday, this means that about 6 per cent of those who survived to adulthood eventually moved to London. It has also been calculated that by the end of the century one adult in six had direct experience of London life. Thus a fairly large percentage of the population was moving over a large distance into a very different urban environment (Wrigley and Schofield 1989: 248–9; Finlay 1981: 9; Wrigley 1967: 49–50).

But in addition to this, overseas migration was occurring at an equal rate. One of the most notable features of the seventeenth century was the rate of migration within the British Isles and emigration to the Americas. The most recent estimates indicate that somewhere in the region of 530,500 people emigrated from England in the seventeenth century. Of these, 180,000 went to Ireland, 190,000 went to the West Indies, 116,000 to the Chesapeake, and 21,000 to New England. Perhaps another 100,000 Irish emigrated to the New World. In Scotland in the early seventeenth century an estimated 90,000 people left. Twenty to thirty thousand went to Ulster, some went to America, many went to Scandinavia and Poland as pedlars, but most became mercenary soldiers in the Thirty Years' War (Canny 1994: 39–75; Wrightson 2000: 221, 159). Just looking at the English figures, most of the emigration to Ireland occurred between 1610 and 1660, and while a few thousand settlers emigrated to Virginia in the 1620s, large-scale Atlantic emigration did not begin until the 1630s. If the population going to Ireland is added to that emigrating to the Americas it means that about 120,000 Englishmen (very few were women – see below) left each decade between 1640 and 1660, which gives the figure of about 6 per cent of the male population over the age of 15 leaving the country every decade. In the 1630s this accounted for 32 per cent of the decade's population growth, which had risen to 51 per cent by the 1640s, and well over 100 per cent for the next two decades, and which reduced the population of England by about 6 per cent. Some left from Bristol, but 80 per cent left through London, meaning that about another 5–6 per cent of the teenage and adult population were moving to London and then going overseas.

Increasing poverty caused by overpopulation is put forward as a simple functionalist argument for this migration, and there is much truth to this. Yet as Abbot E. Smith pointed out over fifty years ago, recruiters for emigrants in Ireland noted that many destitute families chose to remain, and the fact that English emigration continued in large numbers after the home population began to drop (it remained at about 44,000 per year after 1660) and real wages started to rise, shows there was more to the decision than absolute necessity in many cases (Smith 1965: 43–57). It is also significant that of the emigrants to the New World, over 90 per cent went to the Caribbean or Chesapeake rather than New England. In the latter death rates were actually less than in England, and life expectancy better, while in stark contrast malaria and other tropical diseases eventually killed most who went south. Of the 222,000 emigrants to the Caribbean only 35,500 remained by 1700: an adult mortality rate of 84 per cent; and while initial death rates were high in Virginia, mortality rates did decline, but not to the level where the area was able to reproduce itself. There were less people there in 1700 than who had emigrated.

In contrast, the relatively small number of 21,000 emigrants who went to New England in the 1630s had expanded mostly through reproduction to become a population of 91,000 by 1700 (Gemery 1980: 179-231).

This happened because there was less disease and higher living standards in New England and given this, the small number of emigrants going there is striking especially when we consider that the economy there was based on agriculture, when many of the emigrants were obviously from the countryside. While Puritanism played some role in making the New England colonies reluctant to take in a large number of new immigrants each year, this lower rate of emigration indicates that there were positive as well as negative economic factors at work in England influencing decisions about migration. In light of the much higher living standards there based on agriculture, when many of the emigrants were obviously from the countryside, the small number of emigrants is striking, and indicates that there were positive as well as negative economic factors at work in England influencing decisions about migration. These factors were the consumer booms in the consumption of tobacco and then sugar, with cotton also playing a small role. We know that about 20 per cent of emigrants to the Chesapeake were independent self-financing individuals who went with the hope of earning huge fortunes growing tobacco for the English market. The rest were indentured servants who signed a contract for usually 3–4 years labour for the cost of their passage. These people were recruited by agents in England who paid for their servants' transportation, and who made a profit by selling the latter's contracted labour at auction in the New World. Between 75–95 per cent were male, given that the labour involved was heavy field work, but even so women were needed to run households, and female servants actually fetched better prices at auction, but still far fewer women were tempted to go over and form households, which also indicates migration was seen as a way to earn money rapidly (Galenson 1981: 25).

Before 1620 a pound of tobacco in England cost 20–40 shillings, and a full pipe was a luxury, but production expanded so rapidly that the plantation price dropped to a penny a pound by the 1640s. The amount of tobacco imported went up 36 times in just 20 years, from 50,000 pounds in 1618 to 1,800,000 pounds in 1638, and then rose to 9,000,000 pounds in 1668, and had reached 22,000,000 pounds by 1700, of which two-thirds was re-exported to Europe. The initial high prices meant that potential profits were high for free immigrants with capital to invest, and were a great incentive for emigration. One man, James Drax, who arrived at Barbados with £300 during the tobacco boom of the late 1620s, claimed he 'would not look towards England with a purpose to remain there the rest of his life, till he were able to purchase an estate of ten thousand pounds', and indeed by 1654 he was the richest planter in Barbados. For indentured servants, too, there was the lure of high earnings once their contracted period of service ended. It became common for them to serve between four and five years, and upon their release they were paid a 'freedom due', customarily about £10 equivalent in tobacco and then sugar, and once free, unskilled workers could earn a wage of 15–17 pence a day in the 1650s in Barbados or 2–3 shillings in America, compared to only 12 pence in England. By the end of the century wages had risen to 22.5 pence a day. For the many emigrants who were skilled workers, wage levels were much higher than in England. Skilled workers in Barbados earned about 5 shillings per day compared to only 15–18 pence in England. The fall in tobacco prices in the 1640s (before production shifted briefly to cotton and then sugar), and then competition from slave labour, caused wages and opportunities to fluctuate, but the general view from England must have been one of potential rapid opportunity to earn wealth (Beckles 1984: 29; 1986: 13). The dangers of high mortality must have been known to some extent, but since there were no statistics, and the contractors who shipped the indentured labourers out had no interest in conveying any knowledge of the true extent of disease and death, for many labourers and free emigrants alike it must have seemed a tempting gamble compared to the tough competition which existed in England at the time. Emigration only slowed in the late seventeenth century when it actually became cheaper for the first time for planters in America to purchase slaves from Africa rather than indentured servants.

Those middlemen who profited by selling indentured labour and the slaves in the New World were only a small number of the expanding number of the middling sort (20–30 per cent of the population) – artisans, shopkeepers, tradesmen and wholesalers in towns – who earned wealth through the profits from increased demand. This changed the organization of local marketing by greatly increasing the numbers of households involved in distribution. More and more, merchants and retailers such as grocers or mercers became involved in the distribution of goods to different markets over longer distances. London stood at the centre of this expansion in trade. Not only did it import large amounts of grain and coal, its wholesalers and their warehouses became the centre of supply for the whole kingdom – for goods produced in London and foreign imports as well. Imported goods such as spices and silks might first be shipped to London, then to regional ports, and then further inland. The most important centres for distribution were middling and larger towns, as goods were first shipped to merchants in regional port towns, who would then sell them to shopkeepers further inland. Towns such as King's Lynn, Southampton, York, Chester or Shrewsbury expanded their function as trading entrepôts, into which goods were imported and sent inland along the river system. Such urban growth was what led people to move into towns looking for employment in the expanding numbers of artisanal occupations present, but they still became more prosperous as trade grew.

The 1608 muster list for Gloucestershire (without Bristol) clearly shows how important retailing and artisanal industry had become to the economy of the county. Although the list was not exhaustive it still included 19,402 men and 135 women. Even though only 7 per cent of these householders lived in the three towns of Gloucester, Tewkesbury and Cirencester, fully 45 per cent of households on the list were involved in manufacture, transport and retailing. Many households were engaged in textile and clothing manufacture, but still about one quarter or almost 5,000 of the households in the list were involved in retailing of some sort or another. Most of this (25 per cent) was quite clearly concentrated in the three major towns, but there were numerous rural shops and workshops spread throughout the county as well. These figures suggest that by the beginning of the seventeenth century there was sufficient demand even in very rural areas to support a large number of shops and services.

The occupational structure of the trading entrepôt of King's Lynn in the late seventeenth century demonstrates the importance of large-scale wholesale trading in the town. This is shown below in table 1. The importance of urban demand can also be seen by the fact that the basic business of feeding, clothing and providing shelter for people formed the backbone of the urban economy. There were 49 butchers, 30 bakers, 19 brewers, 36 tailors and 32 cordwainers. This means there was at least one butcher for every 38 households in the town, as well as one tailor for every 52 families, indicating that customers would have had a great deal of choice in who to do business with, so there must have been considerable competition in the sale of basic commodities like meat, bread and clothing. About 36 per cent of occupations were primarily concerned with retailing, distribution and transport.

Table 1   Numbers of households broken down by occupational category in King's Lynn for the late seventeenth century.

Category	Number of households	Percentage of total
Clothing/textile	130	17
Victualling	138	17
Maritime	145	18
Building	107	14
Service	72	9
Distribution/sale	63	8
Leather	48	6
Manufacturing	50	6
Agricultural	17	2
Office	22	3
Total	792	100

There were 28 merchants, 28 grocers, 14 mercers, 17 wool and linen drapers, and three fellmongers, most of whom would have been involved in long-distance trading. There were also 112 mariners involved in importing and exporting goods – more than any other single occupation.

Most occupational groups contained wealthy as well as poor artisans, but the wealthiest occupations, in descending order, were merchants, brewers, grocers and mercers. From 1680 to 1687 almost all of the twenty men who served as aldermen or mayors were in the distributive trades. Fourteen were merchants, grocers and woollen drapers; two were brewers, and there was a bookseller, mariner, apothecary and attorney. This was common in other towns as well. In Bristol, between 1558 and 1603, 76 per cent of the mayors had been merchants, and in the seventeenth century all the key positions of mayor, sheriff and chamberlain were dominated by merchants. Although the average rates of profit of trade were not exceptionally high compared to other sources of income (between 7–12 per cent), those wholesalers and merchants who were successful could earn very large amounts. The merchant Dudley North made £20,000 in ten years in the Levant trade, and the Lancaster grocer William Stout accumulated £5,000 from a beginning of only about £100. Success depended on the ability to make connections with other retailers and wholesalers, who would co-operate in offering valuable information on markets and help to buy things in the countryside or in different towns. In this way the middlemen were very dependent on one another, and through this trade many credit relations were created (Muldrew 1998: 56–9).

It is very difficult to estimate what the effects of the civil wars were on the economy because record keeping was disrupted. Certainly transport was disrupted and many towns were besieged and heavily damaged. Many civilians died from disease caused by hardship and massacres in Ireland. It has been estimated that 2.5 per cent of the civilian population lost their lives in England, Scotland and Ireland in the civil wars, considerably more than in the First and Second World Wars combined (Carlton 1998: 278). But at the same time supplying the armies created opportunities for profit, and much heavier levels of taxation were able to be collected in the 1640s than had been the case previously. The years of the Commonwealth also seem to have been relatively prosperous, although little work has been done on this decade. Cromwell's Western Design and the capture of Jamaica, the Navigation Acts and the first Dutch war all certainly set the stage for the course of economic development of the British empire. But after the Restoration there is a great deal of evidence of robust economic growth.

Richard Grassby has calculated that by 1688 there were approximately 2,000 large-scale traders like William Stout in the major and lesser provincial towns. By comparison there were 8,350 in London, over four times as many as there were in the rest of England. By this time about 22–4 per cent of England's population was urban, and half of these households were in London. This shows how central the trading economy of the capital was, as goods imported into London merchants' and tradesmen's warehouses were reshipped throughout the country. The London merchants were also the wealthiest in the country. Six aldermen were worth over £100,000 in Restoration London, and probably forty had assets worth over £30,000, although most were worth less than £500. In contrast, few provincial merchants were worth more than £3,000. In total the combined income of this elite business community was in the range of £4 million per year, excluding the more numerous artisans in towns, which was about a quarter of the total revenues from land by the end of the seventeenth century (Grassby 1995: ch. 8).

In contrast to the first half of the century, the average inventoried value of goods in Kent studied by Whittle and Overton (forthcoming) more than doubled during the Civil War and afterwards. Houses after 1650 had more rooms and a wider variety of goods, as well as more luxurious goods such as upholstered furniture, glass, clocks, mirrors and chests. Plates also replaced platters, chairs replaced benches, and older luxury items such as cushions and carpets declined in number. In contrast to Kent, which benefited from the rapid growth of London, in the more remote economy of Cornwall standards of living remained much lower.

The increase in the number of rural shops and the availability of a wider variety of goods all over the country was a prominent feature of economic growth during the seventeenth century. Although there is no way of knowing the total number of shops, by the period between 1649 and 1672 there were 6,575 substantial shopkeepers who had enough business to justify the expense of issuing their own trade tokens (a form of private currency worth less than a penny). But by 1759 an excise list shows that there were 141,700 shops for a population of just over 6 million, or one for every nine households! We cannot know when this growth occurred, but, as we have seen, the evidence of trade tokens shows that the numbers were already high in the 1650s. Increasing customs revenues show how buoyant trade was in the late seventeenth century. The increasing Atlantic trade and the beginning of trade with India was one of the most notable economic developments of the Restoration. In addition to the growth of tobacco imports, the amount of sugar imported grew from 1 million to over 10 million pounds by the end of the century, while imports of silk went up three-fold between 1622 and 1700, furs over four times, calicoes fourteen times, and iron (largely from Sweden) eighteen times. The Mediterranean trade continued to increase with the importation of fruit, olive oil and coffee (which was drunk in coffee houses from the 1650s), but most of this trade came from the Americas. By the beginning of the eighteenth century what has been called the triangular trade was operating. This involved ships sailing to the coast of Africa to purchase slaves for iron bars or cloth, selling them in the New World for sugar or tobacco, and then sailing back to England to sell these commodities. Increasingly, manufactured goods were also shipped directly to America in exchange for raw materials. In addition plants used for dyestuffs for cloth were harvested in large amounts in the Caribbean. In the eighteenth century the role of India would also increase greatly with the introduction of tea drinking and the increasing fashion for cotton clothes such as mantuas.

Such consumption obviously affected lifestyles, but this is something which had been progressing throughout the century. Perhaps a more significant result of expanding trade, in terms of economic change, was the boom in the creation of joint stock companies in the 1690s, which together with the creation of the Bank of England changed the structure of the English economy. Joint stock companies were not a new development, but an institution which had been in existence since Elizabeth's reign. A joint stock company was a corporation chartered by the crown to engage in trade or settlement of a certain area in which private investors bought a certain amount of stock for an equal percentage of the profits of the company's business. Some of the earliest companies were the Russia Company chartered in

1553, the Levant Company of 1581, and the East India Company chartered in 1600. Companies for settlement included the Munster Plantation Company, the Virginia Company and the Massachusetts Bay Company. Most of these companies were given monopolies on trade or settlement in certain geographical areas, with the rationale being that they needed protection from competition because trading with foreign cultures required specialized knowledge in order to build up stable contacts. In addition, voyages to the east were expensive and risky. This brought stability, but most private traders in London resented such monopolies, and prices might have been lower if there had been freer trade as developed with the Atlantic trade, where greater trust could exist among English merchants using the same law and customs. The East India Company was by far the largest, and it has been estimated that between 1575 and 1630 just over 6,000 individuals, most of whom were merchants and tradesmen, invested about £4 million in joint stock companies in fairly large blocks of around £100 or more per share, of which almost £3 million was invested in the East India Company.

But such shares were not traded very often, if at all, before the 1690s. Between 1689 and 1695, however, the number of joint stock companies in England rose from 11 to about 100 as many new companies were chartered and patents made to use the excess merchant capital which could not be employed in foreign trade because of the French wars. In the early 1690s it was said that the equivalent of the whole stock of the East India Company was changing hands every two years. By 1709 there were probably about 11,000 national creditors, which, despite the huge losses incurred by the collapse of the South Sea Company, rose to 25,000 by 1737. In addition there were numerous other companies created, such as the Hudson's Bay, New River, and Bedford Level Companies. Companies were created in a wide variety of other areas, many of which failed. These included schemes for water supply, convex street lights, a burglar alarm, a machine gun, plastic wood, a musket-proof chariot, and a machine to make salt water fresh for ships.

All of this activity led to the rise of stock jobbing whereby brokers bought and sold shares in coffee houses in the City, and by 1694 traders were already selling futures options in the form of 'calls' and 'puts'. By 1700 it was claimed that jobbers were so thickly clustered in Exchange Alley behind the Royal Exchange in Cornhill that pedestrians could not get through. The development of the stock market was also greatly aided by what has come to be known as the financial revolution with the development of the Bank of England. By the 1680s the value of the circulating coinage probably stood at about £6–7 million, but about half these coins were reduced in value by being clipped on their edges. But King William's wars against Louis XIV required an unprecedented level of taxation which amounted to £3,600,000 a year, or about a half of the circulating currency. Much of this cash was sent to pay for armies abroad where credit was not available. The huge amounts of taxes needed in the 1690s, in fact, led to the collapse of the system of coinage as it existed, which precipitated the great recoinage of 1697, and necessitated the creation of the Bank of England to finance government borrowing. Investors bought shares in the Bank at a set rate of yearly interest, which the bank then lent to the government at interest, payment of which was guaranteed out of future tax revenue. This created the national debt which has been in existence ever since, and established a secure form of *public* paper credit which could attract money from the large cash holdings of merchants seeking a safe investment, and could also tap into the internal, and still largely personal, credit networks in London. The Bank of England together with shares in joint stock companies turned that personal credit into something more negotiable in the form of bank notes and company shares which could be transferred to discount centres on the Continent. The political arithmetician Charles Davenant estimated that by 1698 there was already £15,000,000 worth of assignable instruments in circulation. Most of the investors in these stocks were from the very wealthy London middle class, whose investment in government debt and company stocks went up from 27 per cent of investment assets in 1665–89 to 46 per cent after 1690.

Stock market speculation would reach its infamous apogee with the South Sea Bubble of the 1720s, which came about when a number of speculators and Tory politicians convinced the government that a great part of its debt could be converted to South Sea (for trade to South America) and Hollow Sword Blade Company stock which would be paid for by speculation. The South Sea Company started selling its stock on 14 April 1720 and seven weeks later it was able to sell £5 million of its shares which rose 1,000 per cent in value, worth potentially £50 million. The bubble finally burst when reports of the plague spreading in Europe led to jitters about stops in trade, and by 1 October the value of the stock had fallen to £290 from £1,000, ruining many. Although the political ramifications of the Bubble were enormous, economically the collapse of the company had remarkably little effect on trade or credit. The contrast of the effects of this crisis, as well as the success in dealing with the currency crisis of the 1690s, with the depression of the 1590s cannot be more striking. In the 1690s credit was institutionally transformed to deal with the enormous costs and financial drain of a war on the Continent, with the creation of the stock market, the Bank of England and a national debt. These institutions survived the South Sea Bubble and are still at the centre of the modern economy. In the 1590s the credit system had collapsed because of a lack of cash. It is true that general economic conditions were more favourable at the end of the seventeenth century as exports were more buoyant, inflation had stopped, and real wages were actually rising somewhat. Enough grain was also being produced so that some could be exported in good years, and the poor law was redistributing enough wealth to support 5 per cent of the population (Roseveare 1991).

But the fact that poor relief was needed on an increasingly large scale indicates that the new wealth generated through trade and finance was accumulated in fewer hands, leading to social polarization. Also, not every area of Britain grew equally wealthy. As we have seen, Cornwall lagged behind other areas of the country, and on his tour of Great Britain, while Daniel Defoe praised many towns such as those in Norfolk as being industrious and filled with trade and prosperity, there were others such as Lincoln which he called 'a ragged, decy'd, and still decaying city', or Sudbury, which he claimed was remarkable for nothing other than being 'very populous and very poor'. Also much of rural highland Scotland and Ireland outside the plantations was still almost a subsistence economy, although by 1750 both Edinburgh and Dublin would be thriving Georgian centres of trade of about 40,000 inhabitants each.

Looking at the period as a whole, it is easy to generalize change into trends which stress growth and increasing institutional sophistication, but what really mattered to those involved was their own experience. The perspectives of the individuals caught up in such change were incredibly varied, and are witness to suffering as well as success, and great ambition as well as adherence to custom. Although the figure of Samuel Pepys (who rose from a poor apprentice to one of the most powerful men in the kingdom) enjoying his success in being able to afford a coach and horses while riding through the crowded streets of London for the first time was not uncommon, for others such as the wine merchants caught up in the politics of war with Spain, sheltering from their creditors in the debtor's sanctuary of Ram Alley, to indentured labourers working and dying in the plantations of Barbados and fields of Virginia, or poor colliers trying to survive a winter with wages long in arrears, difficulties abounded.

REFERENCES

Beckles, H. 1984: 'Plantation production and white "proto-slavery"; white indentured servants and the colonization of the English West Indies, 1624–1645', *The Americas*, 41, 21–45.

Beckles, H. 1986: 'Black men in white skins: the formation of a white proletariat in West Indian slave society', *The Journal of Imperial and Commonwealth History*, 15, 225–47.

Brenner, R. 1993: *Merchants and Revolutionaries: Commercial Change, Political Conflict and London's Overseas Traders, 1550–1653*: Cambridge.

Canny, N. 1994: 'English migration into and across the Atlantic during the seventeenth and eighteenth centuries.' In N. Canny, ed., *Europeans on the Move: Studies on European Migration, 1500–1800*: Oxford.

Carlton, C. 1998: 'Civilians.' In J. Kenyon and J. Ohlmeyer, eds., *The Civil Wars: A Military History of England, Scotland and Ireland, 1638–1660*: Oxford.

Challis, C. E. (ed.) 1992: *A New History of the Royal Mint*: Cambridge.

Clay, C. 1984: *Economic Expansion and Social Change: England 1500–1700*, 2 vols: Cambridge.

Davis, R. 1969: 'English foreign trade, 1660–1700.' In E. M. Carus-Wilson and W. E. Minchinton, eds, *The Growth of English Overseas Trade in the Seventeenth and Eighteenth Centuries*: London.

Earle, P. 1991: *The Making of the English Middle Class: Business, Society and Family Life in London, 1660–1730*: London

Erickson, A. L. 1993: *Women and Property in Early Modern England*: London.

Finlay, R. A. P. 1981: *Population and Metropolis: The Demography of London, 1580–1650*: Cambridge.

Galenson, D. 1981: *White Servitude in Colonial America: An Economic Analysis*: Cambridge.

Gemery, H. 1980: 'Emigration from the British Isles to the New World, 1660–1700: inferences from colonial populations', *Research in Economic History*, 5, 179–231.

Grassby, R. 1995: *The Business Community of Seventeenth-Century England*: Cambridge.

Hatcher, J. 1992: *The History of the British Coal Industry Before 1700, Vol. 1: Towards the Age of Coal*: Oxford.

Laslett, P. 1983: *The World We Have Lost Further Explored*, 3rd edn: London.

Muldrew, C. 1998: *The Economy of Obligation: The Culture of Credit and Social Relations in Early Modern England*: London.

Overton, M. 1996: *Agricultural Revolution in England: The Transformation of the Agrarian Economy 1500–1850*: Cambridge.

Overton, M. and Whittle, J. *Production and Consumption*: forthcoming.

Roseveare, H. 1991: *The Financial Revolution, 1660–1760*: London.

Slack, P. 1985: *Poverty and Policy in Tudor and Stuart England*: London.

Smith, A. E. 1965: *Colonists in Bondage: White Servitude and Convict Labour in America, 1607–1776*: Chapel Hill, NC.

Spufford, M. 1974: *Contrasting Communities: English Villagers in the Sixteenth and Seventeenth Centuries*: Cambridge.

Spufford, M. and Went, J. 1995: *Poverty Portrayed: Gregory King and the Parish of Eccleshall*: Keele.

Tawney, A. J. and Tawney, R. H. 1934–5: 'An occupational census of the seventeenth-century', *Economic History Review*, 5, 25–64.

Wood, A. 1999: *The Politics of Social Control: The Peak Country, 1520–1770*: Cambridge.

Woodward, D. 1995: *Men at Work: Labourers and Building Craftsmen in the Towns of Northern England, 1450–1750*: Cambridge.

Wordie, J. R. 1997: 'Deflationary factors in the Tudor price rise', *Past and Present*, 154, 32–70.

Wrightson, K. 1982: *English Society 1580–1680*: New Brunswick, NJ.

Wrightson, K. 2000: *Earthly Necessities: Economic Lives in Early Modern Britain*: New Haven, CT.

Wrigley, E. A. 1967: 'A simple model of London's importance in changing English society and economy, 1650–1750', *Past and Present*, 37, 44–70.

Wrigley, E. A. and Schofield, R. S. 1989: *The Population History of England*: Cambridge.

FURTHER READING

Clay, C. 1984: *Economic Expansion and Social Change: England 1500–1700*, 2 vols: Cambridge.

Erickson, A. L. 1993: *Women and Property in Early Modern England*: London.

Muldrew, C. 1998: *The Economy of Obligation: The Culture of Credit and Social Relations in Early Modern England*: London.

Overton, M. 1996: *Agricultural Revolution in England: The Transformation of the Agrarian Economy 1500–1850*: Cambridge.

Roseveare, H. 1991: *The Financial Revolution, 1660–1760*: London.

Wrightson, K. 1982: *English Society 1580–1680*: London.

Wrightson, K. 2000: *Earthly Necessities: Economic Lives in Early Modern Britain*: New Haven, CT.

Wrigley, E. A. and Schofield, R. S. 1989: *The Population History of England*: Cambridge.

CHAPTER NINE

Literature and History

THOMAS N. CORNS

An Overview

The literary history of Stuart Britain was driven and shaped by political imperatives. Numerous literary kinds matured or were first seen in the seventeenth century. The first English newspapers appeared in the third decade, and the first English journalist of genuine stature, Marchamont Nedham, dominated the 1650s as the voice of the English republic. Though religious polemic had a history stretching into the Tudor period, and the Marprelate controversy of the 1580s established some of the forms and strategies that recurred later, secular pamphleteering was rare in England before 1640; by 1642, its principal sub-genres had been established, and its repertoire of tropes, tricks, conventions and stereotypes was virtually complete. Inception to maturity took less than two years. Autobiography shared with pamphleteering an origin in religious discourse, and though it often retained the role of a sort of spiritual inventory, the greatest examples, among them George Fox's posthumously published *Journal* or Bunyan's *Grace Abounding to the Chief of Sinners* (numerous editions from 1666), engaged with secular politics in a complex and explicit way.

Elizabethan masque had been relatively perfunctory, at least in its verbal content. Jacobean and Caroline performances were not only more accomplished technically but also replete with political meaning, sometimes of a subtle and arguably subversive kind. Under James, the theatre of Shakespeare and Jonson reached its greatest maturity in a drama that engaged uncertainly with the dominant ideology. Under Charles, a critical edge entered as the form moved into a period of relative decadence. At its re-establishment at the Restoration, direct sponsorship and close supervision by the court and its agents aligned the theatre with the politics and the cultural values of a revived cavalierism. Later developments, in the form of the greater ideological diversity of the 1680s and the emergence of a more polite drama in the 1690s, tracked the crises attending the succession of James II and the changing idiom of public life following the Williamite revolution.

Two cultural ideologies dominated the century. The culture of the court, inscribed in the late Tudor period in a celebration of the virgin queen, successively took on the patriarchalism of James I's own political theories and the mystical sacerdotalism of Charles I, the fractured and compromised loyalism of the mid-century, and the ironic, rationalist and sceptical perspectives of the reign of Charles II. Neo-classicism was at the core of the writings of Jonson, Milton and Dryden, towering figures in their own age and in the English literary canon, but it was manifested variously as an internally unstable celebration of imperial dignity, as the defiant articulation of a residual godly republicanism, and as melancholy commemoration of ideological transience. The third great movement of the century, perhaps briefly dominant in the late 1650s, was the culture of Puritanism and its allied political formations. Its origins again lie in the Elizabethan period, in Puritan polemicists like the academic and divine Thomas Cartwright and in the undeferential aggression of the Marprelate tracts. Within this broad tradition may be placed such diverse writers as the Levellers John Lilburne and Richard Overton, the Ranters Abiezer Coppe and Jacob Bauthumley, the Digger Gerrard Winstanley, George Fox and a legion of Quaker writers, many of them women, and the towering figures of Restoration non-conformity, among them John Bunyan. The same spirit both animated Milton's controversial prose and transformed the neo-classical impulses manifested in his late and most important poems.

Throughout the century all regimes and most oppositional groups concurred that literature, particularly in print and performance, had the potential to shift power within the state. From its inception, printing in England had been subject to regulation. Access to the press was perceived and represented, not as a right, but as a privilege within the gift of the crown. A series of measures to control the press evolved over the Tudor and early Stuart period, reaching their greatest complexity in the Star Chamber decree of 1637. The emphasis was not on prosecuting offensive material after publication but on preventing publication through a process of licensing in which the printers' and booksellers' guild, the Stationers Company, was required to register for publication only titles that had passed the scrutiny of the appointed agents of the bishop of London. While such measures were often ignored by all parties for plainly uncontroversial texts, the legislation provided a straightforward basis for prosecution and punishment. While the measures were sometimes significantly challenged in the Caroline period, they were sufficient to restrict severely before 1640 the development of the English newspaper, though manuscript newsbooks enjoyed some success.

Successive parliamentary and republican regimes introduced similar legislation, though of course with new censors exercising different criteria, and pre-publication licensing remained the principal strategy till the Restoration Licensing Act, after a brief period of abeyance in the reign of Charles II, was finally allowed to lapse in 1695. Thereafter, press control was applied largely through the operation of the laws of libel.

Performing arts were also regulated by licensing in a system inherited from Tudor times, though here the responsibility fell to the office of the Master of the Revels. The Long Parliament closed the London theatres in 1642; when two new theatre companies were formed at the Restoration, both operated under royal patent and were managed by men closely aligned with the court; though Master of the Revels retained a responsibility in law, in practice the system anyway excluded oppositional voices.

Just as successive regimes invested considerable energy in limiting their opponents' access to the press, so those activists risked their freedom and well-being in order to publish. Puritan writers in the Elizabethan period often published abroad (as did the equally proscribed Catholics), smuggling texts into England, or else used clandestine presses. The practice re-emerged as central to oppositional activity in the later years of the Personal Rule. The spectacular punishment of William Prynne, Henry Burton and John Bastwick was the culmination of a Star Chamber prosecution for writing and publishing attacks of an astonishingly vitriolic kind against bishops (and by implication against the king). John Lilburne, whipped, pilloried and gagged for distributing such material, reached into his breeches' pockets to pull out other tracts, which he threw to the crowd. After the execution of Charles I royalists invested huge ingenuity at considerable personal risk to print and distribute his apologia, *Eikon Basilike*, which went into thirty-five editions in England alone in 1649, and many others both in English and in translation were printed abroad. Though measures introduced at the Restoration largely precluded open and explicit engagement with the regime of Charles II, old dissenter values pervade the major publications of Bunyan, Fox and Milton, and an explicit critique of Charles and his brother found frequent and eloquent development in the 1670s and 1680s.

All sides seemed to agree with Milton's declaration that books 'are as lively and vigorously productive, as those fabulous Dragons teeth; and being sown up and down, may chance to spring up armed men' (Milton 1953–82: II, 492). Yet it is quite difficult to assess the impact of the press on political developments. Was the printed word as important in the 1630s as, for example, the unrecorded and cautious activities of anti-court conspirators and unpublished Puritan ministers? *Eikon Basilike* may have been an international bestseller, but the regime it challenged survived another eleven years and enjoyed a dialogue with the major states of continental Europe. Levellers, Ranters and Diggers may have had the most colourful and innovative of prose stylists on their side, but their fates were sealed by the repressive apparatuses of the emerging Cromwellian state. Anti-Puritan satire may have had some currency over the winter of 1659 and the spring of 1660, but the major political change was worked out, secretly, between General Monk and Charles II and their respective circles. The Williamite revolution finds polemical justification after the event, but the key decisions were taken by interested parties outside the public sphere. In early modern England all sections of the political nation agreed that literature, widely defined, was a potent component of ideological transformation; clear and certain examples of its operation are harder to find. Arguably it functioned most effectively after the event, confirming and validating major change or else constituting a reservoir of beliefs and values for successive groups of political losers.

Criticism and Historiography

There is nothing new in a hermeneutics that reads seventeenth-century literature in terms of its relationship to seventeenth-century political history. Dr Johnson, the most distinguished critic and scholar of the eighteenth century, recognized that *Macbeth* flattered James I not only in terms of his lineage but also in its endorsement of his profoundly held prejudices about witchcraft, and that Milton's career was shaped by his revolutionary zeal. Indeed, the revival of interest particularly in Milton's prose reflected his (rather dubious) identification as a proto-Whig, a precursor to Locke. Joseph Addison, himself a Whig, remains carefully elusive in his influential series of *Spectator* papers (1712) about Milton's revolutionary politics, and though the long editorial tradition that stretched from the late seventeenth century through the eighteenth and into our own age has largely privileged linguistic, biblical and classical commentary over political readings, there is no mistaking the methodological assumptions of perhaps the most remarkable study of early modern literature to be published in the nineteenth century, David Masson's *Life of John Milton: Narrated in Connexion with the Political, Ecclesiastical, and Literary History of his Time* (Masson 1877–94). In the mid-twentieth century, a remarkable series of major studies charted the substantially forgotten territory on the radical fringes of English Puritanism, establishing the status as author and thinker of Gerrard Winstanley, among others, winkling Milton and Bunyan from the pigeonhole of Protestant respectability where they had generally been filed and returning them to the vibrant context of challenging, undeferential rebelliousness and (in Milton's case) theological heterodoxy (see Wolfe 1941; Hill 1972, 1977, 1988; Lutaud 1976). In the ascendancy of revisionist historiography the contribution of the Marxist tradition specifically in this field is too lightly set aside.

What then was *new* about new historicism, the critical movement that through the 1980s and into the present time has probably dominated early modern literary studies? A crisply argued critique by Wells, Burgess and Wymer represents the achievements of its foremost luminary as something of a triumph for twentieth-century self-fashioning:

> In the Introduction to *Renaissance Self-Fashioning* [Greenblatt 1980] Stephen Greenblatt set up an opposition between his own form of politicized historicism . . . and a caricature of traditional criticism. Greenblatt claims that the latter involves either 'a conception of arts as addressed to a timeless, cultureless, universal human essence' or else a conception of it 'as a self-regarding, autonomous, closed system'. In both forms of traditional criticism 'art is opposed to social life'.
>
> It might be supposed that unfounded generalizations of this kind would have had little impact in the academy. In practice the opposite has happened. Greenblatt is probably the most influential critic currently working in the field of early modern literature. (Wells, Burgess and Wymer 2000: 10–11)

Their last point, certainly, is beyond dispute: dozens of monographs and articles have been published with acknowledgements of methodological indebtedness to *Renaissance Self-Fashioning* somewhere in their first half-dozen footnotes. As a critical movement, though, it has indeed proved difficult to define, its shibboleths remain unformulated, membership is surprisingly open and several critics who would not have chosen the label have been hailed as new historicists, sometimes *avant la lettre*, and its borders with other approaches are remarkably porous. Greenblatt in collaboration with Catherine Gallagher puts the issue with an admirable and disarming candour:

> When years ago we first noticed in the annual job listing of the Modern Language Association that an English department was advertising for a specialist in new historicism, our response was incredulity. How could something that didn't really exist, that was only a few words gesturing toward a new interpretative practice, have become a 'field'? When did it happen and how could we not have noticed? . . . Surely, we of all people should know something of the history and the principles of new historicism, but what we knew about it all was that it (or perhaps we) resisted systematization. We had never formulated a set of theoretical propositions or articulated a program. (Gallagher and Greenblatt 2000: 1)

J. C. Davis's dismissal of Ranterism offers a tempting paradigm: indeed, we can identify people who were contemporaneously termed new historicists, but new historicism as a movement can be dismissed as myth, a media construct (Davis 1986). But that is a temptation worth resisting, in part because some extraordinarily good criticism has been written under the banner of new historicism, not least by Greenblatt himself, whose seminal work contains some remarkable readings; and in part because that phrase 'a new interpretative practice' points us to a larger context in which to place new historicism alongside other historically informed criticism of the last quarter of a century.

At the intersection of criticism and historiography in that period we can identify several characteristics or emphases that mark it off – though we must not exaggerate how sharply – from earlier practices.

First, often in ways that practitioners attribute to the immediate influence of the anthropologist Clifford Geertz, all cultural transactions (very widely defined) may be interpreted as discursive, as part of semiotic systems communicating meaning and values; distinctions between reading literature and interpreting other cultural trans-actions erode and the text is repositioned among what are now perceived as analogous processes. As Geertz puts it,

> The concept of culture I espouse . . . is essentially a semiotic one. Believing, with Max Weber, that man is an animal suspended in webs of significance he himself has spun, I take culture to be those webs, and the analysis of it to be therefore not an experimental science in search of law but an interpretative one in search of meaning. It is explication I am after, construing social expressions on their surface enigmatical. (Geertz 1975: 5)

Unsurprisingly, new historicists love a parade. Those particular kinds of seventeenth-century display that are most tractable to Geertzian hermeneutics – events like royal entries, mayoral processions, court masques – have singular attractions, since they allow the interpretation of symbolic actions alongside close reading of the associated texts.

Such events are often epiphanic of power relationships and new historicists, among other historically informed critics, often absorb into their conceptual framework some of the thinking of Michel Foucault to inform interpretation of hierarchical and repressive social transactions. Though his influence among mainstream historians of early modern Britain is relatively slight, his works, and especially *Surveiller et punir* (translated as *Discipline and Punish*), are frequently cited (Foucault 1975); Wells et al. speak tartly of him as 'the tutelary spirit of New Historicism in its most radical form' (Wells, Burgess and Wymer 2000: 13). An approach that regards punishment as a discursive act inscribed by the state on the body of its victim broadly complements interpretation of literary texts as celebrations or confirmations of power relationships. 'Representation', 'construction' and 'image' recur as favoured terms (see, for example, Corns 1999a; Knoppers 2000; Howarth 1997), though implied scepticism reflects as much the common assumptions of British and American political life in the 1990s and thereafter.

Anecdotes from outside literary discourse play a significant part and literary expli-cation frequently begins or spins off a brief, vivid story: as Gallagher and Greenblatt triumphantly express it, 'The force field of the anecdote pulled even the most canonical works off to the border of history and into the company of nearly forgotten and unfamiliar existences' (Gallagher and Greenblatt 2000: 74). Methodologically, the process has occasioned some misgivings, and mainstream historians have voiced concern how unrepresentative incidents have been used as fulcra on which to turn critical interpretation.

The rise of the anecdote coincides with the eclipse of the canon. Though in practice some texts are more studied, more taught, and frankly more valued than others, contemporary critical theory eschews defining and privileging 'literature' over 'non-literature'. Traditionally canonical works are juxtaposed with other, usually closely contemporary texts in ways that are often illuminating. The procedure reaches its most extreme – and perhaps its most persuasive – manifestation in Nigel Smith's epic account of Civil War writing. Smith, operating with the assurance of one for whom the canon never meaningfully existed, for example comfortably discusses Marvell and Milton in close association with 'the little-known poetry of the Presbyterian minister John Ravenshaw', a figure I only know from this account (Smith 1994: 215).

Recent historically informed criticism is generally much more knowing about the controversies that animate historians. Indeed, Blair Worden and Kevin Sharpe are among the most distinguished revisionist historians of their generation, and both have written impressively on Stuart literary culture. For the most part, however, the relationship between the disciplines has been one of dependency, of critics using history rather than writing it. Latterly, though, Annabel Patterson (1997) and David Norbrook (1999) have produced large arguments that challenge received positions, engaging in the former case with the history of liberal thought and in the latter with the early history of republican ideology. Again, especially in the elusive histories of gender and sexuality, textual evidence may well provide excellent evidence of human behaviour and aspiration in a context where other evidence is substantially missing (see, for example, Bray 1988; Turner 1993; Goldberg 1994).

The Jacobean Period: Courts, Masques and Patriarchy

James I's coronation was preceded in the English fashion with a triumphal entry into London, a pattern that had been developing since the fourteenth century (Manley 1995: 216). A series of arches spanned the route, each designed, in symbolic mode, to celebrate the virtue of the king and the loyalty of its sponsors, in ways highly tractable to historicist interpretation, while panegyrics penned by Jonson, Thomas Dekker and Thomas Middleton reiterated the themes. Three accounts are extant, by Dekker and Middleton and by the builder of the arches, Stephen Harrison, and they provide interesting material for investigation into London's assumptions and aspirations concerning the new king and into how speedily his subjects picked up on the principal themes of his regime, particularly its avowedly irenic perspective (Bergeron 1968). He had later entries of various kinds, after the Gunpowder Plot, to greet his brother-in-law, Christian IV of Denmark, on his son Henry's installation as Prince of Wales, and on the wedding of his daughter Elizabeth to the Elector of the Palatinate, some of which have been interpreted, though there is scope for further work (Smuts 1989: 82, 87).

The masques of the Jacobean period present opportunities for prising open the apparent unanimity of the regime. James, though a considerable horseman, did not

dance, and dance constituted the principal aristocratic involvement in the performance. The speaking and singing parts went to professional actors engaged from the
London drama companies and to professional singers. James's role, however,
remained literally and symbolically central. Within the masquing hall – successive
banqueting houses at Whitehall were adapted for the purpose – while the dramatic
presentation was at one end, the audience was organized hierarchically with the royal
throne occupying a central and elevated position at the other end. The aristocratic
maskers descended from the elaborately designed stage and danced to the king,
whose sightline afforded the best (and possibly the only really satisfactory) view of
the increasingly complex stage and machinery designed for the most part by Inigo
Jones, a rising figure throughout the reign and the undisputed master of Caroline
masque (Orgel 1965).

So the masque was presented to the king and in a sense was a present to the king.
But it also carried meaning, inevitably in a form so concerned with the celebration of
hierarchical power, of a political kind. Barbara Lewalski has termed the masques
presented by Anne of Denmark and her women courtiers 'the Queen's subversive
entertainments' and has read them as discourse which 'subvert[ed] the representation
of James as exclusive locus of power and virtue by means of texts and symbolic actions
which exalt the power and virtue of the Queen and her ladies – and, by extension, of
women generally' (Lewalski 1994: 29).

Similarly, Prince Henry, James's eldest son, is widely perceived as articulating, in a
residual but oppositional form, the more militant version of Protestant politics that
had characterized an important aspect of Elizabethan foreign policy and associated
ideology. As David Norbrook, in an influential account, puts it, 'He had exalted ideas
of monarchy and patronised artists and architects who could express the ideals of
princely magnificence in spectacular forms; but he insisted that splendour should be
accompanied by readiness for action, and should not degenerate into the effeminacy
and unnecessary luxury which critics found in James' court' (Norbrook 1984: 203).
His masques presented to the king, on this account, enter into a dialogue with the
dominant and unswervingly unmilitant perspective, particularly on foreign affairs.
Thus, the masque *Oberon*, written for him by Jonson and performed in 1609, has an
obviously Elizabethan cultural resonance that invites interpretation (Norbrook 1984:
204).

Neither the argument of Lewalski nor Norbrook is uncontroversial. It could be
objected, for example, that the form itself involves a necessary obeisance to
the monarch in which counter-argument, like the antimasque which preceded the
dance, is dismissed, and that the principals, Anne and Henry, remain silent in
the elevated presence of the king, whose word of dismissal brings finality and closure
to the entertainment (and whose resources, ultimately, underwrite the display).
Plainly, there is work to be done. But the masques of prince and queen most certainly
emphasize sharply that the Jacobean court was not monolithic – indeed, that it is
more fitting and useful to think of the Jacobean *courts*. Lewalski, Norbrook and
others effectively demonstrate that clusters of supporters and protégés looked to
Anne or Henry for the encouragement of a cultural idiom and ideology at some
remove from James's official line.

That line included a governmental philosophy of the most patriarchal kind in which
the monarchic role was inscribed in the language of an aggressively hierarchical sexual

politics. Thus, in a speech delivered to the parliament of 1604, he asseverated, with no concessions to consensuality, 'What God hath conioyned then, let no man separate. I am the Husband, and all the whole Isle is my lawfull Wife; I am the Head, and it my Body' (James VI and I 1994: 136). At the human level, one may record no surprise that his real wife came to see advantages in keeping to her own court at Greenwich. More significantly, a political discourse cast in such terms is, interpretatively, ripe for an interpretation which carries over the familiar categories of gender criticism.

James's reign, in terms of its court culture, probably ended with an almost unqualified univocality as Charles, elevated to Prince of Wales in succession to the deceased Henry, and in association with the duke of Buckingham, without dispute the most powerful figure after the king, danced masques that stayed attentively on message; *Pleasure Reconciled to Virtue* (1618), written by Jonson and danced by Charles and Buckingham when the queen was ill, may well have marked an important shift within the larger royal household as 'the Arthurianism of *Oberon* gives way to a decidedly Horatian aesthetic, which relegates martial nature to civilizing nurture' (Corns 1999b: 5).

The Court Culture of Charles I Before the Long Parliament

Contemporaries remarked on the changes in moral climate and cultural practices that distinguished the court of Charles I from that of his father, characterized as 'a major shift from familiarity to formality' (Sharpe 1992: 217). As Lucy Hutchinson, a fierce Puritan, observed in a memoir written after the Restoration, 'The face of the court was much changed in the king, for King Charles was temperate, chaste and serious, so that the fools, and bawds, mimics and catamites of the former Court grew out of fashion' (quoted in Sharpe 1992: 212). In terms of the literary culture of the court the trends produced a more focused and more straightforwardly panegyric production, which was further shaped by Charles's relative indifference to the written word and his enthusiasm for non-verbal cultural modes – this is a great age for English music, and for connoisseurship in the visual arts – and his promotion of text in performance, both in song and in masque.

Ben Jonson, James's poet laureate, retained the title but soon lost the openly expressed patronage he had enjoyed. Jonson wanted keenly to be part of the royal establishment, but he retained always a certain ideological unpredictability, a personal notoriety (he was a prodigious and belligerent drinker), and a lack of co-operation with Inigo Jones's agenda (wholly consonant with the preferences of the new king) of subordinating text to spectacle in court masque. Despite his lack of higher education, Jonson was the most learned creative writer of any significance in the early Stuart period, and his poetry and drama were a manifesto for literary neo-classicism, asserting that English writers could take the standards observed by Greek and Roman masters and meet them in vernacular texts. His, too, was typically a poetry of allusion, couched often in a dense, elliptical idiom. He wrote some excellent lyrics – 'Song To Celia' ('Drink to me only with thine eyes'), delicately turned, remains the most popular song of the period and its early popularity is attested by its currency in many contemporary manuscripts. Yet even that draws heavily on relatively recondite classical sources in the *Greek Anthology* and Philostratus's homoerotic *Epistles* (as modern editors note) (Jonson 1985: 675). Jonson certainly signed up for the Caroline programme, writing in the late 1620s and very early 1630s poems representing the monarch and his consort in appropriate terms. But in a sense Jonsonian praise too often came qualified and sometimes discernibly ironized. The epigram 'To the Ghost of Martial' acknowledged his debt to the Roman master:

> Martial, thou gav'st far nobler epigrams
>   To thy Domitian, than I can my James;
> But in my royal subject I pass thee:
>   Thou flattered'st thine, mine cannot flattered be. (Jonson 1985: 233)

The compliment seems neatly schematized, even including an engaging humility: Martial is better than Jonson, yet his subject, James I, is better than Domitian. But how could one not be better than Domitian, a tyrannical monster? And, of course, the subject of the poem is flattery...

Characteristic Caroline court poetry is much, much simpler. If the poem could be set to music, perhaps by Henry Lawes, an employee and protégé of the king and the finest song-writer of the age, so much the better. In the accomplished but relatively bland poetry of Thomas Carew, the court found its most eloquent expression.

Two themes predominated: the celebration of the 'married chastity' of Charles and Henrietta Maria and their associated fecundity; and the good fortune of England to escape the horrors of the Thirty Years' War, thanks to the sagacity of the king. The former may seem to modern readers a trifle paradoxical. From 1630 onwards Henrietta Maria gave birth to numerous children, five of whom survived infancy. In that self-proclaimed virtuous court, from which the lasciviousness that James had entertained had been strenuously and explicitly banished, the burgeoning sexuality of the monarch and his wife was troped into a kind of Platonic affection, stripped of its carnality though evidently characterized by a lot of sex. The closing sections of the masques of the 1630s virtually tuck Charles and his queen up in bed. Thus, William Davenant's *Britannia Triumphans* offered the bedding of the royal pair as a sort of model for other couples present at the masque: 'Then all with haste to bed, but none to rise!' (Orgel and Strong 1973: 667). While court culture remained explicitly a celebration of royal power, that power often seemed equated with sexual potency. Yet as Ann Coiro (1999) has persuasively demonstrated, the formality and insistent privacy of Charles was perhaps finally compromised by so public a meditation on the most intimate component of that private life.

James had encouraged representation of himself as a peacemaker. The earliest years of his son's reign were marked by disastrous military adventures against Spain and France, culminating in the debacle of the duke of Buckingham's expedition to the Ile de Ré. Thereafter Charles substantially reverted to his father's policy, though like James he remained exposed to criticism from those favouring an active foreign policy in defence of the Protestant cause in the Thirty Years' War. Carew, in a defining expression of the pacifism of the Personal Rule, praised the policy thus:

> But let us that in myrtle bowers sit
> Under secure shades, use the benefit

> Of peace and plenty, which the blessed hand
> Of our good King gives this obdurate Land. (Carew 1964: 75)

Carew set up an antithesis between king and country with an inadvertent prescience: Charles may have been out of step with his people but it was because he is ahead of them, establishing the peaceful conditions that allowed the blissful enjoyment of prosperity and well-being. 'Myrtle' is the plant sacred to Venus; make love, not war, emerges as a Caroline theme, and Carew explicitly counterposed the bloody conflicts of the European theatre of war with the chaste eroticism of court masque.

Carew's poem is 'In Answer of an Elegiacal Letter upon the Death of the King of Sweden from Aurelian Townsend, Inviting me to Write on that Subject'. Townsend, court poet and masque-writer, had sent to Carew an elegy on the death of Gustavus Adolphus, in which he argued that the role of leader of military manifestation of Protestantism had fallen vacant and that Charles I could assume it. The poem apparently remained unprinted in its author's lifetime, but then so too did Carew's response; in the 1630s, court poetry mainly circulated in manuscript. The exchange raises some fascinating issues. Seemingly it demonstrated ideological complexity and a dialogue of ideas within the dominant culture, and a range of opinion and perspective that contrasts with the simpler view of the Caroline court as a self-contained Titanic travelling at full speed towards the icebergs of the Civil War. Indeed, Kevin Sharpe (1987) has developed a wide-ranging critique, which identifies particularly in the masques of the 1630s an idiom of what he terms 'criticism and compliment', a tradition that combines celebration of the achievements of Personal Rule with advice to the king and the articulation of other perspectives and aspirations; the argument complements his wider account of those years, which again characterizes the regime as one, not violently fissured, but actively engaged in a critical process in which a range of voices is heard in the decision-making process (Sharpe 1992).

Certainly, there is a far greater ideological complexity in secular literature produced under the broad patronage of the king than had been conventionally argued. Yet in most of those apparent dialogues the voice heard with finality tends to be that closest to the position of the king. Even the exchange between Townsend and Carew is resolved in Carew's evident victory. Taken together, the pair of poems offers the subtlest of compliments. Of course, Charles *could* be the new Gustavus Adolphus, the hammer of the Counter-Reformation, but he *chooses* not to be, valuing instead the arts of peace and the well-being of his subjects (even against their own judgement).

John Donne had established the intense religious lyric as an early modern form and had taken the English sermon to its greatest achievements. He did so in an ecclesiastical context which resisted engagement with the soteriological controversies which had riven the Dutch church. As such, he acted in concord with James's religious policy avoiding debate and eschewing confrontation with Calvinists or Arminians and he acted with the king's protection and encouragement. Charles, however, welcomed the opportunity to reform the church along ceremonial and broadly Arminian lines. Anglican poets of the 1630s and later invite interpretation in terms of that controversy, and in turn offer case studies in the religious experience of ceremonialists. Herrick's religious verse offers the purest example, though we reserve discussion of that till the next section. George Herbert, the most accomplished religious lyricist of the Caroline period, has been variously interpreted, but his emphases on the beauty of holiness, on preparation for Holy Communion, and on the role of the clergy have a distinctly Laudian air. Caroline church history may well currently be the most active area of investigation in the study of Stuart England; criticism has a rich vein to mine, which in turn should give a new vividness to appreciation of the religious life of the time.

Literature, Civil War and the Royalist Experience of Defeat

The poets active in and around the court of Charles I in the 1620s and 1630s have for long been incorporated into the category of 'Cavalier poetry'. The term is thoroughly misleading, though the critical construct dates back to the earliest days of their publication. Of the poets that wrote Caroline masques, only Davenant published a collection of verse before 1640; very little appeared in print of the verse of Aurelian Townsend, Sir John Suckling, Robert Herrick and Thomas Carew, for whom dissemination took the form of performance (in song) or manuscript circulation. Carew died in 1640, and Suckling perished in exile, possibly by his own hand, in 1642 after leading a failed coup against parliament. The king's court, which through the earlier years of his rule was based primarily in Whitehall, became displaced and eventually dispersed through the battlefields of England, through the country estates to which defeated royalists withdrew, and into exile. Vestigially the court culture clung to the king. William Lawes, brother of Henry and the finest composer of instrumental music then in England, died dutifully serving the king as a gentleman volunteer at the siege of Chester, a waste lamented in subsequent publications of his work. In general, though, the diaspora of the court produced a demand for a print culture that could be carried away. Thus, Carew and Suckling were posthumously printed, in ways that poignantly rehearsed the themes of loss and separation. By its third edition (1651), Carew's poems carry a title page that rehearses a full set of royalist woes: *Poems. With a Maske, by Thomas Carew Esq; One of the Gent. of the privie-Chamber, and Sewer in Ordinary to His late Majesty. The Songs were set in Musick by Mr. Henry Lawes Gent: of the Kings Chappell, and one of his late Majesties Private Musick*. Thus the publisher recalled the dead king and the connections of Carew both with him and with Henry Lawes, who survived his brother but who lived in reduced circumstances in a world without a chapel royal and a private music. A literary movement that had confidently and joyously celebrated the 1630s has become nostalgic and retrospective.

Of course, Carew and Suckling could hardly influence the posthumous application of their verse. Herrick, however, continued to write through the 1640s and his one major collection, *Hesperides*, which appeared in 1648, contains poems on his ejection from his living in Devon, which he held through the patronage of the king, and the removal of Charles to Hampton Court, both of which occurred in 1647. It is a remarkable but puzzling work. Poems celebrate those country festivals, the maypoles, the harvest homes, the maying, the folk rituals of Christmas, sports and pastimes defended by Charles in the 1630s, which were attacked, banned and suppressed by the Puritan regime of the 1640s. It is a matter of critical dispute whether Herrick's work is one of lamentation or defiance (Marcus 1986; Corns 1992); perhaps that critical uncertainty reflects the bewilderment both of the author and of his intended royalist readers in the months before the execution of the king, when renewal of hostilities in the Second Civil War suggested all was not lost, though much, plainly, had gone terribly wrong.

The royalist tradition in the 1640s and 1650s has been singularly well served critically (see Anselment 1988; Potter 1989; Loxley 1997; Wilcher 2001). But fascinating areas of disagreement remain. *Eikon Basilike*, Charles's apologia, was astonishingly successful in terms of its frequent republication and the evident difficulty parliament experienced in suppressing it. Its influence on royalist ways of representing the king and thinking about the regicide have been well documented (see, especially, Skerpan Wheeler in Corns 1999a). Most royalist activists must have had a copy, and its famous frontispiece fixed an abiding image of Charles as martyr. But its real effect, in terms of keeping alive opposition to the emerging Cromwellian ascendancy, is much harder to judge. Again, Herrick, going to press before the execution, in some respects had a simpler problem to negotiate than Richard Lovelace, whose first *Lucasta*, though probably published after the regicide, was delayed in the press, but whose second, posthumous collection, *Lucasta: Posthume Poems* (1659), reflected the grimmer realities of the royalist winter with little to mitigate the gloom. There a certain sleaziness displaces the eroticized heroism of poems like 'To Lucasta, Going to the Wars' and 'To Althea, From Prison'. The second volume opens up the problems royalists faced once republican government became settled (Corns 1992; Hammond 1990). The issues appear in a complex and deliberately oblique way in the later poems of Abraham Cowley, a royalist exile and – significantly – cipher clerk, who returned seemingly to continue a clandestine struggle, but who plainly gave up the royal cause after capture and release (Corns 1992: Smith 1994).

Hesperides is a double volume, the second part of which is a relatively short collection of Herrick's religious poetry. In that context, the latter brings a sort of closure to the book. As Marcus puts it, they can be regarded 'as a retreat into simplicity and a resuscitated Anglican community amidst the uncertainties of war' (Marcus 1993: 180). But that community had been irreparably riven since 1642. While Presbyterian ministers had advanced to significant livings and to positions of power and influence, predominating within the Westminster Assembly of Divines convoked to purge the church of its alleged vestiges of Catholicism and the remains of Laudian ceremonialism, men like Herrick had been systematically ejected from parishes as they fell under the control of parliament's armies. Herrick's Anglicanism is an assiduous memorial to the displaced ecclesiastical regime, marked by a love of ceremony and by a high regard for the priestly role (Corns 1992: 114–28).

Henry Vaughan's religious lyrics, while explicitly in the tradition of George Herbert, have traditionally been viewed as examples of an emerging philosophy of withdrawal from the world, a new Cavalier quietism. Recent critical enquiry, reaching its culmination in the brilliant readings of Wilcher, discloses how much of the world and its woes is carried into that world of rural retreat, and the values of an unreconstitued loyalism are pervasive. Wilcher concludes: 'meditations on the poet's own grief and sinfulness or on the corruption and troubles of mankind in this dark and storm-tossed world are punctuated by yearnings for a release from time through death or through apocalyptic intervention' (Wilcher 2001: 313). Fascinatingly, similarities emerge between Vaughan's ways of coping with the 1650s and defeated radicals' strategies for surviving ideologically in the 1660s.

The baroque culture of the Counter-Reformation achieved relatively little penetration in the England of the 1630s. One could point, perhaps, to the kinds of choral music fostered in the chapel royal of Henrietta Maria (Wainwright 1999: 168–71) or to Charles's enthusiasm for the painting of Rubens, most signally expressed in the canvasses commissioned for and installed in the Banqueting House at Whitehall. Yet though Charles and Henrietta Maria evidently were emotionally very close and despite Charles's enthusiasm for a priestly and ceremonial religious idiom, he and his closest ecclesiastical servant, William Laud, were careful and often energetic in distinguishing their practices from Catholicism. Richard Crashaw, though formally the heir to Donne and Herbert and confrère of Vaughan, stepped over that carefully maintained line, leaving a fellowship in Peterhouse, a high-church college under the mastership of a prominent Laudian, to join the court in exile of Henrietta Maria, converting to Catholicism, and dying in Italy in a minor ecclesiastic office of the Church of Rome. Despite the common ground, his poetry touches a sensibility elsewhere uncelebrated in major English poetry of the early modern period through a writing that is vivid in a wholly baroque manner. To compare Crashaw with Herbert or with Herrick discloses the limitations of high-church Anglicanism and its considerable distance from the devotional practices of the Counter-Reformation.

Puritans, Radicals, Republicans

In the most decisive state intervention to date in the literary culture of England, the Long Parliament on 2 September 1642 passed an ordinance declaring:

> And whereas public sports do not well agree with public calamities, nor public stage plays with the seasons of humiliation, this being an exercise of sad and pious solemnity, and the other being spectacles of pleasure, too commonly expressing lascivious mirth and levity: it is therefore thought fit and ordained by the Lords and Commons in this Parliament assembled, that while these sad causes and set-times of humiliation do continue, public stage plays shall cease and be foreborne. (Wickham, Berry and Ingram 2000: 132)

It may seem obvious that a Puritan parliament should have banned plays in a kill-joy spirit, but the issues are less straightforward than that, and attitudes to drama among those opposing Charles have repaid the close attention given to them, most attentively and influentially by Martin Butler (1984). Of course, some prominent Puritans were fiercely hostile to the playhouses. Most sensationally, William Prynne had published in 1633 *Histrio-Mastix*, a wide-ranging indictment of plays and players, which led to his judicial mutilation and incarceration (since it could be demonstrated also to be an attack on Henrietta Maria, a participant in court dramas).

But the measure of 1642 was not simply Prynne's revenge. Playhouses had been closed temporarily on other occasions, in plague years and in times of solemnn mourning, such as that following the death of Prince Henry. The ordinance echoed previous proclamations of that kind. Moreover, besides a vague threat to public morals, playhouses presented a more immediate and effective danger to public order, in that they were among the very few buildings in London in which a dissident crowd could be assembled. We may recall that participants in the abortive Essex Rebellion of 1601 had attended a performance of Shakespeare's *Richard II* as a preliminary to it (see Wickham, Berry and Ingram 2000: 195, for the pertinent deposition). Butler has convincingly demonstrated that significant activists on parliament's side in the 1630s attended plays, supported companies of players, and would have found in some of the drama they watched gratifying anti-court sentiment. It nevertheless made perfect sense in the earliest weeks of the war to close locations where demonstrations and riots could have originated.

Though the ordinance of 1642 effectively ended the great age of the English theatre, performances did continue. In 1648 parliament returned to the issue, passing legislation of an ideologically less complex and more repressive kind: 'the Acts of stage plays ... is [sic] the occasion of many and sundry great vices and disorders, tending to the high provocation of God's wrath and displeasure'. The new legislation trains an unremitting hostility on the companies of players, who are 'hereby declared to be, and are, and shall be taken to be Rogues, and punishable within the Statutes of the thirty-ninth year of the reign of Queen Elizabeth, and the seventh of the reign of King James, and liable unto the pains and penalties therein contained'; as Glynn Wickham comments, the wording of this ordinance 'has a triumphalist finality' (Wickham, Berry and Ingram 2000: 133–4).

But the Long Parliament reached into other aspects of the cultural and intellectual life of England. Only Oxford and Cambridge, outside London, had printing presses, and after the start of hostilities only Oxford was in royalist control; the printing of royalist material in London was clandestine and generally small scale (though the appearance of the royalist newspaper, *Mercurius Aulicus*, apparently from a London press, was a cause of irritation). But parliament, to establish a legislative framework to its actions, reintroduced the licensing system that had fallen into disuse.

The result was the Licensing Order of 1643, which required texts to be approved by an appointed censor before publication. This provided the stimulus for what is nowadays John Milton's most widely read prose work, *Areopagitica; A Speech of Mr. John Milton For the Liberty of Unlicenc'd Printing, To the Parlament of England* (1644). Milton provides a fascinating case study in the disintegration of the broad Puritan alliance that had confronted the king and the hierarchy of the Church of England and brought England to war. Milton's earliest prose writing was a series of anti-prelatical pamphlets, seconding the efforts of a Presbyterian group, who wrote under the acronym Smectymnuus. The challenge is to identify elements in that group of pamphlets which mark Milton off as potentially more radical than his associates.

Milton's second major initiative had been a group of pamphlets advocating divorce by consent and for reasons of emotional incompatibility. Here, like other heterodox thinkers of the 1640s, he fell foul of the controlling and regulating impulses of Presbyterian opinion, which sought to establish religious uniformity within a reformed Church of England. Teased open, his tracts of 1643–45 reveal the seeds of revolutionary Independency. Puzzlingly, however, he published nothing in 1646–8, till he emerged in *The Tenure of Kings and Magistrates* (1649) as the most eloquent apologist for the judicial process against Charles I. Thereafter, he became a civil servant and official apologist for the republican regime, writing a refutation of *Eikon Basilike*, *Eikonoklastes* (1649), and Latin defences of the regime, directed primarily at a continental European readership.

Milton's complex and elegant prose provides a way into understanding the political assumptions of English republicanism. But the issues are deeply controversial among critics and historians. While recognizing the recurrence of republican values in Milton's prose, I read Milton's republican publications in the light of Blair Worden's contention that 'The regicide was not the fruit of republican theory. Most of its organizers were concerned to remove a particular king, not kingship. They cut off King Charles' head and wondered what to do next' (Worden 1990: 226; Corns 1995). I would distinguish Milton's republicanism from that of younger associates such as John Hall or Marchamont Nedham; the former's seems an opportunistic response to the expedients adopted in 1648–9, rather than something programmic arrived at through reading classical republicanism. But others disagree. Martin Dzelzainis has tracked the relationship between his writings of 1649 and what he identifies as 'his neo-Roman theorizing earlier in the decade', and he finds continuities between his arguments there and his pre-Restoration tract, *The Readie and Easie Way to Establish a Free Commonwealth* (1660), though Milton's large argument emerges in a somewhat generalized form: 'A republic, Milton is saying, is the only form of government fit for adults' (Dzelzainis 2001: 304, 308).

David Norbrook, however, lays down a more far-reaching argument, contending that Milton is part of a larger tradition of English republican thought. Where some historians would see the oppositionalism of the 1620s in terms of arguments about the ancient constitution, Norbrook identifies, especially at the level of literary culture rather than political action, a republican mode that is pervasive, continuous, and sustainedly influenced by classical precedents and paradigms. Those continuities are inscribed across the Milton *oeuvre*: 'It is very difficult to isolate the point in Milton's career when he became a republican. His poetry of the 1630s often followed courtly modes, but . . . he set himself to undermine easier forms of poetic harmony, so that his verse can be connected with more directly oppositional poetry' (Norbrook 1999: 109). Such a view about Milton's early verse is not uncontested (see, for example, Corns 2001b).

Andrew Marvell poses equally demanding interpretative questions in his poetry of the republican period. He had written a dedicatory poem for Lovelace's first *Lucasta*. His first significant political poem, 'An Horatian Ode upon Cromwell's Return from Ireland', has been interpreted as an elegantly balanced and evasive juxtaposition of royalism and republicanism, though the critical consensus has moved closer to reading it as whole-heartedly republican. As David Norbrook, in a convincing essay, put it, 'there is an affirmative note: *if* the forward youths of the realm rally behind the young republic's campaigns, there is a world to win' (Norbrook 1990: 164). Yet in 'Upon Appleton House' he seemed to espouse Fairfaxian retirement, and in his panegyrics of the Protectorate he wrote about Cromwell in ways which appropriated some of the idiom of royalism. Indeed, his work provides an interesting way in to analysis of the proximity of Cromwellian ideology to received notions of the nature of monarchy (though the differences are as important as the similarities).

But more radical voices than Milton's or Marvell's were heard in the 1640s and 1650s. England, however, had not developed a discourse for either democratic politics or speculative theology. In a sense, Levellers had to develop a vocabulary *ex nihilo*, while so-called Ranters like Abiezer Coppe and Jacob Bauthumley faced a crisis of expression that could not be resolved without pushing against the limits of linguistic expression, in so doing producing some of the most remarkable prose of the period. Nigel Smith puts it well:

In the attempt to capture the unattainable and to communicate it some of the most striking and fascinating uses of language in the seventeenth century may be found. Yet, if startling through the 'liberty of the spirit' this language also displayed a wide degree of sensitivity and variation in its attempt to capture the authenticity of God's working within each soul and within the nation. (Smith 1989: 19)

Unmistakably, though, we have a long way to go in understanding the nature, idiom, origins and influences of that cluster of antinomian sects that alarmed respectable Englishmen in the late 1640s and early 1650s. The most significant challenge probably relates to the work of Gerrard Winstanley, whose *oeuvre* contains works of speculative theology, of brilliant journalism, and of political theory; the interrelatedness of those components awaits explication.

From the Restoration to the Williamite Revolution: Winners and Losers

In the short term, the Restoration greatly simplified the literary landscape. After ceremonies of entry and enthronement and a general acclaim in numerous panegyrics for Charles II's return, a court culture of sorts emerged, initially most significantly in the theatre. Meanwhile, that wide range of republican and radical voices, articulated in the previous decade, for the most part, at least intially, fell silent (except, of course, for apostates), before, in a remarkable convergence of disparate ideologies, there emerged by the late 1660s what Neil Keeble (1987) terms the literary culture of nonconformity.

In the most significant gestures of literary patronage of his reign, Charles gave patents to Thomas Killigrew and Sir William Davenant to establish drama companies (respectively, the King's Company and the Duke's Company). In terms of the theatre history, these were heady days, as playhouses developed proscenium arches, perspective stages, changeable backdrops and scenery, and as companies expanded to include women. The drama of the 1660s and 1670s vividly reveals the values and aspirations of the new ascendancy. This was a coterie theatre, playing to a socially exclusive audience, entry to which was controlled both by price and by social practice; the theatre was the place of resort and display for a London elite. It was, too, a knowing audience, aware that the king and his closest associates were sleeping with the actresses. Plays often made allusion to such alliances in their prologues. This is a culture that is fashioning itself as tough, sceptical, worldly-wise, unshockable, and implacably hostile to any residual Puritanism; it reflects the Restoration court. It mirrors, too, the problem of presentation that Charles never really resolved. Once the initial euphoria had been displaced by disasters like the Dutch wars, the comfortable self-delight of the courtiers' world appeared increasingly alien to much of the political nation. The plays serve well to define this issue.

For radical writers the immediate difficulty was explaining defeat. As Neil Keeble suggests, these lines, which Milton wrote for the Chorus in *Samson Agonistes*, vividly depict the 'bewilderment and disillusion which might be caused by this inexplicable disappointment of all for which the Puritans had worked and fought' (Keeble 1990: 228):

> God of our fathers, what is man!
> That thou towards him with hand so various,
> Or might I say contrarious,
> Temper'st thy providence through his short course. (Milton 1997: 380)

The literary opportunities for textually working through that bewilderment were constrained. Radical sectaries had difficulties meeting, let alone proselytizing, from 1660 onwards, and from 1662 the pulpits were closed even to Presbyterians. (Old rivals were finding themselves comrades in adversity.) Political pamphleteering was virtually impossible. However, the ideological crisis could be worked out in memoirs and biographies, for the most part as private, manuscript exercises. Moreover, creative writing, while certainly scrutinized if it came from a notorious hand, received a lighter touch from the process of press control, as indeed it had in the 1640s and 1650s. John Toland, an early biographer of Milton, noted that the licenser who vetted *Paradise Lost* considered suppressing it 'for imaginary Treason' in Book 1, lines 594–9 (Darbishire 1932: 189). The passage in question, a simile referring to how the eclipse of the moon '[p]erplexes monarchs', was of course allowed to stand, and other passages are more tractable still to political reading.

How did the defeated cope? For Lucy Hutchinson, writing the life of her husband, a regicide who died in prison in 1664, the priority is to remember, to memorialize the experiences of the mid-century for the immediate posterity of her children. For John Bunyan, Job, rather than Samson, provided the supporting analogue. George Fox, whose *Journal* was published posthumously in 1694, probably wrote most of it in the 1670s, though the issues remain uncertain. But he retained, in a redefined sort of way, a belief in the local and short-term application of God's providence. Quakers had received less toleration under the Protectorate than may reasonably have been hoped for. Fox can note with grim satisfaction that 'when the King came in they took [Cromwell] up and hanged him: and buried him under Tyburn where he was rolled into his grave with infamy', a fate deserved by his failure to abolish tithes, as promised 'at Dunbar fight': 'And when I saw him hanging there I saw his word justly come upon him' (Fox 1998: 292–3). Quakers probably coped better with the Restoration because, though they had enjoyed very considerable membership growth in the 1650s, they had retained an oppositional edge, outside the circle of the Cromwellian ascendancy.

Once more, Milton affords the richest case study. *Paradise Lost* ends in a vision of futurity in which the godly's expectation is earthly suffering till an indefinitely postponed millennium when the Son of God will return 'to dissolve / Satan with his perverted world' (Milton 1998: 672). But *Paradise Lost*, too, is a memorial to republican values. Certainly, the survival strategies of Adam and Eve in the fallen world provided a paradigm for the godly remnant in late Stuart England (Keeble 1987; Knoppers 1994). But as David Norbrook has most eloquently demonstrated, the epic sustains Milton's republican aspiration: 'the more we try to imagine our way beyond post-Restoration hindsight, the harder it becomes to square a blandly apolitical or defeatist reading of the epic with its author's values' (Norbrook 1999: 433). It is some while since an apolitical reading has been advanced with much conviction. But of course Norbrook is right to remind us of the revolutionary legacy: *Paradise*

Lost is about ideological survival, but the ideology that is protected remains unapologetically anti-clerical and republican.

But the case of John Milton did not end there. By 1671, when he published in a double volume *Paradise Regained* and *Samson Agonistes*, old radicals had begun to recognize that they had survived a decade of persecution, and though they had taken casualties in prison and in more spectacular ways, and though many had turned apostate, there was surely clear evidence that they had come through. By 1672, in the first significant remission of their suffering, Charles issued the Declaration of Indulgence. In the double volume of 1671 Milton showed a reanimated engagement, as the hero of *Samson* leaves the stage to pull down the temple on the ungodly and the hero of *Paradise Regained* contemptuously dismisses Satan and his wiles, confident that his time will come.

Two towering figures carry us to the conclusion of this review: Marvell and Dryden; the former a key figure in the development of a nascent Whig ideology, the latter a loyal supporter of Charles and James II in the developing crises of the 1670s and 1680s.

Critical interest in Marvell has shifted radically in recent times. Famously, he is a poet who fell from critical regard in the nineteenth century to be rediscovered in the early twentieth; his revived reputation was championed by T. S. Eliot, who saw in him 'a fastidious . . . ironist, uncommitted to anything beyond the responsibilities of his art' (quoted in Chernaik and Dzelzainis 1999: 1). But in his own age, and in the century following, it was Marvell the committed Whig satirist that was most valued. While certainly since Eliot's day subtle political readings of his poems of the 1650s abound, the new emphasis on his post-Restoration writing, both poetry and prose, is a welcome corrective. In terms of literary history, he discloses the processes by which the characteristic idioms of the satirical mode developed, while his contribution to intellectual history can best be contextualized in Annabel Patterson's project to chart the development of 'early modern liberalism' in terms of 'how and why liberal claims came to be made in the first place' (Patterson 1997: 15).

Dryden was in the employment of the republic in the late 1650s, and had walked with Milton and Marvell in the funeral procession of Oliver Cromwell, whose death he commemorated in his first poem of significance. His second significant poem welcomed Charles II back to his penitent nation, and thereafter he remained a loyalist, for which he was rewarded with the posts of Poet Laureate and Historiographer Royal, both of which he lost in 1689. His poems of the 1660s disclose the ideological difficulties of constructing a reconciliation between returning royalists and their former opponents. A writer of astonishing versatility, Dryden played a major part in developing a new repertoire for the re-established London stage. His greatest achievement, however, was as a satirist, and *Absalom and Achitophel*, his defence of the royal interest in the Exclusion Crisis, shows a precise judgement of the political temperature, coolly ironic in his assessment of the king's morals, cunningly critical of Monmouth, brilliantly acerbic in his account of the leading Whigs. As Steven Zwicker perceptively concludes, the 'middle way' he seemingly adopted 'was not a philosophical issue . . . but a polemical situation; it was the ground to occupy because it permitted the poet to portray whomever he perceived as his enemies as men who ran to extremes' (Zwicker 1984: 60). The towering achievement of the Williamite period was his translation of the works of Virgil, published in 1697. In his 'brooding and melancholy' (Zwicker 1984: 34) translation of the *Aeneid*, the most complex apologist of the defeated regime obliquely laments the displacement of the regime he had loyally served.

REFERENCES

Anselment, R. A. 1988: *Loyalist Resolve: Patient Fortitude in the English Civil War.* Newark, DE.

Armitage, D., Himy, A. and Skinner, Q. (eds) 1995: *Milton and Republicanism*: Cambridge.

Bergeron, D. M. 1968: 'Harrison, Jonson and Dekker: the magnificent entertainment for King James', *Journal of the Warburg and Courtauld Institutes*, 31, 445–8.

Bray, A. 1988: *Homosexuality in Renaissance England*, 2nd edn: London.

Butler, M. 1984: *Theatre and Crisis 1632–1642*: Cambridge.

Carew, T. 1964: *The Poems of Thomas Carew*, edited by Rhodes Dunlap: Oxford.

Chernaik, W. and Dzelzainis, M. (eds) 1999: *Milton and Liberty.* Basingstoke.

Coiro, A. B. 1999: ' "A ball of strife": Caroline poetry and royal marriage.' In T. N. Corns, ed., *The Royal Image: Representations of Charles I*: Cambridge.

Corns, T. N. 1992: *Uncloistered Virtue: English Political Literature, 1640–1660*: Oxford.

Corns, T. N. (ed.) 1993: *The Cambridge Companion to English Poetry, Donne to Marvell*: Cambridge.

Corns, T. N. 1995: 'Milton and the characteristics of a free commonwealth.' In D. Armitage, A. Himy and Q. Skinner, eds, *Milton and Republicanism*: Cambridge.

Corns, T. N. 1997: 'The poetry of the Caroline court', *Proceedings of the British Academy*, 97, 51–73.

Corns, T. N. (ed.) 1999a: *The Royal Image: Representations of Charles I*: Cambridge.

Corns, T. N. 1999b: 'Duke, prince and king.' In T. N. Corns, ed., *The Royal Image: Representations of Charles I*: Cambridge.

Corns, T. N. (ed.) 2001a: *A Companion to Milton*: Oxford.

Corns, T. N. 2001b: 'On the Morning of Christ's Nativity', 'Upon the Circumcision' and 'The Passion'. In T. N. Corns, ed., *A Companion to Milton*: Oxford.

Darbishire, H. (ed.) 1932: *The Early Lives of Milton*: London.

Davis, J. C. 1986: *Fear, Myth and History: The Ranters and the Historians*: Cambridge.

Dzelzainis, M. 2001: 'Republicanism.' In T. N. Corns, ed., *A Companion to Milton*: Oxford.

Foucault, M. 1975: *Surveillir et punir: naissance de la prison*: Paris.

Fox, G. 1998: *The Journal*, ed. N. Smith: Harmondsworth.

Gallagher, C. and Greenblatt, S. 2000: *Practicing New Historicism*: Chicago.

Geertz, C. 1975: *The Interpretation of Cultures*: London.

Goldberg, J. 1983: *James I and the Politics of Literature: Jonson, Shakespeare, Donne and their Contemporaries*: Baltimore, MD.

Goldberg, J. (ed.) 1994: *Queering the Renaissance*: Durham, NC.

Greenblatt, S. 1980: *Renaissance Self-Fashioning from More to Shakespeare*: Chicago.

Hammond, G. 1990: *Fleeting Things: English Poets and Poems 1616–1660*: Cambridge, MA.

Healy, T. and Sawday, J. (eds) 1990: *Literature and the English Civil War.* Cambridge.

Hill, C. 1972: *The World Turned Upside Down: Radical Ideas during the English Revolution*: London.

Hill, C. 1977: *Milton and the English Revolution*: London.

Hill, C. 1988: *A Turbulent, Seditious, and Factious People: John Bunyan and his Church 1628–1688*: Oxford.

Howarth, D. 1997: *Images of Rule: Art and Politics in the English Renaissance, 1485–1649*: Basingstoke.

James VI and I, 1994: *Political Writings*, ed. J. P. Sommerville: Cambridge.

Jonson, B. 1985: *Ben Jonson*, ed. I. Donaldson: Oxford.

Keeble, N. H. 1987: *The Literary Culture of Nonconformity in Later Seventeenth-Century England*: Leicester.

Keeble, N. H. 1990: ' "The colonel's shadow": Lucy Hutchinson, women's writing and the Civil War.' In T. Healy and J. Sawday, eds, *Literature and the English Civil War*: Cambridge.

Knoppers, L. L. 1994: *Historicizing Milton: Spectacle, Power, and Poetry in Restoration England*: Athens, GA.

Knoppers, L. L. 2000: *Constructing Cromwell: Ceremony, Portrait, and Print, 1645–1661*: Cambridge.

Lewalski, B. K. 1994: *Writing Women in Jacobean England*: Cambridge, MA.

Loxley, J. 1997: *Royalism and Poetry in the English Civil War*: Basingstoke.

Lutaud, O. 1976: *Winstanley: socialisme et christianisme sous Cromwell*: Paris.

Manley, L. 1995: *Literature and Culture in Early Modern London*: Cambridge.

Marcus, L. S. 1986: *The Politics of Mirth: Jonson, Herrick, Milton, Marvell, and the Defense of Old Holiday Pastimes*: Chicago.

Marcus, L. S. 1993: 'Robert Herrick.' In T. N. Corns, ed., *The Cambridge Companion to English Poetry, Donne to Marvell*: Cambridge.

Masson, D. 1877–94: *The Life of John Milton: Narrated in Connexion with the Political, Ecclesiastical, and Literary History of his Time*: London.

Milton, J. 1953–82: *Complete Prose Works of John Milton*, ed. D. M. Wolfe et al.: New Haven, CT.

Milton, J. 1997: *Complete Shorter Poems*, 2nd edn, ed. J. Carey: London.

Milton, J. 1998: *Paradise Lost*, 2nd edn, ed. A. Fowler: London.

Norbrook, D. 1984: *Poetry and Politics in the English Renaissance*: London.

Norbrook, D. 1990: 'Marvell's "Horatian Ode".' In T. Healy and J. Sawday, eds, *Literature and the English Civil War*: Cambridge.

Norbrook, D. 1999: *Writing the English Republic: Poetry, Rhetoric and Politics 1627–1660*: Cambridge.

Orgel, S. 1965: *The Jonsonian Masque*: Cambridge, MA.

Orgel, S. and Strong, R. 1973: *Inigo Jones: The Theatre of the Stuart Court*: Berkeley, CA.

Patterson, A. 1997: *Early Modern Liberalism*: Cambridge.

Potter, L. 1989: *Secret Rites and Secret Writing: Royalist Literature, 1641–1660*: Cambridge.

Sharpe, K. 1987: *Criticism and Compliment: The Politics of Literature in the England of Charles I*: Cambridge.

Sharpe, K. 1992: *The Personal Rule of Charles I*: New Haven, CT.

Smith, N. 1989: *Perfection Proclaimed: Language and Literature in English Radical Religion 1640–1660*: Oxford.

Smith, N. 1994: *Literature and Revolution in England 1640–1660*: New Haven, CT.

Smuts, R. M. 1989: 'Public ceremony and royal charisma: the English royal entry in London, 1485–1642.' In A. L. Beier et al., eds, *The First Modern Society*: Cambridge.

Turner, J. G. (ed.) 1993: *Sexuality and Gender in Early Modern Europe: Institutions, Texts, Images*: Cambridge.

Wainwright, J. P. 1999: 'The king's music.' In T. N. Corns, ed., *The Royal Image: Representations of Charles I*: Cambridge.

Wells, R. H., Burgess, G. and Wymer, R. (eds) 2000: *Neo-Historicism: Studies in Renaissance Literature, History and Politics*: Cambridge.

Wickham, G., Berry, H. and Ingram, W. (eds) 2000: *English Professional Theatre, 1530–1660*: Cambridge.

Wilcher, R. 2001: *The Writing of Royalism 1628–1660*: Cambridge.

Wolfe, D. M. 1941: *Milton and the Puritan Revolution*: New York.

Worden, B. 1990: 'Milton's republicanism and the tyranny of heaven.' In G. Bock, Q. Skinner and M. Viroli, eds, *Machiavelli and Republicanism*: Cambridge.

Zwicker, S. N. 1984: *Politics and Language in Dryden's Poetry: The Arts of Disguise*: Princeton, NJ.

FURTHER READING

Armitage, D., Himy, A. and Skinner, Q. (eds) 1995: *Milton and Republicanism*: Cambridge.

Butler, M. 1984: *Theatre and Crisis 1632–1642*: Cambridge.

Chernaik, W. and Dzelzainis, M., eds, 1999: *Milton and Liberty*: Basingstoke.

Corns, T. N. 1992: *Uncloistered Virtue: English Political Literature, 1640–1660*: Oxford.

Corns, T. N. (ed.) 1999: *The Royal Image: Representations of Charles I*: Cambridge.

Hammond, G. 1990: *Fleeting Things: English Poets and Poems 1616–1660*: Cambridge, MA.

Hill, C. 1972: *The World Turned Upside Down: Radical Ideas during the English Revolution*: London.

Keeble, N. H. 1987: *The Literary Culture of Nonconformity in Later Seventeenth-Century England*: Leicester.

Knoppers, L. L. 2000: *Constructing Cromwell: Ceremony, Portrait, and Print, 1645–1661*: Cambridge.

Lewalski, B. K. 1994: *Writing Women in Jacobean England*: Cambridge, MA.

Loxley, J. 1997: *Royalism and Poetry in the English Civil War*: Basingstoke.

Marcus, L. S. 1986: *The Politics of Mirth: Jonson, Herrick, Milton, Marvell, and the Defense of Old Holiday Pastimes*: Chicago.

Norbrook, D. 1999: *Writing the English Republic: Poetry, Rhetoric and Politics 1627–1660*: Cambridge.

Patterson, A. 1997: *Early Modern Liberalism*: Cambridge.

Potter, L. 1989: *Secret Rites and Secret Writing: Royalist Literature, 1641–1660*: Cambridge.

Sharpe, K. 1987: *Criticism and Compliment: The Politics of Literature in the England of Charles I*: Cambridge.

Smith, N. 1994: *Literature and Revolution in England 1640–1660*: New Haven, CT.

Wilcher, R. 2001: *The Writing of Royalism 1628–1660*: Cambridge.

Zwicker, S. N. 1984: *Politics and Language in Dryden's Poetry: The Arts of Disguise*: Princeton, NJ.

CHAPTER TEN

Art, Architecture and Politics

TIM WILKS

The subject of the fine arts in Stuart Britain was once presented as a succession of stylistic eras and of dominant artistic personalities. Even the best surveys published in the mid-twentieth century digressed into searches for genius and for the even more elusive quality of 'Englishness' in the art of the period (Whinney and Millar 1957; Mercer 1962; Waterhouse 1978). Such preoccupations fail to assist our desire to understand seventeenth-century attitudes to art (the term is used here to refer to the fine and decorative arts in their entirety) or to grasp the political relevance and social significance of art at that time. In pursuit of these concerns, we will attempt to avoid any suggestion of the superiority of one artist over another (however apparent that might seem), or to comment on the merits of particular works, since that would be to stray from the discipline of history into the even more uncertain world of art criticism. However, the expressed preferences of seventeenth-century men and women do require our attention, as they often indicate changes in taste, certain levels of connoisseurship, personal allegiances, and adherence to particular causes or beliefs.

Art and architecture provide valuable material evidence of the past, and testify to the values and concerns of the age in which they were created. Moreover, the social, intellectual, economic and political activity that surrounded the production and transaction of art is now accepted as a rich area of historical investigation. Accordingly, much interest has focused on seventeenth-century British patrons and collectors, who increasingly understood the capacity of art to inform, educate, inspire and impress. This area of study has expanded alongside renewed interest in the principal milieu of the great art patrons and collectors: the Stuart court, which is no longer seen as a backwater of the political nation but as a hub of influence and decision-making (Starkey et al. 1987; Cruickshanks 2000).

Such has been the rapid advance of scholarship in this area, that attention has now spread beyond the principals to those peripheral yet essential figures, without whom art could neither have been acquired nor put to effect. During the Stuart period a cadre of professional advisers emerged, who at various times acted as dealers, connoisseurs, keepers of cabinets and galleries, and agents seeking art to buy or artists to employ. Before even the reign of James I was quite over, the duke of Buckingham's highly effective art agent, Balthasar Gerbier, wrote defiantly and prophetically to his patron from France:

Let enemies and people ignorant of paintings say what they will, they cannot deny that pictures are noble ornaments, a delightful amusement, and histories that one may read without fatigue . . . Our pictures, if they were to be sold a century after our death, would sell for good cash, and for three times more than they have cost. I wish I could only live a century, if they were sold, in order to be able to laugh at those facetious folk who say, *It is monny cast away for bobles and schadows.* (Brewer 1839: II, 370–1)

Gerbier's defence on the grounds that paintings were good long-term investments was eventually proved right by the prices that art came to command in Georgian Britain (Reitlinger 1961: 3–25). What he could not foresee were the successive traumas that the art market would suffer in his lifetime, such that foreign buyers would pay enormous prices – £2,000 for a Raphael; £1,000 for a Correggio (Portier 1996) – when the English parliament disposed of a magnificent royal collection tainted with associations of absolutism and Catholicism, only for much of it to be retrieved later.

Plainly, the arts were greatly affected by the great political and religious controversies of the Stuart period. However, the extent to which art and architecture was influential or provocative within the context of those controversies remains a matter of ongoing debate. Iain Pears has asserted that 'the early collectors such as Arundel and Buckingham should . . . be seen as having acted in a vacuum, their procurement of works of art being a personal business conducted not only independently of the rest of society but even partly at odds with it' (Pears 1998: 106). Yet there is growing awareness of connections between aristocratic interest in the arts and enthusiasm within the middling ranks of society. Old assumptions about the closed nature of the Stuart court are being replaced with a more informed notion of access. No member of the political nation was denied the opportunity to witness the spectacle of the court or to visit houses containing art. Eye-witness accounts are legion, expressions of admiration frequent, of horror very rare. All this suggests that the display of art succeeded, on the whole, in gratifying the many onlookers. Whether it succeeded in any deeper purpose is another matter, as is the possibility that the disapproval of a section of society might have gone largely unrecorded.

Private correspondence concerning artistic matters, as well as the various publications affirming the importance of art and architecture, frequently take on a defensive tone. The threat to art in Stuart Britain was undoubtedly Puritanism. How deeply the country as a whole was inclined to distrust most forms of imagery, show and decoration, not just at the high-point of Puritanism, but for the whole of the seventeenth century and beyond, is a question to which wildly varying answers have been offered. Patrick Collinson's (1988) work stands at one extreme, perceiving the emergence of a fundamentally Protestant society that held far more suspicion than sympathy for the fine arts. A corrective is offered by Edward Chaney (2000), who has shown that Catholic patrons, collectors and art professionals were more numerous than has been supposed, and that they greatly influenced the direction taken by the arts in seventeenth-century Britain.

There was no immediate revolution of style or taste when the Stuarts accompanied by their Scottish followers entered England in 1603. In painting and limning (the art of miniature), a style of portraiture persisted throughout the early Jacobean period that was more iconic than realistic (Strong 1969). Fine detail and often vivid colouring were sought and admired, yet basic techniques of Renaissance art, such as perspective and the use of light and shadow, remained forgotten or ignored. In architecture, buildings that were essentially gothic but overlaid with Mannerist ornament and borrowings from the classical orders still contrived to please through their very peculiarity and intricacy. Within such an essentially insular, visual culture, competent artists such as the painters Robert Peake, Marcus Gheeraerts and William Larkin, the sculptor Maximilian Colt, and the surveyor-builder John Thorpe, found few inventive possibilities.

The only art form to emerge from the Tudor period with anything approaching a strong native tradition was that of the miniature. It relied on techniques and materials quite separate from that of painting, having developed out of the tradition of manuscript illumination. In England it became the art form that provided portable and private images for strengthening bonds between individuals, whereas in Europe the portrait medallion or *Gnadenpfennig* was more established. Nicholas Hilliard, the supreme Elizabethan limner, continued to work well into the reign of James I, but was by then less favoured than Isaac Oliver, whom he had once instructed. Oliver was by far the most accomplished artist of his generation and a figure of wide influence in the arts. In his own art of miniature he instructed his son Peter, who in turn worked closely with the painter-turned-miniaturist John Hoskins and his nephews Alexander and Samuel Cooper. The potency of the miniature and its appropriateness as a diplomatic gift were recognized throughout the seventeenth century. Samuel

Plate 1 Samuel Cooper (attributed), *Oliver Cromwell*, watercolour on vellum, *c*.1655. By courtesy of the National Gallery, London.

Cooper's portraits of Cromwell, for example, were greatly desired by Europe's rulers. By mid-century the miniature had emerged from concealment in bedchambers to be displayed typically in cabinet rooms. Good examples could be valued more highly than large paintings – Richard Cromwell paid £100 for Cooper's unfinished studio sketch of his father, and Abraham van der Doort became so distraught at mislaying one of Charles I's miniatures by Gibson that he committed suicide.

It has always been recognized that good access to continental Europe was critical in the post-Renaissance centuries to the development of visual culture in Britain. The importance of the British traveller encountering the art and architecture of Europe, and seeing its applications and effects, is now seen as a crucial factor alongside that of the influx of continental artists and works of art. Unlike literature and music, the fine arts seem never to have carried very well across the Channel, and carried hardly at all during times of hostility. Consequently, England managed to gain a measure of familiarity with the painting, sculpture and architecture of Europe during the first half of the sixteenth century, but in Elizabeth I's reign became ever more ignorant of it. There continued to be periods in the seventeenth century when large parts of Europe were inaccessible to all except apostates, renegades and the foolhardy. However, isolation from the most important artistic movements on the Continent was never as severe as it had been during the Elizabethan years. Even the hugely disruptive effects of the Civil War and the Interregnum on art patronage and collecting were mitigated to an extent by the cultural experience gained by the many royalist exiles who waited for better times in France, the Low Countries and Italy.

Any consideration of serious art appreciation in Britain would once invariably have begun with Charles I and the so-called 'Whitehall circle'. Much more is now known about the deep and growing interest in art and architecture that existed in the earlier Jacobean period. There is some irony in the fact that James I, who showed little personal interest in the fine arts, by ending hostilities with Spain in 1604, created the conditions for a visual Renaissance in Britain. The numbers of English and Scots gentlemen travelling for education increased sharply, and the routes and destinations of what was to become known as the Grand Tour began to be etched deeper into the cultural tradition of the aristocracy and gentry (Stoye 1989). Those who had spent time on the Continent (especially in Italy and France) encountered sophisticated and persuasive art, and many returned home to become patrons and collectors. With new tastes and new confidence they began seeking to engage foreign artists.

Initially, it was almost impossible to persuade any artist of international repute to come to England. The Florentine sculptor Cellini, would, apart from Holbein, have been the most important foreign recruit of the early Tudor Renaissance, but rejected the English as 'beasts', and a hundred years later it was still commonly assumed throughout Europe that England's climate and inhabitants were equally inhospitable. The first persistent attempt to persuade a highly regarded continental artist to paint in Stuart England was made in 1611 when the court of Henry, Prince of Wales (1594–1612), sought unsuccessfully to secure the services of Michiel Miereveldt, a prominent Dutch portrait painter (Strong 1986: 116). Even after Prince Henry's unexpectedly early death, the new enthusiasm for art in London continued to grow, and other highly competent Dutch painters soon arrived (Hearn 1995: 202–30). Paul van

Somer was in London by December 1616 and wasted little time in creating a memorable portrait in several versions for James I's independent-minded queen, Anne of Denmark, and her mainly female circle.

Other notable Dutch painters who arrived in the later Jacobean years included Jacob van der Doort (whose brother, Abraham, cared for the collections of, first, Prince Henry, and later, Charles I), Abraham van Blyenberch and a young Anthony Van Dyck. The latter's exceptional ability had been recognized even before he emerged from the studio of Rubens. His enticement to London in 1620 to paint especially for the duke of Buckingham was an early sign of the predatory nature of the British patron-collector that became familiar throughout Europe in the following two hundred years. Although these artists did not remain in England for long, they produced work of sophistication and modernity that contributed greatly to the ending of the 'Jacobethan' iconic style. Another Netherlander, Daniel Mytens, did stay on to become 'picture drawer' to the king, and was only supplanted when Van Dyck returned in 1632 after working in Italy.

Prince Henry, and later, Prince Charles and Buckingham, were all guided by Thomas Howard, 14th earl of Arundel (1585–1646), who, more than any other, was responsible for stimulating interest in the fine arts in Britain in the seventeenth century (Howarth 1985). Arundel went on to gain an appreciation of art far deeper than that of any English patron or collector before him. Acquaintance with Italy, which Arundel visited briefly in 1612 and again between 1613 and 1614, proved critical. It inspired him to develop a straightforward fascination with art into something more profound: the pursuit and attainment of *virtù* (the English word 'virtue' fails to capture fully its meaning). All well-educated Britons at least knew what it meant through their reading of Italian Renaissance texts. Arundel felt in Italy he had found a society profoundly influenced by *virtù*, and hoped that England could be likewise conditioned, partly through the introduction of great art. That he did not altogether fail is something that might be deduced from the epithet 'the Father of Vertu', applied to him by Horace Walpole a century later. The perceptive Walpole recognized the real significance of Arundel; that he was not simply a great lord with the wealth, leisure and inclination to employ artists and to accumulate an art collection without precedent in Britain, but one who promoted the fine arts for being exemplary and edifying. On a more pragmatic level, Arundel was concerned that art should be used to its full potential to establish the credibility of Stuart Britain abroad.

The essential contribution which art and architecture could make to the character of a court was understood by the many who were dismayed by the indecorous court of James I and who pinned their hopes on the heir, Prince Henry. It was apparent that throughout Europe the setting, architecture and interiors of courts were being redesigned to take into account major changes in court culture. Accordingly, Prince Henry, who envisioned an heroic role for himself in Europe, set about forming impressive collections of paintings, bronzes, coins and medals, and initiated hugely ambitious building programmes at the palaces of St James's and Richmond that were abandoned after his early death (Strong 1986; Wilks 2001). While the grandest plans were for Richmond, alterations made to St James's included the construction of a picture gallery into which came donations from supporters and European states.

Plate 2   François Dieussart, Thomas Howard, earl of Arundel. Photograph © Edward Chaney.

   Most significantly for the future course of the arts, a group of pictures was bought
in Venice with the aid of the financier Filippo Burlamacchi, and the local knowledge
of the highly cultivated English ambassador in Venice, Sir Henry Wotton, who later
provided his countrymen with the seminal *Elements of Architecture* (1624). This
high-quality purchase, which included at least one painting attributed to Titian, not
only showed the potential of ambassadors as art agents, but also initiated an enduring
British engagement with the colourful and vigorous art of Venice. A second set of
Venetian paintings was soon acquired by Henry Howard, earl of Northampton (Wilks

1997). Another set, and a collection of antique statuary, was bought by Wotton's adept successor, Sir Dudley Carleton, for Robert Carr, earl of Somerset, but after his downfall in 1615 it was split between Arundel and Lord Danvers (Wilks 1989).

Art was acquired to impress, but it was also for solitary contemplation. Partly for this reason it was felt necessary for Prince Henry to have a cabinet of medals and coins such as that formed by the famous Dutch antiquary Abraham Gorlaeus, which was purchased for the enormous sum of £2,200. However, the private enjoyment of art still required a defence against the charge of idleness. Some explanation of the perceived benefits of time spent in a cabinet room was given by another adept ambassador, Sir Thomas Roe. Writing from Constantinople in 1621 to Lucy, countess of Bedford, he recalled how

> I saw you marshalling of antient coynes and medalls, delighting in the records of vertuous tymes, vertuous men and vertuous actions . . . This curiositie of antiquityes, though by some seuere men censured, hath yet diuers uses besides delight, not to be contemned: they are a kind of lay humanitye, teaching and inciting devotion to morall vertue, as well, and more safely then images among the new Romans. (Richardson 1740: 583)

Roe's reference to the dangers of the art being then produced and proffered by papal Rome would have been appreciated by the countess, who in preferring Dutch art to Italian stood against the new tide of aristocratic taste.

Around 1620, Charles (still then Prince of Wales), who had watched Prince Henry, Anne of Denmark and various courtiers build collections, decided to collect art together with the duke of Buckingham. In 1623 the pair (accompanied by other future connoisseurs such as Endymion Porter and Hamilton) visited Spain; their main purpose being to secure a marriage match between Charles and the Infanta. In this they failed, but they at least benefited from exposure to the awesome visual experience of Madrid's palaces. At the court of Philip IV, Charles saw how the authority and power of absolute monarchy was verified by spectacle (Brown 1995: 95–145). If Charles had not already intended to make his own court equal in splendour to any in Europe, then he must have decided upon it in Spain. He returned to England with a haul of prestigious pieces including Titian's *Pardo Venus*, Correggio's *St John the Baptist* and Giambologna's sculptural group, *Samson and the Philistine*.

As a young king, Charles I was impatient in his desire to create a virtuous court in evident contrast to that of his late father. To that end, he was prepared to buy up entire collections and outbid rivals as necessary. When he learned from the Arundels that the ducal house of Gonzaga, in the declining Italian city-state of Mantua, might be persuaded to part with some of its art treasures, he sent Nicholas Lanier, a trusted courtier and art lover, to conduct secret negotiations. Around the same time, the painter Orazio Gentileschi informed Charles of an obtainable collection known to him from his time in Genoa, and gained both permission and funds to send his sons to bargain for it. This was probably always regarded as a secondary target, for once in Italy, Lanier aborted the Gentileschis' mission when it became clear that the Mantuan purchase would proceed.

Although a spillage of mercury aboard ship ruined several paintings, others, attributed to Titian, Correggio, Andrea del Sarto, Raphael, Julio Romano, Dosso Dossi, Domenico Feti, Romanino, Sodoma, Bronzino, Mantegna, Caravaggio and the Carracci, arrived in London in good condition. In 1629 a second Mantuan purchase was made by the Venice-based dealer Daniel Nys, who had assisted with earlier British purchases in Italy. This time, Nys managed to obtain Mantegna's famous set of nine canvases, the *Triumphs of Caesar*, and also many pieces of Roman statuary. It was when the newly adorned Palace of Whitehall found favourable mention in the correspondence of the painter-diplomat, Peter Paul Rubens, that the cost and effort of the coup began to be justified in terms of international prestige (Howarth 1982).

After the arrival of the last Mantuan pieces, Charles I's collecting became much more subdued. He made only one large purchase of pictures during the whole of the 1630s: 23 paintings, again of supreme quality, bought from the dealer William Frizell. It was no coincidence that Charles had begun his long period of personal rule, and was acutely aware of the state royal finances. Moreover, Charles had always associated collecting with his friendship with Buckingham, who was now dead. The royal collection was, in any case, essentially complete, with the galleries and chambers of the principal royal palaces: Whitehall, St James's and Greenwich, all furnished with masterpieces. His old enthusiasm, however, was rekindled in the late 1630s when the collection of Bartolomeo della Nave, and the lesser collections of Priuli and Regnier, became available in Venice. In the event, the king withdrew, allowing the marquis of Hamilton to compete with and eventually outbid Arundel. As a result, a further six hundred prized examples of Renaissance art entered the country.

Charles I remained intensely concerned with other aspects of the arts throughout the 1630s. Van Dyck returned in 1632 to become his painter and was immediately knighted. While in royal service he, with the aid of assistants, still found time to fulfil hundreds of private commissions. These did more than record for posterity the elite of a generation; they reinforced – possibly modified – the aristocracy's conception of itself. Van Dyck's sitters of the 1630s may now appear insouciant, languid or disdainful, but the intention was invariably to imply virtue. It should not be forgotten, moreover, that in 1642 the subjects of these so-called 'cavalier portraits', divided between king and parliament: one sitter, Thomas Chaloner (Hermitage, St Petersburg), even became a regicide.

In 1635 the ceiling of Inigo Jones's Banqueting House at Whitehall finally received Rubens's great canvases celebrating the previous reign. For this commission Rubens was paid £3,000 – more than Van Dyck was paid for seven years of royal commissions (Smuts 1987: 130). As for the royal picture collection, Charles began subtly to change it by exchanging individual works with other collectors. That this was possible at all is an indication of the rapid development of aristocratic collecting. In this way Charles obtained a *St George* by Raphael from the earl of Pembroke in exchange for a book of portrait drawings by Holbein, and gained a *Venus* by Palma Giovane from Endymion Porter for one of the Mantua pictures. Charles also continued to accept works of art as gifts from those familiar with his tastes, such as the sophisticated Lord Ancram, who, in giving him three examples, introduced the king to the work of a contemporary Dutch painter, Rembrandt van Rijn (Millar 1960).

Charles I's attempts to patronize artists (as distinct from collecting art) had mixed results. Just as Prince Henry had earlier found difficulty in attracting leading European artists to England, so Charles I, despite the huge rise in the estimation abroad of England's cultural status, tried and failed to induce successful Italian artists – first

Guercino, then Albani – to come to his court. The sculptor Pietro Tacca, who had long before cast some small bronzes in Florence for Prince Henry, also declined to make the journey (Haskell 1980: 177–9). There were, however, two important Italian arrivals: the history painter Orazio Gentileschi and the 'one-eyed' sculptor, Francesco Fanelli. Though not an Italian, the sculptor François Dieussart was lured from Rome to Arundel House in the 1630s. He, more than any other, was responsible for introducing Baroque sculpture to England, even though Bernini's bust of Charles I caused a sensation when it arrived in England in 1637, having been carved in Rome after Van Dyck's portrait of the king in three positions.

Gentileschi, who arrived in London in 1626, was initially both court painter and one of Buckingham's diplomatic advisers. He was given apartments at York House, Buckingham's residence on the Strand, where Balthasar Gerbier (also fulfilling an occasional diplomatic role) looked after the art collection. After their patron's death a violent enmity developed between the pair, probably initiated by Gentileschi's disparagement of Gerbier's purchases. In contrast, Van Dyck, who entered royal service a few years later, maintained his equanimity; something no doubt made easier by

Plate 3 Robert van Voerst, *Charles I*, 1636, engraving after François Dieussart. © The British Museum.

Gentileschi's lack of any pretension to be a portrait painter. For his part, Van Dyck had no desire to concentrate on anything other than portraits, though he had heralded his return to England by sending Charles I the rapturous mythological painting *Renaldo and Armida*. His later mythological painting, *Cupid and Psyche*, seems only to have been prompted by Henrietta Maria's dissatisfaction with one of the series of canvases on the theme begun by Jacob Jordaens and Rubens in late 1639 for the Queen's House at Greenwich (Finaldi 1999).

The work of Gentileschi, that of Rubens in the Banqueting House and Francis Cleyn in Somerset House, represented a brief golden age for history painting in England. The decorative histories that a generation later were to contribute to the appearance of the Baroque interior in Britain were not especially influential, or indeed applicable beyond the grandest setting, and the genre failed to establish itself. In his English work Gentileschi shed the influence of Caravaggio, adopting instead a more linear, vivid and evenly-lit style that complied with the serenity of the court. Prior to Buckingham's assassination he completed a large ceiling canvas for York House: *Apollo and the Nine Muses*, and thereafter worked mainly for the queen. As well as producing wall-hung, biblical scenes that included *The Finding of Moses, Joseph and Potiphar's Wife* and *Lot and his Daughters*, he created for the ceiling of the Great Hall of the Queen's House at Greenwich a nine-canvas allegory, *Peace Reigning over the Arts*. This theme was especially dear to Charles I, but part of the tragedy of his reign was that he hugely overestimated the extent to which promotion of the arts could engender peace in his kingdom or beyond.

The antipathy of Puritanism to art was expressed in print hardly at all before William Prynne's *Histrio-mastix* (1632), and then only indirectly. Prynne was principally concerned with the immorality of stage plays, yet he found no difficulty in extending his condemnation to most areas of court life. He warns that the subject of 'obscene Pictures' would be discussed, since it was materially relevant to the sinfulness of the theatre. However, Prynne later extrapolates from a standard definition of idolatry to condemn 'the very *art of making Pictures and Images, as the occasion of Idolatory*, together with all stage-portraitures, Images, Vizards, or representations of Heathen Idols, etc.' David Howarth has made the point that *Histrio-mastix* was given notoriety, and was made popular, by archbishop Laud's determination to make an example of Prynne and the savage sentence subsequently imposed upon him by Star Chamber (Howarth 1997: 279). Moreover, the imaginative reading of the authorities that *Histrio-mastix* included an attack on the queen, Henrietta Maria, turned it into just that. Immediately, the entire life of the court, hidden to those ordinary citizens who thronged the streets immediately beyond the walls of royal palaces and the town houses of the aristocracy, became suspect. After Prynne's punishment sympathizers were reluctant to rush into print. But in 1641, following Laud's impeachment, George Salteran published his *Treatise against Images and Pictures in Churches* in which he identified and vilified not just the worship of pictures, but of those who made them and those who displayed them.

A ready defence for the visual arts against the assertions of *Histrio-mastix* was found in Henry Peacham's *The Compleat Gentleman*, published as an expanded third edition in 1634. Erudite reinforcements followed in the form of *De Pictura Veterum* (1637) and its English version, *The Painting of the Ancients* (1638), written by Arundel's librarian, Francis Junius. These emphasized the propriety of contemplating art and sought to fix painting among the respectable arts by citing every known classical reference to it. Puritanism had no essential quarrel with the classical past and tended to disregard pagan imagery. There was, therefore, some hope that a large area of the visual arts could be ring-fenced from the Puritan onslaught, which, if the defensiveness of almost all contemporary literature praising art is an indication, was always expected. Fifty years after Richard Haydocke had censored references to religious imagery in *A Tracte contining the Arts of curious painting, carving and building* (London, 1598), his translation of Lomazzo, Edward Norgate, in *Miniatura or the Art of Limning*, still found need to describe pusillanimously 'this harmless and honest Recreation, of all kinds of painting the most innocent, and which the *Divill* him selfe could never accuse of or infect with Idolatory' (Norgate 1997: 83).

However, these literary efforts were mainly read by those already in sympathy with the cause of art. The Puritan mentality was fundamentally suspicious of aesthetic pleasure however derived, for such worldly satisfaction might be mistaken for an anticipation of salvation. Spectacle, whether in the form of decoration or theatre, was regarded as a distraction from the Word of God. The separate path along which bishops Hooker, Jewel and Andrewes attempted to lead the English church – maintaining a distance from both Rome and Geneva – was ultimately irrelevant in the controversy concerning the appeal to the senses in either the religious or the secular setting, since Charles I and archbishop Laud, for all the niceties of their position, were, in the eyes of Puritans, as much in error as the pope. Where the royal intention was to suggest and inspire virtue through art and architecture, only pride was seen.

Plate 4 Inigo Jones, Queen's Chapel, St James's Palace (west front), London, 1623–5. Photograph © Edward Chaney.

The repair of relations between Charles I and Henrietta Maria in 1629, coincidental with the beginning of the period of personal rule, led to the restoration of the
queen's French household that had been sent packing in 1626. Capuchin friars
arrived to begin services in the queen's chapels at Somerset House and St James's
that caused great interest and a stream of conversions.

The growing influence of the queen led to the decision to allow a papal agent to
reside in London. The first, Gregorio Panzani, arrived in 1635, and the following
year his replacement, George Con, built a papal oratory within his London house
where masses were held six times a day. The tolerant attitude of the king, and his
liking for Con, soon gave rise to hopes (and fears) of a reunion with Rome (Albion
1935: 393–401). Open *rapprochement* with Rome was a political mistake that the
Stuarts made repeatedly. It was only natural for the relationship to have been
smoothed by art. Cardinal Barberini, the pope's nephew, spared neither trouble nor
expense in attempting to influence Charles I and later – as if the Civil War had never
happened – Charles II and James, duke of York. The first batch of papal pictures,
including a work attributed to Leonardo da Vinci, was presented by Panzani in 1636.
Later, Barberini oversaw the commissioning of canvases by Guido Reni for the
Queen's House at Greenwich. This project was thwarted by the Civil War, but after
the Restoration the cardinal took inspiration from it to order some large canvases
from Romanelli. As late as 1677 Barberini was planning to send a fine painting to the
duchess of York (Millar 1984: 73). The inescapable connection between art, religion
and politics was never made plainer than when Henrietta Maria chose to exhibit the
latest art works to have arrived from Rome in her chapel. Those who were uncon-
cerned at having to view them in such surroundings included the likes of secretary
Windebank, who blithely admitted to being a Catholic but not a *Roman* Catholic.

The prodigious spending on art by the likes of Charles I, Buckingham, Arundel,
Pembroke and Hamilton has tended to obscure the fact that the fine and decorative
arts were also present in the houses of lesser individuals. Evidence of art-enriched
households and circles of association beyond the periphery of the court continues to
be uncovered. In 1616 Sir Henry Fanshawe's London house contained 'pictures
. . . both in oyle paintinge and lyminge, and . . . medalls, stones, Prints and Drawings'.
Three years later, John Connock of Calstocke in Cornwall left portraits, and religious
and allegorical pictures to his relatives (Wilks 1997). In 1635 Mark Belford (former
secretary to Sir Henry Wotton in Venice, and briefly thereafter Prince Henry's
household miniaturist) left paintings and miniatures to a circle of friends, including
the free-spending royalist patron Sir Christopher Hatton, and the prominent 'opposition lawyer' Gilbert Barrell. Such individuals were, of course, exceptional; John
Evelyn's comment on Holland in 1641: 'pictures are very common here, there
being scarce an ordinary tradesman whose house is not decorated with them', was
never at any point applicable to Stuart Britain. Even so, interest in art among the
landed gentry and urban elites increased greatly as the century progressed.

When war seemed inevitable, large-scale purchasing of art subsided and building
plans were put to one side. Many foreign artists, deprived of work, left the country.
After the initial exodus, some demand was found to remain. Artists such as the etcher
Wenceslas Hollar returned, while others, such as Gerard Soest, arrived for the first
time. Peter Lely may already have been in London when war broke out. During the
Interregnum he secured his reputation, partly on the strength of a portrait of the

Lord Protector, of which many versions were painted. While a new elite emerged, a secluded life proved the best course for many royalist sympathizers, especially in London. Appalled at the unbridling of the mob and the general uncongeniality of Puritan rule, Edward Norgate set about substantially revising his *Miniatura* in 1648, which had been circulating in manuscript form for about twenty years. In this revision he recommended the practice of limning as 'a sweet and contented retirement from . . . this drunken, perishing, and ending world' (Norgate 1997: 95).

For the arts, the Civil War was not only a period of disruption but also of destruction. Painting and sculpture were mainly at peril in places of worship where, because of their perceived idolatrous and superstitious nature, they caused most offence (Phillips 1973). In March 1643 a Commons Committee accompanied by soldiers went to Somerset House to wreck the Queen's Chapel: as much a venting of frustration as a rational act of pious necessity. Inside, they were confronted by a 'Paradise of glory, forty feet in height', built by François Dieussart to display the holy sacrament, which rose over the altar on pillars, and was painted with the figures of adoring archangels, cherubim and seraphim. They smashed ornaments, defaced images and burned books. Rubens's altarpiece *Crucifixion* was hurled into the River Thames. Later, the allegories that covered the ceiling were over-painted plainly in blue (Huygens 1982: 60). This very visible show of iconoclasm was directed at something Puritan London had long regarded as an affront: the full ritual of Catholicism being practised in the heart of the nation.

Beyond the capital, churches and chapels underwent another post-Reformation purge of decoration and ornament, systematized through the activities of commissioners such as William Dowsing (active in Suffolk and Cambridge) and Richard Culmer (sent to Canterbury because its recalcitrant clergy 'loved their cathedral Jezebel the better because she was painted'). However, even the zealots were not active in every parish, and some medieval carvings, fittings and painted glass survived. Many parliamentarian commanders had the same social background as their royalist opponents, and most stopped short of regarding all art as idolatrous. At Ewelme in Oxfordshire the church's rich Gothic ornament and fittings were saved by the local parliamentarian landowner, Henry Marten (Sherwood and Pevsner 1990: 596–8).

It was a war in which the private house might be burned, looted or entirely left alone, depending on its military value or the mood of the soldiery. When Prince Rupert briefly occupied Denton Hall in Yorkshire, the home of Ferdinando, Lord Fairfax, in June 1644, he ordered that nothing be touched (a gesture attributed to the family portraits kindling memories of old Fairfax family support for the Palatine cause) (Wilson 1985: 47). However, in Kent, Sir William Springate, appointed to search recusants' houses to 'destroy their pictures and trumpery', while visiting the house of another county committee man, 'spied several superstitious pictures, as of the crucifixion of Christ, and of His resurrection and such like, very large, that were of great ornament to the hall . . . He drew out his sword and cut them all out of the frames, and spitting them on his sword's point went into the parlour with them' (Everitt 1973: 148).

Remarkably, it is at this time and in the royalist stronghold of Oxford that a major portrait painter emerged: William Dobson, the first English painter to have fully benefited from the new wave of artists from the Low Countries and Germany (Francis Cleyn, from Rostock, was said to have taught him). Dobson's royalist sitters showed the resoluteness, weariness and stress of a beleaguered existence that was utterly different from the calm assurance that Van Dyck's portraits exuded. Dobson became as intimate with his subjects as Van Dyck had been. The latter had painted himself and Charles I's Gentleman of the Bedchamber, Endymion Porter, as friends and equals. Likewise, Dobson's group portrait of himself, Sir Charles Cotterell and Nicholas Lanier gives mid-century testimony to the social partnership that by then existed between the leading architects of the revival of visual culture and their patrons.

The abandoned palaces of Charles I continued to be protected by the awe of majesty, and the vast art collection remained virtually untouched. However, once the king had been executed, plans for the disposal of the late king's goods were rapidly made. Yet this does not seem to have been impelled by a conscious need to efface the visible remains of a monarchic, absolutist, self-indulgent or profane court culture. The starting premise embodied in the Act of parliament authorizing the disposal, was that the possessions of the king, queen and prince of Wales were justly forfeit and were now the property of the state. However, the king had left debts (largely to his own servants) and these were to be paid out of the proceeds of the sale of his goods. Thus, the royal estate was to be regarded much as the estate of any deceased citizen, that is to say, one with creditors who needed satisfaction. This provided the pretext for the sales that ensued. Significantly, however, parliament

Plate 5   William Dobson, *Portrait of the artist with Nicholas Lanier and Sir Charles Cotterell*, oil, *c.*1645–6. Collection of the duke of Northumberland. Photograph: Photographic Survey, Courtauld Institute of Art.

assigned the first £30,000 as a short-term loan to the treasurers of the navy (Millar 1972). Above all, it was a pressing need for money in 1649 that prompted the sale of Charles I's collections.

The Commonwealth decreed that no works of a superstitious nature were to be sold abroad. Beyond that, despite having overthrown one absolutist regime, it was perfectly prepared to welcome the representatives of others such as France and Spain to buy at the sales. There remained a need to furnish and decorate state apartments, and also Hampton Court and Whitehall, newly become residences of the Lord Protector Cromwell, who lived in some style from 1654 until his death in 1658. Initially, it was decided to keep back £10,000 worth of the royal possessions for the use of the new regime. Later, another £10,000 worth was reserved, and then yet more. Eventually, some sold items were actually bought back for Cromwell. The most important of the reserved items were Mantegna's *Triumphs of Caesar*.

Of all the major collections, only that of Algernon Percy, Earl of Northumberland, would remain untouched at the end of the Protectorate. However, many lesser households, even in London, succeeded in keeping their art. In 1651 the house of Sir Walter Pye contained Venetian paintings and a costly Italian mosaic table, while at the well-furnished house of the merchant Sir Thomas Ingram there were, in the judgement of a sophisticated Dutchman, 'many fine portraits' (Huygens 1982: 58, 63). The case of the leading Covenanter, William, 3rd earl of Lothian, who continued to buy in the Low Countries for his collection at Newbattle in Scotland, is exceptional. He, however, suffered the confiscation of a consignment of pictures intercepted at sea, which was eventually bought by the agent of major-general Lambert, though whether for keeping or for selling on is unclear (Wenley 1993).

It has always been accepted that the arts suffered during the Civil War and Interregnum. However, there is now greater awareness of a community of artists managing to survive, of a continuation of building, and of collections kept intact. Accordingly, the status and role of art during this period is being re-evaluated. There is, however, little evidence of any revolution in the arts accompanying the political upheavals. Unfortunately for those who see minimalist classicism as the style of building most naturally agreeable to the Puritan eye, no broad agreement between leading Puritans or republicans to build in that manner is apparent: East Anglia, for example, is entirely lacking in such architecture (Mowl and Earnshaw 1995). Neither parliament nor Protectorate attempted with any enthusiasm to harness the arts to its cause. Significantly, it was from a group of artists (Peter Lely, Balthasar Gerbier and George Geldorp) that a proposal to paint canvases commemorating parliament's victories emerged, though it was never taken up.

The disagreements that thwarted all attempts to arrive at a long-term political settlement also prevented the state from employing art to its full advantage. If artists had clearly been set the task of inventing a republican iconography or seeking an acceptable Puritan aesthetic, the experiment would have been evident in the representation of Oliver Cromwell. However, the Interregnum allowed a painter such as Robert Walker to come to the fore, who shamelessly borrowed Van Dyck's compositions to pose the Cromwellian elite as the simple replacements of those who had earlier held sway (Peacock 2001: 29). The engraver Pierre Lombart made similar borrowings, most notoriously basing his 'Oliver Cromwell on Horseback' on Van

Dyck's equestrian portrait of Charles I, for which the Council was content to reward him in 1655. The complex subject of Cromwell's portrayal has recently been revisited (Cooper 1999), as has the broader subject of Interregnum culture, which is now seen to have had some lingering effect and to have deprived the Restoration of certain idioms and images (Knoppers 2000).

Horace Walpole quipped that 'the Restoration brought back the Arts, not Taste'. If Charles II was not as fastidious as his father had been in matters of taste, he remained a full believer in the potential of great art to exalt the power and majesty of state. Although Charles returned to his own kingdom before Le Brun and Le Vau began work on Louis XIV's great building programme, he had seen the visual statements of absolutism already introduced by the cardinal-ministers at the Louvre and Saint-Germain. From his period of exile in Holland, Charles was also acquainted with the grandeur of the House of Orange, which itself had followed the French example. Royalist exiles returned with impressions of a Paris which by then boasted the Palais Mazarin (finished internally in 1647) and the somewhat older Palais du Luxembourg of Marie de' Medici.

Charles II displayed an impressive resolve to reconstitute the Stuart royal collection; first, by retrieving what had been lost (to the extent that was possible), and then by buying anew. The Committee for the recovery of goods was in being until 1672, by which time at least 1,000 pictures hung in the various royal palaces. There was even some effort to hang pictures in their old places. Charles also made a determined and ultimately successful effort to retrieve works of art that had been taken to Colombes in France by his mother, Henrietta Maria. From this source came masterpieces by Gentileschi and Baglione, as well as Holbein's *Noli Me Tangere* (Millar 1984: 64–88).

Although Charles II's indolence may rightly be seen to have affected his attitude towards the patronage and collecting of art, it should not be overlooked that he had the Stuart knack of making astounding bulk purchases. His sole venture was in 1660, when he bought for £2,686 a varied collection of pictures of high quality, assembled in Holland by William Frizell (the same dealer who had supplied his father 22 years earlier). The States of Holland at the same time presented a collection of pictures and sculptures, thoughtfully containing contemporary Dutch works by Gerrit Dou and Saenredam, as well as Italian Old Masters, of which one was Lotto's portrait of Andrea Odoni. Once more, the most important collection of Dutch art outside Holland was to be found in London. However, this permanent reminder of the initial goodwill of the Dutch did nothing to dampen colonial and trading rivalry that soon led to the Second Anglo-Dutch War.

Lely maintained his position as the principal society portraitist due partly to his excellence with the brush, but also to his creation of an unmistakably up-market practice. He recreated something of the efficiency and charm of Van Dyck's prewar studio, while establishing a reputation as a proud and difficult individual – unthinkable for an artist fifty years earlier. Having captured much of the top end of the portrait market, Lely held on to it by sustaining a prodigious output, though not without a team of assistants. He was also able to raise his standard prices without resistance time and again throughout his long career. Clearly, a near-monopoly of portrait commissions by one studio was acceptable to Restoration society. There were short periods, however, when satisfaction with Lely seemed threatened by an inclination to use art patronage to signal membership of a clique.

Plate 6   Sir Peter Lely, *Princess Mary* (later Mary II), oil on canvas, 1677. By courtesy of the National Gallery, London.

The Catholic circle of Charles II's queen, Catherine of Braganza, innately suscep-tible to the continental Baroque style of painting, seized upon Jacob Huysmans's opulent and overtly allegorical offerings. Similarly, the French painter Henri Gascar was brought to England in 1670 by Louise de Kérouaille and subsequently favoured by the king's sister, Henrietta Anne, duchess of Orleans, and her Catholic followers. Thus, a fresh introduction of the art of Versailles accompanied the covert promotion of the Treaty of Dover. Although work of these painters was to be found at the very heart of the court (it was the work of Huysmans which was to be seen over the altar in the Queen's Chapel at St James's), it did not succeed in claiming a broader interest within England. Whether its style was too redolent of Catholicism, or whether the style itself was intrinsically disagreeable to the taste of later seventeenth-century England is perhaps too fine a distinction to make. There is some irony in the fact that James, duke of York, in his capacity as admiral, commissioned one of the most convincing artistic productions of this period: Lely's portrait series of victorious sea captains of the Battle of Lowestoft. For these worthy sailors clearly inhabit a world entirely out of keeping with the Baroque ecstasy in which the late Stuarts cocooned themselves.

   The court of Charles II appeared just as oblivious to the external perception of its use of art as that which preceded the Civil War. Charles II was even more indulgent to the forms of Catholicism being exhibited at court than his father had been, and his consort, Catherine of Braganza, was as indiscreet as Henrietta Maria had been about her religion. Even cardinal Barberini resumed the sending of gifts of art to the Stuart court. The probability of the succession of James, duke of York, whose second marriage in 1673 was to Mary of Modena, a Catholic, exacerbated the tensions between the monarchy and the majority of subjects.

A contrasting career to that of Lely's is provided by John Michael Wright (1617–94), who possessed the ability to rival Lely, yet chose to rely largely upon a Catholic network of patronage. This, in the last quarter of the seventeenth century, was insufficient to bring him to a position of national pre-eminence. After serving an apprenticeship in Edinburgh, Wright went to Rome and practised there between about 1642 and 1656. After his return, his most prestigious commission, to paint the portraits of twenty-two London judges and law officials, came in 1670. The draw of Rome exerted itself once more on Wright in 1686, when he became Lord Castlemaine's steward in the embassy sent to announce the accession of James II to Pope Innocent XI.

It was Wright who masterminded the embassy's triumphal entry into Rome involving 330 coaches, the vast banquet that followed, and the publication of a volume lavishly illustrated with engravings, by which Britain was informed of the spectacular proceedings. The centrepiece of the banquet was a baroque table ornament more than 6 feet in height composed of allegorical figures surmounted by the royal arms. At the base lay 'a dismembered Hydra, thereby denoting Rebellion supprest and vanquish't' (Griffiths 1998: 296–7). The plain intention of the whole event was to announce the final triumph, not just of untrammelled monarchy, but also of Catholicism. As ever, the Stuarts sought to confirm their status through spectacle, but the actual precariousness of the regime required such an enactment (the last such before the Glorious Revolution) to take place in Rome.

Lely never found time to make the artist's pilgrimage to Rome, but compensated by building up a fabulous collection, including pictures, statues and bronzes (as both Rubens and Van Dyck had done before), which also became, according to him, 'the best in Europe for prints and drawings' (Dethloff 1996). It drew many admirers to Lely's house in the Piazza of Covent Garden, and proved a good investment, but its real importance was that it provided an invaluable resource for other artists; and to some extent made up for the lack of an English academy of art, which France had possessed since 1648. No serious academy was to appear in England until Kneller's Academy of St Luke was established in 1711. Interestingly, however, the virtuosi organized themselves somewhat earlier: a group of art lovers began meeting in London calling themselves the Virtuosi of St Luke in the late 1680s.

Painting to the last, Lely died in 1680. Thereafter, Godfrey Kneller, who had arrived in England in 1676, steadily achieved his ambition to become accepted as Lely's successor. His innumerable bland portraits have long been unfavourably compared with Lely's and Van Dyck's. If, however, one seeks to grasp Kneller's influence upon later Stuart society, his work should be seen as part of an increasingly sophisticated, multi-stage process of image production, reproduction and dissemination. When Henri Gascar arrived in England he brought with him an engraver, Peter Vandrebanc, to popularize his portraits. This provoked Lely to engage Abraham Blooteling to perform a similar service for him in mezzotint. Also around this time, London's first art auctioneers, Richard Tompson and Alexander Browne, began to publish mezzotints based on the hundreds of Lelys, Van Dycks and Italian masters in Lely's studio. Next, the ambitious newcomer, Kneller, having taken on Vandrebanc to copy his work after Gascar's return to France in 1678, also resorted to mezzotint specialists; first Isaac Beckett then John Smith. It was Smith's reputation above all that was responsible for the mezzotint becoming the only medium since the early seventeenth-century miniature in which England was regarded as pre-eminent in Europe (Griffiths 1998: 217–43).

It is now realized that if we are to comprehend fully the visual culture of Britain in the third quarter of the century, we must pay as much attention to printmaking as to the murals in royal palaces and stately homes painted in the style of Versailles by Antonio Verrio and Louis Laguerre. The phenomenal growth of the print at this time (Griffiths estimates that total production in the period 1675–95 exceeded that of the whole of the earlier part of the century) was made possible by a new influx of foreign artists; first, Dutch, responding to an invitation to seek refuge from Louis XIV's invasion of Holland in 1672; then Huguenots, fleeing from internal persecution in France. Another wave of Dutch artists arrived with William of Orange in 1688. The immigrant workers brought with them knowledge of the mezzotint technique, which had actually been developed in England by Prince Rupert, who shared it only with gentlemen-virtuosi. Once in the hands of professionals, the mezzotint, being faster, cheaper, and offering tonal subtlety that the line-engraving could not match, rapidly gave rise to an industry.

The growth in intaglio print production led to a diversification of genres and also specialization by engravers and publishers. Landscapes and low-lifes, for example, became relatively popular in the 1680s and 1690s, whereas religious subjects were virtually non-existent. It was with the rise of the satirical print, however, that art rudely intruded into the arena of politics as never before. Griffiths (1998: 282) has noted the great increase in illustrated broadsides after the Civil War, seeing this as an indication of the 'growth of visual consciousness in England'. The Popish Plot and the controversies of the reign of James II provided ideal subject matter. It was on such broadsheets, rather than on the walls and ceilings of churches and palaces, that the eyes of late Stuart Britain learned to read visual narratives.

The improvement of architecture was impeded throughout the Stuart age by a dogged adherence to essentially medieval methods of organizing building work (Colvin 1995: 21–8; Airs 1995). A single master would typically offer to 'build by the great', that is, to contract for a complete building. He would then come to his own arrangements with masters of other requisite trades, who would work autonomously within their own areas of skill. Moreover, much of the design details were left to these masters. Such arrangements could, and frequently did, go badly wrong, and it was common wisdom in the seventeenth century that to entrust a building project to a sole 'undertaker' was risky. Alternative ways of contracting, each with their own obvious drawbacks, were 'by the day' (whereby the commissioner of the work would provide materials and simply pay for labour), and 'by the measure' (which involved regular payment according to a measure of what had been satisfactorily completed). The latter method required a surveyor, who did not necessarily have any responsibility for the design, for he was not an architect in any modern understanding of the term. The profession of architect would never be properly established until the autonomy of the master craftsmen was ended.

Plate 7 Romeyn de Hooghe, *Sir Itur ad Astra Scilicet* ('This is the way to the stars, of course'), etching, 1688. © The British Museum.

Grandiose private building, a continuation of the so-called 'prodigy house' construction of the Elizabethan era, continued into the early Stuart years. The extreme was probably reached by Thomas, earl of Suffolk, who ruined himself on the interminable construction of Audley End in Suffolk. Great patrons lent each other their surveyors and also their scarce copies of architectural treatises by Serlio, de L'Orme, Vignola, du Cerçeau and Dietterlin. Picking and choosing from such authorities gave rise to hybrid architecture, which has lately been interpreted as 'Albion's classicism', a deliberate grafting of the classical onto the vernacular (Gent 1995). Contemporaries, however, appeared rather less confident in what they were doing. Even the building of Hatfield House for Robert Cecil, earl of Salisbury, who had call upon England's best, was marked by hesitation and redesigning. Not infrequently, an element of competition entered into country house building, as when the earl of Clanricard infuriated Sir Robert Sidney in 1612 by drawing builders away from Penshurst to his site at Somerhill in Kent. The country house continued to represent the power and wealth of the post-Dissolution landed elite. This peripatetic aristocracy moved not only between country and capital, but also between country houses. These, therefore, were built to impress the continual stream of visitors as well as to dominate their localities.

Also at this time, the most ambitious royal remodelling project of the century, prior to that undertaken by William III at Hampton Court, commenced at Richmond Palace. Even this, as an Italian designer, Costantino de' Servi, was appalled to discover, lacked any central direction. De' Servi (on loan from the court of Tuscany) demanded full authority over the entire project and all the master craftsmen, as he would expect in Italy. The management of the Richmond site was further complicated by the appointment of Inigo Jones as Surveyor of the Prince's Works in 1611. Jones had recently begun to demand recognition as an architect, which was an unprecedented and almost preposterous claim for an Englishman to make. He was probably a joiner by training, but having improved his education and gained some skill as a draughtsman while living abroad, he turned to theatrical design and masque production with huge success. Jones, however, really wanted to design structures that would be permanent, and after obtaining the office of Surveyor of the King's Works in 1615 was able to build as he wished.

Much of our understanding of the subsequent course of the fine and decorative arts in Britain depends on our understanding of Inigo Jones, who occupied a central position throughout the first half of the seventeenth-century. Until fairly recently, the scope of his achievement had been underestimated by modern scholars. Now, he is no longer seen as one who, when not slavishly following the example of Palladio, could only invent 'nonsense architecture' for the settings of Court masques, but as a genuine polymath. (Harris, Orgel and Strong 1973; Harris and Higgott 1989; Peacock 1995). Not only did he provide the visual setting for the theatre of ideas that was the Stuart masque, but he also used it to prime his audiences for his architectural innovations. How much depended on Jones was seen as early as 1606 by his antiquarian friend, Robert Bolton, who expressed the hope that through him 'sculpture, modelling, architecture, picture, theatrical representation and all that is praiseworthy in the elegant arts of the ancients, may one day insinuate themselves across the Alps into our England'.

As one who aspired to establish the profession of architect in Stuart Britain (and thereby to introduce, in the strictest sense, architecture itself), Jones faced two main problems: organizational inefficiency and ignorance of the principles of architecture. He chose not to attempt a national reformation of traditional working practices, which, on his own sites, he could always overcome by force of personality, impressive erudition and his exceptional status as the King's Surveyor. Instead, he concentrated upon introducing principles of classical architecture, which Renaissance Europe had rediscovered in the texts of Vitruvius. Jones's adamantine insistence upon the faithful application of theory, and his heavy reliance on borrowed images and design details, may be partly explained by his self-education. Recent interdisciplinary studies have done much to uncover Jones's intellectual development; these have included analyses of the development of his drawing, his annotations in his library books, and his 'Roman Sketchbook' (Newman 1988; Chaney 2002).

Jones took an uncompromising stance on the question of how much of the grammar of classical architecture to adhere to in contemporary buildings. Although he was the first British architect to reject Gothic and Mannerist influences entirely, and the only one of his generation capable of freeing himself entirely from it, he ignored the latest Baroque architecture appearing in Europe. Instead, he held to the example of Andrea Palladio and his follower, Scamozzi, whose work, though of the second half of the sixteenth century, was for him definitive. His own royal work included the Banqueting House at Whitehall (1619–22), the Queen's Chapel at St James's Palace (1623–5) and the Queen's House at Greenwich (1616–19 and 1630–5). He also

Plate 8   Inigo Jones, Banqueting House, Whitehall, 1619–22. Photograph © Edward Chaney.

remodelled the pre-Fire St Paul's Cathedral and added to its exterior a great, classical portico (1633–42). At Covent Garden he introduced uniform town planning to Britain, designed for the Puritan and anti-court Francis, 4th earl of Bedford, the piazza (1631–7) and the first classical church in England (1631–3).

Few contemporaries were capable of fully understanding what Inigo Jones was about. Indeed, it was just after the Stuart age had closed that he was hailed by Colen Campbell, the author of *Vitruvius Britannicus* (first volume, 1715), and subsequently became a figure revered by the proponents of English Palladianism. Yet, before the Civil War, Jones had in great measure brought the influence of architecture to bear upon the life of the political nation. His Banqueting House dominated the Whitehall skyline; initially serving to enhance the court masques played out within, that affirmed the fundamental assumptions of the Stuart monarchy; later, after Rubens's canvases were installed, serving as a vast presence chamber where foreign dignitaries would first encounter British majesty. In January 1649 it became the obvious backdrop for the final drama of the reign of Charles I, and from one of its windows the king stepped onto the scaffold.

The grandeur of Jones's architectural vision also reinforced Laudianism. The archbishop attempted, with Jones's help, to impose a sense of decorum around the Gothic cathedral of St Paul's, whose yard was filled with booksellers, other vendors and even prostitutes. To the west face of the cathedral Jones added a massive portico with Corinthian columns 57 feet in height that rivalled the Pantheon in Rome. The intention was to surmount it with a line of statues, as on the west front of St Peter's in Rome, but only those of James I and Charles I, cast by Hubert Le Sueur, were ever set up. In 1650 parliament ordered that these prominent symbols of monarchy be thrown down and broken to pieces (Howarth 1989: 92).

In his later years Jones was often only a remote influence, as with the rebuilding of Wilton House for the earl of Pembroke, approving, altering and annotating the designs of competent associates such as John Webb and Isaac de Caus. Even during the more active years of his career, when he advised on all aspects of the visual arts, he delegated tasks. Drawings for smaller private houses exist in Jones's hand, though how many such houses, if any, were built according to his direct instructions, is unknown. These drawings, however, appear to sanction a simple, astylar design of a kind that began to be built in the Interregnum and continued to appear thereafter. It has been termed 'Puritan Minimalist' (Mowl and Earnshaw 1995), but there is little to connect the style with Puritanism, and nothing to indicate that Jones simplified his style to suit Puritan owners. Leaving a design free of columns, pilasters and pediments had less to do with religion than with the double benefits of economy and ease of execution.

Jonesian design spread not through any publication, but through the myriad contacts within the building profession, and through the desires of patrons to have something similar to a Jones building they knew. His closest associates clearly aided the process. Nicholas Stone was recommended by Jones to build the new Gold-smiths' Hall to an astylar design that was within Stone's ability. On completion, the building received much praise from foreign visitors as well as from the citizens of London. Nicholas Stone's son, John, in his turn, received an education in Palladian-ism. His competence and his fidelity to Jones was such that he was able to design such a building as Chesterton House in Warwickshire, completed during the last years of the Protectorate, which loudly echoed the Banqueting House. Originally astylar, its Corinthian orders were superimposed at a later date (when finances of the royalist Peyto family improved), though it would have been no embarrassment without them. However, after the Restoration even the closest of Jones's few disciples, his nephew by marriage, John Webb, partly succumbed to the influence of the Baroque. Now recognized as a significant architect in his own right, Webb eventually practised in a style somewhere between Jones and Wren.

The reign of Charles II was hardly characterized by the kind of virtue epitomized by the earl of Arundel, and yet the arts flourished, as did the sciences. The visual arts were now required as an accompaniment to that wholesale pursuit of pleasure which set in throughout society as a reaction to the austerity of the previous two decades. Such was the strength of the national economy that the double catastrophe of the Plague of 1665–6 and the Great Fire of 1666 was followed by rapid repopulation and a rebuilding of London. The city also expanded its bounds considerably in the last thirty years of the century, and this, together with the rebuilding, fostered the development of architectural ideas and practical skills, which later spread throughout the country (Reddaway 1940; Porter 1998).

Even before the Fire, a Commission for Repairing St Paul's Cathedral was in existence. It included among its number the gentleman-virtuoso John Evelyn, who had just published, optimistically, an English edition of Fréart's *Parallel of the Antient Architecture with the Modern* (1664). The Commission relied heavily upon a brilliant young scholar, Christopher Wren, who had fortunately turned to architecture. For only his second building, the Sheldonian Theatre in Oxford, Wren produced a design with inherent technical difficulties (essentially, how to roof a Roman theatre without using supporting columns), for which he was able to supply an ingenious, practical solution based on scientific principles. No master craftsman without the most explicit guidance could have realized such a design. A grandiosity of intention that brought with it new technical challenges had finally forced the emergence of the architect in Britain.

One thing remained unchanged; the need for any would-be British architect to travel abroad to see examples of great architecture and to commune with the best living architects. Sir Roger Pratt, a returned traveller and one of a new generation of gifted gentleman-architects, declared that there was still nothing remarkable to see in England apart from Jones's Banqueting House and his portico at St Paul's. In 1665, half a century after Jones sought out Scamozzi, Wren travelled to France to learn and to meet Bernini (and possibly also Mansart). As late as 1683–5, when Wren was working on the never-to-be-completed Winchester Palace, the influence of Versailles was still apparent in his designs. This, however, was due as much as anything to the persistent influence of Louis XIV on Wren's patron, Charles II. After his return from France, Wren entered into the enormous task of rebuilding the City after the Great Fire. His proposal for a regular street plan was rejected because of the commercial

Plate 9 Sir Christopher Wren, St Paul's Cathedral (west, upper), London, 1675–1710. Photograph © Edward Chaney.

need to rebuild quickly. Wren and his deputies, Robert Hooke and Edward Woodruff (later Hawksmoor and Dickinson), were responsible for the fifty churches and the cathedral but not for the secular rebuilding. Work upon some of the church towers continued into the early eighteenth century. The cost was found from taxation (Coal Money), and, in a sense, Wren's new London skyline declared the continuance of an episcopalian England.

Though Wren could not ignore the Baroque, which had swept into Britain with the returning royalists, he occasionally designed more purely classical buildings, and even returned to the Gothic if he saw good reason for so doing (as with Tom Tower at Christchurch, Oxford). His principal protégé, Nicholas Hawksmoor, who came to act, curiously, as a two-way conduit of ideas between an ageing Wren and John Vanburgh, had a more genuine feeling for the Baroque. But he, too, drew inspiration from all periods and styles, and helped create an ingenious style that has been termed 'Gothic-Baroque'. To the Palladian enthusiasts of the new century, following the line of Lord Shaftesbury, eclectic design, whether the result of intention or ignorance, was abhorrent (Chaney 2000: 314–19). Shaftesbury went so far as to affirm a moral aesthetic; something that suggests Whigs were, in this regard at least, the offspring of the Puritans.

By the close of the Stuart age, Britain's aristocratic rulers of taste felt confident enough to reject contemporary European taste. The Whigs perceived a broad desire for plainness and restraint in building, which could be taken as a sign that the country had become thoroughly Protestant. By then Inigo Jones's architecture was seen as a distinctly national achievement, and therefore it was possible by following the classical also to be patriotic. Neo-classicism also accorded well with the new age of science. If the national taste had been correctly divined, an aesthetic revolution had indeed taken place since 1603. Britain was a late and somewhat desperate claimant to the Renaissance, but refused to succumb entirely to the sensual pleasures it offered. Many were suspicious of the newly introduced arts, fearing their political rights and their very souls could be lost amid the distractions. The Stuarts and their courtiers, however, saw art as their natural ally, for it had been used so successfully to affirm monarchical and aristocratic authority throughout Europe.

REFERENCES

Airs, M. 1995: *The Tudor and Jacobean Country House: A Building History*. Stroud.
Albion, G. 1935: *Charles I and the Court of Rome*. London.
Brewer, J. (ed.) 1839: *The Court of King James the First*, 2 vols: London.
Brown, J. 1995: *Kings and Connoisseurs: Collecting Art in Seventeenth-Century Europe*. Princeton, NJ.
Chaney, E. 2000: *The Evolution of the Grand Tour*. London.
Chaney, E. (ed.) 2002: *Inigo Jones's 'Roman Sketchbook'*. London.
Collinson, P. 1988: *The Birthpangs of Protestant England: Religious and Cultural Change in the Sixteenth and Seventeenth Centuries*. Basingstoke.
Colvin, H. 1995: *A Biographical Dictionary of British Architects 1600–1840*. New Haven, CT.
Cooper J. 1999: *Oliver the First: Contemporary Images of Oliver Cromwell*. London.
Cruickshanks, E. (ed.) 2000: *The Stuart Courts*. Stroud.
Dethloff, D. 1996: 'The executors' account book and the dispersal of Sir Peter Lely's collection', *Journal of the History of Collections*, 8 (1), 15–51.

Everitt, A. 1973: *The Community of Kent and the Great Rebellion 1640–60*: Leicester.

Finaldi, G. 1999: *Orazio Gentileschi at the Court of Charles I*: London.

Gent, L. (ed.) 1995: *Albion's Classicism: The Visual Arts in Britain 1550–1660*: New Haven, CT.

Griffiths, A. 1998: *The Print in Stuart Britain 1603–1689*: London.

Harris, J. and Higgott, G. 1989: *The Architectural Drawings of Inigo Jones*: London.

Harris, J., Orgel, S. and Strong, R. 1973: *The King's Arcadia: Inigo Jones and the Stuart Court*: London.

Haskell, F. 1980: *Patrons and Painters*: New Haven, CT.

Hearn, K. (ed.) 1995: *Dynasties: Painting in Tudor and Jacobean England 1530–1630*: London.

Howarth, D. 1982: 'Mantua peeces: Charles I and the Gonzaga collections.' In D. Chambers and J. Martineau, eds, *Splendours of the Gonzaga*: London.

Howarth, D. 1985: *Lord Arundel and his Circle*: New Haven, CT.

Howarth, D. 1989: 'Charles I, sculpture and sculptors.' In A. MacGregor, ed., *The Late King's Goods: Collections, Possessions and Patronage of Charles I in the Light of the Commonwealth Sale Inventories*: London.

Howarth, D. 1997: *Images of Rule: Art and Politics in the English Renaissance, 1485–1649*: Basingstoke.

Huygens, L. 1982: *The English Journal 1651–1652*, ed. A. G. H. Bachrach and R. G. Collmer: Leiden.

Knoppers, L. L. 2000: *Constructing Cromwell: Ceremony, Portrait and Print 1645–1661*: Cambridge.

Mercer, E. 1962: *English Art 1553–1625*: Oxford.

Millar, O. 1960: 'Abraham van der Doort's catalogue of the collections of Charles I', *Walpole Society*, 37.

Millar, O. 1972: 'The inventories and valuations of the king's goods 1649–1651', *Walpole Society*, 43.

Millar, O. 1984: *The Queen's Pictures*: London.

Mowl, T. and Earnshaw, B. 1995: *Architecture Without Kings: The Rise of Puritan Classicism under Cromwell*: Manchester.

Newman, J. 1988: 'Italian treatises in use: the significance of Inigo Jones's annotations.' In J. Guillaume, ed., *Les Traités d'architecture de la Renaissance*: Paris.

Norgate, E. 1997: *Miniatura or the Art of Limning*, ed. J. M. Muller and J. Murrell: New Haven, CT.

Peacock, J. 1995: *The Stage Designs of Inigo Jones*: Cambridge.

Peacock, J. 2001: 'Robert Walker (*c.*1607–*c.*1658), *Self-portrait*.' In E. Chaney and G. Worsdale, eds, *The Stuart Portrait: Status and Legacy*: Southampton.

Pears, I. 1998: *The Discovery of Painting: The Growth of Interest in the Arts in England 1680–1768*: New Haven, CT.

Phillips, J. 1973: *The Reformation of Images: Destruction of Art in England 1535–1660*: Berkeley, CA.

Porter, S. 1998: *The Great Fire of London*: Stroud.

Portier, F. 1996: 'Prices paid for Italian pictures in the Stuart age', *Journal of the History of Collections*, 8 (1), 53–69.

Reddaway, T. F. 1940: *The Rebuilding of London after the Great Fire*: London.

Reitlinger, G. 1961: *The Economics of Taste: The Rise and Fall of Picture Prices*: London.

Richardson, S. (ed.) 1740: *The Negotiations of Sir Thomas Roe in His Embassy to the Ottoman Porte from the Year 1621 to 1628 Inclusive*: London.

Sherwood, J. and Pevsner, N. 1990: *Oxfordshire*: Harmondsworth.

Smuts, R. M. 1987: *Court Culture and the Origins of a Royalist Tradition in Early Stuart England*: Philadelphia, PA.

Starkey, D. et al. 1987: *The English Court from the Wars of the Roses to the Civil War*. London.

Stoye, J. 1989: *English Travellers Abroad 1604–1667: Their Influence in English Society and Politics*. New Haven, CT.

Strong, R. 1969: *The English Icon: Elizabethan and Jacobean Portraiture*. London.

Strong, R. 1986: *Henry Prince of Wales and England's Lost Renaissance*. London.

Waterhouse, E. 1978: *Painting in Britain 1530–1790*. Harmondsworth.

Wenley, R. 1993: 'William, third earl of Lothian: covenanter and collector', *Journal of the History of Collections*, 5 (1), 23–40.

Whinney, M. and Millar, O. 1957: *English Art 1625–1714*. Oxford.

Wilks, T. 1989: 'The picture collection of Robert Carr, earl of Somerset (*c*.1587–1645) reconsidered', *Journal of the History of Collections*, 1 (2), 167–77.

Wilks, T. 1997: 'Art collecting at the English court from the death of Henry, Prince of Wales to the death of Anne of Denmark (November 1612–March 1619)', *Journal of the History of Collections*, 9 (1), 31–48.

Wilks, T. 2001: ' "Forbear the heat and haste of building": rivalries among the designers at Prince Henry's court, 1610–1612', *The Court Historian*, 6, 49–65.

Wilson, J. 1985: *Fairfax*. London.

FURTHER READING

Brown, C. 1982: *Van Dyck*. Oxford.

Gent, L. and Llewellyn, N. (eds) 1990: *Renaissance Bodies: The Human Figure in English Culture c.1540–1660*. London.

Howarth, D. (ed.) 1993: *Art Patronage in the Caroline Court: Essays in Honour of Sir Oliver Millar*. Cambridge.

Langley, T. R. 2001: *Image Government: Monarchical Metamorphoses in English Literature and Art, 1649–1702*. Pittsburgh, PA.

Sloan, K. 2000: *'A Noble Art': Amateur Artists and Drawing Masters c.1600–1800*. London.

Summerson, J. 1993: *Architecture in Britain: 1530–1830*. Harmondsworth.

Summerson, J. and Colvin, H. 2000: *Inigo Jones*. Harmondsworth.

Thornton, P. 1978: *Seventeenth-Century Interior Decoration in England, France and Holland*. New Haven, CT.

Whinney, M. 1988: *Sculpture in Britain, 1530–1830*, revd J. Physick. Harmondsworth.

Worsley, G. 1995: *Classical Architecture in Britain*. New Haven, CT.

CHAPTER ELEVEN

Scientific Change: Its Setting and Stimuli

MICHAEL HUNTER

A book on the historiography of Stuart Britain would not be complete without a chapter on the history of science – on changing interpretations of the transformation in people's understanding of the natural world that occurred in this country during this period, and of the relationship between this and the broader social and cultural scene. Obviously, developments in this country formed part of broader trends to be found throughout Europe, but seventeenth-century Britain is generally acknowledged to have played a crucial role in the origins of modern science, particularly at the hands of such figures as Robert Boyle, Robert Hooke and Isaac Newton, in the intellectual environment associated after 1660 with the Royal Society. There have, of course, been revisionist claims to the contrary, arguing that science in a modern sense only emerged in the nineteenth century (Cunningham and Williams 1993), but these have not met with general support. Crucially, late seventeenth-century Britain played a key role in the emergence of a recognizably modern experimental method and in the synthesis of this with mathematics that was exemplified by Newton's *Principia* (1687). It is also at this time that we see the emergence of a distinctive scientific culture characterized by the foundation of the first national institution devoted to such ends and associated with the emergence of such genres for the dissemination of ideas as the journal article.

Yet, perhaps because of their importance, these developments have been the subject of a variety of interpretations, not least concerning the extent to which they can be explained in terms of their context. Views have ranged from highly 'internalist' accounts which have seen the innovative ideas of the time as almost wholly generated by thinkers' responses to the intellectual problems that confronted them, to 'externalist' accounts which have laid predominant stress on the economic, social and institutional context in which such developments occurred, often being 'relativist' – in the sense of seeing ideas as the exclusive product of their cultural setting – or 'reductionist', in wanting to attribute them to underlying economic motivations. Indeed, seventeenth-century England has long been the chief cockpit of attempts to establish links between scientific ideas and their milieu, which have proved of interest to commentators far beyond those with exclusively early modern preoccupations. It is to the debates that have raged on these topics, and to the current state of play on the subject, that this chapter will be devoted.

At the outset, it is worth pointing out in a book devoted to the whole of Britain that the institution which formed the focus of scientific activity for the last fifty years of the Stuart period, the Royal Society, was always a British rather than an exclusively English one. Its early activists included such prominent Scots as Sir Robert Moray and Alexander Bruce, earl of Kincardine, while its first president, William Brouncker, was viscount of Castle Lyons in the Irish peerage. Thereafter, the Society's Fellows were drawn from Scotland and Ireland as well as from England and Wales, and it saw its remit as coextensive with its royal patron's territories, even though its actual meetings took place in London (Hunter 1994). Though a satellite society was set up in Dublin in 1683, this was intended to complement the activities of the Royal Society rather than to rival them, as was the case with the society established at Oxford in the same year (Hoppen 1970). In Scotland there were comparable, if less formal, developments; though, towards the end of the century, the idea was launched of setting up a separate Royal Society there, in the end this failed to materialize (Ouston 1980; Emerson 1988; Withers 1996, 1999). Instead, then as earlier the Royal Society acted as the conduit through which much Scottish work in this field was presented to the world, while a number of Scots were prominent in scientific positions south of the border.

In surveying the historiography of British science in this period, it is appropriate to start with a longstanding fount of interest in the subject which still retains vitality today, namely among practising scientists, many of whom have developed a curiosity about the history of their disciplines. Until the history of science became established as an academic discipline in the twentieth century, this was the sole source of such study, being represented in the late nineteenth century most notably by the studies made by W. W. Rouse Ball and others of the manuscripts of Newton, following the deposit of the scientifically significant component of his archive to Cambridge University Library in 1872 (Ball 1893). This mirrored comparable developments in other countries, where antiquarian motives overlapped with patriotic ones in inspiring editions of the writings of such scientists as Galileo Galilei, Christiaan Huygens and G. W. Leibniz (Hunter 1998). A parallel tradition in this country stemmed from the biological sciences and from the world of museums, as seen in such figures as Charles Singer and R. T. Gunther. In particular, Gunther's *Early Science in Oxford*, though frequently unreliable, remains a treasure trove of information not only on various facets of Oxford science (including the Philosophical Society founded there in 1683), but also on Robert Hooke, many of whose works are there reprinted (Gunther 1923–45).

But the 1930s saw influential new impulses in the field, most notably from two figures who derived their inspiration from rather different traditions. One, Boris Hessen, was a member of the Moscow Academy of Sciences, who formed part of the Soviet delegation to the pioneering International Congress for the History of Science held in London in 1931 (see Werskey 1978: 138ff.). Hessen gave a talk on 'The social and economic roots of Newton's *Principia*' which presented an explicitly Marxist analysis of the sources and context of Newton's ideas (Hessen 1931) – even if possibly not Marxist enough for his Soviet masters, since Hessen seems to have disappeared in the purges a few years later. Hessen's basic claim was that Newton's mathematical physics was driven by the economic concerns of emergent capitalism, which had an interest in improved understanding of such topics as ballistics, hydrostatics and navigation; he also saw Newton's overall philosophical outlook as representing a reactionary stance in the 'class struggle' of his day.

Secondly, there was the American sociologist Robert K. Merton, later to become the grand old man of American sociology, whose investigation of 'Science, technology and society in seventeenth-century England' was published in the journal *Osiris* in 1938, only much later being reprinted in book form (Merton 1970). Merton was a Weberian rather than a Marxist: indeed, his thesis can in some respects be seen as an extension to the intellectual sphere of Max Weber's claims for a link between the Protestant ethic and the spirit of capitalism (for the argument that he was more directly influenced by the Italian sociologist Vilfredo Pareto, see Shapin 1988). Merton had a dual motive. In part, rejecting the 'vulgar materialism' of the Marxist tradition, he wanted to argue for the autonomy of scientific ideas. But he also sought the roots of scientific activity in the cultural values of the period from which it emanated, which in the case of seventeenth-century England he found in 'Puritanism'. This, he thought, entailed a set of religious and ancillary motivations which he saw as promoting science – though his use of the concept of Puritanism was ill-defined, being virtually coterminous with contemporary English Protestantism, in contrast to the more precisionist sense in which the term is normally used. In addition, he sought the roots of scientific activity in an analysis of economic incentives which at times overlaps suprisingly closely with that of Hessen.

These attempts to 'explain' science in terms of its social and economic milieu inspired an intellectualist counter-attack in the period of the Cold War which has been brilliantly explored by Roy Porter (1987). In the writings of such authors as Alexandre Koyré, Herbert Butterfield and A. Rupert Hall, an alternative view was formulated which laid much greater stress on the internal development of scientific ideas, attributing them to the free play of the human intellect rather than to social forces. Their argument, in Porter's paraphrase, was that 'science had not chugged forward following Five Year Plans, but had been transformed in stupendous, unpredictable leaps of reason' (Porter 1987: 295). This tradition has retained vitality ever since – as has its tension with Marxism – and it has resurfaced in some of the recent 'science wars' that we will come to later in this chapter. In the postwar period, in alliance with the older tradition of the study of the subject by scientists already alluded to, it inspired a tradition of editing and exegesis which arguably represented the main contribution to the study of British science of our period in the 1950s and 1960s. These years saw the inauguration of massive editions of Newton's mathematical papers and correspondence (Newton 1959–77, 1967–80), while much erudition was deployed in interpreting his ideas, perhaps most notably by R. S. Westfall (1971); for a survey of this entire literature, see Westfall (1980: 875–94). Another product of this tradition was an epic edition of the correspondence of the Royal Society in its early years in the person of its first secretary, Henry Oldenburg (Oldenburg 1965–86).

Alexandre Koyré was always alert to the metaphysical and religious setting of the ideas he studied, and none of the figures referred to in the previous paragraph was altogether obtuse to their context; but such scholars saw such matters as peripheral to the real business of understanding how brilliant men like Newton rose to the intellectual challenges that confronted them. The 1960s, however, saw a revival of interest in science's links with its milieu. This was stimulated particularly by Christopher Hill and the Ford Lectures that he gave at Oxford in 1962, subsequently published in book form as *Intellectual Origins of the English Revolution*. In its time this was a quite pioneering book for a historian of Hill's ilk: he commented at the outset on the 'curious academic division of spheres of influence in this country', in which 'some "historians", as we call ourselves, are perhaps dimly aware of another world in which historians of science write the history of science for historians of science, and historians of ideas write the history of ideas for the *Journal of the History of Ideas*' (Hill 1965: 15). But the result was almost entirely wrong-headed, indeed forming arguably one of the most misleading books on intellectual history ever published. In it, Hill made a case for the 'Puritan' origins of modern science (in the normal, precisionist sense of the word, in contrast to that used by Merton) largely by suppressing all counter-evidence: in his preface, he stated that he had omitted only information that struck him as 'neutral', but in fact this meant building up a one-sided picture by default (ibid.: vii). The shortcomings of the book have since been widely acknowledged (see Feingold 1984; Cormack 1997). Though Hill has recently unrepentantly reissued the work with a new title and with the addition of some rather miscellaneous extra chapters, the core of the work remains its original, unreconstructed self.

Yet, in the context of the 1960s, Hill's book stimulated extensive debate on such themes, not least in the columns of *Past and Present*. The contributions in question are conveniently collected in Charles Webster's anthology, *The Intellectual Revolution of the Seventeenth Century*, and though many of them now have a rather crude and dated edge, a few remain worth reading as a point of reference for subsequent debates. For instance, in her article, 'Latitudinarianism and science in seventeenth-century England', Barbara Shapiro argued that science was to be linked, not with Puritanism, but with religious moderation (Webster 1974: 286–316): she subsequently expanded this to form the conclusion to her biography of John Wilkins, the example of the linkage of science and Latitudinarianism on which it is in any case mainly based (Shapiro 1969).

These debates formed the starting point of the dominant approaches of the 1970s. One was the work of J. R. Jacob and M. C. Jacob, who essentially developed the 'Puritanism/Science' thesis to suggest that science was not revolutionary but counter-revolutionary. The foundation stone of this thesis was represented by J. R. Jacob's study, *Robert Boyle and the English Revolution*, in which he argued that Boyle was engaged in a 'dialogue with the sects': Jacob saw Boyle's corpuscular philosophy, and the experimental method he used to substantiate it, as being deliberately formulated in answer to the threats to political and social stability represented by the radical sects which sprang up in the aftermath of the Civil War. Jacob claimed that Boyle's view that the universe was composed of inert particles of matter (which he called 'corpuscles') presupposed that their activity was derived from an external God, thus providing support for the existing political and religious hierarchies; on the other hand, the sectaries' claims that matter was itself endowed with activity – their 'vitalism' – had subversively levelling implications. Jacob went on to argue that the Royal Society in its early years was associated with an aggressive, imperialist ethos for science. Disagreeing with Shapiro's view of science as essentially withdrawing from politics, he argued that instead it adopted an ethos which not only 'forestalls those who said at the time that science is injurious to religion' but also gave science 'an ideological edge' (Jacob 1977: 155).

The sequel was provided by Margaret C. Jacob in *The Newtonians and the English Revolution*, focused on the eponymous lectures which Robert Boyle founded in his

will, in which she argued that these, too, were concerned with the threat of subversion. In them, in her reading, Newtonian science was pitted against radical attack,
and its victory ensured that 'England never became a republic of pantheists'
(Jacob 1976: 249). She thus gave a highly politicized view of the significance of the
lectures in bringing together science and religion, contrasting with the more altruistic
view of the synthesis that they effected that had prevailed hitherto. Margaret Jacob
subsequently went on to develop her thesis of science as establishmentarian and
deliberately confronting a subversive subculture in other writings, notably in *The
Radical Enlightenment* (Jacob 1981).

   In fact, these views have met with considerable criticism. There have been some
searching critiques of Margaret Jacob's claims, suggesting that science was more
tangential to the apologetic message of the Boyle Lectures than she implied, and
that the legitimation of science owed more than she was prepared to admit to
agencies other than ecclesiastical polemic, such as scientific lecturing (Russell
1983: 52ff.). She also failed to do justice to the real ideological divisions in the
early eighteenth-century church, especially the vitality of the High Church party;
hence the invocation of science in a religious context remained a more peripheral and
ambiguous phenomenon than her rather triumphalist account implied (Holmes
1978). As Roy Porter has put it, before the nineteenth century science was often 'a
rather minor weapon in the ideological armoury...a weapon peculiarly likely to
backfire' (quoted in Russell 1983: 60), and this evaluation has been echoed in
more recent studies of the Boyle Lectures and their aftermath (Gascoigne 1988).

   Similarly, an examination of the 'ideology' of the early Royal Society suggests that
this was diffuse – even confused – in contrast to the purposefulness claimed for it by
the Jacobs (Hunter 1989: ch. 2). Still more damaging for the 'Jacob thesis' as a whole
has been the demonstration that Boyle's 'dialogue with the sects' was an illusion. In
fact, Boyle seems to have had much in common with men whom some of his
contemporaries would have shunned as 'enthusiasts', and the Jacobs' view oversim-
plified his somewhat idiosyncratic religious outlook, making him appear more conservative than he really was (Hunter 2000: 51–7). In addition, the polarization
between corpuscularianism and vitalism that was central to the Jacob thesis has
been undermined by the demonstration that views on matter theory were far less
clearly polarized than was formerly presumed (Henry 1986).

   The other, parallel development of the 1970s was the appearance of Charles
Webster's book, *The Great Instauration: Science, Medicine and Reform, 1626–60*
(1975), a massive and influential book which is about to be reissued. This completely
altered the terms of reference of the 'science/Puritanism' debate by injecting into it a
vast body of new material – in this case, much of it taken from the Hartlib Papers at
Sheffield University Library, an archive until that time hardly exploited. From this and
other sources, Webster was able to document in detail the schemes for intellectual
and technological reform associated more or less directly with the Puritan regime in
the 1640s and 1650s, accompanying this by some telling asides criticizing previous
historians in the field for applying to it criteria of intellectual achievement which he
considered anachronistic in a seventeenth-century context. In contrast to those who
attached greatest significance to advances in the mathematical and physical sciences,
he argued that 'the signs of significant adjustments in intellectual perspective should
be sought in subjects high in the contemporary estimation, such as medicine,

agriculture and natural history, and in technical subjects relating to the embryonic industries, such as chemistry, metallurgy and mining' (ibid.: 504–5).

Whatever the truth may be about such estimates of a broad shift affecting British culture, the fact of the matter is that contemporaries do seem to have attached a high value to the achievements valued by posterity, as the widespread and immediate acclaim for Newton's *Principia* reveals. They also had a clear conception of 'natural philosophy' as an important area of intellectual activity to which much of the work done by the artisans on whom Webster laid such stress was simply irrelevant. In addition, the terms of reference by which Webster labelled the key developments as 'Puritan' proved on examination to be somewhat vague, albeit defined slightly more precisely in a sequel in which he discriminated between different varieties of religious reformism (Mulligan 1980; Webster 1986). More significant, Webster made very little distinction between idealistic blueprints that never got off the ground and schemes that were actually implemented: this meant that his 'Puritan intellectuals' were given a lot of credit for unrealized – often unrealistic – pipe-dreams, the kind of empty 'projects' that were to be the subject of derision later in the seventeenth century. Webster can also be criticized for largely ignoring the vast – perhaps preponderant – section of the Hartlib archive which was concerned, not with the technological and other improvements that interested him, but with projects for religious reform and reconciliation and for translations of the Bible. This has become clear from the complete publication of the archive in electronic form, and by the research that has been published in conjunction with that (Hartlib Papers 1995; Greengrass, Leslie and Raylor 1994).

Whatever the limitations of Webster's overall thesis, however, there can be no doubt of the significance of *The Great Instauration* for deepening the texture of our understanding of the culture of science in the Interregnum, an important development in its own right. Neither was this the only work published in the late 1970s and early 1980s which enhanced our understanding of the relationship between scientific ideas and their setting. Perhaps the best example of this is Robert G. Frank's *Harvey and the Oxford Physiologists*, subtitled *Scientific Ideas and Social Interaction*, a profound and wide-ranging book, the implications of which have arguably still not been fully absorbed; in it, Frank places the epoch-making developments in understanding of the working of the human body associated with men like Thomas Willis in the setting of the institutional and social networks of Interregnum and Restoration Oxford (Frank 1980). At the same time, a new view of the most famous scientific institution of the period, the Royal Society, was achieved by looking at its actual 'morphology' – its make-up in terms of the contribution to it made by its more or less active, and more or less long-serving, members – and this was accompanied by an attempt at a comprehensive survey of various aspects of the ethos and milieu of science in the years after 1660, based on a wide range of manuscript and printed sources (Hunter 1994, 1981).

All of these earlier contributions to the subject, however, were eclipsed by the appearance in 1985 of Steven Shapin and Simon Schaffer's *Leviathan and the Air-Pump: Hobbes, Boyle and the Experimental Life*, one of the most influential historical works to have been published in the past two decades. This book focused on the controversy between Hobbes and Boyle over the interpretation of the findings that Boyle set out in his *New Experiments Physico-Mechanical, touching the Spring of the*

Air and its Effects (1660). Previous historians had generally dismissed this dispute on the grounds that Hobbes had simply 'misunderstood' the self-evidently correct method of conducting scientific research by controlled experiment that Boyle championed. But Shapin and Schaffer were able to use Hobbes's reservations to problematize the entire outlook on knowledge epitomized by that view, arguing that Boyle was deliberately seeking a new consensus on the basis of 'matters of fact' which could be experimentally demonstrated and corporately agreed, to which the individual interpretation represented by hypothesis and speculation should be treated as tangential. Hence, the whole basis of the 'new' knowledge that Boyle and the Royal Society wanted to vindicate as neutral and disinterested was in fact socially constructed to serve ends specific to the political and social situation of late seventeenth-century England, and particularly the need to rebuild consensus after the damaging effects of the Civil War (at this point, their interpretation overlapped with that of the Jacobs, though it was now given a subtler veneer than previously). By blowing the whistle on this, in their view, 'Hobbes was right' (Shapin and Schaffer 1985: 344).

In the course of this, Shapin and Schaffer presented an ingenious view of the enterprise of Boyle and the Royal Society, particularly the way in which Boyle's provision of an engraving of his air-pump and the laborious prose in which he described his pneumatic experiments – his 'literary technology' – were supposed to enable 'virtual witnessing': those who could not actually be present in his laboratory could imagine exactly what happened there from his painstaking account of it. This was all the more necessary because, as Shapin and Schaffer showed, few air-pumps were ever constructed, and even those that were did not necessarily work as predicted (though such technical difficulties themselves could be and were used by both sides in the controversy to bolster their case). Overall, the entire enterprise was presented as a kind of elaborate game, while, out of the free-for-all of rival interpretations, rules could be seen emerging which defined just who was and who was not considered a legitimate commentator on the 'matters of fact' that Boyle was deemed to prioritize, and who was allowed to join the experimental community of which he formed part.

Leviathan and the Air-Pump was perhaps the classic – and certainly the most historically sophisticated – text in a broader movement of what has been called 'constructivism' in the history of science, by which is meant an outlook 'which regards scientific knowledge primarily as a human product, made with locally situated cultural and material resources, rather than as simply the revelation of a pre-given order of nature' (Golinski 1998: ix). This quotation is taken from Jan Golinski's *Making Natural Knowledge: Constructivism and the History of Science*, an 'avowedly partisan' synthesis of the subject which usefully places Shapin and Schaffer's book in the context of a convergent tradition of interpretation of ideas about the natural world as socially formed; it shows how their work seemed to offer a historical validation to ideas otherwise formulated largely by sociological and other theorists such as Bruno Latour, Barry Barnes and H. M. Collins. It is perhaps this that explains some of the counter-attacks to which the book and its genre have been subject, not least from conservative scholars in the United States as part of the 'science wars' currently raging there. Such authors as Paul R. Gross and Norman Levitt have seen *Leviathan and the Air-Pump* as part of an attempt to undercut the pursuit of truth by presenting all knowledge as relative and socially formed, objecting particularly to Shapin and Schaffer's depiction of scientists – both in the seventeenth century and, implicitly, in the twentieth – as a self-perpetuating and arrogant oligarchy (Gross and Levitt 1994: 63–9; cf. Koertge 1998).

Since the publication of *Leviathan and the Air-Pump* its co-authors have moved on to develop their work in somewhat different ways. In Schaffer's case, this is represented particularly (in the context of seventeenth-century England) by his constructivist reading of Newton's optical experiments: his argument is that, more than anything else, it was the power relationships associated with Newton's dominant position in early eighteenth-century English science which ensured that his ideas were widely accepted (Schaffer 1989). Meanwhile, Steven Shapin went on to write *A Social History of Truth: Civility and Science in Seventeenth-Century England* (1994), which is as ambitious as *Leviathan and the Air-Pump* in its attempt to use historical data to problematize much broader issues in human thought, and which has achieved a similarly wide following as a result.

In this work, Shapin explores the fundamental issue of how we decide what knowledge about the world is trustworthy, arguing that models that have come down to us from the seventeenth century have had a far more lasting influence than is generally recognized, particularly in the light of the claim made in his book that the prime criterion of trustworthiness in the seventeenth century was of social status. Rejecting the anachronistic application of models of professionalization to seventeenth-century science, he seeks to illustrate that, because of his economic independence, a gentleman was deemed trustworthy, whereas a non-gentleman – by definition dependant – was not. The book also makes much of the fact that one of the most trustworthy writers in the period was a quintessential gentleman, Robert Boyle, an entire chapter being devoted to illustrating how Boyle became 'a highly visible pattern for the making of a proper experimental identity. The triple conjunction of birth and wealth, learning, and piety that had been so long recommended by Christian humanist writers was now taken to be exemplified in the remarkable person of the Honourable Robert Boyle' (Shapin 1994: 143).

In a sense, Shapin and Schaffer have founded a historiographical school, the most notable example of which is another work which is already proving influential – Adrian Johns's *The Nature of the Book: Print and Knowledge in the Making*, which its author specifically sees as illustrating the validity of Shapin's approach in an area to which the master did not apply it (Johns 1998: 31). In this book, Johns extends a relativist view of knowledge to the means by which ideas were communicated, arguing that the ways in which books were printed and marketed at the time meant that the ultimate control of what ideas were presented, and the manner in which they reached the public, had far less to do with the authors than with the producers – the printers, booksellers and others involved in the book trade at the time. So far from print offering a reliable means for the transmission of ideas, therefore, he claims to show the printed word as an unpredictable resource, which contemporaries had to learn to live with and to attempt to control. Hence, after a series of rather discursive chapters exploring the world of books in seventeenth-century England, Johns provides two detailed chapters which seek to illustrate the difficulties in disseminating reliable data that had to be confronted by scientists in late seventeenth-century England.

Undoubtedly, we have learned much from works of this kind, which have forced scholars to think more deeply about how ideas were formulated and controlled, the settings in which they were produced, and the broader milieux in which they circulated in terms of printing shops, coffee houses and the like. But one might still feel that such studies have not delivered as much as they promised, and some of the principal reasons for this may be spelled out here, by way of an agenda for future study in the field. At the most obvious level, such historians have been accused of deliberately underrating intellectual factors in favour of social ones. Thus in a study of the 'war' between Hobbes and the Oxford mathematician John Wallis, which ran in parallel with the dispute that forms the focus of *Leviathan and the Air-Pump* but which is there largely ignored, Douglas Jesseph (1999) has argued that it is only in terms of the mathematical issues involved in the debate that one can understand why, after an initial promising start, Hobbes ended up virtually without credibility in the field. Similarly, Alan Shapiro (1996) has taken issue with Simon Schaffer's invocation of Newton's influence as president of the Royal Society in the adoption of his views on light and colour, arguing that in fact the international scientific community came round to his views sooner, and for more purely intellectual reasons, than this implies.

More broadly, it can be argued that, in their anxiety to be able to attribute significance to the counter-revolutionary impulse of post-Civil War England, such historians have conflated developments that in fact unfolded more slowly and over a broader geographical area. Thus the stress on 'fact' has a longer ancestry, even if the purchase of the concept may have reached its peak in the post-Restoration years (Shapiro 1994). A perhaps greater problem about the emphasis on the Hobbes–Boyle dispute in *Leviathan and the Air-Pump* is that it detracts attention from the great, raging debate in seventeenth-century natural philosophy, namely between the mechanical philosophy (of which both Boyle and Hobbes championed different variants) and the Aristotelianism which had dominated European intellectual life for centuries, and the resilience and inventiveness in the early modern period proves to have been grossly underrated (Schmitt 1983). For one thing, the result of this is to distort the intellectual priorities of a man like Boyle and to make him and others like him seem more intellectually conservative than they really were. More significantly, it obscures the process of formulating an alternative view of the world to that of Aristotle, which was clearly one of the leading achievements of this period, as recent scholarship has illuminated. In the course of this, a synthesis of mathematical physics with experimentalism, which had its roots in the work of René Descartes and reached its climax in Newton's *Principa*, became established as a common currency across Europe, transcending the purely local factors which dominate constructivist accounts of intellectual change (Dear 1995). To such longer-term developments in European natural philosophy, the subject-matter of *Leviathan and the Air-Pump* can be seen as almost incidental.

There is also a danger that the focus on Boyle's debate with the intellectualist Hobbes gives a misleading significance to 'matters of fact'. In other contexts – particularly when contrasting himself with others more 'empirical' than him, such as the practical chemists of the day – Boyle laid stress on his hypotheticalism, which was always an adjunct of his fact-collecting, even though he sought to make a distinction between the two. Moreover, it has been argued that the deployment of 'matters of fact' was itself a strategy used by Boyle as part of the European-wide debate between rival systems of natural philosophy which was not ended but redirected by such an appeal (Schuster and Taylor 1997). Similarly with *A Social History of Truth*, in which the emphasis on gentility in guaranteeing assent is laboured almost *ad nauseam*: for, though it may be salutary for this lost system of values to be rehearsed for the benefit of an ill-informed modern audience, it is clear that contemporaries had other criteria in judging knowledge claims, notably of expertise and of intellectual coherence, which are elided here. In other words, Shapin points to a significant criterion by which early modern thinkers decided what was plausible, but he does so at the expense of other considerations which were often more important.

Such theories are also prone to be presentist, pandering to twenty-first-century models of what seems 'rational' behaviour. In particular, these authors have difficulty in doing justice to the power of religion as a motivating force in intellectual activity in the period. There is thus a degree of obtuseness in Steven Shapin's account of Boyle's religiosity, and his disarming admission that 'I do not profess to know *why* Robert Boyle chose a publicly visible life of Christian virtue' (Shapin 1994: 156). It is symptomatic that in *Leviathan and the Air-Pump* Shapin and Schaffer elide Boyle's 'main reason' for refusing to take holy orders, namely, that he lacked a vocation, in favour of the functionalist one that, as a layman, he might claim an impartiality which clergymen lacked. In addition, they never cite Boyle's explicit statement as to why he was anxious to refute Hobbes – his concern about the influence of his 'dangerous Opinions about some important, if not fundamental, Articles of Religion', which he thought might be offset by showing 'that in the Physicks themselves his Opinions, and even his Ratiocinations, have no such great advantage over those of some Orthodox Christian Naturalists' (Hunter 2000: 10, 64). In other words, what Boyle was concerned about was the threat of 'atheism', a pervasive anxiety at the time which cannot be reduced to the threat of social subversion, in that it was seen as liable to lead to cosmic catastrophe at the hands of a jealous God and the collapse of human social institutions altogether.

More broadly, the issue of the relationship between science and religion in the late seventeenth century has long had a rich historiography which shows no sign of abating and which depends on proper understanding of contemporary ideas in their own right, free from anachronistic presumptions about underlying motivations which have all too often characterized a constructivist stance. In particular, such issues as the role of millenarianism in the thought of the day (Webster 1975, 1982); the conviction that the ancients had had a 'prisca sapientia' with both philosophical and moral connotations which it was possible and desirable to emulate (Rattansi and McGuire 1966); and the tension between the use of science for religious apologetic and the common suspicion that it was itself tainted with heterodoxy (Brooke 1991): these need sympathetic teasing-out with full sensitivity to the preoccupations of the time.

A constructivist approach has also proved ill-equipped to give a convincing account of contemporary attitudes towards magic. The Jacobs at least had a clear – if simplistic – rationale of the replacement of magical by mechanistic explanations of the workings of the world, namely that the former were potentially subversive, giving undue authority to unauthorized practitioners; a similar view has been taken in the account of the decline of astrology by Patrick Curry (1989), himself to some extent an acolyte of the Shapin/Schaffer school. Yet this does not map well with the interest in supernatural phenomena of a man like Boyle, who was glad of such evidence to offset a view of the world as an atheistic automaton. The fact that supernatural phenomena might be empirically demonstrable further complicates matters, particularly at a time when the validity of such immaterial entities was being publicly contested. We now know that both Newton and Boyle were fascinated by alchemy, devoting much time to its study in private, though both had to be careful about divulging their interests publicly (Dobbs 1975, 1991; Principe 1998, 2000). It is clear that there was a complex interrelationship between the personal belief in such matters which individuals like these might hold, and public pressures towards adopting certain views rather than others and against divulging beliefs which were at odds with the developing, naturalistic consensus. This needs to be sensitively mapped out, making due allowance for the entire range of factors involved in the decisions that such authors reached as to just how much to publish of their views on such matters, and in what form (Hunter 2000: ch. 10).

There is also a proneness among authors of a constructivist persuasion to make insufficient allowance for contingency. To some extent this appears at an institutional level. Recent studies have tended to revert to traditional stereotypes in their approach to the early Royal Society, taking for granted its purposefulness and simply mapping new objectives onto it. Yet in fact there was a strong element of contingency in the manner in which the Society developed in its early years, which we ignore at our peril if we are to understand the manner in which its institutional evolution occurred (Hunter 1989). Much the same is true of the role of the universities, which appear almost in caricature in the work of the historians dealt with here, perhaps particularly in *A Social History of Truth*, where they are mentioned almost as a by-word for pedantry: yet they clearly played a significant role in intellectual change in the period, if complicated by donnish deployment of the institutional complexity by which such bodies were characterized (Gascoigne 1985; Tyacke 1997).

This is even more the case with the individuals with whom such studies are concerned, who were complex personalities crying out for sympathetic understanding. One of the most disappointing aspects of *A Social History of Truth* is the extent to which its portrait of Boyle reiterates the traditional view of the great man as a purposeful paragon of industry and virtue, which goes back directly (and explicitly) to such contemporaries and early followers as Henry Oldenburg, Gilbert Burnet and Thomas Birch, even if Shapin puts a different gloss on it. He thus almost wilfully ignores one of the principal changes to our view of Boyle in recent years, the discovery of his tortured religious life, which is vividly illustrated by extant sources, and of the extent to which his intellectual personality had an obsessive, even 'dysfunctional', streak which needs to be taken into account properly to understand him (Hunter 2000). A similar myopia is displayed by Adrian Johns, who, having demonstrated to his satisfaction the pervasiveness of piracy and 'usurpation' in science communication at the time, notes with relief of Robert Hooke that, in this light, his 'concern becomes by no means so unusual – let alone, as has sometimes been hinted, paranoid' (Johns 1998: 510).

Now it is easy to understand the reasons for the rejection of such factors, which can seem tiresomely idiosyncratic and elusive compared with broad cultural patterns, as Steven Shapin indicated in a manifesto issued many years ago (Shapin and Barnes 1979). Yet one could argue that here the wish has given birth to the prescription, whereas the extent to which individual thinkers had complex personalities that invite analysis is surely something that cries out for fuller investigation. In the case of perhaps the most brilliant figure of all, Isaac Newton, this has long been clear, and he has been the subject of a number of insightful biographies, perhaps most notably Frank Manuel's *A Portrait of Isaac Newton* (1968), which offered an overtly Freudian reading of the man. In extending such approaches more widely, we may or may not need to have as overt a recourse to psychoanalysis as Manuel did. It is revealing that some of Manuel's most perceptive chapters deal with figures such as Hooke and John Flamsteed, of whom he is highly insightful despite the fact that he does not embark on a detailed psychoanalysis of them to match that of Newton. The pros and cons of the use of psychoanalysis in a historical context were debated at a conference held at Birkbeck College in 1997, in this case with special reference to Robert Boyle (*British Journal for the History of Science* 1999). One thing that emerged from this was that, in many respects, historical sensitivity may be more significant than specific clinical orientation. What seems clear, however, is that we should be aware – as contemporaries were – that some were more prone to obsessive or cantankerous behaviour than others. It is thus revealing that such considerations are invoked by the historian of the 'war' between Hobbes and Wallis which paralleled that between Boyle and Hobbes, who considers that 'the natural interpretation of Wallis' penchant for controversy must be in terms of individual psychological factors rather than some fanciful sociological just-so story in which he appears as the defender of a form of life' (an overt allusion to the Wittgensteinian terms of reference of *Leviathan and the Air-Pump*) (Jesseph 1999: 354).

Happily, the materials for such study are now more readily available than ever, due to a proliferation in recent years of new, complete editions, particularly of the correspondence of various of the figures involved (Boyle 2001; Flamsteed 1995–2001; Hobbes 1994). Hence my primary prescription for the way forward is biography, involving the painstaking investigation of all the interwoven circumstances affecting decisions taken and statements made. Again, the need for this can be illustrated from *The Nature of the Book*, in which Adrian Johns cites at length the complaints about plagiarism and piracy made by Boyle and others without ever trying to assess how reliable they were, and what the circumstances were which underlay them. If this is done, it often brings to light a more complicated, but no less revealing, picture than his (Boyle 1999–2000: I, lxxv ff.).

Armed with such understanding, we will be better able to place the intellectual and other challenges perceived by individuals in a broader picture, which, by doing justice to individual complexity, will supersede the tired clichés which have often characterized generalizations about intellectual change in the past. Indeed, I have argued elsewhere that we need a new way of looking at intellectual change, which gives priority to the thought of individuals, but which combines this with attention to the shared imperatives and polarizations to which they responded (Hunter 1995: 11ff.). There is certainly no reason why a proper attention to the personal make-up and social milieu of those involved in scientific enquiry need detract from a proper understanding of the intellectual goals that these men set themselves. In the case of Boyle, we now have a new edition of his writings as well as his correspondence (Boyle 1999–2000), but the materials for such study have long been available, and if anything are now more so than ever with the onset of Internet dissemination.

The challenge is to produce an interpretation which draws on the richness of understanding of the links between ideas and their context that the work of the past few decades has cumulatively given us, while abandoning the elements of crudity which have characterized some of the analyses surveyed here. In particular, we need to be suspicious of presentist agendas seeking to establish timeless laws of the sociology of scientific knowledge by constructing a distorted image of early modern science to fit the bill: instead, we need to combine a sensitivity to the milieu in which scientific work was carried out and to the individuals who executed it with a deep understanding of their intellectual agenda. How well we rise to it remains to be seen, but this is surely the true challenge to our 'postmodern' generation.

REFERENCES

Ball, W. W. R. 1893: *An Essay on Newton's Principia*: London.
Boyle, R. 1999–2000: *The Works of Robert Boyle*, 14 vols, ed. M. Hunter and E. B. Davis: London.
Boyle, R. 2001: *The Correspondence of Robert Boyle*, 6 vols, ed. M. Hunter, A. Clericuzio and L. M. Principe: London.
British Journal for the History of Science 1999: Special issue: 'Psychoanalysing Robert Boyle', *British Journal for the History of Science*, 32, 257–324.
Brooke, J. 1991: *Science and Religion: Some Historical Perspectives*. Cambridge.
Cormack, L. B. 1997: *Charting an Empire: Geography at the English Universities, 1580–1620*: Chicago, IL.
Cunningham, A. and Williams, P. 1993: 'De-centring the "Big Picture": *The Origins of Modern Science* and the Modern Origins of Science', *British Journal for the History of Science*, 26, 407–32.
Curry, P. 1989: *Prophecy and Power: Astrology in Early Modern England*: Cambridge.
Dear, P. 1995: *Discipline and Experience: The Mathematical Way in the Scientific Revolution*: Chicago, IL.
Dobbs, B. J. T. 1975: *The Foundations of Newton's Alchemy, or, 'The Hunting of the Greene Lyon'*: Cambridge.
Dobbs, B. J. T. 1991: *The Janus Faces of Genius: The Role of Alchemy in Newton's Thought*: Cambridge.
Emerson, R. 1988: 'Sir Robert Sibbald, Kt., the Royal Society of Scotland and the origins of the Scottish Enlightenment', *Annals of Science*, 45, 41–72.
Feingold, M. 1984: *The Mathematicians' Apprenticeship: Science, Universities and Society in England, 1560–1640*: Cambridge.
Feingold, M. 1996: 'When facts matter', *Isis*, 87, 131–9.
Flamsteed, J. 1995–2001: *The Correspondence of John Flamsteed*, ed. E. G. Forbes, L. Murdin and F. Willmoth: Bristol.
Frank, R. G. 1980: *Harvey and the Oxford Physiologists: Scientific Ideas and Social Interaction*: Berkeley, CA.
Gascoigne, J. 1985: 'The universities and the scientific revolution: the case of Newton and Restoration Cambridge', *History of Science*, 23, 391–434.
Gascoigne, J. 1988: 'From Bentley to the Victorians: the rise and fall of British Newtonian natural theology', *Science in Context*, 2, 219–56.
Golinski, J. 1998: *Making Natural Knowlege: Constructivism and the History of Science*: Cambridge.

Greengrass, M., Leslie, M. and Raylor, T. (eds) 1994: *Samuel Hartlib and Universal Reformation: Studies in Intellectual Communication*: Cambridge.

Gross, P. R. and Levitt, N. 1994: *Higher Superstition: The Academic Left and its Quarrels with Science*: Baltimore, MD.

Gunther, R. T. (ed.) 1923–45: *Early Science in Oxford*, 14 vols: Oxford.

Hartlib Papers 1995: *The Hartlib Papers on CDRom*: Ann Arbor, MI.

Henry, J. 1986: 'Occult qualities and the experimental philosophy: active principles in pre-Newtonian matter theory', *History of Science*, 24, 335–81.

Hessen, B. 1931: 'The social and economic roots of Newton's *Principia*.' In N. I. Bukharin et al., eds, *Science at the Crossroads*: London.

Hill, C. 1965: *Intellectual Origins of the English Revolution*: Oxford. Reprinted with additions in 1998 as *Intellectual Origins of the English Revolution Revisited*.

Hobbes, T. 1994: *The Correspondence of Thomas Hobbes*, 2 vols, ed. N. Malcolm: Oxford.

Holmes, G. 1978: 'Science, reason and religion in the age of Newton' [review essay of M. Jacob, *The Newtonians and the English Revolution*]. *British Journal for the History of Science*, 11, 164–71.

Hoppen, K. T. 1970: *The Common Scientist in the Seventeenth Century: A Study of the Dublin Philosophical Society, 1683–1708*: London.

Hunter, M. 1981: *Science and Society in Restoration England*: Cambridge; reprinted 1992, Aldershot.

Hunter, M. 1989: *Establishing the New Science: The Experience of the Early Royal Society*: Woodbridge.

Hunter, M. 1994: *The Royal Society and its Fellows 1660–1700: The Morphology of an Early Scientific Institution*, revd edn: Oxford. Originally published as 'The social basis and changing fortunes of an early scientific institution', *Notes and Records of the Royal Society*, 31 (1976), 9–114.

Hunter, M. 1995: *Science and the Shape of Orthodoxy: Intellectual Change in Late Seventeenth-Century Britain*: Woodbridge.

Hunter, M. (ed.) 1998: *Archives of the Scientific Revolution: The Formation and Exchange of Ideas in Early Modern Europe*: Woodbridge.

Hunter, M. 2000: *Robert Boyle (1627–91): Scrupulosity and Science*: Woodbridge.

Jacob, J. R. 1977: *Robert Boyle and the English Revolution: A Study of Social and Intellectual Change*: New York.

Jacob, M. C. 1976: *The Newtonians and the English Revolution, 1689–1720*: Hassocks.

Jacob, M. C. 1981: *The Radical Enlightenment: Pantheists, Freemasons and Republicans*: London.

Jesseph, D. M. 1999: *Squaring the Circle: The War between Hobbes and Wallis*: Chicago, IL.

Johns, A. 1998: *The Nature of the Book: Print and Knowledge in the Making*: Chicago, IL.

Koertge, N. (ed.) 1998: *A House Built on Sand: Exposing Postmodernist Myths about Science*: New York.

Manuel, F. E. 1968: *A Portrait of Isaac Newton*: Cambridge, MA.

Merton, R. K. 1970: *Science, Technology and Society in 17th-Century England*: New York; originally published in *Osiris*, 4 (1938), 360–632.

Mulligan, L. 1980: 'Puritans and English science: a critique of Webster', *Isis*, 71, 456–69.

Newton, I. 1959–77: *The Correspondence of Isaac Newton*, 7 vols, ed. H. W. Turnbull, J. F. Scott, A. R. Hall and L. Tilling: Cambridge.

Newton, I. 1967–80: *The Mathematical Papers of Isaac Newton*, 8 vols, ed. D. T. Whiteside: Cambridge.

Oldenburg, H. 1965–86: *The Correspondence of Henry Oldenburg*, 13 vols, ed. A. R. Hall and M. B. Hall: Madison, WI.

Ouston, H. 1980: 'York in Edinburgh: James VII and the patronage of learning in Scotland, 1679–88.' In J. Dwyer et al., eds, *New Perspectives on the Politics and Culture of Early Modern Scotland*: Edinburgh.

Porter, R. 1987: 'The scientific revolution: a spoke in the wheel?' In R. Porter and M. Teich, eds, *Revolution in History*: Cambridge.

Principe, L. M. 1998: *The Aspiring Adept: Robert Boyle and his Alchemical Quest*: Princeton, NJ.

Principe, L. M. 2000: 'The alchemies of Robert Boyle and Isaac Newton: alternative approaches and divergent deployments.' In M. J. Osler, ed., *Rethinking the Scientific Revolution*: Cambridge.

Rattansi, P. M. and McGuire, J. E. 1966: 'Newton and the "Pipes of Pan"', *Notes and Records of the Royal Society*, 21, 108–43.

Russell, C. 1983: *Science and Change 1700–1900*: London.

Schaffer, S. 1989: 'Glass works: Newton's prisms and the uses of experiment.' In D. Gooding, T. Pinch and S. Schaffer, eds, *The Uses of Experiment: Studies in the Natural Sciences*: Cambridge.

Schmitt, C. 1983: *John Case and Aristotelianism in Renaissance England*: Montreal.

Schuster, J. A. and Taylor, A. B. H. 1997: 'Blind trust: the gentlemanly origins of experimental science', *Social Studies of Science*, 27, 503–36.

Shapin, S. 1988: 'Understanding the Merton thesis', *Isis*, 79, 594–605.

Shapin, S. 1994: *A Social History of Truth: Civility and Science in Seventeenth-Century England*: Chicago, IL.

Shapin, S. and Barnes, B. 1979: 'Darwin and social Darwinism: purity and history.' In B. Barnes and S. Shapin, eds, *Natural Order: Historical Studies of Scientific Culture*: Beverly Hills, CA.

Shapin, S. and Schaffer, S. 1985: *Leviathan and the Air-Pump: Hobbes, Boyle and the Experimental Life*: Princeton, NJ.

Shapiro, A. 1996: 'The gradual acceptance of Newton's theory of light and color, 1672–1727', *Perspectives on Science*, 4, 59–140.

Shapiro, B. 1969: *John Wilkins: An Intellectual Biography*: Berkeley, CA.

Shapiro, B. 1994: 'The concept "fact": legal origins and cultural diffusion', *Albion*, 26, 1–26.

Tyacke, N. (ed.) 1997: *The History of the University of Oxford, Vol. 4: Seventeenth-Century Oxford*: Oxford.

Webster, C. 1974: *The Intellectual Revolution of the Seventeenth Century*: London.

Webster, C. 1975: *The Great Instauration: Science, Medicine and Reform, 1626–1660*: London.

Webster, C. 1982: *From Paracelsus to Newton: Magic and the Making of Modern Science*: Cambridge.

Webster, C. 1986: 'Puritanism, separatism and science.' In D. C. Lindberg and R. L. Numbers, eds, *God and Nature: Historical Essays on the Encounter between Christianity and Science*: Berkeley, CA.

Werskey, G. 1978: *The Visible College: A Collective Biography of British Scientists and Socialists of the 1930s*: London.

Westfall, R. S. 1971: *Force in Newton's Physics*: London.

Westfall, R. S. 1980: *Never at Rest: A Biography of Isaac Newton*: Cambridge.

Withers, C. W. J. 1996: 'Geography, science and national identity in early modern Britain: the case of Scotland and the work of Sir Robert Sibbald', *Annals of Science*, 53, 29–73.

Withers, C. W. J. 1999: 'Reporting, mapping, trusting: making geographical knowledge in the late seventeenth century', *Isis*, 90, 497–521.

FURTHER READING

Cohen, I. B. (ed.) 1990: *Puritanism and the Rise of Modern Science: The Merton Thesis*: New Brunswick, NJ.

Henry, J. 2002: *The Scientific Revolution and the Origins of Modern Science*, 2nd edn: Basingstoke.

Hunter, M. 1995: *Science and the Shape of Orthodoxy: Intellectual Change in Late Seventeenth-Century Britain*: Woodbridge; esp. chs 4, 5 and 12.

Hunter, M. 2000: *Robert Boyle (1627–91): Scrupulosity and Science*: Woodbridge.

Jacob, J. R. and Jacob, M. C. 1980: 'The Anglican origins of modern science: the metaphysical foundation of the Whig constitution', *Isis*, 71, 251–67.

Manuel, F. E. 1968: *A Portrait of Isaac Newton*: Cambridge, MA.

Porter, R. 1987: 'The scientific revolution: a spoke in the wheel?' In R. Porter and M. Teich, eds, *Revolution in History*: Cambridge.

Shapin, S. 1996: *The Scientific Revolution*: Chicago, IL.

Shapin, S. and Schaffer, S. 1985: *Leviathan and the Air-Pump: Hobbes, Boyle and the Experimental Life*: Princeton, NJ.

Webster, C. 1982: *From Paracelsus to Newton: Magic and the Making of Modern Science*: Cambridge.

Webster, C. 1986: 'Puritanism, separatism and science.' In D. C. Lindberg and R. L. Numbers, eds, *God and Nature: Historical Essays on the Encounter between Christianity and Science*: Berkeley, CA.

Part III

Stuart Britain, 1603–1642

CHAPTER TWELVE

Politics in Early Stuart Britain, 1603–1640

DAVID L. SMITH

Introduction: Problems and Debates

The study of politics in early Stuart Britain has always been haunted by the knowledge of the events that followed during the 1640s and 1650s. Because the middle of the seventeenth century saw the complete collapse of a monarchical system, and then its replacement by a republic, historians have naturally asked whether the British polity was at all stable during the decades that preceded this crisis. For centuries, from soon after the events themselves until the later twentieth century, the answer seemed clear enough: that the English Civil War was a struggle between royal tyranny and parliamentary liberties, the origins of which could be traced back at least to 1603, and probably earlier. The first two Stuart kings of Great Britain, James VI and I, and especially Charles I, harboured aggressively authoritarian ideas of kingship which they were determined to impose on their three kingdoms. These ambitions generated political and religious instability and brought them into conflict with their leading subjects as represented in parliaments. Tensions mounted which culminated in civil wars in all three kingdoms. It was the story, in Geoffrey Elton's famous phrase, of a 'high road to civil war' (Elton 1974–92: II, 164–82).

This account, often labelled the 'Whig' interpretation, was partially superseded from the 1940s onwards by a view heavily influenced by Marxist thought. This suggested that political processes and conflicts were but a reflection of more deep-rooted changes in Britain's economic and social structures. It was argued that underlying the conflict between crown and parliament was a more profound battle between an outmoded territorial elite and rising 'bourgeois' elements whose wealth derived originally from commerce or the professions. Despite their superficial contrasts, this interpretation was closer to the Whig view than the advocates of either generally acknowledged. In particular, both accounts assumed that:

1 the early Stuart political system was innately unstable;
2 it contained inherent tensions, within which lay the origins of the English Revolution;
3 these tensions steadily mounted during the early seventeenth century, making the political history of 1603–40 one of progressively worsening conflict.

The common premises of the Whig and Marxist accounts in turn made it possible to synthesize many of their main points into a single interpretative scheme, as for example in Stone (1972).

From the mid-1970s onwards, however, a growing number of historians felt increasing dissatisfaction with this picture of early Stuart politics. Out of this dissatisfaction emerged the radically new lines of interpretation known as 'revisionism'. The so-called 'revisionists', who included such scholars as Conrad Russell, John Morrill, Mark Kishlansky and Kevin Sharpe, were very diverse and independent historians who never formed any kind of 'school' or advanced any one view of the period. They all had different angles and varied areas of interest within the field. What they did have in common was a rejection of the assumptions summed up in the three points in the previous paragraph. This in turn opened the way for new approaches to early Stuart political history, which attempted to see it in its own terms rather than as a prelude to the civil wars and revolution, and which suggested that the polity was more stable, effective and harmonious than had previously been suggested. In particular, 'revisionism' led to a much less conflict-centred account of political dynamics and of relations between the monarchs and their parliaments (e.g. Sharpe 1978; Russell 1979).

However, as with any major new interpretation, there was a danger of losing the baby with the bath-water. As a result, during the course of the 1980s and 1990s, various forms of 'post-revisionism' appeared. Scholars such as Ann Hughes, Richard Cust, Tom Cogswell and Johann Sommerville have argued that political and ideological conflict within the early Stuart polity should not be underestimated (e.g. Cust and Hughes 1989; Sommerville 1999). Once again, this was not a coherent 'school' of historians, and reflected ongoing historiographical debates in which many of the original 'revisionists' also played a very prominent part. Among the central themes that emerged in the writings of this period were:

1   a deepening awareness of the relationship between politics and religion, and the importance of religious conflict in the origins of the civil wars (Morrill 1993);
2   a greater appreciation of the significance of personal monarchy, and of the monarchs' personalities, in shaping political processes;
3   a rehabilitation of James VI and I's reputation while that of Charles I declined even further (Wormald 1983; Reeve 1989; Russell 1990; Fincham 1993).

These arguments helped to build up a much more nuanced view of early Stuart politics in which principled disagreement was not necessarily incompatible with a broadly harmonious framework. Another characteristic of 'post-revisionism' was to stress the importance of 1625 as a key turning point and to argue against seeing the period 1603–40 as a monolith in which tensions steadily mounted towards the outbreak of civil war.

Since the early 1990s two further historiographical trends have opened up fresh perspectives on early Stuart politics. First, the close relationship between political ideas and political practice, and the impossibility of separating the two, has been explored much more fully (e.g. Peck 1991; Burgess 1992, 1996; Sommerville 1999). This has been closely associated with a much rounder and richer sense of 'political culture' which integrates the history of political processes into analyses of intellectual, literary and cultural developments (e.g. Lake and Sharpe 1994; Amussen and Kishlansky 1995). Among the corollaries of this has been to take the history of the royal court and its political significance much more seriously (e.g. Starkey 1987; Peck 1991). The second trend has been to rebut the Anglocentricity of much earlier historiography and to seek instead to construct a 'British' history that demonstrates the interdependence of the Stuart monarchies (e.g. Ellis and Barber 1995; Bradshaw and Morrill 1996). That interdependence was evident at a number of levels, including the political, and is discussed more fully in chapters 1, 2 and 15 of this book.

All these recent historiographical developments have opened up fresh approaches to early Stuart political history and identified new preoccupations and emphases within it. They point less to traditional themes of liberty versus tyranny, or the conflicts between crown and parliaments, than to the nature of personal monarchy and political culture, the relationship between political practice and the history of ideas, the importance of the court and the politics of access, and the interaction between monarchs and their leading subjects through a series of conciliar structures of which parliament was one. These are the issues and debates that will form the central themes of this chapter, and they will be examined in turn in each of the following sections.

Personal Monarchy in Theory and Practice: James VI and I

Early Stuart Britain, like the majority of states in early modern Europe, was a personal monarchy, and this fact profoundly shaped the nature of its political life. The monarch ruled as well as reigned, and was the apex of the polity as well as the social hierarchy. All public offices were held on commissions from the crown, and courts of law were royal courts exercising justice in the monarch's name. Government was royal government, conducted on behalf of the monarch rather than of an impersonal 'state'. In such a system, the personality of individual monarchs necessarily had an immense impact on political decisions and priorities; their personalities could no more be separated from political affairs than can those of, say, the British prime minister or the United States president today.

This mattered all the more because the crown's powers were very extensive yet poorly defined. These powers, known collectively as the royal prerogative, were divided into two categories, the ordinary and the absolute (what Glenn Burgess has called the 'duplex nature of kingship': Burgess (1992: 155)). The ordinary prerogative powers were defined and limited by the law, and included such powers as the right to appoint to public offices, to dispense justice and to regulate trade. The absolute prerogative powers were discretionary powers: they were not constrained by the laws, although they could not contravene them. These powers could be used in emergencies, such as the making of war, and allowed actions necessary for national security. The monarch's powers were thus 'absolute and legally limited', and contemporaries saw no contradiction in this idea. However, the boundary between the absolute and ordinary prerogatives was not clearly laid down, and a great deal of political life therefore rested, as in the medieval and Tudor periods, on the personal relationships between the monarchs and their leading subjects. It is no wonder, therefore, that the personalities of James VI and I and Charles I, and the issue of their suitability for kingship, have continued to loom large in discussions of early Stuart politics.

Among the most striking features of recent historiography has been the rehabilitation of James VI and I's reputation. Older accounts tended to assume that the early
Stuarts were as bad as each other, and that James's accession to the English throne in
1603 was a very significant step on the 'high road to civil war'. As S. R. Gardiner put
it, James 'sowed the seeds of revolution and disaster' (Gardiner 1883–4: V, 316). The
major problem with this interpretation was that it seemed utterly at odds with James's
widely praised performance as king of Scotland, where he succeeded in raising the
authority of the crown to new heights and brought a greater degree of stability to a
notoriously turbulent polity. The apparent contradiction with the tactless, extravagant, undignified and foolish king that emerged in so much traditional English
historiography prompted Jenny Wormald (1983) to wonder whether James VI and
I was 'two kings or one'. Since then, a series of books and articles have presented an
altogether more positive account of James as king of Great Britain and suggested that
he was a much more skilled political practitioner than had previously been allowed.

The essence of this revised view of James is that his style of kingship generally
fostered political stability rather than the reverse. To be sure, he was at times tactless
and capable of triggering unnecessary confrontations, as for example in 1604 and
again in 1621 when he told the Commons that their privileges were the gracious gift
of his ancestors and could therefore be 'retrenched' if he thought necessary. Members
of the Commons responded by insisting that their privileges were 'the ancient and
undoubted birthright and inheritance of the subjects of England' (Kenyon 1986:
42). But James knew how to defuse such moments of high tension by making
conciliatory gestures, as for example when he opened the 1624 parliament by explicitly inviting members to advise him on foreign policy. At the heart of Jacobean
politics lay a realization that James did not present a serious threat to the future of
parliaments. In 1614 his relations with parliaments reached their lowest ebb with the
dissolution of the Addled Parliament after barely two months. Shortly afterwards,
James complained to the Spanish ambassador Gondomar that 'the House of Commons is a body without a head. The members give their opinions in a disorderly
manner. At their meetings nothing is heard but cries, shouts, and confusion.' He
professed himself 'surprised that my ancestors should ever have permitted such an
institution to come into existence'. But he then added, revealingly: 'I am a stranger,
and found it here when I arrived, so that I am obliged to put up with what I cannot
get rid of' (Gardiner 1883–4: II, 251). Although James might complain about
parliaments, it was never on his agenda to discontinue them permanently.

James's view of parliaments reflected a shrewd political realism that made him climb
down rather than push issues to the point where they caused serious political instability. Perhaps the best example of this pragmatic approach is James's recognition by
1608 that opposition to his vision of a union of the kingdoms of England and
Scotland was so strong, on both sides of the border, that the project had better be
abandoned. Instead, characteristically, he changed tack and adopted a more gradualist
approach which involved sporadic, piecemeal reforms – such as the introduction of
justices of the peace into Scotland in 1609 – that were designed to make the institutions of the two kingdoms more 'congruent' (Morrill 1993: 101) with each other.
This tactical shift showed James's political insight and intelligence at their best. He
also displayed a marked ability to paper over cracks by appealing to an agreed
intellectual framework, as in his famous speech of 21 March 1610. Here he argued

that although kings exercised 'a manner or resemblance of divine power upon earth', nevertheless 'every just king in a settled kingdom is bound to observe that paction made to his people by his laws, in framing his government agreeable thereto' (Kenyon 1986: 12). James was in effect restating the idea of monarchy as both absolute and legally limited that was a commonplace of early seventeenth-century English thought. James also pledged that 'never king was in all his time more careful to have his laws duly observed, and himself to govern thereafter, than I' (ibid.: 12). This was not mere rhetoric. James genuinely respected due process of law and was deeply conscious of his coronation oath to protect the fundamental laws of the realm.

To argue that James was committed to promoting stability and consensus is not to lose sight of his weaknesses as a ruler. His tactlessness undoubtedly got him into political scrapes, even if he then proved adroit at extricating himself. His extravagance, especially in the early years of his reign in England, magnified the crown's already chronic financial problems. The underlying difficulties were structural and long term: inflation had caused the ordinary income of the crown to fall by about 40 per cent in real terms between the 1540s and 1603. James lamented that but for this 'eating canker of want' he would be 'as happy in all other respects as any other king or monarch that ever was since the birth of Christ' (Akrigg 1984: 291). Unfortunately, James weakened a strong case by his lavish expenditure and gift-giving to his favourites. This made parliament reluctant to grant him more money, which led James to harness non-parliamentary expedients, such as impositions (a form of customs duty), with the result that royal finances became a standing political issue. The root of the problem was that the English fiscal system, barely changed in essentials since the fourteenth century, was unable to generate the resources needed to finance government by the seventeenth century, especially in wartime. The one attempt to replace this antiquated system was the Great Contract of 1610, a visionary proposal by which the crown would have surrendered certain rights such as wardship and purveyance in return for a lump sum and then an annual grant of £200,000 raised by a land tax. This scheme anticipated the kind of restructuring implemented in the 1690s, but in 1610 it fell victim to caution, conservatism and a suspicion on both sides that they might be better off under the existing system.

A further problem with James's kingship was his erratic judgement about people. He could be brilliantly shrewd, as when he presciently warned Prince Charles and Buckingham not to promote William Laud in 1621: 'take him to you, but on my soul you will repent it' (Smith 1998: 64). But there were other times when his judgement was very wayward, especially when a sexual infatuation led his heart to rule his head. The most notorious example of this was the meteoric rise of George Villiers from obscurity in 1615 to duke of Buckingham by 1623. James's political and emotional dependence on Buckingham clouded his judgement during his declining years and inspired growing mistrust within parliament and the privy council: James astonished the latter in 1617 by declaring that 'Christ had his John, and I have my George' (Kenyon 1970: 51). By the mid-1620s Buckingham had acquired a virtual stranglehold on patronage and he was probably the most hated man in Britain.

Yet, through it all, James was on balance an effective ruler. His conciliatory and pragmatic approach generally promoted consensus and stability. His avoidance of dogma and reluctance to push policies beyond the point of confrontation enabled him to develop good relations with most of his subjects. The grey areas within this unwritten constitution remained grey, and if James did not resolve them he at least did not make them significantly worse. Many of James's subjects found him quirky, unkempt and at times lacking in judgement, but very few of them disliked him. He was an intellectual in politics, a monarch of great intelligence and genuine political skill. The label 'the wisest fool in Christendom', often attributed to Henri IV of France but possibly coined by Anthony Weldon, catches James's paradoxical qualities very neatly. In contrast to earlier historians, recent research on his reign has tended to emphasize the wisdom and downplay the foolishness. As a result, we are now in a better position to understand why, amid the conflicts of the 1640s, so many contemporaries looked back on James's reign as a golden age, ruled over by 'Great Britain's Solomon'.

Personal Monarchy in Theory and Practice: Charles I

The political history of Charles I's reign presents a very different picture. In a personal monarchy a change of monarch was inevitably a moment of crucial significance for the political system. If older accounts saw 1603, and the arrival of the Stuarts, as a dangerous development, more recently historians have drawn out the importance of Charles's accession in 1625 as a turning point. John Reeve, for example, has argued that Charles was 'fundamentally unsuited to the task of kingship' (Reeve 1989: 173), while Conrad Russell finds 'civil war without him almost impossible to imagine' (Russell 1990: 211). Once again, personality mattered enormously. Charles was a very different person from his father: shy and uncommunicative, he was also much more rigid and was prepared to assert royal powers regardless of the political costs. His determination to define his powers proved deeply problematic in a polity whose operation depended so much on the interpretation of custom and precedent.

In essence, the problems with Charles's kingship resolve themselves into three. The first was that it was possible to follow the letter of the law while flouting its spirit, and a monarch's actions might be theoretically legitimate without being politically advisable. On virtually every occasion, Charles's assertions of his powers were technically correct, but that did not necessarily mean that he chose the most sensible political option. For example, it was technically within Charles's powers to introduce a new Prayer Book in Scotland in 1637, but this initiative precipitated a national rebellion which forced him to recall parliament. As Bill Hinton argued, 'Charles was none the less a tyrant because the law showed the way . . . When therefore Charles I did only what the law allowed, this does not mean that he acted correctly' (Hinton 1956: 86–7).

The second problem was that Charles, like James, was undoubtedly a visionary monarch; but unlike his father he did not know when to compromise his visions and adjust them to political realities. As Kevin Sharpe (1992) has shown, Charles's Personal Rule was founded on an ideal of a benignly ordered commonwealth. However, that ideal proved intensely controversial among Charles's subjects, many of whom bitterly resented what they saw as the crown's authoritarian intrusions in their lives. In a political culture which assumed that the 'ancient constitution' was immutable and that all change was by definition bad, Charles's commitment to reform was necessarily problematic and has prompted Russell's comment that 'Charles, unlike James, suffered from energy' (Russell 1979: 422). Just as the technically defensible could also be politically unwise, so policies that were visionary could also be deeply divisive.

The third problem was perhaps the most difficult to unravel. It arose from Charles's tendency to use powers that he was generally acknowledged to possess, but in what many of his subjects believed were inappropriate circumstances. This was most clearly seen in his attempts to employ his prerogative powers to raise money by means of the Forced Loan (1627) and Ship Money (1634–9). In both cases the legality of such levies deeply divided Charles's subjects, and Ship Money was particularly controversial because from 1635 Charles extended a levy traditionally raised only on coastal regions to the whole nation. Almost all contemporaries agreed that the monarch could implement certain military and financial measures in emergencies to protect national security. But what happened if the monarch chose to exercise such powers outside an emergency? If the monarch asserted that an emergency existed, could anyone else contest that assertion and challenge royal actions at law? These were questions that simply did not have answers within the 'ancient constitution', and they were questions that Charles's policies repeatedly forced his subjects to ask.

Some, like the divines Robert Sibthorpe and Roger Manwaring, asserted that the king was quite within his authority to make these demands and could not be legitimately resisted. But others, including many members of the House of Commons, thought it essential to take steps to prevent what they perceived as the misuse of royal powers. The dilemma they faced was how to achieve that without so defining the king's discretionary powers that they ceased to be discretionary any more. This was the delicate task that parliament attempted to achieve in 1628 by means of the Petition of Right. In the end, despite its self-conscious protestations that it merely rehearsed existing statutes, the Petition did introduce novel restrictions on royal powers to raise Forced Loans, to imprison, and to billet troops on the civilian population. Charles only accepted it with extreme reluctance, as the price for a grant of parliamentary taxation, and later tried to nullify the force of the Petition by ordering its statute number to be removed, thereby casting doubt on whether it could be cited as a statute in courts of law. Such behaviour was widely perceived as indicative of Charles's duplicity and desire to shake off any legal constraints on his use of royal powers.

Similar problems can be seen in Charles's rule over his other kingdoms as well. Throughout, there was a common style of kingship that involved asserting royal authority against representative and legal structures. In Scotland no parliament was summoned between 1621 and the crisis of 1639, apart from a brief ten-day session in June 1633 when Charles visited Scotland to be crowned. Charles chose Holyrood Palace in Edinburgh as the location for his coronation, rather than the traditional locations of Scone or Stirling, thereby emphasizing royal authority, and the coronation service offended many Scots by its Laudian overtones and clear emulation of the English style of coronation (Morrill 1993: 92–5). Charles had already alienated many of his leading Scottish subjects in 1625 by imposing an Act of Revocation that reclaimed all crown and kirk property alienated since 1542. As so often, Charles took a precedent (that Scottish monarchs could reclaim crown lands alienated while they were minors once they came of age) and twisted it into something new: he had never ruled as a minor, and the revocation was back-dated nearly a century and extended to kirk lands as well. From 1625 onwards, the Scottish privy council became increasingly a cipher for decisions taken in London, and lack of consultation with the Scottish parliament or the general assembly of the Kirk helped to precipitate the rebellion against the new Prayer Book in 1638.

It was a similar story in Ireland. There the crown's authority was exercised through a lord deputy rather than directly, and was much less hedged about by laws and customs than in England or Scotland. Sir Thomas Wentworth, lord deputy from 1633, set about using prerogative institutions, such as the court of castle chamber, to by-pass common-law rights of property and ensure that Ireland ceased to be a drain on the English exchequer. There was only one Irish parliament between 1615 and 1640, in 1634–5, and Wentworth categorically refused to bargain away royal author-ity by granting concessions to particular groups. As a result, he achieved the remark-able feat of simultaneously alienating all three of the main elements in Irish society: the (Catholic) Gaelic Irish, the (Catholic) Old English and the (Protestant) New English settlers. Wentworth enjoyed Charles's enthusiastic backing, which made it impossible for the Irish to go over the lord deputy's head by appealing directly to Whitehall as they sometimes had done in earlier decades.

Charles thus did not so much have a 'British policy' as a common style of rule that he pursued in all three of his kingdoms. The key features of this style were a powerful assertion of royal authority at the expense of legal and representative institutions, a lack of respect for the common law and for property rights, and a willingness to manipulate precedents as a way of legitimating innovation. These traits were if anything more marked in Scotland and Ireland than they were in England, and directly reflected Charles's personality and high sense of his own authority. Nowhere was that personality more plainly evident than in Charles's reshaping of the royal court, and this will form the subject of the next section.

The Politics of the Jacobean Court

One of the most significant developments in recent historiography has been much fuller research into the royal court and a recognition of its political significance (e.g. Starkey 1987; Peck 1991; Sharpe 1992; Adamson 1999). The court was not simply a splendid ceremonial setting for the monarch; it was also a vital centre of political intrigue and decision-making, and like the privy council and parliament it served as a 'point of contact' (Elton 1974–92: III, 38–57) between the monarchs and some of their most eminent subjects. Personal access to the monarch became a crucial source of political influence, and the extent to which the monarch participated in the life of the court or held aloof from it shaped the processes by which political priorities and decisions were determined.

In common with other early modern European monarchies the court was wherever the monarch happened to reside. This meant that after 1603 the court was also a 'British' court, even though it was almost invariably in England, often in London. James only paid one visit to Scotland after his accession to the English throne, in 1617, when what he called his 'salmon-like instinct' drew him back to his northern kingdom (Morrill 1993: 99). Charles paid two visits: one in 1633 to be crowned as king of Scotland, the other in 1641 to finalize a settlement with his Scottish subjects after the rebellion of 1638–40. Neither monarch ever visited Ireland. Instead, members of the elites of all three kingdoms had to come to the court based in England if they wished to have direct personal access to their sovereign.

James tried to remedy this problem of absentee kingship in a novel and interesting way. He made a distinction between the outer parts of the court, the privy chamber, whose personnel remained predominantly English, and the inner portions which were separated into a new department, the bedchamber, whose members were almost exclusively Scots. From the perspective of James's Scottish subjects this offered reassurance that they had a voice at the very heart of government and retained intimate access to their monarch. But from the point of view of his English subjects the Scottish dominance of the bedchamber became a major political issue. Among the most eloquent expressions of their deep unhappiness was a 'grievance' submitted to parliament in 1610 by Sir John Holles, the comptroller of the Prince of Wales's household. Holles complained that

> the Scottish monopolise [the King's] princely person, standing like mountains betwixt the beams of his grace and us; and, though it becomes us not to appoint particulars about him, yet we most humbly beseech his Majesty his Bedchamber may be shared as well to those of our nation as to them, that this seven years brand of jealousy [and] distrust may at last be removed. (Starkey 1987: 205)

Resentment of the Scottish presence in the innermost parts of the court was a key reason why successive Jacobean parliaments were so unwilling to grant the king more supply, or to license his raising of impositions. As long as the Scots remained the principal beneficiaries of the king's patronage and generosity, many members of the Commons, like Thomas Wentworth in 1610, asked 'to what purpose to draw a silver stream into the royal cistern if it shall daily run out thence by private cocks' (ibid.: 204).

The king's attempts to create a 'British' court thus helped to undermine his relations with his English parliaments. They also prompted intense public interest in the court in a way that proved deeply unfortunate as, in the mid-1610s, the court's reputation was tarnished by a series of alleged scandals involving sexual license, financial extravagance and corruption. In 1613 the king's current favourite, the Scot Robert Carr, earl of Somerset, was married to Lady Frances Howard, formerly countess of Essex and a member of the Howard family who had come to dominate political life after Robert Cecil's death in 1612. Amid sensational publicity, in 1616 Somerset and his wife were convicted of complicity in the murder of Sir Thomas Overbury, who had attempted to prevent her divorce from Essex. Three years later, her father Lord Treasurer Suffolk was fined and imprisoned for embezzlement of funds on a massive scale. Such events seriously tainted the reputation of the Jacobean court and fuelled the view summed up by Sir Walter Raleigh, that it 'glows and shines like rotten wood' (Smith 1998: 39).

Ironically, what finally replaced the ascendancy of the Howards and also ended the Scottish dominance of the bedchamber was a development that ushered in even greater long-term problems: the rise of Buckingham. As he rose from being a gentleman of the bedchamber in 1615 to a duke by 1623, Buckingham acquired an ever tightening grasp on the machinery of patronage. Central to this was his iron grip on the personnel of the bedchamber, and ironically it was this that finally eroded the predominance of Scots within that department. Whereas in 1614 six of the seven gentlemen of the bedchamber and all ten of the grooms were Scots, by 1625 five of the twelve gentlemen were English, as were three of the eleven grooms. But this was only achieved at the price of packing the bedchamber with Buckingham's relatives and dependants.

That process of packing also damaged some of the more positive aspects of the Jacobean court. Until James's final years, and the ascendancy of Buckingham, the court had functioned pretty well as a 'point of contact'. For all its seediness, promiscuity and corruption, the court provided an open, accessible and diverse political arena. James's Scottish experience had impressed on him the crucial importance of close personal relations with the political elite, and he placed great emphasis on this in *Basilikon Doron* (1599), his book of advice to his eldest son, Prince Henry (1594–1612). James was a natural extrovert, and his gregariousness led him to participate more fully in the life of the court than any monarch since Henry VIII. Intellectually self-assured, James never minded disagreement or debate: John Hacket described conversation at the Jacobean court as a 'trial of wits', while Francis Bacon observed that James 'giveth easy audience' (Smith 1998: 40). Until his later years, when Buckingham's control over patronage became ever stronger, James avoided associating himself with any particular political grouping, with the result that the court had an air of tolerant pluralism that accepted different opinions and encouraged easy communication.

The Politics of the Caroline Court

In his management of the court, as in other areas, Charles I once again presented a marked contrast to his father. His reserved and orderly personality led him to promote formality, ceremony and dignity in the life of the court. Within days of his accession, the Venetian ambassador reported that Charles observed 'a rule of great decorum' (Starkey 1987: 228). The new king invested an immense amount of time and effort in regulating the life of the court in minute detail. Large books of household ordinances were drawn up, prescribing exactly who had access to which parts of the court; supplies were carefully accounted for, and a concerted campaign launched against waste and corruption. Lucy Hutchinson observed that 'the face of the court was much changed in the change of the king, for King Charles was temperate, chaste and serious; so that the fools and bawds, mimics and catamites of the former court grew out of fashion' (Hutchinson 1968: 67). Instead, Charles wanted the court to be 'a place of civility and honour' (Sharpe 1992: 211). He revived the annual ceremonies of the Order of the Garter as a symbol of chivalry and piety, and every stage of Charles's daily routine was accompanied by a heightened dignity and ritual.

The cultural achievement of the Caroline court was very considerable. Charles was a great patron of artists such as Van Dyck and Rubens, and the latter described him as 'the greatest amateur [i.e. lover] of painting among the princes of the world' (Kenyon 1985: 125). Van Dyck's equestrian portraits of Charles, and Rubens's famous ceiling installed in the Banqueting House in Whitehall in 1635, presented an idealized view of kingship in which a benign monarch imposed order upon chaos. This was also a central theme of the many masques that were performed at court, especially during Charles's Personal Rule, with scenery by Inigo Jones and texts by writers such as Thomas Carew and Sir William Davenant. Yet these artistic developments were remote from the country at large, and the king's cultural interests failed to win him many admirers. His liking for the art of the Counter-Reformation fostered anxieties about the spread of popish influences at court, while some of his subjects questioned why he spent such large sums on what they regarded as 'old rotten pictures and broken-nosed marbles' (Daniels and Morrill 1988: 34).

Politically, perhaps the most damaging aspect of the Caroline court was Charles's almost obsessive concern with privacy. A 'distant' style of kingship replaced James's much more 'intimate' style: whereas his father had given 'easy audience', Charles did 'not wish anyone to be introduced to him unless sent for' (Starkey 1987: 228). Access to the privy chamber was confined to nobility, privy councillors and gentlemen of the privy chamber. Twice, in 1626 and again in 1636–7, Charles had all the locks for the palace of Whitehall changed to restrict freedom of access and control who could enter the state apartments. Firm restrictions were placed on those subjects wishing to present petitions to the king, thereby curtailing a longstanding custom that such individuals might approach the monarch in person. Charles also issued a series of proclamations limiting the times when he would touch for 'the King's Evil' (the name often given to scrofula, the tubercular inflammation of the lymph glands in the neck, which by ancient tradition English monarchs were thought able to heal by touching those afflicted). Whereas James had been willing to touch the scrofulous throughout the year, except during the summer months, Charles restricted the practice to Easter and Michaelmas, and thereby greatly diminished the occasions on which he could meet a cross-section of his subjects.

This emphasis on distance was closely linked to a narrowing of the range of political opinion that was able to find voice at court. Until his assassination in August 1628, Buckingham's stranglehold on patronage became if anything tighter than it had been during James's reign. Thereafter, Charles tended to surround himself with an inner circle of yes-men, drawn mainly from the bedchamber, whom he had chosen because they were likely to give him the advice that he wished to receive. Unlike his father, he never felt comfortable in situations involving debate or dialogue, and he tended to equate disagreement – even if sincere or principled – with disloyalty and subversion. Those less well disposed towards the policies of the Personal Rule (the earl of Essex, for example, or viscount Saye and Sele) therefore found themselves marginalized or displaced, and very often policy was decided at court and only then presented to the privy council. This was the context of parliament's demand, in the Nineteen Propositions of June 1642, 'that the great affairs of the kingdom may not be concluded or transacted by the advice of private men, or by any unknown or unsworn councillors' (Gardiner 1906: 250). Charles's style of rule made the court much less effective as a 'point of contact' because it ensured that he only received the advice that he wanted; dissenting voices had great difficulty finding a legitimate channel through which to be heard. This problem was also plainly apparent in his handling of the more formal conciliar structures, the privy council and the great council (parliament), to which we now turn.

The Crown and its Councils: The Privy Council

The conciliar bodies which offered the monarch counsel and advice spread around the crown in a series of concentric circles. The innermost ring was the privy council, which had been formalized as an institution in 1536–40, and which met at least once a week (often more regularly) for most of the year. Monarchs appointed privy councillors at their discretion: nobody sat *ex officio* or as of right, and the monarch determined the size and composition of the council. The outermost ring was formed by the great council, or parliament, which comprised a much wider cross-section of the political elite. It consisted of two Houses, the Lords (containing the hereditary peers and the bishops) and the Commons (containing representatives of the shires and the boroughs, the majority of whom in the early Stuart period were landed gentry). This great council only met sporadically, at irregular intervals, and was summoned, prorogued or dissolved entirely at the monarch's discretion. There was considerable overlap of personnel between the privy council and the great council: together with the court, they formed an organic system of royal government, and once again the personal style of individual monarchs decisively affected how efficiently these institutions operated.

Elizabeth I had preferred to work with a very small privy council, numbering only thirteen by the time of her death. James VI and I allowed it to expand to somewhere between twenty and twenty-eight for much of his reign, and during that period the focus of political deliberations and decision-making shifted somewhat from the council to the more private areas of the court, the privy chamber and bedchamber. James's relaxed approach, dislike of routine business and frequent hunting trips away from London ensured that he probably attended barely fifty privy council meetings between 1603 and 1625. At times, there was a lack of royal direction and control, with the result that factional in-fighting was rife within the Jacobean council. Usually one individual or group dominated: Robert Cecil until 1612, the Howards from 1612 to 1616, and Buckingham thereafter. But James allowed scope for diversity and, crucially, was willing to permit a range of opinions to be heard. For example, in 1616 James quarrelled with Sir Edward Coke, the most eminent of the common law judges, when the latter played a prominent part in bringing the earl and countess of Somerset to justice, and also attempted to prevent Chancery proceedings in cases triable at common law. James dismissed Coke as chief justice of King's Bench and suspended him from the privy council. But it was typical of James's capacity to rebuild bridges that he allowed Coke back onto the council the following year. As a 'point of contact' the Jacobean council functioned effectively enough.

Possibly more impressive was James's management of the Scottish privy council. He continued to take a very keen interest in Scottish affairs and was supplied with regular news bulletins, especially by the earl of Dunbar between 1605 and 1611. James established a highly efficient postal service between London and Edinburgh, and he sent a steady stream of letters to the Scottish privy council, giving instructions and explaining policies. There was more than a grain of truth in his celebrated boast in 1607 that 'This I must say for Scotland, and I may truly vaunt it; here I sit and govern it with my pen, I write and it is done' (Sommerville 1994: 173). Only in his later years, in the controversy over the Five Articles of Perth (1618–21), were there signs that long absence had eroded James's intuitive feel for Scottish political and religious opinion.

Charles I's management of the privy council was once again a direct reflection of his personality and political style. He expanded the council still further, to forty in 1625 and forty-two by 1630. He attended its meetings far more regularly than his father (he was present at over forty of the 131 meetings in 1637, for example), and he tightened up its organization and record-keeping with characteristic thoroughness.

During the Personal Rule the council also assumed an increasingly important role in implementing Charles's reforms of local government. In particular, it oversaw the attempts to create an 'exact militia', the introduction of a new Book of Orders in 1631 that made justices of the peace more accountable to the council, and the collection of Ship Money. But increasingly Charles's naturally authoritarian approach showed through. He relied more and more on an inner 'cabinet council', led by the likes of Laud, Weston, Windebank and Cottington, to formulate policy and take key decisions rather than the full council. As in the court, the fact that Charles preferred to listen to yes-men seriously undermined the council's effectiveness as a 'point of contact'. This was also evident in Charles's by-passing of the Scottish privy council, which became increasingly a cipher for decisions taken at Westminster: he never took as much trouble as James to keep abreast of Scottish opinion, and in the end this contributed to the rebellion in 1638–40 which forced him to recall parliaments in all three of his kingdoms.

The Crown and its Councils: The Great Council

It is important, as many recent writings on this period have shown, to see parliaments as part of this organic system of royal government, as agents of the crown rather than as counterweights to it. In England, parliaments had originally evolved during the thirteenth and fourteenth centuries as an extension of the monarch's council, and they continued to display evidence of their origins into the early modern period. They were not so much a forum for political debate, let alone conflict, as an institution to offer counsel, vote taxes and pass laws. Parliament also had a judicial role and was often referred to as the monarch's High Court: it was integrated into the structure of law courts, and the House of Lords was the highest court of appeal (a function eclipsed in the sixteenth century but vigorously revived from 1621 onwards). The Acts of parliament (statutes) passed by the king-in-parliament were the highest form of human law in England, and by the 1530s were recognized as a supreme and omnicompetent form of edict. The parliamentary trinity of monarch, Lords and Commons was thus the sovereign legislative authority in the kingdom. The monarch alone could not issue anything of comparable force: proclamations could not touch life, limb or property, whereas statute could take away all three if so desired. This meant that the monarch was more powerful when collaborating with parliament than when working alone, and in general the more clearly a monarch understood this principle the more successful he or she was likely to be.

James certainly grasped the sweeping powers of statute. In a speech on 20 June 1616 he observed that he had 'come to that knowledge, that an Act of Parliament can do greater wonders: and that old wise man the Treasourer Burghley was wont to say, hee knew not what an Acte of Parliament could not doe in England' (Sommerville 1994: 209). Indeed, it was precisely because he recognized the supremacy of statute that James sought to enact the union of the kingdoms of England and Scotland by Act of parliament. He understood the importance of working with parliaments, and it was never on his agenda to discontinue them permanently. During his reign there was no uniform escalation of tension between crown and parliaments: the lowest point was reached with the Addled Parliament in 1614, whereas James's last parliament, in 1624, was probably his most harmonious and produced no fewer than seventy-three

Acts. Conrad Russell has written that 'in general, the story of 1621 and 1624 suggests that not very much was wrong with relations between crown and parliament' (Russell 1979: 419).

There were, of course, intractable issues and moments of conflict between James and his parliaments. However, it was striking how much these issues varied during the course of the reign. Impositions, which caused major controversy in the parliaments of 1604–10 and 1614, were rather less prominent in 1621 and 1624; freedom of speech was contested in 1604 and 1621, but not in the other parliaments; foreign policy was discussed heatedly in 1621 and more harmoniously in 1624, but hardly at all earlier in the reign; religion was scarcely an issue for most of the Jacobean parliaments, and only surfaced prominently in 1621 and 1624. All in all, it was a very varied and mixed picture, and one that certainly does not warrant ideas of rising parliamentary assertiveness or the 'winning of the initiative by the House of Commons' (Notestein 1924). James's relations with his parliaments might more appropriately be likened to a turbulent, at times verbally violent, marriage, but one where a divorce was never on the cards.

One of the reasons for James's intermittent difficulties with his English parliaments was his prior experience of the very different parliament of Scotland. There the monarch exercised far greater control over the membership and business of a parliament that consisted of a single chamber, containing peers, burgesses, bishops and officers of state. Furthermore, there was no concept of the supremacy of statute in Scotland, and the monarch did not necessarily need parliament's consent to create laws or raise taxes. In fact it was relatively easy for the monarch to secure the passing of an Act; the really difficult task was to ensure its enforcement at grassroots level. This was the opposite of the situation in England, where the hardest part was to manage the passage of a Bill through parliament, but once an Act had been passed by both Houses and received the royal assent England's highly centralized system of law courts made it straightforward to implement. Indeed, it has been suggested that one reason why James quickly abandoned his plans for an Anglo-Scottish union in 1604–8 in the face of English parliamentary resistance was that he was 'discouraged at falling at what in Scotland would have been the lowest hurdle' (Morrill 1993: 96). Only late in his reign did James's grasp of Scottish politics begin to weaken. He seems to have been genuinely caught out by the level of hostility towards the Five Articles of Perth expressed in the Scottish parliament of 1621. That parliament nearly denied him a large grant of taxation, and suggested that the problems of absentee kingship were at last coming home to roost.

The Irish parliament was different again. Like the English parliament it comprised two Houses, the Lords and the Commons. However, Poynings' Law (1494) stipulated that no Bill could be introduced into the Irish parliament until it had first been approved by the king and privy council in England. The Irish parliament met only once during James's reign, for three sessions in 1613–15. Perhaps the most significant development was the increasing dominance of the Protestant New English, whereas for much of the Tudor period parliament had consisted mainly of the Catholic Old English. The parliament of 1613–15 contained only a hundred Catholics (nearly all Old English rather than Gaelic Irish), but 132 Protestants. Increasingly, the Irish parliament was becoming a mechanism for extending the direct rule of the crown over Ireland, and from 1609 onwards James authorized the systematic

'Anglicization' (colonization) of Ulster by Protestant settlers from England and Scotland. Parliaments thus fulfilled very different roles in each of the Stuarts' three kingdoms, and it would be fair to say that the English parliament was the largest, strongest and most often summoned of the three.

Indeed, it met with particular frequency during the opening years of Charles I's reign – in four of his first five years as king – but that only served to highlight the very rapid deterioration in his relations with parliament. This was all the more ironic because the 1624 parliament had supported Charles in calling for a war against Spain and feted him as, in Sir Benjamin Rudyerd's words, a 'prince bred up in Parliaments' (Kyle 1998: 621). The contrast with James was again immediately apparent when Charles told his first parliament that it did not 'stand with [his] nature to spend much times in words' (Smith 1999: 113). James was loquacious, but relaxed and pragmatic in practice: his parliaments knew where they stood with him, whereas Charles was a man of few words but assertive and authoritarian in his deeds. He tended to regard his parliaments as tests of his subjects' loyalty, and to attribute any signs of disobedience to a minority of 'malevolent' and 'ill-affected' individuals who formed a 'faction of discontented, seditious persons' (Cust 1990). He consistently felt that if he could only remove that minority of ringleaders, all would be well. Ironically, his positive experiences of the parliaments of 1621 and 1624 may have caused him to underestimate the difficulties of managing parliaments, especially during the wars against Spain (1625–30) and France (1627–9). Before the 1626 parliament he appointed six members of the Commons whom he thought 'ill-affected' to be sheriffs, thereby making them ineligible for election; after dissolving parliament in March 1629 he arrested nine members whom he blamed for a sensational attempt to forestall a dissolution by holding the Speaker down in his chair. But such moves became self-fulfilling because they were liable to alienate more moderate opinion both within parliament and in the nation at large.

Charles felt, with some justice, that certain members of the Commons were behaving unreasonably by demanding a continental war that they then refused to finance adequately. With proper funding, he insisted, disasters like the Ile de Rhé expedition of 1627 could have been avoided. Within parliament, however, military setbacks were widely blamed on mismanagement by Buckingham, who was Lord High Admiral. Many members felt that until he was dislodged it was pointless throwing good money after bad. In 1626 parliament launched impeachment proceedings against the duke, and in order to save his favourite Charles dissolved the parliament. However admirable in personal terms, Charles's protection of Buckingham was politically unwise and strikingly different from James's reaction to the impeachments of 1621 and 1624, which was simply to abandon those individuals who had become political liabilities. It appeared that Charles would rather trust Buckingham than accept the advice of his parliament, a view that was reinforced when, shortly afterwards, he began raising revenue by non-parliamentary means in the form of the Forced Loan.

The mistrust between Charles and parliament grew rapidly worse in 1628–9. After acrimonious debates, Charles grudgingly accepted the Petition of Right, but then undermined its force by ordering its statute number to be removed. In 1629 the Commons' mounting anxieties led members to pass three resolutions against religious innovation and the continued collection of tonnage and poundage, another category of customs duties, without parliamentary consent. Infuriated, Charles dissolved the parliament, denouncing the 'undutiful and seditious carriage in the Lower House', and insisting that 'some few vipers amongst them did cast this mist of undutifulness over most of their eyes' (Smith 1999: 118–19). Later, on 27 March, he issued a proclamation declaring it 'presumption for any to prescribe any time unto us for Parliaments' and stating that: 'we shall be more inclinable to meet in Parliament again when our people shall see more clearly into our intents and actions, when such as have bred this interruption shall have received their condign punishment, and those who are misled by them, and by such ill reports . . . shall come to a better understanding of us and themselves' (ibid.: 119). That enigmatic and strangely menacing final sentence was characteristic of Charles's political style.

Eleven years passed until Charles called another parliament in England, and this period of Personal Rule reflected the fact that he had come to prefer ruling without parliaments. By about 1632, if not earlier, he had apparently resolved not to recall parliament unless he had absolutely no choice. In 1637 the Kentish gentleman Sir Roger Twysden wrote in his commonplace book that 'none could expect a Parliament, but on some great necessity not now imaginable' (Fincham 1984: 236). A similar desire to avoid parliaments as much as possible characterized Charles's government of his other kingdoms as well. In Ireland, parliament met for three sessions in 1634–5, but Wentworth decisively alienated the Catholic Old English by refusing to enshrine in statute the 'graces', which granted them significant religious and economic concessions. In Scotland, parliament met for just ten days in June 1633, but otherwise not until the Prayer Book rebellion necessitated its recall in 1639. That lack of consultation undoubtedly contributed to the collapse of Charles's authority in Scotland, and this crisis ultimately forced him to summon another parliament in England in 1640.

In a sense, each of the early Stuart kings got the parliaments he deserved. Under James, parliaments mainly engaged with their monarch on his own theoretical and intellectual level: they defended their privileges and argued about their origins, but they did not fundamentally fear for their survival. With Charles, they faced a more direct threat from a monarch who wished to assert his powers much more actively. This forced them, in turn, to try to define their own position, as in the Petition of Right. Charles's eleven years of rule without parliament represented a far more conscious preference for non-parliamentary government than anything seen in the Jacobean period, and they ensured that when parliament did meet again in 1640 he was faced with a bitter outpouring of pent-up hostility towards recent royal policies.

Conclusion: 'A High Road to Civil War'?

In many ways, recent scholarship has argued against the idea of a 'high road to civil war', but in favour of seeing Charles I's accession as a key turning point in early Stuart political history. His personal manner and preferred policies undoubtedly contributed to the crisis that had befallen the British monarchies by 1640. During the course of that year, Charles's own free decisions led him to lose control over events. The Short Parliament (April–May 1640) refused to grant Charles supply for another campaign against the Scots until their grievances were fully discussed. At that point, Charles had three main alternatives open to him:

1   Make concessions to the Short Parliament as the price for gaining supply, and
    then launch a second, properly funded, campaign against the Scots.
2   Dissolve parliament and then make concessions to the Scots.
3   Dissolve parliament and launch another, inadequately funded, campaign against
    the Scots.

Either of the first two were viable options; the third was not, and that was precisely
the one that Charles chose. A second campaign in the summer of 1640 proved utterly
disastrous: the Scots routed Charles's forces at Newburn, invaded the northeast of
England and occupied Newcastle. They then refused to return home until Charles
reached a settlement with them, acceptable to an English parliament, and in the
meantime demanded £850 a day as their price for not advancing further into England. Charles therefore had no alternative but to summon the Long Parliament to
meet in November 1640; when it did so his financial position was so desperate that in
practice he did not have the freedom to dissolve it even if wanted to. He had thus
ceased to hold the political initiative.

   If Charles's weaknesses were increasingly evident, the underlying strengths of the
political system nevertheless remained considerable. Faith in the capacity of existing
institutions to resolve the crisis was still deeply rooted: Sir Henry Slingsby, for
example, hoped for a 'happy Parliament' in which 'the subject' would be able to
gain 'a total redress of all his grievances' (Smith 1999: 123). Such faith helped to
prevent the outbreak of civil war until the summer of 1642. As the Long Parliament
went on, it became ever clearer that the political problems it faced stemmed primarily
from Charles I's kingship rather than from the constitutional system as such. Perhaps
the clearest evidence of this was the Grand Remonstrance of November 1641, a
comprehensive indictment of Charles's rule containing no fewer than 204 clauses.
Crucially, none of the grievances listed in it pre-dated 1625, and all the remedies it
advocated were designed to neutralize the effects of Charles's perceived misgovernment. Interestingly, even one of Charles's most loyal servants, Edward Hyde, later
earl of Clarendon, took a similar view when he wrote at the start of his *History of the
Rebellion and Civil Wars* that he would not 'lead any man farther back in this journey,
for the discovery of the entrance into these dark ways, than the beginning of this
King's reign' (Macray 1888: I, 3).

   The early Stuart polity gave the monarch very extensive powers and in the end the
monarch had to bear considerable responsibility for the direction of political developments. If, by the early 1640s, the king was widely mistrusted, and if many of his
subjects felt that his powers needed to be defined more precisely, then much of the
blame must lie with Charles I himself. There may not have been a 'high road to civil
war', but on the twisting journey that ultimately led to conflict, 1625 represented a
far more significant staging-post than 1603. For it was under Charles, rather than
James, that the grey areas within the 'ancient constitution' began to be explored and
probed more profoundly than ever before. The fact that the boundaries between royal
powers and the rule of law, and between the crown's authority and parliamentary
privileges, were blurred, and their interaction regulated only by custom and precedent, henceforth became a weakness in the polity rather than an advantage.

   In the process, the early Stuart paradigm of a monarchy that was both 'absolute'
and 'legally limited' began to break down. Faced with a monarch who was widely

thought to be using his 'absolute' powers in inappropriate ways, significant numbers of the political elite came to feel that they had no alternative but to embark on the painful task of imposing tighter legal restrictions upon those powers. This was the background to the Triennial Act of 1641, which required the king to summon parliament at least every three years, and a further Act which denied him the power to dissolve the Long Parliament except with its own consent. The following year, the Houses demanded the right to approve the king's choice of advisers. The final crunch came when the Houses asserted that in a national emergency they had a duty to assume control over the armed forces. By a crushing irony, just as Charles I had earlier claimed that an emergency legitimated sweeping use of his prerogative powers, so the emergency created by the Irish Rebellion of November 1641 enabled his leading critics in parliament to justify taking over military command from the king. Such an encroachment on a long-established part of the royal prerogative was bound to prove intensely controversial; nor could any monarch be expected to accept it without a struggle. By the time the Houses made the devastating claim, on 6 June 1642, that 'the King's supreme and royal pleasure is exercised and declared in this High Court of law and council, after a more eminent and obligatory manner than it can be by personal act or resolution of his own' (Smith 1999: 47), the outbreak of civil war could only be a matter of time.

REFERENCES

Adamson, J. (ed.) 1999: *The Princely Courts of Europe: Ritual, Politics and Culture under the Ancien Régime, 1500–1750*: London.

Akrigg, G. P. V. (ed.) 1984: *Letters of King James VI and I*: Berkeley, CA.

Amussen, S. D. and Kishlansky, M. A. (eds) 1995: *Political Culture and Cultural Politics in Early Modern England: Essays Presented to David Underdown*: Manchester.

Bradshaw, B. and Morrill, J. (eds) 1996: *The British Problem, c.1534–1707: State Formation in the Atlantic Archipelago*: London.

Burgess, G. 1992: *The Politics of the Ancient Constitution: An Introduction to English Political Thought, 1603–1642*: London.

Burgess, G. 1996: *Absolute Monarchy and the Stuart Constitution*: New Haven, CT.

Cust, R. 1990: 'Charles I and a draft declaration for the 1628 parliament', *Historical Research*, 63, 143–61.

Cust, R. and Hughes, A. (eds) 1989: *Conflict in Early Stuart England: Studies in Religion and Politics, 1603–1642*: Harlow.

Daniels, C. W. and Morrill, J. 1988: *Charles I*: Cambridge.

Ellis, S. G. and Barber, S. (eds) 1995: *Conquest and Union: Fashioning a British State 1485–1725*: Harlow.

Elton, G. R. 1974–92: *Studies in Tudor and Stuart Politics and Government*: Cambridge.

Fincham, K. 1984: 'The judges' decision on Ship Money in February 1637: the reaction of Kent', *Bulletin of the Institute of Historical Research*, 57, 230–7.

Fincham, K. (ed.) 1993: *The Early Stuart Church, 1603–1642*: London.

Gardiner, S. R. 1883–4: *History of England from the Accession of James I to the Outbreak of the Civil War, 1603–1642*: London.

Gardiner, S. R. (ed.) 1906: *Constitutional Documents of the Puritan Revolution, 1625–1660*: Oxford.

Hinton, R. W. K. 1956: 'Was Charles I a tyrant?' *The Review of Politics*, 18, 69–87.

Hutchinson, L. 1968: *Memoirs of the Life of Colonel Hutchinson*: London.

Kenyon, J. P. 1970: *The Stuarts*: London.

Kenyon, J. P. 1985: *Stuart England*: Harmondsworth.

Kenyon, J. P. (ed.) 1986: *The Stuart Constitution: Documents and Commentary*: Cambridge.

Kyle, C. R. 1998: 'Prince Charles in the parliaments of 1621 and 1624', *Historical Journal*, 41 (3), 603–24.

Lake, P. and Sharpe, K. (eds) 1994: *Culture and Politics in Early Stuart England*: London.

Macray, W. D. (ed.) 1888: *The History of the Rebellion and Civil Wars in England by Edward, Earl of Clarendon*: Oxford.

Morrill, J. 1993: *The Nature of the English Revolution*: Harlow.

Notestein, W. 1924: 'The winning of the initiative by the House of Commons', *Proceedings of the British Academy*, 11, 125–75.

Peck, L. L. (ed.) 1991: *The Mental World of the Jacobean Court*: Cambridge.

Reeve, L. J. 1989: *Charles I and the Road to Personal Rule*: Cambridge.

Russell, C. 1979: *Parliaments and English Politics, 1621–1629*: Oxford.

Russell, C. 1990: *The Causes of the English Civil War*: Oxford.

Sharpe, K. (ed.) 1978: *Faction and Parliament: Essays on Early Stuart History*: Oxford.

Sharpe, K. 1992: *The Personal Rule of Charles I*: New Haven, CT.

Smith, D. L. 1998: *A History of the Modern British Isles, 1603–1707: The Double Crown*: Oxford.

Smith, D. L. 1999: *The Stuart Parliaments, 1603–1689*: London.

Sommerville, J. P. (ed.) 1994: *King James VI and I: Political Writings*: Cambridge.

Sommerville, J. P. 1999: *Royalists and Patriots: Politics and Ideology in England, 1603–1640*: Harlow.

Starkey, D. (ed.) 1987: *The English Court from the Wars of the Roses to the Civil War*: Harlow.

Stone, L. 1972: *The Causes of the English Revolution, 1529–1642*: London.

Wormald, J. 1983: 'James VI and I: two kings or one?' *History*, 68, 187–209.

FURTHER READING

Bradshaw, B. and Morrill, J. (eds) 1996: *The British Problem, c.1534–1707: State Formation in the Atlantic Archipelago*: London.

Burgess, G. 1992: *The Politics of the Ancient Constitution: An Introduction to English Political Thought, 1603–1642*: London.

Coward, B. 1994: *The Stuart Age: England, 1603–1714*: Harlow.

Cust, R. and Hughes, A. (eds) 1989: *Conflict in Early Stuart England: Studies in Religion and Politics, 1603–1642*: Harlow.

Ellis, S. G. and Barber, S. (eds) 1995: *Conquest and Union: Fashioning a British State 1485–1725*: Harlow.

Hirst, D. 1999: *England in Conflict, 1603–1660: Kingdom, Community, Commonwealth*: London.

Hughes, A. 1998: *The Causes of the English Civil War*: London.

Kenyon, J. P. (ed.) 1986: *The Stuart Constitution: Documents and Commentary*: Cambridge.

Lockyer, R. 1999: *The Early Stuarts: A Political History of England, 1603–1642*: Harlow.

Morrill, J. 1993: *The Nature of the English Revolution*: Harlow.

Morrill, J. (ed.) 1996: *The Oxford Illustrated History of Tudor and Stuart Britain*: Oxford.

Morrill, J. 1999: *Revolt in the Provinces: The People of England and the Tragedies of War, 1630–1648*: Harlow.

Russell, C. 1979: *Parliaments and English Politics, 1621–1629*: Oxford.

Russell, C. 1990: *The Causes of the English Civil War*. Oxford.

Scott, J. 2000: *England's Troubles: Seventeenth-Century Political Instability in European Context*. Cambridge.

Sharpe, K. 1992: *The Personal Rule of Charles I*. New Haven, CT.

Smith, D. L. 1998: *A History of the Modern British Isles, 1603–1707: The Double Crown*. Oxford.

Smith, D. L. 1999: *The Stuart Parliaments, 1603–1689*. London.

Sommerville, J. P. 1999: *Royalists and Patriots: Politics and Ideology in England, 1603–1640*. Harlow.

CHAPTER THIRTEEN

Religion in Early Stuart Britain, 1603–1642

TOM WEBSTER

When James VI of Scotland succeeded Elizabeth to the crowns of England and Ireland it was a watershed in religious history. Although the tendency to see a 'Jacobethan' period of relative continuity has much validity, in religious terms this was a serious change of circumstances and was met by various groups with a sense of trepidation and/or anticipation. In the Scottish Kirk trepidation was the dominant theme, with fears that James might be 'led astray' by the weaker Protestantism and the stronger ceremonialism of the Kirk's sister, the Church of England. As James moved south he was greeted in Northamptonshire with the Millenary Petition said to be supported by 1,000 ministers calling for further reformation in the Church of England. Before his accession he had adopted a conciliatory stance towards the Church of Rome and this produced a petition in 1604 from Roman Catholics pleading for a limited toleration. Similarly in Ireland different groups celebrated. Six days after the death of Elizabeth, Hugh O'Neill, the earl of Tyrone, surrendered, effectively ending the long and bloody Nine Years' War, raising Protestant hopes for an effective colonial government. At the same time, the hopes of urban Catholics were raised by the arrival onto the throne of the son of the good Catholic Mary, Queen of Scots. The townsfolk in the south resumed the public observance of Catholicism, reclaiming and restoring their churches.

The disparate political nations had, from their different perspectives, watched James closely in the later years of Elizabeth. The fact that different groups were hopeful with effectively mutually exclusive hopes shows how close James had kept his cards. Before we trace the fate of those hopes and fears we need to have an idea of the religious spectrum James had inherited. Each kingdom had a single established Protestant church. In each church the dominant theology was Calvinist in terms of the doctrine of grace, accepting the predestination of the saved, the elect, and the damned, the reprobate. From his eternal perspective God had chosen the division of humanity after the Fall and this was determined solely by the sacrifice of Christ rather than any foreseen credit earned by those to be saved. The image of the three churches was built upon a conflictual model, with the negative 'other' being the Roman church. The pope, and sometimes the whole Roman church, was regarded as the Antichrist, that is, a servant of Satan committed to seducing the 'godly' and taking them from true faith to the corruption of a false church. However, despite this common ground, the contrasting contexts produced three very different churches. In Scotland the Kirk was born with a Catholic monarch on the throne and James had worked painfully to overcome the separation of church and state, gradually acquiring recognition for religious authority in the throne. The style of worship was free of a liturgy, focused on the sermon and extempore prayers guided by the Holy Spirit in an iconophobic environment. The Lowlands were dominated by Protestantism but the north and west were slower to convert, with a surviving Catholicism retaining a strong voice. The Church of England had a stronger Erastian tradition, with the monarch as supreme governor. English Calvinism was delivered with a legally requis-ite Book of Common Prayer. The preaching ministry was also very important, but the church courts required fairly strict conformity to the liturgy. Elizabeth's reign had seen the appearance of a powerful voice of ministers and laity pushing for further reform, looking for a service consisting of ceremonies with scriptural grounding rather than those of merely human tradition. This group of reformers within the church were the Puritans. There were Roman Catholics in England and Wales but they were few and mostly passively obedient, suffering from the occasional imposition of the recusancy laws, placing fines on those who failed to attend divine service. The vast majority of English people were Protestants accepting the piety of the Prayer Book. This stood in stark contrast to Ireland, where Protestantism was predominantly the faith of the English and Scottish settlers, referred to as the New English, alone. The older colonists, the descendants of the Norman invaders, who were coming to be known as the Old English, had retained their Catholic faith as had the vast majority, the native Irish.

The contrasting contexts and the different fortunes of the three kingdoms in religious terms make an immediately holistic analysis of the three kingdoms a task performed at the expense of comprehension; cohesion would join with incoherency, as it were. However, moving from one realm to another is more than a necessary evil. Moving from Scotland to Ireland and then to England and Wales has a more positive impact in that it works against the still too prevalent Anglocentrism in the current historiography (Brown 1990; Canny 1995a). In addition, it is intended to modify the current English assessment of James which flatters him, particularly in comparison to his successor, as an astute, almost Machiavellian politician who managed the problems of three kingdoms with reasonable success. By changing the perspective, we change or at least qualify our conclusions.

In Scotland, of course, the Kirk was all too familiar with the government of James. In the years before 1603 he had, with a mixture of patronage and intimidation, rejuvenated the office of bishop, operating as moderators of the presbyteries and gradually accumulating more power (MacDonald 1998). Apart from the crown, the Kirk was the only institution of national governance and, as James saw it, he needed a means to govern from a distance which was more manipulable and less likely to run counter to his wishes than the Presbyterian system. When he moved south this was very much a project far from completion; the Scottish bishops paled next to the powers of their English namesakes. Having said this, their development had been fraught with tension and substantial opposition. After 1603 James continued the project in two ways. He continued to appoint bishops to vacant dioceses, with only three of the thirteen vacant by 1605. He called a general assembly to Aberdeen in 1605 but repeatedly postponed it until, in 1606, radicals began an illegal assembly, expressing fears of an ecclesiastical union with England. James called eight of his most vociferous opponents south and held them as virtual prisoners. With them out of the way, he convened a conference at Linlithgow which was packed with his supporters and accordingly approved of bishops as constant moderators of synods. This meeting was only declared to be a general assembly after it met. After this episode, in order to silence opposition, the assembly met rarely. The power of the assembly was further reduced in 1610 when English-style courts of high commission were established as the ultimate courts of ecclesiastical discipline, a role formerly held by the assembly.

Despite the level of opposition, with the most prominent radicals in exile or effective imprisonment and the general assembly inactive, the next few years were relatively peaceful. From 1617 this harmony ceased. At this point James visited his northern kingdom for the first time since 1603. Having completed his polity pro-gramme, attention was turned to the practice of worship. The first signs were in the service at Holyrood palace. Choristers accompanied James on his trip and an organ was installed in the chapel. These were not to the Kirk's taste and James had to be persuaded at least to postpone the erection of statues of the apostles. The service was conducted according to the English liturgy, and communicants were required to kneel. All these practices were either unscriptural, or papist, or both, but worse was to come.

James had been consulting with his bishops on the question of forms of worship for some time. In 1617 the plans were made public. The five articles were for kneeling at communion, confirmation of children by a bishop, private baptism, private commu-nion in the right circumstances and the celebration of holy days such as Christmas, Good Friday and Easter Sunday. A general assembly was called to pass the proposals; despite increased control over the Kirk, they were swiftly rejected. James responded by calling another general assembly in Perth in 1618. Guards were placed to watch the ministers and threats of deprivation and exile were delivered and the assembly duly 'agreed' to pass what became known as the Five Articles of Perth.

Attempts to implement the innovations were very troubled (Cowan 1967; Mackay 1977). The efforts in the Presbyterian strongholds of the Lowlands met with a little success, at the price of hostility, alienation and the emergence of an underground matrix of resistance. The difference in the opposition to that of polity was two-fold. It was a larger opposition quantitatively and also qualitatively, in that these reforms made an impact on worship, so they were met with much more practical resistance in the refusal to observe the ceremonies, particularly the requirement to kneel at commu-nion. Opposition came to a head in the parliament of 1621, where there was a prolonged struggle over the ratification of the Articles (Goodare 1995). James came very close to defeat, was saved by the bishops and the nobles who owed their titles to the king, but the underlying message was clear. Even in these circumstances, with his attention primarily on European diplomacy and substantial difficulties in England, he contemplated a new campaign of enforcement as late as 1624. At the end of his reign he had a Kirk seriously dissatisfied over liturgical innovations and governmental style, a pattern that was to be repeated and intensified in his son's reign.

The Protestant victory in the Nine Years' War, followed by the Flight of the Earls in 1607, seemed to extend royal writ across the whole of Ireland for the first time. The Church of Ireland saw this as creating an opportunity, indeed a responsibility, to convert the Catholic population with a blend of coercion and persuasion (Clarke and Edwards 1976). Churchmen justified the persecution from the precedent of Augustine's forceful persuasion of the Donatists and the Lord Deputy, Sir Arthur

Chichester, dismissed fears that it would create disloyalty by arguing that it was impossible for Catholic disloyalty to get any worse. Thus in July 1605 the Dublin government issued a proclamation ordering priests to leave and imposing a 12 pence fine on absentees from church. The urgency with which the policy was pursued can be understood in the light of Bishop Lyons's experience in his survey in Cork, where a Catholic counter-culture was emerging from the work of the Jesuits and the Franciscans: he found the royal supremacy rejected, the Prayer Book dismissed as 'the Devil's worship' and ministers described as 'Devils' (Bradshaw 1998: 50). However, London was less inclined to pursue a strategy of coercion, preferring persuasion, seeing the former as impracticable and a danger to international diplomacy. Accordingly, once the post-Gunpowder Plot heat had cooled, Dublin was to quietly drop the rigours of persecution. Although the fervour was revived whenever political circumstances allowed it, the next three decades saw a *de facto* tolerance of Catholicism.

Withdrawal of support was resented by the Protestant community in Ireland and came to be seen as almost a betrayal, an act of theological treachery. The truth is that conversion was a structural impossibility for three reasons. The first was the effective work of the Jesuits after 1596 and their hand in the development of a Counter-Reformation identity, a process aided by Old English priests educated in Louvain returning to work in their home community and, to a slightly lesser degree, among the native Irish. The fact that they were working in sympathetic communities made their expulsion extremely difficult. The second reason was education, in two ways. Teaching throughout the island was dominated by Catholic schools. In terms of the provision of Protestant ministers, the product badly suited the market. Most ministers were English and Anglophonic, taught at Oxford or Cambridge, and others were Scottish with education from their homeland. When Trinity College, Dublin was established in 1591 the ministers rarely moved west to the poorer benefices and hostile congregations. As a result, the Church of Ireland came to serve the Pale and the settlers solely, with an emphasis on anti-popery and a sharp attitude towards the perceived degeneracy of the Catholics. This siege-mentality would hardly serve an evangelical mission. The third reason was that the financial and organizational nature of the church was deeply inadequate, with far too much land and money lost to lay coffers possessed by communities hostile to the success of the church. These factors combined to exacerbate the association of Protestantism with Anglicization, making the church hopelessly entwined with colonialism and boundaries between the two communities gradually hardened (Ford 1995).

The divergence between London and Dublin, the hardening of the identity of the Church of Ireland and the related alienation of the Catholic communities are a theme that runs through the second decade of James's reign. Chichester used a memorandum from James to authorize him to reissue the 1605 proclamation in 1612. The English privy council was prepared to accept exemplary punishment of the occasional titular bishop. The aged bishop of Down and Connor, Cornelius O'Devany, was accordingly indicted for treason as an acolyte of Hugh O'Neill. In 1612 he was executed and this served more to create a martyr than to intimidate Catholics. In the parliament of the following year, with a gerrymandered New English majority, the laws against recusancy were sharpened, bringing them closer to English models. In addition, the first national convocation met in tandem with the parliament. A total of 104 Irish Articles were passed, a confession of faith to be read against the Thirty-Nine

Articles of the Church of England. The Irish version was markedly more Calvinist, eliminating any ambiguity on double predestination, emphasizing Sabbatarianism and omitting any reference to the lawfulness of the consecration of bishops. The articles, the brainchild of James Ussher, expressed a clearer identification of the pope as Antichrist. In practical terms, the consequence was a substantial effort to enforce anti-Catholic legislation over the next few years.

What followed was little in terms of the success of persecution, much less in terms of conversion. Despite changes to the system of enforcement, it was held in check by local conditions, relying upon Catholic local authorities and juries beyond the Protestant areas. Peter Lombard, the titular Catholic archbishop of Armagh, had been pressing for a moderate relationship with James and towards the end of the decade this came into a harmony with London's perspective. As James sought to solve the outbreak of the Thirty Years' War by balancing his connections with Bohemia by a Spanish Match for his son, persecution became impolitic and was put on hold from 1618 onwards. This was matched by an increasing concern about Protestant nonconformity, particularly in Ulster. Christopher Hampton, the royal chaplain who became archbishop of Armagh in 1613, voiced concern particularly about the Presbyterian Scottish communities who sat happily within the amorphous church of the early decades. As attentions turned to them, from a New English perspective James could be seen to be neglecting the Catholic enemy while enforcing conformity upon 'good Protestant' settlers.

In England and Wales, Jacobean religious policies were rather less troubled than in the other two kingdoms, partly because the realm was less sharply divided than Ireland and partly because his governance was less authoritarian than in Scotland. After his accession he proved much more willing than Elizabeth to negotiate with Puritans making demands for further reformation. His response to the Millenary Petition was to convene the Hampton Court Conference in January 1604. The conference brought him together with bishops and some moderate Puritans and he managed the forum with some success. Minor structural defects were acknowledged, lesser liturgical changes were offered (and, most famously, a new translation of the Bible was undertaken), but the greater complaints were dismissed and James took the opportunity to express his hostility to changes to the polity. The reforms, and their limitations, were formalized in the 1604 Canons and it was made plain that they were conditional upon subscription to the Three Articles which recognized the king's authority and accepted the Book of Common Prayer.

The consequence of the conference was a drive against nonconformity, particularly over the next two years. Ministers who subscribed were given a relative tolerance in the way they conducted services, while the more contumacious divines who refused compromise were deprived. From 1604 to 1610 about eighty beneficed ministers were deprived along with an unknown number of curates and lecturers. This was a way of dividing moderate Puritans who accepted royal authority from their radical colleagues who would not. This policy of tolerance, rather than toleration, with the *sine qua non* of a level of obeisance for royal authority, was fairly successful for the next fifteen years. The political nuisance of radical reform was seriously muted, almost divorced from the remaining voluntaristic piety and local campaigns for the 'reformation of manners' which were closer to mainstream interests (Fincham and Lake 1985; Collinson 1991).

Similar policies of divide and rule were adopted towards the English Catholics. James brought his Scottish experience and policies with him. His anti-Catholicism was relatively moderate, focused on the papal authority to depose heretical monarchs, and his initial moderation regarding recusancy laws combined with an appetite for expelling (rather than executing) seminary priests and Jesuits reflected this. His tolerance was turned to a less moderate course by a certain Catholic triumphalism and by the less moderate ethos of his parliament. A small group of radicals responded with the Gunpowder Plot of late 1605. The discovery of the plot created an opportunity for some intense persecution of Catholics. James worked, as far as was possible, to keep the emphasis on the question of loyalty and the resulting oath of allegiance focused on papal claims to depose. In the long term, the separation of moderates and radicals met with some success.

James established a fairly broad spectrum in his episcopacy, ranging from George Abbot, the new archbishop of Canterbury appointed in 1611, a low-church Calvinist with sympathy for the Puritans, to Lancelot Andrewes, an anti-Calvinist with a more sacerdotal, sacramental piety (Fincham 1990). For the early decades the former were the dominant group, with the latter providing a useful stress on the requirements of order and conformity. The advancement of anti-Calvinist bishops was conditional upon a silence regarding their soteriology. Down to 1618, James publicly supported the Calvinist doctrine of grace. In that year English representatives were sent to the Synod of Dort in the Netherlands, a conference intended to defuse the troubles within Protestantism caused by the arrival of Arminianism, to which we will return. At Dort the church supported, with James's approval, a moderate Calvinist orthodoxy.

The year 1618 proved to be the beginning of a change of emphasis in diplomacy with serious consequences for the Church of England. As the Thirty Years' War broke out the conflict was seen by many English Protestants as an apocalyptic war between Catholics and Protestants, with James having a responsibility to support his son-in-law Frederick V of Bohemia against his Spanish opponents. James looked for a diplomatic solution to be promoted by a marriage between his son and the Spanish Infanta. He received public criticism through pulpit and press, exacerbated by some of the hostility coming from principal figures in the church, including his primate. He worked to silence the complaints with proclamations and discipline and, in 1622, with the Declaration for Preachers forbidding divines to discuss matters of state. These circumstances strengthened the hand of the anti-Calvinist divines. With their stress on order and obedience and a willingness to support his hispanophile diplomacy, their influence grew. In addition, their broad definition of Puritanism as a subversive and irreverent threat now chimed with James's fears (Ferrell 1998; McCullough 1998).

These were the circumstances in which Richard Montagu, with the support of anti-Calvinist bishops, published his work *A New Gag for an Old Goose*. In this text Montagu minimized the differences between the Churches of Rome and England, presenting doctrinal Calvinism and Puritanism as virtual synonyms and a serious hindrance to current diplomacy. This was on the back of substantial court preaching redefining Puritanism in similar ways and with James under pressure from his heir, his favourite and the House of Commons for a less hispanophile foreign policy, this was appealing. Despite widespread condemnation, the king looked simply for clarification, which Montagu provided with *Appello Caesarum*. This was even more rebarbative than its predecessor and received approval from James. His death in March 1625 means that we have little idea of his response in the long term, but it means that his successor received a newly empowered anti-Calvinist episcopacy and an outraged and deeply concerned political nation in England.

One matter that has only been dealt with implicitly so far is the way in which James coped with the added task of the challenge of three contrasting religious realms. Of late he has received a certain amount of acclaim for his pursuit of a vision of congruity rather than uniformity, in particular for his northern and southern kingdoms. In terms of suggestions of any institutional imperialism this is convincing (Morrill 1994). In Ireland, given the impossible task of satisfying the contrasting demands of Old and New English, he coped fairly well, although his goals were always driven by mainland English interests. Regarding Anglo-Scottish relations, the median thesis works to a degree, but it should be noted that while the Church of England was taken towards the Kirk in terms of the promotion of the preaching, paternalist bishop, this fails to match the authoritarian imposition of changes in polity and then practice upon the Kirk (MacDonald 1998: esp. 179–87).

When we examine the reign of Charles I between 1625 and 1642 it is necessary to start with England and Wales before we move on to Ireland and Scotland, as the latter have to be understood in the light of the former to be comprehensible. As a part of that we need a brief note on nomenclature. To this point we have employed the term 'anti-Calvinist' to describe the clique which operated under James to offer a different vision of the Church of England. An alternative title is 'Arminian', that is, adherents to the softened Protestantism of the Dutch theologian Jacobus Arminius who re-introduced a degree of free will to the doctrine of grace. The problems with these terms are three-fold. The second term in particular was abusive, as Arminianism was abhorrent to Calvinists. Second, it cannot be shown that all those accused *were* Arminian; indeed, some were willing to deny the claim. Third, these terms focus the controversy too narrowly on soteriology whereas, as we will see, the disputes were much broader than that. A less restricted adjective is 'Laudian', disciples of William Laud. This term is appropriate from the late 1620s but, before that, he was far from being the leader of this group.

In the mid-1620s the main complaint was of Arminianism. In the parliament of 1625 Richard Montagu was attacked as an Arminian and was perceived as represent-ing a fifth column within the church intending to take the Church of England back to Rome. At the same time, leading lay Calvinists convened the York House Conference where allies of Montagu were to be pitted against orthodox Calvinists in debate. The conference ended inconclusively, as well as a failure for the Calvinists, with the powerful favourite, the duke of Buckingham, backing the Arminians. This was made worse by Charles's decision to take Montagu on as a royal chaplain. That is not to say that Charles's support for the Arminians was clear in the early years of his reign. His need for parliamentary supply while he was at war with Spain and then also with France was a limiting factor, although criticisms grew to a climax with the Commons resolution of March 1629 against religious innovations. In these circum-stances the appointments of Samuel Harsnett to York, William Laud to London and Montagu to Chichester in 1628 were extraordinary declarations of support to make (Fincham and Lake 1993: 38–40; Tyacke 1987).

Once Charles withdrew from the Thirty Years' War by the end of 1630, the English parliament was no longer there to provide a chorus of opposition. When Laud became archbishop of Canterbury in 1633, the process really took off. Charles had been promoting divines of a similar outlook, effectively destroying the spectrum his father had created. In October the Jacobean Book of Sports, intended to reduce Sabbatarianism, was reissued and on this occasion ministers were required to read it to their congregations and it was enforced, making it much less easy to ignore than its predecessor. More importantly, a full Laudian programme for divine worship was promoted in a much more universal fashion than previous circumstances had allowed. Ministers were required to wear the full clerical regalia in every service, to bow at the name of Jesus, to use the cross on the child's forehead in baptisms and to employ the Book of Common Prayer with no omissions or additions. This worked hand in hand with the promotion of the 'beauty of holiness', a willingness to allow paintings, statues and stained glass windows in churches (Lake 1993). What made these contro-versial ceremonies and styles worse was that subscription was no longer regarded as a sufficient gesture to conformity; constant and complete conformity was demanded of clergy and laity alike, with many ministers deprived of their benefices and emigration to the Netherlands and New England rising exponentially.

    The policy that offended most Puritans and Prayer Book Protestants was the altar policy. Communion was usually celebrated with the table placed 'tablewise', with the long sides running parallel to the long sides of the chancel and communicants seated around it in a re-enactment of the Last Supper, as far as possible from the Catholic mass. Laudian bishops required the table to be placed 'altarwise' against the east wall of the chancel and railed off. The minister was to stand on one side of the rails and hand the elements to communicants who were required to kneel at the rails. This was seen to be utterly offensive by most English Protestants as, along with Laudian ceremonialism generally, it represented a substantial step towards Catholicism. The whole programme was seen as a 'popish plot' and the religious affiliation of Laud and, eventually, Charles were questioned. That neither were Catholics is not the point; they were perceived to be undercover agents of Antichrist, working to corrupt the Church of England in doctrine and practice, an accusation that was made all the more powerful in the context of the Thirty Years' War.

    In addition to the innovations of Laudianism, the flipside of the regime was disciplinary. The heightened operation of the church courts has been noted, but there were also some particular *causes célèbres* that illustrated the shifting ground of orthodoxy and created martyrs for opponents of Laudianism. The Feoffees for Impropriations was a group of Puritans who raised money and bought back tithes that had fallen into lay hands and then used the money to establish preachers at locations of their choosing. Laud saw them as a subversive Puritan plot and in 1633 they were duly prosecuted in the Court of Exchequer. This was seen by many as an attack on a wholly laudable enterprise. Greater attention was paid to the prosecution of William Prynne, John Bastwick and Henry Burton. These pamphleteers castigated the Laudian reformers for supposedly preparing the church for the invasion of popery. In June 1637 they were convicted in the Star Chamber, given life sentences, each fined £5,000 and sentenced to have their ears chopped off. The consequence was the creation of three Protestant martyrs, for they expressed concerns that many felt but would not express in public. For instance, Prynne was also sentenced to be branded with 'S.L.' on each cheek; the initials stood for 'seditious libeller' but his supporters accepted his claim that they stood for *stigmata Laudis*.

With an established tradition of anti-popery heightened by Laudian innovations, Charles added grist to this mill. Many were uneasy when he married Henrietta Maria, the French Catholic princess, in 1625. It was made worse in that the marriage treaty permitted her to continue to worship, with a Catholic church being built in London for these purposes. In 1634 Charles admitted a papal agent to the court for the first time since 1558. The sight of the papal carriage around London and the reports of numerous conversions among courtiers fed into fears of a popish plot. In the first fifteen years of his reign Charles had turned Protestant concerns regarding the last years of his father's reign into intense fears and had diminished if not destroyed the common ground occupied by the religious part of the political nation and their monarch.

We left the religious state of Ireland in 1625 with Protestant concerns about what they saw as misdirected Anglocentric action against Protestant nonconformity and a *de facto* tolerance of Catholicism, with London's policies driven by considerations of foreign policy. Under the duress of war, Charles hoped to raise money and troops without creating dissatisfied Catholics willing to provide an open back door to Spanish forces. From mid-1626, negotiations were opened where subsidy was to be guaranteed in exchange for 'Graces', the suspension of the disabilities against Catholics (Clarke 1976). Naturally there were Protestant objections which appeared, with the split being captured in sermons by two bishops and by James Ussher, the Lord Primate of Ireland and a member of the Irish privy council. The Graces produced short-term gains and long-term losses, in that the offer provided bait to the Old English which they were unwilling to jeopardize by disobedience but the delivery of which was indefinitely postponed, while the offer also alienated the New English.

As in England, the end of the war created different circumstances. This offered some hope to the Protestants, who took the opportunity to impose discipline on public masses and religious houses in and around Dublin. Such hopes were of short tenure, however, as the arrival of Thomas Wentworth as Lord Deputy in 1632 took the objectives of Irish religious policy in a very different direction (Merritt 1996; McCafferty 1995). In May 1634 his chaplain John Bramhall was appointed as bishop of Londonderry and worked as a go-between for Wentworth and Laud, as Laud's eyes in Ireland and as a proactive reformer in his own right. Upon his arrival, the objectives were made plain. The Church of Ireland was to be structurally reformed in order to be a successful evangelical agent in the long term. This meant that the constitutional, disciplinary and doctrinal basis of the church was to be brought into resemblance with the Church of England as Laud envisaged it. Laud may have expressed no interest in bringing the Irish Church under the jurisdiction of Canterbury, but it should also be noted that, with Bramhall in command, he had no need to.

The events of 1634 set the agenda for the rest of the decade. The Old English were alienated in the parliament. Loss of trust in Charles's promises to deliver the Graces persuaded them to have them enacted in statute. Wentworth played along in order to get more subsidies and then more or less dismissed their legislative efforts. In the concurrent convocation, Bramhall worked on the adoption of the English Thirty-Nine Articles and 1604 Canons. When the Canons were taken into a committee, serious modifications were made to make them more appropriate to the ethos of the Irish Church. Wentworth brusquely intervened, drafted his own version much closer to the English model, and demanded that it should be passed verbatim. Archbishop Ussher supervised a compromise version, with some Irish distinctions. Similarly,

Ussher insisted that passing the Thirty-Nine Articles did not abrogate the Articles of 1615, an effort to save the consciences of his clergy. However, in terms of *realpolitik*, Wentworth's work was done and Ussher withdrew to Drogheda and concentrated on his scholarly work. From this point he was little more than a figurehead, with Bramhall, if not Wentworth, the effective primate.

The reformed disciplinary machinery was completed by the establishment of an English-style court of high commission which had its first meeting in early 1636. New English fears of the intentions of Wentworth and Bramhall were fulfilled by its operation. They shared English fears of the support for Catholicism, and as the courts were used to expel Scottish Presbyterians from the north while allowing the enforcement of recusancy laws to go into abeyance these fears seemed to be accurate. The truth was that Wentworth thought that it was counter-productive to try to enforce ineffectual laws until the church was fully reformed, but of course this was not an understanding that the New English Protestants would share.

Wentworth's innovative strategy made some sense and it is certainly true that earlier forms of evangelical Protestantism had failed in Ireland. However, it was flawed in two ways. It underestimated the scale of the alienation of the Old English. One of the improvements of Wentworth's governance had costs that were not taken into account. For the first time, London and Dublin were working in full accord, with the Lord deputy and the crown in close contact and of the same mind. This meant that it was no longer possible to appeal over the Lord Deputy's head to the monarch. With this space for negotiation gone, with the betrayal over the Graces still rankling and a sense of impotence resultant upon effective exclusion from government, the neglect of the recusancy laws provided relatively small comfort, particularly as the *de facto* tolerance depended upon a governor known to be hostile to Catholicism and seen to be untrustworthy. An effect of this was to enhance the alliance between the Old English and the native Irish, as can be seen from the historical and hagiographic works of the 1630s (Mac Craith 1995). As time would tell, this was by no means a solid alliance but it was to have dire consequences for English rule. The second flaw was that his strategy assumed that the Catholic cultures would remain static, almost waiting to be converted. In fact the Church of Rome sustained, even intensified its initiative. Residential Catholic bishops appeared, religious houses prospered and the number of seminary priests expanded. In these times of unhampered prodigality, success brought internal rivalries with the most important group, the Franciscans, being identified with Spanish and native Irish interests against the Capuchins and the Jesuits closest to French and Old English concerns. Factional disputes over former monastic houses even appeared in the common-law courts.

After five years as Lord Deputy, Wentworth was in a position of self-congratulation. As he saw it, there were sources of confidence in that the authoritarian imposition of his vision, taking confidence from the trust drawn from Charles and his consequent ability to rise above dependence upon the conflicting factions within Irish religious politics, was being achieved, producing resentment rather than resistance. It could be argued that with time he would have eventually fulfilled his ambitions if external factors had not intervened. However, it is more accurate to conclude that the growing dissatisfaction and alienation of all parts of the realm could only have been contained for a limited period and that, sooner or later, the aggression and the recriminations that were to follow would have found a voice.

The particular circumstances that ended the lull before the storm were precipitated by the experience of Caroline rule in Scotland and it is to that which we must turn our attention. In 1625 the Kirk was bruised and resentful after James's authoritarian changes to polity and practice. Charles was to work in similar ways with similar intentions, but his reforms were taken to a crucially higher degree and imposed with greater insensitivity. The first few years, however, were relatively peaceful, Charles's attentions being elsewhere. The proposed Act of Revocation, which was partly intended to improve the Kirk financially, created a furore as an attack on property rights from a position of dubious legality, but the project collapsed upon itself. Newly ordained ministers were, from 1626, required to observe the Five Articles of Perth, but the main characteristic of the 1620s was the 'awakening' in the southwest, an appetite for fasts and voluntary devotions beyond the regularities of the Kirk (Stevenson 1972–4).

From 1629 reforms in government, discipline and liturgy gradually moved up a few gears. Those chosen for the episcopacy tended to be Laudian. A new bishopric of Edinburgh was funded and St Giles was refurbished and while only four of the fourteen bishops could be seen as ceremonialist, they held a disproportionate sector of the power, as privy councillors and lords of the articles. Divisions became clear when, in 1633, Charles came north, eight years late, to have his Scottish coronation (Morrill 1990: 2–4). The ceremony was offensive in many ways, from its timing to its location (Holyrood rather than Scone or Stirling), but the setting and the service were far from the Kirk's preferences. A stage was erected with a communion table at the east end, richly decorated and in front of a tapestry featuring a crucifix, to which the Laudian bishops bowed. Archbishop Spottiswoode and his associates wore rich vestments, in stark contrast to the other bishops who wore simple black gowns. The coronation was part of the eucharist delivered according to the English liturgy and Charles had expanded the coronation oath, pledging to defend episcopacy.

If the traditionalist bishops were shocked, so too was Charles (Macinnes 1991; Lee 1985). He returned to England willing to bring considerable reforms to the Kirk. The first stage was disciplinary; the following year the court of high commission was granted civil powers, drawing on the royal prerogative. In 1636 new Canons were imposed and they were ill-judged in terms of content and mode of delivery. Communion was usually served on long tables in the centre of the church; the Canons required an altar-style placement, with the minister wearing a surplice. The Canons forbade extempore prayer, stock-in-trade for a good minister. In addition, they were imposed simply by royal prerogative, without seeking the approval of parliament or general assembly.

As under James, it was modifications to the practice of divine worship that cut to the quick. Laud had been pressing for liturgical imposition since he visited with James in 1617 and since 1629 he had been closely involved with the preparation of a Book of Common Prayer that was primarily the concern of the Scottish Laudian bishops. Although the liturgy, released in 1637, was not a pure Anglicization, it plainly borrowed substantially from the English liturgy and the public perception was that Laud was behind an attempt to restore Catholicism. Despite the modifications for the Scottish context, the very idea of ceremonial conformity grated against the reformed tradition in Scotland. In addition, it was delivered without consultation with, or ratification by, parliament or general assembly. Charles understood his royal supremacy to place him with absolute authority over the church. However authoritarian, James had at least gone through the pretence of mimicking such consultation. The imposition of the liturgy was a serious blow to national pride, constitutional etiquette and religious principle.

When the Prayer Book was first used, at St Giles Cathedral in Edinburgh on 23 July 1637, it was met with a raucous reception, developing into a popular riot (Stevenson 1973; Brown 1992: 111–19). Similar dissent spread north into Fife and then west. Initially the complaint was focused on the liturgy, but as dissent spread and the privy council lost control, criticism broadened to include the bishops and liturgical reform, expressed in petitions and a supplication circulated across the region. This movement came to a climax with the National Covenant, first signed by noblemen in Greyfriars Kirk in Edinburgh on 28 February 1638. It is a prolix and complex document, cleared by lawyers to avoid treason charges and intended to have a wide appeal. However, there are three elements which should be noted. The first is that the signatories pledged to defend *both* the church and the king, with support for the latter being conditional on godly government. The second is that it amounted to a long-term critique; the Prayer Book provoked a critique of ecclesiastical policy from the 1590s onwards. Third, there was an *implicit* radicalism. By including the 'negative confession' of 1581, by feeding off vitriolic anti-Catholicism and by extolling earlier Presbyterian legislation, the Covenant condemned the Five Articles of Perth, the institution of episcopacy and the liturgy as popish and arbitrary. The prerogative of the king was set against the 'proper' government of parliament, general assembly and the law. Through 1638 and 1639, the National Covenant was sold all over Scotland, supported by active evangelists, adopting apocalyptic tones in their sermons.

The reaction of Charles was initially desultory, with the privy council disinclined to describe the popularity of the dissent and the extent to which they had lost control. Eventually, in November 1638, he called a general assembly in Glasgow, but his efforts at reconciliation were thwarted. He offered some concessions but he made no effort to organize a body of supporters and was seriously out-manoeuvred. The radicals established the agenda and the personnel. By the end of December, bishops were abolished along with the court of high commission; the Five Articles, the Canons and the liturgy were rejected, and the assembly had denounced the royal supremacy and announced that they had the right to call future assemblies of their own volition. In the assembly of 1639, after a year of purging the Kirk and distributing the Covenant, prelacy was defined as against the will of God, with consequences for Scoto-Irish and Anglo-Scottish relations. In about two years a religious revolution had been declared, clear evidence of the level of dissent bred by early Stuart religious policy.

The impact of the revival of the reformed tradition in Scotland was immense but had ramifications in the other two kingdoms which were to have equally spectacular, albeit different consequences. Charles had hoped to control or at least contain the radicals in Scotland, but his initial failure forced him to call, in November 1640, what was to become the Long Parliament in England. He hoped for support and subsidies; he got, from his perspective, a suppurating sore of grievances (Morrill 1993: chs 3, 4). Most of these were indigenous, but disenchanted Puritans had established contact with Scottish radicals and part of the reform agenda was driven by a tense, uneasy alliance with the Covenanters. The appetite for reform was voracious; in addition to the experience of the 1630s, the meeting of Convocation in the spring had remained after the dissolution of parliament (in itself unusual) in order to pass new Canons which amounted to a complete authorization of Laudianism. The result was a consensus within parliament that something had to be done.

In its negative sense, this consensus lasted. Apart from the bishops and privy councillors, Laudianism had few supporters. The scale of reform was heightened by three elements outwith the parliament. The first was the apocalyptic preaching, particularly in parliamentary fasts, with ministers refusing to recognize any middle ground, with a militaristic, almost vengeful, call for reform. The second was the impact of an organized petitioning campaign on religious issues with about 800 parishes registering complaints within the first two years. Many of the petitions were directed against the office of episcopacy as well as the individuals, most famously the 'Root and Branch' petition from London which was delivered on 11 December 1640, with allegedly 15,000 signatures, asking for the abolition of episcopacy. The third element was the press, with hundreds of tracts, pamphlets and treatises published on the nature and polity of the church. There were internal generators of reform too, partly driven by individuals like John Pym and Lord Saye and Sele, but also simply by the bringing together of the political nation, MPs and Lords sharing their experiences of Laudianism. This also worked on a formal level, with investigations into the workings of the dioceses feeding an appetite for scandal.

The consequences of this situation were manifold, some intended and some unintended. Parliament assumed several juridical and administrative capacities which were *ultra vires*. Laud and several of his acolytes were incarcerated or disabled. *Ad hoc* iconoclasm was authorized or tolerated. Divines were considered to be accountable to parliamentary committees and a Protestant free-market economy was allowed to operate with exiled radicals, deprived ministers and even lay preachers tolerated. However, not all MPs and even fewer of the Lords were prepared to embrace the opportunity for radicalism quite so enthusiastically. Less radical reformers, in the Houses and in the country, saw the solution in an idealized Jacobethan golden age, with petitions and speakers pleading for a preservation of a good Prayer Book Protestantism with an episcopacy in the style of Richard Bancroft and George Abbot. By the time of the first recess, taken in response to plague in London in September 1641, a moderate 'Anglican' stance was emerging which was at odds with the more Puritan reformers, many of them recently radicalized.

Events in Scotland and England completely changed the religious power structures in Ireland in the early 1640s (Canny 1995b; Mac Cuarta 1993; Perceval-Maxwell 1994). Wentworth's first responsibility after the National Covenant emerged was to control the Scots in Ulster because, of course, it encouraged their dissent. In May 1639 a secularized oath was imposed upon all Scots resident in Ulster, forcing them to recognize the king's authority in the most abject terms. Many fled to avoid the enforcement of the oath and its main effect was to exacerbate their hatred of Wentworth. In the short term, it created a curious ecumenical consensus in parliament, with religious issues placed on a back-burner to allow Catholics and Protestants to work together to express their opposition to the Lord Deputy. By the autumn of 1641 normal relations were resumed but with divisions seriously sharpened.

The Covenant had a dual impact on the Catholic population. The newly empowered anti-popery of the Kirk and the Long Parliament raised terrifying possibilities for them.

At the same time, the success of the Covenanters was inspiring: it showed that Charles could be forced to acquiesce to religious demands against his will. In the summer and autumn of 1641 there were rumours of Charles entering into negotiations with the earl of Antrim to raise an Irish Catholic army. The veracity of these rumours is still not settled, but their immediate consequence is clear (Ohlmeyer 1993: 96–9; 1992; Ohlmeyer and Maxwell-Perceval 1994). They encouraged a native Irish conspiracy, fostering an action to protect the practical toleration of their Catholicism. The insurgency broke out in October 1641 and was initially intended to disarm the Ulster Protestants, but it was loosely organized and precipitated a massacre of up to 3,000 Protestants. The inexperience of Wentworth's replacements and the weakness of the forces available to them meant that the rebellion could not be curtailed. The Old English were in a difficult position: they were not part of the rising but they were neither trusted nor protected by the government and their property was threatened by the rebels. Consequently, by the start of December they joined the native Irish in an uneasy alliance, thus effectively overturning Dublin's governance of the entire isle.

Rumour and propaganda determined the effects the rebellion had in England. Sir Phelim O'Neill used the rumours of the 'Antrim plot' to claim royal authority, showing a commission with a royal seal to prove it. It was a forgery, but the English parliament had so little trust in Charles that it seemed all too credible. At the same time, reports from refugees in England, published in gory detail immediately, seriously exaggerated the massacres, raising the death toll to 20,000 and holding the king responsible. When the Houses reassembled on 20 October, Pym and his colleagues pressed this damning perception of the rebellion as a large-scale slaughter of the Protestants with royal complicity. On 8 November 1641 Pym brought the Grand Remonstrance before the Commons. This document was produced by several committees over the previous year and amounted to a savage indictment of the actions of Charles's government since his accession, attributing all the calumnies to popish councillors intent upon subverting and weakening good Protestant government. For our purposes, what is important is that this debate, in this situation, sharpened the divisions in the parliament, for the Remonstrance did not see the solution to be a return to Jacobean conditions. Prelacy had been shown to be an inadequate guard against popery and a thorough and complete reformation had to be undertaken to prevent the resurrection of Laudianism in the future. Early in the morning of 23 November, after twelve hours of debate, the Remonstrance was narrowly passed with 159 radicals for it and 148 moderates against.

The polarization of moderates and radicals continued through 1642, encouraged by acts of wisdom and folly by Charles. With much of London sharing the concerns of the Houses brought on by reports of the massacres in Ireland, demonstrators gathered outside parliament calling for the bishops to be excluded. On 27 December they were physically successful. Twelve bishops made the mistake of petitioning for all business conducted in their absence to be revoked; the Lords perceived this as a breach of their privilege and thus accepted a Commons proposal for the bishops to be impeached for high treason, making their remaining members more likely to accept a more radical religious agenda. Thus, in February 1642 parliament passed an Act excluding the bishops from the Lords. In June the Houses delivered to Charles a new set of demands known as the Nineteen Propositions. This included a call to step up the enforcement of the recusancy laws and also to accept parliamentary proposals regarding the reformation of church government and liturgy. The carefully phrased response of Charles along with the radicalism of the proposals made the king a newly attractive leader for the 'middle ground' of the moderates.

Scottish interests were drawn away from English affairs. With disaffection among the Covenanters and negotiations being conducted with Charles from the summer of 1641, the imperative was to cement their earlier achievements. Charles accepted the reforms, including the abolition of episcopacy, in exchange for the withdrawal of Scottish troops from English soil. The Irish Rebellion, with the violence, real and imagined, against Scottish settlers, diverted Scottish military goals and the first of 10,000 troops arrived in April 1642, regaining much of eastern Ulster. Despite these losses, the Irish forces were developing as a governing body in 1642. In May the lay and clerical leaders met in Kilkenny, where an oath establishing the 'Confederate Catholics of Ireland' was formulated, setting up a council and a representative assembly. Old English and native Irish were joined in a pledge to fight 'pro fide, pro rege, pro patria', for faith, king and fatherland. The most powerful government for most of Ireland was Roman Catholic.

We tend to get distracted by the familiarity of the wars of the mid-century or too enthralled by the searches for the causes of them to fully appreciate the scale of the crises engendered by the religious policies of the early Stuarts. The crises differed, of course, geographically and temporally and can be traced to a varying mixture of conflicting mindsets, structural difficulties, failures of communication, changing and conflicting intentions and, on occasion, insecurity, insensitivity and incompetence. When we remove the sense of inevitability from the conflicts of the 1640s and compare and contrast the conditions of 1603 and 1642 then our awareness of the scale of change is sharpened. The conditions at James's accession to the thrones of England and Ireland were not idyllic but he cannot, on the whole, be said to have achieved wholesale improvement. There were existing tensions in Scotland, but his continued reform of polity and then practice in the Kirk stepped the tensions up a gear. In England he deserves credit for the early years of his reign, but towards the end he was losing the trust of the dominant religious consensus. Ireland may have demanded a more sensitive touch and the conversion of the Catholic population may have been beyond the art of the possible, but with his policies being driven by his own, and England's, interests and priorities he succeeded merely in offering opportunities to the Catholic communities and aggravating the Protestant ones.

The debits of James's reign tend to be ignored against those of his son and, to a certain extent, this is deservedly so. However, it should not be forgotten that several of Charles's projects were initiated in his father's later years and that James can be said to have been saved by his timely death. Having said that, it must also be acknowledged that Charles changed difficult situations into crises, grievances into rebellions and was almost inspired in adding new elements of his own to the developing conflict. In Ireland, similarly Anglocentric interests informed, if not determined, the policies, and the imposition of his appetite for Laudian order and ceremonialism on a wholly inappropriate church was ill-considered. This criticism can only be taken so far, however, as the outlooks of London and Dublin, and the Church of Ireland that he inherited, were not exactly burgeoning with success. If existing difficulties play a part in explaining Caroline difficulties in Ireland, the same can be said to a much lesser degree in Scotland. James can be accused of making changes in an authoritarian manner, changes which grated against the Kirk's traditions, but compared to Charles he was almost gentle. It is possible to understand that Charles wanted greater order and that he equated ceremony and decorous rites with a stable secular regime. It is also difficult to do so without an undertone of astonishment at the insensitivity with which it was done or at least with the poor efforts he made to understand the traditions he was altering. The excuse of an alien environment is absent when we evaluate Caroline rule in England. His almost single-minded promotion of divines, divine worship and decoration matched by an ill-judged unwillingness to hear dissent, to compromise or to accept that criticism was coming from anything other than a fanatical few, was to test the loyalty of his subjects severely. Laudianism, and the way it was promoted, created a level of misunderstanding, resentment and insecurity that merely needed to be given a forum to be expressed and intensified. The Long Parliament provided such a forum and placed alongside the Covenanters in Scotland and the Confederates in Ireland, religion was in different revolutionary modes across all of Charles's realms by 1642.

REFERENCES

Bradshaw, B. 1998: 'The English Reformation and identity formation in Wales and Ireland.' In B. Bradshaw and P. Roberts, eds, *British Consciousness and Identity: The Making of Britain, 1533–1707*: Cambridge.
Brown, K. 1990: 'British history: a sceptical comment.' In R. Asch, ed., *Three Nations: A Common History?*: Bochum.
Brown, K. 1992: *Kingdom or Province? Scotland and the Regal Union, 1603–1707*: Basingstoke.
Canny, N. 1995a: 'Responses to centralization c.1530–c.1640.' In A. Grant and K. Stringer, eds, *Uniting the Kingdom? The Making of British History*: London.
Canny, N. 1995b: 'What really happened in 1641?' In J. Ohlmeyer, ed., *Ireland: From Independence to Occupation 1641–1660*: Cambridge.
Clarke, A. 1976: 'Selling royal favours, 1624–32.' In M. Moody, F. X. Martin and F. J. Byrne, eds, *A New History of Ireland, Vol. 3: Early Modern Ireland*: Oxford.
Clarke, A. and Edwards, D. 1976: 'Pacification, plantation, and the catholic question, 1603–23.' In T. W. Moody, F. X. Martin and F. J. Byrne, eds, *A New History of Ireland, Vol. 3: Early Modern Ireland*: Oxford.
Collinson, P. 1991: *The Birthpangs of Protestant England: Religious and Cultural Change in the Sixteenth and Seventeenth Centuries*: Basingstoke.
Cowan, I. B. 1967: 'The five articles of Perth.' In D. Shaw, ed., *Reformation and Revolution: Essays Presented to Hugh Watt*: Edinburgh.
Ferrell, L. A. 1998: *Government by Polemic: James I, the King's Preachers, and the Rhetorics of Conformity, 1603–1625*: Stanford, CA.
Fincham, K. 1990: *Prelate as Pastor: The Episcopate of James I*: Oxford.
Fincham, K. (ed.) 1993: *The Early Stuart Church, 1603–1642*: Basingstoke.
Fincham, K. and Lake, P. 1985: 'The ecclesiastical policy of James I', *Journal of British Studies*, 24, 169–207.
Fincham, K. and Lake, P. 1993: 'The ecclesiastical policies of James I and Charles I.' In K. Fincham, ed., *The Early Stuart Church, 1603–1642*: Basingstoke.
Ford, A. 1995: 'The Church of Ireland, 1558–1634: a puritan church?' In A. Ford, J. McGuire and K. Milne, eds, *As By Law Established: The Church of Ireland Since the Reformation*: Dublin.

Ford, A., McGuire, J. and Milne, K. (eds) 1995: *As By Law Established: The Church of Ireland Since the Reformation*: Dublin.

Goodare, J. 1995: 'The Scottish parliament of 1621', *Historical Journal*, 38, 29–51.

Lake, P. 1993: 'The Laudian style: order, authority and the pursuit of the beauty of holiness in the 1630s.' In K. Fincham, ed., *The Early Stuart Church, 1603–1642*: Basingstoke.

Lee, M., Jr 1985: *The Road to Revolution: Scotland under Charles I, 1625–37*: Urbana, IL.

Mac Craith, M. 1995: 'The Gaelic reaction to the Reformation.' In S. G. Ellis and S. Barber, eds, *Conquest and Union: Fashioning a British State 1485–1725*: Harlow.

Mac Cuarta, B. (ed.) 1993: *Ulster 1641: Aspects of the Rising*: Dublin.

McCafferty, J. 1995: 'John Bramhall and the Church of Ireland in the 1630s.' In A. Ford, J. McGuire and K. Milne, eds, *As By Law Established: The Church of Ireland Since the Reformation*: Dublin.

McCullough, P. 1998: *Sermons at Court: Politics and Religion in Elizabethan and Jacobean Preaching*: Cambridge.

MacDonald, A. R. 1998: *The Jacobean Kirk, 1567–1625: Sovereignty, Polity and Liturgy*: Aldershot.

Macinnes, A. I. 1991: *Charles I and the Making of the Covenanting Movement, 1625–1641*: Edinburgh.

Mackay, P. H. R. 1977: 'The reception given to the five articles of Perth', *Records of the Scottish Church History Society*, 9, 185–201.

Merritt, J. F. (ed.) 1996: *The Political World of Thomas Wentworth, Earl of Strafford, 1621–1641*: Cambridge.

Moody, T. W. and Byrne, F. J. 1976: *A New History of Ireland, Vol. 3: Early Modern Ireland*, ed. T. W. Moody, F. X. Martin and F. J. Byrne: Oxford.

Morrill, J. 1990: 'The National Covenant in its British context.' In J. Morrill, ed., *The Scottish National Covenant in its British Context*: Edinburgh.

Morrill, J. 1993: *The Nature of the English Revolution*: Harlow.

Morrill, J. 1994: 'A British patriarchy? Ecclesiastical imperialism under the early Stuarts.' In A. Fletcher and P. Roberts, eds, *Religion, Culture and Society in Early Modern Britain: Essays in Honour of Patrick Collinson*: Cambridge.

Ohlmeyer, J. 1992: 'The "Antrim plot" of 1641 – a myth?' *Historical Journal*, 35, 905–19.

Ohlmeyer, J. 1993: *Civil War and Restoration in the Three Stuart Kingdoms: The Career of Randal MacDonnell, Marquis of Antrim, 1609–1683*: Cambridge.

Ohlmeyer, J. and Maxwell-Perceval, M. 1994: 'The "Antrim plot" of 1641 – a myth? A response', and J. Ohlmeyer, 'The "Antrim plot" of 1641: a rejoinder', *Historical Journal*, 37, 421–37.

Perceval-Maxwell, M. 1994: *The Outbreak of the 1641 Rebellion in Ireland*: Montreal.

Stevenson, D. 1972–4: 'Conventicles in the kirk, 1619–37', *Records of the Scottish Church History Society*, 18, 99–114.

Stevenson, D. 1973: *The Scottish Revolution 1637–1644: The Triumph of the Covenanters*: Newton Abbot.

Tyacke, N. 1987: *Anti-Calvinists: The Rise of English Arminianism*: Oxford.

FURTHER READING

Canny, N. 1987: *From Reformation to Restoration: Ireland 1534–1660*: Dublin.

Clarke, A. 2000: *The Old English in Ireland 1625–42*: Dublin.

Collinson, P. 1982: *The Religion of Protestants: The Church in English Society, 1558–1625*: Oxford.

Collinson, P. 1983: *Godly People*: London.

Davies, J. E. 1992: *The Caroline Captivity of the Church: Charles I and the Remoulding of Anglicanism*: Oxford.

Donald, P. 1990: *An Uncounselled King: Charles I and the Scottish Troubles, 1637–41*: Cambridge.

Donaldson, G. 1954: *The Making of the Scottish Prayer Book of 1637*: Edinburgh.

Durston, C. and Eales, J. (eds) 1996: *The Culture of Puritanism, 1560–1700*: Basingstoke.

Ford, A. 1985: *The Protestant Reformation in Ireland, 1590–1641*: Frankfurt-am-Main.

Foster, W. R. 1975: *The Church before the Covenants: The Church of Scotland 1596–1638*: Edinburgh.

Gillespie, R. 1997: *Devoted People: Belief and Religion in Early Modern Ireland*: Manchester.

Kearney, H. F. 1989: *Strafford in Ireland 1633–41: A Study in Absolutism*, 2nd edn: Manchester.

Kirk, J. 1989: *Patterns of Reform: Continuity and Change in the Reformation Kirk*: Edinburgh.

Lake, P. 1987: 'Calvinism and the English church, 1570–1635', *Past and Present*, 114.

Maltby, J. 1998: *Prayer Book and People in Elizabethan and Early Stuart England*: Cambridge.

Mullan, D. G. 1986: *Episcopacy in Scotland: The History of an Idea, 1560–1638*: Edinburgh.

Mullan, D. G. 2000: *Scottish Puritanism 1590–1638*: Oxford.

Patterson, W. B. 1997: *King James VI and I and the Reunion of Christendom*: Cambridge.

Sheils, W. J. and Wood, D. (eds) 1989: *The Churches, Ireland and the Irish: Studies in Church History*, 20: Oxford.

Tyacke, N. 2001: *Aspects of English Protestantism, c.1530–1700*: Manchester.

CHAPTER FOURTEEN

Political Thought in Early Stuart Britain

MALCOLM SMUTS

Any history of political thought will implicitly raise fundamental issues concerning sources, methodology and conceptual assumptions. Does 'thought' mean only discussions showing a high degree of theoretical awareness, or should it also encompass less systematic forms of thinking? Many historians now argue that we need to reconstruct the vocabularies and linguistic rules through which political discourse was conducted in the past, rather than concentrating only on a few canonical thinkers. Yet specialists in political thought have in practice continued to focus either on major theorists like Thomas Hobbes or the discourse of lawyers and theologians, two professional groups that had developed especially rigorous procedures for discussing certain kinds of political problems (e.g. Burgess 1993). They have paid little attention to the vocabularies and assumptions revealed by sources like diplomatic correspondence, policy memoranda and newsletters. Nor have they made extensive use of imaginative literature, representational culture and political ritual, although literary scholars and cultural historians have examined ideas expressed through these genres (e.g. McCoy 1996; Sharpe 2000: chs 1, 6 , 11).

The adjective 'political' raises further issues. In the early modern period the word 'politics' was associated with Aristotelian and humanist, rather than feudal or chivalric, discourses, which employed a different vocabulary of lordship and allegiance. Frequently it also implied moral and institutional restraints on power: in Fortescue's definition of England as a *regnum politicum et regale*, *politicum* stands for laws and forms of participation by the king's subjects in governance. Modern historiographical usage has normally equated *political* thought with discussions of liberties and relationships between institutions – especially the crown, parliament and the law – rather than personal or dynastic concepts of power. Debates over the legality of non-parliamentary taxes have always figured prominently in histories of political thought, in ways that ideas about honour, lineage and political virtue have not (cf. McCoy 1996). This orientation reflects modern preoccupations with the rise of the nation-state and origins of liberalism that arguably distort seventeenth-century thought patterns.

Monarchy, Mixed Monarchy and Hereditary Right

The risk of introducing unrecognized biases will perhaps be reduced if we focus discussion around central issues of the period, rather than ideas and discourses. In this way we may leave open the question of just what counts as 'political thought' until we come to concrete instances. The best place to begin, in terms of both chronology and logical priority, is with controversies surrounding the most fundamental early modern political institution. Everyone knew that England was a monarchy in which royal authority gave life to every aspect of secular and ecclesiastical government. They also knew that the crown normally descended by heredity. But the precise nature of English kingship and the rules governing its succession remained disturbingly unsettled throughout the late sixteenth century, in ways that continued to shape later Stuart attitudes.

Difficulties in determining title to the throne stemmed partly from Henry VIII's attempts to regulate the succession through statute and royal wills, as if the crown were a private possession (Nenner 1995). Despite the legitimist rebellion that thwarted Edward VI's bequest of the crown to Jane Grey in 1553, the belief that parliament or a sitting monarch might determine the next successor remained alive. Indeed a statute of 1572 made it treason to *deny* that the queen in parliament might alter the succession. Since any dispute over title to the throne threatened to ignite a confessional war between Protestants and Catholics and foreign intervention, this issue had enormous implications. It quickly became entangled in Mary Stuart's efforts to claim the crown by inciting rebellions, invasions and assassination plots, which in turn raised the question of whether the hereditary heir might be disqualified and punished for crimes against the throne's present occupant, even if she was already queen of another kingdom. Mary's execution in 1587 set an uncomfortable precedent for legally sanctioned regicide.

Elizabeth's gender raised further concerns, since the sixteenth century believed that women possessed weaker powers of reason and self-discipline than men, making them incapable of fully exercising the functions of kingship. It has recently been argued that worries about this problem led the queen's supporters to place greater emphasis on the authority of the council and parliament (McLaren 1999). Elizabeth's gender also magnified anxieties about dangers of faction and evil council, since a weak female sovereign might offer less resistance to ambitious domineering men. Catholic polemics accused the queen of allowing William Cecil or the earl of Leicester to usurp her powers, while in 1579 John Stubbs and Sir Philip Sidney both warned her that if she persisted in her desire to marry the Catholic duke of Anjou, he would erect a popish faction capable of plunging the realm into civil war. The period's imaginative literature is full of stories of weak rulers who cause political disaster by failing to fulfill their duties, reflecting a style of political thought focusing less on abstract rights of authority than ethical analyses of behaviour, which persisted into the Stuart period (McCoy 1996; Sharpe 2000: esp chs 4–5; see also below). Yet it is doubtful that the queen's gender alone fully explains these emphases. They also stemmed from awareness that aristocratic factions and confessional hatreds had ripped apart other European kingdoms and threatened to do the same to England, if those at the helm failed to contain the threat.

The period's uncertainties and the need to safeguard Protestantism encouraged a flexible and pragmatic approach to theories of royal authority. The regime insisted that all subjects owed obedience to the queen, but it also aided rebellions against legitimate Catholic sovereigns in Scotland, the Netherlands and France, while Burghley and other Protestant leaders were certainly prepared to violate law and custom to prevent Mary Stuart from taking the throne. Most educated Elizabethans appear to have believed that England was a 'mixed monarchy', in which royal power was tempered by the common law and the need to obtain parliamentary consent to taxation, a view articulated in the fifteenth century by Sir John Fortescue, in a treatise first translated into English in 1567, then reprinted in 1573 and 1599 (Williamson 1999: 152–3). Although Elizabeth herself never accepted it, and more authoritarian views gained wider currency toward the end of her reign, the argument put forward by James VI and his supporters that England was a pure monarchy, in which the crown descended by indefeasible hereditary right, remained untypical. James's ideas triumphed after 1603 not because they seemed irrefutable but because they became convenient, once it was clear that the hereditary heir also stood the best chance of assuring a smooth succession and continuity in the religious settlement (Nenner 1995: ch. 3). The concept of indefeasible hereditary right also received indirect support from developments in France, where an actual war over the royal succession had recently concluded with a victory for the hereditary heir, Henry IV, the candidate supported by Protestants, anti-Spanish royalists and the English (Salmon 1990). Whereas in the 1570s resistance theory and concepts of limited monarchy had usually served Protestant interests, in the 1590s they were increasingly adopted by militant Catholics. Support for legitimate hereditary kingship, by contrast, provided a basis for solidarity between Calvinists and moderate *politiques*. Unlike their childless predecessors both James and Henry succeeded in producing male heirs to assure stability after their own deaths. These circumstances encouraged a tendency in both kingdoms to magnify the importance of the royal blood and its biological transmission as a mystical source of legitimacy and civic peace. James stressed his descent from Henry VII and Margaret of York as well as Stuart kings of Scotland; he also claimed several ancient Irish kings among his ancestors. People owing allegiance to all these lineages should therefore bury ancient enmities and happily unite under his sovereignty. Francis Bacon carried the argument onto a higher plane by arguing that through dynastic marriages God had erected three great monarchies, in France, Spain and Britain, so that together they might keep the peace of Europe (Spedding and Heath 1966: VI, 265).

Was the Jacobean View of Monarchy Contentious?

Although the Tudors had also emphasized the importance of royal legitimacy in guaranteeing civic peace, the strong Jacobean stress on indefeasible hereditary right had important implications. To James and others it meant not only that parliament lacked the authority to alter the succession, but also that he possessed indelible rights *as a king* that ultimately transcended all particular bodies of law and custom. Historians have disagreed sharply over whether this view was significantly controversial. J. P. Sommerville (1998) sees it as typical of European absolutist thought and argues that it represented one of three competing ideological positions available in the period, the other two being the concept of an ancient constitution that limited the crown and a belief that monarchy derived from an original contract between king and people. By contrast Glenn Burgess (1993, 1996) has argued that Jacobean Englishmen normally believed in *both* divine right monarchy and the rule of law, seeing no contradiction between them. The proper aim of government – and of the law itself – was to maintain harmony between these principles, which were equally essential to political health.

One reason both historians have found evidence for their interpretations is that contemporaries were adept at hedging theoretical claims with qualifications and disclaimers that reduced grounds for contention. If we concentrate on logical contradictions between theories of authority, as Somerville does, we may therefore arrive at a picture of conflict, whereas if we focus instead on how people sought to reconcile divergent views, the method favoured by Burgess, we will find consensus. As an example we might take a message James delivered to the House of Commons in 1610, to soothe alarms raised by the recently published dictionary of legal terminology of the civil lawyer James Cowell, which contained definitions elevating the king's power above the law. The king acknowledged that 'though he did derive his title from the loins of his ancestors, yet the law did set the Crown upon his head', adding that

> it was dangerous to submit the power of a king to definition. But withall he did acknowledge that he had no power to make laws of himself, or to exact any subsidies *de jure* without the consent of his three estates...and lastly...that there was such a marriage and union between the prerogative and the law as they cannot possibly be severed. (Gardiner 1862: 24)

Although this statement conceded nothing at the deepest philosophical level, it shifted emphasis away from contentious arguments about the ultimate theoretical nature of authority to a set of commonplaces to which everyone might assent. Such attempts at defusing conflict usually succeeded, since most people knew better than to pick fights over philosophical abstractions when doing so would have destructive practical consequences.

The desire to avoid damaging ideological disputes is not the same thing, however, as intellectual consensus. Significant tensions did exist between James's views and other ideas current in the period. His statement that 'it is dangerous to submit a King's power to definition' – and his even stronger assertion in 1616 that 'it is presumption and high contempt in a subject to dispute what a King can do' – sits uneasily beside William Camden's claim that the prerogative can and *should* be defined, 'for what is it in the name of a king that imports so much it cannot be limited?' Outright conflict between these views was avoided by distinguishing between an undefinable absolute prerogative beyond the law, and definable prerogative powers to act within it (Burgess 1993: ch. 6). But this still left an uncomfortable frontier between unlimited and limited authority, along which skirmishes continued to arise. Camden went on to argue that powers freely 'released' by past kings can never be rightfully reclaimed by their successors, a view that James would certainly have disputed (McIlwain 1918: 333; Smith Fussner 1957: 209). Worries about where such ideas might lead stimulated the king's decision to close down the Society of Antiquaries. On the other hand, the Commons would not have made a fuss about Cowell had they not already been worried about a tendency to magnify the prerogative until it threatened the rule of law. Although overt ideological disagreement is rare in Jacobean political discourse, signs of wariness and mistrust are relatively common. If this was a society that wished to avoid public contention over political theories, it was also one in which people feared to let down their guard. Their wariness derived partly from a belief that in a mixed monarchy – which is what English government certainly amounted to in practice – the different elements will struggle against each other for supremacy (Smuts 1999: 25–6). In 1604 the Commons drew up an 'Apology' complaining that whereas 'the prerogatives of princes may easily and do daily grow; the privileges of the subject are for the most part at an everlasting stand', while in 1607 Francis Bacon warned the king that 'monarchies in name do often degenerate into aristocracies or rather oligarchies in nature . . . when prerogatives are made envious or subject to construction of laws' (Spedding and Heath 1966: X, 371). These statements reflect similar worries that the balance between royal author- ity and liberty had become precarious – and diametrically opposing views about how this had happened.

The Meanings of Jacobean Divine Right

Understanding this period's political thought therefore requires attention not just to abstract theories, but also to ways in which ideas were developed and applied in particular circumstances. James's theories of kingship had initially evolved in Scot- land, partly in response to the arguments of his tutor James Buchanan and other Presbyterians who wanted to subordinate royal authority to the theoretical sover- eignty of the people and the practical control of their own party. This context has been illuminated by historians of Scottish political thought, which differed from England's in its strongly theological orientation and pronounced cosmopolitanism (Burns 1996; Mason 1994; Williamson 1999). The earliest of James's many pub- lished tracts on political theology, produced around the time of the Armada, were meditations on Bible passages from Revelation and Chronicles that displayed a typically Calvinist use of scripture to comment on current political issues. The king identified the pope as Antichrist, equated Spain and the French Catholic League with the biblical Philistines and portrayed himself as a new David, rallying a godly nation he identified with the inhabitants of 'this isle' rather than Scotland alone. He also described David as a king who always consulted the 'spiritual rulers in his Kirk' before doing anything affecting religion. This model reflected the Presbyterian alliance he had forged in the late 1580s (Burns 1996: 260).

A decade later that alliance had collapsed and in *The Trew Law of Free Monarchies* and *Basilikon Doron* James outlined a significantly different theology of kingship. He referred only in passing to external enemies, concentrating instead on the 'reciproque duties' of kings and subjects. Kings are appointed by God as his representatives on earth and are owed unconditional obedience, but James quickly added that although 'the King is above the law . . . yet a good king will not only delight to rule his subjects by the law, but even will conform himself in his own actions thereunto' (McIlwain 1918: 63). In *Basilikon Doron* he acknowledged that kings who fail to rule lawfully might face rebellion and regicide since, although God never sanctions rebellion, he sometimes allows it to succeed to punish wicked rulers. A theoretical assertion of absolutism was thus hedged about with religious, moral and prudential restrictions. James went on to describe how a Scottish king should reform the vices of his subjects by restraining the nobles' 'oppression' of commoners, limiting seigneurial jurisdic- tions and civilizing the inhabitants of the western isles by planting orderly lowlanders among them. He particularly criticized the Presbyterian doctrine of ministerial parity and the tendency of the clergy to stir up political protest, as dangerous legacies of a Scottish reformation achieved through rebellion rather than lawful authority, as in England or Denmark. 'Some fiery spirited men in the ministry got such a guiding of the people at that time of confusion, as finding the gust of government sweet, they begouth to fantasy to themselves a democratic form of government:... leading people by the nose, to bear the sway of all the rule' (McIlwain 1918: 23). He urged restraining these self-appointed 'tribunes of the people' by rebuilding hierarchical authority in the church. These tracts effectively answered Buchanan on his own terms. For Buchanan was less a rigid Calvinist than a humanist who believed in the Erasmian ideal of government as an agency to promote peace and justice on earth. In *Rerum Scotiacarum Historia* he had emphasized the role of unruly passions and moral weaknesses among leading Scottish political figures in causing the turbulence of Mary's disastrous reign. James turned this line of argument against Presbyterian clergy, factious nobles and advocates of popular sovereignty like Buchanan himself, accusing them of unruly passions while building a case for an orderly reformation of religion and society under a strong king (Mason 1994; Burns 1996: 233–46). This stance provided potential common ground with English supporters of episcopacy like Richard Bancroft, who identified Calvinism with the republicanism of places like Geneva and the Netherlands, and potentially with French Gallicans, who had rallied around King Henry IV and ideas of *iure divino* (Salmon 1990; Burns 1996: 225–30).

In England after 1603 James's predilection for viewing affairs of state through a theological prism significantly enhanced the importance of the court sermon as a vehicle for political argument, and of sermons published by royal command as indicators of official attitudes (McCullough 1998). Since arguments about political theology were significantly more open to participation by Scots and foreign nationals than those conducted within a framework of English law and custom, James's interests helped ensure that court political discourse retained strong British and European dimensions. Because he patronized clergy of differing outlook, court pulpits also continued to express a wide spectrum of Protestant opinion. Many Scots regarded James's dynastic unification of Britain within a framework of apocalyptic thought that looked forward to a climactic confrontation between Protestantism and Catholicism (Williamson 1999). For them, Stuart divine right implied that the dynasty had responsibilities to lead and protect reformed churches throughout Europe. Many English Protestants held similar views and shared an interest in apocalyptic speculations. Dreams of future military victories usually centred on the king's children and Peter McCullough has shown that the clergy appointed to Henry's household in 1610 and to Charles's a few years later were especially prone to apocalyptic discourses and internationalist militancy. Several got into trouble for criticizing James's failure to break with Spain after the start of the Thirty Years' War (McCullough 1998: 183–95).

Such attitudes gave a harder partisan edge to British Protestantism than bishops and privy councillors liked and appeared to conflict with James's policy of peace with Spain. The king's willingness to countenance their expression by court clergy therefore indicates that his own views on European confessional politics remained complex and fluid for some time after 1603. Although capable of voicing remarkably irenic statements when it suited his purposes, James also told Isaac Casaubon in 1611 that he still regarded the pope as Antichrist. Between 1606 and 1616 he supported a campaign of preaching and polemical writing against claims that popes had the authority to depose kings for tyranny or heresy, publishing three pamphlets on the subject under his own name in Latin and English, aimed as much at international audiences as his own subjects (Sommerville 1998; Burgess 1996: 101–2; McIlwain 1918: 45–80). One accused the papacy of fomenting civil wars and predicted that God would soon arouse the kings of Europe from their 'slumber...to take order...that popes hereafter shall no more play upon their patience' (ibid.: 267).

The king's principal target was not Catholic religion, however, but Catholics who stirred rebellion, and this was an argument that potentially cut in two directions. English clergy who disliked apocalyptic enthusiasms equated Jesuits with Puritans, as similar fanatics, while identifying Christian rule with the promotion of moderation, civic order and peace, in ways calculated to appeal to the values James had articulated in *Basilikon Doron*. 'He that soweth sedition between kings or hinders their just peace', proclaimed one clergyman during the king's visit to Scotland in 1617, 'is a firebrand between two kingdoms' (Wilkinson 1617: 14). The same sermon equated peace with a time 'when the superiors govern justly, when inferiors obey willingly... when they whom God hath placed above are obeyed as bishops' (ibid.: 13). Clergy who adopted this line replaced the warlike David with the peaceful Solomon as the favoured scriptural model, countering apocalyptic militancy with different readings of biblical history and God's providential design for building the true church. James's two last treatises show that he eventually embraced this position. *A Meditation on the Lord's Prayer* repudiated the application of chiliastic (apocalyptic) ideas to politics and denounced 'puritans' for presuming to think they knew God's will. This arrogance would lead, he warned, to heresy and chaos. *A Meditation upon the...27th Chapter of Saint Matthew* reveals a change in the underlying style of the king's thought. The royal model is no longer an Old Testament king but Christ as he is mocked by Roman centurions. James reads Matthew's narrative as describing a Roman coronation, pointing out specific parallels between the centurions' actions and ceremonies used in creating emperors: in ridiculing Christ his tormentors unconsciously affirmed his status as a supreme king. In doing so they revealed the close affinities between ceremonial devotion to kings and Christian worship, which 'superstitious foolish puritans' wrongly deny by refusing to kneel when taking the sacrament. The rituals and objects used to mock Christ become symbols of specific facets of kingship, with the plaited crown of thorns standing for the 'intricate pains' kings must endure for the sake of their people (Sharpe 2000: 166). James had here travelled more than half the distance separating his earliest published *Meditation on Revelations* from the Caroline imagery of royal martyrdom found, for example, in the frontispiece to *Eikon Basilike*. He had long insisted that kings are images of God on earth, but in the earlier tracts this idea had normally referred to royal actions in administering justice and ruling a chosen people. In the *Meditation on Matthew* the royal image and its surrounding ritual apparatus take on symbolic meanings that have much closer affinities to the thought of Lancelot Andrewes and some Catholic theologians than to Calvinist divinity (cf. Burns 1996: 232). James's tract gestures unmistakably toward the Caroline tendency to infuse kingship with mystical and sacerdotal meanings.

The 1620s witnessed the triumph of a *certain kind* of divine right theology, associated with a rejection of militant Calvinist internationalism, hostility to

Puritanism, advocacy of liturgical reforms and a determination to promote hierarch-ical order in both secular and ecclesiastical life. In many ways this trend culminated in the campaign to reform the Scottish Church after 1637. The Covenanters responded by employing prophetic and apocalyptic language to appeal for solidarity with English Puritans and in the 1640s chiliastic language flourished in discourses that were almost always hostile to the king's party. These developments reflect the bifurcation of strands of argument that had once seemed equally compatible with Stuart claims.

Common Law Thought

Did a conflict also develop between divine right ideas and belief in an ancient consti-tution? To answer this question we must begin with what John Pocock, in a seminal book of 1957, called 'the common law mind' (Pocock 1987). This was an outlook that sought to resolve political controversies by appeals to legal precedents and concepts of immemorial custom. It rested on a belief in the essential continuity of English legal history over a very long period of time, which alone justified applying ancient precedents to contemporary conditions. Indeed common law minds regarded that continuity as fundamental to England's identity and cohesion. In the late sixteenth century these convictions provided an argument for preserving the basic procedures of English governance against threats posed by Spanish invasions and an uncertain succession. They reinforced – and were reinforced by – a broader conviction that the English were a distinctive people whose ancient traditions might stand comparison with those of any other nation, which also found reflections in the Arthurian imagery of Spenser's poetry, the use of gothic forms in Elizabethan architecture, and the period's fascination with heraldry, genealogy and 'topograph-ical' histories. Although this was in some ways an insular attitude it did not imply lack of interest in wider European culture. It amounted instead to a rejection of the charge that the English had until recently been a barbarous people, who therefore needed to imitate others. They had used reason in their own way to develop distinctive practices, which they had every reason to preserve (cf. Pocock 1987: ch. 3; Burgess 1993: 12–17; Smuts 1999: 20–1).

   The lawyer's concept of immemorial custom might be explained in any of three ways. A few jurists, including Edward Coke at certain moments, argued that the common law had descended intact from remote antiquity, despite upheavals like the Norman Conquest. The more normal view was that English law had developed gradually through the adjustment of universal natural principles of justice to specific-ally English circumstances (Burgess 1993: ch. 2). Legal custom was therefore con-tinuously being altered in detail without changing its fundamental structure, which derived simultaneously from natural law and fundamental English traits. A third view, which might be combined with the second, saw the law as the product of historical concessions by monarchs seeking to secure their authority by agreeing to observe their subjects' customs. It resulted from a process through which a royal power that had once been arbitrary, oppressive and unstable had become settled and rooted in the fabric of English life, so that it normally operated by unforced consent. By limiting the prerogative the law therefore strengthened it.

   Only the first of these interpretations conflicted with James's ideas and he himself adopted elements of the third in a speech to parliament in 1610 (Christianson 1991).

In Scotland he had enlarged the jurisdiction of Scottish common law and after 1603 he supported the extension of English common law over Gaelic regions of Ireland. He had no reason to regard the law as an antagonist, especially since the lawyers themselves, including Coke, readily acknowledged the supremacy of royal authority and the duty of allegiance as fundamental legal principles. But if the principle of the rule of law was uncontroversial, its detailed application did sometimes arouse conflict, for several reasons. Belief in the wisdom enshrined in immemorial custom did not imply that English laws lacked imperfections. As products of history they had inevitably suffered from the corruption inherent in secular affairs and so needed periodic reform. But the question of how much reform, and of precisely what kind, set lawyers arguing against each other, tempting the king to join in. Moreover the creation of a coherent system of legal principles from the accumulated jumble of precedents still remained very much a work in progress. Coke's *Reports* and *Institutes* eventually formed the most impressive monument to this process of codification, but Coke was in some ways an untypical legal thinker, as well as a controversial man cordially disliked by many of his colleagues, whose interpretations did not always go unchallenged (cf. Burgess 1996: ch 6; Smuts 1999: 23–4). Because contemporaries believed the law to be clear and consistent they often became short tempered when arguing cases for which the precedents were actually confused and contradictory.

Jurisdictional disputes pitting the common law courts against Chancery, the conciliar court at Ludlow in the Welsh marches and the church courts, provide examples. These conflicts were a natural by-product of the system of overlapping judicial institutions that had developed since the Middle Ages, but they raised sticky questions about the common law's relationship to other forms of legal authority. They also fed into a bitter personal rivalry pitting Coke, who defended the supremacy of his own court of Common Pleas and its sister, King's Bench, against both Bacon and Lord Chancellor Ellesmere, who upheld the rights of Chancery and the court at Ludlow. James decided he should arbitrate, since each of the competing jurisdictions delivered justice in his name. When he decided for Bacon and Egerton, Coke interpreted his defeat as a violation of the common law itself. Another controversy arose in 1619 when James resurrected the medieval court of the Earl Marshal and Lord Constable, which had jurisdiction over conflicts of honour. Several lawyers protested but the king and privy council were persuaded to overrule them, partly because of precedents gathered by Sir Robert Cotton, one of the kingdom's foremost legal antiquarians, on behalf of the newly appointed Earl Marshal, his patron the earl of Arundel.

These controversies pitted 'common law minds' against each other and were not examples of assaults on the law by absolutists. But some contemporaries perceived them as evidence of a tendency to whittle away at the law's supremacy in ways that left subjects more vulnerable to arbitrary power. These worries increased in 1627, when Charles declared martial law in districts where he was assembling troops, to suppress disorder by conscript soldiers. Although no one denied the king's right to declare martial law during a war on English soil, its use when there was no enemy in the land seemed ominous. The punishment of Henry Burton, Richard Bastwick and John Prynne for seditious libel by Star Chamber in 1637 was also construed as a violation of the common law. A reaction to all these incidents led to the abolition of the prerogative courts, the Earl Marshal's court and the ecclesiastical tribunal of High Commission during the early months of the Long Parliament. This legislation reflected a hardening of attitudes among many lawyers and their supporters, who believed that vindicating the common law required the quashing of customs and precedents that conflicted with its jurisdictional supremacy. On the other hand William Laud wrote to his friend Thomas Wentworth in 1633 that 'the Church . . . is so bound up in the forms of the common law that it is not possible for me, or for any man, to do that good which he would or is bound to do: for . . . they which have gotten so much power in and over the Church will not let go their hold' (Wentworth: StrP8, 32). Wentworth himself had recently complained to another privy councillor, Francis Cottington, about a speech by a royal judge undermining his attempts to collect recusancy fines as president of the Council of the North. If a judge is allowed 'to villify the dispensation of [the king's] justice in the hands of his faithful ministers', he fumed, the lawyers will soon 'leave no latitude at all for his Majesty to govern and manifest his greatness and power, forth by the precepts of their yearbooks' (ibid.: StrP3, 23). While not directly challenging the common law itself, these statements express deep impatience with the limitations lawyers sought to impose on other organs of royal authority.

Public Needs, Private Hopes and the King's Finances

Arguments about law also frequently became entangled in disputes about other kinds of issues. At the outset of his English reign James's eagerness to promote a more thorough unification of England and Scotland led him to propose legislation to replace English and Scottish common law with a new uniform system. He had the support of several English councillors, notably Bacon, who argued from historical examples that the preservation of separate laws and institutions, within states united under a single monarch, almost always perpetuated an inner source of disunity and weakness (Spedding and Heath 1966: X, 335). Since James had decided that the new British law should be closely modelled on that of England, he saw no reason for his subjects to object to its introduction. He failed to appreciate the depth of English fears that any attempt to replace the common law, even with an outwardly similar system, would destroy the kingdom's integrity, and ultimately had to capitulate before a firestorm of protest.

In the long term James's chronic shortage of money proved a more fertile source of contention, raising issues not just about the legalities of taxation but also the basic nature of his relationship to his people. Everyone agreed that subjects had an obligation to supply the king with money to defend the realm and that in cases of urgent necessity, like a foreign invasion, he might compel their contributions. Everyone also agreed that in normal circumstances a king should not take his subjects' property except by parliamentary grant or in ways otherwise sanctioned by law. These principles did not, however, provide clear guidance in cases where the extent of the king's need was itself in dispute. James believed that his subjects had a duty to support not only his bare necessities but his honour, which meant, for example, defraying the cost of major foreign embassies and providing him with resources to reward loyal service. Failure to do so might not immediately jeopardize the kingdom's safety but it would diminish his reputation and ability to attract service, with potentially disastrous eventual consequences. James and his council also knew that previous English kings had sometimes resorted to irregular fiscal expedients; in fact the earl of Northampton set Cotton to work researching the relevant precedents. Cotton concluded his survey, however, by warning against non-parliamentary taxation, as a remedy that had often 'proved more dangerous than the disease' of royal poverty because of the ill-will it provoked.

Unfortunately, pleas that parliament should supply the king's needs raised questions about whether he was truly necessitous, rather than profligate and wasteful. A particularly astute analysis of this problem came in a series of outspoken memoranda to James by the Lord Treasurer, Robert Cecil. Cecil believed the crown's accumulated debts and chronic peacetime deficit posed significant threats to English security, by leaving the king with insufficient reserves for emergencies. 'This is a certain rule, that all princes are poor and unsafe that are not so rich and potent as to defend themselves upon any sudden offence or invasion, and to help their allies and neighbours upon just occasion' (Croft 1987: 283). But Cecil bluntly warned the king that he needed to exercise greater fiscal discipline before seeking new income from his subjects. His generosity in granting pensions and gifts had established a pattern of diverting revenues from 'public and political' needs to feed 'private men's hopes', turning 'the garden of your Majesty's treasure' into 'a common pasture for all that are in need, or have unreasonable desires' (ibid.). Schemes for raising money through prerogative measures compounded the problem, since they were invariably exploited for private gain.

> You have been constrained, for want of means to reward others, to suffer your people to be molested and enquired after, upon every claim and obscure title, some being searched for debts beyond memory of man; some pursued for concealment, some troubled upon new projects and hard inquisitions, not only for the public but also for the use of private men. (Ibid.: 275)

James had become trapped in a destructive cycle, as his generosity undermined his ability to gain supply, encouraging his ministers to resort to irregular schemes for raising money, which in turn multiplied abuses and generated more ill-will. The longer this process continued the more difficult it would become to restore confidence that royal government truly served public needs and so deserved parliamentary grants.

Unfortunately, Cecil and his successors never truly solved the problem he had diagnosed and the perception that the operation of royal government had become distorted to serve 'private wants' continued to generate critical discourse. It easily led to the further supposition that the beneficiaries of abuses might try to block reform by poisoning the king's mind against parliament and its reformist programmes. This suspicion, in turn, fed into discourses about royal favourites that were also shaped by classical and contemporary European sources. The problem of the great favourite, who monopolized control over power and patronage, had become a subject of general European concern in the early seventeenth century (Feros 1999). Although favourites did have a few defenders, they were generally seen as figures who interposed themselves between kings and their people, excluding virtuous men from office and blocking good counsel. These fears reached a climax during Buckingham's ascendancy early in Charles I's reign, a period that all historians regard as one of sharpened polarization (e.g. Burgess 1993: ch. 7). Discussions of the intellectual dimensions of that polarization have concentrated on theological disputes over Arminianism or legal issues arising from the Forced Loan and the imprisonment of loan refusers. This has kept the focus on domestic issues, despite the fact that this was also a period of war, when European events were more important to English politics than at any time since the 1590s. Yet for Charles and his ministers, relations with parliament and arguments over the legalities of taxation were inseparably bound up with strategic concerns arising from the great war in Europe. A brief examination of ideas about international power and military leadership will therefore help to place the debates of the 1620s in context.

Necessities, Reputation, Honour and Virtue

Diplomats and royal ministers centrally concerned with international affairs tended to view financial issues from a perspective in which England's position in Europe mattered at least as much as domestic reform. In their parlance talk of a king's necessities (usually in the plural) meant not just shortages of money, but difficulties in finding resources to defend specific vital interests. They also recognized, however, that a monarch's position depended as much on perceptions of his strengths and weaknesses as on actual resources. A king with a reputation for strength might limit his necessities by attracting allies and deterring attacks, whereas one whose reputation had suffered might find himself deserted by friends as he faced emboldened enemies. The conservation of a king's international reputation was, therefore, not just a matter of pride but a vital strategic concern. Broken parliaments harmed the crown not just by depriving it of revenue but by encouraging the view that the king lacked the support needed to rally his subjects during an international conflict. Richard Weston was not simply scoring a rhetorical point when he told the parliament of 1625 that Charles had 'learned in Spain that nothing brought his father into so much contempt as the coldness between him and his people', since Jacobean diplomats had privately expressed similar views (Jansson 1987: 398; PRO: SP94/21, fo. 162).

The concept of reputation was closely associated with discourses on honour. In the late Elizabethan period, especially in the circle around the earl of Essex, a revival of chivalric concepts of honour had fused with more modern humanist emphases. The gentleman warrior was urged to acquire intellectual skills needed in modern warfare, in ways reflecting emergence of a distinct military profession. Essex's circle also adopted the current European fashion for the Roman historian Tacitus, as an incisive observer of the destruction of political virtue under tyranny. This eclectic range of influences produced an outlook in which emphasis on the importance of noble blood and the chivalric ideal of valour readily combined with humanist concepts of public service and Tacitean analyses of corruption. Essex exalted military exploits by men of ancient lineage like himself, sometimes in language redolent of medieval romances, but he also justified bold actions, like the sack of Cadiz by an English force in 1596, for the way they inspired sacrifice and dedication among the population. The monarch and the nobility, he argued, had a duty to set an example of courage and dedication to 'public' causes, including the defence of religion and liberty abroad. If they did not they might undermine the people's capacity for virtue. The earl's militant ideas did not go unchallenged, especially during the long Jacobean peace, when several writers developed more pacific concepts of political virtue (Williamson

1999). But his values survived in the entourage of Prince Henry, within aristocratic families that had once belonged to his circle and among writers they patronized (McCoy 1996). This last group associated the Jacobean peace with a decline in 'old English honour', especially within the court, where the king's love of ease, duplicitous Spanish diplomacy and the distribution of Spanish pensions all allegedly induced neglect of the kingdom's security. Criticisms that James had allowed the prerogative to serve 'private wants' instead of 'public needs' merged with broader religious and strategic concerns, particularly during negotiations over the Spanish Match.

Charles's entry into the Thirty Years' War with parliament's support in 1625 appeared to signal the restoration of unity and public virtue under a young and vigorous monarch determined to redeem English honour in Europe. The king's speeches and those of his ministers certainly attempted to reinforce this impression. 'This being my first action', Charles exhorted parliament, 'all the eyes of Christendom will be on me; and as I do in this, so it will get me credit and repute abroad and honour at home' (Jansson 1987: 192). When the crown demanded further grants a few months later, viscount Conway argued: 'The honour and safety of the nation and religion are at stake if we now grow cold, and the princes of Germany will divide, the King of France come in as a party to the Catholic League, the King of Denmark make his peace with the Emperor' (ibid.: 387). Like Essex a generation earlier, Charles's councillors warned that a slackening of English service to the 'public cause of Christendom' might trigger a chain reaction of defections by others. Parliament's willingness to approve taxes thus became a crucial test of the *kingdom's* virtue.

Unfortunately this outlook raised especially painful questions as military defeats accumulated, the enormous financial burdens of the war became clear and political discord grew. Since English valour had failed, the fault must lie either at court or with parliament and the country, and debates on this question were not going to promote harmony. Buckingham was especially vulnerable as a favourite who had risen from obscurity, monopolizing offices, excluding men of nobler lineages from influence, enriching himself through crown gifts and even – his critics charged – prostituting honour itself by selling titles of nobility. He was accused of undermining the very principle of virtuous service to the crown, and therefore of threatening the ethical foundations of English governance (McCoy 1996: 144–5). In addition he had a Catholic mother and had married into a recusant family. He was a man in whom all the various forms of corruption of royal governance appeared to converge, 'drawn like lines to one centre'. Charles, on the other hand, saw Buckingham as a virtuous servant traduced for carrying out royal policies; sacrificing him would merely expose royal authority to factious enemies who stirred up malice and envy – the traditional enemies of honour – against those at the head of government. The struggle over Buckingham's impeachment in 1626 was only indirectly about the law and the prerogative. It centred around a debate over the moral causes of the collapse of a healthy relationship between the king and his people, and the resulting humiliation of England on the European stage.

Fears for the security of the rule of law soon came to the fore as well, however, since the dissolution of the 1626 parliament left Charles facing urgent military needs he could only meet through non-parliamentary taxation and other arbitrary actions. Theoretical arguments that the king might act outside the law in cases of necessity suddenly acquired a practical importance they had always previously lacked. The

Forced Loan, arbitrary arrests and billeting of troops on English householders during 1626–7 led, once a new parliament had assembled, to efforts at reaffirming the common law principles the king had violated through the Petition of Right. The deliberations over this document provide the single most impressive example in the period of the common law mind at work. Leading jurists, including Coke, Cotton and John Selden, methodically marshalled precedents in support of the Commons' view that an English king might not take his subjects' property without their consent, arrest and imprison them without speedy trial, billet soldiers in their houses or try them by martial law in time of peace. Burgess has blamed the growing confrontation over the law on Charles's failure to handle the 'consensual language' of Jacobean political discourse 'idiomatically' (Burgess 1993: ch. 7). Yet what was plainly at stake by 1628 was not just clumsy language but tangible evidence that calculations of military necessity had swept aside normal legal constraints. As in France and Spain during the same period, a political logic driven by international competition for reputation and power had dissolved customary restraints on royal actions.

A Triumph of Absolutism?

Did Charles's actions also amount to a deliberate effort to alter government in an absolutist direction? Some contemporaries certainly thought so: warnings about the introduction of 'new counsels' and the threat of a change in 'the form of government' were heard repeatedly in this period. But were they accurate? Did the Forced Loan of 1627 and the breach with parliament two years later result in a further, significant development of ideas that can usefully be described as absolutist, and did those ideas shape Charles's policies? In this period altering forms of government was something people normally accused their enemies of doing, rather than a goal they publicly embraced. Laud's chaplain, Peter Heylin, appears to have been a rare exception. In 1632 he published (anonymously) a work entitled *Augustus: Or an Essay of those Means and Counsels, whereby the Commonwealth of Rome was Altered and Reduced unto a Monarchy*, describing how Augustus changed the mixed polity of the Republic into a pure monarchy by infiltrating the key political organs of the Roman state and subordinating them to his will. The tract may well have been intended as advice to the king. But if so this was absolutism of a particularly subtle and devious kind, since it involved disguising royal power beneath customary forms and procedures. Heylin's detailed prescriptions are also frequently moderate; for example, he opposed the rigorous punishment of seditious libels, since this would only gain the authors sympathy.

The more normal argument of those sympathetic to the king was that he needed to restore the ancient form of government, after distortions caused by the parliamentary faction. People who took this position also believed that English kings had anciently enjoyed a more complete authority than the court's critics believed. A courtier named Francis Kynaston wrote a treatise in the early 1630s in which he set out to correct what he saw as mistaken historical arguments that had led members of the Commons to challenge the crown. He argued that parliament had developed well after the Norman Conquest from the king's great council, and had never enjoyed independent authority. It originally consisted of the Lords alone and Henry III had restricted the rights of commoners to attend it, showing the king's absolute authority to divest them of their privileges. The power to make laws and levy taxes had anciently belonged to the king alone and in the final analysis still did, even though for many centuries kings had chosen to enact statutes through parliament. Law expresses the king's will and 'is rather fortified than created by the subjects' consent'.

In making his case Kynaston compared a king's relationship to his subjects to that between a father and his sons. At some date around 1630 the Kentish gentleman named Sir Robert Filmer finished a much more systematic treatise developing the same analogy. He argued that kings derive their authority from the unlimited right of command that Adam once possessed over all his descendants. Their will is consequently superior to the law and there is no legitimate right of resistance to it. Even more than Kynaston, Filmer was unquestionably an absolutist thinker (Burgess 1996: 37–40). But like Kynaston, he did not publish his treatise, which therefore remained outside the mainstream of political discussion until after the Restoration.

Charles's own public justification for the 1629 dissolution avoided absolutist theories. Instead the king adopted a tone of injured righteousness, complaining that his people needed to 'see more clearly into his intents and actions' instead of being 'misled' by the 'ill reports' spread by demagogues. The statement is typical of Charles's concern throughout his life to vindicate his claim to have acted uprightly, according to his own conscience (Sharpe 2000: ch. 5). He had become convinced that a popular faction, fundamentally hostile to royal authority, had gained control of the Commons and begun to threaten his ability to rule. The situation called not for theoretical arguments but condign punishment of the chief offenders and a firm reassertion of his will to govern.

Yet those centrally involved in royal governance also faced the problems of raising needed revenues and restoring the crown's badly diminished European reputation without parliamentary assistance. They attempted to do so not by flouting the law but by exploiting precedents and stretching the king's legal powers for fiscal purposes. As Burgess has argued, this course of action raised questions about whether the law was, in fact, capable of limiting royal power. Ship Money, in particular, again provided an instance of the king's absolute prerogative to act in defence of the realm being used to justify non-parliamentary taxation (Burgess 1993: 202–10). The argument from necessity was not entirely specious, since a strong navy was critical to the kingdom's safety, and if Charles waited for an emergency before building one, it might be too late. Behind Ship Money lay the European concept of 'reason of state', the idea that a king's duty to defend the *salus populi* meant he had a right to defend his kingdom by whatever means he thought necessary, without giving a public account of his conduct. Contemporaries on both sides of the dispute saw this clearly. Clarendon complained that the real threat posed by the judges' decision in favour of Ship Money in 1637, by the narrowest possible majority of 7 to 5, was that it allowed 'apothegms of state [to be] urged as elements of law', making 'judges as sharp-sighted as secretaries . . . in the mysteries of state' (ibid.: 211). Thomas Wentworth, on the other hand, hoped that the tax had given Charles not just a defensive but an offensive weapon: 'certainly it is most true, howbeit you do no great matters with your fleet, yet when other princes see his Majesty provided to set such strength at sea it shall make him so considerable they will court him on all sides . . . Nothing in reason of state concerns him more' (Strafford: StrP9/30). But Wentworth also knew that

Ship Money had not entirely removed the crown's vulnerability. When some members of the council wanted to use the fleet against Spain he quickly became alarmed: 'I was always so fearful of the Ship Moneys as I could never advise any great action to have been raised from so uncertain a foundation' (ibid.: StrP7/54). In a real emergency a tax that many people regarded as illegal and resented having to pay might become impossible to collect. Until respect for the king increased to a point at which he no longer had to fear challenges to his authority he would remain hampered. Purely theoretical assertions of royal sovereignty were of limited help in dealing with this problem, since what was really needed was to change attitudes and behaviour.

A body of theory did exist in the period addressing this sort of problem, associated with the concept of political prudence. The foremost European exponent of this concept, the Flemish scholar Justus Lipsius, defined prudence as 'a skill to govern external [political] matters quietly and safely' and argued that it required attention to 'two things ... *force and virtue*'. By force Lipsius chiefly meant soldiers and fortifications, although he also recommended the planting of colonies in especially unsettled areas, as the Stuarts had done in Ulster (Lipsius 1594: 66, 72–4). Lipsian virtue referred not to the ruler's own actions but to the attitudes of his subjects. Lipsius further divided it into the two qualities of 'love' and 'authority'. The last term had a meaning similar to reputation: a 'reverent opinion of the King and his estate, imprinted as well in his own subjects as in strangers', consisting 'of admiration and fear' (ibid.: 75, 78–9). Lipsius implicitly disagreed with a famous passage of Machiavelli's *Prince*, which had argued that it was nearly impossible for a ruler to be loved and feared at the same time and that fear was a more reliable support for power. Lipsius thought both emotions essential. He did tacitly agree with Machiavelli, however, in identifying the two greatest threats to a king as his subjects' 'hate' and 'contempt' (ibid.: 78–123, esp. 93, 109).

Although there is no reason to think Lipsius had a significant direct influence on Caroline government, his discussion clarifies commonplace attitudes that Charles and his council demonstrably shared. They worried incessantly about the need to combat contempt and uphold royal authority, especially against 'Puritan' dissidents. But it is also striking how consistently Caroline court literature treated love as a central political theme. In the masques of the 1630s love is at once a metaphysical principle uniting the cosmos, the bond tying Charles to the queen, and the central virtue of political life. This was in part political rhetoric, but it would be a mistake to dismiss it as nothing more, since Charles's councillors continued throughout the 1630s to stress the importance of regaining his subjects' affections. Some, like the earl of Holland, advocated the summoning of a new parliament as the best means of doing so. Others rejected this plea but accepted the basic premise that public affection for the king and voluntary compliance with his commands were signs of political health, whereas the need to resort continually to coercive measures showed that something had gone badly wrong. The stress on 'love' reflected fundamental political assumptions. It also stemmed from recognition that coercion and fear alone were an inadequate basis for strong government in a monarchy as deficient in soldiers and fortifications as Great Britain.

The relevance of this point comes through clearly in disagreements between hardliners and moderates on the council during the crisis with Scotland. Hardliners generally believed both that a decisive military action would quickly overwhelm Scottish resistance, and that England would remain loyal while Charles dealt with his northern subjects. The moderates were more sceptical of the king's military resources and more worried about the breadth and depth of English disaffection. Wentworth's prescriptions for dealing with the crisis included placing garrisons in Berwick and Carlisle, 'which had it been early done perchance the covenanters, [with] so great a power near them, would never have wound themselves up to that insolence they are now come unto' (Wentworth: StrP10b, fo. 55v). While agreeing that the Scottish 'mischief' might prove contagious, he assured himself that 'the subject of England hath so much fear of God and loyalty to our Prince and Excellent Master, [as] not to take the impression of rebellion into their hearts' (ibid.: 73–4). As the crisis deepened, his determination to prevail by force increased, an attitude vividly conveyed by Henry Vane's notes of his comments in the fateful privy council meeting of 5 May 1640:

> Go vigorously on or let them alone . . . The quiet of England will hold out long . . . Go on with an offensive war as you first designed, loosed and absolved from all the rules of government being reduced by extreme necessity, everything is to be done as power will admit . . . You have an army in Ireland you may employ here to reduce this kingdom. Confident as anything under heaven, Scotland shall not hold out five months. (CSPD 1640: 477)

For Wentworth, the greatest danger lay in capitulation to the Scots, since by demonstrating weakness it encouraged contempt and invited future defiance.

By contrast the earl of Northumberland complained in July of 1638:

> In the Exchequer . . . there is found but two hundred pounds . . . the King's magazines are totally unfurnished of arms and all sorts of ammunition; and commanders we have none . . . The people through all England are generally so discontented . . . as I think there is reason to fear that a great part of them will be readier to join the Scots than to draw their swords in the King's service. (Knowler 1739: II, 186)

Although Northumberland disliked the new Scottish liturgy, his fundamental objection was that for a king as weak and unpopular as Charles attempting to prevail by the sword meant courting disaster. Henry Vane the elder evolved from a hardliner into a moderate, as he realized that the king's Scottish policy was weakening his authority over his English subjects. He remained optimistic in February 1640, not only that Charles would prevail, but that he would emerge with a strengthened reputation as a 'just and merciful King'. By August and September his correspondence is full of anguished comments about Scottish sympathizers in the southern kingdom (e.g. CSPD 1639–40: 477, 641–2; CSPD 1640–1: 15, 23). His optimism briefly returned during the king's progress to Edinburgh in 1641, when he felt that Charles had begun to recover his subjects' 'love', 'so that I assure myself by next spring he will be useful to his friends abroad, to the comfort of all reformed churches' (ibid.: 101). Even at this late date Vane continued to view the king's domestic problems in light of larger European conflicts. By the end of November he was again close to despair: 'Three kingdoms in this condition, no money and little affection, should well be thought of, and the Catholic Romish princes abroad all drawing to a peace . . . we cannot be happy if we change not our counsels' (ibid.: 149). 'No money and little affection': a king in this position lacked the means to defend his kingdom. In a real sense he had ceased to reign.

In urging Charles to act as if 'loosed and absolved from the rules of government' Wentworth advocated an absolutist policy in the strict sense of the term, whereas Northumberland and Vane remained wedded to more moderate solutions that might loosely be termed 'constitutionalist'. Yet characterizing their positions in this way does not adequately describe their disagreements, which had less to do with ideas about the constitution than assessments of the impact Charles's actions were having on his ability to govern. Although intensely practical in focus, those assessments possessed intellectual dimensions that need to be included in any full history of the period's political thought. Ideas about divine right, the common law and the ancient constitution certainly mattered in the seventeenth century, but they were never the only ideas that counted in the political arena. Early Stuart political thought was more diversified, more complex and often more practical in orientation than many studies of the subject still suggest.

REFERENCES

Burgess, G. 1993: *The Politics of the Ancient Constitution: An Introduction to Political Thought, 1603–1642*: University Park, PA.

Burgess, G. 1996: *Absolute Monarchy and the Stuart Constitution*: New Haven, CT.

Burns, J. H. 1996: *The Trew Law of Kingship: Concepts of Monarchy in Early Modern Scotland*: Oxford.

Christianson: 1991: 'Royal and parliamentary voices on the ancient constitution, *c.*1604–1621.' In L. Peck, ed., *The Mental World of the Jacobean Court*: Cambridge.

Croft: 1987: 'A collection of several speeches and treatises of the late treasurer Cecil', *Royal Historical Society Camden Treatises Miscellany*, 5, 29: 273–318.

CSPD 1858–97: *Calendar of State Papers Domestic, Reign of Charles I*, 23 vols: London.

Feros, A. 1999: 'Images of evil, images of kings: the contrasting faces of the royal favourite and the prime minister in European political literature, *c.*1580–*c.*1650. In J. H. Elliott and L. W. B. Brockliss, eds, *The World of the Favourite*: New Haven, CT.

Gardiner, S. R. 1862: *Parliamentary Debates in 1610*: London.

Jansson, M. 1987: *Proceedings in Parliament 1625*: New Haven, CT.

Knowler, W. 1739: *The Earl of Strafford's Letters and Despatches*, 2 vols: London.

Lipsius, J. 1594: *The Six Bookes of Politickes*: London.

McCoy, R. 1996: 'Old English honor in an evil time: aristocratic principle in the 1620s.' In M. Smuts, ed., *The Stuart Court and Europe*: Cambridge.

McCullough, P. 1998: *Sermons at Court: Politics and Religion in Elizabethan and Jacobean Preaching*: Cambridge.

McIlwain, C. H. 1918: *The Political Works of James I*: Cambridge, MA.

McLaren, A. N. 1999: *Political Culture in the Reign of Elizabeth I*: Cambridge.

Mason, R. 1994: 'George Buchanan, James VI and the Presbyterians.' In R. Mason, ed., *Scots and Britons*: Cambridge.

Nenner, H. 1995: *The Right to be King*: Chapel Hill, NC.

Pocock, J. G. A. 1987: *The Ancient Constitution and the Feudal Law: A Reissue with a Retrospect*: Cambridge.

Salmon, J. H. M. 1990: 'Catholic resistance theory, Ultramontanism, and the royalist response'. In J. H. Burns, ed., *The Cambridge History of Political Thought 1450–1700*: Cambridge.

Sharpe, K. 2000: *Remapping Early Modern England: The Culture of Seventeenth-Century Politics*: Cambridge.

Smith Fussner, F. 1957: 'William Camden's "Dioscourse Concerning the Prerogative of the Crown"', *Proceedings of the American Philosophical Society*, 101.

Smuts, R. M. 1999: *Culture and Power in England 1585–1685*: Houndsmills.

Sommerville, J. P. 1994: *King James VI and I: Political Writings*: Cambridge.

Sommerville, J. P. 1998: *Royalists and Patriots*: London.

Spedding, R. E. and Heath, D. (eds) 1966: *Works of Francis Bacon*, 14 vols: Stuttgart.

Wilkinson, R. 1617: *Barwicke Bridge*: St Andrewes.

Williamson, A. 1999: 'Patterns of British identity: Britain and its rivals in the sixteenth and seventeenth centuries'. In G. Burgess, ed., *The New British History: Founding a Modern State 1603–1715*: London.

ARCHIVAL DEPOSITS

PRO: Public Record Office, London.

Wentworth: Wentworth Woodhouse Muniments. Sheffield Public Library, Sheffield, England.

FURTHER READING

Burgess, G. 1993: *The Politics of the Ancient Constitution: An Introduction to Political Thought, 1603–1642*: University Park, PA.

Burgess, G. 1996: *Absolute Monarchy and the Stuart Constitution*: New Haven, CT.

Burns, J. H. 1996: *The Trew Law of Kingship: Concepts of Monarchy in Early Modern Scotland*: Oxford.

Croft, P. 1987: 'A collection of several speeches and treatises of the late treasurer Cecil', *Royal Historical Society Camden Treatises Miscellany*, 5, 29: 273–318.

Feros, A. 1999: 'Images of evil, images of kings: the contrasting faces of the royal favourite and the prime minister in European political literature, *c*.1580–*c*.1650. In J. H. Elliott and L. W. B. Brockliss, eds, *The World of the Favourite*: New Haven, CT.

McCoy, R. 1996: 'Old English honor in an evil time: aristocratic principle in the 1620s.' In M. Smuts, ed., *The Stuart Court and Europe*: Cambridge.

McCullough, P. 1998: *Sermons at Court: Politics and Religion in Elizabethan and Jacobean Preaching*: Cambridge.

McLaren, A. N. 1999: *Political Culture in the Reign of Elizabeth I*: Cambridge.

Mason, R. 1994: 'George Buchanan, James VI and the Presbyterians.' In R. Mason, ed., *Scots and Britons*: Cambridge.

Nenner, H. 1995: *The Right to be King*: Chapel Hill, NC.

Peck, L. (ed.) 1991: *The Mental World of the Jacobean Court*: Cambridge.

Pocock, J. G. A. 1987: *The Ancient Constitution and the Feudal Law: A Reissue with a Retrospect*: Cambridge.

Salmon, J. H. M. 1990: 'Catholic resistance theory, Ultramontanism, and the royalist response'. In J. H. Burns, ed., *The Cambridge History of Political Thought 1450–1700*: Cambridge.

Sharpe, K. 2000: *Remapping Early Modern England: The Culture of Seventeenth-Century Politics*: Cambridge.

Sommerville, J. P. 1994: *King James VI and I: Political Writings*: Cambridge.

Sommerville, J. P. 1998: *Royalists and Patriots*: London.

Williamson, A. 1999. 'Patterns of British identity: Britain and its rivals in the sixteenth and seventeenth centuries'. In G. Burgess, ed., *The New British History: Founding a Modern State 1603–1715*: London.

CHAPTER FIFTEEN

The Outbreak of the Civil Wars in the Three Kingdoms

JASON PEACEY

The search for the 'causes' of the civil wars is the 'traditional blood sport of English historians' (Russell 1979: 4), which enthuses and confuses scholars and students alike. It has attracted the most important scholars and historiographical traditions, and produced some of the most provocative history of the twentieth century, much of it written by authors whose colours were firmly nailed to political masts. Its perennial interest lies in understanding the most turbulent period of British history, and in confronting fundamental issues relating to 'causality', the interpretation of evidence, and political motivation. This chapter reconsiders the causes, course and nature of events which began in Edinburgh in 1637 and ended with the outbreak of fighting in 1642. The focus is provided by two recent trends in early modern historiography, 'revisionism' and 'British history', to demonstrate how such ideas have influenced our understanding, the nature of the criticisms they have occasioned, and future directions for research.

Context and Causes: Revisionism and British History

Much traditional analysis emphasized a mixture of what Lawrence Stone called 'preconditions', 'precipitants' and 'triggers', and stressed either 'structural' or 'conjunctural' factors. The 'preconditions' of war were factors which promoted 'disequilibrium' and 'multiple dysfunction' during the early modern period; long-term social developments, economic transformations, ideological divisions, and political tensions, and the emergence of 'new social forces', 'new political relationships', and 'new intellectual currents'. These included a literate lower middle class, and rich property owners, professionals, and merchants – in the counties, the courts, the church and commerce – whose social and economic weight became reflected in political independence. They also included the 'unfinished' nature of the Reformation, the transformation of parliament in the sixteenth century, and the rise of a Puritan opposition. This approach was shared by 'Whigs' and Marxists alike, the former stressing the emergence of a religio-constitutional crisis and the creation of modern political structures, the latter emphasizing conflict between a rising bourgeoisie and a declining feudal class. Where Tawney detected a rising gentry, and Stone a declining aristocracy, Trevor-Roper focused upon the decline of small and middling landowners and the rise of a yeomanry and a professional and trading gentry, and upon the role of the 'mere gentry' in the 'country party' which opposed the 'court'.

Meanwhile, postwar American liberal historians, such as Hexter, returned the focus to high politics, highlighting the collapse of aristocratic military control, the rise of the House of Commons, and the growth of religious and constitutional conflict. Such 'structural' interpretations have been blended with short-term factors, war being conceived to have been precipitated by fiscal and religious policies of the 'personal rule' (1629–40) which made conflict a probability rather than a possibility, and to have been triggered by incidents and fortuitous events after 1640, such as the attempted arrest of the 'five members' in January 1642 (Stone 1972: 114–15).

Since the 1970s, however, received wisdom has been challenged by 'revisionist' scholars, most notably Conrad Russell, who questioned the existence of a 'high road' to war, whether formulated by a 'teleological' or 'scientific' reading of history (Russell 1990a, 1990b). Revisionists stress the absence of demand for war, let alone revolution, suggesting that there was insufficient 'combustible material' in England to ignite a conflict. Those alienated by Stuart policies were few in number, and rebellion was unfeasible without parliament, a pretender, or a foreign army (Russell 1991: 2). Revisionists stress that cohesion and consensus provided the dominant paradigm during the early modern period, and that conflict resulted from factionalism at court and tension in the shires, rather than ideological division or constitutional disagreement. Political innovation was not a cause of the troubles, but a result of the wars, as parliamentarians developed their ideas in an *ad hoc* manner in order to deal with a stubborn and untrustworthy king. There was no split between royalists who favoured arbitrary government and parliamentarians who favoured an 'ascending' theory of political power, and all argued on the basis of the 'rule of law' (Russell 1990a: 131–60).

Revisionism is often portrayed as being hostile to 'structural' interpretations and to the idea of long-term tensions causing the civil war, and as stressing instead short-term factors, contingency and 'accidents', not least the personality of the king, his role as an innovator, and the impact of his blunders. Charles was an 'authoritarian meddler' who was out of touch and bad at communicating, and who mixed insecurities with a strong notion of kingship (ibid.: ch. 8). The ship of state hit the rocks, one might say, because of pilot error rather than mechanical breakdown. In reality, Russell *reworks* structural analyses, recognizing long-term issues while disputing their traditional identification, and the importance attributed to them. Reluctant to use the label 'cause', revisionists seek a more rigid notion of causality which identifies factors which promoted instability, rather than causes of war. For Russell, the crisis of 1637–42 reflected the revival of dormant instabilities by particular policies and incidents. Neither this process, nor the factors which fostered division, *caused* the civil war, or provided people with the motivation to fight, since tensions could have been defused or resolved. This might seem like word play, but revisionism highlights the need for rigorous historical understanding, and for recognition that political, religious, social and economic problems did not necessarily promote crisis.

In modifying the 'preconditions' of war, and the factors which generated tension, revisionists reject the importance of social transformations and ideological conflicts. Instead, Russell identified three long-term causes of *instability*: religious division, 'functional breakdown' and the nature of multiple kingdoms (ibid.: 213–19). The notion of persistent Puritan opposition has been challenged in favour of a 'Calvinist consensus' which was fractured by the 'Arminian' policies of William Laud. Political tensions have been reinterpreted as 'functional breakdown' rather than constitutional crisis, and early modern parliaments have been portrayed as weak rather than strong, and as 'events' rather than an 'institution'. Problems in the 1620s stemmed from the crown's financial weakness and inability to wage war, and although this sprang from resistance to taxation, such opposition reflected attitudes within 'county communities', and parochial rather than national concerns. Tensions dissipated once war was removed from the agenda in the 1630s, and there was no direct correlation between the king's critics in the 1620s and his enemies in the 1640s (ibid.; Russell 1979: 434–6). England was 'in working order' in 1637, problems only resurfacing once rebellion in Scotland returned war to the political agenda (Russell 1991: 1). Tension was produced, in other words, because Britain was a 'multiple kingdom', comprised of countries with distinct cultures, religions and institutions, yet ruled by a single monarch. The problem with multiple kingdoms lay in absentee monarchy, communication breakdown, and the possibility that tension in one country might 'infect' the others. Britain's troubles arose from pressure for further integration, and while James sought to 'nudge' England and Scotland closer in law, religion and government, Charles pursued an impatient policy for union. His excessive haste provoked crisis by sparking counter-revolution (Russell 1990a: ch. 2).

Revisionists such as John Adamson have also modified traditional historiography by highlighting the 'bicameral' nature of politics, and the 'baronial' nature of opposition to Charles. Accepted identification of the leading actors in the troubles has been challenged, with attention shifting from the House of Commons to the nobility, for whom men such as John Pym were clients and employees. Such bicamerality reinforces the idea that parliamentarians sought limited change rather than parliamentary sovereignty, and the idea that their language resembled a medieval 'baronial revolt'. They sought to challenge Charles I, and to supplant his counsellors as if under a protectorate, rather than to place fundamental limitations upon the monarchy. Understanding 'parliamentarian' demands in this way, it is argued, enables a reassessment of the potential for peaceful settlement (Cust and Hughes 1997: 83–110).

For revisionists, therefore, long-term factors caused instability but not war; they were necessary but not sufficient conditions for conflict. Russell has stressed the difficulty of identifying issues which were 'in an absolute and immediate sense' causes of the wars (Russell 1991: 24). The need to assess 'great events' while dismissing 'great causes' has led revisionists to focus upon a narrow time frame. While religious divisions, functional breakdown and the nature of the multiple kingdom created tensions, these deepened only as a result of events after 1637. Russell identified seven key events leading to war, each of which exposed tensions which a wiser king than Charles might have left concealed, and each of which was affected by one or more long-term factor. The events identified by Russell were: the Bishops Wars (1639–40); England's defeat by the Scots; failure to reach a political settlement; failure to dissolve the Long Parliament; polarization and party formation after 1640; failure to negotiate; and the 'diminished majesty' of Charles (Russell 1990a: 13, 24). Replacing the vision of growing crisis towards inevitable conflagration, therefore, revisionism stresses the local context, and substitutes detailed narrative for 'grand narrative'.

By stressing the importance of events after 1637, the limited radicalism of Charles's English 'opponents', and the importance of Britain as a multiple kingdom, revisionism has encouraged, and been encouraged by, the development of 'new British history', the rediscovery of the 'British problem', and the 'three kingdoms context', as pioneered by Russell, John Pocock and John Morrill (Gaunt 1997). Their work has challenged 'Anglocentrism' – the stress upon the centrality of English affairs and the uniqueness and self-sufficiency of her history – and focused instead upon 'external' events which impacted upon England. Crisis occurred because of incidents outside England which did not centre on her religion, constitution, society and economy. Concentrating upon the local context draws attention to events in Scotland and Ireland, and reminds us that England was the last of the three kingdoms to rebel, and had the weakest 'opposition' (Russell 1991: 27). Crucial to the Russellian strand of 'British' history is the 'billiard ball effect': the idea that events in any one kingdom were affected by what was taking place elsewhere, and that such 'external' events could expose and stimulate political, religious and economic tensions. England and Ireland, it is argued, were destabilized by the need to suppress rebellion in Scotland, and each kingdom was divided by the continual intrusion into its affairs of the other two (Russell 1990a: 27). It is suggested that the pressure placed upon the king during the early 1640s was produced in Scotland and Ireland, rather than England, and that Englishmen who sought to coerce Charles became reliant upon the Scots, and committed to their religious programme. This helped create the royalist party, although such religious divisions were still insufficient to cause war until the Anglo-Scottish *rapprochement* after 1640, and the satisfaction of Scottish demands for the removal of the earl of Strafford as Lord Lieutenant in Ireland, provoked the Irish rebellion, which further destabilized English politics. A less fully developed strand of British history, associated with John Morrill, stresses the 'holistic' nature of the troubles in the three kingdoms, and the need to understand events on the basis of a single crisis rather than interacting nations (Morrill 1993: ch. 13).

Both revisionism and 'British history' are broad historiographical schools of thought, and do not always prove mutually compatible, or even reinforce one another. Moreover, both have been subjected to extensive criticism. Revisionists have been accused of literalism in their treatment of sources which express consensual aspirations, and of failing to take seriously other contemporary views. Historians of political thought, religion and society have reasserted the existence of ideological tensions, challenged the notion of a Calvinist consensus, and documented the emergence of new forces in society. Revisionists have also been charged with failing to appreciate the difficulties involved in expressing opposition in the early seventeenth century, and of failing to appreciate the possibility of 'conformist opposition' to policies such as Ship Money. They may also be accused of paying insufficient attention to the world beyond Westminster, of underplaying the role of ideology in favour of pragmatism, and of underestimating the growth of rival conspiracy theories, based upon fears of either a popular Puritan conspiracy to undermine royal authority, or a popish plot to overthrow English liberties; of either parity or popery (Hughes 1998). They may be too quick to dismiss radical minorities, since such groups provided focal points for opposition, and were able to connect their agendas to more general concerns. Ultimately, revisionists may be mistaken in challenging accepted interpretations through analysis of contemporary motivations, aspirations and understandings. Detecting that contemporaries neither wanted nor expected a conflict, while recognizing the existence of recurrent tension, revisionists sometimes resort to somewhat semantic distinctions between causes of tension and causes of war, or else to a picture of contemporaries who failed to appreciate the dangers with which they were faced. More recently, sceptical voices have been raised regarding the possibility of genuinely 'British' history (Gaunt 1997). There may be a tendency for 'tokenism' in studying peripheral regions, and a risk of Anglocentric contextualization which remains obsessed with the English state and the chronologies of English history (Asch 1993: 117–27). It might be argued, however, that English dominance within the three kingdoms makes such 'enriched English history' perfectly appropriate. Russell may overstate Scottish impact upon the English political process, and that rather than Charles's English opponents being prisoners of the Scots, the Covenanters were treated as allies who were only half trusted (Fletcher 1993: 212; Morrill 1993: 260–3).

Assessment of revisionism and 'British history' can be undertaken on many levels and over many time frames, but this chapter focuses upon the period after 1637, and proposes moving the debate towards analysis of English opposition to Charles. A potential threat to recent scholarship lies in re-examining how those alienated by Stuart rule drew together in more or less informal, and more or less oppositional, networks, and in addressing their agenda. They were arguably a small yet aggressive group with a determined political programme, and with a vision which extended beyond Britain to Europe, and which was coloured by the Thirty Years' War and the threat to international Protestantism. Without retreating to a pre-revisionist agenda, and without advocating the existence of a revolutionary momentum, it is nevertheless possible to challenge revisionist conclusions. It is plausible to detect an oligarchic challenge to the Stuarts from within England, not least through New England colonial schemes, while recognizing that the ability to challenge Charles was hampered by the limited support for such an agenda in the nation at large, and the risk of acting treasonably. Such a challenge needed to be broached with great care in order to evade unwelcome attention from the king, and in order to avoid alienating potential supporters. The aim of John Pym and viscount Saye may have been to connect their disaffection with dissatisfaction in the country, and to exploit fears regarding religious innovation and popish plots. While war was not 'inevitable', it was increasingly likely, and superficial stability masked unease, discontent and opposition. This 'coiled spring' of godly zeal was mobilized by men who believed in the popish plot and genuinely sought power (Morrill 1993: 15). This is as much a 'context' of the road to war as events in Scotland and Ireland, and by reassessing the role of Pym and Saye it is possible to re-evaluate the relationship between England and the other Stuart kingdoms.

The Covenanter Rebellion

Within the work of revisionists and new British historians, the Scottish rebellion assumes profound importance. The riot which greeted the introduction of the English Prayer Book, the signing of the Scottish National Covenant, and the policies adopted by the Covenanters, are portrayed as the archetypal 'billiard ball'; the *deus ex machina* of the civil wars which engulfed the three kingdoms in 1642. The rebellion is considered to be an exogenous event impacting upon England, providing an inspiration and example to the king's English opponents, and forcing the king to react in ways which exposed and heightened tensions in all three kingdoms. It is portrayed as the event which heightened divisions which previously existed, but which had never seemed sufficiently serious to cause war. Events in Scotland were a reaction to early Stuart religious policy, and the attempt to impose religious unity across national boundaries, and to undermine a Presbyterian church which was considered threatening to monarchy, not least because of its claim to be divinely sanctioned. The rebellion thus attests to the difficulty of enforcing religious unity in a multiple monarchy, and the danger of an impatient pursuit of unpopular policies, and it has been used to demonstrate how longstanding tensions were transformed by policy blunders in the late 1630s. Charles and his ministers were largely responsible for creating the Covenanter movement, and for turning tension into crisis (Morrill 1990: 90–105).

Critics of revisionism have dismissed as overly simplistic a picture which emphasizes religion at the expense of money and politics. The origins of the Covenanter movement were arguably more diverse and of longer gestation than revisionists allow, and were rooted in the 'revocation' of land titles by Charles, the poverty of the Scottish nobility, and the floundering nature of the Scottish economy. Financial weakness and extravagance rendered ordinary revenues insufficient, and necessitated the use of extraordinary, and deeply unpopular, taxation. Indeed, it is plausible to talk of a crisis of government in Scotland, caused by an absentee court and systematic errors which arose from lack of understanding, clumsiness and failure to secure able advisers. Charles responded to hostility regarding the 'revocation' with harsh treatment of individuals and by weakening the political role of the nobility. By undermining the traditional ruling elite, and by imposing a contentious religious policy through churchmen, Charles reunited an old alliance of disgruntled aristocrats and kirkmen. He touched raw nerves and revived 'simmering' patriotism, a revolutionary ideology of covenanting reformation, and a political theory which sanctioned resistance to monarchs by inferior magistrates. While acknowledging the importance of events in the late 1630s, therefore, it is possible to suggest that mounting opposition and a revolutionary theory made conflict in Scotland increasingly likely (Macinnes 1991).

Just as contentious as the cause of the rebellion has been its impact, given that revisionists have accentuated policy blunders and the infectious nature of the Covenanter movement. Attention has been devoted to the way in which the Scottish privy council misinterpreted the seriousness of the rebellion, and to the fact that they dithered sufficiently to lose control of the situation. More important was the English military response, Charles refusing counsels of compromise despite the difficulties involved in waging war. Although the marquess of Hamilton was despatched to Scotland for talks, this was primarily aimed at buying time and at dividing the Covenanters through selective concessions. Hamilton's lack of preparation for the meeting of the general assembly of the Kirk in Glasgow (November 1638) resulted in his humiliating withdrawal, after which the rebels overthrew the royal supremacy, the bishops, and the high commission (Donald 1990). Furthermore, Charles's military policy transformed events in Scotland into a three kingdoms issue, and had profound repercussions for both England and Ireland. War exposed

the financial weakness of the crown, which hampered the response to the Covenanters, while the need for troops prompted the involvement of the Irish, who were
ordered to mobilize an army. Although Charles was entitled to use troops from one
kingdom in order to quell unrest in another, the idea of employing a Catholic Irish
army to defeat Scottish Protestants was symbolic and destabilizing, not least because
it provoked fears that such an army would be used against domestic opponents. If the
king sought to use such a threat to induce compliance, he succeeded only in
heightening tension once such a threat was perceived to be real (Russell 1991:
128). Meanwhile, the first 'Bishops War' saw only a military standoff, while Irish
assistance failed to materialize. Neither side was yet prepared for a fight, and the
English may have been inclined to make peace in order to limit the polarizing effect of
the conflict. Both sides, indeed, sought compromise, which was duly agreed at
Berwick in June 1639. That this proved to be a victory for the Scots, however, is
evident from the ability of the general assembly to reconvene (August 1639), and of
the Scottish parliament to ratify its decisions (September 1639).

The aborted nature of the first Bishops War, and the continuation of reform in
Scotland, heightened the chances of further military preparations. A new war was
being planned from December 1639, but such a policy clearly required the calling of
a parliament in England, in order to raise the money necessary to mobilize on
a sufficient scale to defeat the Scots. As a result, the Covenanters have been portrayed
as the means by which the 'personal rule' was brought to an end, and England's Short
Parliament (April–May 1640) might be said to have been 'made in Scotland' (Morrill
1990: 106). It was the expectation of a parliament which led to the first significant
drop in Ship Money receipts, and the meeting of parliament which presented an
opportunity for the expression of grievances in England, and which raised the
question of whether granting of money (supply) should precede, or follow, satisfactory response to such complaints. It was stalemate on this issue which ensured the
rapid dissolution of the assembly, an event followed not only by the arrest of leading
critics of the crown, but also by the unorthodox prolongation of the church 'parliament' (convocation), which granted extraordinary clerical taxation and passed controversial new canons.

Perhaps the most contentious way in which the Scots have been considered influential in English affairs is through their politically radical agenda for reform, and their
confederalist vision for Britain (ibid.: 74–8). The Scots reassured the English about
their intentions, yet clearly sought to elicit support from potential allies. Indeed, the
Covenanters appreciated the necessity of challenging royal power in England as well
as in Scotland, and the necessity of exporting their revolution. The Scottish rebellion
thus proved impossible to contain north of the border, and inevitably threatened to
contaminate the other Stuart kingdoms. Russell suggested that 'the ideas, the actions,
and the sheer infectious force of their example all did a great deal to encourage the
English Parliament and its supporters' (Russell 1991: 44). The Scots certainly waged
a propaganda campaign in England, to which Charles failed to respond, but to which
his English opponents warmed. The Covenanters found the English Puritans 'receptive' to their ideas, and contacts were forged with leading opponents of Charles in
order to force the summoning of parliament in England. Moreover, the Scottish
parliament and 'committee of estates' provided a model for the English to follow in
terms of specific policies. In December 1639 it had been decided that parliament

could not be dissolved without its own consent, and after the Scottish parliament reconvened on 2 June 1640, it implemented a profound constitutional revolution, with measures to ensure triennial parliaments, the abolition of the Committee of Articles (by which its predecessors had been dominated by Whitehall), and with the demand for a role in the selection of office-holders (ibid.: 61–2).

There is a degree of consensus regarding the nature of the problem confronting Charles by the summer of 1640. He faced co-ordinated opposition in England and Scotland, and the second Bishops War was triggered by a pre-emptive Scottish invasion (22 August 1640) which was encouraged by the Covenanters' English supporters, who had been engaged in correspondence regarding tactical matters. Whether the embarrassment of the English forces which ensued was a product of strategic errors rather than overwhelming Covenanter strength, and whether it symbolized wider governmental and religious problems, as well as weakened morale and a lack of English support for the king, the defeat at Newburn (28 August 1640) and the Scots' occupation of Newcastle precipitated a new crisis in England. Charles summoned his peers to York, where he faced overwhelming pressure for another parliament from the 'twelve peers'. If the Scots were in the driving seat from 1637 until the calling of the Short Parliament, then the vehicle used to force Charles into the arms of another parliament in October 1640 had dual controls.

However, just as it is possible to challenge the revisionist reading of events within Scotland in order to reassert structural weaknesses, and tensions produced by early Stuart rule, so it is also possible to question the extent to which the English were mobilized by, and responsive to, the Scots. Doubts can be raised regarding the role of the covenanting rebellion as a 'billiard ball'. Russell concedes that Scottish propaganda was circulated by the 'more adventurous' of the English godly, and that we are unable to measure the extent of this network (Russell 1991: 61). However, this is arguably only the tip of a more problematic iceberg threatening the revisionist argument. It is, in fact, possible to detect the existence of profound and long-standing cross-border Puritan connections, and of an Anglo-Scottish Protestant culture based upon both print and personal contacts. Print was a key means for mutual encouragement, and tracts by English Puritans were published in Edinburgh in the 1620s, and read by leading Covenanters during the early 1630s. Personal contacts, meanwhile, were probably more common than written correspondence, which was treasonable, and secretive meetings between English and Scottish Puritans were occurring months before the rebellion. Rather than simply taking their lead from the Covenanters, members of the Anglo-Irish opposition to Charles encouraged the Scots to pursue specific policies, such as 'root and branch' church reform. Such mutual encouragement by opponents of Stuart policy may mean that the Scottish rebellion signalled confidence regarding English support, as much as an attempt to create allies. Personal contacts became increasingly common after the outbreak of rebellion, with Nathaniel Fiennes attending the Scottish general assembly in July 1639, and the Scots being offered encouragement regarding their religious demands, and with Covenanter ministers visiting England (Morrill 1990: 96–100). Having detected that key English figures encouraged the Scots in the late 1630s, it becomes possible to reassess the degree to which the Civil War had English as much as British origins, and reflected English concerns. Beyond this, the attitude of English Puritans towards the Scots remains open to question, particularly regarding the extent to which they rejected the Covenanter vision of confederal uniformity, and the extent to which they had a British vision at all.

The Long Parliament

In addition to assessing the extent to which the Scots acted as the motor of historical developments after 1637, it is also crucial to examine their role after the assembly of the Long Parliament in November 1640. Revisionists are far from being unanimous about the importance of the Scots and Irish in English affairs, or about the attitudes, ideas and motivations of Charles's English opponents, but the most provocative of recent accounts have placed greatest emphasis upon the Scots. Although it is salutary to be reminded that war was still far from 'inevitable', and that negotiations remained feasible during the first year of the parliament, the revisionist case remains open to challenge, in terms of its interpretation of both the situation within England and the influence of Ireland and Scotland. It is possible to question whether the ostensible desire for a negotiated settlement reflected a genuine desire for peace, or rather the realization that neither the king nor his English opponents could yet count on support from sufficient numbers of their countrymen on a battlefield.

The Scots were certainly in a strong position after Newburn, and provided an 'alternative political model' and an 'alternative power base' (Russell 1991: 145). Defeat for Charles and the occupation of Newcastle by Covenanter forces ensured that the rebels could try to dictate the terms of a peace settlement, and that their removal would require either money or political concessions, or both. The possibility of yet another military campaign doubtless encouraged the Scots to undermine the king's power, which explains the lengthy nature of their negotiations with Charles, at Ripon (October 1640) and later at London. Not only was Charles compelled to call parliament, but a quick dissolution would also prove difficult, since money was not likely to be approved before attention was devoted to grievances which had only increased since the Short Parliament. This is clearly an important context for understanding the opening months of the Long Parliament, and some of the policies pushed through would not have been successful in any other situation. What is less easily determined is the extent to which the measures passed while Charles's hands were tied reflected a Scottish agenda, or an agenda favoured by the king's English opponents. Parliament, it has been suggested, was less a means for the English to rectify domestic grievances than the arena in which the Scots and Irish demanded reform, and where the policies implemented reflected the extent to which the English had learnt from, and sought to copy, their brethren in Scotland. For Russell, the first six months of the parliament is predominantly a Scottish story. The policies pursued reflected their need to prevent the king from starting another war without parliamentary consent, and to destroy his religious policy. What we witness during this period, therefore, is the Scots working behind a 'front' of English allies, with a 'shopping list' of demands, including 'root and branch' reform of the church, the abolition of episcopacy, and the impeachment of William Laud (ibid.: 180–2). Likewise, Protestant Irish settlers sought to exert pressure by sending a delegation from the Irish parliament to lobby on issues such as Strafford. Revisionists have also stressed that Scottish demands helped form a royalist party, for while there was consensus on the need for reform, the Scots overplayed their hand with the radicalism of their policy demands. England, in short, was essentially stable and consensual until the disturbance provided by the Scots polarized the political classes, inspiring both imitators (parliamentarians) and opponents (royalists).

There were certainly limits to unanimity among the English on the desirability of reform in 1640. Many future royalists agreed on the need for action regarding recusants, the canons and Ship Money, and some approved of the removal and punishment of prominent courtiers, and on moderate ecclesiastical reform. However, there was little consensus beyond this limited agenda, and the nature of a more substantial settlement proved controversial. Having said this, it is difficult to demonstrate with certainty that policies for 'further reformation' represented a Scottish agenda, rather than an agenda shared by the Covenanters and their English allies. Russell identifies those who were most radical among the English but questions their strength and says that they represent 'something less than a revolutionary head of steam' (ibid.: 204). While revolutionary zeal may indeed have been lacking, it is more difficult to dismiss the existence of pressure within England for genuine reform.

There are grounds for arguing, as even some revisionists have done, that Russell underemphasized the support for reform in England, and that it is crucial to assess the agenda of Pym and Saye, as well as their ability to create a party. It is possible to argue that they were more enthusiastic for church reform than Russell allows, and that annual parliaments were on the agenda in England long before they were introduced in Scotland (Fletcher 1993: 213–14). The king's critics were not mere ciphers for the Scots. Furthermore, the limited size of the reformist faction is less important than their influence, and their ability to foster a wider movement for change. The central difficulty for determining such questions is the absence of documentary evidence regarding relations between the English reformers and their Covenanter allies, which necessitates the extrapolation of intentions from recorded actions. It is difficult to demonstrate definitively that the Scots were making the running, or to make unambiguous claims regarding the attitudes of Pym's group. The debate on revisionism goes to the heart of the problems of historical evidence: the difficulty of understanding events, intentions and motivations in the absence of perfect knowledge of the past; and the danger of relying upon surviving records when not all crucial evidence was recorded.

The revisionist picture may be no more plausible than one which depicts a small but zealous core of reformers who were prepared to treat the Scots as allies rather than masters. Although their attitude seems more conciliatory than that of the Scots, the English reformers probably recognized the need to carry both parliament and the people along with them. Since support for extensive reform was limited, the reformers needed to reveal their demands in such a way as to avoid alienating potential supporters. This is not to say that Pym and Saye opposed negotiations, at least until the late spring of 1641. However, more attention has been paid to the tactics employed by Charles than to those of his critics. The king sought to divide his English and Scottish enemies with both offers and threats, and consistently raised the stakes. His English critics, meanwhile, arguably sought to demand as much reform as they could without losing support or creating enemies within parliament. Settlement was likely to be purchased, from Charles's point of view, by the reform of public office, either through the appointment of specific officers, or by means of new political structures. His opening offer involved nominations to top jobs, and the introduction of a 'moderated episcopacy', in the hope of weakening the constituency of support for 'root and branch' reform. His English critics secured the passage of the Triennial Act to ensure regular parliaments (February 1641), and sought the abolition of high commission and Star Chamber, but were prepared to offer the revival of the 'Great Contract', the attempted financial settlement brokered in 1610, or alternatively a grant of the excise. More important, however, were demands for church reform and the removal of both Strafford and Laud, which were always likely to prove difficult for Charles to accept, and to pose a threat to negotiations.

It can be demonstrated that pressure for action against Strafford and Laud, and for root and branch church reform, came in part from the Irish and the Scots, in order to prevent an accommodation between the king and his English critics. It is not necessary, however, to proceed to an assertion that Pym and Saye pursued such policies in order to reassure the Scots and Irish. In analysing a four-cornered negotiating process, it is easier to identify the pressures being brought to bear by each participant than to make firm conclusions about why politicians adopted particular courses of action. It is possible to recognize an English motivation for church reform, for punitive action against Laud, and for the trial, attainder and execution of Strafford, not least to place pressure on the king, and as a reaction to the 'Army Plot' and the attempt to free Strafford and intimidate parliament.

It can be stated with more confidence that Strafford's fate, together with the death of the earl of Bedford (9 May 1641), scuppered prospects for a negotiated settlement, not least because Charles realized that he could raise a party around Sir Edward Hyde (later earl of Clarendon), Sir John Culpepper and viscount Falkland. Once it became clear that these moderate or 'constitutional royalists' no longer sought further reform, Pym and Saye were arguably able to behave in a more assertive manner, and to raise the political stakes. They asserted parliament's power to influence such appointments with the 'Ten Propositions' (24 June 1641). They also re-floated demands for religious reform and the abolition of the secular power of the bishops (July 1641). The 'Protestation' oath (3 May 1641) provided a means of identifying supporters and opponents of reform, and perhaps reflected and accelerated the polarization process. Furthermore, since the emergence of a 'royalist' party and the impossibility of settlement raised the prospects for a dissolution of parliament, it became necessary to close this option with the so-called 'perpetual parliament' Act (10 May 1641). Charles was effectively told to decide between securing financial stability (through the grant of Tonnage and Poundage) and retaining the bishops' role in the House of Lords, and perhaps even in the church hierarchy.

In order to stress the distance which still needed to be travelled before the country descended into war, revisionists have drawn attention to the length of time between the failure of settlement in England and the outbreak of conflict, and to the importance of the British context for understanding events at Westminster (Russell 1991: 302). However, it is possible to question at least part of their argument. It can be argued, for example, that the dynamic of English politics between May 1641 and August 1642 was as much about preparation for war as it was about reluctance to enter the field of battle. The proto-parliamentarians were arguably ready for war by May 1641, but lacked a party in the country with which to challenge the king, and still lacked a firm grip on the City of London, with its financial resources, and the House of Lords, where support for reform, and for an aggressive policy towards the king, was weakest. The reformers may have recognized that the sense of national crisis which was necessary in order to garner support was yet lacking in the localities in the summer of 1641 (Fletcher 1981: 81).

It is certainly true that events continued to be played out in a British, rather than a purely English, arena, and this has been used to demonstrate both that war could still have been prevented and that the impetus for war continued to come from external pressures. The Scots have been portrayed as having held the key not merely to the emergence of divisions within England, but also to the possible defusing of tension (Russell 1991: ch. 8). The king, therefore, spent the second half of 1641 seeking to remove the Scots from England and to prevent a combination between his Scottish and English critics. He pursued a double strategy of approaching both the Covenanters (around Argyll) and their opponents (around Montrose), the division between whom, and the secretive Cumbernauld band (August 1640), came to light in the spring of 1641, as hopes of an English settlement faded. Once again, however, a possible settlement was hampered not by intrinsic divisions, but by Charles's tactical blunders, and when his attempt to woo the anti-Covenanters had become evident (June 1641), the Covenanters and their English allies drew closer together. Nevertheless, the king's mission to Scotland in the summer of 1641 once again heralded negotiations with the Covenanter regime, and although his tactics were confused and contradictory, he proved willing to make concessions, and to bow to the measures passed in Scotland since 1637. His aim was to contain the revolution, to prevent it from providing a precedent for the English, and to enable him to concentrate on the domestic threat. However, while such negotiations offered a real chance to neuter the Covenanter threat, it arguably did little to solve all of his problems. While domestic critics were weakened by the 'defection' of the Covenanters, this posed a major concern to the English reformers only in so far as they had ever been 'dependent' upon the Scots.

The more aggressive policy pursued by Saye and Pym in the summer of 1641 became clear as a result of the royal journey to Scotland, as parliament addressed the governance of the country in the king's absence. In terms of the radicalism of the king's opponents, it is certainly instructive to observe that calls were initially made for the appointment of a *custos regni* (keeper of the crown), for although this revealed hostility to the monarchical power of Charles I, it did not imply opposition to the monarchy *per se*, and in seeking to remove powers from the king it implied transferring them to another powerful individual. Only when proposals for the *custos regni* failed did the idea emerge to invest parliament with such power. For that portion of the king's absence when parliament went into recess, power was held by the first in a long line of powerful select bodies from within its ranks, the 'recess committee'. There was, however, a greater risk to the settlement being brokered by the king than the attitude of his English opponents regarding the locus of power. This was the king's behaviour in Scotland, and the precarious nature of the situation became evident in early October 1641, when news arrived in England of 'the Incident': the attempt to arrest and kill Hamilton and Argyll, perhaps with the king's consent. This was exploited by Charles's opponents as evidence of his untrustworthiness, but the chances of 'the Incident' having a lasting and profound impact were limited by the rapidly unfolding events in another of Charles's kingdoms.

The Irish Rebellion

As the English were coming to terms with the repercussions of the king's visit to Scotland and of 'the Incident', a Catholic rebellion broke out in Ireland (23 October 1641), which led eventually to the creation of a provisional 'confederate' Catholic government at Kilkenny. The rebels claimed to be acting on orders from the king, which while impossible to prove, was certainly considered plausible. The arrival of news of the rebellion on 1 November has been portrayed as a significant factor in polarizing opinion in England. Ireland offers perhaps the best example of a 'billiard ball', in the sense of an outside event which had an impact upon England. Until the outbreak of the rebellion the campaign for reform in England was running out of steam, and the king had reached agreement with the Scots, both of which lessened the chances of war. The Irish rebellion threw everything into confusion once again (Russell 1990b: ch. 15).

However, the Irish rebellion can itself be related to events unfolding in Scotland and England in the late 1630s and early 1640s. Rather than being seen as a random intervention from without, it was arguably the logical result of the rise of an aggressive and expansionist Covenanter movement, and of Anglo-Scottish *rapprochement* which was explicitly anti-popish in nature. The Irish rebellion can thus be portrayed as a response to the threat posed to Irish Catholicism. It is also possible to recognize that the rebellion might never have taken place without the English crown having been severely weakened, and that Catholic fears and resentment had long-term causes involving the land settlement and the future of Catholicism within a multiple kingdom. The story of early Stuart and particularly Caroline rule was one in which many elements of Irish society became aggrieved. Catholics felt betrayed by the failure to implement the 'Graces', an attempt to prevent Catholic resentment while pursuing war with Spain in the 1620s by means of religious concessions. Strafford's lieutenancy of Ireland in the 1630s, furthermore, saw the imposition of the 'black oath' upon Ulster Scots, creating resentment which later emerged in Covenanter demands for action against the Lord Lieutenant, while the attempt to raise a Catholic army with which to fight the Covenanters helped push grandees such as the earl of Argyll into the Covenanter camp. The Covenanter rebellion, in turn, inspired the Irish by offering an example of what could be achieved by resisting an English government, and by provoking fear regarding the Scottish threat, and resentment over the death of Strafford. Meanwhile, the grievances of the Protestant settlers in Londonderry, epitomized by Sir John Clotworthy, resulted in the delivery of the 'Remonstrance' to the Long Parliament (7 November 1640) and in pressure for the overthrow of Strafford. Furthermore, Charles once again failed to fulfill a promise to implement the 'Graces', made when he had given up hope of an English settlement (April 1641).

Moving from the causes to the impact of the Irish rebellion, the crucial issue was how to deal with the rebels, which raised the problem of how to levy, and who should command, a military force. The Irish rebellion worsened relations between king and parliament not only because of suspicion regarding the king's complicity, but also because it placed them on a collision course over control of the army. This question eventually led to parliament's highly controversial militia ordinance in 1642, and provided one of the final triggers for war. The renewed tension in England was epitomized by the introduction of the 'Grand Remonstrance' (8 November 1641), which was passed amid much acrimony on 22 November, and which not only addressed the people as much as the king, but also provided a detailed catalogue of grievances dating back to 1625, invoked the popish threat, and demanded church reform and the removal of 'evil councillors'.

Although the Irish rebellion had a profound impact upon affairs at Westminster, and upon relations between king and parliament, it is important to stress why this should have been so. In order to understand the significance of the rebellion it is necessary to examine its impact in the country at large, rather than merely on high politics. The Irish rebellion not only created tension, but also exposed existing divisions, and fed into long-standing fears and prejudices. The English reacted as they did because of pre-existing concerns regarding the existence of, and threat from, a popish plot (Shagan 1997). Little over fifty years after the Spanish Armada, and less than forty years after the Gunpowder Plot, such fears were never far from the surface. This is particularly important in the context of the Thirty Years' War, a pan-European conflict in which Ireland was a potential 'back door' through which the forces of Catholicism could gain entry into England. Furthermore, it is crucial to recognize that news of the rebellion, and of the atrocities associated with it, was exploited by the English in order to stoke fears regarding the Catholic threat. The aftermath of the Irish rebellion witnessed the first evidence of the print explosion with which the road to civil war has become synonymous, and reveals the importance of the popular print medium in the process of polarizing the country, and of forming the parties that went to war (Lindley 1972). In this process of exploiting the rebellion the parliamentarians at Westminster were probably instrumental, or at least complicit, using the situation in order to connect their reforming agenda with popular anti-Catholicism, and creating a union of interests between the centre and the localities which had hitherto been absent. If the rebellion fostered polarization and helped create 'parties', then it was partly because certain figures at Westminster recognized its potential to do so.

Given the tension produced by the arguments that raged, and the policies which were pursued, in the wake of the Irish rebellion, and the disastrous attempt to arrest 'Five members' of the Commons and one peer in January 1642, it is perhaps remarkable that England remained at peace for so long, particularly given the king's withdrawal from London. Perhaps it is a testament to the stability of the period, and the reluctance to go to war, that even the most flagrant breach of parliamentary privilege could not trigger fighting. Revisionist analysis stresses that both 'royalists' and 'parliamentarians' retained reasons for avoiding conflict, not the least of which was the desire to avoid being perceived as the aggressor (Russell 1991: 454–62). It is also the case, however, that politicians were seeking to secure positions of strength for the impending conflagration. It is probable that the petitioning campaigns of early 1642 were both organized at the centre, and reflected genuine local feeling, and their publication certainly indicates a systematic attempt to capitalize upon their presenta-tion, and to convey to the world the strength of support for parliament. Sermons and pamphlets were used by both sides in order to rabble-rouse, mobilize and politicize the public, who would have to fight for, and finance, a war. Such works helped to ensure that by the summer of 1642, unlike in the summer of 1641, there existed a close union between the central leadership and the localities, and a sense of national crisis. The desire to promote and test popular support, and to demonstrate its existence, probably explains the renewed importance of the Protestation in early 1642, and in addition to the need to secure, and broadcast, popular support in the country, it was vital to ensure the existence of a solid core of reforming zeal within the House of Lords. This arguably did not exist at any time before February 1642, when Pym's allies in the Lords secured a dominant position in the wake of the impeachment of the twelve bishops (30 December 1641), the removal of the churchmen by the terms of the Clerical Disabilities Act (13 February) and the withdrawal of many royalist peers (Fletcher 1981: 243).

Part of this process of preparing for an ever more likely conflict was the 'phoney' or 'paper' war, in which parliamentarians and royalists traded blows in print in the months preceding the trading of mortar and musket fire. In addition to the many declarations which traversed the country, the early months of 1642 witnessed the refusal to allow Charles entry to the garrison at Hull, and the passage of the militia ordinance, wherein parliament signalled its intent to 'legislate' even in the absence of royal assent. Revisionists have sought to remove another prop supporting Whiggish theories relating to the rise of constitutional crisis, by stressing that the arguments deployed by parliament fell short of a full statement of parliamentary sovereignty, and that parliamentarians adapted their views under pressure, and felt their way in the dark (Russell 1990a: 132–50). Other historians, however, have refocused attention upon early Stuart political argument in order to demonstrate that parliamentarian ideas dated back to the early part of the century, albeit they now served more radical ends (Sommerville 1986). Furthermore, the Nineteen Propositions (1 June 1642) heralded the demand for a significant extension of parliament's powers, even if only during a period of 'imminent dangers'. Indeed, it is possible that certain parliamentarians remained worried about revealing their political colours, and about the degree of support which such views would garner. Consideration of the king's response to the Nineteen Propositions revealed a willingness to compromise which vindicated such fears, and the views of those in the vanguard of parliamentarianism are best found in the statements of writers and theorists such as Henry Parker, rather than in official declarations. That such debates continued for so long is probably a reflection not only of the need to convince potential supporters in parliament and the country, but also of the vital need for both sides to set in place their war machines. Parliament needed to implement the militia ordinance, while royalists needed to secure support upon the proclamation of commissions of array. Both sides needed to raise money, and to seize control of local government, and only when these processes were complete could the king raise his standard at Nottingham (22 August 1642), signalling the onset of war.

Conclusion

Revisionism and 'new British history' have altered seventeenth-century history for good, and undoubtedly for the better. It is unquestionably valuable to recognize that war could have been avoided, and the lengths to which people went to stress their reluctance to allow fighting to break out. It is also worthwhile to return attention to the detailed chronology, to Charles I, and to events within the three kingdoms. It is clearly necessary to understand the nature, dynamic and impact of events throughout Britain, and the nature of the relationships between the Stuart kingdoms. Nevertheless, it is possible to challenge the new British history, and revisionism's understanding of the outbreak of civil war. It may be possible to develop the kind of 'post-revisionist' picture which both learns from and challenges recent scholarship, and which recognizes the existence of culture clashes, ideological divisions, functional breakdown, and British history, as well as the possibility for a patched-up settlement, and the role of contingency and chance, political characters and foibles. It is possible to recognize the importance of political misunderstanding and mistrust, and of a spiral of threats that helped widen a gap that may otherwise have been bridgeable, as well as ideological conflict and structural weakness.

The vital area on which work needs to focus is the 'opposition' to Charles I within England, and future parliamentarian leaders such as Saye and Pym who were most disgruntled with Caroline rule (Fletcher 1981: 408). It is possible to accept that nobody wanted war, or would admit to being prepared to fight, while recognizing that conflict became increasingly difficult to avoid, and something which some people were prepared to contemplate, should other avenues fail. While few wanted war, let alone 'revolution', some undoubtedly sought profound changes regarding religion and political power. Given that such critics of Charles were probably limited in number, and that they ran the risk of being accused of treason, relying upon their public statements may result in misrepresentation of their aims, since there was a risk of pushing too far and too fast, and of failing to carry with them the bulk of the political nation. Their task was arguably to press for reform as quickly as possible while ensuring that they did not run ahead of what was politically acceptable, and that they were seen to be responding to the wishes of the nation at large. Pym and Saye may have had a more radical policy than they were prepared to admit. They may not have sought permanent reform of the constitution, but they certainly sought to secure the means of preventing Charles from doing what he was doing, and perhaps sought to reassert the need for parliamentary control of emergency powers, as a counterweight to the crown. It is not necessary to impute to such men revolutionary intentions, demands for parliamentary sovereignty, or anything other than a 'baronial' agenda in order to recognize the aggressive nature of their actions and intentions. Nevertheless, their agenda was probably more complex, and they may have been aware that the 'language' of baronialism was perfect for a culture dominated by the need for historical justification and precedents, and which feared innovation. There is certainly evidence that contemporaries found the language adopted by such men in public was less forthright than that which was evident in private, and in parliamentary committees. Furthermore, even if Pym and Saye formed a minority, they were powerful and influential, and exploited events of the late 1630s in order to play upon old fears, most notably relating to the existence of a popish plot and the threat to both liberties and parliament. Such issues were inextricably linked, and were certainly portrayed as such, even if only in the sense that certain grandees tapped into religious concerns for ends that were not strictly religious.

By re-evaluating the position of Charles's most severe critics in England it is also possible to question the notion of 'billiard balls' and the 'three kingdoms' approach to the origins of civil war. While the events that led to the outbreak of war were played out in the British arena, the Scots and the Irish did not necessarily dominate them, and the king's English enemies were not necessarily dependent upon, or inspired by, critics in other kingdoms. Events in Scotland and Ireland are crucially important for a full *understanding* of the civil wars, but may not provide the key to *explaining* their occurrence. Events in England may be sufficient for such an explanation, and are certainly more important than they appear in some recent accounts. Even when the English appear to respond to events in Scotland and Ireland, they can be shown to have reacted in ways that were structured by their historical experience, and by the distinctive character of English political culture. Furthermore, while the 'billiard ball' idea relies upon notions of distinct entities that impacted upon each other, it is plausible to challenge the existence of separate English, Irish and Scottish cultures, whether political, religious, social or economic. It is possible to recognize a pan-national Puritanism, and to refigure the rebellions in England, Ireland and Scotland as the product, at least in part, of co-operative effort.

Ultimately, studying the outbreak of the civil wars, and its treatment in recent scholarship, raises profound historiographical questions. Scholars have developed more rigorous understanding of the sources, and of concepts such as 'context', 'causality' and 'inevitability'. However, revisionism has arguably sought to refocus the question of the war's 'causes' by moving the goalposts in order to establish when war became inevitable. This ensures that the focus of attention is shifted to events after 1637, and risks confusing separate inquiries. It would be dangerous to move from a conclusion that war was not inevitable until sometime after the assembly of the Long Parliament, to a conclusion which denied that there were long-term 'causes', or that war became increasingly likely. Recent scholarship also raises the question of how to reach historical understanding when faced with evidence which may be, or even must be, partial and incomplete. This forces the historian to extrapolate intentions from recorded actions, and to make *judgements* regarding the nature of politics and the political process. Revisionism has been accused of underplaying the element of 'ideology' in the politics of Pym and Saye, of being overly literal in its reading of seventeenth-century politics, and over-reliant on surviving records. While this is an understandable and even laudable project, it arguably fails to recognize important elements of practical political life, such as the need for politicians to play their cards close to their chest in order to build alliances and factions, and ensure the passage of particular measures, and the need to garner popular support by means of what the modern world would call 'spin', and the exploitation and manipulation of public opinion. Of course, an approach which claims that what men said was not necessarily what they thought is both realistic and historically problematic, and arguably as dangerous as an approach that is extremely literal. Nevertheless, revisionism can never be said to have sacrificed *judgement* in favour of *evidence*, and the difficult judgements involved in such issues provide one of the keys to the historian's craft, as they form a key part of the human condition.

REFERENCES

Asch, R. (ed.) 1993: *The Three Nations – a Common History?* Bochum.
Cust, R. and Hughes, A. (eds) 1997: *The English Civil War*. London.
Donald, P. 1990: *An Uncounselled King: Charles I and the Scottish Troubles, 1637–1641*: Cambridge.

Fletcher, A. 1981: *The Outbreak of the English Civil War*. London.
Fletcher, A. 1993: 'Power, myths and realities', *Historical Journal*, vol. 36.
Gaunt, P. 1997: *The British Wars, 1637–51*: London.
Hughes, A. 1998: *The Causes of the English Civil War*, 2nd edn: Basingstoke.
Lindley, K. 1972: 'The impact of the 1641 rebellion upon England and Wales, 1641–5', *Irish Historical Studies*.
Macinnes, A. 1991: *Charles I and the Making of the Covenanting Movement, 1625–1641*: Edinburgh.
Morrill, J. (ed.) 1990: *The Scottish National Covenant in its British Context*: Edinburgh.
Morrill, J. 1993: *The Nature of the English Revolution*: London.
Russell, C. 1979: *Parliaments and English Politics, 1621–1629*: Oxford.
Russell, C. 1990a: *The Causes of the English Civil War*. Oxford.
Russell, C. 1990b: *Unrevolutionary England, 1603–1642*: London.
Russell, C. 1991: *The Fall of the British Monarchies 1637–1642*: Oxford.
Russell, C. 1993: 'The Scottish party in English parliaments 1640–2, or, the myth of the English revolution', *Historical Research*.
Shagan, E. 1997: 'Constructing discord: ideology, propaganda and English responses to the Irish rebellion of 1641', *Journal of British Studies*, 36, 1, 4–34.
Sommerville, J. P. 1986: *Politics and Ideology in England, 1603–40*: London.
Stone, L. 1972: *The Causes of the English Revolution, 1529–1642*: London.

FURTHER READING

Bradshaw, B. and Morrill, J. (eds) 1996: *The British Problem, c.1534–1707: State Formation in the Atlantic Archipelago*: Basingstoke.
Burgess, G. (ed.) 1999: *The New British History: Founding a Modern State 1603–1715*: London.
Cust, R. and Hughes, A. (eds) 1997: *The English Civil War*: London.
Donald, P. 1990: *An Uncounselled King: Charles I and the Scottish Troubles, 1637–1641*: Cambridge.
Ellis, S. G. and Barber, S. (eds) 1995: *Conquest and Union: Fashioning a British State, 1485–1725*: London.
Fletcher, A. 1981: *The Outbreak of the English Civil War*. London.
Gaunt, P. 1997: *The British Wars, 1637–51*: London.
Hughes, A. 1998: *The Causes of the English Civil War*, 2nd edn: Basingstoke.
Lindley, K. 1972: 'The impact of the 1641 rebellion upon England and Wales, 1641–5', *Irish Historical Studies*.
Macinnes, A. 1991: *Charles I and the Making of the Covenanting Movement, 1625–1641*: Edinburgh.
Moody, T. W., Martin, F. X. and Byrne, F. J. (eds) 1976: *A New History of Ireland, Vol. 3*: Oxford.
Morrill, J. (ed.) 1990: *The Scottish National Covenant in its British Context*: Edinburgh.
Morrill, J. 1993: *The Nature of the English Revolution*: London.
Russell, C. 1979: *Parliaments and English Politics, 1621–1629*: Oxford.
Russell, C. 1990a: *The Causes of the English Civil War*. Oxford.
Russell, C. 1990b: *Unrevolutionary England, 1603–1642*: London.
Russell, C. 1991: *The Fall of the British Monarchies 1637–1642*: Oxford.
Russell, C. 1993: 'The Scottish party in English parliaments 1640–2, or, the myth of the English revolution', *Historical Research*.

Shagan, E. 1997: 'Constructing discord: ideology, propaganda and English responses to the Irish rebellion of 1641', *Journal of British Studies*, 36, 1, 4–34.

Stevenson, D. 1973: *The Scottish Revolution, 1637–1644: The Triumph of the Covenanters*. Newton Abbot.

PART IV

Stuart Britain, 1642–1660

CHAPTER SIXTEEN

The Wars of the Three Kingdoms, 1642–1649

DAVID SCOTT

For sheer spectacle and violence there are few decades in British or Irish history to rival the 1640s. Between the raising of the royal standard at Nottingham in August 1642, and Charles I's beheading outside the Banqueting House on 30 January 1649, a higher proportion of the English people was killed as a result of the kingdom's 'intestinal broils' than was slaughtered in the trenches during the First World War. The 1640s witnessed the birth and demise of Catholic Ireland's first independent government before 1919 – a struggle for greater political and religious freedom that wiped out about a quarter of the island's entire population. Scotland, too, capitalized on the collapse of English power, exerting a greater influence across the 'Atlantic archipelago' than at any other time in her history, although again at a massive cost in lives, property, and, in the end, to national autonomy.

The wars in and between England, Ireland, and Scotland during the period 1637 to 1653 have generated a huge if rather uneven historical literature. Until the publication of Micheál Ó Siochrú's *Confederate Ireland 1642–1649* (1999) there was no dedicated volume on the political and constitutional history of the Catholic Irish during the 1640s; and the kingdom's Protestants still await a comprehensive study. Scotland during the 1640s has been rather better served thanks to four monographs by David Stevenson on the Covenanter regime and its domestic and Irish opponents, and to John Young's (1996) book, *The Scottish Parliament 1639–1661*. More has probably been written on aspects of the English Civil War than on Caroline Scotland and Ireland put together. But if we are looking for a detailed narrative that spans the entire Civil War era in England then we have to go back to S. R. Gardiner's *History of the Great Civil War* published in the 1880s and 1890s.

Many works on the English Civil War have begun with the remark that the conflict divides historians today just as it did contemporaries. But the major division among historians has been, and still is, about the origins of the war rather than its course or consequences. Some of the most stimulating recent work on the English Civil War – for example, Conrad Russell's *The Fall of the British Monarchies* and Anthony Fletcher's *The Outbreak of the English Civil War* – stops in the summer of 1642. There are no detailed modern studies that bridge the 1642 divide, or pick up where Russell and Fletcher left off, and take the story down to Charles's execution or beyond. What we have instead are a number of books that gloss the period 1640 to 1660, numerous local studies of varying quality, and a series of scholarly works focusing on just a few years of the 1640s.

The historical disjuncture created by the resort to arms in 1642 has been reinforced by recent historiographical trends. Since the late 1970s, 'revisionist' historians have done their best to destroy the notion of a 'high road to civil war'. The implication in most revisionist work is that England's troubles during the 1640s were largely the product of contingent, short-term causes. In this framework, there were no profound connections between the collapse of the Caroline regime in 1640 and the regicide in 1649. The course and outcome of the civil wars were the products of an aberrant political environment; bizarre developments stimulated by the necessity of war. It is hardly surprising therefore that the revisionists have shown little interest in straying beyond 1642.

Revisionism may have reinforced the 1642 barrier. On the other hand, it has done the study of the 1640s an invaluable service in undermining the notion inherent in Whig and Marxist histories that the English Civil War was both self-generated and self-contained. Russell's more recent work on the origins of the Civil War has demonstrated just how hard it is to make sense of the slide into civil war in England without reference to the preceding upheavals in Scotland and Ireland. Some historians, notably John Morrill, would like to take this holistic approach further, and have criticized Russell for invoking the Covenanter and Irish uprisings merely to explain the fall of the English monarchy, rather than treating all three crises as the breakdown of a single system with common, interlocking causes.

This debate is just one aspect of the recent vogue for treating the archipelago as the most useful conceptual framework for understanding the histories of its component peoples – a body of work known as the New British History. An archipelagic perspective seems, on the face of it, peculiarly applicable to the closely intertwined histories of the Stuart monarchies during the 1640s, and promises a major shake-up in the way the mid-seventeenth century is studied. It may not be able to answer all the questions that historians have traditionally asked of the period. Nevertheless, a fully integrated account of the wars of the three kingdoms would bridge the 1642 divide in English history, and perhaps render a more faithful picture of how the wars were experienced and comprehended by contemporaries than the sometimes insular approach to the period that prevailed on both sides of the Irish Sea for most of the last century.

The Wars of the Three Kingdoms

The historian who has proselytized hardest for the merits of British history in relation to the 1640s is John Morrill. In a series of overlapping essays he has advanced several models for conceptualizing the nature of the interactions and relationship between the three Stuart monarchies. After over a decade working on the 'war(s) of the three kingdoms' (Morrill 1999: 67), he remains uncertain whether we can speak of a single archipelagic conflict or history in the period 1637–53. Yet he insists that in constitutional, political, religious and military terms it simply does not make sense to treat the history of mid-seventeenth century England, Scotland and Ireland as three separate histories. The wars and much of their associated politics, he argues, can best be seen as the product of a dialectical process whereby events in each one of the kingdoms shaped the affairs of the other two.

Attractive as the Morrillian approach might seem to some historians, it does not yet enjoy the status of orthodoxy. One obvious objection is that many developments within the component parts of the archipelago can be explained without reference to a British dimension. At the other end of the spectrum, Jane Ohlmeyer, Jonathan Scott and others have argued that a three kingdoms perspective is actually restrictive, and that the only adequate analytical framework is Europe. In other words, the wars need to be viewed as part of the General Crisis of the mid-seventeenth century, or the religious polarization of the Thirty Years' War. If one is looking at the *causes* of the conflicts in Britain and Ireland, then the notion of a European context to the outbreak of the wars has much to recommend it. Irish and Scottish perceptions of the threat from London, for example, or the English reaction to the 1641 Irish uprising, drew heavily on the fears and hopes generated by the confessional and dynastic struggles on the Continent. But suppose we shift our gaze to the mid-1640s, when troops from each kingdom were fighting in at least one of the other two? From this perspective it is hard to see continental developments as the main driving force behind events within the three kingdoms.

To argue that the three kingdoms provide a useful interpretative framework for the 'great events' that occurred within each of them in the 1640s, falls some way short of establishing that there was actually a history of the three kingdoms in this period to be written. In order to confirm the three kingdoms as a definable and legitimate field of study, the advocates of British history must 'illustrate a peculiar framework of shared institutions, of common culture, of specially intimate connexions, or of incorporating ideologies' (Claydon 1997: 222) that might qualitatively differentiate the relations between the three kingdoms from their relations with other European nations. In short, they need to demonstrate that Britain and Ireland formed essentially a single polity – which is no easy task given that they were divided on religious grounds, lacked common political institutions, and were socially, culturally and economically very diverse. An even greater obstacle perhaps is the fact that the English – the largest and most powerful of the Stuart nations – seemingly showed no interest in the idea of 'Britain' (Anglo-Scottish union), however conceived, and made only fitful attempts to extend an English *imperium* to Ireland.

These are indeed formidable obstacles, but not insurmountable. In fact, it is possible that the interactions of the 1640s enhanced, and perhaps even created, many of the mentalities and political dynamics characteristic of a single realm. Paradoxically, the wars strengthened, or rather deepened, the juridical relationship between the three kingdoms. England, Scotland and Ireland already enjoyed a peculiar framework of shared institutions in that they were joined in the person of the king and the authority of his prerogative powers in the governance of each of his kingdoms. They also shared a basic political culture and language inasmuch as the overwhelming majority of Charles's subjects acknowledged him as their rightful sovereign. Once the three kingdoms had descended into war, therefore, each nation's leaders were forced to recognize that the fundamental structures of their individual polities could be sustained or reshaped only by renegotiating their relationship with the crown – the result of which would inevitably lead to a redefining of the monarchy's relationship with the other two kingdoms. Even the most conservative blueprint for settlement – that of the Irish Confederate Catholics in seeking to make the crown the sole link between Ireland and England – would have had profound implications for the relationship between all three kingdoms. The more they sought to right matters in their own kingdoms, the more the Stuart peoples became enmeshed in each other's affairs.

It was the readiness of the king's subjects to reform the regnal union that launched armies within and across the three kingdoms in the 1640s. The collapse of the crown's authority in England, its main powerbase, created a free-for-all in which the Stuart nations sought to coerce or influence their monarch, or to appropriate his prerogative powers, in such a way as to alter their own political environment and, intentionally or not, that of the other kingdoms. This dialectical process clearly did not apply to France, Spain or any other of the European states that sporadically intervened in the conflict. France was involved diplomatically in all three kingdoms; Spain and the papacy in Ireland; the Dutch in England; and so on. Further research in European archives would probably turn up more evidence of such interventions. None of these states was vitally interested in events in Britain and Ireland, and most had one clear priority in sticking their oar in: to obtain troops to fight their own wars on the Continent. The Swedes were desperate for Scottish soldiers; the Spanish for Irish soldiers; and the French showed a fine insensitivity to the niceties of British warfare by recruiting Irish Confederates, Scottish Covenanters and English royalists.

It is striking that while the temporary collapse of English power in the archipelago freed the Scots and the Irish to pursue independent foreign policies, they did so with the aim of consolidating their position within the Stuart monarchy. National interest meant fettering or exploiting the English crown or parliament. It was this objective that consumed the energies of most of the ruling groups within the three kingdoms, that obliged them to intervene in each other's affairs, and that dictated the choice of methods, namely diplomacy and coercion, the political and the military. Politics (under which heading we can include confessional rivalries) and war therefore constitute the essential dynamic of 'British' history in the 1640s. This is not to say that a holistic or comparative account of the three kingdoms could not be constructed around cultural or socio-economic developments. But it appears that such approaches work best over a relatively extended timeframe, and would lack sufficient explanatory power in accounting for the course and outcome of the wars.

The notion of a single crisis in a single system can be sustained in other ways. John Morrill has shown how the exigencies of war forced many individuals and groups in all three kingdoms to think in terms of one conflict and to devise pan-Britannic strategies in response (Morrill 1993: 96–9). Nor was there a shortage of incorporating ideologies in this period. The work of John Adamson on Anglo-Irish relations in the mid-1640s has revealed a strongly imperialistic bent in the Westminster Independents' stance towards Ireland (Adamson 1995: 128–59). Above all, there was the Scottish Covenanters' commitment to religious uniformity and a confederal political settlement between the three kingdoms. It was these two aspirations, plus a desire to protect Scottish colonists in Ireland, that informed Edinburgh's decision to send an army into Ulster in 1642, and to negotiate an alliance with Westminster in September 1643 – the Solemn League and Covenant – that led to a Scottish invasion of northern England in 1644.

There was, undeniably, a strong element of self-interest in the Scots' desire for a 'covenanted uniformity'. The Bishops Wars (1639–40) had taught them that there could be no long-term security for Scotland unless the English crown was constrained from using the resources of the three kingdoms against them. This meant exporting their Presbyterian church government throughout the archipelago, and entrenching Scottish interests at the heart of English and Irish affairs. Yet as Arthur Williamson has made clear, many Scots were disposed to regard the Covenanting movement and godly union in strongly apocalyptic terms, as a precursor to the destruction of popery, and the establishment of God's rule over all the nations (Williamson 1979: 143–5). It was in this expansive frame of mind – as Alexia Grosjean and John Young have argued (Grosjean 1998) – rather than one of nationalist self-interest that the Covenanters made approaches to both the Dutch and the Swedes in the 1640s to 'join with the kingdoms of Scotland, England, and Ireland in this Solemn League and Covenant for opposing popery and prelacy and establishing the true religion' (Young 2001: 90–1). Even when they began to feel threatened by events at Westminster, as they did from 1645, the Covenanters spurned the opportunity to forge separate alliances with continental Protestant powers, insisting that the English parliament be party to any treaty.

Scottish enthusiasm for a confederal settlement was matched by English resistance to the idea – or so we are repeatedly told. The conception of the English as solidly anti-Covenant is so entrenched, however, even in the work of historians such as John Morrill who are keen to play up the 'Britishness' of the wars, that it has discouraged the search for any evidence to the contrary. The failure to take English enthusiasm for closer union seriously is due partly to the lack of work on political and religious Presbyterianism; partly also to our fascination with prejudice. Sneering references to 'gude brother Jockie' have been allowed to drown out those English voices urging respect for 'our dear brethren of Scotland'. One such voice was that of the Presbyterian polemicist Thomas Edwards, who Ann Hughes argues was highly influential in shaping public opinion (Hughes, in Tyacke 1998: 235–55). Edwards argued for a 'nearer union and communion' between the kingdoms, declaring his readiness to 'fall and perish . . . with the kingdom of Scotland and the Presbyterian party in England, standing for the Covenant' (Edwards 1646: 212). In addition, Elliot Vernon's (1999) Cambridge dissertation on metropolitan Presbyterianism has uncovered a powerful group of godly Londoners, styling themselves the 'covenant-engaged citizens', who insisted upon adhering to the Covenant 'in the Scottish sense'. The 'Scottified' English, as their detractors called them, may well have been more numerous and influential than we have hitherto supposed.

We shall never really know the extent of English commitment to closer religious and political union, if only because it was the Scots' enemies – the Independents – who emerged triumphant. It is a tribute to their success in stirring up anti-Scottish feeling in England that historians have tended to adopt a rather pitying attitude towards the Covenanters – as if their ideas for closer union between the two kingdoms were doomed to failure from the very start. Certainly a 'perfect union' would have been impossible given the very distinct political identities of each nation. But a strengthening of cross-border political and ecclesiastical ties was feasible, and would probably have occurred if the first civil war had been won by the English Presbyterians and their Scottish allies.

Anglocentrism

Writing Scotland and Ireland back into the English Civil War commands the support of most scholars. What does not is the assertion that the main focus of any British study must be on events in England. Yet it is difficult to see how a fully integrated, holistic approach to the wars can fail to be anything but Anglocentric. This is awkward, for Anglocentrism has become the New British History's most heinous offence. The understandable desire of English historians to avoid such a charge has lent some recent British scholarship a faint air of political correctness; an unstated but nevertheless detectable desire for 'even-handedness' in assessing the impact of each kingdom upon the course of the wars. Anglocentrism, however, is not a modern nor even, perhaps, an English invention. If English politicians tended to focus on the play of events in England, then so too did many of their Scottish and Irish counterparts. England's size and wealth relative to Scotland and Ireland, and its habit of throwing its weight around in the archipelago as the perennial 'awkward neighbour', made it impossible for the other two kingdoms to ignore. The Covenanters and Confederates may well have regarded the wars as a 'single conflict in several theatres' (Morrill 1999: 82), but they also realized that in the end one theatre counted more than others to the outcome of their domestic crises, and that was England. If they endeavoured to seize control of their respective kingdom's territory and government, it was usually with the ultimate goal of intervening in the quarrel in England and turning it to their own advantage. Equally, if none of the English parties thought a great deal beyond achieving a settlement that would secure their ascendancy in England, it was because they had little need to. Once the Independents had conquered England they were happy to allow the Scots to opt out of the regnal union; and powerful enough to subdue them when they refused to do so. Ireland was a somewhat different matter. It was a dependency of the English crown, and honour alone demanded the reassertion of English hegemony. Besides which, there was the matter of the Protestant blood shed since 1641 to be avenged. But again, once the English had put their own house in order, there was never much doubt that they could and would bring the Irish Catholics to heel.

The more one studies the histories of the three kingdoms during the 1640s the more it appears that the major turning point for each of them was the triumph not simply of the English parliament, but of a radical, chauvinistic faction within it, namely the Independents. The battle of Naseby (June 1645) was above all a victory for the New Model and its Independent backers. The ascendancy in England of this virulently anti-Scottish faction and its army ensured that the inevitable resurgence of English power in the wake of the first civil war threatened not just the Irish Confederates but also the Scottish Covenanters. A Presbyterian or a royalist victory in England would probably have preserved one, possibly both, of the other two kingdoms from English invasion. But in their determination to usurp the king's prerogative, and to make Westminster the seat of power throughout the archipelago, the Independents made settlement with the Covenanters impossible, and the eventual absorption of Ireland into an enhanced English state all but inevitable. How to counter the Independent threat was the motor that drove much of the politics in Britain and Ireland from 1645. Thus the second civil war of 1648 should properly be regarded as merely the English and Welsh phases of a wider conflict – the War of the Engagement – that encompassed all three kingdoms and was a direct response to the Independents' 'conquest' of king, London and parliament. Of all the possible outcomes of the English Civil War, victory for the Independents was the most likely to prolong the wars of the three kingdoms.

The Rise of the Grandees

Although the 1640s witnessed a massive shake-up in political structures and practices throughout the three kingdoms, John Morrill's and John Walter's observation with respect to England – 'a third, popular force did not emerge from the widespread disorders of the 1640s' (Morrill and Walter 1997: 314) – holds true for the entire archipelago.

For a variety of reasons – economic, social and political – the English Civil War never developed into anything resembling a collective assault by the lower orders on seignorial authority. A great deal of what looks like popular disorder in the 1640s, even when directed against members of the gentry, turns out, on closer inspection, to have depended at some level upon official encouragement or licence. The common people, even the more assertive elements among the 'middling sort', generally sought legitimation for their wartime undertakings by enlisting the approval or leadership of the gentry, and blamed their social superiors when it was not forthcoming. These attempts to enlist gentry backing were often framed in the language of deference and hierarchy. The leaders of the West Riding parliamentarians, the Fairfaxes – who, as Andrew Hopper has shown, were initially reluctant to take up arms against the king – were encouraged by the people to the feudal strains of 'A Fairfax, a Fairfax. We will live and die with a Fairfax!' (Hopper 1997: 12).

The role of noblemen as focal points of popular allegiance has led John Adamson to suggest that contemporaries played upon the parallels between the English Civil War and baronial conflicts of the middle ages (Adamson 1997: 83–99). This is not to say (and Adamson has never said it) that the Civil War was merely a re-run of the Wars of the Roses – a clash between overmighty subjects who marshalled their feudal retinues and tenant levies under the slogan 'support your local baron' (Morrill 1999: 187). Just as the common people often couched their appeals for gentry support in studiedly deferential terms, so the parliamentarian and royalist leaderships were obliged to deploy the rhetoric of the people's liberties and the preservation of true religion (however defined) in order to rally the populace to their banners. The mobs that periodically surged around Westminster during the 1640s were at once tools fashioned by parliamentary and civic factions to coerce their rivals, and prime examples of the politicized, confessional crowd that form the subject of John Walter's (1999) study of the Stour Valley 'riots' in 1642.

A central theme among 'post-revisionist' historians such as Richard Cust, Ann Hughes and Peter Lake is the existence in early Stuart England of a politically well-informed and engaged public – a phenomenon closely linked to deeper trends such as increasing social differentiation, the emergence of the middling sort and rising literacy levels. The outbreak of civil war owed much to the growth in political awareness and assertiveness of the people and at the same time accelerated this process. The very fact that the nation's leaders were divided among themselves, and were forced to court the 'popularity' in order to prosecute their quarrel, allowed the ordinary people unprecedented freedom of political choice and expression. Yet in arguing that the outbreak of war widened the scope for popular participation in national politics we are faced with a conundrum. For if the war began with the empowering of the Commons, it ended in 1648 with the vast majority of the people powerless in the face of an unrepresentative and deeply unpopular 'junto' at Westminster. What went wrong? Why did the 1640s not become 'the people's decade'?

Part of the answer lies in the appearance in England of that most feared continental phenomenon: professional standing armies. The experience of battle and the camaraderie it engendered tended to set the soldiery apart from the people, and could also render it open to radical or unrepresentative ideas. Armies, especially when operating away from home territory, often exercised an arrogant authority that generally limited the people's ability to make free political choices. Yet in none of the three kingdoms did politics degenerate into military rule – although England teetered on the brink late in 1648. Most armies were controlled and sustained by oligarchic factions. Indeed, if the 1640s can be associated with any particular form of government it is oligarchy. As the reign of the Westminster Independents clearly shows, there were few more powerful political forces than an elite faction (no matter how unpopular) with a body of regular troops at its disposal and the means to pay them. The 'military aristocracy, or rather oligarchy' at Westminster, wrote one commentator, 'govern by power, not by love' (Walker 1648: 140–1, 143); while another claimed that 'it is notoriously known that . . . the people everywhere dislike what you are now a doing, and are ready to pull you off those benches [in parliament], did not the army you keep up restrain them' (A Letter, 1648: 15).

The 1640s were arguably the last sustained period in British history when power at the centre of government derived more or less directly from the barrel of a gun. Had the Scottish army that invaded England in 1644 been able to perform as effectively on the battlefield as the Covenanters had expected, then their influence in English counsels would have been much greater than it was. The spectacle in August 1647 of the New Model Army – a force of barely 15,000 poorly equipped but veteran soldiers – overawing London, a city of some 400,000 people, is testament to the power that an effective fighting force afforded its political masters. Although it began to pull away from its oligarchic moorings in 1647, the New Model never looked like assuming its idealized perception of itself as the people's army. The ideas and concerns that swayed the majority of the soldiers did not command widespread support. The single most unpopular act committed anywhere in the three kingdoms during the 1640s – the execution of the king – would have been impossible without the backing of the New Model.

Oligarchy was the keynote in Confederate politics during the 1640s. The power vacuum created by the collapse of royal authority over most of Ireland after the 1641 uprising was filled almost exclusively by the Catholic elite. To the extent that the uprising was an expression of popular grievances it was quickly hijacked by a small section of the nobility and gentry for their own ends. Although the Confederate Association claimed to represent and act for all of Ireland's Catholics, in practice there seems to have been no widening of the franchise during the 1640s. The men elected to the confederate general assembly or appointed to the supreme council (the approximate equivalents of a parliamentary legislative and executive) were drawn overwhelmingly from the same landed upper class that had sat in the prewar Irish parliaments at Dublin. Certain sections of Irish society, notably the Catholic clergy, enjoyed greater political influence. But the views of the vast mass of the Irish population were as little consulted at Kilkenny as they had been at Dublin. Popular feeling made a direct impact on confederate policy only when the Catholic church hierarchy roused the people in defence of religion, and even then it needed the backing of Owen Roe O'Neill's Ulster army to make it effective.

The triumph of oligarchy was even more pronounced in Scotland; and unlike the Confederates, the Covenanters intended their experiment in self-government to be permanent. A group of disaffected noblemen and gentry harnessed popular resentment at the king's attempt to foist an English Prayer Book on Scotland to strip him of virtually all authority north of the border. Charles could do little more than watch as they usurped his prerogative powers and abolished episcopacy in favour of an unadulterated Presbyterian church. This restructuring of central government resulted in a massive increase in parliamentary authority, and the creation of a plethora of interlocking executive committees, of which the most important, the Committee of Estates, governed in the intervals between parliaments. Power was exercised by one of two oligarchic inner cores grouped around the Marquess of Argyll and the Duke of Hamilton. The struggle between these two factions to attain voting majorities and pack executive committees did not alter the fundamental nature of covenanting rule (at least until 1649), which Allan Macinnes has dubbed the era of 'oligarchic centralism' (Macinnes 1990: 106–28). As in England, professional armies bolstered oligarchic authority and limited the common people's capacity to shape national causes that they had helped to create. A popular uprising by anti-Engagement Covenanters at Mauchline Moor in June 1648 was suppressed by Hamilton's troopers as surely as the New Model had crushed whatever resistance it had encountered from the Clubmen – the nearest thing to people's armies in the English Civil War.

The Covenanters' bold innovations in central and local government probably served as a model for the English parliamentarians' own experiment in rule by committee – as it may also have done for the Irish Confederates. Perhaps the most stimulating, certainly controversial, work in recent years on political structure at Westminster is that of John Adamson (1987, 1991; Jones 1989: 21–50). Although Mark Kishlansky and others have challenged his interpretation, Adamson's basic premise – that the nobility had a central role in the politics of the 1640s – has quietly gained acceptance. Adamson has conjured up a world at Westminster in which bicameral interests – small networks of like-minded politicians, or 'grandees' – vied for control of parliament in order to impose their own terms for settlement. To achieve their ends the grandees developed a range of methods aimed at swaying the non-aligned majority, circumventing the cumbrous procedural conventions that prevailed in both Houses, and garnering support among the people.

In investigating these methods of management we are inevitably drawn outside the analytical framework established by Whig historians and their preoccupation with the 'great debates' in the Commons, and the guiding genius of Puritan heroes such as John Pym and Oliver Cromwell. Oratory and force of character were important in open debate, but parliament's development of bicameral executive committees to manage the war-effort had the effect of sidelining proceedings on the floor of the Houses. It was in the backroom workings of these committees that real power in terms of policy-making and political patronage often resided. The ascendancy enjoyed by the Independents for most of the period 1645–8 owed much to their control of parliament's revenue committees. With these committees in their pocket the Independent grandees were able to 'draw a general dependency after them, for he that commands the money, commands the men' (Walker 1647: 7). The success of the New Model, which in effect was the Independents' army, was closely linked to the tactical freedom its commanders enjoyed and in particular to its regular receipt of pay; and these in turn were the result of the Independents' domination of key executive committees.

Another important, yet often overlooked, tool of management was propaganda. The Presbyterian grandees, for example, played upon fears of a world turned upside down in order to rally support both inside and outside parliament. Similarly, the Independents' exploitation of reports concerning the 'oppressions' of the Scottish army in northern England was arguably their most effective tactic in forging a majority in the Commons during the mid-1640s. The Scottish minister, Robert Baillie, wrote from London in 1645 that 'some very few guides all now at their pleasure, only through the default of our army...[which] they exaggerate' (Laing 1841: II, 319).

When out-managed by their rivals, the grandees generally resorted to coercion. During the mid-1640s the earl of Essex and other leading Presbyterians proved adept at using the City to pressure their opponents at Westminster. Citizen mobs, Common Council petitions, and rendezvous of the London trained bands, were all brought to bear against the Independents. In extreme circumstances, troops might be deployed to overawe parliament, as the men of the New Model were on several occasions in 1647–8. But the primary political use of armies was to underwrite the grandees' terms for peace. Military force was the only way of bringing Charles to the negotiating table or of imposing a settlement upon a divided nation.

Bicameral factions and grandee management dominated the political scene at Westminster by the winter of 1642–3. Two main interests can be detected – one centred around viscount Saye and Sele, John Pym, and those grandees who had conspired to bring down the Personal Rule in 1640, and who now saw a military alliance with the Scots as an insurance policy against a soft settlement that would leave them exposed to the king's vengeance. Ranged against this faction was a group headed by the earls of Northumberland and Holland, and Denzil Holles, that resented the power of parliament's commander-in-chief, the earl of Essex, and was anxious for a swift, negotiated peace. Jack Hexter's sixty-year-old model of a three party system – war, peace and middle – centred upon the Commons and dominated by 'King Pym' is based upon unsubstantiated assumptions, misreading of the evidence, and almost total neglect of the peers as politicians. It should be discarded forthwith.

Three Kingdoms Politics?

Part of our difficulty in attempting to track the growth and structure of factionalism at Westminster in the 1640s may be that our interpretative framework is too narrow. Once again, some of the answers may lie in taking a more multi-kingdom perspective. In terms of party formation at Westminster, the crucial period seems to be the second half of 1643 under the impact of two major events in 'British' politics: the Solemn League and Covenant, and the king's cessation of arms with the Irish Confederates. Between them, the Covenant and cessation broke and recast the political mould at Westminster.

To the Northumberland–Holles interest, an alliance with the Scots represented a potentially ruinous escalation of the conflict. It would encourage the king to bring in Irish and other foreign troops to redress the balance, thus threatening to drag England into the vastly more destructive wars that had been raging on the Continent. Even more worrying perhaps was the threat from below. Scottish confederal demands would make a settlement even harder to attain, and the longer the fighting went on then the greater the risk that 'the necessitous people of the whole kingdom will presently rise in mighty numbers and . . . set up for themselves to the utter ruin of all nobility and gentry' (HMC 1891: 87). For some of the Northumberland–Holles interest, however, the cessation was even more appalling in its implications, and rendered the idea of a negotiated settlement with the king unthinkable. With Northumberland among their number, they threw in their lot with the pro-Scots alliance faction. Moving in the opposite direction were several groups closely associated with the Saye–Pym interest, notably Essex and his staff officers. Essex still awaits a decent modern study (Vernon Snow's (1970) biography is merely adequate, and virtually ignores the last two years of Essex's career when arguably his political influence was at its height), but it seems that a combination of injured pride and dislike of the Scots' religious demands pushed him into an alliance with Holles and the earl of Holland. Joining Essex in this new coalition were Sir John Clotworthy and other Anglo-Irish MPs, angered that parliament had conceded supreme command of the British forces in Ireland to the Scots. It was here, in the second half of 1643, in reaction to the Covenant and cessation, that the future leaderships of the Independent and Presbyterian factions coalesced – not, as is generally assumed, in the reversal of alliances that occurred late in 1644, when the Scots joined forces with Essex's interest.

Some of the issues on which the Independents and Presbyterians were divided also had archipelagic implications. Lacking an army of their own by 1645, the Presbyterians relied upon the Scottish forces to underwrite their terms, and this meant meeting the Scots half-way on the question of religious uniformity, and allowing them some degree of involvement in English and Irish affairs. Leading Presbyterians thus had a distinctly 'three-kingdoms' policy towards Ireland, inasmuch as they were ready to allow the Scots a hand in subduing the Confederates, and to consider some kind of alliance with the marquess of Ormond – the king's Lord Lieutenant of Ireland. They sought not the reassertion of English hegemony in the archipelago so much as a pragmatic collaboration between the Protestant elites of each kingdom.

The Independent grandees, by contrast, were keener than their rivals to keep England's and Scotland's government 'distinct, without intermixture' (Hamilton 1963: 88), and to subordinate Ireland to English imperial rule. Thus the Scots were to be excluded from Irish affairs, and the minimum of concessions offered to Irish royalists. Peace – or war for that matter – was to be, in Cromwell's words, 'with the English interest in the head of it' (Underdown 1966: 156). The Independent grandees were in many ways the political heirs of Sir Philip Sidney, whose vision for England has been summarized as 'reform at home, leadership for Protestant

Europe, hegemony in the region, and, *sotto voce*, empire across the ocean' (Williamson 1999: 154).

The royalist grandees provide a particularly revealing case study of the impact of 'British' issues on English high politics. Although much more work needs to be done on English royalism, particularly post-1645, it looks as if the basic division among the king's party after the war ran along essentially the same British fault-line that separated the Independents and Presbyterians. Lords Digby and Jermyn headed a faction in Paris that was willing to see Charles restored by Scottish and, if necessary, French force of arms so long as it gave him the opportunity somewhere along the line to recoup, and ideally extend, his lost sovereignty. In opposition to this faction stood a group made up largely of so-called 'Constitutional Royalists', who were anxious to preserve not just Charles's majesty but the whole frame of English law and government – 'the patria' as Sir Edward Hyde revealingly termed it – without which, they argued, the honour and power of the king and the nation would be seriously impaired. A restoration of monarchy by foreign conquest ran entirely counter to such sentiments. On the other hand, this desire to demarcate and preserve an English frame of government, belief in the superiority of England's laws and institutions, and hostility towards the Covenanters, had many echoes in the thinking of the Independent grandees. Indeed, it might well be said that the fundamental division in British politics by 1647 was no longer that of royalist versus parliamentarian–Covenanter, but between Hyde's royalist patriots and leading Independents on the one hand, and the Covenanters, English Presbyterians and pro-Scots royalists on the other.

In the case of politics at Edinburgh during the 1640s, it is very difficult to identify a major cause of disagreement that did not have a strongly British or archipelagic dimension. The quarrel between the 'radical mainstream' under Argyll, and the moderate Covenanters and 'pragmatic royalists' led by Hamilton, seems to have centred upon securing a relationship with the crown – either through Westminster or a reconstructed English court – that best sustained their respective powerbases while protecting Scotland against its southern neighbour. Edinburgh politics showed a marked sensitivity to changes in Anglo-Scottish relations. The rise of the Independents from 1645, and the consequent rejection by the English parliament of a confederal settlement, prompted the most significant realignment in Scottish politics since the Bishops Wars. With the Westminster Independents carrying all before them by late 1645, Hamilton's faction opened secret negotiations with the king about a possible royalist–Covenanter military alliance. What the Hamiltonian Covenanters sought from these furtive talks was a renegotiated union between England and Scotland based not upon the two kingdoms' parliaments – the cornerstone of Covenanter strategy since 1641 – but upon the king and his court. The Scottish (and Irish) reaction to the rise and eventual triumph of the Independents and the New Model led directly to the second civil war.

The problem of how to neutralize or tame the English also shaped the political structure at Kilkenny. Until quite recently, it was believed that the main cause of disunity among leading Confederates was rooted in the ethnic and cultural divide between the Gaelic or native Irish, and the Old English. But in his study of the Confederate Association, Micheál Ó Siochrú (1999) argues against racial origins as a reliable guide to factional allegiance. In fact, he finds little evidence of ethnic divisions in confederate politics at all, with Gaelic Irish and Old English present in every faction. It is clear from his work that the fundamental division among the Irish, *as Confederates*, was ecclesiastical and political in nature and related closely to their minimum terms for helping the king against his enemies in Britain; or in other words, to the kind of settlement to be sought with the English crown. Instead of the traditional names for the two principal factions – the Old Irish and the Old English – he prefers the clerical and peace parties.

What Irish historians have perhaps overlooked, however, is the degree to which the relationship between the kingdoms influenced not just the structure of confederate politics but also the swings in policy and power at Kilkenny. It was surely no accident that the period of dominance enjoyed by the clerical party in Ireland coincided closely with the period of the royalists' greatest weakness in England – that is, from 1645 to 1648. The rise of the clerical party had been linked almost exclusively to Irish or continental developments – in particular the arrival in Ireland of the papal nuncio, Archbishop Rinuccini, in the autumn of 1645. Much of Rinuccini's initial success, as Tadgh Ó hAnnracháin (1995) has revealed, can be attributed to the immense influence he wielded as the Holy See's senior representative in Ireland. But this argument largely ignores a further possibility: that the nuncio's popularity reflected the Confederates' appreciation of the realities of British politics. For at least the first eighteen months of his nunciature, Rinuccini's policy with respect to the English problem was highly credible. He sought to make the Confederates masters of all Ireland so that they could assist the king or defy parliament from a position of maximum military strength. In the context of the royalists' total defeat in England, this strategy made far more sense than that of the peace party, which continued to press for an alliance with a king who had no armies left in Britain, and who was in no position to grant even the smallest of Confederate demands. The collapse of the royalist cause in England lent Rinuccini's strategy a compelling logic, and it may well have been his appeal to both reason and conscience that gave him such a powerful party in Ireland. By the same reckoning, the resurgence of the peace party at Kilkenny early in 1648 was closely linked to the contemporaneous revival of the king's military prospects in England and Scotland.

Allegiance

Recent work on the wars of the three kingdoms has focused on the views of the king's leading subjects, and has all but ignored the strong 'British' dimension to allegiance lower down the social scale. The dominant discourse in popular parliamentarianism in England, for example, was anti-popery – a political vocabulary that drew heavily on the facts and, more often, the fictions generated by the Irish uprising to encourage and legitimize all kinds of activity in support of parliament, from ransacking the houses of Catholic gentry to fighting in its armies. The clothing districts of the west country and Yorkshire provide particularly dramatic evidence of the way rumour and propaganda about events in Ireland helped to politicize the common people and nerve them to take up arms against the king.

For many inhabitants of northern England, on the other hand, fear and hatred of the Scots proved an equally powerful motivation against the parliament. There is much in viscount Saye's claim that the common people in the north 'abhorred to hear of the coming in of the Scots' in 1644 (Scott 2000: 858). The king's *rapprochement* with the Scots in the late 1640s, coupled with the Independents' campaign to rid the northern counties of the ill-disciplined Scottish army, effected a shift in the pattern of popular allegiance in the region – on the one hand, undermining commitment to the royalist cause, on the other, establishing northern England as the Independents' main political powerbase. One of the more striking aspects of the second civil war was the failure of Yorkshire and adjacent counties to rise in considerable numbers for the king. Like his ill-fated predecessor, Henry VI, Charles discovered that using the Scots to fight his quarrels south of the border was likely to lose him the affection of his northern English subjects.

Intriguingly, while fear of an Irish Catholic invasion fuelled support for parliament in many parts of England, in Wales it seems to have fed, by processes as yet unexplained, into popular royalism. The native Welsh were thus unique among the Stuart nations in 1642 in feeling threatened by Irish Catholics and English parliamentarians alike. In an impressive study of popular allegiance that builds upon David Underdown's (1985) seminal work in this area, Mark Stoyle has identified religious traditionalism – an 'addiction' to Prayer Book Protestantism – as the main basis of popular royalism among the Welsh and their Celtic cousins, the Cornish (Stoyle 1994: 238–41). More controversially, he has argued that Welsh and Cornish royalism was an expression of national independence. Indeed, he has suggested that rather than a war of three kingdoms, we should be thinking more in terms of a 'war of five peoples' (Stoyle 1998: 51): English, Irish, Scottish, Welsh and Cornish. Stimulating though this approach is, it needs refinement. The Welsh and Cornish were certainly anxious to preserve their language and distinctive cultural identity. But whether we can go a step further and say that they saw the war as a struggle against English hegemony (as the Confederate Irish did) is debatable.

The sensitivity of the Irish Catholics to events in the other two kingdoms was heightened by awareness of their religious isolation within the Stuart dominions. Although Catholics made up the vast majority of Ireland's population, they had been systematically excluded from power at home, and were regarded with fear and hostility by the predominantly Protestant peoples of Britain. Protestant hysteria about the supposed threat of militant Catholicism in the three kingdoms became a self-fulfilling prophecy, for the Irish were driven to rebellion in 1641 largely because of their fear of the 'Puritan party' in Britain. Very few of the motives behind the uprising – whether it was resentment of Protestant settlers, or economic dislocation caused by Strafford's policies – were entirely without a British dimension. The apprehension among the Irish of a Protestant plot to extirpate their religion and appropriate their land was possibly even more pervasive than corresponding Scottish and English fears of a popish plot. During 1641 a host of alarming rumours circulated among the native Irish – that the 'Puritans' were planning a general massacre of Catholics; that the Scots were preparing to invade Ulster; even that the king had been executed. Indeed, it is ironic that whereas English fears concerning the Irish were rarely born out in fact, Irish fears concerning the Scots and English proved all too well-founded. It was small consolation to the Irish that the unity of their Protestant opponents in Ireland also foundered on the rock of British politics – the Protestants in Ulster and Munster eventually aligning with the English and Scottish parliaments; those in Leinster adhering to the king. The breakdown in the parliamentarian–Covenanter alliance in Britain from 1645 divided the Protestant forces in Ireland still further.

The covenanting movement in Scotland, like the Irish Confederate Association, was a deeply reactive phenomenon. The Scots were rightly concerned that if those holding the reins of power in England were not themselves bridled, then their kingdom would be reduced to the status of an English province. It was this concern and attendant worries over the future of godly religion in Scotland that led such large numbers of Scottish men and women to resist the crown in the late 1630s. Similarly, it was fear of a royalist victory in England, made more immediate by rumours of a court-inspired Irish Catholic invasion, that galvanized the Covenanter heartlands in lowland Scotland again in 1643. The 21,000–strong Covenanter army that marched into England early in 1644 was the single largest body of men under arms anywhere in the archipelago during the 1640s. A higher proportion of Scottish men, relative to the size of Scotland's population, fought in the wars of the three kingdoms than of any other nation.

But the Scottish people were far from united in opposing their king; and in forging an alliance with Westminster the Covenanters triggered a civil war in Scotland. Elements of the episcopal northeast of the country and Catholic northwest rose at one time or another against Edinburgh, but were too divided on clan, religious and cultural lines to topple the Covenanter regime and then march to the king's aid in England. Although the renewed threat of English aggression represented by the rise of the Independents helped to paper over some of the cracks between Covenanters and Scottish royalists, Hamilton's invasion of England in 1648 to rescue the king once again triggered civil war in Scotland – this time in the so-called 'radical south-west' of the country. The militant Presbyterians of Ayrshire would not countenance fighting for an uncovenanted king, and following Cromwell's defeat of Hamilton's army at Preston (August 1648) they marched on Edinburgh and installed a government of their own. The Scots continued to fret and divide over the terms for restoring the Stuart monarchy in Britain until the New Model decided the issue at the battle of Worcester in 1651.

Radicalism

Scottish attempts to contain English power provoked a counter-reaction of similar intensity in England. The Westminster Independents were defined in part by their conviction that the Scots aimed at sacrificing English liberties on the altar of a confederalist church settlement. Although Kishlansky (1979) has debunked the traditional perception of the fledgling New Model as a hotbed of religious and political radicalism, it is clear that from its creation the army was closely associated with the Independents, and shared their desire to end parliament's humiliating reliance upon the Scots. The New Model was radical from the first in the sense that it was anti-Scots. 'How things stand between us and the Scots, I know not', wrote one officer in November 1645, 'but the late jealousies of them had such an influence on this army that I believe it hath ever since look't askwint, casting one eye westward [towards the king's remaining armies] and another eastward [towards the Scottish army]' (BL, Add. MS 72437, fo. 119). The London Independent Thomas Juxon believed that the New Model allowed Oxford to surrender on easy terms in June

1646 because it was eager to try conclusions with the Scots (Lindley and Scott 1999: 128). By the time it clashed with the parliamentary Presbyterians in 1647 the army was already politicized to the extent that it was generally anti-Scots, and favoured a settlement that preserved English liberties and restored the king to his 'honour, crown, and dignity'. It was fear that the Presbyterians were planning to seize the king themselves and use a Scottish army to impose a conservative settlement that drew the New Model deeper into the political fray.

Scottish intervention and confederalist claims were a powerful stimulus not just to political Independency and army radicalism but also to English republican thought. It was in answer to the Scots' assertion of an interest in the king while he was on English soil, that the future regicide, Thomas Chaloner, delivered a highly publicized speech in October 1646 in which he implied that parliament had exclusive authority over the person and powers of the monarch, and that Charles's best interests were incompatible with those of the English people (Chaloner 1646). His arguments were endorsed by several radical polemicists, one of whom, Henry Marten (the only avowedly republican MP at this stage), virtually demanded the king's execution. Like the trauma of civil war, or the logic of the Puritan impulse, the challenge to English self-identity inherent in Scottish confederalism prompted a radical reappraisal of England's government and constitutional make-up.

The most fundamental critique of the ancient constitution came from the Levellers. Phil Baker, in forthcoming research, argues that those later christened by their enemies as Levellers did not emerge as an organized movement with a coherent political programme until the autumn of 1647 – a development that he links to the Presbyterians' attack upon the New Model earlier that year. Future Leveller leaders looked to the army as a bulwark against the influence of the Scots and their English friends, and the burgeoning power of the grandee committeemen that we discussed above. In truth, however, the army needed the 'state junto' in order to sustain it in pay, just as the grandees needed the army to maintain them in power. Not surprisingly, therefore, the Levellers' campaign against a powerful executive made little headway in the ranks.

Although it is right that the Levellers continue to command our attention, the massive literature they have generated is somewhat out of proportion to their positive contribution to events. They were always a tiny minority, even in London, with just a handful of friends in the army and on the radical fringe of the Commons. Yet to many of the people, wedded as they were to notions of hierarchy and *inequality*, and alarmed by the cracks the war had opened in the foundations of society, the Levellers probably represented a frightening new phase in the nation's apparent slide towards anarchy. It was in the fear they aroused, which spread to Scotland and probably Ireland too, rather than through anything they actually did, that the Levellers made perhaps their greatest impact.

The Failure of Settlement

The problems inherent in a composite monarchy had a major bearing on the failure of any group in the three kingdoms to forge a successful settlement with the king – whose consent was deemed vital to a well-grounded peace. Although Charles could and did appeal to his duty to preserve the interests of all his subjects, this was practically impossible given the incompatible religious and constitutional priorities of the prevailing groups in each kingdom by 1645. After his own defeat in the English Civil War, he effectively needed the political and military backing of two of his three kingdoms in order to regain his throne – or of one, if that kingdom was England. The summer of 1646, when the English and Scottish parliaments presented him with the Newcastle Peace Propositions, represented his best opportunity to make his peace with his British kingdoms; the summer of 1647, and the army's Heads of Proposals, his best chance of a settlement in England. In both instances he preferred to sow division among his captors and hold out for better terms. The emergence in 1647 of a radical minority in the army; its split with Cromwell and other senior officers trying to strike a deal with the king; and its convergence with future Leveller leaders, can be traced directly to the resentment and frustration that Charles aroused by trying to play the army off against the Scots.

A proper understanding of the 1640s is impossible without some assessment of Charles's character – his finely-tuned conscience regarding the preservation of his friends and his supremacy in religion; his hatred of religious Presbyterianism and political Independency; his willingness to seek foreign allies and to lie about doing so; and his abiding preference for coercing his opponents rather than conciliating them. These traits obliged those who wanted a settlement that protected them from an untrustworthy monarch to reduce him to 'a necessity of granting' (Russell 1991: 275). Charles had many failings as a politician – in particular, his inability to attune himself fully to the anti-popish reflex of his Protestant subjects. But as a three-kingdoms strategist he had flashes of genius. His signing of the Engagement with the Scots in December 1647, far from being his ultimate folly as Underdown (1971: 88) has argued, represented a shrewd political gamble. By harnessing the reaction in the three kingdoms against the rise of the New Model Army he obtained the means to fight a second civil war.

Charles's 1640s exploits are crying out for an in-depth study. Michael Young's (1997) biography is the best of the current crop, but its treatment of Charles's career post-1642 suffers from the general lack of work on royalist strategy and politics. It also, like its predecessors, loses sight of the fact that right to the very end of his life Charles remained monarch of three kingdoms. Although defeated in England by January 1649, he retained a considerable party in northern Scotland, while the Engagement had fostered an Ormondist–Confederate alliance that left him stronger in Ireland than at any time since 1640. Charles thus held a powerful bargaining counter, for only he could prevent a possible Irish invasion or spare the New Model a bloody reconquest of Ireland. It is therefore difficult to accept the prevailing view of his trial as a premeditated exercise in judicial murder. Both John Adamson and Sean Kelsey have mounted convincing arguments for seeing the trial as an extension of the junto's policy of 'bargaining with menaces' (Adamson 2001). Charles's life was to be spared if he called off the military preparations in Ireland and stood down the fleet he had acquired when half of parliament's navy had revolted in May 1648. Likewise, the familiar picture of Charles during his trial as passive victim or would-be martyr is romantic fiction. His conduct in Westminster Hall was of a piece with his preference for coercion over conciliation. In refusing to recognize the court's jurisdiction he was signalling his refusal to foreswear the use of Scottish and Irish arms against his English enemies. In effect, he was playing out the hand that he had acquired in signing the

Engagement – convinced to the last that no one would dare strike down God's anointed. But he miscalculated. The various parties conjoined in Ormond's Irish alliance, as Adamson has argued, were held together primarily by loyalty to the person of Charles I – remove him and the whole edifice would likely collapse. In light of his intransigence, therefore, regicide became a matter of cold necessity.

A similar set of calculations applied to Charles's relationship with the Scots, and may account for the high proportion of northerners among the regicides. His imperviousness to demands that he abjure the Scots raised the spectre of another Scottish invasion of northern England. The trial managers had been at pains to emphasize that Charles was being tried as king of England, and they apparently reasoned (wrongly, as it transpired) that severing his head would likewise sever the regnal union and thus finally exorcise the threat of Scottish confederalism. These politic considerations aside, Charles's refusal to renounce his perceived design to 'vassalize' the English to the Celtic nations probably removed any lingering doubts in the minds of Cromwell and other regicides that the providential moment for justice against 'that man of blood' had finally arrived.

The regicide illustrates a central theme of this essay: the potential benefits of seeking 'British' answers to questions traditionally asked within a single-nation context. Inevitably, national histories of the 1640s will continue to dominate the bookshelves – and rightly so. They are less problematic than a multiple-kingdom approach, and certainly no less historiographically valid. But an integrated study of the 1637–53 period would provide a valuable additional layer of interpretation, and need not be insensitive to issues and trends peculiar to each kingdom, or over-emphasize convergence and linkage, as the critics of the New British History fear. On balance, there seems much to be gained from an integrated account, for if the British project offers a privileged view anywhere, it is surely over the tangled drama of the wars of the three kingdoms.

REFERENCES

A Letter from an Ejected Member of the House of Commons to Sir Jo: Evelyn 1648: BL, E463/18.
Adamson, J. 1987: 'The English nobility and the projected settlement of 1647', *Historical Journal*, 30.
Adamson, J. 1989: 'Parliamentary management, men-of-business, and the House of Lords, 1640–49.' In C, Jones, ed., *A Pillar of the Constitution: The House of Lords in British Politics, 1640–1784*: London.
Adamson, J. 1991: 'Politics and the nobility in Civil-War England', *Historical Journal*, 34.
Adamson, J. 1995: 'Stafford's ghost: the British context of Viscount Lisle's lieutenancy of Ireland.' In J. Ohlmeyer, ed., *Ireland from Independence to Occupation, 1641–1660*: Cambridge.
Adamson, J. 1997: 'The baronial context of the English Civil War.' In R. Cust and A. Hughes, eds, *The English Civil War*: London.
Adamson, J. 2001: 'The frighted junto: perceptions of Ireland and the last attempts at settlement with Charles I.' In J. Peacey, ed., *The Regicides and the Execution of Charles I*: London.
Chaloner, T. 1646: *An Answer to the Scotch Papers...Concerning the Disposal of the King's Person*, BL, E361/7.

Claydon, T. 1997: 'Review article: problems with the British Problem,' *Parliamentary History*, 16.

Edwards, T. 1646: *The Second Part of Gangraena*, BL, E338/12.

Fletcher, A. 1981: *The Outbreak of the English Civil War*: London.

Gardiner, S. R. 1987: *History of the Great Civil War 1642–1649*, 4 vols: London.

Grosjean, A. 1998: 'Scots and the Swedish state: diplomacy, military service and ennoblement 1611–1660.' Unpublished Ph.D. thesis, University of Aberdeen.

Hamilton, C. L. 1963: 'Anglo-Scottish militia negotiations, March–April 1646', *Scottish Historical Review*, 42.

Historical Manuscripts Commission 1891: *Thirteenth Report*, i.

Hopper, A. J. 1997: ' "The readiness of the people": the formation and emergence of the army of the Fairfaxes, 1642–3', *Borthwick Paper*, 92.

Hughes, A. 1998: 'Popular Presbyterianism in the 1640s and 1650s: the cases of Thomas Edwards and Thomas Hall. In N. Tyacke, ed., 1998: *England's Long Reformation 1500–1800*: London

Jones, C. (ed.) 1989: *A Pillar of the Constitution: The House of Lords in British Politics, 1640–1784*: London.

Kelsey, S. 2001: 'Staging the trial of Charles I.' In J. Peacey, ed., *The Regicides and the Execution of Charles I*: London.

Kishlansky, M. 1979: *The Rise of the New Model Army*: Cambridge.

Laing, D. (ed.) 1841: *The Letters and Journals of Robert Baillie*, 3 vols: Edinburgh.

Lindley, K. and Scott, D. (eds) 1999: *The Journal of Thomas Juxon, 1644–1647*: Camden Society, 5th series, 13.

Macinnes, A. I. 1990: 'The Scottish constitution, 1638–51: the rise and fall of oligarchic centralism.' In J. Morrill, ed., *The Scottish National Covenant in its British Context 1638–51*: Edinburgh.

Morrill, J. 1993: 'The Britishness of the English Revolution 1640–1660.' In R. G. Asch, ed., *Three Nations – a Common History? England, Scotland, Ireland and British History c.1600–1920*: Bochum.

Morrill, J. 1999: 'The war(s) of the three kingdoms.' In G. Burgess, ed., *The New British History: Founding a Modern State 1603–1715*: London.

Morrill, J. and Walter, J. 1997: 'Order and disorder in the English Revolution.' In R. Cust and A. Hughes, eds, *The English Civil War*: London.

Ó hAnnracháin, T. 1995: ' "Far from *terra firma*": the mission of GianBattista Rinuccini to Ireland, 1645–49'. Unpublished Ph.D. thesis, European University Institute.

Ó Siochrú, M. 1999: *Confederate Ireland 1642–1649: A Constitutional and Political Analysis*: Dublin.

Russell, C. 1991: *The Fall of the British Monarchies 1637–1642*: Oxford.

Scott, D. 2000: 'The Barwis affair: political allegiance and the Scots during the British civil wars', *English Historical Review*, 115.

Snow, V. F. 1970: *Essex the Rebel: The Life of Robert Devereux, the Third Earl of Essex, 1591–1646*: Lincoln, NB.

Stoyle, M. 1994: 'The last refuge of a scoundrel: Sir Richard Grenville and Cornish particularism, 1644–6', *Historical Research*, 71.

Stoyle, M. 1998: *Loyalty and Locality: Popular Allegiance in Devon during the English Civil War*: Exeter.

Tyacke, N. (ed.) 1998: *England's Long Reformation 1500–1800*: London

Underdown, D. 1966: 'The parliamentary diary of John Boys, 1647–8', *Bulletin of the Institute of Historical Research*, 39.

Underdown, D. 1971: *Pride's Purge: Politics in the Puritan Revolution*: Oxford.

Underdown, D. 1985: *Revel, Riot and Rebellion: Popular Politics and Culture in England 1603–1660*: Oxford.

Vernon, E. 1999: 'The Sion College conclave and London Presbyterianism during the English Revolution.' Unpublished Ph.D. thesis, Cambridge University.

Walker, C. 1647: *The Mysterie of the Two Juntoes*, BL, E393/29.

Walker, C. 1648: *The History of Independency*, BL, E463/19.

Walter, J. 1999: *Understanding Popular Violence in the English Revolution: The Colchester Plunderers*: Cambridge.

Williamson, A. 1979: *Scottish National Consciousness in the Age of James VI*: Edinburgh.

Williamson, A. 1999: 'Patterns of British identity: "Britain" and its rivals in the sixteenth and seventeenth centuries.' In G. Burgess, ed., *The New British History: Founding a Modern State 1603–1715*: London.

Young, J. 1996: *The Scottish Parliament 1639–1661: A Political and Constitutional Analysis*: Edinburgh.

Young, J. 2001: 'The Scottish parliament and European diplomacy 1641–1647: the Palatine, the Dutch Republic, and Sweden.' In S. Murdoch, ed., *Scotland in the Thirty Years' War*: Brill.

Young, M. 1997: *Charles I*: London.

FURTHER READING

For the New British History and the wars of the three kingdoms, see: B. Bradshaw and J. Morrill, eds, 1996: *The British Problem, c.1534–1707: State Formation in the Atlantic Archipelago*: London; J. Young (ed.) 1997: *Celtic Dimensions of the British Civil Wars*: Edinburgh; P. Gaunt 1997: *The British Wars 1637–1651*: London; J. Adamson 1998: 'The English context of the British Civil Wars', *History Today*, 48, November; G. Burgess (ed.) 1999: *The New British History: Founding a Modern State 1603–1715*: London.

For politics and allegiance in the English Civil Wars, see: D. Underdown 1971: *Pride's Purge: Politics in the Puritan Revolution*: Oxford; M. Kishlansky 1979: *The Rise of the New Model Army*: Cambridge; S. R. Gardiner 1987: *History of the Great Civil War 1642–1649*, 4 vols: London; M. Stoyle 1994: *Loyalty and Locality: Popular Allegiance in Devon during the English Civil War*: Exeter; R. Cust and A. Hughes, eds, *The English Civil War*: London; J. Adamson 2002: *The Noble Revolt*: London.

For Ireland and the Confederate Association, see: P. Corish 1976: 'The rising of 1641 and the Catholic Confederacy, 1641–5' and 'Ormond, Rinuccini, and the Confederates, 1645–9', both in T. W. Moody, F. X. Martin and F. J. Bryne, eds, *A New History of Ireland, Vol. 3: Early Modern Ireland 1534–1691*: Oxford; J. Ohlmeyer 1993: *Civil War and Restoration in the Three Stuart Kingdoms: The Career of Randal MacDonnell, Marquis of Antrim, 1609–1683*: Cambridge; J. Ohlmeyer (ed.) 1995: *Ireland from Independence to Occupation 1641–1660*: Cambridge; M. Ó Siochrú 1999: *Confederate Ireland 1642–1649: A Constitutional and Political Analysis*: Dublin.

For Scotland and the Covenanting movement, see: D. Stevenson 1973: *The Scottish Revolution 1637–1644: The Triumph of the Covenanters*: Newton Abbot; D. Stevenson 1977: *Revolution and Counter-Revolution in Scotland, 1644–1651*: London; D. Stevenson 1987: 'The early Covenanters and the federal union of Britain', in R. Mason, ed., *Scotland and England 1286–1815*: Edinburgh; J. Morrill (ed.) 1990: *The Scottish National Covenant in its British Context 1638–51*: Edinburgh; J. Scally 1996: 'Constitutional revolution, party and faction in the Scottish parliaments of Charles I', in C. Jones, ed., *The Scots and Parliament*: Edinburgh.

CHAPTER SEVENTEEN

Unkingship, 1649–1660

SEAN KELSEY

In the history of the seventeenth century, the early modern era, perhaps even the entire span of time since the rise and consolidation of English, Scottish and Irish monarchies at various stages in the middle ages, one brief epoch has always stood out in the popular imagination as fundamentally different from anything experienced before or after. In 1649, after seven years of civil war, Charles I was executed, and monarchy abolished. For eleven years, a centuries-old system of personal kingship was replaced by a bewildering succession of different governments and constitutional experiments, none of which attained lasting stability. In 1660 the peoples of the Atlantic archipelago decisively rejected government by saints, soldiers and civilian 'republicans' by engineering the restoration of Charles II to the thrones of three kingdoms.

The absence of a crowned head of state made these eleven years unique, and the experience has no close parallel in modern times. But in many ways it was the outpouring of genuinely radical ideas which made the period truly remarkable. For a few short years England was a 'world turned upside down' by war and revolution, its political and intellectual landscape seemingly dominated by a parade of visionaries, madmen and holy fools: men and women such as the prophetess Elizabeth Poole, who passed messages from God to the generals of the New Model Army; the Digger Gerard Winstanley, whose followers established a utopian communism on enclosed common land in Surrey; the Quaker James Nayler, who rode into Bristol astride an ass in blasphemous re-enactment of Christ's entry into Jerusalem; and the bands of Ranters whose lewd, drunken, godless antics so exercised the authorities of the day (Hill 1991).

Even more profound than any of the radical ideas espoused by these ordinary men and women living in such extraordinary times was the proliferation of independent congregations and radical sects which, in the course of the 1650s, slowly emerged as a new establishment in the religious life of the British Isles (Hughes 1992). Their dominance was temporary. The real significance of the era for the longer-term development of English society and Western thought lay in the fact that they found at least some sympathy and support among the supreme governors of three nations. The revolution in England was led by the famous New Model Army, a body of men radicalized by the experiences of war and by the attempts of their own masters in parliament to silence their religious and political opinions. From 1649, friends of the army, those peaceable Protestants who rejected the prewar church, its clergy, service and Prayer Book, enjoyed greater freedom than ever before to worship God as they saw fit, while their new rulers discussed schemes for the fundamental reform of church, state and society. Never before had so much power resided in the hands of men whose minds were open to the possibility of transforming the world, perhaps even the human condition itself, by asserting the principles of Christian liberty, and by exploring the positive advantages of tolerating unorthodox ideas.

These were the men who, on 4 January 1649, proclaimed the sovereignty of the people of England, then placed the tyrannical Charles I on trial and executed him for trying to rob the people of their freedoms. In the nineteenth century it was argued by some that these actions paved the way to the establishment of those civil and religious freedoms finally achieved in the Victorian age. Having established that the law, made by the people's representatives, was superior to the will of any individual, the revolutionaries had anticipated the establishment of modern parliamentary sovereignty and the strict limits it placed on the powers of the monarch. But it was also argued by the Whig and liberal historians of the day that freedom had never been truly safe in the hands of the soldiers who had called the shots in 1649. In truth, these armed revolutionaries, their violent methods so antithetical to the progressive reformism which constituted the genius of the English, were in any case 'predestined to failure' because their ideas were just too far ahead of their time. Their proposals for change were 'often such as to commend themselves to the men of the nineteenth, perhaps even to the men of the twentieth century, rather than to those of the seventeenth' (Gardiner 1988: I, 1–2). After eleven years of increasingly bitter argument between soldiers and civilians about what the revolution was supposed to achieve, the republic collapsed in on itself, giving way to the restored monarchy.

Although they have rejected the rather excessive belief in England's inevitable progress to democracy and freedom manifested by their nineteenth-century predecessors, modern historians of the period between regicide and restoration have nevertheless retained a deep-seated sense that there was a revolution in 1649 – far more obviously so than at any time between 1641 and 1647 – that its protagonists aimed in some respects to change at least their own small portion of the world, if nothing else, and that they had almost entirely failed by 1660. Moreover, the roots of their failure lay in the internal contradictions of the revolution itself. The frustration of their aims was thus very largely inevitable. The army had launched a massive assault against the existing system of government, much of which lay in ruins by the spring of 1649. But the army believed that it was necessary that its cherished programme of religious, social and political reform be enacted by a legitimate civilian authority to ensure that this 'third reformation' commanded some measure of support in the country at large. Several parliamentary regimes were therefore established by the army with a remit to bring about reform. Yet none of them showed much stomach for the fundamental transformation of English society, and all of them eventually fell foul of the army. This was 'the central conflict of the 1650s' (Worden 1974: 12), and it goes a long way towards explaining the ultimate sterility of the English revolution. 'The essence of the problem' faced by every government was 'the incompatibility of the "godly commonwealth" sought by the Army, and the return to stability and tradition which the majority of those involved in politics desired' (Smith 1992: 16).

The first of the revolutionary regimes was the Rump Parliament. Its foundation set the tone for political developments in the ensuing eleven years. It was created in

December 1648 by the forcible exclusion of the army's opponents from the Long Parliament. This 'purge' was a compromise between soldiers who wanted to replace the existing parliament with a radically reformed legislative assembly more representative of the people, and sitting MPs who believed that authority ought to be left in their hands so that they could reform the system themselves. The purge was the prelude to the declaration of popular sovereignty, and then the trial and execution of Charles I. But almost as soon as it had begun, the revolution was thrown into reverse by the deliberate efforts of the Rumpers themselves. It became apparent that the MPs left in place at Westminster by the purge did not share the soldiers' radical visions for the future. On the contrary, many MPs were angry with the army for its use of violence against parliament and felt extremely isolated and exposed in the aftermath of regicide. Consequently they decided to readmit to the Commons many of their colleagues who had opposed the trial and execution of the king, many of whom returned to parliamentary duty largely in order to prevent the revolution going any further (Underdown 1971: 143–207).

The reactionary element at the heart of the Rump Parliament soon became dominant, making it much easier to understand why the army's programme of reform was not translated into practice. Although the Rump abolished the monarchy and founded the English 'free state' or Commonwealth in May 1649, these were cosmetic changes, undertaken for almost entirely pragmatic reasons, largely thanks to 'the absence of a plausible alternative' (Worden 1974: 172). They created what one contemporary called, dismissively yet entirely accurately, a state of 'unkingship', an absence of kingship – they certainly did not reflect any deep-seated, radical commitment to a 'republican' settlement among a majority of MPs. Thereafter, the struggle for control between the minority radicals and majority conservatives within the Rump effectively paralysed an assembly in which a great many godly civilians and soldiers had vested all their hopes of building a new Jerusalem. From 1649 to 1651 the army was preoccupied, fighting in Ireland and Scotland. But as soon as it was free to do so, it set about stirring up the stagnant mill-pond at Westminster, pressing for reform, and for a commitment from the Rumpers to hold fresh elections. When no reform was forthcoming, and when preparations for elections appeared to make it all the more likely that sweeping change would never be obtained, the army's commander, Oliver Cromwell, forced the Rump to dissolve in April 1653.

Although the next phase of revolutionary government appeared far more likely to satisfy radical demands, it proved to be just as compromised by internal contradiction as its predecessor. Meeting in July 1653, Barebone's Parliament was conceived of by many as an assembly of 'saints' or 'elders', loosely modelled on a biblical form of government, the Sanhedrin, its membership brought together as a result of widespread canvassing of opinion among religious radicals, many of whom offered their own nominations. However, it has been demonstrated conclusively that Barebone's was an extremely mixed body of men, very largely hand-picked by the army high command, which brought together radicals and conservatives in very similar proportion to those found in the Rump Parliament (Woolrych 1982). Consequently, Barebone's suffered from the same kinds of internal conflict, brought embarrassingly into the open when one half of the assembly surrendered power back to the army which had set it up, even while the other half discussed some extremely radical proposals for the reform of the church, in December 1653.

Next the army established the Protectorate, promoting its own commander to the position of chief magistrate of England, Scotland and Ireland. But as a sign of the army's continuing commitment to some degree of legalistic propriety, the new constitution divided power between Cromwell, his council and regular parliaments. In this way it merely institutionalized the fatal contradictions within the revolutionary coalition of civilian and military politicians. The whole situation was further complicated by the traumatic events which had brought down the Rump and Barebone's Parliaments. Cromwell faced the impossible task of balancing the conflicting demands of the supporters of each, while simultaneously attempting a policy of 'healing and settling' the wider divisions of the country at large, goals which were thrown very largely into turmoil by the institution of a system of direct military rule over England and Wales in response to a royalist rebellion in 1655.

A lurch in the direction of hardline military reformers and their supporters among the zealous godly minorities in the localities, the rule of the Major-Generals aimed at achieving lasting security through the moral reformation of society. But these objectives were never achieved, and the whole episode merely provoked an equal and opposite reaction from the civilians. In 1657, although they narrowly failed to persuade Cromwell to accept the crown of England, Scotland and Ireland, civilian politicians succeeded in revising the terms on which the Protectorate was set up in order to diminish the influence of the army officers and rein in the increasingly influential Baptists, Quakers and other religious radicals who relied on military protection (Barnard 1997: 35–66; Hutton 2000: 58–113).

When Oliver Cromwell died in September 1658, soldiers and civilians vied to establish control over his successor, his eldest son Richard. The ease, even the popularity, of Richard's succession encouraged the many conservative parliamentarians and even former royalists who comprised the court party – sometimes referred to as the 'new Cromwellians' – to believe that they now had an opportunity to curb the role of the military in the government of the Commonwealth and turn back the tide of religious radicalism. However, their efforts simply served to push the senior army officers led by Charles Fleetwood, and other self-proclaimed defenders of that 'facile catch-phrase' (Woolrych 1957: 136) 'the good old cause' into further acts of political violence. First they turned against the new Lord Protector and his parliament, turning them out of office in April 1659 as soon as they attempted to assert some control over the commanding officers of the army. Then, ironically, they reinstated the few dozen surviving Rumpers, only to find that they were almost as unbiddable as they had been in April 1653.

Dumping the Rumpers yet again in October 1659, Fleetwood and his friends in England and Ireland finally reduced their civilian support to an irreducible minimum. They also did irreparable damage to the army's unity of purpose. Coming to the defence of the Rump, General George Monck in Scotland and Admiral Edward Montagu in command of the fleet now turned against the radical army officers. In December 1659 Monck brought the Rumpers back for a third shot at pacifying the three nations, a task which harvest failure, recession and rising unemployment made all but impossible. The breakdown of local justice, riots and the threat of tax strikes prompted the final disintegration of Commonwealth revenues and its political base in the capital and beyond. Any lingering support in the country at large finally evaporated with the catastrophic dissolution of the alliance struck by Monck and the

Rumpers. Increasingly desperate for some sort of stability, conservatives within the Commonwealth establishment began to contemplate joining forces with royalists and the Long Parliamentarians turned out of the Commons in December 1648, setting in train the events which would lead to the restoration of Charles II (Davies 1955; Hutton 1993: 3–84).

Conflict between soldiers and civilians ruined every attempt at settlement after 1649. But as well as discussing the contradictions internal to successive revolutionary regimes, several modern accounts have also offered a sensitive appraisal of individual revolutionary psychology as the key to the inevitability of their failure. In Oliver Cromwell they have found the perfect embodiment of the revolution's own 'ideological schizophrenia' (Worden 1974: 69). The Lord Protector's modern biographers have described in fine detail the way in which he was torn by his background, his instincts and his experience between a liberal belief in religious toleration, a more authoritarian commitment to the 'reformation' of society along evangelical Protestant lines, and a conservative attachment to the existing social and political order in England (Coward 1991; Gaunt 1996; Davis 2001). The extensive range of Cromwell's surviving letters and speeches, comprising one of the finest sets of sources for the entire period (Abbott 1989), makes it easier to describe the complexity of this one man's world view than that of almost any of his contemporaries – if it also offers a grave temptation, not always successfully resisted, to take the man at his word in everything he ever said or wrote. But it is perfectly clear that Cromwell was not unique in the complexities and self-contradictions of his character, motivation and action.

He and his fellow soldiers could hardly blame civilians for the failure of each attempted settlement, because it was they themselves who had created regimes which perfectly reflected their own internal ideological contradictions. For example, Cromwell and many of his fellow officers may well have had a hand in orchestrating the resignation of the conservatives within Barebone's Parliament because they actually feared the implications of abolishing lay control over church patronage which some of its members were discussing. If the radicals had had their way, they would have called in question one of the main property rights enjoyed by a large proportion of the English gentry, as well as their control over the appointment of the clergy, important aspects of any gentleman's authority within his local community (Woolrych 1982: 344). A strong urge to reform the church and a strong attachment to the principle of private property were by no means incompatible. But it would prove almost impossible to balance the two, making the failure of a radical 'Puritan revolution' inevitable. It was consumed not just by external conflicts between radical reformation and conservative constitutionalism, but by its own inescapable internal contradictions.

The conclusion is inescapable that, paradoxically, 'the revolution' failed to achieve fundamental reform of government and society very largely because so many of the so-called 'revolutionaries' were really nothing of the sort. Like Cromwell, many of the rulers of the Commonwealth, both military and civilian, came from outside the social group which traditionally shouldered the responsibility for national government. But by and large they also came from well within that far larger portion of society which either owned property or had recently acquired it, and which consequently placed enormous value on the existing system of law and social hierarchy which underpinned the dominance of the property-owning classes (Gentles 1997). It would be absurdly deterministic to insist that this necessarily made them incapable of sincere devotion to the cause of religious and political reform. But it did make many of them extremely suspicious of groups advocating the wholesale transformation of society who had little or nothing vested in the existing order of things. Due to the delicate balance of power in the politics of the strategically all-important City of London, such groups exercised a disproportionate influence over the life of the nation at key moments between 1647 and 1660. Some army officers undoubtedly cultivated and exploited connections with the Levellers and others. But not all those who did so were by any means sincere advocates of reform for its own sake.

The language of principle could serve some very pragmatic purposes. For example, in December 1648 and January 1649, with preparations for the trial of Charles I under way, the army officers debated a blueprint for constitutional reform. This Agreement of the People proposed dramatic changes to the electoral system and greater religious freedom, among many other things. But it is doubtful whether the debates at Whitehall were ever intended to achieve the implementation of this revolutionary blueprint, and far more likely that the commanding officers of the army merely paid lip-service to radical ideas in order to pacify John Lilburne, the Levellers, and the more radical elements among the junior officers (Underdown 1971: 198–9). It was the army itself which crushed radicals in its own midst later in 1649 by the suppression of a Leveller mutiny, and by the destruction of the Diggers' communist experiment in Surrey (Manning 1992; Gurney 1994). Similarly, it is now better appreciated that the Rump was not forcibly dissolved in 1653 just because the army had grown impatient with the Rump's failure to reform, but probably also at least in part because MPs had very recently attempted to reduce the pay and reward of those soldiers who had participated in the conquest of Ireland, while it was also rumoured that they were considering removing Cromwell from overall military command (Barber 1992; Woolrych 1982: 69–70). Radical groups in London supported the coup in order to secure the defeat of their factional rivals in the City corporation at Guildhall. Further support for the Lord General's actions came from the powerful new local government authority in Wales, the largely sectarian Commission for the Propagation of the Gospel. The Rump had recently allowed the commission to lapse amid gathering pressure for a moderate church settlement, as well as serious allegations of financial impropriety among the commissioners (Farnell 1967; Worden 1974: 328; Woolrych 1982: 60–1). The pressure for godly reformation which brought about the dissolution of the Rump was very clearly mixed up inextricably with much more prosaic and earthly matters relating to power, office and influence.

This mixture of principle and pragmatism was always in evidence whenever the military intervened in national politics. After all, many of the army's leaders were also members of parliament and government officials, and really ought to be considered as politicians in their own right, rather than as disinterested revolutionaries. Neither were they a particularly brotherly band of men. Divisions, rivalries and conflicts within the army itself often influenced political developments just as much as the tensions between military and civilian governors. Again, the dissolution of the Rump is a case in point. Cromwell only acted under enormous pressure from one particular group of officers, Fifth Monarchists and others, who took seriously the notion of preparing for the imminent return of Christ. As they grew increasingly dissatisfied with the Rump, they may even have begun to question Cromwell's own leadership (Worden 1974: 380–3; Woolrych 1982: 74–7). Their leader was Major-General Thomas Harrison, MP for Wendover, nominal head of the Commission for the Propagation of the Gospel in Wales and patron of the radical millenarian congregations in the City of London. After the fall of the Rump, Harrison was politically ascendant, and had greater influence over what ensued than his principal rival in the army high command, Major-General John Lambert. These two men represented the contrasting tendencies within the military establishment which made Barebone's Parliament just as much of a compromise as the Rump had been. When the moderates walked out in December 1653, just six months into the assembly's eighteen-month term of office, the circumstantial evidence for their collusion with Lambert is strong, and it was he who now contributed more than most to the foundation of the Protectorate, whilst Harrison began his journey into the political wilderness (ibid.: 70–7, 352–61).

Rivalry and conflict such as that between Harrison and Lambert reminds us how difficult it is to talk about the objectives of 'the army' as a whole. Sectional interests within the army often pulled in completely opposite directions. Moreover, its principal officers were men of a complexity to rival that which has fascinated Cromwell's biographers. Lambert himself is a good example of the soldier who was also a provincial English gentleman and a politician. His prominence in English politics depended very much on his appeal to a wide variety of men, some of them violently at odds with one another. Some of his principal political supporters, especially in the local powerbase of his native Yorkshire, lay among the godly minorities who came to political prominence in the regions of England and Wales after 1649. These groups struggled to maintain their authority as 'healing and settling' took hold after 1653 and 'traditional rulers' returned to the business of local government. On the national stage, Lambert would later present himself as the scourge of unrepentant royalism. Yet in private, Lambert also used his influence to make life as easy as possible for those royalist, even recusant, Catholic kinsmen and close friends who themselves came under the lash. After the Restoration some of these men were influential in protecting Lambert from severe punishment (Farr 2000). Lambert had gone down fighting for 'the good old cause', finding himself on the wrong side of a struggle for the soul of the army in 1659–60, which was by then a very different entity from that which had purged the House of Commons back in 1648. Lambert and the Wallingford House group of officers came unstuck at the hands of General George Monck, the parliamentarian commander in Scotland who nearly twenty years earlier had led Charles I's Irish forces into battle against parliament during the first civil war. It is just as misleading to talk of 'the army' as a united and unchanging entity, as it is to imply without question the uniformity of principled reformism among the enormously diverse, ever changing New Model officer corps.

Detailed investigation of the New Model Army and painstaking Namierite reconstruction of successive civilian regimes at Westminster has transformed knowledge of the 1650s in the past thirty years. Oddly, greater appreciation of the complexities of politics in the period sometimes seems barely to have dented the basic belief that 1649 proved to be a kind of 'false dawn' followed by the betrayal of radical dreams. But given the manifold ambiguities of 'the revolution' and its architects, attempting to explain why the revolution failed has begun to seem fairly futile. If they could possibly have helped it, many 'revolutionaries' would undoubtedly have preferred not only to have kept Charles I alive in 1649, but also to have kept intact as much of the ancient constitution as possible, so it is questionable whether they can be said to have 'failed' to establish alternatives. Broadly speaking, many of the most revolutionary changes of all – the abolition of the kingly office, the proclamation of the free state and the establishment of the Protectorate, for example – were undertaken in order to ensure that private property and the rule of law were preserved in the face of those marginal yet frightening forces which threatened them from the fringes of society. The fact that the Protectorate fell, the Commonwealth ended and the kingly office came back would appear largely irrelevant by contrast. Practically every form of early modern government 'failed' in the long run, giving way to new forms in order that property and law might be sustained.

Perhaps we ought not to trouble ourselves any longer with the inappropriate and entirely misleading question of why the revolution 'failed'. The whole issue makes too many assumptions about the nature and desirability of one particular vision of 'progress' in human affairs, notions which, to coin a phrase, 'commend[ed] themselves to the men of the nineteenth, perhaps even to the men of the twentieth century, rather than to those of the seventeenth'. Neither ought they to appeal to the historiographers of the twenty-first century. As has been well said, 'the time is surely ripe for an application to the 1650s of the watchword of those who set about revising the place conventionally allotted to the 1620s in English historiography – that the past be detached from any *a priori* framework and studied in its own terms' (Hirst 1996a: 359). In order to set aside once and for all the mind-set which has belaboured with grinding monotony for a century or more the failure between 1649 and 1660 to effect the kind of real long-term political and constitutional change in England, Scotland and Ireland which nobody really intended in the first place, and in the interest of working our way around to a new understanding of the place of revolution in English political culture, perhaps it would be better simply to concentrate, as many historians have in recent years, on describing and explaining how politics and government *worked* in the absence of kings.

The execution of Charles I was such a dramatic, unprecedented event that it is natural to assume that it was a watershed in the history of the British Isles. In some respects it undoubtedly was, if only because it did such extraordinary violence to the network of political allegiances and temporary coalitions which had just about kept the English parliamentarian cause buoyant throughout the 1640s. Politics could certainly never be the same again. But many historians have noted the remarkable degree of continuity in government before and after regicide. The change from a mixed monarchy to a free state had practically nothing to do with principled objection to the old system, so it is not surprising to discover that most of that system survived the establishment of the Commonwealth. Indeed, in many respects the free state was identical with the old system, and distinguished from it by nothing more than the absence of kings – by its 'unkingship'. The office of king was abolished, but the powers of the crown effectively went into commission when they were vested in a council of state. The House of Lords was abolished also, but its last few remaining leaders were inducted straight into the new government (Kelsey 2002). A constitutional experiment like Barebone's Parliament was much more obviously novel, although an overwhelming majority of its members had plenty of experience as the foot-soldiers of the old system, as JPs, assessment commissioners and in all sorts of other administrative capacities. The Protectorate's deliberate combination of a monarchy, an 'aristocracy' (in the form of the Lord Protector's council, or the upper house appended to parliament in 1657) and elements of democracy demonstrates a rather self-conscious commitment to the search for constitutional forms which contemporaries could at least recognize, even amid their undoubted novelty.

As the debates over the reinstatement of kingship demonstrated, just because the Protectorate was broadly recognizable did not make it legally acceptable. English common law remained the touchstone of constitutional propriety after 1649, just as it had before. Little or nothing which happened during the 1650s challenged this basic fact of early modern English political life. In the face of considerable opposition to regicide among leading judges, the judiciary was remodelled in 1649. But the central courts, the laws which they enforced and most legal process remained almost entirely the same. Generally speaking, beyond its volubility there was nothing special about the debate on legal reform which took place in the 1650s. Certainly it was just as ineffectual as any before or since. Far more important was the survival of the rule of law. The courts stayed open and stayed very much in business. A decade of war necessarily threw up serious challenges to the legal system, and many suits were diverted from the normal course of justice, passing instead through the hands of indemnity commissioners responsible for protecting those whose illegal actions were undertaken on parliament's behalf during the wars (Hughes 1986). Law and politics were damagingly entangled by the engagement oath, and occasional embarrassments such as Cony's case, in which a London merchant disputed the legality of taxation under the Protectorate. But whatever Englishmen might have thought about the legitimacy or otherwise of the revolutionary regimes at Westminster, few were prepared to sacrifice their material interests by refusing to use aggressively the ancient jurisprudential facilities those regimes preserved and maintained. For their part, the common lawyers even extended their dominion, engrossing the lucrative business once handled by church courts, such as tithe disputes, and made other valuable inroads into some equity jurisdictions (Cromartie 1992).

Of necessity, the appearance of many aspects of central authority did indeed change. These ostensibly cosmetic alterations can tell us a great deal about the nature of politics in the period from regicide to restoration. Successive revolutionary regimes devised and deployed a range of images and 'icons' of public authority alternative to those of the old regal system. For example, the Rump replaced the portrait of the king on horseback which had appeared on Charles I's great seal with a group portrait of the parliament in session. The royal coat of arms gave way to an emblem uniting the English cross of St George and the Irish harp of Erin. All such emblems made straightforward claims about the parliamentarian, legalistic, nationalistic nature of authority in the aftermath of regicide. Eschewing the kind of overt and exotic innovation which brought freemasonry, fasces and phrygian bonnets to the heart of American and French political culture in the eighteenth century, England's revolutionary rulers relied instead on the imaginative redeployment of reassuringly familiar elements taken from well within the existing political culture (Kelsey 1997: 85–118). In broad outline, the patterns of politics remained unchanged, also, taking place within a physical and mental environment which remained identifiably court-like, despite the absence of a king. During the Protectorate a seal was introduced which reverted to the old regal style, showing Cromwell seated on horseback, with the City of London in the background. Seated in the palatial surroundings of Hampton Court, the government of 'Oliver P.', as he signed himself, in conscious emulation of 'Charles R.', provided a focus for the emergent conflicts between rival Cromwellian courtiers (Sherwood 1989; Knoppers 2000).

Many 'county studies' have noted a high level of continuity in regional administration across the so-called 'watershed' of 1649. Aside from the commissions for the propagation of the gospel in Ireland, Wales and the north of England, no development in local government after 1649 significantly shifted power away from the old structures. In some respects the latter effectively reasserted themselves in the course of the 1650s, especially with the abolition of the parliamentary county committees in 1650. Recent discussions of the relationship between central and local government have also called in question conventional notions about the intrusion of outside authority into regional and provincial affairs. Where the power of the state grew, as with the new militia and assessment commissions, it tended to do so in collaboration with groups of local people who saw an opportunity to turn the situation to their own, local advantage (Roberts 1998; Braddick 1994: 134–6, 150). In the meantime, the county commissions, quarter sessions and assizes of England functioned as normal, with the addition of one or two new responsibilities. Apart from the efforts of one or two Major-Generals, attempts at 'the reformation of manners' were just as patchy after regicide as they had been before (Hughes 1992: 86–7). It is time to wonder whether there is enough evidence of an especial and unique desire for the reformation of personal behaviour that we ought really to claim that it, too, 'failed' during the 1650s.

Undeniably, the composition of the county benches changed during the 1650s. But such changes were often limited, and sometimes less dramatic than those which took place during other 'revolutionary' phases in English politics, during the later 1620s, the 1640s, the 1660s and the early 1680s. 'New men' were to be found everywhere, especially after 1650–1, but established families also retained their local dominance. As a whole, power was not lost by, but redistributed among, the gentry, whose political standing was, if anything, generally increased in the period with the establishment of a new model militia force and the collection of the monthly taxes, and the creation of local commissions for the regulation of the clergy. These responsibilities fell squarely on the shoulders of the gentry, albeit a higher proportion were drawn from the middle and lower end of the scale. Furthermore, economic and legal developments during the 1650s generally favoured the interests of landowners, and especially those willing to invest in improvement. Despite (or perhaps even because of) the antics of the Diggers on St George's Hill, the period witnessed a fairly decisive shift in government thinking broadly in favour of the enclosers of common land, where beforehand the full weight of the traditional patriarchy had often been aimed at those who would deprive ordinary people of their marginal economic privileges (Fletcher 1986: 14–19; Morrill 1992: 95–107).

The upper reaches of the social order in England grew stronger at the expense of the lower orders during the 1650s. Equally significant in this respect was the general lack of any appreciable alteration to the pattern of landownership. Detailed studies of the southeast and the north of England have demonstrated that, in the long run, the policies of sequestration, composition and forced sales had a relatively limited impact on royalist families, many of whom not only bought back their own property, but did so with the knowledge, even the connivance, of successive revolutionary regimes (Thirsk 1952; Holiday 1970; Blackwood 1978; Philips 1978). As far as most of England's rulers in the 1650s were concerned, the objective in selling confiscated estates was simply to raise money, not to ruin forever either individual royalists or their families, whose continued presence in their communities was valued as a source of social stability. Even the mass liquidation of crown assets did not see the creation of a new landowning class, much of the old crown estates being acquired by existing property owners (Gentles 1973). Like the rule of law, the principle of property could and did become compromised at times by its entanglement with politics. The conditions on which many former royalists held their estates after their surrender to the parliamentarian forces in the 1640s were a political minefield; the decimation tax imposed along with the Major-Generals was an uncomfortably hot potato, because it contravened the property rights of men who had lived peaceably for a decade or more. But, on the whole, the interests of property survived and prospered during the 1650s.

In their essentials it might easily be argued that government and society underwent few if any real changes as a result of regicide. But it is impossible to pretend that life did not change at all after 1649, and indeed it would be absurd to suggest that regicide had no discernible impact on government and society – especially if the focus is broadened to take account of Scotland and Ireland. Perhaps the most significant feature of constitutional change at Westminster after 1649 was the emergence of a new kind of archipelagic polity (Hirst 1996b). Since 1603 the three kingdoms had been united in the person of the king, and fairly superficially through some of the offices and institutions of the royal court. In 1649 the Rump effectively annexed Ireland, the first step in a journey which would lead towards a full political union. The Rump's theoretical dominion there did not become a reality until the completion of an extremely difficult military operation to suppress the Catholic revolt which had broken out in 1641. That operation was not much helped by the hostility of the English and Scottish colonists in the island who had generally disliked the turn of events at Westminster since 1647, when the army had first taken the upper hand. The presence of the parliamentarian army in Ireland after 1649 did at last make the colony safe for Protestant settlers, most of whom came round to a grudging acceptance of the English Commonwealth even if they deeply resented the rule of the military and civilian governors sent from the metropolis. The Catholic majority, on the other hand, was simply blasted into oblivion by a murderous campaign of conquest and the mass confiscation of the rebels' property which paid for it. The 1650s was the beginning of the end for Catholic Ireland, and the end of the beginning for the Protestant ascendancy (Barnard 2000).

Yet even in Ireland the 1650s really marked little more than a redoubling of very long-standing efforts at Anglicization, supplemented with a few new ones distinguished only by their savagery. For Scotland, the effects of the first-ever meaningful military conquest and occupation were in many ways far more shockingly profound. The execution of the Scottish king by a band of English had done little to soothe the tensions between the two nations, but they maintained an uneasy coexistence until the arrival of Charles II in 1650. An English army invaded shortly after. Its miraculous victory at Dunbar on 3 September made worse the mutual jealousies among the different factions in Scottish politics. These divisions gravely weakened Charles II's invasion of England in 1651. Insecure in Scotland, the would-be king failed entirely to raise the support of his English subjects, who were loath to see him placed on his English throne by means of Scottish arms, and his desperate military adventure ended disastrously at Worcester on 3 September. The future security of the Commonwealth dictated the annexation of Scotland, although it was dressed up as a union of equal partners – which in truth it was, in some sense at least, given the co-operation between the English invaders and sections of Scottish society pleased to have an opportunity to engineer the suppression of the traditional aristocratic leadership in the northern kingdom (Dow 1979: 30–51).

The creation of an archipelagic polity through the conquest and occupation of Ireland and Scotland clearly had an enormous impact on the politics of all three nations. It certainly sponsored the growth of classical republican pretensions to the emulation of ancient Rome. More important, certainly from the English point of view, was the continued growth of the military establishment to an unprecedented size (in the region of 50,000 for most of the 1650s), as well as a proportionate growth in the system of taxation to pay for it. The scale of the military presence lays the revolutionary regimes open to the charge of military dictatorship. This is not an easy charge to uphold against any particular feature of government after the execution of Charles I (Woolrych 1990). However, it is worth remembering that the remarkably high level of compliance with the tax demands made by successive regimes (most counties paid 90 per cent or more of direct taxation – the city of Norwich actually managed to pay more than it was asked for over the decade) owed a great deal to the military presence. If force was only rarely used directly to ensure taxes were paid, then threats of force, or, more frequently, the threat of free quarter, which amounted to more or less the same thing, were probably enough to weaken most resistance (Braddick 1994: 140–1, 157–8, 178). Furthermore, it is very difficult to get away from the fact that throughout the 1650s there were men in a position to dictate the pace and direction of political developments in England thanks to nothing more than their command over very large groups of men bearing arms subject to their discipline. Such facts plainly made political life very difficult, poisoning relations between the Lord Protector and his parliaments, for example. The level of conflict between them can be, and has been, overstated. Protectorate parliaments did at least attempt to 'fulfil the traditional and constructive role of an early modern parliament in new and difficult circumstances'. In their success, as in their failure, they had 'much in common with a typical early modern English parliament' (Gaunt 1998: 97). But the perception of dictatorship, regardless of the facts of the matter, greatly raised the temperature of those rather less than constructive debates about the constitutional settlement which wrecked several parliamentary sessions and exasperated the Lord Protector himself.

The rule of the Major-Generals had no real precedent in the history of English government (the likeness between decimation and the punitive bonds exacted by Henry VII notwithstanding), and appears to epitomize the tendency of revolutionary regimes towards military dictatorship. But it was not necessarily the straightforward example of direct military rule from the centre which it might seem, reflecting instead the complex relationship between centre and localities characteristic of the entire early modern period. The system was intended to solve the problem of authority in the regions by strengthening the dominance of the godly in their own neighbourhoods, and it was welcomed by such groups because it gave them the upper hand in a number of long-standing competitions for superiority in local affairs. Equally, the experiment did not fail because of resistance in the counties, but largely because of the inadequacy of support at the centre for an overly ambitious set of objectives (Durston 2001: 229–30). But whatever its complexities, the whole episode of the Major-Generals raised serious questions about the Protector's continued reliance on his old army comrades, their influence over the formation of his policy, and in particular their desire to continue punishing ex-royalists innocent of any crime. These questions were all clearly very important in the emergence of proposals to offer Oliver Cromwell the crown, in order to diminish the connection between legitimate public authority and naked military power (Firth 1909: I, 128–200; Egloff 1990).

Several recent discussions have demonstrated that at least some of the political divisions of the Protectorate era arose not just as a consequence of English military expansion, conquest and entrenchment, but also as a function of the participation of Scots and Irish politicians in the affairs of the metropolis. The conquered lands underwent that 'healing and settling' of differences which so eluded the Lord Protector in his governance of England. In the aftermath of Glencairn's revolt, the balance of power within the government of Scotland was shifted markedly in favour of the native civilians and away from the invading soldiers as a way of reducing tensions. Headed by Roger Boyle, Lord Broghill, the new administration in the north depended much more on local men and local law, paying far greater respect to the condition of society, and religion, as it had pertained before the English military conquest (Dow 1979: 161–228). Broghill's subsequent return to Ireland in 1656 tipped the balance in the power struggles between the established colonial interest and upstart military interlopers in a very similar way. Under the Lord Deputyship of Henry Cromwell, younger son of the Lord Protector, the Old Protestants regained the upper hand, reasserting themselves over the amalgam of swordsmen and religious radicals who had dominated the government of Ireland since the closing stages of the Cromwellian conquest (Barnard 2000: 300–3).

In turn, the inhabitant rulers of the territories ostensibly 'annexed' to England supported the rise of the 'new Cromwellians' in England in order to safeguard the restoration of their authority and interest by helping to entrench conservative revolution in the metropolis. This 'court' party in England consisted of moderate parliamentarians and even former royalists. Greatly resented by many 'old Cromwellians', especially the officers of the original New Model Army, the new Cromwellians were strengthened by the Scots and Irish representatives in the Protectorate parliaments, hand-picked, under the terms of the Instrument of Government, by the Protector and his councillors. These developments helped inform the kingship crisis at Westminster in 1657, an episode reflecting Irish concerns for the status of the union with England and the security of Irish legal, property and commercial interests, just as much as it reflected the concerns of the English lawyers for the status of the chief magistracy in the eyes of English common law (Little 2000).

Conditions pertaining in both Scotland and Ireland would ultimately help ease the passage to Stuart restoration. In Scotland, the religio-political rivalries of Protester

and Resolutioner, as those between the burghs and the shire nobility, had survived
the English occupation, an experience which if anything had merely worsened their
differences. Whatever the true intentions of the English commander-in-chief in
Scotland in 1659, General Monck's purging of religious radicals from his army and
his subsequent intervention in England on behalf of the Rump Parliament was seen
by Presbyterian clericalists in Scotland as an opportunity to reassert themselves over
their Protester opponents. Their triumph, or at least the defeat of their enemies, was
sealed when they threw in their lot with those royalists whom once they had damned
as 'malignant', in helping bring about the restoration of Charles II (Buckroyd 1987).
Similarly, in Ireland the Old Protestants made their precarious position more secure
in 1660. They held no very particular brief for the Stuart cause, yet saw in its revival
an opportunity to break the influence of the radicals, free themselves from the heavy
burden of taxation which partial union with England had imposed on them, and
finally seal the victory of the Protestant interest which would help give rise to the
ascendancy established in full by the end of the century (Clarke 1999).

As well as the archipelagic politics of the age, another aspect of the period of
'unkingship' clearly sets it apart from much of what had gone before. It was not
just novel military commitments by land which kept the tax bill high. After 1649 the
free state also devoted itself to the fastest expansion in maritime power anywhere in
Western Europe since the sixteenth century (Capp 1989). The growth of maritime
power was politically significant. First, it reflected the fact that the free state was, in
some small part, the creation of a 'new merchant' elite in the City of London, a group
of commercial interlopers, aligned with radical elements in the army, who had
challenged and defeated the old trade monopolies exercised by the chartered companies. The massive naval war with the Dutch which began in 1652 was in many ways
the high point of new merchant influence over Commonwealth foreign policy. Yet the
navy and the aggressive foreign policy of which it was the tool were extremely
expensive, a drain on scarce tax resources which exacerbated the long-term crisis in
meeting the wage arrears of the army. Part of the reason the Rump fell foul of the
army was that it had strongly supported the war with the Dutch. When the Rump
was dissolved, it was new merchants who protested most vigorously (Brenner 1993:
633–7).

Ironically, the Dutch war was also immensely popular with many of the religious
radicals who had called for some sort of action to be taken against the Rump for its
failure to enact reform. Millenarians such as Thomas Harrison took seriously the
notion that there was a war on foot for the final overthrow of the devil and all his
works, as part of the preparation for the thousand-year reign of king Jesus, in
accordance with the prophecies of the New Testament Book of Revelation. They
believed that the United Provinces, one-time heroes of the struggle with Antichrist,
were now guilty of collusion with him because they had given refuge to Charles II and
refused to co-operate with the English when they were offered the opportunity of a
strategic union in defence of international Protestantism (Pincus 1996). Consequently, despite Cromwell's efforts to kick-start a diplomatic solution shortly after
the dismissal of the Rump, the Dutch war continued during the rule of Barebone's
Parliament, further undermining Commonwealth finances. The Dutch war thus
contributed just as much to the downfall of the nominated assembly as it had to
that of its predecessor. The foundation of the Protectorate marked a profound

reversal in the diplomatic alignment of the Commonwealth, with the rapid conclusion of peace with the Dutch, an alliance with France and the commencement of war with Spain – a revolution every bit as blessed in the eyes of many as that which had taken place in 1624.

During the 1650s, military and naval expansion altered many aspects of the politics and government of the three nations, not to mention society, and altered dramatically the relationship between the atlantic archipelago and the rest of Europe, indeed the rest of the world. But it is important to keep these changes in perspective. In the accidental aspect of its causes, and the unpredictable nature of its consequences, the revolution of 1649 was *intrinsically* no different to the Henrician reformation or the union of the English and Irish crowns with that of Scotland in 1603, for example. Constitutional arrangements, foreign policy and the division of power and spoils across the archipelago underwent alterations just as revolutionary as those witnessed in the 1650s, if rarely quite so violently, on average about once a generation during the early modern period – maybe more, certainly no less. Regicide remains unique, the lightning flash illuminating an entire century, an age, a culture. But in many respects regicide, and all the other political and constitutional developments which followed, was just as fleeting and just as profound as any of those moments of dynastic transition, religious schism, factional reorientation, change of ministry or foreign policy *détourne* which took place in such dizzying profusion in the early modern era. In many ways, the simple assumption, with which this chapter opened, that the period from 1649 to 1660 was somehow different from all that had gone before and all that would come after has inhibited, rather than encouraged, the kind of scholarly engagement enjoyed by preceding and succeeding eras in the past thirty years or so. Widespread reference to 'the Interregnum' reinforces the commonsense view that this was an eleven-year interlude from the normal course of experience, the resumption of which was a foregone conclusion – a claim which no serious account of the restoration settlements would ever seriously venture. Similar problems beset the universal tendency to refer to the various regimes of the 1650s as 'the Republic'. All historiography depends on shorthand to some extent. But some of the preconceptions built into the label most commonly applied to the years of unkingship have corrupted historical understanding of what happened in England, Scotland and Ireland in that period, and why.

In the seventeenth century, 'monarchy' and 'republic' were terms whose meanings shifted as a function of political conflict. Either might carry overtones of tyranny and anarchy, or else denote models of constitutional perfection, but many loyal subjects of early modern English kings and queens described themselves as denizens of a republic or 'commonwealth'. Indeed, early modern England has been called a 'monarchical republic', a mixed polity in which, rhetorically, law reigned supreme, a place where politics were idealized as aristocratic, conservative and consensual. When, in 1649, despite their best efforts, a small handful of Englishmen were forced to kill Charles I, few if any had had the institution of monarchy in their sights as well, and few believed sincerely in the establishment of popular sovereignty. Despite the famous cliché, there was no deep desire to cut the king's head off with the crown upon it. Indeed, there was no deep desire to kill Charles I at all. Many of his judges in January 1649 believed he remained central to the quest for settlement in English politics, and to the pacification of relations between his three kingdoms. Moreover, if it could be

contrived in safety, the partial restoration of his regality would have helped these same
men to frustrate those among their colleagues who were prepared to support the case
for democratic reform (Kelsey 2003a, 2003b). Consequently, when they set up 'the
Republic' they were very keen to stress its compatibility with all existing law and
government, and that in effect it stood not for anti-kingship, but for 'unkingship'. In
time, and especially with the growth of Commonwealth military power and the
revival of English commercial fortunes, some no doubt came to believe in the
inherent superiority of a state of kinglessness. But much of the hostility to monarchy
which developed in the years which followed the execution of Charles I reflected
practical opposition to those factions at Westminster and Whitehall who wished,
perhaps as early as 1650, to make Oliver Cromwell into a monarch of some description. The Stuart restoration was a personal and political disaster for some, but it did
not necessarily mark the humiliating defeat of men who had failed to wean society
from its childish devotion to kingship. In 1660 even the regicide Henry Marten could
declare that 'I think his Majesty that now is, is King upon the best title under Heaven,
for he was called in by the Representative body of England'.

The attorney general who prosecuted Marten and the other regicides in 1660 did
so in the name of a king to whom he referred as 'caput reipublicae' as well as God's
lieutenant on earth. It seems not unreasonable to suggest that, to take contemporaries at their own meaning of the word, England was already a republic in 1649 and
remained a republic after 1660, a republic in which the role of a sanctified monarch
was central. The constitutional arrangements of the regimes which rose and fell
between 1649 and 1660 were distinguished from their predecessors and their successors by little more than their 'unkingship'. That which historians conventionally
designate 'the Republic' was, in effect, a sequence of kingless republics – experiments
in remodelling mixed monarchy minus the office of king, an office which proved
entirely peripheral to business as usual: prerogative power subject to a very limited,
indirect account, an emphasis on the rule of law, fervent commitment to the preservation of property, a high regard for gentry self-governance and a vigorous defence of
eroding social distinction all continued almost entirely unhindered by the absence of
King Charles II. These key elements of early modern English political culture were
the constituents of a 'vernacular republicanism', a hegemonic ideology which had
next to nothing to do with the relative merits of kingship and unkingship, because it
underpinned and helped to destroy both (Kelsey 1997).

Great opportunities lie in store for the study of unkingship. If not strictly the
'neglected subject' common to so many doctoral dissertations and academic monographs, the epoch from regicide to restoration has still not enjoyed anything like the
kind of attention lavished on the Stuart ages either side of it. For all the continuities
and similarities with earlier and later periods, there remain notable gaps in our
knowledge of governance in England after 1649. Much more work is needed to
contextualize the implementation of the engagement oath of loyalty to the kingless
commonwealth, as well as the formation of the regime's part-time militia forces. Both
policies may help to clarify aspects of the relationship between rulers, ruling and the
ruled during the period of unkingship. Meanwhile, new departures for the study of
politics and government were opened up a long time ago in a ground-breaking study
which examined some of the networks of patronage and influence criss-crossing the
executive and administration in the 1650s, providing useful new lines for enquiry into

the nature of the kingless Commonwealth and the ways in which it worked, few of which have yet been developed (Aylmer 1974). Interest in the period is bound to be revived when Professor Worden completes his multi-volume biography of Oliver Cromwell. The eventual publication of the relevant volumes of the *History of Parliament* will doubtless inspire future generations, as Professor Hirst has urged, to study the 1650s 'in their own terms'. Throughout successive eras of revisionism and post-revisionism in early modern historiographical scholarship, the age of unkingship has remained the last bastion of 'progressive' anachronism, Whig teleology and an assumption that 'revolutions' are somehow radically *different*. But the politics and governance of the period were dominated by much the same issues as dominated the entire early modern history of the atlantic archipelago: bold and imaginative responses to constitutional crisis; the creative reinvention of crown prerogative; paradoxical and unsustainable conjunctions of principle and pragmatism and all the rigmarole of courtly faction; the rule of law and legal impropriety; the interests of property and their abuse; military and political violence, sometimes fuelled by ethnic, more often by religious, hatred; dogged devotion to parliaments and frustration at their inadequacies; a (frequently millenarian) Protestant nationalism capable of justifying and explaining diametrically opposed foreign policy and colonial objectives; an unshakable devotion to social hierarchy, gentry oligarchy and the responsibilities of godly magistracy. Having for so long bashed away contentedly at the proposition that 'the Republic' was the square peg which would never fit the round hole of early modern archipelagic history, it is time to recognize that the hole was square, all along.

REFERENCES

Abbott, W. C. 1989: *The Writings and Speeches of Oliver Cromwell*, 2nd edn, 4 vols: Oxford.

Aylmer, G. E. 1974: *The State's Servants: The Civil Service of the English Republic 1649–1660*: London.

Barber, S. 1992: 'Irish undercurrents to the politics of April 1653', *Bulletin of the Institute of Historical Research*, 65, 315–35.

Barnard, T. C. 1997: *The English Republic 1649–1660*, 2nd edn: London.

Barnard, T. C. 2000: *Cromwellian Ireland*, 2nd edn: Oxford.

Blackwood, B. 1978: *The Lancashire Gentry in the Great Rebellion*: Manchester.

Braddick, M. J. 1994: *Parliamentary Taxation in Seventeenth-Century England: Local Administration and Response*: London.

Brenner, R. 1993: *Merchants and Revolution: Commercial Change, Political Conflict and London's Overseas Traders, 1550–1653*: Cambridge.

Buckroyd, J. 1987: 'Bridging the gap: Scotland, 1659–1660', *Scottish Historical Review*, 66, 1–25

Capp, B. S. 1989: *Cromwell's Navy: The Fleet and the English Revolution, 1648–1660*: Oxford.

Clarke, A. 1999: *Prelude to Restoration in Ireland*: Cambridge.

Coward, B. 1991: *Oliver Cromwell*: Harlow.

Cromartie, A. 1992: 'The rule of law.' In J. Morrill, ed., *Revolution and Restoration: England in the 1650s*: London.

Davies, G. 1955: *The Restoration of Charles II, 1658–1660*: San Marino, CA.

Davis, J. C. 2001: *Oliver Cromwell*: London.

Dow, F. 1979: *Cromwellian Scotland*: Edinburgh.

Durston, C. 2001: *Godly Governors: The Rule of Cromwell's Major Generals*: Manchester.

Egloff, C. S. 1990: 'Settlement and kingship: the army, the gentry, and the offer of the crown to Oliver Cromwell.' Unpublished Ph.D. thesis, Yale University.

Farnell, J. E. 1967: 'The usurpation of honest London householders: Barebone's Parliament', *English Historical Review*, 82, 24–46

Farr, D. 2000: 'Kin, cash, Catholics and cavaliers: the role of kinship in the financial management of major-general John Lambert', *Historical Research*, 74, 44–62

Firth, C. H. 1909: *The Last Years of the Protectorate, 1656–1658*, 2 vols: London.

Fletcher, A. 1986: *Reform in the Provinces: The Government of Stuart England*: New Haven, CT.

Gardiner, S. R. 1988: *History of the Commonwealth and Protectorate*, 4 vols: Adlestrop.

Gaunt, P. 1996: *Oliver Cromwell*: Oxford.

Gaunt, P. 1998: 'Cromwellian parliaments.' In I. Roots, ed., *Into Another Mould: Aspects of the Interregnum*, 2nd edn: Exeter.

Gentles, I. 1973: 'The sale of crown lands during the English Revolution', *Economic History Review*, 2nd series, 26, 614–35.

Gentles, I. 1997: 'The New Model officer corps in 1647: a collective portrait', *Social History*, 22, 127–44.

Gurney, J. 1994: 'Gerrard Winstanley and the Digger movement in Walton and Cobham', *Historical Journal*, 37, 775–802

Hill, C. 1991: *The World Turned Upside Down: Radical Ideas in the English Revolution*: Harmondsworth.

Hirst, D. 1996a: 'Locating the 1650s in England's seventeenth century', *History*, 81, 359–83.

Hirst, D. 1996b: 'The English republic and the meaning of Britain.' In B. Bradshaw and J. Morrill, eds, *The British Problem, c.1534–1707: State Formation in the Atlantic Archipelago*: Basingstoke.

Holiday, P. G. 1970: 'Land sales and repurchases in Yorkshire, 1650–70', *Northern History*, 5, 67–92.

Hughes, A. 1986: 'Parliamentary tyranny? Indemnity proceedings and the impact of the Civil War: a case study from Warwickshire', *Midlands History*, 11, 49–78.

Hughes, A. 1992: 'The frustrations of the godly.' In J. Morrill, ed., *Revolution and Restoration: England in the 1650s*: London.

Hutton, R. 1993: *The Restoration: A Political and Religious History of England and Wales, 1658–1667*, 3rd edn: Oxford.

Hutton, R. 2000: *The British Republic 1649–1660*, 2nd edn: London.

Kelsey, S. 1997: *Inventing a Republic: The Political Culture of the English Commonwealth, 1649–1653*: Manchester.

Kelsey, S. 2001: 'Staging the trial of Charles I.' In J. Peacey, ed., *The Regicides and the Execution of Charles I*: London.

Kelsey, S. 2002: 'The foundation of the council of state.' In C. Kyle and J. Peacey, eds, *Parliament at Work: Power, Patronage and Access, c.1510–1670*: London.

Kelsey, S. 2003a: 'The trial of Charles I', *English Historical Review*.

Kelsey, S. 2003b: 'The death of Charles I', *Historical Journal*.

Knoppers, L. 2000: *Constructing Cromwell: Ceremony, Portrait and Print, 1645–61*: Cambridge.

Little, P. 2000: 'The first unionists? Irish Protestant attitudes to union with England, 1653–9', *Irish Historical Studies*, 32, 44–58.

Manning, B. 1992: *1649, the Crisis of the English Revolution*: London.

Morrill, J. 1992: 'The impact on society.' In J. Morrill, ed., *Revolution and Restoration: England in the 1650s*: London.

Philips, C. 1978: 'The royalist north: the Cumberland and Westmorland gentry, 1642–1660', *Northern History*, 14, 169–92.

Pincus, S. 1996: *Protestantism and Patriotism: Ideologies and the Making of English Foreign Policy, 1650–1668*: Cambridge.

Roberts, S. 1998: 'Local government reform in England and Wales during the Interregnum: a survey.' In I. Roots, ed., *Into Another Mould: Aspects of the Interregnum*, 2nd edn: Exeter.

Sherwood, R. 1989: *The Court of Oliver Cromwell*, 2nd edn: Cambridge.

Smith, D. 1992: 'The struggle for new constitutional and institutional forms.' In J. Morrill, ed., *Revolution and Restoration: England in the 1650s*: London.

Thirsk, J. 1952: 'The sales of royalist lands during the Interregnum', *Economic History Review*, 2nd series, 5, 188–207.

Underdown, D. 1971: *Pride's Purge: Politics in the Puritan Revolution*: Oxford.

Woolrych, A. 1957: 'The good old cause and the fall of the Protectorate', *Cambridge Historical Journal*, 13, 133–61.

Woolrych, A. 1982: *Commonwealth to Protectorate*: Oxford.

Woolrych, A. 1990: 'The Cromwellian Protectorate: a military dictatorship?' *History*, 75, 207–31.

Worden, B. 1974: *The Rump Parliament, 1648–1653*: Cambridge.

FURTHER READING

Ashley, M. P. 1972: *Financial and Commercial Policy Under the Cromwellian Protectorate*, 2nd edn: London.

Aylmer, G. (ed.) 1974: *The Interregnum: The Quest for Settlement*: London.

Aylmer, G. (ed.) 1975: *The Levellers in the English Revolution*: Ithaca, NY.

Barber, S. 1998: *Regicide and Republicanism: Politics and Ethics in the English Revolution, 1646–1659*: Edinburgh.

Barber, S. 2000: *A Revolutionary Rogue: Henry Marten and the English Republic*: Stroud.

Buckroyd, J. 1976: 'Lord Broghill and the Scottish church', *Journal of Ecclesiastical History*, 27, 359–68.

Carlin, N. 1987: 'The Levellers and the conquest of Ireland in 1649', *Historical Journal*, 30, 269–88.

Collins, J. R. 2002: 'The church settlement of Oliver Cromwell', *History*.

Cotterell, M. 1968: 'Interregnum law reform: the Hale Commission of 1652', *English Historical Review*, 83, 689–704.

Egloff, C. 1998: 'The search for a Cromwellian settlement: exclusions from the second Protectorate parliament. Part 1: The process and its architects; Part 2: The excluded members and the reactions to the exclusion', *Parliamentary History*, 17, 178–97, 301–21.

Gentles, I. 1992: *The New Model Army in England, Ireland and Scotland, 1645–1653*: Oxford.

Grainger, J. D. 1997: *Cromwell Against the Scots: The Last Anglo-Scottish War, 1650–1652*: East Linton.

Hirst, D. 1988: 'Concord and discord in Richard Cromwell's House of Commons', *English Historical Review*, 103, 339–58.

Hirst, D. 1991: 'The failure of godly rule in the English republic', *Past and Present*, 132, 33–66.

Howell, R. 1993: 'Cromwell and his parliaments: the Trevor-Roper thesis revisited.' In R. C. Richardson, ed., *Images of Oliver Cromwell: Essays for and by Roger Howell*: Manchester.

Johnson, A. M. 1978: 'Wales during the Commonwealth and Protectorate.' In D. Pennington and K. Thomas, eds, *Puritans and Revolutionaries: Essays in Seventeenth-Century History Presented to Christopher Hill*: Oxford.

Roots, I. 1970: 'Swordsmen and decimators.' In R. H. Parry, ed., *The English Civil War and After, 1642–1658*: London.

Venning, T. 1995: *Cromwellian Foreign Policy*: London.

CHAPTER EIGHTEEN

Religion, 1640–1660

ANN HUGHES

Preliminaries

When the Long Parliament convened in November 1640, its position secured by the Scots army occupying the north of England, religion was a central element in contemporary analyses of the crisis, and more problematically, in contemporary hopes for redress and reform. John Pym, the Commons spokesman for the advanced opposition to Charles I, outlined the kingdom's ills in a two-hour speech on 7 November. He condemned a popish design to 'alter the kingdom both in religion and government', a design abetted by the 'corrupt part of our clergy' (Kenyon 1966: 204). Most members of the parliament, and, apparently, many in the country at large, were agreed on the need to dismantle the ecclesiastical 'innovations' promoted by the king and his archbishop of Canterbury, William Laud: the enforcement of ceremonial, the turning of the communion table 'altar-wise' and railing it off in the chancel, the elevation of clerical authority and the discouraging of godly preachers. No MP opposed the impeachment of Laud in December 1640, and he was placed under restraint. A midlands gentlewoman, Anna Temple, rejoiced that 'altars begin to go down apace and rails in many places'. She hoped to see 'idolatry and superstition rooted out and God's ordinances set up in the purity and power of them' (Hughes 1987: 131), while an enthusiastic MP, Sir John Wray, claimed the whole parliament was 'fully fixed upon the true Reformation of all Disorders and Innovations in Church or Religion' (Morrill 1993: 45). But the positive aspirations of Puritans like Temple and Wray proved more divisive and elusive than the negative attack on Laudianism. The ensuing twenty years were to witness the frustration of long-standing Puritan hopes for the completion, at long last, of the reformation of the English church. As English Protestantism fragmented irrevocably, a remarkable range of religious sects and radical speculations developed – to the marvelling of some and the horror of many; and a robustly self-conscious 'Anglican' commitment to a Protestant but not Puritan Church of England emerged, perhaps for the first time.

An older historiography conceived of this period as one of liberty and emancipation, as a populist Puritan commitment to lay activism and a stress on the individual conscience led inevitably to religious pluralism and toleration. More recently, in the wake of more sceptical views of the Protestant Reformation itself, historians have become more dubious about the accessibility and popularity of zealous Protestantism or Puritanism. It is not necessary here to spend long on the definitional disputes that have often obscured rather than clarified our understanding of religious affiliations. In the Grand Remonstrance, the partisan account of Charles's reign pushed through the House of Commons in November 1641, Pym and his associates highlighted the way in which the label 'Puritan' was both a term of abuse and one welcomed by those who identified themselves as the godly. Clause 64 mourned how 'The Puritans, under which name they include all those that desire to preserve the laws and liberties of the kingdom, and to maintain religion in the power of it, must be either rooted out of the kingdom with force, or driven out with fear' (Gardiner 1906: 216). Clearly we need more than this. For most historians Puritanism should be seen as a zealous, experiential Protestantism, marked by a particularly strong commitment to central tenets of the Reformation such as predestinarian Calvinist theology and the necessity for regular preaching of the word. Puritans worked energetically to construct networks of the godly self-consciously opposing the more complacent or 'profane' in their communities. Theirs was an intellectually challenging and morally demanding faith, which might well be regarded as forbidding, inaccessible and divisive by many who preferred a religious life based on regular participation in the rituals and ceremonies of the 'halfly reformed' English church. When the zealots in the Long Parliament – egged on by the Old Testament-style prophetic sermons established in its early months – moved on from attacks on abuses, altars and Laudian bishops to 'reform the Reformation' in the words of Edmund Calamy, a broad campaign emerged in defence of the Church of England, its bishops and most of all its worship enshrined in the Common Prayer Book (Calamy, quoted in Morrill 1993: 56).

The events of the 1640s and 1650s owe much to long-standing complexities and contradictions within Puritanism itself. Many Puritans claimed a commitment to order and stability; although this was to their own reformed and purified order, whose achievement might well entail disruption and instability. Nonetheless, in the Jacobean church where many bishops shared an adherence to Calvinist theology and lively preaching, Puritans had links with the ecclesiastical establishment. On the other hand, tensions among Puritans were held in precarious check through the 1630s in the face of the Laudian assault. But sharply divergent views on crucial issues of church government and salvation already troubled Puritans in both old and New England before 1640. The choice of exile in New England rather than remaining to defend true religion at home was itself controversial while leading Puritans such as Simeon Ashe became increasingly alarmed at trends in church government in Massachusetts. The power given to the broader congregation as opposed to the minister and elders was questioned and there was some disquiet also over the degree of independence of individual congregations. Here were the seeds of the adherence of men like Ashe to Presbyterian church government after 1640. The campaign for a Presbyterian church in England was, of course, immeasurably strengthened by the success of the Scots rebellion against Charles and by the Scots desire for reforms to bring the English church into line with their own Kirk. On the other hand, the exile congregations in the Netherlands and in New England had inevitably been self-governing and virtually autonomous. Returning exiles, especially from the Netherlands, such as Thomas Goodwin, Philip Nye and Jeremiah Burroughs, were to form the core of 'congregationalist' or Independent resistance to a Presbyterian church settlement in the 1640s. Furthermore the practices of the godly in England itself had increasingly focused on 'voluntary religion' – on 'gadding' from home parishes to godly sermons, on private conferences of dubious legality for discussion of sermons, fasting and prayer. The compromises between lay activism and clerical involvement within such activities would not fit easily within a formal Presbyterianism seen as unduly clericalist. Despite their flight, men like Thomas Goodwin in Holland and John Cotton in Massachu-setts regarded the Church of England as a true, if flawed church, but already in 1630s London and some other cities, small groups of separatists had become convinced that a national church comprehending both the ungodly and the godly was unacceptable.

Provocatively in Massachusetts and more mutedly in London the 1630s had also seen an 'Antinomian' challenge to what was denounced as a legalistic Calvinist divinity. Antinomians like Anne Hutchinson in Boston or Samuel Eaton in London criticized the obsessive introspection, the drive to examine one's life for signs of election that was a product of much Calvinist preaching, as in effect a salvation of works. Legalistic forms of Calvinism almost implied that certain types of conduct guaranteed election. 'Antinomians' stressed instead the overwhelming capacity of God's grace to transform his elect, hence underplaying the relevance of conventional obedience to the moral law. This more mystical strand of religious experience, with the immediate and perfect personal relationship between God and the elect at its core, was in part the product of debates and tensions within Calvinist Puritanism itself, in part derived from spiritual and perfectionist trends within the radical reformation. The potent mixture, characteristic also of much radicalism of the 1640s and 1650s, provoked an alarmed and repressive response from more mainstream Puritans.

Puritanism before 1640 thus comprehended a collective drive for overall reforma-tion and an urge towards immediate personal identification with the divine. Ironically, the realistic prospect of power to achieve a Puritan England had a corrosive impact as Puritans failed dramatically to agree on what they did want and earlier tensions became unbridgeable in the 1640s and 1650s. As well as the prospect of achieving a reformation, the period also brought heady but double-edged opportunities to publicize a variety of religious views and compete for support within a religious market-place where censorship had effectively collapsed and nothing had replaced the old ecclesiastical courts in enforcing church attendance or doctrinal orthodoxy. Significant numbers of parliament's supporters were radicalized by their continuing victories in what was understood to be a godly war, victories which intensified the millenarian elements in English religious culture. Again, while many felt that God was doing extraordinary things in and through his people, there was sharp disagreement over what form his interventions would take.

Most of the critics of Charles's personal rule had conformed under episcopal church government and would, in 1640, have accepted a 'reduced' or modified episcopacy. Throughout 1641 there were discussions aimed at reaching a church settlement led by the widely respected archbishop of Armagh, the Calvinist James Ussher, and Laud's old enemy John Williams, bishop of Lincoln. A Bill, read in the Lords in July 1641, sought to re-establish bishops as diocesan presidents with twelve ministers in each county to act as their assistants to bishops for ordination and disciplinary matters. The Bill also denounced Arminian doctrine and promised reform of abuses. This measure went no further and indeed its proposals had been overtaken by more radical hopes on the one hand, and a more positive episcopalianism on the other.

The difficulties of separating episcopacy as an institution from actual, often Lau-dian bishops, along with the optimism engendered by a reforming parliament, had encouraged more drastic steps. On 11 December 1640 a London petition to the Commons claimed that the 'government of archbishops and lord bishops, deans and archdeacons, etc, with their courts and ministrations in them, have proved prejudicial and very dangerous both to the Church and Commonwealth'. The claim that episcopal government carried divine authority was against the laws of the kingdom and derogatory to the power of the king. Under episcopacy, false doctrine, 'human inventions in God's worship' and lascivious books had been promoted while godly books had been banned and godly ministers harassed. The petitioners thus demanded that the government of the church 'with all its dependencies, roots and branches' be abolished (Gardiner 1906: 137–9). A pamphlet debate for and against Presbyterian church government ensued, although a Bill to abolish episcopacy languished in the Commons throughout 1641 and never reached the Lords.

Action against 'human inventions' was taken at local and central level. In September 1641 the House of Commons, claiming a novel authority to act alone, ordered churchwardens to remove ecclesiastical 'innovations' from parish churches. They were to take down the communion rails, remove the communion table from its 'altar-wise' position in the east of the church and level the chancel steps. All 'crucifixes, scandalous pictures of any one or more persons of the Trinity, and all images of the Virgin Mary' were to go, while bowing at the name of Jesus and Sunday 'sports' were banned. Altar rails had been the object of local attack since 1639, but these resolutions sanctioned further violent iconoclasm in the localities. The Herefordshire Puritan MP Sir Robert Harley pulverized the cross at Wigmore 'to dust', while at Leintwardine he pulled down the cross and beat the stained glass 'small with a hammer' before throwing it in the river (quoted in Russell 1995: 372).

The majority in the Lords were more hesitant. In September 1641 they countered the Commons decisions by reiterating an earlier order that church services as appointed by Act of parliament should be performed without disturbance and without any rites or ceremonies not sanctioned by the laws of the land. This order had been first passed in January 1641 following a Lords' investigation into lay preachers and separatist congregations in London. As yet the vast majority of parliamentary Puritans in both Houses supported a national church. As the Grand Remonstrance insisted:

> it is far from our purpose or desire to let loose the golden reins of discipline and government in the Church, to leave private persons or particular congregations to take up what form of Divine Service they please, for we hold it requisite that there should be throughout the whole realm a conformity to that order which the laws enjoin according to the word of God. And we desire to unburden the consciences of men of needless and superstitious ceremonies, suppress innovations, and take away the monuments of idolatry.

One startling exception was the radical peer Lord Brooke, whose tract against episcopacy published late in 1641 anticipated many of the views associated later in the 1640s with Cromwell. He was unworried by the prospect of religious disunity: in every age 'Divisions, Sects, Schisms and Heresies, must come' and advocated the tolerant approach of the United Provinces: 'how religion doth flourish there is known to most men'. He presented the arguments of the lay preachers and separatists denounced by his fellow peers in an overtly neutral way – 'I am speaking their words, not my own' – but in effect with remarkable sympathy, citing biblical texts supporting the preaching of gifted men. 'They conceive 30, or 40, or an 100 Good men of any one or more congregations, to be as fit Judges of their parts and abilities every way, as one Lord Bishop and his ignorant (perhaps drunken) chaplains' (Greville 1642: 88, 91, 106). Fear of separatism and disorder encouraged caution among most parliamentarians, however, and few positive measures were passed before war broke out; the Grand Remonstrance did not mention 'root and branch' reform but focused on removing the inordinate, temporal power of bishops.

In the House of Commons in July 1641 Sir John Culpepper had opposed the Lords Bill for a church settlement on the grounds that it failed to offer protection for the liturgy of the Book of Common Prayer. Within parliament and in many counties, increasing support was expressed for episcopacy and a more ceremonial worship throughout 1641–2. Over half of English counties sent petitions to parliament in support of episcopacy, more indeed than petitioned for its abolition. The sentiments expressed by Cromwell's county of Huntingdon were typical if unexpected:

> the form of divine service expressed and contained in the book of common prayer, was with great care, piety, and sincerity revised and reduced from all former corruptions and Romish superstitions, by those holy and selected instruments of the reformation of religion within this Church, and was by them restored to its first purity, according as it was instituted and practised in primitive times.

The holy instruments were the bishops, learned and pious men who had ruled the church throughout the Christian world since the 'first planting' of Christianity. They were 'the lights and glorious lamps of God's Church', and their government was sanctioned by God's word. The assaults on episcopacy by bitter troublemakers had brought division and disorder (Lindley 1998: 63–4). Although these petitions were clearly co-ordinated centrally by the emerging royalist party in Westminster, they equally clearly gained genuine and broad support in many counties. In Herefordshire some ministers and parishioners tried to stop Harley destroying their crosses, pictures and decorative glass.

'Anglican' religious commitment was at the heart of much royalist support, as godly Puritanism motivated parliamentarians. Parliament's victory in the Civil War, and the regimes that governed thereafter, brought for Puritans a complex mixture of freedom, opportunity and disillusionment, while Anglicans found in adversity a greater sense of a non-Puritan, non-Laudian Church of England, whose bishops had produced, defended and, under Mary I, died for its government and liturgy embodied in the Book of Common Prayer. The following sections will discuss the attempts to establish a godly national church, the radical challenges to this enterprise and Anglican obstruction and survival.

'The Public Profession of these Nations'

Although the bishops had been excluded from the Lords following demonstrations in the city in December 1641 (confirmed in legislation of February 1642), no formal abolition of episcopacy occurred until October 1646. Parliament's peace propositions from February 1643 called for the king to consent to Bills for the 'utter abolishing' of all archbishops, bishops, deans and other aspects of church government, and for an assembly of divines, plus measures against superstitious innovations, scandalous ministers and popery.

The Grand Remonstrance had also called for 'a general synod of the most grave, pious, learned and judicious divines of this island' to effect reformation, and the resulting Westminster Assembly met for the first time in the summer of 1643. Two ministers from each county, along with a small number of laymen, and from autumn 1643 voluble Scots representatives, worked energetically if not quickly on reformation of doctrine, liturgy and government in the English church. The obvious alternative to episcopal government for a Protestant national church was some variant of Presbyterianism and this solution became more likely after parliament's alliance with the Scots in the summer of 1643. The Solemn League and Covenant, the oath marking that alliance, and taken in theory by all adult males in England, bound parliamentarians to the preservation of the reformed religion in Scotland, against 'our common enemies', and to the reformation of religion in England and Ireland, 'in doctrine, worship, discipline and government, according to the Word of God, and the example of the best reformed Churches'. Adherents vowed to bring the churches in the three kingdoms of Ireland, Scotland and England 'to the nearest conjunction and uniformity in religion, confession of faith, form of Church government, directory for worship and catechising, that we, and our posterity after us, may, as brethren, live in faith and love, and the Lord may delight to dwell in the midst of us' (Gardiner 1906: 268–9).

For the Scots, and the majority in the Assembly, this meant a Presbyterian system of parish committees or elderships, with further neighbourhood and regional committees or assemblies in a pyramid topped by a general assembly. A Presbyterian church, crucially, would be comprehensive and compulsive. Power within the church flowed in two directions: ministers and lay elders were to be elected from parishes to local classes and county assemblies, but the deliberations of those bodies were in turn to be binding on the parishes. Such a structure ran contrary to many of the habits of godly 'voluntary religion' and the practices developed by exiled congregations. Thus a small but well-organized group of 'dissenting brethren', including Thomas Goodwin and Philip Nye, mounted a determined resistance to the broadly Presbyterian majority's plans for church government. There was much more agreement on matters of doctrine and worship, however. A 'Directory of Worship' was published in January 1645 and all parish ministers ordered to use it rather than the Book of Common Prayer. The Directory eschewed the set prayers and formal ceremony of its predecessors, offering ministers a stark framework into which appropriate preaching and prayer was to be inserted. 'Presbyterians' and 'Independents' worked together also on catechisms and a confession of faith endorsed by the assembly.

But church government caused bitter divisions in both assembly and parliament. In January 1644 Goodwin, Nye and three allies issued *An Apologeticall Narration* in which they argued for the autonomous power of single congregations on the basis of the practices of the primitive church and their own experiences in the Netherlands. Rejecting the 'proud and insolent title of Independency' – the label given them by their Presbyterian rivals – they declared 'we believe the truth to lie and consist in a middle way betwixt that which is falsely charged on us, Brownism [or separatism]; and that which is the contention of these times, the authoritative Presbyterial

Government in all the subordinations and proceedings of it' (Goodwin et al. 1644: 23–4). Fears of an authoritarian Presbyterianism, dominated by the clergy, grew also in the parliament, and the first 'Presbyterian' legislation, passed in August 1645, was regarded as wholly inadequate by the ministers of the assembly and their allies among the zealous Presbyterians of the City of London, both lay and clerical. Dispute focused on the location of ultimate authority in the church, with parliament insisting on the supremacy of lay commissioners rather than a general assembly. The most sensitive question was that of a final court of appeal for those excluded from the sacrament of the lord's supper; the power of the parish eldership to exclude parishioners from communion on grounds of scandalous life, or ignorance of fundamental doctrines of religion, was the crucial tool of Presbyterian 'discipline'. For committed Presbyterians it was an essential means of effecting a moral reformation and raising the religious understanding of the people. Prominent laymen like MPs used to controlling others' behaviour, rather than being subject to external judgements, feared public humiliation at the hands of the clergy and were determined not to give up control of the church to a general assembly. The ministers of the assembly responded by attempting to enumerate as many scandals as possible that would disqualify people from the sacrament, in order to limit the freedom of manoeuvre of any lay commissioners – a proceeding almost laughable now but to them deadly serious. Provocative petitioning campaigns from city and assembly continued until the spring of 1646, but produced only bitter rebuffs as parliament declared their petitions to be breaches of privilege. Furthermore the House of Commons declared that its commitment to a Presbyterian system did not tie it to giving an 'arbitrary and unlimited Power and Jurisdiction to near ten thousand Judicatories . . . nor have we yet resolved how a due regard may be had, that tender consciences which differ not in fundamentals of religion, may be so provided for, as may stand with the word of God and the peace of the kingdom' (*Journals of the House of Commons*, 17 April 1646). Only in June 1646 did London ministers, with great reluctance and many qualifications, agree to implement what they regarded as an inadequate Presbyterian structure.

Delays and divisions thus proved fatal to a fully functioning Presbyterian system. Although legislation elaborating the details of church government continued to appear until August 1648, it was never backed by any effective measures for enforcement. Only in London and Lancashire did a provincial assembly operate, with fairly wide participation but on an essentially voluntary basis, while some other areas developed local classes or other, less formal associations among parishes, as we shall see below. The basic 'Erastianism' (or commitment to lay authority) of most godly laymen and the rise of a parliamentary army committed to liberty of conscience had rendered Presbyterian legislation irrelevant. The army's proposed settlement with the king in 1647 – 'The Heads of the Proposals' – developed in co-operation with prominent Independent peers like viscount Saye, insisted 'That the taking of the Covenant be not enforced upon any, nor any penalties imposed on the refusers'. All Acts enforcing the use of the Book of Common Prayer and church attendance were to be repealed, but no overall scheme for a national church was proposed (Gardiner 1906: 321).

Much that the army and its allies wanted was achieved under the Commonwealth or Rump regime of 1649–53, established through the military revolution of

December 1648. In September 1650 all existing legislation imposing penalties for not coming to church was repealed, although the sabbath was to be observed and everyone was to perform 'some religious duty, either of prayer, preaching, reading or expounding the scriptures, or conferring upon the same' on Sundays and official days of thanksgiving or humiliation (ibid.: 394). The religious policies of the Rump illustrated the long-standing tensions within Puritanism with drives for reformation as well as a commitment to liberty. A sizeable minority in the Rump still hankered for a more coherent Presbyterian church, and the Commons passed in August 1650 an Act against 'several Atheistical, Blasphemous and Execrable Opinions'. Less restrictive than a 'Heresy Ordinance' of May 1648, passed after hectic Presbyterian agitation, this Act nonetheless condemned those who denied the divinity of Christ, or the existence of heaven, hell and sin, or who claimed to be God or equal to God. The 'Blasphemy Act' took its place among other measures which were the culmination of aspirations going back to the Elizabethan Puritan movement – against sabbath breaking, swearing and adultery. It also had more timely motives – being directed specifically against a miscellaneous collection of prophets, self-styled messiahs and 'Ranters' who claimed to be free from sin. These emerged in the months following the regicide and the establishing of the Commonwealth and caused an alarm entirely disproportionate to their numbers. After 1650 both adultery and blasphemy could be punishable by death – although very few died for adultery and no one for doctrinal offences.

Oliver Cromwell's Protectorate, established by an 'Instrument of Government', Britain's first written constitution, confirmed a degree of religious liberty remarkable for early modern Europe. Clauses 35–8 of the Instrument declared 'That the Christian religion, as contained in the Scriptures, be held forth and recommended as the public profession of these nations' and raised the prospect of maintenance for 'able and painful teachers' of religion 'less subject to scruple and contention, and more certain than the present' method of compulsory tithes. In the meantime, however, tithes were to be paid. Ministers were also responsible for the 'discovery and confutation of error, heresy and whatever is contrary to sound doctrine'. This 'public profession' was not compulsory: 'That to the Public profession held forth none shall be compelled by penalties or otherwise; but that endeavours be used to win them by sound doctrine and the example of a good conversation.' Instead:

> such as profess faith in God by Jesus Christ (though differing in judgement from the doctrine, worship or discipline publicly held forth) shall not be restrained from, but shall be protected in, the profession of the Faith, and exercise of their religion; so as they abuse not this liberty to the civil injury of others, and to the actual disturbance of the public peace on their parts. Provided this liberty be not extended to Popery nor Prelacy, nor to such as, under the profession of Christ, hold forth and practice licentiousness.

Catholics, provocative Episcopalians and 'Ranters' were thus excluded, but for the rest all legislation 'contrary of the aforesaid liberty shall be esteemed as null and void' (Gardiner 1906: 416).

The Humble Petition and Advice of May 1657 sought, in religious as in other matters, to take the Protectorate in a more conservative direction. Most MPs had been thoroughly alarmed by the Quaker James Naylor's provocative entrance into

Bristol in blasphemous imitation of Christ's entry into Jerusalem. During the debate on Naylor's crime and punishment many MPs shared the views of the army veteran, Major-General Philip Skippon: 'These Quakers, Ranters, Levellers, Socinians and all sorts, bolster themselves under thirty-seven and thirty-eight of Government, which at one breadth, repeals all the acts and ordinances against them. I have heard the supreme magistrate [Cromwell] say it was never his intention to indulge such things, yet we see the issue of this liberty of conscience' (Rutt 1828: 49–50). Thus the Humble Petition spelt out more carefully what was permitted and committed the regime to a more assertive promotion of the 'public profession'. A 'Confession of Faith' was to be agreed by the Protector and the Parliament and 'asserted, held forth and recommended to the people of these nations'. No one was to be permitted 'by opprobrious words or writing maliciously or contemptuously to revile or reproach the Confession of Faith'. There remained freedom of worship for those who 'profess faith in God the Father, and in Jesus Christ his eternal Son, the true God, and in the Holy Spirit, God co-equal with the Father and the Son, One God blessed for ever, and do acknowledge the Holy Scriptures of the Old and New testament to be revealed Will and Word of God. (Kenyon 1966: 355)

From 1646 at least therefore the parliamentarian regimes had been as concerned with securing liberty of conscience and worship outside a national church, as with the nature of the 'public profession'. Bishops and church courts had been removed but no comprehensive national structure was enforced. Throughout the 1640s and 1650s, however, parliaments and Protector did concern themselves with the nature of the ministry and with worship at a parish level. Puritans had long been concerned with the lack of adequate support for a learned, preaching ministry and from the mid-1640s, tithe income sequestered from the church or convicted royalists was used to 'augment' the stipends of approved parish ministers and pastors of some gathered congregations. The Rump established more systematic procedures in June 1649, and Cromwell built on their work with an ambitious reforming ordinance of September 1654 which established Trustees for the Maintenance of Ministers. As often in early modern England, implementation of these arrangements was sometimes haphazard, but after 1654 some thirty Warwickshire ministers were receiving a total of £1,000 per annum in augmentations. The Rump had conducted comprehensive surveys of the standards and maintenance of the parish clergy in 1650, and these made recommendations for some reform of parochial structure through division of large parishes and amalgamation of tiny ones. Again, Cromwell built on this work and some of the changes were implemented after 1654.

This gives some idea of survivals as well as transformations in the 1640s and 1650s. The basic parish structure was left alone, although parish worship now, in theory at least, was organized around the Directory's framework rather than the Book of Common Prayer, and moved to a different rhythm. The great festivals of the Anglican church, particularly Christmas, were denounced as superstitious relics and a more uniform calendar instituted, centred on Sundays and punctuated by extraordinary days of thanksgiving or humiliation as events dictated. Compulsory maintenance of the parish ministry by tithes continued, despite moves in the Barebone's Assembly to abolish them, and despite the pious hopes of the Instrument of Government. The uncertainty of any alternative provision, along with the fact that tithes were a form of property ownership, held by lay people as well as clergymen, prevented change. Lay patronage, too, was tinkered with but not really challenged; its survival meant that a speedy and dramatic transformation in the nature of the parish clergy was never likely – as reformers had discovered from the earliest days of the English Reformation. Procedures for the removal of unsuitable clergy operated on a local level and a national level throughout the 1640s, and Cromwell sought to complete a purge of 'scandalous' ministers by re-establishing county commissioners with clerical assistants in 1654. The impact of these arrangements will be discussed below. Positive measures for the ordination and approval of parish ministers were more haphazard before 1654. The Presbyterian classes of London and other local groupings of clergy ordained, but many aspirant ministers were uncertain where to turn, and it is clear that some sought out bishops living in retirement and obtained traditional episcopal ordination. In March 1654 Cromwell's ordinance for the Approbation of Public Preachers established the 'Triers' – a central group of clergy who approved parish ministers and others in receipt of public maintenance on the basis of local testimonials, certificates of ordination and a call to a parish or other congregation.

What is remarkable about this rather patchy, loosely defined church structure is the degree of co-operation on both a local and national level after 1651, between men who had disagreed very sharply on church government in the mid-1640s and clashed bitterly over regicide and the establishment of a republic in 1648–50. A coercive Presbyterian system was no longer feasible after 1648, so Independents could relax and be gracious. The bitter conflicts of 1644–9, however, were misleading, as the conflicts over church government obscured the extent to which Presbyterians, especially the less doctrinaire of them, and respectable Congregationalists had things in common. Most Congregationalists were not strict separatists and held communion with the parish churches; some indeed, like Philip Nye, held parochial livings alongside their ministry to gathered congregations. They believed in an educated, ordained ministry and were doubtful about the preaching of gifted laymen and, through taking state maintenance, were indirect receivers of tithes. Although the assault by zealous Presbyterians in the 1640s may have forced Independents into an uneasy temporary alliance with more radical groups, they were alarmed by strict separation and more thorough-going doctrinal speculation among groups who endorsed general redemption or Antinomian mysticism. This grouping has been dubbed 'magisterial Independents', as they accepted the right of the civil magistrate to legislate on church matters (as Cromwell did in 1654) – in contrast to both committed Presbyterians and more radical separatists. On doctrine, Independents and Presbyterians had much common ground. William Bridge, one of the signatories of the *Apologeticall Narration*, considered Arminians and Socinians to be heretics and blasphemers. The clause in the Instrument of Government guaranteeing liberty of conscience to those who 'profess faith in God by Jesus Christ' excluded those who rejected the trinity or the divinity of Christ. Parliaments dominated by Independents condemned the Socinian John Biddle in 1654 and the Quaker James Naylor in 1656. The rise of an aggressive Quaker movement generally prompted a closer alliance between Independents and Presbyterians.

Some Presbyterians were irreconcilable. The veteran Scots minister Robert Baillie, writing to Simeon Ashe in 1655, was bitterly contemptuous of the compromises of

Stephen Marshall, then on his deathbed. But a majority abandoned the futile quest for a coercive national church and came to a *rapprochement* with the regimes of the Rump and Cromwell, which at least had a commitment to a preaching ministry and to godly reform. There were thus broad discussions in the later months of the Rump and throughout the Protectorate which aimed at definitions of the 'fundamentals of religion', or producing the Confession of Faith promised by the Humble Petition. These discussions always began with high hopes, but then floundered as some Independents and Baptists came to fear that too narrow a definition of orthodoxy would exclude them from a doctrinal consensus and render them heretics. A broader liberty of conscience than Presbyterians wished for thus survived and no agreed Confession of Faith ever emerged in the later 1650s. The long discussions themselves, however, are testimony to the overlapping interests among the godly.

On practical matters the 'establishment' in the Cromwellian church ranged from Presbyterians to non-separatist Calvinist Baptists. The majority of the Triers, for example, were mostly the mainstream Independents who were closest to Cromwell, like Thomas Goodwin, Nye and John Owen, but moderate Presbyterians such as Marshall, Anthony Tuckney and Thomas Manton also served alongside the most respectable of the Baptists, Henry Jessey and John Tombes. At a local level, many Presbyterians were willing by 1654 to act as assistants to the commissioners charged with ejecting scandalous ministers: the Presbyterian author Samuel Clarke served in London, and Adoniran Byfield, one of the scribes of the Westminster Assembly, in Wiltshire. In Lancashire Presbyterians like Henry Newcome and Robert Constantine acted with the Independent Samuel Eaton and the Baptist John Wigan in signing testimonials for ministers seeking approval from the Triers. Many Lancashire Presbyterians, like Robert Constantine of Oldham had suffered suspension and even imprisonment in 1650–1 over their refusal to take the Engagement of loyalty to the new Commonwealth, but three years later they were secure in their parishes and many accepted additional income – augmentations – from the non-monarchical regimes.

Although there was no legally enforceable organization in the church beyond the parish, the classes and provincial assemblies of Lancashire and London met until shortly after the restoration of Charles II. They operated essentially as voluntary bodies, dependent on the willing participation of ministers and laymen. In other parts of the country in the 1650s a variety of informal associations emerged to offer advice and support to parish ministers. The best known of these, the Worcestershire Association established by Richard Baxter, sought to avoid contentious issues of church government and partisan labels, giving priority to pastoral matters and collegial relationships. This association, perhaps the most successful, comprehended no more than a third of the county's ministers, while more overtly Presbyterian-style enterprises in Devon, Nottingham and Warwickshire involved much smaller numbers. In Cumberland and Westmoreland and in Cheshire, ministers co-operated in often dispiriting campaigns to catechize their parishioners. The Cheshire Presbyterian Adam Martindale described in his autobiography how many of the 'old ignoramuses' contrived to be away from home when he called to catechize them, and bemoaned the large parishes of the northwest which ensured that half his congregation would be dead before he could get round to instructing them.

The association established in Cheshire in October 1653 did not claim any right to 'any pastoral inspection over one another's congregations; but only to be helpful to them in a charitable way'. This body approved elders and ordained ministers, and sought to support parish ministers in their most difficult dilemmas over criteria for admission to the sacrament. Most 'Anglicans' admitted all but the notoriously scandalous and regarded the communion as a symbol of parochial unity, beyond its theological significance, while separatists admitted only those 'visible saints' who had voluntarily joined their congregation. Mainstream Puritans saw admission to the sacrament as a privilege for those who understood the main tenets of true religion, and led lives free from scandal. For godly ministers admission or non-admission was a means of raising standards (and hence catechizing to improve people's knowledge was part of the process) and of disciplining the profane. For parishioners used to a more easy-going regime this replaced a communal celebration with a divisive and potentially humiliating ordeal, and the administration of the sacrament of the Lord's supper was a source of tension within parishes throughout this period. The veteran London Puritan Thomas Gataker complained that many of his parishioners refused to pay their tithes 'because I admit not all promiscuously to the Lords table'. In Earls Colne, the Essex parish of Ralph Josselin, the sacrament was suspended altogether for nine years and only revived after much heart-searching in February 1651. In Martindale's parish one young man was excluded for scandal because his wife was pregnant before their marriage. This very common offence would not have been seen as scandalous by most of Martindale's parishioners and the young man himself responded by joining the Quakers.

But if ministers like Josselin and Martindale were at odds with some of their parishioners, they also had the benefit of intimate and mutually supportive relationships with an inner core or godly elite among their neighbours. The arrangements for the restoration of the sacrament in Earls Colne emerged after conscientious debate among a company of the godly who met weekly with Josselin. In Martindale's parish of Rostherne, 'the people that were most eminent for profession of religion' kept up 'work-day conferences' to discuss disputed questions of divinity. They were to some extent a social as well as a religious elite, able to spare the time in the working week, although on Martindale's own account they were not all able to write. The group's notes and discussions of contentious issues were polished by Martindale into an 'axiomatical catechism' and published as *An Antidote against the Poyson of the Times* (Martindale 1845).

There was broad godly support also for general reformation, for assaults on idleness, drunkenness and swearing, on bridal pregnancy and other sexual offences, on profanation of the sabbath or the popish, superstitious pastimes of maypoles and dancing. In 1643 the Solemn League and Covenant had called for 'real reformation' – implying a broad moral, social and educational transformation: 'our true and unfeigned purpose, desire and endeavour, for ourselves and all others under our power and charge, both in public and in private, in all duties we owe to God and man, [is] to amend our lives, and each one go before another in the example of a real reformation' (Gardiner 1906: 270). Again, the campaigns for moral reformation were longstanding Puritan traditions: the Rump's adultery Act was the culmination of pressure going back to Elizabethan parliaments. Throughout the 1640s and 1650s, however, the drive for a purified society was given added point by the godly's association of profanity and superstition with royalism. Cromwell argued in September 1656 that the cavaliers had the 'badge and character of countenancing profaneness, disorder and wickedness in all places' and it was not coincidental that when the parliament met on 25 December 1656 (a day the profane called Christmas), the debate focused on renewal of punitive taxation on royalists. As Major-General Lambert complained, royalists 'are, haply, now merry over their Christmas pies, drinking the king of Scots health, or your confusion' (quoted in Hughes 1992: 74). As we have seen, catechizing and exclusion of the unsuitable from the sacrament were the specifically religious means of encouraging moral transformation, while there were periodic attempts to spur local governors into action against vice and wickedness. The most determined were those by Cromwell's Major-Generals, who were given wide powers to supervise local governors. Their aim was to 'encourage and promote godliness and virtue, and discourage and discountenance all profaneness and ungodliness', but they had large complex territories to oversee and extensive security preoccupations. Although the energetic young Major-General Charles Worsley died of exhaustion following an unremitting campaign against alehouses in Lancashire it seems that the Major-Generals' impact on local government, like other initiatives, was patchy and short-lived. The godly's highest hopes for the moral purification of England were dashed – inevitably. The fact that all regimes of the 1640s and 1650s had a vision of 'real reformation' and overt commitment to its achievement, is nonetheless important in itself.

A broad range of the godly gained significantly during the 1640s and 1650s: they had the freedom to preach, publish and evangelize, and to nurture their supportive networks free from the demands of bishops and ceremonial uniformity. Many, and not only Independents, were close to the heart of affairs in London and in the provinces. But they had to compete for support in a religious market-place where liberty of conscience was guaranteed by law, and for Presbyterians and others who wished for a comprehensive national church this brought many frustrations. A voluntary discipline was a contradiction in terms – those who chafed under an exacting parochial regime could simply go elsewhere, like Martindale's young man turned Quaker. The most ambitious hopes for Puritan reformation floundered on their own divisions over church government – unnecessarily bitter in the mid-1640s – but also on the open challenges of separatism and radical speculation – and the sullen obstructionism of the less prominent but more numerous groupings who maintained a stubborn adherence to 'prelacy'. These contrasting responses will now be discussed.

Radical Experimentation

It is neither useful nor possible to define the religious radicalism of the period too precisely: radicalism is always comparative and contextual, to be identified in concrete situations and with reference to particular issues. Mainstream and radical Puritans need to be located on a spectrum or rather on a series of spectra because people who were radical on one measure, such as rejection of a compulsory national church, might be orthodox on another, such as commitment to an ordained ministry or to Calvinist predestinarian doctrine. Many radical impulses emerged, as already emphasized, from and against Puritan traditions, while others came from the rather different roots of the enthusiastic mysticism of the radical reformation. Congregationalists such as Thomas Goodwin – the subject of virulent attack in the 1640s by Presbyterian propagandists such as Thomas Edwards, who denounced 'Independents' as the allies and promoters of separatists and heretics – mounted a radical attack on a Presbyterian church settlement, but in many other ways were part of the 'establishment'. The ambiguities of their position are evident in the need to discuss them both here and in the previous section. Mainstream Independents like Thomas Goodwin or Nye can be located with other religious radicals within the politically radical wing of parliamentarianism, supporting the regicide and the establishing of the Commonwealth in 1649, for example. But within this broad alignment there were many bitter cleavages – among supporters of the Rump, the army or those calling for the rule of the Saints in 1652–3; or between opponents and supporters of Cromwell becoming king in 1657, forcing the Protector to cashier hostile Baptist officers from his own regiment. The most distinctive political stance among religious radicals was that of the Fifth Monarchy movement of the early 1650s. The dramas of regicide and revolution encouraged a belief in the prophecies of the Book of Daniel that a fifth monarchy of divine rule would follow the successive overthrow of the world's empires. Impatient with the hesitations of the Rump, fiery London preachers called for its overthrow and for the rule of the Saints – a godly elite – who would prepare the way for King Jesus. While many Protestants were affected by millenarian expectations during these drastic upheavals, most believed in waiting on the Lord rather than hastening godly rule through direct action.

Church government, as we have seen, forms one spectrum along which radical positions can be identified. Where Presbyterians and other mainstream Puritans called for a reformed compulsory national church, radicals argued that the true church in this world was not a mixed body of saints and sinners but a voluntary gathering of the visibly godly. It might well be constituted through a formal covenant or agreement, and have formal methods for admission of members – usually through some public testimony of a saving faith. The Calvinist Baptist churches of the West Country advised that no one was to be admitted to one of their congregations 'without a declaration of an experimental work of the Spirit upon the heart' (White 1971–4: 56). There were diverse positions, however, on the proper relationship of these gathered congregations or 'churches of Christ' to the national church. The mainstream Congregationalists and 'open-communion' Baptists, for example, did not want to be part of a parochially based national church, but they seem to have accepted the necessity for some 'public profession' and themselves participated in its activities as Triers or assistants to county commissioners for scandalous ministers. Many accepted state maintenance as lecturers. The London Fifth Monarchists of the early 1650s combined political extremism with a more moderate stance on church government and were mostly from non-separatist congregations. The Kent Independent John Durant is a striking example of how a man can seem extreme in some contexts, mainstream in others. Durant was one of the lay preachers denounced in the Lords in 1641 as an unqualified wash-ball maker, yet he had clearly been to a university and at some stage was more formally ordained. By 1649 he was pastor of an Independent congregation in Canterbury whose members petitioned for the trial and punishment of the king. Throughout the 1650s, however, he defended orthodox Puritan positions within his congregation – denouncing those who were attracted by 'Arminian' errors on free will, and insisting that the church offices of minister and elder were of divine origin. He accepted public maintenance, and his membership of the Cromwellian establishment was confirmed, as for many others, by service as an assistant to the commissioners for scandalous ministers.

In contrast to Durant or Thomas Goodwin, some congregations were strict separatists, shunning the corruptions of the 'world'. The Calvinist Baptist congregations who consulted together as a West Country association in the 1650s counselled against their members hearing parochial or other 'national' ministers as a 'conforming to the worship of those men which we are commanded to separate from'. They were as strongly opposed to their ministers taking any public or set maintenance 'from those that are without'. Instead ministers should rely on the voluntary contributions of their flock, or earn their living in some everyday calling. Taking money from the 'world' was a 'tye and fetter upon the feet of the ministers of the Gospel', forcing them to preach 'according to the will of men'. It would compromise their capacity to criticize the parish ministers who 'Balaam like run after the reward . . . the way of the ministry of the whore of Babylon'. For these separatist Baptists, tithes were 'a soule offending and oppressing yoke' (White 1971–4: 61–3, 69). Quakers, too, condemned tithes as an anti-Christian burden on the consciences of Christians and an exploitation of the poor. They ridiculed church buildings as 'steeple houses' and parish ministers as corrupt priests, preaching for hire by the 'hour-glass'. All these separatist groups rejected the mainstream Protestant notion of a publicly maintained, highly educated, specifically ordained ministry. Instead they argued that 'gifted men', whatever their background, should be allowed to exercise their god-given gifts in preaching and otherwise leading the congregations. In some gathered congregations, separatist and Baptist, the gifted men who emerged were set apart in some formal way to perform ministerial functions. In the most radical groups, such as the Quakers and some general Baptist congregations, the whole idea of a specialized ministry was rejected and women as well as men were allowed to preach if qualified and inspired.

The early Quakers were far from the quietist pacifists of later stereotypes. Rather, they were aggressive and provocative – competing very systematically for support with other radical groups, especially the Baptists. George Fox, now the best known of their early leaders, described a typical incident from 1655: 'And from Romney I passed to Dover, and near unto Dover there was a governor that was convinced and his wife that had been Baptists: and at Dover I had a meeting where several were convinced and the Baptists were very much offended and envious: but the Lord's power came over all' (Fox 1998: 158). From the other point of view, the records of the General Baptist churches of East Anglia are full of attempts to prevent defections to the Quakers. At Fenstanton in 1654–5 many were 'carried away by those people commonly called quakers', claiming to be guided by the light in their consciences; and when 'we began to speak of the ordinances of God which formerly they believed and practised, as baptism, breaking of bread etc, these they affirmed to be carnal ordinances'. The renegades said 'it was folly to be baptised' and refused to listen to their former brethren (Underhill 1854: 115–16).

The Quakers were practical mystics, co-ordinating the distribution of their printed pamphlets with well-organized evangelizing missions. They interrupted parish ministers in their sermons, and displayed hostile printed broadsides on church doors and other public places. One Cheshire schoolmaster claimed: 'Their religion consists chiefly in censuring others, & railing upon them, especially Ministers, whom they despised and counted as the Dung of the Earth, making it their ordinary practice to disturb them in their Sermons. They denied the Trinity, they denied the Scriptures to be the Word of God; they said they had no Sin' (Burghall 1889: 229–30). Adam

Martindale was 'severall times affronted by some of that gang at mine own church and elsewhere, and pelted with their furious papers', while the Essex minister Ralph Josselin was openly derided by the Quakers. 'There cometh your deluder' one shouted after him in the street, while another cried 'woe to the false prophet' as he went in to church with a fellow minister in September 1656 (Martindale 1845: 117; Macfarlane 1976: 379–80).

The radical congregations had sharply contrasting reactions to Calvinist teaching on salvation. Baptists who agreed on the necessity for adult baptism as the mark of membership of their congregations were sharply divided between 'particular' Baptists who held orthodox Calvinist views and 'general' Baptists who preached universal redemption. Some of the most extreme groups could be seen as prompted in part by Calvinist speculation. Ranters' practical licentiousness could be justified by an Anti-nomian perfectionism that held the elect were free from sin and could not fall from grace. The founders of one of the most remarkable sects of the 1650s, the Muggle-tonians, were Lodowick Muggleton and John Reeve, who had a simple solution to the problem of how to tell who the elect were. They claimed to be the two witnesses of the Book of Revelation, whose testimony guaranteed salvation for their followers. These radicals took Calvinist theology on salvation to distinctive but not illogical conclusions. Others, though, rejected the exclusivity of predestination in favour of general redemption, the doctrine that Christ had died for all who believed in him. As well as the general Baptists, their bitter rivals the Quakers rejected Calvinism. Their doctrine of the 'light within' offered the prospect of salvation to all who accepted the light – a mystical identification with the risen Christ.

In other ways, however, Baptist religious experience differed dramatically from Quaker practice. The Baptists were biblical literalists and obsessive formalists, search-ing the letter of the Bible for guidance on all aspects of their lives and convinced that formal routines such as baptism were an essential mark of the true church. The West Country association approached all problems through analysis of scriptural texts. They planned 'some rule for habit and hair, inasmuch as costly habit of women and long hair of men are both forbidden in the scripture', but floundered over the lawfulness of using astrology in medical treatment and had 'to wait on the Lord for further light in it' because of the ambiguity of scripture (White 1971–4: 54, 65). The Quakers, on the other hand, rejected literalism and formalism. Quaker prose was saturated with biblical quotation in a repetitive, poetic style, yet for Quakers the word of God was not identical with the letter: the Bible had to be apprehended through the prism of the spirit. Where the Baptist obsession with forms often led to a despairing preoccupation among their members with the validity of their baptism and the authenticity of their faith, Quakers offered a straightforward and immediate promise of a mystical and personal identification with Christ. Hence their appeal to disillu-sioned Baptists.

The 1640s and 1650s form a crucial period in English history, a period of liberty when sects like varieties of Baptists and the Quakers were able to evangelize and organize so effectively that they survived the persecution of ensuing decades. Despite the anxieties expressed in the debates on Naylor that liberty had gone too far, some MPs refused to condemn Quakers. The Baptist Lord President of the Council Henry Lawrence and Colonel William Sydenham both affirmed that Quaker doctrine was near 'to that which is a glorious truth, that the spirit is personally in us'

(Rutt 1828: 62). From the early 1640s a minority of radicals like the Leveller William Walwyn had argued for the toleration of erroneous doctrines; Cromwell was overtly committed to a narrower liberty for a variety of groups who sought common religious truths, but his regime in practice went further than this. In theory, as we have seen, the Instrument of Government did not guarantee full religious liberty, yet Cromwell in particular, like Brooke in 1641, was reluctant to persecute those he thought were mistaken, unless they were intolerably provocative. In August 1650 he had issued a moving protest to the doctrinaire Presbyterian ministers of Scotland: 'is it therefore infallibly agreeable to the word of God all that you say? I beseech you in the bowels of Christ think it possible that you may be mistaken' (Abbott 1939: II, 303). Such open-mindedness underlay Cromwell's willingness to listen to George Fox when he rode up to his coach in Hyde Park in 1656 to denounce the 'sufferings of friends . . . contrary to Christ' (Fox 1998: 207–8) and ensured that most radicals suffered limited harassment under his regimes.

The preceding discussion in terms of organized groups is in some ways misleading, for the religious ferment of the time also witnessed many less formal, loose gatherings of 'seekers' who rejected all external forms and organization in favour of personal quests for truth and also many eccentric but momentarily influential charismatic prophets of self-styled messiahs, such as William Franklin, who toured the country with a woman companion Mary Gadbury who believed Franklin to be the Messiah and described herself as the spouse of Christ. The Quakers' remarkably rapid success in the early 1650s was possible because they brought together a range of hitherto scattered mystical 'Seeker' groups in the far northwest.

In London in particular, but also in East Anglia, Kent, the east midlands and the far northwest, there is evidence for small separatist and semi-separatist congregations meeting before 1640, but subject to legal harassment from church and secular authorities. The semi-separatist congregation led by Henry Jacob provided a seed-bed for many of the Baptist and separatist groups that grew larger and bolder during the Civil War, including the church headed by Praisegod Barebone and the partly Baptist congregation led by Henry Jessey. The collapse of ecclesiastical authority, the freedom of press and pulpit and the upheavals of civil war formed a potent environment for sectarian speculation and organization. Despite all the qualifications that cautious historians make, the role of parliament's godly army was crucial. It was a crucible where lay preaching and religious discussion flourished. A range of prominent individual radicals from Paul Hobson, pastor of a London Baptist congregation, to the Quaker James Naylor, had served in parliament's armies, while on a collective level the army both secured liberty of conscience through its national political influence from 1646–7 and protected specific congregations in garrison towns throughout the 1650s.

By the mid-1640s it has been estimated that there were some thirteen independent churches in London, with differing stances towards the national church and nine stricter separatist groups under lay pastors. Eight Calvinist Baptist churches signed a confession of faith in 1646; the most influential was that led by William Kiffin and Thomas Patient (Tolmie 1977).

More radical and aggressive were the general Baptists connected with the congregation led by Thomas Lambe, a charismatic soap boiler. Notorious members of this group included the Leveller Richard Overton and the woman preacher 'Mrs Attaway'. Lambe's church pioneered the missionary expeditions later perfected by Quaker preachers (who indeed often followed the same routes). Samuel Oates, the most famous of these itinerant preachers, was a Norwich man who already had contacts with Essex separatists and helped establish congregations throughout the eastern counties in the 1640s.

By 1660 it has been calculated that there were some 150 particular Baptist congregations and about 100 of general Baptists, with a combined membership of perhaps 25,000 (McGregor 1984). These were concentrated in the south, the west and the midlands and increasingly preoccupied with maintaining their own organization and integrity in the face of the Quaker challenge rather than with evangelizing in the corrupt world. The Baptists were relatively weak in the north, but it was here that the Quakers first emerged to become the most successful of the radical movements of the Interregnum.

It has been suggested that no more than 5 per cent of the population attended radical congregations before the emergence of the Quakers, although numbers will have risen in the later 1650s. However, the energy and singular stances of the radicals ensured they had an impact, both positive and negative, much greater than mere numbers would suggest.

The sects were associated by their alarmed opponents with political extremism and social subversion, and the priority given to voluntary membership of gathered congregations could cut across previous allegiances to families and communities. Most religious radicals held conventional opinions on social and gender hierarchies, yet they also insisted that obedience to God came before worldly loyalties. Equally the sects gave opportunities for participation and leadership to many groups, male and female, who wielded little influence in the outside world. Several congregations were led by charismatic figures from relatively privileged and educated backgrounds; many indeed, like the general Baptist Henry Denne, were renegade parish ministers. But many others, like the Quakers Fox, Naylor and Edward Burroughs, the Ranter and Muggletonian Laurence Clarkson, and the general Baptists Lamb and Oates, were from humbler backgrounds: artisans, small tradesmen or husbandmen. The very poor were rarely prominent in radical congregations, but men and women from the middling sort were numerous and influential. The social implications of religious separatism were complex: internally the sects operated on relatively egalitarian lines and Quakers, in particular, were aggressively critical of the corrupt hierarchies of the world. The Quakers refused conventional marks of social respect such as 'hat-honour' to their social superiors – whom they also addressed with the intimate 'thou' form of the second person. On the other hand, religious radicals were spiritual elitists, claiming to apprehend truths not vouchsafed to outsiders. Their uneasy or hostile relations with more conventional neighbours limited their social influence. Consequently the Quakers, who gained adherents throughout the social spectrum, with a preponderance of people of middling status, also aroused much hostility from what Fox called the 'rude multitude' who stoned them from Warwick in a typical episode (Fox 1998: 171).

The implications of radical religion for gender hierarchy and women's autonomy were equally ambiguous. Women were a majority or large minority of the membership in many congregations, such as the Fenstanton General Baptists. Dorothy Hazzard, widow of a Bristol grocer and later wife to an ordained minister, played a crucial role in the establishing of an Independent congregation in the city around 1640; she was eulogized as a Deborah, a mother in Israel. Many women found in intense, personal religious commitment a self-expression denied in other aspects of their lives. Many churches, however, were uneasy at the prominence and independence of women, and for the orthodox the visibility of women was in itself a sign of sectarian error. The Pauline text 2 Timothy 3 was commonly quoted: 'in the last days perilous times shall come' with the rise of false prophets, 'which creep into houses and lead captive silly women, laden with sins, led away with divers lusts'. Nonetheless scores of women were active as organizers, propagandists and itinerant preachers in the Quakers and in a typically aggressive tract, Priscilla Cotton and Mary Coles (1655) turned 2 Timothy 3 against the scoffers:

> Silly men and even women may see more into the mystery of Christ Jesus than you, for the apostles, that the scribes called illiterate, and Mary and Susanna (silly women as you would be ready to call them, if they were here now) these know more of the Messiah, than all the learned priests and rabbis, for it is the spirit that searcheth all things.

Baptists and even Quakers faced inescapable dilemmas, for they held conventional views on gender hierarchies in the everyday world, but believed that church membership might involve defying the authority of fathers or husbands. Furthermore they held that in these extraordinary times God might well show his power by choosing extraordinary means to work his will. This latter feeling justified the remarkable roles of women as prophets among the Quakers and the Fifth Monarchists. Fifth Monarchist women such as Mary Cary and Anna Trapnel acquired a remarkable public and political influence as the channels – they held – for God's denunciations of the Cromwellian betrayal of the godly cause. In 1654 Trapnel went into a trance in Whitehall, fasting, praying and singing for hours each day. Eminent visitors heard her explain her conversion to become an 'instrument' of God's purposes: 'for particular soules shal not onely have benefit by her, but the Universality of Saints shal have discoveries of God through her' (Trapnel 1654a: 4). Trapnel denounced Cromwell as the 'little horn' from the Book of Daniel who turned on the Saints; she proceeded to a preaching and prophesying tour of Cornwall where she attracted large audiences, split between those who accepted her pronouncements as the word of God, and those who denounced her as a witch or vagrant (Trapnel 1654b).

Radical millenarians appealed to the inspiring words of Joel 2. 28–9: 'I will pour out my spirit upon all flesh; and your sons and your daughters shall prophesy, your old men shall dream dreams, your young men shall see visions. And also upon the servants, and upon the handmaids in those days will I pour out my spirit.' As the unapologetically single daughter of a Stepney artisan, Trapnel was God's handmaid *par excellence*, one of many, however, who dreamed dreams in these decades of revolutionary optimism, that they could establish true religion in England.

Popery and Prelacy

All parliamentarian regimes excluded 'popery' and 'prelacy' from any religious liberty, and this exclusion was underlined by the identification of both with royalist political commitment. Royalist Catholics had two-thirds of their estates put up for sale (although it was often trustees who bought them back on behalf of the family), and they were subject to continuing political harassment and financial penalties. But Cromwell's aversion to religious persecution extended to Anglicans and even Catholics in the absence of aggressive religious or political defiance. Only one Catholic priest was executed during the Protectorate, and he suffered on charges dating back to the 1620s. No major Catholic families renounced their faith, although the heirs of several, such as the Warwickshire Throckmortons, conformed to Protestantism for a while.

As we have seen, a broad commitment to the episcopalian church of England and its liturgy was evident in the petitioning of the early 1640s, and one historian has argued that 'the greatest challenge to the respectable Puritanism of the Parliamentarian majority came from the passive strength of Anglican survivalism' (Morrill 1993: 150). Those who were hostile to the austere, word-based Calvinism of the godly were undoubtedly the most numerous if not necessarily the most visible or alarming of the enemies of Puritan reformation. 'Anglican survivalism' is perhaps too straightforward a designation, however, for a coherent Anglicanism was invented as much as preserved in this period. The Church of England became more tightly defined and more beloved as its central elements came under bitter attack; and as parliament's destruction of episcopacy and the innovations of the 1630s paved the way for unfettered, divisive Calvinist divinity in the parishes, and dangerous 'schismatics and separatists' beyond them.

Anglicanism was a complex amalgam of religious practices and beliefs with a range of adherents. For some intellectuals its essence lay in a theological challenge to Calvinist predestinarian theology, but this was paralleled at a broader level by a conviction that leading a decent life, and regular attendance at parochial worship, was the way to salvation. For many parishioners, grim and impractical Puritan preaching and a divisive approach to the sacrament were deeply unpopular – Martindale's 'old ignoramuses' may well have had a different, rather than an inadequate, grasp of true religion. The petitions of 1641–2 reveal also a broad commitment to the government and liturgy of the church. At an intellectual level, again, there was an increasing stress on the historical integrity of an English episcopal church, independent of the papacy and free from popish corruption, yet not condemning the pope as Antichrist, or the Catholic Church as the antithesis of true religion. The affection for the liturgy of the Common Prayer Book was more widely shared. The sacraments and rituals of the Common Prayer Book seemed to chime in with the natural rhythms of the year. They embodied a vision of a harmonized community and gave meaning to the central rites of passage in a human lifespan. Ritual gestures, set prayers, parish festivals, pictures and music offered a broader emotional and aesthetic experience than the demanding word-based religion of the Puritans.

For the humbler laity we lack personal documentation but get many indications of their resentment of godly reformation. There was much local support for the parish ministers sequestered by parliamentary authority – and for their truculent wives who often refused to surrender their homes to intruders. The inhabitants of Henley in Arden persisted with their maypoles and may games despite the attentions of the Justices in the 1650s, and made it their 'custom' to disturb the godly preachers imposed by the sequestrators. Christmas, outlawed by parliament as a superstitious hangover from pagan and popish times, was widely observed as a festival of neighbourly sociability as well as religious renewal; the Directory was adopted painfully slowly and the illegal Common Prayer Book widely used. Tithe refusers who disliked Puritans like Gataker, were undoubtedly more numerous than those radicals who denounced tithes as a bridle on liberty of conscience. An Anglican nostalgia was a vital element in political movements against parliament in the later 1640s. The Sussex clubmen bemoaned in 1645 'the want of church government whereby our churches are decayed, God's ordinances neglected, orthodox Ministers cast out without cause and never heard, Mechanicks and unknowen persons thrust in', while Glamorgan royalists complained in 1646 that the 'Common Prayer Book hath been commonly traduced' and feared 'its final rejection ... were we not resolved by the help of God to continue it' (Morrill 1976: 198, 201).

We can be more precise about the experience of the bishops and other Anglican clergy during the 1640s and 1650s. Most bishops lived in retirement from 1642. Their experience varied widely, from Laud's execution in January 1645 and Matthew Wren's decades of imprisonment, through the semi-underground attempts of Skinner and Hall to continue ordinations and other diocesan affairs, to the comfortable compromises of the Calvinist bishops Ussher and Brownrigg who preached in London without interference throughout the 1640s (King 1968).

Parliament used a range of local and national commissions to purge the parish clergy on political, religious and moral criteria. Some 2,800 ministers were ejected, with some 28 per cent of livings affected – although this figure obscures regional variations, from 86 per cent of clergy removed in London to only 14 per cent in Yorkshire despite the establishment of a special commission under the parliamentary commander Lord Fairfax. Some of the accusations against the Anglican clergy seem stereotypical: the Suffolk minister William Aldous denounced as a 'common alehousehaunter' was one of many. On the other hand, many clergy were accused of very detailed political and religious offences. Several Suffolk clergy had co-operated with Matthew Wren's altar policy, forcing their congregation to the rails to receive communion, and conforming to 'popish and superstitious innovations'. Others were accused of denouncing the Scots in 1639–49 as a 'treacherous kind of people ... ready to cut our throats for they come for no good' (Holmes 1970: 65–6, 71). In Wiltshire – where the purges came later after parliament took control of the county in 1645 – ministers were accused of being 'very forward in the club business', or of ignoring parliament's fasts in favour of the king's Friday fast. At a 'club' rendezvous a minister urged 'let not the Book of Common Prayer be forgotten'. One Anne Holdway attacked the minister of Newton Solney: 'he extolled the Book of Common Prayer' and said that 'laymen ought not to meddle with the scripture and that women ought not to read the Scripture' (BL, Additional Ms. 22084, ff. 4r, 8r). Such proceedings do indicate that elements among Anglicans' congregations were pre-pared to attack their former ministers.

The impact of these ejections can be overstated. Some 1,180 out of the 2,780 clerics ejected continued to serve in the church in some form; some were pluralists who only lost one of their livings, while others obtained posts subsequent to their ejection. Nonetheless, with natural 'wastage' (death) it is clear that less than half of the ministers in parishes in the 1640s continued into the 1650s (Green 1979). The vacancies in many parishes intensified the widespread sense of religious dislocation. The limited interference with lay patronage, and the determined adherence to the 'old ways', ensured that Anglican practices survived throughout the period, despite intermittent harassment. The diarist John Evelyn heard 'that excellent prelate' James Ussher preach in Lincoln's Inn, London, shortly after his return from exile in February 1652, but also managed to practise Anglican ceremonies and observe Anglican festivals. Evelyn's children were baptized according to the Book of Common Prayer, and his wife had the traditional ritual of churching administered by the sequestered minister of Eltham, whom Evelyn kept as a chaplain. He observed Christmas at home in 1652, while in 1656 he received communion on the day of 'this holy Festival' at the lodgings of the sequestered Anglican minister Dr Wild, along with a full gathering of 'devout and sober' Christians. Only in December 1657, when there was a general crackdown, was there real trouble. At Exeter House Chapel in London, where the Anglican Peter Gunning was officiating, the congregation was seized by soldiers as they were receiving the sacrament. The earl of Rutland, the countess of Dorset, Lady Hatton and others were questioned for observing 'the superstitious time of the nativity, using common prayers and praying for Charles Stuart' (De Beer 1955: 61, 76–9, 185, 203–5).

Anglican myth-makers such as Isaac Walton created an attractive vision of a traditionally harmonious, hierarchical and festive community undermined by Puritan hypocrisy and trouble-making. In his life of the moderate Calvinist Robert Sanderson, the post-Restoration bishop of Lincoln, Walton promoted an accessible, natural, repetitive cycle of worship in place of an off-putting Calvinist divinity that could offer no useful guide to Christian life. He presented Sanderson's opinion 'That the way to restore this Nation to a more meek and Christian temper, was to have the Body of Divinity (or so much of it as was needful to be known) to be put into 52 Homilies or Sermons' each lasting 15 or 20 minutes, with 'needful points' 'so clear and plain, that those of a mean capacity might know what was necessary to be believed, and what God requires to be done', 'and these to be read every Sunday of the year, as infallibly as the blood circulates the body; and then as certainly begun again, and continued the year following'; hence 'it might probably abate the inordinate desire of knowing what we need not' (Walton 1927: 395). Such a vision was attractive to those who resented both mainstream godliness and the excesses and eccentricities of Quakers and other radicals.

Conclusions

Anglicans were, however, divided. Matthew Wren spoke increasingly of a 'tribe' of Laudians, opposed by their supposed friends as well as by the Puritans. The Laudian polemicist Peter Heylyn attacked more moderate figures such as Thomas Fuller as no better than Presbyterians. Many Anglicans like Ussher and Brownrigg were compromised by their acquiescence at least in the Cromwellian church and some, like the future bishop of Norwich Edward Reynolds, had co-operated more enthusiastically with London Presbyterians in the 1650s. Following Oliver Cromwell's death, the fragmentation of the parliamentarian alliance in 1659–60 reopened the religious and political splits among the orthodox godly. These months witnessed radical enthusiasm at a higher level than any time since 1653, as well as an alarmed backlash against the Quakers and other enthusiasts. The restoration of Charles II in May 1660 was the signal for a clear reaction against godly reformation, with a rapid resurgence of profane maypoles and morris dancing. Nonetheless 'Presbyterians' or the orthodox godly had no immediate reason to fear the future, but expected some sort of revival of the compromise proposals on church government and ceremonial. But it transpired that the revolutionary decades had fractured Protestant unity once and for all. In the place of the godly national church most parliamentarians had expected in the early 1640s, a religious market-place had emerged with a loosely defined public profession, a variety of competing sects, and sullen self-conscious traditionalists. The capacity of moderate Episcopalians and Puritans to work together as they had in the Elizabethan and Jacobean church had been fatally compromised, as the intimate but bitter cleavage of Bartholomew's day 1662 amply revealed.

REFERENCES

Abbott, W. C. (ed.) 1939: *The Writings and Speeches of Oliver Cromwell*: Oxford.
Burghall, E. 1889: *Providence Improved*, Record Society of Lancashire and Cheshire, vol. 19.
Coffey, J. 2000: *Persecution and Toleration in Protestant England 1558–1689*: Harlow.
Cotton, P. and Cole, M. 1655: *To the Priests and People of England, we discharge our consciences and give them warning*: London.
De Beer, E. S. (ed.) 1955: *The Diary of John Evelyn*, vol. 1: Oxford.
Fox, G. 1998: *The Journal*, ed. N. Smith: Harmondsworth.
Gardiner S. R. 1906: *The Constitutional Documents of the Puritan Revolution*: Oxford.
Goodwin, T., Nye, P., Simpson, S., Burroughs, J., Bridge, W. 1644: *An Apologeticall Narration*: London.
Green, I. 1979: 'The persecution of "scandalous" and "malignant" parish clergy during the English Civil War', *English Historical Review*, 94, 507–31.
Greville, R., Lord Brooke 1642: *A Discourse Opening the Nature of that Episcopacie, which is exercised in England*, 2nd edn: London.
Hill, C. 1972: *The World Turned Upside Down: Radical Ideas During the English Revolution*: London (many subsequent editions).
Holmes, C. (ed.) 1970: *The Suffolk Committee for Scandalous Ministers*, Suffolk Record Society, vol. 13.
Hughes, A. 1987: *Politics, Society and Civil War in Warwickshire 1620–1660*: Cambridge.
Hughes, A. 1992: 'The frustrations of the godly.' In J. Morrill, ed., *Revolution and Restoration: England in the 1650s*: London.
Kenyon, J. P. 1966: *The Stuart Constitution*: Cambridge.
King, P. 1968: 'The episcopate during the English Civil War', *English Historical Review*, 83.
Lindley, K. 1998: *The English Civil War and Revolution: A Sourcebook*: London.
Macfarlane, A. (ed.) 1976: *The Diary of the Reverend Ralph Josselin*: Oxford.
McGregor, J. F. 1984: 'The Baptists: fount of all heresy.' In J. F. McGregor and B. Reay, eds, *Radical Religion in the English Revolution*: Oxford.
Martindale, A. 1845: *Life of Adam Martindale*, Chetham Society.
Morrill, J. 1976: *The Revolt of the Provinces*: London.
Morrill, J. 1993: *The Nature of the English Revolution*: Harlow.
Russell, C. 1995: *The Fall of the British Monarchies*: Oxford.
Rutt, J. T. (ed.) 1828: *Diary of Thomas Burton esq*: London.
Spurr, J. 1991: *The Restoration Church of England*: New Haven, CT.
Tolmie, M. 1977: *The Triumph of the Saints*: Cambridge.
Trapnel, A. 1654a: *Strange and Wonderful Newes from Whitehall*: London.

Trapnel, A. 1654b: *Report and Plea, or a Narrative Of her Journey into Cornwal . . . Whereunto is annexed A defiance, Against all the reproachful, vile, horrid, abusive and scandalous reports*: London.

Underhill, E. B. 1854: *Records of the Churches of Christ gathered at Fenstanton, Worboys and Hexham, 1644–1720*, Hanserd Knollys Society, vol. 9.

Walton, I. 1927: *The Lives of John Donne . . . and Robert Sanderson*: London.

White, B. R. (ed.) 1971–4: *Association Records of the Particular Baptists of England, Wales and Ireland to 1660*, Baptist Historical Society.

FURTHER READING

Coffey, J. 2000: *Persecution and Toleration in Protestant England 1558–1689*: Harlow.

Hill, C. 1972: *The World Turned Upside Down: Radical Ideas During the English Revolution*: London (many subsequent editions).

Hughes, A. 1992: 'The frustrations of the godly.' In J. Morrill, ed., *Revolution and Restoration: England in the 1650s*: London.

McGregor, J. F. 1984: 'The Baptists: fount of all heresy.' In J. F. McGregor and B. Reay, eds, *Radical Religion in the English Revolution*: Oxford.

Morrill, J. 1993: *The Nature of the English Revolution*: Harlow.

Russell, C. 1995: *The Fall of the British Monarchies*: Oxford.

Spurr, J. 1991: *The Restoration Church of England*: New Haven, CT.

Tolmie, M. 1977: *The Triumph of the Saints*: Cambridge.

CHAPTER NINETEEN

Political Thought During the English Revolution

J. C. DAVIS

Introduction

The 1640s and 1650s were, in John Pocock's phrase, 'the epic years of the English political intellect', a period when English political thinkers made the first of their major contributions to Western political thought. These were the years, after all, of the collapse of Stuart government, of civil war, revolution and the post-revolutionary struggle for stability. Epic deeds elicited epic words.

Until the middle of the last century, orthodox accounts presented both deeds and words as having progressive outcomes. On the one hand, the struggle was depicted as for civil and religious liberty against tyranny and foreign intervention. On the other, it was against social revolution. For some, this meant a triumph over anarchy; for others, the disappointment of their hopes of a better society. Alongside these great events and interacting with them, was an innovative set of discourses about the rule of law, liberty and constitutionalism, religious toleration and rationalism, secularity, sovereignty, rights, obligation and history; a series of steps forward in what was recognized as the developmental progress of Western political thought. Much of that progressive sense has been swept away by revisionist historians in the last quarter of the twentieth century and so far neither anti-revisionists nor post-revisionists have seriously attempted to restore it. The notion of the political thought of the period as, in any sense, a triumphant assertion of liberal or constitutional, let alone of socialist values, has gone. As the political struggles of the English 'Revolution' have become a succession of short-term crises rather than the product of seismic shifts in the socio-political landscape, so too the political arguments of the period seem to have lost any association with deep-rooted social change. As the colours of revolutionary liberation and progressive transformation have faded, it has still proved possible (Scott 2000) to argue that England's only genuine experience of revolution was in the range and substance of its political thought, but with a consequential location of that intellectual revolution not at the heart of events but uneasily on their periphery. The heroes of England's epic years of political thought appear increasingly like impotent commentators on the unrevolutionary events unfolding before them; unhappily compromised or, heroically if irrelevantly, defiant.

In this respect the 'linguistic turn', the attempt to relate political thought to the discursive or linguistic contexts in which it operated and by which it was constrained, betokened at once a redirection and a narrowing of focus. From the late 1950s and mid-1960s, John Pocock and Quentin Skinner were denouncing the anachronism of existing approaches to the history of political thought and insisting that the reconstruction of contemporary conceptual paradigms or patterns of linguistic usage was the key to uncovering authorial intentions. The history of political thought was a study of 'speech acts' to be understood in the context of the linguistic matrices within which they were performed. The assumption was that 'the history of political thought . . . takes the form of a history of political "discourse"' (Pocock 1993: 1). Accordingly, lawyers – and others – carried with them into the political debates of the period 'the common law mind'; Thomas Hobbes became an 'Engagement theorist'; James Harrington, the exponent of a political language, not the advocate of a political programme. It was not a background of social and political transition which illuminated Harrington's thought so much as his engagement with earlier authors: Machiavelli, Selden, Bacon or Hobbes. We were moving a long way from either the sociology of knowledge or the theoretical and practical triumph of political and constitutional idealism towards what might be, rather harshly, described as self-referential intellectual genealogies. Substantial tracts of the epic period of the English political intellect were now held to be comprehensible only in the light of readings of mainly foreign authors: Grotius, Lipsius, Machiavelli, Cicero, Livy, Seneca and Tacitus.

The 'linguistic turn' and its advocates have had a profound influence on the history of political thought in general and of this period in particular. It is important, however, to recognize that the approach has too often been identified, incorrectly, with a turning away from all other contexts but that of language. At its best, the linguistic turn has been complemented by close attention to the political context. Social contextualization, perhaps in reaction to the anachronism of the cruder forms of class affiliation, is still too often dismissed as reductionist. On the other hand, despite the influence of linguistic contextualization, the polarities and categorizations of political ideas – conservative, progressive, radical – are still too often simplistically and anachronistically drawn. Two issues stand out with respect to the agenda which the linguistic approach can expect to confront in the near future. The first concerns the relationship between linguistic modes, strategies and political culture. To put it at its simplest, political language operates at a variety of levels: polemic, rhetoric, philosophy. Are the demands, purposes, contexts and audiences different at each of these levels, or do we wrap them them all together in a generalized history of discourse? Secondly, it was a commonplace of the 1640s that the warring sides were, as Jeremiah Whittacker (preaching to parliament in January 1643) noted, inseparable in terms of language. How can linguistic contextualization help us to understand linguistically uniform partisanship, a war of words in which the adversaries inhabit the same linguistic context?

The Collapse of Government Occasions the Revolution in Political Thought

One of the most sustained and interesting debates has been that over whether ideological conflict or consensus characterized the decades before 1640. Johann Sommerville (1986) argued that there was a distinct absence of consensus on significant issues such as the origins, nature and limits of royal authority, the relationship between law and the crown, and the role of parliament in church affairs. The need to respond to possible articulations of a right to resist on any of these issues led to an aggressive insistence on the divine right of kings. Monarchs were not only irresistible but potentially unlimited. Glenn Burgess, in response, has attempted to demonstrate an early seventeenth-century consensus around the idea that all authority was divinely sanctioned and that the authority of English kings was irresistible but limited; limited, in fact, because irresistible. Building on the work of Deborah Baumgold, Burgess has argued for a common belief in the pacificatory or conflict-resolving capacities of the English constitution and especially of the king-in-parliament (Baumgold 1988; Burgess 1992, 1996). This argument, especially in respect to political writings in print, has been influential. One response has been not to deny Burgess's central contention but to suggest that the language of conflict, so rare in print, makes its appearance in manuscript. Another has suggested that pre-Civil War discourses were too fluid and nuanced to fit either the conflict or consensual models of interpretation.

In many respects, nevertheless, Burgess provides the most satisfactory introduction to the problem of intellectual engagement with the collapse of government and the outbreak of civil war in 1640 to 1642. The fact that most participants made the same claims in similar language is one indication of pre-existent consensus. Another is the range of reactions seeking to address the dilemmas of conscience thrown up by the disintegration of government. The assumption that political authority was essentially authority over conscience provides a context, that of casuistical instruction, which Keith Thomas has identified as central to the nature of political thought in early modern England. This too suggests the arrival of violent conflict in an ideologically unpolarized world, a milieu intellectually under-prepared for it. The resort, in 1642, to extra-constitutional violence, might have been expected to produce resort to alternative languages. That of absolutist patriarchalism had been developed by Sir Robert Filmer, in manuscript at least, between 1628 and 1632. As Markku Peltonen (1995) has shown, a classical language of civic virtue and republican values continued from the early sixteenth century into the 1630s and beyond. Another means of charting the uncertain waters of 1642 might have been recourse to Grotian ideas of necessity and reason of state which have been described as having a breeding-ground in pre-Civil War England (Tuck 1993: 202). However, the collapse of the ideological matrix of legal constitutionalism, subordination under God, providence and prophecy, was still some way off (Sharp 1983: 6; Judson 1949). The English enjoyed a constitution balanced between royal prerogative and subjects' rights. Kings were irresistible but limited. More recently we have come to appreciate that this anti-absolutist consensus was rooted in the practical realities of the royal conscience under God, and of the networks of mediatory and discretionary agencies and practices which made up the *potestas irritans* of the early modern state. We now see the government of Charles I as dependent on 'the voluntary action of elites for whom political authority was a useful resource; it rested on a mutuality of interests' (Braddick 2000: 340; Burgess 1996: 6–7, 18, 39, 41–6, 135, 153, 177). The discretion of lesser magistrates and often relatively humble officeholders was a substantial limitation on the crown. Discretion rather than a theoretical right to resist was a key feature of the system which Mark Goldie (2001) has described as an 'unacknowledged republic'.

Kings were irresistible but limited and the reality of this lay in the mutuality of interests, the participatory and discretionary nature of the early modern dispersed state. But what if the crown was bent not on preserving that mutuality of interests, but on driving through policies and overriding the discretion of local agencies and governors? How then were the limitations on kings to be secured without resistance? The answer in the first nine months of the Long Parliament was by statutory reinforcements. Yet the growing atmosphere of conspiratorial distrust and the Irish rebellion of October 1641 left considerable unease and division about how irresistible kings might be more securely limited. The first exercises in thinking this problem through refrained from engaging with the languages of patriarchalism, classical republicanism, order theory or reason of state. One immediate answer was that, even against the evidence, trust must be placed in a chastened king's willingness to abide by informal and statutory limitations. Another was that irresistibility overrode the breach of limitations. Tyrannical kingship must *in extremis* be endured. Another was that the king was misled by 'evil advisers'. He was not to be resisted but liberated. None of this conceded a right of resistance and this continued to be the official line down to the Solemn League and Covenant of September 1643. It was a position fatally undermined as perceptions of Charles were transformed by the processes of war and the capture of his papers after the battle of Naseby, from the dupe of malignants to their accomplice and then finally to their leader. Charles's perceived willingness to act in complicity with popery played a major part in hardening these attitudes.

It was, however, another response to the problem of reconciling the limited authority of kings with their irresistibility which was pregnant with the potential for new forms of political discourse. This was the denial that, in a civil war, such a reconciliation was possible. If one of the limitations on kings was that they might not wage war on their own people then, like artillery captains who turned their guns on their own side, they should be resisted. In civil war kings became resistible as well as limited and much of the political thought of the 1640s and 1650s was about working through the consequences of this momentous shift. As John Selden observed, the king's use of necessity to justify the raising of his standard against his own people in August 1642 would rob him of his special position within society, since his people could use the same argument – the necessity of self-preservation – to resist his armies (Burns and Goldie 1991: 528). For a while at least, it might be possible to believe that recourse to arms had been the latest in a series of tragic and unnecessary blunders and that negotiations could restore the *status quo ante bellum* both intellectually and practically. There were soon two reasons to doubt this prospect. The first was the king's *Answer to the XIX Propositions* which had been presented to him by parliament in June 1642. The king's reply argued that the English constitution was a tripartite system in which crown, Lords and Commons checked and balanced one another. To that *he* was essential. Ironically, implicit in this argument was the notion that any element in the triumvirate had the duty, as well as the right, of resistance to preserve the balance (Mendle 1985). It was, as we shall see, this point on which Henry Parker seized to justify the first claims to parliamentary sovereignty. The second and more major problem preventing a return to the ideological status quo was that alongside the crisis of counsel went a crisis of religion and to this the status and nature of the church was central. Consequent upon the removal of the bishops and the abolition of the court of high commission, religious and civil order required the re-establishment of ecclesiastical authority. Philip Hunton's identification of government, in 1643, as 'the exercise of a moral power' raised the question as to how, if government collapsed, morality was to be maintained. In this sense, the authorization of a church appropriate to the management of consciences and thereby of morality became not only a crucial ecclesiological issue but *the* central concern of political thought in the 1640s. At its heart was the problem of idolatry, the worship of false gods or the false worship of the true God, whose anger once unleashed could lead to national destruction. It is, in this respect, worth remembering that the right or duty to resist a monarch had been asserted on the narrow grounds of idolatry as early as the 1550s and John Knox's fulminations against the rule of Mary Tudor (Burns and Goldie 1991: 196, 199).

The problem of the church was complicated and intensified by the setting up in 1643 of the Westminster Assembly, an Anglo-Scots forum intended to address it. It was a problem not only of the nature of ultimate governmental and constitutional authority but of yet another dimension of the relationship between a central authority and the government/'state' in the wider sense. The civil parish, like the civic community of the hundred, borough or county was, as Michael Braddick has shown, critical to the process of state formation in early modern England. Local complicity was so fundamental to the state in its confessional, as well as its other modes, as to make 'absolutism' a term applicable to aspirations but barely to civil or religious realities before 1640. In this respect, and against the background of the reassuring legislation of 1641, a conflict mentality was slow to arrive. As Burgess has argued, resistance theory is hard to find in the pamphlet literature of the early 1640s. But religion may well be a different matter. Did religion bind men to obedience (Burgess) or fortify them for resistance (Lamont)? Certainly, the desire to give greater priority to the substance of religion over its forms, the note of anti-formalism struck from November 1640 in the Fast Sermons regularly delivered to parliament made the institutions of government and their claims to obedience pale alongside the need to appease a living and jealous God and to purge the land of idolatry.

The collapse of Stuart government was swift and dramatic, but men's minds took time to adjust. The process of adjustment was marked by uneven and often contradictory development. Three documents illustrate this process. The Grand Remonstrance of December 1641 sought to better advise the king against the machinations of a 'corrupt and ill-affected party' and did so by reciting the abuses of government power under their influence over the previous forty years. A crisis of counsel was to be resolved by the better ordering of the counsels of the king. In March 1641 the Militia Ordinance implicitly recognized the king's unwillingness to accept parliament's vision of such a reordering and the case for the two Houses acting in their own defence without the authority of king-in-parliament. Emergency, reason of state and *salus populi* were all cited as justifications for an extra-constitutional preparation of the sword. In answering the Nineteen Propositions (June 1642) which would have given retrospective sanction to this extension of parliamentary authority to act without him, Charles introduced the notion of a *co-ordination* of government along Polybian lines. Stability could only be maintained if king, Lords and Commons acted as checks upon one another (Mendle 1985; Burns and Goldie 1991: 395). As negotiations gave way to violent confrontation, the question insistently became what would happen if these elements in a mixed monarchy could not act in co-ordination. Who then would have legitimate authority to restore stability, even to the point of using military means to do so? By the end of 1642, Charles Herle was pointing out that the principle of co-ordinate government placed the monarch on a parity of footing with the other Estates, Lords and Commons. Within a year, William Prynne had developed the claim that the Lords and Commons combined must possess greater authority than the king on his own. But by this stage the question was turned inside out. If parliament was supreme, how could the king act as a check upon it? Had an irresistible and unlimited authority been conjured into existence?

After Charles had stigmatized the Militia Ordinance, a case of 'legislation' without him, as absolutist, Henry Parker transformed the political debate not by denying parliamentary absolutism but by justifying it. Since power derived from the people, there must be a public authority capable of checking princes. This must be parliament which was 'the whole kindome it selfe', the epitome of the state. For Parker, the public interest overrode all else and that interest could only be addressed through parliament. Since laws had proved insufficient to defend the general interest and true religion, they should be subservient to parliament which possessed an *absolute* power to declare the law. In every state there had somewhere to be an arbitrary power, if the safety of the state was to be secured. Such power, in England, was legitimately in parliament. This was parliamentary absolutism with a vengeance and it contained the seeds of Parker's later rejection of any monarchical or legal checks on the two Houses. By 1650 he would defend the republic by proclaiming: 'We have conquered the Conqueror' (Mendle 1995: 171).

Parker's *Observations upon some of his Majesties late Answers and Expresses* (July 1642) was full of conditional, if pregnant, statements: 'if the King will not joyne with the people, the people may save themselves'. For Philip Hunton, such sentiments meant that the consciences of individual subjects must individually engage with the issue. This, in Sir Robert Filmer's view, meant anarchy. Moreover, to argue that absolute authority rested only in the people's representatives was, since the defection of many members of both Houses to the king, to beg the question of their represen-tativeness. The invocation of an arbitrary power in the two Houses also raised the question of a potential for parliamentary tyranny. Parker denied such a possibility, but the question became more insistent as parliament's fiscal, administrative and military practices unfolded under the pressures of war between 1642 and 1646. In this sense, the Solemn League and Covenant's determination to recast the war as still a struggle to achieve a well-counselled monarch rather than to change the location of sover-eignty was a flinching away from the brutal logic of Parker's assertion of parliamen-tary absolutism.

It may be true that many fought for the king out of a sense of personal loyalty, rather than in pursuit of ideology, but what is striking in royalist apologetics in this period is their rejection of absolutist claims (Newman in Morrill, Slack and Woolf 1993). The intellectual core of Charles's support – Lord Falkland, Edward Hyde and Edward Bagshaw – presented their cause as a defence of mixed government and the balanced constitution. The critiques of mixed government in 1640–1, by Filmer and Hobbes, were set aside (Burns and Goldie 1991: 349, 531). Nor did divine right, which was in any case a theory of obligation rather than of absolutism, play any significant part in royalist polemic (Zagorin 1954: 189). The central royalist argu-ment was a conventional insistence on the irresistibility of a crown limited within the framework of a mixed system of government. Henry Ferne in a work typical of the political casuistry central to political thought in the period, *The resolving of conscience* (1642), set the tone for much royalist writing. The authority or power of all government came from God; the form of particular governments was decided by men, but once decided it became irresistible (Sharp 1983: 54–94). Clergymen like Ferne, Bramhall and Heylyn, as well as lawyers like Spelman, were prominent in arguing the royalist case, not because the issue was one of the divine right of kings but because the question of allegiance was a matter of conscience and it was appropriate, therefore, that the doctors of conscience should lead the debate. The vulnerability of the royalist position was that justifying the mixed polity of the ancient constitution had as its reference point the mechanics of peace and stability and the reality was now that of war. While it might be held that the king-in-parliament ought to be supreme, the question now was what allegiance was owed to the king out of parliament or parliament bereft of a king.

Liberty and the Problem of Settlement

In many senses, then, the first civil war was fought, as John Pocock has observed, to reconstitute king-in-parliament. But motivating men to kill one another in an increasingly devastating fratricidal conflict meant using the languages of law, liberty and religion, invoking the spectre of conspiratorial, foreign and anti-religious or popish enemies. In a new world of relatively unrestrained discourse, men could interpret and apply these languages in a wide variety of ways. Even so innately conservative a document as the Solemn League and Covenant would later provide Gerrard Winstanley with what he saw as a foundation document justifying the overthrow of 'Kingly Government' not only in its institutional branches but in its social and economic roots. The political thought of the quest for settlement between 1646 and 1649 – one of the under-researched areas of political thought in this period – was faced with two challenges. One was that of reconciling the constituents of a reassembled king-in-parliament. The other was how to still the plurality of discourse unleashed by the unrestrained rhetorical strategies of war. Those stirring preachers to parliament who had insisted that this was a holy, even an apocalyptic, war had clearly raised the threshold of acceptable settlement. Preaching to the Lords in July 1646, Samuel Bolton, Master of Christ's College, Cambridge, advised that the nation was 'now upon the borders of Canaan'. 'The field is fought and won; we only go forth to fetch the trophies of victory.' A year later, when the text was published, he acknowledged that he might have been unduly optimistic. On the other hand, the pacificatory capacities of the mixed constitution had been cruelly exposed and Sir Robert Filmer's *The Anarchy of a Limited or Mixed Monarchy*, which had been held back since 1644, was finally published in 1648 to warn against reconstituting a system and an ethos which had failed. Yet, not only had the pre-Civil War constitution failed to preserve peace, it could also be seen to have failed to protect civil and religious liberty. What had the war been fought for if these prizes were now to be surrendered or rendered insecure? And which of civil or religious liberty might have priority? For civil liberty meant submission to the regularities of law and the protection of legality by limitations on government. But religious liberty might mean submission to an absolute, arbitrary and volatile God (Davis 1992). So 'Freeborn' John Lilburne in *The Freeman's freedom vindicated* (1646) invoked the sovereignty of a God – 'who is circumscribed, governed and limited by no rules, but doth all things merely and only by His sovereign will and unlimited good pleasure' – as the reason for the conscientious citizen's inability to submit unconditionally to civil constitutions and laws (Sharp 1998: 31).

The language of liberty in mid-seventeenth century England had a very different signification to that of a post-liberal culture. Liberty within civil society was in submission, either through law or to God. Christians were, as Milton was to say, like soldiers, with providence their drum and only command (Dzelzainis 1991: 46). Or, as Hobbes put it, all religious believers 'are God's slaves'. The problem with the liberty of submission to this living, providential and apocalyptic God was that he was a breaker of forms, a dispenser with formalities in the pursuit of moral and spiritual substance. Such liberty under God could be difficult to square with submission to the forms and due process of law, or to the formalities of mixed government. It could lead to pragmatism about forms and institutions or, where God was perceived to have given special commissions, it could lead to both pluralism and rigidity about particular forms in church and state. This combination of proliferation and intransigence might then be read as a prescription for anarchy, renewed civil war, failure to achieve settlement, or all three.

The Levellers and others looked for the peace dividend of liberation by the people's representatives, but what that meant in practice was a question productive of yet further debate and division. The dawning recognition that the *status quo ante bellum* might not address this need, left work for the drafters of constitutional blueprints to do. Between 1646 and 1649 their efforts revolved around two concerns. The first was how to balance discretionary kingship, with its attendant risk of tyranny, against the prospect that limitations rigorous enough to justify the parliamentary war effort could look like impotence to the king and his advisers. The most significant attempt to reconcile these requirements was the Heads of Proposals approved by the New Model Army in July 1647 and beginning to be enacted by parliament late in the same year, but fatally rejected by the king and decried by the Levellers. The political thought which formed the intellectual context for these negotiations has yet to be thoroughly investigated.

On the other hand, by the later 1640s the threat of tyranny appeared to many, including many non-royalists, to be coming from the oppressive fiscal, military, administrative, judicial and religious policies of parliament (Sommerville 1986: 80). This threat pushed the Levellers, initially preoccupied with liberty of conscience, into a party with a fully-fledged constitutional programme. By 1647 they were appealing from the Commons to the people and associating themselves with the New Model Army in that appeal. Parker's parliamentary absolutism (of which they had approved) had degenerated into tyranny and the lesson was that even representative governments must be limited. English laws might enshrine English liberties, but their corruption required the surgery of constitutional transformation. The spectre of parliamentary tyranny, like that of a royal despotism, pushed limited or co-ordinated government back on to the agenda. We no longer see the Levellers as a product of secular rationalism, nor as expressive of possessive individualism (Haller 1934: Macpherson 1962). Their thought was rooted in Christian ideas of limited self-propriety and therefore of the limited transfer of authority to any government. Absolute government was illegitimate because men were incapable of transferring God's rights in them to others. Constitutions existed, in substantial measure, to prevent political encroachments on God's sovereignty over us. Meanwhile, many of their practical constitutional proposals related to the participatory and discretionary processes of local, urban and metropolitan governance. Constitutional arrangements, such as regular elections, rotation of office, and accountability, were designed to prevent the exploitation of power for sectional rather than the general interest. For this reason, they disavowed the concept of 'party' and its application to them. They were the voice of the people, the spokesmen of honest households and all government should be an expression of popular sovereignty (Burns and Goldie 1991: 433). Whether this justifies describing them as exponents of 'individual liberty and true democracy' (McMichael and Taft 1989: preface) has been a contentious issue. It might still be possible to argue that they were liberal democrats (Sharp 1998; Wootton, in Burns and Goldie 1991), but not in an unqualified modern sense. An interest in precision on the franchise may have been forced on them by the debates at Putney. After that they consistently proposed a franchise exclusive of women, children, almstakers and servants, as well as one subject to at least temporary political tests. They were promoters of a community of self-ruling citizens which would be corrupted if those incapable of self-rule were allowed full participatory rights. The Agreements of the People therefore were meant to express both the consent of the people, their endorsement of limitations on government, and to provide antidotes to corruption. Nevertheless, by the late 1640s suspicions arose of the corruptibility not only of government and parliament but also of the people. Lawrence Clarkson in 1647 charged the 'commonality' of England with a corruption which led them to choose their own oppressors as their representatives. The following year William Sedgewick warned, in similar vein, of the corruptibility of the people and, by 1649, the Leveller leaders themselves were reflecting ruefully on the gullibility of the people and the ease with which they could be deceived.

A wider sense of the inability of the majority of fallen human beings to manage themselves and their consciences was to be found in the search for a basis for 'true religion'. The Westminster Assembly had produced a Presbyterian design, ratified in the main by parliament, but in practice largely still-born. John Morrill has shown that the Church of England's liturgy, though formally proscribed, continued to claim the loyalty of most parishes. Sectarian congregations probably never accounted for more than 5 per cent of the population. A number of incompatibles uncomfortably jostled one another: the desire for godly decency, for the reformation of manners, for liberty of conscience, for the practice rather than merely the formal observance of true religion, for order and unity, but also for liberty in the service of a living and wilfully unpredictable living God. As William Lamont has most consistently argued, this is but to enumerate the multiple facets of a mental world in which civil and religious were virtually one and the same. Most assumed that God would reward godliness and punish impiety, whether in individuals or nations. In a society reformed on an Erastian basis, it was an important function of the civil authorities to address the consequences of this. The most important of these was that it was difficult to think in terms of a separation between the nation in a civil sense and in the sense of a community of Christian believers, or a church. Few historians would now accept what was a commonplace until the 1960s, that Puritanism promoted an intellectual segregation between nature and grace and therefore a secularization of the sphere of nature, leaving the way open for the development of modern science and secular politics. Instead, we assume that society was seen as a conscientious and therefore religious community held together under the sovereignty of God and, accordingly, under some obligation to pursue divine purposes. The key questions facing contemporaries now appear to us to have been: should Christian liberty embrace a plurality of ways of responding to the prompting of God in action, in worship and in opinion; how might such plurality be prevented from leading to disorder, indecency or to fratricidal conflict driven by holy zeal; under what terms and in what time frame might God have given latitude to humans to determine their own social and political arrangements? Brooding over these discussions in the 1640s and 1650s was the spirit of Richard Hooker, author of *The Laws of Ecclesiastical Polity*. Books six and eight of this work were published in 1648, more than half a century after books one to four. (Book seven was not to appear, much mutilated editorially, until 1661.) Hooker had insisted on the coterminous social identity of the church and the national community. There was a limited core of matters essential to true religion and a wide range of adiaphoristic elements which could be determined with considerable flexibility. But those determinations should be by the whole community rather than by the monarch, king-in-parliament or the ecclesiastical hierarchy. The 1640s witnessed a reaction against the Laudian/Caroline attempt to override the ecclesiological preferences of individual communities, a reaction which, spinning out of control, destabilized the church–community–state of the Hookerian formulation.

Alongside the internecine squabbling of sectarian champions were five positions from which various protagonists chose to address these unintended consequences of the overthrow of Laudianism. One was the hardline Presbyterianism of the Scots and Thomas Edwards. The obligations of consciences could be formally identified. Their liberty was to submit to righteous forms and those who dissented from this should be disciplined. A variation on this was Richard Baxter's concern that the rebinding of church and nation must not bring the church down to the level of the nation. Above all, the godly minority must be protected from corruption and the nation be enabled to follow their lead. There is much of this spirit in the republicanism of John Milton, Henry Vane and Algernon Sidney, and it spills over into the politico-religious elitism of Fifth Monarchism. But an alternative was to move the godly away from political engagement of any kind. They were not of this world. To remain unspotted, they must separate from civil engagement. Roger Williams proposed that church and state should be separated and the civil power possess no authority, disciplinary or otherwise, in matters of belief. The church could remain intact but there should be considerable toleration with respect to permitted ecclesiological forms. For others, most eloquently William Walwyn, any church was inherently a formalistic contrivance, focusing attention on institutional and liturgical forms rather than on the practical and moral substance of Christianity. The antagonism to priestcraft implicit in many mid-seventeenth century responses to church issues was bound up with the idea of the clergy as devisers of idolatrous forms, diverting the godly from submission to the living God. A final position was that which informed the church policy of the Protectorate from 1654 onwards. There must be liberty of conscience for the godly to pursue the will of God, but provision of a non-compulsory national church was also essential to the moral and spiritual health of the nation. Cromwell may have believed that this was a provisional state of affairs and that, in his good time, God

would lead his people into unity of faith, both in belief and practice. As David
Wootton has argued, the scope of liberty of conscience was, for contemporaries,
'the most important political issue of the seventeenth century, alongside, and inseparable from, that of the choice between constitutionalism and absolutism'
(Wootton 1986: 67).

Thus we have moved from seeing this period as one in which liberty, in a modern,
post-liberal sense, secular politics and rational political thought advanced as one, to a
questioning of all three categories. Most instructive has been a recontextualization of
the seventeenth-century language of liberty. In submission to the rule of law or to the
lawful exercise of privilege (civil liberty), or in conscientious submission to the will of
God (religious liberty), the seventeenth-century conscience was sovereign but not
free. Like monarchs it should be irresistible but limited – limited by the will of God.
Hence, the importance of rightly informing, tuning and doctoring conscience: the
importance of casuistry (Thomas, in Morrill, Slack and Woolf 1993).

Similarly, and rather than forming a platform for modern secularity and rationalism, mid-seventeenth century thought is now more likely to be seen as shaped by a
seriousness of religious belief. Ideas of providence governing the life of the community as well as of individuals were ubiquitous. History was commonly believed to be
working to an imminent apocalyptic termination, although the precise timetable and
the interim political arrangements were subjects of intense debate. Consciences had
to be informed by appropriate readings of the meaning of providential interventions
in the life of the nation and of the unfolding of God's historical design. They also had
to be guided through the moral dilemmas presented by successive crises and the
impossibility of conscientiously performing what had been sworn to, sometimes in
formal public oaths, when the circumstances, which might have made such performance possible, had disappeared (Jones 1999). One of the great theoretical struggles of
the period was between a constitutionalism which sought to stabilize the play of
political and religious forces and an anti-formalism which rejected such institutional
priorities, in church or state, as unacceptable limitations on the will of God (Davis
1993). The rejection of a written constitution in December 1648 was on just these
grounds, as was the condemnation of Cromwell as an apostate, who had usurped
the throne of King Jesus, when he adopted the Instrument of Government in
December 1653.

The anti-clericalism of Thomas Hobbes, once seen as a manifestation of his
secularism, now needs to be read in this context (Sommerville 1992: 113–16).
Richard Tuck has shown how its intensification before 1651 mirrors a growing
scepticism not only about ecclesiastical and political forms in general, but about the
capacity of the clergy to serve the common interest, in particular (Tuck, in Phillipson
and Skinner 1993: 122). Anti-clericalism transcended the boundaries of radicalism.
Even so, it should not be confused with irreligion or even with an aversion to all
ecclesiastical forms. Consolidating the Reformation remained a central theme of
political discourse throughout the period.

Divine Republicanism/Divine Liberty 1649–1653

The revolution of 1648–9 was a more confident shutting of the door on a restitution
of the *status quo ante bellum*, in any guise, than it was an opening of the path to a new

political culture. It exposed the brute fact of change and the need for political ideas to accommodate that fact. One aspect of this process was the development of republican theory. It is no longer possible to see that theory as altogether an effect rather than a cause of the regicide (Peltonen 1995). Yet, in the words of John Pocock, the Rump began as 'an experiment in *de facto* government rather than in revolution' and the first task of political thought was to justify submission to the regime as a means of maintaining peace rather than as an exemplary or even prima facie legitimate form (Pocock 1993: 172). This was certainly Anthony Ascham's view of the task and he was not alone. The fact that the unicameral republic declared in 1649 was so singularly protean – not much beyond the military and mortal termination of dialogue with the crown – meant that not only were the defences of republicanism to be worked out, but so too was the form of the republic itself.

It is the varieties of English republicanism, rather than the phenomenon as a whole, which have attracted most attention in the last twenty-five years (though the work of Blair Worden and work in progress by Jonathan Scott offer a more broadly based assessment). Nevertheless, in an important argument, Quentin Skinner has tried to provide a coherent framework for the discussion of republican theory in England following the regicide. His thesis is that the Free State set up in 1649 was defended by Marchamont Nedham, Henry Vane and John Milton in terms of 'neo-Roman republicanism'. This assumed that the liberty of the individual was only secure if embedded in the freedom of a civil association; if it was part of the 'common liberty', 'the liberty of the commonwealth' or 'the Liberties of nations'. Following Machiavelli, Livy and the *Digest* of Roman Law, the neo-Romans assumed that the loss of liberty was the same for the state as for individuals, a fall into slavery. Such servitude resulted either from conquest or from a constitution allowing for discretionary authority. Since politically effective princes exercised such discretion, either as a consequence of conquest or through the sloth of their subjects, no monarchy could be a free state. A republic, or free state, was therefore a realm without a king. For the defenders of 1649, this was primary; the issue of individual liberties, secondary (Skinner 1998). Skinner's approach to this has not gone unchallenged. William Walker (2001) has suggested that the equation of republican states with the absence of monarchy was neither a feature of the thought of Livy and Machiavelli nor of their mid-seventeenth century followers. In Walker's view, there were at least two situations in which the rule of a single person might be acceptable to them: in the foundation of a commonwealth or in the reform of a corrupt one. As Milton knew, God himself was a king. What mattered was not particular forms of government, but a presiding ethos of virtue and merit expressed in Christian, as well as classical, terms. Though with slightly different emphasis, Blair Worden, Jonathan Scott and David Norbrook have all stressed the primacy of moral values over institutional forms in the republicanism of Nedham, Vane, Milton and Sidney. It is these values which link English republican sentiment from the 1580s to the 1650s and beyond. But the creation of a 'Free State' in 1649 also produced a dilemma of conscience for those who, in the oath of the Solemn League and Covenant or elsewhere, had sworn to preserve the life, authority and dignity of the king. At its most unflinchingly providential, the dilemma was resolved by the divinely conferred victories in Ireland and at Dunbar and Worcester. Preaching on a day of thanksgiving for Dunbar held in faraway Massachussetts, John Cotton drew a parallel in the oath set aside to execute Amaziah (2 Chronicles

25:27–8): 'There is A Lawfull and Loyall Conspiracy as well as a Disloyall and Wicked Conspiracy'. God's will, the preservation of the reformed church and a godly Commonwealth *could* override a prior conscientious engagement, but the understanding of this balance and the authority to so act could only be in the hands of a providentially sanctioned minority. Alongside the classical and Machiavellian languages of republican liberty and *virtu* there also existed a set of concerns with casuistry, providential sanction, scriptural – predominantly Old Testament – precursors and Christian virtue.

The most evident blending of the Christian and the classical was to be observed in Vane, Milton and Sidney. For Vane, all civil government was limited by the sovereignty of God over Christian consciences and must not 'intrude into the proper office of Christ'. Magistrates' claims over conscience would remain untenable until the saints, Christ's agents on earth, became magistrates. He would not concede such status to either the members of the Rump or to Cromwell after 1653 (Judson 1969; Parnham 2001). Milton's republicanism was always qualified by doubts as to his fellow-countrymen's fitness for republican self-rule. It was this which permitted him to give the Protectorate, which alienated other commonwealthsmen, some measure of support. Yet, despite his elitism, Milton never unconditionally identified a legitimate elite. His least qualified republican statement, *The Ready and Easy Way* (1659), balanced the sovereignty of a 'standing senate' against the *potestas irritans* of the relatively autonomous agencies of the dispersed state. Closer to the practical exercise of power under the Rump, Algernon Sidney saw despotism not so much as the absence of a constitution as the absence of virtue (Goldie, in Burns and Goldie 1991: 602; Worden, in Burns and Goldie 1991: 459–60). Given the beleaguered state of virtuous republics, and his own experience of civil war and republican imperialism in the years of the Rump, Sidney associated the maintenance of republican virtue with constant warfare. The basis of such a republic he thought of as a plentiful baronage, ideally suited to command armies of freeholders. Republicanism was not, in this view, about stability, but about the conquest of corruption within and aggression without the commonwealth by incessant war (Scott 1988, 1991). Marchamont Nedham occupied something of a middle ground in this variety of republican theorizing. Called on to be a quasi-official defender of the republic before he had turned thirty, Nedham knew that his task was to persuade those with a moral distaste for the outcome of 1648–9. He began where Anthony Ascham and many of the *de facto* theorists of the Engagement controversy began (Sharp 1983: 3; Wallace 1968), with the ephemerality and contingency of all human government. All governments were founded and maintained by the sword. Without submission there could be no protection and therefore prior oaths were no adequate grounds to resist the present government. Nedham, appealing to an audience of moderates, argued that most who had fought for the king had not supported absolute monarchy because such a regime would have been threatening to their estates. The Civil War had not been fought to destroy monarchy but to regulate it. Freedom was to be found where there was security of property; the rule of law; an impartial, cheap and accessible system of justice; free elections to successive parliaments and the vigilant, active participation of a people uncorrupted by luxury (Knachel 1969).

Republican theory in the period of the Rump was therefore extensive in its variety. The republic of *virtu*/virtue, its anti-formalist mode, could embrace classical or providentialist languages. In its more formalist modes it struggled with the identification of virtuous elites, with the establishment of constraints either in the workings of the dispersed state or in the constitutional restraints of regulated government. There was, in this sense, a coalition of republican apologists and activists which was fragmented by the expulsion of the Rump in 1653. Its members were then confronted by a choice between opposition or a further search for the means of regulated government as a basis for the moral values of republicanism.

The overthrow of kingly government and the establishment of a Commonwealth could have other meanings besides those of the republican types we have so far examined. The most obvious of these was Gerrard Winstanley's attempt to establish a distinctive version of commonwealth's government in the digging experiments of 1649–50 and in his *The Law of Freedom* (1651). For most of the twentieth century Winstanley was seen as an outstanding radical, alienated from and challenging his society and its values. For Christopher Hill, his challenge was to the social moderation of the revolution of 1648–9. The degree to which we can apply categories like 'radical' and 'conservative' to seventeenth-century society has been questioned by Conal Condren (1994) and others, and most historians of political thought are now more cautious. We also know more about the life of Winstanley and a number of his followers. His participation in parish politics as a vestryman and officeholder both before and after the digging experiments suggests much greater integration with the parochial communities of London and Surrey than was previously allowed. Closer reading of his published works of 1648, hitherto generally available only in severely truncated extracts, reveals a casuist concern with the problems of allegiance and obligation in the military and political crisis of that year. It became clear to him that the driving force of material necessity prevented the poor from adequately weighing the issues of conscience confronting them. Alternative social and economic structures capable of removing material necessities and liberating consciences for the service of God became essential. The fall of kingly government was part of the unfolding of divine history, and the restoration of 'Creation Right' through communist community had accordingly an apocalyptic dimension. It remains striking that this was combined in Winstanley's thought, not with alienation from the parliamentary revolution, but with the attempt to draw out what he regarded as its full potential. From the Solemn League and Covenant to the Acts establishing a republic, the logic of the struggle, *in parliament's own words*, justified the wholesale social restructuring for which he campaigned. In this respect, Winstanley claimed to be at the heart of the true mainstream of the English Revolution. His two most important points of contact with contemporary political culture were a casuistry densely informed by scriptural readings and a concern to re-establish and secure the self-governing communities which had been placed under intense pressure by socio-economic polarization and the ravages of war. Both were reflected in the arrangements for household, parish, country and nation of his ideal society.

Claims to the authoritative informing of Christian conscience had, however, multiplied by the 1650s, to the point where religious fragmentation might leave the individual conscience in a maze of instability, as portrayed, for example, in Laurence Clarkson's *The Lost Sheep Found* (1660). His escape from the chronic spiritual uncertainty of the 1650s was to subscribe to an authority which could replace the contested scriptures of the Old and New Testaments, the new holy writ of the Muggletonians,

John Reeves's *A Divine Looking-Glass* (1656). But they were not the only ones to seek the stabilization of a prolonged crisis of conscience by the establishment of an authoritative and exclusive basis for casuistry. The Muggletonians attempted to seize the interpretative high ground by producing a third Testament. The Fifth Monarchists, by contrast, advocated the seizure of secular power in order to prepare the ground for the final interpretative consummation, the reign of Jesus Christ directly on earth. To many of them, access to secular power appeared to come with the calling of the Nominated Assembly in mid-1653. The collapse of that experiment and the establishment of the Protectorate in December of that year left them fulminating, and in some cases plotting, against Cromwell's apostasy and usurpation of 'King Jesus'. Their political thought, however, remained rudimentary: wish lists of desired changes moderated by a sense of the imminence of divine government.

Neither Muggletonians nor Fifth Monarchists ever possessed the political means to bring an end to the fragmentation and instability underpinning the sense of a crisis of conscience. Cromwell in the 1650s saw the 'scatterings, divisions and confusions' of sectarian division as akin to a state of war in which competing interpreters of scripture would not hesitate to 'cut the throats of one another, should not I keep the peace'. Their demands for liberty were specious, something they insisted on for themselves but would deny others. Ironically, we can see Thomas Hobbes as addressing exactly this problematic agenda, even if his conclusions were distinctly different to those drawn by Cromwell. We now see *Leviathan* not as a timeless work of political reflection but as engaged with political events and problems as well as with the language and rhetoric through which those problems might be addressed. As client and servant of the royalist Cavendish family, one milieu for interpreting Hobbes's masterwork is that of a court in exile and the struggle between loyalty to the Church of England and a religious pragmatism which might enable the claimant to an Anglo-British throne to work with the Scots for his restoration in all of his kingdoms. Hobbes had tutored the Prince of Wales and his patrons moved in the circle of the sponsor of religious pragmatism, Henrietta Maria. The writing of *Leviathan* was begun at a moment of optimistic faith in the ability of the Scots to restore Charles to the throne in England by force of arms (Tuck 1993: 320–5). It was finished in the aftermath of the crushing defeat of those hopes at the battle of Dunbar. In the wake of that reversal, the Cavendish family had begun to compound with the regime in England in an attempt to preserve their estates and status.

Building on Quentin Skinner's work of the mid-1960s it is now common to see Hobbes as an Engagement theorist, in some sense summative of *de facto* arguments. But, however much we integrate him with the debates of the 1640s and 1650s, there are still a number of respects in which he remains a novel thinker, whose thought ran against the grain of his time and provoked a predictably hostile reaction. This was evident in his exclusion of the sovereign from the social contract and hence from the limitations of contractual obligations; in his denial that 'God's slaves', in submission to providential direction, could thereby be seen to enjoy liberty. It was equally so in his insistence that only the sovereign could justly inform the consciences of his subjects and that, therefore, resistance could never be a matter of conscience, but was only justifiable on grounds of self-preservation. These novel teachings have been traced to a rejection of Aristotelian and Scholastic metaphysics, to a current of scepticism running through late Renaissance thought and, above all, to a Grotian reduction of the universal in human nature to the imperative of self-preservation. But whereas Grotius had held that that imperative could lead to co-operation, Hobbes held that this could never be relied on. Since we never knew the limits of our mutual aggressiveness, pre-emptive strikes could always be prudential, so reinforcing the cycle of potential conflict. Because self-preservation might justify doing anything, fearful individuals, seeking an authority capable of securing their preservation, must have allowed that authority the right to do anything, except to threaten their survival. Mixed, co-ordinate or any form of limited government was an anathema to this theory.

As partisan groups struggled for support, Hobbes's ideas could appear at once both threatening and neutral. Obligation was entirely relative to a regime's capacity to guarantee the security and preservation of its subjects. In the meantime, subjects must allow those who could protect them to inform their consciences, and it was in this respect, as well as in its materialism, that Hobbes's teaching could appear atheistic. In one reading he seemed 'to overthrow the notion of civil society as a natural community engaged in a collective seeking after virtue'. 'The church's understanding was collapsed into the state's will' (Goldie, in Burns and Goldie 1991: 602, 611). Hobbes's problem was how to make this unpalatable medicine acceptable to his conflict-ridden countrymen. The answer, according to one of the most important recent works on Hobbes's intentions in *Leviathan*, was through mounting a most ambitious rhetorical exercise (Skinner 1996). In *Behemoth* Hobbes presented the disaster of civil war as the triumph of rhetoric over reason. In *Leviathan* reason must be served by the same instrument if the English were to be led to accept the laws of nature and escape the state of war. Yet there remains a parenthetical pessimism about a work seeking to impart to them a 'knowledge of what is good for their conservation (which is more than man has)'.

Co-ordinate Government

The Instrument of Government adopted by Oliver Cromwell in December 1653 was an attempt to establish the framework and relationships of co-ordinate government. The balance of the one, the few and the many – Protector, Council and representative assembly – was not, however, left to the contingencies of interaction between them (as had seemed implicit in the king's *Answer to the XIX Propositions*). Rather, the Instrument, working back to the Heads of Proposals, sought to define those relationships and the limitations on the power of each element. Above all, the *Instrument* enshrined the principle that final authority lay with the representative assembly. The people were, under God, the original of all just power and the constitutional consequences of that assumption found expression here. The problem was whether the 'people' would accept the legitimacy of the package as a whole. For many it remained a defiance of the regime to which they had been conscientiously engaged since the early 1640s. For the commonwealthsmen it represented a retreat from the principles of a Free State. For yet others, it was a betrayal of King Jesus.

The exclusion of irreconcilable members from its first parliament in September 1654 further tarnished the Instrument's claims to legitimacy. A Tacitean/Lipsian embracing of the lesser evil was almost a requisite of its defence. Universal consensus on religious and moral issues remained a distant prospect. In the meantime, the provision of a state powerful enough to prevent a relapse into civil war and to protect the nation from external threats might seem justified (Burns and Goldie 1991: 502). The balancing of interests became the essence of this form of constitutionalism, but while Cromwell was head of state it could never be entirely reduced to that. Aspirations associated with him always embraced godliness in the twin senses of reformation of the law, manners and civil society and of continued service under the living God. Michael Hawkes provided just such a Lipsian defence of the Protectorate in *The Right of Dominion and Property of Liberty, Whether Natural, Civil or Religious* (1656). It was not so far from the surprisingly pragmatic advice of Sir Robert Filmer to those uncertain of their conduct in the face of what to them amounted to a conquest. His *Directions for Obedience to Government in Dangerous or Doubtful Times* (1652) was published as royal hopes expired in the shadow of the defeat at Worcester, but it could equally be applied to the Protectorate as an expression of 'possession by the permissive will of God'. As Christopher Feake, by no means the most compliant of Oliver's subjects, put it in 1655: 'either I must own the present Powers, or I must own Anarchy'. His advice to the saints was to accept the present powers for as long as God sustained them and to get on with running their own affairs. In his second speech to his first parliament (12 September 1654), Cromwell responded to querulousness about the regime's legitimacy by pointing to the role of Providence in bringing him to his present position and to the many 'witnesses' to his authority. Prominent among the latter were those local officeholders who made communal self-government a reality: the constables, churchwardens, jurymen, justices, borough officers, lesser magistrates and judges who were the sinews of the dispersed state and had accepted the renewal of their commissions *under his authority*. The Althusian sense of political society as an ascending series of corporate, and to a large extent self-governing, groups was here given expression by a practical politician seeking to stabilize a governmental framework in the aftermath of civil war and revolutionary upheaval.

As the events of 1648–9 and 1653 had shown, the temptation to military intervention could prove overwhelming, but there was a reluctance to convert such intervention into permanent military control. Responsible government was still the goal of those who had begun the struggle as a defence of civil and religious liberties. This meant accountability not to the soldiers but to the 'witnesses' of the dispersed state, those whose active participation in largely unpaid officeholding mediated and shaped the state across the parishes, hundreds, counties and boroughs of the nation (Braddick 2000; Hindle 2000). A central question hanging over the Protectorate was whether these people, or their representatives, would be prepared to swallow the military origins of the constitutional arrangements under which they were called to continue to act, along with the heavy costs of military establishments in England, Wales, Scotland and Ireland.

The most systematic attempt to address these issues was James Harrington's *Oceana* (1656) and its associated publications. Over the last forty years scholars have moved from a preoccupation with Harrington's Agrarian Laws and his imputed role as bourgeoise imperialist to a concern with his use, or abuse, of the language of classical and Machiavellian republicanism. Whereas Algernon Sidney proclaimed the martial virtues of a baronial-led but popularly based republic, Harrington provided an historical analysis of the collapse of the baronage and its military and political consequences. In the sense that his republic was post-baronial, Pocock (1992) was right to describe *Oceana* as a Machiavellian meditation on the end of feudalism. But there is also force in Blair Worden's description of *Oceana* as a meditation on Cromwell's expulsion of the Rump and, in that sense, much more closely engaged with the problems of the 1650s. It is a suggestion reinforced by the recent demonstration of *Oceana*'s close reading of contemporary debates about the military and, in particular, the Militia Bill of October 1656 (Kubik 1998). Harrington's advocacy of a citizen militia and failure to recognize the implications of the military revolution have been taken as evidence that he was in the grip of a classically derived republican language. What he was doing with that language has, however, become the subject of substantial debate. Pocock's thesis in *The Machiavellian Moment* (1975) was that Harrington's work was the means by which such a language was adjusted from the needs of compact city-states to the requirements of extensive agrarian societies and made available for American resistance to imperial and monarchical pretensions in the eighteenth century. Others have argued that a preoccupation with settlement, perhaps in competition with Hobbes, pushed him in the direction of institutional constraints so utopian as to render the self-governing participation of his republican citizens nugatory (Davis 1981; Scott, in Phillipson and Skinner 1993). It is now clear that future readings of Harrington's proposals must engage with his agenda of elaborate rituals designed to restore and maintain the civil and military machinery of governance through the dispersed state of parish, hundred and county. The people were once more to be 'equally possest of the government' and the militia. Provision for participatory officeholding was on an impressive scale. Over two years, half of adult citizens would be required to discharge some public office. This was the rule of 'King PEOPLE'. Oceanic government was co-ordinate not only in the relationship between its central institutions of council and bicameral legislature, but also in the relationship between them and the state in its local and regional forms of expression. Harrington's civil religion needs to be seen in the same light: national provision with a good deal of local mediation and provision for the liberty of Protestant consciences. It is that aspect of Harrington which comes closest to Cromwellian arrangements after 1654.

Harrington remains the most idiosyncratic of mid-seventeenth century English republicans. His concern both with a secular history which furnished England's moment of republican opportunity, and with the political architecture of institutional and ritual formalities by which that moment might be immortalized, distinguish him from his republican contemporaries.

Ritual and Bankruptcy: The Collapse of the Protectorate 1658–1660

The Protectorate collapsed, not because of its enemies, but because of its own mismanagement. Taxes were slashed without matching cuts in the military establishment. When faced with a government incapable of meeting its material needs, the army became again a source of instability. William Sprigge in his *Modest Plea for an Equal Commonwealth* (1659) was not alone in invoking a return to the drawing board: 'We are now Rasa Tabula'. Among the many schemes designed to escape that state, it was a Presbyterian cleric, George Lawson, who provided the most sophisticated and ambitious attempt to address the twin problems of reconciliation and settlement. Following Hooker, Lawson saw church and state as mutually informing. Although not necessarily derived from consent, community was 'a divinely sanctioned society worthy of consent'. Personal majesty could fail, as the fall of Richard Cromwell demonstrated, but real majesty – capacity to form or change a constitution – remained inherent in the community. As a settlement theorist, Lawson argued for an irenic view of both church and state. For the former, he recommended a wide interpretation of the adiaphora and comprehension of the widest range of believers, consistent with 'the English Protestant Interest'. For the latter, he urged a prudential flexibility. In his praise of the post-regicide conformists, Lawson was the last of the *de facto* theorists, but he was first and foremost a casuist, offering guidance to troubled consciences in dangerous times. The prime objects of this conscientious guidance were what Lawson called the *eminenter cives*, the chief inhabitants of parishes, hundreds and shires; those who bore the burden of governance throughout the land. Lawson's *Politica Sacra et Civilis* (1660) expressed what Condren (1989, 1992) has called 'an elaborate doctrine of office'. The same appeal to reassemble the dispersed state or to balance the rule of virtue through the offices and the officeholders of the dispersed state informed the debates of the Harringtonian Rota Club in 1659–60 and the proposals of Milton's *Ready and Easy Way* (1660). Their thought may have been shaped by linguistic, polemical and rhetorical strategies, but it also meshed with the mediating, discretionary and brokered institutions, offices and practices of 'republican' participatory local government – those elements of the 'state' which had survived and functioned through the upheavals of the 1640s and 1650s. The question of settlement then became how to remove the unwelcome accretions and establish a central apparatus accommodated to the needs of sense of legitimacy of this 'unacknowledged republic'. That process had begun under Cromwell, in his negotiations surrounding the Humble Petition and Advice, and in the tax concessions of Cromwell's last years.

As the Cromwellian regime disintegrated after the great Protector's death, it is understandable that, alongside the voices of irenicism and pragmatism, were those seeking revenge, those for whom politics was war by other means. Nevertheless, ultimately for them too the issue was the means of settlement. Prolonged instability had consolidated a world of competing interests and of pluralistically informed consciences. How, in this situation, could divided human minds create a consensually approved legitimacy? The late Harringtonian answer of *A System of Politics* (written in 1661 but published posthumously) was by the reconciliation of interests through the constraining forms of an immortal commonwealth. If, by this stage, this looked like a partisan answer, so too did that which proposed a return to the traditions of the ancient constitution reinforced by divine, patriarchal legitimation. The contested nature of such appeals to the reason of history, interest or scripture raised the question of a shift from rationality to coercion and ritual, from providence and spiritual intuition to Holy Writ authoritatively interpreted. The marquis of Newcastle's advice to Charles II was that, on the one hand, he should secure his control of 'well ordered force' and, on the other, that he should exploit to the full the ritual and ceremonial capacities of the crown: 'though seremony is nothing of itt selfe, it doth Every thing'. The combination of force and ritual 'Governes all, both in peace and warr' (Condren, in Phillipson and Skinner 1993). The alternative of a theocratic state, as for example in Richard Baxter's *A Holy Commonwealth* (1659), in which 'only the voluntary subjects of God' might be granted civil status, held no appeal for Charles, nor for the officeholders of an exhausted nation. In 1660 the prospect of 'stability' and 'normality' had more appeal than that of contested liberty and competing versions of the godly nation.

Conclusion and Prospect

In surveying possible future trends in the study of this period's political thought, we should begin with the influence and importance of the 'linguistic turn'. One of the consequences of this approach is to open the yet unresolved question as to what range of discursive practice, including the non-verbal, symbolic and ritualistic, should come within the focus of the history of political thought. At the very least, the linguistic turn obliges us to look at a range of discursive actors and we can expect more theoretical discussion and research in these areas. We should also see a more systematic effort to unpack the layers of what might be called the 'linguistic dependency' – European, British, English or classical, religious, contemporary – of those who performed political speech acts. In part this will relate to studies of the reading of political and other texts in the period. We need a more sophisticated understanding, both in terms of authorial intention and reader reception, of the various levels of discourse – for example, polemic, rhetoric and philosophy – and the degrees of their penetration. In turn we can expect a further development of the movement away from detailed examination of the canonical works of political thought as timeless classics, towards a closer recovery of their political, as well as discursive, contexts. We should expect more on the links between words and action or the constraints on action. Recent work on petitioning and oaths has suggested some of the way forward here. That the emergence of a Habermassian public sphere in the mid-seventeenth century is a key to understanding this world of subscriptional communities and extended audiences for print and newsbooks seems doubtful (Zaret 2000; Jones 1999). A good example of progress towards a richer contextualization in terms of the socio-political milieu would be the important work done recently on London, including Keith Lindley's *Popular Politics and Religion in Civil War London* (1997).

Associated with this greater emphasis on the contexts of political circumstance and political culture will go a renewed sense of the importance of casuistry and Sir Keith Thomas's perception that a central concern of the political thought of the period is casuistical. When Samuel Hartlib, in 1636, called for collections of casuistical cases to be available in every church in the land, he was making a political and social, as well as moral and spiritual, statement. That Harrington in his *Oceana* could describe the commonwealth as 'nothing else but the national conscience' obliges us to look to the casuist works of the period as one of the contexts for his political thought. The more general question is that of how to deal with the religious context for political thought in a period of religious fragmentation and anti-formalist submission to the shifting dispensations of a living God. We have come a long way from the easy ascription of secular rationality, or even atheism, to those who appeared to be progressive thinkers, but much remains to be done for a world in which men could struggle against absolute rulers in the name and service of an absolute God of 'illimited Prerogative'.

Much more attention will necessarily be paid to political culture and its roots in a new sense, that of the unacknowledged republic, the dispersed state, the 'signs of political life at levels where it was not previously thought to have existed' (Collinson 1989: 22). It may well be here too that the issue of gender and political thought in the period becomes most accessible. Ann Hughes has begun to show the way forward here with her work on the Levellers' polemical use of the 'honest household' (Hughes, in Amussen and Kishlansky 1995: 162–88). Just as the parish needs to be accommodated as a context for some varieties of political thought, so too does the household and, with the household, comes the notion of *oeconomia*, of frugality and luxury. William Walwyn's attack on 'our darling superfluities' parallels the strictures of Milton and Nedham on luxury as undermining a free state and the belief of both Cromwell and Harrington that too great a disparity of wealth was incompatible with a commonwealth. The notion of consumption, emulation and the household as an agency of moral discipline or of luxury and corruption have obvious resonances requiring further research in contextualizing political ideas. An epic period in the historiography of the political thought of the English Revolution awaits us!

ACKNOWLEDGEMENTS

My thanks to Glenn Burgess, Mark Knights, Gaby Mahlberg and Jonathan Scott for their comments on an earlier draft of this chapter.

REFERENCES

Amussen, S. D. and Kishlansky, M. (eds) 1995: *Political Culture and Cultural Politics in Early Modern Europe*: Manchester.
Baumgold, D. 1988: *Hobbes' Political Theory*: Cambridge.
Braddick, M. J. 2000: *State Formation in Early Modern England*: Cambridge.
Burgess, G. 1992: *The Politics of the Ancient Constitution*: London.
Burgess, G. 1996: *Absolute Monarchy and the Stuart Constitution*: New Haven, CT.
Burns, J. H. with Goldie, M. (eds) 1991: *The Cambridge History of Political Thought 1450–1700*: Cambridge.
Collinson, P. 1989: *De Republica Anglorum: Or, History With the Politics Put Back*: Cambridge.
Condren, C. 1989: *George Lawson's Politica and the English Revolution*: Cambridge.
Condren, C. (ed.) 1992: *George Lawson: Politica Sacra et Civilis*: Cambridge.
Condren, C. 1994: *The Language of Politics in Seventeenth-Century England*: London.
Davis, J. C. 1981: 'Pocock's Harrington: grace, nature and art in the classical republicanism of James Harrington', *Historical Journal*, 24, 3, 683–97.
Davis, J. C. 1992: 'Religion and the struggle for freedom in the English revolution', *Historical Journal*, 35, 3, 507–30.
Davis, J. C. 1993: 'Against formality: one aspect of the English revolution', *Transactions of the Royal Historical Society*, 6th series, 3, 265–88.
Dzelzainis, M. (ed.) 1991: *John Milton: Political Writings*: Cambridge.
Goldie, M. 2001: 'The unacknowledged republic: office holding in early modern England.' In T. Harris, ed., *The Politics of the Excluded c.1500–1850*: Basingstoke.

Haller, W. (ed.) 1934: *Tracts on Liberty in the Puritan Revolution*, 3 vols: New York.

Hindle, S. 2000: *The State and Social Change in Early Modern England c.1550–1640*: London.

Jones, D. M. 1999: *Conscience and Allegiance in Seventeenth-Century England: The Political Significance of Oaths and Engagements*: New York.

Judson, M. A. 1949: *The Crisis of the Constitution*: New York.

Judson, M. A. 1969: *The Political Thought of Sir Henry Vane the Younger*: Philadelphia.

Knachel, P. A. 1969: *The Case of the Commonwealth of England Stated by Marchamont Nedham*: Charlottesville, VA.

Kubik, T. R. W. 1998: 'How far the sword? Militia tactics and politics in the *Commonwealth of Oceana*', *History of Political Thought*, 19, 2, 186–212.

Lindley, K. 1997: *Popular Politics and Religion in Civil War London*: Aldershot.

McMichael, J. R. and Taft, B. (eds) 1989: *The Writings of William Walwyn*: Athens, GA.

Macpherson, C. B. 1962: *The Political Theory of Possessive Individualism: Hobbes to Locke*: Oxford.

Mendle, M. 1985: *Dangerous Positions: Mixed Government, the Estates of the Realm, and the Making of the Answer to the xix propositions*: Tuscaloosa, AL.

Mendle, M. 1995: *Henry Parker and the English Civil War: The Political Thought of the Public's Privado*: Cambridge.

Morrill, J., Slack, P. and Woolf, D. (eds) 1993: *Public Duty and Private Conscience in Seventeenth-Century England*: Oxford.

Norbrook, D. 1999: *Writing the English Republic: Poetry, Rhetoric and Politics 1627–1660*: Cambridge.

Parnham, D. 2001: 'Politics spun out of theology and prophecy: Sir Henry Vane on the spiritual environment of public power', *History of Political Thought*, 22, 1, 53–83.

Peltonen, M. 1995: *Classical Humanism and Republicanism in English Political Thought 1570–1640*: Cambridge.

Phillipson, N. and Skinner, Q. (eds) 1993: *Political Discourse in Early Modern Britain*: Cambridge.

Pocock, J. G. A. (ed.) 1992: *James Harrington: The Commonwealth of Oceana and A System of Politics*: Cambridge.

Pocock, J. G. A. (ed.) 1993: *The Varieties of British Political Thought 1500–1800*: Cambridge.

Scott, J. 1988: *Algernon Sidney and the English Republic 1623–1677*: Cambridge.

Scott, J. 1991: *Algernon Sidney and the Restoration Crisis 1677–1683*: Cambridge.

Scott, J. 2000: *England's Troubles*: Cambridge.

Sharp, A. (ed.) 1983: *Political Ideas of the English Civil Wars 1641–1649*: London.

Sharp, A. (ed.) 1998: *The English Levellers*: Cambridge.

Skinner, Q. 1996: *Reason and Rhetoric in the Philosophy of Hobbes*: Cambridge.

Skinner, Q. 1998: *Liberty before Liberalism*: Cambridge.

Sommerville, J. P. 1986: *Politics and Ideology in England 1603–1640*: London.

Sommerville, J. P. 1992: *Thomas Hobbes: Political Ideas in Historical Context*: London.

Tuck, R. 1993: *Philosophy and Government 1572–1651*: Cambridge.

Walker, W. 2001: '*Paradise Lost* and the forms of government', *History of Political Thought*, 22, 2, 270–91.

Wallace, J. M. 1968: *Destiny His Choice: The Loyalism of Andrew Marvell*: Cambridge.

Wootton, D. (ed.) 1986: *Divine Right and Democracy: An Anthology of Political Writing in Stuart England*: Harmondsworth.

Zagorin, P. 1954: *A History of Political Thought in the English Revolution*: London.

Zaret, D. 2000: *Origins of Democratic Culture: Printing, Petitions and the Public Sphere in Early Modern England*: Princeton, NJ.

FURTHER READING

Baskerville, S. 1993: *Not Peace but a Sword: The Political Theology of the English Revolution*: London.

Burns, J. H. with Goldie, M. (eds) 1991/1994: *The Cambridge History of Political Thought 1450–1700*: Cambridge. Especially chs 12–15, 17–18, 20.

Condren, C. (ed.) 1992: *George Lawson: Politica Sacra et Civilis*: Cambridge.

Dzelzainis, M. (ed.) 1991: *John Milton: Political Writings*: Cambridge.

Lamont, W. (ed.) 1994: *Baxter: A Holy Commonwealth*: Cambridge.

McMichael, J. R. and Taft, B. (eds) 1989: *The Writings of William Walwyn*: Athens, GA.

Phillipson, N. and Skinner, Q. (eds) 1993: *Political Discourse in Early Modern Britain*: Cambridge.

Pocock, J. G. A. (ed.) 1992: *James Harrington: The Commonwealth of Oceana and A System of Politics*: Cambridge.

Pocock, J. G. A. (ed.) 1993: *The Varieties of British Political Thought 1500–1800*: Cambridge.

Sabine, G. H. (ed.) 1941/1965: *The Works of Gerrard Winstanley*: New York.

Sharp, A. (ed.) 1983: *Political Ideas of the English Civil Wars 1641–1649*: London.

Sharp, A. (ed.) 1998: *The English Levellers*: Cambridge.

Tuck, R. (ed.) 1991: *Hobbes: Leviathan*: Cambridge.

Tuck, R. and Silverthorne, M. (eds) 1998: *Hobbes: On the Citizen*: Cambridge.

Wootton, D. (ed.) 1986: *Divine Right and Democracy: An Anthology of Political Writing in Stuart England*: Harmondsworth.

PART V

Stuart Britain, 1660–1714

CHAPTER TWENTY

Politics in Restoration Britain

JOHN MILLER

The Restoration Period in Context

The period between Charles II's return to England in May 1660 and James II's flight to France in December 1688 has long been treated as an interlude between two 'revolutions'. For 'Whig' historians of the eighteenth and nineteenth centuries (and beyond), the major 'revolution' was that of 1688–9, 'glorious' because it finally secured England's traditional liberties against the Stuarts' attempts to establish absolute monarchy. It thus made possible an orderly and peaceful progression towards liberal parliamentary democracy, constitutional monarchy and religious liberty. As bloody revolutions convulsed much of Europe in 1848, Lord Macaulay proclaimed triumphantly that Britain alone had avoided a destructive revolution because it had undergone a 'bloodless' 'preserving revolution' at the end of the seventeenth century. In the twentieth century a very different historical approach to the seventeenth century offered a similar view of the Restoration. Marxist or Marxist-influenced historians like Christopher Hill dismissed the Whigs' preoccupation with constitutional and religious developments, arguing that the real motors of historical change were economic and social and that the 'real' revolution of the seventeenth century was that of the 1640s and 1650s. The ordinary people of England, after centuries of subjection, had risen up against their king and the traditional rulers of society. Although in the short term, the old order seemed to be restored in 1660, in the longer term the radical ideas proclaimed between 1640 and 1660 permanently undermined the ideological foundations of the old regime. Belief in the divine right of kings had lost all credibility with Charles I's execution and the Church of England's claims to a religious monopoly could not realistically survive the development of religious pluralism. For the Marxists and neo-Marxists, 1688–9 was a palace coup, substituting one dynasty for another, without the profound social and ideological upheavals of the mid-century. It nevertheless secured at least some of the gains of the 'revolution': not those of the people, whose aspirations were to be cruelly defeated, but those of the landed and mercantile elite, who finally won their struggle for power with the crown and, in the eighteenth century, used their control of the law and the machinery of the state to protect and promote their economic interests (Hill 1980).

Several comments can be made about these seemingly different interpretations. First, they assume the same basic political narrative: Hill differed from Macaulay in arguing that political developments reflected more profound social and economic developments. Second, they were inherently teleological, assuming that history can be seen as a predictable and inexorable *progression*, from a more 'primitive' to a more 'advanced' state, an assumption which owed as much to Darwin as to Marx. Within this mindset, the possibility that things could have turned out differently, and the beliefs of those whose ideas seem historically 'doomed' (for example, proponents of divine-right monarchy), are effectively ignored. Third, both approaches are Anglo-centric. The Revolution of 1688–91 was far from 'bloodless' in Scotland or Ireland. Although Macaulay waxed lyrical about the nineteenth-century British constitution, it should not be forgotten that the process whereby England, Scotland and Ireland became 'Britain' was often contested and painful. Moreover, the model of social and economic development upon which Hill's thesis rested was essentially English: it could not be applied to Scotland or Ireland.

Interpretations of the Acts of Union, between England and Scotland (1707) and Britain and Ireland (1801), have been strongly coloured by late twentieth-century politics. For many Scots the Union was the crowning act of English cynicism and bullying, as England finally asserted its dominance over its smaller neighbour. In that context, the Restoration period sits uneasily between the Scots' heroic resistance to Charles I in 1637–41 and the threats and counter-threats which led up to the Union. The fact that Charles II, unlike his father, did not seek to establish a degree of uniformity (or even congruence) between his three kingdoms ensured that the story of his reign was less one of English interference in Scotland than of Scottish factions competing in London for royal favour. The deep religious divisions left by the civil wars assured that politics in Restoration Scotland were often brutal, with the restored Episcopalian church using a mixture of conciliation and repression in an attempt to keep the Presbyterians quiet. This was, however, a matter of Scottish forces fighting it out among themselves, not the sort of dictation from England which had briefly united the Scots against Charles I. The worst problems Charles faced were minor risings by Presbyterian extremists (Buckroyd 1981). Only in the reign of James II was there an attempt to impose 'English' policies on Scotland, notably the toleration of Catholics and Protestant sectaries, which had the effect of temporarily turning both Episcopalians and Presbyterians – much the largest religious groupings, normally at each other's throats – against the crown.

In Ireland the sense of a lull between two storms was even more apparent. The civil wars and Cromwellian conquest had led to devastation and demographic catastrophe on a scale not seen in England or Scotland. They were followed by a massive transfer of land from Catholics to Protestants and an ambitious attempt at 'ethnic cleansing'. After 1660 Protestant royalists and a few Catholics got their lands back, but in general Charles II had little choice but to work with the new Protestant proprietors. Not only were they the men in possession, but any significant programme of restoring lands to Catholics would have had serious political repercussions in England. Charles may have sympathized with the dispossessed Catholics, but he was a political realist. Maintaining his position in England was always his first priority, so it was vital that Ireland should be kept quiet. With the Catholic majority cowed, deprived of both lands and public office, the key to Charles's Irish policy lay in managing the Protestant elite. This task was made easier by the Irish parliament's voting him 'hereditary revenues' sufficient to cover the costs of governing Ireland: the Dublin parliament did not meet between 1666 and 1689. Despite the Catholics' seeming quiescence, the Protestant elite still felt insecure, relying on a substantial army and militia (both Protestant) to maintain its position. It reacted with alarm, forcefully echoed in the English parliament, to even the most timorous moves to ease the lot of Irish Catholics. In fact, Charles and the duke of Ormond, Lord Lieutenant for much of the reign, saw the Catholics as essentially loyal to the crown, but feared that many Protestants, who had gained land and power under the Republic, were not. Ormond was particularly worried that the Presbyterians of Ulster might make common cause with their co-religionists in Scotland. In the event Ireland remained quiet and, in the 1680s, Charles saw his army in Ireland as a resource to be used in case of trouble in England. All this changed with James's accession. Persuaded by the self-styled leader of the Irish Catholics, the earl of Tyrconnell, that the Protestant elite consisted of 'Cromwellians' utterly opposed to monarchy, James placed more and more power in Ireland in Catholic hands (to the alarm of his Protestant subjects in England and Scotland) (Miller 1977). When James was expelled from England in 1688, Tyrconnell came close to securing the whole of Ireland for the Catholics. Three more years of bloodshed and devastation ended with the virtual completion of the expropriation of the Catholics and the creation of the 'Protestant ascendancy' of the eighteenth century.

The Legacies of the Civil Wars and Interregnum

The fact that historians of Scotland and Ireland have seen the Restoration as an interlude between more dramatic periods has meant that these years have been studied less intensively than those which came before or after. The fact that the concentration of land and power in Ireland in Protestant hands was reversed so spectacularly under James II would suggest that it was not yet secure. Even after renewed military conquest and confiscations from 1690, Protestants on both sides of the Irish Sea remained aware that ultimately the ascendancy rested on English military power. The Cromwellian conquest of Scotland had been notably less brutal than that of Ireland – firm pressure on deluded but redeemable fellow-Protestants rather than the well-merited punishment of savage papists. Nevertheless it was the first English military conquest of Scotland, a warning that in terms of resources and military might the gap between the two kingdoms had grown. This uncomfortable fact lurked below the faction-fighting and posturing which characterized much Scottish politics between the Restoration and the Union.

For many historians of England, too, the Restoration period seemed unimportant – and for some, distasteful. David Ogg, in his magisterial studies of the period 1660–1702 (Ogg 1934, 1955), condemned Charles and James on both moral and political grounds, making none too subtle comparisons between absolutism (at which he thought they were aiming) and fascism. A more balanced approach was apparent in a series of fine biographies (Browning 1951; Kenyon 1958; Haley 1968) which established a sophisticated political narrative and displayed a fine understanding of how politics worked: Kenyon's life of Sunderland, in particular, offered a superb analysis of court politics and decision-making over three reigns. He (and others) also emphasized the importance of the personal and the contingent, the element of luck, above all in the second half of 1688 (Miller 1978). Underlying the Whig view, and even that of Ogg, lay a subconscious certainty, born of hindsight, that however malevolent the Stuarts might be, the tide of history was against them. Shaftesbury and the other Whigs who went into exile after 1681 had no such certainty; nor did those rounded up after Monmouth's defeat in 1685. Nothing showed more clearly the completeness of Charles II's triumph between 1681 and 1685 than the confiscation of the charters of London and other major towns, which made possible the subjugation of the most significant autonomous bodies in the kingdom (Halliday 1998). With the judiciary and legal system firmly under royal control, religious nonconformity driven underground and the state enjoying a near-total monopoly of armed force, it was difficult to see any realistic challenge to the crown from within England: in 1688, as in 1640, the English did not rebel. Instead they were rescued from outside, by William of Orange, his massive Dutch fleet and polyglot army. And even then, had the wind changed or James not lost his nerve, things could have turned out very differently (Israel 1991).

By the late 1970s the picture of seventeenth-century English history as an inevitable progression through civil war and revolution was also being challenged by historians of the early Stuart period. After decades of debate, the assertions that economic and social changes had occurred in the century before 1640 which led inevitably to civil war were at best not proven; after much wrangling and no little ill-will, the combatants retired to lick their wounds and a newer generation turned their attention elsewhere, to the political narrative (expounded most fully by S. R. Gardiner) which the neo-Marxist view had taken for granted. Conrad Russell, John Morrill and others argued that civil war was in many ways much *less* likely in the mid-seventeenth century than in the mid-sixteenth, a time of major agrarian revolts, a disputable succession and bitter opposition to the imposition of Protestantism. In 1640 the succession was secure and England was a Protestant country, although there was ample disagreement about the form of its Protestantism. Moreover, the spate of peasant revolts had long since passed and the autonomous military power of the nobility had melted almost to nothing, at least in England. The most likely source of instability was the complex interrelationship between Charles I's three kingdoms, as he was determined to bring Scotland and Ireland – especially their established churches – into line with England. Both these kingdoms, unlike England, were heavily militarized, with powerful nobilities and habits of settling disputes by violence. It could be argued that the only one of Charles's kingdoms which did *not* rebel between 1637 and 1642 was England: in 1642 the king gathered support in the provinces, like a medieval rebel baron, while parliament controlled the regular machinery of government in London.

The 'revisionist' political narrative, which stresses the contingent and the destabilizing interrelationship between the British monarchies, casts doubt on England's revolutionary potential. For Russell, England was 'unrevolutionary' and the primary 'cause' of the English Civil War was the incompetence, duplicity and ill-luck of 'the man Charles Stuart' (Russell 1990). This view of the English as a 'governable people' has been reinforced by the work of social historians. Studies of riot, crime and the inner workings of parishes and towns have suggested that, while social conflict was by no means absent, for much of the time it was contained or defused. The English state had far weaker powers of coercion than the French state, but also faced far less large-scale popular resistance. One reason was that, under the early Stuarts, the English poor paid virtually nothing in taxation, but that happy situation ended abruptly in the

1640s. The excise (and after 1662 the hearth tax) imposed a severe burden on the poor. There was some violent resistance, a few tax collectors were killed, but most people paid their taxes most of the time (Braddick 1994). The reasons for the relative orderliness and obedience of the English should probably be sought in the strong elements of participation in local government and the legal process. In villages and towns the inhabitants (and especially the 'better sort', in economic and moral terms) held local office, served on juries and shaped the workings of government in the interests of moral order and communal harmony. Even when some aspects of the state – notably the fiscal and military – developed massively, especially after 1688, local self-government continued almost uninterrupted and grew in scope and sophistication.

This picture of the English as an obedient people, who obeyed the laws and paid their taxes, has important implications for the viability of the restored monarchy. The political narrative which underpinned both Whig and neo-Marxist views rested on the assumption of an unstoppable historical process. New ideas or new social groups emerged which posed an ultimately unanswerable challenge to the old order: 'the people' wanted change, 'the people' would not tolerate Stuart misgovernment. And yet if we look at what actually happened, in 1640–2 it was *parliament* which organized the war effort against the king. It encouraged popular direct action against papists, altar rails and courtiers, but that very encouragement was seen as legitimating actions which would normally have seemed unacceptable. In 1688 there was no parliament in being and popular violence was directed primarily against Catholic chapels – and became widespread only after James's first flight from London on the night of 10–11 December. Similarly, relatively few peers or gentry joined William until it became clear that there was a very good chance that he would win. There was an additional reason why the English may have been even less rebellious in 1688 than in 1640–2. Charles II and James II, unlike their father, had standing armies. Charles's normally numbered between 5,000 and 10,000 men; by the end of 1685 James's numbered 20,000, more than Cromwell had had in England during the Protectorate. In addition, the militia had been refurbished at the Restoration and put on a firm legal footing; it was used effectively against political and religious dissidents (although James allowed it to run down, preferring to rely on his army). Last but not least, Charles II's government made strenuous efforts to limit the number of weapons in private hands. Both the first and the last years of the reign saw the homes of the allegedly 'disaffected' being searched for arms, which were confiscated to swell the magazines of the county militias. The net result of all this was to increase the coercive powers of the state and to weaken the capacity of subjects to resist it (Malcolm 1992).

The standing army was one of several legacies of the Interregnum which left the state of Charles II more powerful than that of Charles I. The navy more than trebled in size between 1642 and 1662: in the early 1660s it was much more powerful than the French navy and even able to take on the contemporary naval superpower, the Dutch Republic. Naval power facilitated the expansion of trade, shipping and colonies – profit and power went together – which boosted national wealth, and the crown's income. This had benefited enormously from the radical overhaul of the revenue by parliament in the 1640s (Braddick 1994). First, it had swept away the motley collection of domanial, feudal and prerogative sources of income which the Stuarts had inherited from the Middle Ages. Most were fiscally inefficient and many were politically contentious, allowing predatory individuals to extort large sums from their fellow-subjects. Taxes on land or trade were hampered by under-assessment and the fact that there were huge areas of economic activity that remained untaxed. In 1643 parliament introduced the excise – on goods produced and consumed within England – and the assessment, a property tax with a fixed and predictable yield that would not be undermined by under-assessment and so provided useful and reliable security for government borrowing. Together with the customs, these constituted a rational, efficient and 'modern' fiscal system that saw no further major innovation until the introduction of income tax in the 1790s. Moreover, in 1660 the Convention assessed the crown's annual expenditure, on the administration, army and navy, at £1,200,000 and agreed in principle to provide Charles II with a variety of revenues which would bring in that amount. Initially, the Commons' calculations proved over-optimistic and the yield of these revenues fell well short (even after the hearth tax was added). From the 1670s, however, with foreign trade booming and more efficient revenue collection, yields rose to reach a peak of £1,500,000 per annum by Charles's death. The generosity of James II's 1685 parliament left him in an even stronger financial position, with no need of further parliamentary grants for several years (Chandaman 1975). Charles, thanks to a mixture of debt, improvidence and war, was rarely in so happy a position, but even he was able to survive without parliament in the last four years of his reign – and to build himself a fine new palace at Winchester, which was almost complete when he died. Compared to James I and Charles I, Charles II and especially James II were financially well off. Moreover, their revenues rested squarely on parliamentary grants and so were politically uncontentious: there was no recurrence of the sordid 'projects' and scams of the 1610s and 1630s. (The subsidies that they received from Louis XIV were both small and secret.) If money did indeed constitute the 'sinews of power', the later Stuarts were more powerful than their forebears.

Restoration Politics: The Issues

Thus far we have been concerned mainly with the working of government and have considered the legacy of the civil wars in England mainly in institutional terms. However, to argue that the English were 'governable' or 'unrevolutionary' is not incompatible with the suggestion that they might have been provoked into action by incompetent or predatory rulers, by fears of 'popery' or hopes of creating a new godly order. However confused the divisions of 1640–2 may have been – opinions vary – it is clear that during the first civil war understanding of the issues, and a sense of commitment to one side or the other, became increasingly widespread. Ordinary men and women developed a sense of partisanship and identity, thanks to the press, the pulpit, the movement of armies and word of mouth. With the army's emergence into politics, the regicide and all that followed, the issues of 1642–6 became overlaid by others, but by 1660 the English people were politically more informed, and so potentially more committed, than ever before.

Since the mid-1980s Restoration historians have become interested in the complex ideological legacy of the civil wars and Interregnum. Their interest stemmed partly from an acceptance that 1688 was not inevitable and so that the period was worthy of study in its own right, especially as studies of popular politics showed the existence of first popular royalism and then popular Toryism and Anglicanism. Whig historians had tended to ignore views which seemed backward-looking. Modern historians of the left, seeing class-conflict as natural and inevitable, equated 'popular politics' with 'radical politics' and dismissed popular royalism and Anglicanism as products of indoctrination and repression. Recent studies of the Restoration, while not ignoring the politics of parliament and the court, have focused more on coffee houses and the press, elections and petitions. They have revealed a nation which, by 1681, seemed almost as divided as in 1642. It became clear that what Ogg described as 'the Stuart revenge' of 1681–5 could not have happened without the support of the Tories and indeed was in many ways driven by them (Halliday 1998; Miller 2000). Moreover, having denounced the Whigs for appealing for popular support, the Tories did the same, through the press and loyal addresses – with considerable success (Harris 1987, 1993; Knights 1994).

Much of the recent debate among historians of the Restoration has focused on the nature and concept of 'party' (*Albion* 1993; Harris 1993). They have reconsidered studies by earlier historians who took as their starting point the apparently more developed party politics of the early eighteenth century. James Jones's (1961) pioneering study of the 'first Whigs' sought the origins of later Whiggism, while remaining firmly rooted in the politics of the 'Exclusion Crisis'. Sir John Plumb, in seeking to explain the 'political stability' of the age of Walpole, looked back beyond 1688 for the origins of the 'rage of party' which he, and Geoffrey Holmes, saw as the dominant feature of Anne's reign (Plumb 1967; Holmes 1967). Those who looked back before 1688 for the origins of later partisan divisions have been accused of hindsight and anachronism, of seeing the party divisions of the Restoration as a primitive precursor of those of the eighteenth century, rather than an enduring and painful legacy of the civil wars (Scott 1991) – which indeed continued to be recalled well beyond 1715 (Wilson 1995). Nevertheless, they performed the major service of emphasizing the importance of ideological divisions in mainstream politics, at a time when much of the literature on the Restoration was narrowly constitutional or couched in terms of techniques of management (Kemp 1957; Browning 1951). Such an approach looked at the Restoration primarily in terms of later developments and so saw 1660 as the beginning of a 'long eighteenth century'. So, in a rather different sense, did Jonathan Clark, who argued that England's *ancien régime* continued little changed through the seventeenth and eighteenth centuries – monarchical, aristocratic and Anglican – until it collapsed in the face of religious and political radicalism in 1828–32. In Clark's reading of the period, neither the 'rebellions' of the 1640s nor the 'palace coup' of 1688–9 changed very much: rural society remained conservative and deferential and the prevailing ideologies of divine-right monarchy and non-resistance, as expounded by the Church of England, maintained their hold over the people (Clark 1985, 1986).

Clark's views have been challenged by those historians of the eighteenth century who argue for a vigorous and independently minded popular politics, especially in cities, with deep divisions between Churchmen and Dissenters, Tories and Whigs (Wilson 1995). Similarly, many historians have argued that the Restoration, far from marking the beginning of a 'long eighteenth century', can be understood only in terms of the civil wars and what went before (Scott 1991, 2000; Miller 2000). One recurrent phrase that runs through John Aubrey's *Brief Lives*, a motley patchwork of anecdotes and reminiscences, is 'before the civil wars': for Aubrey, the halcyon days before 1640 represented a lost and different world. Before moving from this to the assertion that after the ideological changes of 1640–60 the world could never be the same again (a view which Clark for one would not accept), we need to be aware that those who saw the civil wars as a radical break with the past mostly did so with revulsion, not enthusiasm. It was not only grumpy old men like Aubrey and the earl of Clarendon, the marquis of Newcastle and Thomas Hobbes, who denounced the civil wars as 'unnatural': so did countless clergymen, aldermen and citizens who well into the eighteenth century kept 30 January, the anniversary of Charles I's execution, as a holy day and celebrated 29 May, the anniversary of his son's return. In Anne's last years, the martyr king's only serious rival as a Tory electoral icon was the High Church hero, Dr Sacheverell.

Both Whig and neo-Marxist historians stressed (quite correctly) the huge flowering of radical political and religious ideas in the 1640s and 1650s and argued that these ideas would inevitably triumph over 'outdated' concepts like the divine right of kings. To Victorian or modern liberals, parliamentary democracy and religious toleration seem self-evidently 'right': surely any rational person in the later seventeenth century would have felt the same? As the previous paragraphs would suggest, many did not. One major reason was the triumphant repackaging of Charles I, in many ways an inadequate king, as a martyr for the church, the monarchy and the legal rights of the subject, through printed accounts of his trial and *Eikon Basilike*, a supposed collection of his prison writings. It should also be remembered that many, probably most of those who had supported parliament in the first civil war, became progressively alienated by Pride's Purge, the regicide and military rule – not to mention the collapse of ecclesiastical authority that allowed the Quakers to flourish. The development of radical ideas may have created some convinced radicals; it also provoked a formidable conservative backlash. By 1660 many who had been unable to trust Charles I were prepared to give his son the benefit of the doubt. In the early 1660s parliament was far more concerned to crack down on radicalism than to restrict the king. As in France after the Fronde, the response to civil war in England seems to have been more reactionary than radical.

But that is not the whole story. Memories of military rule and radical excess could not entirely wipe out memories of Laudian innovation in the church, the brutal punishment of religious dissidents and above all Charles I's associations with 'popery'. Not only was Laud seen as leading the Church of England towards Rome, but his master was seen as far too friendly to Catholics, starting with his wife and the priests at court and extending to the English Catholic gentry, foreign Catholic powers and (worst of all) the Catholics of Ireland, who (in English Protestant eyes) were guilty of the most appalling atrocities against their Protestant neighbours. Unlike the Popish Plot of 1678, which was essentially a fabrication, Charles I's dealings with Catholics were incontrovertible, as seen in the documents captured at Naseby. Moreover, his association with 'popery' was reinforced by the identification of 'popery' with 'arbitrary government' – punishment contrary to law, taxation without consent, the abolition or subjugation of parliament, to which would be added after 1660 the fear of rule by a standing army. The clear demarcation between politics and religion, the secular and the spiritual, which generally prevails in modern Western states, was far less apparent in the seventeenth century. Moreover, the two were further linked by the perceived threat from Louis XIV, who was seen both as the champion of the Counter-Reformation and as aspiring to 'universal monarchy'. Although Whig historians might see Protestantism and parliaments as inherently more progressive than Catholicism and absolutism, and so as bound to triumph in the end, few Englishmen in the 1670s could have shared that confidence. It was easy to link Charles II's friendship towards France with his Catholic connections, including his queen and his brother, together with his perceived aspirations to override Acts of parliament or to ignore, subjugate or dispense with parliament. Perceptions that Charles was inclined towards 'popery and arbitrary government' had little substance in fact – certainly when compared to his father. His brother was quite another matter: an avowed Catholic, he did everything he could to promote Catholicism, dispensing with or suspending laws, appointing Catholics to office contrary to law, bullying those who disagreed with him and rigging (or trying to rig) parliamentary elections: the general election of 1685 was 'managed' from the centre in a manner unprecedented in the seventeenth century – except during the 1650s.

It could plausibly be argued that Restoration politics were dominated by two rival perceptions, shaped and articulated in the course of the civil wars, but having their origins earlier (Scott 2000). In one, which could be labelled 'royalist', or Tory, religious 'fanatics' (earlier called 'Puritans', now Protestant Dissenters), aided and abetted by 'atheists', libertines and other disaffected people, plotted to foment another civil war, to overthrow monarchy and church and to turn the world upside down again. The other, which could be labelled 'parliamentarian', or Whig, denounced the later Stuarts' fondness for 'popery', allowing the Anglican clergy to persecute Dissenters (while failing to persecute Catholics), their closeness to Louis XIV and their refusal to appreciate the religious and geopolitical threat posed by France. As distrust mounted, and parliamentary criticism of the king's policies became more strident, there were complaints about the king's reluctance to summon parliament or to heed its advice; from 1675 there were also allegations that Lord Treasurer Danby was trying to sap the integrity of the Commons by giving places, pensions and other rewards only to those who supported government measures. By 1680 'Whig' MPs were arguing (as some had in 1642) that the king was so misled by 'evil counsellors' that he was 'deranged': his words could be ignored because they did not reflect his real wishes. He should follow the Commons' advice in all things, the only way to recover the trust and love of his people. What would happen if he did not was rarely spelt out, but there was more than a hint that the people might be goaded into rebellion.

Debates in parliament and in the press in 1679–81 show these entrenched positions only too clearly. Both sides stressed the similarities to 1640–2: the Whigs to frighten the king, the Tories to stiffen his resistance. There were other similarities too – an impeached first minister, a rebellion in Scotland – but also (as we shall see) significant differences. For many contemporaries, it was the similarities that were the more striking. The years 1679–85 saw a polarization akin to that of 1642, but it does not follow that the divisions of the first civil war simply carried on through the Restoration. As noted already, the events of 1646–60 had blurred these earlier alignments. Moreover, the divisions of 1642 had been both recent and painful. Then between the zealots on both sides there had been a huge body of moderates, who disliked both Laudian innovation and incipient sectarianism, who distrusted both a king with a track record of duplicity and a group in the Commons who used the smear of anti-popery to inhibit debate and encouraged rioting in the streets. For those whose ideals were an ordered Elizabethan church and a responsible monarch working constructively with parliament, the alternatives that faced them seemed equally unpalatable, but, with the outbreak of hostilities, more and more were forced to choose one or the other.

For moderates on both sides, the Restoration offered a chance to regain the middle ground, to re-establish co-operation between ruler and ruled. True, some royalists wanted revenge, but they were frustrated by the king, whose first priority was to placate his enemies, not to indulge his friends. Only in the later 1670s did the Commons become polarized and the middle ground shrink. After eighteen years without a general election, there were three in two years, often bitterly fought. Voters often judged MPs on their record in parliament; division lists and blacklists circulated. As voting was a public act, electors became identified with one party or the other. The process was carried further by petitions in 1679–80 that the king should allow the recently elected parliament to meet, and 'abhorrences', deploring such attempts to dictate to the king. Subscription to either type of document, or to loyal addresses, carried the process of 'labelling' further. Historians' interpretations of this process have varied. Jonathan Scott sees society as divided between the perceptions described earlier as 'Tory' and 'Whig', but argues that many moved from one to the other: many of the Whigs of 1679 became the Tories of 1681 (Scott 1988). Mark Knights sees the process as one of squeezing the middle ground: as in 1642, leading figures, pressed to commit their votes or to subscribe petitions or abhorrences, found it difficult to sit on the fence (Knights 1994; Miller 2000). What is incontestable is that in 1681–5 party divisions ran through, and distorted, many areas of government and law enforcement. Tory judges, magistrates and juries harassed Whigs and persecuted Dissenters; towns lost their charters. Charles exploited ideological divisions to raise the Stuart monarchy to the zenith of its power. By contrast, James II, like his father in 1640, was to unite his people against him.

King, Parliament and People

From the foregoing, it will be apparent that it is possible to look at Restoration politics in two ways. One would stress the basic 'governability' of the English people: peasant revolts and noble insurrections were things of the past and respect for the law was deep-rooted. The civil wars could be seen as enhancing these characteristics. On one hand, the upheaval created a backlash and a parade of horrors – regicide, soldiers on free quarter, Ranters and Quakers – to set against the more traditional set associated with popery – burnings, massacres, the Inquisition, Gunpowder treason – to which would be added Louis XIV's *dragonnades*. On the other, Charles II's military resources, though still modest by continental standards, were significantly greater than those of his father. A second perspective would emphasize the explosion of political information and popular political awareness in the 1640s, the deep political and religious divisions created by civil war and the development of radical and republican political ideas. As we have seen, the polemical and ideological battles of the mid-seventeenth century continued to be fought well into the eighteenth. 'Revisionist' historians have argued that the early Stuart period was one of consensus. There was basic agreement that England's polity was based on co-operation between king, parliament and people and that relations between them were regulated by custom and the law. This ideal was encapsulated in the concept of the 'ancient constitution', an organic growth in which monarchy, parliament and laws had developed together and supported one another. There was also general agreement on the need for a single, national Protestant church. There is room for debate about how far agreement on the nature of constitution and church broke down in the face of the fiscal and religious policies of Charles I. Nevertheless, he was not faced, as Charles II was, with significant strands of opinion hostile to monarchy or to the very idea of a national church.

If one can find evidence of both consensus and conflict in Restoration political culture, it is also possible to come up with very different assessments of the restored monarchy. Whatever the merits of the 'ancient constitution', by 1642 it had broken down. It had rested on the assumption that the king would rule responsibly, that he would respect the spirit as well as the letter of the law and that he would pay some heed to the wishes and the anxieties of his subjects. Unable either to trust Charles I or to persuade him to heed its advice, parliament was driven to challenge hitherto unchallenged royal prerogatives, to seek to coerce the king and ultimately to fight against him. It was driven to do so because the ancient constitution provided no mechanism to judge between king and parliament, king and people, when mutual trust had broken down. This crucial problem was not so much not resolved at the Restoration as not addressed. The Convention of 1660 and the Cavalier Parliament elected in 1661 undid many of the innovations of 1640–60, on the seemingly unspoken assumption that the ancient constitution would then start working again. True, the Cavalier Parliament left in place much of the legislation of 1641, notably against the prerogative courts and the fiscal devices abused in the 1630s. But neither body showed any eagerness to impose new restrictions on the crown and the Cavalier Parliament was more concerned to prevent radical elements from destabilizing the newly restored monarchy. The militia was re-established, pre-publication censorship was given statutory force, calling the king a papist was made an offence and 'tumultuous' petitioning was made illegal. New laws were passed against unauthorized meetings on 'pretence' of religion, new oaths were imposed, non-conforming clergymen were driven out of the church and those seen as 'disaffected' were purged from municipal corporations (Seaward 1987; Miller 1997). But one central issue was not addressed: in the final analysis, who was supreme – king or parliament?

If that awkward question was not asked in 1660–1, twenty years later it was the central theme of politics. Was it justifiable to debar Charles's brother from succeeding to the throne, on the grounds that, as a Catholic, he would inevitably rule arbitrarily? If Charles would not willingly call parliament to address the ills of the nation, or heed its advice when he called it, how justifiable was it to subject him to mass popular pressure? How far could fear of tyranny, or the right of self-preservation, justify active resistance to the monarch? The various questions boiled down into one: if the interests of the king (or royal family) and those of the people seemed irreconcilable, which was to take precedence? This was exactly the question which had lain at the heart of the political debates of the 1640s: it would seem that the ideological legacy of the civil wars had undermined the Restoration regime, creating a multi-faceted crisis in which many informed contemporaries feared another civil war (Knights 1994).

Such an interpretation is very plausible. One should not lightly dismiss the views of contemporaries, but alternative interpretations are possible. Two questions, in particular, are worth asking. First, was the crisis of 1678–81 (it is a matter of taste whether or not one calls it the 'exclusion crisis') inevitable? Second, was the crisis so serious as to create a real danger of civil war? In an effort to answer these questions we need to return to our two possible ways of viewing the restored regime, one emphasizing consensus, the other conflict. The view that there were serious structural weaknesses in the regime, making renewed political confrontation between king and parliament likely, if not inevitable, prioritizes conflict over consensus. Let us see what can be said on the other side.

First, we need to return to the Restoration settlement. As we have seen, this effectively restored the powers of the crown as they had been at the end of 1641, without prerogative courts or the power to raise money without parliament. Had parliament wished to impose further restrictions on the king it could easily have done so. But it did not, seeming more concerned with guarding against the possibility of insurrection and conspiracy. The most plausible explanation is that revolution from below seemed a much greater threat to the traditional constitutional balance than the possible misuse of royal power. And it seems very probable that it was that *balance* that the Cavalier Parliament, in particular, wished to restore. Historians may say with hindsight that a constitution without a single supreme, sovereign power was unworkable. Contemporaries seem to have believed that the fault lay, not with the constitution itself, but with those who had failed to operate it properly: the 'uncounselled' Charles I or the factious and ambitious demagogues who had led the Long Parliament. If the constitution *was* basically sound, it made good sense to restore it in as traditional a form as was compatible with the changed conditions after a civil war.

Nowhere was the concern for balance more apparent than in parliament's financial provision for Charles II. When he returned the Convention controlled the entire revenue and could easily have retained that control. Instead, it consciously reverted to the traditional principle that the king should 'live of his own', by agreeing to vote him, for life or forever, revenues estimated to bring in enough to cover the cost of government. Given that the power to grant or withhold money was by far parliament's strongest bargaining weapon in its dealings with the king, this resolution was an extraordinary gesture of trust in the new king – and one made by a House of Commons containing far fewer royalists than its successor. The Cavalier Parliament accepted to some extent that the calculations of its predecessor had been flawed, adding the hearth tax to the customs and excises, but thereafter it refused to vote any but temporary revenues, calculating that a king who was a little short of money would be more likely to meet parliament regularly and pay heed to its wishes (Chandaman 1975; Miller 1997). In fact, the Commons' initial generosity limited their bargaining power later in the reign, especially as the revenue's yield began to increase: only in wartime was Charles forced to make substantial concessions (Miller 1982). However, the important point in the context of this discussion was the concern of both parliaments to build up the powers and revenue of the crown, in stark contrast to the behaviour of the Long Parliament, in order to recreate the balance that lay at the heart of the ancient constitution.

The question of the seriousness of the crisis of 1678–81 is rather more problematical, in that it depends on an analysis of what did not happen rather than of what did.

Some comparisons with 1640–2 are salutary. Charles I made repeated substantive concessions to parliament, abandoning key prerogatives (such as the right to call and dismiss parliaments at will) in order to buy time until he could gather sufficient troops to impose his will by force. Charles II made numerous cosmetic concessions, notably his new privy council of 1679, containing most of his leading critics; his father had refused to heed parliament's wishes when choosing advisers. But on the key issues he refused to budge: he vetoed the Militia Bill in 1678 (because he feared it would deprive him of total control over the militia) and refused either to agree to exclude his brother from the succession or to call parliament when faced with a flurry of petitions urging him to do so. Charles I lost effective control of his government to parliament, partly through sheer irresponsibility: when he left for Scotland in the autumn of 1641 he made no effective provision for government in his absence. He also lost control of London. Even as a backlash developed against extremism in parliament in the winter of 1641–2, Charles failed to exploit it, risking everything on his attempt to arrest the Five Members. Charles II maintained full control over his government and his armed forces. He rebuffed or evaded all his new privy council's attempts to persuade him to change the officers of the army or militia or the justices of the peace. Although the election of Whig sheriffs in 1680 and 1681 deprived him of control over London's law courts, Charles's supporters continued to control the City militia. Charles II can be credited with greater shrewdness, or realism, than his father: he never harboured fantasies of reasserting his authority by force and reluctantly, but wisely, agreed in the spring of 1679 to disband the troops raised for war with France the year before. But his position was also inherently stronger. Charles I was driven to call the Long Parliament in 1640 by a Scottish invasion and his relations with parliament reached a crisis as a result of the Irish rising of 1641. Charles II faced a minor revolt in Scotland in 1679, quickly put down; Ireland remained quiet. Whereas there were widespread violent protests, especially in London, in 1641–2, fuelled in large part by fear of royal or popish violence, popular political activity in 1679–81 was surprisingly free from violence, except perhaps in elections. In addition, Charles II had two great, if unseen, assets. First, in 1641 those who took to the streets in London feared being murdered in their beds by the king's popish troops, or having their houses shelled by the mortars in the Tower. In 1679–81 popular anxieties were more distant and hypothetical: of what the king's popish brother might do if ever he became king. Second, the very fact that there had been a civil war and that the world had been turned upside down gravely inhibited the king's critics: most wanted to force a change of policy, not to transform the political, and still less the social, order. In 1680–1, as in 1641–2, a backlash against the king's critics built up, but unlike his father, Charles II was in full control of the government and so in a perfect position to exploit it in the years that followed.

James II

It cannot be stressed enough that in 1685 James II inherited a position of exceptional strength, with a sufficient revenue, a standing army and an unprecedented degree of control over the ruling elites of the corporate towns, which helped him to secure an overwhelmingly Tory House of Commons. His strength was based not only on his material and military resources, but also on the willing co-operation of Tory noblemen, gentlemen, citizens and freeholders, as well as the clergy of the Church of England. That co-operation rested on the assumption, indeed the tacit condition, that James would rule as the Tories wanted, respecting the laws, defending the Church and persecuting Nonconformists. There seemed no need to spell out this condition: for the Tories it was self-evidently in James's best interests to rely on those who had defended his right to the throne and who had been vilified for so doing as 'favourers of popery'. They knew he was a Catholic and expected him to worship as a Catholic, but privately; many would also have no objection to his not enforcing the laws against Catholics, who had (after all) been royalists in the Civil War. They expected him to treat his religion as a personal matter and to rule as if he were an Anglican.

James's first statement as king was that he would support the Church of England because it supported the monarchy. This reassured the Tories but it became apparent that the king's support was conditional on the Churchmen's behaving in what he saw as a loyal manner. Since the 'exclusion crisis' the clergy had repeatedly stressed that active resistance to the monarchy could never be justified; James interpreted this as a commitment to unconditional obedience. However, his Tory parliament would not agree to any formal relaxation of the laws against Catholics and especially the Test Acts of 1673 and 1678, designed to keep Catholics out of public offices and parliament. The Houses were especially perturbed by James's commissioning nearly a hundred Catholic officers in the additional regiments he had raised to oppose Monmouth's rebellion. This could not have happened at a more sensitive time, as Louis XIV's army was forcing his Protestant subjects to attend mass. For James, however, it seemed only just and reasonable that his loyal Catholic subjects should be allowed to worship freely and serve their king. In his eyes, the Tories' failure to recognize this showed that their much-vaunted loyalty would last only as long as he would allow them to monopolize public offices and to persecute those who could not in conscience conform to the Church of England – not only Catholics, but also Protestant Dissenters. James had always made it clear that he disapproved of Dissenters' meetings, not on religious grounds, but because they showed a subversive defiance of the law. Now he seemed to accept their argument that their defiance was forced on them by Anglican intolerance. James still sought toleration and full civil rights for Catholics, but now in the wider context of a general toleration of all Nonconformists, Catholic and Protestant, secured by the repeal, by parliament, of the penal laws (which punished all aspects of non-Anglican worship) and the Test Acts.

How far James was 'sincere' in his advocacy of toleration is a question which is probably impossible to answer (Miller 1978). What is not in doubt is that it alienated the Tories, and especially the Anglican clergy. The Tory reaction and James's electoral success in 1685 had rested on a broad basis of popular Tory support. Without that support it would be hard to secure an amenable parliament. Catholics comprised only a tiny minority of the population. Protestant Dissenters were more numerous, but still a small minority. Both groups had been systematically excluded from public offices since the Restoration, and the Dissenters, while strong in many towns, had few adherents among the landed elite which ruled the shires. There were many Whigs who, while attending their parish church, favoured toleration for Dissenters, but not for Catholics: anti-popery lay at the heart of Whiggism. Many Dissenters, too, would be happy to gain freedom of worship and perhaps admittance to office, but they were reluctant to concede the same to Catholics, believing that once in office they would use their power to persecute Protestants. Only the Catholics and a section of the Dissenters could therefore be relied upon to support the repeal of the penal laws and Test Acts, offering an electoral base far too narrow to secure a parliament that would do what James wished – especially as neither group was legally eligible for office.

James's answer to this problem was two-fold. First, he used his prerogatives to enhance the influence of Catholics and Dissenters. He secured a legal judgement, in the case of *Godden vs Hales*, which provided a pretext to suspend the penal laws, allowing Catholics and Dissenters to worship freely, and to dispense them from the penalties of the Test Acts, so that they could hold municipal and other offices. He used his powers over the personnel of town corporations to remove Tories from office and put Dissenters (and occasionally Catholics) in their places. Second, he did all he could to browbeat and bully Tories and Anglicans into supporting – or at least not opposing – his demands. Magistrates and officials were subjected to all kinds of pressure, including the threat (and sometimes the reality) of having soldiers quartered in their homes. An ecclesiastical commission was set up to silence clergymen who preached against popery and to force the two universities to admit Catholic tutors and students. In 1688 James ordered the bishops to instruct their clergy to read his Declaration of Indulgence (in which he had granted freedom of worship) in the parish churches. Seven bishops refused, claiming that the Declaration was illegal. They were tried for seditious libel, in what was intended to be a show trial, but were acquitted, amid massive popular rejoicing. Some bishops did order their clergy to read the Declaration, but few obeyed. The foremost advocates of non-resistance had refused, *en masse*, to obey an order from the king that seemed to threaten the very being of their church. In the final analysis, they had obeyed God rather than man.

Yet this was a matter of non-obedience, not active resistance: there was no sign of rebellion. Whether James could have secured a parliament that would repeal the penal laws and Test Acts we shall never know, because his preparations were disrupted and then aborted by William III's invasion. Despite assurances that most of James's subjects were disaffected, William brought an army large enough to defeat James's without any help from the English. Although William's propaganda aimed to win over English public opinion, and James became uncomfortably aware that many of his subjects hated him, William's sustained military pressure played a crucial part in James's decision to run away. Despite their reputation on the Continent for rebellion and regicide, the English showed no sign of appearing in arms in 1688 until William's army had safely landed. On the other hand, the Tories and the Anglican clergy had stubbornly refused to co-operate with his preparations for parliament and did virtually nothing to oppose William. Instead their leaders exploited James's discomfiture and pressed him to reverse all the changes he had made since 1685 and to revert to strictly Tory policies. Their plans were foiled by James's totally unexpected decision to run away, leaving them to contend with William, whom they saw as no friend to either the Tories or the church.

It is tempting to see James II's reign as similar to his father's, except that he alienated most sections of his subjects more quickly and more comprehensively. If 'revisionist' studies of the early Stuart period have emphasized the personal and the contingent, similar considerations apply *a fortiori* to James II's reign. Far from giving the final push to the tottering edifice of Stuart personal monarchy, doomed in the face of progressive and liberal ideas, James had seemed in 1685 to possess enormous advantages compared to his father in 1625: a large navy, a significant army, an adequate revenue and a people traumatized by memories of civil war. Even after he had alienated his subjects at an alarming rate, it was by no means inevitable that his regime would collapse ignominiously. William's invasion was an enormously risky – as well as an enormously ambitious – enterprise, made possible by a fortuitous combination of events on the Continent and an even more fortuitous turn in the weather. Unlike some contemporaries, historians nowadays are unaccustomed to ascribing developments to divine providence, at once inevitable and inscrutable. Many are prepared to accept that events could have turned out differently and that the revolution of 1688 was a major, and far from inevitable, turning point in English (and British) history. Recent studies of the Restoration period have served only to emphasize the magnitude of its importance.

REFERENCES

Albion 1993: 'Debate on the nature of party in Restoration England in the autumn 1993', *Albion*, vol. 25, no. 4.
Braddick, M. 1994: *Parliamentary Taxation in Seventeenth-Century England*: Woodbridge.
Browning, A. 1951: *Thomas Earl of Danby*, 3 vols: Glasgow.
Buckroyd, J. M. 1981: *Church and State in Scotland, 1660–81*: Edinburgh.
Chandaman, C. D. 1975: *The English Public Revenue, 1660–88*: Oxford.
Clark, J. C. D. 1985: *English Society, 1688–1832*: Cambridge.
Clark, J. C. D. 1986: *Revolution and Rebellion: State and Society in England in the Seventeenth and Eighteenth Centuries*: Cambridge.
Haley, K. H. D. 1968: *The First Earl of Shaftesbury*: Oxford.
Halliday, P. 1998: *Dismembering the Body Politic: Partisan Politics in England's Towns 1650–1730*: Cambridge.
Harris, T. 1987: *London Crowds in the Reign of Charles II*: Cambridge.
Harris, T. 1993: *Politics Under the Later Stuarts, 1660–1714*: Harlow.
Hill, C. 1980: *Some Intellectual Consequences of the English Revolution*: London.
Holmes, G. 1967: *British Politics in the Age of Anne*: London.
Israel, J. (ed.) 1991: *The Anglo-Dutch Moment: Essays on the Glorious Revolution and its World Impact*: Cambridge.
Jones, J. R. 1961: *The First Whigs: Politics in the Exclusion Crisis*: Oxford.
Kemp, B. 1957: *King and Commons, 1660–1832*: London.
Kenyon, J. P. 1958: *Robert Spencer, Earl of Sunderland*: London.
Knights, M. 1994: *Politics and Opinion in Crisis, 1678–81*: London.
Malcolm, J. L. 1992: 'Charles II and the reconstruction of royal power', *Historical Journal*, 35.
Miller, J. 1977: 'The earl of Tyrconnell and James II's Irish policy', *Historical Journal*, 20.
Miller, J. 1978: *James II: A Study in Kingship*: Hove; revd edn 2000: *James II*: New Haven, CT.
Miller, J. 1982: 'Charles II and his parliaments', *Transactions of the Royal Historical Society*, 5th series, vol. 32.
Miller, J. 1997: *The Restoration and the England of Charles II*: Harlow.
Miller, J. 2000: *After the Civil Wars: English Politics and Government in the Reign of Charles II*: Harlow.

Ogg, D. 1934: *England in the Reign of Charles II*: Oxford.
Ogg, D. 1955: *England in the Reigns of James II and William III*: Oxford.
Plumb, J. H. 1967: *The Growth of Political Stability in England, 1675–1725*: London.
Russell, C. 1990: *The Causes of the English Civil War*: Oxford.
Scott, J. 1988: 'Radicalism and Restoration: the shape of the Stuart experience', *Historical Journal*, 31.
Scott, J. 1991: *Algernon Sidney and the Restoration Crisis, 1677–83*: Cambridge.
Scott, J. 2000: *England's Troubles: Seventeenth-Century English Political Instability in European Context*: Cambridge.
Seaward, P. 1987: *The Cavalier Parliament and the Reconstruction of the Old Regime, 1661–7*: Cambridge.
Wilson, K. 1995: *The Sense of the People: Politics, Culture and Imperialism in England, 1715–85*: New York.

FURTHER READING

Childs, J. 1980: *The Army, James II and the Glorious Revolution*: Manchester.
Childs, J. 1986: *The Army of Charles II*: London.
Cruickshanks, E. (ed.) 1989: *By Force or by Default? The Revolution of 1688–9*: Edinburgh.
Glassey, L. K. J. (ed.) 1997: *The Reigns of Charles II and James VII and II*: London.
Harris, T., Seaward, P. and Goldie, M. (eds) 1990: *The Politics of Religion in Restoration England*: Oxford.
Hutton, R. 1985: *The Restoration, 1658–67*: Oxford.
Hutton, R. 1989: *Charles II*: Oxford.
Jones, J. R. 1972: *The Revolution of 1688 in England*: London.
Miller, J. 1984: 'The potential for "absolutism" in later Stuart England', *History*, 69.
Miller, J. 1991: *Charles II*: London.
Speck, W. A. 1988: *Reluctant Revolutionaries: Englishmen and the Revolution of 1688*: Oxford.
Spurr, J. 2000: *England in the 1670s: 'This Masquerading Age'*: Oxford.
Stater, V. L. 1994: *Noble Government: The Stuart Lord Lieutenancy and the Transformation of English Politics*: Athens, GA.
Western, J. R. 1972: *Monarchy and Revolution: The English State in the 1680s*: London.

CHAPTER TWENTY-ONE

Religion in Restoration England

JOHN SPURR

One wintry Friday in 1674 Agnes Beaumont waited with sinking heart for the neighbour who had promised to let her ride behind him to the Baptist meeting at Gamlinghay, Bedfordshire. This 24-year-old woman, who lived alone with her father on their farm, had joined the congregation in 1672 and currently enjoyed a rich spiritual life: 'there was scarce a corner in the house, or barns, or cowhouse, or stable, or closes, under the hedges, or in the wood, but I was made to pour out my soul to God'. Although the expected neighbour did not turn up, John Bunyan, pastor to the congregation, called in on his way to the meeting. After some hesitation on Bunyan's part, he allowed Agnes to get up behind him on his horse and they set off. 'My heart was puffed up with pride', she later admitted, 'to think I should ride behind such a man as he was.'

> ...there met with us a priest [i.e. a minister of the Church of England] one Mr Lane...and he knew us both, and spoke to us, and looked of us, as we rode along the way as if he would have stared his eyes out; and afterwards did scandalize us after a base manner, and did raise a very wicked report of us, which was altogether false, blessed be God.

For Agnes the meeting that day was 'a feast of fat things'; she sat under the shadow of the Lord, tasted his fruit at his table and had 'a return of prayer'. 'Oh, I had such a sight of Jesus Christ that brake my heart to pieces...A sense of my sins, and of his dying love, made me love him, and long to be with him.' Cold and muddy, but elated, Agnes eventually got home late that night, only to find the door barred against her. Her father 'was very angry with me for riding behind Mr Bunyan, and said I should never come within his doors again, except I would promise him to leave going after that man'. Her pleas had no effect, and she decided to spend the night in the barn and in prayer.

Freezing though it was that night, she felt no cold; she withstood the temptations of Satan, and had 'heart-ravishing visits' from the Lord. Next day, however, her father was adamant that he would not let her into the house unless she promised never to go to the meeting again. Despite her repeated assertion that 'my soul is worth more than so', Agnes eventually gave her promise and returned to her father's house on Sunday. She also returned to her domestic duties, caring for the old man, preparing his meals, and sitting by the fire with him in the evenings. When she confessed how troubled she was by her promise, they wept together. After all, her father himself used to go with her to the meeting until he had been set against it by neighbours, who asked: 'Have you lived to these years to be led away with them? These be they that lead silly women captive into houses, and for a pretence make long prayers.' On the Tuesday night, Agnes was awoken by 'a doleful noise'. Her father was struck with a pain at his heart. Alarmed, Agnes ran half-dressed through the dark snowy night to her brother's farm for help. They had not long returned when their father died. But Agnes's troubles were far from over.

At Baldock fair that same Tuesday, Mr Lane, the Anglican minister who had stared at Agnes and Bunyan as they passed, had spread the slander that Bunyan and she were 'naught[y] together'. This gossip had reached Mr Feery, a local lawyer and a rejected suitor for Agnes's hand, who now accused her of poisoning her father and alleged that Bunyan had put her up to it: 'it will be found petty treason', he told her brother, 'she must be burned'. Agnes and her brother summoned the local doctor to view their father's corpse, then the coroner's jury was assembled. Her life at stake, Agnes was plagued by 'carnal reasoning' or human fears: 'the thoughts of burning would sometimes shake me all to pieces'. She was concerned, too, for Bunyan and 'for the name of God', but at bottom she was resigned to God's will: 'I must leave it with God, who hath the hearts of all men in his hand'. As she went to meet the coroner's jury, 'my heart went out mightily to God to stand by me; and such words as these passed through my heart, "Thou shall not return again ashamed" [Psalm 74: 21]'. She came through the ordeal. Her demeanour, the corpse, and Feery's lack of evidence, all showed that this was a death by natural causes. Local gossip did not acquit Agnes quite so easily. A few weeks later it was rumoured that she had confessed to poisoning her father and had gone mad. She determined to put a stop to this by going to Bigglesworth where she 'walked through and through the market . . . so a great many came to me and said, "We see you are not distracted." And I saw some cry, and some laugh. "Oh," thought I, "mock on; there is a day coming will clear all"' (Beaumont 1992).

Agnes Beaumont's story, unusual as a woman's own account of her experience, is thought-provoking in many ways. This provincial drama raises questions about gender, about the relations of fathers and daughters, about charismatic preachers and disappointed suitors, and about sexual slander and gossip. But, above all, it vividly illustrates the centrality of religion in the lives of some late seventeenth-century individuals. The abiding influence of religion in the reign of the 'merry monarch' and his successors should come as no surprise: the Puritan tradition may have received a setback at the Restoration but it was not eclipsed; this was, after all, the England of Milton, Bunyan and William Penn. The purpose of this chapter is to convey something of the reality of religion in the Restoration and to offer readers a flavour of recent work on the subject. Scholarly attention of late has moved away from narrowly denominational and political history, to concentrate on exploring the religious experience of ordinary people. Stories like Agnes's are testimony to the reality and the costs of religious choice in Restoration England. Her tale is also redolent of a Protestant piety which was widely spread throughout the 'Protestant community' and society at large. And it offers us a glimpse of religious life from the grassroots, from the perspective of a humble female participant rather than that of a clerical leader. So, although this chapter will consider the relevance of religious labels, the appeal of

'Reformation', the predominance of the Church of England, and the political 'problem' of religious diversity, its starting point has to be a much broader question: what did ordinary English people like Agnes and her neighbours want from their religion?

I

There can be no simple answer to our question. After the upheaval of the mid-century, there remained a minority of zealous individuals who sought personal spiritual satisfaction at all costs and a much larger majority of the population who shrank from such 'fanaticism' and 'enthusiasm'. The secrets of most individuals' private or 'closet' devotion are irrecoverable. Almost by definition the surviving diaries of Samuel Pepys, John Evelyn or Ralph Josselin are untypical in their introspective comments about personal religion. Yet we can at least hazard some generalizations. It is clear, for instance, that the English had a taste for sermons: they 'generally place their religion in the pulpit, as the papists do their upon the altar'. City types like Pepys made a habit of 'going from one church to another hearing a bit here and a bit there', they casually dropped in to taste a sermon or made a point of hearing a new preacher, and they were keen to judge the performance, substance and style. In some parishes a second sermon on a Sunday was preferred, even if that meant that the minister had to omit parts of the service.

Hearing sermons was far from passive: congregations followed them in their Bibles; they discussed or repeated them after church; and, although it was becoming less common, many still took notes in church. And what did they learn? It seems likely that the routine weekly preaching of parish ministers concentrated on the central duties of repentance and Christian living. At Deptford parish church in 1670 the Anglican vicar preached on successive Sundays on 'how we are justified by Christ's rising again', 'how justification has reference to works as well as faith' and 'how faith was more than a firm belief or strong persuasion'. Congregations across the land were exhorted to take up holy living in conjunction with a lively faith, to add the power of godliness to its form in fulfilling 'the whole duty of man'. Anglican preachers, especially, discouraged unnecessary speculation and stressed the theological agnosticism of their church. The 'settled doctrine' of the Church of England allowed for a variety of views on speculative subtleties: when Anglicans asked how it was that God worked on the heart of an individual who enjoyed free will, they answered: 'I do not know that we are obliged to trouble ourselves with those nice inquiries' (Wallis 1682: sig.Av, p. 32). What was required was 'plain, practical preaching' on the need for God's assistance and our own efforts. Predestination which had assumed such importance in the early seventeenth century was becoming irrelevant – one gentleman declared that it 'seems lately to be retired to its eternal rest' – and even the labels of Arminian and Calvinist seemed curiously old-fashioned (see Spurr 1991: 314–17).

Some complained that 'to place all or most of our religion in hearing a sermon' undermined prayer and the sacrament. A Cheshire gentleman described 'the sort of people disaffected to the Book of Common Prayer, which frequently stand without the churches, till the common service be read; and then at the singing of the psalm, when the minister goes into the pulpit, then they come into the church and not before' (Leicester 1953: 47). Visiting Bristol diocese in 1683, Bishop Trelawney complained of 'the confused and irregular way of reading the prayers in some ministers, either through their own dissatisfaction with them, or fear of others [being] dissatisfied with them' (Tanner MS 30, fo. 50). Too often the services were reduced to prayers read by the minister and responses by the parish clerk, who supposedly led the congregation, while parishioners mumbled their part or looked on in silence. The laity became more animated by singing. In the country, if not in the more fashion-conscious city, the singing of metrical psalms by the congregation was a staple of weekly worship (see Spaeth 2000: ch. 10; Green 2000: ch. 9).

The sacrament of the Lord's Supper was an even less significant part of the average person's spiritual life than common prayer. Many conforming parishioners remained 'strangely averse' or 'awkward to the sacrament'. Even those who took the church's message seriously and prepared themselves elaborately for a 'worthy reception' of the sacrament, only received communion perhaps two or three times each year. Most received just once a year, probably at Easter, and some insisted on remaining seated rather than kneeling while taking the bread and wine. There were monthly celebrations of the communion in some London churches and cathedrals by the 1680s, but it was the Dissenting congregations that made a habit of more regular celebration and reception.

It is becoming evident that the laity could and did determine their own worship. They participated in both occasional and regular services according to their needs, their other commitments, especially work, and their respect for the minister. They were not shy of making their feelings known, whether they concerned individuals or practices – witness those Wiltshire parishioners who made 'mocks and rhymes at the common prayer' in 1665 (Spaeth 2000: 17).

Reactions to the Prayer Book tell us much about what people may have wanted from their worship. The liturgy certainly suffered from associations with popery: 'I find many of the people have, at the bottom, an ill affection for the prayers and governors of the church, really judging the worship tainted with popery' (Clapinson 1980: 220). When Roger Lowe, a Lancashire apprentice, was chastised by the vicar in church for not standing at the gospel, he roundly denounced standing 'with other ceremonies now in use' as 'mere Romish foppery' and stormed off to a conventicle (Lowe 1938: 7). Anglican worship was full of 'vain inventions' and unwarranted formality. The Prayer Book was said to be 'ineffectual' and 'dry stuff'; 'I have no hope of good by it, as having been bred up under its plenty, and tired with its emptiness, and yet surfeited of it' (Heywood 1937: 107). Anglican worship simply failed to move or to satisfy some. William Stout of Lancaster frequented the worship of the church 'yet not greatly to my satisfaction, considering the formality and indifference there appeared of a sincere repentance, as was enjoined in their common prayer liturgy, and ceremonies and catechisms, [as?] was prayed for and promised' (Stout 1967: 82–3). Dissenters expected to be 'edified', to be confirmed and strengthened in their Christian graces, but in their eyes, the church had signally failed to order the indifferent matters of worship 'unto edifying'.

Others, of course, found Prayer Book services rewarding and were able to construct a deeply satisfying personal piety around the liturgy. We can spy some of this piety in the diaries and autobiographies of individuals like Alice Thornton or John Evelyn, but much of our evidence of this must perforce be indirect, gleaned from the large numbers of books published and sold in the later seventeenth century which instruct their readers in a regime of introspective, almost morbid, self-examination,

penitence and thanksgiving, of private and household devotion, and the other foundations of 'holy living'. The primary purpose was to prepare the individual for the
public worship of the church and participation in the sacrament – as can be seen in the
typical manual like *A Weeks Preparation towards a Worthy Receiving of the Lord Supper*
(1679). While the devotional writers stoked the fires of piety, the church struggled to
provide a public outlet for the consequent devotion. The provision of daily prayers
was increased in the capital. In 1664 Pepys had been surprised to discover that daily
prayers were read at St Dunstans, Fleet Street, but by 1687 there were nearly thirty
parish churches in London offering daily prayers.

Devotion cannot be strictly compartmentalized. Works of moral exhortation and
guidance such as *The Whole Duty of Man* (1657) were popular with Anglicans and
Dissenters. As Ian Green (2000) has demonstrated, the healthy market for devotional
aids of all kinds in Restoration England meant that readers could and did use prayers
and meditations from several different traditions, including Roman Catholicism.
Voluntarism is the key to all this piety. However limited or dangerous, the freedom
to associate explains the form and the intensity of much religious experience. Dissenting congregations, for example, were voluntary associations of like-minded
people who believed themselves to be the godly, and since they lived under the threat
of persecution, it was only natural for them to strengthen their resolve by participation in the communal act of the sacrament. There are some glimpses of voluntary,
extra-parochial groups of Anglicans receiving communion more frequently, such as
the congregation of Anthony Horneck at the Savoy Chapel in London; and in
parishes where monthly communions were available, it is likely that the same small
knot of devout parishioners were the constant receivers. We should perhaps compare
these oases of piety with parishes where the people voted with their feet in the
opposite direction, places like Pewsey in Wiltshire where the irascible and unpopular
rector complained so many 'are addicted to debaucherie & loosnes, if not inclin'd to
Aitheisme that the publike service of God is too much neglected' and more than half
never received communion. In a telling comment, the rector reported that he knew of
'no parishioner that pretends to the name of Papist, Familiast, Anabaptist, Quaker or
other sectarie, unless any will answer to that of Presbyterian' (Spaeth 2000: 179–80).
So, not only did different people seek different things in their religious activities, but
by and large they found what they wanted. What is intriguing, however, is how rarely
lay religious impulses translated directly into the familiar denominational labels.

II

The Puritan Revolution threw up many different groups – some like the Presbyterians
and Independents recognizable descendants from earlier Puritanism, others such as
the Baptists or Quakers distinct or even new sects – but all were still evolving and after
1662 they all had to accommodate themselves to the disagreeable fact of legal
proscription. We can learn much if we concentrate on the experience of their
members rather than on the labels so beloved of their clergy and pastors. Outright
separatists like Agnes Beaumont and her brethren in the Baptist congregation were
'saints by calling, visibly manifesting and evidencing . . . their obedience unto that call
of Christ, who being further known to each other by their confession of the faith
wrought in them by the power of God, declared by themselves . . . do willingly

consent to walk together according to the appointment of Christ' (Matthews 1959: 122). Once they had covenanted together these congregations called themselves simply 'this church of Christ' or 'the congregation of Christ in and about Bedford'. The congregation retained full authority over their affairs. No church hierarchy, nor minister, exercised powers beyond those of the church meeting and within the church, a small group, often the 'elders' or 'deacons', tended to dominate affairs. The congregation chose the pastor on the grounds of his 'gift' of the Holy Spirit rather than formal qualifications and so many were laymen, like Bunyan, and combined their trade or calling with their pastoral duties.

What drew women (who tended to be the majority in the congregations) and men to these churches was the chance to associate with similarly 'experienced' Christians and to shun the worldly. The congregation as a whole exercised 'discipline' in the belief that members could be kept on the straight and narrow by admonition and exhortation, by fellowship and, if need be, by excommunication. The logic of their convictions led many separatist churches to adopt the practice of 'believers' baptism'. Anyone wishing to join the church had to seal their 'covenant' with the congregation by undergoing baptism, often by total immersion in some chilly pond or river. There was, of course, no reason to baptize babies. A handful of congregations left their members freedom of choice in this area. Although described in 1674 as 'for the most part baptized', the congregation meeting at Broadmead in Bristol regarded baptism as an open question, claiming that the pastor should instead 'promote that blessed principle of union among the saints, as saints, though of different persuasions' (Underhill 1847: 213, 211). The implication was that doctrine was less significant than personal righteousness.

These separatist congregations were bound by personal contacts: Anne Wade told the Bristol congregation in 1673 that she was in communion 'with that Church of Christ in Gloucester, walking with Mr Forbes, to who our deceased pastor did, by word of mouth, commend me' (ibid.: 179). These churches maintain a loose affiliation and enjoyed a sense of belonging to a certain tradition. But they often disagreed with each other, not only on baptism, but also on such thorny problems as whether singing was permissible during worship or whether Sunday or Saturday was the sabbath. Neither separatist not Baptist principles of church communion had any necessary correlation with the theologies of salvation which had been so controversial in the 1620s and 1630s. There were therefore both Calvinist and Arminian Baptist congregations. Those who became disillusioned, especially with the varieties of Baptism, often drifted towards the more vaguely defined doctrines of the Quakers.

Not surprisingly these separatists were unequivocal in their rejection of the national Church of England with its parish system, government by bishops, and uniform worship according to the Book of Common Prayer. The choice, claimed the separatists, was between a faith 'bottomed . . . upon tradition, custom, example, etc, or [a faith based] upon the word of God, realized and imprinted upon our hearts through the Spirit' (Underhill 1847: 124). They would have no truck with the Anglicans' 'superstitious and idolatrous worship, that with force and cruelty is maintained in opposition to the true worship and worshippers of God' (Tibbutt 1966: 62). But not all Protestant Dissenters were as single-minded in their views on a national church.

In the aftermath of the ejection of 1,700 parish ministers in 1662, some clergy and congregations felt that they had been forced into separatism. Much as they might dislike the principle of separatism, these individuals cut themselves off from the national church and set up their own congregations. Thomas Jolly, ejected curate of Altham, Lancashire and his congregation resolved to meet privately for worship and exclude any who attended Prayer Book services. It was, however, virtually impossible to isolate members from the community at large. The congregation gathered around the Presbyterian Oliver Heywood in Coley chapelry, Halifax, had a core of committed members who had subscribed a church covenant, but this did not prevent the maintenance of normal social relations with their neighbours. Most such meetings included a number of 'hearers' who were not fully-fledged members of the congregation but who may have been looking for better spiritual sustenance than was on offer in the parish church. In large rural parishes, which contained several chapelries as well as the parish church, the Church of England simply did not provide services every Sunday. The city parishes fared no better: the churches of London 'will not . . . hold their people; and the assemblies of Presbyterians are upon this account nothing else but so many additions, helps, or supplies to the parish defect' (Humphrey 1680: 6).

The rich evidence that survives of lay religious appetites suggests that a large number of people wanted a spiritually satisfying, broadly Puritan piety, but did not wish to suffer persecution or isolation. Time and time again the words and actions of the laity confound the clergy's labels and historians' perceptions of appropriate denominations. At the alehouse one day in 1664, Roger Lowe began to discuss with John Potter 'the manner of God's worship. He was for episcopacy and I for Presbytery. The contention had like to have beene hot, but the Lord prevented. It was two or three days ere we spoke, and I was afraid lest he should do me some hurt' (Lowe 1938: 52). This alehouse quarrel between two laymen is instructive, not simply as a reminder of how passionately people felt about religion, but in its confusion of two forms of church government with two forms of worship. For Lowe, who attended both his parish church and a Nonconformist meeting, Episcopacy and Presbyterianism signified different styles of worship. It has long been appreciated that individual Nonconformists moved from one congregation to another, but it is now clear that many Puritans or Nonconformists also went to their parish church, even if only to the occasional service or to part of a service. 'Dissenters properly so called are not in some dioceses above one in twenty', observed Francis Turner. 'Many absent themselves from our churches out of pure indevotion and laziness. Many frequent the meeting-houses out of curiosity, and many for want of room in their churches and tabernacles at London, or because of their distance from their own parish churches in the country. The stiff and irreconcilable Dissenters appear to be a handful of men in comparison' (Turner 1676: 31–2). Bishop Compton's census in 1676 confirmed that large numbers of parishioners attended both church and conventicle. In Maidstone the local Presbyterians 'usually come to church, and to divine service, one part of the day, and go to a conventicle the other, having a nonconformist teacher in the town, whom they maintain' (Whiteman 1986: xxxix). Bishop Fell's inquiries in Oxfordshire in the 1680s revealed a similar fluidity: the parson of Adderbury explained that though we have very few indeed that wilfully and constantly absent themselves from the offices of the church . . . yet they, many of 'em, will straggle one part of the day thither [to the Presbyterians], when they duly attend the public worship of God on the other, and they seem to be like the borderers betwixt two kingdoms, one can't well tell what prince they are subject to. (Clapinson 1980: 2)

In some cases such apparent fickleness could simply be the result of the legal constraints on all parishioners to attend church. Several commentators suggested that when these obligations were lifted in 1672 and 1687, the congregations at parish churches became very thin; conversely, when they were reimposed the clergy reported good flocks. (Unfortunately for this argument, other observers believed that the church gained in attendance in, say, the late 1680s as Protestant Dissenters sought to show their disapproval of the liberty to papists.) Individuals may have been following the example of some of the leading Nonconformist clergy who maintained communion with the Church of England to show their charity towards that church. Thus the ejected Presbyterian Thomas Manton went to St Paul's Covent Garden to hear the sermons of his successor, Simon Patrick; and Philip Henry attended Anglican services in Shropshire for nearly thirty years. Although *as clergy* these divines were personally excluded from the ministry by the unacceptable requirements of the Act of Uniformity, they did not believe that there was anything to bar them or their lay followers from attending the worship of the Church of England or the sermons of the best Anglican preachers. They feared the dangers of division and separation, which could only end in dispute and confirm suspicions that all Dissenters were quarrelsome, scandalous extremists.

Such Nonconformist clergy often maintained a godly flock of their own. They were, however, careful to make sure that their additional meetings were supplementing, rather than competing with, the parish church – 'only in due subordination to the public' and held at times which did not clash with church services. Richard Baxter, who described himself as a 'half-conformist', persuaded his neighbours 'to join in the public church, and help each other as private men . . . repeating sermons and praying and singing a psalm'. He drew to church the people 'that were averse' and 'sometimes I repeated the parson's sermon, and sometimes taught such as came to my house, between the sermons'. These and other private meetings 'were only spent in such actions as every Christian might do (to repeat a sermon and pray and propose his doubts to his pastor and sing psalms)' (Baxter 1991: II, 156, 188). The ejected minister Adam Martindale heard the sermons of his successor in the parish church, but then in the evening he repeated them 'to an housefull of parishioners of the devoutest sort, adding a discourse of mine own, and praying for a blessing upon all' (Martindale 1845: 173–4). Roger Lowe described how 'after evening prayer there was a few went to Mr Wood's [the ejected curate] to spend the remaining part of the day, I repeated sermon and stayed [for] prayers' (Lowe 1938: 16).

It is apparent that for a considerable number of the population, the Church of England was *in practice* simply one of their religious options, one of the forms of Protestantism available to them. This is one reason why estimating the number of Dissenters is so difficult and why so many people, especially in and about towns or cities, were quite likely to have encountered Nonconformity of some kind. Yet this practice flew in the face of a basic truth about the Church of England. It was not just another church. It differed *in principle* from all the other Protestant denominations because it was the inclusive national church: the whole population was obliged to belong and conform to it; and all parishioners were entitled to its sacraments. After 1662 Nonconformist churches were all by definition 'voluntary'; membership was an individual commitment often at real personal cost. So why was it that so many individuals were able to ignore this fundamental distinction?

One reason lies in the nature of the Church of England. The church was by far the largest, most sophisticated and complex institution in Restoration England. It was tremendously diverse; its clergy differed in their attitudes, theology, allegiance, education and age. The church had absorbed part of the broad tradition of parish Puritanism at the Restoration. Quite a few godly ministers, especially among the younger men, brought themselves to conform to the church, and some, notably Tillotson, Fowler and Kidder, eventually rose to bishoprics. Nor should we overlook the type of conformist epitomized by Ralph Josselin of Earls Colne, the thorough-going Puritan who by evasion, connivance and good luck managed to retain his living without using the surplice or Prayer Book. All of these clergy presumably offered an element of Puritanism, especially Puritan preaching, within the established church. Some ministers were quite happy to omit phrases, rites or even prayers from the liturgy to accommodate their scruples and those of their congregations. Such 'partial conformists' among the clergy would find life more difficult in the 1680s when a new, politicized breed of churchmen sought to weed out these 'ambiguous men', these trimmers, and tarred them as sympathizers with Dissent and closet Whigs.

The teaching of the Church of England was another factor. It was a Protestant church, but of a peculiarly reticent kind. The church contained a wide range of views on the question of episcopacy, from those who thought bishops were established by Christ and were essential to the existence of a true church, to others who regarded them as a useful human institution for the government of the church. This was an important issue not least because of the rival claims of the monarch to be the foundation of the national church. If the Church of England was the territorial church of a godly prince, this left it vulnerable to princely changes of heart – as happened in 1672 and 1687 – but if the church was constituted by the bishops then it had a separate political and spiritual existence and might even defend itself against the prince. The Restoration church had a striking ability to fudge the issue and to allow a range of views on episcopacy to coexist among its clergy and laity.

A third explanation may lie in the church's continuing commitment to 'reforming' the nation. Of course the Anglican ideal of 'Reformation' did not exactly match that of the Dissenters, but there was more in common than has been appreciated. The drive for personal piety and for reformation of manners, the emphasis on providence, and the assumption that the secular authorities should have a role are all common traits. Rather than an event (*the* Reformation) or a process, 'Reformation' is perhaps better regarded as an agenda, and one that continued to inspire English Protestants in the later seventeenth century – although some were perhaps more realistic than their predecessors about the difficulties involved. To fully appreciate its nature and potency, we must trace its roots in common Protestant values and perceptions.

III

Pious Protestants spoke the same language. The idiom in which John Bunyan described his religious experiences in his autobiography *Grace Abounding to the Chief of Sinners* (1666) or in *Pilgrim's Progress* (1678), is very like that of the diaries of Philip Henry, a Presbyterian minister, or of Ralph Josselin, a nominally conformist Anglican clergymen, or of the tale told by Agnes Beaumont. It is a language of consolation and hope: Sir Edward Harley MP reminded his wife that 'an interest in Christ, in whom we are complete, is a remedy for all sorts of crosses and disappointments'. Meditation and introspection are fundamental duties. 'Be you very watchful over yourself that not anything divert your from your morning and evening worship of God in secret and constant reading the scripture and some other good book', he instructed his daughter. 'Warn your sisters from me to do the like' (BL, Addit. MS 70011, fos. 226, 152). Peers, gentlemen, ministers and yeomen, and their wives and daughters, shared in this Bible-based piety, with its emphasis on personal experience of God, its providentialism and deep sense of personal and national sinfulness, and its determination to manifest the individual's calling in a godly life.

Easy relations existed between godly individuals of different denominations. Aristocrats like the godly earl of Anglesey mixed with bishops and leading Nonconformists like John Owen, while gentlemen such as Harley entertained Nonconformist clergy and yet outwardly conformed to the Church of England. Richard Baxter's correspondence is evidence of the toing and froing between the godly whatever their affiliations. 'All acknowledge there is at this day a number of sober peaceable men both ministers and others among the dissenters', wrote Philip Henry in 1671, and he wondered why steps were not taken to reunite them with the church (Henry 1882: 234). Moderate Dissenters and Anglican ministers shared the same priorities, especially in the pulpit.

The tenor of much preaching from both Anglicans and Nonconformists was unashamedly practical. When Philip Henry stressed our duties to our neighbours, this was derided as 'good moral preaching; but let them call it as they will, I am sure it is necessary, and as much now as ever' (ibid.: 136). Theologians within the Church of England were moving away from the standard emphases of the Reformed or Puritan tradition to stress instead that faith 'comprehends . . . all the works of Christian piety' or that predestination is obscure. Although the new theology of the Restoration church did not persuade all Anglicans, it did win the support of Dissenters such as Richard Baxter. In other words, theological alignments crossed denominational allegiances (see Spurr 1991: 296–303).

A similar 'confusion' even affected the Protestant conviction that the great opponent of English Reformation was the Church of Rome. Two important and divisive theological questions arose here: (1) was Rome formally idolatrous and therefore heretical and (2) was the pope to be literally identified as the Antichrist of the Book of Revelation? The old Protestant certainty about both of these weighty questions was beginning to crumble, and again the divisions ran through denominations rather than between them. For almost all Protestants, however, the dubious religious teaching of the Roman Church was exacerbated by its political characteristics. Increasingly the threat was of Jesuits converting good English Protestants, especially among the royal family, and plotting to subvert the laws, liberties and religion of old England. It was common knowledge that papists aspired to domination and would stop at nothing – assassination, regicide, massacre, even spurious religious 'toleration' – to achieve their ultimate end. Anti-popery aimed at the educated market was often disguised as historical or theological tracts about the papacy, Jesuits and the Counter-Reformation, the Armada and the Gunpowder Plot; but increasingly the major anti-Catholic message, whether through sermons, preached or printed, engravings, ballads, the pageantry marking 5 November or even an edifice like London's Monument to the Great Fire, was directed towards the masses.

Protestantism was also under threat from profanity. This was 'an age of so much profaneness and atheism', lamented Bishop Barlow to Sir Edward Harley. In Oxford Anthony Wood, who detested the common 'bantering', 'prating of news' and the refusal 'to be earnest and zealous', claimed that 'people [are] taken with fooleries, plays, poems, buffooning and drolling books', among them Marvell's *Rehearsal Transpros'd* and John Eachard's *The Grounds and Occasions of the Contempt of the Clergy* (1670). The wits and 'scoffers' took aim at the clerical profession and their pretensions. In one 'letter to a witty gentleman' a minister protested that the wits want the people to 'confess we have been fools all this while, and miserably bewitched into vain hopes, by the charming voices of a company of crafty priests'. 'Priestcraft', the self-interested elevation of religion into a mystery by the clerical profession, was a powerful accusation to level against the clergy. Many were only too happy to jeer at the failings of the clergy. For some commentators, profanity was a product of sin, but it was also recognized as a reaction against the misguided zeal and the 'enthusiasm' of the mid-century and the hypocrisy of contemporary pretenders to godliness. Charles II amused himself by 'showing the cheat of such as pretended to be more holy and devout than others, and said they were generally the greatest knaves', and then proceeded to name 'some eminent men of the present age', including bishops (Reresby 1991: 208). Many of the pious found a handy culprit in Thomas Hobbes, whose teachings on human nature and political power were beyond the pale for orthodox Protestants. Others blamed the atheists who were impervious to argument. 'We may praise God that the late godly endeavours against atheism have powerfully settled the tempted Christians in their most holy faith. But divines may write and preach their heart out, yet men whose God is in their belly and their lust, will speak and do what they list.' The doubts of the atheists grew out of their evil lives (Spurr 2000: 228–30).

The Protestant response was to fight reason with reason, but only up to a point. Protestants took a pride in their reasonable religion as opposed to the idolatry of Rome or the superstition of sectaries, but that did not mean that everything was explicable: assent to doctrines on the basis of understanding was not faith but science. Protestants might disagree about the degree of reason needed in the religious quest or about the transformation of reason by faith, but they were convinced that reason is an ally not an enemy of religion.

A second strategy was to insist upon the practical godliness and holy living which was central to all brands of Protestantism and to avoid teachings that were either too difficult for Christians or too prone to misunderstanding. As Ian Green's monumental surveys of early modern catechizing and religious publications have shown, there was a marked change from the mid-seventeenth century:

The realization among the clergy that they had to simplify their message if they were to get it across to children and less-educated adults, and from the 1650s their concern to resist what was seen as a wave of antinomianism, led to a version that continued to stress faith, repentance, and morality, in easily understood terms, but that also offered much firmer guidance on Bible study and tried to sideline or temper what was seen as excessive spiritual angst.

The laity, he suggests, simply selected those aspects that they found congenial, usually those which supported conventional morality. And the result was a version of Protestantism which paved the way for both the secularized prudential religion of the eighteenth century and for the reaction against in the Evangelical Revival (Green 2000: 656–7).

The agenda of Reformation ran alongside these strategies and was broad enough to catch the interest of several different groups. It was visible, for instance, in the persistent ambition of a city like Bristol to establish uniform parish worship, preaching and reading of the word, and the reformation of manners (see Barry in Tyacke 1998). It informed the Anglican lay voluntary societies which emerged in the 1670s and devoted themselves to pious exercises such as hearing sermons, reading the Bible or receiving communion. It was a thread running through the popular devotional manuals. Institutional interest can be detected: when courted by Danby in 1675 the bishops had demonstrated their eagerness to embark upon a moral crusade; and the church also lent its support to Nonconformist initiatives for a new missionary effort in Wales. Yet the church was handicapped by its lack of effective discipline: while Nonconformist congregations could exclude errant members, the church's disciplinary mechanism, and especially its courts, were far from ideal pastoral tools. After the Glorious Revolution, Reformation gained momentum, especially among the laity who now animated the religious societies and the new cross-denominational 'societies for the reformation of manners'. Encouragement came from the entourage of William III and its self-conscious promotion of Reformation: Bishop Burnet's influential *Discourse of Pastoral Care* (1692) was aimed at 'the completing of our Reformation, especially in the lives and manners of men' (sig. A3r).

So far this chapter has deliberately reversed the usual historical perspective to emphasize common ground and unity rather than division and contention among the Protestants of Restoration England. A broad Protestant consensus was evident, but was it strong enough to overcome a legacy of animosity or the new suspicions generated in the pursuit of these goals? After all, English Protestants still had one foot in the past. Trapped by a history of internecine controversy, and by the legal definitions enshrined in the 1662 Act of Uniformity, they were bound to come into conflict with each other. The time has come to take more account of the tensions of the period, and particularly those created by the Church of England's dominance.

IV

In 1662 the Uniformity Act had attempted to cram the lid back on Pandora's box and reimpose religious uniformity in a country which had experienced twenty years of religious freedom and experimentation. It was probably a doomed project from the start. It was the work of the leaders of the Church of England and their parliamentary allies, aided by the mistakes, arrogance and cowardice of others, both clergymen and politicians. The complex interaction of genuine fears, political calculations and mismanagement effectively permitted the enactment of discriminatory laws, known as the Clarendon Code, which were designed to root out all Protestants save the Anglicans. To many this looked like a group of bishops had turned the clergy into a tool of political repression. When he could bestir himself, Charles II attempted to moderate the excesses of this legislation. His efforts culminated in the 1672 Declaration of Indulgence which allowed Protestant Nonconformists freedom of worship if they took out licences. A year later parliament forced a humiliated Charles to cancel the Declaration, but the licences were still extant and many congregations seem – like the Bedfordshire Baptists – to have worshipped in freedom. As Charles's ministers admitted, the Cavalier Parliament no longer had the political will to persecute fellow Protestants and any newly elected Parliament would lean towards toleration. Hindsight suggested to many contemporaries that 1672 had rung the death knell for the dream of uniformity. There would be bursts of severe persecution, especially where a local magistrate took up the cause as in Bristol in 1675, or during the 'Tory Reaction' of 1681–5 when there was intense and widespread harassment. Feared and fearless groups such as the Quakers would suffer greatly: perhaps 15,000 Quakers were prosecuted and 400 died in the filthy gaols of Restoration England. But there was no real hope of extirpating Nonconformity.

Not that this rendered persecution any the less distressing or intimidating. Much recent research has offered insights into the mechanics of persecution. To be effective the laws needed zealous local magistrates, constables and informers, as well as political encouragement from Whitehall: understandably these were a relatively rare combination. However, the lower-level harassment and the social pressure upon Dissenters is more difficult to track and may well have been more common. As Agnes Beaumont's tale reveals, the weight of neighbourly expectation – the reproaches made to her father that undermined his own commitment, and the slander and suspicion of her sexual probity, mental balance and familial duty – could be immense. And how many other cases were there of collusion between the parish minister and the local men of influence? How many other instances of the sordid confusion of sexual jealousy and base avarice? Predictably communities varied and personalities shaped cases. The community often had its say on persecution: a constable might not execute a warrant or neighbours might refuse to buy the distrained goods of convicted local Nonconformists. They might insist on treating Nonconformists as full members of the community to the extent of expecting them to serve in parish offices, even that of churchwarden (see Stevenson in Spufford 1995).

There were alternatives to the policy of rooting out Dissent. The most widely discussed was known as a 'comprehension' and was often mentioned in tandem with toleration. A comprehension would lift various requirements for clerical subscription, so that many of the 'moderate' Nonconformist clergy would return to the church as ministers and bring their followers with them. An indulgence or toleration would then be extended to the sects who remained resolutely outside the enlarged national church. In other words, far from being a human right, toleration was a poor second designed to cover the recalcitrant minority. Unfortunately few of the parties concerned could agree on what they wanted. Those who could not be comprehended feared that once 'the most considerable' Nonconformist ministers had been absorbed into the church, 'their own exclusion and suppression would be unavoidable' (Baxter 1696: II, 433–4). The sober Nonconformists, the Presbyterians, were the main supporters of comprehension. They even attempted to give a gloss of comprehension to such acts as seeking a licence under the indulgence of 1672. True, they were setting up congregations, but only as a supplement or strengthening of the existing churches. Although it has often been asserted that Presbyterianism was moving towards sectarianism, the evidence of this is far from conclusive; and as late as 1689 some Dissenters still aspired to re-union with the church.

The Church of England, on the other hand, was always wary of comprehension. In public and in private the Anglican clergy were consistent opponents of a scheme which would create two standards of entry for ministers of the church. Even those on the liberal wing of the church, such as Stillingfleet or Patrick, refused to countenance what would in effect 'establish a schism in the church by law, and so bring a plague into the very bowels of it'. This did not mean that liberals would not be generous once the former Nonconformists had entered the church's ministry. 'Variety of opinions and unity of opiners are not inconsistent'; the church embraced many theological outlooks; and its latitude of liturgical practice was undeniable (see Spurr 1989). The Anglican clergy nevertheless had a pastoral obligation to preach religious uniformity and so were bound to come into conflict with their Dissenting brethren and parishioners. Anglican preachers often sought to accentuate the common Protestant heritage with sober Nonconformists and to drive a wedge between these moderates and the dangerous 'fanatics' and sectaries. But in the last resort all Dissenters were guilty of dividing Protestantism and thus weakening it in the face of popery – a charge which Dissenters cheerfully threw back at the church. Few Anglican polemicists could restrain themselves from denouncing Dissenters as 'peevish', 'factious', 'seditious', proud and self-interested. Nonconformists could complain that the Church of England had betrayed its principles, or that it was hopelessly mired in its papal past, or that it was simply intolerant and tyrannical.

For all their vitriol in religious controversy, the Anglican ministers were not speaking from a position of strength and self-confidence. In fact the churchmen suffered a profound sense of being beleaguered. They battled against indifference, immorality and disdain because they believed that the English were in danger of squandering their chance to placate an irate God. They felt the sins of the nation deeply, including the sin of schism committed by those who needlessly followed the Nonconformist preachers. Yet they also pleaded with Dissenters to lay animosity aside and unite against the common enemies of popery, profanity and atheism. The Anglican church saw itself as being crucified between two thieves, popery and dissent: 'the common cry is, that the Church of England must go down' (Allen 1677: ep. ded.). Much of the stuffing had been knocked out of the church by Charles's betrayal in 1672 and by the failure of its gentry and other supporters to live up to their professions of loyalty. The clergy's laments about 'false friends' referred not only to the justices who would not prosecute Dissenters and absentees from church, but also to those lay Anglicans who mistook outward conformity, political allegiance to the Stuarts, and even an anti-puritanical lifestyle of drinking and debauchery, for the substance of their religion.

No church or denomination could feel confident in Restoration England. The biggest problem in domestic politics – and to some extent on the international scene too – was how to deal with the reality of religious diversity. This went to the heart of seventeenth-century assumptions about social stability and political authority. The English polity was built upon religious assumptions and institutions. Monarchy, law and parliament were committed to the defence of 'Protestantism' – even though for some that term meant simply a broad piety, while for others it signified the Church of England as re-established in 1662. So integral was the defence of Protestantism to many people's political thinking that 'popery' became synonymous with all and any kind of political threat. Yet as a direct result of 1662, Protestantism in England was divided.

V

What was to be done about religious pluralism? In 1672 Charles II offered one answer when he pointed out that twelve years of persecution had achieved nothing. This pragmatism was appealing to many of his subjects. Since there was a 'natural proneness' or tendency towards what was forbidden, the solution was to allow religious liberty and 'in ten years there shall not be a dissenter left to piss against the wall' (*An Expedient* 1672: 6). Political prudence suggested that manufactures, trade and population figures would all benefit from a freedom of religion. Across the North Sea was a shining example of the practical benefits, not least that no one had 'reason to complain of oppression in conscience; and no man having hopes by advancing his religion, to form a party, or break in upon the state, the differences in opinion make none in affections' (Temple 1972: 106). But there were equally pragmatic counter-arguments. If harmony was so desirable, then the Nonconformists should abandon their stubborn prejudices and defer to the established authorities. If the social consequences of religious freedom were so important, why not recognize that religious liberty will culminate in 'a state of perfect anarchy, in which every man does what is good in his own eyes' (Parker 1671: 7)? Where was liberty to end? Surely the papists would exploit it? And, as the anti-tolerationists gleefully pointed out, the Puritans themselves had been noticeably reluctant to offer freedom of religion during the 1640s and 1650s. In answer to the claim that no one could be coerced into sincere belief, the churchmen simply replied that their aim was outward obedience, not inward assent: the church left every individual the freedom of conscience in belief.

   Some advocates of religious freedom disguised their case as an appeal to liberty, property and religion, legal rights which were infringed by penal laws. Andrew Marvell suggested that 'men ought to enjoy the same propriety and protection in their consciences, which they have in their lives, liberties and estates' (Marvell 1677: 33). Talk of conscience inevitably led to claims based on St Paul's teaching about the need to respect weak and tender consciences. In response, Anglicans dismissed the Dissenters' scruples as prejudice, 'fancy', 'passions and disorderly affections' masquerading as conscience. This 'new gospel of private conscience' could not outweigh the obligation to obey the powers that are ordained by God. We have an obligation of conscience to obey the laws of our sovereign, otherwise our obedience would arise solely out of prudence (and that would open the way to a Hobbesian universe). Many held that conscience could justify the withholding of active obedience if the conscientious were then prepared to suffer the consequences. It was also a commonplace that belief was not subject to will, that no one could command their consciences, nor compel themselves to believe something. Only argument and rational conviction could compel assent. So why did the state and church continue to prosecute Dissenters?

The Church of England for its part was adamant that it simply presented individuals with the opportunity to reconsider their beliefs and examine all of the arguments. The church had a duty to warn people against sin and no sin was more heinous than schism, the baseless separation from a true church. The church also had a pastoral duty to ensure that consciences were properly informed (see Goldie 1991). The church's argument may not now be convincing, but it was more coherent than that of its opponent. Their argument for freedom of conscience was based either on scripture or on the equation of 'conscience' with the free play of human reason. All of them effectively pleaded that the sincerely conscientious should be allowed liberty. In other words, the scruples of the conscientious became the measure of what is permissible, and sincerity of belief mattered more than being right.

One solution was simply to separate church and state. The ex-Cromwellian Sir Charles Wolseley asserted in print in 1668 that 'the civil and ecclesiastical power, are things perfectly in themselves distinct, and ought in their exercise to be kept so' (Wolseley 1668: 25). As Sir William Temple told English readers in 1673, the Dutch managed very well under such a separation of church and state. But this was a minority view. The majority, commonsense view in Restoration England was that the sovereign has authority over all matters, civil and ecclesiastical, since sovereignty by definition can exist in only one person or institution. Alien to modern minds, this position nevertheless had the Bible, patriarchalism and, apparently, experience to recommend it. It assumed an autonomous morality, based on the law of nature and the revealed will of God, but sometimes found it difficult to explain how that morality could exert an influence over the sovereign. In practice, this approach could sound Erastian, as when it seemed to suggest religion and morality were subordinate to the sovereign, or even Hobbesian, if it hinted that the sovereign's will was the only rule of religion and of good and evil.

The argument was still not resolved when events took a decisive turn and the Glorious Revolution threw the whole issue into question. In 1689 religious toleration was not inevitable, nor was it distinct from wider concerns about the religious and moral health of the nation. The Toleration Act was a no more rational or planned piece of legislation than the Act of Uniformity. The 1680 Bills for comprehension and indulgence had been dusted off, but political jockeying and mistakes led to the shelving of comprehension and the legislation of a toleration which covered far more non-Anglican Protestants than had been envisaged. Giving ease to the Dissenters, indulging them from various penalties, had become politically more attractive as comprehension had become increasingly less practicable. There was no sudden leap forward in English thinking about the principle of toleration; the Act's prosaic nature is well caught in Evelyn's description of it as an 'act of indulgence for the dissenters, but not exempting them from paying dues to the Church of England clergy, or serving in offices etc according to law' (Evelyn 1952: IV, 640). And as always the English laity intended to have the last word. The act will 'turn half the nation into downright atheism', complained one churchman, 'the mischief is, a liberty now being granted, more lay hold of it to separate from all manner of worship [and] to perfect irreligion' than to go to conventicles;

and, although the Act allows no such liberty, the people will understand it so, and, say
what the judges can at the assizes, or the Justices of the Peace at their sessions, or we
at our visitations, no churchwarden or constable will present any for not going to
church, though they go nowhere else but the alehouse, for this liberty they will have.
(Prideaux 1875: 154)

VI

The Toleration Act presented all of the different Protestant groups with new challenges. Nonconformity, destined now to remain forever outside the national church,
found it difficult to sacrifice the principle of congregational autonomy in the interests
of mutual co-operation. Attempts at union in the 1690s between Presbyterians and
Congregationalists collapsed, in part due to a growing theological rift over definitions
of the trinity and mutual incomprehension of each other's position on the assurance
of salvation. The Presbyterians increasingly moved towards Arminianism and Unitarianism, teachings which their Puritan forebears abominated, and seemed to have
suffered a loss of spiritual energy as well as members. Indeed, in all quarters of
Dissent there was a palpable air of decline by the end of the century: in 1697 the
Bedford congregation fasted 'that the work of God might be revived among us'
(Tibbutt 1966).

The Revolution of 1688–9 had even more serious consequences for the Church of
England. Having spent so long trumpeting the inalienable principle of hereditary
divine-right monarchy, the clergy were deeply disturbed by the overthrow of James
II. Confronted by the oaths of supremacy and allegiance to William and Mary, a small
but vociferous minority found themselves unable to comply. The deprivation in 1691
of nine bishops, including Archbishop Sancroft and four other of the seven bishops
who had withstood James in June 1688, and about 400 parish clergy was a grievous
blow to the church. Their outspoken criticism of those who took the oaths made
these Nonjurors a serious embarrassment to the new leaders of the Church of
England. Although the Nonjuring schism was not lengthy – the death of the last
Nonjuring bishop, Lloyd of Norwich, in 1710, perhaps marks the end of the rift – the
presence outside the church of a high-minded clique, who constructed a theological
critique of developments within Anglicanism, offered a focus for disaffection.

Two distinct outlooks emerged among the clergy of the post-Revolution Church
of England about the direction the church should take in the new era of religious
toleration. The episcopate was dominated by Whiggish 'Low Churchmen'. They
regarded the church as partially disestablished and argued that it was necessary to
allow diversity within her ranks, to co-operate with laymen and even Dissenters in the
work of moral reformation, religious education and charity. They were prepared to
recognize that, although no provision had been made in the Toleration Act, Dissenters were entitled to set up schools and academies. And some would even connive at
occasional conformity by Dissenters in order to qualify for office under the Test Acts.
The opposite line was taken by the vast majority of the clergy who were 'High
Churchmen'. They yearned for a lost and mythical partnership of church and state.
They believed that only strict conformity from Anglican clergy and laity and restricting Dissenters to the precise letter of the Toleration Act would prevent religious
anarchy and moral degeneration. In the later 1690s the High Churchmen organized

a campaign for the recall of Convocation and when it finally met in 1701 they used it as a platform from which to criticize the leadership of the church. Factionalism pervaded the church, dioceses were divided, preferment became partisan, and the pulpit was prostituted to party ends. The Church of England has rarely been so politicized or divided as it was in the reigns of William III and Queen Anne.

And what of the laity's religion at the end of the seventeenth century? The trend towards the laicization of religion continued unabated. In other words, the English laity took what they wanted from the many different forms of religious expression on offer: for some, religion had already dwindled to little more than a minimal set of ethical principles; for others, religion remained an overwhelming spiritual reality. Perhaps it was the freedom of choice which was the most striking change. People were free to decide how to spend their Sundays and their cash. In 1692, for instance, the Tilehurst Street Baptist Church in Hitchin, Hertfordshire, decided to build its own meeting house. Among the donors was the middle-aged Agnes Beaumont, who gave £2 15 shillings. Agnes was later to marry twice, yet in 1720 when she died at Highgate, London, she asked that she be buried in the yard of the Tilehurst Street Baptist Church near the grave of its former minister, John Wilson. In death, as in life, Agnes Beaumont wished to be close to the ministers and brethren whose fellowship had given such meaning to her religion.

REFERENCES

There are extensive manuscript sources for this subject. Clerical correspondence in the Tanner manuscript in the Bodleian Library, Oxford, offers a great deal to the historian of religion, as do the Harleian and other manuscripts in the British Library. For the Nonconformist perspective, two sources in Dr Williams's Library, London, are indispensable: the letters of Richard Baxter, now calendared by Keeble and Nuttall (see below under Baxter 1991) and the 'Entring Books' of Roger Morrice, soon to be published in five volumes by an editorial team under the leadership of Mark Goldie.

Allen, R. 1677: *England's Distempers*.
Baxter, R. 1696: *Reliquiae Baxterianae*, ed. M. Sylvester: London.
Baxter, R. 1991: *Calendar of the Correspondence of Richard Baxter*, 2 vols, ed. N. H. Keeble and G. F. Nuttall: Oxford.
Beaumont, A. 1992: *The Narrative of the Persecutions of Agnes Beaumont*, ed. V. J. Camden: East Lansing, MI.
Clapinson, M. (ed.) 1980: *Bishop Fell and Nonconformity*, Oxfordshire Record Society, 62.
Claydon, T. 1996: *William III and the Godly Revolution*: Cambridge.
Evelyn, J. 1952: *The Diary of John Evelyn*, 5 vols, ed. E. S. De Beer: Oxford.
Fletcher, A. 1984: 'The enforcement of the Conventicle Acts 1664–1679', *Studies in Church History*, 21.
Goldie, M. 1991: 'The theory of religious intolerance in Restoration England.' In O. Grell, N. Tyacke and J. Israel, eds, *From Persecution to Toleration: The Glorious Revolution and Religion in England*: Oxford.
Green, I. 1996: *The Christian's ABC*: Oxford.
Green, I. 2000: *Print and Protestantism in Early Modern England*: Oxford.
Henry, P. 1825: *The Life of Philip Henry by Matthew Henry*: London.
Henry, P. 1882: *The Diaries and Letters of Philip Henry*, ed. M. H. Lee: London.

Heywood, O. 1937: *Oliver Heywood's Life of John Angier*, ed. E. Axon, Chetham Society, 97.

Humphrey, J. 1680: *Answer to Stillingfleet*.

Jolly, T. 1895: *The Note Book of the Rev. Thomas Jolly*, ed. H. Fishwick, Chetham Society, 33.

Leicester, P. 1953: *Charges to the Grand Jury*, ed. E. M. Halcrow, Chetham Society, 5.

Lowe, R. 1938: *The Diary of Roger Lowe*, ed. W. L. Sachse: London.

Martindale, A. 1845: *The Life of Adam Martindale*, ed. R. Parkinson, Chetham Society, 4.

Marvell, A. 1677: *An Account of the Growth of Popery and Arbitrary Government*: Amsterdam.

Matthews, A. G. (ed.) 1959: *The Savoy Declaration of Faith and Order 1658*: London.

Parker, S. 1671: *Discourse of Ecclesiastical Politie*.

Prideaux, H. 1875: *The Letters of Humphrey Prideaux*, ed. E. M. Thompson, Camden Society, 15.

Reresby, J. 1991: *The Memoirs of Sir John Reresby*, ed. A. Browning; 2nd edn revd M. K. Geiter and W. A. Speck: London.

Spaeth, D. A. 2000: *The Church in an Age of Danger: Parsons and Parishioners, 1660–1740*: Cambridge.

Spufford, M. (ed.) 1995: *The World of Rural Dissenters, 1520–1725*: Cambridge.

Spurr, J. 1989: 'The Church of England, comprehension and the Toleration Act of 1689', *English Historical Review*, 104.

Spurr, J. 1991: *The Restoration Church of England, 1646–1689*: New Haven, CT.

Spurr, J. 1998: *English Puritanism, 1603–1689*: Basingstoke.

Spurr, J. 2000: *England in the 1670s: 'This Masquerading Age'*: Oxford.

Stout, W. 1967: *The Autobiography of William Stout of Lancaster 1665–1752*, ed. J. D. Marshall, Chetham Society, 14.

Temple, W. 1972: *Observations upon the United Provinces of the Netherlands*, ed. G. N. Clark: Oxford.

Tibbutt, H. G. (ed.) 1966: *The Minutes of the First Independent Church (now Bunyan Meeting) at Bedford 1656–1766*, Bedford Historical Record Society, 55.

Turner, F. 1676: *Animadversions*.

Tyacke, N. (ed.) 1998: *England's Long Reformation 1500–1800*: London.

Underhill, E. B. (ed.) 1847: *The Records of a Church of Christ Meeting in Broadmead Bristol 1640–1687*: London.

Wallis, J. 1682: *The Necessity of Regeneration*.

Whiteman, E. A. O. 1986: *The Compton Census of 1676: A Critical Edition*, ed. E. A. O. Whiteman: London.

Wolseley, C. 1668: *Liberty of Conscience*.

FURTHER READING

Claydon, T. 1996: *William III and the Godly Revolution*: Cambridge.

De Krey, G. 1995: 'Rethinking the Restoration: dissenting cases for conscience, 1667–1672', *Historical Journal*, 38.

Goldie, M. A. and Spurr, J. 1994: 'Politics and the Restoration parish: Edward Fowler and the struggle for St Giles Cripplegate', *English Historical Review*, 109.

Green, I. 2000: *Print and Protestantism in Early Modern England*: Oxford.

Harris, T., Goldie, M. and Seaward, P. (eds) 1991: *The Politics of Religion in Restoration England*: Oxford.

Hunter, M. 1985: 'The problem of "atheism" in early modern England', *Transactions of the Royal Historical Society*, 35.

Keeble, N. H. 1987: *The Literary Culture of Nonconformity in Later Seventeenth-Century England*: Leicester.

Ramsbottom, J. 1992: 'Presbyterians and "partial conformity" in the Restoration Church of England', *Journal of Ecclesiastical History*, 43.

Spaeth, D. A. 2000: *The Church in an Age of Danger: Parsons and Parishioners, 1660–1740*: Cambridge.

Spufford, M. (ed.) 1995: *The World of Rural Dissenters, 1520–1725*: Cambridge.

Spurr, J. 1991: *The Restoration Church of England, 1646–1689*: New Haven, CT.

Spurr, J. 1998: *English Puritanism, 1603–1689*: Basingstoke.

Walsh, J., Haydon, C. and Taylor, S. (eds) 1993: *The Church of England c.1689–c.1833: From Toleration to Tractarianism*: Cambridge.

CHAPTER TWENTY-TWO

The Revolution of 1688–1689

Colin Brooks

Introduction

The English polity and political society were deeply divided in 1686–8. The polity would have suffered strains enough had William been unwilling to intervene, or had he been prevented (by Louis XIV or by the weather) from so doing. All those with an interest in public affairs faced up to some difficult questions in 1688. Archbishop Wake later remembered a conversation he had had in early 1688 with a friend who

> fell into discourse, I know not how, concerning the measures of civil obedience. I had never well examined that matter but by the prejudices of my own education . . . had been accustomed to think that all princes were absolute and their subjects were not to contradict them, but merely to obey. I was startled at his discourse, when I heard him hint at something to be done to put a stop to the king's arbitrary proceedings; and began to ask, whether such an attempt could be justified, let the king do what he would? He did not enter any farther into particulars; but in general answered, that he could not tell but that in some cases such endeavours might be lawful. For which I as much wondered at him then, as I have done at my own ignorance and folly since. (Sykes 1959: 34)

Here was the dilemma for the English political nation, the intimation of a fall from innocence and acceptance, into a world of man-made politics, using but not wedded to a providential world view. It was William whose invasion provoked that fall, but it was James's flight that was responsible for precipitating the intense negotiations as to the precise shape of what became known as the Glorious Revolution. Absent William of Orange and no doubt the course of public life in England, in Ireland, Scotland and the Dominions, would have been stormy, probably violent. What would have resulted would not have been the polity as it was in 1689, not to mention 1697 or 1715. English revulsion against James provided the opportunity for William. The reshaping of public values and institutions in the winter of 1688–9 was formed by, and because of, the invasion of William of Orange and was determined according to his taste. But never again would William exercise such leverage over the polity.

William's intervention had been long pondered. His invasion was prompted by a disaffected group, particularly incensed by James II, though opposition to James's way of governing went far beyond those Orangists. Their alienation was combined with a conviction of the righteousness of their cause and a sense of abject helplessness. William, they believed, would be the saviour of English liberty, property and Protestantism. William's public concentration on the holding of a 'free parliament' equally impressed the great mass of Tory and Anglican opinion within the political nation, which was unwilling to accept resistance as justifiable but could not abide James's government. Simultaneously, William did nothing to discourage the party of movement, which believed that the Orangist invasion should prompt not only a change of men and of measures, but also of structures and values. The invasion succeeded because of William's ruthlessness, his exploitation of providence/fortune and his mastery of logistics. William's skilful leadership provoked the demoralization of his adversary, encouraging, as James's vacillation prompted, disaffection and desertion from the king's forces.

The Williamites failed to understand their hero's priorities. William invaded to ensure that, at the least, English resources were not made available to France; at best to deploy those resources, alongside the Dutch Republic, against the over-weening power of France. The impact of William's invasion could not be contained within England. It necessarily had implications for Scotland, where opposition to James's catholicizing had paralleled that in England, and for Ireland, where the matter would be the more complicated by virtue of James's landing there, as a springboard for his return to England. The invasion had its repercussions, too, outside of Europe, especially in the English possessions across the Atlantic and in India. In each case, the Orangist coup in England provided the opportunity and the justification for a reversal of provincial fortunes. In each case, loyalists, Catholics or Jacobites fought back.

The year 1688 was long understood as a check-point where English, even British, liberties were confirmed, a way station on the road to parliamentary democracy. But British celebration of the tri-centenary in 1988 was a low-key affair. In good measure, that was prompted by a fear of offending Irish sensibilities. The political right and the left joined in asserting the unimportance of the Revolution and in denigrating its unsavoury character. Public comment was often ill-informed. Roy Hattersley thought William and Mary's was 'the first equal opportunities' monarchy. Norman St. John Stevas declared that 'no one behaved well, let alone gloriously'. The earl of Perth, as 'a Catholic and a Scot', lamented any celebration of so squalid an event, 'neither "glorious" nor a "revolution"', fearing that 'bloodshed lies ahead and the revival of old hatreds is the best to hope for' (these comments, among many others, were reported in *The Times* during 1988). No great new narrative swept detail along into a compelling explanation of events and an understanding of their significance. No major scholarly biography of William appeared. Collections of essays were the preferred mode.

Recent historical reappraisal has been the product less of a reconsideration of the central questions of 1688 – of sovereignty, succession and political culture in England; of its place in Europe – than of a desire to re-examine the identity of the British state. The course of Irish and Scottish history has been searchingly reviewed, with the Williamite invasion and the subsequent political and religious 'settlements' being used as a test to gauge the nature of their political societies. Such an investigation has not had much to say either about the Williamite invasion itself or about its principal consequences, the restructuring of the English polity and the mobilization of its resources for William's highly personal struggle against Louis XIV.

The sense that British history has not been a given, that the nature and ethos of the polity were for long 'up for grabs', has had a considerable impact on the recent historiography of the late seventeenth century. There has been discussion of the nature of the rule of Charles II and James II, of the potential for absolutism and of the relationship between James's religious policies and his style of government. The role of the radicals and the disaffected in the Revolution and the events around it has been rethought. That started by denying the centrality of John Locke to the events of 1688–9, going on to minimize his contribution to the justification of the post-revolutionary, Whig, regime. It promises now to bring to our attention a broader spectrum of opinion, belief and prejudice outside and on the fringes of the political establishment. Those who might vulgarly be called the losers in any revolutionary situation often acquire posthumous historiographical blessing. The tri-centenary of 1688–9 coincided with a ripple of neo-Jacobite historiography, ruffling a few serene historical sails but having little public impact.

The Revolution was emphatically an event in European history, however much past writers have wanted to concentrate on it as an English, not even a British, phenomenon. The celebrations of 1688 concentrated on Anglo-Dutch cultural links. But in 1688–9 England was invaded, its capital controlled by Dutch soldiers. British history was profoundly affected by the course of European power politics. The struggle to control the meaning of 1688 pitted William, who wanted England to be at the heart of Europe, against a political nation which was profoundly divided as to the necessity and wisdom of such involvement. It was James who sought to avoid European commitment.

The revolution cannot be explained by the events of 1688–9 alone. Extending the examination both backwards, to take in James's reign, the Tory reaction of 1681–5 and the Exclusion Crisis of 1678–81, and forwards, to comprehend William's kingship, the impact of war, and the political battles of the subsequent decades, at once enriches and distorts our understanding of 1688–9. The actors in 1687–9 did not intend to create the public world of the 1690s. The outcome of the Revolution of 1688–9 disappointed the hopes of most. It was a revolution of multiple ironies.

Although the pro-Orangist conspirators begged and planned for William's arrival and many others prayed for relief from James II's kingship, the invasion of November 1688 was unexpected. Many opponents of James believed that things would right themselves, that James would not be able to twist the direction of the polity either substantially or permanently. William showed himself willing to risk a lot, perhaps all. James's collapse caused general surprise. It is salutary to remember how compressed were the events of 1688–9. Before, and perhaps even after, 11 December 1688, it was possible that the English future might be one in which James was a token leader, with an Orangist administration doing the bidding of William. The course of the polity was decided, by tetchy and often overwrought gentlemen, in physical conditions not conducive to calm discussion, between James's flight on 11 December and William and Mary's acceptance of the crown on 13 February.

James II

James was an ambitious and determined man with a mission for his reign: the return to a Catholic England. Just as William had the defence of his country from invasion in

1672 to his credit, so James had, triumphantly, faced up in 1685 to the invasions of both Monmouth and Argyll. His virtual capitulation in November 1688 and his subsequent flight perplexed many. Historians have concentrated on James's psychological state, on the inconclusive counsel he received and on the impact on him of a handful of desertions in mid-November. The indolence of James's elder brother, Charles II, has been compared with his own activity. Yet James's reign proceeded in fits and starts: energy is not a touchstone of success. James was never able to find a consistent approach which both suited his ends and matched, or at least did not contradict, the interests of the more influential of his subjects. The changes of tack which he chose (or into which he was forced) never appeared convincing, always allowed of the worst possible construction. He vacillated between promoting inclusion and demanding exclusion, between using interest and obedience as the cement of the polity. That he wished to lead a regime based not on social hierarchy but on ability, run not by an aristocratic/landed order but by an executive, great merchants and the professional bourgeoisie, was hinted at, but not developed. Nor was he given the necessary time for new identities of interest (for example between Catholic and Protestant Dissenting beneficiaries of a toleration policy) to become apparent.

James favoured Catholicism; his character ensured that he went about it in a particular way. He wished to give more vigour to the machinery of government, partly to enable him to pursue the Catholicizing policy, partly because of a temperamental hostility to the clogs and compromises of representative government. But, although much of the concentration of fire in 1688–9 was on James, the system of governance which was being attacked had been promoted by both Charles II and James II. Miller (1984) has doubted both their desire to create an absolutist regime and the likelihood of that happening, given the conditions – physical, cultural and institutional – of late seventeenth-century Britain. Western (1972), Jones (1972) and Speck (1988), by contrast, have stressed that the refashioning of government in the 1680s gave priority to a standing army, subordinated the judiciary and provincial polities, especially the boroughs, to the royal will, improved administrative efficiency, and rode roughshod over parliament. Concentrating on governance as well as on Catholicism draws us back before 1685, to the Exclusion Crisis and its aftermath. For the Whigs, alienation from the Stuart regime was largely complete by 1681; for the Tories, it occurred in James II's reign. The 'harder' our interpretation of James II's intentions, the more he, and perhaps Charles, appear as the innovators of the era and the more likely we are to see 1688 as a counter-revolution, reactive, restorative and conservative. Charles and James were seeking to mount the crest of a European wave. William, too, and his new-found allies in the political system, would surf with skill. The impetus given to the growth of government – of bureaucracy, the armed forces, tax collection – by the Williamite regime extended the efforts of his predecessors. Such an unwanted continuity was one irony of 1688.

James's determination acknowledged some bounds. Speck (1988: 153) argues that he acted 'impolitically' rather than 'unconstitutionally', perhaps a distinction without a difference. James would not consider changing the succession away from Mary. Energetic in 'packing' parliament (in influencing electoral choice and in determining, by the creation of new peers, the membership of the Lords), he did not seek to change the basis of the composition of the House of Commons, either by enfranchising further boroughs or by deciding not to call representatives from others. In this he was abiding by political custom, not acknowledging constitutional constraint. Nor did he seek, after asking an opinion from his Judges, to use his dispensing powers to enable Catholics to be members of either House of parliament.

Would any parliament, however hand-picked its composition, have done James's bidding? James might have had sufficient supporters (or lackeys) ready and willing to support him. But the abilities and the repute of the potential parliamentarians, and of the substantial slate of new peers envisaged by James, may be doubted. James's senior lawyers were no match for opposing counsel in the judicial tussles of his reign. Had James called such a parliament, and worked with and through it, its reputation as the Grand Inquest of the Nation would have been severely compromised.

At the very least, James wanted Catholicism to be put on an equal footing with Anglicanism. To do that fully would have involved him in a series of measures which would have stretched his acknowledged prerogative powers to the limit; to contemporaries, indeed, without the detachment afforded the historian, they appeared as deliberate transgressions of property rights. There was not much to choose between a land with no parliament and one with a parliament so packed and regimented that it did the king's business and no other. Nor were James's policies – they were more than experiments – in Ireland, Scotland and in the colonies in North America in any way reassuring.

Toleration, as an aid to Catholicism, was to James both a matter of principle and a tactic. He believed that, in an open market, customers would choose the Catholic religion. For market conditions to be established, he needed time. The arrival of a Catholic heir, James Francis Edward, was crucial. His own life and that of his son had to be preserved. Few betting men would have put money on either Mary or Anne providing a Protestant heir (though a male heir for William by a second marriage was a remote possibility). The Protestant line would die of itself. The future lay with Catholicism. The flight of James and his family in December 1688, precipitated by fear on his hearing of the apparently authorized Williamite *Third Declaration*, dwelling on papist horror stories and urging Protestant vigilantism, was intended to protect his son and to preserve those hopes. It was not intended as an acknowledgement of defeat or as an indication that he placed his trust in the France of Louis XIV. But that was the outcome. The consequence was that many a Tory, swallowing hard, placed patriotism above loyalism and connived in a revolution of which he disapproved. Jacobitism would be irredeemably tainted by James's association with France.

William of Orange, William the Stadhouder and William III

William did not intervene to save England, even Britain, from itself. His target was France; European considerations prevailed. He was bent on securing the liberty of the United Provinces against the ambition and irresponsibility of Louis XIV. The Glorious Revolution was, for William, an episode in European history.

William was caught up in the *realpolitik* and the raw emotions of his era. He had no reverence for ceremony, little penchant for softening the harsh surface of public life, other than an acceptance of the need for dissimulation. While his wife was at her devotions preparing for the coronation, William was fuming at the wasted time. William's indifference to political courtesies would cost him dearly. Fearing that the executive process would be clogged were he to take advice from a wide range of the elite, William was 'against taking in a greater number into his councell'. 'In that', noted Halifax, 'hee committed a mistake. – Double the number would have done no hurt, and would have ingaged men of quality' (Foxcroft 1898: II, 204). The ruffled feelings and guilt of the elite would have been assuaged, and William could have got on with his executive cronies. Rejecting 'men of quality', William would find that he had to settle for, and depend upon, men of party.

William's crusade was not against Catholicism. By inclination and pragmatic need a tolerant man, William seriously underestimated the British penchant for religious bigotry. He urged 'moderation' on his reluctant Scottish subjects and refused to 'lay myself under any obligation to be a persecutor' (Cowan, in Israel 1991: 176, 180). He did not appreciate becoming bogged down in Ireland, nor did he savour the outcome. It is ironic that William would subsequently emerge as the patron of Protestant tribalism. Yet William could not entirely avoid identification with the Protestant cause. The banners of his invasion fleet proclaimed it.

William's energies were directed against Louis XIV, who declared war on the United Provinces on 26 November 1688. In his first address to the Convention, William urged it to organize aid for the Dutch Republic as a priority. Halifax judged that 'He hath such a mind to France, that it would incline one to think, hee tooke England onely in his way' (Foxcroft 1898: II, 219). William's conflict with Louis was fed from springs deep within him, released as a result of the humiliating treatment he had received from Louis during the slighting of Orange, his principality in the south of France, in 1681. Europe's conflicts from the 1660s through to 1713 looked forward to a regular, impersonal, state-system. They also looked back to, and perpetuated, monarchies and polities at once personal and unstable. The Orange family had been familiar with *coups d'état* over the course of the preceding century. William was familiar with the necessity, and the tonic effects, of the overthrow of a regime, as in the United Provinces in 1672. He was experienced in the role of national saviour and in the problems caused by subsequent disillusionment, after the euphoria had worn off.

This was a world prodded and set rolling by the imperatives of dynasticism. William's rights and status as Prince of Orange were threatened by Louis XIV. His wife's position in the succession to the English throne was, after mid-1687, threatened by the queen's pregnancy. The birth of an heir to James suggested to the naive that William's grounds for intervention in Britain had fallen. But William's *First Declaration* avowed a determination to uphold his Mary's place in the succession from any spurious claimant: 1688–9 was a 'revolution in the family', between generations and between siblings. The tension between William and Anne was to play an appreciable role in post-revolutionary politics.

The timing of Mary of Modena's pregnancy coincided with a series of French-inspired events which convinced William that he had at least to neutralize England. French policy proved counter-productive. Instead of weakening the resolve and splintering the counsels of the United Provinces, it pushed the merchants of Amsterdam and their fellow traders into William's arms. They offered him substantial financial and material aid. But William had to present his invasion as a British and a family matter, not as part and parcel of the interest of the Dutch Republic. Once installed in England, though, William was all too ready to emphasize his reliance on Dutch advisers and support. Nevertheless, William's preoccupation with France ultimately harmed the interests of the Dutch Republic, especially given his willingness to allow superiority to the British fleet.

Historians continue to disagree as to when William decided that he had to intervene personally and with force; and as to when he decided that intervention had to end with his taking the throne. Pinkham's (1954) argument that William had long been preparing for intervention in England is reflected in recent Jacobite-leaning historiography which has little doubt that William had been playing, in Cruickshanks's (2000: 2) words, 'the most successful confidence trick in British history'. Baxter (1966), by contrast, believed that the surviving evidence, incomplete though it is, suggests that William did not make up his mind to intervene until the spring of 1688. Intervention, invasion and a quest for the throne are different matters. The expeditionary force was gathered together with a decisiveness that suggests long thought, but intervention, even on the scale of November 1688, did not necessarily imply the acquisition of sovereignty. Beddard (1991) argued that William's desire for the crown is only clear from early December 1688. The disappointing initial response to his arrival may have led William to think of a negotiated settlement. Then James's flight provoked another reappraisal.

What William intended, right up to December 1688, to do with James II remains unclear. It may be that he wished literally to overawe James, to breathe down his neck while that monarch recommended to a 'free' parliament that it should apply the nation's resources to the anti-French crusade and that it should restore those rights and privileges which he had sought to annul. Or it may be that from some considerable time before November 1688, William realized that the crown fitted his aims – and that he, already a sovereign, fitted a crown. He certainly insisted throughout his invasion that he embodied lawful authority: he brought, for example, appropriate seals with him. William was not interested in thinking through matters constitutional. He had an open mind as to where he would land when he sailed: he had an open mind, too, as to the constitutional consequences of his intervention.

The outcome of the Revolution was that William, with Mary, was installed on the throne. William played his cards very close to his chest, combining decisiveness and caution. He seemed to throw over that concern for conciliating the Anglican Tories which had previously marked his campaign. Yet, despite urging by Whig men of movement, he refused point-blank to declare himself king. He proceeded, as he and his advisers had long done, by news management and creation. James's flight on 11 December was crucial. William accepted thereafter that he would have, however unwillingly, to take the throne. There was a tension between his need for a *politique* approach and the speed essential for completion of the political project and his return to the field of arms. He gave the English enough rope – and by 6 February 1689 they found themselves not hung, but bound to him.

William would not allow himself to be beholden to anyone, the instrument of an aristocratic coup. He had a ruthless ability to ignore would-be allies. He was fortunate that his military superiority came through multiple desertions followed by James's retreat rather than simply from the desertion of a few senior figures in the army, like Churchill. Similarly, the very success of the provincial risings, and their rapidity, reduced the significance of any individual's provincial *putsch*. There was no Monck in 1688–9. Danby's arrival in London with a posse of armed men did not impress him. William was his own man. Halifax noted his 'great jealousie of being thought to bee governed. That apprehension will give great uneasinesse to men in great places' (Foxcroft 1898: II, 203).

William, perhaps to the surprise of many innocent members of the political nation, would not accept a Regency. If James came back or if the Convention attempted to enforce a Regency, he would return immediately to the Dutch Republic. He wanted ample powers. Late in 1689, he pondered vetoing the Bill of Rights. He fought hard, but ultimately unsuccessfully, throughout his reign to maintain what he considered his justified powers. He wanted to lead a strong government, an executive that would be more forceful, tenacious, self-interested and self-willed than any previous and would-be absolutist government. A weak, divided, navel-gazing Britain was the last thing he wanted.

As regards parliaments, William was indifferent. They might be necessary for the fulfilment of his policies. He always had other options in mind, though he was careful not to compromise his position by too cavalier a revelation of them. It was only to his trusted Dutch advisers that he confessed that he would have been 'able to finish the affair soon' were he 'not by nature so scrupulous'. The *Declaration*'s conclusion, a reference to a free parliament, had been insisted upon by Henry Sidney over William's doubts. 'You will see by the conclusion I am placed entirely at the mercy of Parliament', he wrote to Bentinck late in August 1688 (Schwoerer 1977: 872, 852).

William intended two things. He wanted to ensure that the rights of his wife, Mary, were safeguarded. He was desperate at least to neutralize England in his – Europe's – wars against France; at best, to mobilize England's resources on his own behalf. If either of those things could only be *secured* by his taking the throne, he had few qualms about so doing. The same answer holds if either of those things could be *helped* by his taking the throne. He had not said that he sought the throne. He could not say that. He certainly invaded the country expecting to have to fight James. That is crucial. That he did not have to fight was fortuitous. William did nothing to stop James from leaving his kingdom. William spoke much about the holding of a free parliament and the maintenance of liberties. Beyond that, he kept his options open. His conduct in 1687–9 was by no means faultless. He was often persuaded by interested parties, overestimating the power of some political groups and underestimating others. He had given insufficient thought to how he would extract from British politicians and from their political system the men, money and material which he craved. He kept some cards up his sleeve, but showed others too dramatically: as Schwoerer notes, such commitments meant that he was 'hoist on the petard of his own propaganda' (ibid.: 852). The invasion was William's doing but its outcome was determined by the retreat and then the flight of James.

The Revolution of 1688 in England would be almost bloodless, but that was not for want of William's preparedness. The Revolution of 1689 would be parliamentary but that was not, for William, the heart of the matter. It was not William's intention simply to create or oversee the installation of a parliamentary regime. That, though, is what would happen.

The Political Nation

In the late 1680s few of the British political nation sought or anticipated the kind of polity which would be installed in the country a decade later. Many, of both conservative and radical persuasion, would find much to deplore in the public and political life of Williamite Britain. Their responses would range from connivance and acquiescence, both grudging and grasping, through passivity to alienation. A number would find much to applaud, much on which to congratulate themselves. But even they had had their moments of abject despair as well as of jubilation.

The problem for the Tories, would-be loyalists, lay in disentangling their unwillingness to support the tenor of his rule from their recognition of James as their lawful monarch. James, as much as William, lacking finesse, did little in the last months of 1688 to win back such doubters. The reluctant revolutionary, Danby, declared that he and his kind were

> in arms for a free Parlament, and for the preservation of the Protestant religion and the government as by law established, which the King had very near distroyed, and which the Prince of Orang was com'd to assist them to defend. (Browning 1991: 530)

It is hard to avoid a sense of pity for these men, scorned by James and now apparently to be duped by William. Danby was whistling bravely in the wind, in face of the dawning realization that William's was not his agenda. James's flight cut the ground from under Tory feet. No longer could they act as mediators between William and James. Already deeply scarred by James's lack of rapport with them, sensing that he was as little their king as William might be, they had to stand on their own bottom.

The actions of the Orangist conspirators were not carefully considered. They were unwilling to face up to the distinction between an uprising, assisted by William, and an invasion, a conquest, by William, assisted by members of the political nation. Many of William's Orangist conspirators were reluctant to ask the question: then what? The flight of James seemed to radical ideologues to provide an unrepeatable opportunity for constitutional revision. To the Whig leaders – at once political bosses and aristocratic frondeurs – the invasion, while raising awkward constitutional questions, opened the door to the promised land of power and perks. The latter group outgunned the former. But they were led astray: the flattery of William and his agents in 1687 and 1688 led them wrongly to assume a complete coincidence of interest.

In debates and in pamphlets and broadsides in the first weeks of 1689, irrepressible Whigs danced on the living dead Tories. The exuberant young Orangists vowed to rout the old men in office. But subsequently, their talents found wanting, their *amour propre* bruised, many of them appeared irrelevant to the political battles of the 1690s. Montagu was denied high office by William, as he had been by Charles and James. Taking office in the Treasury, Monmouth swore that 'he would understand the business of it as well as Ld Godolphin in a fortnight' (BL, Halifax Notebook, Addl. Mss.51511, f.26). But Godolphin outlasted such shooting stars of 1687–8. William was invited as the champion of Protestantism and was encouraged to present himself as delivering the English from pernicious, un- or anti-constitutional counsels and measures. William preferred to see himself as the leader of a European league against France. He was invited to help prevent a recurrence of the policies and attitudes which had marked Stuart government for a generation. He himself wished to go beyond that, to take that efficiency as read, to start something new: a continental commitment, at once of measures and ideologies. What William was requiring was responsibility, which few understood. The political nation managed to misjudge both

James and William. They knew what they did not want, but not what they did; nor what William wanted. They were assertive at times when considered responses were needed, reluctant when decisiveness was called for by William, and convoluted when he sought commitment.

It is often argued that, faced with the ill-intending and incompetent James, the British political nation revealed their essential pragmatism. A broad basis of support for (or, at least, acquiescence in) Williamite invasion was required. That meant that the Whigs had to concentrate their attack on James, preferring not to go back beyond 1685, to the years of the early 1680s, when the Anglican Tories, whose collusion and consent the Whigs were now seeking, had been in power. But the exclusion of the parliamentarians of 1685 from the discussions over the 1688–9 New Year apparently signalled that William would look to a Whig-dominated regime. Such a regime was likely to steer a course bringing it directly into collision with the interests and the prejudices of the Anglican Tories. However, after the coronation, William showed himself willing to turn to Nottingham and to continue both Godolphin and the earl of Ranelagh, James II's paymaster, in office.

Two contradictory stimuli prompted supporters of William in the political struggles of 1688–9. The first encouraged them to do all they could to broaden the base of support for a new, Williamite regime. The other provoked them to underline differences of opinion wherever possible, and to bring these differences to public notice. Throughout 1688–9 and for a generation thereafter, we find such a tension, between those who saw the polity as irredeemably divided between two opposing persuasions and those who rejected such a simplification. A number of agitators within parliamentary ranks were joined by publicists in emphasizing division along party lines.

The Anglican Tories were many and well entrenched. But they suffered from a surfeit of loyalties: to the Stuarts, to the Anglican church, to their local position and the social hierarchy, to a view of the seventeenth-century past and a fear of its recurrence. The response of many of the clergy was withdrawal. A number, led by the archbishop of Canterbury himself, refused to recognize the new regime. These non-jurors had little political impact: indeed, they did not seek political clout and this lack of determined linkage with the Jacobites was telling. More Anglican Tories abstained from complicity in, and open approval of, the installation of the new regime. Only three of twenty-six bishops and perhaps a quarter of the peerage were present on 13 February 1689; even the coronation was attended by only ten bishops and some eighty peers.

The revolutionary years revealed once more the openness of political culture, the accessibility of the political elite to proposals from individuals, the ability of seasoned pamphleteers to bring their panaceas to the attention of parliamentarians of whatever political hue. Pamphlets, poems, engravings and squibs abounded. An ebullient print culture offered a plethora of interpretations of past and current events and of suggestions for the future. But the end product, from a mountain of grievance and proposal, has been adjudged a veritable mouse: of these pamphlets, Jones concluded that 'theoretically they are defective and not very interesting . . . the theme through-out was one of restoration and renewal, of protecting existing (or assumed) rights, not of establishing new ones' (Jones 1972: 317). This slights the importance of the means which the radicals suggested for the securing of such rights. The radicals of

1688–9 are one further group being rescued from Edward Thompson's 'enormous condescension of posterity'.

Radicals, mainly outside the Convention, but a number within, and others mixing with parliamentarians, saw 1688 as an 'opportunity' in Machiavellian terms. Their messages were mixed. Some would trust William, the Protestant deliverer, and would look avidly to 'godly reformation'. Others were, though, from the start chary of William: he, after all, had been the leader and beneficiary of the anti-libertarian 'usurpation' of 1672. Nonetheless, this crisis in the history of the world suggested the benefits of strong leadership: the revival of use of the expression 'Prince' is striking. Failed uprisings, Catholic ambition and Stuart revenge had decimated the radicals through the 1680s. Their vitality in 1688–9 is striking but its consequence, as so often, was to push Whig and Tory wings of the establishment briefly together.

In a letter to William of 2 December 1688, Sir Robert Howard insisted that 'theire was noe roome left for trust, and everythinge must be built upon new foundations' (Foxcroft 1898: II, 21). This conviction was the consequence of his hostility to popery, the consistent feature of a chequered career. What distinguished Howard from many of his fellow parliamentarians was that he believed that, with an appropriate structure put in place, trust could and would follow. Others maintained that mistrust was the essential attribute of a citizen-subject facing the wiles of the powerful. Mistrust emerged from the murk of 1688–9 as the crucial element in the make-up of many a parliamentarian.

The Revolution of 1688–1689 and the Polity

Contemporaries well know that the course of English, British and British Atlantic history was less certain than many a subsequent celebrant of 1688 has wished to believe. Although technological and natural constraints remained essentially unaltered in the half-century either side of 1688, events were contingent on accident, quirks of character, weather, royal demography and the determination and perseverance of public figures. The post-revolutionary regime, the polity which it led and the commitments it had embraced, was very different by 1695 from that envisaged in 1688–9.

Subsequent generations were keen to give decisions taken on constitutional issues in 1689 the stamp of permanence, speaking of the 'Revolution settlement'. But that is not the way with questions of power and political structure. The constitution was not, and could not, be settled. Crises over the standing army in 1697–8, the Act of Settlement in 1701, and the abortive constitutional revolution between 1716 and 1719, amply showed that. Yet the outcome of the battle of language, the triumph of 'settlement', served to concentrate attention on the bare bones of the regime, Protestant and parliamentary, established in the aftermath of James's flight – and diverted attention from the flesh put on the regime in its operation in the years after 1689. Emphasis on 1688–9 helped hide the 1690s.

The Revolution began, in British minds, with questions about the constitutionality of a Catholic regime. It became a matter of kingship and sovereignty. Many participants only reluctantly came to constitutional terms with the political decisions which they had made or in which they had been complicit. The need for formal, public documents, as well as pressure from William for quick decisions, forced commitment. Change came spewing forth. In the coronation oath of 1689 an ascending replaced a descending order of power. The new oath, innocent of the contamination of monarchical 'grants', was worked up by the Commons, not by clerics. Even more contentious was the proposal that reference to the church as 'established by law' should give way to 'as shall be established'. Whig failure to carry that point, which would have encouraged a review of the state church, was a premonition of Tory ability to prevail when they were able to insist upon the preservation of the Anglican Church as a single issue. A dissenter noted that 'the House of Commons was stronger by 80 or 100 voices to reform things amiss in the State than in the Church' (Schwoerer 1992: 123–5; Speck 1988: 186).

Parliament would be central to any constitutional revision and political settlement. Yet the political nation, yearning though they were for a parliament in and after 1686, had been concerned at what it might do. Were James, taking a leaf out of the Exclusionists' book, learning from their campaign of instructions, to succeed in summoning a packed parliament, the consequence might be worse than having no parliament at all. There is a nice irony here, for it was precisely such a development that so worried many of the political nation after 1689. In the autumn of 1688, Orangists were embarrassed by the notion of the immediate assembly of a parliament. Were a new parliament to come to an accommodation with James, then William's aid would be the less necessary for the British political nation. Such a parliament might result in the clipping of monarchical prerogatives. At one point, it was suggested that James should summon a parliament but that parliament's consent should be required for any dissolution. Such solutions did not commend themselves to William. He was prepared to use parliament, no more, no less. The grail of a 'free parliament' appeared remote indeed.

The willingness of participants to suggest political action and to involve themselves in *ad hoc* institutions and activities is striking. Unusual forms were turned to usual ends. In the provinces, gentry and peers brought both the militia and the collection of taxes to William. Anne set up an interim administration to maintain order in the east Midlands. Her supporters urged the creation of an Association to protect her. An entirely extra-legal gathering of representatives of the City of London's government joined with members of Charles II's parliaments met in the House of Commons itself. A recall of the last Exclusion Parliament was urged. *De facto* government was instituted in the emergency of 1688–9. Necessity knew no law, created its own practices. If, radicals might well think, such improvisation was legitimate, what might a fully representative body not do?

Orangists, joined here by many opponents of James's government (if not of his kingship), were convinced that a 'free parliament' would have much work to do and would be allowed great scope. In his *Declaration* of 10 October, William had implied that whatever the 'free parliament' agreed, would be enacted. There was no mention of any check on the decisions of the two Houses. Nottingham proposed that the 'free parliament' which all desired should sit for thirty days every year. One of the Convention committees recommended that parliaments should not be dissolved until their business was complete (one of the very few premonitions of the coming centrality of parliament as a legislative body?). Sir Richard Temple revealingly referred to 'your Instrument of Government' (Jones 1988: 148).

How many of the skins of the polity needed to be peeled away before the work of reconstruction could begin? A number of parliamentarians and ideologues, both in England and Scotland, wished to purify the polity. They argued that no resistance had been shown to a true king. By invading religion, liberty and property, James became a tyrant: 'when a King of his own motion Dos Wrong he thereby ceases to be King'. And, of course, he had fled. That left the field open for 'the nation', summoned together, to pronounce upon its future. This opened the way to speculation about fundamentals: 'A parliament makes laws for the administration, but the people, as in a community, make laws for the constitution' in a convention. Such a convention, 'as it has more power than a parliament, and is its creator, must have a larger body... [its] power... must be absolute and uncontrolable'. Sir Robert Howard argued that there was 'no room left for trust' and believed that 'the Right is... wholly in the people, who are Now to new form themselves again, under a Governor yet to be Chosen' (Jones 1988: 250–1; Somers Tracts: 337–9). The Scottish Convention declared (4 April 1689) that James, far from abdicating, had forfeited the crown. Their subsequent Claim of Right talked of his having 'invaded the fundamental constitution of the Kingdom and altered it from a legal limited monarchy, to an arbitrary despotic power'. Such a decisive elimination of James VII, based on his actions not upon his flight, went to parliamentary heads. Sir John Dalrymple wrote that some

> plainly pretend that the King is obliged to redress all their grievances which som proposed as a quality in ther recognising him; and whatever they think a grivance he must redress, otherwys he fails, and they may do right to themselves; whereas the King said only he would redress every thing that was justly grievous wherof they are not sol judges. (Cowan, in Israel 1991: 166)

This nervous and ill-founded sense that what they said went, was soon put in its place by William. A number of the disenchanted veered off into Jacobitism.

Many historians have been intent on seeing 1688–9 as restorative, conservative and consensual. Schwoerer, by contrast, insists upon the breaking of new ground, especially in the Declaration and Bill of Rights. To her, the political nation, led by the Whigs, succeeded in imposing conditions which limited William's kingship: 1688–9 was not a mere 'palace coup' (Schwoerer 1981). Reresby had believed likewise:

> before any person was named to fill the throne they would frame conditions upon which only he should be accepted as King, and tie him up more strictly to the observance of them then other princes had been before. (Browning 1991: 530)

To others, the events of early 1689 were tantamount to Conqueror William graciously extending concessions. Some of those concessions were unwanted by many of the English political nation. William had made it clear that he would not urge the repeal of the Test Acts. But he was committed to 'full liberty of conscience' for Protestant Dissenter and Catholic alike. He would use men of any religion. Prudent William was all too aware of his need to maintain credit with the anti-French yet Catholic powers of Europe. But it was also a matter of principle. What followed was a running battle between William, supported by those who argued for, and would benefit from, extended religious toleration, and those insistent upon maintaining the position of the church as established.

Hostility to Catholicism was as central to 1687–9 as it had been to 1640–2. The potential for persecution remained. The virtues of toleration went largely unappreciated. Yet the English magisterial elite was constrained by the implications of its answers to the last of the Three Questions set by James in 1687–8. Many positive answers were given to the question, 'will you live in peace with neighbours under a Declaration of Indulgence?' In the Convention, Sir Henry Capell acknowledged: 'I know that Papists in communication...with Protestants are good Neighbors enough, but they become inveterate & intollerable where their Church is concerned' (Jones 1988: 236; cf. 207). Such comments might set the tone of public life in the coming century.

Nor was William vengeful. Both in England and Scotland there were attempts to exclude from public life supporters of, and officeholders under, James. William refused to approve the Scottish Incapacity Bill. In England the 'Sacheverell' clause, a Whig-inspired attempt to proscribe all involved in the surrender of borough charters in the 1680s, failed when, to the delight of Tories and churchmen, William's opposition was made clear. William did not want to alienate many who might be useful to him, whose resentment would certainly complicate his rule. He intended to choose his own servants and would not be dictated to, although he knew all too well that some politicians wished to make him 'a Doge of Venice'. He believed that he had been called to the throne by God. He insisted that he would maintain the royal authority although he realized its weakness:

> a K. of England who will governe by Law as hee must do, if hee hath conscience, is the worst figure in Christendome. – Hee hath power to destroy the Nation and not to protect it. (Foxcroft 1898: II, 221)

He recognized the value of a number of men in James's service. The likes of William Blathwayt or, in the administration of the American colonies, Sir Edmund Andros, humiliatingly expelled from New England in 1689 and returning as governor of Virginia in 1692; these were men of considerable efficiency, who shared William's disdain for the compromises of political life.

William was interested in power, in the mobilization of resources, and was less intrigued by constitutional questions. None of the participants in the events of 1687–9 had a sense of the commitments which William would entail on the nation, of what was involved when they recognized that to cashier James was to throw down the gauntlet to Louis XIV. It was these military consequences, and the strong executive which they entailed, which prompted the first flowering of Whig Jacobitism, of radicals prepared to argue that they would be more likely to secure a limited monarchy from a restored and dependent James than from an enthroned and triumphant William. Nonetheless, William's executive was dependent upon parliament, upon the regular voting of men and money.

Hence a consequence of the events of 1687–9 was the further elevation of parliament within the political system and the governance of the realm. The Declaration and the subsequent Bill of Rights may have constrained the monarch: they certainly did nothing to constrain parliament itself. The 'free parliament' became an all-powerful parliament. There was, from 1689, a level of hostility to both its oligarchical nature, and its executive-minded doings. Such hostility may have sprung from no more than a handful of pamphleteers, but the silence of the sources should not be taken to mean that such writers were isolated. Nor, when expressed in situations less elevated than parliament, ought they to be written off as eccentric or motivated by personal grievance.

Subsequent political life, moulded by royal, constitutionalist, local and interest-group agendas, thoroughly changed the structure of the polity, the capacity of government, the pretensions of parliament, and the career structure for ambitious politicians. The polity of, say, the 1720s was clearly one in which the centres of power were stronger than they had been forty years before, though this does not necessarily mean that the provinces and periphery were weaker. Indeed, provided that the game was played by Whig rules, everyone would have a prize. In this respect, local elites in both Britain and its American colonies operated with considerable freedom in the coming century. Even where matters remained uncertain, the wilder flights of fancy were brought crashing to earth. Scottish attempts to decouple the monarchy resulted in Union. The notion of Ireland as a French protectorate (briefly entertained before the birth of James's son, and again in 1691) disappeared.

A consequence of the events of 1687–9 and their aftermath in the war against France was that while William's power remained great, his rights were curtailed. His early hopes were expressed to Halifax: 'Said, the Revenue once settled, hee would take his measures; Note; it is to bee supposed, the Plt was apprehensive of it' (Foxcroft 1898: II, 228).

William was to be confounded. Throughout the 1690s there was an attrition of prerogative powers. And William's power was exercised through his ministers: within parliament, the front benches gained, falteringly but cumulatively, at the expense of the back. William purchased power and resources, specifically money, at the cost of relinquishing rights. He sold those prerogatives on which he had insisted in 1688–9 to maintain his war. Hence Macinnes (1982) sees William as 'the betrayer of English absolutism'. The operating mechanisms of the polity of 1702, the grease and the oil it needed to function, would have shocked the men of 1687–9, and did indeed shock those who had not thrown in their lot with the post-revolutionary world. The brazen assertions of prerogative were giving way to the insidious sapping of corruption. Within a lifetime of 1688–9 the events of that time remained an inspiration to some, a missed opportunity to others, and an embarrassment to what had become a Whig establishment.

Conclusion

It is tempting to be cynical about the participants in the events of 1688–9 and about the claims of subsequent historians. From glorifying, many have passed to scorning its actors and belittling its consequences. Commentators have questioned the integrity and motivation of the participants, and poured cold revisionist water on that sweaty mass of self-congratulation and misinformation which was the historiography of the Revolution. This has proved chilling rather than bracing.

Contemporaries were serious people, grappling with serious issues, liable to self-delusion, often dissimulating, but not given to fancy rhetoric. Convention debates were direct, even brutal: decorum so far broke down that members called each other by name. Contemporaries had invited, or found themselves confronted with, an invading force. They faced the likelihood of civil war: 1688, surprisingly, did not turn into another 1642. William feared that it would; Louis XIV hoped that it would. That such a fate was averted was the responsibility of James, who chose to flee, or, rather, to retreat the better to advance. It was not the case that the English had become too civil in their dealings to contemplate violence one against another.

Instigators of, and participants in, the revolution ought not to suffer historiographical scorn if their intentions were not realized, their hopes dashed, their ambitions aborted. The Orangist claims in the 'Letter of Invitation' that 'nineteen parts of twenty of the people ... are desirous of a change ... and ... would willingly contribute to it' were not merely tactical attempts to reassure William, or wishful thinking (Browning 1953: doc.39; Speck 1987: 455). They were sincerely believed: for how could any but the hardest hearted or evilly inclined concur with James's policies? Much is made of the way in which the actors of the 1680s were shaped by memory of the 1640s and 1650s. But those who welcomed William had in their excitement overlooked the extent then, and the contemporary likelihood, of neutrality, of caution and of legalism.

Harold Macmillan had it right: 'Events, dear boy, events'. Or in seventeenth-century terms, Providence. Providential events threw things out of kilter. But it was not only events like those varying winds which had ultimately brought William to Brixham. It was also individuals: James by his flight, William by his unsuspected determination and conviction. But neither could William himself foresee, in 1687 or 1688, the political world of 1697 or 1698. He left precious few indications of his intentions for the shape of the polity. At what stage, for example, did he decide to take over much of the personnel of James's government? The ends of governance would be very different, but William would not scruple to use the same men. Hence the despairing cry:

> The tyrant gone,
> The tyranny remains.
> ('A Familiar Epistle to King William', Nottingham Univ. Lib., Portland Mss., PWA2032)

April 1689 seems to have been the crucial month, when William continued the likes of Ranelagh and Godolphin in office. Of those politicians on whom William had depended in 1687–8, only Shrewsbury survived, a querulous and marginal figure. Chancellor of the Exchequer Hampden satisfied none. He justified William's demands to parliament with the lame argument that 'His Majesty is a great captain, and since he thinks 65,000 men necessary, I that am but a private man cannot but think there is weight in it' (Horwitz 1972: 31).

Howard's incompetence and peculation at the Exchequer ensured that he would go no further. Halifax could not take the bitterness and the bruises of the new political life. Churchill, chastened in the early 1690s, gave up political intrigue and settled for being indispensable in the field. Of those who made a name for themselves in 1687–9, only Somers was obviously a coming man. A new political generation, that of the Junto, would come to bestride the Whigs and the Westminster world; over against them, the Tories and, by comparison inchoate, those of the Country persuasion. In the unillusioned post-revolutionary world, trust would be magnified as an issue, arbitrary government would be replaced as the bogeyman by corrupt government.

It was for long tempting to insist that the Revolution, in Trevelyan's words, 'enthroned' an 'element of "moderation"' . . . the chaining up of fanaticism alike in politics and in religion' (Trevelyan 1938: 241–2). But moderation did not inform the Revolution settlement. It was gradually, only gradually, spun out from it. The British remained prone to fanaticism, for example to vigilante anti-Catholicism. In the accommodation of 6 February 1689, reached by exhausted and desperate men, there is an element, if not of class war, at least of a fear of the world's being turned upside down. The London people *en masse* had threatened to provoke what they themselves took already to have occurred: the dissolution of government, the return to first principles. As at any moment of unclear succession, there were those who believed that the laws were suspended. This was a matter of self-interest, no doubt, but I see no reason to assume that it was not accompanied by a persuasive analysis of the political and legal consequences of an interregnum. So much unravelling of the tortuously woven skein of civil and propertied government could not be entertained.

Exhaustion came after six weeks of intense argument over language, structures, values and meanings. The balance of opinion in the two Houses of the Convention is difficult to establish – within the nation as a whole, impossible. There were outright Williamites, backing their deliverer. There were those, prepared to experiment, who rejoiced that they were establishing that the hereditary principle was not automatic. There were those worried that parliament might bite off more than it could chew, never mind digest. There were those who feared any change. Some became Jacobites or non-jurors. Others were prepared to sacrifice legitimacy to order. For the earl of Thanet, the Lords' vote on 6 February amounted to 'ye ruin of ye Monarchy of England, for we have made ye Crown elective'. Thanet told Clarendon that 'I know not where it will end. But there is an absolute necessity of having a government, and I doe not see a prospect of any other than this. We must not leave ourselves to ye rabble.' Nottingham agreed: 'I must confess any government is better than none' (Jones 1988: 86; Horwitz 1968: 80).

This was a struggle for control of the political vocabulary. The new oaths to be taken to William and Mary were without the words 'rightful and lawful'. This was a *quid pro quo*, Anglican Tories accepting a change of kingship, the Williamites agreeing to the modified oaths. While the political system was changing gear, parliaments becoming regular, doing a mass of both governmental and private business, old issues would not go away. Resistance was discussed with frightening intensity over a twenty-year period, ultimately considerably embarrassing the Whigs themselves. In 1688–9 there is little sense of the arrival of a new mode of politics, of limited liability. Yet within a generation a new vocabulary took hold. The outcome of the trial of Dr Henry Sacheverell in 1710 was tantamount to an acknowledgement that the Orangist–Whig vocabulary of 1688–9 could not be sustained against either the opposing litanies of the High Anglican Tories or the new world of the imperial state. Violence within the Convention was only narrowly averted on a number of occasions. The generation of 1687–9 remembered the world of Shaftesbury; many that of the late 1640s and 1650s. The worlds of Walpole and of Henry Pelham were unimaginable. William III helped the English political nation to exit from the seventeenth century. But a mixed verdict awaited the new regime and the new politics. One parliamentarian confessed sadly that 'when I gave my voice to make the prince of Orange king, I thought to have seen better times than these'. Such acknowledgement of the vanity of human hopes does not detract from the seriousness of purpose of the political nation of 1688–9. It does serve to remind us of the many ironies of this revolution. Understanding is helped neither by its elevation as glorious nor by its denigration as inglorious.

REFERENCES

Baxter, S. B. 1966: *William III*: London.
Beddard, R. (ed.) 1991: *The Revolutions of 1688*: Oxford.
Browning, A. (ed.) 1953: *English Historical Documents, 1660–1714*: London.
Browning, A. (ed.) 1991: *The Memoirs of Sir John Reresby*, revd edn, ed. M. K. Geiter and W. A. Speck: London.
Burnet, G. 1833: *History of My Own Time*, 6 vols: Oxford.
Cruickshanks, E. 2000: *The Glorious Revolution*: Basingstoke.
Foxcroft, H. C. 1898: *The Life and Letters of Sir George Savile Bart., First Marquis of Halifax*, vol. 2: London.
Hoak, D. and Feingold, M. (eds.) 1996: *The World of William and Mary: Anglo-Dutch Perspectives on the Revolution of 1688–89*: Stanford, CA.
Horwitz, H. 1968: '*Revolution Politicks': The Career of Daniel Finch, 2nd Earl of Nottingham*: Cambridge.
Horwitz, H. (ed.) 1972: *The Parliamentary Diary of Narcissus Luttrell*: Oxford.
Israel, J. (ed.) 1991: *The Anglo-Dutch Moment: Essays on the Glorious Revolution and its World Impact*: Cambridge.
Jones, D. L. (ed.) 1988: *A Parliamentary History of the Glorious Revolution*: London.
Jones, J. R. 1972: *The Revolution of 1688 in England*: London.
Macaulay, T. B. *History of England from the Accession of James II*, various edns.
Macinnes, A. 1982: 'When was the English Revolution?' *History*, 377–92.
Miller, J. 1984: 'The potential for 'absolutism' in later Stuart England', *History*, 69, 187–207.
Pinkham, L. 1954: *William III and the Respectable Revolution*: Cambridge, MA.
Schwoerer, L. G. 1977: 'Propaganda in the Revolution of 1688', *American History Review*, 82, 843–74.
Schwoerer, L. G. 1981: *The Declaration of Rights*: Baltimore, MD.
Schwoerer, L. G. 1992: *The Revolution of 1688–1689: Changing Perspectives*: Cambridge.
Speck, W. A. 1987: 'The Orangist conspiracy against James II,' *History Journal*, 31, 453–62.
Speck, W. A. 1988: *Reluctant Revolutionaries: Englishmen and the Revolution of 1688*: Oxford.
Sykes, N. 1959: *From Sheldon to Secker*: Cambridge.
Trevelyan, G. M. 1938: *The English Revolution*: Oxford.
Western, J. R. 1972: *Monarchy and Revolution: The English State in the 1680s*: London.
Wildman, J. 1748: *A Letter to a Friend*, January 1689, in 'Somers Tracts', *A Collection of Scarce and Valuable Tracts*, 1748, vol. 1.

FURTHER READING

Ashcraft, R. 1986: *Revolutionary Politics and Locke's Two Treatises of Government*: Princeton, NJ.

Ashcraft, R. and Goldsmith, M. M. 1983: 'Locke, revolution principles and the formation of Whig ideology', *History Journal*, 27, 773–800.

Claydon, T. 1996: *William III and the Godly Revolution*: Cambridge.

Cruickshanks, E. (ed.) 1989: *By Force or By Default*: Edinburgh.

Gregg, E. 1980: *Queen Anne*: London.

Grell, O. P. (ed.) 1991: *From Persecution to Toleration*: Oxford.

Harris, T. 1997: 'Reluctant revolutionaries? The Scots and the revolution of 1688–89.' In H. Nenner, ed., *Politics and the Political Imagination in Later Stuart Britain*: Rochester, NY.

Hayton, D. W. and O'Brien, G. 1986: *War and Politics in Ireland, 1649–1730* [essays by J. G. Simms]: London.

Henning, B. D. 1983: *The House of Commons, 1660–1690*, 3 vols: London.

Horwitz, H. 1974: 'Parliament and the Glorious Revolution', *Bulletin of the Institute of Historical Research*, 47, 36–52.

Kenyon, J. P. 1977: *Revolution Principles: The Politics of Party, 1689–1720*: Cambridge.

Miller, J. 1978: *James II: A Study in Kingship*: Hove; revd edn 2000: *James II*: New Haven, CT.

Nenner, H. 1995: *The Right to be King: The Succession to the Crown of England, 1587–1714*: Chapel Hill, NC.

Simms, J. G. 1969: *Jacobite Ireland, 1685–1691*: London; reprinted Dublin, 2000.

Webb, S. S. 1995: *Lord Churchill's Coup: The Anglo-American Empire and the Glorious Revolution Reconsidered*: New York.

CHAPTER TWENTY-THREE

Politics after the Glorious Revolution

MARK KNIGHTS

The Political Sow-Gelder, or the Castration of Whig and Tory (1715), a tract attributed to Daniel Defoe, lamented 'what a woful Condition is Poor England reduced to, that . . . we are brought to this unhappy Dilemma, that we must be either Whig or Tory'. These party labels were, the author lamented, 'names invented in hell and spread about this kingdom to brand honest Men with odious characters and turn the whole nation into confusion'. Defoe reminded readers that a Tory meant a bog-trotter or Irish robber and Whig was a word that had originated in Scotland, meaning either a Presbyterian Covenanter or 'a sort of Butter-Milk or Whey' which was sour, 'not unlike the present temper of the English, for when a Whig and a Tory meet together, they look as sower upon one another as so many Crab-Trees'. Such party bitterness, Defoe noted, ran deep and had become an ingrained feature of everyday life, with disastrous consequences for the nation's honesty and manners: 'the design of Party-Men is not truth but to abuse each other, and like Billingsgate Orators, they that make the greatest noise and call the foulest names, get the better of it'. More-over, the 'Party-Men condemn the contrary Side, purely for opposition-sake'. Lamentably, Defoe suggested, such attitudes had spread right down the social scale and the mob made themselves 'judge' of every case. Written at the time of widespread Jacobite rioting, the tract concluded with an appeal for unity against the enemies of the church and king. If readers disagreed they were invited to use the paper 'as an excellent cleanser of the Posteriors, or a Grand Preservative of the Bottoms of Pies and Tarts, from Oven-Dust and Soil'.

Defoe's tract, its own production a sign that the press had become a powerful presence in partisan struggles, wittily summarizes some of the essential features of post-revolutionary politics. It recognized that the divisions between the Whig and Tory parties had become endemic, and were prevalent among the 'mob', which now considered itself a public umpire. He also noted that the party men (and women, Defoe noted) conducted their discussions about politics as though they were fish-wives railing and cursing in a market. Abusive name-calling seemed to be part of politics. But look beneath the labels, Defoe urged his readers, and let the 'honest' men of both sides come together. And to some extent the castration of Whig and Tory did occur. The passage of the Septennial Act in 1716 reduced the frequency of general elections from at least every three years to every seven. Thus whereas after the revolution, and the subsequent 1694 Triennial Act, Britain witnessed twelve general elections before 1716 (an average of one every two and a half years), electoral fever at a national level thereafter was much less frequent. This chapter explores the nature and impact of the so-called 'rage of party' – the furious hostility between Whig and Tory – during the reign of William III (1689–1702) and at its zenith under Queen Anne (1702–14). It will concentrate primarily on the form of politics rather than on the substantive issues at stake, some of which will be covered in the next chapter since they were of an ideological nature. The issues over which the parties disagreed have also been outlined by a number of other scholars (Speck 1970; Kenyon 1977; Horwitz 1977; Dickinson 1977; Holmes 1987, 1993; Harris 1993). But a very brief overview of some of the points of tension might provide a useful framework for the following discussion. The key flashpoints were religion, the succession, the constitution and war with France.

One of the continuities throughout the later Stuart period was the tension between the church and dissent. Most Dissenters were Whigs, but not all Whigs were Dissenters, for their ranks included many 'low churchmen' who thought Dissenters should be allowed freedom of worship. Most Tories were adherents of the Church of England, which had lost its religious monopoly after the passage of the Toleration Act and often felt threatened by dissent, irreligion and atheism. Some Tories, including leaders such as Sir Edward Seymour and Henry St John, were notable for their absenteeism from church or free-thinking, but a core of Tory support came from those devoted to the established church. The religious tensions between the parties were heightened by issues such as 'occasional conformity' – a term describing Dissenters who took communion according to the rites of the Church of England in order, their opponents alleged, to qualify themselves for political office, entry to which was still restricted by the Test and Corporation Acts. Bills to ban occasional conformity were introduced three times between 1702 and 1705, and again, successfully, in 1711. Religious tensions also reached new heights in 1710, after the parliamentary prosecution of Dr Henry Sacheverell for a sermon in which he attacked Dissenters and 'revolution principles'.

As Sacheverell's trial illustrated, the political principles justifying the revolution of 1688–9 were thus also bones of contention. The Whigs argued that when a king became a tyrant he could be resisted; but the Tories were very uncomfortable with the concept of resistance, since this implied that political power lay originally with the 'people' rather than the king or king-in-parliament. Whigs espoused a variety of different justifications of the revolution, some preferring the idea of an 'ancient constitution' which had been breached, while others thought of a more abstract 'contract' between king and people that James had broken, but they all agreed that the revolution had been just and lawful. Tories, on the other hand, played down the idea that there had been any resistance and many preferred to recognize William as king not by right but as the result of conquest, James's abdication or desertion, divine providence, or obedience to established authority (Goldie 1980). The revolution thus raised fundamental constitutional questions about the powers of the people, church, parliament and monarch, and the parties consequently engaged in ideological exchanges. As Swift put it in the Tory periodical *The Examiner*:

> We charge the [Whigs] with a design of destroying the establish'd church and introducing fanaticism and freethinking in its stead. We accuse them as enemies to Monarchy; as endeavouring to undermine the present form of government and to build a common-

wealth, or some new scheme of their own, upon its ruins. On the other side, their clamors against us, may be summed up in those three formidable words, popery, arbitrary power and the pretender. (*The Examiner*, 3 May 1711; the pretender was James II's son)

Although the accession of Queen Anne was far more acceptable to Tories because of her hereditary claim as the daughter of James II, the succession issue continued to be an ideological sore because, after the death of the duke of Gloucester in 1700, there was no immediate Protestant heir. The 1701 Act of Settlement placed the succession in the Hanoverian line. The Whigs were enthusiastic about this, but the Tory party was to split in 1714 over the acceptability of the Hanoverian George I. The 'Jacobites' were those who were never reconciled to a parliamentary transfer of the crown, either to William or to George, but the Whigs claimed throughout the period that the Tories as a whole were crypto-Jacobites. The need to secure the succession had also necessitated union in 1707 with Scotland, much to the distaste of Tories, who feared that the Scottish Kirk was incompatible with the English episcopacy. The succession issue thus also raised constitutional matters which had to be confronted in 1689, 1701 and 1706–7.

Besides religion, the constitution and the succession, another major fault-line between the parties was the war with France (1689–97, 1702–13), which was in part fought in order to defend William's right to the crown against the exiled Stuarts, whose right to the English crown was supported by Louis XIV. The disagreements between the parties over the war did not revolve so much around the need to defeat France – though Whigs did accuse the Tories of being lukewarm in their resolve – as over how the war should be fought and its dislocation of domestic norms. Tories preferred a sea to a land war and thought that the huge cost of the land war was partly attributable to greedy Whigs, such as those who had been behind the creation of the Bank of England in 1694 and other financial innovations which have cumulatively been termed a 'financial revolution'. An impeachment of the Whig leaders in 1701 owed much to Tory hostility to such apparent profiteering. The Whigs, it was claimed by 1710, gained from a war which they wished to prolong. The parties also fought each other about the nature of the tax burden, which at £3.64 million in the 1690s was double what it had been prior to the Glorious Revolution. It almost doubled again by 1720. Tories by Anne's reign complained that taxation pressed unduly on land.

There was a basic two-party conflict over issues such as religion, the succession, the constitution and the war. Yet the war created new resources at the disposal of the crown and its ministries, and hence a new set of conflict points that are more difficult to pigeon-hole as either Whig or Tory. Opposition to the number of court appointees in the House of Commons or to the court's maintenance of a standing army in peacetime after the peace of Ryswick in 1697 could thus draw support from both Whig and Tory in often rather temporary 'country' alliances. But such 'country' sentiments were more an outlook than a rival party system (Hayton 1984). Indeed, the country programme could also reinforce Whig–Tory identities. The History of Parliament's findings bear out the suggestion that the country programme became more a Tory than a Whig agenda by 1714, a reversal of pre-1689 positions, even though this necessitated some shift in the nature of the demands (Hayton 2002).

The Historiographical Debates about Politics

The divisions between parties thus arose in large measure from the nature of the revolution of 1688–9, the need to defend it and the subsequent impact of the war on which William had embarked. Chapter 22 explores the nature of the revolution and the differing interpretations of it among both contemporaries and historians. Yet controversy has arisen over the meaning of 1689 in a broader sense: what, if anything, did 1689 change? Older interpretations (called the Whig historical tradition) urged that 1689 marked a turning point, from which 'progress' might start to be measured. Such an interpretation stressed the novelty and importance of the passage of the Toleration Act in 1689 in a separation of church and state, the presentation and acceptance of the Bill of Rights as indicative of the framing of a parliamentary monarchy with a stable constitution, and the lapse of pre-publication licensing in 1695 as ushering in a new era of free speech. The historiographical onslaught against this Whig interpretation has thrown down a number of challenges which stress continuity over change and also question what we mean by 'politics'.

Continuity has been seen within 'long seventeenth century' and 'long eighteenth century' perspectives. The first of these, presented in a lively fashion by Jonathan Scott, emphasizes 'the unity of the seventeenth-century experience' (Scott 2000: 24–7). Scott's primary purpose is to remove the artificiality of 1660 as a dividing line, but his argument has consequences for the period after 1689, for his stress on the unity of seventeenth-century experience makes the timing and causation of change unclear. At one time he identifies 1689–94 as the true Restoration settlement and at another stretches this process over the period 1689–1714, years which are said to have witnessed 'fundamental political changes' (ibid.: 26, 46, 492–3). These, Scott suggests, were three-fold: the institutionalization of party politics; a process of state-formation in which parliament played a key role; and a release from the tyranny of memory. Yet, he continues, 'party politics was nothing other than the institutional-ization of that polarity of belief that had been both cause and consequence of the troubles' and was thus really an extension of the long-standing division between church and dissent (ibid.: 493); parliaments had never opposed state power and had shown their capacity to state-build in the 1640s; and republicanism remained alive to shape radical Whiggery. If party politics was nothing really new what, Scott asks, had changed?

A different but equally forceful exposition of the continuity model comes from Jonathan Clark's interpretation of 1660–1832 as a 'long eighteenth century'. Clark marginalizes 1689 as a watershed, arguing (*contra* Scott) that it was the Restoration of the monarchy and church in 1660 that offered 'new answers' to old problems (Clark 2000: 52). The Revolution of 1689 was only 'a stage in the definition of the hegemonic vision of the state in which the church was defended before the monarchy' (ibid.: 82). Consciously challenging 'older ideas that the seventeenth and eighteenth centuries in England witnessed some natural process of secularization', Clark thus identifies a confessional type of politics (ibid.: 29). He therefore minimizes the growth of a fiscal–military state after 1688, finding 'very similar developments in the reigns of James II, Charles II and in the English republic of the 1650s', so that 'the differences were one of scale, not of kind' (ibid.: 42).

Scholars of the late seventeenth and early eighteenth centuries have been rather conspicuous in their failure to engage with Clark, but the issue of continuity and change which he and Scott raise are important ones. Was political conflict under the later Stuarts the politics of religion? Was it anything new? Was 1689–1714, as Plumb (1967) suggested, a period of instability that gave way to one of stability under Walpole (see also the debate in *Albion* 25 (1993))? These questions might be approached by focusing on the nature of party politics, state formation and public memory. The last of these will be covered in the next chapter. This chapter will therefore look briefly at party politics and the state. But it will go on to suggest that we might also examine the politics of the period by studying the language used in debate, by looking at how men argued as much as what they argued about, and that by doing so we can discern moves towards a new political culture.

The Politics of Religion

For all their differences over the process of change, Clark and Scott, along with many other scholars who hold rather different views, share a conviction that the role of religion needs to be made prominent in accounts of the period. Rather than 1689 ushering in an autonomous political sphere, much of the best recent writing has urged that religion and politics continued to be intertwined and that religion lay at the heart of many political struggles. Thus, while Clark may have gone too far in urging us to think of a 'confessional politics', we have been urged to rethink a politics of religion. More detailed and nuanced refutations of 1689 as an important dividing line have thus come from historians who stress the extent to which religious dispute is the key to understanding party conflict. They urge how important providential and biblical ways of thinking continued to be, even in explaining the revolution itself. Such a view certainly does not downplay the vigour of ideological struggle, but it does suggest that such conflict had less to do with the constitution and more to do with religious differences, particularly those between churchmen and Dissenters. On this reading, Whig and Tory were fundamentally religious parties (Rose 1999; Claydon 1996; Harris 1993; see also Bennett 1975 for a study of the High Church Tories). The attractions of this approach are illustrated in Tim Harris's beautifully clear account of party conflict. 'English society during the great rage of party under William and Anne', he writes, 'divided primarily on religious grounds, with the Nonconformists siding overwhelmingly with the Whigs, and High Church Anglicans with the Tories' (Harris 1993: 196; see also p. 8). Religion was not all that the conflict was about, for 'the party struggle, whether in or out-of-doors, was never solely about the conflict between the Church and Dissent; nevertheless, this conflict was a powerful and central feature of that struggle' (ibid.: 203). The continuing strength of popular high church sympathies, which Harris has helped recover and which Geoffrey Holmes explored in several of his works on post-revolutionary politics (Holmes 1975, 1987), has also been paralleled by research into Jacobitism. Conscientious objection either to the Williamite revolution or to the Hanoverian succession has thus been seen as invigorating an alternative politico-religious culture and, once the Whigs appeared to have abandoned their populism by 1714, also offering a language of social protest (Monod 1989; Rogers 1988). Attention to the tensions between church and dissent has also proved fruitful by stressing a powerful antipathy to the political influence and interests of clerics – what contemporaries called 'priestcraft'. Such hostility, it has been persuasively argued, contributed to an 'early enlightenment' that, far from being secular in inspiration, thrived by exploring the boundaries between church and state and between institutional religion and private, rational faith.

Certainly, divisions at local and national level owed a great deal to religious tensions. Party strife was often particularly bitter in constituencies where Dissenters were prominent or numerous and religious tensions do help to explain why party conflicts penetrated institutions such as charitable bodies, which were not formally involved in the national electoral process (De Krey 1985; Rose 1991; Hurwich 1977). Yet 'church' and 'dissent' are terms which carry a bundle of political, social and even economic associations and could also be used as a way of talking, to secure popular conviction and allegiance. An illustration of this comes in a tract called *The Bond-of-Resignation-Man in the True Picture of a Splitter of Freeholds* (1705?). This pamphlet attacked those who split their estates into parcels of freehold property in order to enlarge the electorate and hence to influence the outcome of the polls. Its title would suggest a purely 'political' tract. Yet it was published in the wake of the repeated attempt to enact legislation banning 'occasional conformists'. The author of the tract implied that this widespread practice of 'splitting' was the preserve of the Dissenter. The 'splitter' was thus described as a conventicler who 'spits fire at the ministers of state that are in her Majesty's and the Church's interest' and appropriated 'the name of only true protestant'. The author went on to call this dissenting splitter a republican: he was 'a certain kind of antimonarchical animal, perti per pale, protestant, jew, turk and pagan, the son of the [Whig Junto's] Kit-Kat Club, where the Pope's toe, the Devil's cloven foot and about a hundred and fifty fathers more, besides comers and goers, had to do with his mother the common Jilt [called] the Good Old Cause'. He was, moreover, the arch hypocrite: 'He is continually frighting others with the danger of slavery and arbitrary power, and yet is of the most arbitrary principles himself', for he called his will his conscience. The tract seems proof that politics was discussed in, among other things, religious terms.

But there are dangers here. The use of religious language and the prominence of religious disputes do not necessarily mean that we are dealing with godly politics. Indeed, to say that the dispute was 'primarily religious' seems actually to be intervening in the later Stuart debate, for it was the contention of the high-churchmen that the church *was* in danger, that religion *was* the primary point of conflict, whereas to low-churchmen and Dissenters the slogan of the 'church' was only being used as a cover for other, *political* ends. Thus the author of the low-church but ostensibly non-party *Faults on Both Sides* (1710) was convinced that religion had been manipulated to induce civil war in 1642 and was equally insistent that the occasional conformity Bills of 1703–5 had been devised as 'mischief-making, party-driving' tools designed 'to raise the spirits of the Tory party, to create in the Queen an opinion of their formidable strength and by degrees to model the corporations, weed out the Dissenters and at length to disable them in their electing members of parliament'. If the reader thinks the church is in danger, the author suggests, he or she is like those credulous Tories, 'a looser and less thoughtful sort of people, who look no further than the outside of thing'. Religion was thus used, it was alleged, as a cloak for evil men to trick the gullible. Thus:

it may be very material also to observe to you, that as these names of distinction are taken from words signifying parties differing in their religious sentiments, the world has been led into, and still persists in a mistake, as if the one sort were altogether Dissenters and the other included all that were true church of England men, whereas there has always been a great number of the Whig party, even of the clergy as well as the laiety, who are zealous for the episcopal church government as the Tories themselves; so that they are indeed more truly to be accounted factions in the state than in the church. (Reproduced in *Somers Tracts* 4th collection, 1752, vol. 3)

The outward face of 'religion' could thus be deceptive.

The Politics of the State

A rather different set of definitions and discussion of politics might revolve around the development of the state after 1689. Here we appear to be on more straightforwardly political terrain. One approach to the state stresses 1689 as a turning point in the history of parliament. During the Restoration, parliament sat fitfully, often lay prorogued or adjourned for long periods, and, although there were three elections in as many years between 1679 and 1681, was not subject to electoral scrutiny between 1661 and 1679. No parliament was held in 1684, despite a legal requirement that it should be summoned. Parliament's sitting was even more haphazard during James's reign. Interrupted by the Monmouth rebellion, and then almost immediately dismissed for failing to follow the king's will, it did not sit again before the revolution. This pattern of uncertain, short sessions wreaked havoc with any legislative consistency or success-rate. By contrast, the demands of war with France (1689–97, 1702–13) and the pressure of popular opinion after 1689 ensured annual sessions, the length of which averaged 112 days, almost double the Restoration figure. This greater regularity and longevity had a great impact on legislative initiatives. From 1660 to 1688 parliament passed on average about 26 statutes per session; between 1689 and 1714 this rose dramatically to 64 per session. 'Parliament as a legislature had come of age' (Hoppit 2000: 26; 1996).

This development should make us more alert to changes within parliament and between parliament and the nation. A detailed study of all MPs and their constituencies confirms that party allegiance was being institutionalized. Using twenty-two lists of voting patterns or forecasts, the History of Parliament has shown that MPs' party loyalty to Whig or Tory was very strong. Of the 1,266 members whose names figure on more than one of these lists, 793 (63 per cent) appear as having acted with complete consistency along party lines. And using other sources, of the total 1,875 English and Welsh MPs sitting between 1690 and 1714, only 201 (10.7 per cent) defy classification as Whig or Tory in the context of their electoral or parliamentary behaviour. Only 73 (3.8 per cent) appear to have shifted between one party and another (or to a position of neutrality between the parties). Moreover the study of how the MPs operated in and out of parliament highlights the efficiency of party (particularly Whig) leaders in marshalling votes and planning strategy (Hayton 2002).

Such discipline was evidently much harder to achieve among voters, but studies of pollbooks have also revealed strong party allegiances at any one election (most voters preferred to give both their votes – most had two each – along party lines when possible) and among a dedicated core of voters from one election to another. This evidence has nevertheless produced an interesting debate about the nature of the party divisions at large because of three features of the polls. First, a substantial minority – perhaps about 20 per cent – of voters did switch their allegiance between elections, so-called 'floating voters'. Second, there was an astonishingly high 'turn-over' of voters between elections. For example, only 54 per cent of those who voted in the second general election of 1701 in Westmorland were polled again a few months later in the general election of 1702 and this spasmodic degree of participation does not seem to have been unusual. Third, the numbers of eligible voters were always much higher than the actual number of voters. A low turn-out could hold true even among the gentry in times of crisis – only 30 per cent and 39 per cent of land tax commissioners voted in Hampshire and Suffolk respectively, even in the highly charged political atmosphere of 1710, and as little as 18 per cent in the West Riding of Yorkshire (Holmes 1986: 21–2).

The interpretation of this set of findings has been disputed. Speck argued that they showed voter independence and the influence of propaganda, while others suggest that they reveal some voter independence but also a large measure of deference to landed interests (Speck, Gray and Hopkinson 1975; Holmes 1993: 325–6; Landau 1979; Baskerville, Adman and Beedham 1993; Clark 1985: 15–26). The work of the History of Parliament, which includes surveys of boroughs as well as counties, suggests that many voters could be induced for many reasons and pressures to follow a line, but that there was significant scope for electoral independence, partisan loyalty and widespread participation, even by non-voters in the electoral controversies, especially in the larger freemen constituencies. Only one English county, Dorset, and a dozen English boroughs failed to experience a contested election between 1690 and 1714. Well over a third of all elections were contested and many more were disputed before polling day (Hayton 2002).

The history of parliament is, however, only one dimension of research into the development of the post-revolutionary state, and another approach again questions our definition of politics. The state has recently attracted interest from social historians interested in exploring the connection between the social and the political. There was thus a politics of the parish as much as of parliament, and a politics of poor relief, a politics of neighbourliness, a politics of custom and a politics of gender relations (some of these are explored in Davison et al. 1992; Harris 2001). This redefinition of politics can be invigorating, though the best investigators of 'party' have long been interested in the social, cultural and economic dimensions of partisan rivalries (see, for example, De Krey 1985; Jenkins 1983; Holmes 1981). The integration of political and social history seems a very fruitful approach, particularly from a local perspective and in the light of the expansion of the state and financial and commercial sectors after 1689 (see Brooks 1987; Jones 1988; Gauci 2001; Grassby 1995). The state was also more visible on a mental horizon. Linda Colley (1992) has thus charted the 'growth' of national identity around warfare, popular militarism, Protestantism, commerce, the power of parliament and monarchy, and the closer integration of England and Scotland. She begins her analysis of national identity in 1707, with the Act of Union with Scotland, and although the analysis is developed over the following century and more, some of the characteristics were already present by 1714, enhanced by the politics of war. Political developments after 1689 appear to have strengthened not weakened the state. As we have seen, it was the growth of the resources at the disposal of the crown and government, and which might be used to corrupt electors and representatives, that alarmed some contemporaries.

Oppositional politics could thus take different forms. It could be articulated in a language that stressed the danger to the church or to toleration, but it could also stress the corruption of liberty from court power, corruption introduced by the armed forces, the monied men, electoral manipulation, placemen and court lackeys. The latter idiom is the political vocabulary explored by John Pocock, who sees the employment of terms such as 'virtue', 'honesty' and 'corruption' as offering a language through which opposition carried conviction. 'Politics' in this sense is about how people express and conceive concepts. Yet Pocock's analysis is at its weakest for the period 1689–1714 when there was no fixed 'opposition', for the Whigs and Tories moved in and out of power. Thus during the early 1690s, and then for the early and later years of Queen Anne's reign, the Tories were uppermost; but for the mid-1690s, the mid-1700s and then from 1714 onwards the Whigs were predominant. In the localities the patterns might be similar, but in some boroughs 'power' might lie with the Whigs or Tories, depending on circumstances. Employing a purely 'oppositional rhetoric' was therefore rather a limiting exercise for any party to adopt. If so, we need also to examine how the language of party or partisan politics worked. Paul Halliday (1998: 11) has urged that 'to understand a transformation of political culture, to understand how politics evolved, we need to understand how people talked about politics'. Halliday chose to study the transition from consensual to publicly competitive politics through an examination of the development of legal procedures which arbitrated local contests and hence contained division within a peaceful but dynamic polity. The second half of this chapter will explore some of the ways in which people talked about politics outside the courts and how language itself was one of the principal concerns of partisan politics.

The Politics of Language

Chapter 5 has already explored the expansion of the press and the development of public opinion. But it is worth reminding ourselves that the coffee house and the club were essentially developments of the later Stuart period, for both were sites where the politics of language were important. They were arenas of public discussion about public affairs in part because of the prevalence of a vibrant print culture. While it is true that the number of pamphlets and periodicals during 1640–60 had been unprecedented, pre-publication censorship only finally disappeared from the statute book in 1695. Although regulatory Bills were introduced in parliament thereafter, they all failed. When press legislation was passed in 1712, it was to make money out of the press by taxing it, rather than banning it, and politicians now sought to use, rather than constrain, print for advantage. The press stoked as well as fed a demand and polemical debate now had strong commercial connotations. To be sure, politics, news and trade had always been closely intertwined, but the expansion of overseas markets in the 1680s and the subsequent long war with France meant that news about the conduct of the war had commercial as well as political value. These factors, together with the expansion of the state, and in particular the development of stock investments in the 1690s, amounted to what Jürgen Habermas describes as formation of the 'public sphere'. This was an unprecedentedly civil sphere, revolving around people's public use and expression of their reason, though Habermas might be criticized for idealizing the latter element, for, as we shall see, it was the irrationality and credulity of the public that many commentators lamented.

An additional reason for stressing the importance of language to politics in the period 1689–1714 has to do with the struggle over electoral representation. How a candidate was represented orally or in print affected his credit, reputation and integrity; and how national politics was represented to the constituencies could affect the readiness to turn out to vote or to marshall an electoral 'interest'. The more intense the electoral struggle, the more intense the linguistic one became. For example, in January 1701 sixteen or seventeen Tory Worcestershire gentlemen met together to give their backing to Sir John Pakington. Their Whig opponent, William Walsh, duly spread word that Pakington's selection was an attempt to exclude the freeholders from their birthright. The Tory meeting 'was represented as a strange infringement of the rights and liberties of the freeholders'. This allegation 'made such an impression upon the minds of many as raised a surprising interest for' Walsh, who declared 'he would always stand and fall by the votes of the gentlemen and freeholders' (Glos. RO, Hardwicke Court mss, Lloyd pprs. Box 74, no.18, 'Some observations ... against the next election, which is to be 5 August 1702'). Before the next election in November 1701 Pakington was forced to issue a public statement:

> It being my misfortune to be greatly misrepresented in a libel put up in this place, before the last election by the disingenuous practice of a particular gent[leman], I thought it my duty to undeceive my country and the freeholders and do myself justice. The allegations in that bill were altogether false, for I never attempted anything with the least design of prejudicing the rights of the freeholders ... The happy constitution of England hath always been my care to preserve, and particularly the privileges of the freeholders. (Beaufort mss at Badminton, Coventry pprs. 'Sir John Pakington's answer to the papers put up against him')

Walsh left an answering 'paper' in a coffee house but Pakington scraped a victory at the polls. The incident is instructive. A struggle had occurred over concepts of representation – election or selection? – through a contest over the alleged misrepresentations in a 'libel' produced by the Whigs. And this struggle had pushed Pakington into talking a language of voters' rights and constitutional rectitude. Politics in this case was a contest in which words played an important part.

We should, then, pay close attention to how words were used. The sloganized power of 'the church' has already been noted; and the development of national identity, the state and party allegiance also partly depended on a descriptive as well as an empirical process. Party, particularly in an age of rudimentary organization, was an 'imagined community'. Like national identity, party identity can be forged by how men described themselves and others. Whigs and Tories, Churchmen and Dissenters, coalesced for a host of personal, social, religious and civil reasons; but also because those reasons were expressed and labelled in recognizable ways. The words and terms used mattered enormously. Thus to call a programme 'patriotic' imbued it with positive credentials; but to dismiss it as 'self-interested' rendered it suspect. The

Whigs might be described as defenders of liberties working for the public good or, as the Tories said in the texts of numerous addresses promoted in 1710, bloodthirsty, republican atheists who wanted the war to continue in order to advance their own private interest. A Tory might be labelled a true churchman, or a bigoted hypocrite. Someone who tried to avoid party might be described as honest and independent, or as someone who lacked the courage of his convictions.

Even so, to say that politics was a linguistic struggle may not tell us very much for two reasons. First, a linguistic contest can take many forms. It can be a struggle *over* language – over the meaning or definition of certain words. Or it can be a struggle *about* language – about the abuse of words (such as using words incorrectly in order to insinuate something or lie). Or it might be a struggle *through* language – about the way of talking, the overarching style. Of course, it might also be a combination of these, not least because a contest about language often involves a struggle over the definition of words. But if we claim a linguistic struggle we will need to be clear about which form or forms it took. I argue that it concerned all three. A second objection might be, isn't all politics a linguistic struggle? Isn't that what politics is? The second of these questions is fundamental to the case that Britain's first political parties are peculiarly interesting. To be sure, all politics is about contest through and about language; but what makes the period 1689–1714 distinctive is the combination of changes in the means and modes of communication with very frequent electioneering. This conjunction heightened anxieties, which were not in themselves new, in new ways, since the electoral contest seemed more and more important and yet more and more about misrepresentation. The abuse of words seemed to have become what party politics was about.

The Contest Over Language

We now need to examine what form of struggle took place. It will be argued that it was one over, about and through language. It was over language because words and terms came to mean different things to different sides. This is illustrated by the debate over the Tory addresses promoted in the summer of 1710 to try to persuade the queen to dissolve the parliament that had impeached Dr Henry Sacheverell, the High Church cleric whose trial had reignited controversy over the legitimacy of the revolution of 1689. Both sides published guides to how key words should be defined, using the terminology of dictionaries when they described 'hard words'. The Whig cleric Benjamin Hoadly published *The True Genuine Tory-Addresses to which is added an explanation of some hard terms now in use: for the information of all such as read or subscribe addresses* (1710), which first satirized a Tory address and then picked out key terms such as 'antimonarchical principles', 'hereditary right' and 'republican principles' in order to define them. A Tory reply, by Sacheverell's ally Joseph Trapp, was immediately issued as *The True Genuine Modern Whigg-Address, to which is added an explanation of some hard terms now in use: for the information of all such as read or subscribe addresses* (1710), offering alternative explanations for the same terms. Thus while Hoadly asserted that Tories really meant men who disliked absolute government when they talked of 'anti-monarchical men', Trapp claimed the Tories meant 'such persons as are against the government of a single person'. Hoadly again questioned the Tories' definitions of key terms in *Queries of the Utmost Importance,* in which he asked if, by hereditary right, did they mean something different from parliamentary right, and if not 'why do they abuse the world with distinctions, where there is no difference; why do they use these very words, in order to represent their brethren as persons of pernicious principles when they themselves are forced to own the same?' If, however, the Tories meant hereditary right in a Jacobite sense, 'are not those who understand not their secrets, as certainly misled and perverted by these words, which they honestly understand in the sense in which they have always been used?'

The meaning of many key words was contested and this became important because the truth of any claim became hard to discern. Perhaps the best examples are the two words used to describe the parties, Whig and Tory. By 1699 Whig and Tory had found their way into *A New Dictionary of the Terms Ancient and Modern of the Canting Crew* (1699), which defined Tories as 'zealous sticklers for the prerogative and rights of the Crown in behalf of the monarchy' and the Whigs as 'the republicans or commonwealthsmen, under the name of patriots and lovers of property'. Yet two years later a Whig pamphlet published to advise the electorate how to vote, *The Candidates Try'd* (1701), made a strict equation between Tories and Jacobites to counter the suggestion that the Tories had 'renounced their former Tory principles, even so far as to run into the other extreme, and that instead of submitting all things to royal will and pleasure they are now for depressing the prerogative and exalting the power of the Commons . . . and that they have sufficiently discovered their love for their country by their zeal against corruptions, and mismanagements of the public revenue'. But the greatest controversy lay over the word 'Whig', for the apparent readiness of Whig leaders such as Somers, Montagu and Wharton to enhance the power of the court created real problems of definition. Was a true Whig an 'old Whig', whose origins might be traced back to the opposition to the court in the 1680s, or was he a 'modern Whig', who was ready to embrace the court? Defoe suggested an answer to this distinction in another piece of advice to voters in 1708: 'it is not the Whigs that are chang'd but the Courts . . . so that nothing can be more ridiculous than to hear some men [i.e. the Tories], who serv'd other courts in all that was done wrong, now call themselves the country party for distressing this court that acts right' (*Advice to the Electors of Great Britain*). But to many other observers the definition of a Whig did seem to have shifted. As the fictional Thomas Double put it in a satire, the Whigs 'are not of the same principles we were twenty years ago; we have scarce any thing left but the name of an old whig; such a strange Medley we are compoz'd of, a conjurer woul'd be puzzled to know whether we were men or monsters' (*The True Picture of a Modern Whig reviv'd set forth in a Third Dialogue between Whiglove and Double at Tom's Coffee-house*, 1707). Shifts in the nature of the parties thus led to contests about the meaning of the party labels. This passion for labelling and the simultaneous uncertainty about definitions help explain a complexity of nomenclature that some students of the period find bewildering. The reassurance is that contemporaries often found it hard to explain too, or rather sought to woo and convince voters by playing with the definitions to suit political needs. The party struggle thus partly revolved around a contest over the definition of the very terms that historians use to analyse the period. Once we recognize that the problem with definition was part of the linguistic party struggle then it ceases to be so daunting and becomes far more interesting.

The Contest About Language

It is easy to see how this contest over terms could become one about the abuse of language. The diversity of definition was, it appeared, not the result of accident, but of design. Tom Double was such a literary success when he first appeared in 1701 because he personified the suggestion that outward appearances were wicked deceptions, that inner truth was being deceitfully disguised through the abuse of language. Thus in 1707 Double was depicted as the election agent for Wharton in Yorks, where the Whigs sought to defeat Lord Down in a by-election. Double proclaimed: 'I have hir'd men in all the populous towns of the county, to cry down my lord D— for a persecuting High-Church-man; or if that won't take, to call him a Perkenite, a Jacobite, a Black-List-man, or any other scoundrel names, to render him odious to the people' (*The True Picture*). Labelling was a tool that could be used to ruin the reputation of a candidate or to smear a whole party. The abuse of language was thus part of the political contest. We can see this clearly by looking at the invocation of the term 'moderate' or 'moderation'. Double vilified his opponent with names; but at the same time his preferred candidate was 'to be cry'd up for a pretty moderate gentleman of the Church as by Law establish'd, that loves the Q[uee]n and the M[inist]ry, and will drink a health to her Highness'. The Godolphin–Marlborough–Harley ministry at the time quite explicitly invoked a language of 'moderation'. Yet this moderation was merely a cover, High Church critics warned. Thus Samuel Grascome's *The Mask of Moderation pull'd off* (1704) answered 'a late poisonous pamphlet' by James Owen, *Moderation still a Virtue*, which Grascome thought 'endeavours by nauseous repetitions, impertinent additions and other little arts to delude all and impose upon mankind as well as himself'. Owen had defined moderation as forbearance in things not essential in religion. But, Grascome thundered, 'this is not moderation; but what he would have to be moderation'. Grascome therefore sought to define moderation correctly, 'for there are many things colour'd with the specious name of moderation, which in the issue prove not only encouragements but incentives to wickedness'. The attack on 'moderation' thus became part of the High Church struggle to represent the church as being in danger. *The Memorial of the Church of England* (1705) distinguished between 'that moderation which is a virtue, and a part of the moral duty of every Christian, and the moderation so fashionable, and so much recommended of late, which is nothing but lukewarmness in religion, and indifference in every thing that relates to the service of God, and the interest of his Church'. The contest over the word's meaning and use had become a party matter.

Contemporaries were very sensitive to the idea that language was being abused for party ends. We can find evidence of this at a theoretical level in Locke's *Essay Concerning Human Understanding*, which devoted one of its four parts to 'Words' and suggested that men erred when words were abused. A similar anxiety is evident in the marquis of Halifax's maxim that 'Names to men of sense are no more than fig-leaves; to the generality they are thick coverings that hide the nature of things from them. Fools turn good-sense upon its head, they take names for things and things only for names' (Ralegh 1912: 253). But such concerns also permeated the everyday print exchange of party polemic. Thus Grascome's reflections on how the Low churchmen played with the word 'moderation' led him to conclude that the party debates were fostering an irrational rather than a rational public sphere:

> as in a civil government, when the mad or the mob prevail, that which ought to be the governing part is enfeebled or render'd insignificant, and all things run into disorder and confusion; so in the microcosm, when the affections and passions, humours, discontents, false interests and the like have combin'd in a conspiracy against the governing part of the mind, immediately the understanding is confounded, the will hurry'd away and men run headlong into all irregularities and absurdities. (*Mask of Moderation pull'd off*)

Yet Grascome wrote, he said, in order 'that the plague may not become universal'. The conviction that the poison of rival rhetorics needed an antidote was commonplace. Ironically, of course, the recourse to print to provide such an antidote only meant it more likely that the cycle of reply and counter-response would be perpetuated in an ongoing dialogue.

The public, dialogic nature of politics therefore created an irony. The more intense and vitriolic the political struggle became, the more the representative system relied on a series of misrepresentations. Labels, stereotypes, defamations, slanders, libels, distortions, rumours, half-truths and lies all became standard tools to smear opponents. As the general election of 1713 loomed, Thomas Rawlins, a Norfolk parson, lamented that 'when the choice of persons of the highest merit is necessary for the publick service, what crude and romantick stories are usually spread? What ludicrous and senseless reflections generally made upon candidates of the brightest characters...?' (*Truth and Sincerity Recommended in a sermon against lying*, 1713). Lying, he complained, undermined all discourse and ultimately made man's rational faculty useless. Lying, complained another cleric, Charles Brent, was 'the principal slight and artifice of a cunning man, the tongue and head and heart of a politician'. Claims to speak truth, of impartiality and honesty were thus routine (and marketable) means of establishing the credit of party discourse. They were, of course, also necessary to any system of election rather than selection of candidates.

The Contest Through Language

The abuse of language coincided with abusive language. Persuasiveness in publicly competitive politics, in an arena where the public was not even defined by those who could read but by those who were influenced by public political discourse, meant that securing votes and allegiance was both vital and difficult. This increased the pressures on rhetorical techniques; and it fostered the mastery of scorn, of irony, of detraction, of calumny and of railing. This was often called 'Billingsgate rhetoric', the language of the foul-mouthed market fishwives. This was hardly a new phenomenon, but it did seem to be exacerbated by the rage of publicly competitive rivalries. Printed electoral advice thus attacked the immoderate prints, whose 'gaping admirers sup up the juice of envenom'd Ink as a twist to their coffee'. This was 'an age which super abounds with scandal' and was full of 'scurrilous Billingsgate language' which aimed to raise the mob's fears and 'level the fury of the mob at those particular persons whom they had most mind to destroy' (*Considerations relating to our choice and the qualifications of our members of Parliament*, 1711; *England's Enemies Exposed*, 1701; *The*

Source of Our present fears discovered, 1703). The Whig Arthur Mainwaring accused Jonathan Swift of having been employed to write scandal in his *Examiner*,

> having an inexhaustible fund of malice and calumny, which, according as he was paid, he wou'd right or wrong apply to any subject; and if his image were foul enough, he wou'd not care for the resemblance; but like a common dauber wou'd write the name of his sign, which wou'd serve as well as the likeness with the rabble for whom he was to work. (*Medley*, 12 February 1711)

Yet Swift also accused Mainwaring of writing Billingsgate, prompting Mainwaring to wonder 'how come any words to be Billingsgate in my papers and to be courtly and ministerial in his?' (*Medley*, 18 June 1711). Abusive or scandalous language was thus not the preserve of one party and both sides accused each other of employing it. It too was part of the political struggle.

One response to 'Billingsgate' or the charge of scandal-mongering was merely to invoke the claim to be speaking truthfully and plainly. Thus *The Source of Our present fears discovered* (1703) suggested that

> everything written is either true or false and accordingly ought to meet with encouragement or condemnation. What is true can't be scandalous. Because the word scandal, in the sense of our law, implies a wrongful and generally a malicious aspersion. What is true cannot be the cause of misunderstandings; because, if a right representation be not so understood, it ought to be imputed to want of understanding, and not call'd misunderstanding. For a right representation can't be the cause of a misunderstanding.

But another, by no means mutually exclusive, response was to accuse a political antagonist of being impolite. The moderation that was itself a contested term also became a contested ideal, a way of arguing that could circumscribe the violence of political passion. The history of politeness stretches back beyond 1689; but cultural historians and those interested in the history of political thought have noted a shift in the overall style of language in the later Stuart period (Klein 1994). The classic example of 'polite discourse' is usually taken to be Joseph Addison's and Richard Steele's periodical *The Spectator*, which began in March 1711. It is no coincidence that this explicit appeal to polite manners and rejection of party zealotry should have been written by two Whigs at a time when the passion of the High churchmen seemed almost uncontainable in the wake of the landslide Tory victory at the polls in late 1710. This is not to say that politeness was a style that merely served the Whig party. Both sides invoked it. But it often had a partisan purpose, to discredit the arguments of a rival by invalidating the whole way in which he or she talked – or rather railed. Thus *A Letter to Mr B— a North Wiltshire Clergyman, relating to an address from that archdeaconry to the Queen* (1710) alleged that an address to the queen in 1710, in favour of passive obedience and non-resistance, had slighted Bishop Burnet and was impolite:

> Now this is what I wou'd represent to you as ungenerous and base. In matters of dispute 'tis unbecoming any man to reflect upon those that happen to differ in their opinions from him; and when men come to that, it gives a shrewd suspicion that the cause is weak . . . where we build our notions upon reason and fairly offer our reasons to examination, 'tis not raillery but reason ought to decide it.

Politeness was an idealized, rational, moderate politics. Lawrence Klein thus sees politeness as a way of talking, a vocabulary of 'key words' such as 'politeness', 'manners', 'character', 'civility' and 'breeding' which came into prominence in the later seventeenth century, especially after 1688. But it was not just formulated by the aristocratic third earl of Shaftesbury; it was hammered out in the everyday practice of politics. It did not end political contest; but it could help contain it within a civil polity.

Conclusion

The fears that language was being abused, that passion was predominating over reason, that the bulk of the nation was being misled, and that an impolite mob was uppermost, all came to a head when riots greeted the new King George I in 1715–16. The repeal of the Triennial Act in 1716 by the Whigs thus becomes explicable even if not perhaps justifiable. The Tory ministry, complained one Whig tract, used 'mobbs, riots and tumults' to keep up the spirit of the crowd against truth and right: 'they thought it their interest to govern by the passions of the crowd'. Such passions pushed out reason: 'all reasons founded upon party only, separate from the good of the publick, are such as ought not to weigh with any one; whenever things are carried to such a height as to be looked upon as good or bad, only because done by such a party a man is engag'd in, 'tis plain the publick must be neglected' (*Second Letter to a Friend in Suffolk occasion'd by a report of repealing the Triennial Act*, 1716). Addison approved of the Septennial Act because, he said, it would 'compose our unnatural feuds and animosities, revive an honest spirit of industry in the nation and cut off frequent occasions of brutal rage and intemperance. In short, as it will make us not only a more safe, a more flourishing and a more happy people, but also a more virtuous people' (*Freeholder*, 27 April 1716). Frequent elections were repeatedly condemned for inverting social order, for promoting foul language, disrespect for social superiors and uncivil feuds. Electioneering had debauched the people, who were now thought of not as the bulwark against tyranny which they had been in 1689, but as the credulous tools of evil conspirators. And the abuse of language had been the way in which the grand conspiracy could work its poison into the nation. Significantly, a tract which examined the speeches made in the House of Commons against the Septennial Act condemned them as lying and impolite. 'Nothing is more useful than for some of our parliamentary orators', the commentator observed, 'to amuse themselves and their auditors with Words only, and *no meaning. Breach of Trust, Privilege of the People, and Danger of the Church*, are indifferently applied to all subjects, and serve on all occasions, where there wants ability to debate closely and pertinently.' And another opposition speech was alleged to have been 'made up of railing without reason, of pure Billingsgate without the least mixture of wit' (*A Second Letter to the right Honourable Robert Walpole ... together with some remarks on four speeches (lately publish'd) against the bill for repealing the Triennial Act; as they were spoken in the house of commons April 24. 1716*, 1716).

This chapter has argued that we need to relate politics to public discourse. By focusing on the language used in later Stuart conflicts, and by relating this to the practice of politics, we can show the importance of party politics in shifting and transforming political culture and practice. Such an approach thus helps us understand how and why change did occur in the later seventeenth and early eighteenth centuries. To be sure, political conflict did not disappear in 1716; but by then Britons had found some solutions to the problem of how diverse opinions could be accommodated within a single polity. Indeed, in this sense party politics were creative. If we try to explain why Britain's state grew in strength at a time when the nation seemed most divided we might conclude that party politics aided rather a crucial process of transformation.

REFERENCES

Baskerville, S., Adman, P. and Beedham, K. 1993: 'The dynamics of landlord influence in English county elections, 1701–1734: the evidence from Cheshire', *Parliamentary History*, 12, 126–42.

Bennett, G. V. 1975: *The Tory Crisis in Church and State, 1688–1730*: Oxford.

Brooks, C. 1987: 'John, first baron Ashburnham and the state, *c*.1688–1710', *Bulletin of the Institute of Historical Research*, 60, 64–79.

Clark, J. C. D. 1985: *English Society 1660–1832*: Cambridge.

Clark, J. C. D. 2000: *English Society 1660–1832*, 2nd edn: Cambridge.

Claydon, T. 1996: *William III and the Godly Revolution*: Cambridge.

Colley, L. 1992: *Britons: Forging the Nation, 1707–1837*: New Haven, CT.

Davison, L. et al. 1992: *Stilling the Grumbling Hive: The Response to Social and Economic Problems in England 1688–1750*: Stroud.

De Krey, G. 1985: *A Fractured Society: The Politics of London in the First Age of Party, 1688–1715*: Oxford.

Dickinson, H. T. 1977: *Liberty and Property: Political Ideology in Eighteenth-Century Britain*: London.

Gauci, P. 2001: *The Politics of Trade: The Overseas Merchant in State and Society, 1660–1720*: Oxford.

Goldie, M. 1980: 'The Revolution of 1689 and the structure of political argument', *Bulletin of Research in the Humanities*, 83.

Grassby, R. 1995: *The Business Community of Seventeenth-Century England*: Cambridge.

Halliday, P. 1998: *Dismembering the Body Politic: Partisan Politics in England's Towns 1650–1730*: Cambridge.

Harris, T. 1993: *Politics Under the Later Stuarts: Party Conflict in a Divided Society 1660–1715*: Harlow.

Harris, T. (ed.) 2001: *The Politics of the Excluded, c.1500–1850*: Basingstoke.

Hayton, D. 1984: 'The "country" interest and the party system, 1689–*c*.1720.' In C. Jones, ed., *Party and Management in Parliament, 1660–1784*: Leicester.

Hayton, D. 2002: 'Introduction.' In E. Cruickshanks, S. Handley and D. Hayton, eds, *The History of Parliament: The House of Commons 1690–1714*, vol. 1: Cambridge.

Holmes, G. 1973: *The Trial of Doctor Sacheverell*: London.

Holmes, G. 1975: *Religion and Party in Late Stuart England*: London.

Holmes, G. 1981: 'The achievement of stability: the social context of politics from the 1680s to the age of Walpole.' In J. Cannon, ed., *The Whig Ascendancy*: London.

Holmes, G. 1986: *Politics, Religion and Society in England, 1679–1742*: London.

Holmes, G. 1987: *Politics in the Age of Anne*, revd edn: London.

Holmes, G. 1993: *The Making of a Great Power: Late Stuart and Early Georgian Britain 1660–1722*: Harlow.

Hoppit, J. 1996: 'Patterns of parliamentary legislation, 1660–1800', *Historical Journal*, 39, 109–31.

Hoppit, J. 2000: *A Land of Liberty? England 1689–1727*: Oxford.

Horwitz, H. 1977: *Parliament Policy and Politics in the Reign of William III*: Manchester.

Hurwich, J. 1977: '"A fanatic town": the political influence of Dissenters in Coventry, 1660–1720', *Midland History*, 4, 15–47.

Jenkins, P. 1983: *The Making of a Ruling Class: The Glamorgan Gentry 1640–1790*: Cambridge.

Jones, D. W. 1988: *War and Economy in the Age of William III and Marlborough*: Oxford.

Kenyon, J. P. 1977: *Revolution Principles: The Politics of Party 1689–1720*: Cambridge.

Klein, L. 1994: *Shaftesbury and the Culture of Politeness*: Cambridge.

Landau, N. 1979: 'Independence, deference and voter participation: the behaviour of the electorate in early eighteenth-century Kent', *Historical Journal*, 22, 561–83.

Monod, P. K. 1989: *Jacobitism and the English People, 1688–1788*: Oxford.

Plumb, J. H. 1967: *The Growth of Political Stability in England, 1675–1725*: London.

Ralegh, W. (ed.) 1912: *The Complete Works of George Savile First Marquess of Halifax*: Oxford.

Rogers, N. 1988: 'Popular Jacobitism in provincial context: eighteenth-century Bristol and Norwich.' In E. Cruickshanks and J. Black, eds, *The Jacobite Challenge*: Edinburgh.

Rose, C. 1991: '"Seminarys-of-faction-and-rebellion": Jacobites, Whigs and the London charity schools, 1716–1724', *Historical Journal*, 34, 831–55 .

Rose, C. 1999: *England in the 1690s: Revolution, Religion, and War*: Oxford.

Scott, J. 2000: *England's Troubles: Seventeenth-Century English Political Instability in European Context*: Cambridge.

Speck, W. 1970: *Tory and Whig: The Struggle in the Constituencies, 1701–1715*: London.

Speck, W., Gray, W. and Hopkinson, R. 1975: 'Computer analysis of poll books: a further report', *Bulletin of the Institute of Historical Research*, 48, 64–90.

FURTHER READING

Ball, T., Farr, J. and Hanson, R. L. (eds) 1989: *Political Innovation and Conceptual Change*: Cambridge.

Colley, L. 1982: *In Defiance of Oligarchy: The Tory Party 1714–60*: Cambridge.

Condren, C. 1997: *Satire, Lies, and Politics: The Case of Dr Arbuthnot*: Basingstoke.

Downie, J. 1979: *Robert Harley and the Press: Propaganda and Public Opinion in the Age of Swift and Defoe*: Cambridge.

Goldie, M. 1980: 'The roots of true Whiggism, 1688–1694', *History of Political Thought*, 1, 195–236.

Gunn, J. A. W. 1969: *Politics and the Public Interest in the Seventeenth Century*: London.

Gunn, J. A. W. (ed.) 1972: *Factions No More: Attitudes to Party in Government and Opposition in Eighteenth-Century England: Extracts from Contemporary Sources*: London.

Klein, L. 1989: 'Liberty, manners and politeness in early eighteenth-century England', *Historical Journal*, 32, 583–604.

Klein, L. 1993: 'The political significance of "politeness" in early eighteenth-century Britain.' In G. Shochet, ed., *Politics, Politeness and Patriotism: Folger Institute Center for the History of British Political Thought Proceedings*, vol. 5: Washington, DC.

Klein, L. 1996: 'Coffee house civility 1660–1714: an aspect of post-courtly culture in England', *Huntington Library Quarterly*, 59, 30–51.

Pocock, J. G. A. 1975: *The Machiavellian Moment: Florentine Political Thought and the Atlantic Republican Tradition*: Princeton, NJ.

Pocock, J. G. A. 1985: *Virtue, Commerce, and History: Essays on Political Thought and History, Chiefly in the Eighteenth Century*: Cambridge. Pocock's ideas are challenged in S. Burtt 1992: *Virtue Transformed: Political Argument in England, 1688–1740*: Cambridge; and see also D. Hayton 1990: 'Moral reform and country politics in the late seventeenth-century House of Commons', *Past and Present*, 128, 48–91.

Rogers, N. 1989: *Whigs and Cities: Popular Politics in the Age of Walpole and Pitt*: Oxford.

Skinner, Q. 1974: 'The principles and practice of opposition: the case of Bolingbroke versus Walpole.' In N. McKendrick, ed., *Historical Perspectives: Studies in English Thought and Society in Honour of J. H. Plumb*: London.

Tully, J. (ed.) 1988: *Meaning and Context: Quentin Skinner and His Critics*: Cambridge.

Weil, R. 1999: *Political Passions: Gender, the Family and Political Argument in England, 1680–1714*: Manchester (places the language of debate in a gendered framework).

Wilson, K. 1995: *The Sense of the People: Politics, culture and Imperialism in England, 1715–85*: Oxford.

Zook, M. 1999: *Radical Whigs and Conspiratorial Politics in Late Stuart England*: Philadelphia, PA.

CHAPTER TWENTY-FOUR

Political Thinking between Restoration and Hanoverian Succession

JUSTIN CHAMPION

Wherefore we must be subject, not because of wrath only, but also for conscience sake.

The landscape of the history of political ideas between the Restoration in the 1660s and the successful accession of the Hanoverian monarchy in the decade after 1714 has traditionally been dominated by the powerful and canonical figures of Thomas Hobbes (d. 1679), John Locke (d. 1704) and (perhaps) Sir Robert Filmer. Commonly regarded as an extended preface to the stable culture of the eighteenth-century constitution, when the themes of 'liberty' and 'property' were ascendant over those of hierarchy and order, there has been very little attempt to contextualize and examine the dense fabric of what should be called 'political theology', rather than simply political thought, in the period. One of the central points that this chapter will attempt to reinforce is the persisting power of religious, theological and (perhaps most importantly) ecclesiological arguments. Still at the core of conceptions of the nature and authority of political institutions and principle were the prescriptions revealed to man by God in the form of holy scripture. The fundamental injunction remained that of Romans 13: obey the powers that be. As well as reinforcing the central idea of subordination to established regal authority, and the essential divinity of that authority, the harmonious relationship between church and state – between bishop and king – was a foundational tenet of political theory. Consequently any breach of social or political order or threat to the institutions that defined theological orthodoxy was perceived as seditious.

'Obey the powers that be': Defending Orthodoxy and Order in the Restoration

As a number of historians have underscored, the fundamental understanding of society and politics was hierarchical and divine. This could most effectively be described as a politics of subordination: it applied equally well in a civil and religious context. Priests, especially those of the recently (providentially) restored Church of England, preached true politics. As Robert Nelson put it succinctly in his popular handbook of the festivals and fasts of the Anglican religion, 'the good of the state is hereby more secured, in those instructions men receive from the Ministers of God, in the necessary Duties of Obedience, Justice and Fidelity' (Nelson 1795: 483). Or as the Book of Common Prayer, re-established in 1662, enjoined: every child must learn 'to honour and obey the King, and all that are put in authority under him'. The good Christian must submit to all 'governors, teachers, spiritual pastors and masters' (Waterman 1996: 205). Just as the ecclesiastical polity was the product of Christ's incarnation, so was the civil polity: the significance of the dictum 'no bishop, no king' cannot be too heavily underscored. Priests, then, not only sanctified religion, but politics too. Hierarchy, order and subordination was the dominant form of political ideology, arguably, up until the 1800s. The dictum 'no bishop, no king' carried a high level of political theorizing beneath the apparent clarity of its assertions.

As this chapter will argue, it is possible to recover the dominant ideology from a variety of sometimes ephemeral sources other than the great set pieces of political thought which have formed the canon of theoretical writings commonly studied today. The many sermons, pamphlets and broadsheets written by the unknown and unstudied defenders of orthodoxy and order provide ample evidence that the core theme of Restoration and late Stuart political thought – the divinity of monarchical government and the implied obligation of subordination – was ubiquitous. The tasks of political writers after the restoration of the key institutions of order (bishop and king) in 1660 were to try to annihilate any political legitimacy derived from texts produced during the Commonwealth experiment. The virulence of this pamphlet war can be seen most effectively in the attempts at censoring what were identified as 'dangerous books'.

Roger L'Estrange, licenser to the restored Stationers' Company, defined the moment with the publication of his *Considerations and Proposals in order to the regulation of the Press* (1663), which identified the most subversive of the 'treasonous and seditious pamphlets'. L'Estrange's argument was simple: by extracting seditious passages from contemporary tracts he intended to establish the necessity of regulation. The spirit of malice, hypocrisy and error conjured up in the 'late rebellion' still reigned. Over a hundred titles had been published (he estimated some 30,000 copies); at least a third of these were so-called farewell sermons delivered by ejected ministers which viciously charged both church and king with 'an inclination to popery'. When plotting was still rife and the government was fragile, such texts, directed at the 'common people', were regarded as virtual calls to arms, 'to put swords in their Hands, and to engage them in a direct rebellion'.

L'Estrange identified a set of subversive ideas – the obligation of the covenant, the sovereignty of the people, the continuance of the Long Parliament – that derived from the political discourses of the 1640s and 1650s. As he put it bluntly, 'the books to be supprest are as follows':

> First, all printed papers pressing the murther of the late King. Secondly, all printed justifications of that execrable act. Thirdly, all treatises denying his majesties title to the crown of England. Fourthly, all libels against the person of his sacred Majesty, his blessed Father, or the Royal Family. Fifthly, all discourses manifestly tending to stir up the people against the established government. Sixthly, all positions terminating in this treasonable conclusion, that, His Majesty may be arraign'd, judg'd and executed, by his people.

The precision of the list indicates the persisting fear of republican political arguments. Acknowledging that many of the texts he condemned dated back to the early 1640s (and before), L'Estrange upheld their persisting pernicious nature. The ideological battle being fought in the 1640s was alive and well in the period after the 1660s. Defending the martyred Charles was an essential project for the reconstruction of the authority of the monarchy. To say that the political thinkers and writers of the Restoration were living in the past would not be to accuse them of nostalgia, but of carrying out their intellectual debates on the battlegrounds of political memory. L'Estrange listed the deviant titles along with their printers and useful extracts, sampling their sedition – works like the army's *Remonstrance* (1648), and the periodic *Mercurius Politicus* were named alongside a clutch of libels and treasons. Longer works like Richard Baxter's *Holy Commonwealth* (1659) were condemned with the radical Huguenot resistance text of the sixteenth century (but translated into English in the 1640s), *Vindicae contra tyrannos*, and Milton's *Tenure of Kings and Magistrates* (1649). The message was clear: political sedition was driven by religious dissent. A theme that was reiterated throughout the period.

The conservative response to the continuing perceived threat of disorder in church and state was to reassert the divinity of the status quo. It can be summarized in the title page of a short pamphlet published in the context of the crisis of political authority in 1680: *God and the King: or Monarchy proved from Holy Writ, to be the onley legitimate species of Politick Government, and the only POLITY constituted and appointed by God.* The author (and compiler), Robert Constable MA, dedicated his text to his reverend father, who had provided for his education: designed as a 'brief Collection of the Divine Right of Monarchy', the work reviled the 'phantasied principle of supereminencing the peoples welfare above the kings honour'. The idea that kings were created by 'popular election' was both 'groundless and unreasonable'. Just as kings were sacred and natural rulers, so was Constable's deference to his father: hierarchy and paternalism converged to reinforce principles of natural deference and obedience. As sons obeyed their fathers, so subjects owed obligation to monarchs. In his short pamphlet of some forty pages Constable outlined the central themes of the *de jure divino* account of political government. Traced back to first principle, as established by God at the creation, 'government' by definition implied order and subjection. The notion of a natural chain of hierarchy and subordination manifest in all creation was 'most manifest and particular in the species of rational creatures': Adam was created not only with a rule and dominion over all other creatures in the world, 'but likewise with a monarchical supremacy'. This paternal authority was also regal. Constable contemptuously dismissed any objections which might be drawn from Old Testament history, such as that described in the Book of Samuel which suggested that the people of Israel might have rejected (with divine approval) the monarchy of Saul. Monarchy was continuous from Adam to Christ, although he did not dispute that at certain times to punish the sins and ingratitude of the people God visited 'anarchy' upon Israel. The sacred history of the Old Testament told of usurping traitors – Abimelech, Absalom, Baasha, Zimri, Omri (and more recent history produced the example of Cromwell) – men who were thieves and robbers, who held the title of king not by right and justice, but by conspiracy and deceit.

Constable was concerned to deny the suggestion (again derived from a close reading of biblical history) that the people had some necessary role in anointing kings: the examples of Saul, David and Solomon were the most obvious cases, but those of Jeroboam, Uzziah and Jehoahas had credit too. To deduce such damnable and rebellious consequences and corollaries from sacred history was one of the causes (in Constable's view) of the recent and contemporary crisis of political authority. But men did draw such inferences: first, that although the king was *major universalis* (i.e. more powerful than any one individual) he was *minor universalis* (i.e. subordinate to the collective body of the people); and second, that the people only created their obligation 'by virtue of a stipulation or covenant between himself and the people'. A breach in the trust or terms of this covenant meant that the nation *ad salutem populi* could provide for their own welfare and safety 'either by resistance, deposition, dethronement, or any such means as themselves shall judge'. Constable refuted such opinions by a 'correct' reading of scripture, an interpretation that emphasized that all acts were done by God's approval and providence. When these acts of seemingly popular independence conflicted with divine providence the nations were visited by 'some heavy and sudden judgements'. Such judgements were not confined to the distant past, but also were manifest in the 'horrible sins of rebellion and sacriledge' perpetrated against Charles I. Sin was still sin even if enacted by the whole people rather than a single malefactor. The evidence of the histories of Athens, Lacedemonia and Rome indicated that 'democratical' governments degenerated into 'intestine wars and tragical conflicts' which were only resolved by the re-introduction of monarchy. Birthright and hereditary succession were the sacred antidotes to such specious assertions of covenants and popular sovereignty. Far from being created for the original purpose of the people's welfare, kings were charged with a priority of establishing God's glory and then their own honour. Dealing with the counter-assertion that since the 'Kings honour is subsequent to Gods Glory . . . that when the Kings commands are contrary to Gods, we may resist', Constable insisted that 'we may resist his commands, but not his power'. Kings by definition could simply not do wicked things to their subjects: to resist any acts of a monarch was to resist God, 'who cannot be unjust'. Property, too, as the evidence of the corn of Egypt being tithed by the Pharaoh established, was in the entire control of the king.

Composed in a time of political crisis when memories of the chaos and disorder of the civil wars and catastrophe of the parliamentary execution of Charles I were deliberately invoked and exploited by royalist propagandists, Constable's work was a commonplace and unremarkable, if profoundly robust, defence of *de jure divino* accounts of the powerful political authority of the institution of monarchy. The points to highlight about the nature of the arguments are to be found in the theological dimensions and style of these arguments. Although a lay author, Constable's political thought, like the overwhelming majority of his contemporaries, was driven by the sacred texts of the Old and New Testaments. Grafted onto the fundamentals of a divinely appointed king were more conventional arguments about the absolute nature of legal sovereignty, or the historical rights of conquest, but in essence the political injunctions were straightforward: the king was divine; subjects were bound by conscience to obey.

Priests Preaching Politics

One of the themes that underlay the political thinking of essentially ephemeral works like Constable's was the vilification of religious dissent. Any who claimed rights of conscience against established authority were agents of rebellion and impiety who, under the cloak of religion, engineered political sedition. This bracketing of political and religious deviance was enshrined in the early legislation of the 1660s (known collectively as the Clarendon Code). It was also a staple of the works of a series of clerical authors, who as John Locke put it, beat the 'drum ecclesiastic' vigorously. Peter Heylyn (1600–62), stentorian defender of episcopal authority, royal chaplain, and hagiographer of Archbishop Laud, was a fierce assailant of ungodly Presbyterianism in the 1640s and 1650s. In a series of works from as early as the 1640s like *The Rebells Catechism* (1643), *The stumbling block of disobedience* (1657) and the powerful and reprinted *Aerius Redivivus* (1670, 1672, 1681), Heylyn reviled the disobedient subterfuge of the 'presbyterian' interest. His arguments were simple but powerful. Tracing the origins of political theory of resistance to the theology of Jean Calvin, Heylyn intended to taint all Protestant Dissenters and Nonconformists with the sin of blasphemous insubordination. Especially in *Aerius redivivus*, Heylyn delivered a powerful and detailed analysis of resistance theory, establishing how Calvinist theology exploited a range of classical and pagan sources to construct a semi-republican discourse. The Ephors of Sparta, the Tribunes of Rome and the Demarchi of Athens were neither proper nor legitimate models for the conduct of godly politics. In these series of works, which had a powerful posthumous afterlife, Heylyn laid the conceptual foundations for what could be termed the political theology of Anglican royalism. The point to make about this form of political argument is that it conjured powerful authority because it demanded a primarily religious duty: the background of the awful memories of king-killing and social disorder in the 1640s and 1650s reinforced in a very practical way the dangers and consequences of disobedience.

The fact that powerful churchmen like Heylin saw an intimacy between the rights and powers of the church and state, also riveted this connection, in a very practical way. The pulpit became a compelling instrument for the broadcast of these ideas. The parish priest was one of the most effective political authorities in late Stuart culture. As will be discussed below, the institutions of set-pieced sermons on key days in the political calendar – 30 January (commemorating the execution of Charles I being the most sensitive), 29 May (Restoration Day) or 5 November (Gunpowder Plot) – were one of the most effective forms of disseminating political ideas in the period, communicating with congregations and parish communities orally, but also in the circulation of printed versions of the more popular and valuable sermons, to a broader more 'public' audience. The institutions and authority of the church were deeply bound up in the business of political argument: ecclesiology (or the relationship between church and state, or between believer and subject) was as important as civil and secular arguments about sovereignty and representation.

Importantly, it was also this Anglican royalist connection that contrived the publication of the works of Sir Robert Filmer at the height of the Exclusion Crisis in 1680. Although written much earlier in the century as a reflection of the deeply embedded patriarchal structures of social authority in early seventeenth-century society, famously Filmer's influential book *Patriarcha* was first published in 1680 by the agency of Anglican royalists inspired by the example of Peter Heylyn who had highly valued his friend's work (and indeed an introductory epistle to Filmer's work was written by Heylyn). The example of the powerful bibliographical afterlife of his collected works, published to reinforce royal order against the incipient threat of a second rebellion, is testimony to the continuity of debates in political discourse throughout the second half of the seventeenth century.

Indeed the case of the continuing intellectual purchase of Filmer's work underscores the fact that it would be possible to reconstruct a general map of the contours of political thinking by simply exploring the process of reprinting the important works of earlier decades. Radical Calvinist works of the sixteenth century by figures like Christopher Goodman, John Ponet, John Knox and George Buchanan, who constructed powerful arguments defining the grounds of legitimate resistance to ungodly monarchs as simply injunctions of religious duty, were republished in the 1640s, 1680s and the 1690s. Certainly the evidence of library catalogues shows that there was a wide level of ownership of these classic works right into the eighteenth century. Again the fact that these works were still perceived as having powerful persuasive potential in 1689 as much as 1649 underscores the continuity of political discourse, although not necessarily the continuity of audience or intention. For example, the *Vindicae contra tyrannos* loosely translated in 1648 was understood (if not conceived) as an argument contributing to the regicide. By 1689 it was redeployed as a text defending a particular interpretation of the popular deposition of James II: same text, similar outcomes, but different conceptual arguments. It was not simply the radical works defending the *salus populi* or theories of popular consent that had extended shelf lives – the opposition similarly had a perennial claim on intellectual fashion. So the works of Laud, of Hooker and Heylyn, but most effectively and repeatedly (as we will see below) the *Eikon Basilike* (supposedly) of Charles I, were reprinted for the edification of unborn generations.

The central matter of dispute was then about the nature of obligation. The starting point was that of Romans 13: 'obey the powers that be'. It remained a key injunction of political theology throughout the period. With the restoration of king and bishop in 1660 came a full-blown reassertion of *de jure divino* theories of authority in both church and state. The overwhelming anxieties of the fear of social disorder and religious sectarianism conspired to compromise any attempted defence of what contemporaries called the 'good old cause'. As Cromwell and the regicides were vilified in print and their bodies desecrated in person, one of the key commonplaces of Restoration political theory was the unshakeable conviction that any form of religious, political or social dissent was a fundamental crime against divine order.

After the Revolution

The problems of political thought, then, after the Restoration, were driven by the ideological consequences of the English Revolution: this was a revolution against the established patterns of legitimate government in both church and state. Thus, in one sense the fall, trial and execution of Archbishop William Laud in 1645 was as significant as the 'killing of the king' in 1649. The contemporary view that the chaos of the turbulent years of the 1640s and 1650s had been driven by the insubordination of Protestant Dissenters and republican plotters was powerfully advanced by Thomas Hobbes in his controversial writings of the 1650s and 1670s: *Leviathan* (1651) and *Behemoth* (1679) – works which cast a long pall over the first two decades after 1660. In the first work Hobbes, in attempting to provide a material diagnosis of disorder, and the appropriate remedies, had indicted those civil thinkers who had corrupted the youth with readings from the ancient republican authors. This insight was compounded in the second account, where the role of the self-interested Presbyterians had combined with civil disobedience to provide an ideology corrosive of all order and security. Hobbes's remedial advice, prompted by a combination of his bleak view of human psychology, his reduction of the business of government to that of restraining the anti-social aspirations of most individuals, and his denial of the continuing operation of grace in history, was unpalatable to most contemporary Protestants. For Hobbes, authority was legitimate if it worked; liberty might very reasonably be exchanged for a just measure of protection; in order to work, by necessity, it needed to draw in all sources of power and sovereignty. While his arguments could be exploited by some royalists, keen to refurbish the absolute power of the monarchy, the concomitant insistence that civil sovereignty in all (or indeed any) of its forms also established a superior position over the definition of not only the institutions of the church, but also over the very definition of what was 'true' religion, made his arguments incompatible with the constitution of Anglican royalism.

The phrase 'Godly rule' was then invoked as powerfully by the voice of the Anglican and royalist establishment as by the radical and heterodox. It is not an understatement to suggest that the *de jure divino* account of the 'power of kings' was reinvented in the 1660s against the persisting claims of those interests who still beat the drum of the 'good old cause'. It is sensible to trace this invention back to 1649 and the execution of Charles I. Powerful images of this act of blasphemous desecration were broadcast around the kingdom: the most instrumental device for the projection of the sacral majesty of the Stuart monarchy was the *Eikon Basilike* (1649), a work which exercised tremendous affective power. Indeed the centrality of this book to the formation of a powerful cultural belief in the legitimacy of monarchical rule has been little emphasized in studies of the political ideas of the later seventeenth century. The *Eikon Basilike* was a text with persistent and vibrant cultural power (Madan 1949). Published immediately after the regicide, the work achieved some sixty editions in England, Ireland and abroad in 1649 alone. It was reprinted throughout the remaining part of the seventeenth century, especially at moments when the belief in the divine legitimacy of monarchy required emphasis in the 1660s, 1670s, 1680s and 1690s.

Extracts, verse renderings, imitations and pirated editions supplemented the standard edition. Importantly, the book was prefaced by a frontispiece representing the king as an image of Christ, kneeling before an altar, upon which a crown of thorns and the open Bible lay: the royal brow received divinity from the heavens. This frontispiece, often published separately and distributed as an icon of royal divinity, epitomized the arguments of the text to an audience perhaps unfamiliar with (or unable to read) the printed text (Potter 1989: 161). The visual and imaginative power embedded itself in the political creation of the cult of the royal martyr: the key image that was constructed was the sacred analogy between Charles's and Christ's passion. The parallel between *Christos* and *Carolus* was reinscribed time and time again in the defences of *Eikon Basilike* written by royalists after 1649 (Zwicker 1993: 37–59). Reworking the images of the Davidic monarchy from Psalms, with the typologies of Josiah, Saul and Christ, the *Eikon Basilike* instantiated the scriptural authorization of monarchy. After the Restoration these powerful literary and iconographic images also became embedded as a social practice when the revised Book of Common Prayer incorporated commemoration of Charles's martyrdom as an annual event on 30 January. The second lesson of the Common Prayer for 30 January took Matthew 27, the trial and crucifixion of Christ, as its scriptural theme.

There is evidence to suggest that these days of fasting and humiliation were strictly observed by parts of the community (Stewart 1969). Certainly the sermonizing on 30 January increasingly as the century progressed became an opportunity for recapitulation of the themes of *Eikon Basilike* and Anglican royalism in general. As the only systematic study of the commemorative sermons has argued, after 1670 the January sermon was translated into an instrument of political education, adopting a strident imperative idiom in defence of divine-right theories of government (Randell 1947). The point to be emphasized here is that *Eikon Basilike* was more than simply a book: it was, in the phrase that many modern literary commentators use, a 'holy book of royalist politics' (Zwicker 1993: 37). As we will see below, in the 1690s attacking the authority of *Eikon Basilike* became a key part of the republican attempt to compromise monarchical discourses.

The notion of a sacral monarchy was further reinforced by a series of cultural practices known as the Royal Touch. Both Charles II and his brother James II reinvigorated the ceremony of 'touching'; the latter refurbishing the ritual with additional medieval material in the mid-to-late 1680s. Although it is difficult to derive any subtle political theory from the ceremony beyond the obvious claims of miraculous abilities to cure a minor skin ailment, it is quite clear that the ubiquity of the ceremony, tying as it did the localities with the king, projected powerful representations of the divinity of monarchy right into the core of Restoration society: here was a political theory that produced real effects. This hinterland of political theology was the staple material of the many sermons on 30 January throughout the period.

Writing Against Tyranny and Persecution

Not all wrote in defence of the restored order of kings and priests. Despite the accusations of people like Heylyn and Constable, these oppositional writers were not necessarily republicans. Those who opposed such *de jure divino* arguments, rather than developing anti-monarchical positions, defended their interests by promoting the rights of 'tender' religious conscience. The fact that Charles II, in searching for a platform for social stability, attempted repeatedly (at least up until the early 1670s) to establish some sort of compromise with dissenting communities, meant that the focus of critical hostilities tended to be ecclesiological matters rather than the more obviously constitutional issues of the power of kings or the privileges of parliament. Although, of course, to contemporaries the issues were most likely indistinguishable, because defining the relationship between political authority and private conscience by necessity held implications for the prerogatives of church and state. Once again these discourses were articulated by a myriad of minor figures: ejected clergymen, godly laymen and radical Quaker prophets. To delve into the details of the hundreds of pamphlets produced by these men would be to become submerged in the intricacies of a bewildering range of theological positions upon the strategies the good conscience could adopt in accommodating the dual demands of God and civil society. The point to make is that the impact of 'Anglican royalism' was manifest in the form of penal statutes which established what has been aptly termed a 'persecuting society' (Goldie 1993). It was against this persecution that Dissenters tried to develop an oppositional ideology. By necessity the forms of these arguments were driven by theological anxieties, rather than simply political commitments. Anglican figures, inebriated with absolute conviction that they preserved the one and only line of communication with Christ's true pattern of religious worship, regarded the persecution of dissidents as acts of pious Christian love (citing the impeccable authority of St Augustine). On the other hand, those who suffered (sometimes willingly) saw this persecution as confirmation of the ungodly nature of the established ecclesiastical institutions. The differing dissenting communities adopted different attitudes to the correct form of engagement with such illegitimate government. While some took refuge in the unknown hand of God's providence and counselled caution and a 'waiting upon prophecy', others called for an immediate intervention against the wiles of the popish beast. Just as the fear of dissident subversion underpinned Anglican political arguments, so the 'fear of popery' and the Antichrist shaped and motivated those writers attempting to legitimate their conduct and defend their communities.

It was from these diverse religious contexts that the so-called Country opposition, closely associated with the writings in the 1670s of Andrew Marvell, the 1st earl of Shaftesbury and John Locke, developed a dual attack upon (in the words of one of the famous pamphlets by Andrew Marvell) the 'growth of popery and arbitrary government' that eventually erupted into an explosion of political pamphleteering and polemic during the Exclusion Crisis of 1678–81. Much ink has been spilt on assessing the nature of this constitutional crisis. It still remains an issue of considerable debate whether the successive parliamentary elections, the politicization of the electorate and the popular community beyond, and the royalist *revanche* after the Oxford Parliament were really a potential return to the days of the 1640s. However, the ideological conflict was fought out in traditional terms: Whigs advanced a defence of the rights and liberties of parliament and Protestant conscience, Tories defended the *de jure* claims of the king and the established church. While the Nonconformist cried up the claims of religious conscience, the Anglican episcopacy defended godly order. Just as in the 1640s the political language was drenched in the vocabulary of providence and conspiracy.

As many historians have established, the political crisis did produce radical texts, but perhaps very few new radical arguments. The canonical works of John Locke and Algernon Sidney, as well as the deaths of men like the Protestant apprentice Stephen College and Lord Russell, created a profound tradition of political radicalism which certainly influenced later thinkers, even if it remained submerged to contemporaries. What is clear is that radical discourses failed in the early 1680s and were driven either underground or abroad. The anxiety about social chaos and the strength of political memories recalling the days of the 1640s laid the foundation for a powerful and effective Tory reaction after 1682–3. The strength and authority of this conservative reaction can most effectively be seen in the (almost) untroubled accession of the openly Roman Catholic James II in 1685. The evidence of his coronation and the accompanying iconography of the medal struck in celebration indicates that *de jure divino* assumptions were at the heart of his ambitions. Simply portraying a hand thrust from the heavens holding an imperial diadem (the crown of England), the legend around the coin read: 'A. Militari. AD REGIAM' – from a military crown to an imperial one. As the sermon by Francis Turner reinforced, the king was not elected by the people but appointed by the Lord: he was a 'living sacred image', a reproduction of his martyred father. As one commentator has succinctly pointed out, the king was represented only by laurels on a cushion: an austere and severe representation 'evoking not the happy workings of providence, but the abstract principle of authority and right' (Edie 1990).

Turning from the well-known works of men like Locke and Sidney, it is possible to explore the theme of those political writers who defended 'English Liberties' in a more practical manner. The career of Henry Care (1646–88) provides a useful case study. He earned his radical reputation by the pungency of his pamphleteering campaign against the succession of the Roman Catholic, James duke of York between 1679 and 1683, but when James came to the throne in 1685 Care was to be at the forefront of the campaign to defend the king's policy of establishing a liberty of conscience. Care's radical credentials were excellent: a member of the semi-republican Green Ribbon Club, his weekly *Pacquet of Advice* was prohibited temporarily by the state for its virulence against 'popery' and for 'writing too sharply against the government' in 1680. By 1687 Care was writing with equal vigour in defence of James II's policy of indulgence. His weekly newsletter *Public Occurrences Truly Stated* advertised the benign qualities of the Jacobean regime, defending axioms such as 'no man (keeping within the bounds of the law morall) ought to suffer in his civil rights for his opinions in matters of religion' (Care 1688).

The theme that links these two apparently incompatible positions was Care's commitment to arguments that upheld the toleration of dissident religions. This should serve to remind us that politics and religion were implicitly connected. The mistaken accusation of time-serving hypocrisy originates in a misunderstanding of the relationship between authority and conscience in his polemic. Like many radicals of his time, Care's primary allegiance was to the liberty of religious belief: his political thought was driven by this commitment. Thus his earlier opposition to the succession of James, duke of York was motivated by the belief that as king he would establish a persecuting regime. Care's indictment of 'popish' authority was not because it was theologically insupportable (although he undoubtedly thought Roman Catholic theology was corrupt and mistaken), but because it imposed upon tender conscience.

Again, like many other contemporaries Care's political hostility towards 'popery' was directed not just at the Roman Catholic Church, but also at the intolerance of the Church of England. The prelacy and persecution conducted by the Church of England, under the rubrics of the Clarendon Code, were as 'popish' as Roman Catholicism. Any who claimed the legitimacy of establishing 'an unlawful hierarchy over the consciences of their brethren' were corrupt (Care 1682a). Care believed that liberty of conscience was right because, as he wrote, 'all mortals are full of mistakes, especially in the business of religion, and since there is no such thing as infallibility on earth, why all this bitterness and persecution?' (Care 1682b). Since no authority, political or religious, could be confident that it understood the form of true religion, so each conscience must have an equal ability to find its own beliefs. To punish conscience for sincere belief was unjust, irrational and ungodly. The primacy of this ethical defence of liberty of conscience meant Care was willing to defend any political authority that set out to achieve toleration. This is an important point to help us acknowledge that a commitment to political ideals and values could very rarely escape a prior allegiance to religious principles.

Care's contribution was not merely one that proposed a theoretical defence of the rights of conscience; importantly, he also represents a more practical response to the problem of persecution by law. It was ultimately this pragmatic advice that was to be more effectual than many speculations about the nature of the constitution or the powers of kings. Drawing from his ethical condemnation of intolerance, Care had argued from the early 1680s that the penal statutes were unjust: when James II issued his Declarations of Indulgence in 1687 (and again in 1688) suspending the penalties and establishing a *de facto* toleration, Care defended the morality and indeed legality of the sovereign's actions. Put simply, he argued that the rights of sovereignty in ecclesiastical affairs legitimated the suspensions. In effect he turned the royal supremacy against the advocates of persecution. Once again authority was used to reinforce rather than destroy rights of conscience. Similarly Care defended the exercise of regal jurisdiction in the creation of legal commissions to investigate the actions of the clerical persecutors (Goldie 1993).

This sort of political thinking was practical, contrived to resolve how could (or should) dissidents behave when confronted with persecutors. Attention has been paid in historical writings to the strategies that radical sectarians like the Quakers made, but the example of Care's writings in the 1680s suggests that such forms of engagements with the processes and procedures of the law were far more mainstream. In a number of pamphlets and advice books Care defended *English Liberties* (the title of one of his more successful, and repeatedly reprinted, works, first published in 1680). Little scholarly attention has been paid to these texts, although the first, *English Liberties*, was perennially popular and reprinted later in the seventeenth and eighteenth centuries in both England and America. It might be possible to argue that it was a more influential text in the first instance than the much more famous political writings of Locke. These works were handbooks of advice for the preservation of civil and religious liberties. Written for the 'reader's information', the books were intended to give practical advice on how dissidents might react to the legal charges and judicial procedures that they suffered. *English Liberties* was composed to defend the 'lives, liberties and estates' of the nation. Much of the first half of the book involved reprinting 'magna charta, the petition of right, the *habeas corpus* act; and divers other most useful statutes'. Central to his argument was the claim that the law and correct judicial procedure were the main preservatives of liberty. Care went into detail about the functioning of important processes such as habeas corpus. In the second part of the text he presented similar advice on how to construct legal defences against the many ecclesiastical laws that compromised conscience.

Once again political thinking was conducted in an ecclesiological idiom. In many other works Care developed a strategy for how the conscientious dissident might engage and oppose the threat of legal persecution by gaining knowledge about the function of the law. He was not alone, especially in targeting the ecclesiastical courts. There is evidence that the ecclesiastical courts had been reinvigorated by the Anglican interests as an effective way of punishing dissidents. Imprisonment under the various canon law writs was not subject to the usual counter-pleas of habeas corpus: the imprisoned could be incarcerated until they submitted to the ecclesiastical authorities.

The point to be made here is that this sort of political thinking and writing had profoundly practical objectives.

After the Glorious Revolution

Issues of the nature of monarchy, the powers of parliament and the relationship between church and state (especially the connections between conscience and citizenship) remained unresolved after the second crisis of Stuart government in the late 1680s, which saw James II toppled by an Anglican coup. Contrary to the commonplace historical narrative, the Glorious Revolution of 1688–9 and the consequent constitutional legislation did not see the creation of the modern democratic state. Although historians for many decades have proudly invoked the name and reputation of John Locke as apologist and theorist of a pluralist, tolerant and political theory, more recently some agreement has been contrived to underscore the marginality of his contribution. John Locke's two treatises on government, published in 1690, were composed for the much more radical circumstances of guerrilla war against the popery and arbitrary government of Charles II. As a consequence of Locke's radical defence of individual rights of resistance, his text was deeply unsuitable for any respectable defence of the Revolution of 1689. While his essays on human understanding and the initially anonymous letters on toleration written in the 1690s projected his reputation as a controversial and potentially heretical writer, his political writings remained beyond the pale. A tradition of radical theorizing that did draw from Lockean sources, as well as republican and other radical Whig writings of the Exclusion period, was circulated in the populist form of a series of pamphlets with the names *Vox Populi, Vox Dei* and *Political Aphorisms* throughout the 1690s and 1700s. The explicit defence of theories of popular resistance as 'true maxims of government' meant that in a political environment driven by anxieties about social disorder as much as tyrannical magistrates, these works were of marginal influence.

Political theory still, between 1689 and 1714 (and far beyond), was dominated by a God-centred view of the duties of subjects, the powers of kings and the rights of the Christian church. The traditional assertion that the triumph of the Williamite monarchy (and the associated dominance of the Whiggish cause and interests) led to a civil and secular theory of political society and government, rather than a theological and divine understanding, is both an inaccurate and over-confident assessment. The relationship between God and political authority and civil institutions was the enduring issue of political thinking.

Initially, thinking about the nature of political society, the limits of civil power, the relationship between subject and sovereign, and between conscience and authority, and ultimately between church and state, was prompted by a drive to understand the meaning of the events of 1688–9: an interpretative battle that continued on deep into the intellectual traditions of the long eighteenth century. Dominated by the political memories of 1649, the initial ideological battle was fought out over the implications of the second fall of the Stuart monarchy. Far from being an obvious problem, the constitutional meaning of the termination of James II's rule was profoundly obscure. 'Deposition', 'abdication', 'providential punishment' and 'rebellion' were all words tentatively associated with the historical fact that James was no longer king in 1689. Whether the rule of William and Mary was sanctioned by rights of conquest, parliamentary legitimacy, the providential hand of God, or convoluted hereditary principle, was the subject of sustained, vocal and increasingly violent controversy. Had James been deposed by the people of England as a tyrant for breach of the duties of kingship? Had he merely deserted the kingdom and been replaced by the next legitimate successor (on the authority of parliament)? Was this deposition an indication of the contract between monarchy and people, or merely an act of an impious, seditious and irreligious minority?

After 1689, clergymen still defended the traditional principles of divine right, passive obedience, and the duties of loyalty and subordination with as much authority and power as those who advanced a more consensual or conventional defence of the co-ordinated powers of kings, parliaments and people. The problems of political thought were still driven by issues of conscience: the immediate task in the summer of 1689 was to justify and resolve the need to take an oath of allegiance to the new regime. Failure to take the oath would result in suspension and deprivation from all civil and ecclesiastical office; but taking the oath would mean compromising oaths taken to James II. Resolving this moral problem drove political writers throughout the period. Allegiance to the legitimate actions of the revolution was still a matter of fierce contestation in 1710, when the failure of the Whig administration to combat the virulent polemic of the High churchman Henry Sacheverell in a show trial resulted in a massive electoral victory for the Tory party.

Rethinking Monarchy

Although the Anglican interest might have been regarded as a lost cause after their role in abandoning James II, there was a powerful and co-ordinated attempt to refurbish the authority of monarchy. Commemoration of Charles I's martyrdom on 30 January became a focal point of increasingly royalist propaganda in the 1690s and 1700s. Set-piece sermons before the monarchy or before the separate Houses of parliament became the platforms for the assertion of loyalty, obedience and humiliation, but also moments when a defence of the 'revolution principles' of 1688–9 had to be insinuated into public discourse (Kenyon 1977). While the mainstream of the established church defended the rights of Protestant liberties and the legitimate royal supremacy, the High Church and the Non-Jurors were more vigorous in attempting to assert the continuing legitimacy of *de jure divino* government in church and state, even if it meant *in extremis* defending the legitimacy of the exiled House of Stuart.

At the other political pole, the 'true Whigs' and 'commonwealthsmen' from the early 1690s produced a variety of works calculated to keep the process of revolution going. The 'good old cause' was reinvented almost single-handedly by the editorial labours of John Toland, a heterodox religious figure close to the circle of Shaftesbury, whose theological writings were burnt in Ireland and prosecuted in London. From the mid-1690s Toland was republishing works by republican authors like Edmund Ludlow, John Milton, Algernon Sidney and James Harrington. Carefully designed with editorial material that made the republican agenda engage with the dangers of a priestly tyranny manifest most obviously in the polemics of the High churchmen, Toland adapted the language of the 1650s to the political circumstances of the 1690s. These adaptations were driven by the particular need to defend the legitimacy of a Protestant succession. Indeed Toland became the major apologist for the Hanoverian succession after 1701 – his *Anglia Libera* (1701) presented to the Electress Sophia alongside the *Act of Settlement*, as a defining statement of her power, reinforced the idea of a limited monarchy established to protect the liberties and consciences of all subjects.

The power of this extensive republication can be seen in the reaction to the edition of Milton's prose works and the accompanying *Life* (1698). For many Anglican contemporaries, Milton 'was the great Anti-monarchist' (Von Maltzahn 1995: 241). As we have seen, these regicide works were burnt at the Restoration and again by decree in Oxford in 1683. His political reputation in the 1690s was unambiguously radical and identified in the public sphere with 1649 and the fall of monarchy. Republican writers such as Charles Blount (1654–93) had liberally used Miltonic writings to attack the licensing act and defend a populist interpretation of the settlement of 1689. For example, the *Tenure of Kings and Magistrates* was adapted to the exigencies of Williamite political discourse as *Pro Populo Adversos Tyrannos*, losing in the process most of the biblical and ecclesiological language originally used by Milton. Perhaps the most politically aggressive republication was Milton's *Eikonoklastes* (1649) at Amsterdam in 1690: a book which anatomized the *Eikon Basilike* of the martyred Charles I. At a moment when Anglican royalists were suffering the ideological shock of having condoned (and perhaps even facilitated) yet another practical denial of the principles of divine right with the departure of James II, the republication of *Eikonoklastes* was provocative (Straka 1962). Unsurprisingly, it generated a prolonged and determinedly hostile response in Tory Anglican quarters concerned to preserve the affective power of *Eikon Basilike*. The commonwealth tradition persisted as a powerful set of textual resources throughout the period.

Evidence of how republican languages reached the mainstream can be seen in the example of the radical Whig churchman William Stephens and his 30 January sermon of 1700. Typically, such a sermon did not ordinarily turn to the language of regicide and resistance. On the set day, however, preaching before the House of Commons, Stephens, far from reinforcing the cult of martyrdom, told the Commons 'that the observation of the day was not intended out of any detestation of his murder, but to be a lesson to other Kings and rulers, how they ought to behave themselves towards their subjects, lest they should come to the same end' (Bray 1952: 359). Omitting the prayer for the king and the royal family, Stephens attempted to invert the commonplace practice: 'God forbid that this day of solemn humiliation should be made use of to flatter princes with notions of arbitrary power'. 'Modern tyranny' was rejected in favour of a republican account of the popular and consensual origins of government. The audience was appalled; not only was the usual vote of thanks denied, but a resolution was passed insisting that the selection of future preachers would only include those of suitable seniority and learning in the church. The invitation to print the sermon by authority of the Commons was also withheld.

As one contemporary, 'who took the said sermon in short-hand', put it, Stephens was an 'indelible Disgrace to the present age'. Publishing his reflections upon the sermon 'for the use of the Calves-head Club in order to their conversion', the gentleman condemned the return to republican principles. The 'seditious Hotheaded Crew of Republicans' were returning to the days of 1642. Stephens, 'chaplain in ordinary to the Calves-Head club', was notorious for preaching 'wholesale' republican principles to his parishioners. Rights of resistance, the 'liberty of the subject' and republican readings of Jethro's advice to Moses were not suitable themes either for the commemoration or for 'a true son of the Church of England' (Anon. 1700: 2, 4–5). For this man such 'republican scriblers' were 'numerous, insolent and formidable'. The texts of the 1640s and 1650s, like Milton's, were being promoted: 'are not that vile man's works now reprinted? And for fear they should not do mischief enough that way, is not an abridgement of the most poisonous passages, put all together in the Account of his life?' Having Milton republished was bad enough, but 'are not Ludlow's letters, and Harrington's Commonwealth of Oceana, in every hand?' Reading groups, 'Calves-Head Clubs of commonwealth men, who nightly assemble to promote that interest', prepared the way for sedition. That Stephens intended such a reception, amongst 'his Party', for his sermon was suggested by the fact that the rights of publication were sold for the considerable sum of £25, before the sermon was preached, contrary to his claims that it was published without his knowledge (Worden 1978: 44). Two editions were printed in 1700, with a third added in 1703, under the pretence that it was preached before the Commons in that year.

Stephens's radical political commitments were notorious: a friend of 'commonwealthsmen' like Trenchard, Shaftesbury and Toland, as well as more controversial men like Anthony Collins, his hostility to tyranny was trenchant. It is one of the paradoxes of the political thinking of the period that such a convinced republican could also be a passionate and committed defender of the Hanoverian succession. Yet by the first Sunday after George I's landing in England in 1714, Stephens delivered a sermon to his longstanding parish in Sutton under the title of 'A second delivery from Popery and Slavery'. Addressed to the 'people of England', Stephens blessed heaven for the safe arrival of his 'Majesty'. George I had 'brought light out of darkness, order out of confusion'. Halting the wicked designs of the 'sons of Belial', George had destroyed 'a barbarous, bloody civil, ceremonial war'. The true majesty of the Hanoverian king was contrasted with the 'base ignoble Phantom of Majesty' which would have established a 'treble tyranny over soul, body and property'. A special providence had delivered England from the 'spirit of slavery'. This 'most Glorious second deliverer' was 'our rightful and lawful King George, the preserver and defender of our faith'. By his 'happy accession to the throne of these Kingdoms', liberty, truth and peace were restored 'to this our Israel'. The almost overwhelming gratitude for the regal succession of George was tempered by the careful distinction between lawful and usurping princes, calculated to legitimate the Hanoverian case against that of the pretended claims of the Stuarts. Rightful princes were 'shepherds to their people' whose authority was cultivated by the 'free consent of those nations which they govern'. Such princes established a 'just liberty' which consisted in the 'preservation and improvement of our reason' and resulted in both prosperity and happiness. The sermon, employing in particular Old Testament language from Deuteronomy, Leviticus and Jeremiah, celebrated liberty and freedom: 'how much God Almighty discourages a slavish spirit'. The 'law of liberty' established a tolerant model of government in church and state, 'a moderation, which included condescention, Toleration, Candour, Ingenuity, and fair-dealing'. A prince that pursued such objectives was both religious and just. Clearly, by 1714, the exigencies of political circumstance had encouraged Stephens to adjust the tone of his republican language of 1700 to accommodate and even recommend the 'majesty' of George I.

It would be wrong to suggest, in the face of the persisting power of this common-wealth ideology, that what we can call Tory political thought was insubstantial. Focused upon the rights of the Christian church as represented in the institutions of an apostolic episcopacy and the rights and powers of Convocation, figures like Francis Atterbury, George Hickes and Charles Leslie engaged what they called the 'false brethren' in head-on debate. In a series of popular works – pamphlets and serial journals, as much as systematic writings – these churchmen constructed a powerful ideology that centred upon the key principle of a descending theory of government. In face of the arguments upholding the liberties of the subjects and their estates, or the rights of tender consciences, men like Atterbury advanced the cry of the 'church in danger' as grounds for reinforcing the principles of orthodoxy, conformity and the patriarchalism of Filmer. The conviction among these men that the traditional pat-terns of government were being subverted by a commonwealth conspiracy can be best explored in the controversial figure of yet another churchman, Benjamin Hoadly, who repeatedly attracted the ire of the Tory press in the 1700s and 1710s. Although a turbulent figure on the radical margins of Whig political affiliations, he was a believ-ing Christian, a conforming minister and a moderate episcopalian.

Hoadly, as contemporaries complained, had a reputation as a fierce defender of 'revolution politicks', making a link between his defence of civil liberties, the attack upon a resurgent *de jure divino* conception of society, and true religion. In fighting against the non-juror political theology, Hoadly was engaging with brother priests: those clergymen who reinvigorated divine-right accounts of monarchy and the church, celebrating the royal touch, defending the reputation of Charles I as a royal martyr in Restoration Day and 30 January sermons, were the butt of Hoadly's writings. Vilifying the Caroline divines who defended an absolutist political theology, Hoadly condemned the 'universal madness of Loyalty (falsely so called)' which caused the people to be 'accounted slaves rather than subjects'. In the 1700s he turned specifically to a consideration of the key scriptural text of Romans 13, attempting to recast the classic Pauline injunction 'to obey the powers that be' into a defence of the legitimacy of the revolution of 1689 by employing the Bucerian reading of the text commonly employed by Calvinist theorists of revolution. Just as tyrannical magis-trates might be removed by popular sovereignty, so the example of Solomon's deposition of Abiathar legitimated the civil deprivation of non-juring bishops. Hoa-dly's political thought, then, engaged directly not only with issues of conscience (defining the limits of obligation), but also with directly ecclesiological matters. In return for his efforts, at different moments in the 1700s, Hoadly was burnt in effigy at various places around the country, alongside his books, by devout Anglicans.

That Hoadly was regarded as a problematic political figure as well as a religious deviant is apparent from the representation of his intellectual sources in powerful and popular prints such as 'The Church in Danger', printed in the context of the Whig trial of the extremist High Church cleric Henry Sacheverell. Provoked in the imme-diate sense by his controversy with Ofspring Blackall, bishop of Exeter, Hoadly is portrayed in the engraved print at his desk. On the writing desk before him he has in draft his reply to Blackhall's sermon which lies discarded at the edge of the table. Haunted by a violent hydra armed with an axe, the foreground shows the Devil making off with the vestments and staff, while trampling under foot an episcopal mitre, the Book of Common Prayer, and church ceremonies (represented by an organ). Underscoring the political heritage determining his theological corruption, Hoadly is seated in front of a bookshelf lined with dangerous books: Gilbert Burnet's *Pastoral Letter*, Toland's *Christianity not Mysterious*, Tindal's *The Rights of the Christian Church*, William Coward's *Second Thoughts*, the full canon of republican political writings – Milton, Harrington and Sidney – as well as Hobbes's *Leviathan*, Bacon's 'on Government', Sexby's *Killing no murder*, Locke's 'of Government' and writings by Baxter. In a variant on the engraving 'Guess at my meaning' published in the same year, although the political library was trimmed of the works of Baxter, Coward, Bacon and Sexby, the mixture of Low Church Christian theology (Tindal, Burnet and Toland) and what might be later termed enlightened 'revolution politicks' is profound. It seems, then, that the central languages of political thought in the 1710s were driven by both a vocabulary and a conceptual tradition derived from the 1650s and afterwards.

Conclusion

To understand the nature of political thought between 1660 and 1714 is not ultimately to engage with the great canonical figures of Thomas Hobbes, Robert Filmer, John Locke, James Harrington and Algernon Sidney. It can be best reconstructed by charting the cut and thrust of political and religious exchange among the minor figures, the priests, the pamphleteers, the editors and re-publishers of the canon of earlier texts. After the revolutions of 1649 and 1689, the overwhelming tenor of political thinking was still driven by theological imperative: preserving godly order was a primary ambition. In contesting the legitimate nature of that godly order – in defining the rights, powers and privileges of church institutions as much as in matters of state power and authority – despite the conceptual innovations of Locke and others, most political thinking remained within the carapace of a God-centred world view. The urgent and compelling issues were preservation of a Protestant succession, a legitimate church settlement, and the liberty of tender conscience. The bugbears of 'popery and arbitrary government' that bedevilled earlier seventeenth-century political thinking persisted into the later eighteenth century.

REFERENCES

Anon. 1700: *Reflections upon Mr Stephens's Sermon*.
Bray, W. (ed.) 1952: *The Diary of John Evelyn*, 2 vols: London.
Care, H. 1682a: *A Perfect Guide to Protestant Dissenters*.
Care, H. 1682b: *A Weekly Pacquet of Advice*, vol. 5, no. 8, 13 October.
Care, H. 1688: *Public Occurrances Truly Stated*, no. 8.
Edie, C. A. 1990: 'The public face of royal ritual: sermons, medals and civic ceremony in later Stuart coronations', *Huntington Library Quarterly*, 53, 311–36.
Goldie, M. A. 1993: 'James II and the dissenters' revenge: the commission of enquiry of 1688', *Bulletin of the Institute of Historical Research*, 66, 55–88.
Kenyon, J. P. 1977: *Revolution Principles: The Politics of Party 1689–1720*: Cambridge.
Madan, F. F. 1949: *A New Bibliography of the Eikon Basilike of King Charles the First with a note on Authorship*, Oxford Bibliographical Society, 3.
Nelson, R. 1795: *A Companion for the Festivals and Fasts of the Church of England*, 27th edn.

Potter, L. 1989: *Secret Rites and Secret Writing: Royalist Literature, 1641–1660*: Cambridge.

Randell, H. W. 1947: 'The rise and fall of a martyrology: sermons on Charles I', *Huntington Library Quarterly*, 10, 135–67.

Stewart, B. S. 1969: 'The cult of the royal martyr', *Church History*, 38, 175–87.

Straka, G. 1962: 'The last phase of divine right theory, 1689–1702', *English Historical Review*, 77, 638–58.

Von Maltzahn, N. 1995: 'The Whig Milton, 1667–1700.' In D. Armitage, A. Himy and Q. Skinner, eds, *Milton and Republicanism*: Cambridge.

Waterman, A. M. C. 1996: 'The nexus between theology and political doctrine.' In K. Haakonssen, ed., *Enlightenment and Religion: Rational Dissent in Eighteenth-Century England*: Cambridge.

Worden, A. B (ed.) 1978: *Edmund Ludlow: A Voyce from the Watchtower*, Camden Society.

Zwicker, S. N. 1993: *Lines of Authority: Politics and English Literary Culture 1649–1689*: Ithaca, NY.

FURTHER READING

Ashcraft, R. and Goldsmith, M. M. 1983: 'Locke, revolution principles and the formation of Whig ideology', *Historical Journal*, 26, 773–800.

Clark, J. C. D. 2000: *English Society 1660–1832*, 2nd edn: Cambridge.

Goldie, M. 1980: 'The roots of true Whiggism, 1688–1694', *History of Political Thought*, 1, 195–236.

Goldie, M. 1983: 'John Locke and Anglican royalism', *Political Studies*, 31, 61–85.

Goldie, M. 1989: 'The religious theory of intolerance.' In N. Tyacke, O. Grell and J. Israel, eds, *From Persecution to Toleration*: Oxford.

Goldie, M. 1991: 'The political thought of the Anglican revolution.' In R. Beddard, ed., *The Revolutions of 1688*: Oxford.

Goldie, M. (ed) 1999: *The Reception of Locke's Politics*, 6 vols: London.

Kenyon, J. P. 1977: *Revolution Principles: The Politics of Party 1689–1720*: Cambridge.

Bibliography

A Letter from an Ejected Member of the House of Commons to Sir Jo: Evelyn 1648: BL, E463/18.

Abbott, W. C. (ed.) 1939: *The Writings and Speeches of Oliver Cromwell*: Oxford.

Abbott, W. C. 1989: *The Writings and Speeches of Oliver Cromwell*, 2nd edn, 4 vols: Oxford.

Achinstein, S. 1994: *Milton and the Revolutionary Reader*: Princeton, NJ.

Adamson, J. 1987: 'The English nobility and the projected settlement of 1647', *Historical Journal*, 30.

Adamson, J. 1989: 'Parliamentary management, men-of-business, and the House of Lords, 1640–49.' In C, Jones, ed., *A Pillar of the Constitution: The House of Lords in British Politics, 1640–1784*: London.

Adamson, J. 1990: 'The baronial context of the English Civil War', *Transactions of the Royal Historical Society*, 5th series, vol. 40 (reprinted in R. Cust and A. Hughes, eds, *The English Civil War*, London, 1997).

Adamson, J. 1991: 'Politics and the nobility in Civil-War England', *Historical Journal*, 34.

Adamson, J. 1995: 'Stafford's ghost: the British context of Viscount Lisle's lieutenancy of Ireland.' In J. Ohlmeyer, ed., *Ireland from Independence to Occupation, 1641–1660*: Cambridge.

Adamson, J. 1997: 'The baronial context of the English Civil War.' In R. Cust and A. Hughes, eds, *The English Civil War*: London.

Adamson, J. 1998: 'The English context of the British Civil Wars', *History Today*, vol. 48.

Adamson, J. (ed.) 1999: *The Princely Courts of Europe: Ritual, Politics and Culture under the Ancien Régime, 1500–1750*: London.

Adamson, J. 2001: 'The frighted junto: perceptions of Ireland and the last attempts at settlement with Charles I.' In J. Peacey, ed., *The Regicides and the Execution of Charles I*: London.

Airs, M. 1995: *The Tudor and Jacobean Country House: A Building History*: Stroud.

Akrigg, G. P. V. (ed.) 1984: *Letters of King James VI and I*: Berkeley, CA.

Albion 1993: 'Debate on the nature of party in Restoration England in the autumn 1993', *Albion*, vol. 25, no. 4.

Albion, G. 1935: *Charles I and the Court of Rome*: London.

Allen, R. 2000: ' "Taking up her daily cross": women and the early Quaker movement in Wales, 1653–1689.' In *Women and Gender in Early Modern Wales*: Cardiff.

Amussen, S. D. 1988: *An Ordered Society: Gender and Class in Early Modern England*: New York.

Amussen, S. D. 1995: 'Punishment, discipline and power: the social meanings of violence in early modern England', *Journal of British Studies*, 34 (January), 1–34.

Amussen, S. D. and Kishlansky, M. A. (eds) 1995: *Political Culture and Cultural Politics in Early Modern England: Essays Presented to David Underdown*: Manchester.

Andrews, K. N. 1984: *Trade, Plunder and Settlement: Maritime Enterprise and the Genesis of the British Empire, 1480–1630*: Cambridge.

Andrews, K. R. 1964: *Elizabethan Privateering: English Privateering during the Spanish War, 1585–1603*: Cambridge.

Andrews, K. R. 1991: *Ships, Money and Politics: Seafaring and Naval Enterprise in the Reign of Charles I*: Cambridge.

Anon. 1700: *Reflections upon Mr Stephens's Sermon*.

Anselment, R. A. 1988: *Loyalist Resolve: Patient Fortitude in the English Civil War*: Newark, DE.

Appleby, A. B. 1978: *Famine in Tudor and Stuart England*: Liverpool.

Appleby, A. B. 1979: 'Grain prices and subsistence crises in England and France, 1590–1740', *Journal of Economic History*, 39, 4 (December), 865–87.

Appleby, J. 1978: *Economic Thought and Ideology in Seventeenth Century England*: Princeton, NJ.

Armitage, D. 1997: 'Making the British Empire: Scotland in the Atlantic world, 1542–1717', *Past and Present*, no. 155, May, 99, 34–63.

Armitage, D. 1999: 'Greater Britain: a useful category of historical analysis?' *American Historical Review*, 104, 427–45.

Armitage, D. 2000: *The Ideological Origins of the British Empire*: Cambridge.

Armitage, D., Himy, A. and Skinner, Q. (eds) 1995: *Milton and Republicanism*: Cambridge.

Asch, R. (ed.) 1993: *The Three Nations – a Common History?* Bochum.

Ashcraft, R. 1986: *Revolutionary Politics and Locke's Two Treatises of Government*: Princeton, NJ.

Ashcraft, R. and Goldsmith, M. M. 1983: 'Locke, revolution principles and the formation of Whig ideology', *Historical Journal*, 26, 773–800.

Ashley, M. P. 1972: *Financial and Commercial Policy Under the Cromwellian Protectorate*, 2nd edn: London.

Ashton, R. 1976: *The English Civil War: Conservatives and Revolution, 1603–41*: London.

Astbury, R. 1978: 'The renewal of the Licensing Act in 1693 and its lapse in 1695', *The Library*, 33, 296–322.

Atherton, I. J. 1999a: *Ambition and Failure in Stuart England: The Career of John, first Viscount Scudamore*: Manchester.

Atherton, I. J. 1999b: 'The itch grown a disease: manuscript transmission of news in the seventeenth century'. In J. Raymond, ed., *News, Newspapers, and Society in Early Modern Britain*: London.

Aylmer, G. (ed.) 1974a: *The Interregnum: The Quest for Settlement*: London.

Aylmer, G. 1974b: *The State's Servants: The Civil Service of the English Republic 1649–1660*: London.

Aylmer, G. (ed.) 1975: *The Levellers in the English Revolution*: Ithaca, NY.

Ball, T., Farr, J. and Hanson, R. L. (eds) 1989: *Political Innovation and Conceptual Change*: Cambridge.

Ball, W. W. R. 1893: *An Essay on Newton's Principia*: London.

Barber, S. 1992: 'Irish undercurrents to the politics of April 1653', *Bulletin of the Institute of Historical Research*, 65, 315–35.

Barber, S. 1995: 'Scotland and Ireland under the Commonwealth: a question of loyalty.' In S. G. Ellis and S. Barber, eds, *Conquest and Union: Fashioning a British State, 1485–1725*: London.

Barber, S. 1998: *Regicide and Republicanism: Politics and Ethics in the English Revolution, 1646–1659*: Edinburgh.

Barber, S. 2000: *A Revolutionary Rogue: Henry Marten and the English Republic*: Stroud.

Barker, H. 1999: *Newspapers, Politics and English Society, 1695–1855*: Harlow.

Barnard, T. C. 1975: *Cromwellian Ireland: English Government and Reform in Ireland, 1649–1660*: Oxford. Reprinted with new introduction, 2000.

Barnard, T. C. 1997: *The English Republic 1649–1660*, 2nd edn: London.

Barnard, T. C. 2000: *Cromwellian Ireland*, 2nd edn: Oxford.

Barnard, T. C. and Fenlon, J. (eds) 2000: *The Dukes of Ormonde, 1610–1745*: Woodbridge.

Baron, S. A. 2001: 'The guises of dissemination in early seventeenth-century England: news in manuscript and print.' In B. Dooley and S. Baron, eds, *The Politics of Information in Early Modern Europe*: London.

Baskerville, S. 1993: *Not Peace but a Sword: The Political Theology of the English Revolution*: London.

Baskerville, S., Adman, P. and Beedham, K. 1993: 'The dynamics of landlord influence in English county elections, 1701–1734: the evidence from Cheshire', *Parliamentary History*, 12, 126–42.

Baumgold, D. 1988: *Hobbes' Political Theory*: Cambridge.

Baxter, S. B. 1966: *William III*: London.

Beckles, H. 1984: 'Plantation production and white "proto-slavery"; white indentured servants and the colonization of the English West Indies, 1624–1645', *The Americas*, 41, 21–45.

Beckles, H. 1986: 'Black men in white skins: the formation of a white proletariat in West Indian slave society', *The Journal of Imperial and Commonwealth History*, 15, 225–47.

Beddard, R. (ed.) 1991: *The Revolutions of 1688*: Oxford.

Beer, B. L. 1982: *Rebellion and Riot: Popular Disorder During the Reign of Edward VI*: Kent, OH.

Bellany, A. 1994: '"Raylinge rymes and vaunting verse": libellous politics in early Stuart England, 1603–1628.' In K. Sharpe and P. Lake, eds, *Culture and Politics in Early Stuart England*: Basingstoke.

Bellany, A. 2002: *The Politics of Court Scandal in Early Modern England: News Culture and the Overbury Affair, 1603–1660*: Cambridge.

Bennett, G. V. 1975: *The Tory Crisis in Church and State, 1688–1730*: Oxford.

Bennett, J. M. 1993: 'Women's history: a study in continuity and change', *Women's History Review*, 2, 2, 173–84.

Bennett, M. 1997: *The Civil Wars in Britain and Ireland, 1638–1651*: Oxford.

Bennett, M. 2000: *The Civil Wars Experienced: Britain and Ireland, 1638–51*: London.

Bergeron, D. M. 1968: 'Harrison, Jonson and Dekker: the magnificent entertainment for King James', *Journal of the Warburg and Courtauld Institutes*, 31, 445–8.

Berry, H. 1997: '"Nice and curious questions": coffee houses and the representation of women in John Dunton's *Athenian Mercury*', *The Seventeenth Century*, 12, 257–76.

Birdwood, G. and Foster, W. (eds) 1893: *The First Letterbook of the East India Company*: London.

Birley, R. 1964: *Printing and Democracy*: London.

Bittereli, U. 1986: *Cultures in Conflict: Encounters between European and Non-European Cultures, 1492–1800*: Stanford, CA.

Black, J. 1992: 'War and the English press during the eighteenth century', *Journal of Newspaper and Periodical History*, 8 (2), 65–70.

Black, J. 2001: *The English Press 1621–1861*: Stroud.

Blackwood, B. 1978: *The Lancashire Gentry in the Great Rebellion*: Manchester.

Bossy, J. 1983: 'Postscript.' In J. Bossy, ed., *Disputes and Settlements: Law and Human Relations in the West*: Cambridge.

Bottigheimer, K. S. 1971: *English Money and Irish Land*: Oxford.

Bourne, H. R. F. 1887: *English Newspapers: Chapters in the History of Journalism*, 2 vols: London.

Boyle, R. 1999–2000: *The Works of Robert Boyle*, 14 vols, ed. M. Hunter and E. B. Davis: London.

Boyle, R. 2001: *The Correspondence of Robert Boyle*, 6 vols, ed. M. Hunter, A. Clericuzio and L. M. Principe: London.

Boynton, L. O. 1967: *The Elizabethan Militia 1558–1638*: London.

Braddick, M. J. 1994: *Parliamentary Taxation in Seventeenth-Century England: Local Administration and Response*, Royal Historical Society, Studies in History, 70: Woodbridge.

Braddick, M. J. 1996: *The Nerves of State: Taxation and the Financing of the English State, 1558–1714*: Manchester.

Braddick, M. J. 2000: *State Formation and Social Change in Early Modern England c.1550–1700*: Cambridge.

Braddick, M. J. and Walter, J. (eds) 2001: *Negotiating Power in Early Modern Society: Order, Hierarchy and Subordination in Britain and Ireland*: Cambridge.

Bradshaw, B. 1998: 'The English Reformation and identity formation in Wales and Ireland.' In B. Bradshaw and P. Roberts, eds, *British Consciousness and Identity: The Making of Britain, 1533–1707*: Cambridge.

Bradshaw, B. and Morrill, J. (eds) 1996: *The British Problem, c.1534–1707: State Formation in the Atlantic Archipelago*: Basingstoke.

Bray, A. 1982: *Homosexuality in Renaissance England*: London.

Bray, A. 1988: *Homosexuality in Renaissance England*, 2nd edn: London.

Bray, A. 1996: 'To be a man in early modern society: the curious case of Michael Wigglesworth', *History Workshop Journal*, 41, 155–65.

Bray, W. (ed.) 1952: *The Diary of John Evelyn*, 2 vols: London.

Brenner, R. 1993: *Merchants and Revolution: Commercial Change, Political Conflict and London's Overseas Traders, 1550–1653*: Cambridge.

Brewer, J. (ed.) 1839: *The Court of King James the First*, 2 vols: London.

Brewer, J. 1989: *The Sinews of Power: War, Money and the English State, 1688–1783*: London.

British Journal for the History of Science 1999: Special issue: 'Psychoanalysing Robert Boyle', *British Journal for the History of Science*, 32, 257–324.

Brooke, J. 1991: *Science and Religion: Some Historical Perspectives*: Cambridge.

Brooks, C. 1987: 'John, first baron Ashburnham and the state, c.1688–1710', *Bulletin of the Institute of Historical Research*, 60, 64–79.

Brooks, C. W. 1986: *Pettyfoggers and Vipers of the Commonwealth: The 'Lower Branch' of the Legal Profession in Early Modern England*: Cambridge.

Brooks, C. W. 1998: *Lawyers, Litigation and English Society Since 1450*: London.

Brown, C. 1982: *Van Dyck*: Oxford.

Brown, J. 1995: *Kings and Connoisseurs: Collecting Art in Seventeenth-Century Europe*: Princeton, NJ.

Brown, K. 1990: 'British history: a sceptical comment.' In R. Asch, ed., *Three Nations: A Common History?*: Bochum.

Brown, K. 1992: *Kingdom or Province? Scotland and the Regal Union, 1603–1707*: Basingstoke.

Brown, K. M. 1994: 'The vanishing emperor; British kingship in decline.' In R. A. Mason, ed., *Scots and Britons: Scottish Political Thought and the Union of 1603*: Cambridge.

Brown, K. M. 1999: 'Seducing the Scottish Clio: has Scottish history anything to fear from the New British History?' In G. Burgess, ed., *The New British History: Founding a Modern State, 1603–1715*: London.

Brown, K. M. 2000: *Noble Society in Scotland: Wealth, Family and Culture from Reformation to Revolution*: Edinburgh.

Brown, K. M. 2001: 'The Scottish nobility and the British multiple monarchy (1603–1714).' In R. G. Asch, ed., *Der europäishe Adel im Ancien Régime: Von der Krise der ständishcen Monarchien bis zur Revolution (ca.1600–1789)*: Böhlau.

Browning, A. 1951: *Thomas Earl of Danby*, 3 vols: Glasgow.

Browning, A. (ed.) 1953: *English Historical Documents, 1660–1714*: London.

Browning, A. (ed.) 1991: *The Memoirs of Sir John Reresby*, revd edn, ed. M. K. Geiter and W. A. Speck: London.

Bruijn, J. and Gaastra, F. 1993: *Ships, Sailors and Spices: East India Companies and their Shipping in the 16th and 18th Centuries*: Amsterdam.

Buckroyd, J. 1976: 'Lord Broghill and the Scottish church', *Journal of Ecclesiastical History*, 27, 359–68.

Buckroyd, J. 1987: 'Bridging the gap: Scotland, 1659–1660', *Scottish Historical Review*, 66, 1–25.

Buckroyd, J. M. 1981: *Church and State in Scotland, 1660–81*: Edinburgh.

Burgess, G. 1992: *The Politics of the Ancient Constitution: An Introduction to English Political Thought, 1603–1642*: London.

Burgess, G. 1996: *Absolute Monarchy and the Stuart Constitution*: New Haven, CT.

Burgess, G. (ed.) 1999: *The New British History: Founding a Modern State 1603–1715*: London.

Burghall, E. 1889: *Providence Improved*, Record Society of Lancashire and Cheshire, vol. 19.

Burnet, G. 1833: *History of My Own Time*, 6 vols: Oxford.

Burns, J. H. 1996: *The Trew Law of Kingship: Concepts of Monarchy in Early Modern Scotland*: Oxford.

Burns, J. H. with Goldie, M. (eds) 1991: *The Cambridge History of Political Thought 1450–1700*: Cambridge.

Butler, M. 1984: *Theatre and Crisis 1632–1642*: Cambridge.

Calder, A. 1998: *Revolutionary Empire: The Rise of the English-Speaking Empires from the Fifteenth Century to the 1780s*: London.

Canny, N. 1987: *From Reformation to Restoration: Ireland 1534–1660*: Dublin.

Canny, N. 1991: 'The marginal kingdom: Ireland as a problem in the first British empire.' In B. Bailyn and P. D. Morgan, eds, *Strangers within the Realm: Cultural Margins of the First British Empire*: Chapel Hill, NC.

Canny, N. 1994: 'English migration into and across the Atlantic during the seventeenth and eighteenth centuries.' In N. Canny, ed., *Europeans on the Move: Studies on European Migration, 1500–1800*: Oxford.

Canny, N. 1995a: 'Responses to centralization *c*.1530–*c*.1640.' In A. Grant and K. Stringer, eds, *Uniting the Kingdom? The Making of British History*: London.

Canny, N. 1995b: 'What really happened in 1641?' In J. Ohlmeyer, ed., *Ireland: From Independence to Occupation 1641–1660*: Cambridge.

Canny, N. 1996: *Europeans on the Move: Studies on European Migration, 1500–1800*: Oxford.

Canny, N. (ed.) 1998: *The Origins of Empire: British Overseas Enterprise to the Close of the Seventeenth Century*, vol. 1 of *The Oxford History of the British Empire*: Oxford.

Canny, N. 2001: *Making Ireland British, 1580–1650*: Oxford.

Capp, B. S. 1989: *Cromwell's Navy: The Fleet and the English Revolution, 1648–1660*: Oxford.

Capp, B. S. 1996: 'Separate domains? Women and authority in early modern England.' In P. Griffiths, A. Fox and S. Hindle, eds, *The Experience of Authority in Early Modern England*: London.

Care, H. 1682a: *A Perfect Guide to Protestant Dissenters*.

Care, H. 1682b: *A Weekly Pacquet of Advice*, vol. 5, no. 8, 13 October.

Care, H. 1688: *Public Occurrances Truly Stated*, no. 8.

Carew, T. 1964: *The Poems of Thomas Carew*, edited by Rhodes Dunlap: Oxford.

Carlin, N. 1987: 'The Levellers and the conquest of Ireland in 1649', *Historical Journal*, 30, 269–88.

Carlton, C. 1992: *Going to the Wars: The Experience of the British Civil Wars, 1638–51*: London.

Carlton, C. 1994: *Going to the Wars: The Experience of the British Civil Wars, 1638–51*: London.

Carlton, C. 1998: 'Civilians.' In J. Kenyon and J. Ohlmeyer, eds., *The Civil Wars: A Military History of England, Scotland and Ireland, 1638–1660*: Oxford.

Cavendish, M. 1906: *The Life of William Cavendish, Duke of Newcastle: To which is added The True Relation of my Birth, Breeding and Life; by Margaret, Duchess of Newcastle*, ed. C. Harding Firth: London.

Challis, C. E. (ed.) 1992: *A New History of the Royal Mint*: Cambridge.

Chaloner, T. 1646: *An Answer to the Scotch Papers . . . Concerning the Disposal of the King's Person*, BL, E361/7.

Chandaman, C. D. 1975: *The English Public Revenue, 1660–88*: Oxford.

Chaney, E. 2000: *The Evolution of the Grand Tour*: London.

Chaney, E. (ed.) 2002: *Inigo Jones's 'Roman Sketchbook'*: London.

Chaudhuri, K. N. 1965: *The English East India Company: The Study of an Early Joint Stock Company*: London.

Chaudhuri, K. N. 1978: *The Trading World of Asia and the English East India Company, 1660–1760*: Cambridge.

Chaudhuri, K. N. 1985: *Trade and Civilisation in the Indian Ocean: An Economic History from the Rise of Islam to 1750*: Cambridge.

Chernaik, W. and Dzelzainis, M. (eds) 1999: *Milton and Liberty*: Basingstoke.

Childs, J. 1976: *The Army of Charles II*: London.

Childs, J. 1980: *The Army, James II and the Glorious Revolution*: Manchester.

Childs, J. 1986: *The Army of Charles II*: London.

Childs, J. 1987: *The British Army of William III, 1689–1702*: Manchester.

Childs, J. 1991: *The Nine Years' War and the British Army 1688–1697: The Operations in the Low Countries*: Manchester.

Christianson: 1991: 'Royal and parliamentary voices on the ancient constitution, *c*.1604–1621.' In L. Peck, ed., *The Mental World of the Jacobean Court*: Cambridge.

Clark, A. 1992: *Working Life of Women in the Seventeenth Century*, 3rd edn, with an introduction by A. L. Erickson: London.

Clark, J. C. D. 1985: *English Society: Social Structure and Political Practice during the Eighteenth Century*: Cambridge.

Clark, J. C. D. 1986: *Revolution and Rebellion: State and Society in England in the Seventeenth and Eighteenth Centuries*: Cambridge.

Clark, J. C. D. 2000: *English Society 1660–1832*, 2nd edn: Cambridge.

Clarke, A. 1965: *The Old English in Ireland, 1625–1642*: London. Reprinted Dublin, 2000.

Clarke, A. 1976: 'Selling royal favours, 1624–32.' In M. Moody, F. X. Martin and F. J. Byrne, eds, *A New History of Ireland, Vol. 3: Early Modern Ireland*: Oxford.

Clarke, A. 1978: 'Colonial identity in early seventeenth-century Ireland.' In T. W. Moody, ed., *Nationality and the Pursuit of National Independence*: Belfast.

Clarke, A. 1999: *Prelude to Restoration in Ireland*: Cambridge.

Clarke, A. 2000a: *The Old English in Ireland 1625–42*: Dublin.

Clarke, A. 2000b: 'Patrick Darcy and the constitutional relationship between Ireland and Britain.' In J. H. Ohlmeyer, ed., *Irish Political Thought in the Seventeenth Century*: Cambridge.

Clarke, A. and Edwards, D. 1976: 'Pacification, plantation, and the catholic question, 1603–23.' In M. Moody, F. X. Martin and F. J. Byrne, eds, *A New History of Ireland, Vol. 3: Early Modern Ireland*: Oxford.

Clay, C. 1978: *Public Finance and Private Wealth: The Career of Sir Stephen Fox, 1627–1716*: Oxford.

Clay, C. 1984: *Economic Expansion and Social Change: England 1500–1700*, 2 vols: Cambridge.

Claydon, T. 1996: *William III and the Godly Revolution*: Cambridge.

Claydon, T. 1997: 'Review article: problems with the British Problem,' *Parliamentary History*, 16.

Claydon, T. 2000: 'The sermon, the "public sphere" and the political culture of late seventeenth-century England'. In L. A. Ferrell and P. McCullough, eds, *The English Sermon Revised: Religion, Literature and History 1600–1750*: Manchester.

Clegg, C. S. 2001: *Press Censorship in Jacobean England*: Cambridge.

Cockburn, J. S. 1985: 'Introduction.' In J. S. Cockburn, ed., *Calendar of Assize Records: Home Circuit Indictments, Elizabeth I and James I, Introduction*: London.

Cockburn, J. S. 1988: 'Twelve silly men? The trial jury at assizes, 1560–1670.' In J. S. Cockburn and T. A. Green, eds, *Twelve Good Men and True: The Criminal Trial Jury in England, 1200–1800*: Princeton, NJ.

Cockburn, J. S. 1991: 'Patterns of violence in English society: homicide in Kent 1560–1985', *Past and Present*, 130 (February), 70–106.

Cockburn, J. S. and Green, T. A. (eds) 1988: *Twelve Good Men and True: The English Criminal Trial Jury, 1200–1800*: Princeton, NJ.

Coffey, J. 2000: *Persecution and Toleration in Protestant England 1558–1689*: Harlow.

Cogswell, T. 1989: *The Blessed Revolution: English Politics and the Coming of War, 1621–1624*: Cambridge.

Cogswell, T. 1995: 'Underground verse and the transformation of early Stuart political culture. In M. Kishlansky and S. Amussen, eds, *Political Culture and Cultural Politics in Early Modern England*: Manchester.

Cohen, I. B. (ed.) 1990: *Puritanism and the Rise of Modern Science: The Merton Thesis*: New Brunswick, NJ.

Coiro, A. B. 1999: ' "A ball of strife": Caroline poetry and royal marriage.' In T. N. Corns, ed., *The Royal Image: Representations of Charles I*: Cambridge.

Colley, L. 1982: *In Defiance of Oligarchy: The Tory Party 1714–60*: Cambridge.

Colley, L. 1992: *Britons: Forging the Nation, 1707–1837*: New Haven, CT.

Collins, J. R. 2002: 'The church settlement of Oliver Cromwell', *History*.

Collinson, P. 1982: *The Religion of Protestants: The Church in English Society, 1558–1625*: Oxford.

Collinson, P. 1983: *Godly People*: London.

Collinson, P. 1991: *The Birthpangs of Protestant England: Religious and Cultural Change in the Sixteenth and Seventeenth Centuries*: Basingstoke.

Colvin, H. 1995: *A Biographical Dictionary of British Architects 1600–1840*: New Haven, CT.

Condren, C. 1989: *George Lawson's Politica and the English Revolution*: Cambridge.

Condren, C. (ed.) 1992: *George Lawson: Politica Sacra et Civilis*: Cambridge.

Condren, C. 1994: *The Language of Politics in Seventeenth-Century England*: London.

Condren, C. 1997: *Satire, Lies, and Politics: The Case of Dr Arbuthnot*: Basingstoke.

Connolly, S. J. 1992: *Religion, Law and Power: The Making of Protestant Ireland, 1659–1760*: Oxford.

Cooper J. 1999: *Oliver the First: Contemporary Images of Oliver Cromwell*: London.

Cormack, L. B. 1997: *Charting an Empire: Geography at the English Universities, 1580–1620*: Chicago, IL.

Corns, T. N. 1992: *Uncloistered Virtue: English Political Literature, 1640–1660*: Oxford.

Corns, T. N. (ed.) 1993: *The Cambridge Companion to English Poetry, Donne to Marvell*: Cambridge.

Corns, T. N. 1995: 'Milton and the characteristics of a free commonwealth.' In D. Armitage, A. Himy and Q. Skinner, eds, *Milton and Republicanism*: Cambridge.

Corns, T. N. 1997: 'The poetry of the Caroline court', *Proceedings of the British Academy*, 97, 51–73.

Corns, T. N. (ed.) 1999a: *The Royal Image: Representations of Charles I*: Cambridge.

Corns, T. N. 1999b: 'Duke, prince and king.' In T. N. Corns, ed., *The Royal Image: Representations of Charles I*: Cambridge.

Corns, T. N. (ed.) 2001a: *A Companion to Milton*: Oxford.

Corns, T. N. 2001b: 'On the Morning of Christ's Nativity', 'Upon the Circumcision' and 'The Passion'. In T. N. Corns, ed., *A Companion to Milton*: Oxford.

Cotterell, M. 1968: 'Interregnum law reform: the Hale Commission of 1652', *English Historical Review*, 83, 689–704.

Cotton, A. N. B. 1971: 'London newsbooks in the Civil War: their political attitudes and sources of information.' Unpublished D.Phil. thesis: Oxford University.

Cotton, P. and Cole, M. 1655: *To the Priests and People of England, we discharge our consciences and give them warning*: London.

Couper, W. J. 1908: *The Edinburgh Periodical Press: Being a Bibliographical Account of the Newspapers, Journals, and Magazines issued in Edinburgh from the Earliest Times to 1800*, 2 vols: Stirling.

Cowan, I. B. 1967: 'The five articles of Perth.' In D. Shaw, ed., *Reformation and Revolution: Essays Presented to Hugh Watt*: Edinburgh.

Coward, B. 1991: *Oliver Cromwell*: Harlow.

Coward, B. 1994: *The Stuart Age: England, 1603–1714*: Harlow.

Coward, B. 2002: *The Cromwellian Protectorate 1653–59*: Manchester.

Cranfield, G. A. 1962: *The Development of the Provincial Newspaper 1700–1760*: Oxford.

Cranfield, G. A. 1978: *The Press and Society from Caxton to Northcliffe*: London.

Crawford, P. 1993: *Women and Religion in England 1500–1720*: London.

Crawford, P. 2000: 'Women's dreams in early modern England', *History Workshop Journal*, 49, 129–41.

Cressy, D. 1980: *Literacy and the Social Order: Reading and Writing in Tudor and Stuart England*: Cambridge.

Croft 1987: 'A collection of several speeches and treatises of the late treasurer Cecil', *Royal Historical Society Camden Treatises Miscellany*, 5, 29: 273–318.

Croft 1991: 'The reputation of Robert Cecil: libels, political opinion and popular awareness in the early seventeenth century', *Transactions of the Royal Historical Society*, 6th series, 1, 43–69.

Croft 1995: 'Libels, popular literacy and public opinion in early modern England', *Historical Research*, 68, 266–85.

Cromartie, A. 1992: 'The rule of law.' In J. Morrill, ed., *Revolution and Restoration: England in the 1650s*: London.

Cruickshank, C. G. 1966: *Elizabeth's Army*, 2nd edn: Oxford.

Cruickshanks, E. (ed.) 1989: *By Force or by Default? The Revolution of 1688–9*: Edinburgh.

Cruickshanks, E. (ed.) 2000: *The Stuart Courts*: Stroud.

Cruickshanks, E. 2000: *The Glorious Revolution*: Basingstoke.

CSPD 1858–97: *Calendar of State Papers Domestic, Reign of Charles I*, 23 vols: London.

Cunningham, A. and Williams, P. 1993: 'De-centring the "Big Picture": *The Origins of Modern Science* and the Modern Origins of Science', *British Journal for the History of Science*, 26, 407–32.

Cunningham, B. 2000: *The World of Geoffrey Keating*: Dublin.

Curry, P. 1989: *Prophecy and Power: Astrology in Early Modern England*: Cambridge.

Cust, R. 1986: 'News and politics in early seventeenth-century England', *Past and Present*, 112, 60–90.

Cust, R. 1987: *The Forced Loan and English Politics 1626–1628*: Oxford.

Cust, R. 1990: 'Charles I and a draft declaration for the 1628 parliament', *Historical Research*, 63, 143–61.

Cust, R. 1995: 'Honour and politics in early Stuart England: the case of Beaumont *v.* Hastings', *Past and Present*, 149, 57–94.

Cust, R. (ed.) 1996: *The Papers of Sir Richard Grosvenor, 1st Bart. (1585–1645)*. Record Society of Lancashire and Cheshire 134.

Cust, R. and Hughes, A. (eds) 1989: *Conflict in Early Stuart England: Studies in Religion and Politics, 1603–1642:* Harlow.

Cust, R. and Hughes, A. (eds) 1997: *The English Civil War:* London.

Dahl, F. 1950: 'Amsterdam – cradle of English newspapers', *The Library*, 5th series, 4, 166–78.

Dahl, F. 1952: *A Bibliography of English Corantos and Periodical Newsbooks 1620–1642:* London.

Daniels, C. W. and Morrill, J. 1988: *Charles I:* Cambridge.

Darbishire, H. (ed.) 1932: *The Early Lives of Milton:* London.

Davies, J. D. 1991: *Gentlemen and Tarpaulins: The Officers and Men of the Restoration Navy:* Oxford.

Davies, J. E. 1992: *The Caroline Captivity of the Church: Charles I and the Remoulding of Anglicanism:* Oxford.

Davies, K. M. 1981: 'Continuity and change in literary advice on marriage.' In R. B. Outhwaite, ed., *Marriage and Society: Studies in the Social History of Marriage:* London.

Davis, J. C. 1981: 'Pocock's Harrington: grace, nature and art in the classical republicanism of James Harrington', *Historical Journal*, 24, 3, 683–97.

Davis, J. C. 1986: *Fear, Myth and History: The Ranters and Historians:* Cambridge.

Davis, J. C. 1992: 'Religion and the struggle for freedom in the English revolution', *Historical Journal*, 35, 3, 507–30.

Davis, J. C. 1993: 'Against formality: one aspect of the English revolution', *Transactions of the Royal Historical Society*, 6th series, 3, 265–88.

Davis, J. C. 2001: *Oliver Cromwell:* London.

Davis, R. 1969: 'English foreign trade, 1660–1700.' In E. M. Carus-Wilson and W. E. Minchinton, eds, *The Growth of English Overseas Trade in the Seventeenth and Eighteenth Centuries:* London.

Davis, R. 1972: *The Rise of the English Shipping Industry in the Seventeenth and the Eighteenth Centuries:* Newton Abbot.

Davison, L. 2000: 'Spinsters were doing it for themselves: independence and the single woman in early eighteenth-century rural Wales.' In M. Roberts and S. Clarke, eds, *Women and Gender in Early Modern Wales:* Cardiff.

Davison, L. et al. 1992: *Stilling the Grumbling Hive: The Response to Social and Economic Problems in England 1688–1750:* Stroud.

De Beer, E. S. (ed.) 1955: *The Diary of John Evelyn*, vol. 1: Oxford.

De Beer, E. S. 1968: 'The English newspapers from 1695 to 1702.' In R. Hatton and J. S. Bromley, eds, *William III and Louis XIV: Essays 1680–1720 by and for Mark A. Thomson:* Liverpool.

De Krey, G. 1985: *A Fractured Society: The Politics of London in the First Age of Party, 1688–1715:* Oxford.

De Vries, J. 1993: 'Between purchasing power and the world of goods: understanding the household economy in early modern Europe.' In R. Porter and J. Brewer, eds, *Consumption and the World of Goods:* London.

Dean, D. 1996: *Law-Making and Society in Late Elizabethan England: The Parliament of England, 1584–1601:* Cambridge.

Dear, P. 1995: *Discipline and Experience: The Mathematical Way in the Scientific Revolution:* Chicago, IL.

Dethloff, D. 1996: 'The executors' account book and the dispersal of Sir Peter Lely's collection', *Journal of the History of Collections*, 8 (1), 15–51.

Dickinson, H. T. 1977: *Liberty and Property: Political Ideology in Eighteenth-Century Britain*: London.

Dickson, D. 1987: *New Foundations: Ireland, 1600–1800*: Dublin. 2nd edn 2000.

Dickson, P. G. M. 1967: *The Financial Revolution in England: A Study in the Development of Public Credit 1688–1756*: London.

Dietz, F. C. 1964: *English Public Finance 1485–1641, vol. 2: 1558–1641*: London.

Dobbs, B. J. T. 1975: *The Foundations of Newton's Alchemy, or, 'The Hunting of the Greene Lyon'*: Cambridge.

Dobbs, B. J. T. 1991: *The Janus Faces of Genius: The Role of Alchemy in Newton's Thought*: Cambridge.

Doig, J. A. 1998: 'Political propaganda and royal proclamations in late medieval England', *Historical Research*, 71, 253–80.

Donald, P. 1990: *An Uncounselled King: Charles I and the Scottish Troubles, 1637–1641*: Cambridge.

Donaldson, G. 1954: *The Making of the Scottish Prayer Book of 1637*: Edinburgh.

Dooley, B. 2001: 'News and doubt in early modern culture: or, are we having a public sphere yet?' In B. Dooley and S. Baron, eds, *The Politics of Information in Early Modern Europe*: London.

Dow, F. 1979: *Cromwellian Scotland*: Edinburgh.

Downie, J. A. 1979: *Robert Harley and the Press: Propaganda and Public Opinion in the Age of Swift and Defoe*: Cambridge.

Downing, B. M. 1992: *The Military Revolution and Political Change: Origins of Democracy and Autocracy in Early Modern Europe*: Princeton, NJ.

Dunn, R. S. 1972: *Sugar and Slaves: The Rise of the Planter Class in the English West Indies, 1624–1713*: Chapel Hill, NC.

Durston, C. 2001: *Godly Governors: The Rule of Cromwell's Major Generals*: Manchester.

Durston, C. and Eales, J. (eds) 1996: *The Culture of Puritanism, 1560–1700*: Basingstoke.

Dzelzainis, M. (ed.) 1991: *John Milton: Political Writings*: Cambridge.

Dzelzainis, M. 2001: 'Republicanism.' In T. N. Corns, ed., *A Companion to Milton*: Oxford.

Eales, J. 1988: 'Gender construction in early modern England and the conduct books of William Whateley (1583–1639).' In R. N. Swanson, ed., *Gender and Christian Religion*, Studies in Church History, vol. 34: Woodbridge.

Eales, J. 1990: *Puritans and Roundheads: The Harleys of Brampton Bryan and the Outbreak of the English Civil War*: Cambridge.

Eales, J. 1998: *Women in Early Modern England, 1500–1700*: London.

Earle, P. 1989: 'The female labour market in London in the late seventeenth and early eighteenth centuries', *Economic History Review*, 42, 328–53.

Edie, C. A. 1990: 'The public face of royal ritual: sermons, medals and civic ceremony in later Stuart coronations', *Huntington Library Quarterly*, 53, 311–36.

Edwards, T. 1646: *The Second Part of Gangraena*, BL, E338/12.

Egloff, C. S. 1990: 'Settlement and kingship: the army, the gentry, and the offer of the crown to Oliver Cromwell.' Unpublished Ph.D. thesis, Yale University.

Egloff, C. S. 1998: 'The search for a Cromwellian settlement: exclusions from the second Protectorate parliament. Part 1: The process and its architects; Part 2: The excluded members and the reactions to the exclusion', *Parliamentary History*, 17, 178–97, 301–21.

Eisenstein, E. L. 1968: 'Some conjectures about the impact of printing on western society and thought: a preliminary report', *Journal of Modern History*, 40, 7–29.

Eisenstein, E. L. 1979: *The Printing Press as an Agent of Change*: Cambridge.

Elliot, J. H. 1992: 'A Europe of composite monarchies', *Past and Present*, 137.

Ellis, F. H. (ed.) 1985: *Swift vs. Mainwaring: The Examiner and The Medley*. Oxford.

Ellis, S. G. 1995: 'Tudor state formation and the shaping of the British Isles.' In S. G. Ellis and S. Barber, eds, *Conquest and Union: Fashioning a British State, 1485–1725*: London.

Ellis, S. G. 1998: *Ireland in the Age of the Tudors, 1447–1603*: Harlow.

Ellis, S. G. and Barber, S. (eds) 1995: *Conquest and Union: Fashioning a British State 1485–1725*: Harlow.

Elton, G. R. 1974–92: *Studies in Tudor and Stuart Politics and Government*: Cambridge.

Elton, G. R. 1979: 'Parliament and the Tudors: its functions and fortunes', *Historical Journal*, vol. 22.

Emerson, R. 1988: 'Sir Robert Sibbald, Kt., the Royal Society of Scotland and the origins of the Scottish Enlightenment', *Annals of Science*, 45, 41–72.

Erickson, A. L. 1993: *Women and Property in Early Modern England*: London.

Ertman, T. 1997: *Birth of the Leviathan: Building States and Regimes in Medieval and Early Modern Europe*: Cambridge.

Evans, R. J. W. and Thomas, T. V. (eds) 1991: *Crown, Church and Estates: Central European Politics in the Sixteenth and Seventeenth Centuries*: London.

Everitt, A. 1966: *The Community of Kent and the Great Rebellion 1640–60*: Leicester.

Ewan, E. and Meikle, M. M. (eds) 1999: *Women in Scotland c.1100–c.1750*: East Linton.

Farnell, J. E. 1967: 'The usurpation of honest London householders: Barebone's Parliament', *English Historical Review*, 82, 24–46

Farr, D. 2000: 'Kin, cash, Catholics and cavaliers: the role of kinship in the financial management of major-general John Lambert', *Historical Research*, 74, 44–62

Feingold, M. 1984: *The Mathematicians' Apprenticeship: Science, Universities and Society in England, 1560–1640*: Cambridge.

Feingold, M. 1996: 'When facts matter', *Isis*, 87, 131–9.

Ferguson, W. 1998: *The Identity of the Scottish Nation: An Historic Quest*: Edinburgh.

Feros, A. 1999: 'Images of evil, images of kings: the contrasting faces of the royal favourite and the prime minister in European political literature, *c*.1580–*c*.1650. In J. H. Elliott and L. W. B. Brockliss, eds, *The World of the Favourite*: New Haven, CT.

Ferrell, L. A. 1998: *Government by Polemic: James I, the King's Preachers, and the Rhetorics of Conformity, 1603–1625*: Stanford, CA.

Finaldi, G. 1999: *Orazio Gentileschi at the Court of Charles I*: London.

Fincham, K. 1984: 'The judges' decision on Ship Money in February 1637: the reaction of Kent', *Bulletin of the Institute of Historical Research*, 57, 230–7.

Fincham, K. 1990: *Prelate as Pastor: The Episcopate of James I*: Oxford.

Fincham, K. (ed.) 1993: *The Early Stuart Church, 1603–1642*: Basingstoke.

Fincham, K. and Lake, P. 1985: 'The ecclesiastical policy of James I', *Journal of British Studies*, 24, 169–207.

Fincham, K. and Lake, P. 1993: 'The ecclesiastical policies of James I and Charles I.' In K. Fincham, ed., *The Early Stuart Church, 1603–1642*: Basingstoke.

Firth, C. H. 1909: *The Last Years of the Protectorate, 1656–1658*, 2 vols: London.

Flamsteed, J. 1995–2001: *The Correspondence of John Flamsteed*, ed. E. G. Forbes, L. Murdin and F. Willmoth: Bristol.

Fletcher, A. 1981: *The Outbreak of the English Civil War*: London.

Fletcher, A. 1986: *Reform in the Provinces: The Government of Stuart England*: New Haven, CT.

Fletcher, A. 1993: 'Power, myth and realities', *Historical Journal*, vol. 36.

Fletcher, A. 1994: 'The Protestant idea of marriage in early modern England.' In A. Fletcher and P. Roberts, eds, *Religion, Culture and Society in Early Modern Britain: Essays in Honour of Patrick Collinson*: Cambridge.

Fletcher, A. 1995: *Gender, Sex and Subordination in England 1500–1800*: New Haven, CT.

Fletcher, A. and Stevenson, J. (eds) 1985: *Order and Disorder in Early Modern England*: Cambridge.

Ford, A. 1985: *The Protestant Reformation in Ireland, 1590–1641*: Frankfurt-am-Main.

Ford, A. 1995: 'The Church of Ireland, 1558–1634: a puritan church?' In A. Ford, J. McGuire and K. Milne, eds, *As By Law Established: The Church of Ireland Since the Reformation*: Dublin.

Ford, A. 1997: *The Protestant Reformation in Ireland, 1590–1641*, 2nd edn: Dublin.

Ford, A., McGuire, J. and Milne, K. (eds) 1995: *As By Law Established: The Church of Ireland Since the Reformation*: Dublin.

Foster, W. R. 1975: *The Church before the Covenants: The Church of Scotland 1596–1638*: Edinburgh.

Foucault, M. 1975: *Surveillir et punir: naissance de la prison*: Paris.

Fox, A. 1994: 'Ballads, libel, and popular ridicule in Jacobean England', *Past and Present*, 145, 47–83.

Fox, A. 1997: 'Rumour, news and popular political opinion in Elizabethan and early Stuart England', *Historical Journal*, 40, 3, 597–620.

Fox, A. 2000: *Oral and Literate Culture in England 1500–1700*: Oxford.

Fox, G. 1998: *The Journal*, ed. N. Smith: Harmondsworth.

Foxcroft, H. C. 1898: *The Life and Letters of Sir George Savile Bart., First Marquis of Halifax*, vol. 2: London.

Foyster, E. A. 1996: 'Male honour, social control and wife beating in late Stuart England', *Transactions of the Royal Historical Society*, 6th series, 6, 215–24.

Foyster, E. A. 1999: *Manhood in Early Modern England: Honour, Sex and Marriage*: London.

Frank, J. 1961: *The Beginnings of the English Newspaper 1620–1660*. Cambridge, MA.

Frank, R. G. 1980: *Harvey and the Oxford Physiologists: Scientific Ideas and Social Interaction*: Berkeley, CA.

Fraser, N. 1956: *The Intelligence of the Secretaries of State and their Monopoly of Licensed News 1660–1688*: Cambridge.

Fraser, N. 1992: 'Rethinking the public sphere: a contribution to the critique of actually existing democracy.' In C. Calhoun, ed., *Habermas and the Public Sphere*: Cambridge, MA.

Frearson, M. 1993a: 'London corantos in the 1620s', *Studies in Newspaper and Periodical History*, 1, 3–17.

Frearson, M. 1993b: 'The distribution and readership of London corantos in the 1620s.' In R. Myers and M. Harris, eds, *Serials and their Readers 1620–1914*: Winchester.

Freist, D. 1997: *Governed by Opinion: Politics, Religion and the Dynamics of Communication in Stuart London 1637–1645*. London.

Fulton, T. W. 1911: *The Sovereignty of the Sea: An Historical Account of the Claims for Dominion of the British Seas*: Edinburgh.

Galenson, D. 1981: *White Servitude in Colonial America: An Economic Analysis*: Cambridge.

Gallagher, C. and Greenblatt, S. 2000: *Practicing New Historicism*: Chicago.

Gardiner, S. R. 1862: *Parliamentary Debates in 1610*: London.

Gardiner, S. R. 1883–4: *History of England from the Accession of James I to the Outbreak of the Civil War, 1603–1642*: London.

Gardiner, S. R. (ed.) 1906: *Constitutional Documents of the Puritan Revolution, 1625–1660*: Oxford.

Gardiner, S. R. 1987: *History of the Great Civil War 1642–1649*, 4 vols: London.

Gardiner, S. R. 1988: *History of the Commonwealth and Protectorate*, 4 vols: Adlestrop.

Gascoigne, J. 1985: 'The universities and the scientific revolution: the case of Newton and Restoration Cambridge', *History of Science*, 23, 391–434.

Gascoigne, J. 1988: 'From Bentley to the Victorians: the rise and fall of British Newtonian natural theology', *Science in Context*, 2, 219–56.

Gaskill, M. 2000: *Crime and Mentalities in Early Modern England*: Cambridge.

Gauci, P. 2001: *The Politics of Trade: The Overseas Merchant in State and Society, 1660–1720*: Oxford.

Gaunt, P. 1996: *Oliver Cromwell*: Oxford.

Gaunt, P. 1997: *The British Civil Wars, 1637–51*: London.

Gaunt, P. 1998: 'Cromwellian parliaments.' In I. Roots, ed., *Into Another Mould: Aspects of the Interregnum*, 2nd edn: Exeter.

Gaunt, P. (ed.) 2000: *The English Civil War*: Oxford.

Gay, E. F. 1905: 'The Midland revolt and the inquisitions of depopulation of 1607', *Transactions of the Royal Historical Society*, new series, 18, 195–244.

Geertz, C. 1975: *The Interpretation of Cultures*: London.

Gemery, H. 1980: 'Emigration from the British Isles to the New World, 1660–1700: inferences from colonial populations', *Research in Economic History*, 5, 179–231.

Gent, L. (ed.) 1995: *Albion's Classicism: The Visual Arts in Britain 1550–1660*: New Haven, CT.

Gent, L. and Llewellyn, N. (eds) 1990: *Renaissance Bodies: The Human Figure in English Culture c.1540–1660*: London.

Gentles, I. 1973: 'The sale of crown lands during the English Revolution', *Economic History Review*, 2nd series, 26, 614–35.

Gentles, I. 1992: *The New Model Army in England, Ireland and Scotland, 1645–1653*: Oxford.

Gentles, I. 1997: 'The New Model officer corps in 1647: a collective portrait', *Social History*, 22, 127–44.

Gibbs, G. C. 1992: 'Press and public opinion: prospective.' In J. R. Jones, ed., *Liberty Secured? Britain before and after 1688*: Stanford, CA.

Gillespie, R. 1985: *Colonial Ulster: The Settlement of East Ulster, 1600–1641:* Cork.

Gillespie, R. 1997: *Devoted People: Belief and Religion in Early Modern Ireland*: Manchester.

Glassey, L. K. J. (ed.) 1997: *The Reigns of Charles II and James VII and II*: London.

Goldberg, J. 1983: *James I and the Politics of Literature: Jonson, Shakespeare, Donne and their Contemporaries*: Baltimore, MD.

Goldberg, J. (ed.) 1994: *Queering the Renaissance*: Durham, NC.

Goldie, M. 1980a: 'The revolution of 1689 and the structure of political argument: an essay and an annotated bibliography of the pamphlets on the allegiance controversy', *Bulletin of Research in the Humanities*, 83, 473–564.

Goldie, M. 1980b: 'The roots of true Whiggism, 1688–1694', *History of Political Thought*, 1, 195–236.

Goldie, M. 1983: 'John Locke and Anglican royalism', *Political Studies*, 31, 61–85.

Goldie, M. 1989: 'The religious theory of intolerance.' In N. Tyacke, O. Grell and J. Israel, eds, *From Persecution to Toleration*: Oxford.

Goldie, M. 1991: 'The political thought of the Anglican revolution.' In R. Beddard, ed., *The Revolutions of 1688*: Oxford.

Goldie, M. 1993: 'James II and the dissenters' revenge: the commission of enquiry of 1688', *Bulletin of the Institute of Historical Research*, 66, 55–88.

Goldie, M. (ed.) 1999: *The Reception of Locke's Politics*, 6 vols: London.

Goldie, M. 2001: 'The unacknowledged republic: office holding in early modern England.' In T. Harris, ed., *The Politics of the Excluded c.1500–1850*: Basingstoke.

Golinski, J. 1998: *Making Natural Knowledge: Constructivism and the History of Science*: Cambridge.

Goodare, J. 1995: 'The Scottish parliament of 1621', *Historical Journal*, 38, 29–51.

Goodwin, T., Nye, P., Simpson, S., Burroughs, J. and Bridge, W. 1644: *An Apologeticall Narration*: London.

Goss, J. 1990: *World Historical Atlas, 1662*: London.

Gouge, W. 1634: *Of Domesticall Duties: Eight Treatises*, 3rd edn: London.

Gowing, L. 1996: *Domestic Dangers: Women, Words, and Sex in Early Modern London*: Oxford.

Graham, E., Hinds, H., Hobby, E. and Wilcox, H. (eds) 1989: *Her Own Life: Autobiographical Writings by Seventeenth-Century Englishwomen*: London.

Grainger, J. D. 1997: *Cromwell Against the Scots: The Last Anglo-Scottish War, 1650–1652*: East Linton.

Grant, A. and Stringer, K. (eds) 1995: *Uniting the Kingdom*: London.

Grant, J. 1871: *The Newspaper Press: Its Origin – Progress – and Present Position*, 2 vols: London.

Grassby, R. 1995: *The Business Community of Seventeenth-Century England*: Cambridge.

Green, I. 1979: 'The persecution of "scandalous" and "malignant" parish clergy during the English Civil War', *English Historical Review*, 94, 507–31.

Greenblatt, S. 1980: *Renaissance Self-Fashioning from More to Shakespeare*: Chicago.

Greengrass, M. 1991: 'Introduction: conquest and coalescence.' In M. Greengrass, ed., *Conquest and Coalescence: The Shaping of the State in Early Modern Europe*: London.

Greengrass, M., Leslie, M. and Raylor, T. (eds) 1994: *Samuel Hartlib and Universal Reformation: Studies in Intellectual Communication*: Cambridge.

Gregg, E. 1980: *Queen Anne*: London.

Gregory, J. 1998: 'Gender and the clerical profession in England, 1660–1850.' In R. N. Swanson, ed., *Gender and Christian Religion*, Studies in Church History, vol. 34: Woodbridge.

Gregory, J. 1999: '*Homo religiosus*: masculinity and religion in the long eighteenth century.' In T. Hitchcock and M. Cohen, eds, *English Masculinities 1660–1800*: London.

Grell, O. P. (ed.) 1991: *From Persecution to Toleration*: Oxford.

Greville, R., Lord Brooke 1642: *A Discourse Opening the Nature of that Episcopacie, which is exercised in England*, 2nd edn: London.

Griffiths, A. 1998: *The Print in Stuart Britain 1603–1689*: London.

Griffiths, P., Fox, A. and Hindle, S. (eds) 1996: *The Experience of Authority in Early Modern England*: London.

Grosjean, A. 1998: 'Scots and the Swedish state: diplomacy, military service and ennoblement 1611–1660.' Unpublished Ph.D. thesis, University of Aberdeen.

Grosjean, A. 2000: 'General Alexander Leslie, the Scottish Covenanters and the Riksråd debates, 1638–1640.' In A. I. Macinnes, T. Riis and F. G. Pedersen, eds, *Ships, Guns and Bibles in the North Sea and Baltic States, c.1350–c.1700*: East Linton.

Gross, P. R. and Levitt, N. 1994: *Higher Superstition: The Academic Left and its Quarrels with Science*: Baltimore, MD.

Gunn, J. A. W. 1969: *Politics and the Public Interest in the Seventeenth Century*: London.

Gunn, J. A. W. (ed.) 1972: *Factions No More: Attitudes to Party in Government and Opposition in Eighteenth-Century England: Extracts from Contemporary Sources*: London.

Gunther, R. T. (ed.) 1923–45: *Early Science in Oxford*, 14 vols: Oxford.

Gurney, J. 1994: 'Gerrard Winstanley and the Digger movement in Walton and Cobham', *Historical Journal*, 37, 775–802

Guscott, S. J. 2000: 'Humphrey Chetham (1580–1653): fortune, politics and mercantile culture in seventeenth-century England.' Unpublished Ph.D. thesis: Sheffield University.

Habermas, J. 1974: 'The public sphere: an encyclopedia article', *New German Critique*, 3, 49–55.

Habermas, J. 1989: *The Structural Transformation of the Public Sphere: An Inquiry into a Category of Bourgeois Society*: Cambridge.

Habermas, J. 1992a: 'Further reflections on the public sphere.' In C. Calhoun, ed., *Habermas and the Public Sphere*: Cambridge, MA.

Habermas, J. 1992b: 'Concluding remarks.' In C. Calhoun, ed., *Habermas and the Public Sphere*: Cambridge, MA.

Halasz, A. 1997: *The Marketplace of Print: Pamphlets and the Public Sphere in Early Modern England*: Cambridge.

Haley, K. H. D. 1968: *The First Earl of Shaftesbury*: Oxford.

Haller, W. (ed.) 1934: *Tracts on Liberty in the Puritan Revolution*, 3 vols: New York.

Halliday, P. 1998: *Dismembering the Body Politic: Partisan Politics in England's Towns 1650–1730*: Cambridge.

Hamilton, C. L. 1963: 'Anglo-Scottish militia negotiations, March–April 1646', *Scottish Historical Review*, 42.

Hammond, G. 1990: *Fleeting Things: English Poets and Poems 1616–1660*: Cambridge, MA.

Hancock, D. 1995: *Citizens of the World: London Merchants and the Integration of the British Atlantic Community, 1735–85*: Cambridge.

Harding, R. 1995: *The Evolution of the Sailing Navy, 1509–1815*: London.

Hardman Moore, S. 1998: 'Sexing the soul: gender and the rhetoric of Puritan piety.' In R. N. Swanson, ed., *Gender and Christian Religion*, Studies in Church History, vol. 34: Woodbridge.

Harris, B. 1996: *Politics and the Rise of the Press: Britain and France, 1620–1800*: London.

Harris, J. and Higgott, G. 1989: *The Architectural Drawings of Inigo Jones*: London.

Harris, J., Orgel, S. and Strong, R. 1973: *The King's Arcadia: Inigo Jones and the Stuart Court*: London.

Harris, M. 1987: *London Newspapers in the Age of Walpole*. Rutherford.

Harris, T. 1987: *London Crowds in the Reign of Charles II: Propaganda and Politics from the Restoration until the Exclusion Crisis*: Cambridge.

Harris, T. 1993a: *Politics Under the Later Stuarts: Party Conflict in a Divided Society 1660–1715*: Harlow.

Harris, T. 1993b: 'Tories and the rule of law in the reign of Charles II', *The Seventeenth Century*, 8.

Harris, T. 1997a: 'The parties and the people: the press, the crowd and politics 'out-of-doors' in Restoration England.' In L. K. J. Glassey, ed., *The Reigns of Charles II and James VII and II*: Basingstoke.

Harris, T. 1997b: 'Reluctant revolutionaries? The Scots and the revolution of 1688–89.' In H. Nenner, ed., *Politics and the Political Imagination in Later Stuart Britain: Essays Presented to Lois Green Schwoerer*: Rochester.

Harris, T. (ed.) 2001: *The Politics of the Excluded, c.1500–1850*: Basingstoke.

Harris, T., Seaward, P. and Goldie, M. (eds) 1990: *The Politics of Religion in Restoration England*: Oxford.

Hartlib Papers 1995: *The Hartlib Papers on CDRom*: Ann Arbor, MI.

Haskell, F. 1980: *Patrons and Painters*: New Haven, CT.

Hatcher, J. 1992: *The History of the British Coal Industry Before 1700, Vol. 1: Towards the Age of Coal*: Oxford.

Hay, D. 1975: 'Property, authority and the criminal law.' In D. Hay, P. Linebaugh, J. G. Rule, E. P. Thompson and C. Winslow, eds, *Albion's Fatal Tree: Crime and Society in Eighteenth-Century England*: London.

Hayton, D. 1984: 'The "country" interest and the party system, 1689–c.1720.' In C. Jones, ed., *Party and Management in Parliament, 1660–1784*: Leicester.

Hayton, D. 2002: 'Introduction.' In E. Cruickshanks, S. Handley and D. Hayton, eds, *The History of Parliament: The House of Commons 1690–1714*, vol. 1: Cambridge.

Hayton, D. W. and O'Brien, G. 1986: *War and Politics in Ireland, 1649–1730* [essays by J. G. Simms]: London.

Healy, T. and Sawday, J. (eds) 1990: *Literature and the English Civil War*: Cambridge.

Hearn, K. (ed.) 1995: *Dynasties: Painting in Tudor and Jacobean England 1530–1630*: London.

Henning, B. D. 1983: *The House of Commons, 1660–1690*, 3 vols: London.

Henry, J. 1986: 'Occult qualities and the experimental philosophy: active principles in pre-Newtonian matter theory', *History of Science*, 24, 335–81.

Henry, J. 2002: *The Scientific Revolution and the Origins of Modern Science*, 2nd edn: Basingstoke.

Herd, H. 1952: *The March of Journalism: The Story of the British Press from 1622 to the Present Day*: London.

Herrup, C. B. 1987: *The Common Peace: Participation and the Criminal Law in Seventeenth-Century England*: Cambridge.

Herrup, C. B. 1999: *A House in Gross Disorder: Sex, Law, and the 2nd Earl of Castlehaven*: Oxford.

Hessen, B. 1931: 'The social and economic roots of Newton's *Principia*.' In N. I. Bukharin et al., eds, *Science at the Crossroads*: London.

Hester, M. 1992: *Lewd Women and Wicked Witches: A Study of the Dynamics of Male Domination*: London.

Higgins, P. 1973: 'The reactions of women with special reference to women petitioners.' In B. Manning, ed., *Politics, Religion and the English Civil War*: London.

Hill, C. 1965: *Intellectual Origins of the English Revolution*: Oxford. Reprinted with additions in 1998 as *Intellectual Origins of the English Revolution Revisited*.

Hill, C. 1972: *The World Turned Upside Down: Radical Ideas during the English Revolution*: London.

Hill, C. 1977: *Milton and the English Revolution*: London.

Hill, C. 1980: *Some Intellectual Consequences of the English Revolution*: London.

Hill, C. 1985: 'Censorship and English literature.' In C. Hill, ed., *Collected Essays Volume I: Writing and Revolution in Seventeenth-Century England*: Brighton.

Hill, C. 1988: *A Turbulent, Seditious, and Factious People: John Bunyan and his Church 1628–1688*: Oxford.

Hill, C. 1991: *The World Turned Upside Down: Radical Ideas in the English Revolution*: Harmondsworth.

Hill, C. 1998: 'Protestantism, pamphleteering, patriotism and public opinion.' In C. Hill, ed., *England's Turning Point: Essays on 17th Century English History*: London.

Hindle, S. 1994: 'The shaming of Margaret Knowsley: gossip, gender and the experience of authority in early modern England', *Continuity and Change*, 9, 3, 391–419.

Hindle, S. 1996: 'The keeping of the public peace.' In P. Griffiths, A. Fox and S. Hindle, eds, *The Experience of Authority in Early Modern England*: London.

Hindle, S. 1998: 'Persuasion and protest in the Caddington common enclosure dispute, 1635–39', *Past and Present*, 158 (February), 37–78.

Hindle, S. 2000a: 'The growth of social stability in Restoration England', *The European Legacy*, 5, 4 (August), 563–76.

Hindle, S. 2000b: *The State and Social Change in Early Modern England, c.1550–1640*: London.

Hinton, R. W. K. 1956: 'Was Charles I a tyrant?' *The Review of Politics*, 18, 69–87.

Hipkin, S. 2000: ' "Sitting on his penny rent": conflict and right of common in Faversham Blean, 1595–1610', *Rural History*, 11, 1, 1–35.

Hirst, D. 1975: *The Representative of the People? Voters and Voting in England under the Early Stuarts*: Cambridge.

Hirst, D. 1988: 'Concord and discord in Richard Cromwell's House of Commons', *English Historical Review*, 103, 339–58.

Hirst, D. 1991: 'The failure of godly rule in the English republic', *Past and Present*, 132, 33–66.

Hirst, D. 1996a: 'Locating the 1650s in England's seventeenth century', *History*, 81, 359–83.

Hirst, D. 1996b: 'The English republic and the meaning of Britain.' In B. Bradshaw and J. Morrill, eds, *The British Problem, c.1534–1707: State Formation in the Atlantic Archipelago*: Basingstoke.

Hirst, D. 1999: *England in Conflict, 1603–1660: Kingdom, Community, Commonwealth*: London.

Historical Manuscripts Commission 1891: *Thirteenth Report*, i.

Hitchcock, T. and Cohen, M. (eds) 1999: *English Masculinities 1660–1800*: London.

Hoak, D. and Feingold, M. (eds) 1996: *The World of William and Mary: Anglo-Dutch Perspectives on the Revolution of 1688–89*: Stanford, CA.

Hobbes, T. 1994: *The Correspondence of Thomas Hobbes*, 2 vols, ed. N. Malcolm: Oxford.

Holiday, P. G. 1970: 'Land sales and repurchases in Yorkshire, 1650–70', *Northern History*, 5, 67–92.

Holmes, C. (ed.) 1970: *The Suffolk Committee for Scandalous Ministers*, Suffolk Record Society, vol. 13.

Holmes, G. 1967: *British Politics in the Age of Anne*: London.

Holmes, G. 1973: *The Trial of Doctor Sacheverell*: London.

Holmes, G. 1975: *Religion and Party in Late Stuart England*: London.

Holmes, G. 1978: 'Science, reason and religion in the age of Newton' [review essay of M. Jacob, *The Newtonians and the English Revolution*]. *British Journal for the History of Science*, 11, 164–71.

Holmes, G. 1981: 'The achievement of stability: the social context of politics from the 1680s to the age of Walpole.' In J. Cannon, ed., *The Whig Ascendancy*: London.

Holmes, G. 1986: *Politics, Religion and Society in England, 1679–1742*: London.

Holmes, G. 1987: *Politics in the Age of Anne*, revd edn: London.

Holmes, G. 1993: *The Making of a Great Power: Late Stuart and Early Georgian Britain 1660–1722*: Harlow.

Hoppen, K. T. 1970: *The Common Scientist in the Seventeenth Century: A Study of the Dublin Philosophical Society, 1683–1708*: London.

Hopper, A. J. 1997: ' "The readiness of the people": the formation and emergence of the army of the Fairfaxes, 1642–3', *Borthwick Paper*, 92.

Hoppit, J. 1996: 'Patterns of parliamentary legislation, 1660–1800', *Historical Journal*, 39, 109–31.

Hoppit, J. 2000: *A Land of Liberty? England 1689–1727*: Oxford.

Horwitz, H. 1968: *'Revolution Politicks': The Career of Daniel Finch, 2nd Earl of Nottingham*: Cambridge.

Horwitz, H. (ed.) 1972: *The Parliamentary Diary of Narcissus Luttrell*: Oxford.

Horwitz, H. 1974: 'Parliament and the Glorious Revolution', *Bulletin of the Institute of Historical Research*, 47, 36–52.

Horwitz, H. 1977: *Parliament Policy and Politics in the Reign of William III*: Manchester.

Houlbrooke, R. A. 1986: 'Women's social life and common action in England from the fifteenth century to the eve of the Civil War', *Continuity and Change*, 1, 2, 171–89.

Houston, R. A. 1982: 'The literacy myth? Illiteracy in Scotland 1630–1760', *Past and Present*, 96, 81–102.

Houston, R. A. 1989: 'Women in the economy and society of Scotland, 1500–1800.' In R. A. Houston and I. D. Whyte, eds, *Scottish Society 1500–1800*: Cambridge.

Howarth, D. 1982: 'Mantua peeces: Charles I and the Gonzaga collections.' In D. Chambers and J. Martineau, eds, *Splendours of the Gonzaga*: London.

Howarth, D. 1985: *Lord Arundel and his Circle*: New Haven, CT.

Howarth, D. 1989: 'Charles I, sculpture and sculptors.' In A. MacGregor, ed., *The Late King's Goods: Collections, Possessions and Patronage of Charles I in the Light of the Commonwealth Sale Inventories*: London.

Howarth, D. (ed.) 1993: *Art Patronage in the Caroline Court: Essays in Honour of Sir Oliver Millar*: Cambridge.

Howarth, D. 1997: *Images of Rule: Art and Politics in the English Renaissance, 1485–1649*: Basingstoke.

Howell, R. 1993: 'Cromwell and his parliaments: the Trevor-Roper thesis revisited.' In R. C. Richardson, ed., *Images of Oliver Cromwell: Essays for and by Roger Howell*: Manchester.

Hoyle, R. W. (ed.) 1992: *The Estates of the English crown, 1558–1640*: Cambridge.

Hughes, A. 1986: 'Parliamentary tyranny? Indemnity proceedings and the impact of the Civil War: a case study from Warwickshire', *Midlands History*, 11, 49–78.

Hughes, A. 1987: *Politics, Society and Civil War in Warwickshire 1620–1660*: Cambridge.

Hughes, A. 1992: 'The frustrations of the godly.' In J. Morrill, ed., *Revolution and Restoration: England in the 1650s*: London.

Hughes, A. 1998: *The Causes of the English Civil War*, 2nd edn: Basingstoke.

Hunt, F. K. 1850: *The Fourth Estate: Contributions towards a History of Newspapers, and of the Liberty of the Press*: London.

Hunter, J. P. 1990: *Before Novels: The Cultural Contexts of Eighteenth-Century English Fiction*: New York.

Hunter, M. 1981: *Science and Society in Restoration England*: Cambridge; reprinted 1992, Aldershot.

Hunter, M. 1989: *Establishing the New Science: The Experience of the Early Royal Society*: Woodbridge.

Hunter, M. 1994: *The Royal Society and its Fellows 1660–1700: The Morphology of an Early Scientific Institution*, revd edn: Oxford. Originally published as 'The social basis and changing fortunes of an early scientific institution', *Notes and Records of the Royal Society*, 31 (1976), 9–114.

Hunter, M. 1995: *Science and the Shape of Orthodoxy: Intellectual Change in Late Seventeenth-Century Britain*: Woodbridge.

Hunter, M. (ed.) 1998: *Archives of the Scientific Revolution: The Formation and Exchange of Ideas in Early Modern Europe*: Woodbridge.

Hunter, M. 2000: *Robert Boyle (1627–91): Scrupulosity and Science*: Woodbridge.

Hurwich, J. 1977: '"A fanatic town": the political influence of Dissenters in Coventry, 1660–1720', *Midland History*, 4, 15–47.

Hutchinson, L. 1968: *Memoirs of the Life of Colonel Hutchinson*: London.

Hutton, R. 1985: *The Restoration, 1658–67*: Oxford.

Hutton, R. 1989: *Charles II*: Oxford.

Hutton, R. 1993: *The Restoration: A Political and Religious History of England and Wales, 1658–1667*, 3rd edn: Oxford.

Hutton, R. 1999: *History Today*, vol. 49 (5).

Hutton, R. 2000: *The British Republic 1649–1660*, 2nd edn: London.

Huygens, L. 1982: *The English Journal 1651–1652*, ed. A. G. H. Bachrach and R. G. Collmer: Leiden.

Ingram, M. 1984: 'Ridings, rough music and the "reform of popular culture" in early modern England', *Past and Present*, 105, 79–113.

Israel, J. (ed.) 1991: *The Anglo-Dutch Moment: Essays on the Glorious Revolution and its World Impact*: Cambridge.

Jacob, J. R. 1977: *Robert Boyle and the English Revolution: A Study of Social and Intellectual Change*: New York.

Jacob, J. R. and Jacob, M. C. 1980: 'The Anglican origins of modern science: the metaphysical foundation of the Whig constitution', *Isis*, 71, 251–67.

Jacob, M. C. 1976: *The Newtonians and the English Revolution, 1689–1720*: Hassocks.

Jacob, M. C. 1981: *The Radical Enlightenment: Pantheists, Freemasons and Republicans*: London.

James VI and I, 1994: *Political Writings*, ed. J. P. Sommerville: Cambridge.

James, M. 1986: 'English politics and the concept of honour, 1485–1642.' In M. James, *Society, Politics and Culture: Studies in Early Modern England*: Cambridge.

Jansson, M. 1987: *Proceedings in Parliament 1625*: New Haven, CT.

Jenkins, P. 1983: *The Making of a Ruling Class: The Glamorgan Gentry 1640–1790*: Cambridge.

Jenkins, P. 1986: 'From gallows to prison? The execution rate in early modern England', *Criminal Justice History*, 7, 51–71.

Jenkins, P. 1995: 'The Anglican church and the unity of Britain: the Welsh experience, 1560–1714.' In S. G. Ellis and S. Barber, eds, *Conquest and Union: Fashioning a British State, 1485–1725*: London.

Jesseph, D. M. 1999: *Squaring the Circle: The War between Hobbes and Wallis*: Chicago, IL.

Johns, A. 1998: *The Nature of the Book: Print and Knowledge in the Making*: Chicago, IL.

Johnson, A. M. 1978: 'Wales during the Commonwealth and Protectorate.' In D. Pennington and K. Thomas, eds, *Puritans and Revolutionaries: Essays in Seventeenth-Century History Presented to Christopher Hill*: Oxford.

Jones, A. C. 2002: 'Commotion time: the English risings of 1549.' Unpublished Ph.D. thesis: University of Warwick.

Jones, C. (ed.) 1989: *A Pillar of the Constitution: The House of Lords in British Politics, 1640–1784*: London.

Jones, D. L. (ed.) 1988: *A Parliamentary History of the Glorious Revolution*: London.

Jones, D. M. 1999: *Conscience and Allegiance in Seventeenth-Century England: The Political Significance of Oaths and Engagements*: New York.

Jones, D. W. 1988: *War and Economy in the Age of William III and Marlborough*: Oxford.

Jones, J. R. 1961: *The First Whigs: Politics in the Exclusion Crisis*: Oxford.

Jones, J. R. 1972: *The Revolution of 1688 in England*: London.

Jonson, B. 1985: *Ben Jonson*, ed. I. Donaldson: Oxford.

Judson, M. A. 1949: *The Crisis of the Constitution*: New York.

Judson, M. A. 1969: *The Political Thought of Sir Henry Vane the Younger*: Philadelphia.

Kearney, H. F. 1959: *Strafford in Ireland, 1633–1641*: Manchester. Reprinted Cambridge, 1989.

Kearney, H. F. 1989: *Strafford in Ireland 1633–41: A Study in Absolutism*, 2nd edn: Manchester.

Keeble, N. H. 1987: *The Literary Culture of Nonconformity in Later Seventeenth-Century England*: Leicester.

Keeble, N. H. 1990: ' "The colonel's shadow": Lucy Hutchinson, women's writing and the Civil War.' In T. Healy and J. Sawday, eds, *Literature and the English Civil War*: Cambridge.

Kelly, J. 1987: 'The origins of the act of union: an examination of unionist opinion in Britain and Ireland, 1650–1800', *Irish Historical Studies*, 25.

Kelsall, H. M. and Kelsall, R. K. 1986: 'How people and news got around.' In H. M. Kelsall and R. K. Kelsall, *Scottish Lifestyle 300 Years Ago: New Light on Edinburgh and Border Families*: Edinburgh.

Kelsey, S. 1997: *Inventing a Republic: The Political Culture of the English Commonwealth, 1649–1653*: Manchester.

Kelsey, S. 2001: 'Staging the trial of Charles I.' In J. Peacey, ed., *The Regicides and the Execution of Charles I*: London.

Kelsey, S. 2002: 'The foundation of the council of state.' In C. Kyle and J. Peacey, eds, *Parliament at Work: Power, Patronage and Access, c.1510–1670*: London.

Kelsey, S. 2003a: 'The death of Charles I', *Historical Journal*.

Kelsey, S. 2003b: 'The trial of Charles I', *English Historical Review*.

Kemp, B. 1957: *King and Commons, 1660–1832*: London.

Kenyon, J. P. 1958: *Robert Spencer, Earl of Sunderland*: London.

Kenyon, J. P. 1966: *The Stuart Constitution*: Cambridge.

Kenyon, J. P. 1970: *The Stuarts*: London.

Kenyon, J. P. 1977: *Revolution Principles: The Politics of Party 1689–1720*: Cambridge.

Kenyon, J. P. 1985: *Stuart England*: Harmondsworth.

Kenyon, J. P. (ed.) 1986: *The Stuart Constitution: Documents and Commentary*. Cambridge.

Kidd, C. 1998: 'Protestantism, constitutionalism and British identity under the later Stuarts.' In B. Bradshaw and P. Roberts, eds, *British Consciousness and Identity: The Making of Britain, 1533–1707*: Cambridge.

Kidd, C. 1999: *British Identities before Nationalism: Ethnicity and Nationhood in the Atlantic World, 1600–1800*: Cambridge.

King, P. 1968: 'The episcopate during the English Civil War', *English Historical Review*, 83.

King, P. 1984: 'Decision-makers and decision-making in the English criminal law, 1750–1800', *Historical Journal*, 27, 1, 25–58.

King, P. 1996: 'Punishing assault: the transformation of attitudes in the English courts', *Journal of Interdisciplinary History*, 27, 1 (summer), 43–74.

Kirk, J. 1989: *Patterns of Reform: Continuity and Change in the Reformation Kirk*: Edinburgh.

Kishlansky, K. 1975: *The Rise of the New Model Army*: Cambridge.

Kishlansky, M. 1979: *The Rise of the New Model Army*: Cambridge.

Klein, L. 1989: 'Liberty, manners and politeness in early eighteenth-century England', *Historical Journal*, 32, 583–604.

Klein, L. 1993: 'The political significance of "politeness" in early eighteenth-century Britain.' In G. Shochet, ed., *Politics, Politeness and Patriotism: Folger Institute Center for the History of British Political Thought Proceedings*, vol. 5: Washington, DC.

Klein, L. 1994: *Shaftesbury and the Culture of Politeness*: Cambridge.

Klein, L. 1996: 'Coffee house civility 1660–1714: an aspect of post-courtly culture in England', *Huntington Library Quarterly*, 59, 30–51.

Knachel, P. A. 1969: *The Case of the Commonwealth of England Stated by Marchamont Nedham*: Charlottesville, VA.

Knights, M. 1993: 'London's "monster" petition of 1680', *Historical Journal*, 36, 39–67.

Knights, M. 1994: *Politics and Opinion in Crisis, 1678–81*: London.

Knights, M. 2000: Review of D. Zaret, *Origins of Democratic Culture*, H-Albion, H-Net Reviews, September 2000. URL: http://www.h-net.msu.edu/reviews/showrev.cgi?path =23451969480497.

Knoppers, L. L. 1994: *Historicizing Milton: Spectacle, Power, and Poetry in Restoration England*: Athens, GA.

Knoppers, L. L. 2000: *Constructing Cromwell: Ceremony, Portrait and Print 1645–1661*: Cambridge.

Knowler, W. 1739: *The Earl of Strafford's Letters and Despatches*, 2 vols: London.

Koertge, N. (ed.) 1998: *A House Built on Sand: Exposing Postmodernist Myths about Science*: New York.

Kubik, T. R. W. 1998: 'How far the sword? Militia tactics and politics in the *Commonwealth of Oceana*', *History of Political Thought*, 19, 2, 186–212.

Kupperman, K. O. (ed.) 1995: *America in European Consciousness, 1493–1750*: Chapel Hill, NC.

Kyle, C. R. 1998: 'Prince Charles in the parliaments of 1621 and 1624', *Historical Journal*, 41 (3), 603–24.

Laing, D. (ed.) 1841: *The Letters and Journals of Robert Baillie*, 3 vols: Edinburgh.

Lake, P. 1987: 'Calvinism and the English church, 1570–1635', *Past and Present*, 114.

Lake, P. 1993: 'The Laudian style: order, authority and the pursuit of the beauty of holiness in the 1630s.' In K. Fincham, ed., *The Early Stuart Church, 1603–1642*: Basingstoke.

Lake, P. and Questier, M. 1996: 'Agency, appropriation and rhetoric under the gallows: Puritans, Romanists and the state in early modern England', *Past and Present*, 153 (November), 64–107.

Lake, P. and Questier, M. 2000: 'Puritans, papists, and the "public sphere" in early modern England: the Edmund Campion affair in context', *Journal of Modern History*, 72, 587–627.

Lake, P. and Sharpe, K. (eds) 1994: *Culture and Politics in Early Stuart England*: London.

Lambert, S. 1992: 'State control of the press in theory and practice: the role of the stationers' company before 1640.' In R. Myers and M. Harris, eds, *Censorship and the Control of Print in England and France 1600–1900*: Winchester.

Lamont, W. (ed.) 1994: *Baxter: A Holy Commonwealth*: Cambridge.

Lamont, W. M. 1996: 'The Puritan revolution: a historiographical essay.' In J. G. A. Pocock, ed., *The Varieties of British Political Thought, 1500–1800*: Cambridge.

Landau, N. 1979: 'Independence, deference and voter participation: the behaviour of the electorate in early eighteenth-century Kent', *Historical Journal*, 22, 561–83.

Landsman, N. C. 1998: 'The middle colonies: new opportunities for settlement, 1660–1700.' In N. Canny, ed., *The Oxford History of the British Empire, vol. 1: The Origins of Empire: British Overseas Empire to the Close of the Seventeenth Century*: Oxford.

Langley, T. R. 2001: *Image Government: Monarchical Metamorphoses in English Literature and Art, 1649–1702*: Pittsburgh, PA.

Laqueur, T. 1990: *Making Sex: Body and Gender from the Greeks to Freud*: Cambridge, MA.

Larkin, J. F. and Hughes, P. L. (eds) 1973: *Stuart Royal Proclamations, Vol. 1: Royal Proclamations of King James I, 1603–1625*: Oxford.

Laslett, P. 1983: *The World We Have Lost Further Explored*, 3rd edn: London.

Lawson, P. G. 1986: 'Property crime and hard times in England, 1559–1624', *Law and History Review*, 4, 95–127.

Lawson, P. G. 1988: 'Lawless juries? The composition and behaviour of Hertfordshire juries, 1573–1624.' In J. S. Cockburn and T. A. Green, eds, *Twelve Good Men and True: The English Criminal Trial Jury, 1200–1800*: Princeton, NJ.

Lee, M., Jr 1985: *The Road to Revolution: Scotland under Charles I, 1625–37*: Urbana, IL.

Lee, M., Jr 1990: *Great Britain's Solomon: King James VI and I in his Three Kingdoms*: Urbana, IL.

Lenman, B. and Parker, G. 1980: 'The state, the community and the criminal law in early modern Europe.' In V. A. C. Gatrell, B. Lenman and G. Parker, eds, *Crime and the Law: The Social History of Crime in Western Europe Since 1500*: London.

Levack, B. P. 1987: *The Formation of the British State: England, Scotland and the Union, 1603–1707*: Oxford.

Levack, B. P. 1994: 'Law, sovereignty and the union.' In R. A. Mason, ed., *Scots and Britons: Scottish Political Thought and the Union of 1603*: Cambridge.

Levy, F. J. 1982: 'How information spread among the gentry, 1550–1640', *Journal of British Studies*, 21 (2), 11–34.

Lewalski, B. K. 1994: *Writing Women in Jacobean England*: Cambridge, MA.

Lindley, K. 1972: 'The impact of the 1641 rebellion upon England and Wales, 1641–5', *Irish Historical Studies*.

Lindley, K. 1982: *Fenland Riots and the English Revolution*: London.

Lindley, K. 1998: *The English Civil War and Revolution: A Sourcebook*: London.

Lindley, K. and Scott, D. (eds) 1999: *The Journal of Thomas Juxon, 1644–1647*: Camden Society, 5th series, 13.

Linschoten, J. H. van 1884: *The Voyage of John Huygen van Linschoten to the East Indies from the Old English Translation of 1598*, ed. A. C. Burnell and P. A. Tiele: London.

Linschoten, J. H. van 1955–7: *Itinerario: voyage ofte schipvaert von Jan Huygen van Linschoten naer oost ofte Portugaeles Indien, 1579–92*, 3 vols, ed. H. Kern and H. Terprstra: the Hague.

Linton, D. and Boston, R. 1987: *The Newspaper Press in Britain: An Annotated Bibliography*: London.

Lipsius, J. 1594: *The Six Bookes of Politickes*: London.

Little, P. 2000: 'The first unionists? Irish Protestant attitudes to union with England, 1653–9', *Irish Historical Studies*, 32, 44–58.

Lockyer, R. 1999: *The Early Stuarts: A Political History of England, 1603–1642*: Harlow.

Love, H. 1993: *Scribal Publication in Seventeenth-Century England*: Oxford.

Loxley, J. 1997: *Royalism and Poetry in the English Civil War*: Basingstoke.

Lutaud, O. 1976: *Winstanley: socialisme et christianisme sous Cromwell*: Paris.

Macaulay, T. B. 1913–14: *The History of England from the Accession of James the Second*, 6 vols, ed. C. H. Firth: London.

Macaulay, T. B. *History of England from the Accession of James II*, various edns.

McCafferty, J. 1995: 'John Bramhall and the Church of Ireland in the 1630s.' In A. Ford, J. McGuire and K. Milne, eds, *As By Law Established: The Church of Ireland Since the Reformation*: Dublin.

MacCarthy-Morrogh, M. 1986: *The Munster Plantation: English Migration to Southern Ireland, 1583–1641*: Oxford.

McCavitt, J. 1998: *Sir Arthur Chichester: Lord Deputy of Ireland, 1605–16*: Belfast.

McCoy, R. 1996: 'Old English honor in an evil time: aristocratic principle in the 1620s.' In M. Smuts, ed., *The Stuart Court and Europe*: Cambridge.

MacCraith, M. 1995: 'The Gaelic reaction to the Reformation.' In S. G. Ellis and S. Barber, eds, *Conquest and Union: Fashioning a British State 1485–1725*: Harlow.

MacCuarta, B. (ed.) 1993: *Ulster 1641: Aspects of the Rising*: Belfast.

McCulloch, J. R. 1954: *Early English Tracts on Commerce*: Cambridge.

McCullough, P. 1998: *Sermons at Court: Politics and Religion in Elizabethan and Jacobean Preaching*: Cambridge.

MacCurtain, M. and O'Dowd, M. (eds) 1991: *Women in Early Modern Ireland*: Edinburgh.

MacDonald, A. R. 1998: *The Jacobean Kirk, 1567–1625: Sovereignty, Polity and Liturgy*: Aldershot.

MacDonald, M. and Murphy, T. R. 1990: *Sleepless Souls: Suicide in Early Modern England*: Oxford.

McDowell, P. 1998: *The Women of Grub Street: Press, Politics, and Gender in the London Literary Marketplace 1678–1730*: Oxford.

McEachern, C. 1996: *The Poetics of English Nationhood, 1590–1612*: Cambridge.

McEntee, A. M. 1992: ' "The [un]civill-sisterhood of oranges and lemons": female petitioners and demonstrators, 1642–53.' In J. Holstun, ed., *Pamphlet Wars: Prose in the English Revolution*: London.

Macfarlane, A. (ed.) 1976: *The Diary of the Reverend Ralph Josselin*: Oxford.

Macfarlane, A. 1980: *The Justice and the Mare's Ale: Law and Disorder in Seventeenth-Century England*: Cambridge.

McGinnis, P. and Williamson, A. 2002: 'Britain, race, and the Iberian world empire.' In A. I. Macinnes and J. Ohlmeyer, eds, *The Stuart Kingdoms in the Seventeenth Century: Awkward Neighbours*: Dublin.

McGrath, C. I. 2000: *The Making of the Eighteenth-Century Irish Constitution: Government, Parliament and the Revenue, 1692–1714*: Dublin.

McGregor, J. F. 1984: 'The Baptists: fount of all heresy.' In J. F. McGregor and B. Reay, eds, *Radical Religion in the English Revolution*: Oxford.

McIlwain, C. H. 1918: *The Political Works of James I*: Cambridge, MA.

McInnes, A. 1982: 'When was the English Revolution?' *History*, 377–92.

Macinnes, A. I. 1990: 'The Scottish constitution, 1638–51: the rise and fall of oligarchic centralism.' In J. Morrill, ed., *The Scottish National Covenant in its British Context 1638–51*: Edinburgh.

Macinnes, A. I. 1991: *Charles I and the Making of the Covenanting Movement, 1625–1641*: Edinburgh.

Macinnes, A. I. 1996: *Clanship, Commerce and the House of Stuart, 1603–1788*: East Linton.

Macinnes, A. I. 1999a: 'Politically reactionary Brits?: The promotion of Anglo-Scottish union, 1603–1707.' In S. J. Connolly, ed., *Kingdoms United? Great Britain and Ireland since 1500*: Dublin.

Macinnes, A. I. 1999b: 'Regal union for Britain, 1603–38.' In G. Burgess, ed., *The New British History: Founding a Modern State, 1603–1715*: London.

Macinnes, A. I. 2000: 'Covenanting ideology in seventeenth-century Scotland.' In J. H. Ohlmeyer, ed., *Political Thought in Seventeenth-Century Ireland: Kingdom or Colony*: Cambridge.

Macinnes, A. I. 2001: 'Union for Ireland failed (1703), Union for Scotland accomplished (1706–7).' In D. Keogh and K. Whelan, eds, *Acts of Union: The Causes, Contexts, and Consequences of the Act of Union of 1801*: Dublin.

Macinnes, A. I. and Ohlmeyer, J. 2002 : 'International setting: awkward perspectives.' In A. I. Macinnes and J. Ohlmeyer, eds, *The Stuart Kingdoms in the Seventeenth Century: Awkward Neighbours*: Dublin.

Mack, P. 1992: *Visionary Women: Ecstatic Prophecy in Seventeenth-Century England*: Berkeley, CA.

Mackay, P. H. R. 1977: 'The reception given to the five articles of Perth', *Records of the Scottish Church History Society*, 9, 185–201.

McKenzie, D. F. 1973: '*The Staple of News* and the late plays.' In W. Blissett, J. Patrick and R. W. van Fossen, eds, *A Celebration of Ben Jonson*: Toronto.

McLaren, A. N. 1999: *Political Culture in the Reign of Elizabeth I*: Cambridge.

McMichael, J. R. and Taft, B. (eds) 1989: *The Writings of William Walwyn*: Athens, GA.

Macpherson, C. B. 1962: *The Political Theory of Possessive Individualism: Hobbes to Locke*: Oxford.

Macray, W. D. (ed.) 1888: *The History of the Rebellion and Civil Wars in England by Edward, Earl of Clarendon*: Oxford.

Madan, F. F. 1949: *A New Bibliography of the Eikon Basilike of King Charles the First with a note on Authorship*, Oxford Bibliographical Society, 3.

Maddicott, J. R. 1978: 'The county community and the making of public opinion in fourteenth-century England.' *Transactions of the Royal Historical Society*, 5th series, 28, 27–43.

Malcolm, J. L. 1992: 'Charles II and the reconstruction of royal power', *Historical Journal*, 35.

Maltby, J. 1998: *Prayer Book and People in Elizabethan and Early Stuart England*: Cambridge.

Manley, L. 1995: *Literature and Culture in Early Modern London*: Cambridge.

Manning, B. 1992: *1649, the Crisis of the English Revolution*: London.

Manning, R. B. 1988: *Village Revolts: Social Protest and Popular Disturbances in England 1509–1640*: Oxford.

Manuel, F. E. 1968: *A Portrait of Isaac Newton*: Cambridge, MA.

Marcus, L. S. 1986: *The Politics of Mirth: Jonson, Herrick, Milton, Marvell, and the Defense of Old Holiday Pastimes*: Chicago.

Marcus, L. S. 1993: 'Robert Herrick.' In T. N. Corns, ed., *The Cambridge Companion to English Poetry, Donne to Marvell*: Cambridge.

Martin, J. E. 1983: *Feudalism to Capitalism: Peasant and Landlord in English Agrarian Development*: London.

Martindale, A. 1845: *Life of Adam Martindale*, Chetham Society.

Mason, R. A. 1987: 'Scotching the Brut: politics, history and national myth in sixteenth-century Britain.' In R. A. Mason, ed., *Scotland and England, 1286–1815*: Edinburgh.

Mason, R. A. 1994a: 'George Buchanan, James VI and the Presbyterians.' In R. Mason, ed., *Scots and Britons*: Cambridge.

Mason, R. A. 1994b: 'Imagining Scotland: Scottish political thought and the 'problem' of Britain, 1560–1650.' In R. A. Mason, ed., *Scots and Britons: Scottish Political Thought and the Union of 1603*: Cambridge.

Mason, R. A. 1998: *Kingship and the Commonweal: Political Thought in Renaissance and Reformation Scotland*: East Linton.

Masson, D. 1877–94: *The Life of John Milton: Narrated in Connexion with the Political, Ecclesiastical, and Literary History of his Time*: London.

Mendelson, S. and Crawford, P. 1998: *Women in Early Modern England 1550–1720*: Oxford.

Mendle, M. 1985: *Dangerous Positions: Mixed Government, the Estates of the Realm, and the Making of the Answer to the xix propositions*: Tuscaloosa, AL.

Mendle, M. 1995: *Henry Parker and the English Civil War: The Political Thought of the Public's Privado*: Cambridge.

Mendle, M. 2001a: Review of J. Raymond, ed., *News, Newspapers, and Society in Early Modern Britain*, H-Albion, H-Net Reviews, April 2001. URL: http://www.h-net.msu.edu/reviews/showrev.cgi?path=23833987187733.

Mendle, M. 2001b: 'News and the pamphlet culture of mid-seventeenth-century England.' In B. Dooley and S. Baron, eds, *The Politics of Information in Early Modern Europe*: London.

Mercer, E. 1962: *English Art 1553–1625*: Oxford.

Merritt, J. F. (ed.) 1996: *The Political World of Thomas Wentworth, Earl of Strafford, 1621–1641*: Cambridge.

Merton, R. K. 1970: *Science, Technology and Society in 17th-Century England*: New York; originally published in *Osiris*, 4 (1938), 360–632.

Millar, O. 1960: 'Abraham van der Doort's catalogue of the collections of Charles I', *Walpole Society*, 37.

Millar, O. 1972: 'The inventories and valuations of the king's goods 1649–1651', *Walpole Society*, 43.

Millar, O. 1984: *The Queen's Pictures*: London.

Miller, J. 1977: 'The earl of Tyrconnell and James II's Irish policy', *Historical Journal*, 20.

Miller, J. 1978: *James II: A Study in Kingship*: Hove; revd edn 2000: *James II*: New Haven, CT.

Miller, J. 1982: 'Charles II and his parliaments', *Transactions of the Royal Historical Society*, 5th series, vol. 32.

Miller, J. 1984: 'The potential for 'absolutism' in later Stuart England', *History*, 69, 187–207.

Miller, J. 1991: *Charles II*: London.

Miller, J. 1995: 'Public opinion in Charles II's England', *History*, 80, 359–81.

Miller, J. 1997: *The Restoration and the England of Charles II*: Harlow.

Miller, J. 2000: *After the Civil Wars: English Politics and Government in the Reign of Charles II*: Harlow.

Milton, A. 1998: 'Licensing, censorship, and religious orthodoxy in early Stuart England', *Historical Journal*, 41, 625–51.

Milton, J. 1953–82: *Complete Prose Works of John Milton*, ed. D. M. Wolfe et al.: New Haven, CT.

Milton, J. 1997: *Complete Shorter Poems*, 2nd edn, ed. J. Carey: London.

Milton, J. 1998: *Paradise Lost*, 2nd edn, ed. A. Fowler: London.

Monod, P. K. 1989: *Jacobitism and the English People, 1688–1788*: Oxford.

Montaño, J. P. 1995: 'The quest for consensus: the Lord Mayor's Day Show in the 1670s.' In G. Maclean, ed., *Culture and Society in the Stuart Restoration: Literature, Drama and History*. Cambridge.

Moody, T. W., Martin, F. X. and Byrne, F. J. (eds) 1976: *A New History of Ireland, vol. 3: Early Modern Ireland, 1534–1691*: Oxford.

Moreland, C. and Bannister, D. 2000: *Antique Maps*. London.

Morrill, J. 1976: *The Revolt of the Provinces: Conservatives and Revolutionaries in the English Civil War 1603–42*: Harlow.

Morrill, J. 1990a: 'The National Covenant in its British context.' In J. Morrill, ed., *The Scottish National Covenant in its British Context*. Edinburgh.

Morrill, J. (ed.) 1990b: *The Scottish National Covenant in its British Context*. Edinburgh.

Morrill, J. 1992: 'The impact on society.' In J. Morrill, ed., *Revolution and Restoration: England in the 1650s*. London.

Morrill, J. 1993: 'The Britishness of the English Revolution 1640–1660.' In R. G. Asch, ed., *Three Nations – a Common History? England, Scotland, Ireland and British History c.1600–1920*: Bochum.

Morrill, J. 1993: *The Nature of the English Revolution*: Harlow.

Morrill, J. 1994: 'A British patriarchy? Ecclesiastical imperialism under the early Stuarts.' In A. Fletcher and P. Roberts, eds, *Religion, Culture and Society in Early Modern Britain: Essays in Honour of Patrick Collinson*: Cambridge.

Morrill, J. (ed.) 1996: *The Oxford Illustrated History of Tudor and Stuart Britain*: Oxford.

Morrill, J. 1999a: *Revolt in the Provinces: The People of England and the Tragedies of War, 1630–1648*: Harlow.

Morrill, J. 1999b: 'The war(s) of the three kingdoms.' In G. Burgess, ed., *The New British History: Founding a Modern State 1603–1715*: London.

Morrill, J. and Walter, J. 1997: 'Order and disorder in the English Revolution.' In R. Cust and A. Hughes, eds, *The English Civil War*: London.

Morrill, J., Slack, P. and Woolf, D. (eds) 1993: *Public Duty and Private Conscience in Seventeenth-Century England*: Oxford.

Morrill, J. S. 1975: 'William Davenport and the "silent majority" of early Stuart England', *Journal of the Chester Archaeological Society*, 58, 115–29.

Mousley, A. 1991: 'Self, state, and seventeenth-century news', *Seventeenth Century*, 6, 149–68.

Mowl, T. and Earnshaw, B. 1995: *Architecture Without Kings: The Rise of Puritan Classicism under Cromwell*: Manchester.

Muddiman, J. G. 1920: *Tercentenary Handlist of English and Welsh Newspapers, Magazines and Reviews*: London.

Muddiman, J. G. 1923: *The King's Journalist, 1659–1689*: London.

Muggli, M. Z. 1992: 'Ben Jonson and the business of news', *Studies in English Literature*, 32, 323–40.

Muldrew, C. 1996: 'The culture of reconciliation: community and the settlement of economic disputes in early modern England', *Historical Journal*, 39, 4, 915–42.

Muldrew, C. 1998: *The Economy of Obligation: The Culture of Credit and Social Relations in Early Modern England*: London.

Mullan, D. G. 1986: *Episcopacy in Scotland: The History of an Idea, 1560–1638*: Edinburgh.

Mullan, D. G. 2000: *Scottish Puritanism 1590–1638*: Oxford.

Mulligan, L. 1980: 'Puritans and English science: a critique of Webster', *Isis*, 71, 456–69.

Munter, R. 1967: *The History of the Irish Newspaper 1685–1760*: Cambridge.

Murdoch, A. 1998: *British History, 1660–1832: National Identity and Local Culture*: Basingstoke.

Murdoch, S. 2000: *Britain, Denmark–Norway and the House of Stuart, 1603–1660*: East Linton.

Murdoch, S. (ed.) 2001: *Scotland and the Thirty Years' War, 1618–1648*: Leiden.

Nelson, C. 1993: 'American readership of early British serials.' In R. Myers and M. Harris, eds, *Serials and their Readers 1620–1914*: Winchester.

Nelson, C. and Seccombe, M. 1986: *Periodical Publications 1641–1700: A Survey with Illustrations*. Bibliographical Society, Occasional Paper, no. 2: London.

Nelson, C. and Seccombe, M. 1987: *British Newspapers and Periodicals 1641–1700. A Short-Title Catalogue of Serials Printed in England, Scotland, Ireland, and British America*: New York.

Nelson, R. 1795: *A Companion for the Festivals and Fasts of the Church of England*, 27th edn.

Nenner, H. 1995: *The Right to be King: The Succession to the Crown of England, 1587–1714*: Chapel Hill, NC.

Newman, J. 1988: 'Italian treatises in use: the significance of Inigo Jones's annotations.' In J. Guillaume, ed., *Les Traités d'architecture de la Renaissance*: Paris.

Newton, I. 1959–77: *The Correspondence of Isaac Newton*, 7 vols, ed. H. W. Turnbull, J. F. Scott, A. R. Hall and L. Tilling: Cambridge.

Newton, I. 1967–80: *The Mathematical Papers of Isaac Newton*, 8 vols, ed. D. T. Whiteside: Cambridge.

Norbrook, D. 1984: *Poetry and Politics in the English Renaissance*: London.

Norbrook, D. 1990: 'Marvell's "Horatian Ode".' In T. Healy and J. Sawday, eds, *Literature and the English Civil War*: Cambridge.

Norbrook, D. 1994: '*Areopagitica*, censorship, and the early modern public sphere.' In R. Burt, ed., *The Administration of Aesthetics: Censorship, Political Criticism, and the Public Sphere*: Minneapolis.

Norbrook, D. 1999: *Writing the English Republic: Poetry, Rhetoric and Politics 1627–1660*: Cambridge.

Norgate, E. 1997: *Miniatura or the Art of Limning*, ed. J. M. Muller and J. Murrell: New Haven, CT.

Notestein, W. 1924: 'The winning of the initiative by the House of Commons', *Proceedings of the British Academy*, 11, 125–75.

Ó Buachalla, B. 1987: *Foras Feasa ar Éirinn, History of Ireland: Foreword*: Dublin.

Ó Buachalla, B. 1996: *Aisling Ghearr: Na Stiobhartaigh Agus an tAos Leinn 1603–1788*: Dublin.

Ó hAnnracháin, T. 1995: ' "Far from *terra firma*": the mission of GianBattista Rinuccini to Ireland, 1645–49'. Unpublished Ph.D. thesis, European University Institute.

Ó Siochrú, M. 1999: *Confederate Ireland 1642–1649: A Constitutional and Political Analysis*: Dublin.

Ó Siochrú, M. (ed.) 2001: *Kingdoms in Crisis: Ireland in the 1640s*: Dublin.

O'Brien, P. K. and Hunt, P. A. 1993: 'The rise of a fiscal state in England, 1485–1815', *Historical Research*, 66: 129–76.

O'Callaghan, M. 2000: *The 'Shepheards Nation': Jacobean Spenserians and Early Stuart Political Culture, 1612–1625*: Oxford.

O'Connor, T. (ed.) 2001: *The Irish in Europe, 1580–1815*: Dublin.

Ogg, D. 1934: *England in the Reign of Charles II*: Oxford.

Ogg, D. 1955: *England in the Reigns of James II and William III*: Oxford.

Ohlmeyer, J. 1992: 'The "Antrim plot" of 1641 – a myth?' *Historical Journal*, 35, 905–19.

Ohlmeyer, J. 1993: *Civil War and Restoration in the Three Stuart Kingdoms: The Political Career of Randal MacDonnell First Marquis of Antrim, 1609–83*: Cambridge.

Ohlmeyer, J. and Maxwell-Perceval, M. 1994: 'The "Antrim plot" of 1641 – a myth? A response', and J. Ohlmeyer, 'The "Antrim plot" of 1641: a rejoinder', *Historical Journal*, 37, 421–37.

Ohlmeyer, J. H. (ed.) 1995: *Ireland from Independence to Occupation, 1641–1660*: Cambridge.

Oldenburg, H. 1965–86: *The Correspondence of Henry Oldenburg*, 13 vols, ed. A. R. Hall and M. B. Hall: Madison, WI.

Oldham, J. C. 1985: 'On pleading the belly: a history of the jury of matrons', *Criminal Justice History*, 6, 1–64.

Orgel, S. 1965: *The Jonsonian Masque*: Cambridge, MA.

Orgel, S. and Strong, R. 1973: *Inigo Jones: The Theatre of the Stuart Court*: Berkeley, CA.

Ouston, H. 1980: 'York in Edinburgh: James VII and the patronage of learning in Scotland, 1679–88.' In J. Dwyer et al., eds, *New Perspectives on the Politics and Culture of Early Modern Scotland*: Edinburgh.

Overton, M. 1996: *Agricultural Revolution in England: The Transformation of the Agrarian Economy 1500–1850*: Cambridge.

Overton, M. and Whittle, J. *Production and Consumption*: forthcoming.

Pagden, A. 1995: *Lords of all the World: Ideologies of Empire in Spain, Britain and France c.1500–c.1800*: New Haven, CT.

Parnham, D. 2001: 'Politics spun out of theology and prophecy: Sir Henry Vane on the spiritual environment of public power', *History of Political Thought*, 22, 1, 53–83.

Patterson, A. 1997: *Early Modern Liberalism*: Cambridge.

Patterson, W. B. 1997: *King James VI and I and the Reunion of Christendom*: Cambridge.

Pawlish, H. S. 1985: *Sir John Davies and the Conquest of Ireland: A Study in Legal Imperialism*: Cambridge.

Peacock, J. 1995: *The Stage Designs of Inigo Jones*: Cambridge.

Peacock, J. 2001: 'Robert Walker (*c*.1607–*c*.1658), *Self-portrait*.' In E. Chaney and G. Worsdale, eds, *The Stuart Portrait: Status and Legacy*: Southampton.

Pears, I. 1998: *The Discovery of Painting: The Growth of Interest in the Arts in England 1680–1768*: New Haven, CT.

Peck, L. L. (ed.) 1991: *The Mental World of the Jacobean Court*: Cambridge.

Peck, L. L. 1996: 'Kingship, counsel and law in early Stuart Britain.' In J. G. A. Pocock, ed., *The Varieties of British Political Thought, 1500–1800*: Cambridge.

Peltonen, M. 1995: *Classical Humanism and Republicanism in English Political Thought 1570–1640*: Cambridge.

Perceval-Maxwell, M. 1973: *The Scottish Migration to Ulster in the Reign of James I*: London.

Perceval-Maxwell, M. 1994a: *The Outbreak of the 1641 Rebellion in Ireland*: Montreal.

Perceval-Maxwell, M. 1994b: *The Outbreak of the Irish Rebellion of 1641*: Dublin.

Peters, K. 1998: ' "Women's speaking justified": women and discipline in the early Quaker movement, 1652–56.' In R. N. Swanson, ed., *Gender and Christian Religion*, Studies in Church History, vol. 34: Woodbridge.

Philips, C. 1978: 'The royalist north: the Cumberland and Westmorland gentry, 1642–1660', *Northern History*, 14, 169–92.

Phillips, J. 1973: *The Reformation of Images: Destruction of Art in England 1535–1660*: Berkeley, CA.

Phillipson, N. and Skinner, Q. (eds) 1993: *Political Discourse in Early Modern Britain*: Cambridge.

Pincus, S. 1996: *Protestantism and Patriotism: Ideologies and the Making of English Foreign Policy, 1650–1668*: Cambridge.

Pincus, S. 1998: 'Neither Machiavellian moment nor possessive individualism: commercial society and the defenders of the English Commonwealth, *American Historical Review*, 103.

Pincus, S. A. 2001: *Restoration*: Cambridge.

Pincus, S. C. A. 1995: ' "Coffee politicians does create": coffeehouses and Restoration political culture', *Journal of Modern History*, 67, 819–20.

Pincus, S. C. A. 1996: *Protestantism and Patriotism: Ideologies and the Making of English Foreign Policy, 1650–1668*: Cambridge.

Pinkham, L. 1954: *William III and the Respectable Revolution*: Cambridge, MA.

Plumb, J. H. 1967: *The Growth of Political Stability in England, 1675–1725*: London.

Plumb, J. H. 1969: 'The growth of the electorate in England from 1600 to 1715', *Past and Present*, 45, 90–116.

Pocock, J. G. A. 1975a: 'British history: a plea for a new subject', *Journal of Modern History*, vol. 4.

Pocock, J. G. A. 1975b: *The Machiavellian Moment: Florentine Political Thought and the Atlantic Republican Tradition*: Princeton, NJ.

Pocock, J. G. A. 1985: *Virtue, Commerce, and History: Essays on Political Thought and History, Chiefly in the Eighteenth Century*: Cambridge. Pocock's ideas are challenged in S. Burtt 1992: *Virtue Transformed: Political Argument in England, 1688–1740*: Cambridge; and see also D. Hayton 1990: 'Moral reform and country politics in the late seventeenth-century House of Commons', *Past and Present*, 128, 48–91.

Pocock, J. G. A. 1987: *The Ancient Constitution and the Feudal Law: A Reissue with a Retrospect*: Cambridge.

Pocock, J. G. A. (ed.) 1992: *James Harrington: The Commonwealth of Oceana and A System of Politics*: Cambridge.

Pocock, J. G. A. (ed.) 1993: *The Varieties of British Political Thought 1500–1800*: Cambridge.

Pocock, J. G. A. 1996: 'The Atlantic archipelago and the war of the three kingdoms.' In B. Bradshaw and J. Morrill, eds, *The British Problem, c.1534–1707*: Basingstoke.

Pollock, L. 1989: ' "Teach her to live under obedience": the making of women in the upper ranks of early modern England', *Continuity and Change*, 4, 2, 231–58.

Porter, R. 1987: 'The scientific revolution: a spoke in the wheel?' In R. Porter and M. Teich, eds, *Revolution in History*: Cambridge.

Porter, S. 1998: *The Great Fire of London*: Stroud.

Portier, F. 1996: 'Prices paid for Italian pictures in the Stuart age', *Journal of the History of Collections*, 8 (1), 53–69.

Potter, L. 1989: *Secret Rites and Secret Writing: Royalist Literature, 1641–1660*: Cambridge.

Powell, W. S. 1977: *John Pory 1572–1636: The Life and Letters of a Man of Many Parts*: Chapel Hill, NC.

Prakash, O. (ed.) 1997: *European Commercial Expansion in Early Modern Asia*: London.

Prakash, O. 1998: *The New Cambridge History of India: European Commercial Life in Pre-Colonial India*: Cambridge.

Prestwich, M. 1966: *Cranfield: Politics and Profits under the Early Stuarts*: Oxford.

Price, J. M. 1958: 'A note on the circulation of the London press, 1704–1714', *Bulletin of the Institute of Historical Research*, 31, 215–24.

Principe, L. M. 1998: *The Aspiring Adept: Robert Boyle and his Alchemical Quest*: Princeton, NJ.

Principe, L. M. 2000: 'The alchemies of Robert Boyle and Isaac Newton: alternative approaches and divergent deployments.' In M. J. Osler, ed., *Rethinking the Scientific Revolution*: Cambridge.

Purkiss, D. 1995: 'Women's stories of witchcraft,' *Gender and History*, 7, 3, 408–32.

Quinn, D. B. 1974: *England and the Discovery of America, 1481–1620*: New York.

Quinn, D. B. 1977: *North America from Earliest Discovery to First Settlement*: New York.

Ralegh, Sir Walter 1971: *The History of the World*, ed. C. A. Partrides: London.

Ralegh, W. (ed.) 1912: *The Complete Works of George Savile First Marquess of Halifax*: Oxford.

Randell, H. W. 1947: 'The rise and fall of a martyrology: sermons on Charles I', *Huntington Library Quarterly*, 10, 135–67.

Rattansi, P. M. and McGuire, J. E. 1966: 'Newton and the "Pipes of Pan" ', *Notes and Records of the Royal Society*, 21, 108–43.

Raymond, J. (ed.) 1993: *Making the News: An Anthology of the Newsbooks of Revolutionary England, 1641–1660*: Moreton-in-Marsh.

Raymond, J. 1996: *The Invention of the Newspaper: English Newsbooks 1641–1649*: Oxford.

Raymond, J. 1999a: 'Introduction: newspapers, forgeries, and histories.' In J. Raymond, ed., *News, Newspapers, and Society in Early Modern Britain*: London.

Raymond, J. 1999b: 'The newspaper, public opinion, and the public sphere in the seventeenth century.' In J. Raymond, ed., *News, Newspapers, and Society in Early Modern Britain*: London.

Reddaway, T. F. 1940: *The Rebuilding of London after the Great Fire*: London.

Reeve, L. J. 1989: *Charles I and the Road to Personal Rule*: Cambridge.

Reid, J. G. 1981: *Acadia, Maine and New England: Marginal Colonies in the Seventeenth Century*: Toronto.

Reinmuth, H. S. 1970: 'Border society in transition.' In H. S. Reinmuth, ed., *Early Stuart Studies: Essays in Honour of David Harris Wilson*: Minneapolis.

Reitlinger, G. 1961: *The Economics of Taste: The Rise and Fall of Picture Prices*: London.

Richardson, S. (ed.) 1740: *The Negotiations of Sir Thomas Roe in His Embassy to the Ottoman Porte from the Year 1621 to 1628 Inclusive*: London.

Riley, P. W. J. 1979: *King William and the Scottish Politicians*: Edinburgh.

Roberts, M. 1979: 'Sickles and scythes: women's work and men's work at harvest time', *History Workshop Journal*, 7, 3–28.

Roberts, M. 1985: ' "Words they are women and deeds they are men": images of work and gender in early modern England.' In L. Charles and L. Duffin, eds, *Women and Work in Pre-Industrial England*: London.

Roberts, M. and Clarke, S. (eds) 2000: *Women and Gender in Early Modern Wales*: Cardiff.

Roberts, S. 1983: 'The study of dispute: anthropological perspectives.' In J. Bossy, ed., *Disputes and Settlements: Law and Human Relations in the West*: Cambridge.

Roberts, S. 1998: 'Local government reform in England and Wales during the Interregnum: a survey.' In I. Roots, ed., *Into Another Mould: Aspects of the Interregnum*, 2nd edn: Exeter.

Robertson, J. 1995: 'An elusive sovereignty: the course of the Union debate in Scotland 1698–1707.' In J. Robertson, ed., *A Union for Empire: Political Thought and the Union of 1707*: Cambridge.

Rogers, N. 1988: 'Popular Jacobitism in provincial context: eighteenth-century Bristol and Norwich.' In E. Cruickshanks and J. Black, eds, *The Jacobite Challenge*: Edinburgh.

Rogers, N. 1989: *Whigs and Cities: Popular Politics in the Age of Walpole and Pitt*: Oxford.

Rollison, D. 1992: *The Local Origins of Modern Society: Gloucestershire, 1500–1800*: London.

Roots, I. 1970: 'Swordsmen and decimators.' In R. H. Parry, ed., *The English Civil War and After, 1642–1658*: London.

Roper, M. and Tosh, J. 1991: 'Introduction: historians and the politics of masculinity.' In M. Roper and J. Tosh, eds, *Manful Assertions: Masculinities in Britain Since 1800*: London.

Rose, C. 1991: ' "Seminarys-of-faction-and-rebellion": Jacobites, Whigs and the London charity schools, 1716–1724', *Historical Journal*, 34, 831–55.

Rose, C. 1999: *England in the 1690s: Revolution, Religion, and War*: Oxford.

Roseveare, H. 1991: *The Financial Revolution 1660–1760*: London.

Ross, C. 1981: 'Rumour, propaganda and popular opinion during the Wars of the Roses.' In R. A. Griffiths, ed., *Patronage, the Crown and the Provinces in Later Medieval England*: Gloucester.

Rowell, S. C. 2000: 'The Grand Duchy of Lithuania and Baltic identity, *c.*1500–1600.' In A. I. Macinnes, T. Riis and F. G. Pedersen, eds, *Ships, Guns and Bibles in the North Sea and Baltic States, c.1350–c.1700*: East Linton.

Russell, C. (ed.) 1973: *The Origins of the English Civil War*: Basingstoke.

Russell, C. 1976: 'Parliamentary history in perspective, 1604–29', *History*, vol. 61.

Russell, C. 1979: *Parliaments and English Politics, 1621–1629*: Oxford.

Russell, C. 1983: *Science and Change 1700–1900*: London.

Russell, C. 1987: 'The British Problem and the English Civil War', *History*, vol. 72.

Russell, C. 1990a: *The Causes of the English Civil War*: Oxford.

Russell, C. 1990b: 'The ship money judgements of Bramston and Davenport', reprinted in C. Russell, *Unrevolutionary England, 1603–1642*: London.

Russell, C. 1990c: *Unrevolutionary England, 1603–1642*: London.

Russell, C. 1991: *The Fall of the British Monarchies 1637–1642*: Oxford.

Russell, C. 1993: 'The Scottish party in English parliaments 1640–2, or, the myth of the English revolution', *Historical Research*.

Russell, C. 1994: 'The Anglo-Scottish Union of 1603–43: a success?' In A. Fletcher and P. Roberts, eds, *Religion, Culture and Society in Early Modern Britain: Essays in Honour of Patrick Collinson*: Cambridge.

Russell, C. 1995: *The Fall of the British Monarchies*: Oxford.

Rutt, J. T. (ed.) 1828: *Diary of Thomas Burton esq*: London.

Sabine, G. H. (ed.) 1941/1965: *The Works of Gerrard Winstanley*: New York.

Salmon, J. H. M. 1990: 'Catholic resistance theory, Ultramontanism, and the royalist response'. In J. H. Burns, ed., *The Cambridge History of Political Thought 1450–1700*: Cambridge.

Samaha, J. 1978: 'Hanging for felony: the rule of law in Elizabethan Colchester', *Historical Journal*, 21, 763–82.

Sanders, J. 1998: 'Print, popular culture, consumption and commodification in *The Staple of News*.' In J. Sanders, K. Chedgzoy and S. Wiseman, eds, *Refashioning Ben Jonson: Gender, Politics and the Jonsonian Canon*: Basingstoke.

Scammell, G. V. 1981: *The World Encompassed: The First European Maritime Empires c.800–1650*: London.

Schaffer, S. 1989: 'Glass works: Newton's prisms and the uses of experiment.' In D. Gooding, T. Pinch and S. Schaffer, eds, *The Uses of Experiment: Studies in the Natural Sciences*: Cambridge.

Schmitt, C. 1983: *John Case and Aristotelianism in Renaissance England*: Montreal.

Schnabel, F. forthcoming: 'English crown finance, 1603–42.' Unpublished Ph.D. thesis, Harvard University.

Schofield, R. S. 1968: 'The measurement of literacy in pre-industrial England.' In J. Goody, ed., *Literacy in Traditional Societies*: Cambridge.

Schuster, J. A. and Taylor, A. B. H. 1997: 'Blind trust: the gentlemanly origins of experimental science', *Social Studies of Science*, 27, 503–36.

Schwoerer, L. G. 1977: 'Propaganda in the Revolution of 1688', *American History Review*, 82, 843–74.

Schwoerer, L. G. 1981: *The Declaration of Rights*: Baltimore, MD.

Schwoerer, L. G. 1992a: 'Liberty of the press and public opinion 1660–1695.' In J. R. Jones, ed., *Liberty Secured? Britain before and after 1688*: Stanford, CA.

Schwoerer, L. G. 1992b: *The Revolution of 1688–1689: Changing Perspectives*: Cambridge.

Scott, D. 1999: 'The "Northern Gentlemen", the parliamentary Independents and Anglo-Saxon relations in the Long Parliament', *Historical Journal*, 42

Scott, D. 2000: 'The Barwis affair: political allegiance and the Scots during the British civil wars', *English Historical Review*, 115.

Scott, J. 1986: 'Gender: a useful category of historical analysis', *American Historical Review*, 91, 5, 1053–75.

Scott, J. 1988a: *Algernon Sidney and the English Republic 1623–1677*: Cambridge.

Scott, J. 1988b: 'Radicalism and Restoration: the shape of the Stuart experience', *Historical Journal*, 31.

Scott, J. 1991: *Algernon Sidney and the Restoration Crisis 1677–1683*: Cambridge.

Scott, J. 2000: *England's Troubles: Seventeenth-Century English Political Instability in European Context*: Cambridge.

Scott, J. C. 1985: *Weapons of the Weak: Everyday Forms of Peasant Resistance*: New Haven, CT.

Scott, J. C. 1990: *Domination and the Arts of Resistance: Hidden Transcripts*: New Haven, CT.

Scott, W. R. 1912: *The Constitutions and Finance of English, Scottish and Irish Joint-Stock Companies to 1720*, 3 vols: Cambridge.

Seaver, S. 1985: *Wallington's World: A Puritan Artisan in Seventeenth-Century London*: Stanford, CA.

Seaward, P. 1987: *The Cavalier Parliament and the Reconstruction of the Old Regime, 1661–7*: Cambridge.

Shagan, E. H. 1997: 'Constructing discord: ideology, propaganda, and English responses to the Irish rebellion of 1641,' *Journal of British Studies*, 36, 1, 4–34.

Shapin, S. 1988: 'Understanding the Merton thesis', *Isis*, 79, 594–605.

Shapin, S. 1994: *A Social History of Truth: Civility and Science in Seventeenth-Century England*: Chicago, IL.

Shapin, S. 1996: *The Scientific Revolution*: Chicago, IL.

Shapin, S. and Barnes, B. 1979: 'Darwin and social Darwinism: purity and history.' In B. Barnes and S. Shapin, eds, *Natural Order: Historical Studies of Scientific Culture*: Beverly Hills, CA.

Shapin, S. and Schaffer, S. 1985: *Leviathan and the Air-Pump: Hobbes, Boyle and the Experimental Life*: Princeton, NJ.

Shapiro, A. 1996: 'The gradual acceptance of Newton's theory of light and color, 1672–1727', *Perspectives on Science*, 4, 59–140.

Shapiro, B. 1969: *John Wilkins: An Intellectual Biography*: Berkeley, CA.

Shapiro, B. 1994: 'The concept "fact": legal origins and cultural diffusion', *Albion*, 26, 1–26.

Sharp, A. (ed.) 1983: *Political Ideas of the English Civil Wars 1641–1649*: London.

Sharp, A. (ed.) 1998: *The English Levellers*: Cambridge.

Sharp, B. 1980: *In Contempt of All Authority: Rural Artisans and Riot in the West of England, 1586–1660*: Los Angeles, CA.

Sharp, B. 1985: 'Popular protest in seventeenth-century England.' In B. Reay, ed., *Popular Culture in Seventeenth-Century England*: London.

Sharp, B. 2000: 'The food riots of 1347 and the medieval moral economy.' In A. Randall and A. Charlesworth, eds, *Moral Economy and Popular Protest: Crowds, Conflict and Authority*: London.

Sharpe, J. A. 1981: 'Domestic homicide in early modern England', *Historical Journal*, 24, 29–48.

Sharpe, J. A. 1983: *Crime in Seventeenth-century England: A County Study*: Cambridge.

Sharpe, J. A. 1985a: 'Debate: the history of violence in England, some observations', *Past and Present*, 108 (August), 206–15.

Sharpe, J. A. 1985b: ' "Last dying speeches": religion, ideology and public execution in seventeenth-century England', *Past and Present*, 107 (May), 144–67.

Sharpe, J. A. 1985c: 'The people and the law.' In B. Reay, ed., *Popular Culture in Seventeenth-century England*: London.

Sharpe, J. A. 1999: *Crime in Early Modern England, 1550–1750*, 2nd edn: London.

Sharpe, K. (ed.) 1978: *Faction and Parliament: Essays on Early Stuart History*: Oxford.

Sharpe, K. 1983: 'The personal rule of Charles I.' In H. Tomlinson, ed., *Before the English Civil War*: London.

Sharpe, K. 1987: *Criticism and Compliment: The Politics of Literature in the England of Charles I*: Cambridge.

Sharpe, K. 1992: *The Personal Rule of Charles I*: New Haven, CT.

Sharpe, K. 2000a: 'Celebrating a cultural turn: political culture and cultural politics in early modern England.' In K. Sharpe, ed., *Remapping Early Modern England: The Culture of Seventeenth-Century Politics*: Cambridge.

Sharpe, K. 2000b: *Remapping Early Modern England: The Culture of Seventeenth-Century Politics*: Cambridge.

Sharpe, K. and Lake, P. (eds) 1994: *Culture and Politics in Early Modern England*: Basingstoke.

Sharpe, K. and Zwicker, S. N. (eds) 1987: *Politics of Discourse: The Literature and History of Seventeenth-Century England*: Berkeley, CA.

Sharpe, K. and Zwicker, S. N. (eds) 1998: *Refiguring Revolutions: Aesthetics and Politics from the English Revolution to the Romantic Revolution*: Berkeley, CA.

Sharpe, P. (ed.) 1998: *Women's Work: The English Experience 1650–1914*: London.

Sharpe, P. 1999: 'Dealing with love: the ambiguous independence of the single woman in early modern England', *Gender and History*, 11, 2, 209–32.

Sheils, W. J. and Wood, D. (eds) 1989: *The Churches, Ireland and the Irish: Studies in Church History*, 20: Oxford.

Sherwood, J. and Pevsner, N. 1990: *Oxfordshire*: Harmondsworth.

Sherwood, R. 1989: *The Court of Oliver Cromwell*, 2nd edn: Cambridge.

Shoemaker, R. and Vincent, M. (eds) 1998: *Gender and History in Western Europe*: London.

Siebert, F. S. 1952: *Freedom of the Press in England 1476–1776: The Rise and Decline of Government Controls*: Urbana, IL.

Simms, J. G. 1956: *The Williamite Confiscation in Ireland, 1690–1703*: London.

Simms, J. G. 1969: *Jacobite Ireland, 1685–1691*: London; reprinted Dublin, 2000.

Skinner, Q. 1974: 'The principles and practice of opposition: the case of Bolingbroke versus Walpole.' In N. McKendrick, ed., *Historical Perspectives: Studies in English Thought and Society in Honour of J. H. Plumb*: London.

Skinner, Q. 1996: *Reason and Rhetoric in the Philosophy of Hobbes*: Cambridge.

Skinner, Q. 1998: *Liberty before Liberalism*: Cambridge.

Slack, P. 1980: 'Books of orders: the making of English social policy, 1577–1631', *Transactions of the Royal Historical Society*, 5th series, 30, 1–22.

Slack, P. 1985: *Poverty and Policy in Tudor and Stuart England*: London.

Slack, P. 1992: 'Dearth and social policy in early modern England', *Social History of Medicine*, 5, 1, 1–17.

Slack, P. 1999: *From Reformation to Improvement: Public Welfare in Early Modern England*: Oxford.

Sloan, K. 2000: *'A Noble Art': Amateur Artists and Drawing Masters c.1600–1800*: London.

Smith, A. E. 1965: *Colonists in Bondage: White Servitude and Convict Labour in America, 1607–1776*: Chapel Hill, NC.

Smith, D. 1992: 'The struggle for new constitutional and institutional forms.' In J. Morrill, ed., *Revolution and Restoration: England in the 1650s*: London.

Smith, D. L. 1998: *A History of the Modern British Isles, 1603–1707: The Double Crown*: Oxford.

Smith, D. L. 1999: *The Stuart Parliaments 1603–1689*: London.

Smith, N. 1989: *Perfection Proclaimed: Language and Literature in English Radical Religion 1640–1660*: Oxford.

Smith, N. 1994: *Literature and Revolution in England 1640–1660*: New Haven, CT.

Smith Fussner, F. 1957: 'William Camden's "Dioscourse Concerning the Prerogative of the Crown"', *Proceedings of the American Philosophical Society*, 101.

Smuts, R. M. 1987: *Court Culture and the Origins of a Royalist Tradition in Early Stuart England*: Philadelphia, PA.

Smuts, R. M. 1989: 'Public ceremony and royal charisma: the English royal entry in London, 1485–1642.' In A. L. Beier et al., eds, *The First Modern Society*: Cambridge.

Smuts, R. M. (ed.) 1996: *The Stuart Court and Europe: Essays in Politics and Political Culture*: Cambridge.

Smuts, R. M. 1999: *Culture and Power in England 1585–1685*: Houndsmills.

Smyth, J. 1993: '"Like amphibious animals": Irish Protestants, Ancient Britons, 1691–1707', *Historical Journal*, 36.

Smyth, J. 2001: *The Making of the United Kingdom, 1660–1800*: Harlow.

Snow, V. F. 1970: *Essex the Rebel: The Life of Robert Devereux, the Third Earl of Essex, 1591–1646*: Lincoln, NB.

Snyder, H. L. 1968: 'The circulation of newspapers in the reign of Queen Anne', *The Library*, 5th series, 23, 206–35.

Snyder, H. L. 1976: 'A further note on the circulation of newspapers in the reign of Queen Anne', *The Library*, 5th series, 31, 387–9.

Snyder, H. L. 1977: 'Newsletters in England, 1689–1715: with special reference to John Dyer – a byway in the history of England.' In D. H. Bond and W. R. McLeod, eds, *Newsletters to Newspapers: Eighteenth-Century Journalism*: Morgantown, WV.

Sommerville, C. J. 1996a: *The News Revolution in England: Cultural Dynamics of Daily Information*: New York.

Sommerville, C. J. 1996b: 'Surfing the coffeehouse', *History Today*, 47 (6), 8–10.

Sommerville, J. P. 1986: *Politics and Ideology in England 1603–1640*: London.

Sommerville, J. P. 1992: *Thomas Hobbes: Political Ideas in Historical Context*: London.

Sommerville, J. P. 1994: *King James VI and I: Political Writings*: Cambridge.

Sommerville, J. P. 1999: *Royalists and Patriots: Politics and Ideology in England, 1603–1640*: Harlow.

Sommerville, M. R. 1995: *Sex and Subjection: Attitudes to Women in Early-Modern Society*: London.

Speck, W. A. 1970: *Tory and Whig: The Struggle in the Constituencies, 1701–1715*: London.

Speck, W. A. 1987: 'The Orangist conspiracy against James II,' *History Journal*, 31, 453–62.

Speck, W. A. 1988: *Reluctant Revolutionaries: Englishmen and the Revolution of 1688*: Oxford.

Speck, W. A., Gray, W. and Hopkinson, R. 1975: 'Computer analysis of poll books: a further report', *Bulletin of the Institute of Historical Research*, 48, 64–90.

Spedding, R. E. and Heath, D. (eds) 1966: *Works of Francis Bacon*, 14 vols: Stuttgart.

Spruyt, H. 1996: *The Sovereign State and Its Competitors*: Princeton, NJ.

Spufford, M. 1974: *Contrasting Communities: English Villagers in the Sixteenth and Seventeenth Centuries*: Cambridge.

Spufford, M. 1979: 'First steps in literacy: the reading and writing experiences of the humblest seventeenth-century spiritual autobiographers', *Social History*, 4, 407–35.

Spufford, M. and Went, J. 1995: *Poverty Portrayed: Gregory King and the Parish of Eccleshall*: Keele.

Spurr, J. 1991: *The Restoration Church of England*: New Haven, CT.

Spurr, J. 2000: *England in the 1670s: 'This Masquerading Age'*: Oxford.

Starkey, D. (ed.) 1987: *The English Court from the Wars of the Roses to the Civil War*: Harlow.

Stater, V. L. 1994: *Noble Government: The Stuart Lord Lieutenancy and the Transformation of English Politics*: Athens, GA.

Steele, I. K. 1985: 'Communicating the English Revolution to the colonies, 1688–1689', *Journal of British Studies*, 24, 333–57.

Steensgaard, N. 1973: *Carracks, Caravans and Companies: The Structural Crisis in the European Asian Trade in the Early Seventeenth Century*: Copenhagen.

Stevenson, D. 1972–4: 'Conventicles in the kirk, 1619–37', *Records of the Scottish Church History Society*, 18, 99–114.

Stevenson, D. 1973: *The Scottish Revolution 1637–1644: The Triumph of the Covenanters*: Newton Abbot.

Stevenson, J. 1985: 'The moral economy of the English crowd: myth and reality.' In A. Fletcher and J. Stevenson, eds, *Order and Disorder in Early Modern England*: Cambridge.

Stewart, B. S. 1969: 'The cult of the royal martyr', *Church History*, 38, 175–87.

Stone, L. 1965: *The Crisis of the Aristocracy, 1558–1641*: Oxford.

Stone, L. 1972: *The Causes of the English Revolution, 1529–1642*: London.

Stone, L. 1983: 'Interpersonal violence in English society, 1300–1980', *Past and Present*, 101 (February), 22–33.

Stone, L. 1985: 'Debate: the history of violence in England, a rejoinder', *Past and Present*, 108 (August), 216–24.

Storrs, C. 1999: 'Disaster at Darien: 1698–1700? The persistence of Spanish imperial power on the eve of the demise of the Spanish Habsburgs', *European History Quarterly*, 29.

Stoye, J. 1989: *English Travellers Abroad 1604–1667: Their Influence in English Society and Politics*: New Haven, CT.

Stoyle, M. 1994: 'The last refuge of a scoundrel: Sir Richard Grenville and Cornish particularism, 1644–6', *Historical Research*, 71.

Stoyle, M. 1998: *Loyalty and Locality: Popular Allegiance in Devon during the English Civil War*: Exeter.

Straka, G. 1962: 'The last phase of divine right theory, 1689–1702', *English Historical Review*, 77, 638–58.

Strong, R. 1969: *The English Icon: Elizabethan and Jacobean Portraiture*: London.

Strong, R. 1986: *Henry Prince of Wales and England's Lost Renaissance*: London.

Summerson, J. 1993: *Architecture in Britain: 1530–1830*: Harmondsworth.

Summerson, J. and Colvin, H. 2000: *Inigo Jones*: Harmondsworth.

Sutherland, J. R. 1934: 'The circulation of newspapers and literary periodicals, 1700–30', *The Library*, 4th series, 15, 110–24.

Sutherland, J. R. 1986: *The Restoration Newspaper and its Development*: Cambridge.

Sykes, N. 1959: *From Sheldon to Secker*: Cambridge.

Targett, S. 1994a: 'Government and ideology during the age of Whig supremacy: the political arguments of Walpole's newspaper propagandists', *Historical Journal*, 37, 289–317.

Targett, S. 1994b: ' "The premier scribbler himself": Sir Robert Walpole and the management of public opinion', *Studies in Newspaper and Periodical History*, 2, 19–33.

Tawney, A. J. and Tawney, R. H. 1934–5: 'An occupational census of the seventeenth-century', *Economic History Review*, 5, 25–64.

Tawney, R. H. and Power, E. (eds) 1924: *Tudor Economic Documents*, 3 vols: London.

Thirsk, J. 1952: 'The sales of royalist lands during the Interregnum', *Economic History Review*, 2nd series, 5, 188–207.

Thomas, K. V. 1958: 'Women and the Civil War sects', *Past and Present*, 13, 42–62.

Thompson, A. B. 1998: 'Licensing the press: the career of G. R. Weckherlin during the personal rule of Charles I', *Historical Journal*, 41, 653–78.

Thompson, E. P. 1991: *Customs in Common*: London.

Thornton, P. 1978: *Seventeenth-Century Interior Decoration in England, France and Holland*: New Haven, CT.

Tolmie, M. 1977: *The Triumph of the Saints*: Cambridge.

Trapnel, A. 1654a: *Report and Plea, or a Narrative Of her Journey into Cornwal . . . Whereunto is annexed A defiance, Against all the reproachful, vile, horrid, abusive and scandalous reports*: London.

Trapnel, A. 1654b: *Strange and Wonderful Newes from Whitehall*: London.

Treadwell, V. 1998: *Buckingham and Ireland, 1616–1628: A Study in Anglo-Irish Politics*: Dublin.

Trevelyan, G. M. 1938: *The English Revolution*: Oxford.

Tuck, R. (ed.) 1991: *Hobbes: Leviathan*: Cambridge.

Tuck, R. 1993: *Philosophy and Government 1572–1651*: Cambridge.

Tuck, R. and Silverthorne, M. (eds) 1998: *Hobbes: On the Citizen*: Cambridge.

Tully, J. (ed.) 1988: *Meaning and Context: Quentin Skinner and His Critics*: Cambridge.

Turner, J. G. (ed.) 1993: *Sexuality and Gender in Early Modern Europe: Institutions, Texts, Images*: Cambridge.

Tyacke, N. 1987: *Anti-Calvinists: The Rise of English Arminianism*: Oxford.

Tyacke, N. (ed.) 1997: *The History of the University of Oxford, Vol. 4: Seventeenth-Century Oxford*: Oxford.

Tyacke, N. (ed.) 1998: *England's Long Reformation 1500–1800*: London.

Tyacke, N. 2001: *Aspects of English Protestantism, c.1530–1700*: Manchester.

Tyacke, N. R. N. 1973: 'Puritans, Arminians and counter-revolution.' In C. Russell, ed., *The Origins of the English Civil War*: Basingstoke.

Underdown, D. 1966: 'The parliamentary diary of John Boys, 1647–8', *Bulletin of the Institute of Historical Research*, 39.

Underdown, D. 1971: *Pride's Purge: Politics in the Puritan Revolution*: Oxford.

Underdown, D. 1985a: *Revel, Riot and Rebellion: Popular Politics and Culture in England 1603–1660*: Oxford.

Underdown, D. 1985b: 'The taming of the scold: the enforcement of patriarchal authority in early modern England.' In A. Fletcher and J. Stevenson, eds, *Order and Disorder in Early Modern England*: Cambridge.

Underdown, D. 1996: *A Freeborn People: Politics and the Nation in Seventeenth-Century England*: Oxford.

Underhill, E. B. 1854: *Records of the Churches of Christ gathered at Fenstanton, Worboys and Hexham, 1644–1720*, Hanserd Knollys Society, vol. 9.

Venning, T. 1995: *Cromwellian Foreign Policy*: London.

Vernon, E. 1999: 'The Sion College conclave and London Presbyterianism during the English Revolution.' Unpublished Ph.D. thesis, Cambridge University.

Von Maltzahn, N. 1995: 'The Whig Milton, 1667–1700.' In D. Armitage, A. Himy and Q. Skinner, eds, *Milton and Republicanism*: Cambridge.

Von Stutterheim, K. 1934: *The Press in England*, trans. W. H. Johnson: London.

Wainwright, J. P. 1999: 'The king's music.' In T. N. Corns, ed., *The Royal Image: Representations of Charles I*: Cambridge.

Walker, C. 1647: *The Mysterie of the Two Juntoes*, BL, E393/29.

Walker, C. 1648: *The History of Independency*, BL, E463/19.

Walker, G. 1996: 'Expanding the boundaries of female honour in early modern England', *Transactions of the Royal Historical Society*, 6th series, 6, 235–45.

Walker, R. B. 1974: 'The newspaper press in the reign of William III', *Historical Journal*, 17, 691–709.

Walker, W. 2001: '*Paradise Lost* and the forms of government', *History of Political Thought*, 22, 2, 270–91.

Wallace, J. M. 1968: *Destiny His Choice: The Loyalism of Andrew Marvell*: Cambridge.

Walter, J. 1980: 'Grain riots and popular attitudes to the law: Maldon and the crisis of 1629.' In J. Brewer and J. Styles, eds, *An Ungovernable People: The English and their Law in the Seventeenth and Eighteenth Centuries*: London.

Walter, J. 1989: 'The social economy of dearth in early modern England.' In J. Walter and R. Schofield, eds, *Famine, Disease and the Social Order in Early Modern Society*: Cambridge.

Walter, J. 1999: *Understanding Popular Violence in the English Revolution: The Colchester Plunderers*: Cambridge.

Walter, J. 2001: 'Public transcripts, popular agency and the politics of subsistence in early modern England.' In M. Braddick and J. Walter, eds, *Negotiating Power in Early Modern Society: Order, Hierarchy and Subordination in Britain and Ireland*: Cambridge.

Walter, J. and Schofield, R. 1989: 'Famine, disease and crisis mortality in early modern society.' In J. Walter and R. Schofield, eds, *Famine, Disease and the Social Order in Early Modern Society*: Cambridge.

Walter, J. and Wrightson, K. 1976: 'Dearth and the social order in early modern England', *Past and Present*, 71 (May), 22–42.

Walton, I. 1927: *The Lives of John Donne ... and Robert Sanderson*: London.

Waterhouse, E. 1978: *Painting in Britain 1530–1790*: Harmondsworth.

Waterman, A. M. C. 1996: 'The nexus between theology and political doctrine.' In K. Haakonssen, ed., *Enlightenment and Religion: Rational Dissent in Eighteenth-Century England*: Cambridge.

Weatherill, L. 1986: 'A possession of one's own: women and consumer behaviour in England, 1660–1740', *Journal of British Studies*, 25, 131–56.

Webb, S. S. 1979: *The Governors-General: The English Army and the Definition of Empire, 1569–1681*: Chapel Hill, NC.

Webb, S. S. 1995: *Lord Churchill's Coup: The Anglo-American Empire and the Glorious Revolution Reconsidered*: New York.

Webster, C. 1974: *The Intellectual Revolution of the Seventeenth Century*: London.

Webster, C. 1975: *The Great Instauration: Science, Medicine and Reform, 1626–1660*: London.

Webster, C. 1982: *From Paracelsus to Newton: Magic and the Making of Modern Science*: Cambridge.

Webster, C. 1986: 'Puritanism, separatism and science.' In D. C. Lindberg and R. L. Numbers, eds, *God and Nature: Historical Essays on the Encounter between Christianity and Science*: Berkeley, CA.

Weil, R. 1999: *Political Passions: Gender, the Family and Political Argument in England*: Manchester.

Wells, R. H., Burgess, G. and Wymer, R. (eds) 2000: *Neo-Historicism: Studies in Renaissance Literature, History and Politics*: Cambridge.

Wenley, R. 1993: 'William, third earl of Lothian: covenanter and collector', *Journal of the History of Collections*, 5 (1), 23–40.

Wentworth: Wentworth Woodhouse Muniments. Sheffield Public Library, Sheffield, England.

Werskey, G. 1978: *The Visible College: A Collective Biography of British Scientists and Socialists of the 1930s*: London.

Western, J. R. 1965: *The English Militia in the Eighteenth Century: The Story of a Political Issue 1660–1802*: London.

Western, J. R. 1972: *Monarchy and Revolution: The English State in the 1680s*: London.

Westfall, R. S. 1971: *Force in Newton's Physics*: London.

Westfall, R. S. 1980: *Never at Rest: A Biography of Isaac Newton*: Cambridge.

Whatley, C. A. 2001: *Bought and Sold for English Gold? Explaining the Union of 1707*: East Linton.

Wheeler, J. S. 1999a: *Cromwell in Ireland*: Dublin.

Wheeler, J. S. 1999b: *The Making of World Power: War and the Military Revolution in Seventeenth-Century England*: Stroud.

Whinney, M. 1988: *Sculpture in Britain, 1530–1830*, revd J. Physick: Harmondsworth.

Whinney, M. and Millar, O. 1957: *English Art 1625–1714*: Oxford.

White, B. R. (ed.) 1971–4: *Association Records of the Particular Baptists of England, Wales and Ireland to 1660*, Baptist Historical Society.

Wickham, G., Berry, H. and Ingram, W. (eds) 2000: *English Professional Theatre, 1530–1660*: Cambridge.

Wilcher, R. 2001: *The Writing of Royalism 1628–1660*: Cambridge.

Wildman, J. 1748: *A Letter to a Friend*, January 1689, in 'Somers Tracts', *A Collection of Scarce and Valuable Tracts*, 1748, vol. 1.

Wilkinson, R. 1617: *Barwicke Bridge*: St Andrewes.

Wilks, T. 1989: 'The picture collection of Robert Carr, earl of Somerset (*c*.1587–1645) reconsidered', *Journal of the History of Collections*, 1 (2), 167–77.

Wilks, T. 1997: 'Art collecting at the English court from the death of Henry, Prince of Wales to the death of Anne of Denmark (November 1612–March 1619)', *Journal of the History of Collections*, 9 (1), 31–48.

Wilks, T. 2001: ' "Forbear the heat and haste of building": rivalries among the designers at Prince Henry's court, 1610–1612', *The Court Historian*, 6, 49–65.

Willen, D. 1992: 'Godly women in early modern England: Puritanism and gender', *Journal of Ecclesiastical History*, 43, 4, 561–80.

Williams, J. B. (pseudonym of Muddiman, J. G.) 1908: *A History of English Journalism to the Foundation of the Gazette*: London.

Williams, K. 1977: *The English Newspaper: An Illustrated History to 1900*: London.

Williamson, A. 1979: *Scottish National Consciousness in the Age of James VI*: Edinburgh.

Williamson, A. 1989: 'The Jewish dimension of the Scottish apocalypse: climate, covenant and world renewal.' In Y. Kaplan, H. Mechoulan and R. H. Popkins, eds, *Menasseh Ben Israel and His World*: New York.

Williamson, A. 1999: 'Patterns of British identity: Britain and its rivals in the sixteenth and seventeenth centuries'. In G. Burgess, ed., *The New British History: Founding a Modern State 1603–1715*: London.

Wilson, J. 1985: *Fairfax*: London.

Wilson, K. 1995: *The Sense of the People: Politics, Culture and Imperialism in England, 1715–85*: New York.

Wiseman, S. 1992: ' "Adam, the father of all flesh": porno-political rhetoric and political theory in and after the English Civil War.' In J. Holstun, ed., *Pamphlet Wars: Prose in the English Revolution*: London.

Wiseman, S. 1999: 'Pamphlet plays in the Civil War news market: genre, politics, and "context".' In J. Raymond, ed., *News, Newspapers, and Society in Early Modern Britain*: London.

Withers, C. W. J. 1996: 'Geography, science and national identity in early modern Britain: the case of Scotland and the work of Sir Robert Sibbald', *Annals of Science*, 53, 29–73.

Withers, C. W. J. 1999: 'Reporting, mapping, trusting: making geographical knowledge in the late seventeenth century', *Isis*, 90, 497–521.

Wolfe, D. M. 1941: *Milton and the Puritan Revolution*: New York.

Wood, A. 1997: 'The place of custom in plebeian political culture: England, 1550–1800', *Social History*, 22, 1 (January), 46–60.

Wood, A. 1999: *The Politics of Social Conflict: The Peak Country, 1520–1770*: Cambridge.

Wood, A. 2001: *Riot, Rebellion and Popular Politics in Early Modern England*: London.

Woodward, D. 1995: *Men at Work: Labourers and Building Craftsmen in the Towns of Northern England, 1450–1750*: Cambridge.

Woolf, D. 2001: 'News, history, and the conception of the present in early modern England.' In B. Dooley and S. Baron, eds, *The Politics of Information in Early Modern Europe*: London.

Woolf, D. R. 1990: *The Idea of History in Early Stuart England: Erudition, Ideology, and 'The Light of Truth' from the Accession of James I to the Civil War*: Toronto.

Woolrych, A. 1957: 'The good old cause and the fall of the Protectorate', *Cambridge Historical Journal*, 13, 133–61.

Woolrych, A. 1982: *Commonwealth to Protectorate*: Oxford.

Woolrych, A. 1986: *Commonwealth to Protectorate*: Oxford.

Woolrych, A. 1990: 'The Cromwellian Protectorate: a military dictatorship?' *History*, 75, 207–31.

Wootton, D. (ed.) 1986: *Divine Right and Democracy: An Anthology of Political Writing in Stuart England*: Harmondsworth.

Worden, A. B. (ed.) 1978: *Edmund Ludlow: A Voyce from the Watchtower*, Camden Society.

Worden, B. 1974: *The Rump Parliament, 1648–1653*: Cambridge.

Worden, B. 1987: 'Literature and political censorship in early modern England.' In A. C. Duke and C. Tamse, eds, *Too Mighty to be Free: Censorship and the Press in Britain and the Netherlands*: Zutphen.

Worden, B. 1990: 'Milton's republicanism and the tyranny of heaven.' In G. Bock, Q. Skinner and M. Viroli, eds, *Machiavelli and Republicanism*: Cambridge.

Wordie, J. R. 1983: 'The chronology of English enclosure, 1500–1914', *Economic History Review*, 2nd series, 36, 4, 483–505.

Wordie, J. R. 1997: 'Deflationary factors in the Tudor price rise', *Past and Present*, 154, 32–70.

Wormald, B. H. G. 1993: *Francis Bacon: History, Politics and Science, 1561–1626*: Cambridge.

Wormald, J. 1983: 'James VI and I: two kings or one?', *History*, vol. 68.

Wormald, J. 1991: 'James VI and I, *Basilikon Doron* and *The Trew Law of Free Monarchies*: the Scottish context and the English translation.' In L. L. Peck, ed., *The Mental World of the Jacobean Court*: Cambridge.

Worsley, G. 1995: *Classical Architecture in Britain*: New Haven, CT.

Wright, S. 1985: ' "Churmaids, huswyfes and hucksters": the employment of women in Tudor and Stuart Salisbury.' In L. Charles and L. Duffin, eds, *Women and Work in Pre-Industrial England*: London.

Wrightson, K. 1982: *English Society 1580–1680*: London.

Wrightson, K. 1993: 'The enclosure of English social history.' In A. Wilson, ed., *Rethinking Social History: English Society and its Interpretations*: Manchester.

Wrightson, K. 1996: 'The politics of the parish in early modern England.' In P. Griffiths, A. Fox and S. Hindle, eds, *The Experience of Authority in Early Modern England*: London.

Wrightson, K. 2000: *Earthly Necessities: Economic Lives in Early Modern Britain*: New Haven, CT.

Wrightson, K. and Levine, D. 1995: *Poverty and Piety in an English Village: Terling, 1525–1700*, 2nd edn: Oxford.

Wrigley, E. A. 1967: 'A simple model of London's importance in changing English society and economy, 1650–1750', *Past and Present*, 37, 44–70.

Wrigley, E. A. and Schofield, R. S. 1981: *The Population History of England, 1541–1871*: Cambridge.

Wrigley, E. A. and Schofield, R. S. 1989: *The Population History of England*: Cambridge.

Young, J. 1996: *The Scottish Parliament 1639–1661: A Political and Constitutional Analysis*: Edinburgh.

Young, J. 2001: 'The Scottish parliament and European diplomacy 1641–1647: the Palatine, the Dutch Republic, and Sweden.' In S. Murdoch, ed., *Scotland in the Thirty Years' War*: Brill.

Young, J. R. 1999: 'The Parliamentary Incorporating Union of 1707: political management, anti-Unionism and foreign policy.' In T. M. Devine and J. R. Young, eds, *Eighteenth Century Scotland: New Perspectives*: East Linton.

Young, M. 1997: *Charles I*: London.

Zagorin, P. 1954: *A History of Political Thought in the English Revolution*: London.

Zahedieh, N. 1998: 'Credit, risk and reputation in late seventeenth-century colonial trade', *Research in Maritime History*, no. 15.

Zaret, D. 1992: 'Religion, science, and printing in the public spheres in seventeenth-century England.' In C. Calhoun, ed., *Habermas and the Public Sphere*: Cambridge, MA.

Zaret, D. 2000: *Origins of Democratic Culture: Printing, Petitions and the Public Sphere in Early Modern England*: Princeton, NJ.

Zook, M. 1999: *Radical Whigs and Conspiratorial Politics in Late Stuart England*: Philadelphia, PA.

Zwicker, S. N. 1984: *Politics and Language in Dryden's Poetry: The Arts of Disguise*: Princeton, NJ.

Zwicker, S. N. 1993: *Lines of Authority: Politics and English Literary Culture 1649–1689*: Ithaca, NY.

Index

Abbot, George, archbishop of Canterbury   258, 265
Abercorn, 1st earl of   12
Aberdeen, General Assembly (1605)   254
absolutism   36, 91, 99, 188, 235, 273, 275–6, 284–8, 376–7, 399, 401, 438
  constitutionalism versus   384
  parliamentary   379, 381–2
  use of term   378
Academy of St Luke, established (1711)   204
Achaius   6
Achinstein, S.   96
acts of parliament *see* under topic
Adamson, John   xvii, 292, 314, 317, 319, 327
Adderbury, Oxfordshire   422–3
Addison, Joseph   91, 92, 168, 469, 470
Addled Parliament (1614)   236, 245
adultery   114, 357, 361
Africa   20, 51
agrarian laws, Harrington's   390
agrarian policies
  Caroline   139
  Stuart   138–9
Agreement of the People (1648–9)   336, 382
agricultural labourers   152, 153
  landless   148–9
agriculture
  and cloth making industry   152
  commercialization of   152–3
agronomy, European-style   62–3
Alba   5
Albani   195
Albany   19
alchemy   224
aldermen   153, 160
Aldous, William   370
Aleppo   49
Alexander, Sir William, of Menstrie *see* Stirling, earl of
Alien Act (1705)   20
allegiance   323–5, 379–80, 387
  controversy (1689–94)   95

  see also oath of allegiance
Allestree, Richard, *The Ladies Calling*   123
almshouses   155
Altham, Lancashire   422
Amazon basin   58
ambassadors, as art agents   192–3
Amboina massacre (1623)   48
Americas
  colonization   13, 64
  English settlements in   52
  migration to   156
  news in   93
  trade   161
Amerindians, expulsion   56
Amsterdam   89
anatomy, and gender relations   113
ancien régime approach   xv, 405
ancient constitution thesis   273, 278, 288, 326, 409–10, 456
Ancram, Lord   194
Andrea del Sarto   193
Andrewes, Lancelot, bishop   197, 258, 277
Andros, Sir Edmund   449
Anglesey, earl of   425
Anglicanism
  emergence of   18, 265, 350–4, 369–71, 404, 429
  James II and   440
  lay voluntary societies   427
  Non-Juror schism   432–3
  poetry   175, 177
  purge of bishops   370–1
Anglo-Saxons   5, 11
anglocentrism   xvi, xvii, 5, 11, 18, 235, 254
  challenges to historiographical   293–4, 400
  and new British history   316–17
Anjou, duke of   272
Anne of Denmark   172, 191, 193
Anne, Queen (1702–14)   xiv, 20–1, 42, 122, 405, 406, 433, 440, 441
  interim administration in east Midlands   447
annuities   78

Antichrist   9, 253, 257, 275, 277, 425, 482
Antigua   57
antinomian sects   181, 352, 359, 365, 427
antiquarianism   5, 11
Antrim, County   32
Antrim, earl of   12, 266
Antrim, marquesses of   34
Antrim plot (1641)   266
Antwerp, Spanish blockade   48
Apologeticall Narration   355, 359
Appleby, Andrew   142
apprenticeships   119, 155
arable areas   143
architecture   189, 205–11
   Elizabethan   278
   Gothic   211
   'Gothic–Baroque' style   211
   hybrid: 'Albion's classicism'   206
   Palladian   208–9
   'Puritan Minimalist' style   209
Arctic   12
Argyll, 7th earl of   12
Argyll, 9th earl of   439
Argyll, house of   12
Argyll, marquis and 8th earl of   15, 301, 302,
   319, 322
aristocracy *see* nobility
Aristotelianism   222, 271
Armada, Spanish   426
armaments industry   50
armies
   British expeditionary forces   12
   Charles II's use of Irish   401
   expenses abroad   162
   parliamentary control of   250, 366
   Scots in Northern European   57
   standing   318, 403–4, 411, 439, 457; costs
      of   78–9
   use of Catholic Irish to defeat Scots   296
   see also militia; New Model Army
Arminianism   xv, 175, 258, 259, 282, 292, 359,
   418, 421, 432
   denounced (1641)   352, 363
Arminius, Jacobus   259
'Army Plot'   300
art
   'Englishness' in   187, 278
   expenditure by monarchs   194, 198
   history of   xviii, 187–213
art auctioneers   204–5
art collection   187–93
Arthur, King   5
artisans   158, 161
Arundel, 14th earl of   188, 191, 193, 194, 198,
   279
   bust   192 plate 2
Ascham, Anthony   385, 386
Ashe, Simeon   351, 359–60
Ashton, Robert   xv

Asia   xviii, 45–66
   conflict and crisis (1639–60)   59–60
   fortified trading posts   48
   northwest passage to   52
   pre-1640   46–51: map   47
   Scottish and Irish involvement in   57–9
   transformation   61–2
Assada, nr Madagascar   59
assault
   aggravated   133
   definition of   133
assessment tax   77, 340, 404
assizes   134, 136, 152, 340
   Irish county   32
Astell, Mary   123
Aston, Walter *see* Forfar, Lord
astrology   223
atheism   223–4, 426
Atherton, Ian   x, xix, xxii, 88–110
Atlantic, the   xviii, 45–66
   conflict and crisis (1639–60)   59–60
   north   51–2
   pre-1640   51–7: map   53
   Scottish and Irish involvement in   57–9
   south   52
   trade   161, 162
   transformation   62–4
Attaway, Mrs   366–7
Atterbury, Francis   489
Aubrey, John, *Brief Lives*   405–6
auditing   78
Audley End, Suffolk   206
Aughrim, battle of   36
Augustine, St   255, 482
'auld alliance' (Franco-Scottish)   6, 7, 10
authoritarianism   xv, 14, 233, 245
autobiography   166
Ayrshire   325

Backwell, Edmund   83
Bacon, Sir Francis   10, 242, 273, 275, 279, 280,
   375, 490
Baglione, Giovanni   202
Bagshaw, Edward   379
Baillie, Robert   320, 359–60
Baker, Phil   326
Ball, W. W. Rouse   215
ballads   99, 100, 112, 140, 426
Baltic, the   51
Bancroft, Richard   265, 276
Bank of England
   founded (1694)   20, 69, 81, 85, 161–3
   to finance government borrowing   162–3
   Whigs and the   457
bank notes   162
Bank of Scotland   20
bankruptcy   154
Banqueting House
   by Inigo Jones   207–8 Plate 8

Banqueting House (*Cont.*)
  ceiling by Rubens 194, 196, 208, 242
    Charles I's execution (1649) 311
    see also Whitehall, Palace of
Bantam, Java 49, 61
Baptists 334, 360, 364–8, 416–18, 420–1, 428
  female 366–8, 416–18
  particular and general 365, 367, 421
  West Country 363, 364, 365
Barbados 13, 57, 60, 62, 158
Barberini, Cardinal 198, 204
Barbieri, Francesco *see* Guercino
Barebone, Praisegod 366
Barebone's Parliament (1653) 333, 335, 337,
    338–9, 344, 358, 388
Barlow, Thomas, bishop 426
Barnard, Toby x, xvi, xvii, xviii, 26–44
Barnes, Barry 220
baronialism 292, 305, 317, 319–20, 390–1, 402
baroque 178, 195, 196, 203–4, 209, 211
Barrell, Gilbert 198
Barrington, Lady Joan 122
Barrymore, earls of 34
Barrys *see* Barrymore, earls of
Bartolommeo della Nave 194
Bastwick, John 168, 260, 279
Bate, John 73
Bathurst, Anne 124
Baumgold, Deborah 376
Bauthumley, Jacob 167, 180
Baxter, Richard 360, 383, 423, 425, 490
  A Holy Commonwealth 393, 476
Baxter, S. B. 442
Beaumont, Agnes 416–18, 420, 425, 428, 433
Beckett, Isaac 205
Beddard, R. 442
Bedford, Francis, 4th earl of 208, 300
Bedford Level Company 162
Bedford, Lucy, countess of 193
Bedfordshire 416–18, 428, 432
Belford, Mark 198
Bellany, A. 99
Bellings, Sir Richard 30
benevolences 73
Bengal 59, 61, 62
Bentinck, William *see* Portland, earl of
Bernini, Gianlorenzo 195, 210
Berwick 287, 296
Bess of Hardwick *see* Shrewsbury, countess of
Bible
  and gender relations 112
  King James's Authorised Version (1611) 9, 257
bicameralism 292, 305, 319–20
Biddle, John 359
bills of exchange 73, 83, 152
bills of mortality 101
biological sciences 215
Birch, Thomas 224
Birmingham 156

Birr *see* Parsonstown
bishops
  Anglican (1640s and 1650s) 370–1
  anti-Calvinist 258–9
  bill to re-establish (1641) 352
  deprivation (1691) 432
  excluded from House of Lords (1642) 266,
    300
  Irish Catholic 37
  petitions for abolition of 265, 267, 353
  removal of power of 353–4, 370–1, 377
  in Scotland 254–5, 264, 295, 319
  see also episcopacy
Bishops Wars (1639–40) 14–15, 292, 296, 297,
    315
Black, J. 102
Blackfriars, London 115
Blackhall, Ofspring 489
Blaeu, Joan, *Grand Atlas* 7
Blaeu, Wilhelm 8, 14
  Britannia map 6
blasphemy 357
Blathwayt, William 449
Bloome, Richard (alias Nathaniel Crouch) 18
Blooteling, Abraham 204
Blount, Charles 487
body, humoral model 113
Boece, Hector 6, 7
Bohemia 257
  crisis (1619–24) 12, 55, 94, 96, 258
Bologna, Giovanni da 193
Bolton, Robert 207
Bolton, Samuel 380
Bombay 61
Bond-of-Resignation-Man, The 460
bonds 73
Book of Common Prayer 254, 257, 260, 263,
    332, 351, 354, 369, 370, 418
  in Ireland 256
  not to be enforced 356
  re-established (1662) 475, 480–1
  reactions to 419–20
  in Scotland (1637) 238, 239, 248, 263, 264,
    294, 319
Book of Orders (1631) 245
Borders, Anglo-Scottish 12, 20, 132
Borough, Sir John 13, 16
boroughs
  chartered English 153
  chartered Irish 32, 33
  elections 462, 463
  'Sacheverell' clause 449
  subordinated to James II 439, 449
  taxation 82
borrowing
  early Stuart 73, 77–8
  long-term 78
  see also forced loan (1626)
Boston 352

bourgeoisie 94–5, 290
  see also middle class; 'middling sort'
Bourne, H. R. F. 89, 90, 94
Boyle, Robert 214, 217–18, 223–4, 225
  controversy with Hobbes 219–23, 225
Boyle, Roger *see* Broghill, Lord
Boyne, battle of the 36
Braddick, Michael J. x, xviii, xx, xxi–xxii, 69–87, 378
Bramhall, John, bishop of Londonderry 261, 262, 380
Brazil, Portuguese 60
bread prices 148
Brent, Charles 468
Bridge, William 359
Bristol 52, 55, 121, 156, 157, 160, 358, 418, 421, 427, 428
Britain
  construct from myth-making 5
  and Ireland 3–25
  as a multiple kingdom 292–3
  northern boundaries 5
  the political nation 443–6
  politics in restoration 399–415
  see also England; Great Britain; Ireland; Scotland; Wales
Britannic perspective 11–14, 17
British approaches *see* new British history
British Empire 5, 9, 17, 18, 21
  colonial 65
  economic development 160–4
  fiscal–military mobilization 69, 79, 85
'British problem' 3–25, 293
  defined 10–11
British West Indies 56
Britons 5
broadsheets, illustrated 205, 475
Broghill, Lord 343
Bronzino, Agnolo 193
Brooke, Lord 353, 366
Brooks, Colin x, xvi, xviii, xx, 436–54
Brouncker, William *see* Castle Lyons, viscount of
Browne, Alexander 204–5
Brownrigg, bishop 370, 371
Bruce, Alexander *see* Kincardine, earl of
Brut 5
Brutus 8
Buchanan, George 7, 9, 14, 275, 276, 479
Buckingham, duke of 173, 194, 237, 241–2, 243, 244, 259, 281, 283
  art patronage 187, 191, 193, 195, 198
  expedition to Ile de Ré (1627) 174, 247
bullion trade 49, 55, 61, 63–4, 149
Bullocke, William 121
Bunyan, John 166, 167, 168, 169, 182, 416–18, 421
  Grace Abounding 425
  Pilgrim's Progress 425
bureaucracy 439

Burgess, Glenn 169, 235, 273, 274, 284, 285, 376, 378
Burghley, 1st baron 245, 272
burghs, Scottish 93, 344
Burke, Richard *see* Clanricarde, 4th earl of
Burlamacchi, Filippo 192
Burnet, Gilbert, bishop 224, 469
  Discourse of Pastoral Care 427, 490
Burroughs, Edward 367
Burroughs, Jeremiah 351
Burton, Henry 167, 260, 279
Butler, James *see* Ormonde, 1st duke of
Butler, Martin 178–9
Butlers 34
Butterfield, Herbert 216
by-laws 152–3
Byfield, Adoniran 360
Byzantium 5

cabinet council 245
Caddington 143
Cadiz, sack of (1596) 282
Calamy, Edmund 351
Calcutta 61
calendar, political 478
Calves-Head Club 487–8
Calvin, Jean 478
Calvinism 9, 175, 253, 273, 351, 418, 421
  and anti-Calvinism 258–9, 352, 365, 369, 478
  English 254, 258
  Irish 257
  and political theology 275, 479
  in Ulster 58
Calvin's Case (1608) 10
Cambridge 179
Cambridge University Library 215
Cambridgeshire 139, 151
Camden, William 5, 7, 8, 14, 274
Campbell, Archibald *see* Argyll, earls of
Campbell, Colen 208
Canaries 55
Candidates Try'd, The (1701) 466
Canny, Nicholas x, xviii, xxi, 45–66
Cape Breton 13
Capell, Sir Henry 449
capitalism
  emergent 116, 215
  enclosure protests and development of property rights 141
  and growth of crimes against property 132–3
  Protestant ethic and the spirit of 216
Capuchins 198, 262
Caravaggio, Michelangelo Merisi da 193, 196
caravan trade 49
Care, Henry 483–4
  English Liberties 484
  Pacquet of Advice 483
  Public Occurrences Truly States 483
Carew, George *see* Totness, earl of

Carew, Thomas   174–5, 176, 242
Caribbean
  attempts to settle   54
  dyestuffs for cloth   161
  migration to   157
  Spanish settlements   52
Carleton, Sir Dudley   193
Carlisle   287
Carlisle, earl of   11, 13
Carolinas   63
Carr, Robert *see* Somerset, earl of
Carracci brothers   194
Carter, Ann   121, 138
cartography   5–6, 7, 8, 14, 18
Cartwright, Thomas   167
Cary, Mary   368
Casaubon, Isaac   276
cash, demand for   70–1, 149
Castle Lyons, viscount of   215
Castlehaven trial   102
Castleisland   33
Castlemaine, Lord   204
catechisms   355, 361, 362, 426–7
Catherine of Braganza *see* Catherine, Queen
Catherine, Queen   30, 203–4
Catholic Confederates *see* Confederate Catholics of
    Ireland (1642)
Catholicism   188, 253–70
  Charles I and   198, 242–3, 261, 377, 406
  Charles II and   407
  in England   254, 258
  in Ireland   8, 29–30, 31; de facto
    tolerance   256, 262
  James II and   440
  under William III   449, 452
  see also Roman Catholic Church
Caus, Isaac de   209
causes, necessary and sufficient   xiv, 290–4
Cavalier Parliament (1661)   409, 410, 428
cavaliers   361–2
Cavendish family   388
Cavendish, Margaret *see* Newcastle, duchess of
Cecil, Robert *see* Salisbury, earl of
Cecil, William *see* Burghley, 1st baron
Céitinn, Séathrún *see* Keating, Geoffrey
Cellini, Benvenuto   190
censorship
  by royal prerogative (1682)   90
  Cromwellian   89, 475–6
  and development of the press   93–4
  elimination of   89, 90, 94, 95, 352, 458, 463
  pre-publication licensing   167, 179, 409, 458
  in Scotland   93
  Stuart   89, 91, 101
Central America, Spanish settlements   52
Chalmers, George   88
Chaloner, Thomas   194, 326
Champion, Justin   x, xix, xxi, 474–91
Chancery   279

Chaney, Edward   188
change, continuity and   xxi–xxii, 338–9, 347,
    458–9
chapbooks   112
'charivari'   114, 121, 139
Charlemagne   6
Charles I
  art collection   190, 193–5, 242
  coronation at Holyrood (1633)   239, 240, 263
  court culture   173–6, 242–3
  court in exile   176, 177, 202
  declaration of martial law (1627)   279
  Eikon Basilike   168, 177, 277, 406, 479,
    480–1, 487
  and the Engagement (1647)   15–16, 317,
    327–8, 339, 346, 360, 386, 388
  engraving   195 plate 3
  execution (1649)   16, 311, 332, 333, 338, 399,
    480; *see also* regicide
  financial policies   77
  hands himself over to the army (1646)   15
  and Irish Catholic Confederation   8, 31
  as a martyr   406, 481, 486, 487
  Personal Rule   174–5, 198, 238, 248, 291, 296,
    320, 352–3
  personality   xv, 238–40, 242, 327–8
  and the privy council   244–5
  relations with parliament   239, 247–9,
    298–303, 411
  relations with the Scots   13, 15–16, 248,
    263–5, 286–7, 301, 328
  religious policies   259–68, 295
  and Roman Catholicism   198, 242–3, 261, 377,
    406
  trading policy   59–60
  trial   327–8, 332, 333, 406
  visits to Scotland   240, 301, 411
Charles II
  advice to   392
  art collection   202–4, 209
  control of towns   402
  coronation (1661)   17–18
  court culture   181
  financial policies   78–81, 403–4, 410
  invasion of England (1651)   342
  and Irish Catholics   31, 33, 400–1
  personality   xv, 439
  political and religious tensions   xiii, 168, 183
  proclaimed as king of Great Britain and Ireland
    (1649)   16
  relations with parliament   410, 411
  religious policies   428, 430, 481, 485
  and Roman Catholicism   198, 203–4
  see also Restoration
chastity   112, 114
  married   173
Chaudhuri, K. N.   50
Chesapeake, the   54, 56, 57, 60, 62
  migration to   156, 157

Cheshire   360–1
    petition (1641)   102
Cheshunt, Hertfordshire   138
Chester   159
    siege of   176
Chesterton House, Warwickshire   209
Chetham, Humphrey   83
Chichester, Sir Arthur   30, 255–6
Chidley, Katherine   123
Christchurch, Oxford, Tom Tower   211
Christian IV of Denmark   12, 15, 171
Christianity, spread of   5, 6
church associations   360–1
church attendance   422–3
church courts   254, 260, 279
    women and   114, 120
Church of England
    Anglican   350–4, 369–71, 429
    Canons (1604)   257, 261
    Canons (1636)   263, 299
    claims to monopoly   399, 405, 427–30, 431
    doctrine   418–19
    effects of Revolution (1688–9) on   432–3
    factionalism   432–3
    government disputes   355–63, 382–4, 422–4
    nature of the   424–7, 483
    reformed   179, 474
    root and branch reform   265, 297, 298, 300,
        332
    and Scottish Kirk   28, 253
    Tory adherents   456
    see also Anglicanism
Church of Ireland   33, 34, 35, 39, 256, 267
    Irish Articles (104)   256–7, 262
    reform of   261–2
church property, tax exemptions for   82
Church of Rome see Roman Catholic Church
Church of Scotland see Scottish Kirk
church and state   280, 392, 460, 474, 478
    separation of   254, 383, 431, 458
    'thorough' in   14
    see also ecclesiology
churches,
    independent in London   366–7
    Nonconformist   423–4
Churchill, John see Marlborough, 1st duke of
churching of women   371
Cicero   375
civic virtue, and republican values   376
civil courts   133
civil society, the press and   91
Civil War, English
    accidental nature of   xv, 291, 312
    'high road to'   233–52, 291, 312
civil wars (1642–9)   xiii, 3, 60, 311–30
    effect on economy   160
    effects on art collection   190, 198, 199, 201–2
    effects on status of monarchy   377–8
    key events leading to   292–3

legacies   401–4, 409
    and literature   176–8
    origins of   290–308, 311, 312
    public finances in and after   77–81
    in Scotland   325
    Three Kingdoms approach   xiii, xvi, xx, xxiii
        n.3, 15, 57, 290–308, 311–30
Clanricarde, 4th earl of   12, 206
Clanricarde, marquesses of   34
Clare, County   34
Clarendon Code   428, 478, 483
Clarendon, earl of   249, 285, 300, 322, 379, 406,
    452
    History of the Rebellion and Civil Wars   249
Clark, Alice   116
Clark, Jonathan C. D.   xv, 405, 458, 459
Clarke, Samuel   360
Clarkson, Laurence   367, 382
    The Lost Sheep Found   387
class relationships, mediate and proximate
    structuration   142
Claydon, Tony   xvii
Cleaver, Robert   112
Clegg, C. S.   94, 96
clergy
    contempt of the   426
    local commissions for the regulation of the   340
    marriages   115
    and monarchy   412
    and William III   445
    see also Puritan clergy
Clerical Disabilities Act (1642)   304
Cleyn, Francis   196, 199
cloth finishing industry   151, 152
Clotworthy, Sir John   32–3, 302, 321
Clubmen   319
clubs   319, 463, 483, 487
coal   150
Coal Money   211
coffee   161
coffee houses   88, 92, 95, 96, 98, 161, 222, 405,
    463
    shares in   162
Coggeshall, Essex   153
Cogswell, Tom   94, 99, 234
coin
    collection   193
    James I   9
    James II   482–3
    shortages   80, 83, 149, 151–2
coinage   51
    collapse of system and re-coinage (1697)   162
    value of (1680s)   162
Coiro, Ann   174
Cokayne, Alderman, project   151
Coke, Sir Edward   244, 278, 279, 284
Cold War   216
Coleraine   55
Coles, Mary   368

Coley, Halifax 422
College, Stephen 482
Colley, Linda 462
Collins, Anthony 488
Collins, H. M. 220
Collinson, Patrick 188
Colombes, France 202
colonial administration 83
colonial policy
James I's 13–14
James II's 440
colonization, English 54, 63
Colt, Maximilian 189
Columba, St 6
Columbus, Christopher 46
commissions of array 235, 304
Commissions for the Propagation of the
Gospel 336, 337, 340
Committee of Articles, abolition (1640) 297
Committee of Both Kingdoms 15
Committee of Estates of Scotland 296, 319
petition (1641) on trading rights 59
common law
administration 152
and civil law 10
and divine right monarchy 273, 278–80, 288
English 5, 10–11, 131–6, 279, 339, 343
Scottish 12, 279, 280
common law courts 279
Commons Committee, destruction of art
(1643) 199
Commons, House of 244, 291, 318
Charles I and 239, 284–5, 303
James I and 236, 274–5
James II and 439
polarization 407–8
policy on religious reform (1640–1) 353, 354
as representative of public opinion 98
Commonwealth, English (1649–53) xiii, 3,
16–17, 332, 338, 385
disposal of Charles I's art collection 201
foreign policy 160, 344–5
founded 333
and Ireland 341–2
revenue failures 334–5, 344–5
and Scotland 4, 7, 342
commonwealth tradition 180, 385, 391–4, 487–9
commonwealthsmen 389, 486, 487–8
communist experiment 331, 336, 387
community, ideal types 143
Company of the Royal Fishery of England 19
Company of the Royal Fishery of Great Britain and
Ireland (1661) 19
Company of Scotland 20
company shares 162
compositions, imposition of 82
'comprehension', Bills for (1680) 428–9, 431
Compton, Henry, bishop 422
Con, George 198

conciliar court, Ludlow 279
Condren, Conal 387, 392
conduct books, and gender relations 112–16,
125
confederalism 314–15, 318–19, 322–3, 326
Confederate Catholics of Ireland (1642) 8, 15,
16, 31, 35, 37, 267, 268, 302, 313, 316,
322–3
king's cessation of arms with 321
oligarchy 318–19
confessional politics 458, 459
confessional state, and public office in Ireland 15,
34–5
conformity, 'occasional', bills to ban (1702, 1705,
1711) 456, 460
Congregationalists 351, 359, 362–3, 432
Connacht 5, 8, 12
Connecticut 60
Connock, John, of Calstocke 198
conquistadores 54
conscience
crisis of 388–9
liberty of 356, 357–8, 359, 362, 368, 383–4,
399, 430–3, 448, 483–4
political authority and 376, 379–80, 385,
387–8, 430–3, 477–8, 481–5, 486
conscientious objection 459
consensus
Calvinist 291–2, 293, 427
or conflict 375–7, 402–3, 408–10
conservatism xv, 333, 335, 387, 406, 444, 476,
482–3
conspiracy theories 293, 482
Constable, Robert, God and the King... 476–7,
481
Constantine the Great 5
Constantine, Robert 360
constitution
Britain's first written 357, 384
Christian aspects of 381–2
nineteenth-century British 400
and post-revolutionary politics 457, 458,
485–6
reform 336
tripartite with checks and balances 377, 380,
410
constitutional monarchy xv, 20, 399
constitutional protest, in Scotland 14–17, 296–7
constitutionalism
Gothic 19–21
legal 376
'Norman yoke theory' 18
versus absolutism 384, 390
continuity, and change xv, xxi–xxii, 338–9, 347,
458–9
contracts, commercial 51
contractualism, Lockean xv
Convention (1660), on revenues for Charles II
404, 409, 410

Convocation (1639) 265, 296; recall (1701) 433
Conway, viscount 283
Cony's case (1655) 339
Cooper, Alexander 189
Cooper, Samuel, portrait of Cromwell 189–90 plate 1
Coppe, Abiezer 167, 180
copper 61
corantos 89, 92, 94, 101, 103
Cork 256
Cornish language 324
Corns, Thomas N. x–xi, xviii, 166–86
Cornwall 4, 5, 150, 161, 163, 324, 368
Coromandel coast, India 49, 59, 61
Corporation Acts 456
corporations
chartered 161, 162
Irish 33
Correggio, Antonio 193
corruption 71, 74, 241, 279, 282, 283, 382, 386, 394, 450
cosmopolitanism 275
Cotterell, Sir Charles, portrait 200 plate 5
Cottington, Francis 245, 280
cotton 57, 157, 161
Cotton, A. N. B. 92
Cotton, John 352, 385–6
Cotton, Priscilla 368
Cotton, Sir Robert 279, 281, 284
Council of the North 280
council of state, Lord Protector's 334, 338, 339
Council for Trade and Plantations (1660) 63
councils, royal 243–8
Counter-Reformation 8, 9, 14, 178, 242, 407, 426
in Ireland 256
counties
administration during Protectorate 340
Irish 32
taxation 82
country houses 206
Country Party 290, 452, 457, 482
'country trade' 49, 50, 61
county commissioners 340, 359, 363
county towns 156
court
art and architecture 187–213
and bedchamber 241, 243
costs of 70, 75–6
factionalism 291
gender relations 114–15, 125
masques and patriarchy 171–3
papal agent admitted by Charles I 261
political significance of royal 240–3
politics of Caroline 242–3
politics of Jacobean 240–2
privy chamber 240, 243
scandal 102

Scottish entourage at 76, 241, 400
court of castle chamber 240
court of Common Pleas 279
court culture
of Charles I 166, 173–6, 242–3
of James I 166, 172–3, 191, 240–2
court of the Earl Marshal and Lord Constable 279
court of High Commission 89, 255, 262, 263, 264, 279, 295
abolished 300, 377
Courteen Company 51, 59
courtiers 11, 30, 70, 74
conversions to Catholicism 261
punishment of prominent 298, 299
courts, ecclesiastical 484
courts leet and baron, in Ireland 32
Covenanters, Scottish 3, 7, 11, 14–17, 40, 264–5, 266, 267, 268, 278, 294, 314, 316
effects in Ireland 302
European links 315
experiment in self-government 319
Rebellion 294–8, 301
strength of army 325
support in England 296–9, 315, 321
Covenanting Movement see Covenanters, Scottish
Covent Garden 208
'coverture' 117, 118, 121, 154
Coward, Barry xi, xiii–xxiv
Coward, William 490
Cowell, James 274
Cowley, Abraham 177
Craig of Riccarton, Sir Thomas 10, 13
Cranfield, G. A. 94
Cranfield, Lionel 76, 83
Crashaw, Richard 178
Crawford, Patricia 126
credit
expansion of 149, 152
personal turned into transferrable 162
private networks 83
raising 77–8, 81
to finance trade 51, 73, 149, 152
to finance war 69
crime 130–6
'dark figure' of unprosecuted 132
incidence of 132–3
criminal justice system 131–6
character of seventeenth-century 136
discretion within 135–6
Crispe, Nicholas 51
critical theory 171
Cromwell, Henry, as Lord Deputy of Ireland 343
Cromwell, Oliver 15, 16–17, 59, 89, 180, 182, 201, 319, 321, 328, 394, 479
death of (1658) 183, 334
dissolves Rump (1653) 333, 336–7
legitimacy of regime 79–80, 384, 389–90, 392
national interest 142

Cromwell, Oliver (*Cont.*)
  personality 335
  portrait 189 plate 1
  proposals to offer him the crown 343, 346, 363
  religious policies 361–2, 366, 369, 383
  Western Design (1655–6) 60, 160
  see also Protectorate, Cromwellian
Cromwell, Richard 190, 334, 392
crop rotation 152
Crouch, John, *The Man in the Moon* 102
Crouch, Nathaniel *see* Bloome, Richard
crowd behaviour 136–7, 140
crown assets, alienated or mortgaged 70–1, 74,
  76, 341
Cruickshanks, E. 442
Culmer, Richard 199
Culpepper, Sir John 300, 354
cultural context xviii–xx
culture, the concept of 170
Cumberland 360
Cumbernauld band 301
Cunningham, Sir James 58
currency crisis (1690s) 162, 163
currency exchange, tables of 51
Curry, Patrick 223
Cust, Richard 99, 234, 317
custom
  of disobedience 139, 141–2
  lex loci 141–2
  respect for 137, 462
customs and excise duties 63, 70, 71, 72, 77, 79,
  80, 161, 404, 410
customs farms 70, 78, 83

Dahl, F. 89, 91, 92
Dalrymple, Sir John 448
Danby, earl of, as Lord Treasurer 407, 427, 442,
  444
dance 172
Danes 5, 8
Danvers, Lord 193
Darien scheme 20, 21, 64
Darwin, Charles 400
Davenant, Charles 163
Davenant, Sir William 176, 181, 242
  Britannia Triumphans 174
Davies, Sir John 10
Davis, J. Colin xi, xv, xix, xxi, 170, 374–96
de L'Orme, Philibert 206
de' Medici, Marie 202
de' Servi, Costantino 206–7
debate, public 97–8, 100
debt
  household 155
  investment in the national 83–4, 85
  repayment system 78
  royal 281; becomes national 69, 77–8, 80,
    81, 85, 162
Declaration of Indulgence

(1672) 428, 429, 431
(1688) 183, 413, 449, 484
Declaration for Preachers (1622) 258
defamation 120
Defoe, Daniel 91, 163
  Advice to the Electors of Great Britain 466
  The Political Sow-Gelder (attr.) 455
Dekker, Thomas 171
Delaware valley 63, 64
democracy, progress towards parliamentary 332,
  339, 399, 437
Denmark 12
Denne, Henry 367
Denton Hall, Yorkshire 199
Deptford 418
Derbyshire 150
Derry 55
Descartes, René 222
Devon 360
Devonshire, earl of 30
devotional manuals 420, 427
diaries 104, 115
Dickinson, William 211
Dietterlin 206
Dieussart, François 195, 199
  bust of Charles I 195 plate 3
  bust of Thomas Howard, earl of Arundel 192
    plate 2
Digby, Lord 322
Diggers 167, 168, 331, 336, 340, 387
'Directory of Worship' (1645) 355, 358, 370
disafforestation policies 138
discourse
  politics of xviii–xx
  see also language; political discourse
discretion
  royal 235, 239, 243–4, 376, 381, 385
  within criminal justice system 135–6
dissenters *see* Nonconformists
distributive justice 132
divine right monarchy xv, 18, 273, 376, 399,
  405, 449, 474
  and common law 278–80
  meanings of Jacobean 275–8, 288
  Scots view of 276
  and subordination 474–5, 476–7
  theories of government 480–1, 485–6, 486
divorce, by consent 179
Dobson, Mary 120
Dobson, William 199–200
  portrait with Nicholas Lanier and Sir Charles
    Cotterell 200 plate 5
Dod, John 112
Domitian 174
Donatism 255
Donne, John 175
  sermons 175
Dorset 462
Dorset, countess of 371

Dort, Synod of (1618) 258
Dossi, Dosso 193
Dou, Gerrit 202
Dover, Treaty of 203
Down and Connor, bishop of 256
Down, County 32
dowries 119
Dowsing, William 199
drama 98, 101, 112, 166, 167
  Elizabethan 178–9
  Restoration 112, 166, 181, 183
drama companies 181
Drax, James 158
Dryden, John 166, 183–4
du Cerçeau, Jacques Androuet, the Elder 206
Dublin 39, 93, 261
  centre of trade 163
  Trinity College established (1591) 256
Dublin administration 26, 29, 32, 266
  proclamation ordering priests to leave
    (1605) 256
Dublin, County 34
ducking stool 114, 120
Duke's Company 181
Dunbar, battle of (1650) 342, 385, 388
Dunbar, earl of 244
Dunluce, viscount 12
Durant, John 363
Dutch 58, 314
  artists 190–1, 202, 205
  cultural links with the English 438, 441–2
  ships 14
  trade links 19, 46, 48, 61
Dutch War
  First (1652–4) 16, 59, 63, 160, 344–5
  Second (1666–7) 18, 63, 202; costs of 78
  Third (1672–4) 18, 63; costs of 78
dynastic approach 4–9, 273, 441
Dzelzainis, Martin 180

Eachard, John, The Grounds and Occasions of the
    Contempt of the Clergy 426
Eales, Jacqueline 115
Earle, Peter 116, 154
Earls Colne, Essex 361, 424
East Anglia 151, 152, 364
East India Company 46
  Dutch see Vereenigne Oost-Indische Compagnie
  English 20, 46–51, 55, 57, 61–2, 161; as a
    joint stock company 59, 162
  Scottish 58
  United 61–2
East New Jersey 19
East Sussex, grand jurors 135
Eaton, Samuel 352, 360
Eccleshall, Staffordshire 153
ecclesiology 478, 481, 484–6,
    489–90
economic activity, and social morality 139–40

economic crisis, European mid-seventeenth
    century 50
economic depression (1590s) 148, 149, 163
economic development 148–65
economy, and gender relations 116–19
Edinburgh
  as bishopric 263
  centre of trade 163
  Charles I's coronation (1633) 239, 263
  Charles I's visits 240, 287
  Covenanter regime 325
  Greyfriars Kirk 264
  Holyrood Palace 240, 255, 263
  James II's court in 19
  news trade 93
  St Giles Cathedral 263, 264
  sends army to Ulster (1642) 314
education
  Catholic schools in Ireland 256
  travel for 190, 210
Edward VI 272
Edwards, Thomas 315, 362, 383
Egerton, Sir Thomas, baron Ellesmere 279
Egypt 6, 7
Eikon Basilike (attr. Charles I) 168, 177, 277,
    406, 479, 480–1, 487
Eireannaigh 8
elections 405, 408
  frequency of general 455, 470
  general (1685) 407
  parliamentary 98
  struggle over representation 464
Eliot, T. S. 183
Elizabeth I 29, 37, 190
  chivalric concepts of honour 282–3
  drama 179
  financial policies 74–5, 154
  government of 244
  problems of royal authority 272
  religion under 253, 254
  trading licenses 52
Elizabeth (James I's daughter), wedding 171
Ellesmere, Chancellor see Egerton, Sir Thomas
Elton, Geoffrey R. xiv, 233
Ely, Isle of 139
Elzevirus, Bonaventura and Abraham 7
emblems see iconography
empire,
  concept of 4–5, 8–9, 62
  see also British Empire
employment
  import trade and 64
  lack of 153
enclosure 152, 340
enclosure protests 130, 137, 138–40
  and capitalist development 141
  women in 121
Engagement (1647) 15–16, 317, 327–8, 339,
    346, 360, 386, 388

England
  absorption of Cornwall and Wales   4
  Catholicism in   254, 258
  Charles II's invasion (1651)   342
  dominance of   xvii, 79, 271
  invasion of Scotland (1650)   16
  jurisdiction over Ireland   27–31, 41–2
  northern and the Scots   15, 314, 323–4
  population (seventeenth century)   57, 149–50,
    156, 157
  religion in Restoration   416–35
  Scots invasion: (1644)   314, 318, 324, 325;
    (1648)   16, 292, 325
  support for Covenanters   296–9, 315, 321
  trade in Asia   45–51
  see also union
English language   9
English Revolution see 'Glorious Revolution';
    Revolution (1688–9)
'Englishness', in art   187, 278
episcopacy
  abolished (1646)   354
  Protestant   9, 258, 352–4, 422, 424
  see also bishops
Episcopalian Church, in Scotland   400
Erasmus, Desiderius   276
Erastianism   254, 356, 382, 431
espionage service   11
Essex
  assault indictments (1620–80)   133
  Rebellion (1601)   178
  theft prosecutions (1620–80)   135
Essex, earl of   30, 243, 282–3, 320, 321
Estado da India   46, 49
Europe
  context   xvii–xviii, 313, 314
  England's position in   282–3, 344–5
  influence on art collection   190
  Northern   11
  Protestant   9
  Revolution in context of   438
  Southern   55
European Wars (1689–1713), effects on trade   61
Evangelical Revival   427
Evelyn, John   113, 198, 209, 371, 418, 419, 431
Ewelme, Oxfordshire   199
Examiner, The   456–7, 469
Exchequer
  court of   260
  Stop   78
excise   77, 79, 82, 403, 404
  list (1759)   161
  see also customs and excise duties
excisemen   79–80, 82, 83
Exclusion Crisis (1679–81)   18, 19, 183, 405,
    410, 412, 438, 439
  and the press   90, 93, 95, 478–9, 482
Exclusion Parliament (1681)   447, 482
Exeter House Chapel, London   371

experimental method   xxiii, 214, 217
exploration, Asia and the Atlantic   45–66
export trade, value of (1663–1700)   64

factories, on Gold Coast   51, 57
Fairfax family   317
Fairfax, Ferdinando, Lord   199, 370
Falkland, Lord   300, 379
families   113, 119
  mobility   155–6
Familists   123
famine
  Irish (after 1649)   38
  see also harvest failures
Fanelli, Francesco   195
Fanshawe, Sir Henry   198
fashions, and trade   161
Faults on Both Sides (1710)   460
Feake, Christopher   390
Feery, Mr   417
Fell, John, bishop   422–3
Fell, Margaret   123
felony   134–5
femininity   111, 123
  negative stereotypes   124
Feoffees for Impropriations   260
Fergus son of Earc   6, 8
Fergus son of Ferchar   6
Ferne, Henry   379–80
Feti, Domenico   193
feudal dues   72, 77
feudalism   271, 290, 391
Fiennes, Nathaniel   297
fifteenths and tenths   72–3, 76
Fifth Monarchists   336–7, 363, 383,
    388
  female   123, 368
Filmer, Sir Robert   113, 285, 376, 379, 390, 474,
    490
  Patriarcha   478–9, 489
  The Anarchy of a Limited or Mixed
    Monarchy   380
finances
  Protectorate   391–3
  public, in civil wars and after   77–81, 85
  royal, public needs and private hopes   280–2
  royal transformed into public   77–85
'financial revolution'   162, 457
financial system, of early Stuarts   71–4
financiers   83
fine arts see architecture; arts
fiscal state, the rise of the   69–87, 237, 403–4,
    458
fishing
  in Ireland   58
  in New England   56, 60
  in north Atlantic   51–2, 56, 57, 60, 62
  in North Sea   57
  policies   12–13, 13–14, 19

Five Articles of Perth (1618)   244, 246, 255, 263, 264
Flamsteed, John   225
fleet *see* navy
Fleetwood, Charles   30, 334
Flemish   48
Fletcher, Alexander, of Saltoun   21
Fletcher, Anthony, *The Outbreak of the English Civil War*   xv, 311
Flight of the Earls (1607)   255
food prices (1530–1640)   148
food riots, eighteenth-century   136
Forbes, Mr   421
forced loan (1626)   76, 239, 247, 282, 284
Forfar, Lord   12
Fortescue, Sir John   271, 273
Foucault, Michel   170
Fowler, bishop   424
Fox, George   123, 166, 167, 168, 182, 364, 366, 367
Fox, Sir Stephen, Lord Treasurer   83
Foyster, Elizabeth   xi, xx, 111–29
France   5, 31, 314, 345
    'auld alliance' with Scotland   6, 7, 10
    Irish links with   3
    James II's flight to (1688)   399, 401, 413, 436, 438, 440
    militant Protestant traders   52
    royalists in exile   190
    taxation in   85
    trade with   61
    war of succession   273
    wars against (1627–9)   247, 259
    wars against (1689–97, 1702–13)   457, 461
franchise   382, 462
Franciscans   256, 262
Frank, J.   89, 90, 92
Frank, Robert G.   219
Franklin, William   366
Fréart   209
Frederick V of Bohemia   258
freedom of speech   246, 458
Freist, D.   102
French Catholic League   275
Frizell, William   202
Fuller, Thomas   371
functional approaches   xv, xvi
fur trade   52, 56, 63, 161
futures options   162

Gadbury, Mary   366
Gael   7–8
Gaelic tradition   7–8, 27, 32
Galen of Pergamum   113
Galilei, Galileo   215
Gall   8
Gallagher, Catherine   169, 170–1
Galway   12, 33, 58
Galway, County   34

Gama, Vasco da   46
Gardiner, S. R.   236, 402
    History of the Great Civil War   311
Garnett, Jane   120
Gascar, Henri   203, 204
Gataker, Thomas   361, 370
Gathelus of Athens   6
Geertz, Clifford   170
Geldrop, George   201
gender, and religion   123–5, 367–8, 416–18, 421
gender history, and Stuarts   125–6
gender relations   xx, 111–29
    and conduct books   112–16, 125
    and the economy   116–19
    and politics   119–23, 173, 394, 462
gender socialization   113–14
Gentileschi, Orazio   193, 195–6, 202
gentry
    control over clergical appointments   335
    failure to support Anglicanism   429
    landholding   143
    property rights   335–6
    thesis of rise of the   xiv, 290, 317–20, 340
    travel for education   190
George I   36, 457, 470, 488
Gerbier, Balthasar   187–8, 195, 201
Germany   12
Gheeraerts, Marcus   189
Giambologna *see* Bologna, Giovanni da
Gibson, 190
Gilbert, Humphrey   52
Giovane, Palma   194
Glamorgan   370
Glasgow
    General Assembly (1638)   264, 295
    newspaper   93
Glencairn's revolt   343
'Glorious Revolution' (1688–9)   xiii, 3, 19–21, 399, 431, 453
    fiscal–military mobilization   80–1
    political thought after   485–6
    politics after   455–73
    publishing during   90, 95
    see also Revolution (1688–9)
Gloucester, duke of   457
Gloucestershire   138, 152, 421
    muster list (1608)   159
Gnadenpfennig (portrait medallion)   189
Goa   49
Godden v. Hales   413
Godolphin, Sidney, 1st earl of   444, 445, 451, 467
Gold Coast   51, 57
gold trade   51, 59, 149, 151
Goldie, M.   95, 99, 376
Goldsmiths' Hall   209
Golinski, Jan   220
Gondomar, Diego Sarmiento de Acuña, Conde de   236
Gonzaga family   193

Goodman, Christopher 479
Goodwin, Thomas 351, 352, 355, 360, 362–3
Gookin, Daniel 57
Gordon, Sir Robert, of Stralloch 7
Gorlaeus, Abraham 193
gossip 100, 120, 121
Gothic architecture 211
Gothic perspective 5, 8, 11, 17, 19–21
Goths 5, 8, 11
Gouge, William 112, 113, 114, 115
government
  changes in form xxi–xxii
  co-ordinate 378–9, 389–91
  collapse and revolution in political
    thought 375–80
  continuity before and after regicide 338–9
  democratic form in Scotland 276
  descending theory of 489
  growth of 439
  and laws in union 10
  mixed with a balanced constitution 379, 381–2
  and morality 378, 386–7
  popery and arbitrary 406–7, 409, 482, 490
  representative 439
  as royal government 235–40, 243–4, 273–4
grace
  doctrine of 253, 258, 352, 382–3
  and free will 259
'Graces, the' 31, 261, 262, 302
Graham, James see Montrose, marquis of
grain market
  'books of orders' (1577–1631) 138, 141
  regulation 138, 141
grain riots 137–8, 141
  women in 121
grammar schools 114
Grand Remonstrance (1641) 249, 266, 268, 303,
  351, 353–4, 355, 378
Grand Tour 190
Grascome, Samuel, The Mask of Moderation pull'd
  off 467–8
Grassby, Richard 160
Great Britain
  addition of Ireland (1801) 4, 400
  emergence of xxii, 4, 26–44
  and Ireland 16, 26–44
  see also Britain; England; Ireland; Scotland; Wales
Great Contract (1610) 74, 76, 237, 300
Great Council 245–8
Great Fire (1666) 209
  Monument to the 426
Green, Ian 420, 426–7
Green Ribbon Club 483
Greenblatt, Stephen, Renaissance Self-
  Fashioning 169, 170–1
Greenland 12
Greenwich Palace, Queen's House 194, 196,
  198, 207
Gregory, Jeremy 125

Grey, Jane 272
Griffiths, A. 205
Groot, Hugo de see Grotius
Grosjean, Alexia 315
Gross, Paul R. 220
Grosvenor, Sir Richard 133
Grotius, Hugo 13, 57, 375, 376, 388–9
Guercino 195
guilds, male-dominated 119
Guinea Company 59, 60
  Scottish 58
Gujarat 49, 50, 57, 59, 61, 62
Gunning, Peter 371
Gunpowder Plot (1605) 171, 256, 258, 408, 426
Gunther, R. T. 215
Gustavus Adolphus 175

Habermas, Jürgen xix, 94–5, 97, 99, 104, 464
Hacket, John 242
Hakluyt, Richard, Discourse of Western
  Planting 54
Halasz, A. 96, 97
Halifax, 1st earl of 444, 466
Halifax, 1st marquis of 441, 442, 450, 451, 467
Hall, A. Rupert 216
Hall, John 180
Hall, Joseph, bishop 370
Halliday, Paul 463
Hamilton, 3rd marquis of 12
Hamilton, duke of 319, 322, 325
Hamilton, James see Abercorn, 1st earl of;
  Hamilton, 3rd marquis of
Hamilton, marquis of 193, 194, 198, 295, 301
Hamiltons 27
Hampden, Chancellor of the Exchequer 451
Hampden, John 73–4
Hampshire 462
Hampton, Christopher, bishop of Armagh 257
Hampton Court 176, 201, 206
Hampton Court Conference (1604) 257
Handasyd, Thomas 21
hanging 134, 138
Hanoverians 20, 42, 457, 486–7, 488
Hariot, Thomas 54
Harley, Lady Brilliana 122
Harley, Sir Edward 425, 426, 467
Harley, Sir Robert 91, 353, 354
Harrington, James 375, 392, 394, 486, 490
  A System of Politics 392
  Oceana 390–1, 393, 488
Harris, T. 95, 98, 459
Harrison, Stephen 171
Harrison, Thomas 337, 344
Harsnett, Samuel, archbishop of York 259, 393
harvest failures
  (1586–7, 1594–7, 1622–4) 134, 137–8, 141,
    149, 334
  Scottish (1690s) 64
Hatfield House 206

Hattersley, Roy   437
Hatton, Lady   371
Hatton, Sir Christopher   198
Hawkes, Michael   390
Hawkins, John   51
Hawksmoor, Nicholas   211
Hay, Peter, of Hayston   13
Hay, Sir James *see* Carlisle, earl of
Haydocke, Richard   197
Hazzard, Dorothy   367–8
Heads of Proposals (1647)   327, 356, 381, 389
Heads of Severall Proceedings... (1641)   89
hearth tax   78, 79, 82–3, 153–4, 403, 404, 410
hedges, levelling in enclosure riots   138–9
Henley in Arden   369
Henri IV of France   238, 273, 276
Henrietta Anne, duchess of Orleans   203
Henrietta Maria   174, 178, 196, 198, 202, 261, 388
Henry II, invaded Ireland   26
Henry III   284–5
Henry the Navigator, Prince   58
Henry, Philip   423, 425
Henry, Prince of Wales   171, 172, 190, 191, 193, 242
Henry VI   324
Henry VII   273, 342
Henry VIII
   adoption of Protestantism   29
   attempts to regulate succession   272
   rule of Ireland   26
Herbert, George   175–6, 177
Herberts of Cherbury   33
hereditary right, monarchy and   271–3, 402, 452, 477
Hereford, by-election (1642)   122
Herefordshire   354
Heresy Ordinance (1648)   357
Herle, Charles   379
Hermannides, Rutgerius   17
Herrick, Robert   175, 176, 177
   Hesperides   176, 177
Hertfordshire   134
Hessen, Boris   215
Hext, Sir Edward   134
Hexter, Jack   291, 320
Heydon   135
Heylyn, Peter   284, 371, 380, 478, 479, 481
   Aerius Redivivus   478
Heywood, Oliver   422
Hickes, George   489
High Church Party   218, 486
High Churchmen   405, 432–3
Highlands   12
Hill, Christopher   xv, xviii, xx, 93, 98, 216–17, 387, 399
Hilliard, Nicholas   189
Hindle, Steve   xi, xx, 130–47
Hinton, Bill   238

Hirst, D.   347
Hispanola   54
historiography   xiii–xxiv, 3
   of the civil wars   290–308, 311–30
   of crime   131–6: interactionist   134; neo-positivist   135
   debates about politics   458–9
   and literary criticism   168–71
   modern preoccupations   271
   neo-Jacobite   438, 442
   of popular protest   137, 140
   problems and debates   233–5
   themes   234
   see also new British history; revisionism
history
   beliefs about   384
   and literature   166–86
Hitchin, Hertfordshire, Tilehurst Street Baptist Church   433
Hoadly, Benjamin   489–90
   Queries of the Utmost Importance   465–6
   The True Genuine Tory-Addresses...   465
Hobbes, Thomas   xix, 271, 375, 379, 381, 384, 391, 406, 426, 431, 490
   Behemoth   389, 479–80
   controversy with Boyle   219–23, 225
   influence   474
   Leviathan   388–9, 479–80, 490
   social contract theory   388–9
Hobson, Paul   366
Holbein, Hans, the Younger   190, 194, 202
Holdway, Anne   370
Holinshed, Ralph   5
Holland, art collection in   198, 202
Holland, earl of   286, 320, 321
Hollar, Wenceslas   198
Holles, Denzil   320, 321
Holles, Sir John   241
Hollow Sword Blade Company   163
Holmes, Geoffrey   405, 459
homicide   134
   evidence of   132–3
homosexuality   114
honour
   conflicts of   279
   reputation and virtue   280, 282–4
   Tudor nobility   131
Hooghe, Romeyn de, etching   206 plate 7
Hooke, Robert   211, 214, 215, 224, 225
Hooker, Richard   197
   The Laws of Ecclesiastical Polity   383, 392, 479
Hopper, Andrew   317
Horneck, Anthony   420
Hoskins, John   189
household
   economy   154
   female-headed   117
   number on poor relief   153–4
   occupational categories   159–60

household (*Cont.*)
  patriarchal model   113–14, 119–20
  use of term 'honest'   394
Howard family   241, 244
Howard, Henry *see* Northampton, earl of
Howard, Lady Frances   241
Howard, Sir Robert   446, 448, 451
Howard, Thomas *see* Arundel, 14th earl of
Howarth, David   196
Hudson Bay   52, 63, 64
Hudson's Bay Company   19, 63, 162
Hughes, Ann   xi, xx, xxi, 234, 315, 317, 350–73, 394
Hugli   61
Huguenots   13, 63, 205, 476
Hull   153, 304
humanism   271, 276, 282
Humble Petition and Advice (1657)   357–8, 392
Hunter, Michael   xi, xvi, xx, xxii, 214–29
Huntingdon   354
Huntingdon, earl of   114
Hunton, Philip   377–8, 379
husbandmen   149
Hutchinson, Anne   352
Hutchinson, Lucy   173, 182, 242
Hutton, Ronald   xviii
Huygens, Christiaan   215
Huysmans, Jacob   203
Hyde, Edward *see* Clarendon, earl of
'hyperlexis'   132
hypotheticalism   222–3

Iberia   6, 7
  composite monarchy   46, 52
Iceland   52
iconography   8–9, 121, 339–40, 482–3
identity
  British state   437
  English national   16
  gender   111, 125–6
  growth of national   462–3, 464
  Irish hybrids   41
  national   3–4
ideological approaches   xv, xxi, 166–8, 293, 305, 306, 375–6, 474–91
idolatry   196, 378
Ile de Ré expedition (1627)   174, 247
illiteracy   98
Impartial Protestant Mercury   90
import substitution   50, 54, 62
imports, Asian and American (*c.*1700)   63–4, 150–1, 161
impositions   72, 76, 77, 237, 241, 246
Incapacity Bill, Scotland   449
Inchiquin, earls of   34
'Incident, the' (1641)   301, 302
income tax, introduction (1790s)   404
indentured servants   157, 158
  from the Chesapeake   56, 57, 60, 62

Independents   179, 315, 316–17, 318, 355, 359, 360, 362, 420
  against Presbyterian church in England   325–6, 351–2, 362–3
  control of revenue committees   320
  and Ireland   314, 321
  in northern England   324
India, trade with   49, 59, 61, 62, 161
Indian Ocean   46
indigenous populations, settlers and   56, 57
indigo   57
Indonesia   61
industrialization   116
Infanta of Spain, proposed marriage of Charles I to   193, 257, 258, 283
infantry   69–70
inflation
  (1600–50)   150
  (late sixteenth century)   75, 134, 148–9, 237
Ingram, Sir Thomas   201
Innocent XI, Pope   204
Inns of Court, London   37
Inquisition   408
Instrument of Government (Protectorate)   343, 357, 358, 359, 366, 384, 389
International Congress for the History of Science, London (1931)   215
Interregnum   28, 42, 60
  culture of science in   219
  effects on art collection   190, 198–9, 201–2
  legacies of   401–4
  use of term   345
  see also Commonwealth; Protectorate, Cromwellian
inventories   115, 117, 118, 160
  probate   149, 150
investment
  in government debt and company stocks   162–3, 463–4
  joint stock companies   50, 59, 161, 162
  in the national debt   83–4, 85
  in settlement syndicates   54
Ireland
  added to Great Britain (1801)   4, 400
  as an English dependency   7, 9, 18, 316
  Anglican ascendancy   19, 341, 344
  anglicization policies   xvii, 32, 247, 256, 267, 341–2
  annexation by the Rump   341–2
  Britain and   3–25
  Catholicism in   8, 9–30, 31, 253, 256, 261–2, 267
  characterization of seventeenth-century   40–3
  colonial administration   17
  composition of early   5
  confederate government   37, 267, 268, 302, 311
  Cromwellian rule   341–2, 343
  English Act for the kingly title of (1541)   29

ethnic cleansing 400–1
as a French protectorate 450
history of political and constitutional
    subjection 21, 26–8
involvement in Asia and the Atlantic 57–9
James I's religious policies 255–7, 259
landownership 34–8
law 32
links with Spain and France 3, 314
lord deputies 240
the making of Great Britain and 26–44
migration to and from 156–7
Nine Years War (1594–1603) 27, 253, 255
the Pale 256
plantation projects 8, 27–8, 32, 39, 40, 55, 58
population (seventeenth century) 57, 150
Protestant settlers see New British; New English
Protestantism in 33, 34, 35, 39, 254, 255–7,
    261–2, 267
religious power structure 265–6, 267
Restoration 400–1
rural subsistence economy 163
Scots and English interests in 27–8
settlement 27–8, 35, 41
Stuart policies in 26–44
union with Britain (1801) 400
and William III 436, 441
see also union
Irish, Gaelic 8, 37, 240, 254, 256, 262, 266,
    322–3
lords 12, 32
tradition of kings 6, 7–8, 273
Irish Catholics 8, 19, 29–30, 31, 34–5, 36–8, 406
alliance with Stuarts 36–7
attitudes 39–40
Charles II and 400–1
conversion to Protestantism 34–5
in exile on the Continent 36
see also Confederate Catholics of Ireland; Old
    English of Ireland
Irish language 30
Irish parliament 17, 20–1, 33, 240, 265, 319
allegiance to James I 8, 246–7
clerical and peace parties 322–3
hereditary revenues for Charles II 400
New English majority 256
regular 42–3
sessions (1634–5) 248
Irish Protestants 31, 41–3
ascendancy 35, 401
Charles II and 400–1
and civil rights 36, 39
imported 27, 29–30, 31
see also New English of Ireland
Irish Rebellion (1641) 35, 37, 60, 250, 266, 267,
    324, 377
English reactions to 293, 302–4, 313, 318,
    341–2
Irish uprisings (1640s and 1680s) 39–40

iron 150, 161
Italy 191
artists 190, 191–4, 195, 202, 204
royalists in exile 190
ivory trade 59, 61

Jacob, Henry 366
Jacob, J. R. 217
Jacob, Margaret C. 217–18
Jacobean Book of Sports 260
Jacobean period, courts, masques and
    patriarchy 171–3
Jacobitism 440, 445, 449, 452, 457, 459
Irish 36
Scots support for 19, 448
Jamaica 21, 60, 62
seized (1655) 16, 160
James, duke of York 18–19, 198, 203, 483
second marriage to Mary of Modena 204
see later James II
James, Francis Edward 440
James I of England see James VI and I
James II of England see James VII and II
James IV, and Margaret Tudor 6
James, Mervyn 131
James VI and I
accession to English throne (1603) 4
Basilikon Doron 242, 275–6, 277
diplomacy 11–12, 282, 283
dynastic claims 5–7, 8
financial policies 75–7, 154, 237
frontier policy 12–14
as king of Scotland 236, 279
pamphlets and treatises 277
and parliament 245–6
personal monarchy xiv, 235–8
personality 236–8
plantation policy 55
proclamation on riots (1607) 130–1
religious policies xvi, 253–9, 267
speech to parliament (1610) 274, 278
The Trew Law of Free Monarchies 275
triumphal entry to London 171
visit to Scotland (1617) 240, 255
James VII and II xiii, 438–40
attitude to Ireland 31, 33–4, 35, 39
coronation (1685) 482–3
financial situation 404
flight to France (1688) 399, 401, 413, 436,
    438, 440, 442, 451
landing in Ireland 436
and Louis XIV 36
personality xv, 439–40
policy towards Ireland 401
policy towards Scotland 400
political and religious tensions xiii, 166,
    411–14
religious policies 183, 413, 438–40, 449,
    483–4

Java 49
Jermyn, Lord 322
Jerome, Stephen 121
Jesseph, Douglas 222
Jessey, Henry 360, 366
Jesuits 8, 256, 258, 262, 277, 425–6
Jewel, John, bishop 197
Johns, Adrian, *The Nature of the Book* 221, 224, 225
Johnson, Samuel 168
joint stock companies 50, 59, 161, 163
Jolly, Thomas 422
Jones, Inigo 172, 173, 194, 211, 242
    Queen's Chapel, St James's Palace 197
        plate 4; 207
    as Surveyor of the Prince's Works 207–10
Jones, J. R. 405, 439, 445
Jonson, Ben 97, 103, 166, 171
    Oberon 172
    Pleasure Reconciled to Virtue 173
    as poet laureate 173–4
Jordaens, Jacob 196
Josselin, Ralph 125, 361, 365, 418, 424, 425
journalism 88–9, 94, 166
    party political 91
judges 135, 244, 280, 345, 440
judicial institutions, overlapping 279, 313
judiciary 439
    remodelled (1649) 339
Junius, Francis 196
Junto 451
jurors 135, 136
justices of the peace 245
    Scotland 236
Juxon, Thomas 325

Keating, Geoffrey 7–8
Keeble, Neil 181
Kelsey, Sean xi, xvi, xviii, 327–8, 331–49
Kent 150, 161
Kenyon, J. P. 401
Kérouaille, Louise de 203
Kerry, County 33
Kidder, bishop 424
Kiffin, William 366
Kilkenny, Confederation of 31, 37, 267, 302, 318–19, 322–3
Killigrew, Thomas 181
Kincardine, earl of 215
king
    and church, Scottish National Covenant (1638) 264
    contract with people 273, 456, 486
    de iure 8
    defining the power of a 274
    parliament and people 408–11
    see also monarch
King, Gregory 79, 84–5, 153
king-in-parliament 245, 376–7, 380

King's Bench 279
King's Company 181
King's Evil, touch for the 243, 481
King's Lynn 159
'king's price' 70, 72
kingship
    absentee 240–1, 246, 292
    authoritarian 14, 233–5, 245
    and constitutionality of a Catholic regime 446–7
    'duplex' nature of 235
    James VI and I on 275–7
    and mythology 5
    Scottish line 6
    or unkingship (1649–60) 331–49
    see also monarchy
Kinsale uprising (1601) 27
Kishlansky, Mark xv, 234, 319, 325
Klein, Lawrence 470
Kneller, Godfrey 204–5
Knights, Mark xi, xx, 95, 98, 99, 102, 408, 455–73
Knowsley, Margaret 121
Knox, John 7, 378, 479
Koyré, Alexandre 216
Kynaston, Francis 284

La Rochelle 13
labour, sexual division of 116, 117
Ladbroke, Warwickshire 139
Laguerre, Louis 205
laity 353–4, 355, 356, 364, 419, 421–2, 432, 433
Lake, Peter 97, 100, 317
Lambe, Thomas 366–7
Lambert, John 201, 337, 362
Lamont, William 378, 382
Lancashire 356, 360, 362, 419
land
    assessment of 77, 340, 404
    sequestration, composition and forced sales of royalist 341
    as wealth 71–2
land law 153
land market 153
land taxes 77, 79–80, 85, 237, 457
landownership
    in 1650s 340–1
    decline of small and middling 290
    Irish 34–8, 41, 302, 401
    tenure and wardship 72, 76, 152
Lane, Mr 416, 417
language
    gendered 113, 124
    political labelling and abuse of 466–8, 470
    post-revolutionary politics of 463–70
    rhetorical techniques 468–70
Lanier, Nicholas 193
    portrait 200 plate 5

larceny
  and benefit of clergy   134, 135
  grand   134
  petty   134
Larkin, William   189
Las Casas, Bartolomé de, Fra   54
Latitudinarianism   96, 217
Latour, Bruno   220
Laud, William, archbishop of Canterbury   14,
    178, 196, 197, 237, 245, 259–60, 261, 263,
    265, 280, 292, 406, 478, 479
  impeachment and execution (1645)   298, 300,
    350, 370, 479
Lauderdale, duke of   17, 18
Laudianism   177, 208, 239, 259–60, 265, 267–8,
    371, 406
  altar policy   260, 263, 350
  consequences of overthrow   383–4
law
  codification   279
  differing Scottish and Irish traditions   10–11,
    280
  due process and the monarch   237
  jus regis and lex regis   9–10
  lack of unified legal system   11
  see also common law; Roman law
law courts   235, 339
  as royal courts   235, 245, 246
  and sexual deviance   114–15
Lawes, Henry   174
Lawes, William   176
Lawrence, Henry   365
Lawson, George   391–2
  Politica Sacra et Civilis   392
Lawson, Peter   134
lawyers   271, 279–80, 339, 343, 375, 440
  Irish   34–5
Le Brun, Charles   202
Le Sueur, Hubert   208
Le Vau, Louis   202
lead mining   150
leather industry, and meat consumption   152
Leeward Islands   13
Leghorn   52
Leibniz, G. W.   215
Leicester, earl of   272
Leicestershire   130, 138
Leinster   5, 8, 324
Leith   93
Lely, Peter   198–9, 201, 202, 203, 204
  portrait of Princess Mary   203 plate 6
Leonardo da Vinci   198
Leslie, Charles   489
L'Estrange, Roger   475–6
  Considerations and Proposals in order to the
    regulation of the Press   475
letters of marque   75
Levant Company   46, 161
Levant trade   150, 160

Levellers   16, 18, 123, 130, 167, 168, 180, 326,
    327, 336, 358, 366, 394
  enclosure riots   138–9
  fear of tyranny   381–2
Levitt, Norman   220–1
Lewalski, Barbara   172
libel   99, 100, 140
  laws of   167
liberalism, early modern   171, 183
liberty
  Christian   383, 384, 399, 484
  and the problem of settlement   380–4
  and republicanism (1649–53)   384–9
Licensing Act
  (1662)   90, 167, 487
  (1685)   90; lapsed (1695)   90, 167
Licensing Order (1643)   179
life expectancy   157
Lilburne, John   167, 168, 366
  The Freeman's freedom vindicated   380–1
Limerick   33
limning   188, 189, 197, 199
Lincoln   153, 163
Lincolnshire   139, 151
Lindley, Keith, Popular Politics and Religion in
    Civil War London   393
'linguistic turn'   xviii, 374–5, 393
Linlithgow, General Assembly (1606)   255
Linschoten, Jan Huygen van, Itinerario   48
Lipsius, Justus   286, 375, 390
literacy   98, 317
literary criticism, and historiography   168–71
literature
  and civil war   176–8
  eclipse of the canon   171
  emancipation of English   90–1
  and history   xviii, 166–86
Lithuanians   6
litigation   131–2
liturgy, Laudian   254, 263
living standards   150, 160–1
Livy   375, 385
Lloyd, bishop of Norwich   432
Lloyd, William, bishop of St Asaphs   18
local government   153, 304
  during the Protectorate   340, 362, 392
  participation in legal process   403
  reform   245
local interests, taxation and   81–4, 85
locality, of custom   141–2
Locke, John   xix, 113, 168, 438, 474, 478, 482,
    490
  Essay Concerning Human Understanding   467
  Treatises on Government   485, 490
Lomazzo, Giovanni Paolo   197
Lombard, Peter, archbishop of Armagh   8, 257
Lombart, Pierre   201–2
London
  administration of Ireland   27, 29, 30, 40, 256

London (*Cont.*)
  as capital 5
  confiscation of charter (1680s) 402
  expansion of 152, 156, 158
  financial centre 18, 73, 81
  foreign artists in 190–1
  'monster' petition to the king (1680) 102
  papal agent in 198
  parish churches 420
  politics and religion in 393
  printing press 179
  rebuilding (after 1666) 209–11
  'Root and Branch' petition (1640) 265
  theatres 181, 183
  trading and exploratory centre 45, 50, 62, 64,
    150–1, 156, 158, 344
London, bishop of, agents in censorship 167
London Gazette 90, 92
Londonderry, County 55, 302
Long Parliament 298–301, 306, 377, 410, 475
  Charles's failure to dissolve 292
  closure of London theatres (1642) 167, 178
  Grand Remonstrance (1641) 249, 266, 268,
    303
  purge of (1648) 333, 335
  religion and the 350–4
  Remonstrance (1640) 302
  summoned (1640) 249, 264, 298
  Triennial Act (1641) 250
Lords, House of 21, 244, 245, 284, 300–1, 304
  abolished (1649) 338
  bishops excluded (1642) 266, 300, 304
  impeachment of twelve bishops (1641) 304
  James II and 439
  ruling on conduct of church services
    (1641) 353
lords of manors, Ireland 32
Lord's Supper 361, 362, 419
Lothian, William, 3rd earl of 201
Lotto, Lorenzo 202
Louis XIII 13
Louis XIV
  building plan 202, 210
  Charles II's secret dealings for alliance with 17,
    406–7
  dragonnades 408, 412
  invasion of Holland (1672) 205
  James II and 36, 440
  subsidies from 404
  support for Stuarts 457
  William's wars against 20, 162, 436, 437, 441,
    449, 457
Louth 34
Louvain 256
love, as a political theme 286
Lovelace, Richard 177, 180
Low Churchmen 405, 432, 490
Low Countries
  militant Protestants 52

royalists in exile 190, 351
Lowe, Roger 419, 422, 423
Lowestoft, battle of (1665) 203
Lowlands 17
  Covenanters in 325
  Protestantism in 254, 255
Ludlow, conciliar court 279
Ludlow, Edmund 486, 488
Luke, Sir Samuel 100
luxury goods 45, 50, 52, 150
Lyons, bishop 256

MacAlpine, Kenneth 6
Macassar, Celebes 49
Macaulay, Thomas Babington, Lord 90, 399, 400
McClellands 27
McCullough, Peter 276
MacDonnell, Randal *see* Antrim, earl of
Macdonnells *see* Antrim, marquesses of
Macfarlane, Alan 131
Machiavelli, Niccolò 375, 385
  The Prince 286
Macinnes, Allan I. xi–xii, xvi, xvii, xviii, 3–25,
    319, 450
Mack, Phyllis 123, 124
Mackenzie, Sir George, of Rosehaugh 18
Macmillan, Harold 451
Madeira 55
Madras 61, 62
magic 223
magistrates 133, 135, 343, 359, 376, 386, 413,
    428
  grain market regulation 138
  in Ireland 32
Maidstone 422
Mainwaring, Arthur 469
Mair, John 6–7
Maitland, James *see* Lauderdale, duke of
Major-Generals, rule of the 334–7, 342–3,
    362
Malabar coast 61
Malaysia 61
Maldon, Essex, grain riots (1629) 121, 138
Maltby, J. 102
Manchester 156
Mannerism 189
manners, reformation of 257, 340, 424–7,
    469–70
manorial courts 32, 133, 152, 153
manors 32, 152
Mansart, Jules Hardouin 210
manslaughter 132, 133
Mantegna, Andrea 193, 194, 201
Manton, Thomas 360, 423
Mantua 193–4
Manuel, Frank 225
manufactured goods 48, 63, 80
manufacturing 149
manuscript illumination 189

manuscript news xxii, 88, 97, 98, 99, 100, 101, 167, 376
Manwaring, Roger 239
maps *see* cartography
Marcus, L. S. 177
Margaret Tudor 6–7
Margaret of York 273
market towns 153
Marlborough, 1st duke of 442, 451, 467
Marprelate controversy (1580s) 166, 167
marriage
  at court 122
  of clergy 115
  contracts and female inheritance 154
  fidelity 112
  patriarchal model 114
married women 117, 118, 120, 121
  control of property 115, 117
  role in the economy 117
  submission to husbands 112, 113, 115, 117, 154
Marshall, Stephen 124, 360
Marten, Henry 199, 326, 346
martial law (1627) 279
Martial, Marcus Valerius Martialis 174
Martindale, Adam 360, 361, 364–5, 369, 423
Marvell, Andrew 171, 180, 183, 430, 482
  Rehearsal Transpros'd 426
Marx, Karl 400
Marxism, and revisionism 169, 290
Marxist approaches xiv, xviii, xx, 215, 233–4, 312, 399
Mary I 354, 378
Mary II xiv, 122, 439, 440, 441
  portrait by Lely 203 plate 6
  see also William III and Mary II
Mary of Modena 204, 441
Mary Queen of Scots 9, 253, 272–3
masculinity 111, 119, 124, 125
masques 171–3, 207
  Caroline 166, 172, 173–5, 176, 242, 286
  as discourse 172
  Elizabethan 166
  Jacobean 166, 171–2
Massachusetts, religion in 351, 352, 385
Massachusetts Bay 56, 60
Massachusetts Bay Company 162
Masson, David 169
master craftsmen, and architecture 205–6
Master of the Revels 167
mathematics 214
matter theory 218
Mauchline Moor uprising (1648) 319
Maxwell, Robert *see* Nithsdale, 1st earl of
mayors 153, 160
meat consumption, and leather industry 152
Meath 5, 34
mechanical philosophy 222
mechanization 116

medal collections 193
medicine, humoral model 113
medievalists 97
Mediterranean trade 46, 51, 52, 161
Memorial of the Church of England (1705) 467
men's work 118–19
mercantilism 17, 18, 19, 20, 21
mercenaries, Scots 156
Merchant Adventurers 151
merchants 149, 158, 160, 399
  as creditors 70
  Irish 58
  licenses and concessions 83
  London 45–6, 48, 51, 55, 57, 160, 344
  Scottish 58, 64
  syndicates to promote settlements 54
  Venetian middlemen 46
Mercurius Aulicus 100, 179
Mercurius Britannicus 15
Mercurius Politicus 90, 476
Merton, Robert K. 216
messianism 366
mezzotints 204–5
middle class, London 163
Middle Shires 12
middlemen 46, 158
Middleton, Thomas 171
'middling sort' 143, 158, 317, 367
Midland Rising (1607) 130, 138
Miereveldt, Michiel 190
migration, overseas 156–7
military
  aristocracy 318
  billeting 284, 408, 413
  demands for service 70
  expeditions (prior to 1640) 12, 75
  expenditure 69–71, 76–7, 283, 344
  and fiscal state 458
  garrisons 287, 366
  growth of power 403, 439
  in Ireland 29, 38, 42
  as a profession 78–9, 83, 84
  rule of Cromwell 331–49, 406
militia
  Bill (1656) 391
  Bill (1678) vetoed by Charles II 411
  'exact' 245
  expense of 75, 79
  and land tax 85
  new commissions 340
  ordinance (1642) 302, 304, 378, 379
  re-established (1661) 409
  in Scotland 17
millenarianism 223, 344, 352, 363, 368
Millenary Petition (1603) 253, 257
Miller, John xii, xvi, xx, 98, 399–415, 439
Milton, A. 94

Milton, John 16, 166, 167, 168–9, 171, 394, 417
  Areopagitica 179
  Eikonoklastes 487
  pamphlets 179
  Paradise Lost 182–3
  Paradise Regained 183
  republicanism 179–80, 381, 385, 386, 486, 487
  Samson Agonistes 181–2, 183
  Tenure of Kings and Magistrates 476
  The Readie and Easie Way to Establish a Free Commonwealth 180, 386, 392
miniatures 189–90
ministers
  Approbation of Public Preachers (1654) ordinance 359
  nonconformist deprived (1604–10) 257, 260
  Presbyterian 355, 356
  provision and education for Ireland 256
  purge of 'scandalous' 359
  Puritan reforming 254
  rejection of ordained 364, 475
  Scottish 263
  Trustees for the Maintenance of ordinance (1654) 358
Mint, the 151
Misselden, Edward 151
missionaries 45
  Quaker and Baptist 364, 367
  to native Americans 52–4
  women as 123
moderates 407–8
  defining 467
  and radicals 258–67, 336–7
'modernity'
  and the Stuart press 103–4
  thesis of progress towards xiv, xxii
Moluccan islands 48
Molyneux, William 21
monarch
  and church 254
  office distinguished from person of the king 14, 271
  and parliament 245
  personal access to the 240
  personality xxii, 234, 235–40, 291
  reduction of role 85
  see also king
monarchy
  as absolute and legally limited 235, 237, 249–50, 274–5
  collapse of 233–5, 314, 331–49
  and hereditary right 271–3, 402, 452, 477
  interdependence of Stuart 235, 313–14
  and its councils 243–8
  Jacobean view 273–5
  legitimacy of rule 480–1

  limited 19, 235, 273, 332, 376–7, 449, 487
  mixed 271–3, 275, 345, 346, 378–9
  parliament and xxi, 32, 233–5, 245, 273–4, 281–2, 284–5, 291, 377, 378–9
  parliamentary 458
  patriarchal 172–3, 376–7
  and peace 273
  rethinking 486–90
  right of resistance to 7, 14–16, 378, 448, 478, 485
  universal 407
  use of term 345
  see also absolutism; constitutional monarchy; divine right monarchy; kingship
Monck, General George 168, 334, 337, 344
money market, emergence of 73, 81
Monmouth, James, duke of 183
  rebellion (1685) 402, 412, 439, 444, 461
monopolies 70–1, 76, 161
Montagu, Charles *see* Halifax, 1st earl of
Montagu, Edward, Lord Admiral 334
Montagu, Richard 259
  A New Gag for an Old Goose 258
  Appello Caesarum 258
Montrose, marquis of 301
Montserrat 57
Moore, Susan Hardman 124
moral economy thesis 137, 140, 141
morality
  gender bias and 120
  and government 378, 385
  and religion 424–7, 431
Moray, Sir Robert 215
Morrill, John xv, xvi, 234, 293, 312, 314, 315, 317, 382, 402
Moscow Academy of Sciences 215
Mountjoy *see* Devonshire, earl of
Mountrath 32
Muggleton, Lodowick 365
Muggletons 365, 387–8
Muldrew, Craig xii, xx, xxii, 148–65
Munn, Thomas 49
Munster 5, 8
  plantation 27, 32, 39, 41, 55
  Protestant population 32, 324
  as resource base 55–6, 58, 64
Munster Plantation Company 161
murder, distinguished from manslaughter 132
Murrays of Broughton 27
museums 215
music 173, 176
  choral 178
mutual association 14
Mytens, Daniel 191
myth-making, origins 5, 7

Namier, Sir Lewis Bernstein 337
Naples 9
Naseby, battle of (1645) 316, 377, 406

National Covenant, Scottish (1638) 9–10, 14, 16, 264
  effects of 264–6, 475
National Debt 20, 69, 77–8, 80, 81, 85, 162, 163
national interest 142
  importance of trade to 80
  taxation and the 83–4, 239
national wealth 403–4
  public revenues as proportion of 69
nationalism, development of Irish Catholic 37
nationality, common since the regal union 10
natural philosophy 219, 222
Navigation Laws
  (1651) 16, 63
  (1660, 1671, 1681) 17, 18, 19, 63, 160
navigation system, and trade 79
navy, under Cromwell 334, 344
Navy, Royal 18, 327, 403
  costs of 70, 76, 78–9, 285
  Irish in 42
Naylor, James 331, 357–8, 359, 365, 366, 367
Nedham, Marchamont 15, 16, 17, 90, 166, 180, 385, 386, 394
Nelson, C. 91
Nelson, Robert 474–5
neo-classicism 166–7, 173, 211
neo-Marxist approaches 399, 402, 406
neutralism xv
Nevis 57
New British *see* New English of Ireland
new British history xvi–xviii, 3–4, 290–4, 304, 312–30
  'billiard ball effect' 293, 294–5, 297, 302, 305–6
  holistic approach xvi–xvii, 293, 312–28
new Cromwellians 334–8, 343, 479, 480, 486
New Dictionary of the Terms Ancient and Modern of the Canting Crew, A (1699) 466
New England 13, 62, 449
  English Puritan settlements 52, 56, 57, 60, 294
  migration to 156, 157, 260
  Puritanism in 157, 351
  trade and fishing 56, 57, 60, 63
New English of Ireland 8, 37, 240, 246, 254, 257, 261–2
  MPs 256, 321
new historicism xviii, 169–70
New Jersey 63
New Model Army xv, 15, 16, 316, 318, 331
  Heads of Proposals (1647) 327, 356, 381, 389
  Major-Generals 331–49
  and parliament 15, 320, 325, 332–3
New River Company 162
New World 54, 156–7, 161
New York 18–19
Newbattle 201
Newburn, battle of (1640) 249, 297, 298
Newcastle 150, 156
  Scots occupation of (1640) 249, 297, 298

Newcastle, duchess of 111
Newcastle, marquis of 392, 406
Newcastle Peace Propositions (1646) 327
Newcome, Henry 360
Newfoundland 52, 56, 57, 60, 62
news
  audience for 102, 103
  circulation 101–2
  content and language of 102
  material culture 102–3
  and trade 463
news media, diversity of 100–1
news serials 89
newsbooks
  (1640s) 89–90, 92, 94, 97, 99, 101–2, 103, 167
  Scottish 93
newsletter writers, professional 101, 483
newspapers
  circulation figures 92
  daily, evening and provincial 91
  Irish 93
  Scottish 93
  Stuart 88, 90, 91, 100, 101, 102, 166, 167
  taxation of 91
  see also broadsheets
Newton, Isaac 214, 215, 216, 221, 224
  biographies of 225
  Principia 214, 215, 219, 222
Newton, Rockingham Forest, battle of (1607) 130, 139
Newton Solney 370
Nine Years' War (1688–97) 85
Nine Years' War, Ireland (1594–1603) 27, 253, 255
Nineteen Propositions (1642) 243, 266–7, 304
  Charles I's Answer to 377, 378, 389
Nithsdale, 1st earl of 12
nobility
  early Stuart 131
  Elizabethan 131, 282–3
  martial and chivalric codes become civic and humanist 132
  opposition to Charles I 292
  poverty of Scottish 295
  role of the xv, 290, 317–20
  taming of the 131–2, 295, 402
  travel for education 190
  Tudor 131
Noell, Martin 78, 83
Nominated Assembly (1653) *see* Barebone's Parliament
Non-Jurors 432–3, 445, 452, 486
Nonconformists 355, 420–1, 423–4
  and Churchmen 405, 412–13
  clergy 422–4
  and 'comprehension' 428–9
  female 123
  licenses for 428, 429

Nonconformists (*Cont.*)
  publication by 168
  as 'splitters' 405, 460
  Whig 456, 459
nonconformity
  literary culture of 181
  persecution of 257–8, 402, 406, 409, 412,
    416–18, 481–5
  and sedition 475–6
  tension with church 456, 459–61
  'Tory reaction' (1681–5) 428
Norbrook, David 96, 171, 172, 180, 182, 385
Norfolk 151, 163
Norgate, Edward 197, 199
Normans 5, 8
Norsemen 5
North America
  colonies 440
  plantations 62–3
  trade 52, 151
North, Dudley 160
North Sea 51, 57
Northampton, earl of 192, 280–1
Northamptonshire 121, 130, 138, 142, 253
Northaw, Hertfordshire 138
Northumberland, earl of 201, 287, 288, 320,
    321
Northumbria 5
Norway 12
Norwich 150, 156, 342
  Census of the Poor (1570) 117, 153
Nottingham 360
  raising of royal standard (1642) 304, 311
Nottingham, earl of 445, 447, 452
Nova Scotia 13, 58
novel, birth of the 104
Nua-Gallaibh *see* New English
Nye, Philip 351, 355, 359, 360, 363
Nys, Daniel 194

O hAnnracháin, Tadgh 323
O Siochrú, Micheál, *Confederate Ireland* 311,
    322–3
Oates, Samuel 367
oaths of allegiance 14, 265
  and Catholics 258
  to William and Mary at their coronation
    (1689) 432, 447, 452, 486
obedience 474–9
O'Briens 34
O'Callaghan, M. 97
occupational structure 159–60
O'Devany, Cornelius *see* Down and Connor,
    bishop of
O'Dohertys 27
Odoni, Andrea 202
O'Flaherty, Roderic 18
Ogg, David 401, 405
Ogilby, John 17–18

Ohlmeyer, Jane 313
Old English of Ireland 8, 37, 240, 246, 248, 254,
    256, 261, 262, 266, 322, 344
Oldenburg, Henry 216, 224
oligarchy 318–19
Oliver, Isaac 189
Oliver, Peter 189
O'Neill, Hugh *see* Tyrone, earl of
O'Neill, Owen Roe 319
O'Neill, Sir Phelim 266
opposition
  difficulties of expressing 293–4
  in politics 463
  printed 167
  Puritan 290, 291–2
  to Charles I in England 290–305
Orange, House of 202
Orange, south of France 441
Orangists 436–8, 444, 447
  'Letter of Invitation' 451
order, Stuart ideology of 130–1, 139–40, 474–7
Order of the Garter 242
Orkney, annexation (1612) 12
Orleans, duchess of (Henrietta Anne) 203
Ormonde, duke of, as Lord Lieutenant of
    Ireland 18, 30, 321, 327, 328, 401
Ormonde, dukes of 34
Ormuz 49
Osborne, Thomas *see* Danby, earl of
Osiris 216
Ossory, Lord 30
Overbury affair 102, 241
Overbury, Sir Thomas 241
Overton, M. 150, 161
Overton, Richard 167, 366
Owen, James, *Moderation still a Virtue* 467
Owen, John 360, 425
Oxford 179, 199, 325–6, 426, 487
  Philosophical Society 215
  Royal Society 215, 219
  Sheldonian Theatre 209
Oxford Gazette 90

Paige, John 154–5
painting, history 196
Pakington, Sir John 464
palaces, royal 194, 200
Palatinate, Elector of the 171
Palladianism, English 208–9
Palladio, Andrea 207
pamphlet wars (1640s) 96, 303–4, 475–6
pamphlets 463, 475, 481, 482, 485
  news 89
  polemical (1689–94) 95, 166, 444
panegyrics 171, 173, 181
Panzani, Gregorio 198
papacy, as Antichrist 9, 253, 257, 275, 277,
    425–6, 482
paper credit, secure public 162

paper money 83
Pareto, Vilfredo 216
Paris 322
    Louvre 202
    Palais du Luxembourg 202
    Palais Mazarin 202
parishes 355
    governance of rural 143
    politics of 462
    and poor relief 155, 462
    rural 422
Parker, Henry 304, 377, 379, 381, 430
    *Observations upon some of his Majesties late
        Answers and Expresses* 379
parliament
    act for the disposal of Charles I's assets 200–1
    attempt to arrest 'five members' (1642) 291,
        303, 411
    Charles I's relations with 247–9, 283, 297,
        298–303, 411
    and church government 356–9
    composition of 244
    control of revenues 69, 71, 72–3, 77
    English (1606–7) 10
    evolution of xxii, 245, 284–5, 290, 304, 461
    factionalism 320–3, 346, 406–8
    grant of taxation 74, 76, 78, 79, 239, 273,
        281, 404, 410
    James I's relations with 236–7, 255
    James II and 439–40
    king and people 408–11
    manuscript account of proceedings 102
    and monarchy xxi, 32, 233–5, 245, 273–4,
        281–2, 284–5, 291, 377, 378–9
    and the New Model Army 15, 16, 316, 318,
        331
    Nineteen Propositions (1642) 243
    perpetual parliament act (1641) 300
    post-revolutionary 461
    'recess committee' 301
    revenue committees 320
    war effort against the king (1640–2) 403
    William's 'free' 437, 442, 443, 444, 447–50
    see also Addled Parliament; Barebone's
        Parliament; Cavalier Parliament; Exclusion
        Parliament (1681); Irish parliament; Long
        Parliament; Rump Parliament; Scottish
        parliament; Short Parliament
parliament, members of, English and Welsh
        numbers (1690–1714) 461
parliamentarians 299–301, 303, 317, 323, 354,
        363, 407, 448
parliamentary union of England and Scotland,
        stages towards 4, 10, 20–1
Parsonstown (later Birr) 32
pastoral areas 143
patents 70–1, 162, 181
paternalism, and deference 137, 139–40, 141
Paterson, William 64

Patient, Thomas 366
patriarchy 113, 114, 119, 126, 478–9
    absolutist 376–7
    courts and masques 166, 172–3
Patrick, Simon 423, 429
patrimonialism xxii
patronage xxii, 30, 41, 70–1, 143, 237, 243, 281,
        346
    of the arts 187, 194–5, 202
Patterson, Annabel 171, 183
peace and war, act *anent* (1701) 20
Peacey, Jason xii, xiv, xvi, 290–308
Peacham, Henry, *The Compleat Gentleman* 196
Peak District 142
Peake, Robert 189
Pears, Iain 188
Pelham, Henry 452
Peltonen, Markku 376
Pembroke, earl of 194, 198, 209
penal system, death rate (1580–1630) 136
Penn, William 417
Pennsylvania, Quaker settlements in 63
Penshurst 206
people
    king and parliament 408–11
    see also sovereignty of the people
pepper 46, 49, 50, 61, 151
Pepys, Samuel 19, 163, 418, 420
Pequots 56
Percy, Algernon *see* Northumberland, earl of
performances, public 97, 98
performing arts, regulation by licensing 167
periodicals 91, 463
persecution, of nonconformity 257–8, 402, 406,
        409, 412, 416–18, 481–5
Persia 49
personality, of monarchs xxii, 235–40, 291
Perth, earl of 437
Perth, General Assembly (1618) 244, 246, 255
Peters, Kate 123
Petition of Right (1628) 239, 247–8, 248, 284
petitions
    (1679–80) 408
    campaign (1642) 303, 369
    and popular protest 140, 405
    printed 96–7, 98, 101, 102
    women's participation in 122
Petty, Sir William 19, 80
Pewsey, Wiltshire 420
Peyto family 209
Philip II of Spain 52
Philip IV of Spain 193
Philosophical Society, Oxford 215
philosophy, corpuscular 217–18
Philostratus 173
physics, mathematical and experimentalism 222
Picts 5, 6
pillories 136
Pincus, S. C. A. 96

Pinkham, L.   442
Pinney, Hester   117
piracy   54
place names   13
plague
    (1590s)   149
    (1641) in London   265
    (1665–6)   209
plantation projects   8, 27–8, 32, 39, 40, 55–6, 58,
    286
playhouses   181
plays *see* drama; stage plays
Plumb, Sir John H.   405, 459
Pocock, John G. A.   xvi, 278, 293, 374, 375, 380,
    385, 463
    The Machiavellian Moment   391
poetry
    Caroline court   174
    Cavalier   176–7
    religious   175–6, 177, 178
Poland, Scots pedlars in   57, 156
politeness, history of   469–70
Political Aphorisms   485
political authority
    and conscience   376, 379–80, 385, 387–8,
        430–3, 477–8, 481–5, 486
    monarchy and   272–4, 286
political culture   xix, 234–5, 238, 394
    participatory   131, 136, 445
    towards a new post-revolutionary   459–71
political discourse
    during 1640s and 1650s   374–84, 393–4
    Jacobean compared with modern   271–8, 284
    post-revolutionary   459–71, 482
    Scottish apocalyptic   276
political economy   18, 19, 49, 80
political history, literature and   168–9
political ideas, and political practice   234–5
political party formation   292, 320–3, 405–8,
    445, 458
    institutionalization of party allegiance   461–3
    'rage of party'   455–73
political power, depersonalization of   78, 85
political theology   275–6, 474–91
political thought   xxi, 271–89
    between Restoration and Hanoverian
        succession   474–91
    during the English Revolution   374–96
    Jacobean compared with modern   271
    Scottish   275–6
politics
    (1603–40)   233–52
    after the Glorious Revolution   455–73
    art and architecture   187–213
    association with Aristotelian and humanist
        discourse   271
    bicameral and baronial nature of   292, 305,
        319–20
    and gender relations   119–23, 126, 394, 462

historiographical debates   458–9
interdependence of Irish and English   30–1
oppositional   463
popular and elite   99–100
in Restoration Britain   399–415
and social history   462–3
three kingdoms approach   320–3
see also religious–political dimensions
Polybius   378
Ponet, John   479
Poole, Elizabeth   331
poor, moral economy of the   137
poor relief   153–4, 155, 163
    charity   155
    parish   141, 462
    records   115
    statute (1598)   155
popery, and prelacy   368–71
popish plots
    (1678)   406
    fears of   205, 261, 293, 294, 303, 305, 408,
        430, 475–6, 482
popular protest *see* protest, popular
population
    growth (1550–1650)   57, 149–50, 156–7
    Tudor England   148
Port Royal   13
Porter, Endymion   193, 194, 200
Porter, Roy   216, 218
Portland, earl of   443
portraiture   188–9, 199–200, 202, 204
    'cavalier'   194
ports
    duty to provide ships in wartime   72
    English   45, 56, 71
    Irish   56, 62
Portugal
    exploration   58
    trade   46, 49
Pory, John   101
post-revisionism   xv–xvi, 234, 305, 317–18, 347
postal service   94, 244
postmodernism   226
Potosi   51
Potter, John   422
Pouch, Captain   139
poverty
    estimates   153
    in Ireland   39
    overpopulation and   157
    taxes and   82, 403
    women and   117–18
power, gender relations and   113–14, 119, 126
Poynings' Law (1494)   246
Pratt, Sir Roger   210
prayers   418–19, 420
predestination   253, 365, 418
pregnancy, mitigation in criminal
    proceedings   134

prelacy, and popery   362, 368–71, 483–4
prerogative courts   138, 410
  abolition of   89, 279, 409
Presbyterianism   179, 422
  discipline   356
  in England   351, 355
  in Ireland   28, 355
  in Scotland   20, 28, 254–5, 275–6, 315, 319,
    344, 355, 366, 383, 400
  sectarianism in   429
  see also ministers
Presbyterians
  and 'comprehension'   429
  and Congregationalists   432
  and Independents   321–2, 326, 355–6, 359,
    372, 420
press
  access to the   167
  freedom of the   89, 90, 93–4, 366
  impact on political development   168, 404–5
  innovation in form   91
  legislation (1712)   463
  and popular public opinion   88–110
  post-revolutionary politics   455
  regulation   475–6
Preston, battle of (1648)   325
Pride's Purge   406
'priestcraft'   460
priests, preaching politics   474–5, 477–9
print culture   445, 463
  court in exile and   176
  and public opinion   xxii, 88–110, 303–4
  Puritan cross-border   297
printing
  commercialization of   94, 179
  and dissemination of scientific
    knowledge   221–2
  regulation of   167, 179, 409, 458
prints   205
  intaglio   205
  scurrilous   468, 489–90
Priuli   194
private property   338
  and duty of service   73
  protection by criminal justice system   134–6
private sphere, women in the   112, 119
privateers, English   52, 75
Privy Council
  English   240, 243, 243–5, 256, 279, 287; new
    (1679)   411
  Scottish   239, 244, 245, 264, 295
privy seal loans   73
probate accounts   154
  see also inventories, probate
proclamations   97
  (1650s) discriminatory against Irish
    Catholics   35
profanity   426
progress approach   xiv, 374, 399–400, 458

propaganda   99, 320, 323, 413, 462
  royalist   486
  Scottish   297
property
  crimes against   132–3, 134, 136; incidence
    of   134; prosecution   134–5
  decimation tax   341
  rights   141, 440
  taxation   404
  women's control of   117, 118
  see also private property
Proposals for an incorporating union, Charles II's
    (1669)   17
prosecution
  binding over system   133
  private   131
Protectorate, Cromwellian (1653–9)   xiv, 4,
    16–17
  anglicization policies in Scotland and
    Ireland   xvii, 16, 337
  collapse (1658–60)   391–3
  financial problems   390, 391–3
  Instrument of Government   343, 357, 358,
    359, 366, 384, 389
  military rule over England and Wales   334
  and parliament   334
  and Quakers   182
  seal of royal type   340
protest
  popular   130, 136–42; continuum thesis   140
  social   459–60
Protestant ethic, and the spirit of capitalism   216
Protestantism   5, 52, 253–70
  conversions to in Ireland   34–5, 256
  European defence of   76, 344
  fragmentation of English   350–2
  in Ireland   33, 34, 35, 39, 254, 255–7, 261–2,
    267
  need to safeguard   272–3, 430
  and scientific activity   216
  in Scotland   254, 263–5, 343–4
  values and perceptions   424–7
  and William III   441, 444
  see also Reformation
Protestation oath (1641)   300, 304
Protesters, and Resolutioners   343–4
Providence Island   60
prudence, political   286
Prynne, William   18, 167, 260, 279, 379
  Histrio-Matrix   178, 196
psychoanalysis, use in historical context   225
public office
  commissions from the crown   235
  and confessional status in Ireland   34–5
public opinion
  form and content   98–104, 315, 413
  growth of   xix, xxi, 94–104, 317–18, 404–5,
    408–9, 463
  and the press   88–110, 306

public opinion (*Cont.*)
  Scottish against the court   20
  use of term   94
public profession   354–62, 363, 372
public revenues
  boundaries of   71
  as proportion of national wealth   69
public sphere
  characteristics   95
  creation of a bourgeois   94–8
  Habermas's   xix, 94–5, 99, 393, 464
  men in   112, 119
  plurality   97
  the press and the   91
publication
  licensing   167, 179
  Puritan abroad   167
Publick Intelligencer, The   90
punishment
  capital   134, 136, 138
  corporal   133–4; for women   121, 133
  as a discursive act   170
  exemplary   136
Puritan clergy
  and gender relations   112, 115, 416–18
  and Laudianism   260, 350–2
Puritanism   254–70
  antipathy to art   188, 196–7, 199
  attitude to drama   167, 178
  and court culture   176–7
  cross-border sympathy   297–8, 306
  in literature   167, 169, 181–3
  in New England   157
  as revolutionary   xiv, 420–4
  and scientific cultural values   216–19
  use of the label   351
Puritans   178–81
  anti-Spanish policy in Atlantic   59–60
  Irish fear of   324–5
  in opposition   290, 291–2
'purveyance'   70, 72, 75
Pye, Sir Walter   201
Pym, John   15, 265, 266, 292, 294, 299, 300,
  301, 304, 305, 306, 319, 320, 321, 351
  speech to the Commons (1640)   350

Quakers   334, 358, 359, 364–8, 371, 406, 408,
  420, 421, 484
  female   123–4, 167, 364, 368
  literature   167, 182
  prosecution (1681–5)   428
quarter sessions   133, 143, 152, 340
queen in parliament, succession and   272
Questier, M.   97, 100
quota taxes   77, 82

radicalism   325–6, 331, 362–8, 387, 406, 438,
  444, 482
radicals   178–81, 333, 445–6, 449

moderates and   258–67, 322
  religious   334, 344–5, 352, 362–8
Raleigh, Walter   52–4, 241
Ranelagh, earl of   445, 451
Ranters   xv, 167, 168, 170, 180, 331, 357, 358,
  365, 408
  female   123
Raphael   193, 194
Ravenshaw, John   171
Rawlins, Thomas   468
Raymond, J.   93, 96, 97, 100, 101–2
reading habits   88, 92, 98, 100, 103
recusancy laws   254, 256, 258, 262, 266, 299
Red Sea   49
red wood   51
Reeve, John   365
  A Divine Looking-Glass   388
Reeve, L. J.   238
Reform Act (1832)   98
Reformation   6, 124, 350–1
  as an agenda   424–7
  consolidation of the   xxi, 290, 384
  in Ireland   4
  in Scotland   276
regicide   328, 345, 363, 406, 408
  legally sanctioned   272, 346
  literature and   177, 180, 479
  refusal of Irish and Scots to accept   17
Regnier   194
religion   253–70
  (1640–60)   350–73
  central position of   xxi, 166
  and gender   123–5, 416–18, 421
  laicization of   353–4, 355, 356, 364, 419,
    421–2, 432, 433
  and morality   424–7, 431
  post-revolutionary politics   456–7, 459–61
  public profession   354–62
  in Restoration England   416–35
  and science   223–4
religious houses, dissolution of (1540s)   155
religious innovation
  parliamentary resolution against (1629)   247,
    259
  removal from parish churches (1641)   353
religious liberty *see* conscience, liberty of
religious pluralism   xxi, xxii, 350, 399, 430–3
religious polemic   166, 460–1, 463
religious revolution, Scottish   14, 264–7, 294–5
religious–political dimensions   xiii, xx, xxi, 97,
  188, 234, 290, 335–6, 382–4, 459–61,
  477–9, 483–4
Rembrandt van Rijn   194
Remonstrance (1648)   476
Renaissance
  art   112, 189, 191, 193–4, 211
  scholarship   4, 7
Reni, Guido   198
representation, concepts of   xviii, 464–5, 481

republic
    'unacknowledged' 394
    use of term 345
republican rule xiii, 233–5, 332, 345–6
    failure of 337–8
republican values, and civic virtue 376
republicanism 167, 171, 180, 276, 326, 342,
        390–1, 458, 475
    association with nonconformity 460
    divine and liberty (1649–53) 383, 384–9
    literature 486–7, 490
    Milton's 179–80, 182–3, 381, 385, 386, 486,
        487
    post-Reformation Scottish 7
    'vernacular' 346
Republicans 178–81
reputation 120, 152, 154
    historical 234, 236
    honour and virtue 280, 282–4
Reresby, 448
resistance theory 7, 14–16, 273, 378, 478, 485
Resolutioners, and Protesters 343–4
Restoration (1660) xiii, 17–19, 331, 335, 371–2
    art 202
    defending orthodoxy and order 474–7
    drama 112, 166, 181, 183
    literature 181–4
    politics 399–415; the issues 404–8
    religion in England 416–35
    and slave trade 60
revenue rights, and legitimacy of regimes 79–80
revenues
    ordinary and extraordinary 71–2, 78
    parliamentary and non-parliamentary 71, 72–3,
        410
    political friction in raising 73–4
    pressure to increase 69–71
    proportion from taxation 85
    see also customs and excise duties; public
        revenues
revisionism 93, 171, 234, 347, 374, 413–14
    and the 'British' context xvi–xviii
    and change xxi–xxii
    and the civil wars 291–2, 304, 306, 312
    and the 'cultural' context xviii–xx
    and the ideological context xxi
    and Marxism 169
    methodology xiv, 290–4
    reactions to xvi–xxii
    and the Restoration 402–3, 408–9
    and the social and economic context xx
    value and limitations xiv–xvi
    see also post-revisionism
Revocation, Act of (1625) on crown and kirk
        property 13, 239, 263, 295
Revolution (1688–9) 436–54
    consequences for Church of England 432–3
    political thought 374–96, 479–81
    and the polity 446–50

social and economic causes xx
    see also 'Glorious Revolution'
revolutionary approach xv, 20, 332–3, 335–9,
        345, 402–3
Reynolds, Edward, bishop of Norwich 371
rhymes 140
Richard II 36
Richmond Palace 191, 206–7
Rights, Bill of (1689) 443, 448, 449, 458
Rinuccini, archbishop, papal nuncio in
        Ireland 323
riots
    artisanal in west and gentrified in east 142
    chronology of 140–1
    during Cromwellian regime 334
    technical definition 137
    women's participation in 121
    see also food riots; grain riots
Ripon 298
Roanake Island 54
Roe, Sir Thomas 193
Roman Catholic Church 253, 425–6
    in Ireland 8, 29–30, 262
    see also Catholicism
Roman Catholics, petition (1604) for limited
        toleration 253
Roman law 10, 385
Roman occupation 5, 8
Romanelli, Giovanni Francesco 198
Romanino 193
Romano, Julio 193
Rome, triumphal ambassadorial entry (1686) 204
'Root and Branch' petition (1640) 265, 297,
        298, 300
Rossingham, Edmund 101
Rota Club (1659–60) 392
Royal African Company 62
Royal Company for Fishery in Scotland 19
Royal Exchange, Cornhill, Exchange Alley 162
royal prerogative 18, 20, 250, 263, 409, 447
    attrition of 450
    and the law 274–5, 281, 346, 413
    ordinary powers and absolute powers 235,
        274–5
    and subjects' rights 376, 440
Royal Society
    ideology 214–24
    Scots and Irish contribution xvi, 215
Royal Touch see King's Evil
royalist party 293, 298–9, 303, 304, 317, 322,
        335, 354, 407, 408
royalists
    Anglican 478, 481–2
    Catholic 368–9
    constitutional 300, 322
    court culture 176–7
    defeat 176–8
    in exile 190, 202
    popular 404

royalists (*Cont.*)
    rebellion (1655)   334
    rejection of absolutist claims   379–80
    Scottish   322
    sequestration of land   341
    taxation on   362
Rubens, Peter Paul   178, 191, 194, 196, 199, 242
Rudyerd, Sir Benjamin   247
rule of law   132, 143, 249
    and royal power   273–5, 279, 283–4, 291, 346
    survival of the   338–9
rumour   100, 140, 323
Rump Parliament (1648–53)   332–3, 334, 336–7,
        339, 344
    Adultery Act (1650)   357, 361
    annexation of Ireland   341–2
    Blasphemy Act (1650)   357
    church government   357–62
    as experiment in *de facto* government   385, 386
    expulsion   387
    Heresy Ordinance (1648)   357
    trading policy   59
Rupert, Prince   199, 205
rural economy   141, 152–3
    political geography of   143
    sexual division of labour   117
Russell, Conrad   xiv, xvi, xvii, 234, 238, 246, 291,
        292, 293, 294, 296, 297, 298, 299, 312, 402
    The Fall of the British Monarchies   311
Russell, Lord   482
Russia   11
Russia Company   161
Rutland, earl of   371
Ryswick, peace of (1697)   457

Sabbatarianism   257, 260, 421
Sacheverell, Dr Henry   406, 449, 452, 456, 465,
        486, 489
sacrament *see* Lord's Supper
Saenredam, Pieter   202
St Christopher (St Kitts)   57, 58
St Dunstans, Fleet Street   420
St James's Palace   191, 194
    Queen's Chapel   198, 203; by Inigo
        Jones   197 plate 4, 207
St John, Henry   456
St John Stevas, Norman   437
St Lawrence, Gulf of the   52
St Paul's Cathedral   208, 209
    Wren's   210 plate 9
St Paul's Church, Covent Garden   423
Saint-Germain   202
Salisbury   116
Salisbury, earl of   206, 241, 244, 281
salons   95
salt   52, 58, 82
Salteran, George   196
saltpetre   59, 61
salvation doctrines   365

Sancroft, archbishop   432
Sanderson, Robert, bishop of Lincoln   371
satire   97, 102, 103, 168, 466
    prints   205
    Whig   183
Saville, George *see* Halifax, 1st marquis of
Savoy Chapel, London   420
Saxons   5
Saye and Sele, Lord   60, 243, 265, 294, 299, 300,
        301, 305, 306, 320, 321, 323–4, 356
scaffolds   136
Scamozzi, Vincenzo   207
scandals, court   102, 241
Scandinavia   11, 156
    Scots trade with   57
Schaffer, Simon, *Leviathan and the Air
        Pump*   219–23
schools, bequests to set up   155
Schwoerer, L. G.   443, 448
science
    as counter-revolutionary   217–18, 222
    and religion   223–4, 426
    setting and stimuli for change   214–29
science, history of   xxii, 214–29
    constructivism in   220–3
    'externalist' accounts   214, 216–17
    'internalist' accounts   214, 216
    'reductionist' accounts   214
    'relativistic' accounts   214, 221
'science wars'   216, 220
scolding   114, 120
Scota   6
Scotland
    alliances with United Provinces and Sweden   3
    anglicization policies   xvii, 13–14, 17
    'auld alliance' with France   6, 7, 10
    Catholicism in   254, 263
    Charles I's relations with   248, 263–5, 286–7,
        301, 328, 400
    Covenanter Rebellion   294–8, 325
    Cromwellian occupation   16, 286–7, 341–2
    economy   295
    Forth–Clyde division   5
    independence   18
    invasion by England (1650)   16
    and Ireland   27
    and James VII   448
    justices of the peace   236
    parliamentary incorporation   20–1
    population (1550–1650)   150; seventeenth-
        century   57
    Presbyterianism   20, 28, 254–5, 275–6, 315,
        319, 344, 355, 366, 383, 400
    Protestantism in   254, 263–5
    Protesters and Resolutioners   343–4
    religious revolution   14, 264–7, 294–5
    Restoration   400
    revolt (1679)   411
    rural subsistence economy   163

southwest religious 'awakening' (1620s)   263
  and William III   436, 441
  see also union
Scots
  in American colonization   13
  attitude to union (1707)   400
  conscription to navy   18
  early   5, 6, 7
  foreign policies   314
  invasions of England (1640)   297;
    (1644)   314, 318, 324, 325; (1648)   16, 325
  involvement in Asia and the Atlantic   57–9
  James I's use in diplomatic affairs   11
  migrants   156–7
  origin myths   6, 7
  rebellion (1638–40)   239, 240, 245, 248, 249,
    296
  role in Restoration   341–2, 344, 388
  scientific   215
  trading contacts   57–9
  see also Ulster Scots
Scott, David   xii, xiv, xvi, xvii, xix, 311–30
Scott, James C.   140
Scott, Jonathan   313, 385, 408, 458, 459
Scottish Convention (1689), Claim of Right   448
Scottish Council of Trade   19
Scottish Estates   4, 20, 21
  and the National Covenant (1638)   9–?
Scottish Kirk   9, 253–4, 263
  Charles I and   263–5
  and Church of England   28, 457
  General Assembly   239, 254–5, 296
  and James VI and I   253, 254–5, 259
  reform   278
  revocation of property (1625)   239
Scottish National Covenant (1638)   9–10, 294–5
Scottish parliament   17, 239, 246, 296–7, 319
scribal publication   97
scrofula   243
Scudamore, viscount   101
sculpture   192, 195, 208
  baroque   195
'seacoal'   150
Sean-Gallaibh *see* Old English
Sebright, Mayor   55
Seccombe, M.   91
secularization   104, 382–3, 458
Security, Act of   20
Sedgewick, William   382
sedition   474–8
'Seekers'   366
Selden, John   13, 16, 284, 375, 377
semiotic systems   170
Seneca   375
Senegambia   51
'separates'   100, 101
separatism, religious   352, 353–4, 364–8, 420–4
Septennial Act (1716)   455, 470
Serlio, Sebastiano   206

sermons   97, 98, 101, 254, 303, 351, 418, 426, 475
  at court   276–7
  Donne's   175
  farewell by ejected ministers   475
  Fast Sermons to parliament   378
  and gender relations   112
  republican   487–8
  set-piece   478, 486
servants in husbandry   153
service
  commutation into cash payments   72, 73–4, 85
  private property and duty of   73
Settlement
  Act of (1701)   20–1, 446, 457, 487
  the failure of (in 1640s)   326–8
  liberty and the problem of   380–4, 392
  Restoration (1660)   410
  Revolution (after 1689)   20, 446, 452
Sexby, Edward   490
sexual politics   172–3, 237, 241
Seymour, Sir Edward   456
Shaftesbury, 1st earl of   402, 452, 482, 486, 488
Shaftesbury, 3rd earl of   211, 470
Shakespeare, William   166
  Macbeth   168
  Richard II   178
Shapin, Steven
  A Social History of Truth   221, 223, 224
  Leviathan and the Air Pump   219–23
Shapiro, Alan   222
Shapiro, Barbara   217
Sharpe, Jim   135
Sharpe, Kevin   171, 175, 234, 238
Shetland, annexation (1612)   12
ship money (1634–9)   72, 76, 239, 245, 285–6,
    293, 296, 299
shipbuilding   45, 50
ships
  merchant and warships   70, 75, 76
  tonnage   150
shopkeepers   158
shops, rural   161
Short Parliament (1640)   248–9, 296, 297, 298
Shrewsbury   159
Shrewsbury, 12th earl and duke of   451
Shrewsbury, countess of   118
Shropshire   423
Sibbald, Sir Robert   18
Sibthorpe, Robert   239
Sicily   9
Sidney, Algernon   383, 386, 390, 482, 486, 490
Sidney, Henry   443
Sidney, Sir Philip   272, 321
Sidney, Sir Robert   206
Sierra Leone   51
silk trade   49, 54, 59, 61, 150, 161
silver   49, 51, 149, 151
  Spanish   52, 151–2
Singer, Charles   215

Skimmington, Lady   139
Skinner, bishop   370
Skinner, Quentin   375, 385, 388
Skippon, Philip   358
slander, sexual   416–18
slave trade, African   51, 60, 62, 63, 158, 161
Slingsby, Sir Henry   249
Smectymnuus   179
Smith, Abbot E.   157
Smith, Adam   137
Smith, David L.   xii, xiv, xvi, 233–52
Smith, Henry   112
Smith, John (mezzotints)   205
Smith, Nigel   171, 180–1
Smuts, Malcolm   xii, xix, xxi, 271–89
social contract theory (Hobbes)   388–9
social discipline   136
social and economic context   xx
social history, and politics   462–3
social morality, and economic activity   139–40
social polarization   163
Society of Antiquaries   274
Socinians   358, 359
sociology, American   216
Sodoma, Giovanni Antonio Bazzi   193
Soest, Gerard   198
Solemn League and Covenant (1643)   15–17, 28,
    314–15, 321, 355, 361, 385
  Charles II subscribes (1651)   16
  results of   377, 379, 380, 387
Somerhill, Kent   206
Somers, John, 1st baron   451, 466
Somerset, earl of   193, 241, 244
Somerset House   196, 198, 199
Sommerville, C. J.   88, 103
Sommerville, Johann P.   234, 273, 274, 375–6
Sophia, Electress   487
soteriology   258, 259
Source of Our present fears discovered, The
    (1703)   469
South Carolina   19
South Sea Bubble (1720s)   163
South Sea Company   162, 163
Southampton   159
sovereignty
  parliamentary   377–8
  of the people   333, 345, 382, 475; in
    Scotland   275
  royal   431
  of Stuart ius imperium   10–11
Spain   20, 31, 42, 190, 276, 282
  blockade of Antwerp   48
  Catholic missionaries   52–4
  colonies   54, 60
  and England   54, 345
  fishing off Ireland   58
  Irish links with   3, 314
  proposed marriage of Charles with Infanta   193,
    257, 258, 283

settlements in Caribbean and Central
    America   52
  threat of invasion   10
  war at sea   48, 75
  war with Bohemia   258
  wars against (1625–30)   247, 259
Speck, W. A.   439, 462
Spectator, The   92, 168, 469
Speed, John   5–6, 7, 8, 14
Spelman, Sir Henry   11, 380
Spencer, Robert see Sunderland, earl of
Spenser, Edmund   278
spice trade   48, 49, 50, 61, 150
spinsters   117
Spottiswoode, John, archbishop   263
Sprigge, William, Modest Plea for an Equal
    Commonwealth   391
Springate, Sir William   199
Spurr, John   xii, xxi, 416–35
stage plays, acts against (1642 and 1648)   167,
    178, 179
Stamp Act (1712)   91, 92
Star Chamber
  archives   138
  decree controlling the press (1637)   167, 168,
    279
Star Chamber court   89, 132, 141, 196, 260
  abolished   300
state
  coercive powers increased   403
  'dispersed'   394
  post-revolutionary politics of the   461–3
state formation
  British   xxi, 4, 458, 464–5
  by acquisition or conquest   4
  in early modern Europe   4
Stationers' Company   167, 475–6
Steele, Richard   90, 91, 469
Steensgaard, Niels   49
Stephens, William   487–8
Stevenson, David   311
Stewarts   6, 9; see also Stuarts
Stillingfleet, William, bishop of Worcester   18, 429
Stirling, earl of   13, 58
stock market, development of the   162–3, 463–4
stocks (punishment)   136
Stone, John   209
Stone, Lawrence   131, 133, 234, 290
Stone, Nicholas   209
Stour Valley riots (1642)   317
Stout, William   160, 419
Stoyle, Mark   324
Strafford, Sir Thomas Wentworth, earl of   240,
    241, 248, 280, 285–6, 287, 288, 293, 298,
    300, 302, 324
  as Lord Deputy of Ireland   261–2, 265
structural analysis   291–2, 305
Stuart Britain
  (1603–42)   231–308

(1642–60) 309–96
(1660–1714) 397–491
the changing face of 67–229
as 'early modern' xxii
fine arts in 187–213
religion in early 253–70
and the wider world 1–66
Stuarts
in exile 457, 486
financial history of early 74–7
financial system of early 71–4
as imperial British dynasty 4–8, 9, 273
Irish acceptance of dynasty 8
Irish policies 27–44
jus imperium 10–11, 13–14, 17–18
literary history 166–86
Stubbs, John 272
subculture, thesis of dissident 140
subordination, popular mentalities of 137, 140
subsidies 72, 76, 82
from Louis XIV 404
subsistence, right to 137
subsistence economy, in rural Scotland and
      Ireland 163
succession
of Anne 457
of Charles II's brother 409, 411
of Mary 439
and post-revolutionary politics 457
problems 452
see also hereditary right
Suckling, Sir John 176
Sudbury 163
Suffolk 151, 206, 462
Suffolk, Lord Treasurer 241
Suffolk, Thomas, earl of 206
sugar 150, 157, 158, 161
plantations 60, 62
Sumatra 49
Sunderland, earl of 401
Surat 49, 61
Surrey, communist experiment 331, 336
Sussex clubmen 370
Sutherland, J. R. 90, 91
swearing the peace 133
Sweden 6, 12, 15, 161
Scotland and 3, 14, 314
Swift, Jonathan, *Examiner* 456–7, 469
Sydenham, William 365
symbolism 8–11

Tacca, Pietro 195
Tacitus 282, 375
Talbot, Charles *see* Shrewsbury, 12th earl and duke of
Talbot, Elizabeth *see* Shrewsbury, countess of
Talbot, Richard *see* Tyrconnel, earl of
tariff reform 13
Tawney, Richard Henry 290
tax collection 79–80, 83, 404, 439

taxation 71, 160
concerns about legality 280–2, 283–4, 285, 339
of newspapers 91
parliamentary 77, 79–80, 85, 239, 273, 404
political economy of 80
post-revolutionary 457
reactions to 81–4, 292
refusal to pay 81–3
for wars 162, 344
see also assessment tax; customs and excise; ship
      money; subsidies
taxations populaires (1629–31) 138, 141
tea, Chinese 61, 161
teleology *see* progress approach
Temple, Anna 350
Temple, Sir William 431, 447
Ten Propositions (1641) 300
Terling 143
Test Acts
(1673, 1678) 412, 413, 432, 456
in Ireland 33; (1704) 34, 35
textiles, trade and manufacture 48, 49, 50, 59,
      61, 62, 151, 152, 153, 161
Thanet, earl of 452
theatre *see* drama
theft 134
theologians, discourse of 271
Thirty Years War (1618–48) 3, 12, 50, 76, 94,
      156, 174, 257, 258, 276, 283, 303, 313
Thirty-Nine Articles, of the Church of
      England 256–7, 261
Thomas, Sir Keith 376, 393
Thomond, earls of 34
Thompson, A. B. 94
Thompson, Edward 136–7, 140, 446
Thomson, Maurice 57, 59, 60
Thornborough, James, bishop of Bristol 9
Thornton, Alice 419
Thorpe, John 189
Three Questions, of James II 449
thrift 154
Throckmortons 369
Tillotson, John, archbishop of Canterbury 424
time, modern notions of 104
Tindal, Matthew 490
tithes
disputes over 339, 358, 359, 361, 364, 370
and Feoffees for Impropriations 260
Titian 192, 193
tobacco 56, 57, 60, 62, 151, 157–8, 161
Toland, John 182, 486–7, 488, 490
Anglia Libera 487
toleration
and 'comprehension' 428–9
religious 350, 412–13, 439–40, 483–4, 485
Toleration Act (1689) 431, 432, 456, 458
Tombes, John 360
Tompson, Richard 204–5
tonnage and poundage 72, 77, 247, 300

Tories   xiv, 18, 91, 404, 405, 406, 407, 411–12, 455–7
  alienation to Stuarts   439, 444
  Anglican   445, 459
  electoral contests   464–71
  fortunes   463, 486
  ideology   482, 489–90
  reaction to nonconformity (1681–5)   428, 438
  use of label   466
Totness, earl of   30
towns
  child mortality rates   156
  confiscation of charters (1680s)   402, 408
  distribution centres   158
  English   152
  garrison   287, 366
  Irish   33
  James II's power over corporations   411, 413
  Scottish   93
Townsend, Aurelian   175, 176
tracts, printed   97, 99, 460–1
trade
  Asia and the Atlantic   45–66
  colonial after 1707   64–5
  commissions   63
  economic development   160–4, 403
  entrepôts   158
  French   61
  Irish   36, 38
  and navigation system   79, 344
  negative balance of payments   151–2
  and news   463
  re-export   50, 63–4
  regional domestic   137
  royal charters for Scottish   58
  Scottish–Dutch   19
  statistics (seventeenth-century)   150
  tariffs   80
  triangular   161
trade winds   45
tradesmen   148–9, 152, 158
Trapnel, Anna   123, 368
Trapp, Joseph, *The True Genuine Modern Whig-Address...*   465
travel for education   190, 210
Treasury   83, 85
Trelawney, Sir Jonathan, bishop   418–19
Trenchard, John   488
Trevelyan, G. M.   452
Trevor-Roper, Hugh Redwald   290
trials, criminal   136
Triennial Act (1641)   250, 300; (1694)   455; repeal (1716)   470
'Triers'   359, 360, 363
trust, in business relations   152, 154
Tuck, Richard   384
Tuckney, Anthony   360
Tudors   8, 273

art   189–90
  honour complex   131
  Irish policies   26, 29
  taxation   79
Turner, Francis   422, 483
Twysden, Sir Roger   248
tyranny   282, 377, 386, 409, 448, 456, 486
  of memory   458, 485–6
  parliamentary   379, 381–2
  writing against   476, 479, 481–5, 487–8
Tyrconnel, earl of   27, 30, 256, 401
Tyrone, earl of   27, 29, 253

Ulster   5, 8, 12
  British migration to   55, 156
  plantation of   8, 12, 27–8, 32, 41, 55, 286
  Protestant nonconformity   257
  Protestant population   32, 266
  settlement in   27–8, 39, 247
Ulster Scots   27, 28, 58, 64–5, 265, 324
  'black oath'   302
  Presbyterianism   19, 28, 35, 401
  protection of (1642)   314
Underdown, David   102, 324, 327
Unhedgeall, Thomas   139
Uniformity, Act of (1662)   423, 427, 431
union
  of Britain and Ireland (1801)   4, 400
  Charles II's Proposals for an incorporating union (1669)   17
  commercial of Scotland and England   4, 10
  of England and Scotland: (1608), opposition   236, 246; (1707)   xxii, 4, 64–5, 400, 457, 462; proposed (1645)   322
  incorporating   20–1
  stages towards parliamentary   4, 10, 20–1
  Treaty of (1707)   21
Unitarianism   432
United Provinces   42, 344
  France and   440, 441
  Scotland and   3
  taxation in   85
  trade   46
  see also Dutch; Holland
universities   82, 114
  forced to admit Catholics   413
  role in scientific thought   224
unkingship (1649–60)   331–49
urban development   148–65
Ussher, James, archbishop of Armagh   9, 257, 261–2, 352, 370, 371

vagrancy   155
Van Blyenberch, Abraham   191
Van der Doort, Abraham   190, 191
Van der Doort, Jacob   191
Van Dyck, Anthony   191, 194, 195–6, 200, 242
  plagiarism from   201–2
Van Somer, Paul   190–1

Van Voerst, Robert, engraving of Charles I after Dieussart 195 plate 3
Vanbrugh, Sir John 211
Vandrebanc, Peter 204, 205
Vane, Henry 287, 288, 383, 385, 386
Vaughan, Henry 177
Venice 46, 192
Verenigdne Oost-Indische Compagnie (VOC) 46, 49, 50, 59
Vernon, Elliot 315
Verrio, Antonio 205
Verstegen, Richard (alias Rowlands) 11
Vignola, Giacomo Barozzi da 206
Villiers, George see Buckingham, duke of
Vindicae contra tyrannos (trans. 1640s) 476, 479
violence
    crime 131–6
    domestic 115, 121
    low levels in popular protest 136–42
    spontaneous 133
    Stuart monopoly of 136
    and violation 134
Virgil 183–4
Virginia 56, 57, 156, 157, 449
Virginia Company of London 54, 55, 56, 162
virtue
    honour and reputation 282–4
    republican 386–7
    as virtù 191, 194, 386–7
Virtuosi of St Luke 204
visual arts 173, 187–213
Vitruvius Pollio, Marcus 207
VOC see Verenigdne Oost-Indische Compagnie (VOC)
Von Pufendorf, Samuel 17
voters, party allegiance 461–2
Vox Dei 485
Vox Populi 485
Vyner, Robert 83

Wade, Anne 421
wage levels 158
Wake, William, archbishop 436
Wales 4, 5, 26, 257
    borders 132
    Catholicism in 254
    Commission for the Propagation of the Gospel 336, 337
    division into North, South and Powys 5
    market towns 153
    missionaries in 427
    population (1550–1650) 150; seventeenth-century 57
    Quakers in 123
    royalism in 324
    unmarried women 117
Walker, R. B. 91
Walker, Robert 201

Walker, William 385
Waller, George 16
Wallingford House affair 337
Wallington, Nehemiah 103, 114
Wallis, John 222, 225
Walpole, Horace 91, 191, 202, 405, 452, 459
Walsh, William 464
Walter, John 317
Walton, Isaac 371
Walwyn, William 366, 383, 394
War of Spanish Succession 42
wardship 72, 76, 152, 237
wars
    cost of 69, 149
    and news hunger 94
    of the Three Kingdoms see civil wars
Warwick, earl of 60
Warwickshire 130, 138, 358, 360, 369
Waterford 33
Waterman, William 116
wealth, social distribution of 80, 394
weaponry, costs of 75
weaving 152, 153
Webb, John 209
Weber, Max 170, 216
Webster, Charles 217, 218–19
Webster, Tom xii, xvi, xvii, xxi, 253–70
weights and measures 51
Weldon, Anthony 238
Wells, R. H. 169
Wellwood, William 13
Welsh 5, 317
    in Ireland 33
Welsh language 324
Wentworth, Sir Thomas see Strafford, Sir Thomas Wentworth, earl of
West Country 152, 323, 363, 364, 365
West Indies 20, 56, 57, 62
    forced migrants to 60
    Irish in 58
    migration to 156
    news in 93
Western Isles 12
Western, J. R. 439
Western Rising (1628–32) 138
Westfall, R. S. 216
Westminster Assembly of Divines (1643) 177, 355, 378, 382
Westminster Confession of Faith 355, 360
Westmorland 360, 462
Weston, Richard 245, 282
Wexford 33
Weymouth, George 46
whaling 12
Wharton, Thomas, 1st marquis of 466
Whateley, William 112, 115
Whig historical tradition xiv, xxii, 3, 89, 93, 95, 233–4, 290, 304, 312, 319, 399, 401–2, 404–5, 406, 407, 458

Whigs   xiv, 7, 18, 91, 104, 412, 438, 455–7
    alienation from Stuarts   439, 444, 445
    electoral contests   464–71
    emergence of   183, 405, 407
    in exile   402
    fortunes   463, 486
    ideology   482
    Low Churchmen   432, 459
    and Puritans   211
    sheriffs   411
    use of label   466
    and William III   445, 447, 448, 452
whipping posts   136
'Whitehall circle'   190
Whitehall, Palace of   194, 201, 243
    see also Banqueting House
Whittacker, Jeremiah   375
Whittle, J.   150, 161
Wickham   153–4
Wickham, Glynn   179
widows   117–18
Wigan, John   360
Wilcher, R.   177
Wilkins, John   217
Wilks, Tim   xii, xviii, 187–213
William III   xiv, 93, 206, 433, 440–3
    First Declaration   441, 447, 449
    invasion   413, 414, 436, 438
    personality   440–3
    and the polity   436–8
    Protestantism   427
    religious policies   448–9
    Third Declaration   440
    wars against Louis XIV   20, 162, 440, 441, 444,
        449, 457
William III and Mary II   19–20, 485–6
    acceptance of crown (1689)   438, 442–3, 445
    Irish attitudes to   36, 41, 42
    oaths of allegiance   432, 447, 452, 486
William of Orange   18, 40, 205, 402, 403
    as Stadhouder   440–3
    see also William III
Williamite Revolution, literature and the   166,
    168, 181–4
Williamites   437, 452
Williams, J. B. (pseud. of Muddiman, J. G.)   90
Williams, John, bishop of Lincoln   352
Williams, Roger   383
Williamson, Arthur   315
Willis, Thomas   219
wills   115, 117
Wilson, John   433
Wilton House   209
Wiltshire   370, 419, 420
Winchester Palace   210, 404
Windebank   198, 245
Wine Islands   56
wine trade   52, 54, 58, 150
Winstanley, Gerrard   167, 169, 181, 331, 380

The Law of Freedom   387
Winthrops and Downings   57
witchcraft   114, 120
Wolseley, Sir Charles   431
women
    churching of   371
    collective action   121
    elite   118, 122
    petitions and   102, 122
    as political agents   122
    as queens with royal authority   272
    religious roles   123–4, 367–8, 421
    in theatres   181
    see also married women
women's agency   120
women's experiences   116
women's work   117, 118, 119
Wood, Anthony   426
Woodruff, Edward   211
Woodward, Donald   153
wool trade   21, 45, 48
Wootton, David   384
Worcester, battle of (1651)   325, 342, 385, 390
Worcestershire   138, 464
Worcestershire Association   360
Worden, Blair   171, 180, 347, 385, 391
Wordie, J. R.   141, 149
work, gender relations and   116–17, 118–19,
    126
workhouses   116, 155
Wormald, Jenny   236
worship
    freedom of   413
    law punishing Irish who failed to attend Church
        of Ireland (1560)   33
    penal laws, repeal of   412
    styles of   422
Worsley, Charles   362
Wotton, Sir Henry   198
    Elements of Architecture   192
Wray, Sir John   350
Wren, Christopher   209–11
Wren, Matthew   370, 371
Wright, John Michael   204
Wrightson, Keith   xx
Wymer, R.   169

yeomanry   131, 141, 148, 149, 290
York   156, 159, 297
York, duchess of   198
York House   196
York House Conference (1625)   259
Yorkshire   323, 324, 370
    West Riding   462
Young, John   327
    The Scottish Parliament (1639–1661)   311, 315

Zaret, D.   96–7, 98, 104
Zwicker, Steven   183